Ninth Edition

Drugs and Society

Glen R. Hanson
Professor, Department of Pharmacology and Toxicology
University of Utah
Salt Lake City, Utah
Director, Utah Addiction Center
Senior Advisor
National Institute on Drug Abuse, NIH

Peter J. Venturelli
Chair and Associate Professor of Sociology and Criminology
Department of Sociology
Valparaiso University
Valparaiso, Indiana

Annette E. Fleckenstein
Associate Professor, Department of Pharmacology and Toxicology
University of Utah
Salt Lake City, Utah

JONES AND BARTLETT PUBLISHERS
Sudbury, Massachusetts
BOSTON   TORONTO   LONDON   SINGAPORE

World Headquarters
Jones and Bartlett Publishers
40 Tall Pine Drive
Sudbury, MA 01776
978-443-5000
info@jbpub.com
www.jbpub.com

Jones and Bartlett Publishers Canada
6339 Ormindale Way
Mississauga, Ontario L5V 1J2
CANADA

Jones and Bartlett Publishers International
Barb House, Barb Mews
London W6 7PA
UK

Jones and Bartlett's books and products are available through most bookstores and online booksellers. To contact Jones and Bartlett Publishers directly, call 800-832-0034, fax 978-443-8000, or visit our website, www.jbpub.com.

Substantial discounts on bulk quantities of Jones and Bartlett's publications are available to corporations, professional associations, and other qualified organizations. For details and specific discount information, contact the special sales department at Jones and Bartlett via the above contact information or send an email to specialsales@jbpub.com.

Production Credits
Chief Executive Officer: Clayton Jones
Chief Operating Officer: Don W. Jones, Jr.
President, Higher Education and Professional Publishing: Robert W. Holland, Jr.
V.P., Sales and Marketing: William J. Kane
V.P., Design and Production: Anne Spencer
V.P., Manufacturing and Inventory Control: Therese Connell
Acquisitions Editor: Jacqueline Mark-Geraci
Senior Production Editor: Julie C. Bolduc
Associate Editor: Nicole L. Quinn
Editorial Assistant: Amy L. Flagg
Associate Marketing Manager: Wendy Thayer
Interactive Technology Manager: Dawn Mahon Priest
Composition: NK Graphics, Inc.
Interior Design: Shawn Girsberger
Cover Design: Kristin E. Ohlin
Senior Photo Researcher: Kimberly Potvin
Photo Researcher: Christine McKeen
Cover Image: © Jeremy Woodhouse/Photodisc/Getty Images
Printing and Binding: Courier Kendallville
Cover Printing: Courier Kendallville

Library of Congress Cataloging-in-Publication Data
Hanson, Glen R.
    Drugs and Society / Glen R. Hanson, Peter J. Venturelli, Annette E.
Fleckenstein.—9th ed.
       p. cm.
    Includes bibliographical references and index.
    ISBN 0-7637-3732-1
    1. Drugs.   2. Drugs—Toxicology.   3. Drug abuse.   I. Venturelli,
Peter J., 1949–   .   II. Fleckenstein, Annette E.   III. Title.
    [DNLM: 1. Substance-Related Disorders.   WM 270   H2505d 2006]
RM301.W58   2005
362.29—dc22
                                                2005026062

Printed in the United States of America
09 08 07 06 05   10 9 8 7 6 5 4 3 2 1

BRIEF CONTENTS

iii

CONTENTS

Preface

THIS REVISED EDITION of *Drugs and Society* is intended to convey to students the impact of drug use and/or abuse on the lives of ordinary people. The authors have combined their expertise in the fields of drug abuse, pharmacology, and sociology with their extensive experiences in research, teaching, drug policy-making, and drug policy implementation to create an edition that reflects the most current information and understanding relative to drug abuse issues available in a textbook.

We made the ninth edition of *Drugs and Society* an exceptionally comprehensive text on drug use and drug-related problems. This book is written on a personal level and directly addresses the college student by incorporating individual drug use and abuse experiences and perspectives. For example, many chapters include excerpts from personal interviews conducted with recreational drug users, habitual (often addicted) drug users, and former drug users. Students will find these first-hand accounts both insightful and interesting. This significant improvement makes *Drugs and Society* truly unique. We implemented this approach in response to suggestions from readers, students, and instructors to further stimulate students' interest.

Drugs and Society was written to instruct university students from a wide range of disciplines to gain a realistic perspective of drug-related problems in our society. Students in nursing, physical education and other health sciences, psychology, social work, and sociology will find that our text provides useful current information and perspectives to help them understand these critical issues:

- Social and psychological reasons why drug use and abuse occurs
- The results of drug use and abuse
- How to prevent drug use and abuse
- How drugs can be used effectively for therapeutic purposes

To achieve this goal, we have presented the most current and authoritative views on drug abuse in an objective and easily understood manner. To help students appreciate the multifaceted nature of drug-related problems, this edition exposes the issues from pharmacological, psychological, and sociological perspectives. Besides including the most current information concerning drug use and abuse topics, each chapter includes updated and helpful learning aids for students:

- **Holding the Line:** Vignettes intended to help readers assess governmental efforts to deal with drug-related problems.
- **Case in Point:** Examples of relevant clinical issues that arise from the use of each major group of drugs discussed.
- **Here and Now:** Current events that illustrate the personal and social consequences of drug abuse.
- **Point/Counterpoint:** Features that expose students to different perspectives on drug-related issues and encourage them to draw their own conclusions.
- **Highlighted definitions:** Definitions of new terminology are conveniently located adjacent to their discussion in the text.
- **Learning objectives:** Goals for learning are listed at the beginning of each chapter to help students identify the principal concepts being taught.
- **Summary statements:** Concise summaries found at the end of each chapter correlate with the learning objectives.
- **Chapter questions:** Provocative questions at the end of each chapter encourage students to discuss, ponder, and critically analyze their own feelings and biases about the information presented in the book.
- **Concise and well-organized tables and figures:** Updated features found throughout the book present the latest information to students in an easily understood format.
- **Color photographs and drawings:** These additions graphically illustrate important concepts

and facilitate comprehension as well as retention of information.

Because of these new and updated features, we believe that this edition of *Drugs and Society* continues to be much more "user friendly" than the previous editions and will encourage student motivation and learning.

The ninth edition of *Drugs and Society* includes updated statistics and current examples of the key principles being taught in this text. The new topical coverage includes:

- Information on the abuse of prescription and performance-enhancing drugs
- New information on methamphetamine and Ecstasy problems
- The latest status of over-the-counter stimulants such as ephedrine
- Updated data on abuse levels in young people
- Current topics such as steroids in baseball, Oxy-Contin, restrictions on pain pills, and heroin potency
- "National Household Survey" (National Survey on Drug Use and Health) and "Monitoring the Future" survey data

The material in the text encompasses biomedical, sociological, and social-psychological views. Chapter 1 provides a helpful overview: the current dimensions of drug use (statistics and trends) and the most common currently abused drugs. Chapter 2 comprehensively explains addiction and drug use and abuse from multidisciplinary and theoretical standpoints. The latest biological, psychological, social-psychological, and sociological perspectives are explained. Chapter 3 discusses how the law deals with drug use and abuse of both licit (alcohol, OTC, and prescription) and illicit (marijuana, hallucinogens, and cocaine) drugs.

Chapter 4 helps the student understand the basic biochemical operations of the nervous and endocrine systems and explains how psychoactive drugs and anabolic steroids alter such functions. Chapter 5 instructs students about the factors that determine how drugs affect the body. This chapter details the physiological and psychological variables that determine how and why people respond to drugs used for therapeutic and recreational purposes.

Chapters 6 through 14 deal with specific drug groups that are commonly abused in this country. Those drugs that depress brain activity are discussed in Chapters 6 (sedative-hypnotic agents), 7 and 8 (alcohol), and 9 (opioid narcotics). The drugs that stimulate brain activity are covered in Chapters 10 (amphetamines, cocaine, and caffeine) and 11 (tobacco and nicotine). The last major category of substances of abuse is hallucinogens. Such drugs alter the senses and create hallucinatory and/or distorted experiences. These substances are discussed in Chapters 12 (hallucinogens such as LSD, mescaline, Ecstasy, and PCP) and 13 (marijuana). Chapter 14 discusses inhalants, substances that are particularly popular among youth.

Although most drugs that are abused cause more than one effect (for example, cocaine can be a stimulant and have some hallucinatory properties), the classification we have chosen for this text is frequently used by experts and pharmacologists in the drug abuse field and is based on the most likely drug effect. All of the chapters in this section are similarly organized. They discuss:

- The historical origins and evolution of the agents so students can better understand society's attitudes toward, and regulation of, these drugs;
- Previous and current clinical uses of these drugs to help students appreciate distinctions between therapeutic use and abuse;
- Patterns of abuse and distinctive features that contribute to each drug's abuse potential; and
- Nonmedicinal and medicinal therapies for drug-related dependence, withdrawal, and abstinence.

Chapter 15 explores the topic of drugs and therapy. Like illicit drugs, nonprescription, prescription, and herbal drugs can be misused if not understood. This chapter helps the student to appreciate the uses and benefits of proper drug use as well as to recognize that licit (legalized) drugs can also be problematic.

Chapter 16 explores drug use in several major subcultures: sport/athletic, women, adolescent, college student, HIV-positive, and entertainment. Included in this chapter is a discussion of new media "electronic" drug subcultures that have recently arisen.

Chapter 17 acquaints students with drug abuse prevention. This chapter focuses on the following topics: (1) the most prominent factors affecting an individual's use of drugs, (2) major types of drug prevention programs, (3) major types of drug users that must be recognized before creating a prevention program, (4) the four levels of comprehensive drug prevention programs for drug use and abuse, (5) major family factors that can affect the use of drugs, (6) primary prevention programs in higher education, (7) four recent large-scale prevention programs, and (8) two additional prevention measures that may substitute for the attraction to drug use.

Chapter 18 focuses on treating drug dependence.

The Appendix in this ninth edition includes an explanation of federal agencies with drug abuse missions as well as a detailed description of schedules for drugs of abuse.

Instructor's Aids

The ancillary package for the ninth edition includes the most contemporary technology. For instructors who adopt the ninth edition, an Instructor's ToolKit CD-ROM is available. Designed for classroom use, this CD contains lecture outlines in PowerPoint format, a computerized Test Bank, an Image Bank, and an instructor's manual. Other instructor resources such as web exercises, a transition guide, and lecture outlines can be found on *http://drugsandsociety.jbpub.com*. Content links, practice quizzes, animated flashcards, crossword puzzles, and an online glossary are also available for students. For distance learning options or additional information, call your Jones and Bartlett Publishers Representative at 800-832-0034.

About the Authors

Dr. Glen R. Hanson, a Professor in the Department of Pharmacology and Toxicology at the University of Utah and the director of the Utah Addiction Center, has researched the neurobiology of drug abuse for over 20 years and authored more than 200 scientific papers and book chapters on the

subject. Dr. Hanson has lectured on drug abuse topics throughout the world. He served as the Director of the Division of Neuroscience and Behavioral Research at the National Institute on Drug Abuse (NIDA) after which he became NIDA's acting director from 2001 to 2003. He continues to serve as a NIDA senior advisor. As a component of the National Institutes of Health (NIH), NIDA is the federal agency recognized as the world's premier science organization dealing with drug abuse issues and funds 85% of the drug abuse–related research in the world.

Dr. Peter J. Venturelli has been the coauthor of this text since the second edition of *Drugs and Society* in 1988. In addition to revising this text every three years, Dr. Venturelli's experiences and qualifications in academia and professional life include publishing research in drug and ethnic anthologies, other drug texts, and scholarly journals; authoring more than 43 conference papers at national professional sociological meetings; serving in elected and administrative positions in professional drug research associations; being the recipient of several research grants involving drug use and ethnicity; authoring the latest drug research in sociological encyclopedias; and full-time teaching of undergraduate and graduate students for the past 20 years.

Dr. Annette E. Fleckenstein is an associate professor in the Department of Pharmacology at the University of Utah. She has researched the neurobiology of substance abuse for nearly 10 years, and has authored more than 50 scientific papers and book chapters on the subject. She continues to lecture to undergraduate, graduate, and professional students, as well as to colleagues at professional meetings throughout the country.

Acknowledgments

The many improvements that have made this the best edition yet of the *Drugs and Society* series could not have occurred without the hard work and dedication of numerous people.

We are indebted to the many reviewers who evaluated the manuscript at different stages of development. Much of the manuscript was reviewed and greatly improved by comments from:

Scott Alpert
University of Maryland

Roger Bounds
Northern Arizona University

Douglas Engwall
Central Connecticut State University

Karamarie Fecho
University of North Carolina–Chapel Hill

Myrna Hewitt
University of Massachusetts–Amherst

John Janowiak
Appalachian State University

Mark Kelley
University of Wisconsin–LaCrosse

Keith King
University of Cincinnati

Robin Lewis
Allan Hancock College

Susan Cross Lipnickey
Miami University

Michael Maina
Valdosta University

Jennifer McLean
Corning Community College

Kelly Mosel
Southwest Texas University

James Pahz
Central Michigan University

Kathy Phillips
Eastern Illinois University

Mark Allen Thompson
University of Kansas

Ray Tricker
Oregon State University

The authors would like to express, once again, their gratitude for the comments and suggestions of users and reviewers of previous editions of *Drugs and Society*.

Dr. Fleckenstein acknowledges the support of her family in her participation in the preparation of this revised text.

At Valparaiso University, Dr. Venturelli is very grateful to many staff members and students at the university. Special mention goes to Linda Matera, Nancy Young, Dan Baggs, and Sarah Ndungu. Linda and Nancy are especially thanked for continually searching the web for the latest information. Also gratefully acknowledged are the countless other students and working people who were interviewed for hours on end regarding their observations, knowledge, personal use, and/or experiences with drugs. Dr. Venturelli wants all of these individuals to know that despite the many other family, school, and job demands they faced, the quality of this edition has been substantially enhanced by their effort, loyalty, and dedicated assistance.

At our respective institutions, each of the authors would like to thank a multitude of people too numerous to list individually but who have given us invaluable assistance.

Dr. Hanson is particularly indebted to his wife, Margaret, for her loving encouragement. Without her patience and support this endeavor would not have been possible. She reminds him that what is truly important in this world is service to our family and to each other. Also appreciated are the efforts of Jarom and Liina with writing this revision.

CHAPTER 1

Introduction to Drugs and Society

Did You Know?

- The popular use of legal drugs, particularly alcohol and tobacco, has caused far more deaths, sickness, violent crimes, economic loss, and other social problems than the use of all illegal drugs combined.

- The effect a drug has depends on multiple factors: (1) the ingredients of the drug and its effect on the body, (2) the traditional use of the drug, (3) individual motivation, and (4) the social and physical surroundings in which the drug is taken.

- Attempts to regulate drug use were made as long ago as 2240 B.C. Ancient literature is filled with references regarding the use of mushrooms, *datura*, hemp, marijuana, opium, poppies, and so on.

- In the past, the penalty for cigarette smoking was having the nose cut off in Russia, the lips sliced off in Hindustan (India), and the head chopped off in China (Thio 1983, 1995, 2000).

- Today, drug abuse is a more acute problem and more widespread than in any previous era.

- Designer drugs are instantly created from existing illicit-type drugs both for profit and to circumvent the laws against drugs.

- Drug use — both licit and illicit drugs — is an "equal-opportunity affliction." This means that drug consumption is found across all income levels, social classes, genders, races, ethnicities, lifestyles, and age groups.

- Approximately $102 billion in sales per year of prescription drugs has been reported in the United States.

- In 2003, approximately 46% of the U.S. population aged 12 and older reported using illicit drugs at some point in their lives.

- There is a tendency to eventually become addicted with repeated use of most psychoactive drugs. Eighty-two percent of local jail and state prison inmates have self-reported that they used drugs at some point in their lives.

- Approximately 76% of drug users in the United States are either employed full- or part-time.

- Approximately 41% of convicted inmates had been drinking alcohol, and 36% were using drugs at the time they committed their offense (Harlow 1998).

- Health and wellness can only be achieved when the mind, body, and spirit are free from the unnecessary use and abuse of nonprescribed psychoactive substances.

Introduction

Each year, at an accelerating rate, as technology brings about new changes, our family, community, city, and nation, as well as the entire world, experience social change. These technological changes affect our everyday lives. It is no exaggeration to say that today, more than ever before, technology drives social change. More importantly, this change affects our lives. As an example, let us look at the cellular phone as a recent innovation. Your great-grandparents may have been fortunate to have a black stationary and wired telephone at home to communicate with friends and neighbors living at a distance. Likewise, your grandparents had newer versions of the same telephone with an extension telephone used in other parts of their homes. Your parent(s) had the same type of telephone, but it was more stylized with several extension phones in their homes. Today, your technological reality includes home-based telephones, facsimile machines, pagers, and mobile (cellular) telephones, with Internet capability, instant messaging, speaker capability, caller identification, alarm clock, games, and other software that were never imagined 20 years ago. Further, we now have another generation of mobile phones with which you can have a live, visual conversation with a friend living practically anywhere in the world.

Consider another example. More than likely, your great-grandparents wrote letters on manual typewriters. Your grandparents wrote letters on electric typewriters, whereas your parents started writing letters on electric typewriters and then had to change to computers. Today, you often communicate with family members and friends by email and instant messaging. Although the electronic "gadgets" that surround your life are perceived as normal, a visit to a museum displaying science and technology offers many surprises and, more than likely, an appreciation for how "things were and how much they have changed." This example illustrates how the way we do things is in a continuous state of development. Life is changing so rapidly that there is constant demand to keep pace and remain current with newly developing "gadgets."

What does this have to do with drug use and/or abuse? Just as electronics continually evolve, drugs follow similar paths of evolution. Today, there are thousands of new drugs available that are used either legally or illegally. These drugs are used for medicinal purposes, recreational purposes, or to achieve effects that do not include maintaining health. Other people in society use drugs to cope with pressures emanating from social change. Some people use and eventually abuse drugs to cope with, delay, or even avoid social change.

Despite the wealth of knowledge regarding the dangers of unnecessary drug use, together with the recent laws prohibiting drug manufacture and consumption, and the ensuing stiff penalties for violating such drug laws, many more people today than in the past use legal and illegal types of drugs without any medically approved reason.

Drug Use

Anyone can become dependent and addicted to a drug. For example, the desire to use a drug before drug dependence (addiction) sets in is both seductive and nondiscriminating of its users. Most people do not realize that drug use causes at least three major simultaneous changes:

1. The social and psychological basis of the attraction to a particular drug can be explained as feeling rewarded or satisfied from social pressures that have become postponed, momentarily rectified, or neutralized and defined as nonproblematic.
2. Pharmacologically, the use of such a drug alters body chemistry largely by interfering (affecting) with the proper (homeostatic) functioning. Drugs enhance, slow down, or distort the reception *and* transmission of reality.
3. The desire may satisfy an inborn or genetically programmed need or desire.

(Much more detail regarding this example is presented later in this chapter and in Chapter 2.)

Many argue that our "reality" would become perilous and unpredictable if people were legally free to dabble in their drugs of choice. Many do not realize, however, that if abused, even legal drugs can alter our perception of reality, become severely addicting, and destroy our social relationships with loved ones. Before delving into more detailed information, which is the basis of the other chapters in this book, we begin by examining and answering some key questions related to drug use:

1. What constitutes a drug?
2. What are the most commonly abused drugs?
3. What are designer drugs?
4. How widespread is drug abuse?
5. What is the extent and frequency of drug use in our society?
6. What are the current statistics on and trends in drug use?
7. What types of drug users exist?
8. How does the media influence drug use?
9. What attracts people to drug use?
10. When does drug use lead to drug dependence?
11. When does drug addiction occur?
12. What are the costs of drug addiction to society?
13. What can be gained by learning about the complexity of drug use and abuse?

Dimensions of Drug Use

To determine the perception of drug use in our country, we asked several of our many interviewees presented in this book, "What do you think of drug use in our society?" The following are three of the more typical responses:

I think it is a huge problem, especially when you think about the fact that there are so many people doing drugs. Even in my own family, my sister's kids have had drug problems. My niece became addicted to cocaine, nearly died one night from overdosing, had to leave college for a year and go into rehab. I cannot emphasize enough how this was one of the most beautiful (physically and mentally sharp) and polite nieces I ever had. The rest of the family had no idea why she left school last year. Then, just last week, my sister tearfully announced during a Christmas gathering that Cindee was heavily into drugs while attending her second year of college. We were all shocked by this information. Now, just think how many other kids are addicted to such junk while the people who really care and love them do not have a clue. If the kids are having to deal with this, just stop and think how many other people in other jobs

and professions are battling or have caved into their drugs of choice.

How many workers are there on a daily basis doing jobs that require safety and are "high" on drugs? This is a scary thought. Just think of a surgeon on drugs, or an airline pilot. Yes, we have big monster problems with controlling drug use. *(From Venturelli's research files, 43-year-old female dietician, in Chicago, Illinois, February 9, 2003.)*

A second response to the same question:

Every effort by the government to stop illegal drug use has failed miserably. Even legal drug use, like alcohol and cigarettes, continues despite what the governmental public health media say. People should be left alone about their drug use unless such drug use is potentially harmful to others. I know that if I ever quit using both legal and illegal drugs it will be my own decision, not because the law can punish me. Yes, drug use is a problem for the addicted, but all throughout our history, drug use has been there. So why worry about it now? *(From Venturelli's research files, 24-year-old male graduate student in a Midwestern city, October 3, 1996.)*

A third response to the same question:

My drug use? Whose business is it anyway? As long as I don't affect your life when I do drugs, what business is it but my own? We come into the world alone and leave this world alone. I don't bother anyone else about whether or not so and so uses drugs, unless of course, their drug use puts me in jeopardy (like a bus driver or pilot high on drugs). On certain days when things are slow, I even get a little high on cocaine while trading stocks. These are the same clients who I have had for years and who really trust my advice. Ask my clients whether they are happy with my investment advice. I handle accounts with millions of dollars for corporations and even the board of education! Never was my judgment impaired or adversely affected because of too much coke. In fact, I know that I work even better under a little buzz. Now, I know this stuff has the potential to become addictive, but I don't let it. I know how to use it and when to lay off for a few weeks. *(From Venturelli's research files, 48-year-old male investment broker working in a major metropolitan city in California, June 2, 2000.)*

These three interviews reflect vastly contrasting views and attitudes about drug use. The first and second interviews show the most contrast, whereas the third interview, from an insider's perspective, shows the strong determination and belief that this man maintains about his drug use. Overall, this individual perceives his drug use as being under control. Although much about these viewpoints can be debated, an interesting finding is that such vastly different views about drug use often divide users and non-drug users. Drug users and/or sympathizers of drug use are often considered "**insiders**" with regard to their drug use, whereas, nonusers and/or those who are against drug use are "**outsiders**." These two classifications result in very different sets of values and attitudes about drug usage. Such great differences of opinion and views about drugs and drug use often result from the following sources: (1) prior socialization experiences, such as family upbringing, relations with siblings, and types of peer group association, (2) the amount of exposure to drug use and drug users, (3) the age of initial exposure to drug use, and (4) whether an attitude change has occurred with regard to the acceptance or rejection of using drugs (most of these factors are discussed further in Chapter 2). Keep in mind that in its entirety, this book views four principal factors as affecting

how a drug user experiences a drug: pharmacological, cultural, social, and contextual.

Pharmacological factors. The ingredients of a particular drug affect the functions of the body and the nervous system, which in turn affect social behavior.

Cultural factors. Society's views of drug use, as determined by custom and tradition, affect our initial approach to and use of a particular drug.

Social factors. The motivation for taking a particular drug is affected by needs such as diminishing physical pain; curing an illness; providing relaxation; relieving stress or anxiety; trying to escape reality; self-medicating; heightening awareness; wanting to distort and change visual, auditory, or sensory inputs; or strengthening confidence. Included in the category of social factors is the belief that attitudes about drug use develop from the values and attitudes of other drug users; the norms in their communities, subcultures, peer groups, and families; and the drug user's personal experiences with using drugs. These are also known as *influencing social factors.*

Contextual factors. Specific contexts define and determine personal dispositions toward drug use, as demonstrated by moods and attitudes about such activity. Specifically, these factors encompass the drug-taking social behavior that develops from the physical surroundings where the drug is used. For example, drugs may be taken at fraternity parties, outdoors in a secluded area with other drug users, in private homes, secretly at work, or at rock concerts.

Paying attention to the cultural, social, and contextual factors of drug use leads us to explore the sociology and psychology of drug use. Equally important are the pharmacological factors and consequences that directly focus on how the drugs taken affect the body — primarily the central nervous system (CNS) and the mind.

Although substances that affect both mind and body functioning are commonly called **drugs**, researchers in the field of drug or substance abuse use a more precise term: **psychoactive drugs (substances)**. Why the preference in the use of this term

Examples of drugs that can easily be abused.

Examples of illicit types of drugs that can become costly once drug dependence occurs.

as opposed to *drugs*? Because the term *psychoactive drugs* is more precise in referring to *how* drugs affect the body. This term focuses on the particular effects these substances have on the CNS and emphasizes how they alter consciousness and perception. Because of their effects on the brain, psychoactive drugs can be used to treat physical or mental illness. Because the body can tolerate increasingly larger doses of them, many psychoactive drugs are used in progressively greater and more uncontrollable amounts to achieve the same level of effect. For many substances, a user is at risk of moving from occasional to regular use or from moderate use to heavy to chronic use. Whenever the drug is not supplied, a chronic user may then risk **addiction** (mostly psychological attachment) and experience **withdrawal symptoms** that are either physical and/or psychological in nature whenever the drug is not supplied.

Generally speaking, any substance that modifies the nervous system and states of consciousness is a drug. Such modification enhances, inhibits, or distorts the functioning of the body, thereby affecting patterns of behavior and social functioning. Psychoactive drugs are classified as either **licit** (legal) or **illicit** (illegal). (See Table 1.1 for a list of slang terms used by drug users.) For example, coffee, tea, cocoa, alcohol, tobacco, and **over-the-counter (OTC)** drugs are licit. When licit drugs are used in moderation, they often are socially acceptable. Marijuana, cocaine, and lysergic acid diethylamide (LSD) are examples of illicit drugs. Any use of these drugs is not generally socially acceptable by larger society or legally allowed.

Researchers have made some interesting findings about legal and illegal drug use:

1. The use of such legal substances as alcohol and tobacco is much more common than the use of illegal drugs such as marijuana, heroin, and LSD. Other legal drugs, such as depressants and stimulants, although less popular

KEY TERMS

addiction
generally refers to the psychological attachment to a drug(s); addiction to "harder" drugs such as heroin results in both psychological and physical attachment to the chemical properties of the drug, with the resulting satisfaction (reward) derived from using the drug in question

withdrawal symptoms
psychological and physical symptoms that result when a drug is absent from the body; physical symptoms are generally present in the cases of drug dependence to more addictive drugs such as heroin; physical and psychological symptoms of withdrawal include perspiration, nausea, boredom, anxiety, and muscle spasms

licit drugs
legalized drugs such as coffee, alcohol, and tobacco

illicit drugs
illegal drugs such as marijuana, cocaine, and LSD

over-the-counter (OTC)
drugs sold without a prescription

Table 1.1 Slang Drug Terms
Street Terms Relating to Drugs and Drug Use

What slang drug terms do users employ for their drug use today? This table is a sampling of the many different terms used.

ACAPULCO GOLD: A very potent strain of marijuana from Acapulco, Mexico

ACID: LSD

ACID HEAD: User of LSD, "acid freak"

AIRHEAD: Under the influence of marijuana

ALLEY JUICE: Very cheap wine, "grapes"

ANGEL DUST: Phencyclidine or PCP

ARTILLERY: Equipment for shooting drugs

BACK-UP: Permitting blood to back up into a syringe to ensure the needle is in a vein

BAD TRIP: Unpleasant LSD experience

BAG: Packet of drugs, usually a standard amount for sale

BAG MAN: Person who transports money

BEAN: Capsules for drugs

BEAT: To cheat someone

BENNIES: Benzedrine, "peaches"

BIG C: Cocaine

BIG CHIEF: Mescaline

BIG MAN: Supplier of drugs

BINDLE: A small packet of drug powder

BLACK BEAUTIES: Amphetamines

BLACK HOLLIES: Amphetamines

BLASTED: High on drugs

BLAZE: Marijuana

BLOTTERS: LSD

BLOW: Smoke marijuana, sniff cocaine

BLUE DEVILS: Amo barbital

BLUNTS: A cigar slit open and filled with marijuana

BOMBED OUT: Very much intoxicated by narcotics

BOMBITA: Mixture of cocaine and heroin

BONG: A cylindrical water pipe for smoking narcotics, especially marijuana

BOOST: To steal

BOOZE, JUICE, SAUCE: Alcohol

BREAD: Money

BRICK: A kilogram (2.2 pounds) of tightly compacted marijuana or hashish

BRING DOWN: Come off a drug

BROKER: Go-between for a drug deal

BUDS: Marijuana

BUMMER: Bad experience with drugs

BURN: Cheated by a pusher

BURNOUT: Heavy user of drugs

BUSTED: Arrested on a drug-related charge

BUTTONS: Peyote or mushrooms

BUZZED: Mildly intoxicated

CACTUS: Mescaline or peyote

CANDY: Barbiturates or cocaine

CANDYMAN: Drug supplier

CARTWHEELS: Amphetamines

CHARGED UP: Under the influence of drugs

CHASING THE DRAGON: A particular way of inhaling heroin

CHINA WHITE: A very pure, white heroin

CHIPPING: Occasional use of drugs

Table 1.1   (continued)

CHIPPY: Person who uses drugs infrequently	DRUGGIE: A narcotic user or addict
CLEAN: Drug free; not having drugs in one's possession	DRUNK PILLS: Valium
COASTING: Being high on drugs	DUST: Narcotics in powder form
COCAINE: Also known as blow crack, coke, booth, railers, snow, ringer, divits, toot, cola, rocks, blast, white dust, ivory flakes, nose candy, mobbeles	DUSTING: Sprinkling a narcotic powder on another drug such as PCP or marijuana
	DYNAMITE: High-quality, potent drugs
COKE BROKE: Financially incapacitated from supporting cocaine habit	EASY SCORE: Obtaining drugs without difficulty
COLOMBO: Marijuana grown in Colombia	EIGHTH: One-eighth of a pound of drugs
COME DOWN: The ending of a drug experience	ELEPHANT: PCP
CONNECT: To purchase drugs	EXPERIENCE: Trip on LSD
COOKER: Usually a spoon or bottle cap used to heat drugs for injection	FACTORY: Place where illicit drugs are prepared for sale
COP: To obtain drugs	FIX: An injection of drugs
COP-OUT: To evade an issue	FLASHBACK: Recurrence of previous hallucinations
CRACK: Cocaine prepared for smoking	FLEA POWDER: Poor-quality drugs
CRASH: To sleep off the effects of drugs	FLIP OUT: Become psychotic or irrational
CRYSTALS: Methamphetamine	FLYING: Under the influence of drugs
CUT: To adulterate drugs	FOOTBALL: Amphetamine
CUT OUT: To leave from someplace	FREEBASE: Smoking cocaine from a special water pipe
DAGGA: South African word for marijuana	FREEZE: To renege on a drug transaction
DEALER: Someone who sells illegal drugs	FRONT: To put money out before receiving the merchandise
DEXIES: Dexedrine, or "dex"	
DIME BAG: $10 worth of a narcotic	FUZZ: The police
DOLLIES: Methadone	GANJA: The Jamaican word for marijuana
DOWNS: Depressants such as barbiturates, tranquilizers	GET OFF: Feel a drug's effects
	GET ON: Use drugs for the first time
	GLUEY: A glue sniffer
DRIED OUT: Having gone through a withdrawal program for drugs or alcohol	GOLD: Marijuana, also called Acapulco
DROP: To take drugs orally; a place where money or drugs are left	GOODS: Drugs
	GOOFBALLS: Barbiturates *(continued)*

Table 1.1 *(continued)*

GRAM: A metric measure of weight	HUFFING: Inhaling solvents from a bag
GRASS: Marijuana	HUSTLE: Attempt to obtain drug customers
GUN: Equipment for injecting drugs	HYPE: Narcotic addict
HAPPY DUST: Cocaine	ICE CREAM HABIT: Occasional drug use
HARD STUFF: Narcotics	IN: Connected with drug suppliers
HASH: Marijuana	ISOMERIZER: Used to increase potency of THC in marijuana
HAY: Marijuana	JAG: Extended period of using a drug
HEAD: Someone who uses drugs frequently	JIVE: Marijuana
HEAD SHOP: Store specializing in the sale of drug paraphernalia	JOINT: A marijuana cigarette
HEARTS: Dexedrine	JOY POPPING: Occasional use of drugs
HEAVEN: Cocaine	JUICE: Alcohol
HEAVENLY BLUE: Morning glory seeds; a hallucinogen	JUNK: Heroin, so named because it's never pure when sold on the street
HEAVY BURNER: A person who smokes a lot of dope, a burnout	JUNKIE: An opiate addict
HEELED: Having plenty of money	KEY: Kilogram
HERB: Marijuana	KICK: To stop using drugs
HEROIN: Also known as China white, fix, horse, smack, whack, mother pearl, H, junk	KICKBACK: Relapse back into drug usage
HIGH: To be intoxicated on drugs	KIDDIE DOPE: Usually prescription drugs
HIT: A single dose of drugs	KILLER: Strong drug
HOG: PCP	KILLER WEED: Strong marijuana, or marijuana sprinkled with PCP
HOLDING: In possession of drugs	KILO: 2.2 pounds; also called "key"
HOME GROWN: Locally grown marijuana; local weed; ditch weed	KIT: Equipment used to inject drugs
HOOKED: Addicted	LAUGHING GAS: Nitrous oxide (inhalant)
HOPPED UP: Under the influence of drugs	LEMONADE: Poor-quality drugs
HORSE: Heroin	LETTUCE: Money
HOT: Wanted by authorities	LEAPERS: Amphetamines
HOT SHOT: Fatal injection of drugs	LID: One ounce or less of marijuana
HUFFER: Glue sniffer	LINE: A dose of cocaine arranged in a line on a smooth surface

Table 1.1 (*continued*)

LOAD: A large quantity of drugs	NARC: Narcotic agent
LOADED: High on drugs or alcohol	NEEDLE FREAK: A person who prefers to take drugs with a needle
LOCKER ROOM: Butyl nitrite (inhalant)	NICKEL BAG: A $5 bag of drugs
LSD: Lysergic acid diethylamide; also known as acid, microdots, purple haze, blotters, fry, blaze, tab, dose, gel, pyramid, trips	NORML: National Organization for the Reform of Marijuana Laws; lobbies for lenient drug laws
LUDES: Methaqualone, Quaaludes, Valium	NUGGET: Marijuana
MAINLINE: Inject a drug directly into a vein, "shoot up"	O.D.: Overdosed on drugs
MAINLINER: A person who injects directly into the vein	ON: Under the influence of a drug
MAN: Police	ON A TRIP: Under the influence of drugs
MANICURE: Remove seeds from marijuana	ON ICE: In jail
MARIJUANA: Also known as buds, bhang, dope, goof butt, grass, hash, hay, hemp, herb, jive, pot, rope, stinkweed, stuff, tea, weed, wacky tobaccky, whack	ON THE NOD: Under the influence of narcotics or depressants
MARY JANE: Marijuana	OUT OF IT: Under the influence of drugs
MARIJUANA CIGARETTE: Also known as bone, doobie, joint, J, reefer, spliff	O.Z.: One ounce
	PAKALOLO: Hawaiian term for marijuana
MATCHBOX: Measurement for a small amount of marijuana	PANAMA GOLD, RED: Potent marijuana grown in Panama
MESCALINE: Also known as mess, crystal	PANIC: Drugs not available
MEET: Buyer and seller get together	PAPERS: Rolling papers, used to make marijuana or tobacco cigarettes
MERCHANDISE: Drugs	PARAPHERNALIA: Accessories used to take drugs
METHADONE: Also known as junk, burdock, jungle juice	PCP: Phencyclidine; also known as angel dust, kools sherms, high, wet daddies, dust, juice
MICRODOT: A tablet containing LSD	
MISS EMMA: Morphine	PEACE PILLS: PCP
MONKEY: Drug dependency; a kilogram of a narcotic	PEPSI HABIT: Occasional use of drugs
MULE: A carrier of drugs	PEANUTS: Barbiturates
MUNCHIES: The hunger that follows after using marijuana	PEYOTE: Hallucinogenic cactus, buttons
	PICKUP: Purchase drugs
MUSHROOMS: Also known as magic mushrooms, shrooms, mushies	PIECE: Usually one ounce of drugs
NAILED: Arrested	PINKS: Seconal (barbiturate)

(*continued*)

Table 1.1 (*continued*)

PLANT: A hiding place for drugs	SINSEMILLA OR SINS: A potent type of marijuana without seeds grown in northern California
POPPERS: Amyl nitrite capsules (inhalant)	SKIN POPPING: To inject a drug under the skin
POT: Marijuana	SMACK: Heroin
POTHEAD: Marijuana user	SNAPPERS: Amyl nitrite capsules (inhalant)
POWER HITTER: A device (often plastic) used to deliver a blast of marijuana smoke to the lungs	SNORT: To inhale cocaine through the nostrils
QUACK: Doctor	SNOW: Cocaine
RAINBOWS: Barbiturate	SNOW BIRD: Dependent on cocaine
RAP: (1) To talk with someone; (2) charged with a crime	SPACE CADET: Habitual user of marijuana
RED DEVILS: Seconal (barbiturate)	SPACED OUT: Under the influence of drugs
REEFER: Marijuana	SPACED: Unresponsive to surroundings
RIG: The paraphernalia for injecting drugs	SPEED, CRYSTAL, CRANK, METH, BLACK BEAUTIES, BENNIES, UPPERS, DEXIES, 357 MAGNUMS: Amphetamines
RIDING THE WAVE: Under the influence of drugs	
RIPPED OFF: Robbed	SPEEDBALL: A mixture of cocaine and heroin; "Bombita"
ROACH: The stub of a marijuana cigarette	SPEED FREAK: Person who repeatedly takes amphetamines, usually intravenously
ROACH CLIP: Any tweezers-like device used to hold a marijuana cigarette stub that is too short to hold in the fingers	SPIKE: Needle used to inject drugs
	SPOONS: Paraphernalia associated with cocaine, often worn as jewelry
RUSH: An intense surge of pleasure; butyl nitrite inhalant	STAR DUST: Cocaine
SAUCE: Alcohol	STASH: A place where drugs are hidden
SCAT: Heroin	STEP ON: To dilute drugs
SCHOOL BOY: Codeine	STICK: A marijuana cigarette
SCORE: To locate and purchase a quantity of drugs	STIMULANTS: Pep pills
SCRIPT WRITER: A doctor willing to write a prescription for faked symptoms	STONED: Under the influence of drugs
SET UP: (1) To arrange to have a person arrested for drugs; (2) combination of uppers and downers (barbiturates and amphetamines)	STRAIGHT: Not using drugs
	STRUNG OUT: Heavily addicted to drugs
SHOOTING GALLERY: Place where addicts inject drugs	STUFF: Drugs
SHOOT UP: To inject intravenously	SUPERMAN: LSD blotter with Superman imprint
SHOTGUN: A way of smoking marijuana, by blowing smoke back through the joint into another's mouth	TASTE: A small sample of drugs

Table 1.1 (*continued*)

TEA: Marijuana	UNCLE: Federal agents
THAI STICKS: Marijuana laced with opium	UPPERS: Stimulants, amphetamines
TOBACCO: Also known as butt, chew, weed, cig	VALIUM: Ludes, drunk pills, v's blues
TOKE: Inhaling marijuana or hashish smoke	WACKY TOBACCKY: Marijuana
TOLLEY: Toluene; a cheap, extremely harmful paint solvent (inhalant)	WASTED: Intoxicated, strung out
TOOT: To sniff cocaine	WEED: Marijuana
TOOTER: Small, hollow tube (strawlike) to sniff cocaine	WHITE: Cocaine
	WHITE LIGHTNING: LSD
TO PARTY: Refers to having a good time using alcohol and other drugs	WIRED: Addicted to amphetamines or heroin
TRACKS: A row of needle marks on the skin	WORKS: Equipment for injecting drugs
TRAP: A hiding place for drugs	YELLOW JACKETS: Nembutal, barbiturate
TRIP: Under the influence of drugs	YEN: A strong craving
TURF: A location where drugs are sold	ZIGZAG: A brand of rolling papers used to make marijuana cigarettes
TURKEY: A substitute sold as a specific drug	ZOMBIE: Heavy user of drugs
TURNED ON: Introduced to drugs, or under the influence of drugs	ZONKED: Extremely high on drugs
TWEEZES: A wild variety of psilocybin mushrooms (hallucinogen)	

Source: Office of National Drug Control Policy. *Street Terms.* http://www.whitehousedrugpolicy.gov/streetterms/byalpha.asp. Accessed 5/30/05.

than alcohol and tobacco, are still more widely used than heroin and LSD.

2. The popular use of licit drugs, particularly alcohol and tobacco, has caused far more deaths, sickness, violent crimes, economic loss, and other social problems than the combined use of all illicit drugs.

3. Societal reaction to various drugs changes with time and place. Today, opium is an illegal drug and widely condemned as a *pan-pathogen* (a cause of all ills). In the 18th and 19th centuries, however, it was a legal drug and was popularly praised as a *panacea* (a cure for all ills). Alcohol use was widespread in the United States in the early 1800s, became illegal during the 1920s, and then was legalized a

second time and has been widely used since the 1930s. Cigarette smoking is legal in all countries today. In the 17th century, it was illegal in most countries, and smokers were sometimes harshly punished. For example, in Russia, smokers could lose their noses; in Hindustan (India), they could lose their lips; and in China, they could lose their heads (Thio 1983, 1995, 2000). Today, new emphasis in the United States on the public health hazards from cigarettes again is leading some people to consider new measures to restrict or even outlaw tobacco smoking.

Table 1.2 introduces some of the terminology that you will encounter throughout this text. It is

Table 1.2 Commonly Used Terms

TERM	DESCRIPTION
Gateway drugs	The word *gateway* suggests a path leading to something else. Alcohol, tobacco, and marijuana are the most commonly used drugs. Almost all abusers of more powerfully addictive drugs have first experimented with these three substances.
Medicines	Generally, these drugs are prescribed by a physician to prevent or treat the symptoms of an illness.
Prescription medicines	These drugs are prescribed by a physician. Common examples include antibiotics, antidepressants, and drugs prescribed to relieve pain, induce stimulation, or induce relaxation. These drugs are taken under a physician's recommendation because they are more potent than OTC drugs. The amount spent on prescription medicines is approximately $94 billion per year. Approximately 2.5 billion prescriptions are dispensed by physicians to their patients (Goode 1999, p. 141).
Over-the-counter (OTC)	These drugs are sold without a prescription. Recently, OTC drugs accounted for $15 billion per year in retail sales (Goode 1999). OTC drugs can be purchased at will without first seeking medical advice. Examples include aspirin, laxatives, diet pills, cough suppressants, and sore throat medicines. Often, these drugs are misused or abused (overused).
Drug misuse	The unintentional or inappropriate use of prescribed or OTC drugs. Misuse includes, but is not limited to, (1) taking more drugs than prescribed; (2) using OTC or psychoactive drugs in excess without medical supervision; (3) mixing drugs with alcohol or other drugs, often to accentuate euphoric effects; (4) using old medicines to self-treat new symptoms of an illness or ailment; (5) discontinuing certain prescribed drugs at will or against a physician's recommendation; and (6) administering prescription drugs to family members or friends without medical consultation and supervision.
Drug abuse	Also known as *chemical or substance abuse.* The willful misuse of either licit or illicit drugs for recreation, perceived necessity, or convenience. Drug abuse differs from drug use in that *drug use* is taking or using drugs, whereas *drug abuse* is a more intense and often willful misuse of drugs, often to the point of addiction.
Drug addiction	Drug addiction involves noncasual or nonrecreational drug use. A frequent symptom is intense psychological preoccupation with obtaining and consuming drugs. Most often psychological and — in some cases, depending on the drug — physiological symptoms of withdrawal are often manifested when the craving for the drug is not satisfied. Today, more emphasis is placed on the psychological craving (mental attachment) to the drug than on the more physiological-based withdrawal symptoms of addiction. (See Chapter 4 for more detailed information regarding addiction and the addiction process.)

Source: Goode, E. *Drugs in American Society,* 5th ed. Boston, MA: McGraw-Hill College, 1999.

important that you understand how the definitions vary.

MOST COMMONLY ABUSED DRUGS

In looking at drug use, this book examines the following topics: (1) OTC drugs (the drugs most sub-ject to abuse), (2) prescription drugs, (3) other drugs and compounds not taken for a medical need or necessity but for pleasure or relief from boredom, stress, or anxiety, and (4) some of the most important information that results from drug use (for example, theories of why drugs are used, legality of drugs, addiction, bodily effects of drug use, lifestyles of drug users, and drug abuse treatment and prevention).

To begin, we now briefly examine the major drugs of use and often abuse. The drugs examined next are stimulants, hallucinogens and other similar compounds, depressants, alcohol, nicotine, cannabis (marijuana and hashish), anabolic steroids, inhalants/organic solvents, narcotics/opiates, and designer drugs. A brief overview is provided here, and these same drugs are discussed in much more detail in separate chapters throughout this book.

Stimulants

Although some of these drugs can be considered to be gateway drugs (see definition in Table 1.2), these substances act on the CNS by increasing alertness, excitation, euphoria, pulse rate, and blood pressure. Insomnia and loss of appetite are common outcomes. The user initially experiences pleasant effects, such as a sense of increased energy and a state of euphoria, or "high." In addition, users feel restless and talkative and have trouble sleeping. High doses used over the long term can produce personality changes. Some of the psychological risks associated with chronic stimulant use include violent, erratic, or paranoid behavior. Other effects can include confusion, anxiety and depression, and loss of interest in sex or food. Major stimulants include amphetamines, cocaine and crack, methamphetamine ("meth"), and methylphenidate. Minor stimulants include caffeine, tea, chocolate, and nicotine (the most addictive minor stimulant).

Hallucinogens/Psychedelics and Other Similar Drugs

Either synthetic or grown naturally, these drugs produce very intense alteration of perceptions, thoughts, and feelings. They most certainly influence the complex inner working of the human mind, causing users to refer to these drugs as *psychedelics* (because they cause hallucinations or distortion of reality and thinking). For example, while under their influence, these drugs can affect the sense of taste, smell, hearing, and vision. Tolerance to hallucinogens builds very rapidly, which means that increasing amounts of this drug are needed for similar effects. Hallucinogens include LSD, mescaline, phencyclidine (PCP), psilocybin

or "magic mushrooms," and the more potent (hybrid) varieties of marijuana, hashish, and opium that are smoked as well as a newer type known as ketamine.

Depressants

These drugs depress the CNS. If taken in a high enough quantity, they produce insensibility or stupor. Depressants are also taken for some of the same reasons as hallucinogens, such as to relieve boredom, stress, and anxiety. In addition, the effects of both opioids (drugs that are derived from opium) and morphine derivatives appeal to many people who are struggling with emotional problems and looking for physical and emotional relief and in some cases, to induce sleep. Depressants include alcohol (ethanol), barbiturates, benzodiazepines (such as diazepam [Valium]), and methaqualone (Quaaludes).

Alcohol

Known as a **gateway drug, ethanol** is a colorless, volatile, and pungent liquid resulting from fermented grains, berries, and other fruits. Alcohol is a depressant that mainly affects the CNS. Excessive amounts of alcohol often cause a progressive loss of inhibitions, flushing and dizziness, loss of coordination, impaired motor skills, blurred vision, slurred speech, sudden mood swings, vomiting, irregular pulse, and memory impairment. Chronic heavy use may lead to high blood pressure, arrhythmia (irregular heartbeat), and cirrhosis (severe liver deterioration).

Nicotine

Nicotine is also considered a gateway drug. It is a very addictive, colorless, highly volatile liquid alkaloid found in all tobacco products, including

KEY TERMS

gateway drugs
alcohol, tobacco, and marijuana — types of drugs that, when used excessively, may lead to using other and often stronger and/or more addictive drugs such as hallucinogens, cocaine, crack, and heroin

ethanol
pharmacological term for alcohol

cigarettes, chewing tobacco, pipe tobacco, and cigars. Because nicotine is highly addictive and tobacco use is still socially acceptable under certain circumstances, smokers often start young and have a very difficult time quitting. Long-term use of tobacco products can lead to several different chronic respiratory ailments and cancers.

Marijuana (Cannabis) and Hashish

Cannabis is the most widely used illicit drug in the United States. Marijuana consists of the dried and crushed leaves, flowers, stems, and seeds of the *Cannabis sativa* plant, which readily grows in many parts of the world. Delta 9-tetrahydrocannabinol (THC) is the primary psychoactive, mind-altering ingredient in marijuana that produces euphoria ("a high"). Plant parts are usually dried, crushed, and smoked much like tobacco products. Other ways of ingesting marijuana include crushing the leaves into cookie or brownie batter and baking the batter. Hashish is another cannabis derivative that contains the purest form of resin and contains the highest amount of THC.

Anabolic Steroids

Steroids are a synthetic form of the male hormone testosterone. They are often used to increase muscle size and strength. Medically, steroids are used to increase body tissue or to treat allergies. Steroids are available either in liquid or pill form. Athletes have a tendency to use and abuse these drugs because dramatic results can occur with regard to body mass and muscle tissue. Some side effects include heart disease, liver cancer, high blood pressure, septic shock, impotence, genital atrophy, manic episodes, depression, violence, and mood swings.

Inhalants/Organic Solvents

Inhalants and organic solvents are also often considered gateway drugs and are very attractive to and popular among preteens and younger teenagers. Products used include gasoline, airplane glue, and paint thinner. When inhaled, the vapors from these solvents can produce euphoric effects. Organic solvents can also refer to certain foods, herbs, and vitamins, such as "herbal Ecstasy." [Appendix B lists (1) the most commonly abused drugs in society, (2) their more common street

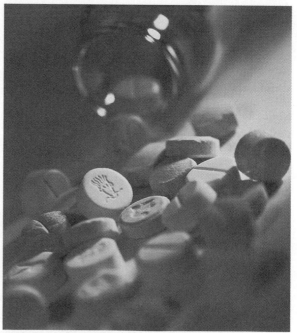

Designer pills made from the illicit drug Ecstasy. This drug has some stimulant properties like amphetamines as well as hallucinogenic properties like LSD.

Inhalants. These volatile chemicals, which include many common household substances, are often the most dangerous drugs, per dose, that a person can take. In addition, inhalants are most often used by young preteens and younger teenagers.

names/terms, (3) medical uses, (4) routes of administration, (5) Drug Enforcement Administration (DEA) schedules, and (6) duration of detection in the body.]

Narcotics/Opiates

These drugs also depress the CNS and if taken in a high enough quantity, they produce insensibility or stupor. Narcotics include opium, morphine, codeine, and meperidine (Demerol).

Designer Drugs/Synthetic Drugs or Synthetic Opioids

In addition to the most commonly abused illicit drug categories just described, innovations in technology have produced new categories known as **designer drugs/synthetic drugs or synthetic opioids**. These relatively new types of drugs are developed by people who seek to circumvent the illegality of a drug by modifying the drug into a new compound. Ecstasy is an example of a designer drug/synthetic

Here and Now

Recent Abuse of Prescription and Performance-Enhancing Drugs

In the United States, young people frequently abuse prescription drugs; the only illicit drug that is abused more frequently is marijuana (USDOJ 2004). An estimated 6.3 million persons were current users of psychotherapeutic drugs taken nonmedically (see Table 1.4). For example, according to the 2000 National Household Survey on Drug Abuse (NHSDA), 10.9% of 12- to 17-year-olds reported nonmedical use of any psychotherapeutic drug at least once during their lifetime compared with 18.3% who reported having abused marijuana.

Three categories of prescription drugs that are currently abused are narcotics, depressants, and stimulants. *Narcotics* (OxyContin, Vicodin, and Percocet) include analgesics or opioids that are generally prescribed for physical pain. Abuse occurs when they are used nonmedically because of their euphoric and numbing effects. *Depressants* (Xanax, Valium, and Librium) are generally used to treat anxiety and sleep disorders. These drugs are abused because of their sedating properties. *Stimulants* (Ritalin, Dexedrine, and Meridia) are used to treat attention deficit disorder (ADD), attention deficit hyperactivity disorder (ADHD), and asthma. These drugs are abused because of their euphoric effects and energizing potential (Publishers Group 2004).

The two drugs in this stimulant category that are most often abused are Ritalin (methylphenidate hydrochloride) and Adderall (amphetamine). These prescription drugs are legitimately prescribed for ADHD, ADD, and narcolepsy (a sleep disorder) (CESAR 2003). When used nonmedically, they are taken orally as tablets or the tablets are crushed into a powder and snorted (a far more popular method). Students often illegally purchase these tablets for $5 each from other students who have a legal prescription for the medication.

> I feel like Dr. Pill. All these brothers [fraternity brothers] are always looking for me at parties so that I can sell them a few tabs. What the heck, I make extra money selling Ritalin, enough to buy essentials like beer and cigarettes. *(From Venturelli's research files, 20-year-old male undergraduate student at a Midwestern university, December 9, 2004.)*

These drugs are often used in conjunction with alcohol or marijuana to enhance the "high" or for staying awake so as to increase comprehension and remain focused while reading or studying for an exam (CESAR 2003). Both prescription drugs are readily available and can be easily obtained by teenagers, who may abuse these drugs to experience a variety of desired effects. Increasingly, younger adolescents are obtaining prescription drugs from classmates, friends, and family members, or are stealing the drugs from school medicine dispensaries and from family members or other people for whom the drug has been legitimately prescribed.

Ritalin and Adderall abusers tend to be high school and college students. "A 2002 national survey found that 3% to 5% of students in grades 8, 10, and 12 reported using Ritalin without medical supervision at least in the past year" (Johnston et al. 2003). Further, in a 2002 study conducted at the University of Wisconsin at Madison, one out of five students reported taking such drugs nonmedically (Nichols 2004).

drug or synthetic opioid. Such drugs are created as **structural analogs** of substances already scheduled and forbidden under the Controlled Substances Act (CSA). Structural analogs are the drugs that result from altered chemical structures of already existing illicit drugs. Generally, these drugs are created by underground chemists whose goal is to make a profit by creating compounds that mimic, change, or intensify the psychoactive effects of controlled substances. The number of designer drugs that are created and sold illegally is very large.

Anyone with knowledge of college-level chemistry can alter the chemical ingredients and produce new designer drugs, although it may be nearly impossible to predict their properties or effects except by trial and error. Currently, three major types of synthetic analog drugs are available through the illicit drug market: analogs of PCP; analogs of fentanyl and meperidine (both synthetic narcotic analgesics) such as Demerol, MPPP (called MPTP, or PEPAP); and analogs of amphetamine and methamphetamine (which have stimulant and hallucinogenic properties) such as **MDMA**, known as "Ecstasy" or "Adam," which is widely used on college campuses as a euphoriant.

The production of these high-technology psychoactive substances is a sign of the new levels of risk and additional challenge to the criminal justice system. As the production and risk associated with the use of such substances increase, the need for a broader, better-informed view of drug use becomes even more important than in the past.

An Overview of Drugs in Society

Many people think that problems with drugs are unique to this era. In reality, drug use and abuse have always been part of nearly all — past and present — human societies. For example, the Grecian oracles of Delphi used drugs, Homer's Cup of Helen induced sleep and provided freedom from care, and the mandrake root mentioned in the first book of the Bible, Genesis, produced a hallucinogenic effect. In Genesis 30:14–16, the mandrake is mentioned in association with bartering for lovemaking:

In the time of wheat harvest Reuben went out, found some mandrakes in the open country, and brought them to his mother Leah. Then Rachel asked Leah for some of her son's mandrakes, but Leah said, "Is it so small a thing to have taken away my husband, that you should take my son's mandrakes as well?" However, Rachel said, "Very well, let him sleep with you tonight in exchange for your son's mandrakes." So when Jacob came in from the country in the evening, Leah went out to meet him and said, "You are to sleep with me tonight; I have hired you with my son's mandrakes." That night he slept with her.

Ancient literature is filled with references to the use of mushrooms, *datura*, hemp, marijuana, opium poppies, and so on. Under the influence of some of these drugs, many people experienced extreme ecstasy or sheer terror. Some old pictures of demons and devils look very much like those described by modern drug users during so-called bummers, or bad trips. The belief that witches could fly may also have been drug-induced because many natural preparations used in so-called witches' brews induced the sensation of disassociation from the body, as in flying or floating.

As far back as 2240 B.C., attempts were made to regulate drug use. For instance, in that year, problem drinking was addressed in the Code of Hammurabi, where it was described as "a problem of men with too much leisure time and lazy dispositions." Nearly every culture has experienced drug abuse, and as part of its historical record, laws were enacted to control the use of certain types of drugs.

HOW WIDESPREAD IS DRUG ABUSE?

As mentioned earlier, drug abuse today is more acute and widespread than in any previous age. The evidence for this development is how often large quantities of illicit drugs are seized in the United States as well as throughout the world (see "Here and Now," Current Global Status of Illicit Drug Use in Selected Countries). Media exposure about illicit drug use is more likely to occur today than in the past. On any given day, you can scan most major national and international newspapers and run across stories about illegal drug manufacture, storage and distribution, use and/or abuse, and convictions. Drug use is an "**equal-opportunity affliction**." This means that no one is immune from the use and/or abuse of both licit and illicit drugs. Research shows that drug consumption is found across the many different income, education, social class, occupation, race and ethnic, lifestyle, and age groups. To date, no one has proved to be immune from drug use and/or abuse. (See "Here and Now," How Widespread Is the Use of Drugs?, on page 24.)

An example of a situation that requires clear thinking without the use of mind-altering drugs.

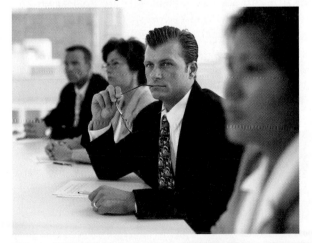

Many of us, for example, are dismayed or surprised when we discover that certain individuals we admire — our family members, close friends, workmates, celebrities, politicians, athletes, clergy, law enforcement personnel, physicians, academics, and even the seemingly upstanding man or woman next door — either admit to, are accused of, or arrested for either licit and/or illicit drug use.

We are also taken aback when we hear that cigarettes, alcohol, and marijuana abuse are commonplace in many public and private junior high schools. Furthermore, most of us know of at least one (and many times more than one) close friend or family member who appears to secretly or not so secretly use drugs.

EXTENT AND FREQUENCY OF DRUG USE IN SOCIETY

Erich Goode (2005), a much-respected sociologist, lists four types of drug use:

1. *Legal instrumental use.* Taking prescribed drugs and OTC drugs to relieve or treat mental or physical symptoms.
2. *Legal recreational use.* Using such licit drugs as tobacco, alcohol, and caffeine to achieve a certain mental or psychic state.
3. *Illegal instrumental use.* Taking drugs without a prescription to accomplish a task or goal, such as taking nonprescription amphetamines to drive through the night or relying excessively on barbiturates to get through the day.
4. *Illegal recreational use.* Taking illicit drugs for fun or pleasure to experience euphoria, such as abusing prescribed methylphenidate (Ritalin) as a substitute for cocaine.

Why has the prevalence of licit and illicit drug use remained consistent since 1988? Why has this trend occurred, when expenditures for fighting the drug war by the federal, state, and local governments have been increasing at the same time?

KEY TERMS

equal-opportunity affliction
refers to the use of drugs, stressing that drug use cuts across all members of society regardless of income, education, occupation, social class, and age

Here and Now

	Current Global Status of Illicit Drug Use in Selected Countries
Afghanistan	World's largest producer of opium; cultivation of opium poppy — used to make heroin — expanded to 30,750 hectares in 2002, despite eradication attempts; potential opium production of 1278 metric tons; source of hashish; many narcotics-processing labs throughout the country; drug trade is a source of instability and some government groups profit from the trade; 80%–90% of the heroin consumed in Europe comes from Afghan opium; vulnerable to narcotics money laundering through informal financial networks.
Argentina	Used as a transshipment country for cocaine headed for Europe and the United States; some money-laundering activity, especially in the Tri-Border Area; domestic consumption of drugs in urban centers is increasing.
Austria	Transshipment point for Southwest Asian heroin and South American cocaine destined for Western Europe.
Bahamas	Transshipment point for cocaine and marijuana bound for the United States and Europe; offshore financial center.
Belgium	Growing producer of synthetic drugs; transit point for U.S.-bound Ecstasy; source of precursor chemicals for South American cocaine processors; transshipment point for cocaine, heroin, hashish, and marijuana entering Western Europe; despite a strengthening of legislation, the country remains vulnerable to money laundering related to narcotics, automobiles, alcohol, and tobacco.
Bolivia	World's third-largest cultivator of coca (after Colombia and Peru) with an estimated 28,450 hectares under cultivation in June 2003 — a 23% increase from June 2002; intermediate coca products and cocaine exported mostly to or through Brazil, Argentina, and Chile to European and U.S. drug markets; eradication and alternative crop programs under the MESA administration have been unable to keep pace with farmers' attempts to increase cultivation; money-laundering activity related to narcotics trade, especially along the borders with Brazil and Paraguay.
Brazil	Illicit producer of cannabis; minor coca cultivation in the Amazon region, used for domestic consumption; government has a large-scale eradication program to control cannabis; important transshipment country for Bolivian, Colombian, and Peruvian cocaine headed for Europe and the United States; also used by traffickers as a way station for narcotics air transshipments between Peru and Colombia; upsurge in drug-related violence and weapons smuggling; important market for Colombian, Bolivian, and Peruvian cocaine; illicit narcotics proceeds earned in Brazil are often laundered through the financial system; significant illicit financial activity in the Tri-Border Area.
Canada	Illicit producer of cannabis for the domestic drug market and export to the United States; use of hydroponics technology permits growers to plant large quantities of high-quality marijuana indoors; transit point for heroin and cocaine entering the U.S. market; vulnerable to narcotics money laundering because of its mature financial services sector.
Colombia	Illicit producer of coca, opium poppy, and cannabis; world's leading coca cultivator (cultivation of coca in 2002 was 144,450 hectares — a 15% decline since 2001); potential production of opium between 2001 and 2002 declined by 25% to 91 metric tons; potential production of heroin declined to 11.3 metric tons; world's largest processor of coca derivatives into cocaine; supplier of about 90% of the cocaine to the U.S. market and the great majority of cocaine to other international drug markets; important supplier of heroin to the U.S. market; active aerial eradication program; a significant portion of non-U.S. narcotics proceeds are either laundered or invested in Colombia through the black-market peso exchange.

Current Global Status of Illicit Drug Use in Selected Countries (*continued*)	
Egypt	Transit point for Southwest Asian and Southeast Asian heroin and opium moving to Europe, Africa, and the United States; transit stop for Nigerian couriers; of concern as a money-laundering site due to its lax financial regulations and enforcement.
Germany	Source of precursor chemicals for South American cocaine processors; transshipment point for and consumer of Southwest Asian heroin, Latin American cocaine, and European-produced synthetic drugs; major financial center.
Greece	Gateway to Europe for traffickers who are smuggling cannabis and heroin from the Middle East and Southwest Asia to the West and precursor chemicals to the East; some South American cocaine transits or is consumed in Greece; money laundering related to drug trafficking and organized crime.
Haiti	Major Caribbean transshipment point for cocaine en route to the United States and Europe; substantial money-laundering activity; Colombian narcotics traffickers favor Haiti for illicit financial transactions; pervasive corruption.
Iran	Despite substantial interdiction efforts, remains a key transshipment point for Southwest Asian heroin to Europe; domestic narcotics consumption remains a persistent problem — according to official Iranian statistics, there are at least 2 million drug users in the country; lax anti-money-laundering regulations.
Israel	Increasingly concerned about cocaine and heroin abuse; drugs arrive in country from Lebanon and, increasingly, from Jordan; money-laundering center.
Mexico	Illicit cultivation of opium poppy (cultivation in 2001: 4400 hectares; potential heroin production: 7 metric tons) and of cannabis (4100 hectares in 2001); government eradication efforts have been key in keeping illicit crop levels low; major supplier of heroin and largest foreign supplier of marijuana and methamphetamine to the U.S. market; remains the primary transshipment country for U.S.-bound cocaine from South America, accounting for 70% of the estimated annual cocaine movement to the United States; major drug syndicates control majority of drug trafficking throughout the country; producer and distributor of Ecstasy; significant money-laundering center.
Netherlands	Major European producer of Ecstasy, illicit amphetamines, and other synthetic drugs; important gateway for cocaine, heroin, and hashish entering Europe; major source of U.S.-bound Ecstasy, large financial sector vulnerable to money laundering.
North Korea	From the 1970s into the 1990s, citizens of the Democratic People's Republic of (North) Korea (DPRK) — many of them diplomatic employees of the government — were apprehended abroad while trafficking in narcotics; in recent years, police investigations in Taiwan and Japan have linked North Korea to large illicit shipments of heroin and methamphetamine, with the attempt by the North Korean merchant ship *Pong Su* to deliver 125 kg of heroin to Australia in April 2003 being the most recent example of Pyongyang's involvement in the drug trade; all indications point to North Korea emerging as an important regional source of illicit drugs targeting markets in Japan, Taiwan, the Russian Far East, and China.
Peru	Until 1996 the world's largest coca leaf producer; emerging opium producer; cultivation of coca in Peru fell 15% to 31,150 hectares between 2002 and the end of 2003; much of the cocaine base is shipped to neighboring Colombia for processing into cocaine, while finished cocaine is shipped out from Pacific ports to the international drug market; increasing amounts of base and finished cocaine, however, are being moved to Brazil and Bolivia for use in the Southern Cone or transshipped to Europe and Africa. *(continued)*

Current Global Status of Illicit Drug Use in Selected Countries (*continued*)	
Russia	Limited cultivation of illicit cannabis and opium poppy and production of methamphetamine, mostly for domestic consumption; government has active illicit crop eradication program; used as transshipment point for Asian opiates, cannabis, and Latin American cocaine bound for growing domestic markets, to a lesser extent Western and Central Europe, and occasionally to the United States; major source of heroin precursor chemicals; corruption and organized crime are key concerns; heroin increasingly popular in domestic market.
Taiwan	Regional transit point for heroin and methamphetamine; major problem with domestic consumption of methamphetamine and heroin; renewal of domestic methamphetamine production is a problem.
United States	Consumer of cocaine shipped from Colombia through Mexico and the Caribbean; consumer of heroin, marijuana, and increasingly methamphetamine from Mexico; consumer of high-quality Southeast Asian heroin; illicit producer of cannabis, marijuana, depressants, stimulants, hallucinogens, and methamphetamine; money-laundering center.
World	*Cocaine:* Worldwide, coca is grown on an estimated 173,450 hectares — almost exclusively in South America with 70% in Colombia; potential cocaine production during 2003 was estimated at 728 metric tons (or 835 metric tons of export-quality cocaine); coca eradication programs continue in Bolivia, Colombia, and Peru; 376 metric tons of export-quality cocaine was seized in 2003, and 26 metric tons was disrupted (jettisoned or destroyed); consumption of export-quality cocaine is estimated to have been 800 metric tons.
	Opiates: Cultivation of opium poppy occurred on an estimated 137,944 hectares in 2003 — mostly in Southwest and Southeast Asia — with 44% in Afghanistan; potentially produced 3775 metric tons of opium, which conceivably could be converted to the equivalent of 429 metric tons of pure heroin; opium eradication programs have been undertaken in Afghanistan, Burma, Colombia, Mexico, Pakistan, Thailand, and Vietnam.

Source: CIA. *The World Fact Book.* Washington, DC: U.S. Government Printing Office, 2004. Available http://www.cia.gov/cia/publications/factbook/fields/2086.html.

There are several possible answers, none of which, by itself, offers a satisfactory response. One perspective notes that practically all of us use drugs in some form, with what constitutes "drug use" being merely a matter of degree. A second explanation is that more varieties of both licit and illicit drugs are available today. One source estimated that approximately 80% of all currently marketed drugs were either unknown or unavailable 20 years ago (Critser 1996). Regarding prescriptions, another source stated, "The retail sales of OTC drugs (aspirin, Tylenol, No-Doz, and so on) totaled $15 billion in 1995"; "$111.1 billion worth of pharmaceutical prescription drugs were sold in 1999" (Pear 2000, A16); "In 2002, 3.34 billion prescriptions were written for Schedule II through Schedule V drugs" (see Chapter 3 for information about drug schedules) (Goode 2005, p. 227).

Pharmacists' records show that in the United States, about $102 billion is spent on psychoactive drug prescriptions (Ananth et al. 2000). In 2002 total worldwide sales for prescription pharmaceuticals were $430 billion (*Pharmacy Times* 2003). In the United States alone, the rate of yearly prescription growth is estimated at approximately 9%–12%. Such figures indicate that it may be more difficult to find people who do *not* use psychoactive drugs compared to individuals who do.

Further, in recent years, a third category of drug sales has joined OTC and prescription drugs: herbal medicines, vitamins, minerals, enzymes, and other natural potions. These drugs were purchased by 123.5 million Americans — totaling $16 billion in 2000 (Spake 2002).

Drug use is so common that even the average household in the United States owns about five drugs, of which two out of the five are prescription drugs, and the other three are OTC drugs. Of the many prescriptions written by physicians, approximately one-third modify moods and behaviors in one way or another. A National Institute on Drug Abuse (NIDA) study and other research indicates that more than 60% of adults in the United States have, at some time in their lives, taken a *psychoactive drug* (one that affects mood or consciousness). More than one-third of adults have used or are using depressants or sedatives. A third explanation is that ". . . in the modern age, increased sophistication has brought with it techniques of drug production and distribution that have resulted in a worldwide epidemic of drug use" (Kusinitz 1988, p. 149). In the 1980s and 1990s, for example, illicit drug cartels proliferated, and varieties of marijuana with ever-increasing potency infiltrated all urban and rural areas as well as the world. Many of these varieties are crossbred with ultrasophisticated techniques and equipment available everywhere.

Finally, even coffee (as discussed in Chapter 10, "Here and Now") has undergone a technological revolution. Higher caffeine content has become available worldwide. This trend has led to the phenomenal growth of the following: (1) franchise duplication of gourmet coffee bars in the United States (such as Starbucks and Three Brothers Coffee), (2) sales of espresso and cappuccino coffee makers for home use, with accompanying coffee grinders, and (3) sales of specialized coffees and teas through a multitude of email coffee/tea clubs.

Approximately 25 years ago, it was difficult to purchase a cup of espresso or cappuccino in a typical restaurant; today, availability of such types of coffees is commonplace. Even at airports, shopping malls, and inner-city coffee shops, it is not unusual to see people lined up waiting to order and purchase their specially made and specially flavored coffee or tea. This is just one example of how caffeine (often seen as a benign drug) has evolved, with many new varieties of coffee beans from exotic islands and countries coming together with more sophisticated electronic equipment, with the result that the idea of simple brewing has been relegated to the past. The standard American "cup of coffee in the morning" has spilled into including coffee during the afternoon and evening. This is a small example of a much-tolerated drug maintaining its own impressive history of development, increased use, complexity in developing many more varieties, and added sophistication.

Drug Use: Statistics, Trends, and the Demographics of Drug Use

An incredible amount of money is spent each year for licit (legal) and illicit (illegal) chemicals that alter consciousness, awareness, or mood. Five classes of these legal chemicals exist:

1. *Social drugs.* Approximately $104 billion is spent for alcohol. Another $51.9 billion is for tobacco products, of which 95% comes from cigarette sales. The other 5% accounts for the $2 billion or so spent on cigars, chewing tobacco, pipe tobacco, roll-your-own tobacco, and snuff tobacco. In addition, $5.7 billion is spent on coffee, tea, and cocoa.

2. *Prescription drugs.* Worldwide, racked up $430 billion in sales for prescription pharmaceuticals in 2002 (*Pharmacy Times* 2003). The United States is the world's largest pharmaceutical market. Annually, Americans spend $176 billion

Often the consumption of drugs (such as caffeine) complements social interaction.

Here and Now

How Widespread Is the Use of Drugs?

In the 1990s, a variety of factors came together in the United States to extend drug abuse beyond just the very rich or the urban poor. The ease of brewing cheaper, more potent strains of speed (methamphetamine, or "meth") and heroin, coupled with the fact that enforcement officials tended to focus on drug abuse and traffic in urban areas on the East and West Coasts, left middle-class and rural populations throughout the country largely overlooked. (See "Youth Drug Use" illustration in the next column.) Suddenly, the illicit drug market was booming where no one had been looking.

By the late 1990s, speed — which had gained popularity in the 1970s among outlaw bikers, college students facing exams, all-night party-goers, and long-haul truckers — was more sought after than ever. Teenagers, middle-class workers, and suburbanites joined the ranks of methamphetamine users. "We've been fighting it really strongly for nearly seven years," Edward Synicky, a special agent with California's Bureau of Narcotics Enforcement, told *Time* magazine in early 1996. "But cocaine gets all the publicity because it's glamorous. And law enforcement in general doesn't put the resources into meth that it should."

Increasingly, the illegal substance was produced in clandestine labs set up by both major drug dealers and individual users. By January 1996, John Coonce, head of the U.S. Drug Enforcement Administration's (DEA's) meth-lab task force, said methamphetamine use was "absolutely epidemic." The surge was attributed largely to powerful Mexican drug syndicates and motorcycle gangs that sold their goods on street corners. Speed acquired the nickname "crank" because it was frequently concealed in motorcycle crankcases.

Clandestine manufacture and use of speed were especially high in the West and Southwest. Speed kitchens flourished in California because it was relatively easy for the Mexican syndicates to smuggle in ephedrine, a key ingredient that is tightly controlled in the United States. From the mid-1980s to the mid-1990s, methamphetamine-related hospitalizations in California rose approximately 366%. In Arizona's Maricopa County, methamphetamine-linked crimes jumped nearly 400%

over a 3-year period in the early 1990s (see the sections The Costs of Drug Use to Society and Drugs, Crime, and Violence in this chapter).

Soon this easy-access drug began spreading across the United States. In 1994, DEA field offices in Houston, Denver, Los Angeles, New Orleans, Phoenix, St. Louis, San Diego, and San Francisco were responsible for approximately 86% of the methamphetamine laboratory seizures in the country. By 1996, however, officials were seizing huge shipments of methamphetamine that originated in Mississippi and Tennessee.

Youth Drug Use

Rural 8th-grade students are more likely to use drugs than their peers in large cities. Here are the results of a survey conducted of the percentage of 8th graders who used drugs during the previous month.

Marijuana
11.6%
8.6%

Amphetamines
5.1%
2.5%

Cocaine
1.5%
1.4%

Crack
1.1%
0.6%

Heroin
0.7%
0.6%

■ Rural towns **(Population less than 50,000)**

☐ Large cities **(Population more than 1 million)**

Source: National Center on Addiction and Substance Abuse at Columbia University. *Monitoring the Future Survey,* Ann Arbor, MI: University of Michigan, 1999.

How Widespread Is the Use of Drugs? (*continued*)

But speed was not the only drug barreling its way across the country. Use of heroin ran rampant as well. In a southeastern Massachusetts fishing community, at least 50 fishermen died of AIDS or other drug-related causes between 1991 and 1996. The captain of one scalloper told a local newspaper, "As a wild guess, I would say that if the fishing industry were to run a blood test and eliminate the people that had drug problems, there would be very few boats sailing with a full crew" (Associated Press 1996). Many skippers cited the ease with which drug users and dealers could find jobs on board ships as one reason for the alarming rise in drug abuse among their ranks.

Even crack cocaine, which was first seen primarily in New York and Los Angeles, infiltrated rural areas. Headlines report that in many U.S. counties, 8th graders in rural areas are using more drugs than urban youth (Briske 2000). According to the DEA, a combination of factors forced some crack distributors to develop new markets in smaller towns and rural areas; Pike County, Mississippi, was hit especially hard. Enforcement officials believed most of the crack in Mississippi came from New Orleans, but some drug shipments originating in South America were flown to remote landing strips in the middle of Mississippi farmland.

Whatever people's reasons for using these dangerous substances, it is clear that an important step toward stemming abuse is to dry up the supply lines to middle America. To accomplish that goal, the law enforcement community must look beyond traditional hotbeds of activity among the urban poor.

Sources: Associated Press. "Survey: Drug Use Pervading New Bedford Fleet." *Maine Sunday Telegram* (21 July 1996).

Briske, P. "Rural Eighth-Graders Using More Drugs Than Urban Kids." *The Times* (27 January 2000): 3. Available at http://www.thetimesonline.com.

National Narcotics Intelligence Consumers Committee, *The NNICC Report, 1994.* Washington, DC: U.S. Drug Enforcement Agency, 1994: 70.

National Public Broadcast (NPR). "All Things Considered." *PM News* (18 September 1996).

Toufonio, A., et al. "There Is No Safe Speed." *Time* (8 January 1990).

Wilkie, C. "Crack Cocaine Moves South." *Boston Globe* (23 June 1996).

each year on prescription drugs (*Pharmacy Times* 2005).

3. ***Over-the-counter (patent) drugs.*** These products account for $23.5 billion in sales, including cough and cold items, external and internal analgesics, antacids, laxatives, antidiarrhea products, sleep aids, sedatives, and so on.

4. ***Nonmedical use of prescription-type drugs.*** In recent years, another alarming statistic related to abuse is the growth of the nonmedical use of prescription-type drugs. In 2001, 36 million Americans (16% of persons aged 12 or older) had used prescription-type drugs nonmedically at least once in their lifetime. This included 9.6 million persons (18%) aged 12 to 25. In 2001, almost 3 million youths aged 12 to 17 (12%) and almost 7 million young adults aged 18 to 25 (23%) had used prescription-type drugs nonmedically at least once in their lifetime. The most common category of prescription-type drugs used nonmedically by youths and young adults in the past year was pain relievers. Pain relievers include codeine, methadone, meperidine (Demerol), Percocet, hydrocodone (Vicodin), and oxycodone (OxyContin) (SAMSHSA January 16, 2003).

5. ***Others.*** The amount spent on inhalants and other miscellaneous drugs, such as nutmeg and morning glory seeds, cannot be estimated.

How much money goes to purchase illicit drugs? The White House Office of National Drug Control Policy conducted a study to determine the amount Americans spent on illicit drugs. It found that between 1988 and 1995, Americans spent $57.3 billion on drugs: $38 billion on cocaine, $9.6 billion on heroin, $7 billion on marijuana, and $2.7 billion on other illegal drugs and on legal drugs that were misused (NIDA 1998).

Further, regarding the extent of drug use, studies carried out by the Social Research Group of George Washington University, the Institute for

Table 1.3 Trend Data on the Prevalence of Illicit Drug Use, 1998–2003

	1998	1999	2000	2001	2002	2003
Used in Past Month						
All ages 12+	6.2	6.3	6.3	7.1	8.3	8.2
12–17	9.9	9.7	9.8	10.8	11.6	11.2
18–25	16.1	16	15.6	18.5	20.2	20.3
26–34	7	7	7.9	9.2	10.8	11.1
35+	3.3	3.2	3.3	3.4	4.6	4.4
Used in Past Year						
All ages 12+	10.6	11.5	11	12.6	14.9	14.7
12–17	16.4	19.79	18.8	20.8	22.2	21.8
18–25	27.4	28.6	27.5	31.59	35.5	34.6
26–34	12.7	13.7	13.7	16.7	19.8	20.1
35+	5.5	5.5	5.5	6.2	8.2	8.1
Used in Lifetime (Ever Used)						
All ages 12+	35.8	39.7	38.9	41.2	46.6	46.4
12–17	21.3	27.6	27.1	28.3	30.9	30.5
18–25	48.1	52.7	51.2	55.6	59.8	60.5
26–34	50.6	52.9	51	53.5	58.2	57.4
35+	31.8	35.4	35.5	38.5	43.9	44.8

This table shows three major trends. First, for all three categories of drug users (used in past month, used in past year, and used in lifetime [ever used]) and within each age group category, there is a very steady and persistent growth in the percentage using illicit drugs from 1998 through 2003. Second, even though in 2002 and 2003 there appeared to be a higher increase (spike) over previous years in the percentage using illicit drugs, *the percentage increases in 2002 and 2003 are not comparable to data for prior years because beginning in 2002 and 2003 the survey questions changed, resulting in what appear to be increases in drug use. As a result, percentage comparisons of these two years with prior years are not possible.* Third, for all three categories of drug users, the heaviest users of drugs are between 18 and 25 years of age.

Illicit drugs include marijuana/hashish, cocaine (including crack), heroin, hallucinogens, inhalants, or any prescription-type psychotherapeutic used nonmedically (sedatives, tranquilizers, stimulants, and analgesics). The figures presented here include use of marijuana, cocaine, hallucinogens, inhalants (except in 1982), heroin, and nonmedical use of sedatives, tranquilizers, stimulants, and analgesics.

Sources: 1998 data: Substance Abuse and Mental Health Services Administration (SAMHSA). *Summary of Findings from the 1998 National Household Survey on Drug Abuse.* Rockville, MD: Office of Applied Studies and Substance Abuse and Mental Health Services Administration, 1999.

1999 and 2000 data: Substance Abuse and Mental Health Services Administration (SAMHSA). *National Household Survey on Drug Abuse, 1999 and 2000.* Rockville, MD: Office of Applied Studies and Substance Abuse and Mental Health Services Administration, 2000.

2001 data: Substance Abuse and Mental Health Services Administration (SAMHSA). *National Household Survey on Drug Abuse, 2000 and 2001.* Rockville, MD: Office of Applied Studies and Substance Abuse and Mental Health Services Administration, 2002.

2002 and 2003 data: Substance Abuse and Mental Health Services Administration (SAMHSA). *Results from the 2003 National Survey on Drug Use and Health: National Findings.* Rockville, MD: Office of Applied Studies, 2004.

Research in Social Behavior in Berkeley, California, and others provide detailed, in-depth data showing that drug use is universal. A major purpose of their studies was to determine the level of psychoactive drug use among people aged 18 through 74, excluding those people hospitalized or in the armed forces. Data were collected to identify people who used specific categories of drugs (that is, caffeine, sleeping pills, nicotine, alcohol, and other psychoactive drugs). Other studies have shown that people in the 18- to 25-year-old age groups are by far the heaviest users and experimenters in terms of past-month and past-year usage (see Table 1.3).

Table 1.3 supports the findings of the Social Research Group of George Washington University. For example, an estimated 60 million Americans aged 12 and older smoked cigarettes in 2003, or 25.4% of the total U.S. population. Statistics also reveal that, in 2003, approximately 118 million Americans (50%) aged 12 and older were drinkers (see Table 1.4).

Table 1.4 National Household Survey on Drug Abuse, 2003

Percentage of population and estimated number of alcohol, tobacco, and illicit drug users in the United States.

	LIFETIME*		PAST MONTH	
	PERCENTAGE	NUMBER OF USERS	PERCENTAGE	NUMBER OF USERS
Alcohol	83.1	197,533,000	50.1	118,066,000
Cigarettes	68.7	163,240,000	25.4	60,434,000
Any illicit drug	46.4	110,205,000	8.2	19,470,000
Marijuana and hashish	40.6	96,611,000	6.2	14,638,000
Smokeless tobacco	19.4	46,065,000	3.3	7,725,000
Nonmedical use of any psychotherapeutic drug[†]	20.1	47,882,000	2.7	6,336,000
Pain relievers	13.1	31,207,000	2.0	4,693,000
Stimulants	8.8	20,798,000	0.5	1,191,000
Methamephetamine	5.2	12,303,000	0.3	607,000
Tranquilizers	8.5	20,220,000	0.8	1,830,000
Sedatives	4.0	9,510,000	0.1	294,000
Hallucinogens	14.5	34,363,000	0.4	1,042,000
LSD	10.3	24,424,000	0.1	133,000
Ecstacy	4.6	10,904,000	0.2	470,000
PCP	3.0	7,107,000	0	56,000
Cocaine	14.7	34,891,000	1.0	2,281,000
Crack	3.3	7,949,000	0.3	604,000
Inhalants	9.7	22,995,000	0.2	570,000

*Lifetime refers to drug use anytime during the lifespan.

[†]Includes pain relievers, tranquilizers, stimulants, and sedatives; does not include over-the-counter drugs.

Source: Substance Abuse and Mental Health Services Administration (SAMHSA). *Overview of Findings from the 2003 National Survey on Drug Use and Health.* Office of Applied Studies, NSDUH Series H-24, DHHS Publication No. SMA 04-3963. Rockville, MD: 2004.

CURRENT PATTERNS OF LICIT AND ILLICIT DRUG USE

Table 1.4 shows that illicit drug use remains an alarming problem. In looking at the use of licit-type and illicit-type drugs, it is estimated that approximately 19.4 million Americans aged 12 or older were current illicit drug users in 2003. This number represents 8.2% of the population aged 12 years old or older (SAMHSA 2004). Table 1.4 also shows that in 2004, 46.4% of the U.S. population aged 12 and older reported using illicit drugs at some point in their lives (SAMHSA 2004). The leading illicit-type drugs (see Figure 1.1) were marijuana (40.6%), hallucinogens (mainly LSD and Ecstasy; 14.5%), cocaine (14.7%), pain relievers (13.1%), and inhalants (9.7%).

Regarding the licit-type drugs used during the same reported year, from highest to lowest the most popular were alcohol (83.1%), tobacco (72.7%), and nonmedical use of psychotherapeutics (20.1%), which includes pain relievers (13.1%), stimulants (8.8%), tranquilizers (8.5%), and sedatives (4%); see Table 1.4.

Figure 1.2 shows the past-month use of illicit drugs among persons aged 12 or older. Again the category "any illicit drug" shows the highest use, followed by use of marijuana, psychotherapeutics, cocaine, hallucinogens, and inhalants.

Nonmedical Use of Pain Relievers

Figure 1.3 shows the number of lifetime nonmedical users of selected pain relievers for 2002 and 2003. There was a significant increase in the number of persons aged 12 or older with lifetime nonmedical use of pain relievers during this time span, from 29.6 million in 2002 to 31.2 million in 2003. Specific pain relievers with statistically significant increases in lifetime use were Vicodin, Lortab, or Lorcet (from 13.1 million to 15.7 million); Percocet, Percodan, or Tylox (from 9.7 million to 10.8 million); hydrocodone (from 4.5 million to 5.7 million); OxyContin (from 1.9 million to 2.8 million); methadone (from 0.9 million to 1.2 million; and Tramadol (from 52,000 to 186,000) (SAMHSA 2004). (See Figure 1.3.)

FIGURE 1.1

Percentage of U.S. residents (aged 12 or older) reporting lifetime use of alcohol, tobacco, and illicit drugs, 2003.

*Nonmedical use only does not include over-the-counter drugs.

Source: Substance Abuse and Mental Health Services Administration (SAMHSA). *Overview of Findings from the 2003 National Survey on Drug Use and Health.* Office of Applied Studies, NSDUH Series H-24, DHHS Publication No. SMA 04-3963. Rockville, MD, 2004.

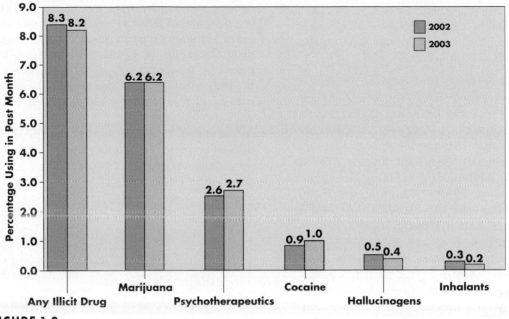

FIGURE 1.2

Past-month use of selected illicit drugs among persons aged 12 or older, 2002 and 2003.

Source: Substance Abuse and Mental Health Services Administration (SAMHSA). *Results from the 2003 National Household Survey on Drug Use and Health: National Findings.* Rockville, MD: Office of Applied Studies (OAS), 2004.

FIGURE 1.3

Number (in millions) of lifetime nonmedical users of selected pain relievers among persons aged 12 or older: 2002 and 2003.

Note: Statistically significant differences (at 0.05 level) between 2002 and 2003 are denoted by "+".

Source: Substance Abuse and Mental Health Services Administration (SAMHSA). *Results from the 2003 National Household Survey on Drug Use and Health: National Findings.* Rockville, MD: Office of Applied Studies (OAS), 2004.

Age Patterns

Figure 1.4 shows the past-month use of illicit drugs by age in 2003. With regard to age patterns, the following trends are apparent:

- Rates of drug use showed substantial variation by age. For example, 3.8% of youths aged 12 or 13 reported current illicit drug use in 2003. As in other years, illicit drug use tended to increase with age among young persons.
- The 18–25 age category used the most types of illicit drugs. Although this report broke out the age categories slightly differently, the 18–20 age group had the highest illicit drug use in 2003 (23.3%), followed by the 16–17 age group (19.2%) and the 21–25 age group (18.3%).
- A breakdown of the types of drug use by 18- to 25-year-olds shows that 17% used marijuana, 6% used prescription-type drugs nonmedically, 2.2% used cocaine, and 1.7% used hallucinogens.

- Among youths, the types of drugs used differed by age in 2003, as was the case in prior years. Marijuana was the most commonly used drug among 16- or 17-year-olds (15.6%), followed by prescription-type drugs used nonmedically (6.1%), hallucinogens (1.9%), and cocaine (1.2%). Only 1.0% of youths aged 16 or 17 used inhalants.
- An estimated 70% of all psychoactive prescription drugs used by people younger than 30 were obtained without the user having a prescription (SAMHSA 2004).

Racial and Ethnic Differences

Figure 1.5 shows average past-month illicit drug use among persons aged 12 or older by racial and ethnic differences in 2002 and 2003. The latest figures reveal the following trends:

- From highest to lowest, groups had the following rates of illicit drug use: American Indians

FIGURE 1.4

Past-month illicit drug use, by age, 2003.

Source: Substance Abuse and Mental Health Services Administration (SAMHSA). *Results from the 2003 National Survey on Drug Use and Health: National Findings.* Rockville, MD: Office of Applied Studies (OAS), 2004.

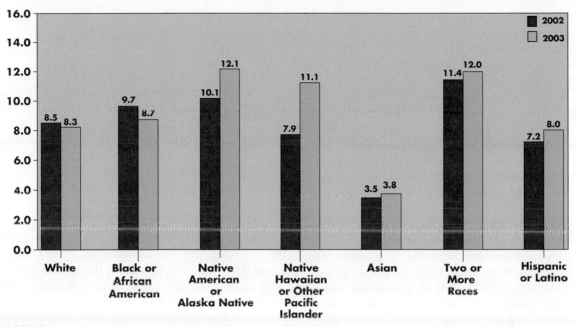

FIGURE 1.5

Past-month illicit drug use among persons aged 12 or older, by race/ethnicity, 2002 and 2003.

....

Source: Substance Abuse and Mental Health Services Administration (SAMHSA). *Results from the 2003 National Household Survey on Drug Use and Health: National Findings.* Rockville, MD: Office of Applied Studies (OAS), 2004.

or Alaska Natives (12.1%), two or more races (12.0%), Native Hawaiians or other Pacific Islanders (11.1%), blacks or African Americans (8.7%), whites (8.3%), Hispanics or Latinos (8.0%), and Asians (3.8%).

- Asians continued to have the lowest percentage of current illicit drug use when this research was conducted, just as many other racial and ethnic group studies on drug use had found previously.
- Among the various racial and ethnic groups, the highest amount of current illicit drug use in youths aged 12 to 17 is found among American Indians/Alaska Natives (19.3%) — higher than the rate among all youths (11.2%) — and the rate among Asian youths (6.5%) is significantly lower compared with the overall rate for all youths.
- Among Hispanic groups, Puerto Ricans were the heaviest users of illicit drugs, followed by Mexicans and Cubans. Central and South Americans had the lowest amount of current illicit drug use.

- Although estimates of current hallucinogen use for all racial/ethnic groups combined showed a decrease between 2002 and 2003, among Hispanics aged 18 to 25 such use did increase significantly, from 0.7% in 2002 to 1.3% in 2003 (SAMHSA 2004).

Gender

In 2003 (SAMHSA 2004), the following were major findings regarding illicit drug use by gender:

- Men are more likely to report current drug use than women (10.0% versus 6.5%).
- The rates of nonmedical use of any prescription-type psychotherapeutics were similar for males (2.7%) and females (2.6%).
- Among youths aged 12 to 17, the rate of current illicit drug use was similar for boys (11.4%) and girls (11.1%). While boys aged 12 to 17 had a higher rate of marijuana use than same-age girls (8.6% versus 7.2%), rates of nonmedical use of any prescription-type psychotherapeutics were 4.2% for girls and

3.7% for boys (not a statistically significant difference).

- Generally, gender and licit/illicit drug use correlate with specific age periods. Men have a tendency to prefer stimulants in their thirties, depressants in their forties and fifties, and sedatives from age 60 on. In comparison to men, women are most likely to use stimulants from age 21 through age 39 and depressants more frequently in their thirties. Women's use of sedatives shows a pattern similar to men's use, with the frequency of use increasing with age. Generally, women tend to take pills to cope with problems, whereas men tend to use alcohol and marijuana for the same purpose.

- People older than 35 are more likely to take pills, whereas younger people prefer alcohol and other licit and illicit types of drugs. Among those using pills, younger people and men are more likely to use stimulants than older people and women, who more frequently take sedatives. (The actual usage rates for all psychoactive drugs are probably 35% higher than the reported data.)

- Among younger people (ages 18 through 32 years), use of stimulants and depressants for nonmedical reasons often results from drug misuse or dependency. Methods for obtaining psychoactive drugs for nonmedical purposes include (1) getting drugs from friends and relatives who have legitimate prescriptions, (2) resorting to drug dealers, and (3) purchasing or shoplifting OTC medications.

Pregnant Women

In looking at this group, we find two major outcomes:

- In 2003 (SAMHSA 2004), among pregnant women aged 15 to 44 years, 4.3% reported using illicit drugs in the month before their interviews during 2002 and 2003. This rate was significantly lower than the rate among women aged 15 to 44 who were not pregnant (10.4%). (These estimates are based on combined 2002 and 2003 data.)

- Pregnant women as less likely to use drugs than similar-age women who are not pregnant.

Education

Illicit drug use rates in 2003 were correlated with educational status:

- Among adults aged 18 or older, the rate of current illicit drug use was lower among college graduates (5.2%) compared with those who did not graduate from high school (9%), high school graduates (8.3%), or those who had taken some college courses (9.2%).

- Adults who had completed 4 years of college were more likely to have tried illicit drugs in their lifetime as compared with adults who had not completed high school (51% versus 38%). This is despite the fact, that while college graduates had used significantly more illicit types of drugs in their *lifetime use*, their *current use*—usually after graduation and movement away from their respective campuses—was significantly less than that among their counterparts who had not completed high school.

College Students

The most significant findings regarding college students and illicit drug use are as follows:

- In the college-age population (persons aged 18 to 22 years), the rate of current illicit drug use was nearly the same among full-time undergraduate college students (21.4%) as for other persons aged 18 to 22 years, including part-time students, students in other grades, and nonstudents (22.5%).

- The rate of current illicit drug use among college students and other 18- to 22-year-olds did not change between 2002 and 2003 (SAMHSA 2004).

Employment

With regard to current employment status, the following are significant findings related to illicit drug use:

- Current employment status was highly correlated with rates of illicit drug use in 2003. An estimated 18.2% of unemployed adults aged 18 or older were current illicit drug users compared with 7.9% of those employed full-time and 10.7% of those employed part-time.

- Although the rate of drug use was higher among unemployed persons compared with those from other employment groups, most drug users were employed. Of the 16.7 million illicit drug users aged 18 or older in 2003, 12.4 million (74.3%) were employed either full- or part-time.

Geographic Area

Several of the more significant findings related to illicit drug use in specific geographic areas follow:

- The rate of illicit drug use in metropolitan areas is higher than the rate in nonmetropolitan counties. Rates were 8.3% in large metropolitan counties, 8.6% in small metropolitan counties, and 7% in nonmetropolitan counties.
- Within nonmetropolitan areas, counties that were urbanized had an illicit drug use rate of 7.9%, while completely rural counties had a significantly lower rate (3.1%).
- Among persons aged 12 or older, the rates of current illicit drug use in the United States were: 9.3% in the West, 8.7% in the Northeast, 7.9% in the Midwest, and 7.4% in the South (SAMHSA 2004).

Criminal Justice Populations/Arrestees

Certain significant findings and correlations are unique to the criminal justice populations:

- In 2003, among the estimated 1.4 million adults aged 18 or older who were on parole or other supervised release from prison during the past year, 24.3% were current illicit drug users, compared with 7.7% of adults not on parole or supervised release.
- Among the estimated 4.8 million adults on probation at some time in the past year, 28% reported current illicit drug use in 2003. This compares with a rate of 7.4% among adults not on probation in 2003.
- Of the 114,589 offenders arrested by federal law enforcement agencies in 2000, 28% were arrested for drug offenses. Of the 35,000 arrests made in 2001 by the U.S. Drug Enforcement Administration (DEA), 38.8% involved cocaine, 9.4% involved heroin, 19.7% involved marijuana, and 32% involved other drugs, including stimulants (e.g., methamphetamine),

depressants (e.g., barbiturates), and hallucinogens (e.g., LSD and PCP) (ONDCP, March 2003).

- In 2001, the Federal Bureau of Investigation (FBI) reported 13,699,254 state and local arrests throughout the United States. Arrests for drug abuse violations accounted for 11.6% of all state and local arrests reported to the FBI during 2001, with 1,586,902 drug-related arrests being reported. The remaining arrests were for all other offenses, such as nonaggravated assaults, fraud, driving while under the influence (DWI), and disorderly conduct (ONDCP, March 2003).
- In a survey of inmates in state and federal correctional facilities, 33% of state prisoners and 22% of federal prisoners said they had committed their current offenses while under the influence of drugs. Drug offenders (42%) and property offenders (37%) reported the highest incidence of drug use at the time of the offense (BJS 2004).
- Offenders most likely to have reported using alcohol were those convicted of DWI (94%), homicide (47%), and assault (47%). Those most likely to be using drugs were offenders who were convicted of drug trafficking (60%), drug possession (57%), fraud (45%), and robbery (44%) (Harlow 1998).
- Women were more likely than men to be in jail for a drug offense. Among female inmates, 27% had violated drug laws; among male inmates, 21% had committed such crimes. Women (24%) were also more than twice as likely as men (11%) to be in jail for fraud or theft (Harlow 1998).

TYPES OF DRUG USERS

Just as a diverse set of personality traits (for example, introverts, extroverts, type A, obsessive-compulsive, and so on) exists, so drug users vary according to their general approach or orientation, frequency of use, and types and amounts of the drugs they consume. Some are occasional or moderate users, whereas others display much stronger attachment to drug use. In fact, some display such obsessive-compulsive behavior that they cannot let a morning, afternoon, or evening pass without using drugs. Some researchers have classified such variability in the frequency and extent of usage as fitting into three basic patterns: experimenters, compulsive users, and "floaters" or "chippers" (members of the last category drift between experimentation and compulsive use).

Experimenters begin using drugs largely because of peer pressure and curiosity, and they confine their use to recreational settings. Generally, they more often enjoy being with peers who also use drugs recreationally. Alcohol, tobacco, marijuana, hallucinogens, and many of the major stimulants are the drugs they are most likely to use. They are usually able to set limits on when these drugs are taken (often preferred in social settings), and they are more likely to know the difference between light, moderate, and chronic use.

Compulsive users, in contrast, ". . . devote considerable time and energy to getting high, talk incessantly (sometimes exclusively) about drug use . . . [and "funny" or "weird" experiences] . . . and become connoisseurs of street drugs" (Beschner 1986, p. 7). For compulsive users, recreational fun is impossible without getting high. Other characteristics of these users include the need to escape or postpone personal problems, to avoid stress and anxiety, and to enjoy the sensation of the drug's euphoric effects. Often, they have difficulty assuming personal responsibility and suffer from low self-esteem. Many compulsive users are from dysfunctional families, have persistent problems with the law, and have serious psychological problems underlying their drug-taking behavior. Problems with personal and public identity, some to excessive confusion about their sexual orientation, boredom, family discord, childhood sexual and/or mental abuse, academic pressure, and chronic depression all contribute to the inability to cope with issues *without* drugs (see "Case in Point," Ignoring the Signs of Drug Abuse: A Hard Lesson Learned).

Floaters or **chippers** focus more on using other people's drugs without maintaining a steady supply of drugs. Nonetheless, chippers, like experimenters, are generally light to moderate consumers of drugs. Chippers vacillate between the need for pleasure seeking and the desire to relieve moderate to serious psychological problems. As a result, although most are on the path to drug dependence, at this stage they drift between experimental drug-taking peers and chronic drug-using peers. In a sense, these drug users are marginal individuals who do not strongly identify with experimenters or compulsive users. (An example of how the various types of drug users are often adversely affected by peers is discussed in more detail in Chapters 2 and 4.)

INFLUENCE OF THE MASS MEDIA ON DRUG USE

Studies continually show that the majority of young drug users come from homes in which drugs are liberally used (Goode 1999; SAMHSA 1996b). These children frequently witness drug use at home. For instance, parents may consume large quantities of coffee to wake up in the morning and other forms of medication throughout the day: cigarettes with morning coffee, antacid tablets for an upset stomach, vitamins for stress, or aspirin for a headache. Finally, before going to bed, the grown-ups may take a few "nightcaps" or a sleeping pill to relax. The following is an interview related to the overuse of drugs:

> Yeah, I always saw my mom smoking early in the morning while reading the newspaper and slowly sipping nearly a full pot of coffee. She took prescription drugs for asthma, used an

KEY TERMS

experimenters
first category of drug use typified as being in the initial stages of drug use; these people often use drugs for recreational purposes

compulsive users
second category of drug use typified by an insatiable attraction followed by a psychological dependence to drugs

floaters or chippers
third category of drug use; these users vacillate between the felt need to use drugs and the desire to relieve moderate to serious psychological problems. This category of drug use has two major characteristics: (1) a general focus mostly on using other people's drugs (often without maintaining a personal supply of the drug) and (2) vacillation between the characteristics of chronic drug users and experimenter types

►Case in Point   Ignoring the Signs of Drug Abuse: A Hard Lesson Learned

Michael Alig missed all of the warning signs of the dangers of drug abuse and addiction. He states, "There is no excuse for killing someone, no reason to justify being wholly or even partly responsible for the death of another human being. I have never been a violent person. I don't even like sports." Now in prison for the accidental death of a friend, Michael recalls the following warning signs he refused to note:

1. Michael was living without any real boundaries. Now that he looks back at his life, he says it was out of control, and his friends were out of control.

2. Michael overdosed many times on many different drugs and would often wake up unaware of where he was, where he had been, who he was with, what he was doing with whomever he was with, what took place while he was on drugs, and so on.

3. One time Michael regained consciousness and was in the presence of "… an entire dinner of cocaine on the floor!" which he admits was too tempting to pass up.

4. People around Michael were constantly warning him to stop using drugs, and these were the same people with whom he was annoyed.

5. Just before his arrest, Michael had overdosed numerous times with naloxone, barely escaping death several times.

6. Michael used heroin with the false sense of euphoric security that all was good.

Now Michael, who was called the King of the Club Kids, believes he has finally learned to accept responsibilities as an adult. After solitary confinement for several months to stop using heroin in prison, he says that his approach to life has completely changed. Michael says, "A smile or a laugh isn't just a reaction to the most extreme situations anymore, but to my average daily experiences like eating a piece of sour candy, or seeing a fat boy in the prison yard with the crack of his butt exposed for everyone to see." Michael believes it will take a lot of time for his brain to rewire itself toward enjoying the simple pleasures of life. He states, "Now it will be the small, subtle life experiences that will be my reinforcements … [besides] parties in jail are dangerous." Today, Michael is approximately 34 years of age.

Reconstructed by author from source: Michiana Point of View/Michael Alig. "Alig Missed Signs Along the Road to Tragedy." *The South Bend Tribune* (10 January 1999): B-3.

inhaler, and took aspirin for headaches. When she accused me of using drugs at concerts, I would pick up her pack of cigarettes and several prescription bottles and while she was raging on me, I would quietly wave all her drugs close up in front of her face. She would stop nagging within seconds and actually one time I think she wanted to laugh but turned away toward the sink and just started washing cups and saucers. The way I figure it, she has her drugs, and I have mine. She may not agree with my use of my drugs but then she is not better either. It's great to have a drug-using family ain't it? *(From Venturelli's research files, male, age 20, college student, June 12, 2000.)*

Some social scientists believe that everyday consumption of legal drugs — caffeine, prescription and OTC drugs, and alcohol — is fueled by the pace of modern lifestyles and greatly accelerated by the influence of today's increasingly sophisticated mass media.

If you look around your classroom building, the dormitories at your college, or your own home, evidence of mass media and electronic equipment can be found everywhere. Cultural knowledge and information are transmitted via media through electronic gadgets we simply "can't live without" to the point at which they help us define and shape our everyday reality.

Although more than 70% of adults are regular newspaper readers, television remains the most influential medium. Ninety-eight percent of households have at least one television set and 74% have two or more television sets. In the average American household, a television is on 7 hours and 12 minutes

Amanda Geiger never saw the drunk driver.

Friends Don't Let Friends Drive Drunk.

U.S. Department of Transportation

Ad Council

Although the media are often accredited for glamorizing dangerous drug use, many successful prevention campaigns have used TV, radio, and print media as outlets. Since the Advertising Council began the campaign "Friends Don't Let Friends Drive Drunk," 79% of Americans have stopped an intoxicated friend from getting behind the wheel.

per day (Nielsen 1998). Advertisers invest huge amounts of money in television commercials because of the popularity of the medium. For example, the alcohol industry spends more than $1 billion on yearly advertising (Critser 1996; Kilbourne 1989; Robert Wood Johnson Foundation 2001). "The advertising budget for one beer — Budweiser — is more than the entire budget for research on alcoholism and alcohol abusers" (Kilbourne 1989, 13).

In 1995, this advertising resulted in spirits, wine, and beer sales totaling $103.9 billion, with the largest sales — those of beer — reaching $62.6 billion (Critser 1996). Further, even "spending on consumer advertising [for prescription drugs] rose to $1.8 billion in 1999, from $1.3 billion in 1998" (Pear 2000). Such sales figures clearly indicate that advertising is both highly effective and very lucrative in promoting drinking and drug use.

Radio, newspapers, and magazines are also saturated with advertisements for OTC drugs that constantly offer relief from whatever illness you may have. There are pills for inducing sleep and those for staying awake, as well as others for treating indigestion, headache, backache, tension, constipation, and the like. Using these medicinal compounds can significantly alter mood, level of consciousness, and physical discomfort. Experts warn that such drug advertising is likely to increase.

In the early 1990s, the Food and Drug Administration (FDA) lifted a 2-year ban on consumer advertising of prescription drugs; since then, there has been an onslaught of new sales pitches. In their attempts to sell drugs, product advertisers use the authority of a physician or health expert or the seemingly sincere testimony of a product user. Adults are strongly affected by testimonial advertising because these drug commercials can appear authentic and convincing to large numbers of viewers, listeners, or readers.

The constant barrage of commercials, including many for OTC drugs, relays the message that, if you are experiencing restlessness or uncomfortable symptoms, taking drugs is an acceptable and normal response. As a result, television viewers, newspaper and magazine readers, and radio listeners are led to believe or unconsciously select the particular brand advertised when confronted with dozens upon dozens of drug choices for a particular ailment. In effect, this advertising reaffirms the belief that drugs are necessary when taken for a real or an imagined symptom.

Drug Use and Drug Dependence

Why are so many people attracted to drugs and the effects of recreational drug use? Like the ancient Assyrians, who sucked on opium lozenges, and the Romans, who ate hashish sweets some 2000 years ago, many users claim to be bored, in pain, frustrated, unable to enjoy life, or alienated. Such people turn to drugs in the hope of finding oblivion, peace, inner connections, outer connections (togetherness), or euphoria. The fact that many OTC drugs never really cure the ailment, especially if taken for social and psychological reasons, and the fact that frequent use of most drugs increases the risk of addiction do not seem to be deterrents. People continue to take drugs for many reasons, including the following:

1. Searching for pleasure and using drugs to heighten good feelings.
2. Taking drugs to temporarily relieve stress or tension or provide a temporary escape for people with anxiety.
3. Taking drugs to temporarily forget one's problems and avoid or postpone worries.
4. Viewing certain drugs (such as alcohol, marijuana, and tobacco) as necessary to relax after a tension-filled day at work.
5. Taking drugs to fit in with peers, especially when peer pressure is strong during early and late adolescence; seeing drugs as a *rite of passage*.
6. Taking drugs to enhance religious or mystical experiences (very few cultures teach children how to use specific drugs for this purpose).
7. Taking drugs to relieve pain and some symptoms of illness.

It is important to understand why historically many people have been unsuccessful in eliminating the fascination with drugs. To reach such an understanding, we must address questions dealing with (1) why people are attracted to drugs, (2) how experiences with the different types of drugs vary (here, many attitudes are conveyed from the "inside" — the users themselves), (3) how each of the major drugs affects the body and the mind, (4) how patterns of use vary among different groups, and (5) what forms of treatment are available for the addicted. In Chapter 2, explanations and responses to such questions are addressed from a more theoretical (explanatory) level. In Chapters 8 through 16, each of the major types of drugs is separately examined.

WHEN DOES USE LEAD TO ABUSE?

Views about the use of drugs depend on one's perspective. For example, from a pharmacological perspective, if a patient is suffering severe pain because of injuries sustained from an automobile accident, high doses of a narcotic such as morphine or Demerol should be given to control discomfort. While someone is in pain, no reason exists not to take the drug. From a medical standpoint, once healing has occurred and pain has been relieved, drug use should cease. If the patient continues using the narcotic because it provides a sense of well-being or he or she has become dependent to the point of addiction, the pattern of drug intake is then considered abuse. Thus, the *amount* of drug taken or the frequency of dosing does not necessarily determine abuse (even though individuals who abuse drugs usually consume increasingly higher doses). Most important is the *motive* for taking the drug, which is the principal factor in determining the presence of abuse.

Initial drug abuse symptoms include: (1) excessive use, (2) constant preoccupation about the availability and supply of the drug, (3) refusal to admit excessive use, and (4) reliance on the drug. All of these four factors frequently result in producing the initial symptoms of withdrawal whenever the user attempts to stop taking the drug. As a result, the user often begins to neglect other responsibilities or ambitions in favor of using the drug.

Even the legitimate use of a drug can be controversial. Often, physicians cannot decide even among themselves what constitutes legitimate use of a drug. For example, MDMA ("Ecstasy") is currently prohibited for therapeutic use, but in 1985, when the DEA was deciding MDMA's status, some 35 to 200 physicians (mostly psychiatrists) were using the drug in their practice. These clinicians claimed that MDMA relaxed inhibitions and enhanced communication and was useful as a psychotherapeutic adjunct to assist in dealing with psychiatric patients (Levinthal 1996; Schecter 1989). From the perspective of these physicians, Ecstasy was a useful medicinal tool. However, the DEA did not agree and made Ecstasy a Schedule I drug (see Chapter 3). In a legal sense, Schedule I excludes any legitimate use of the drug in therapeutics; consequently, according to this ruling, anyone taking Ecstasy is guilty of drug abuse (Goode 1999).

If the problem of drug abuse is to be understood and solutions are to be found, identifying the causes of the abuse is most important. When a drug is being abused, it is not legitimately therapeutic; that is, it does not improve the user's physical or mental health. If such drug use is not for therapeutic purposes, what is the motive for taking the drug?

There are many possible answers to this question. Initially, most drug abusers perceive some psychological advantage when using these compounds. For many, the psychological lift is significant enough that they are willing to risk social exclusion, health problems, dramatic changes in personality, arrest, incarceration, and fines to have their drug. The psychological effects that these drugs cause may entail an array of diverse feelings. Different types of drugs have different psychological effects. The type of drug an individual selects to abuse may ultimately reflect his or her own mental state.

For example, people who experience chronic depression, feel intense job pressures, are unable to focus on accomplishing goals, or have a sense of inferiority may find that a stimulant such as cocaine or amphetamines appears to provide a solution to such dilemmas. These drugs cause a spurt of energy, a feeling of euphoria, a sense of superiority, and imagined self-confidence. In contrast, people who experience nervousness and anxiety and want instant relief from the pressures of life may choose a depressant such as alcohol or barbiturates. These agents sedate, relax, provide relief, and even have some amnesiac properties, allowing users to suspend or forget their problems. People who perceive themselves as creative or who have artistic talents may select hallucinogenic types of drugs to "expand" their minds, heighten their senses, and distort the confining, often perceived monotonous nature of reality. As individuals come to rely more on drugs to inhibit, deny, accelerate, or distort their realities, they run the risk of becoming psychologically dependent on drugs — a process described in detail in Chapters 2, 4, and 6.

Some have argued that taking a particular drug to meet a psychological need, especially if a person is over 21 years of age, is not very different from taking a drug to cure an ailment. The belief here is that physical needs and psychological needs are really indistinguishable. In fact, several drug researchers and writers, including Szasz (1992) and Lenson (1995), believe that drug taking is a citizen's right and a personal matter involving individual decision making. They see drug taking as simply a departure from consciousness. Lenson states that taking drugs for recreational purposes is simply an additional form of diversity among many other acceptable forms of diversity, such as racial, religious, gender, and sexual orientation. (For additional elaboration on these views, see Venturelli 2000.) Obviously, within drug use research, this topic remains strongly debatable.

DRUG DEPENDENCE

Although Chapters 2 and 18 discuss addiction and drug dependence in detail, here we introduce some underlying factors that lead to drug dependence. Our discussion emphasizes *drug dependence* instead of *addiction* because the term *addiction* is both controversial and relative (an issue that came to the forefront during the 1996 presidential election, for example). Even when drug dependence becomes full-fledged, addiction remains debatable, with many experts unable to agree on one set of characteristics that constitutes addiction. Furthermore, the term *addiction* is viewed by some as a pejorative that adds to the labeling process (see Chapter 2, labeling theory).

The main characteristics necessary for drug dependence are as follows:

- Both physical and psychological factors precipitate drug dependence. Recently, closer attention has been focused on the mental (psychological) attachments than on physical addiction to drug use as principally indicative of addiction — mostly, the craving aspect in wanting the drug for consumption.
- More specifically, *psychological dependence* refers to the need that a user may feel for continued use of a drug to experience its effects. *Physical dependence* refers to the need to continue taking the drug to avoid withdrawal symptoms, which often include feelings of discomfort and illness.
- There is a tendency to eventually become addicted with repeated use of most psychoactive drugs.
- Generally, *addiction* refers to mind and body dependence. In the process of dependence, addiction can be viewed as one stage within the dependence phase.

The process of addiction involves five separate phases (Figure 1.6): relief, increased use, preoccu-

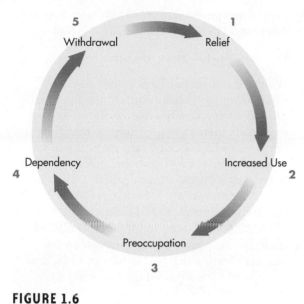

FIGURE 1.6
Stages of Drug Dependence

pation, dependency, and withdrawal. Initially, the **relief phase** refers to the relief experienced by using a drug, which allows a potential addict to escape one or more of the following feelings: boredom, loneliness, tension, fatigue, anger, and anxiety. The **Increased use phase** involves taking

KEY TERMS

relief phase
satisfaction derived from escaping negative feelings in using the drug

increased use phase
taking increasing quantities of the drug

preoccupation phase
constant concern with the supply of the drug

dependency phase
synonym for addiction

withdrawal phase
physical and/or psychological effects derived from not using the drug

NIDA
National Institute on Drug Abuse, the principal federal agency responsible for directing drug use and abuse-related research

greater quantities of the drug. The **preoccupation phase** consists of a constant concern with the substance — that is, taking the drug becomes "normal" behavior. The **dependency phase** is synonymous with addiction. In this phase, more of the drug is sought without regard for the presence of physical symptoms, such as coughing and/or shortness of breath in cases of cigarette and marijuana addiction, blackouts from advanced abuse, and moderate to severe soreness of nasal passages and inflammation from snorting cocaine. The **withdrawal phase** involves such symptoms as itching, chills, tension, stomach pain, or depression from the nonuse of the addictive drug and/or an entire set of psychological concerns mainly involving an insatiable craving for the drug (Monroe 1996).

The Costs of Drug Use to Society

Society pays a high price for drug addiction. Many of the costs are immeasurable — for example, broken homes, illnesses, shortened lives, and loss of good minds from industries and professions. The dollar costs are also enormous. The National Institute on Drug Abuse (**NIDA**) has estimated that the typical narcotic habit costs the user $100 or more per day to maintain, depending on location, availability of narcotics, and other factors. If a heroin addict has a $100-a-day habit, he or she needs about $36,500 per year just to maintain the drug supply. It is impossible for most addicts to get this amount of money legally; therefore, many support their habits by resorting to criminal activity or working as or for drug dealers.

Most crimes related to drugs involve theft of personal property — primarily, burglary and shoplifting — and, less commonly, assault and robbery (often mugging). Estimates are that a heroin addict must steal three to five times the actual cost of the drugs to maintain the habit, or roughly $100,000 per year. Especially with crack and heroin use, a large number of addicts resort to pimping and prostitution. No accurate figures are available regarding the cost of drug-related prostitution, although some law enforcement officials have estimated that prostitutes take in a total of $10 to $20 billion per year. It has also been estimated that nearly three out of every four prostitutes in major cities have a serious drug dependency.

Another significant concern arises from the recent increase in clandestine laboratories throughout the country that are involved in synthesizing or processing illicit drugs. Such laboratories produce amphetamine-type drugs, heroin-type drugs, designer drugs, and LSD and process other drugs of abuse such as cocaine and crack. The **DEA** reported that 390 laboratories were seized in 1993, a figure that increased to 967 in 1995. Another example of the phenomenal growth of methamphetamine laboratories can be found in Missouri. From 1995 to 1997, seizures of such labs in Missouri increased by 535% (Steward and Sitarmiah 1997). "In Dawson County in western Nebraska . . . 'The percentage of meth-related crimes is through the roof' . . . as reiterated by an investigator with the county sheriff's office. . . . In the state as a whole, officials discovered 38 methamphetamine laboratories in 1999; last year they discovered 179" (Butterfield 2002, p. A23).

The reasons for such dramatic increases relate to the enormous profits and relatively low risk associated with these operations. As a rule, clandestine laboratories are fairly mobile and relatively crude (often operating in a kitchen, basement, or garage) and are run by individuals with only elementary chemical skills.

Another interesting discovery is that these laboratories are not always stationary in locations such as garages, barns, homes, apartments, and so on. Though these stationary "labs" predominate, especially in the production of methamphetamine, recently mobile labs have made an appearance:

Cooking in cars and trucks helps producers in two ways: It eludes identification by law enforcement; and motion helps the chemical reaction [of methamphetamine production]. Motels are a new production setting. . . . Clandestine labs are also set up in federal parklands, where toxic

byproducts pose a danger to hikers and campers. (ONDCP 2002, p. 58)

Recently, the following was reported:

With portable meth labs popping up everywhere from motel bathrooms to the back seat of a Chevy, it was only a matter of time before they made their way onto campus. Last November, a custodian notified campus police at . . . [university in Texas] . . . about what appeared to be a lab set up in a music practice room in the . . . [university's] . . . Fine Arts Center. "We found beakers of red liquid, papers and other residue, and the room had this horrible odor . . ." Students were on vacation, so the practice room, which had its windows blackened out, would have afforded the occupant a few days to cook. [One campus police official] . . . speculates that this is just the beginning: "Labs are popping up on campuses all over the country. It's just too easy now. You can get the recipe on the Internet. Still, how could someone be so brazen as to set up an operation next to the French horn section?" (Jellinek 2003, p. 54)

Because of a lack of training, inexperience, and the danger of experiencing the effects of methamphetamine while making the drug, the chemical "cooking" procedures are performed crudely, sometimes resulting in adulterants and impure products. Such contaminants can be very toxic, causing severe harm or even death to the unsuspecting user as well as a greater likelihood of sudden explosion (Drug Strategies 1995). Fortunately, when looking at all the illicit drugs produced by such underground laboratories, such outbreaks of physically harmful drugs do not occur very often. Partial proof of this is found in the small number of news media stories of deaths or poisonings from illicit drugs. Nevertheless, because profit drives these clandestine labs, which obviously have no government supervision, impurities or "cheap fillers" are always possible so that greater profits can be made. Here, caution is very advisable in that drug purchasers do not have any guarantees when purchasing powerful illicit drugs.

Society continues paying a large sum even after users, addicts, and drug dealers are caught and sentenced because it takes from $75 to $1500 per

KEY TERMS

DEA
Drug Enforcement Administration, the principal federal agency responsible for enforcing U.S. drug laws

day to keep one person incarcerated. Supporting programs such as methadone maintenance costs much less. New York officials estimate that methadone maintenance costs about $3000 per year per patient. Some outpatient programs, such as those in Washington, D.C., claim a cost as low as $8 to $12 per day (not counting cost of staff and facilities), which is much less than the cost of incarceration.

A more long-term effect of drug abuse that has substantial impact on society is the medical and psychological care often required by addicts due to disease resulting from their drug habit. Particularly noteworthy are the communicable diseases spread because of needle sharing within the drug-abusing population, such as hepatitis and HIV. An estimated 800,000 to 900,000 people in the United States are infected with HIV, which eventually causes AIDS. Further, there are 300,000 Americans who do not know they are HIV positive (Begley 2001). The current worldwide estimate is that 42 million adults and children were infected with HIV by 2002 (Associated Press 2002, p. A8).

In the United States, HIV is spread primarily through unprotected sexual intercourse and sharing of needles used for injecting drugs. HIV in the injecting-drug-user subpopulation appears to be transmitted in small (minuscule) amounts of contaminated blood left on shared needles. The likelihood of a member of the drug-abusing population contracting HIV correlates with the frequency of injection and the amount of needle sharing (NIDA 1995). Care for these AIDS patients lasts from months to years in intensive care units at a cost to the public of billions of dollars. Many cities throughout the United States now have publicly funded programs that distribute new, uncontaminated needles to drug addicts free of charge to prevent spreading HIV and hepatitis B and C with contaminated needles.

Also of great concern is drug abuse by women during pregnancy. Some psychoactive drugs can have profound, permanent effects on a developing fetus. The best documented is fetal alcohol syndrome (FAS), which can affect the offspring of alcoholic mothers (see Chapter 7). Cocaine and amphetamine-related drugs can also cause irreversible congenital changes when used during pregnancy (see Chapter 10). All too often, the affected offspring of addicted mothers become the responsibility of welfare organizations. In addition to the costs to society just mentioned, other costs of drug abuse include drug-related deaths, emergency room visits and hospital stays, and automobile fatalities.

DRUGS, CRIME, AND VIOLENCE

There is a long-established close association between drug abuse and criminality. The beliefs (hypotheses) for this association range along a continuum between two opposing views: (1) criminal behavior develops as a means to support addiction, and (2) criminality is inherently linked to the user's personality and occurs independently of drug use (Drug Strategies 1995; McBride and McCoy 2003). In other words, does addiction to drugs cause a person to engage in criminal behavior such as burglary, theft, and larceny to pay for the drug habit? On the other hand, does criminal behavior stem from an already existing criminal personality such that drugs are used as an adjunct to commit such acts? In other words, are drugs used in conjunction with crime to sedate and give the added confidence needed to commit daring law violations?

The answers to these questions have never been clear because findings that contradict one view in favor of the other continue to mount on both sides. Part of the reason for the controversy about the relationship between criminal activity and drug abuse is that studies have been conducted in different settings and cultures, employing different research methods, and focusing on different addictive drugs. As a result, too many factors are involved to allow us to distinguish the cause from the result. We know that each type of drug has unique addictive potential and that interpretation of exactly when a deviant act is an offense (violation of law) varies. Furthermore, we know that people think differently while under the influence of drugs. Whether criminalistic behavior is *directly* caused by the drug use or whether prior socialization and peer influence work in concert to cause criminal behavior remains unclear. Certainly, we think it would be safe to view prior socialization, law-violating peers, and drugs as strong contributing factors for causing criminal behavior.

Although this controversy about the drugs and crime connection continues to challenge our thinking, the following findings are clear:

1. The National Institute of Justice's (NIJ's) Arrestee Drug Abuse Monitoring (ADAM) program conducted urine tests on males in 23 cities and on females in 21 cities. Male arrestees who tested positive for an illicit drug at the time of arrest ranged from 51.4% in San Jose to 80.5% in Manhattan. Female arrestees who tested positive ranged from 37.6% in San Antonio to 80.5% in Manhattan. Rates among juvenile male detainees ranged from 41.6% in Indianapolis to 65.6% in Washington, D.C. Thus approximately 50% of arrestees used drugs immediately before committing an offense. The 1997 Bureau of Justice Statistics (BJS) Survey of State and Federal Prison Inmates corroborated this finding, reporting that 51% of prison inmates committed their offense while under the influence of drugs or alcohol (Schmidt 1999).

2. The same survey indicated that 82% of inmates in local jails self-reported that they used a drug at some point in their lives.

3. Twenty-eight percent of state and federal prison inmates reported being under the influence of drugs at the time of their offense in 1997 (see Table 1.5). Thirty-three percent were incarcerated for drug offenses, 27% for violent offenses, 24% for property offenses, and 19% for public-order offenses — loitering, disturbing the peace, public intoxication, and so on. One outcome of these findings is that approximately one out of every four major crimes committed — violent offenses, property, and drug offenses — involves an offender who is under the influence of drugs.

4. Another, more recent study also shows a dramatic increase in the correlation between drug use and crime. This study by the Robert Wood Johnson Foundation (2001, 45) reported that with regard to homicide, theft, and assault, at least half of the adults arrested for such major crimes tested positive for drugs at the time of their arrest. "Among those convicted of violent crimes, approximately half of state prison inmates and 40 percent of federal prisoners

had been drinking or taking drugs at the time of their offense."

5. Approximately one out of every six major crimes is committed because of the offender's need to obtain money for drugs.

In regard to the connection between drug use and crime, the following findings can be summarized: (1) drug users in comparison to non-drug users are more likely to commit crimes, (2) arrestees are

Table 1.5 **Percentage of State and Federal Prison Inmates Who Reported Being Under the Influence of Drugs at the Time of Their Offense, 1997**

TYPE OF OFFENSE	PERCENTAGE*
Total of All Inmates	28
Violent Offenses	27
Murder	
Sexual assault	
Robbery	
Assault	
Property Offenses	24
Burglary	
Larceny/theft	
Motor vehicle theft	
Fraud	
Other	
Drug Offenses	33
Possession	
Trafficking	
Other	
Public-Order Offenses	19
Weapons	
Other	

*Percentage compiled by averaging the percentages of federal and state prison inmates.

Source: BJS, *Substance Abuse and Treatment,* State and Federal Prisoners, Washington, DC: U.S. Government Printing Office, 1999.

often under the influence of a drug while committing crimes, and (3) drugs and violence (more than likely cocaine, crack, and other stimulant-type drugs) often go hand in hand.

Drug-related crimes are undoubtedly overwhelming the U.S. judicial system. Just recently, it was discovered that "in the last few years, the number of gang-related web sites has grown to tens of thousands, with about 20% to 30% run by actual gang members, said Detective Chuck Zeglin of the Los Angeles Police Department's career criminal apprehension section" (Associated Press 2001).

According to the U.S. Department of Justice, alcohol consumption is associated with 27% of all murders, almost 33% of all property offenses, and more than 37% of robberies committed by young people. In fact, nearly 40% of the young people (often younger than 21 years of age) in adult correctional facilities reported drinking before committing a crime.

Drug Cartels

Here are some recent trends in the world of drugs, violence, and crime:

> Shortly before 10:00 p.m. on August 3, 1997, as fans gathered in the bars and eateries near the Plaza Monumental bullring in Ciudad Juarez [in Chihuahua, Mexico], four suspected drug traffickers strolled into the popular Max Fim restaurant, pulled out their guns, and squeezed off 130 rounds into the post-fight Sunday night crowd, killing three men and two women and wounding another four people. On their way out, the assailants paused long enough to claim another victim — an off-duty law enforcement officer who had run into the street from the bar next door, gun drawn, to check out the commotion. (Rylander 1999, 1)

In another news report:

> . . . one indication of the export of money laundering, more than $53 million in cash was seized by U.S. customs agents at Southwest border checkpoints between 1994 and 1996. The U.S. government suggested that drug profits of as much as $50 billion a year — $6 billion more than was appropriated in fiscal 1998 for Texas state government — flowed through Texas into

Mexico. The estimate included electronic transfers, exchange house operation, and bulk cash. (Rylander 1999, 3)

And in another news report:

> Drugs present the leading crime challenge in the border region, but other crimes are also a problem. Every 24 hours in 1997, an average of 60 violent crimes and 654 property offenses were committed in the border region. (Rylander 1999, 3)

And finally,

> Bogotá, Colombia — A car bomb exploded Thursday in an affluent Bogotá neighborhood, killing at least eight people and injuring more than 30. It was the worst terrorist act in the Colombian capital since the downfall of the Medellin drug cartel in 1993. No one immediately claimed responsibility for the explosion, but political analyst Alejo Vargas said the style of the attack — with no apparent targets other than civilian — had all the markings of the drug cartels. (Brodzinsky 1999, 33)

These news briefs are just a small sampling of the types of crimes and violence perpetrated by drug dealers. It is clear that production, merchandising, and distribution of illicit drugs have developed into a worldwide operation worth hundreds of billions of dollars (Goldstein 1994). These enormous profits have attracted organized crime, in both the United States and abroad, and all too frequently even corrupt law enforcement agencies (McShane 1994). For the participants in such operations, drugs can mean incredible wealth and power. For example, dating back to 1992, Pablo Escobar was recognized as a drug kingpin and leader of the cocaine cartel in Colombia, and he was acknowledged as one of the world's richest men and Colombia's most powerful man (Wire Services 1992). With his drug-related wealth, Escobar financed a private army to conduct a personal war against the government of Colombia (Associated Press 1992) and until his death in 1993, he was a serious threat to his country's stability.

In December 1999, the notorious Juarez drug cartel was believed to be responsible for burying more than 100 bodies (22 Americans) in a mass grave at a ranch in Mexico. All of the deaths were believed to be drug-related. According to a news story on this gruesome discovery, the alleged perpetrator, Vincente Carrillo Fuentes, is one among dozens of drug lords and lieutenants wanted by U.S. law enforcement agents (Associated Press 1999). This same news release indicated that the drug trade would not end until drug cartels are eliminated. Such occurrences, which are often reported by the mass media, indicate the existence of powerful and dangerous drug cartels that are responsible for the availability of illicit drugs around the world.

Drug-related violence takes its toll at all levels, as rival gangs fight to control their "turf" and associated drug operations. Innocent bystanders often become unsuspecting victims of the indiscriminate violence. For example, a Roman Catholic cardinal was killed on May 24, 1993, when a car he was a passenger in was inadvertently driven into the middle of a drug-related shoot-out between traffickers at the international airport in Guadalajara, Mexico. Five other innocent bystanders were killed in the incident (Associated Press 1993). In many other incidents, unsuspecting people have been injured or killed by drug users who, while under the influence of drugs, commit violent criminal acts.

DRUGS IN THE WORKPLACE: A COSTLY AFFLICTION

"He was a good, solid worker, always on the job — until he suddenly backed his truck over a 4-inch gas line." If the line had ruptured, there would have been a serious explosion, according to the driver's employer. The accident raised a red flag. ". . . under the company's standard policy, the employee was tested for drugs and alcohol. He was positive for both." (Edelson 2000, 3)

Most adults spend the majority of their hours each day in some type of family environment. For most adults employed full-time, the second greatest number of hours is spent in the workplace. Generally, once drug use becomes habitual, drug use often continues at work. The National Household Surveys, for example, found evidence of significant

"HE'S THE TYPICAL AMERICAN MOUSE— LIKES A DRINK BEFORE DINNER, SMOKES A LITTLE, WATCHES TV..."

Source: © Sidney Harris, *American Scientist* magazine. ©2005 by Sidney Harris.

drug use in the workplace. In the surveys, 65.6% of full-time workers reported alcohol use within the past month. Some 9.7% of full-time workers reported marijuana use within the past year. Part-time employees did not differ much in their use of alcohol and marijuana (SAMHSA 1996a). Based on studies of drug use within a 30-day period before being surveyed, approximately 64% of full-time employees reported alcohol use, while 7% reported illicit drug use (NORC 1999). This costs American businesses billions of dollars annually in lost productivity and increased healthcare costs. Over the past several years, many large businesses have instituted substance abuse programs to respond to the problems created by alcohol and other drugs in the workplace. Highlights from the National Council on Alcoholism and Drug Dependence, Inc. (1999), indicate the following:

1. *Men* in the following occupations report the highest rates of illicit drug use: entertainers, food preparation and service, cleaning services, and construction. Among *women*, workers involved in food preparation, social work, and the legal professions, including lawyers and legal assistants, report the highest rates of illicit drug use. Heavy alcohol use follows similar patterns, although automobile mechanics,

vehicle repairers, light truck drivers, and laborers also have high rates of alcohol use, but not necessarily high rates of illicit drug use.

2. The lowest rates of illicit drug use are found among workers in the following occupations: police and detectives, administrative support personnel, teachers, and child care workers. The lowest rates of heavy alcohol use are among data clerks, personnel specialists, and secretaries. Here, we find that workers in occupations that require a considerable amount of public trust (police officers, teachers, and child care workers) report the lowest rates of illicit drug use.

3. Seventy percent of all current adult illegal drug users ages 18 through 49 are employed full-time. Ninety percent of alcoholics work. This means that one out of every six employees uses alcohol and/or other illicit drugs.

4. Approximately 70% of large companies test for drug use. Approximately 50% of medium companies and 22% of small companies perform such testing. Of those companies that drug test, more than 90% use urine analysis, less than 20% use blood analysis, and less than 3% use hair analysis.

5. Most companies that administer drug tests test for marijuana, cocaine, opiates, amphetamines, and PCP.

6. Age is the most significant predictor of marijuana and cocaine use. Younger employees (18 to 24 years old) are more likely to report drug use than older employees (25 years or older).

7. With regard to marijuana and cocaine use among younger employees (ages 18 to 34), no significant differences in marijuana and cocaine use rates have been found across educational categories.

8. In general, unmarried workers report roughly twice as much illicit drug and heavy alcohol use as married workers. Among food preparation workers, transportation drivers, and mechanics, and in industries such as construction and machinery (not electrical), the discrepancy between married and unmarried workers is especially notable.

9. Workers who report having three or more jobs in the previous 5 years are twice as likely to be current or past-year illicit drug users as those who held two or fewer jobs over the same period.

10. Workers in occupations that affect public safety, including truck drivers, firefighters, and police officers, report the highest rate of participation in drug testing.

11. "Among full-time workers, heavy drinkers and illicit drug users are more likely than those who do not drink heavily or use illicit drugs to have skipped work in the past month or have worked for three or more employers in the past year" (Robert Wood Johnson Foundation 2001, 45).

12. Most youths do not cease drug use when they begin working.

In summarizing this research on employees who abuse alcohol or other drugs, five major findings emerge: (1) these workers are three times more likely than the average employee to be late to work; (2) they are three times more likely to receive sickness benefits; (3) they are 16 times more likely to be absent from work; (4) they are five times more likely to be involved in on-the-job accidents (note that many of these hurt others, not themselves); and (5) they are five times more likely to file compensation claims.

Employee Assistance Programs

Many industries have responded to drugs in the workplace by creating **drug testing** and **employee assistance programs (EAPs)**. Drug testing generally involves urine screening that is undertaken to identify which employees are using drugs and which employees may have current or potential drug problems. EAPs are employer-financed programs administered by a company or through an outside contractor. More than 400,000 EAPs have been established in the United States. These programs are designed to aid in identifying and resolving

KEY TERMS

drug testing
urine, blood screening, or hair analysis used to identify those who may be using drugs

employee assistance programs (EAPs)
drug assistance programs for drug-dependent employees

productivity problems associated with employees' emotional or physical concerns, such as those related to health, marital, family, financial, and substance abuse. EAPs have also expanded their focus to combat employee abuse of OTC and prescription drugs in addition to illicit psychoactive substances. Overall, the programs attempt to formally reduce problems associated with impaired job performance.

Recently, however, what has been occurring is that "as the economy falters and hiring slows, many employers have decided not to spend money on testing job applicants for drug use . . . [as reported by *Knight-Ridder Newspapers* on May 11, 2003]" (Join Together Online 2003). Part of the reason is the current state of U.S. economy, especially when the bottom line continues to be cutting costs and increasing profits, and as is known, the cost of drug testing continues to escalate. The other reason cited for companies that are beginning to scale back on drug testing is "[younger-generation management personnel] . . . are moving into the upper echelons of corporate America now that kind of take the stance that if it's not affecting the person's performance, it's not an issue" (Join Together Online 2003). These two reasons alone may have a profound impact on workplace drug testing in the near future.

Venturing to a Higher Form of Consciousness: The Holistic Self-Awareness Approach to Drug Use

Throughout this book, we continually approach drug use from a multidisciplinary perspective, blending pharmacological, psychological, and sociological perspectives and interpretations of the most commonly used licit and illicit drugs. Most chapters discuss the major drugs and their common usage and abuse patterns and emphasize this multiapproach in an effort to more fully comprehend how drugs affect both the mind and the body.

As you proceed through this book, it will become apparent that whenever drug use leads to abuse, it rarely results from a single, isolated cause. Instead, it is often caused or preceded by multiple factors, which may include combinations of the following:

- Hereditary (genetic) factors
- Psychological conditioning
- Peer group pressures
- Inability to cope with stress and anxiety of daily living
- Quality of role models
- Degree of attachment to a family structure
- Level of security with gender identity and sexual orientation
- Personality traits
- Perceived ethnic and racial compatibility with larger society and socioeconomic status (social class)

Gaining knowledge of the reasons for drug use, the effects of drugs, and their addictive potential is the purpose of this text. As authors, we strongly endorse and advocate a **holistic self-awareness approach** that emphasizes a healthy balance among mind, body, and spirit. Health and wellness can be achieved only when these three domains of existence are free from any unnecessary use of psychoactive substances. The holistic philosophy is based on the idea that the mind has a powerful influence on maintaining health. All three — mind, body, and spirit — work as a unified whole to promote health and wellness. Similarly, we are in agreement with holistic health advocates who emphasize the following viewpoint:

Holistic Health is based on the law of nature that a whole is made up of interdependent parts. The earth is made up of systems, such as air, land, water, plants and animals. If life is to be sustained, they cannot be separated, for what is happening to one is also felt by all the other systems. In the same way, an individual is a whole made up of interdependent parts, which are the physical, mental, emotional, and spiri-

KEY TERMS

holistic self-awareness aproach
emphasizes that nonmedical and often recreational drug use interferes with the healthy balance between the mind, the body, and the spirit

tual. While one part is not working at its best, it impacts all the other parts of that person. . . . A common explanation is to view wellness as a continuum along a line. The line represents all possible degrees of health. The far left end of the line represents premature death. On the far right end is the highest possible level of wellness or maximum well-being. The center point of the line represents a lack of apparent disease. This places all levels of illness on the left half of the wellness continuum. The right half shows that even when no illness seems to be present, there is still a lot of room for improvement. . . . Holistic Health is an ongoing process. As a lifestyle, it includes a personal commitment to be moving toward the right end of the wellness continuum. No matter what their current status of health, people can improve their level of well-being. Even when there are temporary setbacks, movement is always headed toward wellness. (Walter 1999, pp. 1–2)[1]

This book works toward this direction by presenting a blend of different perspectives about drug information to more fully comprehend how drugs work and their effects on the mind, body, and spirit.

The different perspectives expand upon limited and narrow points of view so that drug information can be viewed and understood from pharmacological, psychological, and sociological perspectives. As mentioned earlier, understanding drug use is important not only for comprehending our own health, but also for understanding (1) why and how others are attracted to drugs; (2) how to detect drug use in others; (3) what to do (remedies and solutions) when family members and/or friends abuse drugs; (4) how to help and advise drug abusers about the pitfalls of substance use; (5) what the best educational, preventive, and treatment options available are for victims of drug abuse; and (6) what the danger signals are that can arise in yourself and others you care about when drug use exceeds normal and necessary use. Once knowledge is gained about drug use and/or abuse, holistic health awareness

results in self-awareness, and self-awareness leads to self-understanding and assurance. Self-awareness initially begins by understanding your own drug use practices as well as those of close family and friends. By practicing this approach regarding the use of psychoactive substances, you will be better equipped to understand not only yourself, but also others who may be in need.

Discussion Questions

1. Give an example of a drug-using friend and describe how he or she may be affected by pharmacological, cultural, social, and contextual factors.

2. Discuss and debate whether marijuana is or is not addictive.

3. In reviewing the ancient historical uses of drugs, do you think drug use today is different from back then? Explain your answer.

4. Why do Americans use so many legal drugs (for example, alcohol, tobacco, and OTC drugs)? What aspects of our society promote extensive drug use?

5. Table 1.3 shows that drug use continued to increase from 1999 to 2001. Cite two reasons why you think this trend has occurred despite the media campaigns against drug use promoted by private organizations, state and nationally sponsored media campaigns, and the efforts of law enforcement organizations.

6. Because many experimental drug users do not gravitate toward excessive drug use, should experimenters be left alone or perhaps just given legal warnings or fines?

7. Do the mass media really promote drug use, or do they merely reflect our extensive use of drugs? Provide some evidence for your position.

8. When do you think drug use leads to abuse? When do you think drug use does not lead to abuse?

9. What do you believe is the relationship between excessive drug use and crime? Does

1. From Walter, Susan. *The Illustrated Encyclopedia of Body-Mind Disciplines.* New York: The Rosen Publishing Group, 1999. Used with permission.

drug use *cause* crime or is crime simply a manifestation of personality?

10. What principal factors are involved in the relationship between drugs and crime?

11. Should all employees be randomly tested for drug use? If not, which types of employees or occupations should be randomly tested?

12. Should all students be randomly drug tested at their schools and universities? Why or why not?

13. Do you think the approach advocated by the authors regarding a holistic self-awareness approach toward drug use is a viable approach and can be successfully used for stopping drug use? Why or why not? What improvements can be made to strengthen this approach?

Key Terms

insiders 6

outsiders 6

drugs 6

psychoactive drugs (substances) 6

addiction 7

withdrawal symptoms 7

licit drugs 7

illicit drugs 7

over-the-counter (OTC) 7

gateway drugs 15

ethanol 15

designer drugs/synthetic drugs or synthetic opioids 17

structural analogs 18

MDMA 18

equal-opportunity affliction 19

experimenters 34

compulsive users 34

floaters or chippers 34

relief phase 39

increased use phase 39

preoccupation phase 39

dependency phase 39

withdrawal phase 39

NIDA 39

DEA 40

drug testing 45

employee assistance programs (EAPs) 45

holistic self-awareness approach 46

Summary

1 Pharmacological, cultural, social, and contextual issues are the four principal factors responsible for determining how a drug user experiences drug use. Pharmacological factors take into account how a particular drug affects the body. Cultural factors examine how society's views, as determined by custom and tradition, affect use of a particular drug. Social factors include the specific reasons why a drug is taken and how drug use develops from social factors, such as family upbringing, peer group alliances, subcultures, and communities. Contextual factors account for how drug use behavior develops from the physical surroundings in which the drug is taken.

2 Initial understanding of drug use includes the following key terms: drug, gateway drugs, medicines and prescription medicines, over-the-counter (OTC), drug misuse, drug abuse, and drug addiction.

3 Mentions of drug use date back to the Bible, including ancient literature that goes back to 2240 B.C. Under the influence of drugs, many people experienced feelings ranging from extreme ecstasy to sheer terror. At times, drugs were used to induce sleep and provide freedom from care.

4 Drug users are found in all occupations and professions, at all income and social class levels, and in all age groups. No one is immune to drug use. Thus, drug use is an equal-opportunity affliction.

5 According to sociologist Erich Goode (1999), drugs are used for four reasons: (1) legal instrumental use, (2) legal recreational use, (3) illegal instrumental use, and (4) illegal recreational use.

6 The most commonly used licit and illicit drugs (rated from highest to lowest frequency of use) are alcohol, cigarettes, marijuana, nonmedical use of any psychotherapeutic (e.g., prescription pain relievers, tranquilizers, stimulants, or sedatives), smokeless tobacco, cocaine, hallucinogens, inhalants, and crack. The most commonly abused illicit drugs (also from highest to lowest frequency of use) are cannabis (marijuana and hashish), cocaine, hallucinogens, methamphetamine, and crack.

7 The three types of drug users are experimenters, compulsive users, and floaters. Experimenters try drugs because of curiosity and peer pressure. Compulsive users use drugs on a full-time basis and seriously desire to escape from or alter reality. Floaters or chippers vacillate between experimental drug use and chronic drug use.

8 The mass media tend to promote drug use through advertising. The constant barrage of OTC drug commercials relays the message that, if you are experiencing some symptom, taking drugs is an acceptable option.

9 The following are the major findings of the connection between drugs and crime: (1) drug users are more likely to commit crimes, (2) arrestees are often under the influence of drugs while committing their crimes, and (3) drugs and violence often go hand in hand.

10 The five phases of drug addiction are relief, increased use, preoccupation, dependency, and withdrawal.

11 Employee assistance programs (EAPs) are employer-financed programs administered by a company or through an outside contractor. They are designed to aid in identifying and resolving productivity problems associated with employees' emotional or physical concerns, such as those related to health, marriage, family, finances, and substance abuse. Recently, EAPs have expanded their focus to combat employee abuse of OTC and prescription drugs as well as illicit psychoactive substances.

12 The holistic self-awareness philosophy is based on the idea that the mind has a powerful influence on maintaining health. The three domains — mind, body, and spirit — work best when unobstructed by unnecessary drug use, and all three domains work as a unified whole to promote health and wellness.

References

Ananth, P., C. Annis, C. Gonzalez, K. McRae, R. Longoria, and A. Medina. "Prescription Smoothies?" Stanford Learning Lab, *Web Journal,* Department of Human Biology, 2000. Available http://sll-8Stanford.edu/webjournal.

Associated Press. "Program to Fight Drug Smuggling Costs U.S. a Lot, Produces Little." *Salt Lake Tribune* 244 (17 August 1992): A-1.

Associated Press. "Mexican Cardinal, Six Others Killed in Cross-Fire as Drug Battles Erupt in Guadalajara." *Salt Lake Tribune* 246 (25 May 1993): A-1.

Associated Press. "Discovery of Mexican Graves Unlikely to Slow Flow of Drugs." *The Times* (5 December 1999): A-13.

Associated Press. "Gang Members Go Online to Recruit, Discuss Crimes." *Fox News Channel: Top Stories* (5 September 2001): 1. Available http://www.foxnews.com/story/0,2833,33661,00.html.

Associated Press. "Virus Spread, But There Is Hope." *The Post Tribune* (27 November 2002): A8.

Begley, S. "AIDS at 20." Special Report. *Newsweek* (11 June 2001): 35–37.

Beschner, G. "Understanding Teenage Drug Use." In *Teen Drug Use,* edited by G. Beschner and A. Friedman, 1–18. Lexington, MA: D.C. Heath, 1986.

Briske, P. "Rural Eighth-Graders Using More Drugs Than Urban Kids." *The Times* (27 January 2000): 3. Available http://www.thetimesonline.com.

Brodzinsky, S. "Car Bomb Kills 8 in Colombia Neighborhood." *USA Today,* Arlington edition (12 November 1999).

Bureau of Justice Statistics (BJS). *Prisoners: Drugs and Crime Facts.* U.S. Department of Justice, Office of Justice Programs (OJP): 2004. Available http://www.ojp.usdoj.gov/bjs/dcf/duc.htm.

Butterfield, F. "As Drug Use Drops in Big Cities, Small

Towns Confront Upsurge." *New York Times,* National (11 February 2002): A23. Available http://www.nytimes.com/2002/02/11/national/11crim.html.

Center for Substance Abuse Research (CESAR). "Ritalin and Adderall Abused by Students as Party Drugs and Study Aids" (December 2003). Available http://www.cesar.umd.edu.

Center for Substance Abuse Research (CESAR). "One-Fifth of Underage Youth Have Driven Under the Influence of Alcohol or Illicit Drugs" (24 January 2005). Available http://www.cesar.umd.edu.

Critser, G. "Oh, How Happy We Will Be: Pills, Paradise, and the Profits of the Drug Companies." *Harper's Magazine* (June 1996): 39–48.

Drug Strategies. *Keeping Score: What We Are Getting for Our Federal Drug Control Dollars 1995.* Washington, DC: 1995. Available 080/edres/colleges/boss/depts/cesar/drugs/ks1995.

Edelson, E. "Drug Use in the Workplace Plummets." *APB News, Inc.* (7 February 2000): 3. Available http://www.pbnews.com/safetycenter/business/2000/02/07/drugtests0207_01.html.

Goldstein, A. "Lessons from the Street." In *Addiction from Biology to Drug Policy.* New York: Freeman, 1994.

Goode, E. *Drugs in American Society,* 6th ed. New York: McGraw Hill, 2005.

Goode, E. *Drugs in American Society,* 5th ed. Boston, MA: McGraw-Hill College, 1999.

Harlow, C. W. "Profile of Jail Inmates." Bureau of Justice Statistics. NCJ-164620, April 1998, revised June 1998. Available http://www.ojp.usgov/bjs/pub/ascii/pji.txt.

Jellinek, J. "Musical Meth Lab Uncovered." *Rolling Stone,* Issue 916 (20 February 2003): 54.

Johnston, L. D., P. M. O'Malley, J. G. Bachman, and J. E. Schulenberg. *Monitoring the Future: National Survey Results on Drug Use, 1975-2002, Volume I: Secondary School Students.* Bethesda, MD: National Institute on Drug Abuse, 2003.

Join Together Online. "Workplace Drug Testing Slows with Economy." *Join Together Online,* Boston University School of Public Health (22 May 2003): 1. Available http://www.jointogether.Org/jtodirect.

Kilbourne, J. "Advertising Addiction: The Alcohol Industry's Hard Sell." *Multinational Monitor* (June 1989): 13–16.

Kusinitz, M. "Drug Use Around the World." In *Encyclopedia of Psychoactive Drugs,* edited by S. Snyder. Series 2. New York: Chelsea House, 1988.

Lenson, D. *On Drugs.* Minneapolis, MN: University of Minnesota Press, 1995.

Levinthal, C. F. *Drugs, Behavior, and Modern Society.* Boston, MA: Allyn and Bacon, 1996.

McBride, D. C., and C. B. McCoy. "The Drugs–Crime Rela-

tionship: An Analytical Framework." In *Drugs, Crime, and Justice,* edited by L. K. Gaines and B. Kraska, 100–119. Prospect Heights, IL: Waveland Press, 2003.

McShane, L. "Cops Are Crooks in N.Y.'s 30th Precinct." *Salt Lake Tribune* 238 (18 April 1994): A-5.

Monroe, J. "What Is Addiction?" *Current Health* 2 (January 1996): 16–19.

Morrow, D. J. "Worldwide Drug Sales Up 4% in 98." *New York Times* (23 March 1999): C5.

National Council on Alcoholism and Drug Dependence, Inc. (NCADD). *Alcohol and Other Drugs in the Workplace: An Overview.* New York: National Council on Alcoholism and Drug Dependence, Inc. August 1999. Available http://www.ncadd.org.

National Institute on Drug Abuse (NIDA). "Costs to Society." *NIDA Infofax.* Bethesda, MD: U.S. Department of Health and Human Services, 1998. Available http://www.nida.nih.gov.

National Institute on Drug Abuse (NIDA). "NIDA Plays Key Role in Studying Links Between AIDS and Drug Abuse." *NIDA Notes* 10, no. 3 (May/June 1995): 1.

National Institute on Drug Abuse (NIDA). *Principles of Drug Addiction Treatment,* National Institutes of Health Publication No. 99-4180, October 1999.

National Opinion Research Center (NORC). *Substance Abuse and Mental Health Characteristics by Employment Status.* Substance Abuse and Mental Health Services Administration (SAMHSA) and Office of Applied Studies (OAS). Rockville, MD: National Clearinghouse for Alcohol and Drug Information, June 1999.

Nichols, K. "The Other Performance-Enhancing Drugs." *The Chronicle of Higher Education,* LI (17 December 2004): A11.

Nielsen Media Research. *1998 Report on Television.* Northbrook, IL: Nielsen, 1998.

Office of National Drug Control Policy (ONDCP). "Drug Data Summary." Drug Policy Information Clearinghouse, Rockville, MD: March 2003. Available www.whitehousedrugpolicy.gov.

Office of National Drug Control Policy (ONDCP), *Pulse Check: Trends in Drug Abuse.* Washington, DC: Executive Office of the President, Office of National Drug Control Policy, 2002.

Pear, R. "Marketing Tied to Increase in Prescription Drug Sales." *New York Times* (20 September 2000): A16.

Pharmacy Times. Generic Pharmacy RX Report, a Supplement to *Pharmacy Times.* "Pharmaceutical Fraud." (December 2005): 5.

Pharmacy Times, Generic Rx Product Report. "Did You Know." (Spring 2003): 3.

Publishers Group, LLC. "Prescription Drugs." Plymouth, MN: 2004. Available http://www.streetdrugs.org/prescription.htm.

Robert Wood Johnson Foundation. *Substance Abuse: The*

Nation's Number One Health Problem. Prepared by the Schneider Institute for Health Policy for the Robert Wood Johnson Foundation, Brandeis University. Princeton, NJ: Robert Wood Johnson Foundation, February 2001.

Rylander, C. K. (Texas Comptroller of Public Accounts). "Bordering the Future: Crime—Line of Fire." *Window on State Government* (7 April 1999). Available http://www.window.state.tx.us/borer/ch10/ch10html.

Schecter, M. "Serotonergic-Dopaminergic Mediation of 3, 4-Methylenedioxy-Methamphetamine (MDMA, Ecstasy)." *Pharmacology, Biochemistry and Behavior* 31 (1989): 817–824.

Schmidt, G. *Drug Data Summary.* Office of National Drug Control Policy (ONDCP). Rockville, MD: Drug Policy Information Clearinghouse, NCJ-172873, April 1999.

Spake, A. "Natural Hazards." In *Annual Editions: Drugs, Society, and Behavior 2002/2003,* edited by H. T. Wilson, 101–106. Guilford, CT: McGraw-Hill/Dushkin, 2002.

Spiess, M., and D. Fallow. *Drug Related Crime.* Office of National Drug Control Policy (ONDCP). Rockville, MD: Drug Policy Information Clearinghouse, NCJ-181056, March 2000.

Steward, P., and G. Sitarmiah. "America's Heartland Grapples with Rise of Dangerous Drug." *The Christian Science Monitor* (13 November 1997): 1, 18.

Substance Abuse and Mental Health Services Administration (SAMHSA). *Overview of Findings from the 2003 National Survey on Drug Use and Health.* Office of Applied Studies, NSDUH Series H-24, DHHS Publication No. SMA 04-3963. Rockville, MD: 2004.

Substance Abuse and Mental Health Services Administration (SAMHSA). *National Household Survey on Drug Abuse: Population Estimates 2001.* Rockville, MD: U.S. Department of Health and Human Services, Substance Abuse and Mental Health Services Administration, 2003.

Substance Abuse and Mental Health Services Administration (SAMHSA). *Nonmedical Use of Prescription-Type Drugs among Youths and Young Adults.* The NHSDA Report, National Household Survey on Drug Abuse, 16 January 2003.

Substance Abuse and Mental Health Services Administration (SAMHSA), Office of Applied Studies (OAS). *National Household Survey on Drug Abuse: Main Findings 1994.* Rockville, MD: NIDA, 1996a.

Substance Abuse and Mental Health Services Administration (SAMHSA), Office of Applied Studies (OAS). *The Relationship Between Family Structure and Adolescent Substance Use.* Rockville, MD: U.S. Department of Health and Human Services, July 1996b.

Szasz, T. *Our Right to Drugs: The Case for a Free Market.* Westport, CT: Praeger, 1992.

Teter, C. J., S. E. McCabe, C. J. Boyd, and S. K. Guthrie. "Illicit Methylphenidate Use in an Undergraduate Student Sample: Prevalence and Risk Factors." *Pharmacotherapy* 23 (2003): 609–617.

Thio, A. *Deviant Behavior,* 2nd ed. Boston: Houghton Mifflin, 1983: 332–333.

Thio, A. *Deviant Behavior,* 4th ed. New York: Harper-Collins College, 1995.

Thio, A. *Deviant Behavior,* 6th ed., New York: Pearson Education, 2000.

United States Department of Justice (USDOJ). "Information Brief: Prescription Drug Abuse and Youth." Johnstown, PA. National Drug Intelligence Center, 2004. Available http://www.usdoj.gov/ndic/pubs/1765/.

Venturelli, P. J. "Drugs in Schools: Myths and Reality." *Annals of the American Academy of Political and Social Science* 567, edited by W. Hinkle and S. Henry. Thousand Oaks, CA: Sage Publications, 2000: 72–87.

Walter, S. "Holistic Health." *The Illustrated Encyclopedia of Body–Mind Disciplines,* edited by N. Alison, 1–2. New York: The Rosen Publishing Group, Inc., 1999. Available http://ahha.org/rosen.htm.

Wire Services. "Cocaine Kingpin Escapes After Bloody Shootout." *Salt Lake Tribune* 244 (23 July 1992): A-1.

CHAPTER 2

Explaining Drug Use and Abuse

Did You Know?

- Contrary to public perception, addiction is a complex disease.
- Most drugs of abuse include both physical and psychological addictions.
- The prevailing concept or model of addiction in America is the disease model.
- Drug addiction develops as a process and not as a sudden occurrence.
- There exists an excessive amount of variation in values and attitudes regarding drug use.
- Like the United States, nearly all other countries are experiencing increasing amounts of drug use within certain subcultures of people who use or abuse drugs.
- Every culture has experienced problems with drug use or abuse. As far back as 2240 B.C., Hammurabi, the Babylonian king and lawgiver, addressed the problems associated with excessive use of alcohol.
- Today, drugs are more potent than they were years ago.
- Drug use and especially drug dealing are becoming major factors in the growth of crime among the young.
- Seven in 10 drug users work full-time.
- According to biological theories, drug abuse has an innate physical beginning stemming from

physical characteristics that cause certain individuals either to experiment with or to crave drugs to the point of abuse.

- Abuse of drugs by some people may represent an attempt to relieve underlying psychiatric disorders.
- "Addiction to pleasure" theory assumes that it is biologically normal to continue a pleasure stimulus (such as drug use), once begun.
- A strong relationship exists between severe drug addiction and mental illness.
- Sigmund Freud believed that addiction to drugs was an outgrowth of habitual (compulsive) masturbatory activity.
- Such personality traits as extreme forms of introversion and extroversion may explain why many people abuse drugs.
- Drug use is generally learned from others.
- When drug use becomes consistent and habitual, it usually occurs in the peer group setting, with people we like.
- No single theory can explain why most people use drugs.
- Some theories advocate that an individual's alliance with drug-using peers largely results from an inability to cope with rapid societal change.
- People who perceive themselves as drug users are more likely to develop serious drug abuse problems.

On completing this chapter you will be able to:

◎ List three to five major contributing factors responsible for addiction.

◎ List and briefly explain three models used to describe addiction.

◎ List six reasons why drug use or abuse is a more serious problem today than it was in the past.

◎ List and briefly describe the genetic and biophysical theories that biologically explain how drug use often leads to abuse.

◎ Explain how drugs of abuse act as positive reinforcers.

◎ Explain the relationships between some mental disorders and possible effects of certain drugs.

◎ Explain four ways that genetic factors directly or indirectly contribute to drug abuse.

◎ Explain the relationship between introverted or extroverted personality patterns and possible effects of stimulants or depressants.

◎ Briefly define and explain reinforcement or learning theory and some of its applications to drug use and abuse.

◎ List and briefly describe the four sociological theories broadly known as social influence theories.

◎ Describe symptoms and indicators of possible drug use or abuse in childhood behavior patterns.

◎ List and describe three factors in the learning process that Howard Becker believes first-time users go through before they become attached to using illicit, psychoactive drugs.

◎ Define the following concepts as they relate to drug use: primary and secondary deviance, master status, and retrospective interpretation.

◎ Explain how Reckless's containment theory accounts for the roles of both internal and external controls regarding the attraction to drug use.

◎ Understand how making low-risk and high-risk drug choices directly affects drug use.

Drugs and Society Online is a great source for additional drugs and society information for both students and instructors.
Visit **http://drugsandsociety.jbpub.com** to find a variety of useful tools for learning, thinking, and teaching.

Introduction

Chapter 1 provided an overview of drug use. In this chapter, we focus on the major explanations of drug use and/or abuse. The questions we explore are these: Why would anyone voluntarily consume drugs when they are not medically needed or required? Why are some people attracted to altering their minds? Why are others uneasy and uncomfortable with the euphoric effects of recreational drug use? Why do people subject their bodies and minds to the harmful effects of repetitive drug use, eventual addiction, and relapse back into drug use? What logical reasons could explain such apparently irrational behavior?

Following are three perspectives regarding drug use.

First perspective:

Yes, I use a lot of drugs. I like the high from weed [marijuana], the buzz from coke [cocaine], and liquor also. I like psychedelic drugs but can't do them often because one, they are harder to get, and two, I work all the time and go to school at night. Psychedelics require big-time commitment and I just don't have that amount of time anymore to play around with intense mind trips. I think I am biologically attracted to drugs. What else would explain the desire to get high all the time? Some of my friends are worse than me. They don't just hang with the desire to continually want to get high, they just do it. One friend of mine does not accomplish much; my other two friends are coke addicts but they say they are not addicted, they claim to just like it. I don't think a day goes by, unless I am sick with the flu or something, that I don't get at least a little buzzed on some drug. My wife does not do any drugs, but hey, she's cool with my drug use as long as I keep working every day. *(From Venturelli's research files, graduate student and full-time insurance claims adjuster, age 28, July 12, 2000.)*

Second perspective:

You are asking the wrong person about drug use. I am against such drugs as marijuana, cocaine, tobacco, and LSD. My friends feel the same. I occasionally drink when I am with friends or at a party, but even one or two drinks make me feel out of it. I just don't like to feel as if I am losing control of reality, I like reality too much. . . . I think people who use drugs liberally are in some way addicted to the feeling of being high. They are not aware of how great it is to be in control of their thinking. *(From Venturelli's research files, male graduate university student, age 28, March 6, 1996.)*

Third perspective:

Yes, I have friends who try to tell me to slow down when we are smoking weed and drinking. I just like to get high until I am about to pass out. If I could, I would be high all day without any time out. Never think about quitting or slowing down when it comes to drugs. The only time I am happy is when I am completely zonked out. I guess I am a little attached to these drugs — I am addicted to them! *(From Venturelli's research files, male public high school student in a small Midwestern city, age 15, September 9, 1996.)*

The preceding excerpts show extensive variations in values and attitudes regarding drug use. The perspective of the first interviewee represents a type of drug user who is powerfully attracted to drug use. He appears to believe that his attraction to drugs has a biological basis and he wants to feel the effects of drugs on a daily basis. The perspective of the second interviewee represents a type of user who shuns any alteration of his reality. Finally, the perspective of the third interviewee represents a type of drug user who is unaware of the pitfalls of drug addiction and is recklessly involved with substance abuse. These three views represent only a small fraction of the reasons and motivations that push people to either use or not use drugs.

Why the differences in drug use? In this chapter, we offer answers to this question by examining the motivations underlying drug use. We offer different major theoretical explanations about what causes people to initially use and often eventually abuse drugs.

To accomplish these goals, this chapter frames these and literally dozens of other perspectives *within* the major biological, psychological, and sociological perspectives. Similar to the United States, nearly all other countries are experiencing increasing amounts of drug use within certain subcultures. Moreover, as we attempt to offer major scientific and theoretical explanations for drug use, we should be able to develop a much more comprehensive understanding of why drugs are so seductive, why so many people succumb, become addicted, and inflict damage to themselves and others as they become hijacked by the nonmedical use of drugs. Not only does this hold true for members of our society, but also for countless numbers of others throughout the world.

Drug Use: A Timeless Affliction

Historical records document drug use as far back as 2240 B.C., when Hammurabi, the Babylonian king and lawgiver, addressed the problems associated with drinking alcohol. Even before then, the Sumerian people of Asia Minor, who created the cuneiform (wedge-shaped) alphabet, included references to a "joy plant" that dates from about 5000 B.C. Experts indicate that the plant was an opium poppy used as a sedative (O'Brien et al. 1992).

As noted in Chapter 1, virtually every culture has experienced problems with drug use or abuse. Today's drug use problems are part of a very long and rich tradition.

> These [intoxicating] substances have formed a bond of union between men of opposite hemispheres, the uncivilized and the civilized; they have forced passages which, once open, proved of use for other purposes; they produced in ancient races characteristics which have endured to the present day, evidencing the marvelous degree of intercourse that existed between different peoples just as certainly and exactly as a chemist can judge the relations of two substances by their reactions. (Louis Lewin, *Phantasica*, in Rudgley 1993, p. 3)

The quest for explaining drug use is more important than ever as the problem continues to evolve. There are many reasons why drug use and abuse are even more serious issues now than they were in the past:

1. From 1960 to the present, drug use has become a widespread phenomenon.
2. Today, drugs are much more potent than they were years ago. The drug content of marijuana in 1960 was 1% to 2%; today, due to new cultivation techniques, it varies from 4% to 6%.
3. Whether they are legal or not, drugs are extremely popular. Their sale is a multibillion dollar a year business, with a major influence on many national economies.
4. More so than years ago, both licit and illicit drugs are introduced and experimented with by youth at an increasingly younger age. These drugs are often supplied by older siblings, friends, and acquaintances.
5. Through the media, people in today's society are more affected by direct advertising, especially by drug companies that are "pushing" their newest drugs. Similarly, advertisements and sales promotions (coupons) for alcohol, coffee, tea, and vitamins are targeted to receptive consumer audiences as identified through sophisticated market research.
6. Today, there is greater availability and wider dissemination of drug information. Literally thousands of web sites provide information on drug usage, chat rooms devoted to drug enthusiasts, and instructions on how to make or purchase drugs on the Internet. On a daily basis, hundreds of thousands of "spam" emails are automatically sent regarding information on purchasing OTC drugs and prescription drugs without medical authorization (medical prescription).
7. Crack and other manufactured drugs offer potent effects at low cost, vastly multiplying the damage potential of drug abuse (Inciardi et al. 1993; ONDCP 2003).
8. Drug use endangers the future of a society by harming its youth and potentially destroying the lives of many young men and women. When gateway drugs, such as alcohol and tobacco, are used at an early age, a strong probability exists that the use will progress to other drugs, such as marijuana, cocaine, and

amphetamines. Early drug use will likely lead to a lifelong habit, which usually has serious implications for the future.

9. Drug use and especially drug dealing are becoming major factors in the growth of crime rates among the young. Membership in violent delinquent gangs is growing at an alarming rate. Violent gun shootings, drive-by killings, carjacking, and "wilding" occur frequently in cities (and increasingly in small towns).

10. The fact that 7 in 10 drug users work full-time (*USA Today* 1999) increases the possibility of near or serious accidents caused by workers, especially because today we have become highly dependent on technology. For example, the operation of sophisticated machines and electronic equipment requires that workers and professionals be free of the effects of mind-altering drugs. Imagine that on a daily basis, a certain percentage of air traffic controllers are under the influence of mind-altering drugs while working or that a certain percentage of school-bus drivers are under the effects of marijuana and/or cocaine.

With remarkable and unsurpassed excellence in scientific, technological, and electronic accomplishments, one might think that in the United States, drug use and abuse would be considered irrational behavior. One might also think that the allure of drugs would diminish on the basis of the statistically high proportions of accidents, crimes, domestic violence and other relationship problems, and early deaths that result from the use and abuse of both licit and illicit drugs. Yet, as the latest drug use figures show (see Chapter 1), knowledge of these effects is often not a deterrent to drug use.

Considering these costs, what explains the continuing use and abuse of drugs? What could possibly sustain and feed the attraction to use mind-altering drugs? Why are drugs used when the consequences are so well documented and predictable?

In answering these questions, we need to recall from Chapter 1 some basic reasons why people take drugs:

1. People may be searching for pleasure.
2. Drugs may relieve stress or tension or provide a temporary escape for people with excessive anxieties or severe depression.

3. Peer pressure is a strong influence, especially for young people.
4. In some cases, drugs may enhance religious or mystical experiences.
5. Drugs are used for enhancing recreational pursuits such as the popular use of Ecstasy at raves and music festivals.
6. Some believe that illicit use of drugs can enhance work performance, such as the use of cocaine by stockbrokers, office workers, and lawyers.
7. Drugs can relieve pain and symptoms of an illness.

Although these reasons may indicate some underlying causes of excessive or abusive drug use, they also suggest that the variety and complexity of explanations and motivations are almost infinite. For any one individual, it is seldom clear when the drug use shifts from nondestructive use to abuse and addiction. When we consider the wide use of such licit drugs as alcohol, nicotine, and caffeine, we make the following discoveries: (1) More than 88% of the U.S. population use different types of drugs on a daily basis (Drug Strategies 1995; SAMHSA 1998); (2) more than half (53%) have tried an illicit drug by the time they finish high school; and (3) nearly four out of every five students (75%) have consumed alcohol (more than just a few sips) by the end of high school, and nearly half (47%) had done so by 8th grade (Johnston et al. 2003).

Further, as we will see in later chapters, some drugs can mimic many of the hundreds of moods people can experience. We can, therefore, begin to understand why the explanations for drug use and abuse are multiple and depend on both socialization experiences and biological differences. As a result of these two factors, which imply hundreds of variations, explanations for drug use cannot be forced into one or two theories.

Researchers have tackled the drug use and abuse question from three major theoretical positions: biological, psychological, and sociological perspectives. Although the remainder of this chapter discusses these three major types of theoretical explanations, before delving into them, we begin with a discussion of the motivation or "engine" responsible for the consistent attraction to rec-

reational and/or nonmedical use of drugs —
namely, addiction.

The Origin and Nature of Addiction

Humans can develop a very intense relationship
with chemicals. Most people have chemically altered their mood at some point in their lives, if
only by consuming a cup of coffee or a glass of
white wine, and a majority do so occasionally. Yet
for some individuals, chemicals become the center of their lives, driving their behavior and determining their priorities, even to the point at which
catastrophic consequences to their health and
social well-being ensue. Although the word *addiction* is an agreed-upon term referring to such
behavior, little agreement exists as to the origin,
nature, or boundaries of the concept of addiction.
It has been classified as a very bad habit, a failure
of will or morality, a symptom of other problems,
or a chronic disease in its own right.

Although public perception of drug abuse and
addiction as a major social problem has waxed
and waned over the past 20 years, the social costs
of addiction have not: The total criminal justice,
health, insurance, and other costs in the United
States are roughly estimated at $90 to $185 billion
annually, depending on the source. Despite numerous prevention efforts, the "War on Drugs," and a
falloff in the heavy drug use of the 1960s and
1970s, lessons learned in one decade seem to
quickly pass out of awareness.

For example, the rate of lifetime use of any illicit
drug other than marijuana among 12th graders
in 1991 was approximately 27%; in 2004, it had
increased to approximately 29% (Johnston et al.
2004). For marijuana, the highest initiation rates
are now seen in grades 7 through 11, although in
2003 6.1% of 8th graders reported that they had
tried marijuana by the end of 6th grade (Johnston
et al. 2003). Another study found that more than
one-fourth (28%) of high school students had consumed more than a few sips of alcohol before age
13, compared to 18% who had smoked a whole cigarette and 10% who had tried marijuana *before* that
age (CDCP 2004). From these major studies, it is
apparent that both licit and illicit types of drugs
continue to penetrate into increasingly younger
age groups.

DEFINING ADDICTION

Addiction can be described as a complex disease.
In 1964, the World Health Organization (WHO)
of the United Nations defined it as "a state of periodic or chronic intoxication detrimental to the
individual and society, which is characterized by
an overwhelming desire to continue taking the
drug and to obtain it by any means" (pp. 9–10).
Accordingly, addiction is characterized as compulsive, at times uncontrollable, drug craving,
seeking, and use that persist even in the face of
extremely negative consequences (NIDA 1999).
This relentless pursuit of a drug of choice occurs
despite the fact that the drug is usually harmful
and injurious to bodily and mental functions.

The word *addiction*, derived from the Latin verb
addicere, refers to the process of binding to things.
Today, the word largely refers to a chronic adherence to drugs. This can include both physical and
psychological dependence. *Physical dependence* is
the body's need to constantly have the drug or
drugs, and *psychological dependence* is the mental
inability to stop using the drug or drugs.

The *Diagnostic and Statistical Manual of Mental
Disorders*, 4th edition *(DSM-IV-TR)*, published by
the American Psychiatric Association (2000), dif-
ferentiates among intoxication by, abuse of, and
addiction to drugs. Although *substance abuse* is considered maladaptive, leading to recurrent adverse
consequences or impairment, it is carefully dif-
ferentiated from true addiction, called *substance
dependence*, the essential feature of which is continued use despite significant substance-related problems known to the user. Many of the following
features are usually present:

- **Tolerance.** The need for increased amounts
  or diminished effect of same amount.
- **Withdrawal.** The experience of a characteristic
  withdrawal syndrome for the specific substance,
  which can be avoided by taking closely related
  substances. Unsuccessful attempts to cut down.
- **Compulsive.** An increasing amount of time
  spent in substance-related activities, such as obtaining, using, and recovering from its effects.

MODELS OF ADDICTION

Various models attempt to describe the essential nature of drug addiction. Newspaper accounts of "inebriety" in the 19th and early 20th centuries contain an editorializing undertone that looks askance at the poor morals and lifestyle choices followed by the inebriate. This view has been termed the **moral model**, and although it may seem outdated from a modern scientific standpoint, it still characterizes an attitude among many traditional North Americans and members of many ethnic groups.

The prevailing concept or model of addiction in America is the **disease model**. Most proponents of this concept specify addiction to be a chronic and progressive disease, over which the sufferer has no control. This model originated in part from research performed by Jellinek, one of the founders of addiction studies (1960), among members of Alcoholics Anonymous (AA). He observed a seemingly inevitable progression in his subjects, which they made many failed attempts to arrest. This philosophy is currently espoused by the recovery fellowships of AA and Narcotics Anonymous (NA) and the treatment field in general. It has even permeated the psychiatric and medical establishments' standard definitions of addiction. There are many variations within the broad rubric of the disease model. This model has been bitterly debated: viewpoints range from fierce adherence to equally fierce opposition, with intermediate views casting the disease concept as a convenient myth (Smith et al. 1985).

Those who view addiction as another manifestation of something gone awry with the personality system adhere to the **characterological or personality predisposition model**. Every school of psychoanalytic, neopsychoanalytic, and psychodynamic psychotherapy has its specific "take" on the subject of addiction (Frosch 1985). Tangentially, many addicts are also diagnosed with **personality disorders** (formerly known as "character disorders"), such as impulse control disorders and sociopathy. Although few addicts are treated by **psychoanalysis** or psychoanalytic psychotherapy, a characterological type of model was a formative influence on the drug-free, addict-run, "therapeutic community" model, which uses harsh confrontation and time-extended, sleep-depriving group encounters. People who follow the therapeutic community model conclude that addicts must have withdrawn behind a **"double wall" of encapsulation**, where they failed to grow, making such techniques necessary.

Others view addiction as a "career," a series of steps or phases with distinguishable characteristics. One career pattern of addiction includes six phases (Clinard and Meier 1992; Waldorf 1983):

1. Experimentation or initiation
2. Escalation (increasing use)
3. Maintenance or "taking care of business" (optimistic use of drugs coupled with successful job performance)
4. Dysfunction or "going through changes" (problems with constant use and unsuccessful attempts to quit)
5. Recovery or "getting out of the life" (arriving at a successful view about quitting and receiving drug treatment)
6. Ex-addict (having successfully quit)

KEY TERMS

moral model
the belief that people abuse alcohol because they choose to do so

disease model
the belief that people abuse alcohol because of some biologically caused condition

characterological or personality predisposition model
the view of chemical dependency as a symptom of problems in the development or operation of the system of needs, motives, and attitudes within the individual

personality disorders
a broad category of psychiatric disorders, formerly called "character disorders," that includes the antisocial personality disorder, borderline personality disorder, schizoid personality disorder, and others; these serious, ongoing impairments are difficult to treat

psychoanalysis
a theory of personality and method of psychotherapy originated by Sigmund Freud, focused on unconscious forces and conflicts and a series of psychosexual stages

"double wall" of encapsulation
an adaptation to pain and avoidance of reality, in which the individual withdraws emotionally and further anesthetizes himself or herself by chemical means

FACTORS CONTRIBUTING TO ADDICTION

Many, perhaps millions, of individuals use or even occasionally abuse drugs without compromising their basic health, legal, and occupational status and social relationships. Why do a significant minority become caught up in abuse and addictive behavior? The answer stems from the fact that many (i.e., not a single) factors generally contribute to an individual becoming addicted. Table 2.1 represents a compilation of factors identified as complicit in the origin or "etiology" of addiction, taken from the fields of psychology, sociology, and addiction studies.

In addition to the social and cultural factors listed in Table 2.1, other "cultural" risk factors for development of abuse include the following:

- Drinking at times other than at meals
- Drinking alone
- Drinking defined as an antistress and anti-anxiety potion
- Patterns of solitary drinking
- Drinking defined as a rite of passage into an adult role
- Recent introduction of a chemical into a social group with insufficient time to develop informal social control over its use (Marshall 1979)

It is important to recall that the "mix" of risk factors differs for each person. It varies according to social, cultural, and age groups and individual and family idiosyncrasies. Most addiction treatment professionals believe that it is difficult, if not impossible, to tease out these factors before treatment, when the user is still "talking to a chemical," or during early treatment, when the brain and body are still recuperating from the effects of long-term abuse. Once a stable sobriety is established, one can begin to address any underlying problems. An exception is the mentally ill chemical abuser, whose treatment requires special considerations from the outset.

In addition to the factors just listed, a number of age-dependent stressors and conflicts sometimes promote drug misuse. Risk factors that apply especially to adolescents include the following:

- Peer norms favoring use
- Misperception of peer norms (users set the tone)

- Power of age group (peer norms versus other social influences)
- Conflicts that generate anxiety or guilt, such as dependence versus independence, adult maturational tasks versus fear, new types of roles versus familiar safe roles
- Teenage risk taking, sense of omnipotence or invulnerability
- Use defined as a rite of passage into adulthood
- Use perceived as glamorous, sexy, facilitating intimacy, fun, and so on

Risk factors that apply especially to middle-aged individuals include the following:

- Loss of meaningful role or occupational identity due to retirement
- Loss, grief, or isolation due to loss of parents, divorce, or departure of children ("empty nest syndrome")
- Loss of positive body image
- Disappointment when life expectations are not met

Even in each of these age groups, a mix of factors is at play. The adolescent abuser might have risk factors that were primarily neurological vulnerabilities, such as undiagnosed attention deficit hyperactivity disorder. Alternatively, he or she may experience failure and rejection at school, disappoint his or her parents, or be labeled odd, lazy, or unintelligent (Kelly and Ramundo 1993).

In response to the information presented in Table 2.1, a student who was a recovering alcoholic commented: "You're an alcoholic because you drink!" He had a good point: The mere presence of one, two, or more risk factors does not create addiction. Drugs must be available, they must be used, and they must become a pattern of adaptation to any of the many painful, threatening, uncomfortable, or unwanted sensations or stimuli that occur in the presence of genetic, psychosocial, or environmental risk factors. Prevention workers often note the presence of multiple messages encouraging use: the medical use of minor tranquilizers to offset any type of psychic discomfort; the marketing of alcohol as sexy, glamorous, adult, and facilitative of social interaction; and so forth.

Table 2.1 Risk Factors for Addiction

RISK FACTOR	LEADING TO THIS EFFECT
Biologically Based Factors (genetic, neurological, biochemical, and so on)	
• A less subjective feeling of intoxication	• More use to achieve intoxication (warning signs of abuse absent)
• Easier development of tolerance; liver enzymes adapt to increased use	• Easier to reach the addictive level
• Lack of resilience or fragility of higher (cerebral) brain functions	• Easy deterioration of cerebral functioning, impaired judgment, and social deterioration
• Difficulty in screening out unwanted or bothersome outside stimuli (low stimulus barrier)	• Feeling overwhelmed or stressed
• Tendency to amplify outside or internal stimuli (stimulus augmentation)	• Feeling attacked or panicked; need to avoid emotion
• Attention deficit hyperactivity disorder and other learning disabilities	• Failure, low self-esteem, or isolation
• Biologically based mood disorders (depression and bipolar disorders)	• Need to self-medicate against loss of control or pain of depression; inability to calm down when manic or to sleep when agitated
Psychosocial/Developmental "Personality" Factors	
• Low self-esteem	• Need to blot out pain; gravitation to outsider groups
• Depression rooted in learned helplessness and passivity	• Need to blot out pain; use of a stimulant as an • antidepressant
• Conflicts	• Anxiety and guilt
• Repressed and unresolved grief and rage	• Chronic depression, anxiety, or pain
• Post-traumatic stress syndrome (as in veterans and abuse victims)	• Nightmares or panic attacks
Social and Cultural Environment	
• Availability of drugs	• Easy frequent use
• Chemical-abusing parental model	• Sanction; no conflict over use
• Abusive, neglectful parents; other dysfunctional family patterns	• Pervasive sense of abandonment, distrust, and pain; difficulty in maintaining attachments
• Group norms favoring heavy use and abuse	• Reinforced, hidden abusive behavior that can progress without interference
• Misperception of peer norms	• Belief that most people use or favor use or think it's "cool" to use
• Severe or chronic stressors, as from noise, poverty, racism, or occupational stress	• Need to alleviate or escape from stress via chemical means
• "Alienation" factors: isolation, emptiness	• Painful sense of aloneness, normlessness, rootlessness, boredom, monotony, or hopelessness
• Difficult migration/acculturation with social disorganization, gender/generation gaps, or loss of role	• Stress without buffering support system

The Vicious Cycle of Addiction

First, the man takes a drink, then the drink takes a drink, then the drink takes the man.

(Traditional Chinese proverb)

Drug addiction develops as a process: It is not a sudden occurrence. The body makes simple physiological adaptations to the presence of alcohol and other drugs. For instance, brain cell tolerance and increased metabolic efficiency of the liver can develop, necessitating consumption of more of the chemical to achieve the desired effect. Physical dependence can also develop, in which cell adaptations cause withdrawal syndromes to occur in the absence of the chemical.

Other factors can promote the cycle of addiction. For instance, abuse impairs cerebral functioning, including memory, judgment, behavioral organization, ability to plan, ability to solve problems, and motor coordination. Thus, poor decision making, impaired and deviant behavior, and overall dysfunction result in adverse social consequences, such as accidents, loss of earning power and relationships, and impaired health. Such adverse social and health consequences cause pain, depression, and lowered self-esteem, which may result in further use of the drug as an emotional and physical anesthetic. The addict often adapts to this chronically painful situation by erecting a defense system of denial, minimization, and rationalization; the chemical blunting of reality may exacerbate this denial of reality. It is unlikely, at this point, that the addict or developing addict will feel compelled to cease or cut back on drug use on his or her own (Tarter et al. 1983).

Family, friends, and colleagues often unwittingly "enable" the maintenance and progression of addiction by making excuses for addicts, literally and figuratively bailing them out, taking up the slack, denying and minimizing their problems, and otherwise making it possible for addicts to avoid facing the reality and consequences of what they are doing to themselves and others. Although these friends may be motivated by simple naïveté, embarrassment, or misguided protectiveness, there are often hidden gains in taking up this role, known popularly as "codependency" (Beattie 1987). Varieties of cultural and organizational factors also operate in the workplace or school that allow denial of the existence or severity of abuse or dependency. This triad of personal denial, peer and kin denial and codependency, and institutional denial represents a formidable impediment to successful intervention and recovery (Myers 1990).

NONDRUG ADDICTIONS?

The addictive disease model and the 12-step recovery model followed by AA and NA have seemed so successful for both addicts and their families and friends that other unwanted syndromes have been added to the list of "addictions." The degree to which the concept of addiction fits these syndromes varies. Gambling, for example, shows progressive worsening, loss of control, relief of tension from the activity, and continuance despite negative (often disastrous) consequences experienced by the addicted gambler. Some recovering gamblers even claim to have experienced a form of withdrawal. Gamblers Anonymous is a fellowship that has formed to assist its members. Clearly, gambling as an activity has much in common with chemical addictions, but it is debatable whether it belongs in the category of addiction (the *DSM-IV* does not include it, for example).

Many other groups have followed in the footsteps of Gamblers Anonymous, including those related to eating (Overeaters Anonymous) and sexual relationships (The Augustine Fellowship, Sex and Love Addicts Anonymous). In recent years, any excessive or unwanted behaviors, including excess shopping, chocolate consumption, and even

Gambling, like drug use, can easily become addictive.

Internet use, have been labeled "addictions," which has led to satirical reporting in the press. Addiction professionals lament the overdefinition, which they believe trivializes the seriousness and suffering of rigorously defined addictions.

Major Theoretical Explanations: Biological

As noted in Chapter 1, biological explanations have tended to use genetic theories and the disease model to explain drug addiction. The view that alcoholism is a sickness dates back approximately 200 years (Conrad and Schneider 1980; Heitzeg 1996). The disease perspective is upheld by Jellinek's (1960) view that alcoholism largely involves a loss of control over drinking and that the drinker experiences clearly distinguishable phases in his or her drinking patterns. For example, concerning alcoholism, the illness affects the abuser to the point of loss of control. Thus, the disease model views drug abuse as an illness in need of treatment or therapy.

According to biological theories, drug abuse has a beginning stemming from physical characteristics that cause certain individuals either to experiment with or to crave drugs to the point of abusive use. **Genetic and biophysiological theories** explain addiction in terms of genetics, brain dysfunction, and biochemical patterns.

Biological explanations emphasize that the **central nervous system** (CNS) reward sensors in some people are more sensitive to drugs, making the drug experience more pleasant and more rewarding for these individuals (Khantzian; Mathias 1995). In contrast, others find the effects of drugs of abuse very unpleasant; such people are not likely to be attracted to these drugs (Farrar and Kearns 1989).

Most experts acknowledge that biological factors play an essential role in drug abuse. These factors likely determine how the brain responds to these drugs and why such substances prove addictive. It is thought that by identifying the nature of the biological systems that contribute to drug abuse problems, improved prevention and treatment methods can be developed (Koob 2000).

All the major biological explanations related to drug abuse assume that these substances exert their **psychoactive effects** by altering brain chemistry or neuronal (basic functional cell of the brain) activity. Specifically, the drugs of abuse interfere with the functioning of **neurotransmitters**, chemical messengers used for communication between brain regions (see Chapter 4 for details). The following sections detail three principal biological theories that help explain why some drugs are abused and why certain people are more likely to become addicted when using these substances.

ABUSED DRUGS AS POSITIVE REINFORCERS

Biological research has shown that stimulating some brain regions with an electrode causes very pleasurable sensations. In fact, laboratory animals would rather self-administer stimulation to these brain areas than eat or engage in sex. It has been demonstrated that drugs of abuse also activate these same pleasure centers of the brain (Weiss 1999).

It is generally believed that most drugs with abuse potential enhance pleasure centers by causing the release of specific brain neurotransmitters such as **dopamine** (Bespalov et al. 1999). Brain cells become accustomed to the presence of these neurotrans-

KEY TERMS

genetic and biophysiological theories
explanations of addiction in terms of genetic brain dysfunction and biochemical patterns

central nervous system
one of the major divisions of the nervous system, composed of the brain and the spinal cord

psychoactive effects
how drug substances alter and affect the brain's mental functions

neurotransmitters
the chemical messengers released by nervous (nerve cells) for communication with other cells

dopamine
the brain transmitter believed to mediate the rewarding aspects of most drugs of abuse

mitters and crave them when they are absent, leading the person to seek more drugs (Spanagel and Weiss 1999). In addition, it has been proposed that overstimulation of these brain regions by continual drug use "exhausts" these dopamine systems, and leads to depression and an inability to experience normal pleasure (Volkow 1999).

DRUG ABUSE AND PSYCHIATRIC DISORDERS

Biological explanations are thought to be responsible for the substantial overlap that exists between drug addiction and mental illness. Because of the similarities, severe drug dependence itself is classified as a form of psychiatric disorder by the American Psychiatric Association (see the discussion of the *DSM-IV-TR* classifications later in this chapter). For example, abuse of drugs can in and of itself cause mental conditions that mimic major psychiatric illness, such as schizophrenia, severe anxiety disorders, and suicidal depression (APA 2000). It is believed that these similarities occur as a result of common chemical factors that are altered both by drugs of abuse and during episodes of psychiatric illness (NIDA 1993). Several important potential consequences of this relationship may help us understand the nature of drug abuse problems.

1. *Psychiatric disorders and drug addiction sometimes occur simultaneously.* This conclusion is supported by the fact that substance abuse-related problems often coexist with other mental diseases such as conduct disorder, schizophrenia, and mood disorders (APA 2000). Due to the common mechanisms, drug abuse is likely to expose or worsen psychiatric illnesses, making management of these problems considerably more difficult (APA 2000).
2. *Therapies that are successful in treating psychiatric disorders may be useful in treating mental problems caused by drugs of abuse.* It is likely that many of the therapeutic lessons we learn about dealing with psychiatric illnesses can be useful in drug abuse treatment, and vice versa.
3. *Abuse of drugs by some people may represent an attempt to relieve underlying psychiatric disorders.* Such people commonly use CNS depressants

such as alcohol to relieve anxiety, whereas CNS stimulants such as cocaine are frequently used by patients with depression disorders (Grinspoon 1993). In such cases, if the underlying psychiatric problem is relieved, the likelihood of successfully treating the drug abuse disorder improves substantially.

GENETIC EXPLANATIONS

One biological theory receiving scrutiny suggests that inherited traits can predispose some individuals to drug addiction. Such theories have been supported by the observation that increased frequency of alcoholism and drug abuse exists among children of alcoholics and drug abusers (APA 2000; Uhl et al. 1993). Using adoption records of some 3000 individuals from Sweden, researchers Cloninger, Gohman, and Sigvardsson conducted one of the most extensive research studies examining genetics and alcoholism. They found that ". . . children of alcoholic parents were likely to grow up to be alcoholics themselves, even in cases where the children were reared by nonalcoholic adoptive parents almost from birth" (Doweiko 2002). Such studies estimate that drug vulnerability due to genetic influences accounts for approximately 38% of all cases, whereas environmental and social factors account for the balance (Uhl et al. 1993).

Other studies attempting to identify the specific genes that may predispose the carrier to drug abuse problems have suggested that a brain target site (called a receptor — see Chapter 4 for details) for dopamine is altered in a manner that increases the drug abuse vulnerability (Radowitz 2003; Wyman 1997). Studies that test for genetic factors in complex behaviors such as drug abuse are very difficult to conduct and interpret. It is sometimes impossible to design experiments that distinguish among genetic, social, environmental, and psychological influences in human populations. For example, inherited traits are known to be major contributors to psychiatric disorders, such as schizophrenia and depression. Many people with one of these illnesses also have a substance abuse disorder (APA 2000). A high incidence of an abnormal gene in a cocaine-abusing population, for example, not only may be linked to drug abuse behavior but also may be associated with depression or another psychiatric disorder (Uhl et al. 1992).

Theoretically, genetic factors can directly or indirectly contribute to drug abuse vulnerability in several ways:

1. Psychiatric disorders that are genetically determined may be relieved by taking drugs of abuse, thus encouraging their use.
2. In some people, reward centers of the brain may be genetically determined to be especially sensitive to addictive drugs; thus, the use of drugs by these people would be particularly pleasurable and would lead to a high rate of addiction.
3. Character traits, such as insecurity and vulnerability, that often lead to drug abuse behavior may be genetically determined, causing a high rate of addiction in people with those traits.
4. Factors that determine how difficult it is to break away from drug addiction may be genetically determined, causing severe craving or very unpleasant withdrawal effects in some individuals. People with this predisposition are less likely to abandon their drug of abuse.

The genetic theories for explaining drug abuse may help us to understand the reasons that drug addiction occurs in some individuals but not in others. In addition, if genetic factors play a major role in drug abuse, it might be possible to use genetic screening to identify those people who are especially vulnerable to drug abuse problems and to help such individuals avoid exposure to these substances.

Major Theoretical Explanations: Psychological

Psychological theories mostly deal with mental or emotional states, which are often associated with or exacerbated by social and environmental factors. Psychological explanations of addiction include one or more of the following: escape from reality, boredom (Burns 1997), inability to cope with anxiety, destructive self-indulgence to the point of constantly desiring intoxicants, blind compliance with drug-abusing peers, self-destructiveness, and conscious

and unconscious ignorance regarding the harmful effects of abusing drugs. Freud established early psychological theories. He linked "primal addictions" with masturbation and postulated that all later addictions, including those involving alcohol and other drugs, were caused by ego impairments.

Freud said that drugs compensate for insecurities that stem from parental inadequacies, which themselves may cause difficulty in adequately forming bonds of friendships. He claimed that alcoholism (see Chapter 8) is an expression of the death instinct, as are self-destruction, narcissism, and oral fixations. Although Freud's views represent interesting intuitive insights often not depicted in other theories, his theoretical concerns are difficult to observe and test, and they do not generate enough concrete data for verification.

DISTINGUISHING BETWEEN SUBSTANCE ABUSE AND MENTAL DISORDERS

The American Psychiatric Association has established widely accepted categories of diagnosis for behavioral disorders, including substance abuse. As standardized diagnostic categories, the characteristics of mental disorders have been analyzed by professional committees over many years and today are summarized in the *DSM-IV-TR*. In addition to categories for severe psychotic disorders and more common neurotic disorders, experts in the field of psychiatry have established specific diagnostic criteria for various forms of substance abuse. All patterns of drug abuse that are described in this text have a counterpart description in the *DSM-IV (Revised)-TR* for medical professionals. For example, the *DSM-IV (Revised)-TR* discusses the mental disorders resulting from the use or abuse of sedatives, hypnotics, or antianxiety drugs; alcohol; narcotics; amphetamine-like drugs; cocaine; caffeine; nicotine (tobacco); hallucinogens; phencyclidine (PCP); inhalants; and cannabis (marijuana). This manual of psychiatric diagnoses discusses in detail the mental disorders related to the drug use, the side effects of medications, and the consequences of toxic exposure to these substances (APA 2000).

Because of the similarities between, and the coexistence of, substance-related mental disorders and primary psychiatric disorders, it is sometimes difficult to distinguish between the two problems. However, for proper treatment to be rendered, the cause of psychological symptoms must be determined. According to *DSM-IV* criteria, substance use (or abuse) disorders can be identified by the occurrence and consequence of dependence, abuse, intoxication, and withdrawal. These important distinguishing features of substance abuse disorders are discussed in detail in Chapter 5 and in conjunction with each drug group.

According to the *DSM-IV (Revised)-TR*, the following information can also help distinguish between substance-induced and primary mental disorders: (1) personal and family medical, psychiatric, and drug histories; (2) physical examinations; and (3) laboratory tests to assess physiological functions and determine the presence or absence of drugs. However, the possibility of a primary mental disorder should not be excluded just because the patient is using drugs — remember, many drug users use drugs to self-medicate their primary psychiatric problems. The coexistence of underlying psychiatric problems in a drug user is suggested by the following circumstances: (1) The psychiatric problems do not match the usual drug effects (e.g., use of marijuana usually does not cause severe psychotic behavior); (2) the psychiatric disorder was present before the patient began abusing substances; and (3) the mental disorder persists for more than 4 weeks after substance use ends. The *DSM-IV (Revised)-TR* makes it clear that elucidating the relationship between mental disorders and substances of abuse is important for proper diagnosis, treatment, and understanding (APA 2000).

THE RELATIONSHIP BETWEEN PERSONALITY AND DRUG USE

Since medieval times, personality theories of increasing sophistication have been used to classify long-term behavioral tendencies or traits that appear in individuals, and these traits have long been considered to be influenced by biological or chemical factors. Although such classification systems have varied widely, nearly all have shared two commonly observed dimensions of personality: introversion and extroversion. Individuals who show a predominant tendency to turn their thoughts and feelings inward rather than to direct attention outward have been considered to show the trait of *introversion*. At the opposite extreme, a tendency to seek outward activity and share feelings with others has been called *extroversion*. Of course, every individual shows a mix of such traits in varying degrees and circumstances.

In some research studies, introversion and extroversion patterns have been associated with levels of neural arousal in brainstem circuits (Apostolides 1996; Carlson 1990; Gray 1987) and these forms of arousal are closely associated with effects caused by drug stimulants or depressants. Such research hypothesizes that people whose systems produce high levels of sensitivity to neural arousal may find high-intensity external stimuli to be painful and may react by turning inward. With these extremely high levels of sensitivity, such people may experience neurotic levels of anxiety or panic disorders. At the other extreme, individuals whose systems provide them with very low levels of sensitivity to neural arousal may find that moderate stimuli are inadequate to produce responses. To reach moderate levels of arousal, they may turn outward to seek high-intensity external sources of stimulation (Eysenck and Eysenck 1985; Gray 1987; Rousar et al. 1995).

Because high- and low-arousal symptoms are easy to create by using stimulants, depressants, or hallucinogens, it is possible that these personality patterns of introversion or extroversion affect how a person reacts to substances. For people whose experience is predominantly introverted or extroverted, extremes of high or low sensitivity may lead them to seek counteracting substances that become important methods of bringing experience to a level that seems bearable.

THEORIES BASED ON LEARNING PROCESSES

How are drug use patterns learned? Research on learning and conditioning explains how human beings acquire new patterns of behavior by the close association or pairing of one significant reinforcing stimulus with another less significant or neutral stimulus. Also known as **social learning theory** (Bandura 1977; explained more fully in the "Social Learning Theory" section later in this chapter), this theory emphasizes that learned associations occur in the presence of other people using drugs coupled with other, often preconceived associations with the attitudes of society and friends about drug use (Gray 1999). In this method of learning, people form expectations and become used to certain behavior patterns. This specific process of learning is known as conditioning, and it explains why pleasurable activities may become intimately connected with other activities that are also pleasurable, neutral, or even unpleasant. In addition, people can turn any new behavior into a recurrent and permanent one by the process of **habituation** — repeating certain patterns of behavior until they become established or habitual.

The basic process by which learning mechanisms can lead a person into drug use is also described in Bejerot's **"addiction to pleasure" theory** (Bejerot 1965, 1972, 1975). This theory assumes that it is biologically normal to continue a pleasure stimulus once started. Several research findings support this theory, indicating that "a strong, biologically based need for stimulation appears to make sensation-seeking young adults more vulnerable to drug abuse" (Mathias 1995, p. 1; also supporting this view is Khantzian n.d.). A second research finding complementing this theory states, "Certain areas of the brain, when stimulated, produce pleasurable feelings. Psychoactive substances

are capable of acting on these brain mechanisms to produce these sensations. These pleasurable feelings become reinforcers that drive the continued use of the substances" (Gardner 1992, p. 43). People at highest risk for drug use and addiction are those who maintain a constant preoccupation with getting high, seek new or novel thrills in their experiences, and are known to have a relentless desire to pursue physical stimulation or dangerous behaviors and are classified as **sensation-seeking individuals**.

Drug use may also be reinforced when it is associated with receiving affection or approval in a social setting, such as within a peer group relationship. Initially, the use of drugs may not be very important or pleasurable to the individual. However, eventually the affection and social rewards experienced when drugs are used become associated with the drug. Drug use and intimacy may then become perceived as very worthwhile.

I don't know how to explain why but an attractive part of cocaine use is the instant feeling of intimacy with others who are also snorting this drug. You just don't want to leave the scene when the lines are cut on the glass surface and people are taking turns snorting coke. Even after I have had four or five lines and the conversation is very friendly and engaging, leaving the scene because someone is waiting for you at home or even if you have to meet with someone that night does not matter. Usually, everyone is feeling high, a lot of feelings of togetherness, and open to intimate conversation. I never saw anyone getting violent or anything like that, but I hear that it can happen especially if you have a grudge against someone before doing the coke. I think that coke just makes you more open and if you are an angry person then it will just bring it out in you. My experiences have been that everyone is just so friendly and everyone just pretends not to be overly anxious to do the next line. Actually, everyone is kind of pretending, because what they really want is more powder up their nose and an unending amount of time for talking the night away. *(From Venturelli's research files, 26-year-old male graduate student, residing in Chicago, Illinois, May 18, 2000.)*

KEY TERMS

social learning theory
the theory that places emphasis on how an individual learns patterns of behavior from the attitudes of others, society, and peers

habituation
repeating certain patterns of behavior until they become established or habitual

"addiction to pleasure" theory
the theory assuming that it is biologically normal to continue a pleasure stimulus once begun

sensation seeking individuals
types of people who characteristically are continually seeking new or novel thrills in their experiences

By the conditioning process, a pleasurable experience such as drug taking may become associated with a comforting or soothing environment. When this happens, two different outcomes may result. First, the user may feel uncomfortable taking the drug in any other environment. Second, the user may become very accustomed or habituated to the familiar environment as part of the drug experience. The user may not experience the same level of rush or high in this environment and in response may take more drugs or seek a different environment.

Finally, through this process of conditioning and habituation, a drug user becomes accustomed to unpleasant effects of drug use such as withdrawal symptoms. Such unpleasant effects and experiences may become habituated — neutralized or less severe in their impact — so that the user can continue taking drugs without feeling or experiencing the negative effects of the drug.

SOCIAL PSYCHOLOGICAL LEARNING THEORIES

Other extensions of reinforcement or learning theory focus on how positive social influences by drug-using peers reinforce the attraction to drugs. Social interaction, peer camaraderie, social approval, and drug use work together as positive reinforcers to sustain drug use (Akers 1992). Thus, if the effects of drug use become personally rewarding "or become reinforcing through conditioning, the chances of continuing to use are greater than for stopping" (Akers 1992, p. 86). It is through learned expectations or association with others who reinforce drug use that individuals learn the pleasures of drug taking (Becker 1963, 1967). Similarly, if drug use leads to poor and disruptive social interactions, drug use may cease.

Note that positive reinforcers, such as peers, other friends and acquaintances, family members, and drug advertisements, do not act alone in inciting and sustaining drug use. Learning theory as defined here also relies on some variable amounts of imitation and trial-and-error learning methods.

Finally, **differential reinforcement** — defined as the ratio between reinforcers favorable and disfavorable for sustaining drug use behavior—must be considered. The use and eventual abuse of drugs can vary with certain favorable or unfavorable reinforcing experiences. The primary determining conditions are listed here:

1. The amount of exposure to drug-using peers versus non-drug-using peers
2. The general preference for drug use in a particular neighborhood or community
3. The age of initial use (younger adolescents are more greatly affected than older adolescents)
4. The frequency of drug use among peers

Major Theoretical Explanations: Sociological

Sociological explanations for drug use share important commonalities with psychological explanations under social learning theories. The main features distinguishing psychological and sociological explanations are that psychological explanations focus more on how the internal states of the drug user are affected by social relationships within families, peers, and other close and more distant relationships, whereas sociological explanations focus on how factors external to the drug user affect drug use. Such outside forces include the types of families, adopted lifestyles of peer groups, and types of neighborhoods and communities in which avid drug users reside. The sociological perspective views the motivation for drug use as largely determined by the types and quality of bonds (attachment versus detachment) that the drug user or potential drug user has with significant others and with the social environment in general. The degree of influence and involvement with external factors affecting the individual compared with the influence exerted by internal states distinguishes sociological from psychological analyses.

As previously stated, no one biological and psychological theory can adequately explain why most people use drugs. People differ from one another in terms of personality, motivational factors, upbringing, learned priority of values and attitudes, and problems faced. Because of these differences, many responses and reasons exist why people take drugs, which results in a plurality of theoretical explanations. Further, the diverse perspectives of biology, psychology, and sociology offer their own explanations for drug use and abuse.

There are two sets of sociological theories: social influence and social structural. **Social influence theories** focus on microscopic explanations that concentrate on the roles played by significant others and their impact on an individual. **Structural influence theories** focus on macroscopic explanations of drug use and the assumption that the organizational structure of society has a major independent impact on an individual's use of drugs. The next sections examine these theories.

SOCIAL INFLUENCE THEORIES

The theories presented in this section are (1) social learning, (2) role of significant others in socialization, (3) labeling, and (4) subculture theories. These theories share a common theme: An individual's motivation to seek drugs is caused by social influences or social pressures.

Social Learning Theory

Social learning theory explains drug use as learned behavior. Conventional learning occurs through imitation, trial and error, improvisation, rewarded behavior, and cognitive mental associations and processes (Liska and Messner 1999). Social learning theory focuses directly on how drug use and abuse are learned through interaction with other drug users.

KEY TERMS

social influence theories
social psychological theories that view a person's day-to-day social relations as a primary cause for drug use

structural influence theories
theories that view the structural organization of a society, peer group, or subculture as directly responsible for drug use

This theory emphasizes the pervasive influence of *primary groups* — that is, groups that share a high amount of intimacy and spontaneity and whose members are emotionally bonded. Families and long-term friends are examples of primary groups. In contrast, *secondary groups* share segmented relationships in which interaction is based on prescribed role patterns. An example of a secondary group is the relationship between you and a salesclerk in a grocery store or relationships between employees scattered throughout a corporation. Social learning theory addresses a type of interaction that is highly specific. This type of interaction involves learning specific motives, techniques, and appropriate meanings that are commonly attached to a particular type of drug.

The following are examples of first-time users learning drug-using techniques from their social circles:

> The first time I tried smoking weed, nothing much happened. I always thought it was like smoking a cigarette. When the joint came around the first time, I refused it. The next time it came around, I noticed everyone was looking at me. So, I took the joint and started to inhale, then exhale. My friend sitting next to me said something to the effect, "Dude, hold it in; don't waste it. This is good weed and we don't have that much between us." Right after that, we did some "shotguns." This is where someone exhales directly into your mouth — lips to lips. My friend filled my lungs with his exhaled weed breath. After the first comment about holding it in, I started to watch how everyone was inhaling and realized that you really don't smoke weed like an ordinary cigarette; you have to hold in the smoke. *(From Venturelli's research files, male, age 16, second-year high school student in a small Midwestern town, February 15, 1997.)*

> I first started using drugs, mostly alcohol and pot, because my best friend in high school was using drugs. My best friend Tim [a pseudonym] learned from his older sister. Before I actually tried pot, Tim kept telling me how great it was to be high on dope; he said it was much better than beer. I was really nervous the first time I tried pot with Tim and another

friend, even though I heard so much detail about it from Tim. The first time I tried it, it was a complete letdown. The second time (the next day, I think it was), I remember I was talking about a teacher we had and in the middle of the conversation, I remember how everything appeared different. I started feeling happy and while listening to Tim as he poked jokes about the teacher, I started to hear the background music more clearly than ever before. By the time the music ended and a new CD started, I knew I was high. *(From Venturelli's research files, 22-year-old male student at a private liberal arts college in the Midwest, February 15, 1997.)*

First time I tried acid [LSD], I didn't know what to expect. Schwa [a pseudonym] told me it was a very different high from grass [marijuana]. After munching on one "square" [one dose of LSD] — after about 20 minutes — I looked at Schwa and he started laughing and said, "Feelin' the effects, Ki-ki?" I said, "Is this it? Is this what it feels like? I feel weird." With a devious grin . . . Schwa said, "Yep. We are now on the runway, ready to take off. Just wait a little while longer, it's going to get better and better. Fasten your seat belts!" *(From Venturelli's research files, male, age 33, May 6, 1996.)*

Learning to perceive the effects of the drug is the second major outcome in the process of becoming a regular user. Here, the ability to feel the authentic effects of the drug is being learned. The more experienced drug users in the group impart their knowledge to naive first-time users. The coaching information they provide describes how to recognize the euphoric effects of the drug.

I just sat there waiting for something to happen, but I really didn't know what to expect. After the fifth "hit," I was just about ready to give up ever getting high. Then suddenly, my best buddy looked deeply into my eyes and said, "Aren't you high yet?" Instead of just answering the question, I immediately repeated the same words the exact way he asked me. In a flash, we both simultaneously burst out laughing. This uncontrollable laughter went on for what appeared to be over 5 minutes. Then he said, "You silly ass, it's not like an alcohol high, it's

a 'high high.' Don't you feel it? It's a totally different kind of high." At that very moment, I knew I was definitely high on the stuff. If this friend would not have said this to me, I probably would have continued thinking that getting high on the hash was impossible for me. *(From Venturelli's research files, 17 year old male attending a small, private liberal arts college in the Southeast, May 15, 1984.)*

Once drug use has begun, continuing the behavior involves learning the following sequence: (1) identifying where and from whom the drug can be purchased, (2) maintaining steady contact with drug dealers, (3) developing a preoccupation with maintaining the secrecy of use from authority figures and casual non–drug-using acquaintances, (4) reassuring yourself that the drug use is pleasurable, (5) using with more frequency, and (6) replacing non–drug-using friends with drug-using friends.

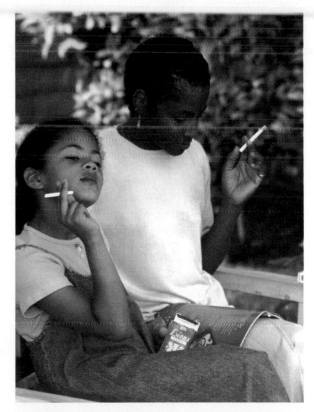

This child is role-playing largely by imitating the habits of a significant other.

Role of Significant Others

After a pattern of drug use has been established, the learning process plays a role in sustaining drug-taking behavior. Edwin Sutherland (1947; Liska and Messner 1999), a pioneering criminologist in sociology, believed that the mastery of criminal behavior depended on the frequency, duration, priority, and intensity of contact with others who are involved in similar behavior (Heitzeg 1996). This theory can also be applied to drug-taking behavior.

In applying Sutherland's principles of social learning to drug use, which he called differential association theory, the focus is on how other members of social groups reward criminal behavior and under what conditions this deviance is perceived as important and pleasurable.

Becker's and Sutherland's theories explain why adolescents may use psychoactive drugs. Essentially, both theories say that the use of drugs is learned during intimate interaction with others who serve as a primary group. (See "Here and Now," Symptoms of Drug and Alcohol Abuse, for information on how the role of significant others can determine a child's disposition toward or away from illicit drug use.)

Learning theory also explains how adults and the elderly are taught the motivation for using a particular type of drug. This learning occurs through influences such as drug advertising, with its emphasis on testimonials by avid users, by medical experts, and by actors and actresses portraying physicians or nurses. Listeners, viewers, and readers who experience such commercials promoting a particular brand name of over-the-counter drugs are bombarded with the necessary motives, preferred techniques, and appropriate attitudes for consuming drugs. When drug advertisements and medical experts recommend a particular drug for specific ailments, in effect they are authoritatively persuading viewers, listeners, or readers that taking a drug will soothe or cure the medical problem presented.

Are Drug Users More Likely to Be Devious?

Social scientists — primarily sociologists and social psychologists — believe that many social development patterns are closely linked to drug use. Based on the age when an adolescent starts to consume alcohol and other drugs, predictions can be made about his or her sexual behavior, academic performance, and other behaviors, such as lying, cheating, fighting, and using marijuana. Similar predictions can be made when the adolescent begins using marijuana. A more detailed study (SAMHSA 2000) shows that there is a strong relationship between adolescent behavior problems and alcohol use.

Figure 2.1 shows that past-month adolescent heavy drinking and emotional/behavioral problems often arise concurrently. Adolescents who drink heavily between the ages of 12 to 17 are more likely to report behavior problems, such as aggressiveness and delinquent and criminal behaviors (SAMHSA 2000).

Figure 2.2 shows that children who began drinking or experimenting with alcohol at or before the 7th grade were more likely at 23 years of age to report smoking (data not shown), marijuana use, and involvement with criminal activities, such as arrest and committing a felony. According to the authors of this longitudinal study, which was conducted in California and Oregon, "Early drinkers do not necessarily mature out of a problematic lifestyle as young adults. Interventions for these high-risk youth should start early and address their other public health problems, particularly their tendency to smoke and use other illicit drugs" (Ellickson et al. 2003, p. 949; CESAR 2003).

Other studies show that early intense use of alcohol or marijuana represents a move toward less conventional behavior, greater susceptibility to peer influence, increased delinquency, and lower achievement in school. In general, drug abusers have 14 characteristics in common:

1. Their drug use usually follows clear-cut developmental steps and sequences. Use of legal drugs, such as alcohol and cigarettes, almost always precedes use of illegal drugs.
2. Use of certain drugs, particularly habitual use of marijuana, is linked to **amotivational syndrome**, which some researchers believe is a

KEY TERMS

amotivational syndrome
the assertion by some drug researchers that heavy use of marijuana causes a lack of motivation in achieving goal-directed behavior

Here and Now

Symptoms of Drug and Alcohol Abuse

Following are profiles of children who are less likely and more likely, respectively, to use and abuse drugs.

Less Likely to Use Drugs

- Child comes from a strong family.
- Family has a clearly stated policy toward drug use.
- Child has strong religious convictions.
- Child is an independent thinker, not easily swayed by peer pressure.
- Parents know the child's friends and the friends' parents.
- Child often invites friends into the house and their behavior is open, not secretive.
- Child is busy and productive and pursues many interests.
- Child has a good, secure feeling of self.
- Parents are comfortable with their own use of alcohol, drugs, and pills; set a good example in using these substances; and are comfortable in discussing their use.
- Parents set a good example in handling crisis situations.
- Child maintains at least average grades and good working relationships with teachers.

Symptoms Exhibited by the Child Who May Be Using Drugs

EDITOR'S NOTE: A child will usually display more than one of the symptoms below when experimenting with drugs. Please remember that any number of the symptoms could also be the result of a physical impairment or disorder.

More Likely to Use Drugs

- Abrupt change in behavior (for example, from very active to passive, loss of interest in previously pursued activities such as sports or hobbies).
- Diminished drive and ambition.
- Moodiness.
- Shortened attention span.
- Impaired communication such as slurred speech or jumbled thinking.
- Significant change in quality of school work.
- Deteriorating judgment and loss of short-term memory.
- Distinct lessening of family closeness and warmth.
- Suddenly popular with new friends who are older and unknown to family members.
- Isolation from family members (hiding in bedroom or locking bedroom door).
- Sneaking out of the house.
- Sudden carelessness regarding appearance.
- Inappropriate overreaction to even mild criticism.
- Secretiveness about whereabouts and personal possessions.
- Friends who avoid introduction or appearance in the child's home.
- Use of words that are odd and unfamiliar.
- Secretiveness or desperation for money.
- Rapid weight loss or appetite loss.
- "Drifting off" beyond normal daydreaming.
- Extreme behavioral changes such as hallucination, violence, unconsciousness, and so on that could indicate a dangerous situation close at hand and needing fast medical attention.
- Unprescribed or unidentifiable pills.
- Strange "contraptions" (for example, smoking paraphernalia) or hidden articles.
- Articles missing from the house. Child could be stealing to receive money to pay for drugs.

Source: L.A.W. Publications, *Let's All Work to Fight Drug Abuse* (Addison, TX: C & L Printing Company, 1985), 38. Used with permission of the publisher. Santa Barbara Alcohol and Drug Program, 1996.

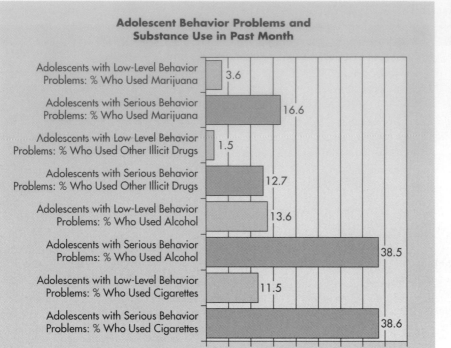

Adolescent Behavior Problems and Substance Use in Past Month

Adolescents with Low-Level Behavior Problems: % Who Used Marijuana — 3.6

Adolescents with Serious Behavior Problems: % Who Used Marijuana — 16.6

Adolescents with Low-Level Behavior Problems: % Who Used Other Illicit Drugs — 1.5

Adolescents with Serious Behavior Problems: % Who Used Other Illicit Drugs — 12.7

Adolescents with Low-Level Behavior Problems: % Who Used Alcohol — 13.6

Adolescents with Serious Behavior Problems: % Who Used Alcohol — 38.5

Adolescents with Low-Level Behavior Problems: % Who Used Cigarettes — 11.5

Adolescents with Serious Behavior Problems: % Who Used Cigarettes — 38.6

FIGURE 2.1

Adolescent behavior problems and substance use in past month.

Source: SAMHSA. "Study Shows Strong Relationship Between Adolescent Behavior Problems and Alcohol Use." (1 March 2000). Available www.samhsa.gov/news/docsshowone.cfm?newsid=175.

FIGURE 2.2

Percentage of grade 7 nondrinkers, experimenters, and drinkers exhibiting problem behaviors at age 23.

*Felonies were defined as buying/selling/holding stolen goods, taking a joy ride without the vehicle owner's permission, breaking into property, arson or attempted arson.

Note: Nondrinkers never had a drink, not even a few sips. Experimenters drank less than three times in the past year, and not in the past month. Drinkers drank three or more times in the past year or drank in the past month. Subjects were assessed in grade 7, again at grade 12, and again at age 23.

Source: Adapted by CESAR (Center for Substance Abuse Research) from P. L. Ellickson, J.S. Tucker, D.J. Klein, "Ten-Year Prospective Study of Public Health Problems Associated with Early Drinking," *Pediatrics* 111(5):949–955, 2003.

general change in personality.[1] This change is characterized by apathy, lack of interest, and inability or difficulty accomplishing goals. The latest research also clearly shows that marijuana use is often responsible for attention and short-term memory impairment and confusion (NIDA 1996).

3. Immaturity, maladjustment, or insecurity usually precede the use of marijuana and other illicit drugs.

4. Those more likely to try illicit drugs, especially before age 12, usually have a history of poor school performance and classroom disobedience.

5. Delinquent or repetitive deviant activities usually precede involvement with illicit drugs.

6. A set of values and attitudes that facilitates the development of deviant behavior exists before the person tries illicit drugs.

7. A social setting in which drug use is common, such as communities and neighborhoods in which peers use drugs indiscriminately, is likely to reinforce and increase the predisposition to drug use.

8. Drug-induced behaviors and drug-related attitudes of peers are usually among the strongest predictors of subsequent drug involvement.

9. Children who feel their parents are distant from their emotional needs are more likely to become drug addicted (see "Here and Now," Does Divorce Affect Adolescent Drug Use?).

10. The younger people are when they begin using drugs, the higher the probability of continued and accelerated drug use. Likewise, the older people are when they start using drugs, the lower the probability of accelerated use and addiction. The period of greatest risk of initiation and habitual use of illicit drugs is usually over by the early twenties.

11. The family structure has changed, with substantially more than half of all women in the United States now working outside the home. A higher divorce rate has led to many children being raised in single-parent households. How the lack of a stay-at-home parent or how membership in a single-family household affects the quality of child care and nurturing is difficult to assess.

12. Mobility obstructs a sense of permanency, and it contributes to a lack of self-esteem. Often, when children are repeatedly moved from one location to another, their community becomes nothing more than a group of strangers. They may have little pride in their home or community and have no commitment to society.

13. Among minority members, a major factor involved in drug dependence is a feeling of powerlessness due to discrimination based on race, social standing, or other attributes. Groups subject to discrimination have a disproportionately high rate of unemployment and below-average incomes. In the United States, approximately 14 million children are reared in poverty (Henslin 2003). The adults they have as role models may be unemployed and experience feelings of powerlessness. Higher rates of delinquency and drug addiction occur in such settings.

14. Abusers who become highly involved in selling drugs begin by witnessing that drug trafficking is a lucrative business, especially in rundown neighborhoods. In some communities, selling drugs seems to be the only available route to real economic success (Jones 1996; Shelden, Tracy, and Brown 2001).

Labeling Theory

Although controversy continues over whether labeling is a theory or a perspective (Akers 1968, 1992; Heitzeg 1996; Plummer 1979), this text takes the position that labeling is a theory (Cheron 2001; Hewitt 1994; Liska and Messner 1999), because it explains something very important with respect to drug use. Although labeling theory does not fully explain why initial drug use occurs, it does detail the processes by which many people come to view themselves as socially deviant from others. Note that the terms *deviant* (in cases of individuals) and *deviance* (in cases of behavior) are sociologically

---

[1] Some argue that perhaps a general lack of ambition (*lethargic behavior*) may *precede* rather than *result from* marijuana use or that amotivational syndrome is present in some heavy marijuana users even before the initial use of this drug, and when the drug is used, the syndrome becomes more pronounced. In any case, some researchers believe that the steady use of marijuana and amotivational syndrome occur together.

Here and Now

Does Divorce Affect Adolescent Drug Use?

As an example of how drug users may be affected by socialization, a study conducted by Needle (Needle et al. 1990; NIDA 1990; Siegel and Senna 1994) found higher drug use among adolescents whose parents divorce. According to the study, children who are adolescents when their parents divorce exhibit more extensive drug use and experience more drug-related health, legal, and other problems than their peers. This study linked the extent of teens' drug use to their age at the time of their parents' divorce. Teenagers whose parents divorce were found to use more drugs and experience more drug-related problems than two other groups of adolescents: those who were aged 10 or younger when their parents divorced, and those whose parents remained married.

This study has important implications for drug abuse prevention efforts. Basically, it says that not everyone is at the same risk for drug use. People at greater risk can be identified, and programs should be developed to meet their special needs.

In this research project, drug use among all adolescents increased over time. However, drug use was higher among adolescents whose parents had divorced when their children were either preteens or teenagers.

Drug use was highest for those teens whose parents divorced during their children's adolescent years. Such families also reported more physical problems, family disputes, and arrests.

The research results showed that distinct gender differences existed in the way that divorce affected adolescent drug use, whether the divorce occurred during the offspring's childhood or adolescent years. Males whose parents divorced reported more drug use and drug-related problems than females. Females whose caretaking parents remarried experienced increased drug use after the remarriage. By contrast, males whose caretaking parents remarried reported a decrease in drug-related problems following the remarriage.

The researchers caution that these findings may have limited applicability, as most of the families studied were white and had middle to high income levels. Needle also notes that the results should not be interpreted as an argument in favor of the nuclear family. Overall, divorce affects adolescents in complex ways and remarriage can influence drug-using behavior, particularly when disruptions occur during adolescence; such turmoil can "trigger" a desire for extensive recreational licit and illicit drug use, often leading to drug abuse.

---

defined as involving the violation of significant social norms held by conventional society. The terms are not used in a judgmental manner, nor are the individuals judged to be immoral or "sick"; instead, the terms refer to an absence of the patterns of behavior expected by conventional society.

Labeling theory says that other people whose opinions we value have a determining influence over our self-image (Best and Luckenbill 1994; Goode 1997; Liska and Messner 1999). (For an example of how labeling theory applies to real-life situations, see "Case in Point.")

KEY TERMS

labeling theory
the theory emphasizing that other people's perceptions directly influence one's self-image

Implied in this theory is the idea that we exert only a small amount of control over the image we portray. In contrast, members of society, especially those we consider to be significant others, have much greater influence and power in defining or redefining our self-image. The image we have of ourselves is vested in the people we admire and look to for guidance and advice. If these people come to define our actions as deviant, then their definition becomes incorporated as a "fact" of our reality.

We can summarize labeling theory by saying that the labels we use to describe people have a profound influence on their self-perceptions. For example, imagine a fictitious individual named Billy. Initially, Billy does not see himself as a compulsive drug user but as an occasional recreational drug user. Let us also assume that Billy is very humor-

▶Case in Point

This excerpt, from the author's files, illustrates labeling theory.

After my mom found out, she never brought it up again. I thought the incident was over — dead, gone, and buried. Well, . . . it wasn't over at all. My mom and dad must have agreed that I couldn't be trusted anymore. I'm sure she was regularly going through my stuff in my room to see if I was still smoking dope. Even my grandparents acted strangely whenever the news on television would report about the latest drug bust in Chicago. Several times that I can't ever forget were when we were together and I could hear the news broadcast on TV from my room about some drug bust. There they all were whispering about me. My grandma asking if I "quitta the dope." One night, I overheard my mother reassure my dad and grandmother that I

no longer was using dope. You can't believe how embarrassed I was that my own family was still thinking that I was a dope fiend. They thought I was addicted to pot like a junkie is addicted to heroin! I can tell you that I would never lay such a guilt trip on my kids if I ever have kids. I remember that for 2 years after the time I was honest enough to tell my mom that I had tried pot, they would always whisper about me, give me the third degree whenever I returned late from a date, and go through my room looking for dope. They acted as if I was hooked on drugs. I remember that for a while back then I would always think that if they think of me as a drug addict, I might as well get high whenever my friends "toke up." They should have taken me at my word instead of sneaking around my personal belongings. I should have left syringes laying around my room!

Source: Interview with a 20-year-old male college student at a private university in the Midwest, conducted by Peter Venturelli on November 19, 1993.

ous, unpretentious, and very outspoken about his drug use and likes to exaggerate the amount of marijuana he smokes on a daily basis. Slowly, Billy's friends begin to perceive him as a "real stoner." According to labeling theory, what happens to Billy? Because of being noticed when "high," his self-presentation, and the comments he makes about the pleasures of drug use, his friends may begin to reinforce the exaggerated drug use image. At first, Billy may enjoy the reflected image of a "big-time" drug user, but after nearly all of his peers maintain a constant exaggerated image, his projected image may turn negative, especially when his friends show disrespect for his opinions. In this example, labeling theory predicts that Billy's perception of himself will begin to mirror the consistent perception expressed by his accusers. If he is unsuccessful in eradicating the addict image or, in this example, the "stoner" image, Billy will reluctantly concur with the label that has been thrust on him. Or, to strive for a self-image as an occasional marijuana user, Billy may abandon his peers so that he can become acceptable once more in the eyes of other people.

An important originator of labeling theory is Edwin Lemert (Lemert 1951; Liska and Messner 1999; Williams and McShane 1999), who distinguished between two types of deviance: primary and secondary deviance. **Primary deviance** is inconsequential deviance, which occurs without having a lasting impression on the perpetrator. Generally, most first-time violations of law, for example, are primary deviations. Whether the suspected or accused individual has committed the deviant act does not matter. What matters is whether the individual identifies with the deviant behavior.

Secondary deviance develops when the individual begins to identify and perceive himself or herself as deviant. The moment this transition occurs,

KEY TERMS

primary deviance
any type of initial deviant behavior in which the prepetrator does not identify with the deviance

secondary deviance
any type of deviant behavior in which the perpetrator identifies with the deviance

deviance shifts from being primary to secondary. Many adolescents casually experiment with drugs. If, however, they begin to perceive themselves as drug users, then this behavior is virtually impossible to eradicate. The same holds true with OTC drug abuse. The moment an individual believes that he or she feels better after using a particular drug, the greater the likelihood that he or she will consistently use the drug.

Howard Becker (1963) believed that certain negative status positions (such as alcoholic, mental patient, ex-felon, criminal, drug addict, and so on) are so powerful that they dominate others (Pontell 1996; Williams and McShane 1999). In the earlier example, if people who are important to Billy call him a "druggie," this name becomes a powerful label that takes precedence over any other status positions Billy may occupy. This label becomes Billy's **master status** — that he is a mindless "stoner." Even if Billy is also an above-average biology major, an excellent musician, and a dependable and caring person, such factors become secondary because his primary status has been recast as a "druggie." Furthermore, once a powerful label is attached, it becomes much easier for the individual to uphold the image dictated by members of society and simply to act out the role expected by significant others. Master status labels distort an individual's public image because other people expect consistency in role performance.

Once a negative master status has been attached to an individual's public image, labeling theorist Edwin Schur asserted that retrospective interpretation occurs. **Retrospective interpretation** is a form of "reconstitution of individual character or identity" (Schur 1971, p. 52). It largely involves *redefining* a person's image within a particular social stereotype, category, or group (see cartoon as an illustration). In the eyes of his peers, Billy is now an emotional, intelligent, yet weird or "freaky" stoner.

Finally, William I. Thomas's (1923) contribution to labeling theory can be summarized in the following theorem: "If men define situations as real, they are real in their consequences" (p. 19). Thus, according to this dictum, when someone is perceived as a drug user, the perception functions as the reality of that person's character and in turn shapes his or her self-perception.

This cartoon illustrates the reflective process in retrospective interpretation that often occurs in daily conversations when we think that our unspoken thoughts are undetectable and hidden. In reality, however, these innermost thoughts are clearly conveyed through body language and nonverbal gestures.

Source: Reproduced with permission of Alex Silvestri.

Subculture Theory

Subculture theory speaks to the role of peer pressure and the behavior resulting from peer group influences. In all groups, there are certain members who are more popular and respected and, as a result, exert more social influence than other peer members. Often, these more socially endowed members are group leaders, task leaders, or emotional leaders who possess greater ability to influence others. Drug use that results from peer pressure demonstrates the extent to which these

KEY TERMS

master status
major status position in the eyes of others that clearly identifies an individual — for example, doctor, professor, alcoholic, heroin addict

retrospective interpretation
social psychological process of redefining a person in light of a major status position — for example, homosexual, physician, professor, alcoholic, convicted felon, or mental patient

subculture theory
theory that explains drug use as a peer-generated activity

more popular and respected leaders can influence and pressure others to initially use or abuse drugs. These three excerpts from interviews illustrate subculture theory:

> When I was 9 or 10, three of my best friends would all take turns sneaking alcohol out of our parents' houses. Then in one of our garages, we would drink the liquor and smoke cigarettes. It was like a street corner thing but it was in a garage. In high school, we would look for the "party-people" and hang out with them. Usually on a Friday or some other school day, we would cut classes and drink and get high at someone's house that would be available. We were a tight-ass group — the goal would be to find a party somewhere. In high school we just hung out together and were known on campus as "the party animals." *(From Venturelli's research files, 21-year-old male college student in a small town in the Midwest, November 23, 2000.)*

> I first started messing around with alcohol in high school. In order to be part of the crowd, we would sneak out during lunchtime at school and get "high." About 6 months after we started drinking, we moved on to other drugs. . . . Everyone in high school belongs to a clique, and my clique was heavy into drugs. We had a lot of fun being "high" throughout the day. We would party constantly. Basically, in college, it's the same thing. *(From Venturelli's research files, 19-year-old male student at a small, religiously affiliated private liberal arts college in the Southeast, February 9, 1985.)*

The third interview illustrates how friendship, coupled with subtle and not-so-subtle peer pressure, influences the novice drug enthusiast:

> There I was on the couch with three of my friends, and as the joint was being passed around, everyone was staring at me. I felt they were saying, "Are you going to smoke with us or will you be a holdout again?" *(From Venturelli's research files, 20-year-old male university student, April 10, 1996.)*

In sociology, charismatic leaders are viewed as possessing status and power, defined as distinction in the eyes of others. In drug-using peer groups, such leaders have power over inexperienced drug users. Members of peer groups are often persuaded to experiment with drugs if the more popular members say, "Come on, try some, it's great" or "Trust me, you'll really get off on this, come on, just try it." In groups where drugs are consumed, the extent of peer influence coupled with the art of persuasion and camaraderie are powerfully persuasive and cause the spread of drug use.

A further extension of subculture theory is the *social and cultural support perspective.* This perspective explains drug use and abuse in peer groups as resulting from an attempt by peers to solve problems collectively. In the neoclassic book *Delinquent Boys: The Culture of the Gang* (1955), Cohen pioneered a study that showed for the first time that delinquent behavior is a collective attempt to gain social status and prestige within the peer group (Liska and Messner 1999; Siegel and Senna 1994; Williams and McShane 1999). Members of certain peer groups are unable to achieve respect within the larger society. Such status-conscious youths find that being able to commit delinquent acts and yet evade law enforcement officials is admirable in the eyes of their delinquent peers. In effect, Cohen believed, delinquent behavior is a subcultural solution for overcoming feelings of status frustration and low self-esteem largely determined by lower class status.

Although the emphasis of Cohen's perspective is on explaining juvenile delinquency, his notion that delinquent behavior is a subcultural solution can easily be applied to drug use and abuse primarily in members of lower-class peer groups. Underlying drug use and abuse in delinquent gangs, for example, results from sharing common feelings of alienation and escape from a society that appears noncaring, noninclusive, distant, and hostile.

Consider the current upsurge in violent gang memberships (see Chapter 16 for more details on adolescents and gangs). In such groups, not only is drug dealing a profitable venture, but drug use also serves as a collective response to alienation and estrangement from conventional middle-class society. In cases of violent minority gang members, the alienation results from racism, poverty, effects of migration and acculturation, and effects of minority status in a white, male-dominated society such as the United States (Glick and Moore 1990; Moore 1978, 1993; Sanders 1994; Thornberry 2001).

STRUCTURAL INFLUENCE THEORIES

Structural influence theories focus on how elements in the *organization* of a society, group, or subculture affect the motivation and resulting drug use behavior that is for nonmedical — most often recreational — drug use. The belief is that no single factor in the society, the group, or the subculture produces the attraction to drug use, but rather that the organization itself or the lack of organization largely causes this behavior to occur.

Social disorganization and social strain theories (Liska and Messner 1999; Werner and Henry 1995) identify the different kinds of social change that are disruptive and explain how, in a general sense, people are adversely affected by the change. Social disorganization theory asks, What in the structure and organization of the social order (the larger social structure) causes people to deviate? Social strain theory attempts to answer the question, What in the structure and organization of the family, the peer, and employee social structure causes someone to deviate? This theory suggests that frustration results from being unable to secure the means to achieve sought-after goals, such as the goal of securing good income without much education, a well-paying job without prior training, and so on. Such perceived shortcomings compel an individual to deviate to achieve desired goals.

An example of feeling stressed and experiencing strain from an overly demanding society.

Overall, social disorganization theory describes a situation in which, because of rapid social change, previously affiliated individuals no longer find themselves integrated into a community's social, commercial, religious, and economic institutions. When this type of alienation occurs, community members whose parents were perhaps more affiliated find themselves more disconnected and feel a lack of effective attachment to the social order. As a result, these disconnected or "disaffiliated" people find deviant behavior to be an attractive alternative.

Developing trusting relationships, stability, and continuity are essential for proper socialization. As is discussed later in this chapter, when major identity development and transformation occur in the teen years, some stability in the immediate environment is very important. Yet, especially today, in our postindustrial and technological society, as well as in most other Westernized types of societies, there are more destabilizing and disorienting factors affecting us as a result of rapid technological development and social change (Gergen 2000; Ritzer 1999, 2000).

Although on the surface most people appear to have little or no difficulty adapting to rapid technological social change, many people find themselves forced to maintain a frantic pace merely to "keep up" on a daily basis. The drive to keep up with social and technological innovation is more demanding today than ever before (Gergen 2000). The constant need to keep pace with change and the increasing multiplicity of realities, and ever more contradictory realities, produced by such change often appears barely controllable and somewhat chaotic. Some individuals who are unable to cope with the constant demand for change and the required adjustment to all this change have difficulty securing a stable self-identity. For example, consider the large numbers of people who need psychological counseling and therapy because they find themselves unable to cope with personal, family, and work-related problems and conflicts. In a recent study, a prediction was made that "32% of all American adults will experience some form of mental disorder during their lives" (Cohen 1997, p. 47). The following interview shows how such confusion and lack of control can easily lead to drug use.

Interviewee: The world is all messed up.

Interviewer: Why? In what way?

Interviewee: Nobody gives a damn anymore about anyone else.

Interviewer: Why do you think this is so?

Interviewee: It seems like life just seems to go on and on. . . . I know that when I am under the influence, life is more mellow. I feel great! When I am high, I feel relaxed and can take things in better. Before I came to Chalmers College [a pseudonym], I felt home life was one great big mess; now that I am here, this college is also a big pile of crap. I guess this is why I like smoking dope. When I am high, I can forget my problems. My surroundings are friendlier; I am even more pleasant! Do you know what I mean? *(From Venturelli's research files, interview with a 19-year-old male marijuana user attending a small, private, liberal arts college in the Southeast, February 12, 1984.)*

Similarly, an interview illustrates how a work environment can affect drug use:

I had one summer job once where it was so busy and crazy that a group of us workers would go out on breaks just to get high. We worked the night shift and our "high breaks" were between 2:00 and 5:00 in the mornings. *(From Venturelli's research files, first-year female college student, age 20, July 28, 1996.)*

Current Social Change in Most Societies

Does social change per se cause people to use and abuse drugs? In response to this question, social change — defined as any measurable change caused by technological advancement that disrupts cultural values and attitudes about everyday life — does not by itself cause widespread drug use. In most cases, social change materialistically advances a culture by profoundly affecting the manner of how things are accomplished. At the same time, *rapid* social change disrupts day-to-day behavior anchored by tradition, which has a tendency to fragment such conventional social groups as families, neighborhoods, and communities. By **conventional behavior**, we mean behavior that is largely dictated by custom and tradition and that

evaporates or goes into a state of flux because of the speed of social change.

Examples include the number of youth subcultures that proliferated during the 1960s (Yinger 1982) and other more recent lifestyles and subcultures, such as pro-life groups, pro-choice groups, Mothers Against Drunk Driving (MADD), gay rights groups, rappers, punk rockers, metalers, grunge, taggers, skinheads, satanists, new wave, and rave enthusiasts (Wooden 1995). Furthermore, two other subcultures, teenagers and the elderly, both have become increasingly independent and, in some subgroups, alienated from other age groups in society (see Figure 2.3).

Simply stated, today's social institutions no longer embrace, influence, and lead people as they did in the past. Consequently, people are free to explore different means of expression and types of recreation. For many, this liberating experience leads to new and exciting outcomes; for others, this freedom from conventional societal norms and attitudes creates an attraction to drug use and abuse.

The following two excerpts, gathered from interviews, illustrate social disorganization and strain theory:

Honest to God, I know things occur much faster than they did 20 years ago. Change is happening faster and occurs more often. What helps is doing some drugs at night at home. I either drink alcohol or do lines of coke. Two different highs but I like them both. This is about the only recreation I have except for the TV at night, after working all darn day nonstop writing letters, answering phone calls, attending meetings, having to go on-site for inspections, and many other things I do each day. *(From Venturelli's research files, interview with a 29-year-old male home security systems manager, Chicago, Illinois, June 23, 2000.)*

I am into my own life because everyone is doing this. I see nearly everyone doing well around here. It's only those who are too stupid

KEY TERMS

conventional behavior
behavior largely dictated by custom and tradition, which is often disrupted by the forces of rapid technological change

*Represents a newly developed and separate stage of identification and expression from the prior era.

FIGURE 2.3

Levels of technological development and resulting subcultures.

to succeed who are poor. I have had a rough time making it lately. Cocaine and speed help, but I know it's not the answer to all my problems. For now, drugs help me to put up with all the shit going on in my life. *(From Venturelli's research files, interview with a 25-year-old male residing in the Southeast and receiving various forms of welfare, March 10, 1985.)*

There is no direct link between social change and drug use. However, plenty of proof exists that certain dramatic changes occur in the organization of society, and many eventually lead certain groups to use and abuse drugs. Figure 2.3 illustrates how the number of life-cycle stages increases

depending on a society's level of technological development. Overall, it implies that, as societies advance from preindustrial to industrial to our current postindustrial type of society, new subcultures emerge at an increasing rate of development. (See Fischer 1976, for similar thinking.) In contrast to industrial and postindustrial societies, preindustrial societies do not have as many separate and distinct periods and cycles of social development. What is shown in Figure 2.3 and implied here is that the greater the number of distinct life cycles, the greater the fragmentation between the members of different stages of development. Generation gaps (conflicting sets of values and attitudes between age cohorts) cause much ignorance and lack of insight between age-group subcultures. This often leads to separation and fragmentation across age groups who develop distinct lifestyle patterns that can easily conflict.

Control Theory

The final major structural influence theory, control theory, emphasizes influences outside the self as the primary cause for deviating to drug use and/or abuse. **Control theory** places importance on positive socialization. **Socialization** is the process by

KEY TERMS

control theory
theory that emphasizes when people are left without bonds to other groups (peers, family, social groups), they generally have a tendency to deviate from upheld values and attitudes

socialization
the growth and development process responsible for learning how to become a responsible, functioning human being

which individuals learn to internalize the attitudes, values, and behaviors needed to become participating members of conventional society. Generally, control theorists believe that human beings can easily become deviant if left without the social controls provided by groups and organizations. Thus, theorists who specialize in control theory emphasize the necessity of maintaining bonds to family, school, peer groups, and other social, political, and religious organizations (Liska and Messner 1999; Thio 1998).

In the 1950s and 1960s, criminologist Walter C. Reckless (1961; Liska and Messner 1999; Siegel and Senna 1991) developed the containment theory. According to this theory, the socialization process results in the creation of strong or weak internal and external control systems. The degree of self-control, high or low frustration tolerance, positive or negative self-perception, successful or unsuccessful goal achievement, and either resistance or adherence to deviant behavior determine internal control. Environmental pressures, such as social conditions, may limit the accomplishment of goal-striving behavior; such conditions include poverty, minority group status, inferior education, and lack of employment.

The external, or outer, control system consists of effective or ineffective supervision and discipline, consistent or inconsistent moral training, and positive or negative acceptance, identity, and self-worth. Many believe that latchkey children have a higher risk of becoming delinquent due to their sporadic supervision and the uneven levels of attention they receive. Alcoholic parents, as well as parents or guardians who are dependent on other types of drugs, are often at risk for raising children with delinquent tendencies because these parents are more apt to be inconsistent with discipline as a result of their drug addiction(s).

In applying this theory to the use or abuse of drugs, we could say that if an individual has a weak external control system, the internal control system must take over to handle external pressure. Similarly, if an individual's external control system is strong, his or her internal control system will not be seriously challenged. If, however, either the internal or external control system is contradictory (weak internal versus strong external), or in the worst-case scenario in which both internal and external controls are weak, drug abuse is much more likely to occur.

Table 2.1 shows the likelihood of drug use resulting from either strong or weak internal and external control systems. It indicates that if both internal and external controls are strong, the use and abuse of drugs are much less likely to occur.

Travis Hirschi (1971; Liska and Messner 1999), a much-respected sociologist and social control theorist, believes that delinquent behavior tends to occur when people lack (1) attachment to others, (2) commitment to goals, (3) involvement in conventional activity, and (4) belief in a common value system. If a child or adolescent is unable to become circumscribed within the family setting, school, and nondelinquent peers, then the drift to delinquent behavior is most likely inevitable.

We can apply Hirschi's theories to drug use as follows:

1. Drug users are less likely than nonusers to be closely tied to their parents.
2. Good students are less likely to use drugs.
3. Drug users are less likely to participate in social clubs and organizations and engage in team sport activities.
4. Drug users are very likely to have friends whose activities are congruent with their own attitudes (drug users "hang with" other drug users and delinquents "hang with" other delinquents).

Table 2.1 Likelihood of Drug Use

INDIVIDUAL INTERNAL CONTROL	EXTERNAL SOCIAL CONTROL	
	Strong	Weak or Nonexistent
Strong	Least likely (almost never)	Less likely (probably never)
Weak	More likely (probably will)	Most likely (almost certain)

Source: Reproduced with permission of Peter J. Venturelli.

The following excerpt illustrates how control theory works:

> I was 15 when my mother confronted me with drug use. I nearly died. We have always been very close and she really cried when she found my "dug out" [paraphernalia that holds a quantity of marijuana] and a "one hitter" [a tubular device for smoking very small quantities of this drug] in her car. My fear was that she would inquire about my drug use with our next-door neighbors, whose children were my best friends. The neighbor residing on the left of our house was one of my high school teachers who knew me from the day I was born. The neighbor on the right side of our house was our church pastor. For a while after she confronted me, I just sneaked around more whenever I wanted to get high. After a few months, I became so paranoid of how my mother kept looking at me when I would come in at night that I eventually stopped smoking weed. Our family is very close and the town I live in (at that time the population was 400) was filled with gossip. I could not handle the pressure, so I quit. *(From Venturelli's research files, female postal worker, age 22, residing in a small Midwestern town, February 9, 1997.)*

In conclusion, control theory depicts how conformity with supportive groups may prevent deviance. It suggests that control is either internally or externally enforced by family, school, and peer group expectations. In addition, individuals who are not equipped with an internal system of self-control reflecting the values and beliefs of conventional society or who feel personally alienated from major social institutions may deviate without feeling guilty for their actions, often because peer pressure results in a suspension or modification of internal beliefs.

Danger Signals of Drug Abuse

How does one know when the use of drugs moves beyond normal use? Many people are prescribed drugs that affect their moods. Using these drugs wisely can be important for both physical and emotional health. Sometimes, however, it may be difficult to decide when use of drugs to handle stress or anxiety becomes inappropriate. It is important that your use of drugs does not result in addiction. The following are some danger signals that can help you evaluate your drug use behavior:

1. Do people who are close to you often ask about your drug use? Have they noticed any changes in your moods or behavior?
2. Do you become defensive when a friend or relative mentions your drug or alcohol use?
3. Do you believe you cannot have fun without alcohol or other drugs?
4. Do you frequently get into trouble with the law, school officials, family, friends, or significant others because of your alcohol or other drug use?
5. Are you sometimes embarrassed or frightened by your behavior under the influence of drugs or alcohol?
6. Have you ever switched to a new doctor because your regular physician would not prescribe the drug you wanted?
7. When you are under pressure or feel anxious, do you automatically take a sedative, a drink, or both?
8. Do you turn to drugs after becoming upset, after confrontations or arguments, or to relieve uncomfortable feelings?
9. Do you take drugs more often or for purposes other than those recommended by your doctor?
10. Do you often mix drugs and alcohol?
11. Do you drink or take drugs regularly to help you sleep or even to relax?
12. Do you take a drug to get going in the morning?
13. Do you find it necessary or nearly impossible to not use alcohol and/or other drugs to have sex?
14. Do you find yourself not wanting to be around friends who do not use drugs or drink on a regular basis?
15. Have you ever seriously thought that you may have a drug addiction problem?
16. Do you make promises to yourself or others that you will stop getting drunk or using drugs?
17. Do you drink and/or use drugs alone, often secretly?

A higher number of "yes" answers indicates a greater likelihood that you are abusing alcohol and/or drugs. Many places offer help at the local level, such as programs in your community listed in the phone book under "Drug Abuse." Other resources include community crisis centers, telephone hotlines, and the National Mental Health Association.

LOW-RISK AND HIGH-RISK DRUG CHOICES

As will become readily apparent throughout this text, some very real risks are associated with recreational drug use. Low-risk and high-risk drug choices refer to two major levels of alcohol and other drug use. **Low-risk drug choices** refer to values and attitudes that keep the use of alcohol and other drugs in control. **High-risk drug choices** refer to values and attitudes that lead to using drugs habitually and addictively, resulting in emotional, psychological, and physical health problems. Low-risk choices include abstinence from all drugs or remaining in true control of the quantity and frequency of drugs taken.

Low-risk choices require self-monitoring your consumption of alcohol and other drugs to reduce your risk of an alcohol and other drug-related problem. Both "low-risk" and "high-risk" are appropriate descriptive concepts that allow us to focus on the health and safety issues involved in drug use and refer to developing and maintaining completely different values and attitudes in your approach to alcohol and other drugs.

This chapter described numerous factors influencing drug use and reasons why people start using or abusing drugs. There are also numerous theories that attempt to explain initial and habitual use. Some people can easily become addicted to alcohol and other drugs because of inherited characteristics, personality, mental instability or illness, and vulnerability to present situations. Others who have more resistance to alcohol and drug addiction may have stronger convictions and abilities to cope with different situations.

Maintaining a Low-Risk Approach

To minimize the risk of alcohol and drug-related problems, we suggest you remain aware of the following:

1. Investigate your family drug history. Does anyone in your family have a history of alcohol or drug abuse? How many members of your family who have alcohol or drug problems are blood relatives? In other words, are you more likely to become dependent on alcohol or drugs because of inherited genes or because of the values and attitudes to which you are exposed?
2. Do you particularly enjoy the effects of alcohol and other drugs? Do you spend a lot of time thinking about how "good" it feels to be high?
3. Does it seem as if the only time you really have fun is when you are using alcohol and other drugs?
4. Keep in mind the following, which is covered throughout this text:
   - **Body size.** A small person typically becomes more impaired by drug use than a larger person.
   - **Gender.** Women typically become more impaired than men of the same size, especially with regard to alcohol use.
   - **Other drugs.** Taking a combination of drugs generally increases the risk of impairment and, in some combinations, accidental death.
   - **Fatigue or illness.** Fatigue increases impairment from alcohol and increases the risk for impairment.
   - **Mind-set.** As you set out to drink or use other drugs, are you expecting heavy use of alcohol or heavy involvement with drugs to the point of inebriation or severe distortion of reality as the evening's outcome? More importantly, what view do you hold regarding moderate use of drugs versus heavy use of drugs?
   - **Empty stomach.** Taking drugs on an empty stomach increases impairment from most drugs.

KEY TERMS

low-risk drug choices
developing values and attitudes that lead to controlling the use of alcohol and drugs

high-risk drug choices
developing values and attitudes that lead to using drugs both habitually and addictively

Also keep in mind that most excessive drug use comes with the following risks:

1. It is against all school policies.
2. It is unlawful behavior (risky with the law).
3. Excessive alcohol and other drug use usually leads not only to public attention, but also to criminal justice attention (police and the courts). Jail time or prison, fines, costly forced rehabilitation programs, and community service work are possible outcomes.
4. The defense costs involved in even simple drug possession charges are often $3000 to $8000 (often beyond an individual's ability to pay for such legal services).
5. A criminal record is a public record and can be acquired or suddenly come to the attention of school officials (especially loan officers and/or government loan personnel), credit bureaus, as well as any other community members.

We leave you with the question: *Are excessive drug use and the resulting drug dependence still worth such risks?* This question is critical, especially when we know that the more often drugs are consumed, the greater the potential not only for drug dependence and addiction, but also for damage to health, personal well-being, family and interpersonal relationships, and community respect.

Discussion Questions

1. Define the terms *addiction, tolerance, dependence*, and *withdrawal.*

2. Describe and contrast the disease and characterological (personality predisposition) models of addiction.

3. List several biological, social, and cultural factors that may be responsible for addiction to drugs.

4. In addition to better cultivation techniques, cite several other possible reasons why the potency of the average marijuana joint has increased since 1960.

5. Given that more than 88% of the U.S. population members are daily drug users of some form, do you think we need to reexamine our strict drug laws, which may be punishing a sizable number of drug users in our society who simply want to use illicit drugs?

6. Is there any way to combine the biological and sociological explanations for why people use drugs so that the two perspectives do not conflict? (Sketch out a synthesis between these two sets of theoretical explanations.)

7. What is the relationship between mental illness and drug abuse? Why is this relationship important?

8. Do you accept the "rats in a maze" concept that psychology offers for explaining why people come to abuse drugs? (This view primarily states that people are like automatons or robots and that reinforcement explains why certain people become addicted to drugs.) Explain your answer.

9. In reviewing the psychological and sociological theories, which best explain drug use? Defend your answer.

10. Does differential association theory take into account non–drug-using individuals whose socialization environment was drug-infested?

11. Do you believe drug users are socialized differently and that these alleged differences account for drug use? Defend your answer.

12. Can divorce be blamed for adolescent drug use? Why or why not? If so, to what extent?

13. Do the current and alarming drug abuse statistics reflect the failure of social change in our society? Why do you agree or disagree with this statement?

14. Is making low-risk choices regarding drug use a more realistic approach for drug moderation than advocating "Just say no" to drug use? Why or why not?

Key Terms

moral model 58

disease model 58

characterological or personality predisposition model 58

personality disorders 58

psychoanalysis 58

"double wall" of encapsulation 58

genetic and biophysiological theories 62

central nervous sytem 62

psychoactive effects 62

neurotransmitters 62

dopamine 62

social learning theory 66

habituation 66

"addiction to pleasure" theory 66

sensation-seeking individuals 66

differential reinforcement 67

social influence theories 68

structural influence theories 68

amotivational syndrome 70

labeling theory 74

primary deviance 75

secondary deviance 75

master status 76

retrospective interpretation 76

subculture theory 76

conventional behavior 79

control theory 80

socialization 80

low-risk drug choices 83

high-risk drug choices 83

Summary

1 Chemical dependence has been considered a major social problem throughout U.S. history.

2 People define chemical addiction in many ways. The essential feature is a chronic adherence to drugs despite significant negative consequences.

3 The major models of addiction are the moral model, the disease model, and the characterological or personality predisposition model.

4 Transitional periods, such as adolescence and middle age, are associated with unique sets of risk factors.

5 Addiction is a gradual process during which a minority of drug users become caught up in vicious cycles that worsen their situation, cause psychological and biological abnormalities, and increase their drug use. Addiction tends to progress, although this step is not inevitable.

6 Drug use is more serious today than in the past because (1) drug use and abuse have increased dramatically since 1960; (2) today's illicit drugs are more potent than in the past; (3) the media present drug use as rewarding; (4) drug use physically harms members of society; and (5) drug use and dealing by violent gangs are increasing at alarming rates.

7 Genetic and biophysiological theories explain addiction in terms of genes, brain dysfunction, and biochemical patterns.

8 Drugs of abuse interfere with the functioning of neurotransmitters, chemical messengers used for communication between brain regions. Drugs with abuse potential enhance the pleasure centers by causing the release of a specific brain neurotransmitter such as dopamine, which acts as a positive reinforcer.

9 The American Psychiatric Association classifies severe drug dependence as a form of psychiatric disorder. Drug abuse can cause mental conditions that mimic major psychiatric illnesses, such as schizophrenia, severe anxiety disorders, and suicidal depression.

10 Four genetic factors can contribute to drug abuse: (1) Many genetically determined psychiatric disorders are relieved by drugs of abuse, which in turn encourages their use; (2) high rates of addiction result from people who are genetically sensitive to addictive drugs; (3) such character traits as insecurity and vulnerability, which are often genetically determined, can lead to drug abuse behavior; and (4) the inability to break from a particular type of drug addiction may be genetically determined, especially when severe craving or very unpleasant withdrawal effects dominate.

11 Introversion and extroversion patterns have been associated with levels of neural arousal in brain stem circuits. These forms of arousal are closely associated with effects caused by drug stimulants or depressants.

12 Reinforcement or learning theory says that the motivation to use or abuse drugs stems from how the "highs" from alcohol and other drugs reduce anxiety, tension, and stress. Positive social influences by drug-using peers also promote drug use.

13 Social influence theories include social learning, the role of significant others, labeling, and subculture theories. Social learning theory explains drug use as a form of learned behavior. Significant others play a role in the learning process involved in drug use and/or abuse. Labeling theory says that other people we consider important can influence whether drug use becomes an option for us. If key people we admire or fear come to define our actions as deviant, then the definition becomes the "fact" of our reality. Subculture theories trace original drug experimentation, use, and/or abuse to peer pressure.

14 There are a number of consistencies in socialization patterns found among drug abusers, which range from immaturity, maladjustment, and insecurity to exposure and belief that selling drugs is a very lucrative business.

15 Sociologist Howard Becker believes that first-time drug users become attached to drugs because of three factors: (1) They learn the techniques of drug use; (2) they learn to perceive the pleasurable effects of drugs; and (3) they learn to enjoy the drug experience.

16 Primary deviance is deviant behavior that the perpetrator does not identify with; hence, it is inconsequential deviant behavior. Secondary deviance is deviance that one readily identifies with.

17 Both internal and external social control should prevail concerning drug use. Internal control deals with internal psychic and internalized social attitudes. External control is exemplified by living in a neighborhood and community in which drug use and abuse are severely criticized or not tolerated as a means to seek pleasure or avoid stress and anxiety.

18 Low-risk and high-risk drug use choices refer to the process of developing values and attitudes toward alcohol and other drugs. Low-risk drug choices encompass values and attitudes leading to a controlled use of alcohol and drugs — from total abstinence to very moderate use. High-risk choices encompass values and attitudes leading to using drugs both habitually and addictively.

References

Akers, R. L. "Problems in the Sociology of Deviance: Social Definition and Behavior." *Social Forces* 6 (June 1968): 455–465.

Akers, R. L. *Drugs, Alcohol, and Society: Social Structure, Process, and Policy.* Belmont, CA: Wadsworth, 1992.

American Psychiatric Association (APA). "Substance-Related Disorders." *Diagnostic and Statistical Manual of Mental Disorders DSM-IV-TR*, 4th ed. Revised. A. Francis, Chair. Washington, DC: American Psychiatric Association, 2000: 191–295.

Apostolides, M. "Special Report: The Addiction Revolution: Old Habits Get New Choices." *Psychology Today* 29 (September/October 1996): 33–43, 75–76.

Bandura, A. *Social Learning Theory.* Englewood Cliffs, NJ: Prentice Hall, 1977.

Beattie, M. *Codependent No More.* San Francisco: Harper, 1987.

Becker, H. S. *Outsiders: Studies in the Sociology of Deviance.* New York: Free Press, 1963.

Becker, H. S. "History, Culture, and Subjective Experience: An Exploration of the Social Basis of Drug-Induced Experiences." *Journal of Health and Social Behavior* 8 (1967): 163–176.

Bejerot, N. "Current Problems of Drug Addiction." *Lakartidingen* (Sweden) 62, 50 (1965): 4231–4238.

Bejerot, N. *Addiction: An Artificially Induced Drive.* Springfield, IL: Thomas, 1972.

Bejerot, N. "The Biological and Social Character of Drug Dependence." In *Psychiatrie der Gegenwart, Forschung und Praxis,* 2nd ed., edited by K. P. Kisker, J. E. Meyer, C. Muller, and E. Stromogrew, Vol. 3: 488P518. Berlin: Springer-Verlag, 1975.

Bespalov, A., A. Lebedev, G. Panchenko, and E. Zvartau. "Effects of Abused Drugs on Thresholds and Breaking Points of Intracranial Self-Stimulation in Rats." *European Neuropsychopharmacology: The Journal of the European College of Neuropharmacology* 9 (1999): 377–383.

Best, J., and D. F. Luckenbill. *Organizing Deviance,* 2nd ed. Englewood Cliffs, NJ: Prentice-Hall, 1994.

Burns, D. B. "The Web of Caring: An Approach to Accountability in Alcohol Policy." In *Designing Alcohol and Other Drug Prevention Programs in Higher Education.* U.S. Department of Education. Newton, MA: Higher Education Center for Alcohol and Other Drug Prevention, 1997. Available http://www.edc.org/hec/pubs/theorybook/burns.html.

Carlson, N. *Psychology: The Science of Behavior,* 3rd ed. Boston: Allyn and Bacon, 1990.

Center for Substance Abuse Research (CESAR). "Early Alcohol Users More Likely to Report Substance Use and Criminal Activity as Young Adults" (September 2003). Available http://www.cesar.umd.edu.

Centers for Disease Control and Prevention (CDCP). "Youth Risk Behavior Surveillance — United States, 2003." *Morbidity and Mortality Weekly Report* 53, SS-2 (2004): 1–96.

Cheron, J. M. *Symbolic Interactionism: An Introduction, an Interpretation, an Integration,* 7th ed. Englewood Cliffs, NJ: Prentice-Hall, 2001.

Clinard M. B., and R. F. Meier. *Sociology of Deviant Behavior,* 8th ed. Fort Worth, TX: Harcourt Brace Jovanovich, 1992.

Cohen, A. K. *Delinquent Boys: The Culture of the Gang.* Glencoe, IL: Free Press, 1955.

Cohen, G. D. "No Job for a Grown-Up." *Utne Reader* (January/February 1997): 47.

Conrad, P., and J. W. Schneider. *Deviance and Medicalization.* St. Louis, MO: Mosby, 1980.

Doweiko, H. E. *Concepts of Chemical Dependency,* 5th ed. Pacific Grove, CA: Brooks/Cole, 2002.

Drug Strategies. "Keeping Score: What We Are Getting for Our Federal Drug Control Dollars 1995." Washington, DC. 1995. Available 000/cdics/colleges/boss/depts/cesar/drugs/ks1995.

Ellickson, P. L., J. S. Tucker, and D. J. Klein. "Ten-Year Prospective Study of Public Health Problems Associated with Early Drinking." *Pediatrics* 111, 5 (2003): 949–955.

Eysenck, H. J., and M. W. Eysenck. *Personality and Individual Differences: A Natural Science Approach.* New York: Plenum Press, 1985.

Farrar, H., and G. Kearns. "Cocaine: Clinical Pharmacology and Toxicology." *Journal of Pediatrics* 115 (1989): 665–675.

Fischer, C. S. *The Urban Experience.* New York: Harcourt Brace Jovanovich, 1976.

Frosch, W. A. "An Analytic Overview of the Addictions." In *The Addictions: Multidisciplinary Perspectives and Treatments,* edited by H. Milman and H. Shaffer. Lexington, MA: Lexington Books/D.C. Heath, 1985.

Gardner, E. L. "Brain Reward Mechanisms." In *Substance Abuse: A Comprehensive Textbook,* 2nd ed., edited by J. H. Lowinson, P. Ruiz, R. B. Millman, and J. G. Langrod, pp. 60–69. Baltimore: Williams & Wilkins, 1992.

Gergen, K. *The Saturated Self: Dilemmas of Identity in Contemporary Life.* New York, NY: Basic Books, Inc., 2000.

Glick, R., and J. Moore, eds. *Drugs in Hispanic Communities.* New Brunswick, NJ: Rutgers University Press, 1990.

Goode, E. *Deviant Behavior,* 5th ed. Upper Saddle River, NJ: Prentice Hall, 1997.

Gray, J. A. *The Psychology of Fear and Stress,* 2nd ed. Cambridge, UK: Cambridge University Press, 1987.

Gray, P. *Psychology,* 3rd ed. New York: Worth, 1999.

Grinspoon, L. "Update on Cocaine." *Harvard Mental Health Letter* 10 (September 1993): 1–4.

Heitzeg, N. A. *Deviance: Rulemakers and Rulebreakers.* Minneapolis, MN: West Publishing, 1996.

Henslin, J. M. *Essentials of Sociology: A Down-to-Earth Approach,* 5th edition. Boston: Pearson/Allyn and Bacon, 2003.

Hewitt, J. P. *Self and Society: A Symbolic Interactionist Social Psychology,* 6th ed. Boston: Allyn and Bacon, 1994.

Hirschi, T. *Causes of Delinquency,* 2nd ed. Los Angeles: University of California Press, 1971.

Inciardi, J. A., D. Lockwood, and A. E. Pottieger. *Women and Crack Cocaine.* New York: Macmillan, 1993.

Jellinck, E. M. *The Disease Concept of Alcoholism.* Highland Park, NJ: Hillhouse Press, 1960.

Johnston, L. D., P. M. O'Malley, and J. G. Bachman. University of Michigan News and Information Services; 17 Dec. 1999, *Citing the National Survey on Drug Abuse, The Monitoring the Future Study.* The University of Michigan Institute for Social Research, National Institute on Drug Abuse, U.S. Department of Human Services, National Institutes of Health, 1999.

Johnston, L. D., P. M. O'Malley, and J. G. Bachman. *Monitoring the Future National Results on Adolescent Drug Use: Overview of Key Findings, 2002.* Rockville, MD: National Institute on Drug Abuse (NIDA), 2003.

Johnston, L. D., P. M. O'Malley, J. G. Bachman, and J. E. Schulenberg. *Monitoring the Future: National Survey Results on Drug Use, 1975–2003, Vol. 1: Secondary School Students 2003.* Bethesda, MD: National Institute on Drug Abuse, 2003.

Johnston, L. D., P. M. O'Malley, J. G. Bachman, and J. E. Schulenberg. *Monitoring the Future: National Results on Adolescent Drug Use: Overview of Key Findings*. Bethesda, MD: National Institute on Drug Abuse, 2004.

Jones, J. *Hep-Cats, Narcs, and Pipe Dreams: A History of America's Romance with Illegal Drugs*. Baltimore, MD: Johns Hopkins University Press, 1996.

Kelly, K., and P. Ramundo. *You Mean I'm Not Lazy, Stupid, and Crazy?!* New York: Scribner, 1993.

Khantzian, E. J. "Addiction: As a Disease" (no date). Available http://www.counselormagazine.com/pfv.asp?aid=addiction.asp.

Koob, G. "Drug Addiction." In *Neurobiology of Disease* 7, 5 (October 2000): 543–545.

Lemert, E. M. *Social Psychology: A Systematic Approach to the Theory of Sociopathic Behavior*. New York: McGraw-Hill, 1951.

Liska, A. E., and S. F. Messner. *Perspectives on Crime and Deviance*. Upper Saddle River, NJ: Prentice Hall, 1999.

Marshall, M. "Conclusions." In *Beliefs, Behavior, and Alcoholic Beverages: A Cross-Cultural Survey*, edited by M. Marshall, 451–457. Ann Arbor, MI: University of Michigan Press, 1979.

Mathias, R. "Novelty Seekers and Drug Abusers Tap Same Brain Reward System, Animal Studies Show." *NIDA Notes* 10, 4 (July/August 1995): 1–5.

Moore, J. *Homeboys: Gangs, Drugs and Prison in the Barrios of Los Angeles*. Philadelphia: Temple University Press, 1978.

Moore, J. "Gangs, Drugs, and Violence." In *Gangs: The Origins and Impact of Contemporary Youth Gangs in the United States*, edited by S. Cummings and D. J. Monti, 27–46. Albany: State University of New York Press, 1993.

Myers, P. L. "Sources and Configurations of Institutional Denial." *Employee Assistance Quarterly* 5 (B) (1990): 43–54.

National Institute on Drug Abuse (NIDA). *Principles of Drug Addiction Treatment*. New York: The Lindesmith Center, 1996.

National Institute on Drug Abuse (NIDA). "Study Finds Higher Use Among Adolescents Whose Parents Divorce." *NIDA Notes* 5 (Summer 1990): 10.

National Institute on Drug Abuse (NIDA). "Double Trouble: Substance Abuse and Psychiatric Disorders." *NIDA Notes* 8 (November/December 1993): 20.

National Institute on Drug Abuse (NIDA). "Attention and Memory Impaired in Heavy Users of Marijuana." Rockville, MD: Office of the National Institute on Drug Abuse, 20 February 1996. Available http://www.health.org/pressrel/heavymar/html.

National Institute on Drug Abuse (NIDA). *2002 Monitoring the Future*, Data Tables. Table 2 — Trends in Annual and 30-Day Prevalence. Rockville, MD: Office of the National Institute on Drug Abuse, 20 June 2003.

Needle, R. H., S. S. Su, and W. J. Doherty. "Divorce, Remarriage, and Adolescent Substance Use: A Prospective Longitudinal Study." *Journal of Marriage and the Family* 52 (1990): 157–159.

O'Brien, R., S. Cohen, G. Evans, and J. Fine. *The Encyclopedia of Drug Abuse*, 2nd ed. New York: Facts on File, 1992.

Office of National Drug Control Policy (ONDCP). *Drug Facts: Cocaine*. White House Drug Policy. Rockville, MD: November 2003. Available http://www.whitehousedrugpolicy.gov/publications/factsht/cocaine/.

Plummer, K. "Misunderstanding Labelling Perspectives." *Deviant Interpretations*, edited by D. Downes and P. Rock, 85–121. London: Robertson, 1979.

Pontell, H. N. *Social Deviance*, 2nd ed. Upper Saddle River, NJ: Prentice Hall, 1996.

Radowitz, J. V. "Smoking and Drug Abuse Traits Linked to Genes." *The Independent's*, 18 June 2003, Independent Digital (UK) Ltd. Available http://news.independent.co.uk/uk/health/story.jsp?story=416515.

Reckless, W. C. "A New Theory of Delinquency." *Federal Probation* 25 (1961): 42–46.

Ritzer, G. *Enchanting a Disenchanted World: Revolutionizing the Means of Consumption*. Thousand Oaks, CA: Pine Forge Press, 1999.

Ritzer, G. *The McDonaldization of Society*, 3rd ed. Thousand Oaks, CA: Pine Forge Press, 2000.

Rousar, E., K. Brooner, M. W. Regier, and G. E. Bigelow. "Psychiatric Distress in Antisocial Drug Abusers: Relation to Other Personality Disorders." *Drug and Alcohol Dependence* 34 (1995): 149–154.

Rudgley, R. *Essential Substances: A Cultural History of Intoxicants in Society*. New York: Kodansha International, 1993.

Sanders, W. B. *Gangbangs and Drive-bys: Grounded Culture and Juvenile Gang Violence*. New York: Aldine De Gruyter, 1994.

Schur, E. M. *Labeling Deviant Behavior*. New York: Harper & Row, 1971.

Shelden, R. G., S. K. Tracy, and W. B. Brown. *Youth Gangs in American Society*, 2nd ed. Belmont, CA: Wadsworth/Thomson Learning, 2001.

Siegel, L. J., and J. J. Senna. *Juvenile Delinquency: Theory, Practice and Law*. St. Paul, MN: West Publishing, 1994.

Smith, D., E. Milkman, and S. Sunderwirth. "Addictive Disease: Concept and Controversy." In *Addictions: Multidisciplinary Perspectives and Treatments*, edited by H. Milkman and H. J. Shaffer. Lexington, MA: Lexington Books/D.C. Heath, 1985.

Spanagel, R., and F. Weiss. "The Dopamine Hypothesis of Reward: Past and Current Status." *Trends in Neuroscience* 22 (1999): 521P27.

Substance Abuse and Mental Health Services Administration (SAMHSA). *National Household Survey on Drug Abuse: Fact Sheet* (August 1998). Available http://www.samhsa.gov/PRESS/99/990818fs.htm.

Substance Abuse and Mental Health Services (SAMHSA). *Study Shows Strong Relationship Between Adolescent Behavior Problems and Alcohol Use*. Rockville, MD: U.S. Department of Health and Human Services Press Release, 1 March

2000. Available http://www.health.org/PRESSREL/mar00/1.htm.

Sutherland, E. *Principles of Criminology*, 4th ed. Philadelphia: Lippincott, 1947.

Tarter, R. E., A. Alterman, and K. L. Edwards. "Alcoholic Denial: A Biopsychosociological Interpretation." *Journal of Studies on Alcohol* 45 (1983): 214–218.

Thio, A. *Deviant Behavior*, 5th ed. New York: Addison Wesley Longman, 1998.

Thomas, W. I., with D. S. Thomas. *The Child in America*. New York: Knopf, 1923.

Thornberry, T. P. "Risk Factors for Gang Membership." In *The Modern Gang Reader*, 2nd ed., edited by J. Miller, C. L. Maxson, and M. W. Klein, 32–42. Los Angeles: Roxbury, 2001.

Uhl, G., K. Blum, E. Noble, and S. Smith. "Substance Abuse Vulnerability and D-2 Receptor Genes." *Trends in Neurological Sciences* 16 (1993): 83–88.

Uhl, G., A. Persico, and S. Smith. "Current Excitement with D-2 Dopamine Receptor Gene Alleles in Substance Abuse." *Archives of General Psychiatry* 49 (February 1992): 157–160.

USA Today. "Seven in 10 Drug Users Work Full-Time" (1999). Available http://www.usatoday.com/life/health/addiction/lhadd091.htm.

Volkow, N. *Changes in Human Brain Systems After Longterm Cocaine Use* (1 February 1999). Available http://165.112.78.61/meetsum/ccb/volkow.html.

Waldorf, D. "Natural Recovery from Opiate Addiction: Some Social-Psychological Processes of Untreated Recover." *Journal of Drug Issues* 13 (1983): 237–280.

Weiss, F. *Cocaine Dependence and Withdrawal: Neuroadaptive Changes in Brain Reward and Stress Systems* (1999). Available http://165.112.78.61/meetsum/ccb/weiss.html.

Werner, E., and S. Henry. *Criminological Theory: An Analysis of Its Underlying Assumptions*. Fort Worth, TX: Harcourt Brace College Publishers, 1995.

Williams III, F. P., and M. D. McShane. *Criminological Theory*, 3rd ed. Upper Saddle River, NJ: Prentice Hall, 1999.

Wilson, W. J. *The Truly Disadvantaged*. Chicago: University of Chicago Press, 1990.

Wooden, W. S. *Renegade Kids, Suburban Outlaws. From Youth Culture to Delinquency*. Belmont, CA: Wadsworth/Thomson Learning, 1995.

World Health Organization Expert Committee on Addiction-Producing Drugs. *World Health Organization Technical Report* 273 (1964): 9–10.

Wyman, J. "Promising Advances Toward Understanding the Genetic Roots of Addiction." *NIDA Notes* 12 (July/August 1997): 1–5.

Yinger, M. J. *Countercultures. The Promise and the Peril of a World Turned Upside Down*. New York: Free Press, 1982.

CHAPTER 3

Drug Use, Regulation, and the Law

Did You Know?

- O Some patent medicines sold at the turn of the twentieth century contained opium and cocaine and were highly addictive.

- O Before World War II, all drugs, except those classified as narcotics, were available without prescription.

- O Enforcement of drug use policies and drug laws differs across different countries.

- O In 2003, an estimated 19.5 million Americans aged 12 or older were current illicit drug users.

- O The United States spends approximately $2.5 billion per year on drug interdiction.

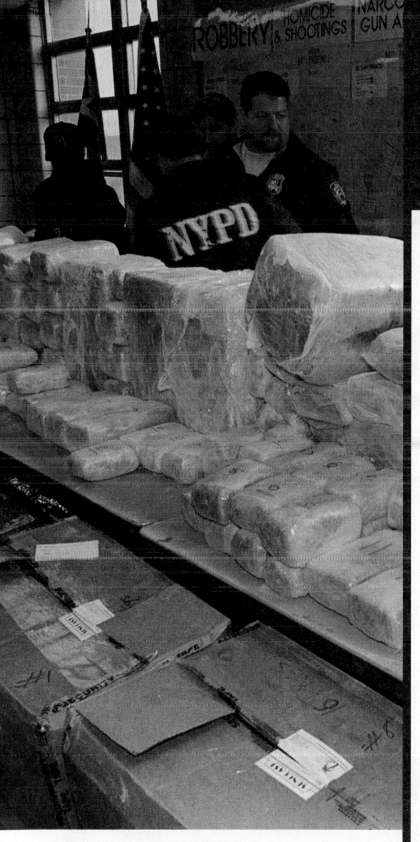

On completing this chapter you will be able to:

◎ Identify the major criteria that determine how society regulates drugs.

◎ Explain the significance of the Pure Food and Drug Act of 1906 and why it was important in regulating drugs of abuse.

◎ Describe the changes in drug regulation that occurred because of the Kefauver-Harris Amendment of 1962.

◎ Identify and explain the stages of testing for an investigational new drug.

◎ Discuss the special provisions (exceptions) made by the Food and Drug Administration (FDA) for drug marketing.

◎ Outline the procedures used by the FDA to regulate nonprescription drugs.

◎ List the three principal factors that influence the formation of laws regulating drug abuse.

◎ Outline the major approaches used to reduce substance abuse.

◎ Describe the three major strategies for combating drug use and abuse.

◎ Explain the main arguments for and against legalizing drugs.

◎ List the most common types of drug testing.

◎ Describe four major factors required for workable drug policies (pragmatic drug policies).

Drugs and Society Online is a great source for additional drugs and society information for both students and instructors.
Visit **http://drugsandsociety.jbpub.com** to find a variety of useful tools for learning, thinking, and teaching.

Introduction

Society mandates that it maintains control over which drugs are permissible and which drugs are prohibited. Through legislation, we decide which drugs are licit and illicit. We decide which licit drugs are readily available "over-the-counter" (OTC) and which can be obtained "by prescription only." Thus, drug laws prohibit indiscriminate use of what society defines as a drug. As we saw in Chapter 1, licit and illicit drugs can produce vastly different effects on both the mental and the bodily functions. Chapters 4 and 5 focus on how and why different types of drugs affect our bodies. In this chapter, you will come to better understand how society attempts to control drug use and abuse.

Drug regulation brings to mind numerous questions. For example, why are the laws against drug use so controversial? When were these laws first created? In regulating and prohibiting the free marketing of either licit or illicit drug use, how does U.S. society compare with other societies? Do these other societies have fewer drug users as a result of being more lenient or restrictive toward drug abusers? Do our drug laws coincide with the opinions of most U.S. citizens? Are nonpunitive approaches toward drug use feasible? Do drug laws realistically diminish drug use? What common attitudes prevail regarding the enactment and enforcement of drug laws?

This chapter attempts to respond to many of these questions by delving into the relationship between drug use and the law. It examines the development of drug regulations in the United States that apply to both the manufacture of drugs and the control of their use. Although many think that the regulation of drug manufacturing and drug abuse lie at the opposite ends of the spectrum, regulation of drug manufacturing and abuse of drugs actually evolved from the same process.

Cultural Attitudes About Drug Use

Currently, cultural attitudes in the United States regarding the use of drugs blend beliefs in individuals' rights to live their lives as they desire with society's obligation to protect its members from the burdens imposed by uncontrolled behavior. The history of drug regulation consists of regulatory swings in response to attempts by government to balance these two factors while responding to public pressures and perceived public needs. For example, 100 years ago, most people expected the government to protect citizens' rights to produce and market new foods and substances; they did not expect or desire the government to regulate product quality or claims. Instead, the public relied on private morals and common sense to obtain quality and protection in an era of simple technology. Unfortunately, U.S. society had to learn by tragic experience that its trust was not well placed; many unscrupulous entrepreneurs were willing to risk the safety and welfare of the public in an effort to maximize profits and acquire wealth. In fact, most medicines of these earlier times were not merely ineffective but often dangerous.

Because of the advent of high technology and the rapid advancements society has made, we now rely on highly trained experts and government "watchdog" agencies for consumer information and protection. Out of this changing environment have evolved two major guidelines for controlling drug development and marketing:

1. Society has the right to protect itself from the damaging effects of drug use. This concept not only is closely aligned with the emotional and highly visible issues of drug abuse, but also includes protection from other drug side effects. Thus, although we expect the government to protect society from drugs that can cause addiction, we also expect it to protect us from drugs that cause cancer, cardiovascular disease, or other threatening medical conditions.

2. Society has the right to demand that drugs approved for marketing be safe and effective to the general public. If drug manufacturers promise that their products will relieve pain, those drugs should be analgesics; if they promise that their products will relieve depression, those drugs should be antidepressants; if they promise that their products will relieve stuffy noses, those drugs should be decongestants.

The public, through the activities of regulatory agencies and statutory enactments, has attempted to require that drug manufacturers produce safe and effective pharmaceutical products. Closely linked to these efforts is the fact that society uses similar strategies to protect itself from the problems associated with the specific drug side effect of dependence or addiction, which is associated with drug abuse.

The Road to Regulation and the FDA

In the late 1800s and early 1900s, sales of uncontrolled medicines flourished and became widespread. Many of these products were called patent medicines, which signified that the ingredients were secret, not that they were patented. The decline of patent medicines began with the 1906 Pure Food and Drug Act, which required manufacturers to indicate the amounts of alcohol, morphine, opium, cocaine, heroin, and marijuana extract on the label of each product. It became obvious at this time that many medicinal products on the market labeled "nonaddictive" were, in fact, potent drugs "in sheep's labeling" and could cause severe dependence. However, most government interest at the time centered on regulation of the food industry, not drugs.

Even though federal drug regulation was based on the free-market philosophy that consumers could make choices for themselves, it was decided that the public should have information about possible dependence-producing drugs to ensure that they understood the risks associated with using these products. The Pure Food and Drug Act made misrepresentation illegal, so that a potentially addicting patent drug could not be advertised as "non–habit forming." This step marked the beginning of new involvement by governmental agencies in drug manufacturing.

Shortcomings in the Pure Food and Drug Act quickly became obvious. For example, the law did not allow the government to stop the distribution of dangerous preparations, including those designed to reduce weight. One such product contained dinitrophenol, a compound that purportedly increased metabolic rate and was responsible for many deaths (FDA History Office 2003).

The Pure Food and Drug Act was modified, albeit not in a consumer-protective manner, by the Sherley Amendment in 1912. The distributor of a cancer "remedy" was indicted for falsely claiming on the label that the contents were effective. The case was decided in the U.S. Supreme Court in 1911. Justice Holmes, writing for the majority opinion, said that, based on the 1906 act, the company had not violated any law because legally all it was required to do was accurately state the contents and their strength and quality. The accuracy of the therapeutic claims made by drug manufacturers was not controlled. Congress took the hint and passed the Sherley Amendment to add to the existing law the requirement that labels should not contain "any statement . . . regarding the curative or therapeutic effect . . . which is false and fraudulent." However, the law required that the government prove fraud, which turned out to be difficult (and is still problematic). This amendment did not improve drug products but merely encouraged pharmaceutical companies to be more vague in their advertisements (Temin 1980).

PRESCRIPTION VERSUS OTC DRUGS

The distinction between prescription and OTC drugs is relatively new to the pharmaceutical industry. All nonnarcotic drugs were available OTC before World War II. It was not until a drug company unwittingly produced a toxic product that killed 107 people that the FDA was given control over drug safety in the 1938 Federal Food, Drug, and Cosmetic Act (Hunter et al. 1993). The bill had been debated for several years in Congress and showed no promise of passage. Then, a pharmaceutical company decided to sell a liquid form of a sulfa drug (one of the first antibiotics) and found that the drug would dissolve well in a chemical solvent, diethylene glycol (presently used in antifreeze products). The company marketed the antibiotic as Elixir Sulfanilamide without testing the solvent for toxicity. Under the 1906 Pure Food and Drug Act, the company could not be prosecuted for the toxicity of this form of drug or for not testing the formulation of the drug on animals first. It could only be prosecuted for mislabeling the product on the technicality that *elixir* refers to a solution in alcohol, not a solution in diethylene glycol. Again, it was apparent that the laws in place provided woefully inadequate protection for the public.

The 1938 act differed from the 1906 law in several ways. It defined *drugs* to include products that affected bodily structure or function even in the absence of disease. Companies had to file applications with the government for all new drugs showing that they were safe (not effective — just safe) for use as described. The drug label had to list all ingredients and include the quantity of each, as well as provide instructions regarding correct use of the drug and warnings about its dangers. In addition, the act eliminated a Sherley Amendment requirement to prove intent to defraud in drug misbranding cases (FDA Backgrounder 2002).

Before passage of the 1938 act, you could go to a doctor and obtain a prescription for any nonnarcotic drug or go to the pharmacy directly if you had already decided what was needed. The labeling requirement in the 1938 act allowed drug companies to create a class of drugs that could not be sold legally without a prescription. It has been suggested that the actions by the FDA were motivated by the frequent public misuse of two classes of drugs developed before passage of the 1938 law: sulfa antibiotics and barbiturates. People often took too little of the antibiotics to cure an infection and too much of the barbiturates and became addicted.

The 1938 Food, Drug, and Cosmetic Act allowed the manufacturer to determine whether a drug was to be labeled *prescription* or *nonprescription*. The same product could be sold as prescription by one company and as OTC by another. After the Durham-Humphrey Amendment was passed in 1951, almost all new drugs were placed in the prescription-only class. The drugs that were patented and marketed after World War II included potent new antibiotics and phenothiazine tran-

quilizers such as Thorazine. Both the FDA and the drug firms thought these products were potentially too dangerous to sell OTC. The Durham-Humphrey Amendment established the criteria, which are still used today, for determining whether a drug should be classified as prescription or nonprescription. Basically, if a drug does not fall into one of the following three categories, it is considered nonprescription:

1. The drug is habit-forming.
2. The drug is not safe for self-medication because of its toxicity.
3. The drug is a new compound that has not been shown to be completely safe.

In 1959, Senator Estes Kefauver initiated hearings concerned with the enormous profit margins earned by drug companies due to the lack of competition in the market for new, patented drugs. Testimony by physicians revealed that an average doctor in clinical practice often was not able to evaluate accurately the efficacy of the drugs he or she prescribed. The 1938 law did not give the FDA authority to supervise clinical testing of drugs; consequently, the effectiveness of drugs being sold to the public was not being determined. Both the Kefauver and Harris Amendments put forth in Congress were intended to deal with this problem but showed no likely signs of becoming law until the thalidomide tragedy occurred.

During the Kefauver hearings, the FDA received an approval request for Kevadon, a brand of thalidomide that the William Merrell Company hoped to market in the United States. **Thalidomide** had been used in Europe as a sedative for pregnant women. Despite ongoing pressure from the firm, medical officer Frances Kelsey refused to allow the request to be approved because of insufficient safety data (FDA History Office 2003). By 1962, the horrifying effects of thalidomide on developing fetuses became known. There are two approximately 24-hour intervals early in pregnancy when thalidomide can alter the development of the arms and legs of an embryo. If a woman takes thalidomide on one or both of these days, the infant could be born with abnormally developed arms and/or legs (called **phocomelia**, from the Greek words for flippers, or "seal-shaped limbs"). Even though Kevadon was never approved for marketing in this

KEY TERMS

thalidomide
a sedative drug that, when used during pregnancy, can cause severe developmental damage to a fetus

phocomelia
a birth defect; impaired development of the arms, legs, or both

Characteristic limb deformities caused by thalidomide.

country, Merrell had distributed more than 2 million tablets in the United States for investigational use — use that the law and regulations left mostly unchecked. Once thalidomide's deleterious effects became known, the FDA moved quickly to recover the supply from physicians, pharmacists, and patients. For her efforts, Kelsey received the President's Distinguished Federal Civilian Service Award in 1962, the highest civilian honor available to government employees.

Although standard testing probably would not have detected the congenital effect of thalidomide and the tragedy would likely have occurred anyway, these debilitated infants stimulated passage of the 1962 Kefauver and Harris Amendments. They strengthened the government's regulation of both the introduction of new drugs and the production and sale of existing drugs. The amendments required, for the first time, that drug manufacturers demonstrate the efficacy as well as the safety of their drug products. The FDA was empowered to

retract approval of a drug that was already being marketed. In addition, the agency was permitted to regulate and evaluate drug testing by pharmaceutical companies and mandate standards of good drug-manufacturing policy.

THE RISING DEMAND FOR EFFECTIVENESS IN MEDICINAL DRUGS

To evaluate the effectiveness of the more than 4000 drug products that were introduced between 1938 and 1962, the FDA contracted with the National Research Council to perform the Drug Efficacy Study. This investigation started in 1966 and ran for 3 years. The council was asked to rate drugs as either effective or ineffective. Although the study was supposed to be based on scientific evidence, this information often was not available, which meant that conclusions sometimes relied on the clinical experience of the physicians on each panel; these judgments were not always based on reliable information.

A legal challenge resulted when the FDA took an "ineffective" drug off the market and the manufacturer sued. This action finally forced the FDA to define what constituted an adequate and well-controlled investigation. Adequate, documented clinical experience was no longer satisfactory proof that a drug was safe and effective. Each new drug application now had to include information about the drug's performance in patients compared with the experiences of a carefully defined control group. The drug could be compared with (1) a placebo, (2) another drug known to be active based on previous studies, (3) the established results of no treatment, or (4) historical data about the course of the illness without the use of the drug in question. In addition, a drug marketed before 1962 could no longer be grandfathered in. If the company could not prove the drug had the qualifications to pass the post-1962 tests for a new drug, it was considered a new, unapproved drug and could not legally be sold.

REGULATING THE DEVELOPMENT OF NEW DRUGS

The amended Federal Food, Drug, and Cosmetic Act in force today requires that all new drugs be registered with and approved by the FDA. The FDA is mandated by Congress to (1) ensure the rights and safety of human subjects during clinical testing of experimental drugs; (2) evaluate the safety and efficacy of new treatments based on test results and information from the sponsors (often health-related companies); and (3) compare potential benefits and risks to determine whether a new drug should be approved and marketed. Because of FDA regulations, all pharmaceutical companies must follow a series of steps when seeking permission to market a new drug (see Figure 3.1).

Regulatory Steps for New Prescription Drugs

Step 1: Preclinical Research and Development A chemical must be identified as having potential value in the treatment of a particular condition or disease. The company interested in marketing the chemical as a drug must run a series of tests on at least two or more animal species. Careful records must be kept of side effects, absorption, distribution, metabolism, excretion, and the dosages of the drug necessary to produce the various effects. Carcinogenic, mutagenic, and teratogenic variables are tested. The dose-response curve must be determined along with potency, and then the risk and benefit of the substance must be calculated (see Chapter 5). If the company still believes there is a market for the substance, it forwards the data to the FDA to obtain an investigational new drug

(IND) number for further tests. No more than 5 in 5000 tested compounds pass these preclinical trials and are proposed for clinical studies (FDA 2002).

Step 2: Clinical Research and Development Animal tests provide some information, but ultimately tests must be done on the species for which the potential drug is intended — that is, humans. These tests usually follow three phases.

Phase 1 is called the *initial clinical stage*. Small numbers of volunteers (usually 20–100), including both healthy people and patients, are recruited to establish drug safety and dosage ranges for effective treatment and to examine side effects. Formerly, much of this research was done on prison inmates, but because of bad publicity and the possibility of coercion, fewer prisoners are used today. Medical students, paid college student volunteers, and volunteers being treated at free clinics are more often used after obtaining informed consent. The data from Phase 1 clinical trials are collected, analyzed, and sent to the FDA for approval before beginning the next phase of human subject testing.

Phase 2 testing is called the *clinical pharmacological evaluation stage*. The effects of the drug are tested to eliminate investigator bias and to determine side effects and the effectiveness of the treatment. Because the safety of the new drug has not been thoroughly established, a few patients (per-

FIGURE 3.1

Steps required by the FDA for reviewing a new drug.

haps 100–300 volunteers) with the medical problem the drug is intended to treat participate in these studies. Statistical evaluation of this information is carried out before proceeding with Phase 3 testing.

Phase 3 is the *extended clinical evaluation stage*. By this time, the pharmaceutical company has a good idea of both drug effectiveness and dangers. The drug can be offered safely to a wider group of participating clinics and physicians, who cooperate in the administration of the potential drug — when medically appropriate — to thousands of volunteer patients who have given informed consent.

This stage makes the drug available on a wide experimental basis. Sometimes, by this point, there has been publicity about the new drug, and people with the particular disease for which the drug was developed may actively seek out physicians licensed to experiment with it.

During Phase 3 testing, safety checks are made and any side effects are noted that might show up as more people are exposed to the drug. After the testing program concludes, careful analysis is made of the effectiveness, side effects, and recommended dosage. If there are sufficient data to demonstrate that the drug is safe and effective, the company submits a new drug application (NDA) as a formal request that the FDA consider approving the drug for marketing. The application usually comprises many thousands of pages of data and analysis, and the FDA must sift through it and decide whether the risks of using the drug justify its potential benefits. The FDA usually calls for additional tests before the drug is determined to be safe and effective and before granting permission to market it.

Step 3: Permission to Market At this point, the FDA can allow the drug to be marketed under its patented name. It may cost $500 million and take an average of 8.5 years to develop a new drug in the United States (FDA 2002). The situation is similar elsewhere, although in some countries the clinical evaluations are less stringent and require less time.

Once the drug is marketed, it continues to be closely scrutinized for adverse effects. This postmarketing surveillance is often referred to as *Phase 4* and is important because, in some cases, nega-

tive effects may not show up for a long time. For example, it was determined in 1970 that diethylstilbestrol (DES), when given to pregnant women to prevent miscarriage, causes an increased risk of a rare type of vaginal cancer in their daughters when these children enter their teens and young adult years. The FDA subsequently removed from the market the form of DES that had been used to treat pregnant women. As described earlier, the thalidomide tragedy resulted in passage of the law that gave the FDA this authority.

Exceptions: Special Drug-Marketing Laws There is continual concern that the process used by the FDA to evaluate prospective drugs is laborious and excessively lengthy. Hence, an amendment was passed to accelerate the evaluation of urgently needed drugs. The so-called fast-track rule has been applied to the testing of certain drugs used for the treatment of rare cancers, AZT (zidovudine) for the treatment of AIDS (the review process only required 2 years; Hunter et al. 1993), and some other drugs. As a result, they have reached the market after a much reduced testing program.

A second amendment, the Orphan Drug Law, allows drug companies to receive tax advantages if they develop drugs that are not very profitable because they are useful in treating only small numbers of patients, such as those who suffer from rare diseases. A *rare disease* is defined as one that affects fewer than 200,000 people in the United States or one for which the cost of development is not likely to be recovered by marketing.

The federal government and the FDA are continually refining the system for evaluating new drugs to ensure that new effective therapeutic substances can be made available for clinical use as soon as it is safely possible. Some of these modifications reflect the fact that patients with life-threatening diseases are willing to accept greater drug risks to gain faster access to potentially useful medications. Attempts to accelerate the drug review are exemplified by the Prescription Drug User Fee Act of 1992. This law required drug manufacturers to pay fees to the FDA for the evaluation of NDAs. Congress required the FDA to use these fees to hire more reviewers so as to expedite the reviews. Since passage of this act, the number of new drug approvals has increased from 63 in 1991 to 131 in 1996 (FDA History Office 2003).

The Regulation of Nonprescription Drugs

The Durham-Humphrey Amendment to the Food, Drug, and Cosmetic Act made a distinction between prescription and nonprescription (OTC) drugs and required the FDA to regulate OTC drug marketing. In 1972, the FDA initiated a program to evaluate the effectiveness and safety of the nonprescription drugs on the market and to ensure that they included appropriate labeling (for more details, see Chapter 15). Each so-called active ingredient in the OTC medications was reviewed by a panel of drug experts including physicians, pharmacologists, and pharmacists. Based on the recommendations of these panels, the ingredients were placed in one of the following three categories:

I. Generally recognized as safe and effective for the claimed therapeutic indication
II. Not generally recognized as safe and effective or unacceptable indications
III. Insufficient data available to permit final classification

By 1981, the panels had made initial determinations about over 700 ingredients in more than 300,000 OTC drug products and submitted more than 60 reports to the FDA.

In the second phase of the OTC drug review, the FDA evaluated the panels' findings and submitted a tentative adoption of the panels' recommendations (after revision, if necessary), following public comment and scrutiny. After some time and careful consideration of new information, the agency issued a final ruling and classification of the ingredients under consideration.

THE EFFECTS OF THE OTC REVIEW ON TODAY'S MEDICATIONS

The review process for OTC ingredients has had a significant impact on the public's attitude about

OTC products and their use (both good and bad) in self-medication. It was apparent from the review process that many OTC drug ingredients did not satisfy the requirements for safety and effectiveness. In fact, in 1990 alone, the FDA banned 223 uses of nonprescription drug ingredients, ruling that the ingredients were ineffective against problems ranging from acne to swimmer's ear. Consequently, it is almost certain that, in the future, there will be fewer active ingredients in OTC medicines, but these drugs will be safer and more effective than ever before.

In addition, with heightened public awareness, greater demand has been brought to bear on the FDA to make better drugs available to the public for self-medication. In response to these pressures, the FDA has adopted a **switching policy**, which allows the agency to review prescription drugs and evaluate their suitability as OTC products. The following criteria must be satisfied if a drug is to be switched to OTC status:

1. The drug must have been marketed by prescription for at least 3 years.
2. Use of the drug must have been relatively high during the time it was available as a prescription drug.
3. Adverse drug reactions must not be alarming, and the frequency of side effects must not have increased during the time the drug was available to the public.

In general, this switching policy has been well received by the public. The medical community and the FDA are generally positive about OTC switches as well. There are some concerns, however, that the wider access to more effective drug products will lead to increased abuse or misuse of OTC products. Hence, emphasis is placed on adequate labeling and education to ensure that consumers have sufficient information to use OTC products safely and effectively.

The Regulation of Drug Advertising

Much of the public's knowledge and impressions about drugs, especially those available OTC, come from advertisements. It is difficult to ascertain the

KEY TERMS

switching policy
an FDA policy allowing the change of suitable prescription drugs to over-the-counter status

amount of money currently spent by the pharmaceutical industry to promote its products. Because of the intense competition among OTC drugs, it is likely that as much as 15% to 20% of the dollar sales for these products is spent on advertising to the general public and that the advertising budget equals a sum of approximately $10 billion annually. For prescription drugs, it is likely that the costs of advertising, promoting, and marketing exceed $10 billion annually (Woolsey 1994).

There is no doubt that these promotional efforts by pharmaceutical manufacturers have a tremendous impact on the drug-purchasing habits of the general public and health professionals. Not surprisingly, drug use based on misleading or false advertising claims, rather than facts, can result in unsatisfactory drug therapy and can be extremely dangerous. Regulations governing the advertising of nonprescription drugs are set and enforced by the Federal Trade Commission (FTC). These rules are less stringent than those for prescription medicines (Woolsey 1994).

PRESCRIPTION ADVERTISING

The economics of prescription drugs are unique because a second party, the health professional, dictates what the consumer, the patient, will purchase. Currently, many pharmaceutical companies advertise medications directly to the public. Direct advertising of prescription drugs to consumers has experts concerned that patients will put pressure on physicians to prescribe inappropriately. For example, in 1992 more than $100 million was spent by pharmaceutical companies for public advertising (TV, newspapers, magazines, and so on) of nicotine patches for people trying to quit smoking. Some medical experts argue that, as a consequence, many consumers perceive the patches as a quick cure for their tobacco dependence and ignore the fact that they work only as part of a serious behavior modification program. Critics claim this lack of consumer understanding led to incorrect use of the patches and has resulted in fatal heart attacks (Hwang 1992).

A large amount of prescription drug promotion is directed at health professionals and controlled by the FDA. The approaches employed by manufacturers to encourage health professionals to prescribe their products include advertising in prestigious medical journals, direct mail advertising, and some radio and television advertising. All printed and audio materials distributed by drug salespeople are controlled by FDA advertising regulations. Perhaps the most effective sales approach is for drug representatives to personally visit health professionals; this tactic is harder to regulate.

Many health professionals rely on drug company salespeople for the so-called latest scientific information concerning drugs and their effects. Although these representatives of the drug industry can provide an important informational service, it is essential that health professionals remember that these people make a living by selling these products, and often their information is biased accordingly.

Many people in and out of the medical community have questioned the ethics of drug advertising and marketing in the United States and are concerned about the negative impact that deceptive promotion has on target populations. One of the biggest problems in dealing with misleading or false advertising is defining such deception. Probably the best guideline for such a definition is summarized in the Wheeler-Lea Amendment to the FTC Act:

> The term *false advertisement* means an advertisement, other than labeling, which is misleading in a material respect; and in determining whether any advertisement is misleading, there shall be taken into account not only representations . . . but the extent to which the advertisement fails to reveal facts.

Tough questions are being asked as to how much control should be exerted over the pharmaceutical industry to protect the public without excessively infringing on the rights of these companies to promote their goods. The solutions to these problems will not be simple. Nevertheless, efforts to keep drug advertisements accurate, in good taste, and informative are worthwhile and are necessary if the public is expected to make rational decisions about drug use (see "Here and Now," What's in an Ad?).

FEDERAL REGULATION AND QUALITY ASSURANCE

No matter what policy is adopted by the FDA and other drug-regulating agencies, there will always

Here and Now

The Federal Food, Drug, and Cosmetic Act requires that all drug advertisements contain information in brief summary relating to side effects, contraindications, and effectiveness. The current advertising regulations specify that this information disclosure needs to include all the risk information in a product's approved labeling. Typically, print advertisements include a reprinting of the risk-related sections of the approved labeling (also called full prescribing information or the package insert). Sponsors, however, can write this risk information in language appropriate for the targeted audience. The FDA encourages this approach.

In addition to the specific disclosure requirements, advertisements cannot be false or misleading or omit material facts. They also must present a fair balance between effectiveness and risk information.

In addition, all prescription drug broadcast advertisements must abide by two specific requirements. First, broadcast advertisements must include the product's most important risk-related information in the audio or audio and visual parts of the advertisement. Second, broadcast advertisements must contain either a brief summary of the advertised product's risk information or, alternatively, make adequate provision for disseminating the product's approved labeling in connection with the ad. Thus, the regulations for broadcast advertisements recognize this medium's inherent limitations by providing an alternative mechanism for meeting the act's information disclosure requirement (FDA, Division of Drug Marketing, Advertising and Communications, 2003).

According to Harvard University, the pharmaceutical industry spends most advertising funds on drugs used as therapy for chronic conditions and drugs with a low occurrence of side effects. In 2000, more than $15 billion was spent by the industry on drug promotion: this represented 14% of sales (Harvard press release, 2002).

---

be those who criticize their efforts and complain that they do not do enough or that they do too much. On the one hand, the FDA has been blamed for being excessively careful and requiring too much testing before new drugs are approved for marketing. On the other hand, when new drugs are released and cause serious side effects, the FDA is condemned for being sloppy in its control of drug marketing.

What is the proper balance, and what do we, as consumers, have the right to expect from the government? These are questions each of us should ask, and we have a right to share our answers with government representatives.

Regardless of our individual feelings, it is important to understand that the current (and likely future) federal regulations do not ensure drug safety or effectiveness for everyone. Too many individual variables alter the way each of us responds to drugs, making such universal assurances impossible. Federal agencies can only deal with general policies and make general decisions. For example, what if the FDA determines that a given drug is reasonably safe in 95% of the population and

effective in 70%? Are these acceptable figures, or should a drug be safe in 99% and effective in 90% before it is deemed suitable for general marketing? What of the 5% or 1% of the population who will be adversely affected by this drug? What rights do they have to be protected?

There are no simple answers to these questions. Federal policies are inevitably compromises that assume that the clinician who prescribes the drug and/or the patient who buys and consumes it will be able to identify when use of that drug is inappropriate or threatening. Unfortunately, sometimes drug prescribing and drug consuming are done carelessly and unnecessary side effects occur or the drug does not work. Then the questions surface again: Are federal drug agencies doing all they can to protect the public? Should the laws be changed?

It is always difficult to predict the future, especially when it depends on sometimes fickle politicians and erratic public opinion. Nevertheless, with the dramatic increase in new and better drugs becoming available to the public, it is not likely that federal or state agencies will diminish their role in regulating drug use. Now more than ever, the public demands safer and more effective drugs. This public attitude will likely translate into even greater involvement by regulatory agencies in issues of drug development, assessment, and marketing.

Another reason for increased regulation in the future is that many of the larger pharmaceutical companies have become incredibly wealthy. Several of the most profitable companies have become subsidiaries of powerful corporations that are driven more by profit margins than by philanthropic interests. In such an environment, governmental agencies are essential to ensure that the rights of the public are protected.

Drug Abuse and the Law

The laws that govern the development, distribution, and use of drugs in general and drugs of abuse in particular are interrelated. There are, however, some unique features concerning the manner in which federal agencies deal with the drugs of abuse that warrant special consideration. A summary of drug abuse laws in the United States is shown in Table 3.1.

Coffee, tea, tobacco, alcohol, marijuana, hallucinogens, depressants (such as barbiturates), and narcotics have been subject to a wide range of controls, varying from none to rigid restrictions. A few countries have instituted severe penalties, such as strangulation for smoking tobacco or opium, and strict bans on alcohol. In other countries, these substances have been deemed either legal or prohibited, depending on the political situation and the desires of the population. Historically, laws have been changed when so many people demanded access to a specific drug of abuse that it would have been impossible to enforce a ban (as in the revocation of Prohibition) or when the government needed tax revenues that could be raised by selling the drug (one argument for legalizing drugs of abuse today). A current example is the controversy over decriminalization or legalization of marijuana (see Chapter 13).

Table 3.1 Federal Laws Associated with the Control of Narcotics and Other Abused Drugs

DATE	NAME OF LEGISLATION	SUMMARY OF COVERAGE AND INTENT OF LEGISLATION
1914	Harrison Act	First federal legislation to regulate and control the production, importation, sale, purchase, and free distribution of opium or drugs derived from opium.
1922	Narcotic Drug Import and Export Act	Intended to eliminate the use of narcotics except for medical and other legitimate purposes.
1924	Heroin Act	Made it illegal to manufacture heroin.
1937	Marijuana Tax Act	Provided controls over marijuana similar to those that the Harrison Act provides over narcotics.
1942	Opium Poppy Control Act	Prohibited growing opium poppies in the United States except under license.
1956	Narcotics Control Act	Intended to impose very severe penalties for those convicted of narcotics or marijuana charges.
1965	Drug Abuse Control Amendments (DACA)	Adopted strict controls over amphetamines, barbiturates, LSD, and similar substances, with provisions to add new substances as the need arises.
1966	Narcotic Addict Rehabilitation Act (NARA)	Enhanced federal efforts to treat and rehabilitate narcotic addicts through three programs provided for voluntary and pretrial civil commitment and sentencing to treatment of convicted addicts.

(continued)

Table 3.1 (continued)

DATE	NAME OF LEGISLATION	SUMMARY OF COVERAGE AND INTENT OF LEGISLATION
1970	Comprehensive Drug Abuse Prevention and Control Act	Directed the Secretary of Department of Health, Education, and Welfare (now the Department of Health and Human Services) to make scientific and medical determinations relative to scheduling of controlled substances.
1972	Drug Abuse Office and Treatment Act	Created the Special Action Office for Drug Abuse Prevention (SAODAP) within the Executive Office of the President; authorized the establishment of the National Institute on Drug Abuse (NIDA) within the National Institute of Mental Health (NIMH) to become operational in 1974 and responsible for developing a national community-based treatment system; and permitted the maintenance treatment of narcotic addicts.
1973	Methadone Control Act	Placed controls on methadone licensing.
1973	Drug Enforcement Administration (DEA)	Remodeled the Bureau of Narcotics and Dangerous Drugs to become the DEA.
1974	Comprehensive Alcohol Abuse and Alcoholism Prevention, Treatment, and Rehabilitation Act Amendments	Statutorily established the Alcohol, Drug Abuse and Mental Health Administration (ADAMHA), charged with supervising and coordinating the functions of NIDA, National Institute on Alcohol Abuse and Alcoholism (NIAAA), and NIMH; programs and responsibilities of SAODAP were moved to NIDA.
1974	Narcotic Addict Treatment Act	Required separate DEA registrations for physicians who want to use approved narcotics in drug abuse treatment and separate approvals of registrants by the U.S. Department of Health and Human Services and by state agencies.
1986	Analogue (Designer Drug) Act	Made illegal the use of substances similar in effects and structure to substances already scheduled.
1986	Executive Order 12564	Mandated a drug-free federal workplace program; NIDA became the lead agency, creating its Office of Workplace Initiatives.
1988	Anti-Drug Abuse Act	Established the Office of National Drug Control Policy (ONDCP) in the Executive Office of the President to oversee all federal policies regarding research about control of drug abuse.
1992	ADAMHA Reorganization Act	Transferred the three institutes that constitute ADAMHA (NIDA, NIAAA, and NIMH) to the National Institutes of Health (NIH), and incorporated ADAMHA's service programs into the new Substance Abuse and Mental Health Services Administration (SAMHSA).
2000	Drug Addiction Treatment Act	Allowed qualified physicians to dispense or prescribe specially approved Schedule III, IV, and V narcotics for the treatment of opioid addiction in treatment settings other than the traditional opioid treatment program (i.e., methadone clinic).

The negative experiences that Americans had at the turn of the 20th century with addicting substances such as opium led to the **Harrison Act of 1914**. It marked the first legitimate effort by the federal government to regulate and control the production, importation, sales, purchase, and distribution of addicting substances. The Harrison Act served as the foundation and reference for subsequent laws directed at regulating drug abuse issues.

Today, the ways in which law enforcement agencies deal with substance abuse are largely determined by the Comprehensive Drug Abuse Prevention and Control Act of 1970. This act divided substances with abuse potential into categories based on the degree of their abuse potential and their clinical usefulness. The classifications, which are referred to as *schedules*, range from I to V. *Schedule I* substances have high abuse potential and no currently approved medicinal use; they cannot be prescribed by health professionals. *Schedule II* drugs also have high abuse potential but are approved for medical purposes and can be prescribed with restrictions. The distinctions between *Schedule II* through *V* substances reflect the likelihood of abuse occurring and the degree to which the drugs are controlled by governmental agencies. The least addictive and least regulated of the substances of abuse are classified as Schedule V drugs (see "Here and Now," Controlled Substance Schedules). Penalties for illegal use and/or trafficking of these agents vary according to the agent's schedule, amount possessed, and number of previous drug-associated offenses (see Table 3.2, page 105).

DRUG LAWS AND DETERRENCE

As previously discussed, drug laws often do not serve as a satisfactory deterrent against the use of illicit drugs. People have used and abused drugs for thousands of years despite governmental restrictions. It is very likely they will continue to do so despite stricter laws and greater support for law enforcement.

As the amount of addiction increased during the mid-1960s, many ill-conceived programs and laws were instituted as knee-jerk reactions, with little understanding about the underlying reasons for the rise in drug abuse. Unpopular, restrictive laws rarely work to reduce the use of illicit drugs. Even as laws become more restrictive, they usually have little impact on the level of addiction; in fact, in some cases addiction problems actually have increased. For example, during the restrictive years of the 1960s and 1980s, drugs were sold everywhere to everyone — in high schools, colleges, and probably every community. In the 1980s especially, increasingly large volumes of drugs were sold throughout the United States. Billions of dollars were paid for those drugs. Although no one knows precisely how much was exchanged, the amount likely approached $80 to $100 billion per year for all illegal drugs, of which the two biggest subcategories were an estimated $30 billion for cocaine and $24 billion for marijuana.

Because of the large sums of money involved, drugs have brought corruption to all levels of society. Other problems associated with the implementation of drug laws are an insufficient number of law enforcement personnel and inadequate detention facilities; consequently, much drug traffic goes unchecked. In addition, the judiciary system sometimes gets so backlogged that many cases never reach court. Plea bargaining is often used to clear the court docket. Many dealers and traffickers are back in business on the same day they are arrested. This apparent lack of punishment seriously damages the morale of law enforcers, legislators, and average citizens.

It is estimated that nearly 1 million drug-related arrests occur each year. This problem represents a tremendous cost to society in terms of damaged lives and family relationships; being arrested for a drug-related crime seriously jeopardizes a person's opportunity to pursue a normal life. Drug taking is closely tied to societal problems, and it will remain a problem unless society provides more meaningful experiences to those who are most susceptible

KEY TERMS

Harrison Act of 1914
the first legitimate effort by the U.S. government to regulate addicting substances

Here and Now

Controlled Substance Schedules

Controlled substances classified as Schedule I, II, III, IV, or V drugs are described below.

Schedule I

- The drug or other substance has a high potential for abuse.
- The drug or other substance has no currently accepted medical use in treatment in the United States.
- There is a lack of accepted safety for use of the drug or other substance under medical supervision.

Schedule II

- The drug or other substance has a high potential for abuse.
- The drug or other substance has a currently accepted medical use in treatment in the United States or a currently accepted medical use with severe restrictions.
- Abuse of the drug or other substance may lead to severe psychological or physical dependence.

Schedule III

- The drug or other substance has less of a potential for abuse than the drugs or other substances in Schedules I and II.
- The drug or other substance has a currently accepted medical use in treatment in the United States.

- Abuse of the drug or other substance may lead to moderate or low physical dependence or high psychological dependence.

Schedule IV

- The drug or other substance has a low potential for abuse relative to the drugs or other substances in Schedule III.
- The drug or other substance has a currently accepted medical use in treatment in the United States.
- Abuse of the drug or other substance may lead to limited physical dependence or psychological dependence relative to the drugs or other substances in Schedule III.

Schedule V

- The drug or other substance has a low potential for abuse relative to the drugs or other substances in Schedule IV.
- The drug or other substance has a currently accepted medical use in treatment in the United States.
- Abuse of the drug or other substance may lead to limited physical dependence or psychological dependence relative to the drugs or other substances in Schedule IV.

Source: U.S. Code, January 24, 1995.

---

to drug abuse. Improved education and increased support should be given to preteens because that is the age when deviant behavior starts. In cases in which drug education programs have been successful in involving students, the amount of drug taking and illegal activity seems to have decreased (see Chapter 17).

FACTORS IN CONTROLLING DRUG ABUSE

Three principal issues influence laws regarding drug abuse:

1. If a person abuses a drug, should he or she be treated as a criminal or as a sick person afflicted with a disease?
2. How is the user (supposedly the victim) distinguished from the pusher (supposedly the criminal) of an illicit drug, and who should be more harshly punished—the person who creates the demand for the drug or the person who satisfies the demand?
3. Are the laws and associated penalties effective deterrents against drug use or abuse, and how is effectiveness determined?

Table 3.2 **Federal Trafficking Penalties**

DRUG/SCHEDULE	QUANTITY	PENALTIES	QUANTITY	PENALTIES
Cocaine (Schedule II)	500–4999 g mixture	**First Offense:** Not less than 5 years, and not more than 40 years. If death or serious injury, not less than 20 years or more than life. Fine of not more than $2 million if an individual, $5 million if not an individual.	5 kg or more mixture	**First Offense:** Not less than 10 years, and not more than life. If death or serious injury, not less than 20 years or more than life. Fine of not more than $4 million if an individual, $10 million if not an individual.
Cocaine base (Schedule II)	5–49 g mixture		50 g or more mixture	
Fentanyl (Schedule II)	40–399 g mixture		400 g or more mixture	
Fentanyl analog (Schedule I)	10–99 g mixture		100 g or more mixture	
Heroin (Schedule I)	100–999 g mixture	**Second Offense:** Not less than 10 years, and not more than life. If death or serious injury, life Imprisonment. Fine of not more than $4 million if an individual, $10 million if not an individual.	1 kg or more mixture	**Second Offense:** Not less than 20 years, and not more than life. If death or serious injury, life imprisonment. Fine of not more than $8 million if an individual, $20 million if not an individual.
LSD (Schedule I)	1–9 g mixture		10 g or more mixture	
Methamphetamine (Schedule II)	5–49 g pure or 50–499 g mixture		50 g or more pure or 500 g or more mixture	
PCP (Schedule II)	10–99 g pure or 100–999 g mixture		100 g or more pure or 1 kg or more mixture	**Two or More Prior Offenses:** Life imprisonment.

		PENALTIES
Other Schedule I and II drugs	Any amount	**First Offense:** Not more than 20 years. If death or serious injury, not less than 20 years, or more than life. Fine $1 million if an individual, $5 million if not an individual.
Flunitrazepam (Schedule IV)	1 g or more	**Second Offense:** Not more than 30 years. If death or serious injury, not less than life. Fine $2 million if an individual, $10 million if not an individual.
Other Schedule III drugs	Any amount	**First Offense:** Not more than 5 years. Fine $250,000 if an individual, $1 million if not an individual.
Flunitrazepam (Schedule IV)	30–999 mg	**Second Offense:** Not more than 10 years. Fine $500,000 if an individual, $2 million if not an individual.
All other Schedule IV drugs	Any amount	**First Offense:** Not more than 3 years. Fine $250,000 if an individual, $1 million if not an individual.
Flunitrazepam (Schedule IV)	Less than 30 mg	**Second Offense:** Not more than 6 years. Fine $500,000 if an individual, $2 million if not an individual.
All Schedule V drugs	Any amount	**First Offense:** Not more than 1 year. Fine $100,000 if an individual, $250,000 if not an individual.
		Second Offense: Not more than 2 years. Fine $200,000 if an individual, $500,000 if not an individual. *(continued)*

Table 3.2 *(continued)*

DRUG	QUANTITY	FIRST OFFENSE	SECOND OFFENSE
Marijuana	1000 kg or more mixture; or 1000 or more plants	• Not less than 10 years, not more than life • If death or serious injury, not less than 20 years, not more than life • Fine of not more than $4 million if an individual, $10 million if other than an individual	• Not less than 20 years, not more than life • If death or serious injury, mandatory life • Fine of not more than $8 million if an individual, $20 million if other than an individual
Marijuana	100–999 kg mixture; or 100–999 plants	• Not less than 5 years, not more than 40 years • If death or serious injury, not less than 20 years, not more than life • Fine of not more than $2 million if an individual, $5 million if other than an individual	• Not less than 10 years, not more than life • If death or serious injury, mandatory life • Fine of not more than $4 million if an individual, $10 million if other than an individual
Marijuana	More than 10 kg hashish; 50–99 kg mixture More than 1 kg of hashish oil; 50–99 plants	• Not more than 20 years • If death or serious injury, not less than 20 years, not more than life • Fine of $1 million if an individual, $5 million if other than an individual	• Not more than 30 years • If death or serious injury, mandatory life • Fine of $2 million if an individual, $10 million if other than individual
Marijuana	1–49 plants; less than 50 kg mixture	• Not more than 5 years • Fine of not more than $250,000, $1 million other than individual	• Not more than 10 years • Fine of $500,000 if an individual, $2 million if other than individual
Hashish	10 kg or less		
Hashish oil	1 kg or less		

Source: U.S. Drug Enforcement Administration. http://www.usdoj.gov/dea/agency/penalties.htm. Accessed 2/19/05.

In regard to the first issue, drug abuse may be considered both an illness and a crime. It is a psychiatric disorder, an abnormal functional state, in which a person is compelled (either physically or psychologically) to continue using the drug (American Psychiatric Association 1994). It becomes a crime when the law, reflecting social opinion, makes abuse of the drug illegal. Health issues are clearly involved because uncontrolled abuse of almost any drug can lead to physical and psychological damage. Because the public must pay for health-care costs or societal damage, laws are created and penalties are implemented to prevent or correct drug abuse problems (see Table 3.2 on federal trafficking penalties).

Concerning the second issue, drug laws have always been more lenient on the user than the seller of a drug of abuse. Actually, it is often hard to separate user from pusher, as many drug abusers engage in both activities. Because huge profits are often involved, some people may not use the drugs they peddle and are only pushers; the law tries to deter use of drugs by concentrating on these persons but has questionable success. Organized crime is involved in major drug sales, and these "drug rings" have proven hard to destroy.

In regard to the third issue, considerable evidence indicates that, in the United States, criminal law has only limited success in deterring drug abuse. During 2004, approximately 39% of 12th graders used an illicit drug during the prior 12 months; marijuana was used by 34%, LSD by 2%, and cocaine by 5% (Johnston et al. 2005). The total number of Americans aged 12 and older using illegal drugs in 2003 has been estimated by the National Survey on Drug Use and Health to be 19.5 million. This estimate represents 8.2% of the population aged 12 years and older (SAMHSA 2004). It is clear that the drug abuse problem is far from being resolved, and many feel that some changes should be made in how we deal with this problem.

Strategies for Preventing Drug Abuse

The U.S. government and the public became concerned about the increasing prevalence of drug use during the 1960s, when demonstrations and nationwide protests against the Vietnam War proliferated as youth (mostly college students) rebelled against what they viewed as an unnecessary and unjust war. During the 1960s and early 1970s, for the first time, large numbers of middle- and upper-middle-class youth began using licit and illicit gateway drugs on a massive scale. In response, the government developed strategies for combating drug use and abuse. Important strategies it employed were **supply reduction**, **demand reduction**, and **inoculation**. More recently, the use of **drug courts** has become a major strategy.

SUPPLY REDUCTION STRATEGY

Early attempts at drug abuse prevention included both the Harrison Narcotic Act of 1914 and the 18th Amendment (Prohibition) to the U.S. Constitution. Both laws were intended to control the manufacture and distribution of classified drugs, with legislators anticipating that these restrictions would compel people to stop using drugs. The laws enforced supply reduction, which involves a lessened, restrictive, or elimination of available drugs.

Supply reduction drug prevention policy attempts to curtail the supply of illegal drugs or their precursors and exert greater control over other, more therapeutic drugs. Part of the supply reduction policy includes **interdiction**, which is defined as decreasing the amounts of these agents that are carried across U.S. borders by using foreign crop eradication measures and agreements, by imposing stiff penalties for drug trafficking, and by controlling alcoholic beverages through licensing.

The United States dedicates enormous resources to interdiction programs. For fiscal year 2004, the federal drug control budget for interdiction was $2.49 billion (USDOJ 2004). Although seizures of large caches of illicit drugs are reported routinely in the national press, there is no indication that the availability of drugs has diminished substantially. One can argue that as long as a strong demand for these psychoactive agents exists, demand will be satisfied if the price is right. Even if interdiction successfully reduces the supply of one drug of abuse, if demand persists, that drug is usually replaced by another drug with similar abuse potential (for example, substitution of amphetamines for cocaine; see Chapter 10).

KEY TERMS

supply reduction
a drug reduction policy aimed at reducing the supply of illegal drugs and controlling other therapeutic drugs

demand reduction
attempts to decrease individuals' tendencies to use drugs, often aimed at youth, with emphasis on reformulating values and behaviors

inoculation
a method of abuse prevention that protects drug users by teaching them responsibility

drug courts
a process that integrates substance abuse treatment, incentives, and sanctions and places nonviolent, drug-involved defendants in judicially supervised rehabilitation programs

interdiction
the policy of cutting off or destroying supplies of illicit drugs

DEMAND REDUCTION STRATEGY

The demand reduction approach attempts to minimize the actual demand for drugs. Through programs and activities often aimed at youth, emphasis is placed on reformulating values, attitudes, skills, and behaviors conducive to resisting drug use. (Chapter 17 provides extensive information about methods and techniques for reducing drug use.) As part of this strategy, support for medical and group drug treatment programs for abusers is encouraged. Although this approach does not address drug supply, it does attempt to curb and eventually eliminate the need to purchase drugs by reducing the buyer's demand.

Drug abuse is a complex and very individual problem, with many causes and aggravating factors. Even so, experience has shown that prevention and demand reduction are better strategies and, in the long run, less costly than interdiction or penalties administered via the criminal justice system (Goldstein 1994).

The following are some suggestions and strategies as to how demand for drugs can be reduced:

1. The top priority of any prevention program, if it is to provide a long-term solution, must be reduction of drug demand by youth. Children must be the primary focus in any substance abuse program. Achieving success requires stabilizing defective family structures, implementing school programs that create an antidrug attitude, establishing a drug-free environment, and promoting resistance training to help youth avoid drug involvement. In addition, children should be encouraged to become involved in alternative activities that can substitute for drug-abusing activity. Potential drug abusers need to be convinced that substance abuse is personally and socially damaging and unacceptable.

2. Education about drug abuse must be carefully designed and customized for the target population or group. For example, education based on scare tactics is not likely to dissuade adolescents from experimenting with drugs. Adolescents are at a point in their lives when they feel invincible, and graphically depicting the potential health consequences of drug and alcohol abuse has little impact. A discussion about the nature of addiction and the addiction process is more likely to influence their attitudes. Adolescents need to understand why people use drugs to appreciate the behavior patterns in themselves. Other important topics that should be discussed are how drug abuse works and why it leads to dependence. To complement drug education, adolescents also should be taught coping strategies that include effective decision-making and problem-solving skills.

3. Attitudes toward drug abuse and its consequence must be changed. The drug use patterns of many people, both young and old, are strongly influenced by their peers. If individuals believe that drug abuse is glamorous and contributes to acceptance by friends and associates, the incidence of drug abuse will remain high. In contrast, if the prevailing message in society is that drug abuse is unhealthy and not socially acceptable, the incidence will be much lower.

4. Replacement therapy has been shown to be a useful approach to weaning the individual off of drugs of abuse. The most common example of this strategy is the use of the narcotic methadone to treat the heroin addict (see Chapter 9). Use of methadone prevents the cravings and severe effects of withdrawal routinely associated with breaking the heroin habit. Unfortunately, most heroin addicts insist that they be maintained on methadone indefinitely. Even though methadone is easier to control and is less disruptive than heroin, one drug addiction has been substituted for another, which draws criticism. Replacement therapy certainly is not the entire answer to all drug abuse problems, but it often can provide a window of opportunity for behavioral modification so that a long-term solution to the abuse problem is possible.

INOCULATION STRATEGY

The inoculation method of abuse prevention aims to protect drug users by teaching them responsibility. The emphasis is on being accountable, rational, and responsible about drug use, and informing users about the effects of drugs on both mind and bodily function. Nonalcohol parties and responsible drinkers who use designated drivers are outcomes of applying inoculation strategy.

DRUG COURTS

Drug courts are designed to deal with nonviolent, drug-abusing offenders. Since 1989, when the first drug courts were established, more than 1300 jurisdictions across the country have implemented or are planning to implement a drug court program (Office of Justice Programs 2003). Drug courts integrate mandatory drug testing, substance abuse treatment, sanctions, and incentives in a judicially supervised setting. These courts hold offenders accountable for their actions and provide them with the support and tools necessary to rebuild their lives and become productive members of the community.

Drug courts can have a positive impact. For example, over 250,000 offenders have participated in more than 500 drug court programs nationwide since the early 1990s. Approximately 70% of these offenders are still enrolled in or have successfully graduated from drug court programs. This is nearly double the expected retention rate from traditional treatment programs. Jurisdictions that have implemented drug court programs also report significantly lower arrest, conviction, and drug usage rates for both drug court participants and graduates. Research indicates that drug courts are cost-effective. The average costs for drug court program participation and services generally range between $8 and $14 per day. The average jail/prison costs are generally calculated at a minimum rate of $40 per day, not including the costs for jail/prison construction (Office of Justice Programs 2003).

Current and Future Drug Use

During the administrations of former Presidents Ronald Reagan and George H. W. Bush (1980–1992), the official policy of the U.S. federal government included a "get tough" attitude about drug abuse. Slogans such as "Just Say No" and "War on Drugs" reflected the frustration of a public that had been victimized by escalating crime (many incidents were drug-related); personally touched by drug tragedies in families, at work, or with associates and friends; and economically strained by dealing with the cost of the problem.

The "War on Drugs" has had some success. According to the 2003 National Survey on Drug Use and Health, an estimated 19.5 million Americans overall (8.2% of the U.S. population age 12 and older) were current users of illicit drugs. (SAMHSA 2004). This remains significantly less than in decades past. Still, much remains to be accomplished in the fight against substance abuse. For example:

- Approximately one-third of all deaths in the United States are attributable to drug use (Werthamer and Chatterji 1998).
- The economic cost to society of drug abuse remains staggering. It includes treatment and prevention costs, as well as costs associated with crime, loss of job productivity, social welfare, and lost wages.
- Between 1992 and 1998, the overall cost of drug abuse to society increased at a rate of 5.9% each year. By 1998, the cost in terms of productivity, health care, the criminal justice system, reducing the supply of drugs, and social welfare was $143.4 billion.
- The Office of National Drug Control Policy (ONDCP) conducted a survey to determine how much money was spent on illegal drugs that might otherwise support legitimate savings or spending by the user: It estimated that between 1988 and 1995, Americans spent $57.3 billion on illegal drugs that would otherwise support legitimate savings of spending by the user (NIDA Infofax 1999).
- The number of first-time users is staggering. For instance, in 2002, an estimated 2.6 million persons first used marijuana. This means that each day, an average of 7000 Americans tried marijuana for the first time. In addition, approximately 1.1. million persons used cocaine for the first time (SAMHSA 2004).
- Millions of dollars have been spent in an attempt to educate young people regarding the dangers of substance abuse. Despite the introduction of "Drug-Free School Zones" throughout the country, in 2003 approximately 16% of youths reported that they had been approached by someone selling drugs in the past month (SAMHSA 2004).

An example of the many public awareness advertisements cautions against drinking and driving.

Fighting the "War on Drugs" is clearly difficult and complex. Progress has been made. Nonetheless, significant problems still exist and require attention of politicians, clinicians, law enforcement agencies, families, counselors, and all concerned citizens.

DRUG LEGALIZATION DEBATE

The persistence of the drug abuse problem and the high cost in dollars and frustration of waging the "War on Drugs" have energized the ongoing debate regarding legalizing the use of drugs of abuse. Proponents of legalization are no longer limited to libertarians and so-called academic intellectuals. Increasingly, this group includes representatives of a distressed law enforcement system. For example, discontented judges whose courts are swamped with drug cases and police officers who spend much of their on-duty time trying to trap and arrest every drug dealer and user on the street are publicly declaring that the drug laws are wasteful and futile.

Several arguments are commonly cited by individuals and groups promoting the legalization of all substances of abuse. For instance, proponents often contend that if drugs were legalized, violence and crime would become less frequent. These individuals point out that users often commit crimes to pay for illicit drugs: If these drugs were legal, then the tremendous profits associated with drugs because of their illegal status would disappear and, once gone, the black market and criminal activity associated with drugs would be eliminated. Furthermore, legalization would decrease law enforcement costs by eliminating the backlog of drug-related court cases and reduce populations in overcrowded prisons.

Conversely, opponents of drug legalization believe that legalization would lead to increased availability of drugs, which would in turn lead to increased use. They point out that the use of drugs, especially methamphetamine, phenylcyclidine (PCP), and cocaine, is often associated with violent criminal behavior. Numerous studies demonstrate the links among drugs, violence, and crime; the link between alcohol, a legal substance, and crime is also well documented. According to legalization opponents, drug use would merely increase the incidence of crime, even if the drugs were legally purchased. Accordingly, the economic (as well as social) cost to society would increase.

Legalization proponents claim that making illicit drugs licit would not cause more of these substances to be consumed, nor would addiction increase. They note correctly that many people use drugs in moderation. Furthermore, many would choose not to use drugs, just as many abstain currently from tobacco and alcohol. Opponents contend that if drugs were made licit and more widely available, usage and addiction rates would increase. These individuals contend that legalizing drugs sends a message that drug use (like tobacco and alcohol) is acceptable and encourages drug use among people who currently do not use drugs.

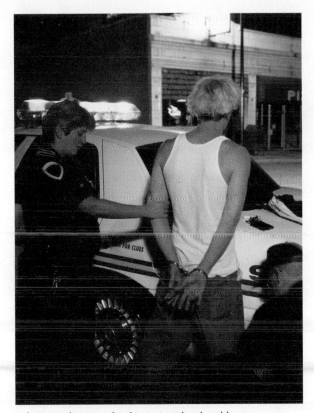

Substance abuse can lead to serious legal problems.

Proponents claim that drug legalization would allow users the right to practice a diversity of consciousness; ". . . the practice of getting high has existed from the dawn of time, and all efforts to eradicate it are based on an incomplete understanding of human nature" (Lenson 1995). Just as diversity of race, ethnicity, sexual orientation, religion, and other varied lifestyles are allowed, legalization of drugs would permit citizens in our society to alter their consciousness without legal repercussions as long as they do not harm or threaten the safety and security of others. Moreover, proponents argue that education, health care, road building, and a wide array of other worthwhile causes would benefit from the taxes that could be raised by legalizing and then taxing drugs. They argue that the United States has spent billions of dollars to control drug production, trafficking, and use with few, if any, positive results. They contend that the money spent on drug control should be shifted to other, more productive endeavors.

Opponents believe that health and societal costs would increase with drug legalization. It has been predicted that drug treatment costs, hospitalization for long-term, drug-related diseases, and treatment of the consequences of drug-associated family violence would further burden our already strapped healthcare system. Such a policy would increase costs to society due to greater medical and social problems resulting from greater availability and increased use of drugs. The two most frequently abused substances, alcohol and tobacco, are both legal and readily available today. These two substances cause more medical, social, and personal problems than all the illicit drugs of abuse combined. Many question whether society really wants to legalize additional drugs with abuse potential.

Despite some of the compelling arguments for legalization of drugs of addiction, the majority of law enforcement professionals, politicians, federal agencies, and medical associations oppose legalization of some or all drugs of abuse. In addition, polls indicate that most voters object to legalization or decriminalization of illicit drugs (Knight-Ridder News Service 1992). A major Gallup survey of public attitudes showed that 54% of respondents opposed drug legalization, and another 31% were moderately opposed to it; only 14% favored it (CNN/*USA Today*/Gallup Poll 1995).

Although arguments for both sides warrant consideration, extreme policies are not likely to be implemented; instead, a compromise will most probably be adopted. For example, areas potentially ripe for compromise include the following (Kalant 1992):

Selective legalization. Eliminate harsh penalties for those drugs of abuse that are the safest and least likely to cause addiction, such as marijuana.

Control of substances of abuse by prescription or through specially approved outlets. Have the availability of the illegal drugs controlled by physicians and trained clinicians, rather than by law enforcement agencies.

Discretionary enforcement of drug laws. Allow greater discretion by judicial systems for prosecution and sentencing of those who violate drug laws. Such decisions would be based on perceived criminal intent.

In conclusion, drug legalization remains a highly divisive issue in the United States. Although legalization would lessen the number of drug violators involved in the criminal justice system, the problems associated with legalizing current illicit drugs cause most members in our society to view this idea with disfavor. As stated earlier, opponents of legalization argue that we already have massive problems with licit drugs such as tobacco and alcohol. According to them, legalizing additional types of drugs would produce a substantial increase in the rate of addiction and in the social and psychological problems associated with drug use. Proponents favoring legalization assert that, despite the current drug laws and severe penalties for drug use, people continue to use illicit drugs.

A compromise between legalization and current criminalization of illicit drug use might include **selective legalization**. Such an approach would probably legalize marijuana, whereas other drugs such as heroin and cocaine would remain illegal. A second type of compromise might call for medical practitioners to control drug availability instead of law enforcement agencies. A third compromise might involve discretionary enforcement of drug laws, which would allow judicial systems to exercise greater discretion in prosecution and sentencing of drug law violators, based largely on perceived criminal intent.

DRUG TESTING

In response to the demand by society to stop the spread of drug abuse and its adverse consequences, drug testing has been implemented in some situations to detect drug users (Catlin et al. 1992; Jaffe 1995). The most common types of drug testing use Breathalyzers and laboratory studies of urine, blood, and hair specimens. Urine and blood testing are preferred for detecting drug use. Hair

specimen testing must overcome technical problems before hair can be used as a definitive proof of drug use, including complications from hair treatment (e.g., hair coloring) and environmental absorption (Jaffe 1995).

The drugs of abuse most frequently tested for are marijuana, cocaine, amphetamines, narcotics, sedatives, PCP, and anabolic steroids. Drug testing is often mandatory in some professions in which public safety is a concern (such as airline pilots, railroad workers, law enforcement employees, and medical personnel) and for employees of some organizations and companies as part of general policy (such as the military, many federal agencies, and some private companies). Drug testing is also often mandatory for participants in sports at all levels — whether in high school, college, international, and professional competition — to prevent unfair advantages that might result from the pharmacological effects of these drugs and to discourage the spread of drug abuse among athletes. Likewise, drug testing is used routinely by law enforcement agencies to assist in the prosecution of those believed to violate drug abuse laws. Finally, drug testing is used by health professionals to assess the success of drug abuse treatment — that is, to determine whether a dependent patient is diminishing his or her drug use or has experienced a relapse in drug abuse habits.

Drug testing to identify drug offenders is usually accomplished by analyzing body fluids (in particular urine), although other approaches (such as analysis of expired air for alcohol) are also used. To understand the accuracy of these tests, several factors should be considered.

1. *Testing must be standardized and conducted efficiently.* To interpret testing results reliably, it is essential that fluid samples be collected, processed, and tested using standard procedures. Guidelines for proper testing procedures have been established by federal regulatory agencies as well as scientific organizations. Deviations from established protocols can result in false positives (tests that indicate a drug is present when none was used), false negatives (tests that are unable to detect a drug that is present), or inaccurate assessments of drug levels.

KEY TERMS

selective legalization
an approach that would legalize marijuana, whereas other drugs such as heroin and cocaine would remain illegal

2. *Sample collection and processing must be done accurately and confidentially.* In many cases, drug testing can have punitive consequences (for example, athletes cannot compete or employees are fired if results are positive). Consequently, drug users often attempt to outsmart the system. Some individuals have attempted to avoid submitting their own drug-containing urine for testing by filling specimen bottles with "clean" urine from artificial bladders hidden under clothing or in the vagina or by introducing "clean" urine into their own bladders just before collection (Catlin et al. 1992). To confirm the legitimacy of the specimen, it often is necessary to have the urine collection witnessed directly by a trustworthy observer. To ensure that the fluid specimens are not tampered with and that confidentiality is maintained, samples should be immediately coded and movement of each sample from site to site during analysis should be documented and confirmed.

Just as it is important that testing identify individuals who are using drugs, it is also important that those who have not used drugs not be wrongfully accused. To avoid false positives, all samples that test positive in screening (usually via fast and inexpensive procedures) should be analyzed again using more accurate, sensitive, and sophisticated analytical procedures to confirm the results.

3. *Confounding factors that interfere with the accuracy of the testing can be inadvertently or deliberately present.* For example, normal dietary consumption of pastries containing poppy seeds is sufficient to cause a positive urine test for the narcotic morphine. The use of bicarbonate alkalinizes the urine and increases the rate of elimination of some drugs, such as methamphetamine, thereby diminishing the likelihood of a positive test (Catlin et al. 1992). Excessive intake of fluid or use of diuretics increases the volume of urine formed and decreases the concentration of drugs, making them more difficult to detect.

The dramatic increase in drug testing since 1985 has caused experts to question its value in dealing with drug abuse problems. Unfortunately, drug testing often is linked exclusively to punitive consequences, such as disqualification from athletic competition, loss of job, or even fines and imprisonment. Use of drug testing in such negative ways does little to diminish the number of drug abusers or deal with their personal problems.

However, drug testing programs can have positive consequences by identifying drug users who require professional care. After being referred for drug rehabilitation, the offender can be monitored using drug testing to confirm the desired response to therapy. In addition, tests can identify individuals who put others in jeopardy because of their drug abuse habits when they perform tasks that are dangerously impaired by the effects of these drugs (for example, airline pilots, train engineers, and truck drivers).

The widespread application of drug testing to control the illicit use of drugs in the general population would be extremely expensive, difficult to enforce, and almost certainly ineffective. In addition, such indiscriminate testing would likely be viewed as an unwarranted infringement on individual privacy and declared unconstitutional. However, the use of drug testing to discourage inappropriate drug use in selected crucial professions that directly impact public welfare appears to be publicly tolerated and has been shown to be effective (Bryson 1992). Even so, it is probably worthwhile to periodically revisit the issue of drug testing and analyze its benefits and liabilities relative to "public safety" and "individual privacy" issues.

PRAGMATIC DRUG POLICIES

Several principles for a **pragmatic drug policy** emerge from a review of past drug policies and an understanding of the drug-related frustrations of today. To create drug policies that work, the following suggestions are offered:

1. It is important that the government develop programs that are consistent with the desires of the majority of the population.

KEY TERMS

pragmatic drug policy
developing drug laws reflecting the desires of the majority of the citizenry; stressing drug education and treatment; developing nondiscriminatory policies

2. Given the difficulties and high cost of efforts to prevent illicit drugs from reaching the market, it is logical to deemphasize interdiction and instead stress programs that reduce demand. To reduce demand, drug education and drug treatment must be top priorities.

3. Government and society need to better understand the role played by law in their efforts to reduce drug addiction. Antidrug laws by themselves do not eliminate drug problems; indeed, they may even create significant social difficulties (for example, as did the Prohibition laws banning all alcohol use). Used properly and selectively, however, laws can reinforce and communicate expected social behavior and values (for example, laws against public drunkenness or against driving a vehicle under the influence of alcohol).

4. Programs should be implemented that employ "public consensus" more effectively to campaign against drug abuse. For example, antismoking campaigns demonstrate the potential success that could be achieved by programs that alter drug abuse behavior. Similar approaches can be used to change public attitudes about drugs through education without making moral judgments and employing crusading tactics. Our society needs to engage in more collaborative programs in which drug-using individuals and their families, communities, and helping agencies work together.

Discussion Questions

1. Describe the FDA approval process for assessing the safety and efficacy of a newly developed drug. What are its advantages and disadvantages?

2. Name the principal legislative initiatives that mandate that drugs be proven safe or effective.

3. What are the principal advantages and disadvantages of switching products from prescription to OTC status?

4. What could account for the vast differences in attitudes and opinions regarding drug use and the law voiced by drug users/abusers and nonusers of drugs?

5. Would decriminalization of illicit drug use increase or decrease drug-related social problems? Justify your answer.

6. Compare and contrast supply reduction, demand reduction, and inoculation strategies for dealing with drug abuse.

7. List the principal arguments for and against legalizing drugs of abuse such as marijuana and cocaine.

Key Terms

thalidomide 94

phocomelia 94

switching policy 98

Harrison Act of 1914 103

supply reduction 107

demand reduction 107

inoculation 107

drug courts 107

interdiction 107

selective legalization 112

pragmatic drug policy 113

Summary

1 Societies have evolved to believe that they have the right to protect themselves from the damaging impact of drug use and abuse. Consequently, governments, including that of the United States, have passed laws and implemented programs to prevent social damage from inappropriate drug use. In addition, such societies have come to expect that drugs be effective.

2 The 1906 Pure Food and Drug Act was not a strong law, but it required manufacturers to

include on labels the amounts of alcohol, morphine, opium, cocaine, heroin, and marijuana extract in each product. It represented the first real attempt to make consumers aware of the active contents in the drug products they were consuming.

3 The 1938 Federal Food, Drug, and Cosmetic Act gave the FDA control over drug safety.

4 The 1951 Durham-Humphrey Amendment to the Food, Drug, and Cosmetic Act made a formal distinction between prescription and nonprescription drugs.

5 The Kefauver-Harris Amendment of 1962 required manufacturers to demonstrate both the efficacy and the safety of their products.

6 All drugs to be considered for marketing must first be tested for safety in animals. Following these initial tests, if the drug is favorably reviewed by the FDA, it is given IND status. It then generally undergoes three phases of human clinical testing before receiving final FDA approval.

7 In 1972, the FDA initiated a program to ensure that all OTC drugs were safe and effective. Specific panels were selected to evaluate the safety and effectiveness of more than 700 OTC drug ingredients. Each of the ingredients was classified into a particular category: I, II, or III.

8 The switching policy of the FDA allows the agency to review prescription drugs and evaluate their suitability as OTC products.

9 Three of the principal questions that influence laws on drug abuse address the following issues: Should drug abusers be treated as criminals or patients? How can drug users and drug pushers be distinguished from one another? What types of laws and programs are effective deterrents against drug abuse?

10 Controversy exists as to how to best reduce substance abuse. A principal strategy used by governmental agencies to achieve this objective is interdiction; the majority of money used to fight drug abuse is spent on trying to stop and confiscate drug supplies. Experience has proved that interdiction is often ineffective. To reduce drug abuse, demand for these substances must be diminished. Youth must be a top priority in any substance abuse program. Treatment that enables drug addicts to stop their habits with minimal discomfort should be provided. Finally, education should be used to change attitudes toward drug abuse and its consequences. Potential drug abusers need to be convinced that substance abuse is personally and socially damaging and is unacceptable.

11 Major strategies for combating drug use and abuse are supply reduction, demand reduction, and inoculation. Supply reduction involves using drug laws to control the manufacturing and distribution of classified drugs. Demand reduction aims to reduce the actual demand for drugs by working mainly with youth and teaching them to resist drugs. Inoculation aims to protect potential drug users by teaching them responsibility and explaining the effects of drugs on bodily and mental functioning.

12 Drug courts are designed to deal with nonviolent, drug-abusing offenders. They require substance abuse treatment and implement sanctions in a judicially supervised program. This emerging strategy has had positive social and economic impacts.

13 In response to the demand by society to stop the spread of drug abuse and its adverse consequences, drug testing has been implemented in some situations to detect drug users. Common drug testing uses Breathalyzers and analysis of urine, blood, and hair specimens. Urine and blood testing are the preferred methods of testing for drug use. Hair specimen testing must overcome a number of technical problems before it can be used as a definitive proof of drug use, including complications caused by hair treatment and environmental absorption.

References

American Psychiatric Association. *Diagnostic and Statistical Manual of Mental Disorders*, 4th ed. Washington, DC: APA, 1994: 175–272.

Bryson, R. "Railroads Try to Derail Drug Abuse." *Salt Lake Tribune* 244 (9 June 1992): D-5.

Catlin, D., D. Cowan, M. Donike, D. Fraisse, H. Oftebro, and S. Rendic. "Testing Urine for Drugs." *Journal of Automated Chemistry* 14 (1992): 85–92.

CNN/*USA Today*/Gallup Poll. "Drugs and Drug Abuse." *Gallup Poll Survey* G0105147, 14–17 September 1995.

FDA. "FDA and the Drug Development Process: How the Agency Ensures That Drugs Are Safe and Effective" (2002). Available http://www.fda.gov/opacom/fact sheets/justthefacts/17drgdev.html.

FDA, Division of Drug Marketing, Advertising and Communications (2003). Available http:// www.fda.gov/cder/ddmac/FAQS.HTM.

FDA History Office. "A Brief History of the Center for Drug Evaluation and Research" (2003). Available http://www.fda.gov/cder/about/history/Histext.htm.

FDA Backgrounder. "Milestones in U.S. Food and Drug Law History" (2002). Available http://www.fda.gov/opacom/backgrounders/miles.html.

Goldstein, A. "Lessons from the Street." In *Addiction from Biology to Drug Policy*. New York: Freeman, 1994.

Harvard Press Release, 2002. "Direct-to-Customer Advertising of Prescription Drugs Grows Rapidly but Remains a Small Share of Promotional Efforts." Available http://www.hsph.harvard.edu/press/releases/press02132002.html.

Hunter, J. R., D. L. Rosen, and R. DeChristoforo. "How FDA Expedites Evaluation of Drugs." *Welcome Trends in Pharmacy* (January 1993): 2–9.

Hwang, S. "Nicotine Patch Reignites Fight Over Drug Ads." *Wall Street Journal* 73 (30 June 1992): B1.

Jaffe, J. H., ed. *Encyclopedia of Drugs and Alcohol.* New York: Simon and Schuster, Macmillan, 1995.

Johnston, L. D., P. M. O'Malley, J. G. Bachman, and J. E. Schulenberg. *Monitoring the Future: National Results on Adolescent Drug Use: Overview of Key Findings, 2004.* NIH

Publication No. [yet to be assigned]. Bethesda, MD: National Institute on Drug Abuse, 2005.

Kalant, H. "Formulating Policies on the Non-medical Use of Cocaine." In *Cocaine: Scientific and Social Dimensions*. Ciba Foundation Symposium 166, 261–276. New York: Wiley, 1992.

Knight-Ridder News Service. "Time to Make Drugs Legal? Many Say Yes." *Salt Lake Tribune* 244 (11 July 1992): A1.

Lenson, D. *On Drugs*. Minneapolis, MN: University of Minnesota Press, 1995.

NIDA Infofax. "Costs to Society." Publication 13564 (November 1999).

Office of Justice Programs, USDOJ (2003). Available http://www.ojp.gov/aag/messages/drug-court052003.htm

Substance Abuse and Mental Health Services Administration (SAMHSA). *Results from the 2003 National Survey on Drug Use and Health: National Findings*. Office of Applied Studies, NSDUH, Series H-25, DHHS Publication No. SMA 04-3964. Rockville, MD: 2004.

Temin, P. *Taking Your Medicine: Drug Regulation in the United States*. Cambridge, MA: Harvard University Press, 1980.

United States Department of Justice (USDOJ). Bureau of Justice Statistics Drugs and Crime Facts: Drug Control Budget (2004). Available www.ojp.usdoj.gov/bjs/dcf/dcb.htm.

Werthamer, L., and P. Chatterji. "Prevention Intervention Cost-Effectiveness and Cost Benefit." NIDA. (1998). Available http://www.drugabuse.gov/about/organization/despr/hsr/dapre/WerthamerPreventive.html.

Woolsey, R. "A Prescription for Better Prescriptions." Issues in Science and Technology (Spring 1994): 59–66.

CHAPTER 4

Homeostatic Systems and Drugs

Did You Know?

- ○ The brain is composed of 10–100 billion neurons that communicate with one another by releasing chemical messengers called *neurotransmitters*.

- ○ Many drugs exert their effects by interacting with specialized protein regions in cell membranes called *receptors.*

- ○ Some natural chemicals produced by the body have the same effect as narcotic drugs; these chemicals are called *endorphins.*

- ○ The body likely produces natural substances that have effects similar to those produced by marijuana and diazepam (Valium).

- ○ Drugs that affect the neurotransmitter dopamine usually alter both mental state and motor activity.

- ○ The pleasant sensations that encourage continual use of most drugs of abuse are due to stimulation of dopamine activity in the limbic system.

- ○ The hypothalamus is the principal brain region for control of endocrine systems.

- ○ The anabolic steroids often abused by athletes are chemically related to testosterone, the male hormone, and stimulate increased muscle mass.

- ○ Anabolic steroids are considered controlled drugs by the Drug Enforcement Administration and have been classified as Schedule III substances.

On completing this chapter you will be able to:

◎ Explain the similarities and differences between the nervous and endocrine systems.

◎ Describe how a neuron functions.

◎ Describe the role of receptors in mediating the effects of hormones, neurotransmitters, and drugs.

◎ Distinguish between receptor agonists and antagonists, and describe how their effects relate to those of neurotransmitters.

◎ Describe the different features of the principal neurotransmitters associated with drug addiction.

◎ Outline the principal components of the central nervous system, and explain their general functions.

◎ Identify which brain areas are most likely to be affected by drugs of abuse.

◎ Distinguish between the sympathetic and parasympathetic nervous systems.

◎ Identify the principal components of the endocrine system.

◎ Explain how and why anabolic steroids are abused and the health impact attributed to abuse.

Introduction

Why is your body susceptible to the influence of drugs and other substances? Part of the answer is that your body is constantly adjusting and responding to its environment in an effort to maintain internal stability and balance. This delicate process of dynamic adjustments — **homeostasis** — is necessary to optimize bodily functions and is essential for survival. These continual compensations help to maintain physiological and psychological balances and are mediated by the release of endogenous regulatory chemicals (such as **neurotransmitters** from neurons and **hormones** from glands). Many drugs exert intended or unintended effects by altering the activity of these regulatory substances, which changes the function of the nervous or **endocrine system**. For example, all drugs of abuse profoundly influence mental states by altering the chemical messages of the neurotransmitters in the brain, and some alter endocrine function by affecting the release of hormones. By understanding the mechanisms of how drugs alter these body processes, we are able to recognize drug benefits and risks and devise therapeutic strategies to deal with related problems.

This chapter is divided into two sections. The first is a brief overview that introduces the basic concept of how the body is controlled by nervous systems and explains why drugs influence the elements of these systems. The second section is intended for readers who desire a more in-depth understanding of the anatomical, physiological, and biochemical basis of homeostatic functions. In this second section, the elements of the nervous system are discussed in greater detail, followed by an examination of its major divisions: the central, peripheral, and autonomic nervous systems (CNS, PNS, and ANS). The components and operation of the endocrine system are also discussed in specific relation to drugs. The use of anabolic steroids is given as an example.

1: Overview of Homeostasis and Drug Actions

The body continuously adjusts to both internal and external changes in the environment. To cope with these adjustments, the body systems include elaborate self-regulating mechanisms. The name given to this compensatory action is *homeostasis*, which refers to the maintenance of internal stability or equilibrium. For example, homeostatic mechanisms control the response of the brain to changes in the physical, social, and psychological environments, as well as regulate physiological factors such as body temperature, metabolism, nutrient utilization, and organ functions. The two principal systems that help human beings maintain homeostasis are the nervous system and the endocrine system (described in Section 2). They are independent yet work together in a coordinated manner.

Introduction to Nervous Systems

All nervous systems consist of specialized nerve cells called **neurons**. The neurons are responsible for conducting the homeostatic functions of the brain and other parts of the nervous system by receiving and sending information. The transfer of messages by neurons includes electrochemical processes that consist of the following steps (see Figure 4.1):

1. The *receiving region* of the neuron (B) is affected by a chemical message (A) that either excites (causes the neuron to send its own message) or inhibits (prevents the neuron from sending a message) it.

KEY TERMS

homeostasis
maintenance of internal stability; often biochemical in nature

neurotransmitters
chemical messengers released by neurons

hormones
chemical messengers released into the blood by glands

endocrine system
relating to hormones, their functions, and sources

neurons
specialized nerve cells that make up the nervous system and release transmitters

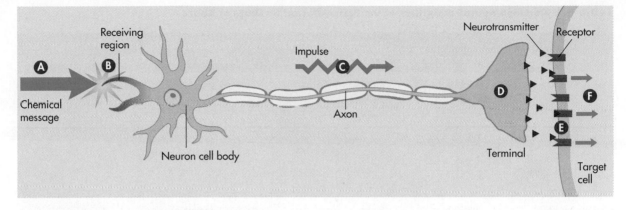

FIGURE 4.1

The process of sending messages by neurons. The receiving region (B) of the neuron is activated by an incoming message (A) near the neuronal cell body. The neuron sends an electricity-like impulse down the axon to its terminal (C). The impulse causes the release of neurotransmitters from the terminal to transmit the message to the target (D). This is done when the neurotransmitter molecules activate the receptors on the membranes of the target cell (E). The activated receptors then cause a change in intracellular functions to occur (F).

2. If the message is excitatory, a chemical impulse (much like electricity) moves from the receiving region of the neuron, down its wire-like processes (called axons) to the sending region (called the terminal) (C). When the electrochemical impulse reaches the terminal, chemical messengers called neurotransmitters are released (D) (for examples see Table 4.1, page 122).

3. The neurotransmitters travel very short distances and bind to specialized and specific receiving proteins called **receptors** on the outer membranes of their target cells (E).

4. Activation of receptors by their associated neurotransmitters causes a change in the activity of the target cell (F). The target cells can be other neurons or cells that make up organs (such as the heart, lungs, kidneys, and so on), muscles, or glands.

Neurons are highly versatile and, depending on their functions, can send discrete excitatory or inhibitory messages to their target cells. Neurons are distinguished by the types of chemical substances they release as neurotransmitters to send their messages. The neurotransmitters represent a wide variety of molecules that are classified according to their functional association as well as their ability to stimulate or inhibit the activity of target neurons, organs, muscles, and glands. They are discussed in greater detail in Section 2.

An example of a common neurotransmitter used by neurons in the brain to send messages is the substance dopamine. When released from neurons associated with the pleasure center in the brain, dopamine causes substantial euphoria by activating its receptor on target neurons (Panzarino 2004). This effect is relevant to drugs of abuse because the addictive properties of these substances relate to their ability to stimulate dopamine release from these neurons (for example, amphetamine or cocaine) and thus cause pleasant euphoric effects in the user (Dackis and O'Brien 2001; Swan 1998).

It is important to understand that many of the desired and undesired effects of **psychoactive** drugs

KEY TERMS

axons
an extension of the neuronal cell body along which electrochemical signals travel

receptors
special proteins in a membrane that are activated by natural substances or drugs to alter cell function

psychoactive
drugs that affect mood or alter the state of consciousness

Table 4.1 Common Neurotransmitters of the Brain Affected by Drugs of Abuse

NEUROTRANSMITTER	TYPE OF EFFECT	MAJOR CENTRAL NERVOUS SYSTEM CHANGES	DRUGS OF ABUSE THAT INFLUENCE THE NEUROTRANSMITTER (DRUG ACTION)
Dopamine	Inhibitory–excitatory	Euphoria Agitation Paranoia	Amphetamines, cocaine (activate)
GABA (gamma-aminobutyric acid)	Inhibitory	Sedation Relaxation Drowsiness Depression	Alcohol, diazepam-type, barbiturates (activate)
Serotonin	Inhibitory	Sleep Relaxation Sedation	LSD (activate)
Acetylcholine	Excitatory–inhibitory	Mild euphoria Excitation Insomnia	Tobacco, nicotine (stimulate)
Endorphins	Inhibitory	Mild euphoria Blockage of pain Slow respiration	Narcotics (activate)

(which alter the mental functions of the brain), such as the drugs of abuse, are due to their ability to alter the neurotransmitters associated with neurons. Some of the transmitter messenger systems most likely to be affected by drugs of abuse are listed in Table 4.1 and are discussed in greater detail in Section 2.

2: Comprehensive Explanation of Homeostatic Systems

For those desiring a more complete understanding of the consequences of drug effects on the homeostatic systems of the body, this section provides an in-depth discussion of the anatomical and physiological nature and biological arrangements of the nervous and endocrine systems. Because drugs of abuse are most likely to exert their psychoactive effects on neurons and their receptor targets, the nervous system is presented first and in greater depth, followed by a less detailed description of endocrine function.

The Building Blocks of the Nervous System

The nervous system is composed of the brain, spinal cord, and all the neurons that connect to other organs and tissues of the body (see Figure 4.7). Nervous systems enable an organism to receive information about the internal and external environment and to make the appropriate responses essential to survival. Considerable money and effort are currently being dedicated to explore the mechanisms whereby the nervous system functions and processes information, resulting in frequent new and exciting discoveries.

THE NEURON: THE BASIC STRUCTURAL UNIT OF THE NERVOUS SYSTEM

The building block of the nervous system is the nerve cell, or *neuron*. Each neuron in the CNS (brain and spinal cord) is in close proximity with other neurons, forming a complex network. The human brain contains 10–100 billion neurons, each

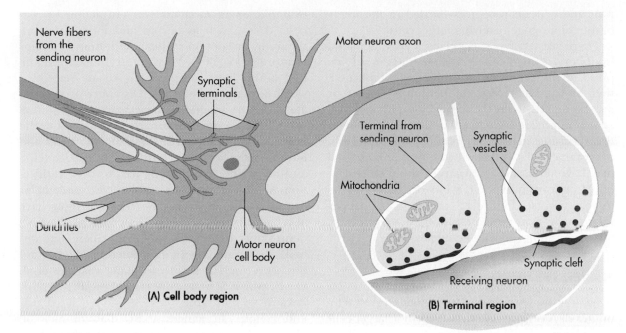

Nerve fibers from the sending neuron

Synaptic terminals

Motor neuron axon

Dendrites

Motor neuron cell body

(A) Cell body region

Terminal from sending neuron

Synaptic vesicles

Mitochondria

Synaptic cleft

Receiving neuron

(B) Terminal region

FIGURE 4.2

(A) Each neuron may have many synaptic connections. They are designed to deliver short bursts of a chemical transmitter substance into the synaptic cleft, where the substance can act on the surface of the receiving nerve cell membrane. Before release, molecules of the chemical neurotransmitter are stored in numerous vesicles, or sacs. (B) A close-up of the synaptic terminals, showing the synaptic vesicles and mitochondria. *Mitochondria* are specialized structures that help supply the cell with energy. The gap between the synaptic terminal and the target membrane is the *synaptic cleft*.

of which is composed of similar components but with different shapes and sizes. Neurons do not form a continuous network. They always remain separate, never actually touching, although they are in close proximity. The typical point of communication between one neuron and another is called a **synapse**. The gap (called the **synaptic cleft**) between neurons at a synapse may be only 0.00002 millimeter wide, but it is essential for proper functioning of the nervous system (see Figure 4.2).

The neuron has a cell body with a nucleus and receiving regions called **dendrites**, which are short, treelike branches that pick up information from the environment and surrounding neurons.

The axon of a neuron is a threadlike extension that receives information from the dendrites near the cell body, in the form of an electrochemical impulse; then, like an electrical wire, it transmits the impulse to the cell's terminal. Although most axons are less than 1 inch in length, some may be

quite long; for example, some axons extend from the spinal cord to the toes.

At the synapse, information is transmitted chemically to the next neuron, as shown in Figure 4.1. A similar synaptic arrangement also exists at sites of communication between neurons and target cells in organs, muscles, and glands; that is, neurotransmitters are released from the message-sending neu-

KEY TERMS

synapse
site of communication beween a message-sending neuron and its message-receiving target cell

synaptic cleft
a minute gap between the neuron and target cell, across which neurotransmitters travel

dendrites
short branches of neurons that receive transmitter signals

rons and activate receptors located in the membranes of message-receiving target cells.

There are two types of synapses: excitatory and inhibitory. The *excitatory synapse* initiates an impulse in the receiving neuron when stimulated, thereby causing release of neurotransmitters or increasing activity in the target cell. The *inhibitory synapse* diminishes the likelihood of an impulse in the receiving neuron or reduces the activity in other target cells. A receiving neuron or target cell may have thousands of synapses connecting it to other neurons and their excitatory or inhibitory information (see Figure 4.2, part A). The final cellular activity is a summation of these many excitatory and inhibitory synaptic signals.

THE NATURE OF DRUG RECEPTORS

Receptors are special proteins located in the membranes of receiving neurons and other target cells (see Figure 4.3). They help regulate the activity of cells in the nervous system and throughout the body. These selective protein sites on specific cells act as transducers to communicate the messages caused by *endogenous messenger substances* (chemicals produced and released within the body), such as neurotransmitters and hormones. The receptors process the complex information each cell receives as it attempts to maintain metabolic stability, or *homeostasis*, and fulfill its functional role (Kandel et al. 2000a). Many drugs used therapeutically and almost all drugs of abuse exert their effects on the body by directly or indirectly interacting (either to activate or antagonize) with these receptors.

Understanding how receptors interact with specific drugs has led to some interesting results. For

example, **opiate receptors** (sites of action by narcotic drugs, such as heroin and morphine) are naturally present in animal and human brains (Fattore et al. 2004). Why would human and animal brains have receptors for opiate narcotics, which are plant chemicals? Discovery of the opiate receptors suggested the existence of internal (endogenous) neurotransmitter substances in the body that normally act at these receptor sites and have effects like narcotic drugs, such as codeine and morphine. This finding led to the identification of the body's own opiates, the **endorphins** (Sabatowski et al. 2004). Specific receptors have also been found for other drugs such as the CNS depressant diazepam (Valium), which activates benzodiazepine receptors (Bateson 2004), and the active ingredient in marijuana (Fattore et al. 2004), which activates the cannabinoid receptor. Because of these discoveries, it is speculated that endogenous substances exist that mimic the effects of Valium and marijuana and help provide natural sedation and relaxation for the body. These are discussed in greater detail in Chapters 6 and 13.

Much remains unknown about how receptors respond to or interact with drugs. Using molecular biology techniques, many of these receptors have been found to initiate a cascade of linked chemical reactions, which can change intracellular environments to produce either activation or inactivation of cellular functions and metabolism (Kandel et al. 2000b).

Receptors that have been isolated and identified are protein molecules; it is believed that the shape of the protein is essential in regulating a drug's interaction with a cell. If the drug is the proper shape and size and has a compatible electrical charge, it may substitute for the endogenous messenger substance and activate the receptor protein by causing it to change its shape, or conform.

AGONISTIC AND ANTAGONISTIC EFFECTS ON DRUG RECEPTORS

A drug may have two different effects on a receptor when interaction occurs: **agonistic** or **antagonistic**. As shown in Figure 4.4, an agonistic drug interacts with the receptor and produces some type of cellu-

KEY TERMS

opiate receptors
receptors activated by opioid narcotic drugs such as heroin and morphine

endorphins
neurotransmitters that have narcotic-like effects

agonistic
a type of substance that activates a receptor

antagonistic
a type of substance that blocks a receptor

FIGURE 4.3

Cell membranes consist of a double layer of phospholipids. The water-soluble layers are pointed outward and the fat-soluble layers are pointed toward each other. Large proteins, including receptors, float in the membrane. Some of these receptors are activated by neurotransmitters to alter the activity of the cell.

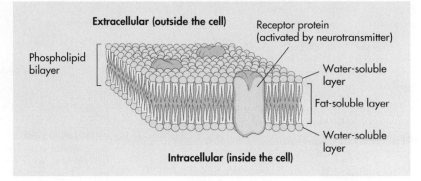

lar response, whereas an antagonistic drug interacts with the receptor but prevents that response.

An agonistic drug mimics the effect of a messenger substance (such as a neurotransmitter) that is naturally produced by the body and interacts with the receptor to cause some cellular change. For example, narcotic drugs are agonists that mimic the naturally occurring endorphins and activate opiate receptors. An antagonist has the opposite effect: It inhibits the sequence of metabolic events that a natural substance or an agonist drug can stimulate, usually without initiating an effect itself. Thus, the drug naloxone (created to treat heroin overdoses) is an antagonist at the opiate receptors and blocks the effects of narcotic drugs, such as heroin, as well as the effects of the naturally occurring endorphins.

NEUROTRANSMITTERS: THE MESSENGERS

Many drugs affect the activity of neurotransmitters by altering their synthesis, storage, release, or deactivation. By changing these processes, a drug may modify or block information transmitted by these neurochemical messengers. Thus, by altering the amount of neurotransmitters, such drugs can act indirectly, like agonists and antagonists, even though they do not directly change neurotransmitter receptors. They do influence the activity of these receptors by altering the amount of neurotransmitters available to naturally alter receptor function.

Experimental evidence shows that many different neurotransmitters exist, although much remains to be learned about their specific functions. These biochemical messengers are selectively released from specific neurons. Transmitters frequently altered by drugs of abuse include acetylcholine (ACh), norepinephrine, epinephrine, dopamine, serotonin, gamma-aminobutyric acid (GABA), and the endorphins (peptides). Because of the unique shapes and chemical features, each neurotransmitter affects only its specific receptors (Bloom 1995). Drugs can also affect these receptors if they are sufficiently similar in shape to the neurotransmitters. Figure 4.5 summarizes some of

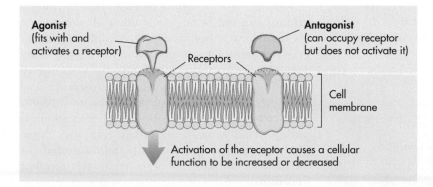

FIGURE 4.4

Interaction of agonist and antagonist with membrane receptor. When this receptor is occupied and activated by an agonist, it can cause cellular changes.

Acetylcholine
Chemical type: Choline product
Location: CNS—Basal ganglia, cortex, reticular activating
                    system
                    PNS—Neuromuscular junction, parasympathetic
                    system
Action: Excitatory (nicotine receptor) and inhibitory
                (muscarinic receptor)

Norepinephrine
Chemical type: Catecholamine
Location: CNS—Limbic system, cortex, hypothalamus,
                    reticular activating system, brain stem, spinal cord
                    PNS—Sympathetic nervous system
Action: Usually inhibitory; some excitation

Epinephrine
Chemical type: Catecholamine
Location: CNS—Minor
                    PNS—Adrenal glands
Action: Usually excitatory

Dopamine
Chemical type: Catecholamine
Location: CNS—Basal ganglia, limbic system,
                    hypothalamus
Action: Usually inhibitory

Serotonin (5HT)
Chemical type: Tryptophan-derivative
Location: CNS—Basal ganglia, limbic system, brain stem,
                    spinal cord, cortex
                    Other—Gut, platelets, cardiovascular
Action: Usually inhibitory

GABA
Chemical type: Amino acid
Location: CNS—Basal ganglia, limbic system, cortex
Action: Usually inhibitory

Endorphins
Chemical type: Peptide (small protein)
Location: CNS—Basal ganglia, hypothalamus, brain stem,
                    spinal cord
                    Other—Gut, cardiovascular system
Action: Inhibitory (narcotic-like effects)

Key: CNS—Central nervous system
          PNS—Peripheral nervous system

FIGURE 4.5

Features of common neurotransmitters.

the important features about the common neurotransmitters.

Neurotransmitters are inactivated after they have done their job by diffusion or, metabolism (by enzymes), or they are taken back up into the neuron by selective transporter proteins. If a deactivating enzyme or the reuptake is blocked by a drug, the effect of the transmitter may be prolonged or intensified.

KEY TERMS

muscarinic
a receptor type activated by ACh; usually inhibitory

nicotinic
a receptor type activated by ACh; usually excitatory

Acetylcholine

Large quantities of acetylcholine (ACh) are found in the brain. ACh is one of the major neurotransmitters in the autonomic portion of the PNS, which is discussed later in the chapter.

Neurons that respond to ACh are distributed throughout the brain. Depending on the region, ACh can have either excitatory or inhibitory effects. The receptors activated by ACh have been divided into two main subtypes based on the response to two drugs derived from plants: muscarine and nicotine. Muscarine (a substance in mushrooms that causes mushroom poisoning) and similarly acting drugs activate **muscarinic** receptors. Nicotine, whether experimentally administered or inhaled by smoking tobacco, stimulates **nicotinic** receptors.

Catecholamines

Catecholamines include the neurotransmitter compounds norepinephrine, epinephrine, and dopamine, all of which have similar chemical structures. Neurons that synthesize catecholamines convert the amino acids phenylalanine or tyrosine to dopamine. In some neurons, dopamine is further converted to norepinephrine, and finally to epinephrine.

After release, most of the catecholamines are taken back up into the neurons that released them, to be used over again; this process is called *reuptake*. An enzymatic breakdown system also metabolizes the catecholamines to inactive compounds. The reuptake process and the activity of metabolizing enzymes, especially monoamine oxidase (MAO), can be greatly affected by some of the drugs of abuse. If these deactivating enzymes or reuptake systems are blocked, the concentration of norepinephrine and dopamine may build up in the brain, causing a significantly increased effect. Cocaine, for example, prevents the reuptake of norepinephrine and dopamine in the brain, resulting in continual stimulation of neuron catecholamine receptors.

Norepinephrine and Epinephrine Although norepinephrine and epinephrine are structurally very similar, their receptors are selective and do not respond with the same intensity to either transmitter or to **sympathomimetic** drugs. Just as the receptors to ACh can be separated into muscarinic and nicotinic types, the norepinephrine and epinephrine receptors are classified into alpha and beta categories. Receiving cells may have alpha- or beta-type receptors, or both. Norepinephrine acts predominantly on alpha receptors and with less action on beta receptors.

The antagonistic (blocking) action of many drugs that act on these catecholamine receptors can be selective for alpha receptors, whereas others block only beta receptors. This distinction can be therapeutically useful. For example, beta receptors tend to stimulate the heart, whereas alpha receptors constrict blood vessels; thus, a drug that selectively affects beta receptors can be used to treat heart ailments without directly altering the state of the blood vessels.

Dopamine Dopamine is a catecholamine transmitter that is particularly influenced by drugs of abuse

(Carelli 2004). Most, if not all, drugs that elevate mood, have abuse potential, or cause psychotic behavior alter the activity of dopamine in some way, particularly in brain regions associated with regulating mental states. In addition, dopamine is an important transmitter in controlling movement and fine muscle activity, as well as endocrine functions. Thus, because many drugs of abuse affect dopamine neurons, they can also alter all of these functions.

Serotonin

Serotonin (5-hydroxytryptamine, or 5HT) is synthesized in neurons and elsewhere (for example, in the gastrointestinal tract and platelet-type blood cells) from the dietary source of tryptophan. Tryptophan is an essential amino acid, meaning that human beings do not have the ability to synthesize it and must obtain it through diet. Like the catecholamines, serotonin is degraded by the enzyme MAO; thus, drugs that alter this enzyme affect levels of not only catecholamines but also serotonin.

Serotonin is also found in the upper brain stem, which connects the brain and the spinal cord (see Figure 4.6). Axons from serotonergic neurons are distributed throughout the entire CNS. Serotonin generally inhibits action on its target neurons. One important role of the serotonergic neurons is to prevent overreaction to various stimuli, which can cause aggressiveness, excessive motor activity, exaggerated mood swings, insomnia, and abnormal sexual behavior. Serotonergic neurons also help regulate the release of hormones from the hypothalamus. Because many drugs of abuse affect serotonin systems, use of these drugs can interfere with these systems.

Alterations in serotonergic neurons, serotonin synthesis, and degradation have been proposed to be factors in mental illness and to contribute to the side effects of many drugs of abuse. In support

KEY TERMS

catecholamines
a class of biochemical compounds including the transmitters norepinephrine, epinephrine, and dopamine

sympathomimetic
agents that mimic the effects of norepinephrine or epinephrine

FIGURE 4.6

Functional components of the central nervous system. Limbic structures include the hypothalamus, thalamus, medial forebrain bundle, and frontal lobe of the cerebrum and are important for controlling emotions and other mental states.

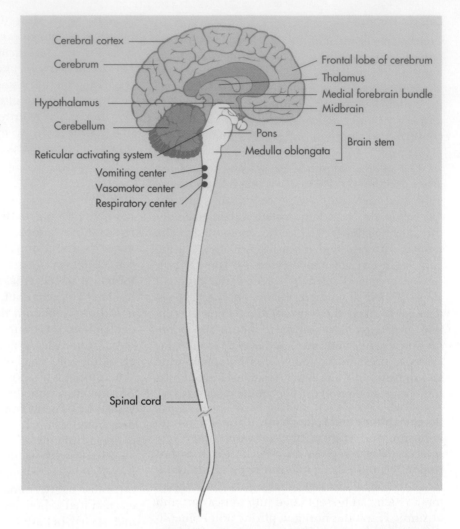

of this hypothesis is the fact that drugs such as psilocybin and lysergic acid diethylamide (LSD), which have serotonin-like chemical structures, are frequently abused because of their hallucinogenic properties and can cause psychotic effects (see Chapter 12).

KEY TERMS

CNS

the central nervous system, including the brain and spinal cord

PNS

the peripheral nervous system, including neurons outside the CNS

Major Divisions of the Nervous System

The nervous system can be divided into two major components: the central (**CNS**) and peripheral (**PNS**) nervous systems. The CNS consists of the brain and spinal cord (see Figure 4.6), which receive information through the input nerves of the PNS. This sensory information allows the CNS to evaluate the specific status of all organs and the general status of the body. After receiving and processing this information, the CNS reacts by regulating muscle and organ activity through the output nerves of the PNS (Lefkowitz et al. 1995).

The PNS is composed of neurons whose cell bodies or axons are located outside the brain or spinal cord. It consists of input and output nerves to the CNS. The PNS input to the brain and spinal cord conveys sensory information such as pain, pressure, and temperature, whereas its output activities are separated into somatic types (control of voluntary muscles) and autonomic types (control of unconscious functions, such as essential organ and gland activity).

THE CENTRAL NERVOUS SYSTEM

The human brain is an integrating (information processing) and storage device whose abilities are unequaled by the most complex computers. It can not only handle a great deal of information simultaneously from the senses, but can also evaluate and modify the response to the information rapidly. Although the brain weighs only 3 pounds, its 10–100 billion neurons give it the potential to perform a multitude of functions. The following are some important brain regions influenced by drugs of abuse.

The Reticular Activating System

The reticular activating system (RAS) is an area of the brain that receives input from all of the sensory systems as well as from the cerebral cortex. The RAS is found at the junction of the spinal cord and the brain (see Figure 4.6). One of its major functions is to control the brain's state of arousal (sleep versus awake).

Because of its complex, diffuse network structure, the RAS is very susceptible to the effects of drugs. It is sensitive to the effects of LSD, potent stimulants such as cocaine and amphetamines, and CNS depressants such as alcohol and barbiturates.

Norepinephrine and ACh are important neurotransmitters in the RAS. High levels of epinephrine, norepinephrine, or stimulant drugs, such as amphetamines, activate the RAS. In contrast, drugs that block the actions of another transmitter, ACh, called **anticholinergic** drugs (for example, antihistamines), suppress RAS activity, causing sleepiness.

The Basal Ganglia

The basal ganglia are the primary centers for involuntary and finely tuned motor functions involving, for example, posture and muscle tone. Two important neurotransmitters in the basal ganglia are dopamine and ACh. Damage to neurons in this area may cause *Parkinson's disease*, the progressive yet selective degeneration of the main dopaminergic neurons in the basal ganglia.

A close association exists between control of motor abilities and control of mental states. Both functions rely heavily on the activity of dopamine-releasing neurons. Consequently, drugs that affect dopamine activity usually alter both systems, resulting in undesired side effects. For example, heavy use of tranquilizers (such as chlorpromazine [Thorazine]), in the treatment of psychotic patients can produce Parkinson-like symptoms. If such drugs are administered daily over several years, problems with motor functioning may become permanent. Drugs of abuse, such as stimulants, increase dopamine activity, causing enhanced motor activity as well as psychotic behavior.

The Limbic System

The limbic system includes an assortment of linked brain regions located near to and including the hypothalamus (see Figure 4.6). Besides the hypothalamus, the limbic structures include the thalamus, medial forebrain bundle, and front portion of the cerebral cortex. Functions of the limbic and basal ganglia structures are inseparably linked; drugs that affect one system often affect the other as well.

The primary roles of limbic brain regions include regulating emotional activities (such as fear, rage, and anxiety), memory, modulation of basic hypothalamic functions (such as endocrine activity), and activities such as mating, procreation, and caring for the young. In addition, reward centers are also believed to be associated with limbic structures. For this reason, it is almost certain that the mood-elevating effects of drugs of abuse are mediated by the limbic systems of the brain.

For example, studies have shown that, when given the option, laboratory animals will self-administer most stimulant drugs of abuse (such as amphetamines and cocaine) through a cannula surgically

KEY TERMS

anticholinergic
agents that antagonize the effects of acetylcholine

placed into limbic structures (such as the medial forebrain bundle and frontal cerebral cortex). This self-administration is achieved by linking injection of the drug into the cannula with a lever press or other activity by the animal (Porrino 2004). It is thought that the euphoria or intense "highs" associated with these drugs result from their effects on these brain regions. Some of the limbic system's principal transmitters include dopamine, norepinephrine, and serotonin; dopamine activation appears to be the primary reinforcement that accounts for the abuse liability of most drugs (DiChiara et al. 2004).

The Cerebral Cortex

The unique features of the human cerebral cortex give human beings a special place among animals. The cortex is a layer of gray matter made up of nerves and supporting cells that almost completely surrounds the rest of the brain and lies immediately under the skull (see Figure 4.6). It is responsible for receiving sensory input, interpreting incoming information, and initiating voluntary motor behavior. Many psychoactive drugs, such as psychedelics, dramatically alter the perception of sensory information by the cortex and cause hallucinations that result in strange behavior.

The most developed part of the cortex is called the *associative cortex*. The associative areas of the brain do not directly receive input from the environment, nor do they directly initiate output to the muscles or the glands. Instead, these cortical areas may store memories, control complex behaviors, help process information, and help make decisions. Some psychoactive drugs disrupt the normal functioning of these areas, thereby interfering with an individual's ability to deal effectively and rationally with complex issues.

The Hypothalamus

The hypothalamus (see Figures 4.6 and 4.7) is located near the base of the brain. It integrates information from many sources and serves as the

CNS control center for the ANS and many vital support functions. It also serves as the primary point of contact between the nervous and endocrine systems. Because the hypothalamus controls the ANS, it is responsible for maintaining homeostasis in the body; thus, drugs that alter its function can have a major impact on systems that control homeostasis. The catecholamine transmitters are particularly important in regulating the function of the hypothalamus, and most drugs of abuse that alter the activity of norepinephrine and dopamine are likely to alter the activity of this brain structure.

The Autonomic Nervous System

Although the cell bodies of the neurons of the **ANS** are located within the brain or spinal cord, their axons project outside of the CNS to involuntary muscles, organs, and glands; thus, the ANS is considered part of the PNS. The ANS is an integrative, or regulatory, system that does not require conscious control (that is, you do not have to think about it to make it function). It is usually considered primarily a motor or output system. A number of drugs that cannot enter the CNS because of the blood–brain barrier are able to affect the ANS only. The ANS is divided into two functional components: the sympathetic and the parasympathetic nervous systems (Lefkowitz et al. 1995). Both systems include neurons that project to most visceral organs and to smooth muscles, glands, and blood vessels (see Figure 4.7).

The two components of the ANS generally have opposite effects on an organ or its function. The working of the heart is a good example of sympathetic and parasympathetic control. Stimulation of the parasympathetic nervous system slows the heart rate, whereas stimulation of the sympathetic nerves accelerates it. These actions constitute a constant biological check-and-balance, or regulatory system. Because the two parts of the ANS work in opposite ways much of the time, they are considered physiological antagonists. These two systems control most of the internal organs, the circulatory system, and the secretory (glandular) system. The sympathetic system is normally active at all times; the degree of activity varies from moment

KEY TERMS

ANS
the autonomic nervous system, which controls the unconscious functions of the body

to moment and from organ to organ. The parasympathetic nervous system is organized mainly for limited, focused activity and usually conserves and restores energy rather than expends it. For example, it slows the heart rate, lowers blood pressure, aids in absorption of nutrients, and is involved in emptying the urinary bladder. Table 4.2 lists the structures and/or functions of the sympathetic and parasympathetic nervous systems and their effects on one another.

The two branches of the ANS use two different neurotransmitters. The parasympathetic branch releases ACh at its synapses, whereas the sympathetic neurons release norepinephrine. An increase in epinephrine in the blood released from the adrenal glands (see the next section) or the administration

FIGURE 4.7

Autonomic pathways of the parasympathetic and sympathetic nervous systems and the organs affected.

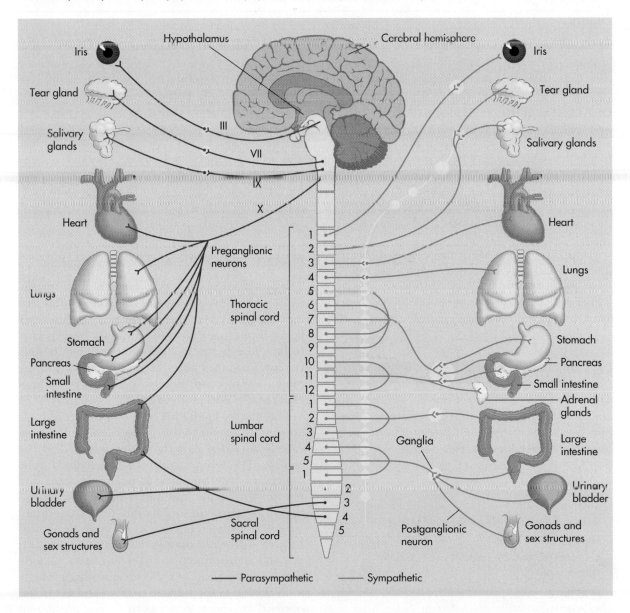

Table 4.2 Sympathetic and Parasympathetic Control

STRUCTURE OR FUNCTION	SYMPATHETIC	PARASYMPATHETIC
Heart rate	Speeds up	Slows
Breathing rate	Speeds up	Slows
Stomach wall	Slows motility	Increases motility
Skin blood vessels (vasomotor function)	Constricts	Dilates
Iris of eye	Constricts (pupil enlarges)	Dilates
Vomiting center	Stimulates	—

of drugs that enhance norepinephrine activity causes the body to respond as if the sympathetic nervous system had been activated. As previously mentioned, such drugs are referred to as *sympathomimetics*. Thus, taking amphetamines (which enhance the sympathetic nervous system by releasing norepinephrine and epinephrine) raises blood pressure, speeds up heart rate, slows down motility of the stomach walls, and may cause the pupils of the eyes to enlarge; other so-called "uppers," such as cocaine, have similar effects.

Drugs that affect ACh release, metabolism, or interaction with its respective receptor are referred to as *cholinergic* drugs. They can either mimic or antagonize the parasympathetic nervous system, according to their pharmacological action.

The Endocrine System

The endocrine system consists of glands, which are ductless (meaning that they secrete directly into the bloodstream) and release chemical substances called **hormones** (see Figure 4.8). These

KEY TERMS

hormones
regulatory chemicals released by endocrine systems

steroids
hormones related to the corticosteroids released from the adrenal cortex

androgens
male sex hormones

hormones are essential in regulating many vital functions, including metabolism, growth, tissue repair, and sexual behavior, to mention just a few. In contrast to neurotransmitters, hormones tend to have a slower onset, a longer duration of action, and a more generalized target. Although a number of tissues are capable of producing and releasing hormones, three of the principal sources of these chemical messengers are the pituitary gland, the adrenal glands, and the sex glands.

ENDOCRINE GLANDS AND REGULATION

The pituitary gland is often referred to as the *master gland*. It controls many of the other glands that make up the endocrine system by releasing regulating factors and growth hormone. Besides controlling the brain functions already mentioned, the hypothalamus helps control the activity of the pituitary gland and thereby has a very prominent effect on the endocrine system.

The adrenal glands are located near the kidneys and are divided into two parts: the outer surface, called the *cortex*, and the inner part, called the *medulla*. The adrenal medulla is actually a component of the sympathetic nervous system and releases adrenaline (another name for *epinephrine*) during sympathetic stimulation. Other important hormones released by the adrenal cortex are called *corticosteroids* or just **steroids**. Steroids help the body respond appropriately to crises and stress. In addition, small amounts of male sex hormones (chemically related to the steroids), called **androgens**, are released by the adrenal cortex. The androgens

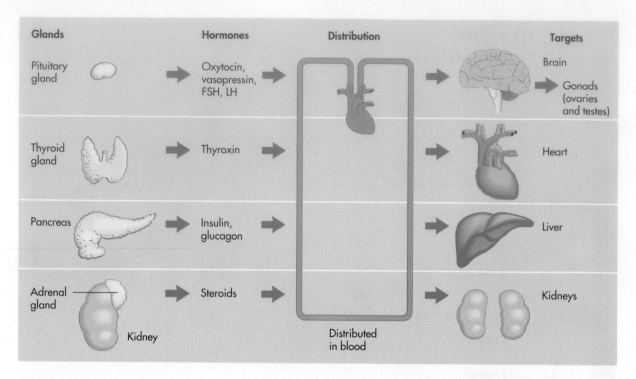

Glands	Hormones	Distribution	Targets

Pituitary gland → Oxytocin, vasopressin, FSH, LH → → Brain / Gonads (ovaries and testes)

Thyroid gland → Thyroxin → → Heart

Pancreas → Insulin, glucagon → → Liver

Adrenal gland / Kidney → Steroids → Distributed in blood → Kidneys

FIGURE 4.8

Examples of some glands in the endocrine system.

produce anabolic effects that increase the retention and synthesis of proteins, causing growth in the mass of tissues such as muscles and bones (Bhasin et al. 1996).

Sex glands are responsible for the secretion of male and female sex hormones that help regulate the development and activity of the respective reproductive systems. The organs known as *gonads* include the female ovaries and the male testes. The activity of the gonads is regulated by hormones released from the pituitary gland (see Figure 4.8) and, for the most part, remains suppressed until puberty. After activation, estrogens and progesterones are released from the ovaries, and androgens (principally testosterone) are released from the testes. These hormones are responsible for the development and maintenance of the secondary sex characteristics. They influence not only sex-related body features but also emotional states, suggesting that these sex hormones enter the brain and significantly affect the functioning of the limbic systems.

For the most part, drugs prescribed to treat endocrine problems are intended as replacement therapy. For example, diabetic patients suffer from

a shortage of insulin produced by the pancreas, so therapy consists of insulin injections. Patients who suffer from dwarfism receive insufficient growth hormone from the pituitary gland; thus, growth hormone is administered to stimulate normal growth. Because some hormones can affect growth, muscle development, and behavior, they are sometimes abused to enhance athletic performance or "body building."

THE ABUSE OF HORMONES: ANABOLIC STEROIDS

Androgens are the hormones most likely to be abused in the United States. In 2004, these drugs were self-administered by 2.5% of high school seniors in this country (Johnston 2004). Testosterone, the primary natural androgen, is produced by the testes. Naturally produced androgens are essential for normal growth and development of male sex organs as well as secondary sex characteristics such as male hair patterns, voice changes, muscular development, and fat distribution. The androgens are also necessary for appropriate growth

▶Case in Point   Winning — But at What Cost?

Steroids' ability to make athletes run faster, be stronger, and endure longer are no longer disputed. What is disputed is the question of "at what cost?" The message being sent by today's star athletes all too often is unsettling. Ken Caminiti, a former Major League Baseball player, admitted that he was on steroids when he won the National League's Most Valuable Player Award in 1996. In 2003, Caminiti proclaimed that he did not regret his steroid use and believed it was necessary to be competitive and make the big money. He also declared that at least half of the players in baseball were using such drugs. Caminiti was not able to control his own drug use and as late as September 2004 he was still doing drugs. On October 11, 2004, at the age of 41, he died from a heart attack. Although the precise cause of the heart attack was not identified, it is thought by many that his use of drugs of abuse, such as steroids, led to his premature demise.

Sources: CNNsi.com. "Caminiti Comes Clean" (28 May 2003); MSNBC News, "Caminiti, 41, Dies of Heart Attack." Available msnbc.msn.com/id/0222740/.

spurts during adolescence (*Drug Facts and Comparisons* 2005). Accepted therapeutic use of the androgens is usually for replacement in males with abnormally functioning testes.

Androgens clearly have an impressive effect on development of tissue (Kolata 2002). In particular, they cause pronounced growth of muscle mass and a substantial increase in body weight in young men with deficient testes function. Because of these effects, androgens are classified as **anabolic** (able to stimulate the conversion of nutrients into tissue mass) **steroids** (they are chemically similar to the steroids).

In addition, many athletes and trainers have assumed that, when taken in very high doses, androgens can enhance muscle growth and increase strength above that achieved by normal testicular function (Kolata 2002). Because of this effect, male and female athletes, as well as nonathletes who are into body building and sports, have been attracted to these drugs in hopes of enlarging muscle size, improving their athletic performances, and enhanc-

Anabolic steroids can cause pronounced growth of muscle mass.

KEY TERMS

anabolic steroids
compounds chemically like the steroids that stimulate production of tissue mass

ing their physiques (see Chapter 16) despite their negative side effects (see "Case in Point").

Several studies have suggested that anabolic hormones can have especially substantial negative effects. Athletic trainers and managers claim to be seeing an increase in severe injuries such as tears of muscles and ligaments due to aggravated trauma created by overmuscled bodies (Verducci 2002). These drugs can also affect the limbic structures of the brain. Consequently, they may cause excitation and a sense of superior strength and performance in some users. These effects, coupled with increased aggressiveness, could encourage continual use of these drugs. Other CNS effects, however, may be disturbing to the user. Symptoms that may occur with very high doses include uncontrolled rage (referred to as "roid rage"), headaches, anxiety, insomnia, and perhaps paranoia (*Drug Facts and Comparisons* 2005). Because of concern about the abuse potential and side effect profile of the anabolic steroids, these drugs are controlled as Schedule III substances.

DESIGNER STEROIDS

In an attempt to circumvent the restriction on steroid use, some athletes have been using the "designer" steroid known as tetrahydrogestrinone (THG). Until the recent ban enacted by the FDA, products containing THG were classified as nutritional supplements, making THG readily available without prescription or restriction. In 2003, the FDA decided that, because THG was closely related to the two controlled anabolic steroids gastrinone and trenbolone, its use and sale would be tightly controlled. Because of concerns that athletes are using THG to enhance performance, professional athletic organizations and the International Olympic Committee now test their athletes for this drug (Gardner 2003) and disqualify them from competition if THG is detected.

Conclusion

All psychoactive drugs affect brain activity by altering the ability of neurons to send and receive messages. Consequently, drugs of abuse exert their addicting effects by stimulating or blocking the activity of CNS neurotransmitters or their receptors.

Thus, to understand why these drugs are abused and the nature of their dependence, how neurons and their neurotransmitter systems function must be studied. In addition, many scientists believe that elucidating how substances of abuse affect nervous systems will lead to new and more effective methods for treating drug addiction.

Discussion Questions

1. What are the similarities and differences between neurotransmitters and hormones?

2. Why is it important for the body to have chemical messengers that can be quickly released and rapidly inactivated?

3. Why are receptors so important in understanding the effects of drugs of abuse?

4. Why is it not surprising that drugs that affect the catecholamine transmitters also affect the endocrine system?

5. What are some mechanisms whereby a drug of abuse can increase the activity of dopamine transmitter systems in the brain?

6. Why might a drug of abuse that damages the associative cortex make the user especially vulnerable to addiction?

7. Was classifying anabolic steroids as Schedule III drugs justified? What do you think will be the long-term consequence of this action?

Key Terms

homeostasis **120**

neurotransmitters **120**

hormones **120**

endocrine system **120**

neurons **120**

axons **121**

receptors **121**

psychoactive **121**

Summary

1 The nervous and endocrine systems help mediate internal and external responses to the body's surroundings. Both systems release chemical messengers to achieve their homeostatic functions. These messenger substances are called neurotransmitters and hormones, and they carry out their functions by binding to specific receptors. Many drugs exert their effects by influencing these chemical messengers.

2 The neuron is the principal cell type in the nervous system. This specialized cell consists of dendrites, a cell body, and an axon. It communicates with other neurons and organs by releasing neurotransmitters, which can cause either excitation or inhibition at their target sites.

3 The chemical messengers from glands and neurons exert their effects by interacting with special protein regions in membranes called receptors. Because of their unique construction, receptors interact only with molecules that have specific shapes. Activation of receptors can alter the functions of the target system.

4 Agonists are substances or drugs that stimulate receptors. Antagonists are substances or drugs that bind to receptors and prevent them from being activated.

5 A variety of substances are used as neurotransmitters by neurons in the body. The classes of transmitters include the catecholamines, serotonin, acetylcholine, GABA, and peptides. These transmitters are excitatory, inhibitory, or sometimes both, depending on which receptor is being activated. Many drugs selectively act to either enhance or antagonize these neurotransmitters and their activities.

6 The central nervous system consists of the brain and spinal cord. Regions within the brain help to regulate specific functions. The hypothalamus controls endocrine and basic body functions. The basal ganglia are primarily responsible for controlling motor activity. The limbic system regulates mood and mental states. The cerebral cortex helps interpret, process, make decisions, and respond to input information.

7 The limbic system and its associated transmitters, especially dopamine and serotonin, are major sites of action for the drugs of abuse. Substances that increase the activity of dopamine cause a sense of well-being and euphoria, which encourages psychological dependence.

8 The autonomic nervous system is composed of the sympathetic and parasympathetic systems; neurons associated with these systems release noradrenalin and acetylcholine as their transmitters, respectively. These systems work in an antagonistic fashion to control unconscious, visceral functions such as breathing and cardiovascular activity. The parasympathetic nervous system usually helps conserve and restore energy in the body, whereas the sympathetic nervous system is continually active.

9 The endocrine system consists of glands that synthesize and release hormones into the blood. Distribution via blood circulation carries these chemical messengers throughout the body, where they act on specific receptors. Some of the principal structures include the pituitary, adrenals, and gonads (testes and ovaries).

10 Anabolic steroids are structurally related to the male hormone testosterone. They are often abused by both male and female athletes trying to build muscle mass and enhance performance. The continual use of high doses of anabolic steroids can cause annoying and dangerous side effects. The long-term effects of low, intermittent doses of these drugs have not been determined. Because of concerns voiced by most medical authorities, anabolic steroids are controlled substances and have been classified as Schedule III substances.

References

Bateson, A. "The Benzodiazepine Site of the GABA A Receptor: An Old Target with a New Potential." *Sleep Medicine* 5 (2004): S9–S59.

Bhasin, S., T. W. Storer, N. Berman, C. Callegari, B. Clevenger, J. Phillips, T. Bunnell, R. Tricker, A. Shirazi, and R. Casaburi. "The Effects of Supraphysiologic Doses of Testosterone on Muscle Size and Strength in Normal Men." *New England Journal of Medicine* 335 (1996): 1–7.

Bloom, F. "Neurotransmission and the Central Nervous System." In *The Pharmacological Basis of Therapeutics*, 9th ed., edited by J. Harman and T. Limbird, 267–293. New York: McGraw-Hill, 1995.

Carelli, R. "Nucleus Accumbens Cell Firing and Rapid Dopamine Signaling During Goal-Directed Behavior in Rats." *Neuropharmacology* 47 Supplement 1 (2004): 180–189.

Dackis, C., and C. O'Brien. "Cocaine Dependence: A Disease of the Brain's Reward Centers." *Journal of Substance Abuse Treatment* 21 (2001): 111–117.

DiChiara, G., V. Bassareo, S. Fenu, M. DeLuca, et al. "Dopamine and Drug Addiction: The Nucleus Accumbens Shell Connections." *Neuropharmacology* 47 Supplement 1 (2004): 227–241.

Drug Facts and Comparisons. 59th ed. St. Louis: Walters Kluwar Health, 2005: 322–336.

Fattore, L., G. Cossu, M. Spano, S. Deiana, P. Fadda, M. Scherma, and W. Fratta. "Cannabinoids and Rewards: Interactions with Opioid Systems." *Critical Reviews in Neurobiology* 16 (2004): 147–158.

Gardner, A. "Controversy Grows Over Designer Steroid. Feds Ban THG: Grand Jury Subpoenas Top Athletes." *Healthscout* (30 October 2003): 10F2.

Gonzalez, G., and T. Kosten. "Treatment of Heroin (Diamorphine) Addiction, Current Approaches and Future Prospects." *Drugs* 62 (2002): 1331–1343.

Grotenhermen, F. "Pharmacokinetics and Pharmacodynamics of Cannabinoids." *Clinical Pharmacokinetics* 42 (2003): 327–360.

Johnston, L. P. "Overall Teen Drug Use Continues Gradual Decline, But Use of Inhalants Rises." Press Release (21 December 2004). Available www.monitoringthefuture.org.

Kandel, E., J. Schwartz, and T. Jessell. "Overview of Synaptic Transmission." In *Principles of Neural Science*, 4th ed., 175–186. New York: McGraw-Hill, 2000a.

Kandel, E., J. Schwartz, and T. Jessell. "Modulation of Synaptic Transmission: Second Messengers." In *Principles of Neural Science*, 4th ed., 229–252. New York: McGraw-Hill, 2000b.

Kolata, G. "With No Answers on Risks: Steroid Users Still Say 'Yes'." *The New York Times* (2 December 2002). Available nytimes.com.

Lefkowitz, R., B. Hoffman, and P. Taylor. "Neurotransmission, the Autonomic and Somatic Motor Nervous Systems." In *The Pharmacological Basis of Therapeutics*, 9th ed., edited by J. Hardman and T. Limbird, 361–396. New York: McGraw-Hill, 1995.

Panzarino, P. "Depression" (December 2004). Available http://www.medicinenet.com/depression/article.htm.

Porrino, L., J. Daunais, H. Smith, and M. Nadar. "The Expanding Effects of Cocaine: Studies in Nonhuman Primate Model of Cocaine Self-Administration." *Neuroscience Biobehavioral Reviews* 27 (2004): 893–920.

Sabatowski, R., D. Shafer, S. Kasper, H. Brunsch, and L. Radbruh. "Pain Treatment: A Historical Overview." *Current Pharmaceutical Design* 10 (2004): 701–716.

Swan, N. "Like Other Drugs of Abuse, Nicotine Disrupts the Brain's Pleasure Circuit." *NIDA Notes* 13 (1998): 12.

Verducci, T. "The Injury Toll." (May 28, 2002). Available CNNSI.com.

CHAPTER 5

How and Why Drugs Work

On completing this chapter you will be able to:

◎ Describe some of the common unintended drug effects.

◎ Explain why the same dose of a drug may affect individuals differently.

◎ Explain the difference between potency and toxicity.

◎ Describe the concept of a drug's "margin of safety."

◎ Identify and give examples of additive, antagonistic, and potentiative (synergistic) drug interactions.

◎ Identify the pharmacokinetic factors that can influence the effects caused by drugs.

◎ Cite the physiological and pathological factors that influence drug effects.

◎ Explain the significance of the blood–brain barrier to psychoactive drugs.

◎ Define *threshold dose*, *plateau effect*, and *cumulative effect*.

◎ Discuss the role of the liver in drug metabolism and the consequences of this process.

◎ Define *biotransformation*.

◎ Describe the relationships among tolerance, withdrawal, rebound, physical dependence, and psychological dependence.

◎ Discuss the significance of placebos in drug therapy and drug abuse.

◎ Describe drug craving, and explain how it may cause relapse to a drug addiction.

Drugs and Society Online is a great source for additional drugs and society information for both students and instructors.
Visit **http://drugsandsociety.jbpub.com** to find a variety of useful tools for learning, thinking, and teaching.

Introduction

A common belief is that drugs can solve most of life's serious physical, emotional, and medical problems. Although medications are essential to treatment for many diseases, excessive reliance on drugs causes unrealistic expectations that may lead to dangerous — even fatal — consequences. For example, drug addiction and dependence often follow from such unrealistic drug expectations. Obviously, not every person who uses drugs inappropriately becomes a drug addict, nor are patients who use drugs as prescribed by the doctor immune from becoming physically and mentally dependent on their medications. In fact, because of individual variability, it is difficult to predict accurately which drug users will or will not have drug problems such as addiction and dependence.

In this chapter, we consider the factors that account for the variability of drug responses — that is, what determines how the body responds to drugs and why some drugs work while others do not. First, we review the general effects of drugs, both intended and unintended. The correlation between the dose and response to a drug is addressed next, followed by a discussion of how drugs interact with one another. The section on *pharmacokinetic* factors considers how drugs are introduced into, distributed throughout, and eliminated from the body, along with physiological and pathological variables that modify how drugs affect the body. The final sections in the chapter consider concepts important to understanding drug abuse, such as tolerance, physical versus psychological dependence, and addiction.

The Intended and Unintended Effects of Drugs

When physicians prescribe drugs, their objective is usually to cure or relieve symptoms of a disease.

KEY TERMS

side effects
unintended drug responses

withdrawal
unpleasant effects that occur when use of a drug is stopped

Frequently, however, drugs cause unintended effects that neither the physician nor the patient expected. These are called **side effects**.

A response that is considered a side effect in one situation may, in fact, be the therapeutic objective in another. For example, the antihistamines found in many over-the-counter (OTC) drugs have an intended main effect of relieving allergy symptoms, but they often cause annoying drowsiness as a side effect; in fact, their labels include warnings that they should not be used while driving a car. These antihistamines are also included in OTC sleep aids, in which their sedating action is the desired main effect.

Side effects can influence many body functions and occur in any organ (see Figure 5.1). Side effects of prescription and nonprescription drugs are estimated to seriously injure 2.1 million people and kill 100,000 people in the United States each year (MacDonald 1998). The following are basic kinds of side effects that can result from drug use:

Nausea or vomiting.

Changes in mental alertness such as sedation or nervousness.

Dependence, which compels people to continue using a drug because they want to achieve a desired effect or because they fear unpleasant reactions, called **withdrawal**, that occur when use of the drug is discontinued.

Allergic reactions (hypersensitive reactions or sensitization) often experienced as rashes or breathing difficulty.

Changes in cardiovascular activity altering the activity of the heart or blood pressure.

This partial list of side effects demonstrates the types of risks involved whenever any drug (prescription, nonprescription, illicit, and even some herbal products) is used. Consequently, before taking a drug, whether for therapeutic or recreational use, you should understand its potential problems and determine whether the benefits justify the risks. For example, it is important to know that morphine is effective for relieving severe pain, but it also depresses breathing and retards intestinal activity, causing constipation. Likewise, amphetamines can be used to suppress appetite for losing

FIGURE 5.1

Common side effects with drugs of abuse. Almost every organ or system in the body can be negatively affected by the substances of abuse.

Organ	Side Effect	Drug
Brain	Insomnia	Amphetamines, caffeine
	Drowsiness	Alcohol
	Hallucinations	LSD
	Psychosis	Cocaine, PCP
Eyes	Blurred vision	PCP
	Red eyes	Marijuana
Lungs	Emphysema	Tobacco, marijuana
	Cancer	
Heart	Heart attacks	Amphetamines,
	Arrhythmias	cocaine
Liver	Cirrhosis	Alcohol
Kidneys	Increased urine	Alcohol, caffeine
Stomach	Nausea	Narcotics
Intestines	Constipation	Narcotics

weight, but they also increase blood pressure and stimulate the heart. Cocaine is a good local anesthetic, but it can be extremely addicting and can cause tremors or even seizures. The greater the danger associated with using a drug, the less likely that the benefits will warrant its use.

Adverse effects of drugs of abuse are particularly troublesome in the United States. Studies have suggested that tens of billions of dollars are spent each year in the United States on medical care and premature deaths due to the use of addicting substances (Rice 1999).

The Dose-Response Relationship of Therapeutics and Toxicity

All effects — both desired and unwanted — are related to the amount of drug administered. A small concentration of drug may have one effect, whereas a larger dose may create a greater effect or a different effect entirely. Because some correlation exists between the response to a drug and the quantity of the drug dose, it is possible to calculate **dose-response** curves (see Figure 5.2).

Once a dose-response curve for a drug has been determined in an individual, it can be used to predict how that person will respond to different doses of the drug. For example, the dose-response curve for user B in Figure 5.2 shows that 600 mg of aspirin will relieve only 50% of his or her headache. It is important to understand that not everyone responds the same way to a given dose of drug. Thus, in Figure 5.2, although 600 mg of aspirin gives 50% relief from a headache for user B, it relieves 100% of the headache for user A and none of the headache for user C. This variability in response makes it difficult to predict the precise drug effect from a given dose.

Many factors can contribute to the variability in drug responses (Bourne 1998). One of the most important is **tolerance**, or reduced response over time to the same dosage, an effect that is examined carefully in a later section of this chapter. Other factors include the size of the individual, stomach contents if the drug is taken by mouth, different levels of enzymatic activity in the liver (which changes the drug via metabolic action), acidity of the urine (which affects the rate of drug elimination), time of day, and state of the person's health. Such multiple interacting factors make it

KEY TERMS

dose-response
correlation between the amount of a drug given and its effects

tolerance
changes in the body that decrease response to a drug even though the dose remains the same

FIGURE 5.2

Dose-response curve for relieving a headache with aspirin in three users. User A is the most sensitive and has 100% headache relief at a dose of 600 mg. User B is the next most sensitive and experiences 50% headache relief with a 600-mg dose. The least sensitive is user C: with a 600-mg dose, user C has no relief from a headache.

difficult to calculate accurately the final drug effect for any given individual at any given time.

MARGIN OF SAFETY

An important concept for developing new drugs for therapy, as well as for assessing the probability of serious side effects for drugs of abuse, is called the **margin of safety**. The margin of safety is determined by the difference between the doses necessary to cause the intended (therapeutic or

KEY TERMS

margin of safety
range in dose between the amount of drug necessary to cause a therapeutic effect and that needed to create a toxic effect

potency
amount of drug necessary to cause an effect

toxicity
capacity of one drug to damage or cause adverse effects in the body

recreational) effects and the toxic unintended effects. The larger the margin of safety, the less likely that serious adverse side effects will occur when using the drug to treat medical problems or even when abusing it. Drugs with relatively narrow margins of safety, such as phencyclidine (PCP) or cocaine, have a very high rate of serious reactions in populations who abuse these substances.

There is no such thing as the perfect drug that goes right to the target in the body, has no toxicity, produces no side effects, and can be removed or neutralized when not needed. Unfortunately, most effective drugs are potentially dangerous if the doses are high enough or if they are used recklessly. Pharmacologists refer to the perfect drug as a "magic bullet"; so far, no magic bullets have been discovered. Even relatively safe drugs available on an OTC basis can cause problems for some prospective users. Not surprisingly, all drugs of abuse can cause very serious side effects, especially when self-administered by users who are unfamiliar with the potential toxicities of these substances. The possibility that adverse effects will occur should always be considered before using any drug.

POTENCY VERSUS TOXICITY

Most of us know that some drugs of abuse are more dangerous than others. For example, it is common knowledge that abuse of the narcotic drug heroin is more likely to be lethal than abuse of another narcotic drug, codeine. One important feature that makes heroin more dangerous than codeine is its high potency. **Potency** is a way of expressing how much of a drug is necessary to cause an effect, whether it be desired or toxic. The smaller the dose required to achieve a drug action, the greater the drug potency.

The concept of potency can also be used to describe a drug's ability to create a therapeutic effect. More potent medications require lower doses to be effective. Knowledge of a drug's potency is essential if it is to be used properly and safely.

Toxicity is the capacity of a drug to upset or even destroy normal body functions. Toxic compounds are often called *poisons*, although almost any compound — including sugar, table salt, aspirin, and vitamin A — can be toxic at sufficiently high doses. If a foreign chemical is introduced into the body, it may disrupt the body's normal functions. In many instances, the body can compensate for this disruption, perhaps by metabolizing and rapidly eliminating the chemical, and little effect is noted. Sometimes, however, the delicate balance is altered and the person becomes sick or even dies. If the body's functional balance is already under stress from disease, the introduction of a drug may have a much more serious effect than its use in a healthy person who can adjust to its toxicity.

A drug with high potency often is toxic even at low doses; therefore, the amount given must be carefully measured and the user closely monitored. If caution is not taken, serious damage to the body or death can occur. Very potent drugs that are abused, such as heroin, are particularly dangerous because they are often consumed by unsuspecting users who are ignorant of the drug's extreme toxicity (see "Here and Now," Unexpected Heroin Potency, page 144). Potency depends on many factors, such as the drug's absorption, its distribution in the body, individual metabolism, the form of excretion, the rate of elimination, and its activity at the site of action (Franklin and Franz 2000).

Drug Interaction

A drug's effects can be dramatically altered when other drugs are also present in the body; this effect is known as **drug interaction** (Hussar 2000). A typical example of multiple drug use occurs when you treat your common cold. Because of your many cold-related symptoms, you may consume an assortment of pain relievers, antihistamines, decongestants, and anticough medications all at the same time.

Multiple drug use can create a serious medical problem because many drugs influence the actions of other drugs (Hussar 2000). Even physicians may be baffled by unusual effects when multiple drugs are consumed. Frequently, drug interactions are misdiagnosed as symptoms of a disease. Such errors in diagnosis can lead to inappropriate treatment and serious health consequences. Complications can arise that are dangerous, even fatal. The interacting substance may be another drug, or it may be some substance in the diet or in the environment,

such as a pesticide. Because of the increasing popularity of herbal products, we are also observing that herbs can interact with both prescription and nonprescription drugs. These interactions are not surprising because some of the herbs themselves contain drugs that occur naturally. Consequently, an herb that causes sedation almost certainly will enhance the depressing effects of either prescription or nonprescription sleep aids. Drug interaction is an area in which more research and public education are required.

Depending on the effect on the body, drug interaction may be categorized into three types: *additive, antagonistic (inhibitory)*, and *potentiative (synergistic)*.

ADDITIVE EFFECTS

Additive interactions are the summation of effects of drugs taken concurrently. An example of an additive interaction results from using aspirin and acetaminophen (Tylenol) at the same time. The pain relief provided is equal to the sum of the two analgesics, which could be achieved by a comparable dose of either drug alone. Thus, if a 300-mg tablet of Bayer Aspirin were taken with a 300-mg tablet of Tylenol, the relief would be the same as if two tablets of either Bayer Aspirin or Tylenol were taken instead.

ANTAGONISTIC (INHIBITORY) EFFECTS

Antagonistic interactions occur when one drug cancels or blocks the effect of another drug. For example, if you take antihistamines to reduce nasal congestion, you may be able to antagonize some of the drowsiness often caused by these drugs by using a central nervous system (CNS) stimulant such as caffeine.

KEY TERMS

drug interaction
the presence of one drug alters the action of another drug

additive interactions
effects created when drugs are similar and actions are added together

antagonistic interactions
effects created when drugs cancel one another

Here and Now

Unexpected Heroin Potency

Between 7 and 11 people have died from heroin overdoses this year in Austin, Texas, leading health officials to believe that a more potent form of the drug smuggled from Colombia could be the problem. Although the medical examiner's office had not finished its investigation, it did not want to wait to release the warning because heroin use has increased at college parties. Even though alcohol seems to be the general drug of choice at the University of Texas, officials believe it is important for students to be aware of what is going on around them.

Source: Lai, D. "More Potent Heroin May Be in Austin" (9 February 2005). Available Dailytexanonline.com/news/2004/02/26StateLocal/more-potent.Heroin.May.Be.In.Austin-619716.shtml.

Often, drug abusers who use two drugs at the same time are trying to antagonize the unpleasant side effects of the first drug by administering the second. It has been reported that many of those currently abusing cocaine also use alcohol (Harris et al. 2003). The combined use of these two drugs may be a major factor in drug-related problems and death in emergency rooms (Coffin et al. 2003). Nevertheless, it appears that some users may coadminister these drugs in an attempt to antagonize the disruptive effects of alcohol with the stimulant action of the cocaine (O'Brien 2001).

POTENTIATIVE (SYNERGISTIC) EFFECTS

The third type of drug interaction is known as *potentiation*, or **synergism**. Synergism occurs when the effect of a drug is enhanced by the presence of another drug or substance. A common example is the combination of alcohol and diazepam (Valium) (see Table 5.1). It has been estimated that as many as 3000 people die each year from mixing alcohol with CNS depressants such as Valium. Alco-

hol, like Valium, is a CNS depressant. When depressants are taken together, CNS functions become impaired and the person becomes groggy. A person in this state may forget that he or she has taken the pills and repeat the dose. The combination of these two depressants (or other depressants, such as antihistamines) can interfere with the CNS to the point where vital functions such as breathing and heartbeat are severely impaired.

Although the mechanisms of interaction among CNS depressants are not entirely clear, these drugs likely enhance one another's direct effects on inhibitory chemical messengers in the brain (see Chapter 4). In addition, interference by alcohol with liver-metabolizing enzymes contributes to the synergism that arises with the combination of alcohol and some depressants, such as barbiturates (Hobbs et al. 1995).

DEALING WITH DRUG INTERACTIONS

Although many drug effects and interactions are not very well understood, it is important to be aware of them. A growing body of evidence indicates that many of the drugs and substances we deliberately consume will interact and produce unexpected and sometimes dangerous effects (see Table 5.1). It is alarming to know that many of the foods we eat and some chemical pollutants also

KEY TERMS

synergism
ability of one drug to enhance the effect of another; also called *potentiation*

Table 5.1 **Common Interactions with Substances of Abuse**

DRUG	COMBINED WITH	CONSEQUENCE OF INTERACTION
Sedatives		
Diazepam (Valium), triazolam (Halcion)	Alcohol, barbiturates	Increase sedation
Stimulants		
Amphetamines, cocaine	Insulin Antidepressants	Decrease insulin effect Cause hypertension
Narcotics		
Heroin, morphine	Barbiturates, Valium Anticoagulant Antidepressants Amphetamines	Increase sedation Increase bleeding Cause sedation Increase euphoria
Tobacco		
Nicotine	Blood pressure medication Amphetamines, cocaine	Elevate blood pressure Increase cardiovascular effects
Alcohol	Cocaine	Produces cocaethylene, which enhances euphoria and toxicity

interfere with and modify drug actions. Pesticides, traces of hormones in meat and poultry, traces of metals in fish, nitrites and nitrates from fertilizers, and a wide range of chemicals — some of which are used as food additives — have been shown, under certain conditions, to interact with some drugs (Correia 1998).

It is essential that the public be educated about the interactions most likely to occur with drugs that are prescribed, self-administered legitimately (for example, OTC drugs and herbal products), or taken recreationally (for example, drugs of abuse). People need to be aware that OTC and herbal drugs are as likely to cause interaction problems as prescription drugs. For example, an OTC or herbal decongestant that contains mild CNS stimulants (e.g., pseudoephedrine) taken with potent CNS stimulants, such as cocaine and amphetamines, can cause interactions that fatally affect the heart and brain. If any question arises concerning the possibility of drug interaction, individuals should talk to their physicians, pharmacists, or other healthcare providers.

Most drug abusers are multiple drug (polydrug) users with little concern for the dangerous interactions that might potentially occur. It is common, for example, for drug abusers to combine multiple CNS depressants to enhance their effects, to combine a depressant with a stimulant to *titrate* a CNS effect (to determine the smallest amount that can be taken to achieve the desired "high"), or to experiment with a combination of stimulants, depressants, and hallucinogens just to see what happens. The effects of such haphazard drug mixing are impossible to predict, difficult to treat in emergency situations, and all too frequently fatal.

Pharmacokinetic Factors That Influence Drug Effects

Although it is difficult to predict precisely how any single individual will be affected by drug use, the following major factors represent different aspects of the body's response that should be considered when attempting to anticipate a drug's effects (Galinsky and Svensson 2000; Rollins 2000).

1. How does the drug enter the body? (administration)
2. How does the drug move from the site of administration into the body's system? (absorption)
3. How does the drug move to various areas in the body? (distribution)
4. How and where does the drug produce its effects? (activation)
5. How is the drug inactivated, metabolized, and/or excreted from the body? (biotransformation and elimination)

These issues relate to the **pharmacokinetics** of a drug and are important considerations when predicting the body's response.

FORMS AND METHODS OF TAKING DRUGS

Drugs come in many forms. How a drug is formulated — solution, powder, capsule, or pill — influences the rate of passage into the bloodstream and consequently its efficacy.

The means of introducing the drug into the body will also affect how quickly the drug enters the bloodstream and how it is distributed to the site of action, as well as how much will ultimately reach its target and exert an effect (Galinsky and Svensson 2000) (see Figure 5.3). The principal forms of drug administration are *oral ingestion, inhalation, injection,* and *topical application.*

Oral Ingestion

One of the most common and convenient ways of taking a drug is orally. This type of administration usually introduces the drug into the body by way of the stomach or intestines.

Following oral administration, it is difficult to control the amount of drug that reaches the site of action, for three reasons:

1. The drug must enter the bloodstream after passing through the wall of the stomach or intestines without being destroyed or changed to an inactive form. From the blood, the drug must diffuse to the target area and remain there in sufficient concentration to have an effect.
2. Materials in the stomach or intestines, such as food, may interfere with the passage of some drugs through the gut lining and thus prevent drug action. For example, food in your stomach will diminish the effects of alcohol by altering its absorption.
3. The liver might metabolize orally ingested drugs too rapidly, before they are able to exert an effect. The liver is the major detoxifying organ in the body, which means it removes chemicals and toxins from the blood and usually changes them into an inactive form that is easy for the body to excrete. This function is essential to survival, but it creates a problem for the pharmacologist in developing effective drugs. The liver is especially problematic to oral administration because the substances absorbed from the digestive tract usually go to the liver before being distributed to other parts of the body and their site of action. For this reason, cocaine taken orally is not very effective.

Inhalation

Some drugs are administered by inhalation into the lungs through the mouth or nose. The lungs include large beds of capillaries, so chemicals ca-

Drugs can be introduced into the body using various mechanisms such as pills, capsules, oral liquids, topicals, or injections.

Method of Administration	Onset	Duration	Effect
Smoking			
cocaine	fast (~15 sec)	brief (10–15 min)	potent and strong
heroin	fast (~20 sec)	short (1–2 hr)	potent and strong
Intravenous			
cocaine	fast (20 sec)	short (30 min)	potent and strong
heroin	fast (1–2 min)	short (1–2 hr)	potent and strong
Snorting			
cocaine	moderate (~10 min)	short (45 min)	less potent
heroin	moderate (~15 min)	short (1–2 hr)	less potent
Oral			
cocaine (coca leaf)	slow (30 min)	moderate (~2–4 hr)	minor
methadone	slow (30–60 min)	long (24 hr)	less euphoria/ used for treatment

FIGURE 5.3

Relationship between the method of drug administration and drug effects.

pable of crossing membranes can enter the blood as rapidly as they can via intravenous (IV) injection and can be equally as dangerous (Meng et al. 1999). Ether, chloroform, and nitrous oxide anesthetics are examples of drugs that are therapeutically administered by inhalation. Nicotine, cocaine, methamphetamine, and heroin are drugs of abuse that can be inhaled as smoke (Mathias 1997). One serious problem with inhalation is the potential for irritation to the mucous membrane lining of the lungs; another is that the drug may have to be continually inhaled to maintain the concentration necessary for an effect. Inhalation of illicit drugs of abuse is common to prevent contracting AIDS, which can be transmitted by IV injection with contaminated needles (Meng et al. 1999; *NIDA Notes* 1999).

Injection

Some drugs are given by injection: **intravenously (IV)**, **intramuscularly (IM)**, or **subcutaneously (SC)**. A major advantage of administering drugs by IV is the speed of action; the dosage is delivered rapidly and directly, and often less drug is needed because it reaches the site of action quickly. This method can be very dangerous if the dosage is

calculated incorrectly or the drug effects are unknown. In addition, impurities in injected materials may irritate the vein; this issue is a particular problem in the drug-abusing population, in which needle sharing frequently occurs. The injection itself injures the vein by leaving a tiny point of scar tissue where the vein is punctured. If repeated injections are administered into the same area, the elasticity of the vein is gradually reduced, causing the vessel to collapse.

Intramuscular injection can damage the muscle directly if the drug preparation irritates the tissue or indirectly if the nerve controlling the muscle is damaged. If the nerve is destroyed, the muscle will degenerate (atrophy). A subcutaneous injection may damage the skin at the point of injection if a particularly irritating drug is administered. Another

KEY TERMS

intravenous (IV)
drug injection into a vein

intramuscular (IM)
drug injection into a muscle

subcutaneous (SC)
drug injection beneath the skin

danger of drug injections arises when contaminated needles are shared by drug users. This danger has become a serious problem in the spread of infectious diseases such as AIDS and hepatitis.

Topical Application

Those drugs that readily pass through surface tissue such as the skin, the lining of the nose, and under the tongue can be applied topically, for systemic (whole-body) effects. Although many drugs do not appreciably diffuse across these tissue barriers into the circulation, there are notable exceptions. For example, a product to help quit smoking, a nicotine transdermal patch (Nicoderm), is placed on the skin; the drug passes through the skin and enters the body to prevent tobacco craving and withdrawal. In addition, several drugs of abuse, such as heroin and cocaine, can be "snorted" into the nose and rapidly absorbed into the body through the nasal lining.

DISTRIBUTION OF DRUGS IN THE BODY AND TIME-RESPONSE RELATIONSHIPS

Following administration (regardless of the mode), most drugs are distributed throughout the body in the blood. The circulatory system consists of many miles of arteries, veins, and capillaries and includes 5 to 6 liters of blood. Once a drug enters the bloodstream by passing through thin capillary walls, it is rapidly diluted and carried to organs and other body structures. It requires approximately 1 minute for the blood, and consequently the drugs it contains, to circulate completely throughout the body.

Factors Affecting Distribution

Drugs have different patterns of distribution depending on the following chemical properties (Correia 1998; Nicholas and Benet 1998):

- Their ability to pass across membranes and through tissues

- Their molecular size (large versus small molecules)
- Their solubility properties (do they dissolve in water or in fatty [oily] solutions?)
- Their tendency to attach to proteins and tissues throughout the body

These distribution-related factors are very important because they determine whether a drug can pass across tissue barriers in the body and reach its site of action. By preventing the movement of drugs into organs or across tissues, these barriers may interfere with drug activity and limit the therapeutic usefulness of a drug if they do not allow it to reach its site of action. Such barriers may also offer protection by preventing entry of a drug into a body structure where it can cause problems.

Blood is carried to the nerve cells of the brain in a vast network of thin-walled capillaries. Drugs that are soluble in fatty (oily) solutions are most likely to pass across these capillary membranes (known as the **blood–brain barrier**) into the brain tissue. Most psychoactive drugs, such as the drugs of abuse, are able to pass across the blood–brain barrier with little difficulty. However, many water-soluble drugs cannot pass through the fatty capillary wall; such drugs are not likely to cross this biological barrier and affect the brain.

A second biological barrier, the placenta, prevents the transfer of certain molecules from the mother to the fetus. A principal factor that determines passage of substances across the placental

Transdermal nicotine patches are popular smoking cessation aids.

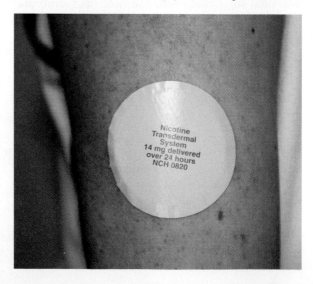

barrier is molecule size. Large molecules do not usually cross the placental barrier, whereas small molecules do. Because most drugs are relatively small molecules, they usually cross from the maternal circulation into the fetal circulation; thus, most drugs (including drugs of abuse) taken by a woman during pregnancy enter and affect the fetus.

Required Doses for Effects

Most drugs do not take effect until a certain amount has been administered and a crucial concentration has reached the site of action in the body. The smallest amount of a drug needed to elicit a response is called its **threshold dose**.

The effectiveness of some drugs may be calculated in a *linear* (straight-line) fashion — that is, the more drug that is taken, the more drug that is distributed throughout the body and the greater the effect. However, many drugs have a maximum possible effect, regardless of dose; this is called the **plateau effect**. OTC medications, in particular, have a limit on their effects. For example, use of the nonprescription analgesic aspirin can effectively relieve your mild to moderate pain, but aspirin will not effectively treat your severe pains, regardless of the dose taken. Other drugs may cause distinct or opposite effects, depending on the dose. For example, low doses of alcohol may appear to act like a stimulant, whereas high doses usually cause sedation.

Time-Response Factors

An important factor that determines responses is the time that has elapsed between when a drug was administered and the onset of its effects. The delay in effect after administering a drug often relates to the time required for the drug to disseminate from the site of administration to the site of action. Consequently, the closer a drug is placed to the target area, the faster the onset of action.

The drug response is often classified as immediate, short-term, or **acute**, referring to the response after a single dose. The response can also be **chronic**, or long-term — a characteristic usually associated with repeated doses. The intensity and quality of a drug's acute effect may change considerably within a short period of time. For example, the main intoxicating effects of a large dose of alcohol generally peak in less than 1 hour and then gradually taper off. In addition, an initial stimulating effect by alcohol may later change to sedation and depression.

The effects of long-term, or chronic, use of some drugs can differ dramatically from the effects noted with their short-term, or acute, use. The administration of small doses may not produce any immediately apparent detrimental effect, but chronic use of the same drug (frequent use over a long time) may yield prolonged effects that do not become apparent until years later. Although for most people there is little evidence to show any immediate damage or detrimental response to short-term use of small doses of tobacco, its chronic use has damaging effects on heart and lung functions (Westmaas and Brandon 2004). Because of these long-term consequences, research on tobacco and its effects often continues for years, making it difficult to unequivocally prove a correlation between specific diseases or health problems and use of this substance. Thus, the results of tobacco research are often disputed by tobacco manufacturers with vested financial interests in the substance and its public acceptance.

Another important time factor that influences drug responses is the interval between multiple administrations. If sufficient time for drug metabolism and elimination does not separate doses, a drug can accumulate within the body. This drug buildup due to relatively short dosing intervals is referred to as a **cumulative effect**. Because of the resulting high concentrations of drug in the body, unexpected prolonged drug effects or toxicity can occur when multiple doses are given within short

KEY TERMS

threshold dose
minimum drug dose necessary to cause an effect

plateau effect
maximum drug effect, regardless of dose

acute
immediate or short-term effects after taking a single drug dose

chronic
long-term effects, usually after taking multiple drug doses

cumulative effect
buildup of a drug in the body after multiple doses taken at short intervals

intervals. This situation occurs with cocaine or methamphetamine addicts who repeatedly administer these stimulants during "binges" or "runs," increasing the likelihood of dangerous effects.

INACTIVATION AND ELIMINATION OF DRUGS FROM THE BODY

Immediately after drug administration, the body begins to eliminate the substance in various ways. The time required to remove half of the original amount of drug administered is called the **half-life** of the drug. The body eliminates the drug either directly without altering it chemically or (in most instances) after it has been metabolized (chemically altered) or modified. The process of changing the chemical or pharmacological properties of a drug by metabolism is called **biotransformation** (Correia 1998). **Metabolism** usually makes it possible for the body to inactivate, detoxify, and excrete drugs and other chemicals, although, metabolism can sometimes actually cause a drug such as heroin to become *more* active.

The liver is the primary organ that metabolizes drugs in the body. This complex biochemical laboratory contains hundreds of enzymes that continuously synthesize, modify, and deactivate biochemical substances such as drugs. The healthy liver is also capable of metabolizing many of the chemicals that occur naturally in the body (such as hormones). After the liver enzymes metabolize a drug (the resulting chemicals are called **metabolites**), the products usually pass into the urine or feces for final elimination. Drugs and their metabolites can appear in other places as well, such as sweat, saliva, or expired air (Galinsky and Svensson 2000).

The kidneys are probably the next most important organ for drug elimination because they remove metabolites and foreign substances from the body. The kidneys constantly eliminate substances from the blood. The rate of excretion of some drugs by the kidneys can be altered by making the urine more acidic or more alkaline. For example, nicotine and amphetamines can be cleared faster from the body by making the urine slightly more acidic, and salicylates and barbiturates can be cleared more rapidly by making it more alkaline. Such techniques are used in emergency rooms and can be useful in the treatment of drug overdosing.

The body may eliminate small portions of drugs through perspiration and exhalation. Approximately 1% of consumed alcohol is eliminated in the breath and thus may be measured with a Breathalyzer; this apparatus is used by police officers in evaluating suspected drunk drivers. Most people are aware that consumption of garlic will change body odor because garlic is excreted through perspiration. Some drugs are handled in the same way. The mammary glands are modified sweat glands, so it is not surprising that many drugs are concentrated and excreted in milk during lactation, including antibiotics, nicotine, barbiturates, caffeine, and alcohol. Excretion of drugs in a mother's milk can pose a particular concern during nursing, as the excreted drugs can be consumed by and affect the infant.

The Breathalyzer takes advantage of the fact that alcohol is partially eliminated from the body in the breath.

KEY TERMS

half-life
time required for the body to eliminate and/or metabolize half of a drug dose

biotransformation
process of changing the chemical properties of a drug, usually by metabolism

metabolism
chemical alteration of drugs by body processes

metabolites
chemical products of metabolism

PHYSIOLOGICAL VARIABLES THAT MODIFY DRUG EFFECTS

As previously mentioned, individuals' responses to drugs vary greatly, even when the same doses are administered in the same manner. This variability can be especially troublesome when dealing with drugs that have a narrow margin of safety. Many of these variables reflect differences in the pharmacokinetic factors just discussed and are associated with diversity in body size, composition, or functions. They include the following factors (Nies and Spielberg 1995).

Age Changes in body size and makeup occur throughout the aging process, from infancy to old age. Changes in the rates of drug absorption, biotransformation, and elimination also arise as a consequence of aging. As a general rule, young children and elderly people should be administered smaller drug doses (calculated as drug quantity per unit of body weight) due to their immature or compromised body processes.

Gender Variations in drug responses due to gender usually relate to differences in body size, composition, or hormones (male versus female types for example, androgens versus estrogens). Most clinicians find many more similarities than differences between males and females relative to their responses to drugs.

Pregnancy During the course of pregnancy, unique factors must be considered when administering drugs. For example, the physiology of the mother changes as the fetus develops and puts additional stress on organ systems, such as the heart, liver, and kidneys. This increased demand can make the woman more susceptible to the toxicity of some drugs. In addition, as the fetus develops, it can be very vulnerable to drugs with **teratogenic** (causing abnormal development) properties. Consequently, it is usually advisable to avoid taking any drugs during pregnancy, if possible.

PATHOLOGICAL VARIABLES THAT MODIFY DRUG EFFECTS

Individuals with diseases or compromised organ systems need to be particularly careful when taking drugs. Some diseases can damage or impair organs that are vital for appropriate and safe responses to drugs. For example, *hepatitis* (inflammation and damage to the liver caused by a viral infection) interferes with the metabolism and disposal of many drugs, resulting in a longer duration of drug action and increased likelihood of side effects. Similar concerns are associated with kidney disease, which causes compromised renal activity and diminished excretion capacity. Because many drugs affect the cardiovascular system (especially drugs of abuse, such as stimulants, tobacco, and alcohol), patients with a history of cardiovascular disease (heart attack, stroke, hypertension, or abnormal heart rhythm) should be particularly cautious when using drugs. They should be aware of medicines that stimulate the cardiovascular system, especially those that are self-medicated, such as OTC decongestants and diet aids. These drugs should either be avoided or used only under the supervision of a physician.

Adaptive Processes and Drug Abuse

Your body systems are constantly changing so that they can establish and maintain balance in their physiological and mental functions; such balance is necessary for optimal functioning of all organ systems, including the brain, heart, lungs, gastrointestinal tract, liver, and kidneys. Sometimes, drugs interfere with the activity of the body's systems and compromise their normal workings. These drug-induced disruptions can be so severe that they can even cause death (see "Here and Now," The Death Toll of Substance Abuse). For example, stimulants can dangerously increase the heart rate and blood pressure and cause heart attacks, whereas CNS depressants can diminish brain activity, resulting in unconsciousness and a loss of breathing reflexes.

To protect against potential harm, the organ systems of the body can adjust to disruption. Of particular relevance to drugs of abuse are the adaptive

KEY TERMS

teratogenic
something that causes physical defects in the fetus

Here and Now

The Death Toll of Substance Abuse

Deaths resulting from using substances of abuse are increasing throughout the world. It is estimated that approximately 7 million people are killed each year by the drugs they abuse. Tobacco heads the list, causing almost 5 million deaths annually. Next is alcohol, causing almost 2 million deaths worldwide each year. Use of the illicit drugs results in approximately 223,000 annual deaths. It is expected that these grim numbers will become worse as there is increased use of these substances around the world.

Source: Alcoholism and Drug Abuse Weekly. "Deaths from Substance Use Are Increasing Worldwide." 15 (2003): 8.

processes known as *tolerance* and **dependence** (both psychological and physical types) and the related phenomenon of *withdrawal* (see Figure 5.4).

Tolerance and dependence are closely linked, most likely to result from multiple drug exposures, and thought to be caused by similar mechanisms. Tolerance occurs when the response to the same dose of a drug decreases with repeated use (O'Brien 2001). Increasing the dose can sometimes compensate for tolerance to a drug of abuse. For the most part, the adaptations that cause the tolerance phenomenon are also associated with altered physical and psychological states that lead to dependence. The user develops dependence in the sense that if the drug is no longer taken, the symptoms of the body become overcompensated and unbalanced, causing withdrawal. In general, withdrawal symptoms are opposite in nature to the direct effects of the drug that caused the dependence (O'Brien 2001).

Although tolerance, dependence, and withdrawal are all consequences of adaptation by the body and its systems, they are not inseparable processes. It is possible to become tolerant to a drug without developing dependence, and vice versa (see Table 5.2). The following sections provide greater detail about these adaptive drug responses, which are very important for many therapeutic drugs and almost all drugs of abuse (O'Brien 2001).

KEY TERMS

dependence
physiological and psychological changes or adaptations that occur in response to the frequent administration of a drug

TOLERANCE TO DRUGS

The extent of tolerance and the rate at which it is acquired depend on the drug, the person using the drug, the dosage, and the frequency of administration. Some drug effects may be reduced more rapidly than others when drugs are used frequently. Tolerance to effects that are rewarding or reinforcing often causes users to increase the dosage. Sometimes, abstinence from a drug can reduce tolerance, but with renewed use, the tolerance often builds quickly. It is important to remember that the body does not necessarily develop tolerance to all effects of a drug equally.

The exact mechanisms by which the body becomes tolerant to different drug effects are not completely understood, but may be related to those mechanisms that cause dependence (American Psychiatric Association 2000). Several processes have been suggested as candidates. Drugs such as barbiturates stimulate the body's production of metabolic enzymes, primarily in the liver, and cause drugs to be inactivated and eliminated faster. In addition, evidence suggests that a considerable degree of CNS tolerance to some drugs develops independent of changes in the rate of metabolism or excretion. This process reflects the adaptation of drug target sites in nervous tissue, so that the effect produced by the same concentration of drug decreases over time.

Another type of drug response that can appear to be tolerance, but is actually a learned adjustment, is called *behavioral compensation*. Drug effects that are troubling may be compensated for or hidden by the drug user. Thus, alcoholics learn to

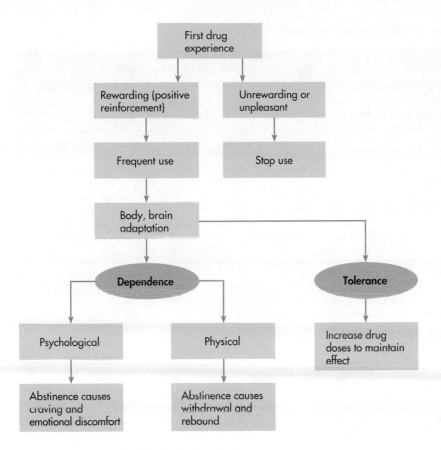

FIGURE 5.4

The relationship and consequences of adaptive processes to drug use. The processes discussed in the text are highlighted in the figure.

speak and walk slowly to compensate for the slurred speech and stumbling gait they usually experience. To an observer, it might appear as though the pharmacological effects of the drug are diminished, but they are actually unchanged. Consequently, this type of adaptation is not a true form of tolerance.

Other Tolerance-Related Factors

The tolerance process can affect drug responses in several ways. We have discussed the effect of tolerance that diminishes the action of drugs and causes the user to compensate by increasing the dose. The following are examples of two other ways that processes related to tolerance can influence drug responses.

Reverse Tolerance (Sensitization)   Under some conditions, a response to a drug is elicited that is the opposite of tolerance. This effect is known as **reverse tolerance**, or sensitization. If you were sensi-

tized, you would have the same response to a lower dose of a drug as you initially did to the original, higher dose. This condition seems to occur in users of morphine and some hallucinogens, as well as amphetamines and cocaine (Lessov and Phillips 2003; Rubino et al. 2001).

Although the causes of reverse tolerance are still unclear, some researchers believe that its development depends on how often, how much, and in which setting the drug is consumed. It has been speculated that this heightened response to drugs of abuse may reflect adaptive changes in the nervous tissues (target site of these drugs). The reverse tolerance that occurs with cocaine use

KEY TERMS

reverse tolerance
enhanced response to a given drug dose; opposite of tolerance

Table 5.2 Tolerance, Dependence, and Withdrawal Properties of Common Drugs of Abuse

DRUG	TOLERANCE	PSYCHOLOGICAL DEPENDENCE	PHYSICAL DEPENDENCE	WITHDRAWAL SYMPTOMS (INCLUDE REBOUND EFFECTS)
Barbiturates	■■	■■	■■■	Restlessness, anxiety, vomiting, tremors, seizures
Alcohol	■■	■■	■■■	Cramps, delirium, vomiting, sweating, hallucinations, seizures
Benzodiazepines	■	■■	■■	Insomnia, restlessness, nausea, fatigue, twitching, seizures (rare)
Narcotics (heroin)	■■■	■■	■■■	Vomiting, sweating, cramps, diarrhea, depression, irritability, gooseflesh
Cocaine, amphetamines	■*	■■■	■■	Depression, anxiety, drug craving, need for sleep ("crash"), anhedonia
Nicotine	■	■■	■■	Highly variable; craving, irritability, headache, increased appetite, abnormal sleep
Caffeine	■	■	■	Anxiety, lethargy, headache, fatigue
Marijuana	■	■	■	Irritability, restlessness, decreased appetite, weight loss, abnormal sleep
LSD (lysergic acid diethylamide)	■■	■	—	Minimal
PCP (phencyclidine)	■	■	■	Fear, tremors, some craving, problems with short-term memory

■■■ Intense   ■■ Moderate   ■ Some   — Not significant
*Can sensitize.

may be responsible for the psychotic effects or the seizures caused by chronic use of this drug (O'Brien 2001).

Cross-Tolerance Development of tolerance to a drug sometimes can produce tolerance to other similar drugs. This phenomenon, known as **cross-**

tolerance, may be due to altered metabolism resulting from chronic drug use. For example, a heavy drinker will usually exhibit tolerance to barbiturates, other depressants, and anesthetics because the alcohol has induced (stimulated) his or her liver metabolic enzymes to inactivate these other drugs more rapidly. Cross-tolerance might also occur among drugs that cause similar pharmacological actions. For example, if adaptations have occurred in nervous tissue that cause tolerance to one drug, such changes might produce tolerance to other similar drugs that exert their effects by interacting with that same nervous tissue site.

KEY TERMS

cross-tolerance
development of tolerance to one drug causes tolerance to related drugs

DRUG DEPENDENCE

Drug dependence can be associated with either physiological or psychological adaptations. Physical dependence reflects changes in the way organs and systems in the body respond to a drug, whereas psychological dependence is caused by changes in attitudes and expectations. In both types of dependence, the individual experiences a need (either physical or emotional) for the drug to be present for the body or the mind to function normally.

Physical Dependence

In general, the drugs that cause physical dependence also cause a drug withdrawal phenomenon called the **rebound effect**. This condition is sometimes known as the *paradoxical effect* because the symptoms associated with rebound are nearly opposite to the direct effects of the drug. For example, a person taking barbiturates or benzodiazepines will be greatly depressed physically but during withdrawal may become irritable, hyperexcited, and nervous and generally show symptoms of extreme stimulation of the nervous system, and perhaps even life-threatening seizures. These reactions constitute the rebound effect.

Physical dependence may develop with high-intensity use of such common drugs as alcohol, barbiturates, narcotics, and other CNS depressants. However, with moderate, intermittent use of these drugs, most people do not become physically dependent. Those who do become physically dependent experience damaged social and personal skills and relationships and impaired brain and motor functions.

Withdrawal symptoms resulting from physical dependency can be prevented by administering a sufficient quantity of the original drug or one with similar pharmacological activity. The latter case, in which different drugs can be used interchangeably to prevent withdrawal symptoms, is called **cross-dependence**. For example, barbiturates and other CNS depressants can be used to treat the abstinence syndrome experienced by the chronic alcoholic. Another example is the use of methadone, a long-acting narcotic, to treat withdrawal from heroin (Zickler 1999). Such therapeutic strategies allow the substitution of safer and more easily managed drugs for dangerous drugs of abuse and

play a major role in treatment of drug dependency.

Psychological Dependence

The World Health Organization states that **psychological dependence** instills a feeling of satisfaction and psychic drive that requires periodic or continuous administration of the drug to produce a desired effect or to avoid psychological discomfort. This sense of dependence usually leads to repeated self-administration of the drug in a fashion described as abuse. Such dependence may be found either independent of or associated with physical dependence. Psychological dependence does not produce the physical discomfort, rebound effects, or life-threatening consequences that can be associated with physical dependence. Even so, it does produce intense cravings and strong urges that frequently lure former drug abusers back to their habits of drug self-administration. In many instances, psychological aspects may be more significant than physical dependence in maintaining chronic drug use. Thus, the major problem with cocaine or nicotine dependence is not so much the physical aspect, because withdrawal can be successfully achieved in a few weeks; rather, strong urges often cause a return to chronic use of these substances because of psychological dependence.

How does psychological dependence develop? If the first drug trial is rewarding, a few more rewarding trials will follow until drug use becomes a conditioned pattern of behavior. Continued positive psychological reinforcement with the drug leads, in time, to primary psychological dependence. Primary psychological dependence, in turn, may produce uncontrollable compulsive abuse of any psychoactive drug in certain susceptible people and cause physical dependence. The degree of

KEY TERMS

rebound effect
form of withdrawal; paradoxical effects that occur when a drug has been eliminated from the body

cross-dependence
dependence on a drug can be relieved by other similar drugs

psychological dependence
dependence that results because a drug produces pleasant mental effects

drug dependence is contingent on the nature of the psychoactive substance, the quantity used, the duration of use, and the characteristics of the person and his or her environment.

Even strong psychological dependence on some psychoactive substances does not necessarily result in injury or social harm. For example, typical dosages of mild stimulants such as coffee usually do not induce serious physical, social, or emotional harm. Even though the effects on the CNS are barely detectable by a casual observer, strong psychological dependence on stimulants like tobacco and caffeine-containing beverages may develop; however, the fact that their dependence does not typically induce antisocial behavior distinguishes them from most forms of dependence-producing drugs.

Psychological Factors

The general effect of most drugs is greatly influenced by a variety of psychological and environmental factors. Unique qualities of an individual's personality, his or her past history of drug and social experience, attitudes toward the drug, expectations of its effects, and motivation for use are extremely influential. These factors are often referred to collectively as the person's **mental set**. The setting, or total environment, in which a drug is taken may profoundly modify its effect.

The mental set and setting are particularly important in influencing the responses to psychoactive drugs (drugs that alter the functions of the brain). For example, ingestion of LSD, a commonly abused hallucinogen, can cause pleasant, even spiritual-like experiences in comfortable, congenial surroundings. In contrast, when the same amount of LSD is consumed in hostile, threatening surroundings, the effect can be frightening, taking on a nightmarish quality.

KEY TERMS

mental set
the collection of psychological and environmental factors that influence an individual's response to drugs

placebo effects
effects caused by suggestion and psychological factors independent of the pharmacological activity of a drug

THE PLACEBO EFFECT

The psychological factors that influence responses to drugs, independent of their pharmacological properties, are known as **placebo effects**. The word *placebo* is derived from Latin and means "I shall please." The placebo effect is most likely to occur when an individual's mental set is susceptible to suggestion. A placebo drug is a pharmacologically inactive compound that the user thinks causes some therapeutic change.

In some persons or in particular settings, a placebo substance may have surprisingly powerful consequences (Solomon 2002). For example, a substantial component of most pain is perception. Consequently, placebos administered as pain relievers and promoted properly can provide dramatic relief. Therefore, in spite of what appears to be a drug effect, the placebo is not considered a pharmacological agent because it does not directly alter any body functions by its chemical nature.

The bulk of medical history may actually be a history of confidence in the cure — a history of placebo medicine — because many effective cures of the past have been shown to be without relevant pharmacological action, suggesting that their effects were psychologically mediated. In fact, even today, some people argue that placebo effects are a significant component of most drug therapy, particularly when using OTC medications or herbal products. It is important when testing new drugs for effectiveness that drug experiments be conducted in a manner that allows a distinction to be drawn between pharmacological and placebo effects. Such studies can usually be done by treating one group with the real drug and another group with a placebo that looks like the drug, and then comparing the responses to both treatments.

Addiction and Abuse: The Significance of Dependence

The term *addiction* has many meanings (see Chapter 2). It is often used interchangeably with *dependence* or *drug abuse* (drug addiction).

The traditional model of the addiction-producing drug is based on opiate narcotics and requires the individual to develop tolerance and both physical and psychological dependence. This model often is not satisfactory because only a few commonly abused drugs fit all of these parameters. It is clearly inadequate for many drugs that can cause serious dependency problems but that produce little tolerance, even with extended use (see Table 5.2).

Because it is difficult to assess the contribution of physical and psychological factors to drug dependency, determining whether all psychoactive drugs truly cause drug addiction poses a challenge. To alleviate confusion, it has been suggested that the term *dependence* (either physical or psychological) be used instead of *addiction*. However, because of its acceptance by the public, the term *addiction* is not likely to disappear from general use.

Some have speculated that the only means by which drug dependence can be eliminated from society is to prevent exposure to those drugs that have the potential to be abused. Because some drugs are such powerful, immediate reinforcers (i.e., they cause a rapid reward), it is feared that rapid dependence (psychological) will occur when anyone uses them. Although it may be true that most people, under certain conditions, could become dependent on some drug with abuse potential, in reality most people who have used psychoactive drugs do not develop significant psychological or physical dependence. For example, approximately 87% of those who use alcohol experience minimal personal injury and few negative social consequences. Of those who have used stimulants, depressants, or hallucinogens for illicit recreational purposes, only 10% to 20% become dependent (O'Brien 2001). The following sections discuss some possible reasons for the variability.

HEREDITARY FACTORS

The reasons why some people readily develop dependence on psychoactive drugs and others do not are not well understood. Of importance may be heredity, which predisposes some people to drug abuse (Kreek at al. 2004), and the interaction of genetic vulnerability with high-risk environments (see "Here and Now," Children of Addicted Parents). For example, studies of identical and fraternal twins have revealed that a greater similarity in the rate of alcoholism for identical twins than for fraternal twins occurs if alcohol abuse begins before the age of 20 years (McGue et al.

1992; Vanyukov and Tarter 2000). Because identical twins have 100% of their genes in common whereas fraternal twins share only 50% of their genes, these results suggest that genetic factors can be important in determining the likelihood of alcohol dependence (Wyman 1997). It is possible that similar genetic factors contribute to other types of drug dependence as well (Kreek et al. 2004).

DRUG CRAVING

Frequently, a person who becomes dependent develops a powerful, uncontrollable desire for drugs during or after withdrawal from heroin, cocaine, alcohol, nicotine, or other addicting substances. This desire for drugs is known as *craving*. Because researchers do not agree as to the nature of craving, there does not exist a universally recognized scientific definition or an accepted method to measure this psychological phenomenon; however, it is thought to be distinct from the phenomenon of withdrawal. Some drug abuse experts claim that craving is the principal cause of drug abuse; others believe that it is not a cause but a side effect of drugs that produce dependence. Craving is often assessed by (1) questioning patients about the intensity of their drug urges; (2) measuring physiological changes such as increases in heart and breathing rates, sweating, and subtle changes in the tension of facial muscles; and (3) determining patients' tendency to relapse into drug-taking behavior (Hester and Garavan 2004).

Evidence indicates that at least two levels of craving can exist. For example, cocaine users experience an acute craving when using the drug itself, but the ex-cocaine abuser can have chronic cravings that are triggered by familiar environmental cues that elicit positive memories of cocaine's reinforcing effects.

Although it is not likely that craving itself causes drug addiction, it is generally believed that, if pharmacological or psychological therapies could be devised that reduced or eliminated drug craving, treatment of drug dependence would be more successful. Thus, many researchers are attempting to identify drugs or psychological strategies that interfere with the development and expression of the craving phenomenon.

Here and Now

Children of Addicted Parents

Substance abuse, alcoholism, and associated trauma seem to have both genetic and environmental components, the interaction of which can have serious consequences. For example, alcoholism tends to run in families. Thus, children of alcoholics are at high risk to become alcohol users themselves because of their genetic vulnerability as well as because of the traumatic environments to which they are often exposed. Levels of conflict in families characterized by alcoholism are much higher than in families with no alcoholism. The environment to which children with alcoholic parents are exposed may include a lack of communication, emotional and physical violence, isolation, and financial problems. At least half of all cases of child maltreatment are linked to a prevalence of substance abuse and alcoholism in the home. It has also been reported that children who receive prenatal exposure to drugs are two to three times more likely to be neglected or abused.

Source: "Children of Addicted Parents" (9 February 2005). Available Hopenetworks.org/addiction/children%20of%20Addicts.htm.

OTHER FACTORS

If a drug causes a positive effect in the user's view, it is much more likely to be abused than if it causes an aversive experience (see Figure 5.4). Perhaps genetic factors influence the brain or personality so that some people find taking drugs an enjoyable experience (at least initially), whereas others find the effects very unpleasant and uncomfortable (**dysphoric**). Other factors that could contribute significantly to drug use patterns include (1) peer pressure (especially in the initial drug experimentation); (2) home, school, and work environments (Swadi 1999); and (3) mental state. It is estimated that 30% to 60% of drug abusers have some underlying psychiatric illness, such as personality disorder, major depression, bipolar disorder, or schizophrenia (Leshner 1999). In some cases, the drug user may be attempting to relieve symptoms associated with the mental disorder by self-medicating with the substance of abuse (Addington 1997).

It is difficult to identify all of the specific factors that influence the risk of drug abuse for each individual. (Some of the possible influences are discussed in Chapter 2.) If such factors could be identified, treatment would be improved and those at greatest risk for drug abuse could be determined and informed of their vulnerability.

KEY TERMS

dysphoric
characterized by unpleasant mental effects; the opposite of euphoric

Discussion Questions

1. What is the significance of drug "potency" in the therapeutic use and the abuse of drugs?

2. How can drug interactions be both detrimental and beneficial? Give examples of each.

3. Why would a drug with a relatively narrow "margin of safety" be approved by the Food and Drug Administration for clinical use? Give an example.

4. What are possible explanations for the fact that you (for example) may require twice as much of a drug to get an effect as does your friend?

5. Why might the blood–brain barrier prevent a drug from having abuse potential?

6. Contrary to your advice, a friend is going to spend $20 on Ecstasy. What significance will the pharmacokinetic concepts of threshold, half-life, cumulative effect, and biotransformation have on your friend's drug experience?

7. How would the factors of tolerance, physical dependence, rebound, and psychological dependence affect a chronic heroin user?

8. Why would the lack of physical dependence on LSD for some drug abusers make it less likely to cause addiction than cocaine, which does cause physical dependence?

Key Terms

side effects **140**

withdrawal **140**

dose-response **141**

tolerance **141**

margin of safety **142**

potency **142**

toxicity **142**

drug interaction **143**

additive interactions **143**

antagonistic interactions **143**

synergism **144**

pharmacokinetics **146**

intravenous (IV) **147**

intramuscular (IM) **147**

subcutaneous (SC) **147**

blood–brain barrier **148**

threshold dose **149**

plateau effect **149**

acute **149**

chronic **149**

cumulative effect **149**

half-life **150**

biotransformation **150**

metabolism **150**

metabolites **150**

teratogenic **151**

dependence **152**

reverse tolerance **153**

cross-tolerance **154**

rebound effect **155**

cross-dependence **155**

psychological dependence **155**

mental set **156**

placebo effects **156**

dysphoric **158**

Summary

1 All drugs have intended and unintended effects. The unintended actions of drugs can include effects such as nausea, altered mental states, dependence, a variety of allergic responses, and changes in the cardiovascular system.

2 Many factors can affect the way an individual responds to a drug: dose, inherent toxicity, potency, and pharmacokinetic properties such as the rate of absorption into the body, the way it is distributed throughout the body, and the manner in which and rate at which it is metabolized and eliminated. The form of the drug as well as the manner in which it is administered can also affect the response to a drug.

3 Potency is determined by the amount of a drug necessary to cause a given effect. Toxicity is the ability of the drug to affect the body adversely. A drug that is very toxic is very potent in terms of causing a harmful effect.

4 A drug's margin of safety relates to the difference in the drug doses that cause a therapeutic or a toxic effect. The bigger the difference, the greater the margin of safety.

5 Additive interactions occur when the effects of two drugs are combined; for example, the analgesic effects of aspirin plus acetaminophen are additive. Antagonistic effects occur when the effects of two drugs cancel; for example, the stimulant effects of caffeine tend to antagonize the drowsiness caused by antihistamines. Synergism (potentiation) occurs when one drug enhances the effect of another; for example, alcohol enhances the CNS depression caused by Valium.

6 Pharmacokinetic factors include absorption, distribution, biotransformation, and elimination of drugs.

7 Many physiological and pathological factors can alter the response to drugs. For example, age, gender, and pregnancy are all factors that should be considered when making drug-related decisions. In addition, some diseases can alter the way in which the body responds to drugs. Medical conditions associated with the liver, kidneys, and cardiovascular system are of particular concern.

8 For psychoactive drugs to influence the brain and its actions, they must pass through the blood–brain barrier. Many of these drugs are fat-soluble and able to pass through capillary walls from the blood into the brain.

9 The threshold dose is the minimum amount of a drug necessary to have an effect. The plateau effect is the maximum effect a drug can have, regardless of dose. The cumulative effect is the buildup of the drug in the body due to multiple doses being taken within short intervals.

10 The liver is the primary organ for the metabolizing of drugs and many naturally occurring substances in the body, such as hormones. By altering the molecular structure of drugs, the metabolism usually inactivates drugs and makes them easier to eliminate through the kidneys.

11 Biotransformation is the process that alters the molecular structure of a drug. Metabolism contributes to biotransformation.

12 Drug tolerance causes a decreased response to a given dose of a drug. It can be caused by increasing metabolism and elimination of the drug by the body or by a change in the systems or targets that are affected by the drug.

13 Physical dependence is characterized by the adaptive changes that occur in the body due to the continual presence of a drug. These changes, which are often chemical in nature, reduce the response to the drugs and cause tolerance. If drug use is halted after physical dependence has occurred, the body is overcompensated, causing a rebound response. Rebound effects are similar to the withdrawal that occurs because drug use is stopped for an extended period. Psychological dependence occurs because drug use is rewarding, bringing euphoria, increased energy, and relaxation, or because stopping drug use produces craving.

14 Suggestion can have a profound influence on a person's drug response. Health problems with significant psychological aspects are particularly susceptible to the effects of placebos. For example, because the intensity of pain is related to its perception, a placebo can substantially relieve pain discomfort. Other placebo responses may likewise be due to the release of endogenous factors in the body.

15 A powerful, uncontrollable desire (craving) for drugs can occur with chronic use of some drugs of abuse. Although craving by itself may not cause drug addiction, if it can be eliminated, treatment of substance abuse is more likely to be successful.

References

Addington, J., and V. Duchak. "Reasons for Substance Use in Schizophrenia." *Acta Psychiatry Scandinavia* 96 (1997): 329–333.

American Psychiatric Association. "Substance Related Disorders." In *Diagnostic and Statistical Manual of Mental Disorders*, 4th ed., *Text Revision*, 191–295. Washington, DC: APA, 2000.

Bourne, H. R. "Drug Receptors and Pharmacodynamics." In *Basic and Clinical Pharmacology*, 7th ed., edited by B. Katzung, 9–33. Stamford, CT: Appleton and Lange, 1998.

Coffin, P., S. Galea, J. Ahern, A. Leon, D. Vlahov, and K. Tardiff. "Opiates, Cocaine and Alcohol Combinations in Accidental Overdose Deaths in New York City, 1990–1998," *Addiction* 98 (2003): 739–747.

Correia, M. "Drug Biotransformation." In *Basic and Clinical Pharmacology*, 7th ed., edited by B. Katzung, 50–61. Stamford, CT: Appleton and Lange, 1998.

Franklin, M., and D. Franz. "Drug Absorption, Action and Disposition." In *Remington: The Science and Practice of Pharmacy*, edited by Alfonso Gennaro, 1098–1126. Baltimore, MD: Lippincott Williams & Wilkins, 2000.

Galinsky, R., and C. Svensson. "Basic Pharmacokinetics." In *Remington: The Science and Practice of Pharmacy*, edited by Alfonso Gennaro, 1127–1144. Baltimore, MD: Lippincott Williams & Wilkins, 2000.

Goeders, N. "The Impact of Stress on Addiction." *European Neuropsychopharmacology* 13 (2003): 435–441.

Harris, D., E. Everhart, J. Mendelson, and R. Jones. "The Pharmacology of Cocaethylene in Humans Following Cocaine and Ethanol Administration." *Drug and Alcohol Dependence* 72 (2003): 169–182.

Hester, R., and H. Garavan. "Executive Dysfunction in Cocaine Addiction: Evidence for Discordant Frontal, Cingulate, and Cerebellar Activity." *Journal of Neuroscience* 24 (2004): 11017–11022.

Hobbs, W. R., T. Rall, and T. Verdoorn. "Hypnotics and Sedatives: Ethanol." In *The Pharmacological Basis of Therapeutics*, 9th ed., edited by J. Hardman and L. Limbird, 386–396. New York: McGraw-Hill, 1995.

Hussar, D. "Drug Interactions." In *Remington: The Science and Practice of Pharmacy*, edited by Alfonso Gennaro, 1746–1761. Baltimore, MD: Lippincott Williams & Wilkins, 2000.

Kreek, M., S. Schlussman, G. Bart, K. Laforge, and E. Butelman. "Evolving Perspectives on Neurobiological Research on the Addictions: Celebration of the 30th Anniversary of NIDA." *Neuropharmacology* 47 Supplement 1 (2004): 324–344.

Leshner, A. "Drug Abuse and Mental Disorder: Comorbidity Is Reality." *NIDA Notes* 14 (1999): 3, 4.

Lessov, C., and T. Phillips. "Cross-sensitization Between the Locomotor Stimulant Effects of Ethanol and Those of Morphine and Cocaine in Mice." *Alcohol Clinical Experimental Research* 27 (2003): 16–21.

MacDonald, S. "Use with Care: Medicines Can Cure or Kill." *Salt Lake Tribune* (September 3, 1998): B-1.

Mathias, R. "Rate and Duration of Drug Activity Play Major Roles in Drug Abuse, Addiction and Treatment." *NIDA Notes* 12 (March/April 1997): 8–11.

McGue, M., R. Pickens, and D. Svikis. "Sex and Age Effects on the Inheritance of Alcohol Problems: A Twin Study." *Journal of Abnormal Psychology* 101 (January 1992): 3–17.

Meng, Y., M. Dukat, D. Bridgen, B. R. Martin, and A. H. Lichtman. "Pharmacological Effects of Methamphetamine and Other Stimulants via Inhalation Exposure." *Drugs and Alcohol Dependence* 53 (1999): 111–120.

Nicholas, H., and L. Benet. "Pharmacokinetics and Pharmacodynamics: Dose Selection and the Time Course of Drug Action." In *Basic and Clinical Pharmacology*, 7th ed., edited by B. Katzung, 34–49. Stamford, CT: Appleton and Lange, 1998.

NIDA Notes. "Infectious Diseases and Drug Addiction." 14 (1999): 15.

Nies, A., and S. Spielberg. "Principles of Therapeutics." In *The Pharmacological Basis of Therapeutics*, 9th ed., edited by J. Hardman and L. Limbird, 43–62. New York: McGraw-Hill, 1995.

O'Brien, C. "Drug Addiction and Drug Abuse." In *The Pharmacological Basis of Therapeutics*, 9th ed., edited by J. Hardman and L. Limbird, 557–577. New York: McGraw-Hill, 1995.

O'Brien, C. "Drug Addiction and Drug Abuse." In *The Pharmacological Basis of Therapeutics*, 10th ed., edited by J. Hardman and L. Limbird, 621–644. New York: McGraw-Hill, 2001.

Rice, D. P. "Economic Costs of Substances of Abuse, 1995." *Proceedings of the Association of American Physicians* 111 (1999): 119–125.

Richtand, N., S. Woods, S. Berger, and S. Strakowski. "D3 Receptor, Behavior Sensitization, and Psychosis." *Neuroscience Behavioral Review* 25 (2001): 427–443.

Rollins, D. "Clinical Pharmacokinetics." In *Remington: The Science and Practice of Pharmacy*, edited by Alfonso Gennaro, 1145–1155. Baltimore, MD: Lippincott Williams & Wilkins, 2000.

Rubino, T., D. Vigano, P. Massi, and D. Parolaro. "The Psychoactive Ingredient of Marijuana Induces Behavioral Sensitization." *European Journal of Neuroscience* 14 (2001): 884–886.

Solomon, S. "A Review of Mechanisms of Response to Pain Therapy: Why Voodoo Works." *Headache* 42 (2002): 656–662.

Swadi, H. "Individual Risk Factors for Adolescent Substance Use." *Drug and Alcohol Dependence* 55 (1999): 209–224.

Vanyukov, M. M., and R. E. Tarter. "Genetic Studies of Substance Abuse." *Drug and Alcohol Dependence* 59 (2000): 101–123.

Westmaas, J., and T. Brandon. "Reducing Risk in Smokers." *Current Opinions on Pulmonary Medicine* 10 (2004): 284–288.

Wilens, T. "Attention-Deficit/Hyperactivity Disorder and the Substance Use Disorders: The Nature of the Relationship, Subtypes of Risk, and Treatment Issues." *Psychiatric Clinic of North America* 27 (2004): 283–301.

Wyman, J. "Promising Advances Toward Understanding the Genetic Roots of Addiction." *NIDA Notes* 12 (July/August 1997): 11, 12.

Zickler, P. "High-Dose Improves Treatment Outcome." *NIDA Notes* 14 (1999): 4, 5.

CHAPTER 6

CNS Depressants: Sedative-Hypnotics

Did You Know?

- Alcohol temporarily relieves anxiety and stress because of its central nervous system (CNS) depressant effects.

- At low doses, a CNS depressant relieves anxiety. At high doses, it becomes a sleep aid.

- Benzodiazepines (Valium-like drugs) are much safer than barbiturates.

- Benzodiazepines are by far the most frequently prescribed CNS depressants.

- Most people who are dependent on benzodiazepines obtain their drugs legally by prescription.

- Long-term users of Valium can experience severe withdrawal symptoms if drug use is stopped abruptly.

- Our bodies probably produce a natural antianxiety substance that functions like drugs such as Valium, triazolam (Halcion), and alprazolam (Xanax).

- Antihistamines are CNS depressants and the principal active ingredients in over-the-counter (OTC) sleep aids.

- The short-acting CNS depressants are the most likely to be abused.

- GHB (gamma-hydroxybutyrate) is a Schedule I "club drug" that occurs naturally in the body and can be easily synthesized by using information available on the Internet.

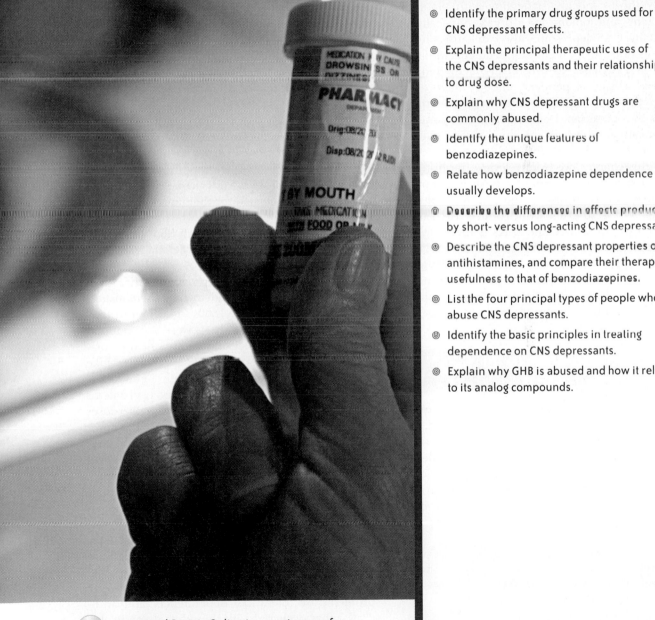

On completing this chapter you will be able to:

- ◎ Identify the primary drug groups used for CNS depressant effects.

- ◎ Explain the principal therapeutic uses of the CNS depressants and their relationship to drug dose.

- ◎ Explain why CNS depressant drugs are commonly abused.

- ◎ Identify the unique features of benzodiazepines.

- ◎ Relate how benzodiazepine dependence usually develops.

- ◎ Describe the differences in effects produced by short- versus long-acting CNS depressants.

- ◎ Describe the CNS depressant properties of antihistamines, and compare their therapeutic usefulness to that of benzodiazepines.

- ◎ List the four principal types of people who abuse CNS depressants.

- ◎ Identify the basic principles in treating dependence on CNS depressants.

- ◎ Explain why GHB is abused and how it relates to its analog compounds.

Drugs and Society Online is a great source for additional drugs and society information for both students and instructors.
Visit **http://drugsandsociety.jbpub.com** to find a variety of useful tools for learning, thinking, and teaching.

Introduction

Central nervous system (CNS) depressants are some of the most widely used and abused drugs in the United States. Why? When taken at low doses, they all produce a qualitatively similar "high" by their disinhibitory effects on the brain. In addition, they relieve stress and anxiety and even induce sleep — effects that appeal to many people, particularly those who are struggling with emotional problems and looking for a break, physically and mentally. CNS depressants also can cause a host of serious side effects, including problems with tolerance and dependence. Ironically, many individuals who become dependent on depressants obtain them through legitimate means: a prescription given by a physician. Depressants are also available on the street, although this illicit source does not account for the bulk of the problem.

In this chapter, we briefly review the history of CNS depressants, in terms of both development and use, and then discuss the positive and negative effects these drugs can produce. Each of the major types of depressant drugs is then reviewed in detail: *benzodiazepines* (Valium-like drugs), *barbiturates*, and other minor categories. We conclude with an examination of abuse patterns related to depressant drugs, and discuss how drug dependence and withdrawal are treated.

An Introduction to CNS Depressants

Why are CNS depressants problematic? First, in contrast to most other substances of abuse, CNS depressants are usually not obtained illicitly and self-administered but rather are prescribed under the direction of a physician. Second, use of CNS depressants can cause very alarming — even dangerous — behavior if not monitored closely; most problems

KEY TERMS

barbiturates
potent CNS depressants, usually not preferred because of their narrow margin of safety

benzodiazepines
the most popular and safest CNS depressants in use today

associated with these drugs occur due to inadequate professional supervision. Third, several seemingly unrelated drug groups have some ability to cause CNS depression. When these drugs are combined, bizarre and dangerous interactions can result (see Chapter 5 for a discussion on drug interactions). Particularly problematic is the combination of alcohol with other CNS depressants. Finally, CNS depressants can cause disruptive personality changes that are unpredictable and sometimes very threatening.

This chapter will help you understand the nature of the CNS depressant effects. In addition, the similarities and differences among the commonly prescribed CNS depressant drugs are discussed.

THE HISTORY OF CNS DEPRESSANTS

Before the era of modern drugs, the most common depressant used to ease tension, cause relaxation, and help forget problems was alcohol. These effects undoubtedly accounted for the immense popularity of alcohol and help explain why this traditional depressant is the most commonly abused drug of all time. (Alcohol is discussed in detail in Chapters 7 and 8.)

Attempts to find CNS depressants other than alcohol that could be used to treat nervousness and anxiety began in the 1800s with the introduction of bromides. These drugs were very popular until their toxicities became known. In the early 1900s, bromides were replaced by **barbiturates**. Like bromides, barbiturates were initially heralded as safe and effective depressants; however, problems with tolerance, dependence, and lethal overdoses soon became evident. It was learned that the doses of barbiturates required to treat anxiety also could cause CNS depression, affecting respiration and impairing mental functions (Hobbs et al. 1995). The margin of safety for barbiturates was too narrow, so research for safer CNS depressants began again.

It was not until the 1950s that the first **benzodiazepines** were marketed as substitutes for the dangerous barbiturates. Benzodiazepines were originally viewed as extremely safe and free from the problems of tolerance, dependence, and withdrawal that occurred with the other drugs in this category (Mondanaro 1988). Unfortunately, benzodiazepines have since been found to be less than ideal antianxiety drugs. Although relatively safe when used for short periods, long-term use can cause dependence and withdrawal problems much like those associated with their depressant predecessors (*Drug Facts and Comparisons* 2005). These problems have become a major concern of the medical community, as is discussed in greater detail later in the chapter.

Many of the people who become dependent on CNS depressants such as benzodiazepines began using the drugs under the supervision of a physician. Some clinicians routinely prescribe CNS depressants for patients with stress, anxiety, or apprehension without trying nonpharmacological approaches, such as psychotherapy or counseling. This practice sends an undesirable and often detrimental message to patients — that is, CNS depressants are a simple solution to their complex, stressful problems. The following quote illustrates the danger of this practice:

> I am still, unfortunately, lost in "'script addiction." . . . I have gone on-line asking for pills. I could really identify with the one posting about doctors who continue to write the 'scripts to increase/continue the patient "flow." This is exactly what is happening with me and my doctor. (*From America Online Alcohol and Drug Dependency and Recovery message board.*)

During the 1970s and 1980s, there was an epidemic of prescriptions written for CNS depressants. For example, in 1973, 100 million prescriptions were written for benzodiazepines alone. Approximately twice as many women as men were taking these drugs at this time; a similar gender pattern continues today. During this period, many homemakers made CNS depressants a part of their household routine, as described in the lyrics of the song "Mother's Little Helper" on the Rolling Stones' album *Flowers:*

> Things are different today
> I hear every mother say
> "Mother needs something today to calm
>   her down"
> And though she's not really ill,
> There's a little yellow pill.
> She goes running for the shelter

> Of her "mother's little helper"
> And it helps her on her way,
> Gets her through her busy day.

As the medical community became more aware of the problem, the use of depressants declined (Latner 2000). Today, efforts are being made by pharmaceutical companies and scientists to find new classes of CNS depressants that can be used to relieve stress and anxiety without causing serious side effects such as dependence and withdrawal.

THE EFFECTS OF CNS DEPRESSANTS: BENEFITS AND RISKS

The CNS depressants are a diverse group of drugs that share an ability to reduce CNS activity and diminish the brain's level of awareness. Besides the benzodiazepines, barbiturate-like drugs, and alcohol, depressant drugs include **antihistamines** and opioid narcotics such as heroin (see Chapter 9).

Depressants are usually classified according to the degree of their medical effects on the body. For instance, **sedatives** cause mild depression of the CNS and relaxation. This drug effect is used to treat extreme anxiety and often is referred to as **anxiolytic**. Many sedatives also have muscle-relaxing properties that enhance their relaxing effects.

Depressants are also used to promote sleep. **Hypnotics** (from the Greek god of sleep, *Hypnos*) are CNS depressants that encourage sleep by inducing drowsiness. Often when depressants are used as hypnotics, they produce **amnesiac** effects as

KEY TERMS

antihistamines
drugs that often cause CNS depression and are used to treat allergies

sedatives
CNS depressants used to relieve anxiety, fear, and apprehension

anxiolytic
drug that relieves anxiety

hypnotics
CNS depressants used to induce drowsiness and encourage sleep

amnesiac
causing the loss of memory

FIGURE 6.1

Dose-dependent effects of CNS depressants.

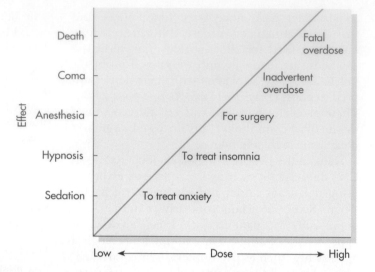

well. As already mentioned, the effects produced by depressants can be very enticing and encourage inappropriate use.

The effects of the CNS depressants tend to be dose-dependent (see Figure 6.1). Thus, if you were to take a larger dose of a sedative, it might have a hypnotic effect. Often, the only difference between a sedative and a hypnotic effect is the dosage; consequently, the same drug may be used for both purposes by varying the dose. By increasing the dose still further, an anesthetic state can be reached. **Anesthesia**, a deep depression of the CNS, is used to achieve a controlled state of unconsciousness so that a patient can be treated, usually by surgery, in relative comfort and without memory of an unpleasant experience. With the exception of benzodiazepines, if the dose of most of the depressants is increased much more, coma or death will ensue because the CNS becomes so depressed that vital centers controlling breathing and heart activity cease to function properly (*Drug Facts and Comparison* 2005).

As a group, CNS depressant drugs used in a persistent fashion cause tolerance. Because of the diminished effect due to the tolerance, users of these drugs continually escalate their doses.

Under such conditions, the depressants alter physical and psychological states, resulting in dependence. The dependence can be so severe that abrupt drug abstinence results in severe withdrawals that include life-threatening seizures (*Drug Facts and Comparison* 2005). Because of these dangerous pharmacological features, treatment of dependence on CNS depressants must proceed very carefully (O'Brien 2001). This issue is discussed in greater detail at the end of this chapter and in Chapter 5.

Types of CNS Depressants

All CNS depressants are not "created equal." Some have wider margins of safety; others have a greater potential for nonmedicinal abuse. These differences are important when considering the therapeutic advantages of each type of CNS depressant. In addition, unique features of the different types of depressants make them useful for treatment of other medical problems. For example, some barbiturates and benzodiazepines are used to treat forms of epilepsy or acute seizure activity, whereas opioid narcotics are used to treat many types of pain. Some of these unique features will be dealt with in greater detail when the individual drug groups are discussed. The benzodiazepines, barbiturate-like drugs, antihistamines, and the naturally occurring gamma-hydroxybutyrate (GHB) are discussed in this chapter. Other CNS

anesthesia

a state characterized by loss of sensation or consciousness

CNS depressants can be used as hypnotics to initiate sleep.

depressants, such as alcohol and opiates, are covered in Chapters 7, 8, and 9.

The unique features of the CNS depressants help determine the likelihood of their abuse. For example, abuse is more likely to occur with the short-acting depressant agents than with those agents that have long-lasting effects. Currently, nonmedicinal use of the sedatives occurs in 3% to 5% of the population. This abuse is most likely to be caused by the benzodiazepines that have a short half-life ("Common Substances of Abuse" 2000).

BENZODIAZEPINES: VALIUM-TYPE DRUGS

Benzodiazepines are by far the most frequently prescribed CNS depressants for anxiety and sleep. In fact, 4 of the top-selling 40 prescription drugs in the United States during 2003 were benzodiazepines (Internet Drug Index 2004). Because of their wide margin of safety (death from overdose is rare), benzodiazepines have replaced barbiturate-like drugs for use as sedatives and hypnotics (Landis and Bryant 1999). Benzodiazepines were originally referred to as *minor tranquilizers*, but this terminology erroneously implied that they had pharmacological properties similar to those of antipsychotic drugs (*major tranquilizers*), when they are actually very different. Consequently, the term *minor tranquilizer* is usually avoided by clinicians.

The first true benzodiazepine, chlordiazepoxide (Librium), was developed for medical use and marketed about 1960. The very popular drug Valium came on the market about the same time. In fact, Valium was so well received that from 1972 to 1978 it was the top-selling prescription drug in the United States. Its popularity has since declined considerably, and in 2003 sales of its generic form, diazepam, ranked only 117th in the United States (Internet Drug Index 2004).

Because of dependence problems, the benzodiazepines are now classified as Schedule IV drugs. In recent years, considerable concern has arisen that benzodiazepines are overprescribed because of their perceived safety; it has been said, somewhat facetiously, that the only way a person could die from using benzodiazepines would be to choke on them. Clinicians are concerned about this overconfident attitude toward benzodiazepines and warn patients against prolonged and unsupervised administration of these drugs (Lader 1999).

Medical Uses

Benzodiazepines are used for an array of therapeutic objectives, including the relief of anxiety, treatment of neurosis, relaxation of muscles, alleviation of lower back pain, treatment of some convulsive disorders, induction of sleep (hypnotic), relief from withdrawal symptoms associated with narcotic and alcohol dependence, and induction of amnesia, usually for preoperative administration (administered just before or during surgery or very uncomfortable medical procedures) (Longo and Johnson 2000).

Mechanisms of Action

In contrast to barbiturate-type drugs, which cause general depression of most neuronal activity, benzodiazepines selectively affect those neurons that have receptors for the neurotransmitter gamma aminobutyric acid (GABA) (*Drug Facts and Comparisons* 2005). GABA is a very important inhibitory transmitter in several regions of the brain: the limbic system, the reticular activating system, and the motor cortex (see Chapter 4). In the presence of benzodiazepines, the inhibitory effects of GABA are increased. Depression of activity in these brain regions likely accounts for the ability of benzodiazepines to alter mood (a limbic function), cause drowsiness (a reticular activating system function), and relax muscles (a cortical function). The specific GABA-enhancing effect of these drugs explains the selective CNS depression caused by benzodiazepines.

Of considerable interest is the observation that these Valium-like drugs act on specific receptor sites that are linked to the GABA receptors in the CNS. As yet, no endogenous substance has been identified that naturally interacts with this so-called benzodiazepine site. It is very likely, however, that a natural benzodiazepine does exist that activates this same receptor population and serves to reduce stress and anxiety by natural means. Because benzodiazepines have specific target receptors, it has been possible to develop a highly selective antagonist drug, flumazenil (Romazicon). This drug is used to treat benzodiazepine overdoses, but must be used carefully because its administration can precipitate withdrawal in people taking benzodiazepines (Hebel 2000).

Types of Benzodiazepines

Because benzodiazepines are so popular and thus profitable, new related drugs are routinely released into the pharmaceutical market. Currently, approximately 14 benzodiazepine compounds are available in the United States.

Benzodiazepines are distinguished primarily by their duration of action (see Table 6.1). As a general rule, the short-acting drugs are used as hypnotics to treat insomnia, thus allowing the user to awake in the morning with few aftereffects (such as a hangover). The long-acting benzodiazepines tend to be prescribed as sedatives, giving prolonged relaxation and relief from persistent anxiety. Some of the long-acting drugs can exert a relaxing effect for as long as 2 to 3 days. One reason for the long action in some benzodiazepines is that they are converted by the liver into metabolites that are as active as the original drug (*Drug Facts and Comparisons* 2005). For example, Valium has a half-life of 20 to 80 hours and is converted by the liver into several active metabolites, including oxazepam (which itself is marketed as a therapeutic benzodiazepine; see Table 6.1).

Side Effects

Reported side effects of benzodiazepines include drowsiness, lightheadedness, lethargy, impairment of mental and physical activities, skin rashes, nau-

Table 6.1 Half-lives of Various Benzodiazepines

DRUG	HALF-LIFE (HOURS)
Alprazolam (Xanax)	12–15
Chlordiazepoxide (Librium)	5–30
Clonazepam (Klonopin)	18–50
Clorazepate (Tranxene)	30–100
Diazepam (Valium)	20–50
Estazolam (ProSom)	10–24
Flurazepam (Dalmane)	2–4
Halazepam (Paxipam)	14
Lorazepam (Ativan)	10–20
Midazolam (Versed)	1–12
Oxazepam (Serax)	5–21
Quazepam (Doral)	25–41
Temazepam (Restoril)	10–17
Triazolam (Halcion)	1.5–5.5
Zolpidem (Ambien; not a true benzodiazepine)	2–5

Source: G. McEvoy. "Benzodiazepines." In *AHFS Drug Information*, 2352–2381. Bethesda, MD: American Society of Health-System Pharmacists, 2003.

sea, diminished libido, irregularities in the menstrual cycle, blood cell abnormalities, and increased sensitivity to alcohol and other CNS depressants (McEvoy 2003). In contrast to barbiturate-type drugs, only very high doses of benzodiazepines have a significant impact on respiration. There are few verified instances of death resulting from overdose of benzodiazepines alone (Longo and Johnson 2000). Almost always, serious suppression of vital functions occurs when these drugs are combined with other depressants, most often alcohol (*Drug Facts and Comparisons* 2005).

Although their long-term effectiveness has been challenged, benzodiazepines are often used to treat persistent disorders such as chronic insomnia (Gorman 2003). Benzodiazepines have less effect on **REM sleep** (rapid eye movement, the restive phase) than do barbiturates. Consequently, sleep under the influence of benzodiazepines is more likely to be restful and satisfying. However, prolonged use of hypnotic doses of benzodiazepines may cause rebound (see Chapter 5) increases in REM sleep and insomnia when the drug is stopped especially if used for long periods of time.

On rare occasions, benzodiazepines can have **paradoxical effects**, producing unusual responses, such as nightmares, anxiety, irritability, sweating, and restlessness (*Drug Facts and Comparisons* 2005). Bizarre, uninhibited behavior — extreme agitation with hostility, paranoia, and rage — may occur as well. One such case was reported in 1988 in Utah. A 63-year-old patient who was taking Halcion (a relatively short-acting benzodiazepine) murdered her 87-year-old mother. The suspect claimed that the murder occurred because of the effects of the drug and that she was innocent of committing a crime. Her defense was successful, and she was acquitted of murder. After her acquittal, the woman initiated a $21 million lawsuit against Upjohn Pharmaceuticals for marketing Halcion, which she claimed was a dangerous drug. The lawsuit was settled out of court for an undisclosed amount. This tragic episode came to a surprising conclusion in 1994 when the daughter committed suicide (Associated Press 1994).

Critics' complaints that Halcion causes unacceptable "amnesia, confusion, paranoia, hostility and seizures" (Associated Press 1994, p. D-3) prompted the Food and Drug Administration (FDA) to closely evaluate this benzodiazepine. Despite the fact that several other countries have banned Halcion, the FDA concluded that its benefits outweigh the reported risks; however, the FDA also concluded that "In no way should this [the FDA's conclusion] suggest that Halcion is free of side effects. It has long been recognized and emphasized in Halcion's labeling that it is a potent drug that produces the same type of adverse effects as other CNS sedative hypnotic drugs" ("New Halcion Guidelines" 1992, p. 14; *PDR* 1997). Although the FDA did not require that Halcion be withdrawn, it did negotiate changes in the labeling and package inserts with Halcion's manufacturer, Upjohn Pharmaceuticals. These changes emphasize appropriate Halcion use in treatment of insomnia and

additional information about side effects, warnings, and dosage. As a result of these concerns, sales of Halcion plummeted, causing it to fall from the 18th largest-selling prescription drug in 1987 to not even being 1 of the top 200 most-prescribed drugs in 2003 (Internet Drug Index 2004).

There is no obvious explanation for the strange benzodiazepine-induced behaviors. It is possible that, in some people, the drugs mask inhibitory centers of the brain and allow expression of antisocial behavior that is normally suppressed and controlled.

Related concerns have also been made public about another very popular benzodiazepine, alprazolam (Xanax). In 1990, Xanax became the first drug approved for the treatment of *panic disorder* — repeated, intense attacks of anxiety that can make life unbearable (McEvoy 2003). Reports that long-term use of Xanax can cause severe withdrawal effects and a stubborn dependency on the drug raised public concerns about use of benzodiazepines in general. For example, how many people are severely dependent on these CNS depressants? What is the frequency of side effects such as memory impairment, serious mood swings, and cognitive problems? And how many patients using the benzodiazepines would be better served with nondrug psychotherapy? Clearly, use of the benzodiazepines to relieve acute stress or insomnia can be beneficial, but these drugs should be prescribed at the lowest dose possible and for the shortest time possible or withdrawal problems can result, as illustrated in the following quote:

> I was put on alprazolam (Xanax) two and a half years ago by [my] doctor. Now told by another doctor that it is for short-term use only and I am trying to get off slowly, but having difficulty. [I] have never used other drugs and do not have any information on the withdrawal process. (*From America Online Alcohol and Drug Dependency and Recovery message board.*)

Tolerance, Dependence, Withdrawal, and Abuse

As with most CNS depressants, frequent, chronic use of benzodiazepines can cause tolerance, dependence (both physical and psychological), and withdrawal (*Drug Facts and Comparisons* 2005). Such side effects are usually not as severe as those of most other depressants, and they occur only after using the drugs for prolonged periods (*Drug Facts and Comparisons* 2005). In addition, for most people, the effects of the benzodiazepines are not viewed as reinforcing; thus, compared with other depressants, such as barbiturates, benzodiazepines are not especially addicting (O'Brien 2001). However, these drugs should be prescribed with caution for patients with a history of drug abuse (Longo and Johnson 2000).

Withdrawal can mimic the condition for which the benzodiazepine is given; for example, withdrawal symptoms can include anxiety or insomnia (Charney et al. 2001). In such cases, a clinician may be fooled into thinking that the underlying emotional disorder is still present and may resume drug therapy without realizing that the patient has become drug-dependent. This can happen after as little as 1 month of treatment ("Common Substances of Abuse" 2000). In situations in which users have consumed high doses of benzodiazepine over the long term, more severe, even life-threatening withdrawal symptoms may occur (*Drug Facts and Comparisons* 2005); depression, panic, paranoia, and convulsions (Gatzonis et al. 2000) have been reported (see Table 6.2). Severe withdrawal can often be avoided by gradually weaning the patient from the benzodiazepine (McEvoy 2003). Long-term use of benzodiazepines (periods exceeding 3 to 4 months) to treat anxiety or sleep disorders has not been shown to be therapeutically useful for most patients (McEvoy 2003). Even so, this approach is a common indiscriminate practice. As one user explains:

> I went through a trauma 4 years ago, and the doctor prescribed a very high dose of Ativan. Well, I soon became addicted, both emotionally and physically . . . How do I get off? . . . This stuff is very addicting and my body can't really function without it. (*From America Online Alcohol and Drug Dependency and Recovery message board.*)

It is very unusual to find nontherapeutic drug-seeking behavior in a patient who has been properly removed from benzodiazepines, unless that individual already has a history of drug abuse (Longo and Johnson 2000). Research has shown that when benzodiazepines are the primary drug of abuse, these CNS depressants are usually self-administered to prevent unpleasant withdrawal symptoms in dependent users. If benzodiazepine-dependent users are properly weaned from the drugs and withdrawal has dissipated, there is no evidence that craving for the benzodiazepines occurs because people usually do not consider the benzodiazepines particularly reinforcing (Kosten and Hollister 1998). An exception to this conclusion appears to be former alcoholics. Many people

Table 6.2 Abstinence Symptoms That Occur When Long-Term Users of Benzodiazepines Abruptly Stop Taking the Drug

DURATION OF ABSTINENCE	SYMPTOMS
1–3 days	Often no noticeable symptoms
3–4 days	Restlessness, agitation, headaches, problems eating, and inability to sleep
4–6 days	The preceding symptoms plus twitching of facial and arm muscles and feeling of intense burning in the skin
6–7 days	The preceding symptoms plus seizures

Source: W. Hobbs, T. Rall, and T. Verdoorn. "Hypnotics and Sedatives." In *The Pharmacological Basis of Therapeutics,* 9th ed., edited by J. Hardman and L. Limbird, 361–396. New York: McGraw-Hill, 1995.

Rohypnol is a benzodiazepine outlawed in the United States.

with a history of alcoholism find the effects of benzodiazepines rewarding; consequently, almost one-fourth of prior alcoholics use benzodiazepines chronically (Johansson et al. 2003).

Benzodiazepines are commonly used as a secondary drug of abuse and combined with illicit drugs. For example, it is very common to find heroin users who are dependent on benzodiazepines as well as narcotics (Walker and Ettenberg 2001).

Another frequent combination is the use of benzodiazepines with stimulants such as cocaine (DeMaria et al. 2000). Some addicts claim that this combination enhances the pleasant effects of the stimulant and reduces the "crashing" that occurs after using high doses. (More is said about benzodiazepine abuse later in this chapter.)

It should also be mentioned that benzodiazepines are occasionally used to make people vulnerable to sexual assaults referred to as *date rapes* (Charney et al. 2001). The use of CNS depressants to commit these acts of violence is discussed in greater detail later in the chapter, but such assaults have sometimes involved the use of the **club drug** Rohypnol. Rohypnol (sometimes called *Rophie, Roche,* or *Forget Me*) is the proprietary name for flunitrazepam, a benzodiazepine. Rohypnol, which has been outlawed in the United States, comes as a tablet that can be dissolved in beverages without leaving an odor or taste and impairs short-term memory, making victims unable to recall details of the assault (*NIDA Notes* 2000; Publishers Group 2002).

BARBITURATES

Barbiturates are barbituric acid derivatives that are used in medicine as sedatives and hypnotics. Barbituric acid was first synthesized by A. Bayer (of aspirin fame) in Germany in 1864. The reason that he chose the name *barbituric acid* is not known. Some have speculated that the compound was named after a girl named Barbara whom Bayer knew. Others think that Bayer celebrated his discovery on the Day of St. Barbara in a tavern that artillery officers frequented. (St. Barbara is the patron saint of artillery soldiers.)

The first barbiturate, barbital (Veronal), was used medically in 1903. The names of the barbiturates all end in -*al*, indicating a chemical relationship to barbital, the first one synthesized. Historically, barbiturates have played an important role in therapeutics because of their effectiveness as sedative-hypnotic agents, which allowed them to be routinely used in the treatment of anxiety, agitation, and insomnia. However, because of their narrow margin of safety and their abuse liability, barbiturates have been largely replaced by safer drugs, such as benzodiazepines. Despite the reduced therapeutic use of the barbiturates in 2004, 6.5% of high school seniors recreationally used a barbiturate (Johnston 2004).

Uncontrolled use of barbiturates can cause a state of acute or chronic intoxication. Initially, there may be some loss of inhibition, euphoria, and behavioral stimulation — a pattern often seen with moderate consumption of alcohol. When taken to relieve extreme pain or mental stress, barbiturates may cause delirium and produce other side effects that can include nausea, nervousness, rash, and diarrhea. The person intoxicated with barbiturates may have difficulty thinking and making judgments, may be emotionally unstable, may be uncoordinated and unsteady when walking, and may slur speech (not unlike the drunken state caused by alcohol).

KEY TERMS

club drug
drug used at all-night raves, parties, dance clubs, and bars to enhance sensory experiences

When used for their hypnotic properties, barbiturates cause an unnatural sleep. The user awakens feeling tired, edgy, and quite unsatisfied, most likely because barbiturates markedly suppress the REM phase of sleep. (REM sleep is necessary for the refreshing renewal that usually accompanies a good sleep experience.) Because benzodiazepines suppress REM sleep (as do all CNS depressants) less severely than barbiturates, use of these agents as sleep aids is generally better tolerated.

Continued misuse of barbiturate drugs has a cumulative toxic effect on the CNS that is more life-threatening than misuse of opiates. When taken in large doses or in combination with other CNS depressants, barbiturates may cause death from respiratory or cardiovascular depression. Because of this toxicity, barbiturates have been involved in many drug-related deaths, both accidental and suicidal. Repeated misuse induces severe tolerance of and physical dependence on these drugs. Discontinuing use of short-acting barbiturates in people who are using large doses can cause dangerous withdrawal effects such as life-threatening seizures. Table 6.3 summarizes the range of effects of barbiturates and other depressants on the mind and body.

Concern about the abuse potential of barbiturates caused the federal government to include some of these depressants in the Controlled Substances Act. Consequently, the short-acting barbiturates, such as pentobarbital and secobarbital, are classified as Schedule II drugs, whereas the long-acting barbiturates, such as phenobarbital, are less rigidly controlled as Schedule IV drugs.

Effects and Medical Uses

Barbiturates have many pharmacological actions. They depress the activity of nerves and skeletal, smooth, and cardiac muscles and affect the CNS in several ways, ranging from mild sedation to coma, depending on the dose. At sedative or hypnotic dosage levels, only the CNS is significantly affected. Higher anesthetic doses cause slight decreases in blood pressure, heart rate, and flow of urine. The metabolizing enzyme systems in the liver are important in inactivating barbiturates; thus, liver damage may result in exaggerated responses to barbiturate use (Charney et al. 2001).

Table 6.3 **Effects of Barbiturates and Other Depressants on the Body and Mind**

	BODY	MIND
Low dose	Drowsiness	Decreased anxiety, relaxation
	Trouble with coordination	Decreased ability to reason and solve problems
	Slurred speech	
	Dizziness	Difficulty in judging distance and time
	Staggering	
	Double vision	Amnesia
	Sleep	
	Depressed breathing	Brain damage
	Coma (unconscious and cannot be awakened)	
	Depressed blood pressure	
High dose	Death	

Low doses of barbiturates relieve tension and anxiety, effects that give several barbiturates substantial abuse potential. The drawbacks of barbiturates are extensive and severe:

- They lack selectivity and safety.
- They have a substantial tendency to create tolerance, dependence, withdrawal, and abuse.
- They cause problems with drug interaction.

As a result, barbiturates have been replaced by benzodiazepines in most treatments. Because of this decreased use, these drugs tend not to be readily available and are not frequently abused in this country (USDOJ 2003). The long-acting phenobarbital is still frequently used for its CNS depressant activity to alleviate or prevent convulsions in some epileptic patients and seizures caused by strychnine, cocaine, and other stimulant drugs. Thiopental (Pentothal) and other ultrashort- and short-acting barbiturates are used as anesthesia for minor surgery and as preoperative anesthetics in preparation for major surgery.

Mechanism of Action and Elimination

The precise mechanism of action for barbiturates is unclear. Like benzodiazepines, they likely interfere with activity in the reticular activating system, the limbic system, and the motor cortex. However, in contrast to benzodiazepines, barbiturates do not seem to act at a specific receptor site; they probably have a general effect that enhances the activity of the inhibitory transmitter GABA (Charney

et al. 2001). Because benzodiazepines also increase GABA activity (albeit in a more selective manner), these two types of drugs have overlapping effects. Because the mechanisms whereby they exert their effects are different, it is not surprising that these two types of depressants also have different pharmacological features.

The fat solubility of barbiturates is another important factor in the duration of their effects (Charney et al. 2001). Barbiturates that are the most fat-soluble move in and out of body tissues (such as the brain) rapidly and are likely to be shorter-acting. Fat-soluble barbiturates also are more likely to be stored in fatty tissue; consequently, the fat content of the body can influence the effects on the user. Because women have a higher body-fat ratio than men, their reaction to barbiturates may be slightly different.

Withdrawal from barbiturates after dependence has developed causes hyperexcitability because of the rebound of depressed neural systems. Qualitatively (but not quantitatively), the withdrawal symptoms are similar for all sedative-hypnotics (Trevor and Lay 1998).

Table 6.4 gives details on the barbiturates that are abused most frequently.

OTHER CNS DEPRESSANTS

Although benzodiazepines and barbiturates are by far used the most frequently to produce CNS depressant effects, many other agents, representing

Table 6.4 Details on the Most Frequently Abused Barbiturates

DRUG	NICKNAMES	EFFECTS
Amobarbital (Amytal Sodium)	Blues, blue heavens, blue devils	Moderately rapid action
Pentobarbital (Nembutal Sodium)	Nembies, yellow jackets, yellows	Short-acting
Phenobarbital (Luminal Sodium)	Purple hearts	Long-acting barbiturate particularly well suited for treatment of epilepsy
Secobarbital (Seconal Sodium)	Reds, red devils, red birds, Seccy	Short-acting with a prompt onset of action
50% amobarbital and 50% secobarbital (Tuinal)	Tooeys, double trouble, rainbows	Results in a rapidly effective, moderately long-acting sedative

an array of distinct chemical groups, can similarly reduce brain activity. Although the mechanisms of action might be different for some of these drugs, if any CNS depressants (including alcohol) are combined, they will interact synergistically and can suppress respiration in a life-threatening manner. Thus, it is important to avoid such mixtures if possible. Even some over-the-counter (OTC) products, such as cold and allergy medications, contain drugs with CNS depressant actions.

Nonbarbiturate Drugs with Barbiturate-like Properties

This category of depressants includes agents that are not barbiturates but have barbiturate-like effects (Charney et al. 2001). All of these drugs cause substantial tolerance, physical and psychological dependence, and withdrawal symptoms. The therapeutic safety of these CNS depressants more closely resembles that of barbiturates than benzodiazepines; consequently, like barbiturates, these agents have been replaced by the safer and easier-to-manage benzodiazepines.

Because these drugs have significant abuse potential, they are restricted much like other CNS depressants. In this group of depressants, methaqualone is a Schedule II drug; glutethimide and methyprylon are Schedule III drugs; and chloral hydrate is a Schedule IV drug. Each classification is based on the drug's relative potential for physical and psychological dependence. Abuse of Schedule II drugs may lead to severe or moderate physical dependence or high psychological dependence, and abuse of Schedule III drugs may cause moderate physical and psychological dependence. Schedule IV drugs are considered much less likely to cause either type of dependence.

Chloral Hydrate Chloral hydrate (Noctec), or "knockout drops," has the unsavory reputation of being a drug that is slipped into a person's drink to make him or her unconscious. In the late 1800s, the combination of chloral hydrate and alcohol was given the name *Mickey Finn* on the waterfront of the Barbary Coast of San Francisco when sailors were in short supply. An unsuspecting man would have a friendly drink and wake up as a crew member on an outbound freighter to China.

Chloral hydrate is a good hypnotic, but it has a narrow margin of safety. This compound is a stomach irritant, especially if given repeatedly and in fairly large doses. Addicts may take enormous doses of the drug; as with most CNS depressants, chronic, long-term use of high doses will cause tolerance and physical dependence (Hobbs et al. 1995; McEvoy 2003).

Glutethimide Glutethimide (Doriden) is another example of a barbiturate-like drug that can be abused and that causes severe withdrawal symptoms. It also induces blood abnormalities in sensitive individuals, such as a type of anemia and abnormally low white cell counts. Nausea, fever, increased heart rate, and convulsions occasionally occur in patients who have been taking this sedative regularly in moderate doses.

Methyprylon Methyprylon (Noludar) is a short-acting nonbarbiturate that is used as a sedative and hypnotic. Its effects are similar to those of Doriden, and it is capable of causing tolerance, physical dependence, and addiction, much like barbiturates.

Methaqualone Few drugs have become so popular so quickly as methaqualone. This barbiturate-like sedative-hypnotic was introduced in India in the 1950s as an antimalarial agent. Its sedative properties, however, were soon discovered. It then became available in the United States as Quaalude, Mequin, and Parest.

After several years of street abuse, methaqualone was classified as a Schedule II drug. Since 1985, methaqualone has not been manufactured in the United States because of adverse publicity.

Common side effects of methaqualone include fatigue, dizziness, anorexia, nausea, vomiting, diarrhea, sweating, dryness of the mouth, depersonalization, headache, and paresthesia of the extremities (a pins-and-needles feeling in the fingers and toes). Hangover is frequently reported.

Antihistamines

Antihistamines are drugs used in both nonprescription and prescription medicinal products. The most common uses for antihistamines are to relieve the

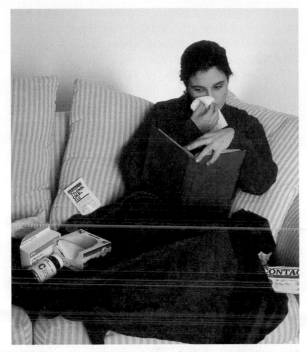

Antihistamines are found in OTC medicines used to relieve cold and allergy symptoms.

symptoms associated with the common cold, allergies, and motion sickness (see Chapter 15). Although frequently overlooked, many antihistamines cause significant CNS depression and are used both as sedatives and hypnotics (*Drug Facts and Comparisons* 2005). For example, the agents hydroxyzine (Visteril) and promethazine (Phenergan) are prescribed for their sedative effects, whereas diphenhydramine is commonly used as an OTC sleep aid.

The exact mechanism of CNS depression caused by these agents is not totally known but appears to relate to their blockage of acetylcholine receptors in the brain (they antagonize the muscarinic receptor types). This anticholinergic activity (see Chapter 4) helps cause relaxation and sedation and can be viewed as a very annoying side effect when these drugs are being used to treat allergies or other problems.

Therapeutic Usefulness and Side Effects Antihistamines are viewed as relatively safe agents. Compared with other more powerful CNS depressants,

antihistamines do not appear to cause significant physical or psychological dependence or addiction problems, although drugs with anticholinergic activity, such as the antihistamines, are sometimes abused, especially by children and teenagers (Halpert et al. 2002). However, tolerance to antihistamine-induced sedation occurs quite rapidly. Reports of significant cases of withdrawal problems when use of antihistamines is stopped are rare. This situation may reflect the fact that these agents are used as antianxiety drugs for only minor problems and for short periods of time (often only for a single dose).

One significant problem with antihistamines is the variability of responses they produce. Different antihistamines work differently on different people. Usually therapeutic doses cause decreased alertness, relaxation, slowed reaction time, and drowsiness. But it is not uncommon for some individuals to be affected in the opposite manner — that is, an antihistamine can cause restlessness, agitation, and insomnia. There are even cases of seizures caused by toxic doses of antihistamine, particularly in children (Serafin and Babe 1995). Side effects of antihistamines related to their anticholinergic effects include dry mouth, constipation, and inability to urinate. These factors probably help to discourage high-dose abuse of these drugs. However, OTC antihistamines are still sometimes taken for recreational purposes despite the unpleasant side effects (Hughes et al. 1999).

Even though antihistamines are relatively safe in therapeutic doses, they can contribute to serious problems if combined with other CNS depressants. Many OTC cold, allergy, antimotion, and sleep aid products contain antihistamines and should be avoided by patients using the potent CNS depressants.

GHB (Gamma-Hydroxybutyrate): The Natural Depressant

GHB is a colorless, tasteless, and odorless substance found naturally in the body resulting from the metabolism of the inhibitory neurotransmitter GABA (see Chapter 4; Lingenhoehl et al. 1999). It was first synthesized nearly 30 years ago by a French researcher who intended to study the CNS effects of GABA (Poldrugo and Addolorato 1999).

GHB is often stored as a clear, colorless, odorless liquid.

It was initially believed that GHB exerted its effects by enhancing CNS GABA systems, although this mechanism has recently been questioned (Carter et al. 2003). There is some evidence that GHB is itself a neuromodulator with its own receptor targets in the brain (Carter et al. 2003). Because of its central depressant effects, GHB has been used in Europe as an adjunct for general anesthesia, a treatment for insomnia and narcolepsy (a daytime sleep disorder), and a treatment for alcoholism and alcohol withdrawal and narcotic dependence (Kam and Yoong 1998). During the 1980s, GHB became available without a prescription in health food stores and was used principally by body builders to stimulate the release of growth hormone with the intent to reduce fat and build muscle ("Club Drugs" 2000; Publishers Group 2002). More recently, this substance has been gaining popularity for recreational use due to what has been described as a pleasant, alcohol-like, hangover-free high with aphrodisiac properties (Morgenthaler and Joy 1994). In 2004, 2% of high school seniors were reported to have used GHB (Johnston 2004). Because of its frequent use by young people at nightclubs and bars, GHB has become known as a *club drug* (USDOJ 2003).

GHB is generally taken orally after being mixed with a liquid or beverage. It has a rapid onset and, when large doses are consumed, can cause unconsciousness and coma in 15 to 40 minutes. These dangerous effects typically require emergency room treatment. Often, the recovery is also rapid with persons regaining consciousness in 2 to 4 hours (Publishers Group 2002).

Due to concerns about GHB abuse and side effects, an advisory warning that this substance is unsafe was first issued by the FDA in 1990. In 1997, the FDA released another warning that GHB was not approved for clinical use in the United States and was a potentially dangerous substance. Finally, due to the rising illicit use of GHB and resultant problems, this drug was made a Schedule I Controlled Substance by the DEA in March 2000 ("Gamma Hydroxybutyric Acid" 2000).

Despite claims about its benign nature (Dean et al. 1997), evidence is mounting that in high doses, GHB can be dangerous and even deadly. There have been more than 70 documented deaths attributed to GHB overdoses as of 2001 (USDOJ 2003). It has been reported that GHB use can cause significant side effects, such as hormonal problems, sleep abnormalities, drowsiness, nausea, vomiting, and changes in blood pressure (Teter and Guthrie 2001). Both users and clinicians seem to agree that GHB is most dangerous when combined with other drugs, especially other CNS depressants such as alcohol ("Gamma Hydroxybutyric Acid" 2000).

Because GHB is illegal in the United States, it is currently available only through the underground "gray market" as a "bootleg" product manufactured by kitchen chemists and with suspicious quality and purity. As of 2000, the FDA had investigated 124 cases involving large-scale interstate manufacture and distribution of GHB (Leshner 2000). The lack of reliability of these GHB-containing products and the highly variable responses of different people to this substance increase the likelihood of problems when using this depressant.

Instructions on how to make GHB are readily available on multiple Internet sites. It is typically portrayed as a relatively benign substance, but one for which proper dosing is critical for "safe" use. Some distributors attempt to evade enforcement by selling legal chemicals required to make GHB to customers rather than GHB itself (USDOJ 2002b). Sales of GHB can be profitable. For example, in 2001, two brothers were sentenced to prison for 4 years for selling GHB "date rape" kits over the Internet. The brothers collected approximately $200,000 in less than a year before being apprehended (USDOJ 2002a).

There is some debate as to whether the use of GHB can cause dependence and withdrawal. Some evidence suggests that chronic high-dose use of GHB may lead to prolonged abuse and a withdrawal syndrome consisting of insomnia, anxiety, and tremors that typically resolves in 3 to 12 days (Craig et al. 2000; Galloway et al. 1997; Mioto and Roth 2001). Another major concern with this substance is its use in cases of date rape. Because GHB can be stored as a clear, colorless, odorless liquid, it is easily added undetected to a beverage such as an alcoholic drink (*NIDA Notes* 2000). Its amnesiac and sedative properties disable users and make them vulnerable to sexual assault (Leshner 2000). Despite attempts to vigorously prosecute these cases, because the victims frequently are unable to recall details of the attack and the drug disappears so quickly from the bloodstream (its half-life is 2 to 3 hours), rape under the influence of GHB can be difficult to prove.

Because GHB is illegal, other GHB-related drugs have become readily available as substitutes, although they are only "legal" if they are included in products technically not intended for human use. These products are supposedly promoted as chemical solvents and typically make a disclaimer that the products are not for human consumption even though the label often implies that the product may be ingested. For example, the label on one industrial solvent stated "Warning! Accidental ingestion . . . will produce GHB in your body. If you ingest some by mistake, don't take alcohol or any other drug" (USDOJ 2002b). The most com-monly used of these GHB analogs are gamma-butyrolactone (GBL) and 1,4-butanediol (BD) (USDOJ 2002b). Because these compounds are converted into GBH in the body, they can cause serious side effects (see "Case in Point").

Patterns of Abuse with CNS Depressants

The American Psychiatric Association (APA) considers dependence on CNS depressants to be a psychiatric disorder. According to its widely used *Diagnostic and Statistical Manual of Mental Disorders,* fourth edition (DSM-IV-TR) (American Psychiatric Association 2000), a *substance dependence disorder* is present when three of the following criteria are satisfied at any time in a 12-month period:

1. The person needs greatly increased amounts of the substance to achieve the desired effect or experiences a markedly diminished effect with continual use of the substance.
2. Characteristic withdrawal occurs when drug use is stopped, which encourages continued use of the substance to avoid the unpleasant effects.
3. The substance is consumed in larger amounts over a longer period of time than originally intended.
4. The person shows persistent desire or repeated unsuccessful efforts to decrease or control substance use.
5. A great deal of time is spent obtaining and using the substance or recovering from its effects.

▶**Case in Point**   BD in "Natural" Sleep Aid

On January 27, 2000, a Utah man died as a consequence of excessive consumption of a product called Zen. The man purchased the product from a local health food store but was unaware that it contained the GHB analog 1,4-butanediol (BD). After frequent use, he realized that he had become dependent on the product and was trying to wean himself off when he died. In April 2002, the man's widow reached an undisclosed settlement with the manufacturer claiming consumers were not warned that this active ingredient is converted into GHB in the body.

Source: Department of Justice, 2002.

6. All daily activities revolve around the substance — important social, occupational, or recreational activities are given up or reduced because of substance use.

7. The person withdraws from family activities and hobbies to use the substance privately or spend more time with substance-using friends.

8. The person continues use of the substance despite recognizing that it causes social, occupational, legal, or medical problems.

A review of the previous discussion about the properties of CNS depressants reveals that severe dependence on these drugs can satisfy all these *DSM-IV* criteria; thus, according to the APA, dependence on CNS depressants is classified as a form of mental illness.

The principal types of people who are most inclined to abuse CNS depressants include the following:

1. Those who seek sedative effects to deal with emotional stress, to try to escape from problems they are unable to face. Sometimes, these individuals are able to persuade clinicians to administer depressants for their problems; at other times, they self-medicate with depressants that are obtained illegally.

2. Those who seek the excitation that occurs, especially after some tolerance has developed. Instead of depression, they feel exhilaration and euphoria.

3. Those who try to counteract the unpleasant effect or withdrawal associated with other drugs of abuse, such as some stimulants, lysergic acid diethylamide (LSD), and other hallucinogens.

4. Those who use sedatives in combination with other depressant drugs such as alcohol and heroin. Alcohol plus a sedative gives a faster high but can be dangerous because of the multiple depressant effects and synergistic interaction. Heroin users often resort to barbiturates if their heroin supply is compromised.

As mentioned earlier, depressants are commonly abused in combination with other drugs (*Drug Facts and Comparisons* 2005). In particular, opioid narcotic users take barbiturates, benzodiazepines, and other depressants to augment the effects of a weak batch of heroin or to counteract a rapidly

shrinking supply. Chronic narcotic users also claim that depressants help to offset tolerance to opioids, thereby requiring less narcotic to achieve a satisfactory response by the user. It is not uncommon to see joint dependence on both narcotics and depressants.

Another common use of depressants is by alcoholics to soften the withdrawal from ethanol or to help create a state of intoxication without the telltale odor of alcohol. Interestingly, similar strategies are also used therapeutically to help detoxify the alcoholic. For example, long-acting barbiturates or benzodiazepines are often used to wean an alcohol-dependent person away from ethanol. Treatment with these depressants helps to reduce the severity of withdrawal symptoms, making it easier and safer for alcoholics to eliminate their drug dependence.

Finally, as already mentioned, CNS depressants are used in conjunction with alcohol to commit sexual assaults. Because these drugs are sedating, remove inhibitions, and can induce a temporary state of amnesia, they are sometimes secretly added to an alcoholic beverage to incapacitate the intended victim of a date rape. Recent statistics suggest that about 40% of women who are sexually assaulted have alcohol in their blood, 20% have cannabinoids (from marijuana use), 8% have cocaine, 8% have a benzodiazepine, 4% have amphetamines, 4% have GHB, less than 2% have opioid narcotics, and 1% have barbiturates (Elsohly and Salamone 1999).

In general, those who chronically abuse the CNS depressants prefer (1) the short-acting barbiturates, such as pentobarbital and secobarbital; (2) the barbiturate-like depressants, such as glutethimide, methyprylon, and methaqualone; or (3) the faster-acting benzodiazepines, such as diazepam (Valium), alprazolam (Xanax), or lorazepam (Ativan).

Dependence on sedative-hypnotic agents can develop insidiously. Often, a long-term patient is treated for persistent insomnia or anxiety with daily exposures to a CNS depressant. When an attempt to withdraw the drug is made, the patient becomes agitated, unable to sleep, and severely anxious; a state of panic may be experienced when deprived of the drug. These signs are frequently mistaken for a resurgence of the medical condition being treated and are not recognized as part of a withdrawal syndrome to the CNS depressant. Consequently, the patient frequently resumes use of the CNS depressant, and the symptoms of withdrawal subside. Such conditions generally lead to a gradual increase in dosage as tolerance to the sedative-hypnotic develops. The patient becomes severely dependent on the depressant, both physically and psychologically, and the drug habit becomes an essential feature in the user's daily routines. Only after severe dependence has developed does the clinician often realize what has taken place. The next stage is the unpleasant task of trying to wean the patient from the drug (**detoxification**) with as little discomfort as possible.

The prevalence of abuse of illicit CNS depressants appeared to peak in the early 1980s for 12th graders. Illegal use of these drugs then decreased dramatically until 1992, at which time abuse appears to have rebounded (see Table 6.5).

TREATMENT FOR WITHDRAWAL

All sedative-hypnotics, including alcohol and benzodiazepines, can produce physical dependence and a barbiturate-like withdrawal syndrome if taken in sufficient dosage over a long period. Withdrawal symptoms include anxiety, tremors, nightmares, insomnia, anorexia, nausea, vomiting, seizures, delirium, and maniacal activity.

Detoxification of patients is often done in groups to help provide support during this difficult time.

The duration and severity of withdrawal depend on the particular drug taken. With short-acting depressants, such as pentobarbital, secobarbital, and methaqualone, withdrawal symptoms tend to have a faster onset of action and be more severe. They begin 12 to 24 hours after the last dose and peak in intensity between 24 and 72 hours later. Withdrawal from longer-acting depressants, such as phenobarbital and diazepam, develops more slowly and is less intense; symptoms peak on the fifth to eighth day (Trevor and Lay 1998).

Not surprisingly, the approach to detoxifying a person who is dependent on a sedative-hypnotic depends on the nature of the drug itself (that is, to which category of depressants it belongs), the severity of the dependence, and the duration of action of the drug. The general objectives of detoxification are to eliminate drug dependence (both physical and psychological) in a safe manner while minimizing discomfort. Having achieved these objectives, it is hoped that the patient will be able to remain free of dependence on all CNS depressants.

Often, the basic approach for treating severe dependence on sedative-hypnotics is substitution with either pentobarbital or the longer-acting phenobarbital for the offending, usually shorter-acting, CNS depressant. Once substitution has occurred, the long-acting barbiturate dose is gradually reduced. Using a substitute is necessary because abrupt withdrawal for a person who is physically dependent can be dangerous, causing life-threatening seizures. This substitution treatment uses the same rationale as the treatment of heroin withdrawal by methadone replacement. Detoxification also includes supportive measures such as vitamins, restoration of electrolyte balance, and prevention of dehydration. The patient must be watched closely during this time because he or she will be apprehensive, confused, and unable to make logical decisions (O'Brien 1995).

If the person is addicted to both alcohol and barbiturates, the phenobarbital dosage must be in-

KEY TERMS

detoxification
elimination of a toxic substance, such as a drug, from the body and its effects

Table 6.5 Lifetime Prevalence of Abuse of CNS Depressants for 12th Graders

	1992	1995	1998	1999	2002	2004
Any illicit drug	40.7%	48.4%	54.1%	54.7%	53.0%	51.1%
Barbiturates	5.5%	7.4%	8.7%	8.9%	9.5%	9.9%
All depressants (including benzodiazepines)	6.1%	7.6%	9.2%	NA	11.4%	10.4%

Source: L. Johnston. *Drug Abuse Survey*. Lansing, MI: University of Michigan, 2004. Available www.monitoringthefuture.org.

creased to compensate for the double withdrawal. Many barbiturate addicts who enter a hospital to be treated for withdrawal are also dependent on heroin. In such cases, the barbiturate dependence should be addressed first because the associated withdrawal can be life-threatening. Detoxification from any sedative-hypnotic should take place under close medical supervision, typically in a hospital (O'Brien 1995).

It is important to remember that elimination of physical dependence is not a cure. The problem of psychological dependence can be much more difficult to handle. If an individual is abusing a CNS depressant because of emotional instability, personal problems, or a very stressful environment, eliminating physical dependence alone will not solve the problem and drug dependence is likely to recur. These types of patients require intense psychological counseling and must be trained to deal with their difficulties in a more constructive and positive fashion. Without such psychological support, benefits from detoxification will only be temporary, and therapy will ultimately fail.

■ DEPRESSANTS

Natural Substances

Some plants that contain naturally occuring CNS depressants are included in herbal products or made into herbal teas for relaxation or as treatment for sleep problems (Kuribara et al. 2000). Probably the best known of this group is the kava kava plant (*Piper methysticum*). Drinks and bars containing extracts from kava kava root are legally available in many health food stores, are especially popular in Polynesian populations, and are sometimes used in religious ceremonies. The extract is prepared from the part of the kava kava plant beneath the surface of the ground. Small amounts of kava kava can produce euphoria and increased sociability, whereas larger doses cause substantial relaxation, lethargy, relaxed lower limbs, and eventually sleep (Boerner et al. 2003). Some users may experience visual and auditory hallucinations that can last 1 to 2 hours. Some users report that kava kava drinks can make the mouth numb much like topical local anesthetics used by dentists.

A second type of common herb that contains CNS depressants belong to the *Datura* family of plants. Although these botanicals are typically associated with hallucinogenic effects, in smaller amounts they sometimes can cause sedation and even induce sleep. Examples of these plants include *Datura inoxia* (Devil's weed) and *Datura strammonium* (jimson weed or thornapple). The active ingredients in these plants are typically anticholinergic drugs such as atropine or scopolamine. In lower doses, these herbs, especially if they contain scopolamine, have been used to encourage sleep. In fact, the actions of the herbs are somewhat similar to the OTC antihistamine-containing sleep aids, which also work due to their anticholinergic actions. In higher doses, both atropine and scopolamine can cause hallucinogenic effects. The anticholinergic actions of these herbs can be quite annoying and include constipation, dry mouth, and blurred vision, just to mention a few.

Discussion Questions

1. Why have benzodiazepine drugs replaced the barbiturates as the sedative-hypnotic drugs most prescribed by physicians?

2. Which features of CNS depressants give them abuse potential?

3. Why is long-term use of the benzodiazepines more likely to cause dependence than short-term use?

4. Why are some physicians careless when prescribing benzodiazepines for patients suffering from severe anxiety?

5. Currently, sleep aid products are available OTC. Should the FDA also allow sedatives to be sold without a prescription? Support your answer.

6. Are there any real advantages to using barbiturates as sedatives or hypnotics? Should the FDA remove them from the market?

7. What types of people are most likely to abuse CNS depressants? Suggest ways to help these people avoid abusing these drugs.

8. What is the appeal for using GHB? Why is it used to commit sexual assaults?

9. What dangers are associated with treating individuals who are severely dependent on CNS depressants?

10. Why are CNS depressants often combined with alcohol, and what is the consequence?

Key Terms

barbiturates 164

benzodiazepines 164

antihistamines 165

sedatives 165

anxiolytic 165

hypnotics 165

amnesiac 165

anesthesia 166

REM sleep 169

paradoxical effects 169

club drug 171

detoxification 179

Summary

1 Several unrelated drug groups cause CNS depression, but only a few are actually used clinically for their depressant properties. The most frequently prescribed CNS depressants are benzodiazepines, which include drugs such as Valium, Ambien, and Xanax. Barbiturates once were popular but, because of their severe side effects, they are no longer prescribed by most clinicians. Much like barbiturates, drugs such as chloral hydrate, glutethimide, and methaqualone are little used today. Finally, some OTC and prescription antihistamines, such as diphenhydramine, hydroxyzine, and promethazine, are used for their CNS depressant effects.

2 The clinical value of CNS depressants is dose-dependent. When used at low doses, these drugs relieve anxiety and promote relaxation (*sedatives*). When prescribed at higher doses, they can cause drowsiness and promote sleep (*hypnotics*). When administered at even higher doses, some of the depressants cause anesthesia and are used for patient management during surgery.

3 Because CNS depressants can relieve anxiety and reduce stress, they are viewed as desirable by many people. If used frequently over long periods, however, they can cause tolerance that leads to dependence.

4 The principal reason that benzodiazepines have replaced barbiturates in the treatment of stress and insomnia is that benzodiazepines have a greater margin of safety and are less likely to alter sleep patterns. Benzodiazepines enhance the GABA transmitter system in the brain through a specific receptor, whereas the effects of barbiturates are less selective. Even though benzodiazepines are safer than barbiturates, dependence and significant withdrawal problems can result if the former drugs are used indiscriminately.

5 Often, benzodiazepine dependence occurs in patients who suffer stress or anxiety disorders and are under a physician's care. If the physician is not careful and the cause of the stress is not resolved, drug treatment can drag on for weeks or months. After prolonged benzodiazepine therapy, tolerance develops to the drug; when benzodiazepine use is stopped, withdrawal occurs, which itself causes agitation. A rebound response to the drug might resemble the effects of emotional stress (agitation), so use of benzodiazepine is continued. In this way, the patient becomes severely dependent.

6 The short-acting CNS depressants are preferred for treatment of insomnia. These drugs help the patient get to sleep and then are inactivated by the body; when the user awakens the next day, he or she is less likely to experience residual effects than with long-acting drugs. The short-acting depressants are also more likely to be abused because of their relatively rapid onset and intense effects. In contrast, the long-acting depressants are better suited to treating persistent problems such as anxiety and stress. The long-acting depressants are also used to help wean dependent people from their use of short-acting compounds such as alcohol.

7 Many antihistamines cause sedation and drowsiness due to their anticholinergic effects. Several of these agents are useful for short-term relief of anxiety and are available in OTC sleep aids. The effectiveness of these CNS depressants is usually less than that of benzodiazepines. Because of their anticholinergic actions, antihistamines can cause some annoying side effects. These agents are not likely to be used for long periods; thus, dependence or serious abuse usually does not develop.

8 The people most likely to abuse CNS depressants include individuals who (1) use drugs to relieve continual stress; (2) paradoxically feel euphoria and stimulation from depressants; (3) use

depressants to counteract the unpleasant effects of other drugs of abuse, such as stimulants; and (4) combine depressants with alcohol and heroin to potentiate the effects.

9 The basic approach for treating dependence on CNS depressants is to detoxify the individual in a safe manner while minimizing his or her discomfort. This state is achieved by substituting a long-acting barbiturate or benzodiazepine, such as phenobarbital or Valium, for the offending CNS depressant. The long-acting drug causes less severe withdrawal symptoms over a longer period of time. The dependent person is gradually weaned from the substitute drug until he or she is depressant-free.

10 GHB is a naturally occurring substance related to the neurotransmitter GABA that has been used for its sedating, euphorigenic, and muscle-building properties. It has also been used to debilitate victims of date rape during sexual assaults. Because of concerns that this substance is frequently abused, GHB was classified as a Schedule I drug in 2000. However, GHB analogs can be purchased legally with the disclaimer they "are not for human consumption."

11 Some plants such as kava kava that contain naturally occurring CNS depressants are included in herbal teas for relaxation or treatment of insomnia.

References

American Psychiatric Association. "Substance Related Disorders." In *Diagnostic and Statistical Manual of Mental Disorders Text Revision*, 4th ed., 191–295. Washington, DC: APA, 2000.

Associated Press. "Woman Who Used Halcion Defense Hangs Self." *Salt Lake Tribune* 248 (1994): D-3.

Boerner, R., H. Sommer, W. Berger, U. Kuhn, U. Schmidt, and M. Manner. "Kava Kava Extract LI 150 Is as Effective as Opipramol and Buspirone in Generalized Anxiety Disorder." *Phytomedicine* 10 Supplement 4 (2003): 38–49.

Brockhaven, F., C. Khan, and F. Zitman. "Dependence Potential of Antidepressants Compared to Benzodiazepines." *Progress in Neurpsychopharmacology Biological Psychiatry* 26 (2002): 939–943.

Carter, L., L. Flores, H. Wu, C. Weibin, A. Unzeitig, A. Coop, and C. France. "The Role of GABA-B Receptors in the Discriminative Stimulus Effects of GHB in Rats: Time Course and Antagonism Studies." *Journal of Pharmacology and Experimental Therapeutics* 305 (2003): 668–674.

Charney, D., S. Mihic, and R. Harris. "Hypnotics and Sedatives." In *The Pharmacological Basis of Therapeutics*, 10th ed., edited by J. Hardman and L. Limbird, 399–427. New York: McGraw-Hill, 2001.

"Club Drugs." NINA Infofax (22 May 2000). Available http://165.112.78.61/Infofax/clubdrugs.html.

"Common Substances of Abuse." *Diagnosis and Treatment of Drug Abuse in Family Practice* (22 May 2000). Available www.165.112.78.61/Diagnosis-Treatment/substances.html.

Craig, K., H. Gomez, J. McMannus, and T. Bania. "Severe Gamma-Hydroxybutyrate Withdrawal: A Case Report and Literature Review." *Journal of Emergency Medicine* 18 (2000): 65–70.

Dean, W., J. Morgenthaler, and S. Fowkes. *GHB: The Natural Mood Enhancer: The Authoritative Guide to Its Responsible Use.* Petaluma, CA: Smart Publications, 1997.

DeMaria, P., R. Sterling, and S. Weinstein. "The Effect of Stimulant and Sedative Use on Treatment Outcome of Patients Admitted to Methadone Maintenance Treatment." *American Journal of Addiction* 9 (2000): 145–153.

Drug Facts and Comparisons, 59th ed. St. Louis, MO: Wolters Kluwar Health, 2005: 1166–1187.

Elsohly, M., and S. Salamone. "Prevalence of Drugs Used in Cases of Alleged Sexual Assault." *Journal of Analytical Toxicology* 23 (1999): 141–146.

Galloway, G., S. Frederick, F. Staggers, M. Gonzales, S. Stalcup, and D. Smith. "Gamma-Hydroxybutyrate: An Emerging Drug of Abuse That Causes Physical Dependence." *Addiction* 92 (1997): 89–96.

"Gamma Hydroxybutyric Acid (GHB, Liquid X, Goop, Georgia Home Boy)." *DEA Bulletin* DEA/ODE #000612 (12 June 2000).

Gatzonis, S., E. Angelopoulos, E. Daskalopoulou, V. Mantouvalos, A. Chioni, C. Zournas, and A. Siafanas. "Convulsive Status Epilepticus Following Abrupt High-Dose Benzodiazepine Discontinuation." *Drug and Alcohol Dependence* 59 (2000): 95–97.

Gorman, J. "Treating Generalized Anxiety Disorder." *Journal of Clinical Psychiatry* 64 (2003): 24–29.

Halpert, A., M. Olmstead, and B. Beninger. "Mechanism and Abuse Liability of the Antihistamine Dimenhydrinate." *Neuroscience Biobehavioral Review* 26 (2002): 61–67.

Hebel, S. "Antidotes, Flumazenil." *Facts and Comparisons*. St. Louis, MO: Wolters Kluwer, 2000: 386–387.

Hobbs, W., T. Rall, and T. Verdoorn. "Hypnotics and Sedatives." In *The Pharmacological Basis of Therapeutics*, 9th ed., edited by J. Hardman and L. Limbird, 361–396. New York: McGraw-Hill, 1995.

Hughes, G., J. McElnay, C. Hughes, and P. McKenna. "Abuse/Misuse of Non-prescription Drugs." *Pharmacy World Science* 21 (1999): 251–255.

Internet Drug Index. "The Top 200 Prescriptions for 2003 by Number of US Prescriptions Dispensed" (December 2004). Available http://www.rxlist.com/top200.htm.

Johansson, B., M. Berglund, M. Hanson, C. Pohlen, and I. Persson. "Dependence on Legal Psychotropic Drugs Among Alcoholics." *Alcohol, Alcoholism* 38 (2003): 613–618.

Johnston, L. "Overall Teen Drug Use Continues Gradual Decline, But Use of Inhalants Rise" (21 December 2004). Available www.monitoringthefuture.org.

Kam, P., and F. Yoong. "Gamma-Hydroxybutyric Acid: An Emerging Recreational Drug." *Anesthesia* 53 (1998): 1195–1198.

Kosten, T., and L. Hollister. "Drugs of Abuse." In *Basic and Clinical Pharmacology*, 7th ed., edited by B. Katzung, 516–531. Stamford, CT: Appleton & Lange, 1998.

Kuribara, H., E. Kishi, M. Okada, and Y. Maruyama. "Anxiolytic Effect of Two Oriental Herbal Drugs in Japan Attributed to Honokiol from Magnolia Bark. *Journal of Pharmaceutical Pharmacology* 52 (2000): 1425–1429.

Lader, M. "Limitations on the Use of Benzodiazepines in Anxiety and Insomnia: Are They Justified?" *European Neuropsychopharmacology* 9 Supplement 6 (1999): S399–405.

Landis, B., and S. Bryant. "Mental Health Disorders." In *Pharmacotherapeutics, a Primary Care Clinical Guide*, edited by E. Youngkin, 747–799. Stamford, CT: Appleton & Lange, 1999.

Latner, A. "The Top 200 Drugs of 1999." *Pharmacy Times* 66 (2000): 16–32.

Leshner, A. E. "Club Drug Alert." *NIDA Notes* 14 (2000): 3 (posted 22 May 2000). Available www.165.112.78.61/NIDA_Notes/NNVOL14N6/DirRepVol14N6.html.

Lingenhoehl, K., R. Brom, J. Heid, P. Beck, W. Froestl, K. Kaupman, B. Bettler, and J. Mosbacher. "Gamma-Hydroxybutyrate Is a Weak Agonist Against Recombinant GABA (B) Receptors." *Neuropharmacology* 38 (1999): 1667–1673.

Longo, L., and B. Johnson. "Addiction: Part I. Benzodiazepines, Side Effects, Abuse Risks and Alternatives." *American Family Physician* 61 (2000): 2121–2128.

McEvoy, G., ed. *American Hospital Formulary Service Drug Information.* Bethesda, MD: American Society of Hospital Pharmacists, 2003.

Mioto, K., and B. Roth. "GHB Withdrawal." Austin, TX: Texas Commission on Alcohol and Drug Abuse, March 2001.

Mondanaro, J. *Chemically Dependent Women*. Lexington, MA: Lexington Books/D. C. Heath, 1988.

Morgenthaler, J., and D. Joy. *Special Report on GHB*. Petaluma, CA: Smart Publication, 1994.

"New Halcion Guidelines." *American Druggist* (January 1992): 14.

NIDA Notes. "What Are Club Drugs?" 14 (22 May 2000). Available http://165.112.78.61/NIDA_Notes/Nnvol14N6/whatare.html.

O'Brien, C. "Drug Addiction and Drug Abuse." In *The Pharmacological Basis of Therapeutics*, 9th ed., edited by J. Hardman and L. Limbird, 557–577. New York: McGraw-Hill, 1995.

O'Brien, C. "Drug Addiction and Drug Abuse." In *The Pharmacological Basis of Therapeutics*, 10th ed., edited by J. Hardman and L. Limbird, 621–642. New York, NY: McGraw-Hill, 2001.

Physicians' Desk Reference. 50th ed. (*PDR*). Montvale, NJ: Medical Economics, 1997.

Poldrugo, F., and G. Addolorato. "The Role of Gamma-Hydroxybutyrate Acid in the Treatment of Alcoholism: From Animal to Clinical Studies." *Alcohol, Alcoholism* 34 (1999): 15–34.

Publishers Group. "Street Drugs." Plymouth, MN: 2002. Available www.Streetdrugs.org.

Serafin, W., and K. Babe "Histamine, Bradykinin and Their Antagonists." In *The Pharmacological Basis of Therapeutics*, 9th ed., edited by J. Hardman and L. Limbird, 581–600. New York: McGraw-Hill, 1995.

Teter, C., and S. Guthrie. "A Comprehensive Review of MDMA and GHB: Two Common Club Drugs." *Pharmacotherapy* 21 (2001): 1486–1513.

Trevor, A., and W. Lay. "Sedative-Hypnotic Drugs." In *Basic and Clinical Pharmacology*, 7th ed., edited by B. Katzung, 354–371. Stamford, CT: Appleton & Lange, 1998.

U.S. Department of Justice (USDOJ). "National Drug Threat Assessment 2003." National Drug Intelligence Center, Product No. 2003-Q0317-001, January 2003.

U.S. Department of Justice (USDOJ). "Drugs, Youth and the Internet." Product No. 2002-R0430-002, August 2002a.

U.S. Department of Justice (USDOJ). "Information Bulletin. GHB Analogs." Product No. 2002-L0424-0034, 2002b.

Walker, B., and A. Ettenberg. "Benzodiazepines Modulation of Opiate Reward." Experimental Clinical Psychopharmacology 9 (2001): 191–197.

CHAPTER 7

Alcohol: Pharmacological Effects

Did You Know?

- Ethanol leads all other substances of abuse in treatment admissions.
- Ethanol is the only alcohol used for human consumption; the other alcohols are poisonous.
- Some wild animals and insects become drunk after seeking out and consuming alcohol-containing fermented fruit.
- The first recorded beer brewery was in existence in 3700 B.C.
- Alcohol-related deaths outnumber deaths related to other drugs of abuse (except tobacco) by a four to one margin.
- Low daily consumption of alcohol can reduce cardiovascular disease in older men and postmenopausal women.
- Women experience a higher blood alcohol level than men when consuming the same amount of alcohol per body weight.

- The lethal level of alcohol is between 0.4% and 0.6% by volume in the blood.
- The liver metabolizes alcohol at a constant rate, unaffected by the amount ingested.
- Among alcoholics, liver disorders account for approximately 10% to 15% of deaths.
- Fetal alcohol syndrome (FAS) is characterized by facial deformities, growth deficiencies, and mental retardation.
- The incidence of FAS is one in three infants born to alcoholic mothers.
- The damaging effects of alcohol tend to be greater for women than for men.
- Alcoholism is commonly associated with severe malnutrition.

On completing this chapter you will be able to:

◎ Explain how common alcohol (ethanol) is a drug.

◎ Explain the pharmacokinetic properties of alcohol and describe how they influence the effects of the drug.

◎ Explain the role of alcohol in "polydrug" abuse.

◎ Identify the possible physical effects of prolonged heavy ethanol consumption.

◎ Explain the potential cardiovascular benefits of moderate alcohol use.

◎ Describe FAS and its effects.

◎ Explain how prolonged consumption of alcohol affects the brain and nervous system, liver, digestive system, blood, cardiovascular system, sexual organs, endocrine systems, and kidneys, and how it leads to mental disorders and damage to fetuses.

◎ Explain why malnutrition is so common among alcoholics.

 Drugs and Society Online is a great source for additional drugs and society information for both students and instructors.
Visit **http://drugsandsociety.jbpub.com** to find a variety of useful tools for learning, thinking, and teaching.

Introduction

In this chapter and the next, we examine several aspects of alcohol use. This chapter focuses on how alcohol affects the body from a pharmacological perspective. Chapter 8 studies the social effects of this drug—mainly the effects and consequences of alcohol on an individual's personal and social life.

As a licit drug, alcohol is extensively promoted socially through advertising (King 2003). In fact, in 2002 more than $1 billion was spent on alcohol advertising in the media trying to convince prospective consumers of the benefits of alcohol-containing beverages (Washington 2003; see "Here and Now," Alcohol Ads Are for Kids). But more important, drinking is perceived as acceptable. The popularity of this drug is clear: In 2004, 76.8% of high school seniors had used alcohol sometime during their life; 70.6% used it during the previous year; 2.8% used alcohol daily; and 60.3% had been drunk sometime during their life (Johnston 2004). College youth also consume large quantities of alcohol and many authorities believe alcohol is the leading drug problem among this population (Center on Alcohol Marketing and Youth 2003), with 67% of full-time college students reporting alcohol use in the previous 30 days (CESAR FAX 2003).

This chapter focuses on the many adverse effects of alcohol on the human body. Overall, it provides you with a foundation to understand the pharmacological nature of alcohol. We hope that such an understanding of how this drug affects the various

Because of frequent advertising, use of alcohol is perceived as normal and acceptable.

organ systems of the body will lead to more responsible use and less abuse of alcohol. Because of its widespread consumption, alcohol leads all other addicting substances as a reason for treatment admissions. Almost 50% of the patients entering treatment for drug dependence in 1997 had abused alcohol (SAMHSA News 2000).

Here and Now

Alcohol Ads Are for Kids

A recent report from the Center on Alcohol Marketing and Youth at Georgetown University revealed that in 2001 and 2002 underage youth were more likely to hear radio ads promoting beer and other alcoholic beverages than people of legal drinking age. This is partially due to the fact that the alcohol radio advertising most often was placed on radio stations with "youth" music formats that routinely have a disproportionately large listening audience of 12- to 20-year-olds. These data suggest that the alcohol industry targets the underage population for its alcoholic products.

Source: Center on Alcohol Marketing and Youth. "Radio Daze: Alcohol Ads Tune in Underage Youth." Georgetown University (2 April 2003): 1, 2.

The Nature and History of Alcohol

Alcohol has been part of human culture since the beginning of recorded history. The technology for alcohol production is ancient. Several basic ingredients and conditions are needed to produce this substance: sugar, water, yeast, and warm temperatures.

The process of making alcohol, called **fermentation**, is a natural one. It occurs in ripe fruit and berries and even in honey that bees leave in trees. These substances contain sugar and water and are found in warm climates, where yeast spores are transported through the air. Animals such as elephants, baboons, birds, wild pigs, and bees will seek out and eat fermented fruit. Elephants under the influence of alcohol have been observed bumping into one another and stumbling around. Intoxicated bees fly an unsteady beeline toward their hives. Birds eating fermented fruit become so uncoordinated that they cannot fly or, if they do, crash into windows or branches. In fact, fermented honey, called **mead**, may have been the first alcoholic beverage.

The Egyptians had breweries 6000 years ago; they credited the god Osiris with introducing wine to humans. The ancient Greeks used large quantities of wine and credited a god, Bacchus (Dionysus), with introducing the drink. Today, we use the words *bacchanalia* and *dionysian* to refer to revelry and drunken events. The Hebrews were also heavy users of wine. The Bible mentions that Noah, just nine generations removed from Adam, made wine and became drunk.

Alcohol is produced by a single-celled microscopic organism, one of the yeasts, that breaks down sugar by a metabolic form of combustion, thereby releasing carbon dioxide and forming water and ethyl alcohol as waste products. Carbon dioxide creates the foam on a glass of beer and the fizz in champagne. Fermentation continues until the sugar supply is exhausted or the concentration of alcohol reaches the point at which it kills the yeast (12%–14%). Thus, 12% to 14% is the natural limit of alcohol found in fermented wines or beers.

The **distillation** device, or *still*, was developed by the Arabs around A.D. 800 and was introduced into medieval Europe around A.D. 1250. By boiling the fermented drink and gathering the condensed vapor in a pipe, a still increases the concentration of alcohol, potentially to 50% or higher. Because distillation made it easier for people to get drunk, it greatly intensified the problem of alcohol abuse. However, even before the invention of the still, alcoholic beverages had been known to cause problems in heavy users that resulted in severe physical and psychological dependence. But not until the past century did the concept of alcoholism as a disease develop (Mann et al. 2000). (See "Here and Now," A Century of Alcohol.)

Alcohol as a Drug

Alcohol (more precisely designated as **ethanol**), as a natural product of fermentation, is an extremely popular social beverage, the second most widely used and abused psychoactive drug (after caffeine), and widely misunderstood (Pociluyko 2003). Its impact on college students has been particularly disturbing, with reports stating that binge drinking among such individuals is commonplace; alcohol use has resulted in assaults (approximately 600,000/year), injuries (500,000/year), and even deaths (1400/year; NIAAA 2002). This psychoactive substance depresses the central nervous system (CNS) while influencing almost all major organ systems of the body. Alcohol is also an addictive drug in that it may produce a physical and behavioral dependence (*DSM-IV-TR* 2000).

KEY TERMS

fermentation
biochemical process through which yeast converts sugar to alcohol

mead
fermented honey often made into an alcoholic beverage

distillation
heating fermented mixtures of cereal grains or fruits in a still to evaporate and be trapped as purified alcohol

ethanol
consumable type of alcohol that is the psychoactive ingredient in alcoholic beverages; often called *grain alcohol*

Here and Now

A Century of Alcohol

An overwhelming need to consume alcohol (known today as alcoholism) was first described in the literature by Benjamin Rush in 1784, but the concept that excessive use of alcohol is a disease didn't really evolve until the past 100 years. This perspective was encouraged by the "temperance movement" of the late 19th century. Because of the ill effects of alcohol, temperance legally became "Prohibition" in 1919. *Prohibition* (alcohol made illegal) was initially successful in reducing consumption, but consumption began to rebound in the late 1920s. However, it has been suggested that Prohibition was repealed in 1933 not because it failed to reduce alcohol use but because of shifting policy during the Great Depression that argued liquor manufacturing would create jobs and provide taxes on alcoholic beverages that could fund government programs.

The second half of the 20th century saw the emergence of the belief that genetics plays a major role in alcoholism. This concept suggests that because of inherited traits, some families and individuals are more vulnerable to alcohol addiction than others. Researchers today are energetically moving forward to identify which genes might contribute to the development and expression of the addiction in an effort to improve prevention and treatment for alcoholism.

Source: Quindien, A. "America's Most Pervasive Drug Problem Is the Drug That Pretends It Isn't." *Salt Lake Tribune* (20 April 2000): A-11.

Although tradition and attitude are important factors in determining the use patterns of this substance, the typical consumer rarely appreciates the diversity of pharmacological effects caused by alcohol, the drug. The pharmacological action of alcohol accounts for both its pleasurable and CNS effects as well as its hazards to health and public safety.

ALCOHOL AS A SOCIAL DRUG

Why is alcohol often perceived as an acceptable adjunct to such celebrations as parties, birthdays, weddings, and anniversaries, and as a way of relieving stress and anxiety? Social psychologists refer to the perception of alcohol as a **social lubricant**. This term implies that drinking is misconceived as safely promoting conviviality and social interaction, and as an activity that bolsters confidence by repressing inhibitions and strengthening extroversion (Pociluyko 2003). Why do many people have to be reminded that alcohol is a drug like marijuana or cocaine and may have serious consequences for some people? Four reasons explain this misconception:

1. The use of alcohol is legal.
2. Through widespread advertising, the media promote the notion that alcohol consumption is as normal and safe as drinking fruit juices and soft drinks.
3. The distribution, advertisement, and sale of alcoholic beverages are widely practiced.
4. Alcohol use has a long tradition, dating back to 3000 B.C. (Royce 1989).

IMPACT OF ALCOHOL

Although many consider the effects of alcohol enjoyable and reassuring, the adverse pharmacological impacts of this drug are extensive, and its effects are associated with more than 100,000 deaths each year in the United States (Hanson and Li 2003; Special Report 1997). It is estimated that at some time during their lives, almost 50% of all Americans will be involved in an alcohol-

KEY TERMS

social lubricant
belief that drinking (misconceived as safe) represses inhibitions, strengthens extroversion, and leads to increased sociability

related traffic accident. The pharmacological effects of alcohol abuse cause severe dependence, which is classified as a psychiatric disorder according to *The Diagnostic and Statistical Manual of Mental Disorders,* fourth edition revised (*DSM-IV-TR* 2000) criteria. These effects also disrupt personal, family, social, and professional functioning and frequently result in multiple illnesses and accidents, violence, and crime (Hanson and Li 2003). Alcohol consumed during pregnancy can lead to devastating damage to offspring and is a principal cause of mental retardation in newborns (Hanson and Li 2003). After tobacco, alcohol is the leading cause of premature death in America. In the United States, approximately $167 billion is spent annually dealing with the social and health problems resulting from the pharmacological effects of alcohol (Quindien 2000). Of course, such estimates fall short in assessing the emotional upheaval and human suffering caused by this drug.

Despite all of the problems that alcohol causes, our free society has demanded access to this drug. At the same time, it is unthinkable to ignore the tremendous negative social impact of this drug. There are no simple answers to this dichotomy, yet clearly governmental and educational institutions could do more to protect members of society from the dangers associated with alcohol. The best weapons we have against the problems caused by alcohol are education, prevention, and treatment (see Chapter 17).

The Properties of Alcohol

Technically, alcohol is a chemical structure that has a hydroxyl group (OH, for one oxygen and one hydrogen atom) attached to a carbon atom (Pociluyko 2003). Of the many types of alcohol, several are important in this context. The first is **methyl alcohol** (*methanol* or *wood alcohol*), which is made from wood products. Its metabolites are poisonous. Small amounts (4 mL) cause blindness by affecting the retina, and larger amounts (80–150 mL) are usually fatal. Methyl alcohol is added to ethyl alcohol (*ethanol* or *grain alcohol*, the drinking type) intended for industrial use so that people will not drink it. A similar mixture is also sometimes added to illegally manufactured ("bootleg") liquor.

Different alcoholic beverages have a wide range of alcohol content.

Another type of poisonous alcohol, **ethylene glycol**, is used in antifreeze. A third type, **isopropyl alcohol**, is commonly used as rubbing alcohol and as an *antiseptic* (a solution for preventing the growth of microorganisms). These two types of alcohol are also poisonous if consumed. Pure ethyl alcohol (ethanol) is recognized as an official drug in the U.S. Pharmacopeia, although the various alcoholic beverages are not listed for medical use.

Alcohol can be used as a solvent for other drugs or as a preservative. It is used to cleanse, disinfect, and harden the skin and to reduce sweating. A 70% alcohol solution is an effective bactericide (Pociluyko 2003). However, it should not be used on open wounds because it will dehydrate the injured tissue and worsen the damage. Alcohol may be deliberately injected in or near nerves to treat severe pain; it causes local anesthesia and deterioration of the nerve.

In all alcoholic beverages—beer, wine, liqueurs or cordials, and distilled spirits—the psychoactive agent is the same, but the amount of ethanol varies (see Table 7.1). The amount of alcohol is

KEY TERMS

methyl alcohol
wood alcohol

ethylene glycol
alcohol used as antifreeze

isopropyl alcohol
rubbing alcohol, sometimes used as an antiseptic

Table 7.1 The Concentration of Ethanol in Common Alcoholic Beverages

TYPE OF BEVERAGE	CONCENTRATION OF ETHANOL
U.S. beers	4%–6%
Wine coolers	10%–12%
Cocktail and dessert wines	17%–20%
Liqueurs	22%–50%
Distilled spirits	40%–50%

expressed either as a percentage by volume or, in the older proof system, as a measurement based on the military assay method. To make certain that they were getting a high alcohol content in the liquor, the British military would place a sample on gunpowder and touch a spark to it. If the alcohol content exceeded 50%, it would burn and ignite the gunpowder. This test was "proof" that the sample was at least 50% alcohol. If the distilled spirits were "under proof," the water content would prevent the gunpowder from igniting. The percentage of alcohol volume is one-half the proof number. For example, 100-proof whiskey has a 50% alcohol content.

The Physical Effects of Alcohol

How does alcohol affect the body? Figure 7.1 illustrates how alcohol is absorbed into the body. After a drink, alcohol has direct contact with the mouth, esophagus, stomach, and intestine, acting as an irritant and an **anesthetic** (blocking sensitivity to pain). In addition, alcohol influences almost every organ system in the body after entering the blood-

KEY TERMS

anesthetic
a drug that blocks sensitivity to pain

blood alcohol concentration (BAC)
concentration of alcohol found in the blood, often expressed as a percentage

stream. Alcohol diffuses into the blood rapidly after consumption by passing (absorption process) through gastric and intestinal walls. Once the alcohol is in the small intestine, its absorption is largely independent of the presence of food, unlike in the stomach, where food retards absorption.

The effects of alcohol on the human body depend on the amount of alcohol in the blood, known as the **blood alcohol concentration (BAC)**. This concentration largely determines behavioral and physical responses to alcoholic beverages. Relative to behavior, circumstances in which the drinking occurs, the drinker's mood, and his or her attitude and previous experience with alcohol all contribute to the reaction to drinking. People demonstrate individual patterns of psychological functioning that may affect their reactions to alcohol as well. For instance, the time it takes to empty the stomach may be either reduced or accelerated as a result of anger, fear, stress, nausea, and the condition of the stomach tissues.

The blood alcohol level produced depends on the presence of food in the stomach, the rate of alcohol consumption, the concentration of the alcohol, and the drinker's body composition. Fatty foods, meat, and milk slow the absorption of alcohol, allowing more time for its metabolism and reducing the peak concentration in the blood. When alcoholic beverages are taken with a substantial meal, peak BACs may be as much as 50% lower than they would have been had the alcohol been consumed by itself. When large amounts of alcohol are consumed in a short period, the brain and other organs are exposed to higher peak concentrations. Generally, the more alcohol in the stomach, the greater the absorption rate. There is, however, a modifying effect of very strong drinks on the absorption rate. The absorption of drinks stronger than 100 proof is inhibited. This effect may be due to blocked passage into the small intestine or irritation of the lining of the stomach, causing mucus secretion, or both. (See "Here and Now," Half-Truths About Alcohol.)

Diluting an alcoholic beverage with water helps to slow down absorption, but mixing with carbonated beverages increases the absorption rate. The carbonation causes the stomach to empty its contents into the small intestine more rapidly, causing

1. **Mouth**—Alcohol is consumed orally.

2. **Stomach**—Alcohol goes right into the stomach. A little of the alcohol passes through the wall of the stomach and into the bloodstream. Most of the alcohol continues down into the small intestine.

3. **Small intestine**—Alcohol goes from the stomach into the small intestine. Most of the alcohol is absorbed through the walls of the intestine and into the bloodstream.

4. **Bloodstream**—The bloodstream carries the alcohol to all parts of the body, such as the brain, heart, and liver.

5. **Liver**—As the bloodstream carries the alcohol around the body, it passes through the liver. The liver changes the alcohol to water, carbon dioxide, and energy. The process is called *oxidation*. The liver can oxidize (change into water, carbon dioxide, and energy) only about one-half ounce of alcohol per hour. Thus, until the liver has time to oxidize all of the alcohol, the alcohol continues passing through all parts of the body, including the brain.

6. **Brain**—Alcohol goes to the brain almost as soon as it is consumed. It continues passing through the brain until the liver oxidizes all the alcohol into carbon dioxide, water, and energy.

FIGURE 7.1

How alcohol is absorbed in the body.

....

Source: National Institute on Alcohol Abuse and Alcoholism. *Alcohol Health and Research World.* Washington, DC: U.S. Department of Health and Human Services, 1988.

a more rapid "high." The carbonation in champagne has the same effect.

Once in the blood, distribution occurs as the alcohol uniformly diffuses throughout all tissues and fluids, including fetal circulation in pregnant women. Because the brain has a large blood supply, its activity is quickly affected by a high alcohol concentration in the blood. Body composition— the amount of water available for the alcohol to be dissolved in—is a key factor in BAC and distribution. The greater the muscle mass, the lower the BAC that will result from a given amount of alcohol. This relationship arises because muscle has more fluid volume than does fat. For example, if two men each weigh 180 pounds but one man has substantially more lean mass than the other man, the former will have a lower blood alcohol level after consuming 4 ounces of whiskey. The leaner man will show fewer effects. A woman of a weight equivalent to a man will have a higher blood alcohol level because women generally have a higher percentage of fat. Thus, they are affected more by identical drinks.

Alcoholic beverages contain almost no vitamins, minerals, protein, or fat—just large amounts of carbohydrates (Pociluyko 2003). Alcohol cannot

Here and Now

Half-Truths About Alcohol

Much is known about alcohol, but much more needs to be learned to effectively and safely manage its use. There are several half-truths that are commonly believed by the general public that should be clarified:

Belief: Alcohol, if used in moderation, is healthy for everyone.

Fact: Moderate drinking benefits only men older than 50 years of age and women who are post-menopausal. Even for these populations, the benefits appear to be minimal in persons who already have healthy lifestyles.

Belief: Pound for pound, women hold their liquor as well as men.

Fact: Because women have proportionally less body water and tend to metabolize alcohol more slowly than men, women become more intoxicated with comparable dose consumption per body weight.

Belief: A drink before bed induces sleep.

Fact: After moderate drinking, onset of sleep may be faster, but the sleep itself becomes restless, marked by frequent wakings and inability to get back to sleep.

Belief: If you don't feel drunk, it is okay to drive.

Fact: People are typically unable to determine accurately how much alcohol is in their system. For most states in the United States, 0.08%–0.1% alcohol in the blood is the legal threshold for driving (i.e., it is against the law to drive with this blood alcohol content or higher), but studies have shown that driving performance is significantly impaired at half this concentration.

Sources: "Your Health: Alcohol: The Whole Truth, Seven Half-Truths About Drinking, Exposed." *Consumer Reports* 64 (December 1999): 60–61; "FAQs on Alcohol Abuse and Alcoholism." NIAAA (2000). Available http://silk.nih.gov/silk/niaaa1/questions/q-a.htm#questions2; Greenfield 2002.

be used by most cells; it must be metabolized by an enzyme, **alcohol dehydrogenase**, which is found almost exclusively in the liver. Alcohol provides more calories per gram than does carbohydrate or protein and only slightly less than does pure fat. Because it can provide many calories, the drinker's appetite may be satisfied; as a result, he or she may not eat properly, causing malnutrition (Achord 1995). The tolerance that develops to alcohol is comparable to that observed with barbiturates (see Chapter 6). Some people have a higher tolerance for alcohol and can more easily disguise intoxication.

KEY TERMS

alcohol dehydrogenase
principal enzyme that metabolizes ethanol

ALCOHOL AND TOLERANCE

Repeated use of alcohol results in tolerance and in reduction in many of alcohol's pharmacological effects. As with other psychoactive drugs, tolerance to alcohol encourages increased consumption to regain its effects and can lead to severe physical and psychological dependence (O'Brien 2001). Tolerance to alcohol is similar to that seen with CNS depressants, such as the barbiturates and benzodiazepines. It consists of both an increase in the rate of alcohol metabolism (due to stimulation of metabolizing enzymes; see Chapter 5) and a reduced response by neurons and transmitter systems (particularly by increasing the activity of the inhibitory neurotransmitter, gamma-aminobutyric acid [GABA]) to this drug. Development of tolerance to alcohol is extremely variable; some users can consume large quantities of this drug with minor pharmacological effects. The tolerance-inducing changes caused by alcohol can also alter the body's response to other drugs (referred to as *cross-tolerance*; see Chapter 5) and can specifically reduce the effects of some other CNS depressants (O'Brien 2001).

Many chronic alcohol users learn to compensate for the motor impairments of this drug by modifying their patterns of behavior. These adjustments are referred to as **behavioral tolerance**. Examples of this adjustment include individuals altering and slowing their speech, walking more deliberately, or moving more cautiously to hide the fact that they have consumed debilitating quantities of alcohol.

ALCOHOL METABOLISM

Almost 95% of consumed alcohol is inactivated by liver metabolism. The liver metabolizes alcohol at a slow and constant rate and is unaffected by the amount ingested. Thus, if one can of beer is consumed each hour, the BAC will remain constant without resulting in intoxication. If more alcohol is consumed per hour, the BAC will rise proportionately because large amounts of alcohol that cannot be metabolized spill over into the bloodstream.

POLYDRUG USE

It is a common practice to take alcohol with other drugs, such as tobacco and even illegal substances (Hanson and Li 2003); this mode of consumption is known as **polydrug use**. Mixing alcohol with other types of drugs can intensify intoxication. This probably helps explain why marijuana users are more likely to combine their marijuana use with alcohol than with other drugs (Liquori et al. 2002). In a recent report, almost one-half of those seeking treatment for alcoholism also were treated for abuse of other drugs (SAMHSA News 2000).

The reasons why individuals combine alcohol with other drugs of abuse are not always apparent. The following explanations have been proposed (Hettema et al. 1999):

1. Alcohol enhances the reinforcing properties of other CNS depressants.
2. It decreases the amount of an expensive and difficult-to-get drug required to achieve the desired effect.

3. It helps to diminish unpleasant side effects of other drugs of abuse, such as the withdrawal caused by CNS stimulants (NIAAA 1993).
4. There is a common predisposition to use alcohol and other substances of abuse.

Clearly, coadministration of alcohol with other substances of abuse is a common practice that can be very problematic and result in dangerous interactions.

SHORT-TERM EFFECTS

The impact of alcohol on the CNS is most similar to that of sedative-hypnotic agents such as barbiturates. Alcohol depresses CNS activity at all doses (Pociluyko 2003), producing definable results.

At low to moderate doses, **disinhibition** occurs; this loss of conditioned reflexes reflects a depression of inhibitory centers of the brain. The effects on behavior are variable and somewhat unpredictable. To a large extent, the social setting and mental state determine the individual's response to such alcohol consumption. For example, alcohol can cause one person to become euphoric, friendly, and talkative but can prompt another to become aggressive and hostile. Low to moderate doses also interfere with motor activity, reflexes, and coordination. Often this impairment is not apparent to the affected person ("Your Health" 1999).

In moderate quantities, alcohol slightly increases the heart rate; slightly dilates blood vessels in the arms, legs, and skin; and moderately lowers blood pressure. It stimulates appetite, increases production of gastric secretions, and markedly stimulates urine output.

KEY TERMS

behavioral tolerance
compensation for motor impairments through behavioral pattern modification by chronic alcohol users

polydrug use
the concurrent use of multiple drugs

disinhibition
loss of conditioned reflexes due to depression of inhibitory centers of the brain

At higher doses, the social setting has little influence on the expression of depressive actions of the alcohol. The CNS depression incapacitates the individual, causing difficulty in walking, talking, and thinking. These doses tend to induce drowsiness and cause sleep. If large amounts of alcohol are consumed rapidly, severe depression of the brain system and motor control area of the brain occurs, producing incoordination, confusion, disorientation, stupor, anesthesia, coma, and even death.

The lethal level of alcohol is between 0.4% and 0.6% by volume in the blood (Pociluyko 2003). Death is caused by severe depression of the respiration center in the brain stem, although the person usually passes out before drinking an amount capable of producing this effect. Although

an alcoholic may metabolize the drug more rapidly than a light drinker, the toxicity level of alcohol stays about the same. In other words, it takes approximately the same concentration of alcohol in the body to kill a nondrinker as to kill someone who drinks on a regular basis. The amount of alcohol required for anesthesia is very close to the toxic level, which is why it would not be a useful anesthetic. See Table 7.2 for a summary of the psychological and physical effects of various BAC levels.

As a general rule, it takes as many hours as the number of drinks consumed to sober up completely. Despite widely held beliefs, drinking black coffee, taking a cold shower, breathing pure oxygen, and so forth will not hasten the sobering process. Stimulants such as coffee may help keep

Table 7.2 Psychological and Physical Effects of Various Blood Alcohol (Concentration Levels)

NUMBER OF DRINKS*	BLOOD ALCOHOL CONCENTRATION	PSYCHOLOGICAL AND PHYSICAL EFFECTS
1	0.02%–0.03%	No overt effects, slight mood elevation
2	0.05%–0.06%	Feeling of relaxation, warmth; slight decrease in reaction time and in fine muscle coordination
3	0.08%–0.09%	Balance, speech, vision, hearing slightly impaired; feelings of euphoria, increased confidence; loss of motor coordination
3–4	0.10%	Legal intoxication in all states; driving is illegal with this level (however, many states are changing or have changed the legal limit to 0.08%)
4	0.11%–0.12%	Coordination and balance becoming difficult; distinct impairment of mental faculties, judgment
5	0.14%–0.15%	Major impairment of mental and physical control; slurred speech, blurred vision, lack of motor skills
7	0.20%	Loss of motor control—must have assistance in moving about; mental confusion
10	0.30%	Severe intoxication; minimum conscious control of mind and body
14	0.40%	Unconsciousness, threshold of coma
17	0.50%	Deep coma
20	0.60%	Death from respiratory failure

Note: For each hour elapsed since the last drink, subtract 0.015% blood alcohol concentration, or approximately one drink.

*One drink = one beer (4% alcohol, 12 oz) or one highball (1 oz whiskey).

Source: Modified from data given in Ohio State Police Driver Information Seminars and the National Clearinghouse for Alcohol and Alcoholism Information, 5600 Fishers Lane, Rockville, MD 85206.

the drunk person awake but will not improve judgment or motor reflexes to any significant extent.

The Hangover

A familiar consequence of overindulgence is fatigue combined with nausea, upset stomach, headache, sensitivity to sounds, and ill temper—the *hangover* (Wiese 2000). These symptoms are usually most severe many hours after drinking, when little or no alcohol remains in the body. No simple explanation exists for what causes the hangover. Theories include accumulation of acetaldehyde (a metabolite of ethanol), dehydration of the tissues, poisoning due to tissue deterioration, depletion of important enzyme systems needed to maintain routine functioning, an acute withdrawal (or rebound) response, and metabolism of the impurities in alcoholic beverages.

The body loses fluid in two ways through alcohol's **diuretic** action, which sometimes results in dehydration: (1) the water content, such as in beer, increases the volume of urine, and (2) the alcohol depresses the center in the hypothalamus of the brain that controls release of a water conservation hormone (*antidiuretic hormone*). With less of this hormone, urine volume is further increased. Thus, after drinking heavily, especially the highly concentrated forms of alcohol, the person is thirsty. However, this effect by itself does not explain the symptoms of hangover.

The type of alcoholic beverage you drink may influence the hangover that results. Some people are more sensitive to particular alcohol impurities than others. For example, some drinkers have no problem with white wine but an equal amount of some red wines gives them a hangover. Whiskey, scotch, and rum may cause worse hangovers than vodka or gin, given equal amounts of alcohol, because vodka and gin have fewer impurities. There is little evidence that mixing different types of drinks per se produces a more severe hangover. It is more likely that more than the usual amount of alcohol is consumed when various drinks are sampled.

A common treatment for a hangover is to take a drink of the same alcoholic beverage that caused the hangover. This practice is called "taking the hair of the dog that bit you" (from the old notion that the burnt hair of a dog is an antidote to its bite). This treatment might help the person who is physically dependent, in the same way that giving heroin to a heroin addict eases the withdrawal symptoms. The "hair of the dog" method may work by depressing the centers of the brain that interpret pain or by relieving a withdrawal response. In addition, it may affect the psychological factors involved in having a hangover; distraction or focusing attention on something else may ease the effects.

Another remedy is to take an analgesic compound such as an aspirin–caffeine combination after drinking. This treatment is based on the belief that aspirin helps control headache; the caffeine may help counteract the depressant effect of the alcohol. In reality, these ingredients have no effect on the actual sobering-up process. In fact, products such as aspirin, caffeine, and Alka-Seltzer can irritate the stomach lining to the point where the person feels worse.

DEPENDENCE

Because of the disinhibition, relaxation, and sense of well-being mediated by alcohol, some degree of psychological dependence often develops, and the use of alcoholic beverages at social gatherings may become routine. It is estimated that in the United States, more than 8 million persons meet the criteria for alcohol dependence and an additional 5.6 million meet the diagnostic criteria for alcohol abuse (Hanson and Li 2003). Unfortunately, many people become so dependent on the psychological influences of alcohol that they become compulsive, continually consuming it. These individuals can be severely handicapped because of their alcohol dependence and often become unable to function normally in society. People who have become addicted to this drug are called alcoholics.

Because of the physiological effects, physical dependence also results from the regular consumption of large quantities of alcohol. This consequence becomes apparent when ethanol use is

KEY TERMS

diuretic
a drug or substance that increases the production of urine

abruptly interrupted and withdrawal symptoms result. The severity of the withdrawal can vary according to the length and intensity of the alcohol habit. The prototypic withdrawal patterns are as follows (NIDA Diagnosis 2000):

Stage 1 (minor): Restlessness, anxiousness, sleeping problems, agitation, tremors, and rapid heartbeat

Stage 2 (major): "Minor" symptoms plus hallucinations, whole-body tremors, increased blood pressure, and vomiting

Stage 3 (delirium tremens): Fever, disorientation, confusion, seizures, and fatality in 3% to 5% of cases

Recovery from alcohol dependence is a long-term process. Because of the severe withdrawal and the need for behavioral adjustments, most people relapse several times before long-term abstinence is achieved. Even people who have not used alcohol for years may relapse under very stressful circumstances (NIDA Diagnosis 2000). The treatment of alcoholism is discussed in more detail in Chapter 8.

The Effects of Alcohol on Organ Systems and Bodily Functions

As mentioned earlier, BAC depends on the size of the person, presence of food in the stomach, rate of drinking, amount of carbonation, and ratio of muscle mass to body fat. Furthermore, alcohol has pervasive effects on the major organs and fluids of the body (Worman 2000). In fact, the effects of this substance on body functions potentially can be so profound and destructive that alcoholism (*severe dependence*) is now considered a disease (Mann et al. 2000). The pervasive effects of alcohol on bodily organs are discussed in greater detail in the next section.

BRAIN AND NERVOUS SYSTEM

Every part of the brain and nervous system is affected—and in extreme cases can be damaged—by alcohol (Figure 7.2 000). Alcohol suppresses subcortical inhibitions of the cortical control cen-

ters, resulting in disinhibition. In higher doses, it depresses the cerebellum, causing slurred speech and staggering gait. Very high doses depress the respiratory centers of the medulla, resulting in death (Fleming et al. 2001). Furthermore, alcohol alters the production and functioning of transmitters such as dopamine, serotonin, GABA, and brain endorphins (Hettema et al. 1999). A recent report suggests that even cannabinoid receptors (see Chapter 13)—the targets of the active ingredients in marijuana—are affected by alcohol (ASAM News 2003). These neurochemical effects contribute to the fact that alcohol consumption can aggravate underlying psychiatric disorders such as depression and schizophrenia (Bertolote et al. 2004) and may suggest novel ways to develop more effective therapies (ASAM News 2003).

Heavy drinking over many years may result in serious mental disorders and irreversible damage to the brain and peripheral nervous system, leading to permanently compromised mental function

A normal liver (*top*) as it would be found in a healthy human body. An abnormal liver (*bottom*) that exhibits the effects of moderate to heavy alcohol consumption.

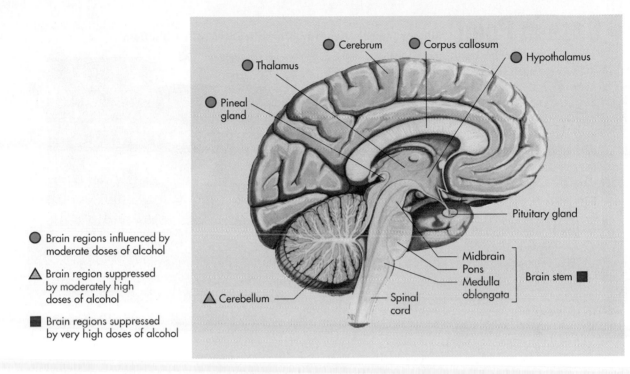

Brain regions influenced by moderate doses of alcohol

Brain region suppressed by moderately high doses of alcohol

Brain regions suppressed by very high doses of alcohol

FIGURE 7.2

The principal control centers of the brain affected by alcohol consumption. Note that all areas of the brain are interconnected

and memory and alterations in other brain systems (Preidt 2003).

LIVER

Among alcoholics, liver disorders are responsible for 10% to 15% of deaths (Worman 2000). There are three stages of alcohol-induced liver disease (Worman 2000). In the first stage, known as *alcoholic fatty liver,* liver cells increase the production of fat, resulting in an enlarged liver. This direct toxic effect on liver tissue is known as the **hepatotoxic effect**. This effect is reversible and can disappear if alcohol use is stopped. Several days of drinking five or six alcoholic beverages each day produces fatty liver in males. For females, as few as two drinks of hard liquor per day several days in a row can produce the same condition. After several days of abstaining from alcohol, the liver returns to normal.

The second stage develops as the fat cells continue to multiply. Generally, irritation and swelling that result from continued alcohol intake cause **alcoholic hepatitis**. At this stage, chronic inflammation sets in and can be fatal. This second stage is also reversible if the intake of alcohol ceases.

Unlike stages 1 and 2, stage 3 is not reversible. Scars begin to form on the liver tissue during this stage. These scars are fibrous, and they cause

KEY TERMS

hepatotoxic effect
a situation in which liver cells increase the production of fat, resulting in an enlarged liver

alcoholic hepatitis
the second stage of alcohol-induced liver disease in which chronic inflammation occurs; it is reversible if alcoholic consumption ceases

►Case in Point   Mickey Mantle Dies from Complications of Alcoholism

Mickey Mantle, the legendary centerfielder for the New York Yankees, died August 14, 1995, at the age of 63, from complications of alcoholism. During his heyday as a baseball star, his heavy drinking was discreetly hidden from adoring fans. It wasn't until well after his retirement from baseball that Mantle checked himself into a treatment clinic and admitted publicly that he had been severely dependent on alcohol for most of his life. He sought professional treatment only after doctors warned Mantle that his drinking habits had almost destroyed his liver. Despite heroic attempts to save Mantle's life with a liver transplant in June of the same year, a cancer from the diseased liver spread rapidly, resulting in death only two months later.

Mickey Mantle

Sources: Knight-Ridder/Tribune News Service, 14 August 1995, p. 814K6829; "Mickey Mantle" (24 April 2004). Available fixed reference.org/en/20040424/wikipedia/Mickey_Mantle.

hardening of the liver as functional tissue shrinks and deteriorates. This condition of the liver is known as **cirrhosis** and often is fatal. (See "Case in Point," Mickey Mantle Dies from Complications of Alcoholism.)

The liver damage caused by heavy alcohol consumption can cause problems when taking drugs that affect liver function. For example, the over-the-counter analgesic acetaminophen (Tylenol) can have a deleterious effect on the liver, especially when the function of this organ has already been compromised by alcohol (Ramack 2004).

DIGESTIVE SYSTEM

The digestive system consists of gastrointestinal structures involved in processing and digesting food and liquids; it includes the mouth, pharynx, esophagus, stomach, and small and large intestines. As alcohol travels through the digestive system, it irritates tissue and can even damage the tissue lining as it causes acid imbalances, inflammation, and acute gastric distress. Often, the result is *gastritis* (an inflamed stomach) and heartburn. The more frequently consumption takes place, the greater the irritation. One out of three heavy drinkers suffers from chronic gastritis. Furthermore, the heavy drinker has double the probability of developing cancer of the mouth and esophagus because alcohol passes these two organs on the way to the stomach.

Prolonged heavy use of alcohol may cause ulcers, hiatal hernia, and cancers throughout the digestive tract. The likelihood of cancers in the mouth, throat, and stomach dramatically increases (15 times) if the person is also a heavy smoker (Lee et al. 2005). The pancreas is another organ associated with the digestive system that can be damaged by heavy alcohol consumption. Alcohol can cause pancreatitis, pancreatic cirrhosis, and alcoholic diabetes (Hayakawa et al. 2002; NIAAA 1997).

KEY TERMS

cirrhosis
scarring of the liver and formation of fibrous tissues; results from alcohol abuse; irreversible

BLOOD

High concentrations of alcohol diminish the effective functioning of the *hematopoietic* (blood-building) system. They decrease production of red blood cells, white blood cells, and platelets. Problems with clotting and immunity to infection are not uncommon among alcohol abusers. Often, the result is lowered resistance to disease. Heavy drinking appears to affect the bone marrow, where various blood cells are formed. The suppression of the bone marrow can contribute to anemia, in which red blood cell production cannot keep pace with the need for those cells. Heavy drinkers are also likely to develop alcoholic bleeding disorders because they have too few platelets to form clots (NIAAA 1997; Schafer 1999).

CARDIOVASCULAR SYSTEM

The effects of ethanol on the cardiovascular system have been extensively studied, but much remains unknown. Ethanol causes dilation of blood vessels, especially in the skin. This effect accounts for the flushing and sensation of warmth associated with alcohol consumption.

The long-term effects of alcohol on the cardiovascular system are dose-dependent. Some studies have suggested that regular light to moderate drinking (two or fewer glasses of wine per day) actually reduces the incidence of heart diseases such as heart attacks, strokes, and high blood pressure by 20% to 40% in some populations. The type of alcoholic beverage consumed does not appear to be important as long as the quantity of alcohol consumed is moderate (1–2.5 ounces per day; "Your Health" 1999). Although the precise explanation for this coronary benefit is not known, it appears to be related to the effects of moderate alcohol doses in relieving stress and increasing the blood concentration of high-density lipoproteins (HDL). HDL is a molecular complex used to transport fat through the bloodstream, and its levels are negatively correlated with cardiovascular disease. In addition, moderate levels of alcohol decrease the formation of blood clots that can plug arteries and deprive tissues of essential oxygen and nutrients. The populations most likely to benefit from the protective properties of moderate levels of alcohol are men older than 50 years of age and postmenopausal women. Moderate drinking on a daily average is approximately one drink (e.g., a glass of wine) for women and two drinks for men. Drink-

ing more than this amount can result in increased health risks that more than offset the benefits (Biotech Week 2004).

The cardiovascular protective effect of moderate drinking may be at least partially race-specific. A recent report suggests that alcohol use that prevents cardiovascular disease in white males may actually increase heart disease in black men (Fuchs 2004).

Because of the potential for developing addiction to alcohol and the increased health risk with heavy drinking, most doctors would not encourage a nondrinker to start to consume alcohol in an attempt to gain a health benefit. In addition, even in those populations most likely to benefit from moderate alcohol consumption, the benefit is likely to disappear in persons who already have healthy lifestyles that include low-fat diets, stress and weight management techniques, and regular exercise ("Your Health" 1999). In general, most clinicians believe that alcohol use kills more people (approximately 100,000/year) than it saves, and those it kills tend to be younger (Hanson and Li 2003; Special Report 1997).

Chronic intense use of alcohol changes the composition of heart muscle by replacing it with fat and fiber, resulting in a heart muscle that becomes enlarged and flabby. Congestive heart failure from **alcoholic cardiomyopathy** often occurs when heart muscle is replaced by fat and fiber. Other results of alcohol abuse that affect the heart are irregular heartbeat or *arrhythmia*, high blood pressure, and stroke. A common example of damage is "holiday heart," so called because people drinking heavily over a weekend turn up in the emergency room with a dangerously irregular heartbeat. Chronic excessive use of alcohol by people with arrhythmia causes congestive heart failure. Malnutrition and vitamin deficiencies associated with prolonged heavy drinking also contribute to cardiac abnormalities (Fairfield and Fletcher 2002).

KEY TERMS

alcoholic cardiomyopathy
congestive heart failure due to the replacement of heart muscle with fat and fiber

SEXUAL ORGANS

Although alcohol lowers social inhibition, its use interferes with sexual functioning. As Shakespeare said in *Macbeth*, alcohol "provokes desire, but it takes away the performance." Continued alcohol use causes *prostatitis,* which is an inflammation of the prostate gland. This condition directly interferes with a man's ability to maintain an adequate erection during sexual stimulation. Another frequent symptom of alcohol abuse is atrophy of the testicles, which results in lowered sperm count and diminished hormones in the blood (Dhawan and Sharma 2002).

ENDOCRINE SYSTEM

As mentioned in Chapter 4, endocrine glands release hormones into the bloodstream. The hormones function as messengers that directly affect cell and tissue function throughout the body. Alcohol abuse alters endocrine functions by influencing the production and release of hormones, and affects endocrine regulating systems in the hypothalamus, pituitary, and gonads. Because of alcohol abuse, levels of *testosterone* (the male sex hormone) may decline, resulting in sexual impotence, breast enlargement, and loss of body hair in men. Women experience menstrual delays, ovarian abnormalities, and infertility (NIAAA 1997).

KIDNEYS

Frequent abuse of alcohol can severely damage the kidneys. The resulting decrease in kidney function diminishes this organ's ability to process blood and properly form urine and can result in serious metabolic problems. Another conse-

quence of impaired kidney function in alcoholics is that they tend to experience more urinary tract infections than do nondrinkers or moderate drinkers (NIAAA 1997).

MENTAL DISORDERS AND DAMAGE TO THE BRAIN

Long-term heavy drinking can severely affect memory, judgment, and learning ability (Uckerman et al. 2003). **Wernicke-Korsakoff's syndrome** is a characteristic psychotic condition caused by alcohol use and the associated nutritional and vitamin deficiencies. Patients who are brain-damaged cannot remember recent events and compensate for their memory loss with *confabulation* (making up fictitious events that even the patient accepts as fact).

THE FETUS

In pregnant women, alcohol easily crosses the placenta and often damages the fetus in cases of moderate to excessive drinking. It can also cause spontaneous abortion due to its toxic actions. Another tragic consequence of high alcohol consumption during pregnancy is **fetal alcohol syndrome (FAS)**, which is characterized by facial deformities, growth deficiency, mental retardation, and joint and limb abnormalities (Eustace et al. 2003; Larroque and Kaminski 1998). The growth deficiency occurs in embryonic development, and the child usually does not "catch up" after birth. The mild to moderate mental retardation does not appear to lessen with time, apparently because the growth impairment affects the functional development of the brain as well.

The severity of FAS appears to be dose-related: The more the mother drinks, the more severe the fetal damage. A safe lower level of alcohol consumption has not been established for pregnant women (Larroque and Kaminski 1998). Birthweight decrements have been found at levels corresponding to about two drinks per day, on average. Clinical studies have established that alcohol itself clearly causes the syndrome; it is not related to the effects of smoking, maternal age, parity (number of children a woman has borne), social class, or poor nutrition. One study reports

KEY TERMS

Wernicke-Korsakoff's syndrome
a psychotic condition connected with heavy alcohol use and associated vitamin deficiencies

fetal alcohol syndrome (FAS)
a condition affecting children born to alcohol-consuming mothers that is characterized by facial deformities, growth deficiency, and mental retardation

Fetal alcohol syndrome is characterized by facial deformities, as well as growth deficiency and mental retardation.

that 30%–45% of women who are moderate to heavy alcohol consumers will give birth to a child with FAS (*Life Science Weekly* 2004).

GENDER DIFFERENCES

Research has demonstrated that there are important pharmacological differences in how males and females respond to the consumption of alcohol. For example, it requires less alcohol to cause the same effects in women as in men (Baraona et al. 2001). This difference persists even after adjusting for the quantity of alcohol according to the differences in gender size. It is thought that at least part of the greater sensitivity of women to the effects of this drug is due to their tendency to metabolize alcohol more slowly than their male counterparts (Baraona et al. 2001). Other differences relate to their response to treatment. Gender differences in treatment outcomes likely reflect factors such as women's tendency to have a later onset of alcohol use and associated problems, a more positive family history, more marital disruption (Gomberg 2003), and more associated psychiatric disorders, such as depression, anxiety, and stress (*Women's Health Weekly* 2003). Although the reasons for these differences are unclear, they must be considered as researchers and clinicians try to elucidate the causes, consequences, and most effective treatments for alcoholism.

MALNUTRITION

As previously mentioned, malnutrition is a frequent and extremely serious consequence of severe alcoholism that tends to occur most often in less affluent alcoholics. It has been suggested that malnutrition exaggerates the damage that alcohol causes to the body's organs, especially the liver (Lieberman 2003). Malnutrition apparently arises so frequently in this population because many alcoholics find it difficult to eat a balanced diet with adequate caloric intake. Many alcoholics consume between 500 and 1000 kilocalories per day (2000 kilocalories per day is considered normal for an average man). In addition, most of the calories consumed by alcoholics come from alcohol, which contains 7 kilocalories/gram (less than fat, which contains 9 kilocalories/gram). The malnutrition problem is aggravated because alcohol's calories are empty—that is, alcohol does not contain other nutrients such as vitamins, minerals, protein, or fat (Pociluyko 2003). Because alcoholics may be deriving 50% or more of their usual caloric intake from alcoholic beverages, profound deficiencies in important nutrients result, leading to serious degeneration of health.

Discussion Questions

1. What evidence indicates that alcohol is a drug like marijuana, cocaine, or heroin?

2. Explain how alcohol is manufactured.

3. In the Western world, alcohol use has a long history. List and discuss some of these historical events, and describe how they affect present attitudes.

4. Explain how the effect of alcohol on brain function compares to that caused by other CNS depressants.

5. Explain how alcohol affects the mouth, stomach, small intestine, brain, liver, and bloodstream.

6. List at least five factors that affect the absorption rate of alcohol in the bloodstream.

7. Explain why alcohol is commonly consumed together with other drugs.

8. List three short-term effects of alcohol abuse.

9. Explain why moderate use of ethanol may prevent heart attacks.

10. Describe the symptoms and causes of a hangover.

11. What characterizes FAS?

12. How does gender affect responses to alcohol?

13. Why is malnutrition a common occurrence in alcoholics, and what are its consequences?

Key Terms

fermentation 189

mead 189

distillation 189

ethanol 189

social lubricant 190

methyl alcohol 191

ethylene glycol 191

isopropyl alcohol 191

anesthetic 192

blood alcohol concentration (BAC) 192

alcohol dehydrogenase 194

behavioral tolerance 195

polydrug use 195

disinhibition 195

diuretic 197

hepatotoxic effect 199

alcoholic hepatitis 199

cirrhosis 200

alcoholic cardiomyopathy 201

Wernicke-Korsakoff's syndrome 202

fetal alcohol syndrome (FAS) 202

Summary

1 Alcohol is considered a drug because it is a CNS depressant, and it affects both mental and physiological functioning.

2 Three types of poisonous alcohols are methyl alcohol, made from wood products; ethylene glycol, used as antifreeze; and isopropyl alcohol, used as an antiseptic. A fourth type, ethanol, is the alcohol used for drinking purposes.

3 The blood alcohol level produced depends on the presence of food in the stomach, the rate of alcohol consumption, the concentration of alcohol, and the drinker's body composition.

4 Alcohol depresses CNS activity at all doses. Low to moderate doses of alcohol interfere with motor activities, reflexes, and coordination. In moderate quantities, alcohol slightly increases heart rate; slightly dilates blood vessels in the arms, legs, and skin; and moderately lowers blood pressure. It stimulates appetite, increases production of gastric secretions, and at higher doses markedly stimulates urine output. The CNS depression incapacitates the individual, causing difficulty in walking, talking, and thinking.

5 Alcohol is commonly used in combination with other drugs (1) to enhance reinforcing properties; (2) to reduce the amount of expensive or hard-to-get drug required for an effect; (3) to reduce unpleasant side effects; or (4) because a predisposition for use of alcohol and other drugs exists.

6 Moderate daily alcohol use can reduce cardiovascular diseases in men older than 50 years of age and in postmenopausal women.

7 Long-term heavy alcohol use directly causes serious damage to nearly every organ and function of the body.

8 Prolonged heavy drinking causes various types of muscle disease and tremors. Heavy alcohol consumption causes irregular heartbeat. Heavy drinking over many years results in serious mental disorders and permanent, irreversible damage to the brain and peripheral nervous system. Memory, judgment, and learning ability can deteriorate severely.

9 Women who are alcoholics or who drink heavily during pregnancy have a higher rate of spontaneous abortions. Infants born to drinking mothers have a high probability of being afflicted with FAS. These children have characteristic patterns of facial deformities, growth deficiency, joint and limb irregularities, and mental retardation.

10 Alcohol has pervasive effects on the major organs and fluids of the body. Every part of the brain and nervous system is affected and can be damaged by alcohol. Among alcoholics, liver disorders include alcoholic fatty liver, alcoholic hepatitis, and cirrhosis. Alcohol also irritates tissue and damages the digestive system. Heavy use of alcohol seriously affects the blood, heart, sexual organs, endocrine system, and kidneys.

11 Malnutrition is a common occurrence in severe alcoholism. It is the result of decreased caloric intake by alcoholics and the diminished consumption of essential nutrients due to the nutritional deficiency of alcoholic beverages.

References

Achord, J. L. "Alcohol and the Liver." *Scientific American and Medicine* 2 (1995): 16–25.

ASAM News. "Cannabinoid System May Help Regulate Drinking." 18 (2003): 12.

Baraona, E., C. Abittan, K. Dohmen, M. Moretti, G. Pazzote, Z. Chayes, C. Schaefer, and C. Lieber. "Gender Differences in Pharmacokinetics of Alcohol." *Alcohol Clinical Experimental Research* 25 (2001): 502–507.

Bertolote, J., A. Fleishmann, D. DeLeo, and D. Wasserman. "Psychiatric Diagnoses and Suicide: Revisiting the Evidence." *Crisis* 25 (2004): 147–155.

Biotech Week. "Excess Drinking Shortens Life by 30 Years." *Morbidity and Mortality Weekly Report from U.S. CDC* 53 (20 October 2004): 866–870.

"Centerpiece: Alcohol in Perspective." *Wellness Letter* 9 (February 1993): 4–6.

Center on Alcohol Marketing and Youth. "Drops in the Bucket: Alcohol Industry 'Responsibility' Advertising on Television in 2001." *Georgetown University* (February 3, 2003): 1, 2.

CESAR FAX. "College Students Less Likely Than Other High School Graduates to Use Illicit Drugs and Cigarettes; More Likely to Use Alcohol." *University of Maryland* (March 10, 2003): 1.

Dhawan, K., and A. Sharma. "Prevention of Chronic Alcohol and Nicotine-Induced Azospermia, Sterility and Decreased Libido, by a Novel Tri substituted Benzoflavone Moiety." *Life Science* 71 (2002): 3059–3069.

Diagnostic and Statistical Manual of Mental Disorders, 4th ed., revised (*DSM-IV-TR*). Washington, DC: American Psychiatric Association, 2000.

Eustace, L., D. Kang, and D. Coombs. "Fetal Alcohol Syndrome: A Growing Concern for Health Care Professionals." *Journal of Obstetrical and Gynecological Neonatal Nursing* 32 (2003): 215–221.

Fairfield, K., and R. Fletcher. "Vitamins for Chronic Disease Prevention in Adults: Scientific Review." *Journal of the American Medical Association* 288 (2002): 1720.

Fleming, M., S. Mihic, and R. Harris. "Ethanol." In *The Pharmacological Basis of Therapeutics* 10th ed., edited by J. Hardman and L. Limbird 429–446. New York: McGraw-Hill, © 2001.

Fuchs, F. "Association Between Alcoholic Beverage Consumption and Incidence of Coronary Heart Disease in Whites and Blacks—The Atheroschlerosis Risk in Communities Studies." *American Journal of Epidemiology* 160 (2004): 466–474.

Gomberg, E. "Treatment for Alcohol-Related Problems: Special Populations: Research Opportunities." *Recent Developments in Alcoholism* 16 (2003): 313–333.

Greenfield, S. "Women and Alcohol Use Disorders." *Harvard Review Psychiatry* 10 (2002): 76–85.

Hanson, G. R., and T. K. Li. "Public Health Implications of Excessive Alcohol Consumption." *Journal of the American Medical Association* 289 (2003): 1031, 1032.

Hayakawa, T., S. Naruse, M. Kitagawa, H. Ishiguro, C. Jin, and T. Kondo. "Clinical Evidence of Pathogenesis in Chronic Pancreatitis." *Journal of Hepatobilliary Pancreatic Surgery* 9 (2002): 669–674.

Hettema, J., L. Corey, and K. Kendler. "A Multivariate Genetic Analysis of the Use of Tobacco, Alcohol and Caffeine in a Population Sample of Male and Female Twins." *Drug and Alcohol Dependency* 57 (1999): 9–78.

Hobbs, W., T. Rall, and T. Verdoorn. "Hypnotics and Sedatives: Ethanol." In *The Pharmacological Basis of Therapeutics,* 9th ed., edited by J. Hardman and L. Limbird, 361–396. New York: McGraw-Hill, 1995.

Johnston, L. "Overall Teen Drug Use Continues Gradual Decline: But Use of Inhalants Rise" (21 December 2004). Available www.monitoringthefuture.org.

King, N. "Radio Daze: Alcohol Ads Tune in Underage Youth." Pamphlet from the Center on Alcohol Marketing and Youth, Georgetown University, 2233 Wisconsin Ave., Suite 525, Washington, DC (2 April 2003).

Larroque, B., and M. Kaminski. "Prenatal Alcohol Exposure and Development at Preschool Age: Main Results of a French Study." *Alcoholism: Clinical and Experimental Research* 22 (1998): 295–303.

Lee, C., J. Lee, D. Wu, H. Hsu, E. Kao, H. Huang, et al. "Independent and Combined Effects of Alcohol Intake, Tobacco Smoking and Betel Quid Chewing on the Risk of Esophageal Cancer in Taiwan." *International Journal of Cancer* 113 (2005): 475–482.

Lieberman, C. "Relationship Between Nutrition, Alcohol Use, and Liver Disease." *Alcohol Research and Health* 27 (2003): 220–231.

Life Science Weekly. "Fetal Alcohol Syndrome Is Still a Threat, Says Publication." (28 September 2004).

Liquori, A., C. Gatto, and D. Jarrett. "Separate and Combined Effects of Marijuana and Alcohol on Mood, Equilibrium and Simulated Driving." *Psychopharmacology* 163 (2002): 399–405.

Mann, K., D. Herman, and A. Heinz. "One Hundred Years of Alcoholism: The Twentieth Century." *Alcohol and Alcoholism* 35 (2000): 10–15.

National Institute on Alcohol Abuse and Alcoholism (NIAAA). "Changing the Culture of Campus." *Alcohol Alert* 58 (October 2002): 1.

National Institute on Alcohol Abuse and Alcoholism (NIAAA). Publication 21 (1997). Available http://silk.nih.gov/silk/niaaa1/publication/iss21-1.htm.

National Institute on Alcohol Abuse and Alcoholism (NIAAA). *8th Special Report to Congress on Alcohol and Health.* (September 1993): 121.

NIDA Diagnosis. "Diagnosis and Treatment of Drug Abuse in Family Practice." (May 2000). Available 165.112.78.61/Diagnosis-treatment/Diagnosis6.html.

On completing this chapter you will be able to:

◎ Cite some of the latest statistics on the use of alcohol.

◎ Cite the countries with the highest and lowest rates of alcohol consumption.

◎ Discuss major ways alcohol is costly to our society.

◎ Discuss the main events of the temperance movement and the Prohibition era.

◎ Define alcoholism, and identify the general characteristics of an alcoholic.

◎ Cite some of the cultural differences for defining problem drinkers.

◎ Explain how culture influences the views about alcohol.

◎ List four cultural factors that affect our views about consuming alcohol.

◎ List four findings about alcohol consumption and college students.

◎ Provide at least three reasons why the effects of alcohol consumption differ in women and men.

◎ Understand the differences between codependency and enabling behaviors.

◎ List two major factors that alcohol treatment must consider.

Drugs and Society Online is a great source for additional drugs and society information for both students and instructors.
Visit **http://drugsandsociety.jbpub.com** to find a variety of useful tools for learning, thinking, and teaching.

Introduction

As a clerk here at this store, I see all kinds of people buying alcohol. Sometimes, you can tell who more than likely have big problems with alcohol by just looking at them. One man comes in about three times a week, usually at night. He buys fifths, half gallons, and pints of vodka. He is usually well dressed and works at some office job somewhere here in town. I know someone who knows him, and a lady friend of his says that if you call him up after 10 at night, his speech is slurred, and she knows for a fact that he keeps pints under his car seat while driving during the day. This lady friend lives right next door to him and she sees him going to and from work and taking swigs from his stash so-to-speak. *(From Venturelli's research files, interview with a 50-year-old female liquor store clerk in a small Midwestern town, August 9, 1999.)*

I even knew a professor who would buy pints of whiskey as soon as we would open in the morning. He would drive off and go to your university [referring to the author's university] to teach. He was a heck of a nice fella, always ready with a joke and very pleasant to talk to, but I knew he had a problem with this stuff. *(From Venturelli's research files, interview with a 50-year-old female liquor store clerk in a small Midwestern town, August 9, 1999.)*

I vividly recall at age 10 seeing at least three or four middle-aged men arrive at my father's tavern as soon as the doors were opened at 8:00 A.M. on most mornings, desperately looking for the morning's first drink of alcohol. I recall my dad would crack a raw egg into an 8-ounce glass. Draft beer and the raw egg filled the glass half full. The reason for the raw egg

was to get some breakfast protein and the reason for the half full glass of beer was because their hands were very shaky and they had to steady the drink to their mouths. Immediately following what my dad referred to as a "full" breakfast were at least several double shots of Jim Beam whiskey. These alcoholic customers had to have the drinks so that they could feel "normal" for the rest of the day. Some would even be dressed in formal attire ready to go off to their office jobs. *(Venturelli, personal observation, May 18, 2000.)*

Alcohol Consumption in the United States

Similar to nearly all societies past and present, alcohol has always been a part of American society. The preceding quotes illustrate how an individual can consume an excessive amount of a psychoactive and addictive substance without necessarily coming to the attention of anyone except perhaps a neighbor, a lone liquor store employee, or even a bar owner and his young son. Furthermore, this same depressant chemical is often not perceived as a drug by many Americans. It is considered more of a social substance, something that is "always" found at social gatherings and is even expected at such gatherings.

Consider these findings from the National Household Survey on Drug Abuse in 2003:

- Approximately 50% of Americans aged 12 or older (119 million people) indicated that they were current drinkers of alcohol in 2003. The same study showed that 22.6% (54 million people) participated in **binge drinking** at least once in the 30 days before the 2003 National Survey on Drug Use and Health (SAMHSA 2004a, 2004b), and approximately 16 million (6.8%) were **heavy drinkers**. The results of this survey are shown in Figure 8.1.
- Among young people, the prevalence of current alcohol use in 2003 increased with age, from 2.9% at age 12 to about 70% of persons 21 or 22 years old (Figure 8.1). The prevalence of alcohol use then decreased with increasing age, from 61.7% among 26- to 29-year-olds to

KEY TERMS

binge drinkers
consuming five or more drinks on one occasion

heavy drinkers
people who drink five or more alcoholic beverages on one occasion for five or more days within any given 30-day period

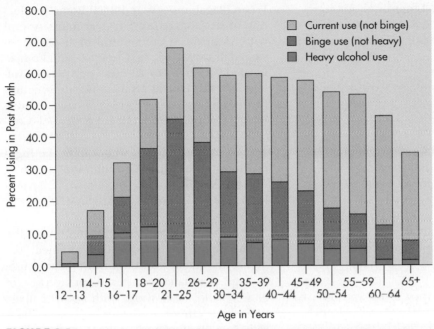

FIGURE 8.1

Current, binge, and heavy alcohol use among persons aged 12 or older, by age.

....

Source: Substance Abuse and Mental Health Services Administration (SAMHSA). *Results from the 2003 National Survey on Drug Use and Health: National Findings.* Rockville, MD: Office of Applied Studies, 2004.

46.2% among 60- to 64-year-olds and 34.4% among people aged 65 or older.

- The highest prevalence of both binge and heavy drinking in 2003 was found among young adults aged 18 to 25, with the peak rate of both measures occurring at age 21. The rate of binge drinking was 41.6% for young adults aged 18 to 25 and 47.8% at age 21. Heavy alcohol use was reported by 15.1% of person's aged 18 to 25 and by 18.7% of persons aged 21.

- While 57.7% of the population aged 45 to 49 in 2003 were current drinkers, 23.2% of persons within this age range were binge drinkers and 0.8% drank heavily. Rates of binge and heavy drinking were relatively low among people aged 65 or older.

- Among youths aged 12 to 17, an estimated 17.7% used alcohol in the month before the survey interview. Among all youths, 10.6% were binge drinkers and 2.6% were heavy drinkers.

Once again, these trends indicate that despite all the laws, increased campaigns and advertisements against drug and alcohol abuse, and continually increasing enforcement expenditures since 1994, the number of underage drinkers has not changed much (SAMHSA 2002).

Current Statistics and Trends in Alcohol Consumption

A recent Gallup Poll indicated that 64% of the adult population drinks alcohol, whereas 26% reported excessive alcohol consumption patterns (Newport 2000). An all-time high of 36% of the population reported that drinking alcohol has caused family problems, and 77% of those questioned indicated that in comparison to all other drug problems, alcohol creates the most family problems in our society (Newport 2000).

In looking at more detailed figures about consumption patterns, we find the following (summarized largely from Newport 2000, unless otherwise designated):

- Sixty percent of men prefer to drink beer, whereas women prefer wine.
- As men age, their preference for beer steadily decreases.
- Overall, as both men and women age, they say wine is their favorite alcoholic beverage.
- Lower-income drinkers prefer beer, whereas higher-income drinkers prefer wine.
- The highest rate of family drinking problems is among 18- to 29-year-olds.
- Currently, 42% of the population report family disputes caused by excessive drinking; 17% reported this problem in 1996.
- Sixty-four percent claim they drink and 36% report that they abstain. In 1999, 61% drank and 39% abstained.
- In 1999, 42% of all alcohol drinkers claimed to primarily drink beer, 34% wine, and 19% hard liquor.
- Of the total number of drinkers, 24% reported that they drink more than they should.
- To date, alcohol has been tried by 53% of 8th graders, 70% of 10th graders, 81% of 12th graders, and 89% of college students. Occasions of *heavy drinking* (five or more drinks in a row at least once before this survey was administered) occurred in 14% of the nation's 8th graders, 24% of the nation's 10th graders, and 32% of the nation's 12th graders.
- Estimated spending for healthcare services was $18.8 billion for alcohol problems and medical consequences of alcohol consumption and $9.9 billion for other types of drug problems.
- An estimated $82 billion was lost in potential productivity due to both alcohol and other drug abuse.
- Throughout the world, Luxembourg tops the list for recorded alcohol consumption per year, at 12.6 liters per person, followed by Germany at 12.1 liters and France at 11.5 liters. The lowest levels are found in Turkey, Krygyzstan, Turkmenistan, Israel, and Armenia, which all have levels below 3 liters per person.

- When illegal imports and illicit home production of alcohol are taken into account, several countries exceed the amount of alcohol consumed in Luxembourg, Germany, and France. Latvia leads at 16 to 20 liters per person, followed by Slovenia at 18 liters per person, and in descending order Estonia, Russia, Lithuania, Macedonia, and Greece (Alcohol Concern 2000).
- Legally (21 and older), whites have the highest rate of alcohol consumption at 86%; African Americans are second at 72%, and Hispanics are third at 69% (SAMHSA/OAS 1999b).
- In contrast to common assumptions, the higher the level of education attained, the higher the likelihood of current alcohol use. College graduates registered an average of 93% alcohol use, those with some college 91%, high school graduates 86%, and those with less than a high school degree 76% (SAMHSA/OAS 1999b).
- Drinking is commonly believed to be associated with poverty, yet according to a Gallup Poll, the people most likely to drink have higher incomes, are younger than age 65, do not attend church, live in regions of the United States other than the South, and are more likely to identify themselves as liberals.
- Research shows that much of the economic burden of alcohol and drug problems falls on the population of taxpayers who do not abuse alcohol and drugs. Government, private insurance, and other members of households bear most of these costs (NIDA 2000).

PERCENTAGES OF THE DRINKING POPULATION: A PYRAMID MODEL

What percentage of our society drinks alcohol? A pyramid can be constructed based on the amount of alcohol consumed, the pattern of drinking, or the "problem" or "illness" dimension (e.g., by attempting to calculate what proportion of Americans are "abusers" or "dependent"; the criteria for each were discussed in Chapter 7). For example, at the beginning of this chapter, the first two interviews discussed people who bought and consumed liquor and are prime examples of alcohol drinkers who probably imbibe approximately 1 quart per day. This, by most definitions, is a clear diagnostic criterion for a diagnosis of alcoholism. Interestingly, all three of the chapter's opening examples indicate that the alcohol drinkers are apparently functional, or at least they manage to create this impression.

The pyramid shown in Figure 8.2 has a base of 35% who are **teetotalers**, then a layer of about 13% who occasionally drink, and a top 52% who drink fairly regularly. Some 11 million Americans, or 5.5% of Americans aged 12 or older, had five or more drinks on the same occasion at least five different days in the past month, which is one possible definition of heavy drinking. Different definitions of what constitutes heavy drinking exist. Thus, if we define *heavy drinking* differently—for example, as more than two drinks per day—we come up with a much larger slice of the pyramid—three times as large.

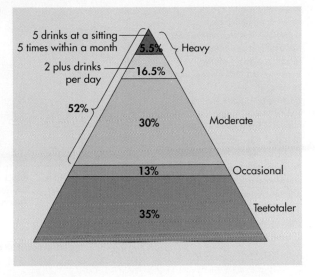

FIGURE 8.2

Broad distribution of drinking behaviors.

Dual Problems: Underage and Adult Drinking

As we saw in Figure 8.1, concerning age, alcohol consumption does not have any boundaries. Although since 1988, all states have had a legal drinking age of 21, a high percentage of the underage population drinks alcohol.

Overall, we can see the larger "picture" regarding the percentages of persons aged 12 or older reporting past-month alcohol use, by level of use and age group in 2003, by considering the following data:

Underage Alcohol Use (SAMHSA 2004a, 2004b)

1. About 10.9 million persons aged 12 to 20 reported drinking alcohol in the month before the survey interview in 2003 (29% of this age group). Nearly 7.2 million (19.2%) were binge drinkers, and 2.3 million (6.1%) were heavy drinkers. These figures were essentially the same as those obtained from the 2003 survey.

2. More males than females aged 12 to 20 reported binge drinking (21.7% versus 16.5%) and heavy drinking (7.9% versus 4.3%) in 2003.

3. Among persons aged 12 to 20, past-month alcohol use rates ranged from 18.2% among

Asians and blacks to 33.2% among whites. Binge drinking was reported by 22.8% of underage whites, 20.8% of underage American Indians or Alaska Native, and 16.9% of underage Hispanics; only 9.6% of underage Asians and 9.1% of underage blacks reported binge drinking.

4. Across geographic regions in 2003, underage current alcohol use rates were higher in the Northeast (32%) and Midwest (31.7%) than in the South and West (26.7% and 27.6%, respectively).

Alcohol Use: Age 12 or Older by Ethnicity and Race (SAMHSA 2004a, 2004b)

5. Figure 8.3 shows the percentage of current, binge, and heavy alcohol use among persons aged 12 or older by race and ethnicity in 2003. Whites were more likely than any other racial or ethnic group to report current use of alcohol in 2003. An estimated 54.4% of whites

KEY TERMS

teetotalers

individuals who drink no alcoholic beverages whatsoever; a term in common usage in decades past

FIGURE 8.3

....

Sources: A and B: Substance Abuse and Mental Health Services Administration (SAMHSA). *Results from the 2003 National Survey on Drug Use and Health: National Findings.* Rockville, MD: Office of Applied Studies.
C: Office of Applied Studies (OAS). "Driving Under the Influence (DUI) Among Young Persons." *National Survey on Drug Use and Health (NSDUH).* Rockville, MD: Substance Abuse and Mental Health Services Administration, 2004.

A. Current, binge, and heavy alcohol use among persons aged 12 or older, by race/ethnicity, 2003

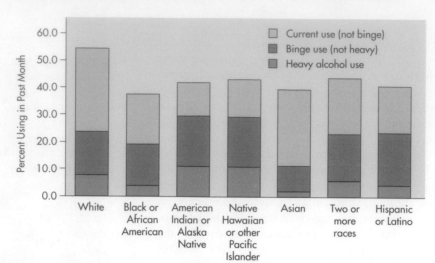

B. Driving under the influence of alcohol in the past year, by age, 2003

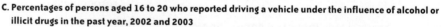

C. Percentages of persons aged 16 to 20 who reported driving a vehicle under the influence of alcohol or illicit drugs in the past year, 2002 and 2003

reported past-month use. The rates were 44.5% for persons reporting that they belonged to two or more races, 43.3% for Native Hawaiians or other Pacific Islanders, 42% for American Indians or Alaska Natives, 41.5% for Hispanics, 39% for Asians, and 37.9% for blacks.

6. The rate of binge drinking was lowest among Asians (11%). Rates for other racial or ethnic groups were 19.0% for blacks, 23.6% for whites, 24.2% for Hispanics, 29.6% for American Indians and Alaska Natives, and 29.8% for Native Hawaiians and other Pacific Islanders.

Education and Alcohol Use

7. The rate of past-month alcohol use increased with increasing levels of education. Among adults aged 18 or older with less than a high school education, 36.7% were current drinkers in 2003. By comparison, 66.5% of college graduates were current drinkers. Binge drinking and heavy drinking were least prevalent among college graduates, however.

College Students and Alcohol Use

8. Young adults aged 18 to 22 enrolled full-time in college were more likely than their peers not enrolled full-time (i.e., part-time college students and persons not enrolled in college) to use alcohol, binge drink, and drink heavily. Past-month alcohol use was reported by 64.9% of full-time college students compared with 54.6% of persons aged 18 to 22 who were not currently enrolled full-time. Binge and heavy use rates for college students were 43.5% and 17.6%, respectively, compared with 38.7% and 13.4%, respectively, for other persons aged 18 to 22.

9. Among persons aged 18 to 22, full-time college students were more likely to be heavy drinkers than than their nonstudent peers (17.6% versus 13.4%). However, at later ages (26 or older), those who had graduated from college were less likely to drink heavily than those who had not graduated (4.4% versus 6.5%).

Employment Status and Alcohol Use

10. Rates of current alcohol use were 61.2% for full-time employed adults aged 18 or older in 2003 compared with 57% of their unemployed peers. The patterns were different for binge and heavy alcohol use: Rates were higher for unemployed persons (35% and 13.3%, respectively, for binge and heavy use) than for full-time employed persons (28.9% and 8.6% respectively).

11. Most binge and heavy alcohol users were employed. Among the 51.1 million adult binge drinkers in 2003, 40.6 million (79.5%) were employed either full- or part-time. Similarly, 12.4 million (79.9%) of the 15.5 million adult heavy drinkers were employed.

Driving Under the Influence of Alcohol

12. An estimated 13.6% of persons aged 12 or older drove under the influence of alcohol at least once in the 12 months before the interview in 2003 (a decrease from the 14.2% rate found in 2003). These percentages represent 32.3 million persons in 2003 and 33.5 million persons in 2002.

13. Rates of driving under the influence (DUI) varied by age group in 2003. About 9.7% of 16- or 17-year-olds, 20.1% of 18- to 20-year-olds, and 28.7% of 21- to 25-year-olds reported driving under the influence of alcohol (see Figure 8.3 [b]). Beyond age 25, these rates declined with increasing age.

14. In 2002 and 2003, more than 4 million individuals (21%) aged 16 to 20 reported driving under the influence of alcohol or illicit drugs in the past year (see Figure 8.3 [c]) (OAS 2004). In this age group, 17% reported past-year DUI involving alcohol, 14% reported DUI involving illicit drugs, and 8% reported DUI involving a combination of alcohol and illicit drugs used together.

15. Males were nearly twice as likely as females (18.2% versus 9.3%) to drive under the influence of alcohol.

Alcohol and the Very Young

Alcohol has been tried by 53% of 8th graders, 70% of 10th graders, 81% of 12th graders, and 89% of college students (NIDA 1999). In 2002, the proportions of 8th, 10th, and 12th graders who admitted drinking an alcoholic beverage in the 30-day period before the survey were 20%, 35%, and 49% respec-

►Point/Counterpoint   Lower the Legal Drinking Age?

If we look across the world, we find that the United States appears to be the only country in the world that sets the minimum legal drinking age at 21. A number of countries such as Ireland, Finland, and Sweden specify a minimum age of 18, and other countries such as Germany, France, Italy, the Netherlands, Portugal, and the United Kingdom specify a minimum age of 16. Still other countries, such as Belgium, Denmark, Greece, Spain, and Austria, do not specify any legal age for alcohol consumption (Harkin and Klinkenberg 1995).

Arguments *against* lowering the legal limit for consuming alcohol are as follows:

1. A higher minimum legal drinking age (MLDA) is effective in preventing alcohol-related deaths and injuries among youth. When the MLDA is lowered, injury and death rates increase, and when the MLDA is increased, death and injury rates decline (Wagenaar 1993).

2. A higher MLDA results in fewer alcohol-related problems among youth, and the 21-year-old MLDA saves the lives of more than 1000 youth each year. Conversely, when the MLDA is lowered, motor vehicle crashes and deaths among youth increase. At least 50 studies have evaluated this correlation (Wagenaar 1993).

3. Research shows that when the MLDA is 21, people younger than age 21 drink less overall and continue to do so through their early twenties (O'Malley and Wagenaar 1991).

4. Higher MLDAs reduce traffic fatalities involving drivers 18 to 20 years old by 13%. These laws have saved an estimated 18,220 lives since 1975 (NHTSA 1999).

Arguments *for* lowering the legal limit for consuming alcohol are as follows:

1. A study of a large sample of young people between the ages of 16 and 19 in Massachusetts and New York after Massachusetts raised its drinking age revealed that the average, self-reported daily alcohol consumption in Massachusetts did not decline in comparison with New York (Hanson 1999).

2. Comparison of college students attending schools in states that had maintained, for at least 10 years, a minimum drinking age of 21 with those in states that had similarly maintained minimum drinking ages below 21 revealed few differences in drinking problems (Hanson 1999).

3. A study of all 50 states and the District of Columbia found "a positive relationship between the purchase age and single-vehicle fatalities." Thus, single-vehicle fatalities were found to be more frequent in those states with high purchase ages (Hanson 1999).

4. Comparison of drinking before and after the passage of raised minimum age legislation has generally revealed little impact on behavior. For example, a study that examined college students' drinking behavior before and after an increase in the minimum legal drinking age from 18 to 19 in New York found the law had no impact on underage students' consumption rates, intoxication rates, drinking attitudes, or drinking problems. These studies were corroborated by other researchers at a different college in the same state (Hanson 1999).

5. An examination of East Carolina University students' intentions regarding their behavior following passage of the 21-year-age drinking law revealed that only 6% intended to stop drinking, 70% planned to change their drinking location, 21% expected to use a false or borrowed identification to obtain alcohol, and 22% intended to use other drugs. Anecdotal statements by students indicated the belief by some that it "might be easier to hide a little pot in my room than a six pack of beer" (Hanson 1999).

Research and the information from sources in this chapter indicate that with regard to under-21 alcohol

—continued on next page

violations, the United States continues to have serious problems. Thus, we are not any better than most countries regarding the percentage of minors consuming alcohol, despite our unique minimum age–21 requirement for alcohol consumption. What about the idea that instead of prohibiting alcohol consumption to those under age 21 (which to date continues to be ineffective), we need to teach moderation at an early age so that the percentage of youth who decide to consume alcohol can learn to do so responsibly?

Because the age 21 requirement has not deterred our nation's youth from consuming alcohol and in light of younger and younger age groups consuming alcohol, do you think it is time to reconsider lowering the age limit of alcohol consumption so that:

1. We are in alignment with the remainder of the world.

2. We can eliminate costly, burdensome, and unnecessary underage drinking violations. These infractions with the law include fines, legal costs, imprisonment, court time, legal expenses, and introducing our nation's youth into the criminal justice system (which many believe should remain "lean and mean" so

that it can effectively prohibit and prosecute serious law violators).

3. We can teach responsible drinking and drinking in moderation, and alcohol consumption can be promoted and taught to be a "normal" part of behavior when eating or socializing with friends (like consuming coffee or fruit juice). Such prevention measures can clearly emphasize that excessive alcohol consumption is a sign of immaturity and lack of self-respect.

How successful do you think a campaign calling for lowering the legal drinking age would be with (1) family members, (2) your school, (3) community, (4) city/town, and (5) American society in general? Would it be successful? If yes, why? If no, why? Have you had any experiences in foreign countries where alcohol consumption was not severely restricted? If so, what did you observe?

In essence, do you think we should try to change the current drinking laws, in light of the fact that the current laws continue to be ineffective? Why are we not like other nations with regard to age limits on the use of alcohol? How important is it for the United States to be like other nations?

Sources: Hanson, D. J. "The Legal Drinking Age: Science vs. Ideology" (1999). Available http://www.student.potsdam.edu/alcohol-info/InMyOpinion/ScienceIdeology.html.

Harkin, A. M., with assistance of L. Klinkenberg. *Profiles of Alcohol in the Member States of the European Region of the World Health Organization.* Copenhagen: WHO Regional Office for Europe, May 1995.

National Highway Traffic Safety Administration (NHTSA), National Center for Statistics and Analysis. *Drunk Driving Facts.* Washington, DC: NHTSA, 1999.

O'Malley, P. M., and Wagenaar, A. C. "Effects of Minimum Drinking Age Laws on Alcohol Use, Related Behaviors and Traffic Crash Involvement Among American Youth: 1976–1987." *Journal of Studies on Alcohol 52* (1991): 478–491.

Wagenaar, A. C. "Minimum Drinking Age and Alcohol Availability to Youth: Issues and Research Needs." In *Economics and the Prevention of Alcohol-Related Problems,* edited by M. E. Hilton and B. Bloss, 175–200. National Institute on Alcohol Abuse and Alcoholism (NIAAA) Research Monograph No. 25, NIH Pub. No. 93-3513. Bethesda, MD: NIAAA, 1993.

tively (Johnston et al. 2003). Even more alarming is that 14% of 8th graders, 24% of 10th graders, and 32% of 12th graders reported an occasion of heavy drinking within a 2-week period before a nationwide survey (NIDA 1999). (See "Point/Counterpoint," Lower the Legal Drinking Age?)

Since the early 1990s to the present, however, 8th, 9th, and 10th graders have reported marijuana to be the drug they use the most frequently, followed by

alcohol (Johnston et al. 2003). Although much more is said in Chapter 13, the noteworthy finding here is that on a daily basis for this group of minors, marijuana usage now exceeds alcohol usage.

With regard to the three major types of alcohol (beer, wine coolers, and liquor) used by junior high and high school students, we find that from 9th through 12th grades, alcohol consumption increases dramatically (*Pride USA Survey* 1998).

In looking at 12th graders' consumption of alcohol, white underage students are much more likely to binge drink (36%) compared with African American students (12%) and Hispanic students (28%). Finally, boys in 12th grade are more likely to drink alcohol on a daily basis compared with girls of the same grade and age: Daily use among boys is reported at 6.4%, whereas the rate among girls is reported at 1.4%. Boys are more likely than girls to drink large quantities of alcohol in a single sitting: 39% of 12th-grade males reported drinking five or more drinks in a row 2 weeks prior to being surveyed, but only 24% of the 12th-grade females drank the same amount. When reviewing the statistics, keep in mind that females differ from males in terms of their alcohol drinking capacities (see Chapter 7 for more details).

ECONOMIC COSTS OF ALCOHOL ABUSE

The economic costs of alcohol abuse to society are staggering. The following are some of the current results of alcohol abuse:

- From a global perspective, when including illness, accidents, and crimes connected to alcohol, the costs add up to more than $250 billion yearly (Reuters Limited 1999).

Figure 8.4 shows the following (NIAAA 2000):

- The estimated cost of alcohol abuse and alcoholism (not including other drugs) to the United States was approximately $184.6 billion in 1998. (This cost rises approximately 12.5% yearly.)

FIGURE 8.4

Economic costs of alcohol abuse, United States, 1998 (total estimated cost: $184.6 billion).

Source: Harwood, H., D. Fountain, and G. Livermore. *The Economic Costs of Alcohol and Drug Abuse in the United States, 1992.* Report prepared for the National Institute on Drug Abuse and the National Institute on Alcohol Abuse and Alcoholism, National Institutes of Health, U.S. Department of Health and Human Services. NIH Pub. No. 98-4327. Rockville, MD: National Institute on Drug Abuse, 1998.

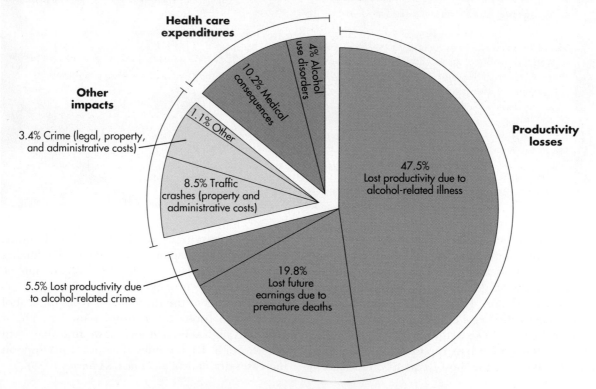

- This 1998 estimate amounted to roughly $683 for every man, woman, and child living in the United States in 1998.
- More than 70% of the estimated costs of alcohol abuse were attributed to lost productivity ($134.2 billion), most of which resulted from alcohol-related illness or premature death.
- Most of the remaining estimated costs were expenditures for healthcare services to treat alcohol use disorder and the medical consequences of alcohol consumption ($26.3 billion, or 14.3% of total), property and administrative costs of alcohol-related motor vehicle crashes ($15.7 billion, or 8.5%), and various criminal justice system costs of alcohol-related crime ($6.3 billion, or 3.4%).

Regarding how the burden of the costs of alcohol abuse is distributed across various segments of society, Figure 8.5 shows the following (published in NIAAA 2000, reference Harwood 2000; Harwood et al. 1998):

- Much of the economic burden of alcohol abuse falls on segments of the population *other than* the alcohol abusers themselves.

- Approximately 45% of the estimated total cost is borne by alcohol abusers and their families, almost all of which is due to lost or reduced earnings.
- Approximately 20% of the total estimated cost of alcohol abuse is borne by the federal government and 18% by state and local governments.
- Nearly three-fourths of the costs borne by the federal government take the form of reduced tax revenues resulting from alcohol-related productivity losses, and most of the remaining federal burden relates to healthcare costs. The burden on state and local governments (reductions in tax revenue) resulting from such productivity losses accounts for just over half, while 38% is for criminal justice and motor-vehicle related costs. Private insurance arrangements (including life, health, auto, fire, and other kinds of insurance) shoulder the burden for 10% of the total estimated cost, primarily in the area of healthcare costs and motor vehicle crashes.
- Six percent of the total costs are borne by victims of alcohol-related crimes (including

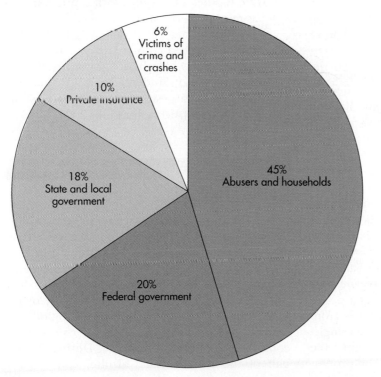

FIGURE 8.5

Distribution of the costs of alcohol abuse.

....

Source: Harwood, H., D. Fountain, and G. Livermore. *The Economic Costs of Alcohol and Drug Abuse in the United States, 1992.* Report prepared for the National Institute on Drug Abuse and the National Institute on Alcohol Abuse and Alcoholism, National Institutes of Health, U.S. Department of Health and Human Services. NIH Pub. No. 98-4327. Rockville, MD: National Institute on Drug Abuse, 1998.

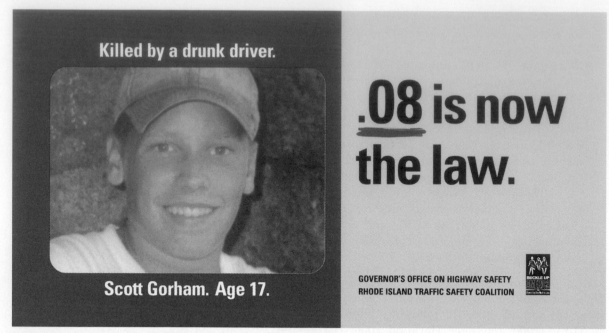

Killed by a drunk driver.

Scott Gorham. Age 17.

.08 is now the law.

GOVERNOR'S OFFICE ON HIGHWAY SAFETY
RHODE ISLAND TRAFFIC SAFETY COALITION

Current advertisement used to promote lowering the minimum legally acceptable blood alcohol concentration (BAC) while operating a motor vehicle in the United States.

homicide) and by nondrinking victims of alcohol-related motor vehicle crashes.

Other findings in a published report by the National Institute on Alcohol Abuse and Alcoholism (NIAAA 2000) disclose the following:

- Each year, more than 107,400 people die because of alcohol-related abuse.
- Productivity losses resulting from alcohol-related illness were estimated at $87.6 billion for 1998.
- Total costs attributed to alcohol-related motor vehicle crashes were estimated to be $24.7 billion.
- Expenditures for alcohol-related crime totaled $6.2 billion, and $17.4 billion for illicit drugs.
- Alcohol abuse is estimated to have contributed to 25% to 30% of violent crime.
- Alcohol is officially linked to at least half of all highway fatalities, and that figure includes only legal intoxication. In most states, the cutoff for the blood alcohol level ranges from 0.08% to 0.1%. In as many as 70% of all single-vehicle fatal crashes on weekend nights, the driver was legally intoxicated, and this propor-

tion holds during most weekends throughout the United States. Interestingly, this single issue has been the only alcohol problem that has inspired very vocal and effective groups to lobby for stricter enforcement of laws against alcohol impaired automobile driving. Groups such as MADD (Mothers Against Drunk Driving) and SADD (Students Against Drunk Driving) are the largest prevention organizations in the nation (Alcoholism Kills 2000).

History of Alcohol in America

DRINKING PATTERNS

From a peak in 1830, when the amount of alcohol ingested by the average American was 7.1 gallons per year, use declined continuously until 1871–1880, when the average was 1.72 gallons. Numbers then rose to a high in 1906–1910 to 2.6 gallons, then fell to 1.96 gallons just before Prohibition, 1916–1919. Under Prohibition, less than a gallon of absolute alcohol per person was consumed annually, on average. During the last half of the 20th century, alcohol consumption stayed constant, within the 2 to 3 gallon range. Wine and beer gained in popularity, while the popularity of "spirits" (hard liquor) declined (Lender 1985).

HISTORICAL CONSIDERATIONS

Alcoholic beverages have played an important role in the history of the United States as well as in most countries throughout the world. Most likely, fermentation was the first method for making alcohol, dating to 4200 B.C. As early as A.D. 100, it appears that brandy was the first distilled beverage. In Ireland and Scotland, whiskey was first distilled in the 1400s, and gin began appearing in the 1600s, after being initially distilled by a Flemish physician. Other types of liquor also have distinct origins. For example, rum was first invented in Barbados in the 1650s. Bourbon was first made near Georgetown, Kentucky, in the late 1700s. In the United States, the first distillery was created in the 1600s in the area that is now New York City.

In colonial America, alcohol was viewed very favorably. From an economic standpoint, the manufacturing of rum became New England's largest and most profitable industry in the so-called triangle trade. It acquired this name because Yankee traders would sail with a cargo of rum to the West Coast of Africa, where they bargained the "demon" for slaves. From there, they sailed to the West Indies, where they bartered the slaves for molasses. Finally, they took the molasses back to New England, where it was made into rum, thus completing the triangle. For many years, New England distilleries flourished and the slave trade proved highly lucrative (see Figure 8.6). This process continued until 1807, when an act of Congress prohibited the importation of slaves.

From a social standpoint, the consumption of alcohol was seen as a part of life. The colonial tavern "was a key institution, the center of social and political life" (Levine 1983, p. 66). In the 17th and 18th centuries, alcohol flowed freely at weddings, baptisms, and funerals. Especially in the 18th century, people drank at home, at work, and while traveling. In the 19th century, largely because of the temperance movement, taverns became stigmatized and were viewed as dens where the lower classes, immigrants, and mostly men would con-

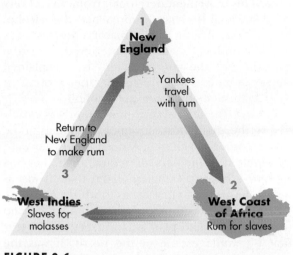

FIGURE 8.6
Slave trade triangle.

gregate. "Any drinking, [Lyman Beecher] argued, was a step toward 'irreclaimable' slavery to liquor" (Lender and Martin 1987). People in the 19th century began to report that they were addicted to alcohol. Here is where the temperance movement had its effects in bringing about a change in attitudes regarding drinking.

From the Temperance Movement (1830–1850) to the Prohibition Era (1920–1933)

The time from the temperance movement to the Prohibition era was a very turbulent period in the history of alcohol in America. The period of heaviest drinking in America began during Jefferson's term of office (1800–1808). The nation was going through uneasy times, trying to stay out of the war between Napoleon and the British allies. The transient population had increased, especially in the seaport cities, and the migration westward had begun. Heavy drinking had become a major form of recreation and a "social lubricant" at elections and public gatherings. The temperance movement never began with the intention of stopping alcohol consumption but with the goal of encouraging moderation. In fact, in the 1830s, at the peak of this early campaign, temperance leaders (many of whom drank beer and wine) recommended abstinence only from distilled spirits, not from the other forms of alcohol such as beer or wine. This movement developed from several very vocal spiritual leaders who preached that alcohol harms "the health and physical energies of a nation" and that alcohol interfered with the spreading of the gospel. Later, as is explained shortly in more detail, the temperance movement went against all other forms of alcohol.

Because the temperance movement was closely tied to the abolitionist movement as well as to the African American church, African Americans were preeminent promoters of temperance. Leaders such as Frederick Douglass stated that "it was as well to be a slave to master, as to whisky and rum. When a slave was drunk, the slaveholder had no fear that he would plan an insurrection; no fear that he would escape to the north. It was the sober, thinking slave who was dangerous, and needed the vigilance of his master to keep him a slave" (Douglass 1892, p. 133).

Over the next decades, partly in connection with religious revivals, the meaning of *temperance* was gradually altered from "moderation" to "total abstinence." All alcoholic beverages were attacked as being unnecessary, harmful to health, and inherently poisonous. Over the course of the 19th century, the demand gradually arose for total prohibition (Austin 1978).

By the late 19th and early 20th centuries, a number of countries either passed legislation or created alcohol restrictions. Most of these laws and restrictions eventually failed. In the United States, attempts to control, restrict, or abolish alcohol were made, but they all met with abysmal failure. From 1907 to 1919, 34 states passed prohibition laws. Finally, on a national scale, the 18th Amendment to the Constitution was ratified in 1919 in an

Al Capone ("Scarface") (*center*), the undisputed leader of Chicago's gang scene during Prohibition, made millions of dollars in his bootlegging operations until he was convicted of tax evasion in 1931 and eventually imprisoned in Alcatraz.

attempt to stop the rapid spread of alcohol addiction. In January 1920, alcohol was outlawed. As soon as such a widely used substance became illegal, criminal activity to satisfy the huge demand for alcohol flourished. Illegal outlets developed for purchasing liquor. Numerous not-so-secret **speakeasies** developed as illegal establishments where people could buy and consume alcoholic beverages, despite the laws of Prohibition. **Bootlegging** was a widely accepted activity. In effect, such "dens of sin" filled the vacuum for many drinkers during Prohibition.

During the temperance movement and Prohibition period, doctors and druggists prescribed whiskey and other alcohol known as **patent medicines** (see "Case in Point," The Great American Fraud: Patent Medicines).

By 1928, doctors made an estimated $40 million per year writing prescriptions for whiskey. Patent medicines flourished, with alcohol contents as high as 50%. Whisko, a "nonintoxicating stimulant," was 55 proof (or 27.5% alcohol). Another, Kaufman's Sulfur Bitters, was labeled "contains no alcohol" but was 40 proof (20% alcohol) and did not contain sulfur. There were dozens of others, many of which contained other types of drugs, such as opium.

Both Prohibitionists and critics of the law were shocked by the violent gang wars that broke out

KEY TERMS

speakeasies
places where alcoholic beverages were illegally sold during the Prohibition era

bootlegging
making, distributing, and selling alcoholic beverages during the Prohibition era

patent medicines
the ingredients in these uncontrolled "medicines" were secret, often consisting of large amounts of colored water, alcohol, cocaine, or opiates

▶Case in Point   The Great American Fraud: Patent Medicines

In the late 1800s and early 1900s, before the days of FDA legislation, the sales of uncontrolled medicines flourished and became widespread. Many of these products were called *patent medicines*, which signified that the ingredients were secret, not that they were patented. The law of the day seemed to be more concerned with someone's recipe being stolen than with preventing harm to the naive consumer. Some of these patent medicines included toxic ingredients such as acetanilide in Bromo-Seltzer and Orangeine and prussic (hydrocyanic) acid in Shiloh's Consumption Cure.

Most patent medicines appear to have been composed largely of either colored water or alcohol, with an occasional added ingredient such as opium or cocaine. Hostetter's Stomach Bitters with 44% alcohol could easily have been classified as liquor. Sale of Peruna (28% alcohol) was prohibited to Native Americans because of its high alcoholic content. Birney's Catarrh Cure contained 4% cocaine. Wistar's Balsam of Wild Cherry (see Figure 8.7), Dr. King's Discovery for Consumption, Mrs. Winslow's Soothing Syrup, and several others contained opiates as well as alcohol.

The medical profession of the mid- and late 19th century was ill prepared to do battle with the ever-present manufacturers and distributors of patent medicines. Qualified physicians during this time were rare. Much more common were medical practitioners with poor training and little scientific understanding. In fact, many of these early physicians practiced a brand of medicine that was generally useless and frequently more life-threatening than the patent medicines themselves.

In 1905, *Collier's Magazine* ran a series of articles called the "Great American Fraud," which warned of the abuse of patent medicines. This brought the problem to the public's attention (Adams 1905). *Collier's* coined the phrase "dope fiend" from "dope," an African word meaning "intoxicating substance." The American Medical Association (AMA) joined in and widely distributed reprints of the *Collier's* story to inform the public about the dangers of these medi-

cines, even though the AMA itself accepted advertisements for patent medicines that physicians knew were addicting. The publicity created mounting pressure on Congress and President Theodore Roosevelt to do something about these fraudulent products. In 1905, Roosevelt proposed that a law be enacted to regulate interstate commerce of misbranded and adulterated foods, drinks, and drugs. This movement received further impetus when Upton Sinclair's book *The Jungle* was published in 1906—this nauseatingly realistic exposé detailed how immigrant laborers worked under appalling conditions of filth, disease, putrefaction, and other extreme exploitations at Chicago's stockyards.

Two substances used in patent medicines helped shape attitudes that would form the basis of regulatory policies for years to come: the opium derivatives (narcotic drugs, such as heroin and morphine) and cocaine (see Chapter 3).

FIGURE 8.7

This poster advertises one of the patent medicines that contained liberal doses of opium and a high concentration of alcohol. This medicine was widely used to treat tuberculosis ("consumption") around the turn of the century, when more than 25% of all adult deaths were attributable to this disease. The U.S. government finally forced the remedy off the market by 1920.

between rivals seeking to control the lucrative black market in liquor. More important, a general disregard for the law developed. Corruption among law enforcement agents was widespread and organized crime began and grew to be an enormous illegitimate business. In reaction to these developments, political support rallied against Prohibition, resulting in its repeal in 1933 by the 21st Amendment. Early in the 20th century, women suffragettes had been prominent temperance organizers; paradoxically, flappers organized against Prohibition and were vital in gathering the signatures for its repeal.

Three main developments occurred as a result of Prohibition. First, alcohol use began to diminish for the first 2 or 3 years after Prohibition was in effect. This trend had begun several years before the law was passed. More importantly, after 3 years of steady decline, the use of distilled liquors rose every year afterward. Further, even minors were becoming addicted to alcohol during this period.

Second, enforcement of laws against alcohol use was thwarted by corrupt law enforcement officials, enforcement was uneven (in some areas of the United States, enforcement was lax, while in other areas very strict), and law enforcement experienced more than 50% turnover in its ranks. Corruption of law enforcement officials stands out as a paramount concern. Reportedly, 10% of law enforcement was "on the take" and had to be continually discharged.

Third, among the Western Europeans who emigrated to the United States *en masse* during this period, the consumption of alcohol was culturally prescribed. Prohibition against alcohol usage to the Italian, German, French, Polish, Irish, and other European-based immigrants was perceived as unnecessary and an infringement to the right to common existence. One 93-year-old Italian American "émigré" to Chicago exemplified some of these attitudes:

> Well, when we were not allowed to drink because of the government, I thought it was a stupid law. Many of us here in the neighborhood [a fading Italian American community in Chicago's West Side and the original home of Venturelli] made lots of money as "alki cookers."

> We would make the alcohol in our bathtubs and sell to other people or even to those mafia types. Oh, it was horrible cheap and crappy alcohol; if you drank too much the night before, it gave you headaches sometimes for days. On Sunday afternoons, if you walked through this neighborhood in the hot summer days, you could smell the alcohol oozing from people's windows. Nearly everyone my mother's and father's age and older at the time made extra money as alki cookers. It was actually a good law [referring to Prohibition] for making a few bucks to help out the family expenses. No one around here gave a damn about the law, because too many were "on the take" so-to-say . . . and it was not just us [referring to the local Italian Americans]. At least for us when we meet together and eat for fun, alcohol is like the air we breathe. Who the hell is going to change that, especially something so deep? *(From Venturelli's research files, interview with a 93-year-old male, May 26, 2000.)*

Defining Alcoholics

As discussed in Chapter 7 and at the beginning of this chapter, creating absolute definitions or categories of behavior that represent an alcoholic *type* is very difficult because all behaviors vary enormously from one person to the next; thus most behaviors range along a continuum. Adding to this confusion is the fact that some disagreement exists among experts on what the exact criteria should be regarding the definition of an alcoholic. In other words, when is a person an alcoholic? Is it the daily drinker or the inebriated weekend drinker? What if the person is able to maintain a job and provide for his or her family? How does this type of alcoholic compare with an unemployed resident of skid row? In the minds of many Americans, an alcoholic is a derelict who frequents skid rows, train stations, and bus terminals; panders for money; and sleeps on a park bench at night. Yet, this stereotypical image of an alcoholic represents only a few percent of the millions of Americans who qualify as alcoholic by any of the accepted medical definitions. The more typical alcoholic, in fact, is the example of the professor or businessman purchasing alcohol at a liquor store (described at the opening of this chapter). In effect, most alcoholics are secret or hidden drinkers who look very much like everyday working people.

CULTURAL DIFFERENCES

Although much more will be presented later in this chapter about the pervasive role that culture plays in drinking behavior, we begin with a quote highlighting cultural differences in interpreting alcohol consumption:

> Even definitions of a "problem drinker" differ from one culture to the next. In Poland, loss of productivity tends to demonstrate a drinking problem, while Californians emphasize drunk driving as an important and sometimes key indicator . . . [Among Italian Americans, an inability to provide for one's family because of heavy drinking qualifies a person as an alcoholic.] . . . Some methods of assessing problem-drinking look to behavior that leads to a brush with the law. However, drunkenness may or may not lead to disruptive behavior. In the Netherlands, alcoholic beverage consumption is similar to that in Finland and Poland, but there is much less disruptive or public drinking. In these nations, the actual amount of alcohol consumed is not indicated by the arrest figures, the actual amount consumed, and the number of physical ailments caused by excessive alcohol consumption. Secondly, the social response to drunkenness may not be arrest and conviction. Ireland, for example, has traditionally used psychiatric institutions to control drunkenness. (Osterberg 1986, p. 83)

Estimates vary, but it is believed that approximately three-fourths of problem drinkers are men and one-fourth are women. The proportion of women has risen in recent years. This increase occurred for two reasons: (1) Women as problem drinkers are more visible and numerous because they now make up about half of the workforce, and (2) women are more likely to acknowledge the problem and seek treatment, especially if they are in white-collar occupations. Thus, female problems drinkers may now be more visible and more self-assured as well as more numerous.

Next, in attempting to define alcoholism, we turn to models that speak of the state of addiction. Alcoholism is a state of physical and psychological addiction to ethanol, a psychoactive substance (see also Chapter 7). It was once viewed as a vice and dismissed as sinful, but over the years, there has been a shift from this perspective to one that views alcoholism as a disease. The "sinfulness" perspective failed to focus on the fact that alcoholism is an addiction—"an illness"—and not the result of a lack of personal discipline and morality.

Attempts to expand the basic definition of alcoholism to include symptoms of the condition and psychological and sociological factors have been difficult; no one definition satisfies everyone. The World Health Organization defines *alcohol dependence syndrome* as a syndrome characterized by a state, psychic and usually also physical, resulting from drinking alcohol. This state is characterized by behavioral and other responses that include a compulsion to drink alcohol (like an unquenchable thirst) on a continuous or periodic basis to experience its psychic effects and sometimes to avoid the discomfort of its absence; tolerance may or may not be present (NIAAA 1980).

Another more classic explanation of alcoholism that remains popular is, "Alcoholism is a chronic behavioral disorder manifested by repeated drinking of alcoholic beverages in excess of the dietary and social uses of the community, to an extent that interferes with the drinker's health or his social or economic functioning" (Keller 1958, p. 78). Another definition emphasizes, "Alcoholism is a chronic, primary, hereditary disease that progresses from an early, physiological susceptibility into an addiction characterized by tolerance changes, physiological dependence, and loss of control over drinking. [In this definition], [P]sychological symptoms are secondary to the physiological disease and not relevant to its onset" (Gold 1991, p. 99).

In summary, the preceding definitions either list or hint at the following major components of *alcoholism* (NIAAA "Frequently Asked Questions"):

Craving: An overwhelming compulsion to drink even when not feasible, such as at work, driving a car, mowing a lawn, and so on.

Very impaired or loss of control: An inability to limit one's drinking once drinking has begun—for example, one drink only before going to bed is impossible to control.

Physical dependence: The presence of withdrawal symptoms when attempting to abstain from usage. Such symptoms as nausea, sweating, shakiness, and anxiety about the availability of alcohol are common.

Tolerance: A need to continually increase the amount of alcohol consumed to maintain its effects (or to maintain the "buzz").

ALCOHOL ABUSE AND ALCOHOLISM

When attempting to understand the meaning of chronic drinking, one additional clarification that should be made is to distinguish between **alcohol abuse** and **alcoholism**. The two explanations of drinking behavior differ as a matter of degree. When speaking of *alcohol abuse*, the craving, loss of control, and physical dependence just listed as primary manifestations are less prominent and not as pronounced as in alcoholism. There is diminished ability to fulfill obligations and goals; more occasions of drinking at the wrong time, such as while driving; legal problems such as driving under the influence; and relationship problems. Note that many of these problems that result from alcohol abuse are also experienced by alcoholics, but not all manifestations of alcoholics are experienced by alcohol abusers. For example, an alcoholic may repeatedly argue with family members two or three times per week, whereas an alcohol abuser

KEY TERMS

alcohol abuse
uncontrollable drinking that leads to alcohol craving, loss of control, and physical dependence but with less prominent characteristics than found in alcoholism

alcoholism
a state of physical and psychological addiction to ethanol, a psychoactive substance

may have fewer occurrences of the same type of alcohol-inspired arguments with a family member. Thus, even though the alcohol abuser has fewer occasions of uncontrollable drinking than the alcoholic, the drinking remains largely uncontrollable when it occurs. For many years, people with drinking problems were lumped together under the label *alcoholic,* and *alcohol abusers* were assumed to be suffering from the same illness. Today, because of greater understanding about addiction and addictive behaviors, the distinction between the two terms leads to a more precise understanding of excessive alcohol abuse (see "Here and Now," Are You "on the Road" to Alcoholism?).

TYPES OF ALCOHOLICS

Although written more than 3 decades ago, Jellinek's (1960) original personality-typology (characterizations) differentiating the types of alcoholics remains very important for adding more preciseness in understanding alcohol abuse and its outcomes. Jellinek's categories are as follows:

Alpha alcoholism. Mostly a psychological dependence on alcohol to bolster an inability to cope with life. The alpha type constantly needs alcohol and becomes irritable and anxious when it is not available.

Beta alcoholism. Mostly a social dependence on alcohol. Often, although not exclusively, this type is a heavy beer drinker who continues to meet social and economic obligations. Some nutritional deficiencies can occur, including organic damage such as gastritis and cirrhosis.

Gamma alcoholism. The most severe form of alcoholism. This type of alcoholic suffers from emotional and psychological impairment. Jellinek believed this type of alcoholic suffered from a true disease and progresses from a psychological dependence to physical dependence. Loss of control over when alcohol is consumed and how much is taken characterizes the latter phase of this type of alcoholism.

Delta alcoholic. Called the maintenance drinker (Royce 1989). The person loses control over drinking and cannot abstain for even a day or

Here and Now

Are You "On the Road" to Alcoholism?

Answer the following questions with either a simple "yes" or "no."

1. Do you frequently drink because you have problems or need to relax?

2. When out with friends, do you become irritated or bored when the evening does not lead to the use of alcohol and/or drugs?

3. Do you drink when you get mad at other people, such as your friends or parents?

4. Do you often prefer to drink alone?

5. Are your grades suffering because of the time you spend drinking?

6. Do you stop drinking "for good" and then start again?

7. Have you begun to drink in the morning, before school or work?

8. Do you often gulp your drinks?

9. Do you have loss of memory because of your drinking?

10. Do you lie about the amount you drink?

11. Do you ever get into trouble when you are drinking?

12. Do you get drunk when you drink, even when you do not plan to?

13. Do you think you are cool when you can hold your liquor?

If you answered more than one as "yes," you may have a drinking problem that will become increasingly problematic, moving in the direction of alcoholism.

Sources: Reformulated from The A.A. Grapevine, Inc., A.A. World Services, Inc., 1988, 1998. Available http://www.acoholics-anonymous.org/ef9doc1.html.

two. Many wine-drinking countries such as France and Italy contain delta-type alcoholics who sip wine throughout most of their waking hours. Being "tipsy" but never completely inebriated is typical of the delta alcoholic.

Epsilon alcoholic. This type of alcoholic is characterized as a binge drinker. The epsilon-type drinker drinks excessively for a certain period (for days and sometimes weeks) but then abstains completely from alcohol until the next binge period. The dependence on alcohol is both physical and psychological. Loss of control over the amount consumed is another characteristic of this type of alcoholic.

Zeta alcoholic. This category was added to Jellinek's types to describe the moderate drinker who becomes abusive and violent. Although this type is also referred to as a "pathological drinker" or "mad drunk," zeta types may not be addicted to alcohol.

Other classifications differentiate alcoholics by their reaction to the drug as quiet, sullen, friendly, or angry types. Another method is to classify alcoholics according to drinking patterns: people with occupational, social, escape, and emotional disorders.

Cultural Influences

This section explains how views of alcohol are culturally determined—that is, how culture encodes the thoughts, attitudes, values, and beliefs about alcohol and how it influences our behavior regarding the use and abuse of alcohol.

> I was just drinking beer a lot and hardly ever drank the hard stuff. I was drinking about a six-pack after work each night. My wife never said anything much about my drinking. Then as time went on, I remember that I would start drinking beer earlier and earlier after work.

Then came the six-pack and an extra quart of beer each night while sitting home trying to relax after a pressure-filled day at the office. Well, little did I realize then, I was having a drinking problem and it was only beer! I could not believe that I was sort of a beer alcoholic. Back then, I never thought that silly ole' beer could get a person hooked. *(From Venturelli's research files, male, age 32, member of Alcoholics Anonymous, April 12, 2000.)*

Or,

Q: Do you consider yourself a heavy drinker?
A: No, I only drink beer.
Q: But, you are often drunk at night?
A: Yea, but it's only beer.

These two interviews illustrate a belief shared by many Americans, which is that the milder alcohols such as beer, wine, and wine coolers are often placed outside the domain of potentially addictive types of beverages. Some may even believe that the distilled spirits such as vodka, gin, and whiskey are the only types of addictive alcoholic beverages. Finally, the comment that "I don't use and never would use drugs; I only drink" can easily be heard being espoused by a large portion of Americans (probably a majority), who place alcohol in a completely separate category from drugs. However, each 12-ounce bottle of beer is equal to 1 ounce of liquor. Thus, two beers equal a double shot of bourbon or vodka.

CULTURE AND DRINKING BEHAVIOR

Another way of looking at how culture influences us is to stand outside of our culture and see how people behave when intoxicated in our culture and in a variety of other cultures in an effort to understand the real relationship among culture, alcohol, and human beings. A major contribution to our knowledge of intoxicated behavior from an outside perspective comes from the field of cultural anthropology.

How, or in what way, does culture affect the way we view alcohol? Why would our culture differ from other cultures in the use and abuse of alcoholic beverages? We focus on these two questions in this section.

Many cultural social interactions demand drinking together.

Throughout the world, cultures create a climate for the development of attitudes toward most behaviors. Like other behaviors, the use of alcohol is embedded within our culture. Culture does more than contain the attitudes and feelings that people have toward alcohol use: It dictates the variety, the attachment, and the intensity of attitudes that are held toward other people's behavior. For example, in the 1930s, American college students acquired a "reverence for strong drink" (Room 1984, p. 8). Although for decades many people believed that college students "majored in drinking," during the 1930s, students grew to consider heavy use as romantic and adult, resonating with the romantic, heavy-drinking expatriate community of writers in Paris, such as Ernest Hemingway.

American culture in general views ethanol-containing beverages as sexy, mature, sophisticated, facilitating socializing, and enhancing status. Today, many of these beliefs are communicated through the mass media, and advertising is a key medium of communication. Advertising uses positive images to persuade observers to purchase a particular brand of alcohol. For example, what messages are found in newspapers and especially magazines about drinking certain types of wine, bourbon, gin, scotch, and the numerous types of domestic and imported beers? What attitudes are generally conveyed when a sexy, glamorous woman is dressed in formal evening attire standing next to her man in front of a perfectly glowing fireplace, smiling confidently as he stares into her eyes and sips his special-label cognac?

CULTURE AND DISINHIBITED BEHAVIOR

The concept of **drunken comportment** was first formulated by MacAndrew and Edgerton (1969). Drunken comportment refers to the behavior demonstrated while under the influence of alcohol within the norms and expectations of a particular culture. Instead of simply labeling drinking behavior as "drunken behavior," this concept sensitizes us to how drinking behavior is influenced by cultural norms and expectations. For example, in the United States, drinking is comported to mean time out away from duties and obligations. "The symbolism of alcohol in American culture contains this motif of release and remission, as in the emergence of TGIF [Thank God It's Friday]" (Gusfield 1986, p. 203). Another example is that in some cultures, drinking occurs during celebrations and festivities, and as part of religious ceremony.

In France and Italy, drinking alcohol occurs while eating with family members. Alcohol is a **disinhibitor**, which refers to depression of the cerebral cortex functions. When this occurs, it results in a suspension of rational or thoughtful constraints on impulsive behavior. *Inhibitions* (inner raw feelings and attitudes) are normally controlled through rationality and logical thought processes. The popular image of office Christmas parties at which too much alcohol is consumed and parties that get out of control because of overconsumption of alcohol are examples. People at such events can easily become uncontrollable, loud, impulsive, and just plain irrational. In such situations, outbreaks of arguing and physical and verbal abuse are more likely to occur. Such behavior is disinhibited behavior.

Although all of us know that the alcohol content that is usually measured in terms of alcohol proof (see Chapter 7 for more details) has an independent effect on the user, two additional factors contribute to the effects of alcohol: **set and setting** (Goode 1999; Zinberg 1984; Zinberg and Robertson 1972). *Set* is the individual's expectation of what a drug will do to his or her personal-

ity. *Setting* is both the physical environment and the social environment in which the drug is consumed. How important are these two distinctions? Some psychologists contend that both set and setting can overshadow the pharmacological effects of most drugs. In fact, set and setting are far more influential in determining a drug user's experience even when the less immediately addictive drugs, such as alcohol and marijuana, are used, in contrast to more potent addictive drugs, such as cocaine and heroin. Good examples of this are when people who drink alcohol say "I felt that drink right away" or "I drank a lot last night but I had something on my mind and dude, I was just not in the partying mood."

A review of various ethnographic studies (Marshall 1983) reveals **pseudointoxicated** behavior among Tahitians, Rarotongans, Chippewa, Dakota, Pine Ridge and Teton Sioux, Aleuts, Baffin Island Inuits, and Potawatomi—that is, people *acting* drunk before or seconds after the bottle is opened, or as the drink is consumed. The frequency of use or the amount consumed has less effect on how drinkers comport themselves; instead, the cultural values, beliefs, mental maps, and norms cause a particular behavioral outcome. Using the terminology of psychology, we would say that it is not the biochemical effects on the brain alone that account for disinhibitory behavior but rather the belief that one has been drinking a substance that

KEY TERMS

drunken comportment
behavior exhibited while under the direct influence of alcohol determined by the norms and expectations of a particular culture

disinhibitor
a psychoactive chemical that depresses thought and judgment functions in the cerebral cortex, which has the effect of allowing relatively unrestrained behavior (as in alcohol inebriation)

set and setting
set refers to the individual's expectation of what a drug will do to his or her personality; *setting* is the physical and social environments where the drug is consumed

pseudointoxicated
acting drunk even before alcohol has had a chance to cause its effects

has a disinhibitory effect; that is, the mental (cognitive) appraisal of the physiological state allows disinhibited behavior. In using the terminology of sociology and revising a famous sociological axiom, we could say that "what we believe to be (or personally define as true) is true in its consequences or in the obtained results." Thus, if you believe you are drunk and you act drunk, then you are drunk.

Cultures vary in how they evaluate alcohol consumption. Some religions in the United States view drinking as evil, whereas other religions view alcohol as a gift from God and use it in religious ceremonies. In some subcultures, excessive use of alcohol is an indication of manhood, strength, and virility; in other subcultures, excessive alcohol use in public is disgusting and embarrassing. Even drug education has different perspectives. Do we emphasize total abstinence or teach people how to drink in moderation? Why such vastly different approaches? Because our culture includes contradictory practices on this front.

Similarly, the views we maintain about alcohol abuse and addiction vary. For example, is alcoholism a disease? Is it prescribed by certain customs within ethnic groups? Does it result from some type of personality flaw? The three concepts discussed in this section—drunken comportment, set and setting, and pseudointoxication—demonstrate that social and cultural contexts exert their influences independently of the effects of alcohol consumption.

CULTURE PROVIDES RULES FOR DRINKING BEHAVIOR

Many cultures, such as traditional Italian and Jewish cultures, permit moderate drinking within the family, especially at meals, but disapprove of drunken behaviors. Note that many differences separate these groups. For example, Italians use wine as a food item, whereas it has only ritual value among Orthodox Jews. In one study of Scandinavian nations, by contrast, drinking was considered absolutely separated from work. Where drinking at work was permitted, however, it was allowed to go on to the point of intoxication (Makela 1986). Finnish, Polish, and Russian cultures are associated with binge drinking, whereas

French culture is linked with sipping. In the United States, we encounter a vast variety of subgroups: Some heavy drinkers may live in a community in which it is not considered excessive to drink with their friends out of paper bags on the street in the morning. In other communities, all outdoor drinking is either done in parks, restaurants, bars, or outdoor cafes. Some people may belong to a "workplace culture of drinking" at a post office, construction site, or law firm where "three-martini lunches" are not unheard of. Perhaps this type of drinking is not much different from the habits of teenage peer groups. To be "treated" for this behavior might seem as strange as going into rehab for acting "normal."

CULTURE PROVIDES CEREMONIAL MEANING FOR ALCOHOL USE

The first notable work on ceremonial use and ethnic drinking practices was undertaken by Bales (1946), who attempted to explain the different rates of drinking between Jews (low) and Irish (high) in terms of symbolic and ceremonial meanings. For Jews, drinking had familial and sacramental significance, whereas for the Irish it represented male convivial bonding.

A high rate of heavy drinking was observed among the Irish in the 1800s. It was said that these individuals drank because they were Irish. Today, some descendants of the Irish continue to live the stereotype; for them, it represents Irishness—they drink because they are Irish. A button displayed on St. Patrick's Day proclaimed, "Today I'm Irish, Tomorrow I'm Hung Over," and a *New York Post* supplement declared this event to be "Three Days of Drinking and Revelry." Jews, on the other hand, think that Jews cannot be alcoholic. That is, they believe that if a person is Jewish, even though he or she drinks a lot, true alcoholism is impossible. If the individual gives up denial, however, and admits to alcoholism, then he or she cannot be Jewish (Blume et al. 1980).

CULTURE PROVIDES MODELS OF ALCOHOLISM

Chapter 2 discussed models of addiction, such as the disease model. U.S. citizens define alcoholism as a disease far more often than French Canadians or French people (Babor et al. 1986). Some South Bronx Hispanics have ascribed alcoholism to "spells," spirits (Garrison and Podell 1981), the evil eye (*mal ojo*), or witchcraft (*brujeria*). The entire addiction may also be ignored or bypassed; ulcers, divorce, or car accidents that an alcohol counselor may recognize as alcoholism-based may instead be traced directly to supernatural influence. One way or another, if it is attributed to a supernatural cause, a supernatural solution may be called upon to cure this problem. Thus, many seek the help of a folk curer (*espiritista, santero,* and so on). Some African Americans interpret their problems as a punishment from God, and they may subscribe to a moral model that conflicts with a disease or other psychiatric or addictive model.

CULTURAL STEREOTYPES OF DRINKING PATTERNS MAY BE MISLEADING

African American drinking patterns run the gamut from middle class cocktail lounges (as seen in liquor ads in *Ebony*), to blue-collar wakes and birthday parties, to the "bottle-gang" of homeless poor. By class, middle-class African American women drinkers are not dramatically different from middle-class white women drinkers: They are typically moderate drinkers, with few nondrinkers and heavy drinkers. Poorer African American female groups have a larger proportion of non-drinkers; among those who do drink, more are heavy drinkers. Breaking it down further, being married, older, and church-affiliated has also been associated with nonacceptance of heavy drinking (Gary and Gary 1985; Kinney 2000). At initially established black colleges and universities, blacks have lower levels of alcohol and other types of drug consumption than are observed at colleges and universities with a majority of white students. At all colleges and universities, white students drink significantly more than African American students (Kinney 2000).

Gordon, who studied a Connecticut city in 1981, examined three Hispanic groups, all new to the United States and all blue-collar. In this group, Dominicans drank less after migration. They emphasized suave or sophisticated drinking,

and they saw drunkenness as indecent (without respect). Alcoholics were seen as "sick," perhaps from some tragic experience. Guatemalans drank substantially more after migration: One-third of males were often drunk and binged most weekends. Being drunk was considered glamorous and sentimentalized—like Humphrey Bogart under the hanging light bulb, alone in a hotel room. These individuals boasted of hangovers, even when they did not have one. The Guatemalan Alcoholics Anonymous (AA) group was alien to Puerto Ricans. Puerto Ricans broke down into middle-class American-style moderate drinkers, depressed and wife-abusing alcoholic welfare recipients, and various sorts of polydrug abusers, including those who entered into the mainland "druggie" youth culture (Gordon 1981). Among Hispanics in general, men were twice as likely to be involved in heavy drinking than both white and African American males (Kinney 2000). In fact, African American students have the lowest lifetime, annual, and 30-day prevalence rates for alcohol use; they also tend to have the lowest rates for daily drinking (NIDA 1999).

Even when looking at physiological responses to alcohol, ethnicity appears to matter. The long-term effects of alcohol dependence are reported to cause more damage to the immune systems of African Americans than other ethnic groups. The greater sensitivity to alcohol and its damaging effects puts this group at an increased risk for infection and, in many cases, at a greater likelihood of death (Rostler 2000).

Blane (1977) surveyed Italian American drinking patterns, comparing recent arrivals (those born abroad but living in the United States for more than 10 years), children of immigrants, and grandchildren of immigrants. Among males, the percentage of daily drinkers declined from 92% to 15% as one moved through the generations, as did wine and cordial consumption. Any heavy use (five drinks at one sitting) rose from one-fifth to three-fifths, and once-a-week heavy use went from one-eighth to one-third. With women, daily drinking declined from 73% to 9%, wine and cordial use was more than halved (although still significantly "Italian"), occasional heavy use rose from 6% to 32%, and weekly heavy use increased from 3% to 10% (Blane 1977).

As information on cultural differences in alcohol use and abuse has become known throughout the alcohol abuse field, administrative agencies have attempted to incorporate these insights into professional standards of practice, under the rubric of "cultural competence." Prevention and treatment programs are to be evaluated from the standpoint of their competence in providing services to the cultural populations they serve. To avoid stereotyping, these considerations include understanding of such variables as ethnic acculturation and skills at eliciting information on the cultural background of clients (OSAP 1992). Prevention issues such as consumption of gateway drugs and media advocacy have been refined to target ethnic at-risk populations. For example, urban African American youths are bombarded with aggressive marketing of 40-ounce malt liquors, known as "40s." Consumption of 40s is celebrated in rap lyrics such as "Tap the Bottle." The alcohol content of malt liquors ranges from 5.6% to 8%, compared with 3.5% for regular beers. This large, inexpensive bottle of potent brew offers a cheap high, often leading to alcohol abuse. Moreover, in the mid-1990s, 40s drinking increasingly became associated with marijuana smoking, going together like cookies and milk, used before school or at "hooky parties."

CULTURE PROVIDES ATTITUDES REGARDING ALCOHOL CONSUMPTION

Although cultures often maintain generalized (normative) attitudes regarding alcohol use and abuse, significant differences in attitudes also exist within cultures (Arkin and Funkhouser 1992; Inciardi 1992). The United States is characterized as culturally ambivalent regarding alcohol use (Kinney 2000). That is, alcohol consumption enormously varies across our culture. Different geographic regions, diverse religious beliefs, and racial and ethnic differences result in confusing attitudes about drinking alcohol. Other factors that contribute to diversity in attitudes include social upbringing, peer group dynamics, social class, income, education, and occupational differences.

What specific impact do such attitudes have on drinking? As just mentioned, attitudes are responsible for making alcohol consumption acceptable or unacceptable—or even relished as a form of behavior. For example, in one segment of impoverished African American groups, alcohol use and abuse are so common that they have become accepted behavior. The following excerpt describes an accepted use of alcohol consumption:

> A party without liquor or a street rap without a bottle is often perceived as unimaginable. These attitudes about drinking are shaped as youth grow up seeing liquor stores in their communities next to schools, churches, and homes. Liquor stores and bootleg dealers frequently permeate the black residential community, where in traditionally white communities they are generally restricted to commercial or business zones. With liquor stores throughout the fabric of black residential life, black youth grow up seeing men drinking in the streets and relatives drinking at home. (Harper 1986)

Contrast this attitude with orthodox religious and fundamentalist communities in which the use of alcohol and other drugs is strictly prohibited:

> I was raised in a very religious, Seventh-Day Adventist family. My father was a pretty strong figure in our little church of 18 members. My mother stayed home most of the time, living in a way like an Old Testament kind of biblical life, so-to-speak. We were strict vegetarians, and all of us in the family had to be very involved with church life. The first time I ever saw alcohol outside of always hearing how corrupting it was to the mind and the body, was when I was 7. One day the father of a friend of mine—the only non-Adventist family friend I was allowed to play with—was drinking a beer in the kitchen when we walked in. I asked, "What's that?" The father's reply was "This is beer, dear John." I looked strangely at him and pretended to be amused at the father's answer. Actually, inside I remember being very surprised and scared at the same time for I was always told that people who drink alcohol were not doing what God wanted them to do in life. *(From Venturelli's*

research files, 18-year-old male university student, May 21, 1993.)

From these contrasting examples, we can see that the values expressed through group and family attitudes regarding drug use are very significant in determining the extent of alcohol consumption.

College and University Students and Alcohol Use

Over the years, alcohol use and consumption rates among college students have remained largely stable, although rates for other drugs show a lot more variance. For example, marijuana use has dramatically risen, fallen, and then risen again. There do exist some interesting findings about college students and alcohol consumption:

- College students drink an estimated 4 billion cans of beer annually.
- The total amount of alcohol consumed by college students each year is 430 million gallons, enough for every college and university in the United States to fill an Olympic-size swimming pool.
- As many as 360,000 of the nation's 12 million undergraduates will die from alcohol-related causes while in school. This is more than the number who will receive master's and doctorate degrees (Alcoholism Kills 2000).
- Nearly half of all college students are binge drinkers.
- The number of college women who drink to get drunk has more than tripled in the past 10 years, rising from 10% to 35%.
- On America's college campuses, alcohol is a factor in 40% of all academic problems and 28% of all dropouts.
- Seventy-five percent of male students and 55% of female students involved in acquaintance rape had been drinking or using drugs at the time.
- For college men, alcohol consumption is inversely related to the size of the institution; that is, male students at smaller institutions consume far more than those at larger institu-

tions. (Lack of social activities could be a precipitating factor.)
- Nearly one-quarter of students report failing a test or project because of the aftereffects of drinking or doing drugs.
- Although only 2 in 20 college students are arrested for driving under the influence, "...27% of students said they drove while under the influence of alcohol ... [and this] ... translates to 2.1 million students." (Hitt 2001, p. 1).
- A related consequence of alcohol abuse is motor vehicle accidents. For young people under the age of 25, motor vehicle accidents rate as the number one cause of death (Presley et al. 1996).
- Findings from the CORE Institute survey (see paragraph following this list) indicate that 300,000 of today's college students will die of alcohol-related causes, such as drunk driving accidents, liver disorders, sexually transmitted diseases from improper sexual protection (lack of condoms leading to HIV), cancers from alcohol abuse, and severely damaged organs from chronic drinking (see Chapter 7; Phoenix House 2000).
- Although the average cost for book purchases for classes is about $450 per year, the average student spends about $900 on alcohol each year (Phoenix House 2000).
- On the positive side, there is a small but very significant downward trend in alcohol use on America's campuses. In 1985, the percentage of college students who had consumed alcohol in the previous 30 days was approximately 80%. By 1990, that number had declined to 74.5% and it continues to decline each year. However, counterbalancing this positive trend, the use of other illegitimate-type drugs continues to increase. Further, the latest studies show that although overall alcohol consumption is slowly decreasing, binge drinking remains high on most campuses throughout the United States (Wechsler et al. 2000b).

The CORE Institute survey is a validated survey instrument that has been administered to more than 1 million students—by far the largest sample of college students surveyed. The available figures

Alcohol consumption is routine at many social activities for college students.

from this survey (Presley et al. 1996) indicate that on average, approximately 83% of college students consumed alcohol within the year this survey was given. The average number of drinks that students consumed was 5.1 per week (Presley et al. 1996). Approximately 42% engaged in binge drinking 2 weeks before the CORE survey was administered. Of all the drugs reported, alcohol was the most heavily abused on college campuses, followed by tobacco (44%) and marijuana (31%).

BINGE DRINKING

Binge drinking is defined as consumption of five or more drinks in one sitting or five or more drinks in short succession. The widely reported study by Wechsler and colleagues (1994 and 2000a) brought this issue to the public's attention. One report, which surveyed 17,592 students at 140 campuses, revealed that 44% engaged in binge drinking, which impacted on many areas of students' lives—both their own and those of others whose lives were disrupted by this behavior (giving rise to the term *secondhand drinking*).

As mentioned in the previous section, 42% to 50% of all college students often binge drink.[1]

_____

1. The variation depends on the methodology of testing (self-report versus survey) and type of campuses (private versus public institutions, alcohol policies and extent of police enforcement, size of campuses, urban versus rural campuses, commuter versus dormitory, college versus university).

This type of alcohol consumption remains very worrisome to anyone supporting, nurturing, protecting, caring for, and responsible for the behavior of young people in this subculture. In addition, health professionals see this as a serious form of alcohol abuse.

One may question whether all five-drink episodes qualify as *binge drinking*, a term that calls to mind a weekend of drinking, or Jellinek's epsilon alcoholism. However, 11.1% of males and 7.4% of females reported three or more episodes of memory loss during the past year due to drug or alcohol use, of which the overwhelming majority were alcohol-related, both because alcohol is the major drug consumed by students and because it produces amnesiac episodes. Amnesiac episodes are accepted as symptoms of problem drinking behavior.

In one national survey of 17,600 students at 140 4-year colleges and universities, which is regularly conducted by the Harvard School of Public Health (Wechsler et al. 2000b, p. 1), the findings were as follows:

- "Overall, 44% of the students were binge drinkers. Among men, 50% were binge drinkers; among women, the figure was 39%."
- "The main reason given for binge drinking was 'to get drunk.'"
- "Being white, involved in athletics, or a resident of a fraternity or sorority made it more likely that a student would be a binge drinker."
- "White students were over twice as likely to be binge drinkers compared to other racial/ethnic groups."
- "Students who said that religious participation is not very important to them were more than twice as likely to be binge drinkers compared to other students."
- "Students who said that athletic participation was very important or important to them were also one-and-a-half times more likely to be binge drinkers."
- "Residents of fraternities or sororities were four times as likely to be binge drinkers compared to other students."

Another study revealed the following:

- Community college students were less likely to engage in binge drinking: 29.9% had binged in the previous 2 weeks compared with 40.4% of their peers at 4-year schools.

- Approximately one-fourth of all males enrolled at 4-year colleges reported three or more binge episodes during the previous 2 weeks.
- Students who lived on campus were more likely to binge drink than those who lived off campus. Furthermore, older, working, off-campus students were less likely to engage in such behavior, lowering their scores in this regard relative to the standard college student.
- Native American students had the highest frequency of drinking episodes, binge drinking, and memory loss, followed (in order) by white, Hispanic, African American, and Asian students.

GENDER AND COLLEGIATE ALCOHOL USE

The findings from the CORE survey consistently indicate greater frequency of male drinking, frequency of male binge drinking, and consequences of drinking. In a review of the literature addressing gender and student drinking patterns, Berkowitz and Perkins (1987) found a historical pattern of male-dominated college drinking patterns. The transition into college is associated with a doubling of the percentages of those who drink for both genders. Both men and women drink to enhance sociability or social interaction, to escape negative emotions or release otherwise unacceptable ones, and to simply get drunk. "Drinking to get drunk"

It is not unusual to overconsume alcohol when college students are "partying."

is generally considered more of a male pursuit. Indeed, males are more frequently associated with binge drinking and negative public consequences than female drinkers. Severe drunkenness and a customary rowdiness or drunken comportment are normative for male drinkers who binge, with the results including fighting, property damage, and troubles with authorities. The latter were twice as likely to be male problems.

Unsurprisingly, drinking is inversely related to academic achievement. With heavier drinkers, grades suffered for both male and female students. According to the studies cited by Berkowitz and Perkins (1987) for binge drinkers, the impact on impaired academic performance is just as great for women drinkers. More recent information (De Jong 1995; Presley et al. 1996; Wechsler 2000a, 2000b) corroborates this finding and shows similar consequences among male and female binge drinkers in terms of health problems, personal injury, and unplanned sexual activity. Over the past few decades, however, drinking behaviors (amount and percentage of drinking) have been becoming more similar between males and females.

Alcohol Consumption Patterns of Women

Women are affected by alcohol differently than are men. Women possess greater sensitivity to alcohol, have a greater likelihood of addiction, and develop alcohol-related health problems sooner than men.[2] Why do women respond differently than men to alcohol? Three reasons are (1) women have a smaller body size (men are generally larger than women); (2) women absorb alcohol sooner than men because on average they possess more body fat and body fat does not dilute alcohol as well as water (male bodies contain more water); and (3) women possess less of a metabolizing enzyme that functions to get rid of (process out) alcohol.

In Great Britain, for example, the proportion of women drinking has risen steadily since 1984. This

2. Even currently accepted definitions of binge drinking differ by gender. For men, binge drinking consists of *five* or more drinks; for women, binge drinking consists of *four* or more drinks in one sitting.

increase in drinking still holds true for all age groups with the exception of women older than 65 (Alcohol Concern 2000). Other notable facts regarding women and drinking can be summarized as follows (*About.com* 1998):

- Although men begin drinking earlier in life, women are more likely than men to start drinking heavily later in life.
- Women are more easily affected by alcohol consumption, both its effects and diseases related to alcoholism—cirrhosis of the liver, stomach cancer, and so on.
- Women's alcohol consumption is often similar to that of people they are close to, such as a lover or husband.
- Full-time working, professionally oriented women drink at the end of their working day, whereas women who stay at home drink alcohol throughout the day.

- More women in alcohol treatment come from sexually abusive homes (70%), in comparison to men (12%).
- Today, women are more visible and their behavior, especially alcohol consumption, is more observable (e.g., drinking in bars, purchasing alcohol).

Figure 8.8 shows the prevalence of reported alcohol consumption among women of childbearing age (18 to 44 years). The highest consumption of alcohol for these women was found in Wisconsin (19.4%), Iowa (18.9%), and Pennsylvania (18.8%). The lowest consumption was found in Tennessee (4.0%), Kentucky (5.2%), and West Virginia (5.3%). As a group, alcohol-abusing women are more likely to drink alone at home. A high incidence of alcohol abuse is found in women who are unemployed and looking for work, whereas less alcohol abuse is likely in women who are em-

FIGURE 8.8

Prevalence of reported frequent alcohol consumption* among childbearing-age women (18 to 44 years)—United States, Behavioral Risk Factor Surveillance System, 1995.

*Consumption of an average of seven or more drinks per week or five or more drinks on at least one occasion during the preceding month.

Source: Centers for Disease Control and Prevention (CDC) Wonder. Available http://wonder.cdc.gov/wonder/prevguid/moo47306/graphic.htm.

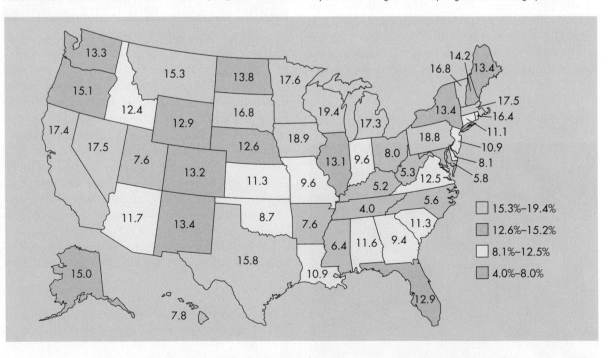

ployed part-time. Divorced or separated women, women who never marry, and those who are unmarried and living with a partner are more likely to use and abuse alcohol than married women. Other high-risk groups are women in their twenties and early thirties and women with heavy-drinking husbands or partners. Other researchers (Wilsnack et al. 1986; Williams et al. 1997) found that women who experience depression or encounter problems with fertility or menopausal changes also demonstrate heavier drinking behavior.

Looking at specific age groups, the following conclusions were drawn by the National Institute on Alcohol Abuse and Alcoholism (1990, 1992) and by Waters at Northern Arizona University (1999):

1. The course of alcohol addiction progresses at a faster rate among women than among men.
2. For many women, heavy drinking came after a health problem such as depression or reproductive difficulties.
3. Women in the 21- to 34-year-old age group were least likely to report alcohol-related problems if they had stable marriages and were working full-time. In other words, young mothers with full-time occupations reported less reliance on alcohol in comparison to childless women without full-time work.
4. Women tend to marry men whose drinking habits match their own.
5. In the 35- to 49-year-old age group, the heaviest drinkers were divorced or separated women without children in the home.
6. In the 50- to 64-year-old age group, the heaviest drinkers were women whose husbands or partners drank heavily.
7. Women 65 years and older constitute less than 10% of drinkers with drinking problems.

More alcohol consumption is also found in women who closely work in traditionally so-called masculine occupations and levels of management, such as executives and traditional blue-collar occupations.

In April 1995, former First Lady Betty Ford made the following statement: Today, we know that when a woman abuses alcohol or other drugs, the risk to her health is much greater than it is for a man. Yet there is not enough prevention, intervention, and treatment targeting women. It is still much harder for women to get help. That needs to change. (SAMHSA 1995, p. 14)

In fact, women risk serious health consequences when they choose to use alcohol and other drugs. Alcohol, in particular, can often be devastating to women's health.

Not only does alcohol have a greater immediate effect on women, but its long-term risks are also more dangerous. Some surveys now show that more alcohol consumption occurs among girls 12 to 17 years old than among boys of the same age. This places young women at a risk of delaying the onset of puberty, a condition that can wreak havoc in terms of adolescent maturation.

Finally, women are more likely to combine alcohol with prescription drugs than men are. When the use of other drugs enters into the equation, ovulation may become inhibited and fertility may be adversely affected. Women also risk early menopause when they consume alcohol.

THE ROLE OF ALCOHOL IN DOMESTIC VIOLENCE

Much attention became focused on domestic violence in the mid-1990s through high-profile criminal cases such as those involving the Menendez brothers and O. J. Simpson. The increased emphasis on decreasing domestic violence has inspired much research into its causes and effects as well as into common traits of abusers. Recent studies have found a significant relationship between the incidence of battering and the abuse of alcohol; furthermore, the abuse of alcohol overwhelmingly emerges as a primary predictor of marital violence (De Jong 1995; Drug Strategies 1999). A study of 2000 American couples conducted in 1993 showed that rates of domestic violence were as much as 15 times higher in households in which the husband was described as "often" being drunk, as opposed to "never" drunk (Collins and Messerschmidt 1993). The same study found that alcohol was present in more than half of all reported incidences of domestic abuse.

Domestic violence also creates significant problems for its victims later in life. A study of 472 women by the Research Institute on Addictions found that 87% of female alcoholics had been physically or sexually abused as children (Drug Strategies 1999; Miller and Downs 1993). The insidiousness of domestic violence may exist because of the consistent abuse of alcohol that is associated with both abusers and victims. Given these disturbing statistics, more research and counseling programs focused on the prevention of alcoholism and subsequent domestic violence is necessary before the very foundations of identity, security, and happiness are forever destroyed. As one reformed alcoholic explains:

> I had gone too far. I had abused my family, I had beaten my wife. I had driven them off, all for a drink. (*From Venturelli's research files, 50-year-old male, October 1996.*)

ALCOHOL AND SEX

Alcohol use is linked to an overwhelming proportion of unwanted sexual behaviors, including **acquaintance and date rape**, unplanned pregnancies, and sexually transmitted diseases, including HIV infections (Abbey 1990; WHO/OMS 1998). Factors that immediately come to mind include disinhibition concerning restraints on sexuality, poor judgment, and unconsciousness or helplessness on the part of victims. The links between unwanted sex and substance abuse are subtler than many imagine, however. Although disinhibition, impulsivity, and helplessness are certainly major considerations, other elements come into play, as illustrated in the following paragraphs.

KEY TERMS

acquaintance and date rape
unplanned and unwanted forced sexual attack from a friend or a date partner

codependency
behavior displayed by either addicted or nonaddicted family members (codependents) who identify with the alcohol addict and cover up the excessive drinking behavior, allowing it to continue and letting it affect the codependent's life

enablers
those close to the alcohol addict who deny or make excuses for enabling the excessive drinking

Recall the drunken comportment thesis that was introduced in the section on culture and drinking behavior. Some nonreligious ceremonial drinking settings incorporate expectations of disinhibited behaviors, such as at holiday office parties. Drinking is a signal or cue that it is acceptable to be amorous, even sexually aggressive, and that the intoxicated object of one's affections will not object and is disinhibited.

Intoxicated people are not as capable of attending to multiple cues. When cues are ambiguous, drunken men are more likely to miss the ambiguity and to interpret cues as meaning that sex will occur and should be initiated (men are generally more likely to interpret friendly cues as sexual signals, but intoxication makes this misunderstanding more likely). In addition, possible dangers implicit in a private setting, on a date, with a drunken male will not be picked up as often or as easily by the intoxicated and potentially victimized female (Abbey 1990).

Alcohol and the Family: Destructive Types of Support and Organizations for Victims of Alcoholics

CODEPENDENCY AND ENABLING

Codependency and enabling generally occur together. **Codependency** (which some call *co-alcoholism*) refers to a relationship pattern, and *enabling* refers to a set of specific behaviors (Doweiko 1999). Codependency is defined as the behavior displayed by either addicted or nonaddicted family members (codependents) who identify with the alcohol addict and *cover up* the excessive drinking behavior. An example of codependency is when a family member remains silent when empty bottles of vodka (for example) are discovered under a bed or in the garage.

Enablers are those close to the alcohol addict who deny or make excuses for enabling the excessive drinking. Often, both codependency and enabling are done by the same person. An example is the husband who calmly conspires and phones his wife's place of employment and reports that his wife has stomach flu when the reality is that she is too drunk or hung over to even realize it is time to go to work.

Such a husband is both codependent and an enabler. He lies to cover up his wife's addiction and enables her not to face her irresponsible drinking behavior. In this example, the husband is responsible for perpetuating the spouse's addiction. Even quiet toleration of the alcoholic's addiction enables the drinker to continue the drinking behavior.

CHILDREN OF ALCOHOLICS (COAS) AND ADULT CHILDREN OF ALCOHOLICS (ACOAS)

Alcoholism is a disease of the family. Not only is there a significant genetic component that is passed from generation to generation, but also the drinking problems of a single-family member affect all other family members. The family environment and genetics can perpetuate a vicious and destructive cycle. (George Washington University Medical Center 2003, pp. 1–2)

Children of alcoholics are at high risk for developing problems with alcohol and other drugs; they often do poorly at school, live with pervasive tension and stress, have high levels of anxiety and depression and experience coping problems. (George Washington University Medical Center 2003, pp. 1–2)

It is estimated that out of 260 million Americans, 14 million Americans—7.4% of the population—meet the diagnostic criteria for alcohol abuse or alcoholism (Grant et al. 1997). There are 28.6 million COAs in the United States, and 6.6 million are younger than the age of 18 (Alcoholism Kills 2000; NCADI 1992). Approximately 25% of American children are exposed before the age of 18 to at least one person in the family who is either an alcoholic or an alcohol abuser (George Washington University Medical Center 2003). Children of alcoholics are at high risk of developing the same attachment to alcohol. Alcoholics are more likely than nonalcoholics to have an alcoholic parent, sibling, or other relative.

Within the last decade, both COAs and ACOAs have been studied extensively. Here are some findings concerning these two groups:

1. COAs are two to four times more likely to develop alcoholism. In addition, both COAs and ACOAs are more likely to marry into families in which alcoholism is prevalent.
2. Approximately one-third of alcoholics come from families in which one parent was or is an alcoholic.
3. Both physiological and environmental factors appear to place COAs and ACOAs at greater risk of becoming alcoholics.
4. COAs and ACOAs exhibit more symptoms of depression and anxiety than do children of nonalcoholic parents.
5. Young children of alcoholics exhibit an excessive amount of crying, bed-wetting, and sleep problems, such as nightmares.
6. Teenagers display excessive perfectionism, hoarding, staying by themselves (loners), and excessive self-consciousness.
7. Phobias develop, and difficulty with school performance is not uncommon.

Treatment of Alcoholism

Chapter 18 provides an overview of treatment and rehabilitation of addicts. Although treatment of alcoholism and treatment of other addictions have somewhat separate historical roots and consequently gave rise to separate therapy systems, governmental authorities, and counselor certifications, they have now merged in most states in the United States. In addition to recognizing that alcohol is a drug addiction, epidemiologically few "pure" alcoholics and drug addicts exist any more. Most addicts drink in addition to their other drug addictions (making them *polydrug users*); many alcoholics abuse other drugs; and some move through stages of heroin, methadone, and alcohol use, in that order. Alcoholism and its treatment have a few special features:

1. While addicts remain in denial, the socially acceptable nature of drinking, or even of heavy drinking, makes it easier to maintain denial as a psychological defense. As an example, it is more difficult to remain in denial of crack addiction.

2. Although all addictions are **relapsing syndrome** and most addicts have a tendency to relapse, the social environment that permits or even encourages drinking and the ready availability of alcohol make it easy to relapse without a radical shift in lifestyle. Again, the alcoholic is buffered within a subcultural (social and cultural) cloud of use. Alcoholics Anonymous remains particularly vigilant in looking for signs of relapse, advising the alcoholic to "keep the memory regarding the misery of addiction green," to HALT (which stands for do not get too **h**ungry, **a**ngry, **l**onely, or **t**hirsty/**t**ired, as these are possible relapse triggers), and not to become isolated from others but to stay in the support system, making phone calls and attending "90 meetings in 90 days."

3. Alcohol rehabilitation differs from other addiction treatments mainly in its medical ramifications. Alcoholism is devastating to the liver, muscles, nutritional system, gastrointestinal system, and brain. Alcoholics who have become "dry" only recently may still suffer from pancreatitis, weakness, impaired cognitive capacities, and so forth. The fact that treatment is so structured, simplified, and made into a slogan ("Don't drink and go to meetings," "Keep coming: It works") makes it possible for the bleary and confused, recently dried-out alcoholic to follow (an AA term for this condition is *mokus*). Although the cognitive impairment tends to clear up somewhat over a period of 6 months (unless clear cortical wasting has occurred, a condition known as "wet brain"), the alcoholic is often physi-

cally ravaged to an extent that requires years to mend the damage, if it is ever possible.

4. The alcoholic is typically more emotionally fragile than other addicts in treatment.

5. The other major medical ramification is withdrawal. Withdrawal from alcohol and withdrawal from barbiturates are the two most severe withdrawal syndromes. Before modern medical management techniques, many individuals succumbed to **acute alcohol withdrawal syndrome**.

GETTING THROUGH WITHDRAWAL

An alcoholic who is well nourished and in good physical condition can go through withdrawal as an outpatient with reasonable safety. However, an acutely ill alcoholic needs medically supervised care. A general hospital ward is best for preliminary treatment.

The alcohol withdrawal syndrome is quite similar to that described in Chapter 6 for barbiturates and other sedative hypnotics. Symptoms typically appear within 12 to 72 hours after total cessation of drinking but can appear whenever the blood alcohol level drops below a certain point. The alcoholic experiences severe muscle tremors, nausea, and anxiety. In extremely acute alcohol syndromes, a condition known as **delirium tremens** occurs, in which the individual hallucinates, is delirious, and suffers from a high fever and rapid heartbeat. Delirium tremens, commonly called DTs, is an uncommon but life-threatening condition.

Alcohol withdrawal syndrome reaches its peak intensity within 24 to 48 hours. About 5% of the alcoholics in hospitals and perhaps 20% to 25% who suffer the DTs without treatment die. Phenobarbital, chlordiazepoxide (Librium), and diazepam (Valium) are commonly prescribed to prevent withdrawal symptoms. Simultaneously, the alcoholic may need treatment for malnutrition and vitamin deficiencies (especially the B vitamins). Pneumonia is also a frequent complication. After the alcoholic patient is over the acute stages of intoxication and withdrawal, administration of CNS depressants may be continued for a few weeks, with care taken not to transfer dependence on alcohol to dependence on the depressants. Long-

KEY TERMS

relapsing syndrome
returning to the use of alcohol after quitting

acute alcohol withdrawal syndrome
symptoms that occur when an individual who is addicted to alcohol does not maintain his or her usual blood alcohol level

delirium tremens
the DDTs; the most severe, even life-threatening form of alcohol withdrawal, involving hallucinations, delirium, and fever

term treatment with sedatives (such as Librium or Valium) does not prevent a relapse of drinking or assist with behavioral adaptation. A prescription of disulfiram (Antabuse) may be offered to encourage patients to abstain from alcohol; it blocks metabolism of acetaldehyde, so that drinking any alcohol will result in a pounding headache, flushing, nausea, and other unpleasant symptoms. The patient must decide about 2 days in advance to stop taking Antabuse before he or she can drink. Antabuse is an aid to other supportive treatments, not the sole method of therapy.

HELPING THE ALCOHOLIC FAMILY RECOVER

Alcoholism is a pervasive family disease. The family is a system, not of planets or subatomic particles, but of people who affect one another and who play certain roles, all maintaining a balance in the system. We are all familiar with the stereotype of families in which the oldest child is the "hero," the middle child is "forgotten," and the youngest is the "baby." Whatever the roles of the individuals, when the family includes an alcoholic, it means that a member of the system is ill. The system adapts to dysfunction by rearranging itself around the problem. The family is like a mobile, a sculpture with interdependent parts that revolve around one another. We are not talking about adjusting to a person with a broken leg or diabetes, but someone who is in denial—manipulative, lying, and blaming other family members. By adjusting around the addiction, the family members enable the addict to progress further along the disease path. Roles become exaggerated and distorted. Persons may be blamed, scapegoated, or lost and forgotten. One major adaptation is related to the person who "takes up the slack" by assuming extra responsibilities and taking on the role of a parent or even spouse.

Early family therapy systems research described how the family often acts as a unit. It focused on the disturbed communication patterns within families and the process by which the family throws up a scapegoat, often in the form of a child who is presented as the "identified patient" (Kolevzon and Green 1985). The concept of the "super-responsible one" was first described by Virginia Satir in 1964. In

Even after the alcoholic is ready for rehabilitation, the other family members will also need treatment and support.

modern, popular writing on addiction in the family and codependent roles of children that are carried into adulthood, all of these roles are depicted as especially characteristic of addicted families (Wegscheider 1991). Because such roles are so common, many individuals may identify with them and ascribe a variety of ills to their being addict offspring. Many individuals do suffer tremendously from the legacy of family addiction, and some have indeed been cast in one of these roles as a by-product of addiction in the family. Acting as if only one kind of family or one kind of addicted family exists, which transcends cultural backgrounds, is not much better than saying that all languages or religions are the same, however. For example, "executive authority" over younger children can be the normal role of the eldest female child in African American families as part of a broader pattern of role flexibility (Brisbane 1985, 1986). When an older child plays a parental part in the family, it may represent culturally routine behavior or it may be indicative of a response to addiction in the family.

There is some gain or perceived benefit to the person playing a role, and to the system as a whole, in the individual's actions, although this gain may seem very indirect and, in fact, be injurious in the long run. Although the super-responsible person may be overburdened and resentful, he or she also feels important, heroic, and capable. Over a period, this role solidifies. Perhaps the hero becomes unable to remember or imagine it any other way. If the alcoholic enters or promises to enter into recovery, it may threaten the benefits to the family member. One of many examples is a wife in a subservient role who relishes, at some level, the power, control, and authority she enjoys with an alcoholic husband or the recognition she receives in martyrdom—perhaps her only recognition in life. Another example is the child who is given executive authority, prematurely, in the family. Without knowing it, the family members may resist change, not only for what they may have to give up but also because change is always feared. Thus, they may undermine recovery.

The role systems found in alcoholic families can be enmeshed so that everyone is hyperresponsive to and dependent on one another: disorganized, chaotic, or exploded into nothingness. The old-fashioned, middle-class alcoholic family is commonly enmeshed. If religion represents a barrier to divorce, and hence removal of the alcoholic, this situation is even more likely to arise.

A family counselor can help the family members understand the roles they are playing and start a process of change. This recognition allows family members to develop their own identities separate from the roles they have been playing. Two of the techniques used in understanding roles and relationships are **psychodrama** (or **role playing**) and the **genogram**, a kind of family tree in which behavioral relationships as well as biological relationships are explored.

The family counselor can help the family members figure out their patterns of thinking, which involves certain modes of information processing. In the alcoholic family, these patterns typically involve denial, minimization, rationalization, shame, blame, and projection. Counselors also rely on certain self statements (see "Here and Now," The "Top Tens" of Helping Alcoholics and Their Families).

In addition, the family counselor can help the family members understand their patterns of communication. Alcoholic family communication is almost certainly a type of abnormal communication, characterized by either simple absence of communication (chaotic, destructive, manipulative, blaming) or a combination of communication methods. What the family does in the public view, visible to the outside world ("front stage"), differs from what goes on when the family is done ("back stage"). Some individuals may be cut off from communication or embroiled in endless argument and acrimony. Teaching people how to communicate their feelings and opinions in a direct, honest, and nonhurtful way begins the healing process.

The alcoholic family is injured, traumatized, often in debt, and collectively suffering from **post-traumatic stress disorder**. Impacted grief, loss, pain, and rage are present. Healing will not take place overnight and will not occur just because the alcoholic stops drinking. The child, in particular, may have been wounded by violence, neglect, and inconsistent parenting, and may have been witness to sex, violence, or depression.

KEY TERMS

psychodrama
a family therapy system developed by Jacques Moreno in which significant interpersonal and intrapersonal issues are enacted in a focused setting using dramatic techniques

role playing
a therapeutic technique in which group members play assigned parts to elicit emotional reactions

genogram
a family therapy technique that records information about behavior and relationships on a type of family tree to elucidate persistent patterns of dysfunctional behavior

post-traumatic stress disorder
a psychiatric syndrome in which an individual who has been exposed to a traumatic event or situation experiences persistent psychological stress that may manifest itself in a wide range of symptoms, including reexperiencing the trauma, numbing of general responsiveness, and hyperarousal

Discussion Questions

1. Why do you think alcohol has always been part of our existence as human beings?

2. Cite five positive and five negative outcomes of alcohol use. Do you think negatives outweigh the positives? If so, why? If not, why not?

3. Look at the pyramid of drinkers shown in Figure 8.2. How do you think the percentages

Here and Now

The "Top Tens" of Helping Alcoholics and Their Families

10 "Don'ts"

Don't "persecute" the addict. Confront lovingly.

Don't have the goal of "saving the family."

Don't start sentences with "you never," or "you always."

Don't live in the past or in the future.

Don't make excuses for the alcoholic.

Don't let the alcoholic be the center of your life.

Don't clean up after the alcoholic (literally or figuratively).

Don't protect the alcoholic from the consequences of his or her behavior.

Don't blame, excuse, justify, or rationalize.

Don't join in drinking.

10 "Do's"

Set limits, using "I" words (I need to stop)

Set limits empathetically (I know, you want me to _____, but I can't).

Detach, lovingly, from the addict's problems.

Teach parenting skills.

Concentrate on the here and now.

Talk about violence and abuse.

Remember that you didn't cause it, you can't cure it, and you can't control it.

Take life a day at a time.

Give "self" assignments, taking care of yourself.

Accept the right to have your feelings and for others to have their feelings.

10 Alcoholic Family Self-Statements

In an Actively Alcoholic Family

"Don't talk" (about how you feel, about what's going on).

"Don't trust."

"Don't feel."

"Alcoholism isn't the cause of our problems."

"Keep the status quo at all costs."

In a Family Having a Hard Time Becoming Used to Sobriety

"We liked you better drunk."

"You're always away at AA meetings."

"Who are these people you're always having coffee with?"

"I felt important feeding my brothers and sisters, Mom."

"I felt important going to the school on Open School Night, Dad."

10 Roles for Spouses of Alcoholics

Rescuer

Long-suffering martyr

Blamer, conscience

Fellow drinker

Placater

Overextended, superresponsible one

Composed computer

Sick hypochondriac

Scapegoat ("it's all your fault")

Avoider

10 Roles for Children of Alcoholics

Family hero*

Scapegoat*

Lost child*

Mascot*

Placater

Sick role

Parental child or pseudoparent to younger children

Pseudoparent to alcoholic parent

Pseudospouse to sober parent

Place of refuge (for younger children)

*Wegscheider, S. *Another Chance.* Palo Alto, CA: Science and Behavior Books, 1991.

Source: Inservice Training Program, Essex County, New Jersey, Professional Advisory Committee on Alcohol and Drug Abuse. November 1993. Prepared by Peter L. Myers, Ph.D. *Helping the Alcoholic Family Recover.*

will change 10 years, 20 years, and 30 years from now? Support your projections.

4. In light of having read Chapters 7 and 8, what are three positive and three negative outcomes regarding lowering the legal drinking age to 18?

5. Do you personally believe in the strong independent effects of set and setting and pseudo-intoxication? Can these psychological processes have more effects on the alcohol user than the alcohol itself? Wherever possible, give personal examples.

6. Why do you think the temperance movement and Prohibition failed? Cite three main reasons that also support the text material.

7. It is believed that gays and homeless people tend to abuse alcohol more than the straight (heterosexual) and nonhomeless populations. What are three reasons why you think each of the members of these two subcultures have a tendency to overconsume alcohol?

8. Why do you think children desire to consume alcohol with their peers?

9. After reviewing the different definitions of what is an alcoholic, what definition do you believe suits you best? Write out a clear definition of what you think is a "real" alcoholic.

10. What specific criteria would you include when teaching college students to drink in moderation during freshman orientation?

11. Should alcohol be available on college campuses for those 21 years of age or over? Why or why not?

12. Recall and discuss the question of how you may have unknowingly acted as an enabler for a family member or a friend. Can you cite the reason why you acted like this?

Key Terms

binge drinking   210

heavy drinkers   210

teetotalers   213

speakeasies   222

bootlegging   222

patent medicines   222

alcohol abuse   226

alcoholism   226

drunken comportment   229

disinhibitor   229

set and setting   229

pseudointoxicated   229

acquaintance and date rape   238

codependency   238

enablers   238

relapsing syndrome   240

acute alcohol withdrawal syndrome   240

delirium tremens   240

psychodrama   242

role playing   242

genogram   242

post-traumatic stress disorder   242

Summary

1 Approximately 50% of Americans aged 12 or older (119 million people) indicated that they were current drinkers of alcohol in 2003. Approximately 23% participated in binge drinking at least once in the 30 days before the 2003 National Survey on Drug Use and Health, and approximately 16 million (6.8%) were heavy drinkers.

2 Luxembourg ranks first in terms of consumption of alcohol, followed by Germany and France. The lowest levels of drinking are found in Turkey, Kyrgyzstan, Turkmenistan, Israel, and Armenia.

3 Globally, alcohol costs add up to more than $250 billion yearly when including illness, accidents, and crime connected to alcohol. Much of the economic burden of alcohol abuse falls on segments of the population *other than* the alcohol abusers themselves. Approximately 45% of the estimated total cost is borne by alcohol abusers and their families, almost all of which is due to lost or reduced earnings. Approximately 20% of the total estimated cost of alcohol abuse is borne by the federal government and 18% by state and local governments. Each year, more than 107,400 people die because of alcohol-related abuse. Productivity losses resulting from alcohol-related illness were estimated at $87.6 billion for 1998 (NIAAA 2000). Total costs attributed to alcohol-related motor vehicle crashes were estimated to be $24.7 billion. Expenditures for alcohol-related crime totaled $6.2 billion, and $17.4 billion for illicit drugs. Alcohol abuse is estimated to have contributed to 25% to 30% of violent crime. Finally, alcohol is officially linked to at least half of all highway fatalities, and that figure includes only legal intoxication. In most states, the cutoff for the illegal blood alcohol level ranges from 0.08% to 0.1%.

4 The temperance movement was a response to the heaviest drinking period in America during Jefferson's term in office (1800–1808). The original goal of this movement was to promote moderate use of alcohol. Largely because it was unsuccessful, the temperance movement began advocating total abstinence. Over the course of the 19th century, reformers sought to have complete prohibition enacted into law. Shortly after Prohibition laws were created making alcohol use illegal, organized crime monopolized the production and sale of alcohol as an illicit drug.

5 There are several accepted definitions of alcoholism. Alcohol addiction involves both a physical and psychological dependence on ethanol. Most definitions include chronic behavioral disorders, repeated drinking to the point of loss of control, health disorders, and difficulty functioning socially and economically.

6 The definition of who is a problem drinker varies from one culture to the next. In Poland, a person becomes a problem drinker when there is a loss of productivity. Californians find that drunken driving violations are a key indication.

For Italian Americans, an inability to provide for one's family because of heavy drinking qualifies a person as a problem drinker.

7 Culture influences our view of alcohol and alcohol consumption. Culture dictates the self-definition, attachment, and intensity of our behavior. For example, with regard to drinking, much of how we feel after ingesting alcohol is determined by social and psychological experiences. In addition to the amount consumed, *drunken comportment* refers to society's expectations regarding drinking behavior. *Set and setting* refer to the expectation and the environment where alcohol is consumed. *Pseudointoxication* refers to the psychological belief regarding how one feels under the effects of alcohol—that is, how inebriated the drinker imagines the effect of the consumed alcohol.

8 The broader ways in which culture influences the consumption of alcohol are the following: (1) Culture provides rules for drinking behavior; (2) culture provides ceremonial meaning for alcohol use; (3) culture provides models of alcoholism; and (4) culture provides attitudes regarding alcohol consumption.

9 Regarding alcohol and college students, (1) college students consume an estimated 4 billion cans of beer annually; (2) nearly half of all college students are binge drinkers; (3) one consequence of alcohol abuse is motor vehicle accidents (the number one cause of death in people younger than age 25 is motor vehicle accidents); and (4) 75% of male students and 55% of female students involved in acquaintance rape had been drinking or using drugs at the time.

10 In comparison to men, women possess greater sensitivity to alcohol, are more likely to become addicted, and develop health problems earlier in life than men. Three main reasons why women are more sensitive and are more easily affected by alcohol use are (1) men have larger bodies than women; (2) women absorb alcohol sooner than men because women have more body fat (fat does not dilute alcohol) and men's bodies contain more water; and (3) women possess less of a metabolizing enzyme that functions to get rid of (process out) alcohol.

11 Codependency and enabling generally occur together. *Codependency* is the behavior that a family member or close friend displays to cover up the excessive drinking. *Enabling* refers to anyone who helps the excessive drinker deny or makes excuses for the excessive drinking.

12 Alcoholism treatment must take into consideration physical withdrawal *and* denial.

References

Abbey, A. "Sex and Substance Abuse: What Are the Links?" *Eta Sigma Gamman* 22 (Fall 1990): 16–18.

Adams, S. H. "The Great American Fraud." *Collier's* 36, 5 (1905): 17–18; 10 (1905): 16–18; 16 (1906): 18–20.

Alcohol Concern 2000. *Alcohol Concern Fact Sheet* 27, London (3 August 2000). Available www.alcoholconcern. org.uk/information/factsheets/factsheet27.htm.

Alcoholism Kills. "Alcoholism Facts." (May 2000). Available http://www.alcoholismkills.com/alcoholi.htm.

Arkin, E. B., and J. E. Funkhouser, eds. *Communicating About Alcohol and Other Drugs: Strategies for Reaching Populations at Risk,* OSAP Prevention Monograph No. 5. Rockville, MD: Office of Substance Abuse Prevention, U.S. Department of Health and Human Services, 1992.

Austin, G. A. "Perspectives on the History of Psychoactive Substance Use." *National Institute on Drug Abuse Research Issues* 23. Washington, DC: U.S. Department of Health, Education, and Welfare, 1978.

Babor, T. F., M. Hesselbrock, S. Radouce-Thomas, L. Feguer, J. P. Ferrant, and K. Choquette. "Concepts of Alcoholism Among American, French-Canadian, and French Alcoholics." In *Alcohol and Culture: Comparative Perspectives from Europe and America,* edited by T. F. Babor, 98–109. New York: Academy of Sciences, 1986.

Bales R. F. "Cultural Differences in Rates of Alcoholism." *Quarterly Journal of Studies on Alcohol* 6 (1946): 489–499.

Berkowitz, A. D., and H. W. Perkins. "Recent Research on Gender Differences in Collegiate Alcohol Use." *Journal of American College Health* 36 (September 1987): 12–15.

Blane, H. "Acculturation and Drinking in an Italian American Community." *Journal of Studies on Alcohol* 38 (1977): 1324–1344.

Blume, S., D. Dropkin, and L. Sokolow. "The Jewish Alcoholic: A Descriptive Study." *Alcohol, Health, and Research World* 4 (1980): 21–26.

Brisbane, F. L. "Understanding the Female Child Role of Family Hero in Black Alcoholic Families." *Bulletin of the NY State Chapter of the National Black Alcoholism Council* 4 (April 1985).

Brisbane, F. L. "A Self-Help Model for Working with Black Women of Alcoholic Parents." *Alcoholism Treatment Quarterly* 2 (Fall 1985b/Winter 1986): 47–53.

Collins, J. J., and M. A. Messerschmidt. "Epidemiology of Alcohol-Related Violence." *Alcohol, Health, and Research World* 17 (1993): 93–100.

De Jong, J. "Scope of the Problem: Gender and Drinking." *Catalyst (Higher Education Center for Alcohol and Other Drug Prevention)* 1 (Spring 1995): 1.

Douglass, F. *Life and Times of Frederick Douglass.* New York: Collier Books, 1892 (1967): 147–148.

Doweiko, H. E. *Concepts of Chemical Dependency,* 4th ed. Monterey, CA: Brooks/Cole, 1999.

Drug Strategies. "Alcohol and Crime." *Millennium Hangover: Keeping Score on Alcohol.* Washington, DC (1999): 5. Available http://www.drugstrategies.org/keepingscore 1999/crime.html.

Garrison, V., and J. Podell. "Community Support Systems Assessment for Use in Clinical Interviews." *Schizophrenia Bulletin* 7 (1981): 1.

Gary, L. E., and R. B. Gary. "Treatment Needs of Black Alcoholic Women." *Alcoholism Treatment Quarterly* 2 (1985): 97–113.

George Washington University Medical Center. "Resources: Fact Sheets." *Ensuring Solutions to Alcohol Problems.* Washington, DC: George Washington University Medical Center, 2003. Available http://www.ensuring%solutions. org/ages/refash.html.

Gold, M. S. *The Good News About Drugs and Alcohol.* New York: Villard Books, 1991.

Goode, E. *Drugs in American Society.* Boston: McGraw-Hill College, 1999.

Gordon, A. J. "The Cultural Context of Drinking and Indigenous Therapy for Alcohol Problems in Three Migrant Hispanic Cultures." *Journal of Studies on Alcohol* supplement 9 (1981): 217–240.

Grant, B. F., T. C. Harford, P. Chou, R. Pickering, D. A. Dawson, E. S. Stinson, and J. Noble. "Prevalence of DSM-IV Alcohol Abuse and Dependence: United States." *Alcohol Health Research World* 18 (1997): 243–248.

Gusfield, J. R. *Symbolic Crusade: Status Politics and the American Temperance Movement,* 2nd ed. Chicago: University of Illinois, 1986.

Harper, F. D. *The Black Family and Substance Abuse.* Detroit, MI: Detroit Urban League, 1986.

Harwood, H. *Updating Estimates of the Economic Costs of Alcohol Abuse in the United States: Estimates, Update Methods and Data.* Report prepared by The Lewin Group for the National Institute on Alcohol Abuse and Alcoholism, 2000.

Harwood, H., D. Fountain, and G. Livermore. *The Economic Costs of Alcohol and Drug Abuse in the United States, 1992.* NIH Pub. No. 98-4327. Rockville, MD: National Institute on Drug Abuse, 1998.

Hitt, E. "Alcohol Abuse Takes Major Toll on College Students." *Yahoo! News,* Reuters Limited (24 October 2001). Available http://dailynews.yahoo.com/h/nm/20011024/hl/lacohol_2.html.

Inciardi, J. A. *The War on Drugs II.* Mountain View, CA: Mayfield, 1992.

Jellinek, E. M. *The Disease Concept of Alcoholism.* New Haven, CT: College and University Press, 1960.

Johnston, L. D., P. M. O'Malley, and J. G. Bachman. *Monitoring the Future: National Results on Adolescent Drug Use, Overview of Key Findings 2002.* Bethesda, MD: National Institute on Drug Abuse, 2003.

Keller, M. "Alcoholism: Nature and Extent of the Problem: Understanding Alcoholism." *Annals American Academy Political and Social Science* 315 (1958): 1–11.

Kinney, J. *Loosening the Grip,* 6th ed. Boston: McGraw-Hill, 2000.

Kolevzon, M. S., and R. G. Green. *Family Therapy Models.* New York: Springer, 1985.

Lender, M. E. *Drinking in America.* New York: Free Press, 1985.

Lender, M. E., and J. K. Martin. *Drinking in America,* rev. ed. New York: Free Press, 1987.

Levine, H. G. "The Good Creature of God and the Demon Rum." In *Research Monograph No. 12: Alcohol and Disinhibition: Nature and Meaning of the Link,* 111–161. Rockville, MD: National Institute on Alcohol Abuse and Alcoholism, 1983.

MacAndrew, C., and R. B. Edgerton. *Drunken Comportment: A Social Explanation.* Chicago, IL: Aldine, 1969.

Makela, K. "Attitudes Towards Drinking and Drunkenness in Four Scandinavian Countries." In *Alcohol and Culture: Comparative Perspectives from Europe and America. Annals of the New York Academy of Science* 472, edited by T. F. Babor. New York: New York Academy of Sciences, 1986.

Marshall, M. "Four Hundred Rabbits: An Anthropological View of Ethanol as a Disinhibitor." In *Alcohol and Disinhibition: Nature and Meaning of the Link.* Washington, DC: U.S. HHS, PHS, ADAMHA, NIAAA Research Monograph No. 12, 1983.

Miller, B. A., and W. R. Downs, "The Impact of Family Violence on the Use of Alcohol by Women." *Alcohol, Health, and Research World* 17 (1993): 137–143.

National Clearinghouse for Alcohol and Drug Information (NCADI). *The Fact Is . . . Alcoholism Tends to Run in Families.* OSAP Prevention Resource Guide. Rockville, MD: NCADI, 1992.

National Institute on Alcohol Abuse and Alcoholism (NIAAA). *10th Special Report to the U.S Congress on Alcohol and Health: Highlights from Current Research.* Washington, DC: US Government Printing Office, June 2000.

National Institute on Alcohol Abuse and Alcoholism (NIAAA). *Facts About Alcohol and Alcoholism.* Washington, DC: U.S. Government Printing Office, 1980.

National Institute on Alcohol Abuse and Alcoholism (NIAAA). *Seventh Special Report to the U.S. Congress on Alcohol and Health.* Washington, DC: U.S. Government Printing Office, 1990.

National Institute on Alcohol Abuse and Alcoholism (NIAAA). *Tenth Special Report to the U.S. Congress on Alcohol and Health.* NIH Publication No. 97-5017. Bethesda, MD: National Institute on Alcohol Abuse and Alcoholism, 1997.

National Institute on Alcohol Abuse and Alcoholism (NIAAA). "Frequently Asked Questions on Alcohol Abuse and Alcoholism." Available http://www.niaaa.nih.gov/faq/q-a.htm.

National Institute on Drug Abuse (NIDA). *National Survey Results on Drug Use from the Monitoring the Future Study, 1975–1998. Volume 1: Secondary School Students.* Washington, DC: U.S. Government Printing Office, 1999.

National Institute on Drug Abuse (NIDA). "Presenter's Comments." In *Alcohol and Disinhibition: Nature and Meaning of the Link.* Washington, DC: U.S. HHS, PHS, ADAMHA, NIAAA Research Monograph No. 12, 1983.

National Institute on Drug Abuse (NIDA) and National Institute on Alcohol Abuse and Alcoholism (NIAAA). "The Economic Costs of Alcohol and Drug Abuse in the United States: 1992, Executive Summary." Available http://www.nida.nih.gov/EconomicCosts/Chapter1.html.

Newport, F. "Alcohol and Drinking." Princeton, NJ: The Gallup Organization, November 13–15, 2000. Available http://www.gallup.com/poll/indicators/indalcohol.asp.

Office of Applied Studies (OAS), Substance Abuse and Mental Health Services Administration (SAMHSA), "The NHSDA Report: Alcohol Use." Rockville, MD: Substance Abuse and Mental Health Services Administration 2001. Available http://www.drugabusestatistics.samhsa.gov/.

Office of Applied Studies (OAS). "Driving Under the Influence (DUI) Among Young Persons." National Survey on Drug Use and Health (NSDUH). Rockville, MD: Substance Abuse and Mental Health Services Administration (SAMHSA), 2004.

OSAP. *Cultural Competence for Evaluators.* Washington, DC: Office for Substance Abuse Prevention, U.S. HHS, PHS, ADAMHA, DHHS Publication No. (ADM) 92-1884, 1992.

Osterberg, E. "Alcohol-Related Problems in Cross-National Perspective." *Alcohol and Culture: Comparative Perspectives from Europe and America. Annals of the New York Academy of Sciences,* 472 (1986): 10–21.

Phoenix House. School Daze? (2000). Available http://www.factsontap.org/collexp/Stats.htm.

Presley, C., P. Meilman, and R. Lyerla. *Recent Statistics on Alcohol and Other Drug Use on American College Campuses: 1995–1996.* Carbondale, IL: CORE Institute, Southern Illinois University at Carbondale, 1996. Available http://www.siu.edu/departments/coreinst/public_html/recent.html.

Pride USA Survey, 1994–95, 1995–96, and 1996–97 (1998). Available http://members.aol.com/hta/drgedrscs/page3.html.

Reuters Limited. "Global Costs of Alcohol Abuse Top $250 Billion." *Yahoo News. Health Headlines* (27 December 1999): 1–2. Available http://dailynews.yahoo.com/h/nm/19991227/hl/adb_3.html.

Room, R. "A Reverence for Strong Drink: The Lost Generation and the Elevation of Alcohol in American Culture." *Journal of Studies on Alcohol* 43 (1984): 540–545.

Rostler, S. "Alcoholism Put Blacks at Greater Risk of Infection." *Reuters Health Headlines* (28 April 2000). Available http://dailynews.yahoo.com/h/nm/a2000048/hl/alcoholism_1.html.

Royce, James E. *Alcohol Problems and Alcoholism,* rev. ed. New York: Free Press, 1989.

Satir, V. *Conjoint Family Therapy.* Palo Alto, CA: Science and Behavior Books, 1964.

Substance Abuse and Mental Health Services Administration (SAMHSA). *1998 Fact Sheet. National Household Survey on Drug Abuse* (August 1999a). Available http://samhsa.gov/press/99/990818fs.htm.

Substance Abuse and Mental Health Services Administration (SAMHSA). *National Household Survey on Drug Abuse: Main Findings 1997* (1999b). Available http://silk.niaaa1database/dkpat2.txtsilk/niaaa/database/dkpat2.txt.

Substance Abuse and Mental Health Services Administration (SAMHSA). *Making the Link: Alcohol, Tobacco, and Other Drugs and Women's Health.* Rockville, MD: U.S. DHHS Publication No. ML011, Spring 1995.

Substance Abuse and Mental Health Services Administration (SAMHSA). *Overview of Findings from the 2003 National Survey on Drug Use and Health.* Rockville, MD: Office of Applied Studies, Department of Health and Human Services, 2004a.

Substance Abuse and Mental Health Services Administration (SAMHSA). *Results from the 2003 National Survey on Drug Use and Health: National Findings.* Rockville, MD: Office of Applied Studies, 2004b.

About.com. "Alcoholism: Greater Risks for Women" (4 November 1998). Available http://alcoholism.about .com/health/alcoholism/library/weekly/aa981104htm.

Waters, T. "Women and Drugs." Criminal Justice course CJ-325. Drug Issues and the Law, Northern Arizona University (1999). Available http://jan.ucc.nau.edu/ %7etfw/cj325/class/women/lesson11.html.

Wechsler, H., A. Davenport, G. Dowdall, B. Moeykens, and S. Castillo. "Health and Behavioral Consequences of Binge Drinking in College: A National Survey of Students at 140 Campuses." *Journal of the American Medical Association* 272 (7 December 1994).

Wechsler, H., J. Eun Lee, M. Kuo, and H. Lee. "College Binge Drinking in the 1990s: A Continuing Problem: Results of the Harvard School of Public Health 1999 College Alcohol Study." 1999 College Alcohol Study (CAS) Binge Drinking Survey, Harvard School of Public Health (2000a). Available http://www.hsph.harvardu. edu/organizations/cas/test/rpt2000rpt.shtml.

Wechsler, H, G. W. Dowdall, A. Davenport, and W. De Jong. "Binge Drinking on Campus: Results of a National Study." Harvard School of Public Health, *Higher Education Center for Alcohol and Other Drug Prevention,* U.S. Department of Education (2000b). Available http:// www.edc.org/hec/pubs/binge.htm.

Wegscheider, S. *Another Chance.* Palo Alto, CA: Science and Behavior Books, 1991.

WHO/OMS. "Trends in Substance Use and Associated Health Problems." *Trends in Substance Use.* Fact Sheet No. 127 (1998). Available http://www.who.int/inffs/ en/fact127.html.

Williams, G. D., F. S. Stinson, D. A. Parker, T. C. Harford, and V. Noble. "Demographic Trends, Alcohol Abuse and Alcoholism, 1985–1995." *Epidemiologic Bulletin No. 15. Alcohol, Health, and Research World* 11 (1997): 80–83.

Wilsnack, S. C., R. W. Wilsnack, and A. D. Klassen. "Epidemiological Research on Women's Drinking, 1978–1984." In *Women and Alcohol: Health-Related Issues.* Research Monograph No. 16. DHHS Pub. No. (ADM). Washington, DC: U.S. Government Printing Office, 1986.

Zinberg, N. E. *Drug, Set, and Setting: The Basis for Controlled Intoxicant Use.* New Haven, CT: Yale University Press, 1984.

Zinberg, N. E., and J. A. Robertson. *Drugs and the Public.* New York: Simon & Schuster, 1972.

CHAPTER 9

Narcotics (Opioids)

Did You Know?

- O The release of natural substances called *endorphins* can mimic the effects of narcotics such as heroin.

- O By the end of the 19th century, almost 1 million Americans were addicted to opiates, primarily due to the use of patent medicines that contained opium products.

- O Narcotics are among the most potent analgesics available today.

- O The natural opioid system appears to contribute to alcoholism.

- O There is evidence that accupuncture reduces pain by activating a natural opioid system.

- O Extreme tolerance to narcotics can develop with continual use, causing as much as a 35-fold increase in dosage to maintain the effects.

- O Almost one-half of all heroin addicts have been exposed to the AIDS virus.

- O Heroin supplies today are more potent and cheaper than those available in the 1980s.

- O Many young people believe that heroin is safe as long as it is not injected.

- O Only 10% of heroin addicts receive adequate treatment for their drug dependence.

- O One designer drug, made from the narcotic fentanyl, is 6000 times more potent than heroin.

- O Some heroin addicts have to be treated with the narcotic methadone for the rest of their lives to keep them from abusing heroin.

- O Buprenorphine was recently approved for the treatment of narcotic addiction by physicians in their primary care practices.

- O One contaminant of illegal narcotic manufacturing, called *MPTP*, can cause irreversible, severe Parkinson's disease in a matter of days.

- O Dextromethorphan (a common over-the-counter cough medicine chemically related to codeine), when taken in high doses, can cause phencyclidine (PCP)-like hallucinations.

Learning ◎bjectives

On completing this chapter you will be able to:

◎ Describe the principal pharmacological effects of narcotics and their main therapeutic uses.

◎ Identify the major side effects of narcotics.

◎ Identify the abuse patterns for heroin.

◎ Outline the stages of heroin dependence.

◎ Describe the association of AIDS with heroin abuse.

◎ List the withdrawal symptoms that result from narcotic dependence, and discuss the significance of tolerance.

◎ Describe and compare the use of methadone and buprenorphine in treating narcotic addiction.

◎ Identify the unique features of fentanyl that make it appealing to illicit drug dealers but dangerous to narcotic addicts.

◎ Describe how "designer" drugs have been associated with narcotics.

◎ Describe why dextromethorphan in cough medicines is abused.

Drugs and Society Online is a great source for additional drugs and society information for both students and instructors.
Visit **http://drugsandsociety.jbpub.com** to find a variety of useful tools for learning, thinking, and teaching.

Introduction

The term *narcotic* in general means a central nervous system (CNS) depressant that produces insensibility or stupor. The term has also come to designate those drugs and substances with pharmacological properties related to opium and its drug derivatives. All opioid narcotics activate opioid receptors and have abuse potential. In addition, the narcotics are effective pain relievers (**analgesics**) and anticough medications and are effective in the treatment of diarrhea.

In this chapter, we introduce the opioid narcotics with a brief historical account. The pharmacological and therapeutic uses of these drugs are discussed, followed by a description of their side effects and problems with tolerance, withdrawal, and addiction. Narcotic abuse is presented in detail, with special emphasis on heroin. In addition, treatment approaches for narcotic addiction and dependence are included. This chapter concludes with descriptions of other commonly used opioid narcotics and related drugs.

What Are Narcotics?

The word *narcotic* has been used to label many substances, from opium to marijuana to cocaine. The translation of the Greek word *narkoticos* is "benumbing or deadening." The term *narcotic* is sometimes used to refer to a CNS depressant, producing insensibility or stupor, and at other times to refer to an addicting drug. Most people would not consider marijuana among the narcotics today, although for many years it was included in this category. Although pharmacologically cocaine is not a narcotic either, it is still legally classified as such. Perhaps part of this con-

KEY TERMS

analgesics
drugs that relieve pain without affecting consciousness

opioid
relating to the drugs that are derived from opium

antitussive
drugs that block coughing

fusion is due to the fact that cocaine, as a local anesthetic, can cause a numbing effect.

For purposes of the present discussion, the term *narcotic* is used to refer to those naturally occurring substances derived from the opium poppy and their synthetic substitutes. These drugs are referred to as the **opioid** (or opiate) narcotics because of their association with opium. They have similar pharmacological features, including abuse potential, pain-relieving effects (referred to as *analgesics*), cough suppression (**antitussive**), and reduction of intestinal movement often causing constipation. Some of the most commonly used opioid narcotics are listed in Table 9.1.

The History of Narcotics

The opium poppy, *Papaver somniferum,* from which opium and its naturally occurring narcotic derivatives are obtained, has been cultivated for millennia. A 6000-year-old Sumerian tablet has an ideograph for the poppy shown as "joy" plus "plant," suggesting that the addicting properties of this substance have been appreciated for many centuries. The Egyptians listed opium along with approximately 700 other medicinal compounds in the famous Ebers Papyrus (~1500 B.C.).

The Greek god of sleep, Hypnos, and the Roman god of sleep, Somnus, were portrayed as carrying containers of opium pods, and the Minoan goddess of sleep wore a crown of opium pods.

During the so-called Dark Ages that followed the collapse of the Roman Empire, Arab traders actively engaged in traveling the overland caravan routes to China and to India, where they introduced opium. Eventually, both China and India grew their own poppies.

OPIUM IN CHINA

The opium poppy had a dramatic impact in China, causing widespread addiction (Karch 1996). Initially, the seeds were used medically, as was opium later. However, by the late 1690s, opium was being smoked and used for diversion. The Chinese government, fearful of the weakening of national vitality by the potent opiate narcotic, outlawed the sale of opium in 1729. The

Table 9.1 Commonly Used Opioid Narcotic Drugs and Products

NARCOTIC DRUGS	COMMON NAMES	MOST COMMON USES
Heroin	Horse, smack, junk (street names)	Abuse
Morphine	(Several)	Analgesia
Methadone	Dolophine	Treat narcotic dependence
Meperidine	Demerol	Analgesia
Oxycodone	Percodan, OxyContin	Analgesia
Propoxyphene	Darvon	Analgesia
Codeine	(Several)	Analgesia, antitussive
Loperamide	Imodium A-D	Antidiarrheal
Diphenoxylate	Lomotil	Antidiarrheal
Opium tincture	Paregoric	Antidiarrheal

penalty for disobedience was death by strangulation or decapitation.

Despite these laws and threats, the habit of opium smoking became so widespread that the Chinese government went a step further and forbade its importation from India, where most of the opium poppy was grown. In contrast, the British East India Company (and later the British government in India) encouraged cultivation of opium. British companies were the principal shippers to the Chinese port of Canton, which was the only port open to Western merchants. During the next 120 years, a complex network of opium smuggling routes developed in China with the help of local merchants, who received substantial profits, and local officials, who pocketed bribes to ignore the smugglers.

Everyone involved in the opium trade, but particularly the British, continued to profit until the Chinese government ordered the strict enforcement of the edict against importation. Such actions by the Chinese caused conflict with the British government and helped trigger the Opium War of 1839 to 1842. Great Britain sent in an army, and by 1842, 10,000 British soldiers had won a victory over 350 million Chinese. Because of the war, the island of Hong Kong was ceded to the British, and an indemnity of $6 million was imposed on China to cover the value of the destroyed opium and the cost of the war. In 1856, a second Opium War broke out. Peking was occupied by British and French troops, and China was compelled to make further concessions to Britain. The importation of opium continued to increase until 1908, when Britain and China made an agreement to limit the importation of opium from India (Austin 1978).

Famous cartoon, showing a British sailor shoving opium down the throat of a Chinese man, which dates back to the Opium War of 1839–1842.

AMERICAN OPIUM USE

Meanwhile, in 1803, a young German named Frederick Serturner extracted and partially purified the active ingredients in opium. It was 10 times more potent than opium itself and was named *morphine* after Morpheus, the Greek god of dreams. This discovery increased worldwide interest in opium. By 1832, a second compound had been purified and named *codeine*, after the Greek word for "poppy capsule" (Maurer and Vogel 1967).

The opium problem was aggravated further in 1853, when Alexander Wood perfected the hypodermic syringe and introduced it first in Europe and then in America. Christopher Wren and others had worked with the idea of injecting drugs directly into the body by means of hollow quills and straws, but the approach was never successful or well received. Wood perfected the syringe technique with the intent of preventing morphine addiction by injecting the drug directly into the veins rather than by oral administration (Golding 1993). Unfortunately, just the opposite happened: Injection of morphine increased the potency and the likelihood of dependence (Maurer and Vogel 1967).

The hypodermic syringe was used extensively during the Civil War to administer morphine to treat pain, dysentery, and fatigue (Kosten and Hollister 1998). A large percentage of the soldiers who returned home from the war were addicted to morphine. Opiate addiction became known as the "soldier's disease" or "army disease."

By 1900, an estimated 1 million Americans were dependent on opiates (Abel 1980). This drug problem was made worse because of (1) Chinese laborers, who brought with them to the United States opium to smoke (it was legal to smoke opium in the United States at that time); (2) the availability of purified morphine and the hypodermic syringe; and (3) the lack of controls on the large number of patent medicines that contained opium derivatives (Karch 1996). Until 1914, when the Harrison Narcotic Act was passed (regulating opium, coca leaves, and their products), the average opiate addict was a middle-aged, Southern,

Chinese laborers often smoked heroin at the turn of the 20th century.

With the development of the hypodermic needle and its use during the Civil War, heroin addiction became more likely and more severe.

white woman who functioned well and was adjusted to her role as a wife and mother. She bought opium or morphine legally by mail order from Sears and Roebuck or at the local store, used it orally, and caused very few problems. A number of physicians were addicted as well. One of the best-known morphine addicts was William Holsted, a founder of Johns Hopkins Medical School. Holsted was a very productive surgeon and innovator, although secretly an addict for most of his career. He became dependent on morphine as a substitute for his cocaine dependence (Brecher 1972).

Looking for better medicines, chemists found that modification of the morphine molecule resulted in a more potent compound. In 1898, diacetylmorphine was placed on the market as a cough suppressant by Bayer. It was to be a "heroic" drug, without the addictive potential of morphine—it thus received the name *heroin*.

Heroin was first used in the United States as a cough suppressant and to combat addiction to other substances (Hubbard 1998). However, its inherent abuse potential was quickly discovered. When injected, heroin is more addictive than most of the other narcotics because of its ability to enter the brain rapidly and cause a euphoric surge (DiChiara and North 1992). Heroin was banned from U.S. medical practice in 1924, although it is

Bayer Pharmaceutical introduced two new products in the late 1800s: aspirin and heroin.

Heroin use was particularly high among soldiers fighting in Vietnam.

still used legally as an analgesic in other countries (Karch 1996).

The Vietnam War was an important landmark for heroin use in the United States (Hubbard 1998). It has been estimated that as many as 40% of the U.S. soldiers serving in Southeast Asia at this time used heroin to combat the frustrations and stress associated with this unpopular military action. Although only 7% of the soldiers continued to use heroin after returning home, those who were addicted to this potent narcotic became a major component of the heroin-abusing population in this country (Golding 1993).

Heroin smoking became popular in the mid-1980s in response to the AIDS epidemic. This was due to a fear of HIV infection when using infected needles to administer the drug intravenously (Hubbard 1998). The effect resulting from inhalation is as intense as that caused by injection, although a very pure drug is required for smoking. Smoking continues to be a favorite form of heroin administration today.

Pharmacological Effects

Even though opioid narcotics have a history of being abused, they continue to be important therapeutic agents.

NARCOTIC ANALGESICS

The most common clinical use of the opioid narcotics is as analgesics to relieve pain. These drugs are effective against most varieties of pain, including *visceral* (associated with internal organs of the body) and *somatic* (associated with skeletal muscles, bones, skin, and teeth) types. Used in sufficiently high doses, narcotics can even relieve the intense pain associated with some types of cancer (Way et al. 1998).

The opioid narcotics relieve pain by activating the same group of receptors that are controlled by the endogenous substances called *endorphins* (Kreck et al. 2004). As discussed in Chapter 4, the endorphins are peptides (small proteins) that are released in the brain, in the spinal cord, and from the adrenal glands in response to stress and painful experiences. When released, the endor-

phins serve as transmitters and stimulate receptors designated as opioid types. Activation of opioid receptors by either the naturally released endorphins or administration of the narcotic analgesic drugs blocks the transmission of pain through the spinal cord or brain stem and alters the perception of pain in the "pain center" of the brain. Because the narcotics work at all three levels of pain transmission, they are potent analgesics against almost all types of pain.

Interestingly, the endorphin system appears to be influenced by psychological factors as well. It is possible that pain relief caused by administration of placebos or nonmedicinal manipulation such as acupuncture is due in part to the natural release of endorphins. This relationship suggests that physiological, psychological, and pharmacological factors are intertwined in pain management through the opioid system, which makes it impossible to deal with one without considering the others.

Although the narcotics are very effective analgesics, they do cause some side effects that are particularly alarming; thus, their clinical use usually is limited to the treatment of moderate to severe pain (*Drug Facts and Comparisons* 2005). Other, safer drugs, such as the aspirin-type analgesics (see Chapter 15), are preferred for pain management when possible. Often, the amount of narcotic required for pain relief can be reduced by combining a narcotic, such as codeine, with aspirin or acetaminophen (the active ingredient in Tylenol). Such combinations reduce the chance of significant narcotic side effects while providing adequate pain relief (McEvoy 2003).

Morphine is a particularly potent pain reliever and often is used as the analgesic standard by which other narcotics are compared (*Medical Letter* 1998). With continual use, tolerance develops to the analgesic effects of morphine and other narcotics, sometimes requiring a dramatic escalation of doses to maintain adequate pain control (*Drug Facts and Comparisons* 2005).

Because pain is expressed in different forms with many different diseases, narcotic treatment can vary considerably. Usually, the convenience of oral narcotic therapy is preferred but often is inadequate for severe pain. For short-term relief from intense pain, narcotics are effective when injected subcutaneously or intramuscularly. Narcotics can also be given intravenously for persistent and potent analgesia or administered by transdermal patches for sustained chronic pain (Karch 1996). Despite the fact that most pain can be relieved if enough narcotic analgesic is properly administered, physicians frequently underprescribe narcotics. Because of fear of causing narcotic addiction or creating legal problems with federal agencies such as the Drug Enforcement Administration (DEA) (see "Here and Now," Are Restrictions on Pain Pills Too Painful?), cancer patients in the United States are often inadequately treated for their pain (Hall and Sykes 2004). An important rule of narcotic use is that adequate pain relief should not be denied because of concern about the abuse potential of these drugs (Hall and Sykes 2004). Indeed, addiction to narcotics is rare in patients receiving these drugs for therapy unless they have a history of drug abuse or have an underlying psychiatric disorder (*Medical Letter* 1998).

Occasionally, there are outbreaks of abuse of commonly prescribed narcotic products such as OxyContin. This product includes the opiate oxycodone, which has the approximate narcotic potency of morphine and can be obtained with relative ease. Authorities claim that the illegal pills come from doctors' offices, from dealers who fake illness to get legal prescriptions or who are writing phony orders, and from others who steal the supplies from pharmacies. OxyContin has been called "oxys," "O.C.," and "killers" on the street and is popular with narcotic abusers because of its rapid and potent effect. On the street, the drug can cost 10 times its prescription price. Because of its potent ability to suppress respiration, OxyContin appears to have been involved in overdose deaths throughout the country, although there is some evidence that other drugs were also involved in many of these cases.

OTHER THERAPEUTIC USES

Opioid narcotics are also used to treat conditions not related to pain. For example, these drugs suppress the coughing center of the brain, so they are effective antitussives. Codeine, a natural opioid narcotic, is commonly included in cough medicine. In addition, opioid narcotics slow the movement of materials through the intestines, a property that can be used to relieve diarrhea or can cause the side effect of constipation (*Drug Facts and Comparisons* 2005). Paregoric contains an opioid narcotic substance and is commonly used to treat severe diarrhea.

When used carefully by the clinician, opioid narcotics are very effective therapeutic tools. Precautions for avoiding unnecessary problems with these drugs include the following (Way and Way 1992):

Here and Now

Are Restrictions on Pain Pills Too Painful?

Because of a spiraling increase in the abuse of prescription "painkillers," the DEA has warned doctors who specialize in pain management that they risk special investigation if they do not comply with DEA guidelines. For example, the DEA recommends avoiding the use of opioid analgesics for the treatment of pain in patients who have a history of abusing these drugs. In addition, the DEA frowns upon the practice of doctors writing prescriptions for these pain drugs that can be filled on a future date. These and other restrictive DEA policies are viewed by some pain doctors as overregulation. Some are concerned that physicians will hesitate to prescribe even needed pain medication for fear of being investigated and charged with breaking the law. They worry that the DEA's actions are sending a chilling message that could result in withholding opioid narcotics from millions of patients who cannot be adequately treated by other drugs.

Source: Kaufman, M. "New DEA Statement Has Pain Doctors More Fearful." *The Washington Post* (30 November 2004): A-17).

1. Before beginning treatment, therapeutic goals should be clearly established.
2. Doses and duration of use should be limited as much as possible while permitting adequate therapeutic care.
3. If other, safer drugs (for example, nonnarcotic analgesics such as ibuprofen or aspirin) adequately treat the medical condition, narcotics should be avoided.

MECHANISMS OF ACTION

As mentioned, the opioid receptors are the site of action of the naturally occurring endorphin peptide transmitters and are found throughout the nervous system, intestines, and other internal organs. Because narcotic drugs such as morphine and heroin enhance the endorphin system by directly stimulating opioid receptors, these drugs have widespread influences throughout the body.

For example, the opioid receptors are present in high concentration within the limbic structures of the brain. Stimulation of these receptors by narcotics causes release of the transmitter, dopamine, in limbic brain regions. This effect contributes to the rewarding actions of these drugs and leads to dependence and abuse (Zocchi et al 2003).

SIDE EFFECTS

One of the most common side effects of the opioid narcotics is constipation. Other side effects include drowsiness, mental clouding, respiratory depression (suppressed breathing is usually the cause of death from overdose), nausea and vomiting, itching, inability to urinate, a drop in blood pressure, and constricted pupils (*Drug Facts and Comparisons* 2005). This array of seemingly unrelated side effects is due to widespread distribution of the opioid receptors throughout the body and their involvement in many physiological functions (Gourlay 2004). With continual use, tolerance develops to some of these undesirable narcotic responses (Low et al. 2004).

Drugs that selectively antagonize the opioid receptors can block the effects of natural opioid systems in the body and reverse the effects of narcotic opiate drugs (*Drug Facts and Comparisons*

2005). When an opioid antagonist such as the drug naloxone is administered alone, it has little noticeable effect. The antiopioid actions of naloxone become more apparent when the antagonist is injected into someone who has taken a narcotic opioid drug. For example, naloxone will cause (1) a recurrence of pain in the patient using a narcotic for pain relief, (2) the restoration of consciousness and normal breathing in the addict who has overdosed on heroin, and (3) severe withdrawal effects in the opioid abuser who has become dependent on narcotics ("Opioids" 1996).

An interesting recent use of opioid antagonists is to treat alcohol dependence. The Food and Drug Administration (FDA) has approved the use of naltrexone (a narcotic antagonist) to relieve the craving of alcoholics for excessive alcohol consumption (*Drug Facts and Comparisons* 2005). Early research suggests that this drug may have an important effect on the future therapeutic approach taken with alcoholism. Only time and experience will reveal whether the benefits are truly as dramatic as originally thought. The initial findings suggest that the natural opioid (endorphin) system likely contributes to the dependence seen in alcoholics.

Abuse, Tolerance, Dependence, and Withdrawal

All the opioid narcotic agents that activate opioid receptors have abuse potential and are classified as scheduled drugs (see Table 9.2). Their patterns of abuse are determined by the ability of these drugs to cause tolerance, dependence, and withdrawal effects.

The process of tolerance literally begins with the first dose of a narcotic, but tolerance does not become clinically evident until after 2 to 3 weeks of frequent use (either therapeutic- or abuse-related). Tolerance occurs most rapidly with high doses given in short intervals. Doses can be increased as much as 35 times so as to regain the narcotic effect. Physical dependence invariably accompanies severe tolerance (Reisine and Pasternak 1995). Psychological dependence can also develop with continual narcotic use because these

Table 9.2 Schedule Classification of Some Common Narcotics

NARCOTIC	SCHEDULE*
Heroin	I
Morphine	II, III
Methadone	II
Fentanyl	II
Hydromorphone	II
Meperidine	II
Codeine	II, III, V
Buprenorphine	III
Pentazocine	IV
Propoxyphene	IV
Narcotics combined with nonsteroidal anti-inflammatory drugs	III

*According to the Drug Enforcement Administration classification, Controlled Substances Act.

drugs can cause euphoria and relieve stress. Such psychological dependence leads to compulsive use (Way and Way 1992). Because all narcotics affect the same opioid systems in the body, developing tolerance to one narcotic drug means the person has cross-tolerance to all drugs in this group.

The development of psychological and physical dependence makes breaking the narcotic habit very difficult. Abstinence from narcotic use by a long-term addict can cause severe withdrawal effects such as exaggerated pain responses, agitation, anxiety, stomach cramps and vomiting, joint and muscle aches, runny nose, and an overall flu-like feeling. Although these withdrawal symptoms are not fatal, they are extremely aversive and encourage continuation of the narcotic habit (McEvoy 2003). Overall, the narcotics have similar actions; there are differences, however, in their potencies, severity of side effects, likelihood of being abused, and clinical usefulness.

HEROIN ABUSE

This is the key to a heroin high: Nothing matters . . . when one is high on smack, one looks at the outside world and only has one thought: Who . . . (cares)? You feel as if you've been wrapped in the most pleasing, warm and comfortable blanket in the world. At high doses, you fall in and out of consciousness, and getting this "nod" is what the veteran user prays for every time he shoots up: to sleep the sleep of angels is the ultimate goal of the heroin addict. (Drugs, Youth and the Internet 2002, p. 23)

This quote illustrates the powerful attraction of heroin and helps explain why it is so frequently abused.

Heroin is currently classified as a Schedule I drug by the DEA. It is not approved for any clinical use in the United States, is one of the most widely abused illegal drugs in the world (Best et al. 1996), and is reported to account for more than $110 billion in global sales each year (Gannett News Service 1997). It is also thought to be associated with some of the highest mortality rates and most emergency room visits of any of the illegal drugs of abuse in the United States (NIDA Infofacts 2005). Heroin was illicitly used more than any other drug of abuse in the United States (except for marijuana) until 20 years ago, when it was unseated by cocaine (DiChiara and North 1992). A recent resurgence in its use, especially in adolescents and young adults (Epstein and Gfroerer 1998), has created great concern among authorities (Stockman 2003).

From 1970 through 1976, most of the heroin reaching the United States originated from the Golden Triangle region of Southeast Asia, which includes parts of Burma, Thailand, and Laos. During that period, the United States and other nations purchased much of the legal opium crop from Turkey in an effort to stop opium from being converted into heroin. From 1975 until 1980, the major heroin supply came from opium poppies grown in Mexico. The U.S. government furnished the Mexican government with helicopters, herbicide sprays, and financial assistance to destroy the poppy crop. Changes in political climates have shifted the source of supply back to the Golden Triangle and Latin American countries (e.g., Colombia; Seper 2003) and more recently to Afghanistan (BBC News 2004).

Heroin Combinations

Heroin is typically smuggled into the United States from one of four foreign sources: Mexico, South America, Southeast Asia (e.g., Burma), or Southwest Asia (e.g., Afghanistan). It is carried into the United States hidden in commercial and private vehicles driven from Mexico or Canada or carried by couriers traveling on commercial flights (National Drug Threat Assessment 2003). Pure heroin is a white powder. Other colors, such as brown Mexican heroin, result from unsatisfactory processing of morphine or from adulterants (DEA 2000). Heroin is usually "cut" (diluted) with lactose (milk sugar) to give it bulk and thus increase profits (DEA 2000). When heroin first enters the United States, it may be up to 95% pure; by the time it is sold to users, its purity may be as low as 3% or (recently) as high as 30%–60% (Epstein and Gfroerer 1998; Stockman 2003). If users are unaware of the variance in purity and do not adjust doses accordingly, the results can be extremely dangerous and occasionally fatal (NIDA Infofacts 2005).

Heroin has a bitter taste, so sometimes it is cut with quinine, a bitter substance, to disguise the fact that the heroin content has been reduced. Quinine can be a deadly adulterant. Part of the "flash" from direct injection of heroin may be caused by this contaminant. Quinine is an irritant, and it causes vascular damage, acute and potentially lethal disturbances in heartbeat, depressed respiration, coma, and death from respiratory arrest. Opiate poisoning causes acute pulmonary edema as well as respiratory depression. To counteract the constipation caused by heroin, sometimes mannitol is added for its laxative effect.

Another potentially lethal combination emerges when heroin is laced with the much more potent artificial narcotic fentanyl. This adulterated heroin

Crude heroin is dark, whereas purified heroin is a white powder.

can be extremely dangerous due to its unexpected potency (NIDA Research Report Series 2004).

Frequently, heroin is deliberately combined with other drugs when self-administered by addicts (National Trends in Drug Abuse 2000). According to the National Institute on Drug Abuse (NIDA)–sponsored Drug Abuse Warning Network (DAWN) survey of emergency rooms in the United States, 41% of the reported heroin abuse cases involved other drugs of abuse in combination with this narcotic. Heroin is most frequently used with alcohol, but it is often combined with CNS stimulants, such as cocaine (National Trends in Drug Abuse 2000). Some crack cocaine smokers turn to heroin to ease the jitters caused by the CNS stimulant (Leland 1996). It also has been reported that heroin addicts use cocaine to withdraw or detoxify themselves from heroin by gradually decreasing amounts of heroin while increasing amounts of cocaine. This drug combination is called **speedballing**, and addicts claim the cocaine provides relief from the unpleasant withdrawal effects that accompany heroin abstinence in a dependent user.

Profile of Heroin Addicts

An estimated 600,000 active heroin addicts live in the United States, a figure that has remained relatively stable despite changes in the number of infrequent and moderate users (NIDA Infofax 2000). Heroin addicts often search for a better and

KEY TERMS

speedballing
combining heroin and cocaine

purer drug; however, if they do find an unusually potent batch of heroin, there is a good chance they will get more than they bargained for. Addicts are sometimes found dead with the needle still in the vein after injecting heroin (Thompson 1995). In such cases, the unsuspecting addict may have died in reaction to an unusually concentrated dose of this potent narcotic. Thousands of deaths occur annually in the United States from heroin over-doses (Leland 1996). Death associated with heroin injection is usually due to concurrent use of alcohol or barbiturates—not the heroin alone—and frequently occurs after an addict has gone weeks or months without the drug and injects the same amount of heroin he or she used before, not realizing that tolerance has worn off (Rombey 2003b).

Hard-core addicts often share a common place where they can stash supplies and equipment for their heroin encounters. These locations, called *shooting galleries*, serve as gathering places for addicts (Bourgois 1999). Shooting galleries can be set up in homes, but are usually located in less established locations such as abandoned cars, cardboard lean-tos, and weed-infested vacant lots. An entrance charge often is required of the patrons. Conditions in shooting galleries are notoriously filthy, and these places are frequented by intravenous heroin users with blood-borne infections that can cause AIDS or hepatitis. Because of needle sharing and other unsanitary practices,

shooting galleries have become a place where serious communicative diseases are spread to a wide range of people of different ages, races, genders, and socioeconomic statuses (Bearak 1992; Bourgois 1999). Some addicts become resigned to their fate. One user, after testing positive for HIV, responded, "I've seen lots of guys die already. They turned into skeletons and their teeth fell out . . . I hope I die before I get that far. Maybe I'll be lucky and just die one night up in the gallery" (Bearak 1992, p. A4).

The heroin in shooting galleries is typically prepared by adding several drops of water to the white powder in an improvised container (such as a metal bottle cap), and lightly shaking the container while heating it over a small flame to dissolve the powder. The fluid is then drawn through a tiny wad of cotton to filter out the gross contaminants into an all-too-often used syringe where it is ready for injection (Bearak 1992).

Some addicts become fixated on the drug's paraphernalia, especially the needle. They can get a psychological "high" from playing with the needle and syringe. The injection process and syringe plunger action appear to have sexual overtones for them. As one reformed user explained, "I think what I miss more than heroin sometimes is just the ritual of shooting up." A current user concurred, explaining, "You get addicted to the needle . . . Just the process of sticking something into your vein, having such a direct involvement with your body . . . " ("Mary" 1996, p. 42).

Heroin and Crime

In 1971, the Select Committee on Crime in the United States released a report on methods used to combat the heroin crisis that arose in the 1950s and 1960s. This report was a turning point in setting up treatment programs for narcotic addicts. The report stated that drug arrests for heroin use had increased 700% since 1961, that there were as many as 4000 deaths per year from heroin, and that the cost of heroin-related crimes to U.S. society was estimated to exceed $3 billion per year. Other studies since that time have linked heroin addiction with crime (Gossop et al. 2000).

Although many young heroin addicts come from affluent or middle-class families (Weiss 1995), research shows most heavy users are poorly edu-

Heroin paraphernalia is usually simple and crude but effective: a spoon on which to dissolve the narcotic and a makeshift syringe with which to inject it.

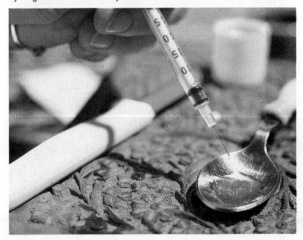

cated with minimal social integration. Because of these disadvantages, heroin addicts often have a low level of employment, exist in unstable living conditions, and socialize with other illicit drug users (Bourgois 1999; Hall et al. 1993). Clearly, such undesirable living conditions encourage criminal activity. However, three other factors also likely contribute to the association between heroin use and crime:

1. The use of heroin and its pharmacological effects encourage antisocial behavior that is crime-related. Depressants such as heroin diminish inhibition and cause people to engage in activities they normally would not. The effects of heroin and its withdrawal make addicts self-centered, demanding, impulsive, and governed by their "need" for the drug.
2. Because heroin addiction is expensive, the user is forced to resort to crime to support the drug habit (Weiss 1995).
3. A similar personality is driven to engage in both criminal behavior and heroin use. Often, heroin addicts start heroin use about the same time they begin to become actively involved in criminal activity. In most cases, the heroin user has been taking other illicit drugs, especially marijuana, years before trying heroin (Hall et al. 1993).

These findings suggest that for many heroin addicts, the antisocial behavior causes the criminal behavior rather than the criminal behavior resulting from the heroin use. Thus, the more a drug such as heroin is perceived as being illegal, desirable, and addictive, the more likely it will be used by deviant criminal populations. However, typically heroin users are not violent, although they may participate in criminal activity to fund their drug habit. Violence is more likely associated with heroin trafficking and distribution because of the criminal groups involved in this activity (National Drug Threat Assessment 2003).

Patterns of Heroin Abuse

It has become apparent that problems with narcotics are no longer confined to the inner cities, but have infiltrated suburban areas and small towns and afflict both rich and poor (see "Here and Now," Heroin Use in a Small Town). The following are recent heroin trends (see Table 9.3):

- Heroin use among adolescents and young adults, after holding steady at high levels in the late 1990s, slightly declined in 2001 and 2002 (Johnston 2004; see Table 9.3).
- Heroin has become purer (60%–70% purity) and cheaper ($10/bag [~100 mg]) than ever before (CEWG 2002).

Here and Now

Heroin Use in a Small Town

Heroin is supposed to be a "big town" drug. Tell that to Sandi Daost, whose 19-year-old son Robby died from a heroin overdose after months of going in and out of rehab centers trying to stay clean. He grew up in the typical small town—Springville, Utah. The family believed that Robby finally had kicked the habit. He had been clean for 7 months and laughed and joked with the family again. He had a job and a cute girlfriend, and was attending church with his family. One Sunday, he told his mother he was going to play golf with a friend. Robby didn't go golfing, but made his last trip to meet his heroin connection. He was found in his bed the next morning, dead from a heroin overdose. The citizens of Springville were bewildered and shocked. Robby was only one of at least six heroin overdose deaths in this small town from 1999 to 2004. All were young men in their late teens or early 20s. We expect this type of thing in Los Angeles or New York, but no one seems to have an answer to "why in Springville?"

Sources: Rombey 2003a, 2003b.

Table 9.3 **Prevalence of Heroin and Other Opioid Abuse Among High School Seniors**

| Year | ANNUAL USE | | LIFETIME USE | |
	Heroin	Other Opioids	Heroin	Other Opioids
1989	0.6%	4.4%	1.3%	8.3%
1992	0.6%	3.3%	1.2%	6.1%
1995	1.1%	4.7%	1.6%	7.2%
1999	1.1%	6.7%	2.0%	10.2%
2002	1.0%	7.0%	1.7%	10.1%
2004	0.9%	9.5%	1.5%	13.5%

Source: Johnston, L. "Monitoring the Future" (2004). Available www.monitoringthefuture.org.

- Thanks to the greater purity, new users are able to administer heroin in less efficient ways, such as smoking and snorting, and avoid the dangers of intravenous use (National Trends in Drug Abuse 2000).
- Many youth believe that heroin can be used safely if it is not injected (Epstein and Gfroerer 1998).
- Because of its association with popular fashions and entertainment, heroin has been viewed as glamorous and chic, especially by many young people, despite its highly publicized lethal consequences ("Heroin '96" 1996; Kennedy 1996). More recently, "heroin chic" has been falling out of fashion within the glamour business because of its very negative consequences (Quinion 2005).
- Emergency room visits due to narcotic overdoses have significantly increased since the beginning of the 1990s (CEWG 2002), going from 41,687 visits in 1994 to 90,232 in 2001 (CESAR FAX 2003b).

The reasons for these disturbing changes in heroin use patterns and attitude are not immediately apparent. It has been speculated that because antidrug efforts in the late 1980s and early 1990s targeted cocaine, they inadvertently encouraged drug users to replace cocaine with heroin. Another possible reason for increased heroin use in the late 1990s is that many drug dealers previously selling cocaine switched to heroin to make greater profits ("Heroin '96" 1996), making heroin even more readily available. Whatever the reasons, it has become imperative to educate all populations about the dangers of this potent drug and reverse the present trend of escalating use and complacency about the dangers.

Stages of Dependence

Initially, the effects of heroin are often unpleasant, especially after the first injection (May 1998). It is not uncommon to experience nausea and vomiting after administration; gradually, however, the euphoria overwhelms the aversive effects (Quinion 2005). There are two major stages in the development of a psychological dependence on heroin or other opioid narcotics:

1. In the rewarding stage, euphoria and positive effects occur in at least 50% of users. These positive feelings and sensations increase with continued administration and encourage use.
2. Eventually, the heroin or narcotic user must take the drug to avoid withdrawal symptoms that start about 6 to 12 hours after the last dose. At this stage, it is said that "the monkey is on his back." This stage is psychological dependence. If one grain of heroin (about 65 milligrams) is taken over a 2-week period on a daily basis, the user becomes physically dependent on the drug.

Methods of Administration

Many heroin users start by sniffing the powder or injecting it into a muscle (intramuscular) or under the skin ("skin popping"). Because of the increased purity and decreased cost, many of today's heroin users are administering their drug by smoking and snorting (CEWG 2002).

Most established heroin addicts still prefer to **mainline** the drug (intravenous injection) (CEWG 2002). The injection device can be made from an eyedropper bulb, part of a syringe, and a hypodermic needle. Mainlining drugs causes the thin-walled veins to become scarred and, if done frequently, the veins will collapse. Once a vein is collapsed, it can no longer be used to introduce the drug into the blood. Addicts become expert in locating new veins to use: in the feet, the legs, the neck, even the temples. When addicts do not want "needle tracks" (scars) to show, they inject under the tongue or in the groin (NIDA Infofax 2000; "Opioids" 1996).

Heroin Addicts and AIDS

As noted previously, because needle sharing is common among heavy heroin users, the transmission of deadly communicable diseases such as AIDS is a major problem (see Chapter 17). More than 50% of intravenous heroin users have been exposed to the AIDS virus (Baglole 2003). Fear of contracting this deadly disease has contributed to the increase of administering this drug by smoking and snorting (Hubbard 1998). However, many heroin users who start by smoking and snorting eventually progress to intravenous administration due to its more intense effects (Leland 1996).

Heroin and Pregnancy

In some places, heroin alone or in combination with methadone represents the drug of choice for approximately 80% of addicted pregnant women (Fabris et al. 1998). In the United States, as many as 10,000 infants are born each year to women

A heroin addict "mainlining" his drug.

who chronically used either heroin or other opioid drugs during their pregnancies (Paule 1998). There is no evidence that prenatal exposure to opioid drugs causes overt structural damage, although incidents of smaller birthweights or even reduced head size have been reported in infants born to mothers using opioid drugs; these findings have not been universally confirmed (Bennett 1999; Paule 1998). The most devastating consequence of heroin or opioid use during pregnancy appears to be physical dependence in the newborn, resulting in withdrawal symptoms usually immediately after birth. Treatment for such withdrawal problems generally includes low doses of a long-lasting opioid narcotic to reduce the intensity of the symptoms and then a gradual tapering of the dose to eventually wean the infant from the drug. For heroin, this typically takes up to 2 weeks (Paule 1998).

KEY TERMS

mainline
to inject a drug of abuse intravenously

Withdrawal Symptoms

After the effects of heroin wear off, the addict usually has only a few hours in which to find the next dose before severe withdrawal symptoms begin. A single "shot" of heroin lasts only 4 to 6 hours. It is enough to help addicts "get straight" or relieve the severe withdrawal symptoms called *dope sickness* but is not enough to give a desired "high" (Bearak 1992). Withdrawal symptoms start with a runny nose, tears, and minor stomach cramps. The addict may feel as if he or she is coming down with a bad cold (Hubbard 1998; NIDA Infofax 2000). Between 12 and 48 hours after the last dose, the addict loses all of his or her appetite, vomits, has diarrhea and abdominal cramps, feels alternating chills and fever, and develops goose pimples all over (going "cold turkey"). Between 2 and 4 days later, the addict continues to experience some of the symptoms just described, as well as aching bones and muscles and powerful muscle spasms that cause violent kicking motions ("kicking the habit"). After 4 to 5 days, symptoms start to subside, and the person may get his or her appetite back (NIDA Infofax 2000). However, attempts to move on in life will be challenging because compulsion to keep using the drug remains strong.

The severity of the withdrawal varies according to the purity and strength of the drug used and the personality of the user. The symptoms of withdrawal from heroin, morphine, and methadone are summarized in Table 9.4. Withdrawal symptoms from opioids such as morphine, codeine, meperidine, and others are similar, although the timeframe and intensity vary (O'Brien 1995).

TREATMENT OF HEROIN AND OTHER NARCOTIC DEPENDENCE

The ideal result of treatment for dependency on heroin or other narcotics is to help the addict live a normal, productive, and satisfying life without drugs. Unfortunately, fewer than 10% of heroin addicts receive adequate treatment for their addiction (Maxwell 1998). Of those who are treated, relatively few heroin users become absolutely "clean" from drug use; thus, therapeutic compromise is often necessary (Millstein 1992; Payte 1998; see Figure 9.1). In the real world, treatment of heroin

dependency is considered successful if the addict does the following:

1. Stops using heroin
2. No longer associates with dealers or users of heroin
3. Avoids dangerous activities often associated with heroin use (such as needle sharing, injecting unknown drugs, and frequenting shooting galleries)
4. Improves employment status
5. Refrains from criminal activity
6. Is able to enjoy normal family and social relationships (McLellan et al. 1993)

For more than 30 years, many heroin addicts have achieved these goals by substituting a long-lasting synthetic narcotic, such as methadone, for the short-acting heroin (Zickler 1999). The maintenance ("substitute") narcotic is made available to heroin-dependent people through drug treatment centers under the direction of trained medical personnel. The dispensing of the substitute narcotic is tightly regulated by governmental agencies. The rationale for the substitution is that a

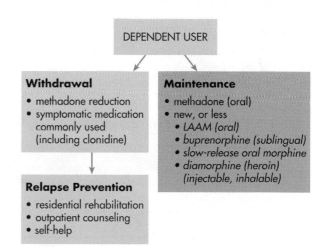

FIGURE 9.1
Treatment of Heroin Addiction
The principal aspects of treating heroin addiction include minimizing the very aversive withdrawal effect (usually with drug adjuncts); preventing relapse (usually with behavioral modification); and if necessary, providing maintenance support with other opioid-like drugs that have longer action than heroin.

long-acting drug such as methadone can conveniently be taken once a day (*Medical Letter* 1998) to prevent the unpleasant withdrawal symptoms that occur within 4 hours after each heroin use (see Table 9.4). Although the substitute narcotic may also have abuse potential and be scheduled by the DEA (see Table 9.2), it is given to the addict in its oral form; thus, its onset of action is too slow to cause a rush like that associated with heroin use, which means that its abuse potential is substantially less (*Medical Letter* 1998). In addition, the cost to society is dramatically reduced. According to one study, an untreated heroin addict costs the community $21,000 for 6 months, but the cost of methadone maintenance for a person dependent on heroin is only $1750 for the same period (Grinspoon 1995; Hubbard 1998; see "Here and Now," The Cycle of Relapse Without Drug Maintenance).

Currently, methadone is approved by the FDA for "opiate maintenance therapy" in the treatment of heroin (or other narcotic) dependency (Hubbard 1998). Proper use of methadone has been shown to effectively decrease illicit use of narcotics and other undesirable behavior related to drug dependence (Lucky 1998).

Another drug called LAAM (*l*-alpha-acetylmethadol) has been clinically tested and also approved to treat narcotic addiction (Eissenberg et al. 1999). LAAM is a very long-acting narcotic and is more convenient because it requires only three administrations per week to block heroin withdrawal symptoms (Eissenberg et al. 1999). However, due to its potential for damaging the liver, LAAM treatment has decreased dramatically.

A third narcotic, buprenorphine, which is used as an analgesic, was recently approved for treatment of narcotic dependence (Hanson 2003). Because buprenorphine is both an opioid agonist and antagonist, it has minimal potential for dependence and ease of management, which makes this drug a desirable substitute for heroin (Robinson 2002). Efforts are being made to provide education and training to primary care physicians so they will be able to use buprenorphine to treat patients addicted to narcotics in their own offices (Landers 2003). This novel strategy opens the door to physicians heretofore not involved in the treatment of drug addiction to become familiar with substance abuse management and hopefully increase the opportunities to diagnose and treat these patients.

Table 9.5 compares the three major opioid drugs used for maintenance therapy. Other drugs used for similar maintenance therapy of heroin addicts include slow-release oral morphine and even heroin itself for addicts who do not respond to the other maintenance opioid drugs (Bammer 1999).

Some people, including some professionals involved in drug abuse therapy, view heroin or narcotic addiction as a "failure of the will" and see methadone treatment as substituting one addiction for another (Goldstein 1994). As a result, unrealis-

Table 9.4 **Symptoms of Withdrawal from Heroin, Morphine, and Methadone**

Symptoms	TIME IN HOURS		
	Heroin	Morphine	Methadone
Craving for drugs; anxiety	4	6	24–48
Yawning, perspiration, runny nose, tears	8	14	34–48
Pupil dilation, goose bumps, muscle twitches, aching bones and muscles, hot and cold flashes, loss of appetite	12	16	48–72
Increased intensity of preceding symptoms, insomnia, raised blood pressure, fever, faster pulse, nausea	18–24	24–36	≥ 72
Increased intensity of preceding symptoms, curled-up position, vomiting, diarrhea, increased blood sugar, foot kicking ("kicking the habit")	26–36	36–48	—

Here and Now

The Cycle of Relapse Without Drug Maintenance

The lack of supportive drug maintenance with long-acting narcotics, such as methadone or LAAM, to relieve withdrawal for patients severely dependent on heroin often results in a cycle of events during treatment that eventually causes relapse of addiction and tremendous frustration. For example, L.S., a long-term heroin addict, 3 months after completing a withdrawal program manifested a dramatic elevation in mood. This sudden and unexpected improvement in behavior contrasted with the irritability and impulsivity he had expressed since stopping the heroin use. L.S. appeared stable and pleasant. What appeared to the casual observer to be a therapeutic success was actually a bad sign suggesting L.S. was returning to his heroin habit. This positive phase was short-lived as L.S. began selling his possessions, missed work, and stayed home for extended periods due to an escalating heroin dependence. Oftentimes this relapse cycle seen in L.S. is repeated several times before the patient finally realizes that his or her life will not stabilize without maintenance drug therapy with methadone or LAAM to help manage withdrawal from heroin.

Source: Payte, J. T. "The Evolution of Methadone Treatment Programs." *Connection* (a semiannual newsletter published by the Association for Health Services Research) (June 1998): 1–2.

tic treatment expectations are sometimes imposed on heroin addicts, leading to high failure rates. For example, many methadone treatment programs may distribute inadequate methadone doses to maintain heroin or narcotic abstinence (Strain et al. 1999); alternatively, narcotic-dependent patients may be told their methadone will be terminated within 6 months regardless of their progress in the program. Such ill-advised policies often drive clients back to their heroin habits and demonstrate that many professionals who treat heroin and narcotic dependency do not understand that methadone is not a cure for heroin addiction but is a means to achieve a healthier, more normal lifestyle (Millstein 1992; Swan 1994).

It also is essential to understand that even proper treatment does not guarantee resolution of heroin or narcotic addiction (see "Case in Point," Death by Heroin Habit). To maximize the possibility of successful treatment, clients must also participate in regular counseling sessions to help modify the drug-seeking behavior and receive on-site care

Table 9.5 Comparison of Narcotic Substitutes Used in Opiate Maintenance Therapy

PROPERTIES	METHADONE	LAAM	BUPRENORPHINE
Administration	Oral	Oral	Oral or sublingual
Frequency of doses	Daily	Three times per week	Daily
Other uses	Analgesic	None	Analgesic
Physical dependence	Yes	Yes	Little
Causes positive subjective effects	Yes	Some	Yes
Abuse potential	Yes	Limited	Limited

Source: Swan, N. "Two NIDA-Tested Heroin Treatment Medications Move Toward FDA Approval." *NIDA Notes* (March/April 1993): 45.

►Case in Point   Death by Heroin Habit

Together, Theresa LaMarca, 22, and Damien Conners, 26, walked out onto the railroad tracks in their neighborhood and sat down in front of an oncoming Amtrak train. Both were killed instantly. Although papers sensationalized the story, calling the New Jersey couple a "real-life Romeo and Juliet," it soon became apparent that the real reason behind the double suicide was not doomed love, but a $300-a-day painkiller and heroin habit. The couple, after exhausting of all of their financial resources and being evicted from their apartment, began cashing forged checks. A few days after the forgeries were discovered, the two committed suicide. Both LaMarca and Conners had managed to free themselves of drugs after treatment, but apparently only temporarily. In the end, they paid for their drug addiction with their lives.

Source: Johnson, J. "New Jersey Couple's Suicide Highlights Failure of US 'Drug War'" (3 June 2002). Available www.wsws.org/articles/2002/jun2002/nj-j03.shtml.

from professionals, including job training, career development, education, general medical care, and family counseling. These supplemental services dramatically improve the success rate of narcotic dependence treatment (Grinspoon 1995; McLellan et al. 1993).

Other Narcotics

A large number of nonheroin narcotics are used for medical purposes. However, many are also distributed in the streets, such as morphine, methadone, codeine, hydromorphone (Dilaudid), meperidine (Demerol), and other synthetics (hydrocodone [Vicodin] and oxycodone [Oxy-Contin]). A few of the most commonly abused opioids are discussed briefly in the following sections. Except where noted, they are all Schedule II or III drugs.

MORPHINE

As noted earlier, morphine is the standard by which other narcotic analgesic agents are measured (Way et al. 1998). It has been used to relieve pain since it was first isolated in 1803. Morphine has about half the analgesic potency of heroin but 12 times the potency of codeine. It is commonly used to relieve moderate to intense pain that cannot be controlled by less potent and less dangerous narcotics. Because of its potential for serious side effects, morphine is generally used in a hospi-

tal setting where emergency care can be rendered, if necessary. Most pain can be relieved by morphine if high enough doses are used (Reisine and Pasternak 1995; Way et al. 1998); however, morphine is most effective against continuous dull pain.

The side effects that occur when using therapeutic doses of morphine include drowsiness, changes in mood, and inability to think straight. In addition, therapeutic doses depress respiratory activity; thus, morphine decreases the rate and depth of breathing and produces irregular breathing patterns. Like the other narcotics, it can create an array of seemingly unrelated effects throughout the body, including nausea and vomiting, constipation, blurred vision, constricted pupils, and flushed skin (Way et al. 1998).

The initial response to morphine is varied. In normal people who are not suffering pain, the first exposure can be unpleasant, with nausea and vomiting being the prominent reactions. However, continual use often leads to a euphoric response and encourages dependence. When injected subcutaneously, the effects of heroin and morphine are almost identical; this situation occurs because heroin is rapidly metabolized in the body into morphine. After intravenous administration, the onset of heroin's effects is more rapid and more intense than that of morphine because heroin is more lipid-soluble and enters the brain faster. Because heroin is easier to manufacture and is more potent, it is more popular in illicit trade than morphine. Even so, morphine also has substantial abuse potential and is classified as a Schedule II substance (McEvoy 2003).

Tolerance to the effects of morphine can develop very quickly if the drug is used continuously. For example, an addict who is repeatedly administering the morphine to get a "kick" or maintain a "high" must constantly increase the dose. Such users can build up to incredible doses. One addict reported using 5 grams of morphine daily; the normal analgesic dose of morphine is 50 to 80 milligrams per day (Jaffe and Martin 1990). Such high doses are lethal in a person without tolerance to narcotics.

METHADONE

Methadone was first synthesized in Germany in 1943, when natural opiate analgesics were not available because opium could not be obtained from the Far East during World War II. Methadone was first called *Dolophine*, after Adolph Hitler; one company still uses that trade name. (On the street, methadone pills have been called *dollies*.) As previously described, methadone is often substituted for heroin in the treatment of narcotic-dependent people (*Drug Facts and Comparisons* 2005). It is an effective analgesic, equal to morphine if injected and more potent if taken orally (Way et al. 1998).

The physiological effects of methadone are the same as those of morphine and heroin. As a narcotic, methadone produces psychological dependence, tolerance, and then physical dependence and addiction if repeated doses are taken (Belluck 2003). It is effective for about 24 to 36 hours; therefore, the addict must take methadone daily to avoid narcotic withdrawal. It is often considered as addictive as heroin if injected; consequently, because methadone is soluble in water, it is formulated with insoluble, inert ingredients to prevent it from being injected by narcotic addicts.

Among methadone's most useful properties are cross-tolerance with other narcotic drugs and a less intense withdrawal response. If it reaches a sufficiently high level in the blood, methadone blocks heroin euphoria. In addition, withdrawal symptoms of patients physically dependent on heroin or morphine and the postaddiction craving can be suppressed by oral administration of methadone.

The effective dose for methadone maintenance is 50 to 100 milligrams per day to treat severe withdrawal symptoms (Way et al. 1998; Zickler 1999).

The value of substituting methadone for heroin lies in its longer action. Because addicts no longer need heroin to prevent withdrawal, they often can be persuaded to leave their undesirable associates, drug sources, and dangerous lifestyles. The potential side effects from methadone are the same as those from morphine and heroin, including constipation and sedation; yet if properly used, methadone is a safe drug (Way et al. 1998).

When injecting methadone, some people feel the same kind of euphoria that can be obtained from heroin. Methadone addicts receiving maintenance treatment sometimes become euphoric if the dose is increased too rapidly. There are cases of people who injected crushed methadone pills and developed serious lung conditions from particles that lodged in the tissue, creating a condition somewhat like emphysema. The number of deaths from methadone overdose has approached those from heroin in some major cities like New York. Many of these deaths involved young children who took methadone that parents in maintenance programs had brought home or teenagers who tried to shoot up with street methadone or methadone in combination with other drugs. Methadone overdoses can be reversed by the antagonist naloxone if the person is treated in time.

FENTANYLS

The fentanyls belong to a family of very potent narcotic analgesics (>200 times the potency of morphine) that are often administered intravenously for general anesthesia. These synthetic opioid narcotics include drugs such as sufentanil and alfentanil (Way et al. 1998). Fentanyls are also used in transdermal systems (patches on the skin) in the treatment of chronic pain (Duragesic). Occasionally, reports surface of individuals abusing a fentanyl patch by licking, swallowing, or even smoking it (Marquardt and Tharratt 1994).

It is estimated that some 100 different active forms of fentanyl could be synthesized; up to now, about 10 derivatives have appeared on the street. They are considered to be "designer" drugs (see Chapter 1). Because of their great potency and ease of production, the fentanyls have sometimes been used to replace heroin. Fentanyl-type drugs can appear in the same forms and colors as heroin, so there is nothing to alert users that they have been sold a heroin substitute (Henderson 1988). Due to their powerful effects, these drugs are especially dangerous, and incredibly small doses can cause fatal respiratory depression in an unsuspecting heroin user (Way 2003). (One "designer" fentanyl, 3-methyl fentanyl, is 6000 times more potent than heroin.) More than 100 deaths have been reported in the United States due to overdoses from fentanyl-related drugs. Most have occurred in California and New York (Karch 1996; Way et al. 1998). Because these drugs are sometimes very difficult to detect in the blood owing to the small quantities used, there is no reliable information regarding the extent of fentanyl abuse.

HYDROMORPHONE

Hydromorphone (Dilaudid) is prepared from morphine and used as an analgesic and cough suppressant. It is a stronger analgesic than morphine and is used to treat moderate to severe pain. Nausea, vomiting, constipation, and euphoria may be less marked with hydromorphone than with morphine (Karch 1996; Way et al. 1998). On the street, it is taken in tablet form or injected.

OXYCODONE (OXYCONTIN)

Oxycodone is a moderate narcotic analgesic that in the past few years has been increasingly abused as the proprietary product OxyContin and created considerable controversy (see "Here and Now," OxyContin Controversy Rages). OxyContin is a long-lasting version of this drug and considered to be an important and effective therapy for the treatment of severe pain from cancer or other lingering diseases (*Medical Letter on the CDC and FDA* 2003). A dramatic rise in the abuse of OxyContin has been a considerable cause for alarm by officials. This is underscored by the report that in 2004, 5% of high school seniors used this drug (Johnston 2004). Concern has been further heightened with reports of drug rings, including physicians illegally distributing OxyContin (DEA 2002); more than 100 deaths in 2002 linked to an overdose of this product (Marsa 2003); and a 352% increase in the visits to hospital emergency rooms associated with OxyContin use (Substance Abuse Letter 2003). However, these reports of adverse events associated with OxyContin use must be put into perspective by the knowledge that the vast majority of these emergency events are associated with drug abuse or physical causes (e.g., cancer) other than the effects of OxyContin (*Biotech Week* 2003). As a result, the FDA and DEA control OxyContin at the same level as morphine.

Here and Now

OxyContin Controversy Rages

Controversy surrounds the drug OxyContin, with some hailing its painkilling abilities even as others emphasize its potentially deadly effects. At a 3-day conference on drug abuse prevention, protesters held up signs referring to friends and family members who they claimed had died as a result of OxyContin overdose, in the hopes of raising awareness about the potential problems associated with the drug. One protester described a young man who had gone through withdrawal and depression after being prescribed the drug as a painkiller, and who eventually died from an accidental overdose. Others recognized the beneficial effects of the drug, noting that OxyContin had relieved pain that other drugs could not alleviate in their loved ones. Most individuals attending the conference felt that the problem was not OxyContin or prescriptions, but rather persuading communities to work together to create solutions to the abuse of this drug.

Source: Bloodsworth, D. "Crowd Protests" (20 November 2003) Available www.oxyabusekills.com/crowdprotests.html.

MEPERIDINE

Meperidine (Demerol) is a synthetic drug that frequently is used as an analgesic for treatment of moderate pain; it can be taken in tablet form or injected. Meperidine is about one-tenth as powerful as morphine, and its use can lead to dependence (Way et al. 1998). This drug is sometimes given too freely by some physicians because tolerance develops, requiring larger doses to maintain its therapeutic action. With continual use, it causes physical dependence. Meperidine addicts may use large daily doses (3–4 grams per day). Repeated use of high doses of meperidine can cause seizures (Way et al. 1998).

BUPRENORPHINE

Buprenorphine, a mild-to-moderate narcotic analgesic has been available as a Schedule V pain reliever for years. After extensive research, this drug was approved in 2002 as an effective medication for the treatment of narcotic abuse and dependence (Hanson 2003). Buprenorphine has been shown to be effective in relieving the cravings for narcotic pain relievers with minimal tendency to cause addiction itself (Landers 2003; *NIDA Notes* 2002). Although buprenorphine has a history of minimal risk, when used properly, there have been isolated reports of occasional deaths especially when combined with other CNS depressant drugs (Forensic Drug Abuse Advisor 2003). Despite its significant safety record and its minimal propensity for abuse, because its new FDA-approved indication would cause it to be dispensed to patients with drug abuse histories, the DEA revised its classification of buprenorphine to a Schedule III drug. Of particular importance is the fact that buprenorphine (Subutex and Suboxone, a combination of buprenorphine and naloxone) has been approved for the treatment of opiate dependence in an office setting. This means for the first time a drug used to treat addiction can be prescribed by trained primary care physicians, in the offices of private doctors. This is the first step in what may become a revolution in addiction treatment, allowing patients to discreetly receive help from a family doctor for their substance abuse problem (CESAR FAX 2003a;

Landers 2003). Currently, more than 2000 physicians have been certified to prescribe it for treatment of opioid drug dependence (Hanson 2003).

MPTP: A "DESIGNER" TRAGEDY

Attempts to synthesize illicit designer versions of meperidine by street chemists have proved tragic for some unsuspecting drug addicts. In 1976, a young drug addict with elementary laboratory skills attempted to make a meperidine-like drug by using shortcuts in the chemical synthesis. Three days after self-administering his untested drug product, the drug user developed a severe case of tremors and motor problems identical to Parkinson's disease, a neurological disorder generally occurring in the elderly. Even more surprising to attending neurologists was that this young drug addict improved dramatically after treatment with levodopa, a drug that is very effective in treating the symptoms of traditional Parkinson's disease. After 18 months of treatment, the despondent addict committed suicide. An autopsy revealed he had severe brain damage that was almost identical to that occurring in classical parkinsonian patients (Davies et al. 1979). It was concluded that a by-product resulting from the sloppy synthesis of the meperidine-like designer narcotic was responsible for the irreversible brain damage.

This hypothesis was confirmed by a separate and independent event on the West Coast in 1981, when a cluster of relatively young heroin addicts (ages 22–42) in the San Francisco area also developed symptoms of Parkinson's disease. All of these patients had consumed a new "synthetic heroin" obtained on the streets, which was produced by attempting to synthesize meperidine-like drugs (Aminoff 1998; Langston et al. 1983). Common to both incidents was the presence of the compound MPTP, which was a contaminant resulting from the careless synthesis. MPTP is metabolized to a very reactive molecule in the brain that selectively destroys neurons containing the transmitter dopamine in the motor regions of the basal ganglia (see Chapter 4). Similar neuronal damage occurs in classical Parkinson's disease over the course of 50 to 70 years, whereas ingestion of MPTP dramatically accelerates the degeneration to a matter of days (Goldstein 1994). As tragic as the MPTP incident was, it was heralded as an important scientific breakthrough: MPTP is now used by researchers as a tool to study why Parkinson's disease occurs and how to treat it effectively (Aminoff 1998).

CODEINE

Codeine is a naturally occurring constituent of opium and the most frequently prescribed of the narcotic analgesics. It is used principally as a treatment for minor to moderate pain and as a cough suppressant. Maximum pain relief from codeine occurs with 30 to 50 milligrams. Usually, when prescribed for pain, codeine is combined with either a salicylate (such as aspirin) or acetaminophen (Tylenol). Aspirin-like drugs and opioid narcotics interact in a synergistic fashion to give an analgesic equivalence greater than what can be achieved by aspirin or codeine alone. Although not especially powerful, codeine may still be abused. Codeine-containing cough syrup is currently classified as a Schedule V drug. Because the abuse potential is considered minor, the FDA has ruled that codeine cough products can be sold without a prescription; however, the pharmacist is required to keep them behind the counter and must be asked in order to obtain codeine-containing cough medications. Despite the FDA ruling, about 50% of the states have more restrictive regulations and require that codeine-containing cough products be available only by prescription (Way et al. 1998).

Although codeine dependence is possible, it is not very common; most people who abuse codeine developed narcotic dependence previously with one of the more potent opioids. In general, large quantities of codeine are needed to satisfy a narcotic addiction; therefore, it is not commonly marketed on the street.

PENTAZOCINE

Pentazocine (Talwin) was first developed in the 1960s in an effort to create an effective analgesic with low abuse potential. When taken orally, its analgesic effect is slightly greater than that of codeine. Its effects on respiration and sedation are similar to those of the other opioids, but it does not prevent withdrawal symptoms in a narcotic addict. In fact, pentazocine will precipitate withdrawal symptoms if given to a person on methadone maintenance (Reisine and Pasternak 1995). Pentazocine is not commonly abused because its effects can be unpleasant, resulting in dysphoria. It is classified as a Schedule IV drug.

PROPOXYPHENE

Propoxyphene (Darvon, Dolene) is structurally related to methadone, but it is a much weaker analgesic, about half as potent as codeine (Way et al. 1998). Like codeine, propoxyphene is frequently given in combination with aspirin or acetaminophen. Although it was once an extremely popular analgesic, the use of propoxyphene has declined as its potency has been questioned. Some research suggests this narcotic is no more effective in relieving pain than aspirin (Reisine and Pasternak 1995). To a large extent, new, more effective nonnarcotic analgesics have replaced propoxyphene. In very high doses, it can cause delusions, hallucinations, and convulsions. Alone, propoxyphene causes little respiratory depression; however, when combined with alcohol or other CNS depressants, this drug can depress respiration.

Narcotic-Related Drugs

Although not classified as narcotics, the following drugs are either structurally similar to narcotics (dextromethorphan) or are used to treat narcotic withdrawal (clonidine) or overdose (naloxone).

DEXTROMETHORPHAN

Dextromethorphan is a synthetic used in cough remedies since the 1960s and can be purchased without prescription. Although its molecular structure resembles that of codeine, this drug does not have analgesic action nor does it cause typical narcotic dependence (*Drug Facts and Comparisons* 2005).

Although not considered a major drug abuse problem, sporadic recreational use of dextromethorphan-containing cough medicines has been reported in the United States and other countries sometimes resulting in deadly consequences (see "Here and Now," Dextromethorphan:

No Coughing Matter). The abuse typically occurs among adolescents and young adults. The relatively few cases of addiction reveal a pattern of high-dose use for months to even years. The principal symptoms of abuse include altered perceptions, sense of floating, hallucinations, visual distortions, and even paranoia and psychotic reactions. Its effects have been described to be similar to those of phencyclidine (PCP) and the general anesthetic ketamine (Cranston 1999). There is some suggestion that both physical and psychological dependence can occur with dextromethorphan, resulting in withdrawal when its use is discontinued (Cranston 1999). Dextromethorphan is sometimes mixed with drugs such as alcohol, amphetamines, and cocaine to give unusual psychoactive interactions. As of 2005, the DEA had taken no steps to restrict the use of dextromethorphan in over-the-counter (OTC) products.

Some people are becoming aware of dextromethorphan abuse potential from web sites on the Internet. A growing number of these sites have promoted dextromethorphan as a "powerful" OTC mind-altering drug. Included on these sites are personal experiences of users as well as directions on how to use the drug, predictions about what to expect, warning signs of adverse reactions, and instructions as to how to extract dextromethorphan from OTC cough medicines (The Vaults of Erowid 2005).

CLONIDINE

Clonidine (Catapres) was created in the late 1970s. It is not a narcotic analgesic and has no direct effect on the opioid receptors; instead, it stimulates receptors for noradrenaline, and its principal use is as an oral antihypertensive (*Drug Facts and Comparisons* 2005). Clonidine is mentioned here because it is a nonaddictive, noneuphoriagenic prescription medication with demonstrated efficacy in relieving some of the physical effects of opiate withdrawal (such as vomiting and diarrhea). However, clonidine does not alter narcotic craving or the generalized aches associated with withdrawal (O'Brien 1995). The dosing regimen is typi-

Here and Now

Dextromethorphan: No Coughing Matter

Dextromethorphan, a key active ingredient in cough suppressants, is the reason why many young people are using OTC cough medicines to get high. The substance—also known as robo, skittles, dxm, dex, and tussein—is found in at least 80 OTC products. Dextromethorphan usually produces a disassociative feeling (roboing, robo rolling, robo tripping) or a feeling of intoxication, but its abuse can also lead to psychotic behavior. When large amounts of dextromethorphan are taken, the drug attaches to receptors in the central nervous system—the same receptors to which PCP attaches. In the long term, this effect can cause depression, memory problems, and suicidal tendencies. Dextromethorphan abuse can also result in death: In 2003, 14 people younger than age 18 died as a result of dextromethorphan use, with many more overdoses reported nationwide.

Source: Magnus, E. "Addicted to Cough Medicine." *MSNBC News* (27 March 2004). Available www.msnbc.msn.com/id/4608341/.

cally a 7- to 14-day inpatient treatment for opiate withdrawal. Length of treatment can be reduced to 7 days for withdrawal from heroin and short-acting opiates; the 14-day treatment is needed for the longer-acting methadone-type opiates. Because tolerance to clonidine may develop, opiates are discontinued abruptly at the start of treatment. In this way, the peak intensity of withdrawal will occur while clonidine is still maximally effective (Kleber 1998; McEvoy 2003).

One of the most important advantages of clonidine over other treatments for opiate withdrawal detoxification is that it shortens the time for withdrawal to 14 days compared with several weeks or months using standard procedures, such as methadone treatment (Kleber 1998). The potential disadvantage of taking clonidine is that it can cause serious side effects of its own, the most serious being significantly lowered blood pressure, which can cause fainting and blacking out (*Drug Facts and Comparisons* 2005). Overall, its lack of abuse potential makes clonidine particularly useful in rapid treatment of narcotic dependence; however, the long-term benefit is controversial (Gowing et al. 2003).

NALOXONE/NALTREXONE

Naloxone and the related drug naltrexone are relatively pure narcotic antagonists. These drugs attach to opiate receptors in the brain and throughout the body. They do not activate but rather prevent narcotic drugs, such as heroin and morphine, from having an effect. By themselves, these antagonists do not cause much change, but potently block or reverse the effects of all narcotics. Because of its antagonistic properties, naloxone is a useful antidote in the treatment of narcotic overdoses; its administration reverses life-threatening, narcotic-induced effects on breathing and the cardiovascular system (*Washington Times* 2003). However, if not used carefully, this antagonist will also block the analgesic action of the narcotics and initiate severe withdrawals in narcotic-dependent people (Way et al. 1998). Its use has been proposed to prevent addicts from experiencing the effects of heroin (Mathias 2003); however, most individuals dependent on heroin are not interested in using this drug because it can precipitate withdrawal symptoms.

An interesting use of naloxone has been to combine it with buprenorphine in small quantities (Suboxone). As long as this product is taken as prescribed, the quantity of naloxone is too small to have an antagonistic effect. However, if Suboxone is consumed in high doses, such as would occur if it were being abused, there would be sufficient naloxone to block the opioid effect (CESAR FAX 2003a). There has been interest in employing this drug to reduce the craving for alcohol in the treatment of chronic alcoholism. It has been approved by the FDA for this purpose (*Drug Facts and Comparisons* 2005).

■ NATURAL SUBSTANCES

Narcotics

Although many herbal preparations can cause drowsiness or have some analgesic properties, few of these actually contain opioid narcotic drugs. The naturally occurring opioid drugs include morphine, codeine, heroin, papaverine, and thebaine and are found only in the opium poppy, *Papaver somniferum*. Although several varieties of opium-yielding poppies exist, they are typically winter crops in the Southern Hemisphere and do best in climates that have warm days and cool nights. All of the plants thrive in sandy soil. Most of the active drugs are found in the seepage from the seed heads located beneath the flower petals of the poppy flowers, although small amounts of these active ingredients are found in other parts of the plant such as the stem and leaves. The poppy flowers persist until the end of October in the Southern Hemisphere. Although this species of plant can survive in the United States if the environment is rigidly controlled, the vast majority of the supplies of the naturally occurring narcotic drugs are brought into the country, either legally and sold as legitimate pharmaceuticals, or smuggled across borders and sold as illicit narcotics.

Discussion Questions

1. Why do narcotics have high abuse potential?

2. What are the principal clinical uses of the opioid narcotics?

3. What is the relationship between endorphin systems and the opioid narcotics?

4. Why was there a substantial increase in heroin abuse in the United States throughout the 1990s?

5. Why does heroin addiction contribute to criminal activity?

6. What are the principal withdrawal effects when heroin use is stopped in addicts?

7. How does "methadone maintenance" work for the treatment of narcotic dependence? Explain a possible drawback to this approach.

8. How does buprenorphine compare to methadone as treatment for narcotic addictions?

9. What is considered to be successful treatment for heroin addiction?

10. How does morphine compare with heroin?

11. Why is dextromethorphan potentially addicting, and what should the federal government do to stop its abuse?

12. What value does naloxone have in treating narcotic addiction or alcoholism?

Key Terms

analgesics 252

opioid 252

antitussive 252

speedballing 260

mainline 264

Summary

1 The term *narcotic* refers to naturally occurring substances derived from the opium poppy and their synthetic substitutes. These drugs are referred to as the opioid (or opiate) narcotics because of their association with opium. For the most part, the opioid narcotics possess abuse potential, but they also have important clinical value and are used to relieve all kinds of pain (they are analgesic), suppress coughing (they are antitussive), and stop diarrhea.

2 The principal side effects of the opioid narcotics, besides their abuse potential, include drowsiness, respiratory depression, nausea and vomiting, constipation, inability to urinate, and sometimes a drop in blood pressure. These side effects can be annoying or even life-threatening, so caution is required when using these drugs.

3 Heroin is the most likely of the opioid narcotics to be severely abused; it is easily prepared from opium and has a rapid, intense effect.

4 When narcotics such as heroin are first used by people not experiencing pain, the drugs can cause unpleasant, dysphoric sensations. However, euphoria gradually overcomes the aversive effects. The positive feelings increase with narcotic use, leading to psychological dependence. After psychological dependence, physical dependence occurs with frequent daily use, which reinforces the narcotic abuse. If the user stops taking the drug after physical dependence has occurred, severe withdrawal symptoms result.

5 Tolerance to narcotics can occur rapidly with intense use of these drugs. This tolerance can result in the use of incredibly large doses of narcotics that would be fatal to a nontolerant person.

6 Methadone and LAAM are frequently used to help narcotic addicts stop using heroin or one of the other, highly addicting drugs. Oral methadone relieves the withdrawal symptoms that would result from discontinuing narcotics. Methadone can also cause psychological and physical dependence, but it is less addicting than heroin and easier to control. Another long-acting narcotic, buprenorphine, was recently FDA-approved for narcotic maintenance programs. Buprenorphine is distinct from methadone in that it has been approved for use in primary care settings.

7 Fentanyls are very potent synthetic opioid narcotics. They can be easily synthesized and converted into drugs that are as much as 3000 to 6000 times more potent than heroin itself. Detection and regulation of these fentanyl derivatives by law enforcement agencies are very difficult. The fentanyl-type drugs are used as heroin substitutes and have killed many narcotic addicts because of their unexpected potency.

8 Attempts to create designer narcotics have led to the synthesis of very potent fentanyl-like drugs that are responsible for a number of overdose deaths. In addition, attempts to synthesize a meperidine (Demerol) designer drug resulted in the inadvertent creation of MPTP, a very reactive compound that causes a dramatic onset of Parkinson's disease in its users.

9 Dextromethorphan is a codeine-related drug used as an antitussive in OTC cough medicines. In very high doses, dextromethorphan can cause PCP-like hallucinations and sensory distortions. The sporadic abuse of this drug has not been substantial enough to result in its removal or special control by federal agencies.

References

Abel, E. L. *Marijuana: The First Twelve Thousand Years.* New York: Plenum, 1980.

Aminoff, M. "Pharmacologic Management of Parkinsonism and Other Movement Disorders." In *Basic and Clinical Pharmacology*, 7th ed., edited by Bertram Katzung, 450–463. Stamford, CT: Appleton and Lange, 1998.

Austin, G. A. *Perspective on the History of Psychoactive Substance Use.* NIDA Research Issues No. 24. Washington, DC: U.S. Department of Health, Education, and Welfare, 1978.

Baglole, J. "Vancouver's Heroin 'Fix.'" *The Wall Street Journal* (1 April 2003): D-8.

Bammer, G., A. Dobler-Mikola, M. Fleming, J. Strang, and A. Uchtenhagen. "The Heroin Prescribing Debate: Integrating Science and Politics." *Science* 284 (1999): 1277–1278.

BBC News. "Afghanistan Retakes Heroin Crown" (March 2003). Available news.bbc.co.uk/1/hi/business/2814861.stm.

Bearak, B. "Junkies Playing Roulette with Needles." *Salt Lake Tribune* (29 November 1992): A-4.

Belluck, P. "Methadone, Once the Way Out, Suddenly Grows as a Killer Drug." *The New York Times* (9 February 2003): 8.

Bennett, A. "Perinatal Substance Abuse and the Drug-exposed Neonate." *Advanced Nurse Practitioner* 7 (1999): 32–36.

Best, S., A. Oliveto, and T. Kosten. "Opioid Addiction: Recent Advances in Detoxification and Maintenance Therapy." *CNS Drugs* 6 (October 1996): 301–314.

Biotech Week. "Purdue Pharma: OxyContin Rarely the Sole Cause of Drug Abuse Deaths." (19 March 2003): 1.

Bourgois, P. "Participant Observation Study of Indirect Paraphernalia Sharing/HIV Risk in a Network of Heroin Injection." NIDA web site (17 November 1999). Available http://165.112.78.61/CEWG/ethno.html.

Brecher, E. M. *Licit and Illicit Drugs.* Boston: Little, Brown, 1972.

Catania, H., and Drug Policy Alliance. (2003). *About Methadone*, 2nd ed. Available http://www.drugpolicy.org/docUploads/about methadone.pdf.

CESAR FAX. "Buprenorphine Now Available for Treating Heroin Dependence in U.S." *University of Maryland* 12 (31 March 2003a): 1.

CESAR FAX. "US Emergency Department Visits Involving Narcotic Analgesics Have Doubled in Five Years." *University of Maryland* 12 (7 April 2003): 1.

CEWG, vol. 1. "Highlights and Executive Summary." NIDA, NIH Publications No. 03-5109A, December 2002.

Cranston, J. "Abuse of Dextromethorphan." *Archives of Family Medicine* 8 (1999): 99.

Davies, G., A. Williams, S. Markey, M. Ebert, E. Caine, C. Reickert, and I. Kopin. "Chronic Parkinsonism Secondary to Intravenous Injection of Meperidine Analogues." *Psychiatry Research* 1 (1979): 249–254.

DEA. "Domestic Strategic June 2002 Highlights." *DEA 02047* (September 2002): 1.

DEA. "Heroin." Chapter from *Drugs of Abuse* (2000). Available www.health.org/pubs/qdocs/heroin/doaher.html.

DiChiara, G., and A. North. "Neurobiology of Opiate Abuse." *Trends in Pharmacological Sciences* 13 (May 1992): 185–193.

Drug and Alcohol Abuse Resource Center. "Drug Addiction Information" (January 2005). Available www.addict-help.com/.

Drug Facts and Comparisons. St. Louis, MO: Wolters Kluwer, 2005: 488, 489, 616, 617, 942–977; 1424–1428.

Drugs, Youth and the Internet. "Heroin/Opiates." U.S. Department of Justice, Product # 2002-R0430-002 (August 2002): 21–24.

Eissenberg, T., M. Stitzer, G. Bigelow, A. Buchalter, and S. Walsh. "Relative Potency of Levo-alpha-acetyl-methadol and Methadone in Humans Under Acute Dosing Conditions." *Journal of Pharmacology and Experimental Therapeutics* 289 (1999): 936–945.

Epstein, J., and J. Gfroerer. "Data Point to Increase in Numbers of Young Heroin Users." *Connection* (a semiannual newsletter published by the Association for Health Services Research) (June 1998): 3.

Fabris, C., G. Prandi, C. Perathoner, and A. Soldi. "Neonatal Drug Addiction." *Panminerva Medica* (1998): 239–243.

Forensic Drug Abuse Advisor. "Buprenorphine-Related Deaths." 15 (February 2, 2003): 1, 2.

Gannett News Service. "Addiction Fueling $400 Billion Global Illegal Drug Industry." *Salt Lake Tribune* 255 (14 November 1997): A-15.

Golding, A. "Two Hundred Years of Drug Abuse." *Journal of the Royal Society of Medicine* 86 (May 1993): 282–286.

Goldstein, A. *Addiction from Biology to Drug Policy.* New York: Freeman, 1994: 137–154.

Gossop, M., J. Marsden, D. Stewart, and A. Rolfe. "Reductions in Acquisitive Crime and Drug Use After Treatment of Addiction Problems: 1-Year Follow-up Outcomes." *Drug and Alcohol Dependence* 58 (2000): 165–172.

Gourlay, G. "Advances in Opioid Pharmacology." *Supportive Care for Cancer* (21 December 2004).

Gowing, L., M. Farrell, R. Ali, and J. White. "Alpha 2 Adrenergic Agonists for the Management of Opioid Withdrawal." *Cochrane Database Systems Review* 2 (2003).

Grinspoon, L. "Psychotherapy for Methadone Patients—Part II." *Harvard Mental Health Letter* 12 (October 1995): 7.

Hall, E., and N. Sykes. "Analgesia for Patients with Advanced Disease." *Postgraduate Medical Journal* 80 (2004): 148–154.

Hall, W., J. Bell, and J. Carless. "Crime and Drug Use Among Applicants for Methadone Maintenance." *Drug and Alcohol Dependence* 31 (1993): 123–129.

Hanson, G. R. "Opening the Door to Mainstream Medical Treatment of Drug Addiction." *NIDA Notes* 17 (January 2003): 3, 4.

Henderson, G. "Designer Drugs: Past History and Future Prospects." *Journal of Forensic Sciences* 33 (1988): 569–575.

"Heroin '96: What Americans Need to Know." *Prevention Pipeline* 8 (November/December 1996): 20.

Hubbard, R. "Focus on Heroin: Increase in Users and Changing Treatment System Present New Challenges for Services Researchers." *Connection* (a semiannual newsletter published by the Association for Health Services Research) (June 1998): 1–2.

Jaffe, J., and M. Martin. "Opioid Analgesics and Antagonists." In *The Pharmacological Basis of Therapeutics,* 8th ed., edited by A. Gilman, T. Rall, A. Nics, and P. Taylor, 522–573. New York: Pergamon, 1990.

Johnston, L. "Monitoring the Future" (2004). Available www.Monitoringthefuture.org.

Johnston, L. "Overall Teen Drug Use Continues Gradual Decline, but Use of Inhalants Rises" (21 December 2005). Available www.monitoringthefuture.com.

Karch, S. "Narcotics." In *The Pathology of Drug Abuse,* 281–408. New York: CRC, 1996.

Kleber, H. "Detoxification." *National Conference on Drug Addiction Treatment: From Research to Practice. Abstract.* (21 April 1998). Available http://165.112.78.61/Meetsum/ Tx/Txinfo31.html.

Kosten, T., and L. Hollister. "Drugs of Abuse." In *Basic and Clinical Pharmacology,* 7th ed., edited by Bertram Katzun, 516–531. Stamford, CT: Appleton & Lange, 1998.

Kreek, M., S. Schlussman, G. Bart, K. Laforge, and E. Butelman. "Evolving Perspectives on Neurobiological Research on the Addictions: Celebration of the 30th Anniversary of NIDA." *Neuropharmacology* 47 supplement 1 (2004): 324–344.

Landers, P. "Fighting Addiction with a Pill." *The Wall Street Journal* (20 February 2003): D-1.

Langston, J., P. Ballard, J. Tetrud, and I. Irwin. "Chronic Parkinsonism in Humans Due to a Product of Meperidine-Analogue Synthesis." *Science* 219 (1983): 979–980.

Law, P., H. Loh, and L. Wei. "Insights into the Receptor Transcription and Signaling: Implications in Opioid Tolerance and Dependence." *Neuropharmacology* 47 supplement 1 (2004): 300–311.

Leland, J. "The Fear of Heroin Is Shooting Up." *Newsweek* (26 August 1996): 55–56.

Lucky, B. "MTQS Study Highlights Possibilities and Challenges for Performance Measurement." *Connection* (a semiannual newsletter published by the Association for Health Services Research) (June 1998): 4.

Marquardt, K., and R. S. Tharratt. "Inhalation Abuse of Fentanyl Patch." *Clinical Toxicology* 32 (1994): 75–78.

Marsa, L. "Drug Mix Proves Deadly." *Los Angeles Times* (3 March 2003): A-1.

"Mary." *Rolling Stone* 30 (1996): 42–43.

Mathias, R. "New Approaches Seek to Expand Naltrexone Use in Heroin Treatment." *NIDA Notes* 17 (January 2003): 8.

Maurer, D., and V. Vogel. *Narcotics and Narcotic Addiction,* 3rd ed. Springfield, IL: Thomas, 1967.

Maxwell, J. "Unmet Treatment Needs Among Heroin Addicts Raise Ethical Issues." *Connection* (a semiannual newsletter published by the Association for Health Services Research) (June 1998): 5.

May, H. "Heroin Easy to Get in S.L., but Hard to Leave Behind." *Salt Lake Tribune* 257 (1998): D-1.

McEvoy, G., ed. "Opiate Agonists and Antagonists." In *American Hospital Formulary Service Drug Information,* 2022–2097. Bethesda, MD: American Society of Hospital Pharmacists, 2003.

McLellen, T., O. Arndt, D. Metzger, G. Woody, and C. O'Brien. "The Effects of Psychosocial Services in Substance Abuse Treatment." *Journal of the American Medical Association* 269 (21 April 1993): 1953–1959.

Medical Letter. Opioid Analgesics. 40 (1998): 81–82.

Medical Letter on the CDC and FDA. "FDA Warns OxyContin Maker over Safety Statement in Ads." (16 February 2003).

Millstein, R. "Methadone Revisited" *NIDA Notes* 7 (July/August 1992): 3–4.

National Drug Threat Assessment 2003. "Heroin." U.S. Department of Justice, Product No. 2003-Q0317-001 (January 2003): 41–50.

National Trends in Drug Abuse. "Information About Heroin from ONDCP Pulse Check." *Newsweek* (26 August 1996): 54. Available www.health.org/pubs/ondcptrends/heroin.html (6 April 2000).

NIDA Infofax. "Heroin." *National Institute on Drug Abuse Infofax* (April 2000). Available http://165.112.78.61/Infofax/heroin.html.

NIDA Infofax. "Heroin" (January 2005). Available www.drugabuse.gov/Infofax/heroin.html.

NIDA Notes. "Buprenorphine Approval Expands Options for Addiction Treatment." 17 (2002): 13.

NIDA Research Report Series. "Heroin Abuse and Addiction" (December 2004). Available www.drugabuse.gov/ResearchReports/heroin/heroin5.html.

Nowak, R. "Cops and Doctors: Drug Busts Hamper Pain Therapy." *Journal of NIH Research* 4 (May 1992): 27–29.

O'Brien, C. "Drug Addiction and Drug Abuse." In *The Pharmacological Basis of Therapeutics,* 9th ed., edited by J. Hardman and L. Limbird, 557–577. New York: McGraw-Hill, 1995.

"Opioids." *Medical Letter* 38 (10 May 1996).

Paule, M. G. "Maternal Drug Abuse and Adverse Effects on Neurobehavior of Offspring." In *Handbook of Developmental Neurotoxicology,* edited by W. Slikker and L. Chang, 617–629. New York: Academic Press, 1998.

Payte, J. T. "The Evolution of Methadone Treatment Programs." *Connection* (a semiannual newsletter published by the Association for Health Services Research) (June 1998): 1–2.

Quinion, M. "Heroin Chic." *World Wide Words* (January 2005). Available www.worldwidewords.org/turnsofphrase/tp-herl.htm.

Reisine, T., and G. Pasternak. "Opioid Analgesics and Antagonists." In *The Pharmacological Basis of Therapeutics,* 9th ed., edited by J. Hardman and L. Limbird, 521–555. New York: McGraw–Hill, 1995.

Roberts, M. "Heroin's Grasp on Portland." *The Sunday Oregonian* (12 July 1998): A-1.

Robinson, S. "Buprenorphine: An Analgesic with an Expanding Role in the Treatment of Opioid Addiction." *CNS Drug Review* 8 (Winter 2002): 377–390.

Rombey, D. "Heroin Is Silent Scourge of Sheltered Springville." *Deseret News* (9 June 2003a): A-1.

Rombey, D. "Heroin Takes Toll on Families." *Deseret News* (10 June 2003b): A-1.

Seper, J. "Colombia Policy Cited for Rise in Heroin Use; Investigators Hit Focus on Cocaine." *Washington Times* (26 May 2003): A-1.

Stockman, F. "Heroin Is Surpassing Cocaine as Users' Choice." *Boston Globe* (26 May 2003): A-1.

Strain, E., G. Bigelow, I. Liebson, and M. Stitzer. "Moderate- vs. High-dose Methadone in the Treatment of Opioid Dependence: A Randomized Trial." *Journal of the American Medical Association* 281 (1999): 1000–1005.

Substance Abuse Letter. "Growing Painkiller Abuse Concerns Federal Officials." *Pace Publications* 8 (2003): 1.

Swan, N. "Research Demonstrates Long-Term Benefits of Methadone Treatment." *NIDA Notes* 9 (1994): 1, 4–5.

Thompson, C. "Deadly, Super-Pure Heroin Spreading." *Salt Lake Tribune* 250 (22 June 1995): A-13.

The Vaults of Erowid. "Dextromethorphan" (6 January 2005). Available www.erowid.org/chemicals/dxm/dxm.shtml.

Washington Times. "Addicts to Give Anti-overdose Drugs." (5 March 2003): B-3.

Wax, P., C. Becker, and S. Curry. "Unexpected Gas Casualties in Moscow: A Medical Toxicology Perspective." *Annals of Emergency Medicine* 41 (2003): 700–705.

Way, W., H. Fields, and E. L. Way. "Opioid Analgesics and Antagonists." In *Basic and Clinical Pharmacology*, 7th ed., edited by Bertram Katzung, 496–515. Stamford, CT: Appleton & Lange, 1998.

Way, W., and E. Way. "Opioid Analgesics and Antagonists." In *Basic and Clinical Pharmacology*, 5th ed., edited by B. Katzung, 420–436. Norwalk, CT: Appleton & Lange, 1992.

Weiss, E. "Seattle Scene Represents Nation's Rising Heroin Use." *All Things Considered*, National Public Radio (2 January 1995).

Zickler, P. "High-Dose Methadone Improves Treatment Outcomes." *NIDA Notes* 14 (1999): 81–82.

Zocchi, A., et al. "Dopamine Responsiveness to Drugs of Abuse: A Shell-Core Investigation in the Nucleus Accumbens of the Mouse." *Synapse* 50 (2003): 293–302.

CHAPTER 10

Stimulants

Did You Know?

- The first therapeutic use of amphetamines was in inhalers to treat nasal congestion.

- Methylphenidate (Ritalin) is a type of amphetamine used to treat hyperactive (attention deficit hyperactivity disorder) children.

- One of the most common Food and Drug Administration (FDA)–approved uses of amphetamines is as an appetite suppressant to treat obesity.

- Illegal methamphetamine can be easily made from drugs found in common over-the-counter (OTC) decongestants and some herbal products.

- Methamphetamine labs are a danger to the neighborhood because they use extremely toxic and explosive chemicals as part of the synthesis process.

- Ecstasy is referred to as a "club drug" owing to its frequent use at "raves," nightclubs, and bars.

- Ecstasy can be addicting, especially when smoked or injected intravenously.

- The original Coca-Cola was a cocaine-containing tonic developed in the late 1800s.

- In the early 1980s, cocaine was viewed as a relatively harmless, glamorous substance by the media and some medical experts in this country.

- Smoking "freebased" or "crack" cocaine is more dangerous and more addicting than other forms of administration.

- Many people who abuse cocaine or methamphetamine have underlying mental illness.

- Using high doses of amphetamines or cocaine can cause behavior that resembles schizophrenia.

- Caffeine is the most frequently used stimulant in the world.

- OTC decongestant drugs usually contain mild central nervous system (CNS) stimulants that can be habit-forming.

- Herbal stimulants promoted as "natural highs" contain CNS stimulants that can cause high blood pressure, seizures, and strokes.

- Ephedrine found in natural herbal products has caused fatal cardiovascular problems in unsuspecting athletes and was recently removed from the list of FDA-approved OTC products.

On completing this chapter you will be able to:

◎ Explain how amphetamines work.

◎ Identify the FDA-approved uses for amphetamines.

◎ Recognize the major side effects of amphetamines on brain and cardiovascular functions.

◎ Identify the terms *speed*, *ice*, *run*, *high*, and *tweaking* as they relate to amphetamine use.

◎ Explain what "designer" amphetamines are and how Ecstasy compares to methamphetamine.

◎ Explain what "club drugs" are.

◎ Trace the changes in attitude toward cocaine abuse that occurred in the 1980s and explain why they occurred.

◎ Compare the effects of cocaine with those of amphetamines.

◎ Identify the different stages of cocaine withdrawal.

◎ Discuss the different approaches to treating cocaine dependence.

◎ Identify and compare the major sources of the caffeine-like xanthine drugs.

◎ List the principal physiological effects of caffeine.

◎ Compare caffeine dependence and withdrawal to that associated with the major stimulants.

◎ Understand the potential dangers of using herbal stimulants such as ephedra.

◎ Identify the role of the FDA in regulating herbal stimulants.

Drugs and Society Online is a great source for additional drugs and society information for both students and instructors.
Visit **http://drugsandsociety.jbpub.com** to find a variety of useful tools for learning, thinking, and teaching.

Introduction

Stimulants are substances that cause the user to feel pleasant effects such as a sense of increased energy and a state of euphoria, or "high." This effect is likely due to the ability of these drugs to release dopamine (Deslandes et al. 2002). The user may also feel restless and talkative and have trouble sleeping. High doses administered over the long term can produce personality changes or even induce violent, dangerous, psychotic behavior. The following is a quote from a former methamphetamine user: "Meth produces the same high as cocaine, but for longer time at a cheaper price . . . You get very violent coming down. And you get violent trying to get the drug. Users tend to take guns—they tend to carry guns." (Prevention Pipeline 1997).

Many users self-medicate psychological conditions (for example, depression) with stimulants. Because the initial effects of stimulants are so pleasant, these drugs are repeatedly abused, leading to dependence.

In this chapter, you will learn about two principal classifications of stimulant drugs. Major stimulants, including amphetamines and cocaine, are addressed first, given their prominent role in current drug abuse problems in the United States. The chapter concludes with a review of minor stimulants—in particular, caffeine. The stimulant properties of over-the-counter (OTC) sympathomimetics and "herbal highs" are also discussed. (Because nicotine has unique stimulant properties, it is covered separately in Chapter 11 on tobacco.)

Major Stimulants

All major stimulants increase alertness, excitation, and euphoria; thus, these drugs are referred to as **uppers**. The major stimulants are classified as either Schedule I ("designer" amphetamines) or Schedule II (amphetamine and cocaine) controlled substances because of their abuse poten-

tial. Although these drugs have properties in common, they also have unique features that distinguish them from one another. The similarities and differences of the major stimulants are discussed in the following sections.

AMPHETAMINES

Amphetamines are potent synthetic central nervous system (CNS) stimulants capable of causing dependence due to their euphorigenic properties and ability to eliminate fatigue. Despite their addicting effects, amphetamines can be legally prescribed by physicians. Consequently, amphetamine abuse occurs in people who acquire their drugs by both legitimate and illicit means (McCaffrey 1999).

The History of Amphetamines

The first amphetamine was synthesized by the German pharmacologist L. Edeleano in 1887, but it was not until 1910 that this and several related compounds were tested in laboratory animals. Another 17 years passed before Gordon Alles, a researcher looking for a more potent substitute for ephedrine (used as a decongestant at the time), self-administered amphetamine and gave a firsthand account of its effects. Alles found that when inhaled or taken orally, amphetamine dramatically reduced fatigue, increased alertness, and caused a sense of confident euphoria (Grinspoon and Bakalar 1978).

Because of Alles's impressive findings, the Benzedrine (amphetamine) inhaler became available in 1932 as a nonprescription medication in drugstores across America. The Benzedrine inhaler, marketed for nasal congestion, was widely abused for its stimulant action but continued to be available OTC until 1949. Because of a loophole in a law that was passed later, not until 1971 were all potent amphetamine-like compounds in nasal inhalers withdrawn from the market (Grinspoon and Bakalar 1978; McCaffrey 1999).

Owing to the lack of restrictions during this early period, amphetamines were sold to treat a variety of ailments, including obesity, alcoholism, bed-wetting, depression, schizophrenia, morphine and codeine addiction, heart block, head injuries, seasickness, persistent hiccups, and caffeine mania.

KEY TERMS

uppers
CNS stimulants

Holding the Line **Air Force Defends Amphetamine Use**

Lawyers for two pilots, charged with accidentally bombing Canadian forces during the Afghanistan invasion in 2002, claim their clients' judgment may have been impaired by amphetamines routinely prescribed for them by Air Force doctors. The Air Force defended the practice by saying they have been doing it since World War II and the doses dispensed are small and would only have a "very mild stimulant effect" to keep the pilots awake. It is not clear whether the amphetamines caused this deadly mistake, nor is it well established that use of amphetamines helps pilots do their job more effectively.

Source: The Age. "Air Force Rushes to Defend Amphetamine Use" (January 18, 2003). Available www.theage.com.au/articles/2003/01/17/1042520778665.

Today, most of these uses are no longer approved as legitimate therapeutics but would be considered forms of drug abuse.

World War II provided a setting in which both the legal and "black market" use of amphetamines flourished (Grinspoon and Bakalar 1978). Because of their stimulating effects, amphetamines were widely used by the Germans, Japanese, and British in World War II to counteract fatigue. By the end of World War II, large quantities of amphetamines were readily available without prescription in seven types of nasal inhalers.

In spite of warnings about these drugs' addicting properties and serious side effects, the U.S. armed forces issued amphetamines on a regular basis during the Korean War and, in fact, continue to make it available to pilots in the Air Force to relieve fatigue (CBS News 2003; see "Holding the Line," Air Force Defends Amphetamine Use). Amphetamine use became widespread among truck drivers making long hauls; it is believed that among the earliest distribution systems for illicit amphetamines were truck stops along major U.S. highways. High achievers under continuous pressure in the fields of entertainment, business, and industry often relied on amphetamines to counteract fatigue. Homemakers used them to control weight and to combat boredom from unfulfilled lives. At the height of the U.S. epidemic in 1967,

some 31 million prescriptions were written for **anorexiants** (diet pills) alone.

Today, a variety of related drugs and mixtures exist, including amphetamine substances such as dextroamphetamine (Dexedrine), methamphetamine (Desoxyn), and amphetamine itself. Generally, if doses are adjusted, the psychological effects of these various drugs are similar, so they will be discussed as a group. Other drugs with some of the same pharmacological properties are phenmetrazine (Preludin), and methylphenidate (Ritalin). Common slang terms for amphetamines include *speed, crystal, meth, bennies, dexies, uppers, pep pills, diet pills, jolly beans, copilots, hearts, footballs, white crosses, crank,* and *ice.*

How Amphetamines Work

Amphetamines are synthetic chemicals that are similar to natural neurotransmitters such as norepinephrine (noradrenaline), dopamine, and the stress hormone epinephrine (adrenaline). The amphetamines exert their pharmacological effect by increasing the release and blocking the metab-

KEY TERMS

anorexiants
drugs that suppress appetite for food

olism of these catecholamine substances as well as serotonin (see Chapter 4), both in the brain and in nerves associated with the sympathetic nervous system. Because amphetamines cause release of norepinephrine from sympathetic nerves, they are classified as sympathomimetic drugs. The amphetamines generally cause an arousal or activating response (also called the *fight-or-flight response*) that is similar to the normal reaction to emergency situations or crises.

Amphetamines also cause alertness so that the individual becomes aroused, hypersensitive to stimuli, and feels "turned on." These effects occur even without external sensory input. This activation may be a very pleasant experience in itself, but a continual high level of activation may convert to anxiety, severe apprehension, or panic.

Amphetamines have potent effects on dopamine in the reward (pleasure) center of the brain (see Chapter 4). This action probably causes the "flash" or sudden feeling of intense pleasure that occurs when amphetamine is taken intravenously. Some users describe the sensation as a "whole-body orgasm," and many associate intravenous methamphetamine use with sexual feelings. The actual effect of these drugs on sexual behavior is quite variable and dependent on dose (McCaffrey 1999).

What Amphetamines Can Do

A curious condition commonly reported with heavy amphetamine use is **behavioral stereotypy**, or getting *hung up*. This term refers to a simple activity that is done repeatedly. An individual who is "hung up" will get caught in a repetitious thought or act for hours. For example, he or she may take objects apart, like radios or clocks, and carefully categorize all the parts, or sit in a tub and bathe all day, persistently sing a note, repeat a phrase of music, or repeatedly clean the same object. This phenomenon seems to be peculiar to potent stimulants such as the amphetamines and

cocaine. Similar patterns of repetitive behavior also occur in psychotic conditions, which suggests that the intense use of stimulants such as amphetamines or cocaine alters the brain in a manner like that causing psychotic mental disorders (*DSM-IV-TR* 2000) and can lead to violent behavior.

Chronic use of high doses of amphetamines causes dramatic decreases in the brain content of the neurotransmitters dopamine and serotonin that persist for months, even after drug use is stopped (Gehrke et al. 2003). These decreases have been shown to reflect damage to the CNS neurons that release these transmitters. It is not clear why this neuronal destruction occurs, although there is evidence that the amphetamines can stimulate production of very reactive molecules, called *free radicals,* which in turn damage brain cells (Fumagalli et al. 1999).

Approved Uses

Until 1970, amphetamines were prescribed for a large number of conditions, including depression, fatigue, and long-term weight reduction. In 1970, the Food and Drug Administration (FDA), acting on the recommendation of the National Academy of Sciences, restricted the legal use of amphetamines to three medical conditions: (1) narcolepsy, (2) attention deficit hyperactivity disorder (ADHD), and (3) short-term weight reduction programs (*DSM-IV-TR* 2000).

Narcolepsy Amphetamine treatment of narcolepsy is not widespread because this condition is a relatively rare disorder. The term **narcolepsy** comes from the Greek words for "numbness" and "seizure." A person who has narcolepsy falls asleep as frequently as 50 times a day if he or she stays in one position for very long. Taking low doses of amphetamines helps keep narcoleptic people alert.

Attention Deficit Hyperactivity Disorder This common behavioral problem in children and adolescents involves an abnormally high level of physical activity, an inability to focus attention, and frequent disruptive behavior. Four to six of every 100 grade-school children have ADHD (Lesesne et al. 2003). The drug commonly used to treat children with ADHD is the amphetamine-related

KEY TERMS

behavioral stereotypy
meaningless repetition of a single activity

narcolepsy
a condition causing spontaneous and uncontrolled sleeping episodes

methylphenidate or Ritalin (discussed later in this chapter).

Weight Reduction By far the most common use of amphetamines is for the treatment of obesity. Amphetamines and chemically similar compounds are used as anorexiants to help obese or severely overweight people control appetite. Amphetamines are thought to act by affecting the appetite center in the hypothalamus of the brain, which causes the user to decrease food intake. The FDA has approved short-term use of amphetamines for weight loss programs but has warned of their potential for abuse. Many experts believe that the euphoric effect of amphetamines is the primary motivation for their continued use in weight reduction programs. It is possible that many obese people have a need for gratification that can be satisfied by the euphoric feeling this drug produces. If the drug is taken away, these individuals return to food to satisfy their need and sometimes experience "rebound," causing them to gain back more weight than they lost. Some persons who become addicted to amphetamine-like substances begin illicit use of these drugs by trying to prevent weight gain or to lose weight on their own without the guidance of a physician (*DSM-IV-TR* 2000).

Side Effects of Therapeutic Doses

The two principal side effects of therapeutic doses of amphetamines are (1) abuse, which has already been discussed at length, and (2) cardiovascular toxicities. Many of these effects derive from the amphetamine-induced release of epinephrine from the adrenal glands and norepinephrine from the nerves associated with the sympathetic nervous system. The effects include increased heart rate, elevated blood pressure, and damage to vessels, especially small veins and arteries (Swan 1996; Drug War Facts 2004). In users with a history of heart attack, coronary arrhythmia, or hypertension, amphetamine toxicity can be severe or even fatal.

Current Misuse

Because amphetamine drugs can be readily and inexpensively synthesized in makeshift laboratories for illicit sale, can be administered by several routes, and cause a more sustained effect, these drugs are more popular than cocaine in many

parts of the United States (DEA 2002; Johnston 2004). Surveys suggest that there was a decline in the abuse of amphetamines in the late 1980s and early 1990s in parallel with a similar trend in cocaine abuse (Johnston 1996). However, in 1993, the declines were replaced by a rise in the number of persons abusing amphetamines. By 2001, approximately 5.6% of high school seniors used amphetamines at least each month. Currently, approximately 4.6% of high school seniors in the United States are regularly using amphetamines (Johnston 2004).

Because of the potential for serious side effects, U.S. medical associations have asked all physicians to be more careful about prescribing amphetamines. Presently, use is recommended only for narcolepsy and some cases of hyperactivity in children (Hoffman and Lefkowitz 1995; *Drug Facts and Comparisons* 2005). In spite of FDA approval, most medical associations do not recommend the use of amphetamines for weight loss. Probably less than 1% of all prescriptions now written are for amphetamines, compared with 8% in 1970.

Amphetamine abusers commonly administer a dose of 10 to 30 milligrams. Besides the positive effects of this dose—the "high"—it can cause hyperactive, nervous, or jittery feelings that encourage the use of a depressant such as a benzodiazepine, barbiturate, or alcohol to relieve the discomfort of being "wired" (Hoffman and Lefkowitz 1995).

A potent and commonly abused form of amphetamine is **speed**, an illegal methamphetamine available as a white, odorless, bitter-tasting crystalline powder for injection. Methamphetamine is a highly addictive stimulant that is cheaper and much longer lasting than cocaine (Swan 1996). The profit for the speed manufacturer is substantial enough to make illicit production financially attractive. Because the cost ranges from $20 to $300 per gram, it is sometimes known as the "poor man's cocaine" (U.S. Department of Justice 2003a). Methamphetamine is relatively easy and inexpensive to make. The illicit manufacturers are

KEY TERMS

speed
an injectable methamphetamine used by drug addicts

usually individuals without expertise in chemistry. Such people, referred to as "cookers," produce methamphetamine batches by using cookbook-style recipes (often obtained in jail or over the Internet). The most popular recipe uses common OTC ingredients—ephedrine, pseudoephedrine, and phenylpropanolamine—as **precursor chemicals** for the methamphetamine. To discourage the illicit manufacture of this potent stimulant, the Comprehensive Methamphetamine Control Act was passed in October 1996. This law increases penalties for trafficking in methamphetamine and in the precursor chemicals used to create this drug and gives the government authority to regulate and seize these substances (Hatch 1999).

Due to the ease of production and the ready availability of chemicals used to prepare methamphetamine, this drug has become particularly problematic in the United States. Traditional methamphetamine users have been white, male, blue-collar workers over 26 years of age, although currently there also is a disturbingly high rate of use in adolescents (3%–5% annual use; Johnston 2004) and use by young women is on the rise in some regions of the United States (Ramboy 2004). There is higher abuse of this drug in the western United States, illustrated by the fact that 43.8%, 36.9%, and 38.5% of all arrestees during 2003 in Honolulu, San Diego, and Phoenix, respectively, tested positive for methamphetamine. In contrast, methamphetamine abuse is much less common on the East Coast; thus, few of the arrestees in New York during this same time period had evidence of this stimulant in their blood or urine (CEWG 2004). In general, production and trafficking are rampant throughout the West and Midwest areas,

with the highest levels occurring in California, Arizona, and Utah. However, the methamphetamine problem is moving across the country, with Iowa and Missouri being particularly affected, and there are increasing reports of its use in the South and some Northeast areas (CEWG 2004).

Today, so-called meth or speed labs are frequently raided by law enforcement agencies across the country as local drug entrepreneurs try to grab a share of the profits. In 2001, the law enforcement agencies shut down more than 7000 illegal methamphetamine labs, most of which were in the western United States (DEA 2004). The laboratory operators are usually well armed, and the facilities are frequently booby-trapped with explosives. Not surprisingly, these operations pose a serious threat to their neighbors (U.S. Department of Justice 2003a) and to residents, especially children, in the structure that contains the lab (U.S. Department of Justice 2002). Law enforcement personnel and firefighters are also at risk when dealing with methamphetamine labs owing to ignitable, corrosive, reactive, and toxic chemicals at the site that might explode, start a fire, emit toxic fumes, or cause serious injury (see "Holding the Line," Lives on the Line). The toxic chemicals can create fumes that contaminate neighboring buildings, the water supply, or soil. These labs are especially dangerous when they are set up in poorly ventilated rooms (Kennedy 1999; see "Here and Now," Chemical Toxins Associated with Meth Labs).

Patterns of High-Dose Use Amphetamines can be taken orally, intravenously, or by smoking. The intensity and duration of effects vary according to the mode of administration. The "speed freak" uses chronic, high doses of amphetamines intravenously and is often infected with HIV (see Chapter 16) (NIDA Research Report 2000). Another approach to administering amphetamines is smoking **ice**, which can cause effects as potent, but perhaps more prolonged and erratic, than intravenous doses. The initial effect (after 5 to 30 minutes) of these potent stimulants is called the **rush** and includes a racing heartbeat and elevated blood pressure, metabolism, and pulse. During this phase, the user has powerful impressions of pleasure and enthusiasm. The next stage is the **high** (4 to 16 hours after drug use) when the per-

KEY TERMS

precursor chemicals
chemicals used to produce a drug

ice
a smokable form of methamphetamine

rush
initial pleasure after amphetamine use that includes racing heartbeat and elevated blood pressure

high
4 to 16 hours after drug use; includes feelings of energy and power

Holding the Line   **Lives on the Line**

Law enforcement and firefighting personnel can be at serious risk when responding to emergencies associated with residences that contain "meth labs." Because the chemicals required to produce this drug are toxic and extremely hazardous, authorities need to be especially cautious when dealing with fire or cleanup at a suspected residence.

On January 6, 2003, firefighters rushed to a mobile home fire in Deep Gap, North Carolina, and encountered intense toxic fumes that caused severe respiratory ailments and chest pains to five of the crew. They later discovered the poisonous gases came from chemicals being used to make methamphetamine. In another incident, two undercover drug investigators experienced similar hazards standing some 50 yards from cleanup of a "meth lab" in a rundown house in Davidson County, North Carolina. The strong vapors seriously irritated their noses and throats, making it difficult to breathe. The detectives were rushed to the hospital for treatment. These are all too common accidents occurring across the country as emergency personnel put themselves in harm's way trying to deal with the environmental disasters resulting from meth labs.

Toxic chemicals are often found in meth labs.

Source: Associated Press. "State Authorities Battling to Contain Spread of Meth Labs" (February 10, 2003).

---

son feels aggressively smarter, energetic, talkative, and powerful and may initiate and complete highly ambitious tasks. The amphetamine addict tries to maintain the high for as long as possible with continual drug use leading to extended mental and physical hyperactivity; this is referred to as a **run** or **binge** and can persist from 3 to 15 days. Persistent use of these drugs, such as methamphetamine, to maintain the high for long periods of time is called **tweaking**. The tweaker often has neither slept nor eaten much for 3 to 15 days and can be extremely irritable and paranoid and have an elevated body temperature, a condition known as **hyperpyrexia**. This is a potentially dangerous stage for medical personnel or law enforcement officers because if the tweaker becomes agitated, he or she can respond violently to the efforts of others to help. To relieve some of the side effects of the extensive use of methamphetamine, tweakers often use a depressant such as alcohol, barbiturates, benzodiazepines, or opioid narcotics. The consequences of such a drug combination are to intensify negative feelings and worsen the dangers of the drug. Tweakers are frequently involved in domestic violence and frequently injure their children and partners (NDIC 2003). Withdrawal follows for 30 to 90 days, including feelings of depression and lethargy. During this phase, craving can be intense and the abuser may even become suicidal. Because a dose of methamphetamine often relieves these symptoms, a high percentage of addicts in treatment return to abusing this stimulant (Prevline 1999).

KEY TERMS

run
intense use of a stimulant, consisting of multiple administrations over a period of days

binge
similar to a run, but usually of shorter duration

tweaking
repeated administration of methamphetamine to maintain the high

hyperpyrexia
elevated body temperature

Here and Now

Chemical Toxins Associated with Meth Labs

Methamphetamine labs can be set up almost anywhere and pose a serious threat to occupants as well as to law officers and emergency personnel. The following are some of the chemicals often present and their toxic potentials.

Chemicals	Toxic Reactions
sodium hydroxide	irritant to skin and eyes
ammonia	induces vomiting and nausea
ether, acetone, and alcohol	flammable
chloroform	carcinogen and volatile
mercuric chloride	poisonous (used as insecticide)
cyanide gas	extremely poisonous if breathed
acids	potent irritants
iodine	irritant; causes nausea, headaches, and dizziness
phosphene gas	poison, flammable (used as nerve gas)

Sources: Kennedy, K. "Meth Mania: Even Cops Duck for Cover." *Salt Lake Tribune* (28 June 1999): B-1; Information Brief. "Iodine in Methamphetamine Production." U.S. Department of Justice (July 2002): Product # 2002-L0490-002.

After the first day or so of a run, unpleasant symptoms become prominent as the dosage is increased. Symptoms commonly reported at this stage are teeth grinding, disorganized patterns of thought and behavior, stereotypy, irritability, self-consciousness, suspiciousness, and fear. Hallucinations and delusions can occur that are similar to a paranoid psychosis and indistinguishable from schizophrenia (*DSM-IV-TR* 2000). The person is likely to show aggressive and antisocial behavior for no apparent reason. Severe chest pains, abdominal discomfort that mimics appendicitis, and fainting from overdosage are sometimes reported. "Cocaine bugs" represent one bizarre effect of high doses of potent stimulants such as amphetamines: The user experiences strange feelings, like insects crawling under the skin. The range of physical and mental symptoms experienced from low to high doses is summarized in Table 10.1.

Toward the end of the run, the adverse symptoms dominate. When the drug is discontinued because the supply is exhausted or the symptoms become too unpleasant, an extreme crash can oc-

cur, followed by prolonged sleep, sometimes lasting several days. On awakening, the person is lethargic, hungry, and often severely depressed. The amphetamine user may overcome these unpleasant effects by smoking ice or injecting speed, thereby initiating a new cycle (*DSM-IV-TR* 2000).

Continued use of massive doses of amphetamine often leads to considerable weight loss, sores in the skin, poor oral hygiene, nonhealing ulcers, liver disease, hypertensive disorders, cerebral hemorrhage (stroke), heart attack, kidney damage, and seizures (Hall and Hando 1993; Kinkead and Romboy 2004). For some of these effects, it is impossible to tell whether they are caused by the drug, poor eating habits, or other factors associated with the lifestyle of people who inject methamphetamine.

Speed freaks are generally unpopular with the rest of the drug-taking community, especially "acid-heads" (addicts who use lysergic acid diethylamide [LSD]), because of the aggressive, unpredictable behavior associated with use of potent stimulants. In general, drug abusers who take high doses of these agents, such as amphetamines or

Table 10.1 Summary of the Effects of Amphetamines on the Body and Mind

	BODY	MIND
Low dose	Increased heartbeat.	Decreased fatigue
	Increased blood pressure	Increased confidence
	Decreased appetite	Increased feeling of alertness
	Increased breathing rate	Restlessness, talkativeness
	Inability to sleep	Increased irritability
	Sweating	Fearfulness, apprehension
	Dry mouth	Distrust of people
	Muscle twitching	Behavioral stereotypy
	Convulsions	Hallucinations
	Fever	Psychosis
	Chest pain	
	Irregular heartbeat	
High dose	Death due to overdose	

cocaine, are more likely to be involved in violent crimes than those who abuse other drugs (McCaffrey 1999). Consequently, these individuals may live together in "flash houses" that are solely occupied by chronic amphetamine or stimulant addicts. Heavy users are generally unable to hold steady jobs because of their drug habits and often have a parasitic relationship with the rest of the illicit drug-using community.

Although claims have been made that amphetamines do not cause physical dependence, it is almost certain that depression (sometimes suicidal), lethargy, muscle pains, abnormal sleep patterns, and, in severe cases, suicide attempts occur after high chronic doses as part of withdrawal (Cantwell and McBride 1998; NIDA Diagnosis 2000). During withdrawal from amphetamine use, the dependent user often turns to other drugs for relief (Cantwell and McBride 1998). Rebound from the amphetamines is opposite to that experienced with withdrawal from CNS depressants (see Chapter 6).

Although the effects of amphetamines on the unborn fetus are not fully understood, recent studies suggest that methamphetamine-exposed newborn infants may experience withdrawal symptoms and growth retardation (Smith et al. 2003). There is evidence that repeated high-dose use of amphetamines, such as methamphetamine, by adolescents or adults causes long-term and perhaps permanent damage to both dopamine and serotonin systems of the brain (Hanson et al. 2004). This brain damage may result in persistent episodes of psychosis (Yui et al. 1999) as well as long-lasting memory and motor impairment (Volkow et al. 2001; Hanson et al. 2004). Abuse of amphetamines often seriously damages personal relationships with friends, associates, and even family members. Particularly disturbing is the increasing methamphetamine use by young mothers. Consequently, children are being exposed to dangerous levels of this drug in many forms (see "Here and Now," Small Towns, Big Problems: The Female Methamphetamine Epidemic).

Here and Now

Small Towns, Big Problems: The Female Methamphetamine Epidemic

Methamphetamine is causing a drug-related epidemic never before experienced in this country. Its abuse and devastating social effects are popping up in communities across the country and greatly taxing public social services in unanticipated ways. For example, 10 years ago social workers in Missoula, Montana, rarely heard of people abusing methamphetamine—let alone had to deal with these addicts. That situation has now changed. Today local and state governments find themselves overrun by the methamphetamine plague.

One of the most striking aspects of this drug's abuse in Montana is its effect on, and appeal to, young adult women. Typically, state figures show that the number of women seeking treatment for drug addiction are considerably lower than the number of men in the same situation; in 2004, however, roughly equal numbers of men and women sought help for methamphetamine as their primary addiction. Clearly, the destructive influence of methamphetamine abuse is taking an enormous toll on homes and families. In Missoula alone, almost half of the 137 children placed in the care of Family Services were removed from their homes due to use of methamphetamine by their mothers. Likewise, Montana's criminal justice system for women offenders is being overwhelmed. In 2004, the Montana State Prison for Women was filled for the first time, principally due to the methamphetamine epidemic in this population.

Women who are addicted to methamphetamine often do not do well in conventional drug treatment. Because of the potent addicting properties of this drug, they typically struggle with the requirements of probation or parole and often end up back in prison. While it is not clear why this stimulant is so seducing to young women, it is apparent that "this drug is a massive black hole. It's swallowing these people alive. It takes a miracle to put these families back together again."

Source: "Escalation in Methamphetamine Use Also Leads to Escalation in Social Service." *Health & Medicine Week* (14 February 2005).

Treatment

Presently, the most effective treatments for amphetamine addiction are behavioral interventions to help modify thinking patterns, change expectations, and increase coping with life's stressors. Amphetamine support groups also appear to be successful as adjuncts to behavioral therapies. There currently are no well-established pharmacological treatments for amphetamine dependency. Approaches used for cocaine have been tried with little success. Antidepressant medication may help relieve the depression that occurs during early stages of withdrawal (NIDA Research Report 2000).

Amphetamine Combinations

As just mentioned, amphetamines are frequently used in conjunction with a variety of other drugs such as barbiturates, benzodiazepines, alcohol, and heroin (Nuckols and Kane 2003). Amphetamines intensify, prolong, or otherwise alter the effects of LSD, and the two types of drugs are sometimes combined. The majority of speed users have also had experience with a variety of psychedelics or other drugs. In addition, people dependent on opiate narcotics frequently use amphetamines or cocaine. These combinations are called **speedballs**.

"Designer" Amphetamines

Underground chemists can synthesize drugs that mimic the psychoactive effects of amphetamines. Although the production of such drugs diminished in the early 1990s, their use by American teens surged in the late 1990s and early 2000s but decreased in 2003 and 2004 (Johnston 2004). These substances have become known as "designer drugs" (Christophersen 2000).

Designer amphetamines sometimes differ from the parent compound by only a single element. These "synthetic spinoffs" pose a significant abuse problem because often several different designer amphetamines can be made from the parent compound and still retain the abuse potential of the original substance.

For many years, the production and distribution of designer amphetamines were not illegal, even though they were synthesized from controlled substances. In the mid-1980s, however, the DEA actively pursued policies to curb their production and sale. Consequently, many designer amphetamines were outlawed under the Substance Analogue Enforcement Act (1986), which makes illegal any substance that is similar in structure or psychological effect to any substance already scheduled, if it is manufactured, possessed, or sold with the intention that it be consumed by human beings (Beck 1990).

The principal types of designer amphetamines are:

- Derivatives from amphetamine and methamphetamine that retain the CNS stimulatory effects, such as methcathinone ("cat").
- Derivatives from amphetamine and methamphetamine that have prominent hallucinogenic effects in addition to their CNS stimulatory action, such as MDMA (Ecstasy).

Because the basic amphetamine molecule can be easily synthesized and readily modified, new amphetamine-like drugs continue to appear on the streets. Although these designer amphetamines are thought of as new drugs when they first appear, in fact most were originally synthesized from the 1940s to the 1960s by pharmaceutical companies trying to find new decongestant and anorexiant drugs to compete with the other amphetamines. Some of these compounds were found to be too toxic to be marketed but have been rediscovered by "street chemists" and are sold to unsuspecting victims trying to experience a new sensation. Table 10.2 lists of some of these designer amphetamines.

Some designer drugs of abuse that are chemically related to amphetamine include DOM (STP), methcathinone (called *cat* or *bathtub speed*), MDA, and MDMA (or methylenedioxymethamphetamine, called *Ecstasy, X, E, XTC,* or *Adam*). All of these drugs are currently classified as Schedule I agents.

MDMA (Ecstasy) Among the designer amphetamines, MDMA continues to be the most popular. It gained widespread popularity in the United States throughout the 1980s, and its use peaked in 1987 despite its classification as a Schedule I drug in 1985 by the DEA. At the height of its use, 39% of the undergraduates at Stanford University reported having used MDMA at least once (Randall 1992a). In the late 1980s and early 1990s, use of MDMA declined in this country, but about this time it was "reformulated": This reformulation was not in a pharmacological sense but in a cultural context.

The "rave" scene in England provided a new showcase for MDMA or Ecstasy (Randall 1992a). Partygoers attired in "Cat in the Hat" hats and psychedelic jumpsuits paid $20 to dance all night to heavy electronically generated sound mixed with computer-generated video and laser light shows. An Ecstasy tablet could be purchased for the sensory enhancement caused by the drug (Randall 1992b). At one time, it was estimated that as many as 31% of English youth from 16 to 25 years old had used Ecstasy (Grob et al. 1996). The British rave counterculture and its generous use of Ecstasy were exported to the United States in the

KEY TERMS

speedballs
combinations of amphetamine or cocaine with an opioid narcotic, often heroin

Table 10.2 "Designer" Amphetamines

AMPHETAMINE DERIVATIVE	PROPERTIES
Methcathinone ("cat")	Properties like those of methamphetamine and cocaine
Methylenedioxy**methamphetamine** (MDMA, "Ecstasy")	Stimulant and hallucinogen
Methylenedioxy**amphetamine** (MDA)	More powerful stimulant and less powerful hallucinogen than MDMA
4-Methylaminorex	CNS stimulant like amphetamine
N,N-Dimethyl**amphetamine**	One-fifth potency of amphetamine
4-Thiomethyl-2, 5-dimethoxy**amphetamine**	Hallucinogen
Para-methoxymeth**amphetamine**	Weak stimulant

early 1990s. High-tech music and video trappings were encouraged by low-tech laboratories that illegally manufactured the drug and shipped it into this country. Ecstasy rapidly became the drug of choice for many young people in the United States (Cloud 2000). The availability of Ecstasy tablets dramatically escalated in the United States as demonstrated by the report that the DEA seized approximately 400,000 of these tablets in 1997, which increased to more than 9 million tablets seized in 2000 (Aarons 2000). Most of these illegal drugs originate in European countries such as the Netherlands and are smuggled into the United States (U.S. Department of Justice 2003b). The association of Ecstasy with raves has continued; however, increased MDMA use is occurring in older populations and the drug is being sold at schools, in shopping malls, and on street corners and marketed with other drugs such as crack cocaine, methamphetamine, and heroin (U.S. Department of Justice 2003b). Because of its frequent association with raves, clubs, and bars,

Dancers at a "rave" often consume Ecstasy for sensory enhancement.

MDMA has been referred to as a **club drug** (Leshner 2000). At its peak in 2000, Ecstasy was being used by 9% of all U.S. high school seniors. During the next few years, however, the popularity of this drug declined; in 2004, only 6% of high school seniors reported use (Johnston 2004).

Some have compared the rave culture of the past decade and its use of MDMA to the acid-test parties of the 1960s and the partygoers' use of LSD and amphetamines (Cloud 2000; Randall 1992a). This drug is said by some not to cause dependence, but intense use appears to be able to cause addiction. For instance, Karen, an 18-year-old, sometimes sneaks off with her friends to take Ecstasy. After the effects take hold, they smile at each other, oblivious to their surroundings. At night, they get together again to take more of the drug because they like how it makes them feel (Cloud 2000). In addition, incidents of medical emergencies caused by MDMA reported by hospitals from 1999 to 2001 almost doubled, suggesting that during this period more intense use of this drug caused severe dependence (U.S. Department of Justice 2003b). Despite the potential for serious consequences caused by MDMA use, many teenagers see little risk experimenting with this drug (CNN 2003).

MDMA was first inadvertently discovered in 1912 by chemists at E. Merck in Darmstadt, Germany (Grob et al. 1996). No pharmaceutical company has ever manufactured MDMA for public marketing, and the FDA has never approved it for therapy. MDMA was first found by the DEA on the streets in 1972 in a drug sample bought in Chicago (Beck 1990). The DEA earnestly began gathering data on MDMA abuse a decade later, which led to its classification as a Schedule I substance in 1985 despite the very vocal opposition by a number of psychiatrists who had been giving MDMA to patients since the late 1970s to facilitate communication, acceptance, and fear reduction (Beck 1990). Even today, some health professionals believe that MDMA should be made available to clinicians for the treatment of some psychiatric disorders such as fear and anxiety (Benedetti 2002; Cloud 2000). In fact, with FDA approval, small trial studies are being conducted to test the safety of this drug (*USA Today* 2004). MDMA and related designer amphetamines are somewhat

Ecstasy tablets are often imprinted with cartoon figures.

unique from other amphetamines in that, besides causing excitation, they have prominent hallucinogenic effects (Leshner 2000; see Chapter 12). These drugs have been characterized as combining the properties of amphetamine and LSD (Schifano et al. 1998). The psychedelic effects of MDMA are likely caused by release of the neurotransmitter serotonin. After using hallucinogenic amphetamines, the mind is often flooded with irrelevant and incoherent thoughts and exaggerated sensory experiences and is more receptive to suggestion.

MDMA is often viewed as a "smooth amphetamine" and does not appear to cause the severe depression, "crash," or violent behavior (U.S. Department of Justice 2003b) often associated with frequent high doses of the more traditional amphetamines. MDMA was originally thought to be nonaddictive; however, recent reports suggest that addiction does occur when high doses of this drug are used (Jansen 1999). Many users tend to be predominantly positive when describing their initial MDMA experiences (Cloud 2000). They claim the drug causes them to dramatically drop their defense mechanisms or fear responses while they feel an increased empathy for others (Benedetti

KEY TERMS

club drug
drug used by young adults at dance parties such as raves

2002). Combined with its stimulant effects, this action often increases intimate communication and association with others (Cloud 2000; Goldstein 1995). However, heavy users often experience adverse effects, such as loss of appetite, grinding of teeth, muscle aches and stiffness, sweating, rapid heartbeat, hostility, anxiety, and altered sleep patterns (Gamma et al. 2000; Morland 2000; Parrott et al. 2000). In addition, fatigue can be experienced for hours or even days after use. In high doses, MDMA can cause paranoid psychosis, panic attacks, and seizures (Schifano et al. 1998). There is evidence that these high doses can seriously damage serotonin neurons in the brain and cause long-term memory deficits and psychological disturbances in some people (Lyles and Cadet 2003; Parrot 2001).

Along with the increases in MDMA-related emergencies, there has been an increase in MDMA-related deaths. Although the 76 MDMA-linked deaths in the United States during 2001 are tragic, compared to other drugs of abuse such as cocaine and heroin, this number is relatively small (DEA.org 2003). The leading causes of deaths associated with MDMA use appear to be complications from either hyperthermia (related to heatstroke), metabolic problems, or underlying heart problems (DEA.org 2003).

Methylphenidate: A Special Amphetamine

Methylphenidate (Ritalin) is related to the amphetamines but is a relatively mild CNS stimulant that has been used to alleviate depression. Research now casts doubt on its effectiveness for treating depression, but it is effective in treating narcolepsy (a sleep disorder). As explained previously, Ritalin has also been found to help calm children suffering from attention deficit hyperactivity disorder (ADHD) and is currently the drug of choice for this indication. The stimulant potency of Ritalin lies between that of caffeine and amphetamine. Although it is not used much on the street by hard-core drug addicts, there are frequent reports of use by high school and college students because of claims that it helps them to "study better," "party harder," and experience a buzz (Hinkle and Winckler 1996; Khan 2003). Recent statistics from the Monitoring the Future Survey suggest that in 2004 5.1% of high school seniors used this drug for nonmedical purposes

(Johnston 2004). Because of its potential for abuse, some critics claim its medical use in the treatment of childhood ADHD may increase the likelihood that patients will later abuse drugs. However, this has not been found to be the case (Barkley et al. 2003). High doses of Ritalin can cause tremors, seizures, and strokes. Ritalin has been classified as a Schedule II drug, like the other prescribed amphetamines. Its principal mechanism of action is to block the reuptake of dopamine and noradrenaline into their respective neurons.

COCAINE

In the so-called War on Drugs, cocaine eradication is considered to be a top priority. The tremendous attention directed at cocaine reflects the fact that from 1978 to 1987 the United States experienced the largest cocaine epidemic in history. Antisocial and criminal activities related to the effects of this potent stimulant have been highly visible and widely publicized.

As recently as the early 1980s, cocaine use was not believed to cause dependency because it did not cause gross withdrawal effects, as do alcohol and narcotics (Goldstein 1994). In fact, a 1982 article in *Scientific American* stated that cocaine was "no more habit forming than potato chips" (Van Dyck and Byck 1982). This perception has clearly been proven false: Cocaine is so highly addictive that it is readily self-administered not only by human beings but also by laboratory animals (Fischman and Johanson 1996). Surveys suggest that during 2000, 2.7 million chronic, and 3.0 million casual, cocaine users lived in the United States (ONDCP 2003).

There is no better substance than cocaine to illustrate the "love-hate" relationship that people can have with drugs. Many lessons can be learned by understanding the impact of cocaine and the social struggles that have ensued as people have tried to determine their proper relationship with this substance.

The History of Cocaine Use

Cocaine has been used as a stimulant for thousands of years. Its history can be classified into three eras, based on geographic, social, and therapeutic considerations. Learning about these eras can help us understand current attitudes about cocaine.

The First Cocaine Era

The first cocaine era was characterized by an almost harmonious use of this stimulant by South American Indians living in the regions of the Andean Mountains and dates back to about 2500 B.C. in Peru. It is believed that the stimulant properties of cocaine played a major role in the advancement of this isolated civilization, providing its people with the energy and motivation to realize dramatic social and architectural achievements while being able to endure tremendous hardships in barren, inhospitable environments. The *Erythroxylon coca* shrub (cocaine found in the leaves) was held in religious reverence by these people until the time of the Spanish conquistadors (Golding 1993).

An Andean chews coca leaves.

The first written description of coca chewing in the New World was by the explorer Amerigo Vespucci in 1499:

> They were very brutish in appearance and behavior, and their cheeks bulged with the leaves of a certain green herb which they chewed like cattle, so that they could hardly speak. Each had around his neck two dried gourds, one full of that herb in their mouth, the other filled with a white flour-like powdered chalk. . . . [This was lime, which was mixed with the coca to enhance its effects.] When I asked . . . why they carried these leaves in their mouth, which they did not eat, . . . they replied it prevents them from feeling hungry, and gives them great vigor and strength. (Aldrich and Barker 1976, p. 3)

It is ironic that there are no indications that these early South American civilizations had any significant social problems with cocaine, considering the difficulty it has caused contemporary civilizations. There are three possible explanations for their lack of negative experiences with coca:

1. The Andean Indians maintained control of the use of cocaine. For the Incas, coca could only be used by the conquering aristocracy, chiefs, royalty, and other designated honorables (Aldrich and Barker 1976).
2. These Indians used the unpurified, and less potent, form of cocaine in the coca plant.
3. Chewing the coca leaf was a slow, sustained form of oral drug administration; therefore, the effect was much less potent than snorting, intravenous injection, or smoking techniques most often used today.

The Second Cocaine Era

A second major cocaine era began in the 19th century. During this period, scientific techniques were used to determine the pharmacology of cocaine and identify its dangerous effects. It was also during this era that the threat of cocaine to society—both its members and institutions—was first recognized (DiChiara 1993; Musto 1998). At about this time, scientists in North America and Europe began experimenting with a purified, white, powdered extract made from the coca plant.

The "refreshing" element in Vin Mariani was coca extract.

Sigmund Freud was an early advocate of cocaine, which he referred to as a "cure-all."

In the last half of the 19th century, Corsican chemist Angelo Mariani removed the active ingredients from the coca leaf and identified cocaine. This purified cocaine was added into cough drops and into a special Bordeaux wine called Vin Mariani (Musto 1998). The Pope gave Mariani a medal in appreciation for the fine work he had done. The cocaine extract was publicized as a magical drug that would free the body from fatigue, lift the spirits, and cause a sense of well-being, and the cocaine-laced wine became widely endorsed throughout the civilized world (Fischman and Johanson 1996). Included in a long list of luminaries who advocated this product for an array of ailments were the Czar and Czarina of Russia; the Prince and Princess of Wales; the Kings of Sweden, Norway, and Cambodia; commanders of the French and English armies; President McKinley of the United States; H. G. Wells; August Bartholdi (sculptor of the Statue of Liberty); and some 8000 physicians.

The astounding success of this wine attracted imitators, all making outlandish claims. One of these cocaine tonics was a nonalcoholic beverage named Coca-Cola, which was made from African kola nuts and advertised as the "intellectual beverage and temperance drink"; it contained 4 to 12 milligrams per bottle of the stimulant (DiChiara 1993). By 1906, Coca-Cola no longer contained detectable amounts of cocaine, but caffeine had been substituted in its place.

In 1884, the esteemed Sigmund Freud published his findings on cocaine in a report called "Uber Coca." Freud recommended this "magical drug" for an assortment of medical problems, including depression, hysteria, nervous exhaustion, digestive disorders, hypochondria, "all diseases which involve degeneration of tissue," and drug addiction.

In response to a request by Freud, a young Viennese physician, Karl Köller, studied the ability of cocaine to cause numbing effects. He discovered that it was an effective local anesthetic that could be applied to the surface of the eye and permit painless minor surgery to be conducted. This discovery of the first local anesthetic had tremendous worldwide impact. Orders for the new local anesthetic, cocaine, overwhelmed pharmaceutical companies.

Soon after the initial jubilation over the virtues of cocaine came the sober realization that with its benefits came severe disadvantages. As more people used cocaine, particularly in tonics and patent medicines, the CNS side effects and abuse liability became painfully evident. By the turn of the 20th century, cocaine was being processed from the coca plant and purified routinely by drug companies. People began to snort or inject the purified form of this popular powder, which increased both its effects and its dangers. The controversy over cocaine exploded before the American public in newspapers and magazines.

As medical and police reports of cocaine abuse and toxicities escalated, public opinion demanded that cocaine be banned. In 1914, the Harrison Act misleadingly classified both cocaine and coca as narcotic substances (cocaine is a stimulant) and outlawed their uncontrolled use.

Although prohibited in patent and nonprescription medicines, prescribed medicinal use of cocaine continued into the 1920s. Medicinal texts included descriptions of therapeutic uses for cocaine to treat fatigue, vomiting, seasickness, melancholia, and gastritis. However, they also included lengthy warnings about excessive cocaine use, "the most insidious of all drug habits" (Aldrich and Barker 1976).

Little of medical or social significance occurred for the next few decades (Fischman and Johanson 1996). The medicinal use of cocaine was replaced mostly by the amphetamines during World War II because cocaine could not be supplied from South America. (Cocaine is not easily synthesized so even today, the supply of cocaine, both legal and illegal, continues to come from the Andean countries of South America.) During this period, cocaine continued to be employed for its local anesthetic action, was available on the "black market," and was used recreationally by musicians, entertainers, and the wealthy. Because of the limited supply, the cost of cocaine was prohibitive for most would-be consumers. Cocaine abuse problems remained of minor concern until the 1980s.

The Third Cocaine Era

With the 1980s came the third major era of cocaine use. This era started much like the second in that the public and even the medical community were naive and misinformed about the drug. Cocaine was viewed as a glamorous substance and portrayed by the media as the drug of celebrities. Its use by prominent actors, athletes, musicians, and other members of a fast-paced, elite society was common knowledge. By 1982, more than 20 million Americans had tried cocaine in one form or another, compared with only 5 million in 1974 (Green 1985).

The following is an example of a report from a Los Angeles television station in the early 1980s, which was typical of the misleading information being released to the public:

> Cocaine may actually be no more harmful to your health than smoking cigarettes or drinking alcohol; at least that's according to a 6-year study of cocaine use [described in *Scientific American*]. It concludes that the drug is relatively safe and, if not taken in large amounts, it is not addictive. (Byck 1987)

With such visibility, an association with prestige and glamour, and what amounted to an indirect endorsement by medical experts, the stage was set for another epidemic of cocaine use. Initially, the high cost of this imported substance limited its use. With increased demand came increased supply, and prices tumbled from an unaffordable $100 per "fix" to an affordable $10. The epidemic began.

By the mid-1980s, cocaine permeated all elements of society. No group of people or part of the country was immune from its effects. Many tragic stories were told of athletes, entertainers, corporate executives, politicians, fathers and mothers, high school students, and even children using and abusing cocaine. It was no longer the drug of the laborer or even the rich and famous. It was everybody's drug and everybody's problem (Golding 1993). As one user recounted:

> I think I was an addict. I immediately fell in love with cocaine. I noticed right away it was a drug that you had power with, and I wanted more and more. (From Venturelli's research files, interview with a 22-year-old male, 1995.)

Cocaine Production

Because cocaine is derived from the coca plant, which is imported from the Andean countries, the

Here and Now

Bloody "Drug War" Fought in Streets of Mexico

Drug cartels ship hundreds of tons of cocaine to the United States. Because of the billions of dollars that can be made from this illegal market, gangs fight each other for control of the production and merchandising of this substance. This competition frequently turns violent as appeared to be the case in the small Mexican border city of Nuevo Laredo, where nine people were found tortured and killed in April 2003. These assassinations were thought to be the result of a power struggle within the cartels.

Source: Weiner, T. "9 Linked to Drug War Found Slain Outside Mexican Border City." *The New York Times* (3 April 2003): A5.

United States' problems with this drug have had a profound effect on several South American countries. With the dramatic rise in U.S. cocaine demand in the early 1980s, coca production in South America increased in tandem. The coca crop is by far the most profitable agricultural venture in some of these countries. In addition, it is easily cultivated and maintained (the coca plant is a perennial and remains productive for decades) and can be harvested several times a year (on average, two to four). The coca harvest has brought many jobs and some prosperity to these struggling economies.

It has been claimed that the U.S. coca eradication program has seriously damaged the fragile economies of poor Latin American countries, such as Bolivia and Peru, causing anti-American sentiment especially in poor rural communities that depend on money from their coca crops (Caesar 2002). In addition, the spraying of herbicides from U.S.-piloted aircraft to destroy coca harvests is suspected of posing health hazards to the native populations (DeYoung 2003). Because of these problems, there is evidence that the attempts by the U.S. government to control cocaine abuse by eliminating coca crops have not been as successful as hoped (Hall 2003).

Trafficking of cocaine is very profitable and often very dangerous (see "Here and Now," Bloody "Drug War" Fought in Streets of Mexico). Because of the highly addictive nature of cocaine and the profits associated with the illegal purchasing and selling of this drug, criminal groups frequently engage in violent struggles for control of the cocaine market (Weiner 2003).

Cocaine Processing

Cocaine is one of several active ingredients from the leaves of *Erythroxylon coca* (its primary source). The leaves are harvested two or four times per year and used to produce coca paste, which contains as much as 80% cocaine. The paste is processed in clandestine laboratories to form a pure, white hydrochloride salt powder (Hatsukami and Fischman 1996). Often, purified cocaine is **adulterated** (or "cut") with substances such as powdered sugar, talc, arsenic, lidocaine, strychnine, and methamphetamine before it is sold on the streets. Adverse responses to street

Cocaine is often sold in a form that appears like small rocks.

cocaine are sometimes caused by the additives, not the cocaine itself. The resultant purity of the cut material ranges from 10% to 85%.

Cocaine is often sold in the form of little pellets, called *rocks*, or as flakes or powder. If it is in pellet form, it must be crushed before used. Such exotic names as Peruvian rock and Bolivian flake are bandied about to convince the buyer that the "stash" is high grade. Other street names used for cocaine have included *blow, snow, flake, C, coke, toot, white lady, girl, cadillac, nose candy, gold dust,* and *stardust.*

CURRENT ATTITUDES AND PATTERNS OF ABUSE

Given contemporary medical advances, we have greater understanding of the effects of cocaine and its toxicities and the dependence it produces. The reasons for abusing cocaine are better understood as well. For example, it has been suggested that some chronic cocaine users are self-medicating psychiatric disorders, such as depression, attention deficit disorders, or anxiety (Gunnarsdottir et al. 2000). Such knowledge helps in identifying and administering effective treatment. The hope is that society will never again be fooled into thinking that cocaine abuse is glamorous or an acceptable form of entertainment.

Attempts are being made to use this understanding (either recently acquired or merely relearned) to educate people about the true nature of cocaine. Such education was likely responsible for trends of declining cocaine use observed from 1987 to 1991 (see Figure 10.1). Decreases occurred in virtually every age group evaluated during this period. Surveys during this time revealed that, in general, cocaine use became less acceptable; these changes in attitude almost certainly contributed to the dramatic reduction in use. From 1992 to 1999 cocaine use rose, but since then it has leveled off (Johnston 2004).

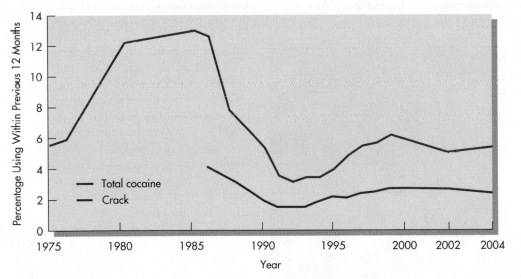

FIGURE 10.1

Trends in cocaine and crack use by high school seniors, 1975–1999. These data represent the percentages of high school seniors surveyed who reported using cocaine during the year.

Note: Crack cocaine did not become widely available until 1986.

Sources: Johnston, L., et al. "Monitoring the Future National Results on Adolescent Drug Use Overview of Key Findings 2002." University of Michigan (2003): NIH Publication #03-5374; Johnston, L. News Release (21 December 2004). Available www.monitoringthefuture.org.

Cocaine Administration

Cocaine can be administered orally, inhaled into the nasal passages, injected intravenously, or smoked. The form of administration is important in determining the intensity of cocaine's effects, its abuse liability, and the likelihood of toxicity (Nathan et al. 1998).

Oral administration of cocaine produces the least potent effects; most of the drug is destroyed in the gut or liver before it reaches the brain. The result is a slower onset of action with a milder, more sustained stimulation. This form is least likely to cause health problems and dependence (Grinspoon 1993). South American Indians still take cocaine orally to increase their strength and for relief from fatigue. Administration usually involves prolonged chewing of the coca leaf, resulting in the consumption of about 20 to 400 milligrams of the drug (DiChiara 1993). Oral use of cocaine is not common in the United States.

"Freebasing" paraphernalia. A water pipe is often used to smoke freebased cocaine, or "crack." Cocaine administered by smoking is very potent and fast-acting; the effect lasts for 10 to 15 minutes, after which depression occurs. This is the most addicting form of cocaine.

"Snorting" involves inhaling cocaine hydrochloride powder into the nostrils, where deposits form on the lining of the nasal chambers and approximately 100 milligrams of the drug passes through the mucosal tissues into the bloodstream (DiChiara 1993). Substantial CNS stimulation occurs in several minutes, persists for 30 to 40 minutes, and then subsides. The effects occur more rapidly and are shorter-lasting and more intense than those achieved with oral administration, because more of the drug enters the brain more quickly. Because concentrations of cocaine in the body are higher after snorting than after oral ingestion, the side effects are more severe. One of the most common consequences of snorting cocaine is rebound depression, or "crash," which is of little consequence after oral consumption. As a general rule, the intensity of the depression correlates with the intensity of the euphoria (Goldstein 1995).

According to studies performed by the National Institute on Drug Abuse, 10% to 15% of those who try intranasal (snorting) cocaine go on to heavier forms of dosing, such as intravenous administration. Intravenous administration of cocaine is a relatively recent phenomenon because the hypodermic needle was not widely available until the late 1800s. This form of administration has contributed to many of the cocaine problems that appeared at the turn of the 20th century. Intravenous administration allows large amounts of cocaine to be introduced very rapidly into the body and causes severe side effects and dependence. Within seconds after injection, cocaine users experience an incredible state of euphoria. The "high" is intense but short-lived; within 15 to 20 minutes, the user experiences dysphoria and is heading for a "crash." To prevent these unpleasant rebound effects, cocaine is readministered every 10 to 30 minutes. Readministration continues as long as there is drug available (NIDA 1998).

This binge activity resembles that seen in the methamphetamine "run," except it is usually shorter in duration. When the cocaine supply is exhausted, the binge is over (Zickler 2001). Several days of abstinence may separate these episodes; the average cocaine addict binges once to several times a week, with each binge lasting 4 to 24 hours. Cocaine addicts claim that all thoughts turn toward cocaine during binges;

everything else loses significance. This pattern of intense use is how some people blow all of their money on cocaine.

Freebasing is a method of reducing impurities in cocaine and preparing the drug for smoking. It produces a type of cocaine that is more powerful than normal cocaine hydrochloride. One way to "freebase" is to treat the cocaine hydrochloride with a liquid base such as sodium carbonate or ammonium hydroxide. The cocaine dissolves, along with many of the impurities commonly found in it (such as amphetamines, lidocaine, sugars, and others). A solvent, such as petroleum or ethyl ether, is added to the liquid to extract the cocaine. The solvent containing the cocaine floats to the top and is drawn off with an eyedropper; it is placed in an evaporation dish to dry, and crystalized cocaine residue is then crushed into a fine powder, which can be smoked in a special glass pipe (*DSM-IV-TR* 2000).

The effects of smoked cocaine are as intense or more than those achieved through intravenous administration (Fischman and Johanson 1996). The onset is very rapid, the euphoria is dramatic, the depression is severe, the side effects are dangerous, and the chances of dependence are high (Bradberry 2002; Grinspoon 1993). The reason for these intense reactions to inhaling cocaine into the lungs is that the drug passes rapidly through the lining of the lungs and into the many blood vessels present; it is then carried almost directly to the brain.

Freebasing became popular in the United States in the 1980s due to the fear of diseases such as AIDS and hepatitis, which are transmitted by sharing contaminated hypodermic needles. But freebasing involves other dangers. Because the volatile solvents required for freebasing are very explosive, careless people have been seriously burned or killed during processing (Seigel 1985). Street synonyms used for freebased cocaine include *baseball, bumping, white tornado, world series,* and *snowtoke.*

"Crack"

Between 1985 and 1986, a special type of freebased cocaine known as **crack** or "rock" appeared on the streets (Hatsukami and Fischman 1996). By 1988, approximately 5% of high school students had tried crack. As of 1992 this number had fallen

to 2.6%, as of 1999 it rose to 4.6%, but by 2004 it declined again to 3.9% (Johnston 2004). Crack is inexpensive and can be smoked without the dangerous explosive solvents mentioned earlier in the discussion of freebasing. It is made by taking powdered cocaine hydrochloride and adding sodium bicarbonate (baking soda) and water. The paste that forms removes impurities as well as the hydrochloride from the cocaine. The substance is then dried into hard pieces called rocks, which may contain as much as 90% pure cocaine. Other slang terms for crack include *base, black rock, gravel, Roxanne,* and *space basing.*

Like freebased cocaine, crack is usually smoked in a glass water pipe. When the fumes are absorbed into the lungs, they act rapidly, reaching the brain within 8 to 10 seconds. An intense "rush" or "high" results, and later a powerful state of depression, or "crash," occurs. The high may last only 3 to 5 minutes, and the depression may persist from 10 to 40 minutes or longer in some cases. As soon as crack is smoked, the nervous system is greatly stimulated by the release of dopamine, which seems to be involved in the rush. Cocaine prevents resupply of this neurotransmitter, which may trigger the crash.

Because of the abrupt and intense release of dopamine, smoked crack is viewed as a drug with tremendous potential for addiction (*DSM-IV-TR* 2000) and is considered by users to be more enjoyable than cocaine administered intravenously (Fischman and Johanson 1996). In fact, some people with serious cardiovascular disease continue using crack despite knowing their serious risk for heart attacks and strokes (Fischman and Foltin 1992).

Crack and cocaine marketing and use are often associated with criminal activity (*DSM-IV-TR* 2000) such as robberies and homicides (Swan 1995).

In general, crack use has been more common among African American and Hispanic populations than among white Americans. Of special concern is the use of crack among women during pregnancy. Children born under these circumstances have been referred to as **crack babies**. Even though the effects of crack on fetal development are not fully understood, many clinicians and researchers have predicted that these crack babies will impose an enormous social burden as they grow up. However, other experts have expressed concern that the impact of cocaine on the fetus is grossly overstated and have suggested that behavioral problems seen in these children are more a consequence of social environment than direct pharmacological effects (Vidaeff and Mastrobattista 2003). This issue is discussed in greater detail later in this section.

It is not coincidental that the popularity of crack use paralleled the AIDS epidemic in the mid-1980s. Because crack administration does not require injection, theoretically the risk of contracting HIV from contaminated needles is avoided. Even so, incidence of HIV infection in crack users is still very high because many crack smokers also use cocaine intravenously, thereby increasing the chances of their becoming HIV infected (see Chapter 16). Another reason for the high incidence of HIV infection (as well as other sexually transmitted diseases, such as syphilis and gonorrhea) among crack users is the dangerous sexual behavior in which these people engage (Castilla et al. 1999). Not only is crack commonly used as payment for sex, but its users are also much less inclined to be cautious about their sexual activities while under the influence of this drug (Ladd and Petry 2003).

Major Pharmacological Effects of Cocaine

Cocaine can have profound effects on several vital systems in the body (*Drug Facts and Comparisons* 2005). With the assistance of modern technology, the mechanisms whereby cocaine alters body functions have become better understood today. Such knowledge may eventually lead to better treatment of cocaine dependence.

KEY TERMS

crack babies
infants born to women who use crack cocaine during pregnancy

Most of the pharmacological effects of cocaine use stem from enhanced activity of catecholamine (dopamine, noradrenaline, adrenaline) and serotonin transmitters. It is believed that the principal action of the drug is to block the reuptake and inactivation of these substances following their release from neurons. Such action prolongs the activity of these transmitter substances at their receptors and substantially increases their effects. The summation of cocaine's effects on these four transmitters causes CNS stimulation (Woolverton and Johnston 1992). The increase of noradrenaline activity following cocaine administration increases the effects of the sympathetic nervous system and alters cardiovascular activity.

CNS Effects Because cocaine has stimulant properties, it has antidepressant effects as well. Some users self-administer cocaine to relieve severe depression or the negative symptoms of schizophrenia (Markou and Kenny 2002), but in general its short-term action and abuse liability make cocaine unsatisfactory for the treatment of depression disorders. The effects of stimulation appear to increase both physical and mental performance while masking fatigue. High doses of cocaine cause euphoria (based on the form of administration) and enhance the sense of strength, energy, and performance. Because of these positive effects, cocaine has intense reinforcing properties, which encourage continual use and dependence (Nathan et al. 1998).

Cocaine addicts can often distinguish between the two phenomena of the rush and the high associated with cocaine administration. Both the rush and the high peak about 3 minutes after use. The rush seems to be associated with elevated heart rate, sweating, and feelings of "speeding" or "being out of control"; the high includes feelings of euphoria, self-confidence, well-being, and sociability. Drug craving also occurs rapidly and is evident as soon as 12 minutes after administration. Interestingly, brain scans of cocaine users have demonstrated that specific brain regions are associated with these drug effects; thus, the rush and craving are linked with different regions of the limbic system in the brain (see Figure 4.6; Stocker 1999).

The feeling of exhilaration and confidence caused by cocaine can easily become transformed into irritable restlessness and confused hyperactivity (*DSM-IV-TR* 2000). In addition, high chronic doses alter personality, frequently causing psychotic behavior that resembles paranoid schizophrenia (*DSM-IV-TR* 2000; Nathan et al. 1998). For example, in an interview with Peter Venturelli, a 17-year-old female explained that a cocaine-abusing friend ". . . was so coked up that he carved the word 'pain' in his arm and poured coke on it. He thought it symbolized something." In addition, cocaine use heightens the risk of suicide, major trauma, and violent crimes (*DSM-IV-TR* 2000). In many ways, the CNS effects of cocaine resemble those of amphetamines, although perhaps with a more rapid onset, a more intense high (due partially to the manner in which the drugs are administered), and a shorter duration of action (*DSM-IV-TR* 2000).

Besides dependence, other notable CNS toxicities that can be caused by cocaine use include headaches, temporary loss of consciousness, seizures, and death (*Drug Facts and Comparisons* 2005).

Cardiovascular System Effects Cocaine can initiate pronounced changes in the cardiovascular system by enhancing the sympathetic nervous system, increasing the levels of adrenaline, and causing vasoconstriction (Zickler 2002). The initial effects of cocaine are to increase heart rate and elevate blood pressure. While the heart is being stimulated and working harder, the vasoconstriction effects deprive the cardiac muscle of needed blood (Fischman and Johanson 1996). Such a combination can cause severe heart arrhythmia (an irregular contraction pattern) or heart attack. Other degenerative processes have also been described in the hearts and blood vessels of chronic cocaine users (Kloner and Rezkalla 2003). In addition, the vasoconstrictive action of this sympathomimetic can damage other tissues, leading to stroke, lung damage in those who smoke cocaine, destruction of nasal cartilage in those who snort the drug, and injury to the gastrointestinal tract (Goldstein 1995).

Local Anesthetic Effects Cocaine was the first local anesthetic used routinely in modern-day medicine (Musto 1998). There is speculation that in ancient times, Andes Indians of South America used cocaine-filled saliva from chewing coca leaves as a local anesthetic for surgical procedures (Aldrich and Barker 1976). However, this assumption is contested by others (Byck 1987). Even so, cocaine is still a preferred local anesthetic for minor pharyngeal (back part of the mouth and upper throat area) surgery due to its good vasoconstriction (reduces bleeding) and topical, local numbing effects. Although relatively safe when applied topically, significant amounts of cocaine can enter the bloodstream and, in sensitive people, cause CNS stimulation, toxic psychosis, or, on rare occasions, death (Harris and Batki 2000; *Medical Letter* 1996).

Cocaine Withdrawal

Considerable debate has arisen as to whether cocaine withdrawal actually happens and, if so, what it involves. With the most recent cocaine epidemic and the high incidence of intense, chronic use, it has become apparent that nervous systems do become tolerant to cocaine and that, during abstinence, withdrawal symptoms occur (*DSM-IV-TR* 2000). In fact, because of CNS dependence, the use of cocaine is less likely to be stopped voluntarily than is the use of many other illicit drugs (Sofuoglu et al. 2003). Certainly, if the withdrawal experience is adverse enough, a user will be encouraged to resume the cocaine habit.

The extent of cocaine withdrawal is proportional to the duration and intensity of use. The physical withdrawal symptoms are relatively minor compared with those caused by long-term use of CNS depressants and by themselves are not considered to be life-threatening (Woolverton and Johnston 1992). Short-term withdrawal symptoms include depression (chronic cocaine users are 60 times more likely to commit suicide than nonusers), sleep abnormalities, craving for the drug, agitation, and *anhedonia* (inability to experience pleasure). Long-term withdrawal effects include a return to normal pleasures, accompanied by mood swings and occasional craving triggered by cues in the surroundings (*DSM-IV-TR* 2000; Mendelson and Mello 1996).

Of particular importance to treatment of chronic cocaine users is that abstinence after bingeing appears to follow three unique stages, each of which must be dealt with in a different manner if relapse is to be prevented. These phases are classified as phase 1, or "crash" (occurs 9 hours to 4 days after drug use is stopped); phase 2, or withdrawal (1 to 10 weeks); and phase 3, or extinction (indefinite). The basic features of these phases are outlined in Table 10.3 (*DSM-IV-TR* 2000).

Treatment of Cocaine Dependence

Cocaine dependency is classified as a psychiatric disorder by the American Psychiatric Association (*DSM-IV-TR* 2000) and is resulting in a growing number of persons seeking treatment for drug addiction (Platt et al. 2002). Treatment of this condition has improved as experience working with these patients has increased. Even so, success rates vary for different programs (Nathan et al. 1998). The problem with program assessments is that they often do not take into account patients who drop out. Also, no clear-cut criteria for qualifying success have been established. For example, is success considered to be abstaining from cocaine for 1 year, 2 years, 5 years, or forever?

No one treatment technique has been found to be significantly superior to others or universally effective (Mendelson and Mello 1996; *SAMHSA News* 1999), nor is there a particularly effective medication to treat cocaine addiction (Platt et al. 2002). Consequently, substantial disagreement exists as to what is the best strategy for treating cocaine dependency. There is a major ongoing effort by federal agencies and scientists to find effective therapy for cocaine addiction. Most treatments are directed at relieving craving. Major differences in treatment approaches include (1) whether outpatient or inpatient status is deemed appropriate, (2) which drugs and what dosages are used to treat patients during the various stages of abstinence, and (3) what length of time the patient is isolated from cocaine-accessible environments.

It is important to treat each individual patient according to his or her unique needs. Some questions that need to be considered when formulating a therapeutic approach include the following:

Why did the patient begin using cocaine, and why has dependency occurred?

What is the severity of abuse?

How has the cocaine been administered?

What is the psychiatric status of the patient; are there underlying or coexisting mental disorders, such as depression or attention deficit disorder?

Table 10.3 Cocaine Abstinence Phases

	PHASE 1: "CRASH"	PHASE 2: WITHDRAWAL	PHASE 3: EXTINCTION
Time since last binge	24–48 hours	1–10 weeks	Indefinite
Features	*Initial*	*Initial*	
	Agitation, depression, anorexia, suicidal thoughts	Mood swings, sleep returns, some craving, little anxiety	Normal pleasure, mood swings, occasional craving, cues trigger craving
	Middle Fatigue, no craving, insomnia	*Middle and late* Anhedonia, anxiety, intense craving, obsessed with drug seeking	
	Late Extreme fatigue, no craving, exhaustion		

Source: Gawin, F. "Cocaine Addiction: Psychology and Neurophysiology." *Science* 251 (1991): 1580–1586.

What other drugs are being abused along with the cocaine?

What is the patient's motivation for eliminating cocaine dependence?

What sort of support system (family, friends, coworkers, and so on) will sustain the patient in the abstinence effort?

Outpatient Versus Inpatient Approaches The decision as to whether to treat a patient who is dependent on cocaine as an outpatient or an inpatient is based on a number of factors. For example, inpatient techniques allow greater control than outpatient treatment; thus, the environment can be better regulated, the training of the patient can be more closely supervised, and the patient's responses to treatment can be more closely monitored. In contrast, the advantages of the outpatient approach are that supportive family and friends are better able to encourage the patient, the surroundings are more comfortable and natural, and potential problems that might occur when the patient returns to a normal lifestyle are more likely to be identified. In addition, outpatient treatment is less expensive.

Cocaine-dependent patients should be matched to the most appropriate strategy based on their personalities, psychiatric status, and the conditions of their addiction (Mendelson and Mello 1996). For instance, a cocaine addict who lives in the inner city, comes from a home with other drug-dependent family members, and has little support probably would do better in the tightly controlled inpatient environment. However, a highly motivated cocaine addict who comes from a supportive home and a neighborhood that is rel-

atively free of drug problems would probably do better on an outpatient basis.

Therapeutic Drug Treatment Several drugs have been used to treat cocaine abstinence, some of which are themselves active on dopamine systems, but none has been found to be universally effective (Smith et al. 1999). Table 10.4 lists some drugs that have been used in each of the three principal phases of cocaine abstinence. Besides relieving acute problems of anxiety, agitation, and psychosis, drugs can diminish cocaine craving; this effect is achieved by giving drugs such as bromocriptine or levodopa that stimulate the dopamine transmitter system or the narcotic buprenorphine. As mentioned, the pleasant aspects of cocaine likely relate to its ability to increase the activity of dopamine in the limbic system. When cocaine is no longer available, the dopamine system becomes less active, causing depression and anhedonia, which result in a tremendous craving for cocaine. The intent of these cocaine substitutes is to stimulate dopamine activity and relieve the cravings. Although this approach sometimes works initially, it is temporary. In the third phase of cocaine abstinence, antidepressants such as desipramine are effective for many cocaine-dependent patients in relieving underlying mood problems and occasional cravings.

The beneficial effects of these drugs are variable and not well studied. There is some debate over their use. Drugs are, at best, only adjuncts in the treatment of cocaine dependence (Carroll et al. 1994). Successful treatment of cocaine abuse requires intensive counseling; strong support from family, friends, and coworkers; and a highly motivated patient. It is important to realize that a complete "cure" from cocaine dependence is not

Table 10.4 **Medications Used in Treatment of Cocaine Abstinence at Various Phases**

PHASE	DRUG	DRUG GROUP (RATIONALE)
1. Crash	Benzodiazepines	Depressants (relieve anxiety)
2. Withdrawal	Bromocriptine, levodopa	Dopamine agonists (relieve craving)
3. Extinction	Desipramine, imipramine	Antidepressants (relieve depression and craving)

Source: Mendelson, J., and N. Mello. "Management of Cocaine Abuse and Dependence." *New England Journal of Medicine* 334 (1996): 965–972.

likely: ex-addicts cannot return to cocaine and control its use (Kleber 1992).

Recovery from Cocaine Dependence Although numerous therapeutic approaches exist for treating cocaine addiction, successful recovery is not likely unless the individual will substantially benefit by giving up the drug. Research has shown that treatment is most likely to succeed in patients who are middle-class, employed, and married; for example, 85% of addicted medical professionals recover from cocaine addiction. These people can usually be convinced that they have too much to lose in their personal and professional lives by continuing their cocaine habit. In contrast, a severely dependent crack addict who has no job, family, home, or hope for the future is not likely to be persuaded that abstinence from cocaine would be advantageous, so therapy is rarely successful (Grinspoon 1993). Unfortunately, there currently is no uniformly effective pharmacological treatment available to deal with long-term cocaine addiction, although intensive research to identify such therapeutic agents is under way (*SAMHSA News* 1999).

Polydrug Use by Cocaine Abusers Treatment of most cocaine abusers is complicated by the fact that they are *polydrug* (multiple drug) users. It is unusual to find a person who abuses only cocaine. For example, many cocaine abusers also use alcohol (Pennings et al. 2002). In general, the more severe the alcoholism, the greater the severity of the cocaine dependence. Alcohol is used to relieve some of the unpleasant cocaine effects, such as anxiety, insomnia, and mood disturbances (Pennings et al. 2002). This drug combination can be dangerous for several reasons:

1. The presence of both cocaine and alcohol (ethanol) in the liver results in the formation of a unique chemical product called cocaethylene, which is created in the reaction of

ethanol with a cocaine metabolite. Cocaethylene is often found in high levels in the blood of victims of fatal drug overdoses and appears to enhance the euphoria as well as the cardiovascular toxicity of cocaine (Pennings et al. 2002).

2. Both cocaine and alcohol can damage the liver; thus, their toxic effects on the liver are likely to add together when the drugs are used in combination (Pennings et al. 2002).

3. The likelihood of damaging a fetus is enhanced when both drugs are used together during pregnancy (Pennings et al. 2002).

4. Cardiovascular stress is increased in the presence of both drugs (Pennings et al. 2002).

Like users of amphetamines, cocaine abusers frequently coadminister narcotics, such as heroin; this combination is called a *speedball* and has been associated with a high risk for HIV infection (Mendelson and Mello 1996). Cocaine users sometimes combine their drug with other depressants, such as benzodiazepines, or marijuana to help reduce the severity of the crash after their cocaine binges. Codependence on cocaine and a CNS depressant can complicate treatment but must be considered.

Cocaine and Pregnancy

One of the consequences of widespread cocaine abuse is that since the mid-1980s approximately 1 million babies in the United States have been born to mothers who used cocaine during pregnancy (Medical References 2003). Cocaine use during pregnancy is highest in poor, inner-city regions. In the United States, more than $1 billion is spent annually for care of cocaine-using women during their pregnancies. Many of these **cocaine babies** are abandoned by their mothers and left to the welfare system for care.

It is still not clear exactly what types of direct effects cocaine has on the developing fetus (Vidaeff and Mastrobattista 2003). Some early studies have been criticized because (1) the pregnant populations examined were not well defined and properly matched, (2) use of other drugs (such as alcohol) with cocaine during pregnancy was often ignored, and (3) the effects of poor nutrition, poor living conditions, and a traumatic lifestyle were not consid-

KEY TERMS

cocaine babies
infants born to women who used cocaine during their pregnancy

Infants born to crack-using mothers are often premature.

ered when analyzing the results. Due to these problems, much of the earlier work examining prenatal effects of cocaine is flawed and the conclusions are questionable (Vidaeff and Mastrobattista 2003).

It is known that cocaine use during pregnancy can cause vasoconstriction of placental vessels, thereby interfering with oxygen and nutrient exchange between mother and child, or contraction of the uterine muscles, resulting in trauma or premature birth. Current data also suggest that infants exposed to cocaine during pregnancy are more likely to suffer a small head (microencephaly), reduced birthweight, and increased irritability and subtle learning and cognitive deficits (Medical References 2003; Singer et al. 2004). Recent findings also suggest that children who had experienced prenatal cocaine exposure have problems with some motor skills, subtle deficits in I.Q., and some minor problems with language development, attention span, and ability to gather and use information (Medical References 2003). Clearly, individuals exposed to cocaine during fetal development can function in society, but they frequently require special help. It remains to be seen how these individuals will cope as adults (Leshner 1999).

Here and Now

Cocaine and Pregnancy

Public health concerns have recently been raised about the long-term cognitive development of cocaine babies. A research study published by Case Western Reserve University School of Medicine and local Cleveland-area hospitals reported that children who were exposed to cocaine prenatally experienced effects on their cognitive development but not on their motor development.

The study also found that prenatal exposure to cocaine was linked to lower birthweight and younger gestational age at delivery. Children exposed to cocaine prenatally were found to have a mental retardation rate almost five times higher than the general population, and they were twice as likely to have mild delays in brain function.

Source: Cocaine.org. "At 2 Years, Cocaine Babies Suffer Cognitive Development Effects" (16 April 2002).

Minor Stimulants

Minor stimulants enjoy widespread use in the United States because of the mild lift in mood provided by their consumption. The most popular of these routinely consumed agents are methylxanthines (commonly called *xanthines*), such as caffeine, which are consumed in beverages made from plants and herbs. Other minor stimulants are contained in OTC medications, such as cold and hay fever products; these will be mentioned briefly in this chapter but discussed at greater length in Chapter 15. Because of their frequent use, some dependence on these drugs can occur; however, serious dysfunction due to dependence is infrequent. Consequently, abuse of xanthines such as caffeine is not viewed as a major health problem by most health experts (Daly and Fredholm 1998).

CAFFEINELIKE DRUGS (XANTHINES)

Caffeine is the world's most frequently used stimulant and perhaps its most popular drug (Demos 2001). Beverages and foods containing caffeine are consumed by almost all adults and children living in the United States today (see Table 10.5). In this country, the average daily intake of caffeine is approximately 200 mg (the equivalent of approximately 2 cups of coffee), with as many as 30% of Americans consuming 500 mg or more per day (*DSM-IV-TR* 2000). The most common sources of caffeine include coffee beans, tea plants, kola nuts, maté leaves, guaraná paste, and yoco bark.

Although the consumption of caffeine-containing drinks can be found throughout history, the active stimulant caffeine was identified by German and French scientists in the early 1820s. Caffeine was described as a substance with alkaloid (basic) properties that was extracted from green coffee beans and referred to as *kaffebase* by Ferdinand Runge in 1820 (Gilbert 1984). In the course of the next 40 to 60 years, caffeine was identified in several other genera of plants, which were used as sources for common beverages. These included

tea leaves (originally the drug was called *thein*); guaraná paste (originally the drug was called *guaranin*); Paraguay tea, or maté; and kola nuts. Certainly, the popularity of these beverages over the centuries attests to the fact that most consumers find the stimulant effects of this drug desirable.

The Chemical Nature of Caffeine

Caffeine belongs to a group of drugs that have similar chemical structures and are known as the **xanthines**. Besides caffeine, other xanthines are *theobromine* (means "divine leaf"), discovered in cacao beans (used to make chocolate) in 1842, and *theophylline* (means "divine food"), isolated from tea leaves in 1888. These three agents have unique pharmacological properties (which are discussed later), with caffeine being the most potent CNS stimulant.

Beverages Containing Caffeine

To understand the unique role that caffeine plays in U.S. society, it is useful to gain perspective on its most common sources: unfermented beverages.

Coffee Coffee is derived from the beans of several species of coffea plants. The *Coffea arabica* plant grows as a shrub or small tree and reaches 4 to

Table 10.5 Caffeine Content of Beverages and Chocolate

BEVERAGE	CAFFEINE CONTENT (MG/CUP)	AMOUNT
Brewed coffee	90–125	5 oz
Instant coffee	35–164	5 oz
Decaffeinated coffee	1–6	5 oz
Tea	25–125	5 oz
Cocoa	5–25	5 oz
Coca-Cola	45	12 oz
Pepsi-Cola	38	12 oz
Mountain Dew	54	12 oz
Chocolate bar	1–35	1 oz

KEY TERMS

xanthines
the family of drugs that includes caffeine

6 meters in height when growing wild. Coffee beans are primarily cultivated in South America and East Africa and constitute the major cash crop for exportation in several developing countries.

The name *coffee* was likely derived from the Arabian word *kahwa* or named after the Ethiopian prince Kaffa. From Ethiopia, the coffee tree was carried to Arabia and cultivated (Kihlman 1977); it became an important element in Arabian civilization and is mentioned in writings dating back to A.D. 900.

Coffee probably reached Europe through Turkey and was likely used initially as a medicine. By the middle of the 17th century, coffeehouses had sprung up in England and France—places to relax, talk, and learn the news. These coffeehouses turned into the famous "penny universities" of the early 18th century where, for a penny a cup, you could listen to some of the great literary and political figures of the day.

Coffee was originally consumed in the Americas by English colonists, although tea was initially preferred. Tea was replaced by coffee following the Revolutionary War. Because tea had become a symbol of English repression, the switch to coffee was more a political statement than a change in taste. The popularity of coffee grew as U.S. boundaries moved west. In fact, daily coffee intake continued to increase until it peaked in 1986, when annual coffee consumption averaged 10 pounds per person. Although concerns about the side effects associated with caffeine use have since caused some decline in coffee consumption, this beverage still plays a major role in the lifestyles of most Americans (McMahon 2001), with approximately 167 million being coffee drinkers in 2003 (Kluger 2004).

Tea Tea is made from the *Camellia sinensis* plant, which is native to China and parts of India, Burma, Thailand, Laos, and Vietnam. Tea contains two xanthines: caffeine and theophylline. As with coffee, the earliest use of tea is not known.

Although apocryphal versions of the origin of tea credit Emperor Shen Nung for its discovery in 2737 B.C., the first reliable account of the use of tea as a medicinal plant appears in an early Chinese manuscript written around A.D. 350. The popular use of tea slowly grew. The Dutch brought the first tea to Europe in 1610, where it was accepted rather slowly; with time, it was adopted by the British as a favorite beverage and became an integral part of their daily activities. In fact, the tea trade constituted one of the major elements of the English economy. Tea revenues made it possible for England to colonize India and helped to bring on the Opium Wars in the 1800s, which benefited British colonialism (see Chapter 9).

The British were constantly at odds with the Dutch as they attempted to monopolize the tea trade. Even so, the Dutch introduced the first tea into America at New Amsterdam around 1650. Later, the British gained exclusive rights to sell tea to the American colonies. Because of the high taxes levied by the British government on tea being shipped to America, tea became a symbol of British rule.

Soft Drinks The second most common source of caffeine is soft drinks. In general, the caffeine content per 12-ounce serving ranges from 30 to 60 milligrams (see Table 10.5). Soft drinks account for most of the caffeine consumed by U.S. children and teenagers; for many people, a can of cola has replaced the usual cup of coffee. Recently, caffeine has been added to juices and even water. These caffeine-containing products have alluring names such as "Surge," "Jolt," "Aqua Buzz," "Krank H2O," and "XTC" and are designed to target teenage consumers (*Consumer Reports* 1997). Americans consumed 574 cans of soft drinks—70% of which were caffeinated—for every man, woman, and child in 2003 (Kluger 2004).

Social Consequences of Consuming Caffeine-Based Beverages It is impossible to accurately assess the social impact of consuming beverages containing caffeine, but certainly the subtle (and sometimes not so subtle) stimulant effects of the caffeine present in these drinks have had some social influence. These beverages have become integrated into social customs and ceremonies and recognized as traditional drinks.

Today, drinks containing caffeine are consumed by many people with ritualistic devotion first thing in the morning, following every meal, and at frequent interludes throughout the day known as "coffee breaks" or "tea times." The immense popularity of these products is certainly a consequence of the stimulant actions of caffeine. Both the dependence on the "jump-start" effect of caffeine and the avoidance of unpleasant withdrawal consequences in the frequent user ensure the continual popularity of these products.

These effects are illustrated by the following comments from college students:

Tina (freshman, psychology major): "I get headaches if I do not have my . . . Coca-Cola. The tension builds up in my head and I feel nauseous . . . As soon as I drink Coke, it goes away. I'm definitely addicted."

Eric (senior, geology major): "I wake up and feel like I could fall asleep walking down the street. That's how I tell I need [coffee]."

Jesse (senior, biology major): "I have worked at a coffeehouse for 2 years. I see customers come in dragging their feet . . . Once [customers] get it, though, they go 'Now I can get through my day.' Some people are more . . . on the edge if they don't get it [coffee]."

(Source: http://www.thejack.nau.edu/ 0913/lige2.html/, 1996)

Other Natural Caffeine Sources

Although coffee and tea are two of the most common sources of natural caffeine in the United States, other caffeine-containing beverages and food are popular in different parts of the world. Some of the most common include guaraná from Brazil; maté from Argentina, Southern Brazil, and Paraguay; and kola nuts from West Africa, West Indies, and South America (Kihlman 1977).

Chocolate

Although chocolate contains small amounts of caffeine (see Table 10.5), the principal stimulant in chocolate is the alkaloid theobromine, named after the cocoa tree, *Theobroma cacao.* (*Theobroma* is an Aztec word meaning "fruit of the gods.") The Aztecs thought very highly of the fruit and seed pods from the cacao tree, and they used the beans as a medium of exchange in bartering. The Mayan Indians adopted the food and made a warm drink from the beans that they called *chocolatl* (meaning

"warm drink"). The original chocolate drink was a very thick concoction that had to be eaten with a spoon. It was unsweetened because the Mayans apparently did not know about sugar cane.

Hernando Cortés, the conqueror of Mexico, took some chocolate cakes back to Spain with him in 1528, but the method of preparing them remained a secret for nearly 100 years. It was not until 1828 that the Dutch worked out a process to remove much of the fat from the kernels to make a chocolate powder that was the forerunner of the cocoa we know today. The cocoa fat, or cocoa butter as it is called, was later mixed with sugar and pressed into bars. In 1847, the first chocolate bars appeared on the market. By 1876, the Swiss had developed milk chocolate, which is highly popular in today's confectioneries.

OTC Drugs Containing Caffeine

Although the consumption of beverages is by far the most common source of xanthines, a number of popular OTC products contain significant quantities of caffeine. For example, many OTC analgesic products contain approximately 30 milligrams of caffeine per tablet (Anacin). Higher doses of 100 to 200 milligrams per tablet are included in stay-awake (NoDoz, Caffedrine) and "picker-upper" (Vivarin) products (PDR *Nonprescription Drugs* 2003). The use of caffeine in these OTC drugs is highly controversial and has been criticized by clinicians who are unconvinced of caffeine's benefits. Some critics believe that the presence of caffeine

OTC caffeine products frequently contain the equivalent of 2–3 cups of coffee and are used to stay awake.

in these OTC drugs is nothing more than a psychological gimmick to entice customers through mild euphoric effects provided by this stimulant.

Despite this criticism, it is likely that caffeine has some analgesic (pain-relieving) properties of its own (Dunwiddie and Masino 2001). Recent studies suggest that 130 milligrams, but not 65 milligrams, of caffeine is superior to a placebo in relieving nonmigraine headaches. In addition, the presence of caffeine has been shown to enhance aspirin-medicated relief from surgical pain (such as tooth extraction). Based on such findings, more clinicians are recommending the use of caffeine in the management of some types of headaches and minor to moderate pains (Zhang 2001).

Physiological Effects of the Xanthines

The xanthines significantly influence several important body functions. Although the effects of these drugs are generally viewed as minor and short-term (Goldstein 1994), when used in high doses or by people who have severe medical problems, these drugs can be dangerous. The following sections summarize the responses of the major systems to xanthines.

CNS Effects Among the common xanthines, caffeine has the most potent effect on the CNS, followed by theophylline; for most people, theobromine has relatively little influence. Although the CNS responses of users can vary considerably, in general 100 to 200 milligrams of caffeine enhances alertness, causes arousal, and diminishes fatigue (Daly and Fredholm 1998). Caffeine is often used to block drowsiness and facilitate mental activity, such as when cramming for examinations into the early hours of the morning. In addition, caffeine stimulates the formation of thoughts but does not improve learning ability in the wide-awake student. The effects of caffeine are most pronounced in unstimulated, drowsy consumers (Goldstein 1994). The CNS effects of caffeine also diminish the sense of boredom (*Consumer Reports* 1997). Thus, people engaged in dull, repetitive tasks, such as assembly-line work, or nonstimulating and laborious exercises, such as listening to a boring professor, often consume caffeine beverages to help compensate for the tedium. Most certainly, xanthine drinks are popular because they cause these effects on brain activity.

Adverse CNS effects usually occur with doses greater than 300 milligrams per day. Some of these include insomnia, increased tension, anxiety, and initiation of muscle twitches. Doses over 500 milligrams can be dysphoric (unpleasant) and can cause panic sensations, chills, nausea, and clumsiness. Extremely high doses of caffeine, from 5 to 10 grams, frequently result in seizures, respiratory failure, and death (*DSM-IV-TR* 2000).

Cardiovascular and Respiratory Effects Drugs that stimulate the brain usually stimulate the cardiovascular system as well. The response of the heart and blood vessels to xanthines is dependent on dose and previous experience with these mild stimulants. Tolerance to the cardiovascular effects occurs with frequent use (*DSM-IV-TR* 2000). With low doses (100–200 milligrams), heart activity can either increase, decrease, or do nothing; at higher doses (more than 500 milligrams), the rate of contraction of the heart increases. Xanthines usually cause minor vasodilation in most of the body. In contrast, the cerebral blood vessels are vasoconstricted by the action of caffeine. In fact, cerebral vasoconstriction likely accounts for this drug's effectiveness in relieving some minor vascular headaches caused by vasodilation of the cerebral vessels.

Among the xanthines, theophylline has the greatest effect on the respiratory system, causing air passages to open and facilitate breathing. Because of this effect, tea has often been recommended to relieve breathing difficulties, and theophylline is frequently used to treat asthma-related respiratory problems.

Other Effects The methylxanthines have noteworthy—albeit mild—effects on other systems in the body. They cause a minor increase in the secretion of digestive juices in the stomach, which can be significant to individuals suffering from stomach ailments such as ulcers. These drugs also increase urine formation (as any heavy tea drinker undoubtedly knows).

Caffeine Intoxication

Consuming occasional low doses of the xanthines (equivalent of two to three cups of coffee per day) is relatively safe for most users (Kluger 2004). However, frequent use of high doses causes psychological as well as physical problems called **caffeinism**. This condition is found in about 10% of the adults who consume coffee (*DSM-IV-TR* 2000; Heishman and Henningfield 1992).

The CNS components of caffeine intoxication are recognized as a "psychoactive substance-induced psychiatric disorder" in *DSM-IV-TR* (2000) criteria established by the American Psychiatric Association. The essential features of this disorder are restlessness, nervousness, excitement, insomnia, flushed face, diuresis, muscle twitching, rambling thoughts and speech, and stomach complaints. These symptoms can occur in some sensitive people following a dose as low as 250 milligrams per day. Caffeine doses in excess of 1 gram per day may cause muscle twitching, rambling thoughts and speech, heart arrhythmias, and motor agitation. With higher doses, hearing ringing in the ears and seeing flashes of light can occur.

Some researchers suggest consuming large quantities of caffeine is associated with cancers of the bladder, ovaries, colon, and kidneys. These claims have not been reliably substantiated (Nawrot et al. 2003).

One problem with many such studies is that they assess the effect of coffee consumption on cancers rather than the effect of caffeine itself. Because coffee contains so many different chemicals, it is impossible to determine specifically the effect of caffeine in such research (Gurin 1994). Other reports claim that caffeine promotes cyst formation in women's breasts. Although these conclusions have been challenged, many clinicians advise patients with breast cysts to avoid caffeine (Margen 1994). Finally, some reports indicate that very high doses of caffeine given to pregnant laboratory animals can cause stillbirths or offspring with low birthweights or limb deformities. Studies found that moderate consumption of caffeine (less than 300 milligrams per day) did not significantly affect human fetal development (Mills et al. 1993); however, intake of more than 300 milligrams per day during pregnancy has been associated with an increase in spontaneous fetal loss (*Consumer Reports* 1997). Expectant mothers are usually advised to avoid or at least reduce caffeine use during pregnancy (Margen 1994).

Based on the information available, no strong evidence exists to suggest that moderate use of caffeine leads to disease (Nawrot et al. 2003). There are, however, implications that people with existing severe medical problems—psychiatric disorders (such as severe anxiety, panic attacks, and schizophrenia), cardiovascular disease, and possibly breast cysts—are at greater risk when consuming caffeine. Realistically, other elements, such as alcohol and fat consumption and smoking, are much more likely to cause serious health problems (Gurin 1994).

Caffeine Dependence

Caffeine causes limited dependence, which, for most people, is relatively minor compared with that of the potent stimulants; thus, the abuse potential of caffeine is much lower and dependence is less likely to interfere with normal daily routines (Kluger 2004). Despite this, caffeine use is thought to be able to produce a significant addiction (*Biotech Week* 2004). Consequently, 50% of those consuming one to three cups of coffee each day develop headaches when withdrawing and 10% become significantly depressed, anxious, or fatigued without their coffee. Some people experience elements of withdrawal every morning before their first cup (*Consumer Reports* 1997). However, caffeine is so readily available and socially accepted (almost expected) that the high quantity of consumption has produced many modestly dependent users (Griffiths and Chausmer 2000). The degree of physical dependence on caffeine is highly variable but related to dose. With typical caffeine withdrawal, adverse effects can persist for several days (see Table 10.6). Although these symptoms are unpleasant, they usually are not severe enough to prevent most people from giving up their coffee or cola drinks if motivated. It is noteworthy that two-thirds of those patients who are treated for caffeinism relapse into their caffeine-consuming habits (Heishman and Henningfield 1992).

KEY TERMS

caffeinism
symptoms caused by taking high chronic doses of caffeine

Table 10.6 Caffeine Withdrawal Syndrome

SYMPTOM	DURATION
Headache	Several days to 1 week
Decreased alertness	2 days
Decreased vigor	2 days
Fatigue and lethargy	2 days
Nervousness	2 days

Source: Based on Holtzman, S. "Caffeine as a Model Drug of Abuse." *Trends in Pharmacological Sciences* 11 (1990): 355–356.

Table 10.7 Common OTC Sympathomimetics

DRUG	OTC PRODUCT (FORM)
Ephedrine	Before removed, was used as a decongestant (oral, nasal spray or drops)
Levodesoxyephedrine	Decongestant (nasal inhalant)
Naphazoline	Decongestant (nasal spray or drops)
Oxymetazoline	Decongestant (nasal spray or drops)
Phenylephrine	Decongestant (oral, nasal spray or drops, eye drops)
Pseudoephedrine	Decongestant (oral)
Tetrahydrozoline	Decongestant (eye drops)
Xylometazoline	Decongestant (nasal spray or drops)

Source: Based on Knodel, L. C. "Cough, Cold and Allergy Products." In *Nonprescription Product. Formulations and Features*, '97–'98. Washington, DC: American Pharmaceutical Association, 1997.

Variability in Responses

Caffeine is eventually absorbed entirely from the gastrointestinal tract after oral consumption. In most users, 90% of the drug reaches the bloodstream within 20 minutes and is distributed into the brain and throughout the body very quickly (Sawynok and Yaksh 1993). The rate of absorption of caffeine from the stomach and intestines differs from person to person by as much as sixfold. Such wide variations in the rate at which caffeine enters the blood from the stomach likely account for much of the variability in responses to this drug.

OTC SYMPATHOMIMETICS

Although often overlooked, the sympathomimetic decongestant drugs included in OTC products such as cold, allergy, and diet aid medications have stimulant properties like those of caffeine (Appelt 1993). For most people, the CNS impact of these drugs is minor, but for those people who are very sensitive to these drugs, they can cause jitters and interfere with sleep. For such individuals, OTC products containing the sympathomimetics should be avoided before bedtime.

The common OTC sympathomimetics are shown in Table 10.7 and include ephedrine. In the past, OTC agents were packaged to look like amphetamines (called *look-alike drugs*) and legally sold on the "street," usually to children or high school students. Although much less potent than amphetamines (even though they can be used as precursor chemicals to make methamphetamine), these minor stimulants can be abused and have caused deaths. Attempts to regulate look-alike drugs resulted in passage of the federal and state Imitation Controlled Substances Acts. These statutes prohibit the packaging of OTC sympathomimetics to look like amphetamines.

These laws have not resolved the problem, however. Other products containing the OTC sympathomimetics are promoted on the street as "harmless speed" and "OTC uppers." It is likely that use of such products can lead to the abuse of more potent stimulants.

HERBAL STIMULANTS

Some OTC sympathomimetics occur naturally and are also found in herbal stimulants or "dietary supplements" sold by mail and in novelty stores, beauty salons, health food stores and online and sometimes by health professionals, including physicians (Fessenden and Drew 2003; Gugliotta 2000). These pills have been sold under names such as "Cloud 9," "Ultimate Xphoria," and "Herbal Ecstasy"; and contained stimulants such as ephedrine, ephedra, or *ma huang* (Gugliotta 2000; *Pharmacy Times* 1996; Sprague et al. 1998). These products were particularly promoted to high school and college students as natural highs to be used as diet aids, energy boosters, or performance enhancers for athletics (Mihoces 2001). Excessive use of these products can cause seizures, heart attacks, and strokes (Gugliotta 2000). In fact, several deaths and many cases of severe reactions have been reported in the United States from excessive use of these products (*Washington Times* 2003). A recent death of a major league baseball player (see "Here and Now," Diet Pills Are Russian Roulette for Athletes) resulted in particularly

strong pressure to ban OTC products, including dietary supplements, containing either the herb ephedra or the active ingredient ephedrine (Shipley 2003). In response to these pressures, the FDA recently banned the use of ephedrine or ephedra in OTC products; however, it will be difficult to actually remove herbal stimulants from the marketplace because of a 1994 federal law that prohibits such action until the FDA conclusively proves the dangers of these substances (Rubin 2003). There have been numerous lawsuits filed against herbal companies that manufactured products containing *ma huang* and the drug ephedrine. These legal actions claim that such products have caused serious illness and even death. Several of these lawsuits have been settled out of court reportedly for millions of dollars (Gugliotta 2000). Even before the FDA ban, because ephedrine can be converted into metham-

Here and Now

Diet Pills Are Russian Roulette for Athletes

Steve Bechler, a 23-year-old pitcher for the Baltimore Orioles of the American League, died in 2003 after collapsing on the field during running drills due to "multiple organ failure resulting from heat stroke," says the autopsy report. Ephedrine was found in Bechler's body and likely contributed to his death. He was reported to be using an ephedrine supplement called Xenadrine RFA-1. Although advised not to use it by his trainer, Bechler was taking this ephedrine-containing product to get his weight down after being criticized by coaches for being too heavy and not performing well in preseason drills. A teammate explained that heavy athletes like Bechler are under a lot of pressure to control their weight to make big-league teams. Although at the time of Bechler's death use of ephedrine was not prohibited by Major League Baseball, it was prohibited by the National Football League in 2002. The NFL's ban came after Korey Stringer, a lineman for the Minnesota Vikings who was taking an ephedrine product, died after collapsing during a training camp workout in 2001.

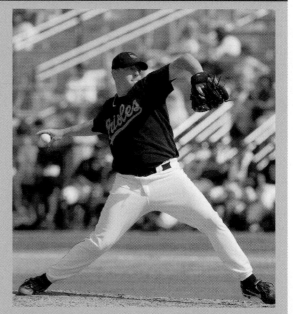

Steve Bechler was a pitcher for the Baltimore Orioles.

Source: Shipley, A. "Bechler's Diet Pills Draw Scrutiny." *The Washington Post* (19 February 2003): D-1.

phetamine, the Comprehensive Methamphetamine Act passed in 1996 regulated the amount of ephedrine that could be purchased or sold at one time (Sprague et al. 1998).

Discussion Questions

1. Should the FDA continue to approve amphetamines for the treatment of obesity? Why?

2. How are methamphetamine and Ecstasy similar, and how do they differ?

3. Should children be taken from mothers who are addicted to methamphetamine?

4. What have past experiences taught us about cocaine? Do you think we have finally learned our lesson concerning this drug?

5. Why does the method of cocaine administration make a difference in how a user is affected by this drug? Use examples to substantiate your conclusions.

6. Why do people use crack cocaine, and what are the major toxicities caused by use of high doses of this stimulant?

7. How is cocaine dependence treated? What are the rationales for the treatments?

8. How does caffeine compare with cocaine and amphetamine as a CNS stimulant?

9. Because of caffeine's potential for abuse, do you think the FDA should control it more tightly? Defend your answer.

10. Do you feel that herbal stimulants, such as ephedra and *ma huang*, should have been removed from OTC products?

Key Terms

uppers 282

anorexiants 283

behavioral stereotypy 284

narcolepsy 284

speed 285

precursor chemicals 286

ice 286

rush 286

high 286

run 287

binge 287

tweaking 287

hyperpyrexia 287

speedballs 291

club drug 293

adulterated 298

freebasing 301

crack 301

crack babies 302

cocaine babies 306

xanthines 308

caffeinism 312

Summary

1 Amphetamines, originally developed as decongestants, are potent stimulants. Some amphetamines have been approved by the FDA as (1) diet aids to treat obesity; (2) treatment for narcolepsy; and (3) treatment for attention deficit hyperactivity disorder in children.

2 In therapeutic doses, amphetamines can cause agitation, anxiety, and panic owing to their effects on the brain; in addition, they can cause an irregular heartbeat, increased blood pressure, heart attack, or stroke. Intense, high-dose abuse of these drugs can cause severe psychotic behavior, stereotypy, and seizures as well as the severe cardiovascular side effects just mentioned.

3 Speed refers to the use of intravenous methamphetamine. Ice is smoked methamphetamine. A run is a pattern of intense, multiple dosing over a period of days that can cause serious neurological, psychiatric, and cardiovascular consequences.

4 Tweakers are individuals who repeatedly self-administer methamphetamine to maintain the high. They often have not slept or eaten for days, are very irritable, and sometimes are paranoid or even violent.

5 "Designer" amphetamines are chemical modifications of original amphetamines. Some designer amphetamines, such as Ecstasy, retain abuse potential and are marketed on the street under exotic and alluring names.

6 In the early 1980s, cocaine was commonly viewed by the U.S. public as a relatively safe drug with glamorous connotations. By the mid-1980s, it became apparent that cocaine was a very addicting drug with dangerous side effects.

7 The CNS and cardiovascular effects of both amphetamines and cocaine are similar. However, the effects of cocaine tend to occur more rapidly, be more intense, and wear off more quickly than those of amphetamines.

8 The intensity of the cocaine effect and the likelihood of dependence occurring are directly related to the means of administration. Going from least to most intense effect, the modes of cocaine administration include chewing, snorting, injecting, and smoking (or freebasing).

9 Crack is cocaine that has been converted into its "freebase" form and is intended for smoking.

10 Cocaine withdrawal goes through three main stages: (1) the "crash," the initial abstinence phase consisting of depression, agitation, suicidal thoughts, and fatigue; (2) withdrawal, including mood swings, craving, anhedonia, and obsession with drug seeking; and (3) extinction, when normal pleasure returns and cues trigger craving and mood swings.

11 Treatment of cocaine dependence is highly individualistic and has variable success. The principal strategies include both inpatient and outpatient programs. Drug therapy often is used to relieve short-term cocaine craving and to alleviate mood problems and long-term craving. Psy-

chological counseling and support therapy are essential components of treatment.

12 Caffeine is the most frequently consumed stimulant in the world. It is classified as a xanthine (methylxanthine) and is added to a number of beverages, including water. It is also included in some OTC medicines such as analgesics and "stay-awake" products. Caffeine causes minor stimulation of cardiovascular activity, kidney function (it is a diuretic), and gastric secretion.

13 Dependence on caffeine can occur in people who regularly consume large doses. Withdrawal can cause headaches, agitation, and tremors. Although unpleasant, withdrawal from caffeine dependence is much less severe than that from amphetamine and cocaine dependence.

14 OTC sympathomimetics such as ephedrine have been consumed in high doses and used as "legal" highs. Although not as potent as the major stimulants, the recreational use of these drugs can be dangerous. Because of those potential dangers, the FDA has prohibited the use of ephedrine in OTC products.

References

Aarons, R. "Task Force Combats Ecstasy Smuggling." *U.S. Customs Today* (October 2000): 1.

The Age. "Air Force Rushes to Defend Amphetamine Use" (18 January 2003). Available www.theage.com.au/articles/2003/01/17/1042520778665.

Aldrich, M., and R. Barker. In *Cocaine: Chemical, Biological, Social and Treatment Aspects,* edited by S. J. Mule, 3–10. Cleveland, OH: CRC, 1976.

Appelt, G. "Weight Control Products." In *Handbook of Nonprescription Drugs,* 10th ed., edited by T. Covington, 339–349. Washington, DC: American Pharmaceutical Association, 1993.

Barkley, R., M. Fischer, L. Smallish, and K. Fletcher. "Does the Treatment of ADHD with Stimulants Contribute to Drug Use/Abuse? A 13-Year Prospective Study." *Pediatrics* 111 (2003): 97–109.

Beck, J. "The Public Health Implications of MDMA Use." In *Ecstasy,* edited by S. Peroutka, 77–103. Norwell, MA: Kluwer, 1990.

Benedetti, W. "Ecstasy Supporters Hope FDA-Approved Study Will Vindicate Drug." *Seattle Post-Intelligencer*

(9 May 2002). Available http://seattlepi.nwsource. com/lifestyle/69629_ecstasystudy.shtml.

Biotech Week. "Caffeine Withdrawal Recognized as a Disorder" (20 October 2004).

Bradberry, C. "Dynamics of Extracellular Dopamine in the Acute and Chronic Actions of Cocaine." *Neuroscientist* 8 (2002): 315–322.

Byck, R. "Cocaine Use and Research: Three Histories." In *Cocaine: Chemical and Behavioral Aspects,* edited by S. Fisher, 3–17. London: Oxford University Press, 1987.

Caesar, M. "US Finds Anger in South America." *Toronto Globe and Mail* (31 August 2002).

Cantwell, B., and A. McBride. "Self Detoxification by Amphetamine-Dependent Patients: A Pilot Study." *Drug and Alcohol Dependence* 49 (1998): 157–163.

Carroll, K., B. Rounsaville, L. Gordon, C. Nich, P. Jatlow, R. Bisighini, and F. Gawin. "Psychotherapy and Pharmacotherapy for Ambulatory Cocaine Abusers." *Archives of General Psychiatry* 51 (1994): 177–187.

Castilla, J., G. Barrio, M. Belza, and L. de la Fuente. "Drug and Alcohol Consumption and Sexual Risk Behaviour Among Young Adults: Results from a National Survey." *Drug, Alcohol and Dependence* 56 (1999): 47–53.

CBS News. "Airman Order Was to 'Hold Fire,'" CBSNEWS.com (17 January 2003): Available www. cbsnews.com/stories/2003/03/20/attack.

Christophersen, A. "Amphetamine Designer Drugs—An Overview and Epidemiology." *Toxicology Letters* 112–113 (2000): 127–131.

Cloud, J. "The Lure of Ecstasy." *Time* 155 (5 June 2000): 60.

CNN. "Survey: Teens See Little Risk in Ecstasy" (11 February 2003). Available http://edition.cnn.com/2003/ HEALTH/parenting/02/11/drug.survey/.

Community Epidemiology Work Group (CEWG). Available www.drugabuse.gov/infofax/methamphetamine.html.

Consumer Reports. "Coffee Clutch: Should You Worry About All That Caffeine?" 62 (1997): 52–53.

Daly, J., and B. Fredholm. "Caffeine—An Atypical Drug of Dependence." *Drug and Alcohol Dependence* 51 (1998): 199–206.

DEA. "Drug Intelligence Brief." (October 2002): Publication DEA-02046.

DEA. "Maps of Methamphetamine Lab Seizures" (2005). Available www.dea.gov/concern/map_lab_seizures.html.

DEA.org. "Ecstasy Statistics" (19 July 2003): Available http://theDEA.org/statistics.html.

Demos, K. "One Cup of Coffee May Temporarily Harden Arteries." *Yahoo News* (4 September 2001). Available http:// dailynews.yahoo.com/h/nm/20010904/hl/coffee_1.html.

Deslandes, P., D. Pache, and R. Sewell. "Drug Dependence: Neuropharmacology and Management." *Journal of Pharmacy and Pharmacology* 54 (2002): 885–895.

DeYoung, K. "U.S.: Coca Cultivation Drops in Colombia." *Washington Post* (28 February 2003): A-19.

DiChiara, G. "Cocaine: Scientific and Social Dimensions." *Trends in Neurological Sciences* 16 (1993): 39.

Drug Facts and Comparisons. St. Louis, MO: Walters Kluwars, 2005: 917–941, 2081.

Drug War Facts. "Methamphetamine" (2004). Available www.drugwarfacts.org/methamph.htm.

DSM-IV-TR. "Substance-Related Disorders." In *Diagnostic and Statistical Manual of Mental Disorders,* 4th ed., Text Revision, A. Francis, chairperson, 223–250. Washington, DC: American Psychiatric Association, 2000.

Dunwiddie, T., and S. Masino. "The Role and Regulation of Adenosine in the Central Nervous System." *Annual Review of Neuroscience* 24 (2001): 31–55.

Fessenden, F., and C. Drew. "Bottom Line in Mind, Doctors Sell Ephedra." *The New York Times* (31 March 2003).

Fischman, M., and R. Foltin. "Self-Administration of Cocaine by Humans: A Laboratory Perspective." In *Cocaine: Scientific and Social Dimensions,* edited by Ciba, 165–180. New York: Wiley, 1992.

Fischman, M., and C. Johanson. "Cocaine." In *Pharmacological Aspects of Drug Dependence: Towards an Integrated Neurobehavior Approach Handbook of Experimental Pharmacology,* edited by C. Schuster and M. Kuhar, 159–195. New York: Springer-Verlag, 1996.

Fumagalli, F., R. Gainetdinov, Y. Wang, K. Valenzano, G. Miller, and M. Caron. "Increased Methamphetamine Neurotoxicity in Heterozygous Vesicular Monoamine Transporter 2 Knock-Out Mice." *Journal of Neuroscience* 19 (1999): 2424–2431.

Gamma, A., E. Lehman, R. Pasqual-Marqui, D. Hell, and F. Vollenweider. "Mood State and Brain Electric Activity in Ecstasy Users." *Clinical Neuroscienc and Neuropsychology* 11 (January 2000): 157–162.

Gehrke, B., S. Harrod, W. Cass, and M. Bardo. "The Effect of Neurotoxic Doses of Methamphetamine on Methamphetamine-Conditioned Place Preference in Rats." *Psychopharmacology (Berlin)* 166 (2003): 249–257.

Gilbert, R. "Caffeine Consumption." In *The Methylxanthine Beverages and Foods: Chemistry, Consumption, and Health Effects,* edited by G. Spiller. New York: Liss, 1984.

Golding, A. "Two Hundred Years of Drug Abuse." *Journal of the Royal Society of Medicine* 86 (May 1993): 282–286.

Goldstein, A. *Addiction from Biology to Drug Abuse.* New York: Freeman, 1994.

Goldstein, F. "Pharmacological Aspects of Substance Abuse." In *Remington's Pharmaceutical Sciences,* 19th ed., edited by A. R. Genaro, 780–794. Easton, PA: Mack, 1995.

Green, E. "Cocaine, Glamorous Status Symbol of the 'Jet Set,' Is Fast Becoming Many Students' Drug of Choice." *Chronicle of Higher Education* 13 (November 1985): 1, 34.

Griffiths, R., and A. Chausmer. "Caffeine as a Model of Dependence: Recent Developments in Understanding Caffeine Withdrawal, the Caffeine Dependence Syndrome and Caffeine Negative Reinforcement." *Nihon Shinkei Seishin Yakurigaku Zasshi* 20 (2000): 223–231.

Grinspoon, L. "Update on Cocaine, Parts 1 and 2." *Harvard Mental Health Letter* 10 (August-September 1993): 1–4.

Grinspoon, L., and J. Bakalar. "The Amphetamines: Medical Use and Health Hazards." In *Amphetamines: Use, Misuse and Abuse,* edited by D. Smith, 18–33. Boston: Hall, 1978.

Grob, C., R. Poland, L. Chang, and T. Ernst. "Psychobiological Effects of 3.4-Methylenedioxymethamphetamine in Humans: Methodological Considerations and Preliminary Observations." *Behavioral Brain Research* 73 (1996): 103–107.

Gugliotta, G. "Ephedra Lawsuits Show Big Increase." *The Washington Post* (23 July 2000): A-1.

Gunnarsdottir, E., R. Pingitore, B. Spring, L. Konopka, J. Crayton, T. Milo, and P. Shirazi. "Individual Differences Among Cocaine Users." *Addiction Behavior* 25 (2000): 641–652.

Gurin, J. "Coffee and Health." *Consumer Reports* (October 1994): 650–651.

Hall, K. "Peru: Peru's Coca Farmers Hoping to Boost Crops' Market." *Macon Telegraph (GA)* (23 July 2003).

Hall, W., and J. Hando. "Illicit Amphetamine Use Is a Public Health Problem in Australia." *Medical Journal of Australia* 159 (1993): 643–644.

Hanson, G. R., K. Rau, and A. Fleckenstein. "The Methamphetamine Experience: A NIDA Partnership." *Neuropharmacology* 47 (2004): 92–100.

Harris, D., and S. Batki. "Stimulant Psychosis: Symptom Profile and Acute Clinical Course." *American Journal of Addiction* 9 (2000): 28–37.

Hatch, O. "Methamphetamines" (5 August 1999). Available www.orrinhatch.org/leading/legislation/meth.html.

Hatsukami, D., and M. Fischman. "Crack Cocaine and Cocaine Hydrochloride." *Journal of the American Medical Association* 276 (1996): 1580–1588.

Heishman, S., and J. Henningfield. "Stimulus Functions of Caffeine in Humans: Relation to Dependence Potential." *Neuroscience and Behavior Review* 16 (1992): 273–287.

Hinkle, J., and S. Winckler. "Vitamin R: The Expansion of Ritalin Abuse." *PRN (Pharmacy Recovery Network)* 4 (April/June 1996): 1.

Hoffman, B., and R. Lefkowitz. "Catecholamines, Sympathomimetics Drugs, and Adrenergic Receptor Antagonists." In *The Pharmacological Basis of Therapeutics,* 9th ed., edited by J. Hardman and L. Limbird, 199–248. New York: McGraw–Hill, 1995.

Jansen, K. "Ecstasy (MDMA)." *Drug and Alcohol Dependence* 53 (1999): 121–124.

Johnston, L. *University of Michigan Annual National Surveys of Secondary Students.* Lansing, MI: University of Michigan, 1996. Available from author at 412 Maynard, Ann Arbor, MI.

Johnston, L. "Monitoring the Future." *Drug Trends in 1999 Among American Teens.* Lansing, MI: University of Michigan, 1999. Available from author at 412 Maynard, Ann Arbor, MI.

Johnston, L. "Overall Teen Drug Use Continues Gradual Decline, But Use of Inhalants Rises" (21 December 2004). Available www.monitoringthefuture.org.

Kennedy, K. "Meth Mania: Even Cops Duck for Cover." *Salt Lake Tribune* (28 June 1999): B-1.

Khan, M. "Drugs Used to Enhance Studying Draw Concern." *Miami Herald* (8 July 2003).

Kihlman, B. *Caffeine and Chromosomes.* Amsterdam: Elsevier, 1977.

Kinkead, L., and Romboy, D. "Meth Emergency." *Deseret Morning News* 153 (14 November 2004): A1, A15–A17.

Kleber, H. "Treatment of Cocaine Abuse: Pharmacotherapy." In *Cocaine Scientific and Social Dimensions,* edited by Ciba, 195–206. Ciba Foundation Symposium 166. New York: Wiley, 1992.

Kloner, R., and S. Rezkalla. "Cocaine and the Heart." *New England Journal of Medicine* 348 (2003): 487–488.

Kluger, J. "The Buzz on Caffeine." *Time* (20 December 2004).

Ladd, G., and N. Petry. "Antisocial Personality in Treatment-Seeking Cocaine Abusers: Psychosocial Functioning and HIV Risk." *Journal of Substance Abuse Treatment* 24 (2003): 323–330.

Lesesne, C., S. Visser, and C. White. "Attention-Deficit/Hyperactivity Disorder in School-Aged Children: Association with Maternal Mental Health and Use of Health Care Resources." *Pediatrics* 111 (2003): 1232–1237.

Leshner, A. "Research Shows Effects of Prenatal Cocaine Exposure Are Subtle, but Significant." *NIDA Notes* 14 (1999): 3–4.

Leshner, A. "A Club Drug Alert." *NIDA Notes* 14 (2000): 3–5.

Lyles, J., and J. Cadet. "MDMA Neurotoxicity: Cellular and Molecular Mechanisms." *Brain Research Review* 42 (2003): 155–168.

Margen, S. "Caffeine: Grounds for Concern." *U.C. Berkeley Wellness Letter* 10 (March 1994): 4.

Markou, A., and P. Kenny. "Neuroadaptations to Chronic Exposure to Drugs of Abuse: Relevance to Depression Symptomology Even Across Psychiatric Diagnostic Categories." *Neurotoxicology Research* 4 (2002): 297–313.

McCaffrey, B. "Methamphetamine." *ONDCP, Drug Policy Information Clearinghouse.* NCJ-1756677 (May 1999): 1–3.

McMahon, P. "Cause Coffee's Produce a Cup with an Agenda." *USA Today* (26 July 2001): A-1.

Medical Letter. "Acute Reaction to Drugs of Abuse." (1996): 43.

Medical References. "Cocaine Use During Pregnancy."

Quick Reference: Drugs and Alcohol (25 July 2003). Available www.marchofdimes.com/printable articles/681_1169.asp?printable=true.

Mendelson, J., and N. Mello. "Management of Cocaine Abuse and Dependence." *New England Journal of Medicine* 334 (1996): 965–972.

Mihoces, G. "Ephedra: Is It Safe or Lethal." *USAToday*.com (8 November 2001).

Mills, J., L. Holmes, J. Aarons, J. Simpson, Z. Brown, L. Peterson, M. Conley, B. Graubard, and R. Knopp. "Moderate Caffeine Use and the Risk of Spontaneous Abortion and Intrauterine Growth Retardation." *Journal of the American Medical Association* 269 (1993): 593–602.

Morland, J. "Toxicity of Drug Abuse—Amphetamine Designer Drugs (Ecstasy): Mental Effects and Consequences of Single Dose Use." *Toxicology Letters* 112–113 (2000): 147–152.

Musto, D. "International Traffic in Coca Through the Early 20th Century." *Drug and Alcohol Dependence* 49 (1998): 145–156.

Nash, M. "How We Get Addicted." *Time* (5 May 1997): 69–76.

Nathan, K., W. Bresnick, and S. Battei. "Cocaine Abuse and Dependence." *CNS Drugs* 10 (1998): 43–59.

National Institute on Drug Abuse (NIDA). "Comparing Methamphetamine and Cocaine." *NIDA Notes* 13 (June 1998).

National Institute on Drug Abuse. "Cocaine Abuse and Addiction." *NIDA Research Report*. NIH Publication No. 99-4342 (May 1999).

Nawrot, P., S. Jordan, J. Eastwood, J. Rotstein, A. Hugenholtz, and M. Feeley. "Effects of Caffeine on Human Health." *Food Additives and Contaminants* 20 (2003): 1–30.

NDIC. "North Carolina Drug Threat Assessment: Methamphetamine." (April 2003). Available www.usdoj.gov/ndic/pubs3/3690/meth.htm

NIDA Diagnosis. "Diagnosis and Treatment of Drug Abuse in Family Practice" (May 2000). Available 165.112.78.61/ Diagnosis-Treatment/Diagnosis6.html.

NIDA Research Report. "Methamphetamine Abuse and Addiction" (22 May 2000). Available 165.112.78.61/ ResearchReports/Methamph/methamp5.html.

Nuckols, C., and J. Kane. "Methamphetamine Addiction: 'Speed' Still Kills." *Counselor* 4 (2003): 14–18.

ONDCP. "Cocaine." ONDCP Drug Policy Information Clearinghouse (2003). Available www.whitehousedrugpolicy.gov/publications/factsht/cocaine/.

Parrott, A. "Human Psychopharmacology of Ecstasy (MDMA)." *Human Psychopharmacology* 16 (2001): 557.

Parrott, A., E. Sisk, and J. Turner. "Psychobiological Problems in Heavy 'Ecstasy' (MDMA) Polydrug Users." *Drug and Alcohol Dependence* 60 (2000): 105–110.

Pennings, E., A. Leccese, and F. Wolff. "Effects of Concurrent Use of Alcohol and Cocaine." *Addiction* 97 (2002): 773–783.

Pharmacy Times. "New York County Bans Herbal Stimulants." 62 (1996): 8.

Physicians' Desk Reference for Nonprescription Drugs, 24th ed. Montvale, NJ: Medical Economics, 2003.

Platt, D., J. Rowlett, and R. Spealman. "Behavioral Effects of Cocaine and Dopaminergic Strategies for Preclinical Medication Development." *Psychopharmacology* 163 (2002): 265–282.

Prevention Pipeline. "Methamphetamine Update." *The Prevention Pipeline* 10 (September/October 1997): 13–16.

Prevline. "Methamphetamine." *Quick Docs. Prevline, Prevention Online* (1999). Available http://www.health.org.

Randall, T. "Ecstasy-Fueled 'Rave' Parties Become Dances of Death for English Youths." *Journal of the American Medical Association* 268 (1992a): 1505–1506.

Randall, T. "'Rave' Scene, Ecstasy Use, Leap Atlantic." *Journal of the American Medical Association* 268 (1992b): 1506.

Rubin, R. "For FDA, Banning Ephedra Is Not as Easy as It Sounds." *USA Today* (3 March 2003): D-7.

SAMHSA News. "Abuse Treatment Guidelines Released." 17 (Summer 1999): 17.

Sawynok, J., and T. Yaksh. "Caffeine as an Analgesic Adjuvant: A Review of Pharmacology and Mechanisms of Action." *Pharmacological Reviews* 45 (1993): 43–85.

Schifano, F., L. Furia, G. Forza, N. Minicuci, and R. Bricolo. "MDMA ('Ecstasy') Consumption in the Context of Polydrug Abuse: A Report on 50 Patients." *Drug and Alcohol Dependence* 52 (1998): 85–90.

Seigel, R. K. "Treatment of Cocaine Abuse." *Journal of Psychoactive Drugs* 17 (1985): 52.

Shipley, A. "Bechler's Diet Pills Draw Scrutiny." *The Washington Post* (19 February 2003): D-1.

Singer, L., et al. "Cognitive Outcomes of Preschool Children with Prenatal Cocaine Exposure." *Journal of the American Medical Association* 291 (2004): 2448–2456.

Smith, M., A. Hoeping, K. Johnson, M. Trzcinska, and A. Kozikovski. "Dopaminergic Agents for the Treatment of Cocaine Abuse." *Drug Discovery Technology* 4 (1999): 322–332.

Smith, L., M. Yonekura, T. Wallace, N. Berman, J. Kuo, and C. Berkowityz. "Effects of Prenatal Methamphetamine Exposure on Fetal Growth and Drug Withdrawal Symptoms in Infants Born at Term." *Journal of Developmental Pediatrics* 24 (2003): 17–33.

Sofuoglu, M., S. Dudish-Poulsen, S. Brown, and D. Hatsukami. "Association of Cocaine Withdrawal Symptoms with More Severe Dependence and Enhanced Subjective Response to Cocaine." *Drug and Alcohol Dependence* 69 (2003): 273–282.

Sprague, J., A. Harrod, and A. Teconchuk. "The Pharmacology and Abuse Potential of Ephedrine." *Pharmacy Times* (May 1998): 72–80.

Stocker, S. "Cocaine Activates Different Brain Regions for

Rush Versus Craving." *NIDA Notes* 13 (1999): 7–10.

Swan, N. "31% of New York Murder Victims Had Cocaine in Their Bodies." *NIDA Notes* 10 (March/April 1995): 4.

Swan, N. "Response to Escalating Methamphetamine Abuse Build on NIDA-Funded Research." *NIDA Notes* 11 (November/December 1996): 1–12.

U.S. Department of Justice. "Children at Risk." *Information Bulletin* (July 2002): Product Number 2002-L0424-001.

U.S. Department of Justice. "Methamphetamine." *National Drug Threat Assessment* (April 2003a): Product Number 2003-Q0317-001, 13–25.

U.S. Department of Justice. "National Drug Threat Assessment 2003." *National Drug Intelligence Center* (January 2003b): Product No. 2003-Q0317-001, 51–58.

USA Today. "Study to Test Ecstasy on Terminal Cancer Patients." Health and Behavior (28 December 2004). Available www.usatoday.com/news/health/2004-12-27-ecstasy_x.htm.

Van Dyck, C., and R. Byck. "Cocaine." *Scientific American* 246 (1982): 128–141.

Vidaeff, A., and J. Mastrobattista. "In Utero Cocaine Exposure: A Thorny Mix of Science and Mythology." *American Journal of Perinatology* 20 (2003): 165–172.

Volkow, N., L. Chang, G. Wong, J. Fowler, and D. Francesch.

"Loss of Dopamine Transporters in Methamphetamine Abusers Recovers with Protracted Abstinence." *Journal of Neuroscience* 21 (2001): 9414–9418.

Washington Times. "Yet Another Warning Against Ephedra." (5 February 2003): A-5.

Weiner, T. "9 Linked to Drug War Found Slain Outside Mexican Border City." *The New York Times* (3 April 2003): A-5.

Woolverton, W., and K. Johnston. "Neurobiology of Cocaine Abuse." *Trends in Pharmacological Sciences* 13 (1992): 193–200.

Yui, K., et al. "Methamphetamine Psychosis: Spontaneous Recurrence of Paranoid-Hallucinating States and Monoamine Neurotransmitter Function." *Journal of Clinical Psychopharmacology* 17 (1999): 34–43.

Zhang, W. "A Benefit–Risk Assessment of Caffeine as an Analgesic Adjuvant." *Drug Safety* 24 (2001): 1127–1142.

Zickler, P. "Methamphetamine, Cocaine Abusers Have Different Patterns of Drug Use, Suffer Different Cognitive Impairments." *NIDA Notes* 16 (December 2001): 11.

Zickler, P. "Cocaine's Effect on Blood Components May Be Linked to Heart Attack and Stroke." *NIDA Notes* 17 (2002): 5.

CHAPTER 11

Tobacco

Did You Know?

- Approximately 29.8% of the U.S. population aged 12 and older reports current use of a tobacco product.

- Tobacco use is the leading preventable cause of death in the United States.

- Tobacco kills more than 440,000 United States citizens each year.

- Tobacco farming is among the top 10 largest legal cash crops in the United States.

- Nicotine is one of thousands of chemicals found in cigarette smoke.

- Nearly 4000 young people in the United States will begin smoking today.

- Several smoking cessation aids are available, including nicotine gum, patches, nasal spray, and inhalers. In addition, antidepressants are now used to help with smoking cessation.

On completing this chapter you will be able to:

- ⊚ Describe the social and economic costs of smoking in the United States.

- ⊚ Describe the history of tobacco use.

- ⊚ Explain how the quality of leaf tobacco has changed since the mid-1950s.

- ⊚ Describe the pharmacological effects of nicotine.

- ⊚ List several disease states caused by cigarette smoking.

- ⊚ Explain the consequences of environmental tobacco smoke on nonsmokers.

- ⊚ List several reasons individuals smoke.

- ⊚ List several strategies that aid in smoking cessation.

- ⊚ List the four primary aspects of tobacco control laws at the state level.

Drugs and Society Online is a great source for additional drugs and society information for both students and instructors.
Visit **http://drugsandsociety.jbpub.com** to find a variety of useful tools for learning, thinking, and teaching.

Tobacco Use: Scope of the Problem

Tobacco use is the leading preventable cause of death in the United States, accounting for approximately 440,000 deaths (NCI 2004). The impact of nicotine addiction in terms of morbidity, mortality, and economic costs to society is staggering. Nationally, smoking resuls in more than 5.6 million years of potential life lost each year. Approximately 80% of adult smokers started smoking before age 18. Accordingly, more than 6.4 million children living today will die prematurely because of a decision they will make as adolescents (CDC 2005).

In addition to these enormous health consequences, there is a significant economic burden. Tobacco use results in an annual cost of $75 billion in direct medical costs (CDC 2005). These high costs will likely continue and increase in the future because it is estimated that each day, nearly 4000 people younger than age 18 start smoking (CDC 2005), and many of them will become addicted.

Although much of this chapter deals with tobacco use in the United States, it is noteworthy that tobacco is used throughout the world and that markets for tobacco sales abroad have expanded in recent years. "Tobacco is the fourth most common risk factor for disease worldwide" (WHO 2005). The World Health Organization (WHO) estimates that tobacco kills 5 million people each year. By about 2020 and if current smoking trends continue, that number will rise to approximately 10 million per year. It is estimated that 50% of current smokers, or approximately 650 million individuals, will eventually die from tobacco-related illnesses (WHO 2005).

CURRENT TOBACCO USE IN THE UNITED STATES

In 2003, 70.8 million Americans, or 29.8% of the population aged 12 or older, reported current use of a tobacco product. Among these individuals, 1.6 million smoked tobacco in pipes, 7.7 million used smokeless tobacco, 12.8 million smoked cigars, and 60.4 million smoked cigarettes (SAMHSA 2004). Approximately 35.9 percent of males and

The WHO estimates that by 2030, tobacco will kill 10 million people per year worldwide. Early exposure increases the chance that young people will become regular adult smokers.

24.0% of females aged 12 or older were past-month users of any tobacco product (SAMHSA 2004).

In 2003, past-month cigarette smoking rates peaked at age 20. Specifically, rates increased from 1.7% at age 12 to 26.4% at age 17. At age 20, the rate was 44.1%. After age 22, rates generally declined with age: 30.9% for 30- to 34-year-olds; 31.1% for 40- to 44-year-olds; 25.0% for 50- to 54-year-olds; 16.5% for 60- to 64-year-olds; and 10.0% for persons aged 65 or older (SAMHSA 2004).

Past-month tobacco use among individuals aged 12 or older by U.S. region is as follows: approximately 32.6% of the population in the Midwest region, 31.8% in the South region, 24.7% in the West region, and 28.7% in the Northeast region. Level of educational attainment was also correlated with tobacco usage: 35.3% of adults aged 18 or older who did not complete high school smoked cigarettes, whereas only 14% of college graduates smoked. Additional information on the groups that use tobacco is discussed later in this chapter (SAMHSA 2004).

In 1999, the Substance Abuse and Mental Health Services Administration (SAMHSA) began reporting information on the use of specific cigarette brands. According to the 2003 SAMHSA survey, among past-month cigarette smokers aged 12 or older, the most commonly smoked brands were Marlboro (41.3%), Newport (10.8%), and Camel (7.0%).

THE HISTORY OF TOBACCO USE

Like alcohol, tobacco has a long history of use in the Americas and is indigenous to the United States. In fact, tobacco was one of the New World's contributions to the rest of humanity. The word *tobacco* may have come from *tabacco*, which was a two-pronged tube used by the natives of Central America to take snuff. Columbus reported receiving tobacco leaves from the natives of San Salvador in 1492. However, the native peoples had been smoking the leaves for many centuries before Columbus arrived. Practically all native people, from Paraguay to Quebec, used tobacco. The Mayans regarded tobacco smoke as divine incense that would bring rain in the dry season. The oldest known representation of a smoker is a stone carving from a Mayan temple, which shows a priest puffing on a ceremonial pipe. The Aztecs used tobacco in folk medicine and religious ritual.

Indeed, Native Americans used tobacco in every manner known: smoked as cigars and cigarettes (wrapped in corn husks) and in pipes; as a syrup to be swallowed or applied to the gums; chewed and snuffed; and administered rectally as a ceremonial enema (O'Brien et al. 1992; Schultes 1978).

In the 1600s, Turkey, Russia, and China all imposed death penalties for smoking. In Turkey, smoking was introduced in the 1600s, spread in popularity, and instantly created two camps. On the one hand, poets praised tobacco as one of four elements of the world of pleasure: tobacco, opium, coffee, and wine. On the other hand, priests were violently opposed to this substance. They created the legend that tobacco grew from Mohammed's spittle, after he was bitten by a viper, sucked out the venom, and spat.

Murad (Amurath) IV, known as Murad the Cruel, who reigned during 1623–1640, executed many of his subjects caught smoking:

> Whenever the Sultan went on his travels or on a military expedition, his halting-places were always distinguished by a terrible increase in the number of executions. Even on the battlefield, he was fond of surprising men in the act of smoking, . . . he would punish them by beheading, hanging, quartering, or crushing their hands and feet and leaving them helpless between the lines. . . . Nevertheless, in spite of all the horrors of this lust [smoking] that seemed to increase with age, the passion for smoking still persisted. . . . Even the fear of death was of no avail with the passionate devotees of the habit. (Corti 1931)

The Romanov tsars publicly tortured smokers and exiled them to Siberia. The Chinese decapitated anyone caught dealing in tobacco with the "outer barbarians." Yet smoking continued to grow to epidemic proportions. Despite their opposition to anything foreign, the Chinese became the heaviest smokers in Asia, thus facilitating the later spread of opium smoking. Thus, no nation whose population has learned to use tobacco products has been successful in outlawing use or getting people to stop.

Snuffing first became fashionable in France during the reign of Louis XIII and spread throughout the European aristocracy. Snuffing was regarded as daintier and more elegant than constantly exhaling smoke. King Louis XIV, however, detested all forms of tobacco and would not permit its use in his presence. (He would have banned it, but he needed the tax revenue that tobacco brought in.) His sister-in-law, Charlotte of Orleans, was one of the few at court who agreed with him. As she wrote to her sister, "It is better to take no snuff at all than a little; for it is certain that he who takes a little will soon take much, and that is why they call it 'the enchanted herb,' for those who take it are so taken by it that they cannot go without it." Napoleon is said to have used seven pounds of snuff per month (Corti 1931).

POPULARITY IN THE WESTERN WORLD

When tobacco reached Europe, it was at first merely a curiosity, but its use spread rapidly. Europeans had no name for the process of inhaling smoke, so they called this "drinking" smoke. Perhaps the first European to inhale tobacco smoke was Rodrig de Jerez, a member of Columbus's crew. He had seen people smoking in Cuba and brought the habit to Portugal. When he smoked in Portugal, his friends, seeing smoke coming from his mouth, believed he was possessed by the devil. As a result, he was placed in jail for several years (Heimann 1960; O'Brien et al. 1992).

In 1559, the French ambassador to Portugal, Jean Nicot, grew interested in this novel plant and sent one as a gift to Catherine de Medici, Queen of France. The plant was named *Nicotiana tabacum* after him.

The next several hundred years saw a remarkable increase in the use of tobacco. Portuguese sailors smoked it and left tobacco seeds scattered around the world. Over the next 150 years, the Portuguese introduced tobacco to trade with India, Brazil, Japan, China, Arabia, and Africa. Many large tobacco plantations around the world were started by the Portuguese at this time.

An early Christian religious leader, Bishop Bartolome de las Casas (1474–1566), reported that Spanish settlers in Hispaniola (Haiti) smoked rolled tobacco leaves in cigar form like the natives. When the bishop asked about this disgusting habit, the settlers replied that they found it impossible to give up.

As the use of tobacco spread, so did the controversy about whether it was bad or good. Tobacco use inspired the first major drug controversy of global dimensions. As a medicine, tobacco was at first almost universally accepted. Nicholas Monardes, in his description of New World plants (dated 1574), recommended tobacco as an infallible cure for 36 different maladies. It was described as a holy, healing herb—a special remedy sent by God to humans.

Opponents of tobacco use disputed its medical value. They pointed out that tobacco was used in the magic and religion of Native Americans. Tobacco was attacked as an evil plant, an invention of the devil. King James I of England was fanatically opposed to smoking. In an attempt to limit tobacco use, he raised the import tax on tobacco and also sold the right to collect the tax (Austin 1978; O'Brien et al. 1992).

Nevertheless, tobacco use increased. By 1614, the number of tobacco shops in London had mushroomed to more than 7000, and demand for tobacco usually outstripped supply. Tobacco was literally worth its weight in silver; to conserve it, users smoked it in pipes with very small bowls. Use of tobacco grew in other areas of the world as well.

In 1642, Pope Urban VIII issued a formal decree forbidding the use of tobacco in church under penalty of immediate excommunication. This decree was in response to the fact that priests and worshippers had been staining church floors with tobacco juice. One priest in Naples sneezed so hard after taking snuff that he vomited on the altar in full sight of the congregation. In response, Pope Innocent X issued another edict against tobacco use in 1650, but the clergy and the laity continued to take snuff and smoke. Finally, in 1725, Pope Benedict XIII, himself a smoker and "snuff-taker," annulled all previous edicts against tobacco (Austin 1978).

HISTORY OF TOBACCO USE IN AMERICA

Tobacco played a significant role in the successful colonization of the United States (Langton 1991). In 1610, John Rolfe was sent to Virginia to set up a tobacco industry. At first, the tobacco planted in Virginia was a native species, *Nicotiana rustica,* that was harsh and did not sell well. But in 1612, Rolfe managed to obtain some seeds of the Spanish tobacco species **Nicotiana tabacum**, and by 1613, the success of the tobacco industry and the Virginia colony was ensured.

The history of tobacco smoking in the United States is rich in terms of the tremendous number of laws, rules, regulations, and customs that have arisen around the habit of smoking. Many states have had laws prohibiting the use of tobacco by young people as well as women of any age. In the 1860s, for instance, it was illegal in Florida for anyone younger than the age of 21 to smoke cigarettes. A 20-year-old caught smoking could be taken to court and compelled to reveal his source (the cigarette "pusher"). In Pennsylvania, as in South Carolina, any child not informing on his or her cigarette supplier was a criminal.

KEY TERMS

Nicotiana tabacum
primary species of tobacco cultivated in the United States

Up to the turn of the 20th century, chewing and snuffing were the most common ways of using tobacco in the United States. In 1897, half of all tobacco was prepared for chewing. Law required that spittoons be placed in all public buildings until 1945 ("Cigars" 1988).

Cigars became popular in the United States in the early 1800s. Cigar manufacturers fought the introduction of cigarettes for many years. They spread rumors that cigarettes contained opium, were made with tobacco from discarded cigar butts, and were made with paper made by Chinese lepers, and so on. By about 1920, cigarette consumption started to exceed that of cigars. The introduction of the cigarette-rolling machine in 1883 spurred cigarette consumption because cigarettes became cheaper than cigars. By 1885, 1 billion cigarettes per year were being produced. Americans consumed more than 815 billion cigarettes in 1988. More recent estimates show that the number of cigarettes manufactured in the United States rose from 667 billion in 1983 to 695 billion in 1991 to 702 billion in 1992–1993. Although domestic consumption has dropped, the increases result from foreign demand of U.S. tobacco leaf and U.S. cigarette manufacturers offering discounted cigarettes and lower prices on premium brands.

Tobacco Production

Tobacco is one of the top 10 cash crops in the United States, with a farm value in 2003 of $1.6 billion (Economic Research Service, USDA 2004). Although there are more than 60 species of plants, *Nicotiana tabacum* is the primary species of tobacco cultivated in the United States. Its mature leaves are 1 to 2.5 feet long. The nicotine content ranges from 0.3% to 7%, depending on the variety, leaf position on the stalk (the higher the position, the more nicotine), and growing conditions. The flavor of tobacco comes from nicotianin, also called *tobacco camphor.*

After harvesting and drying, tobacco leaves are shredded, blown clean of foreign matter and stems, remoisturized with glycerine or other chemical agents, and packed in huge wooden barrels called *hogsheads.* These barrels are placed in storehouses for 1 to 2 years to age, during which time the tobacco becomes darker and loses moisture, nicotine, and other volatile substances. When aging has been completed, moisture is again added and the tobacco is blended with other varieties.

There are many types of tobacco, with varying characteristics of harshness, mildness, and flavor. **Bright**, also called **flue-cured**, or **Virginia**, is the most common type used in cigarettes. (Flue-cured tobacco is heated in curing sheds to speed the drying process.) Developed just before the Civil War, this technique made tobacco smoke more readily inhalable.

The amount of leaf tobacco in a cigarette has declined by roughly 25% since 1956. There are at least two reasons for this drop. The first reason is the use of reconstituted sheets of tobacco. Parts of the tobacco leaves and stems that were discarded in earlier years are now ground up, combined with many other ingredients to control factors such as moisture, flavor, and color, and then rolled out as a flat, homogenized sheet of reconstituted tobacco. This sheet is shredded and mixed with regular leaf tobacco, thus reducing production costs. Nearly one-fourth of the tobacco in a cigarette comes from tobacco scraps made into reconstituted sheets.

A second technological advance has further reduced the amount of tobacco needed. This

Use of spittoons (on floor at ends of table) was considered a preferment in public conduct.

process, called **puffing**, is based on freeze-drying the tobacco and then blowing air or an inert gas, such as carbon dioxide, into it. The gas expands, or puffs up, the plant cells so they take up more space, are lighter, and can absorb additives better.

Tobacco additives are not controlled by the Food and Drug Administration (FDA) or any other government agency. Additives may include extracts of tobacco, as well as nontobacco flavors such as licorice, cocoa, fruit, spices, and floral compositions. (Licorice was first used in tobacco as a preservative around 1830 and became appreciated only later as a sweetener.) Synthetic flavoring compounds also may be used.

In the 1870s, a "cigarette girl" could roll about four cigarettes per minute by hand. When James Duke leased and improved the first cigarette-rolling machine in 1883, he could make about 200 cigarettes per minute. This advance was the last link in the chain of development leading to the modern American blended cigarette. Today's machines make more than 3600 uniform cigarettes per minute.

Tar and nicotine levels in cigarettes have dropped considerably over the past 40 years (Bartecchi et al. 1995; Palfai and Jankiewicz 1991). Most cigarettes today are low-tar and low-nicotine types. The filtertip, in which the filter is made of cellulose or in some cases charcoal, has also become common; the vast majority of all cigarettes sold currently in the United States are filtertips. The filter does help remove some of the harmful substances in smoke, but most, such as carbon monoxide, pass through into the mouth and lungs. Sixty-nine cancer-causing substances have been identified out of the 4800 substances used in cigarettes (CDC 2003). The health consequences of many more substances found in cigarettes have not been adequately analyzed.

In 1999, domestic cigarette manufacturers sold 411 billion cigarettes domestically, 10.3% less than the previous year (FTC 2001). Declines in sales

have been attributed to health concerns, aggressive anti-smoking campaigns, price increases, and decreased social acceptance of smoking. Figure 11.1 shows the relationship between smoking rates and major smoking and health events.

Government Regulation

In the early 1960s, attitudes toward tobacco use began to change in the United States. Before this time, tobacco was perceived as being devoid of any negative consequences. After years of study and hundreds of research reports about the effects of smoking, the Advisory Committee to the U.S. Surgeon General reported in 1964 that cigarette smoking is a cause of lung cancer and laryngeal cancer in men, a probable cause of lung cancer in women, and the most important cause of chronic bronchitis. The committee stated that "cigarette smoking is a health hazard of sufficient importance in the United States to warrant appropriate remedial action." In 1965, Congress passed legislation setting up the National Clearinghouse for Smoking and Health. This organization has the responsibility of monitoring, compiling, and reviewing the world's medical literature on the health consequences of smoking.

Reports were published by this clearinghouse in 1967, 1968, and 1969. The statistical evidence presented in 1969 made it difficult for Congress to avoid warning the public that smoking was dangerous to their health. Since November 1, 1970, all cigarette packages and cartons have had to carry this label: "Warning: The Surgeon General Has Determined That Cigarette Smoking Is Dangerous to Your Health." In 1984, Congress enacted legislation requiring cigarette advertisements and packages to post four distinct warnings (see Figure 11.2), which are to be rotated every 3 months.

Further pressure on Congress prompted laws to be passed that prohibited advertising tobacco on radio and television after January 2, 1971. The intent was to limit the media's ability to make smoking seem glamorous and sophisticated. The loss in revenue to radio and television was enormous.

The 1979 publication *Smoking and Health: A Report of the Surgeon General* gave what was then up-to-date information on research about the effects of

KEY TERMS

puffing
a method of reducing the amount of tobacco in cigarette production

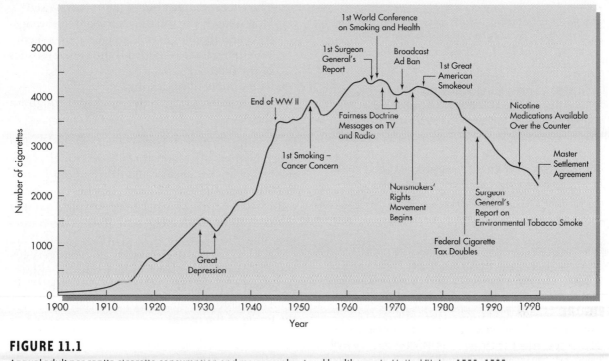

FIGURE 11.1

Annual adult per capita cigarette consumption and major smoking and health events, United States, 1900–1998.

Sources: United States Department of Agriculture; 1986 Surgeon General's Report.

tobacco on cardiovascular disease, bronchopulmonary disease, cancer, peptic ulcer, and pregnancy. It also emphasized the increase in smoking by women and girls over the preceding 15 years. The 1981 U.S. Surgeon General's report, *The Changing Cigarette,* gave further information, and the 1985 report, *The Health Consequences of Smoking,* gave research findings showing the relationship of smoking, cancer, and chronic lung disease in the workplace.

Over the years, private insurance companies, as well as state and federal agencies, have paid billions of dollars to cover healthcare costs presumably resulting from diseases caused by tobacco use. A series of lawsuits have forced large tobacco companies to compensate for some of these losses. In a landmark settlement in 1998, 46 states reached an agreement with five major tobacco companies to pay a settlement estimated at exceeding $200 billion. As part of the 1998 agreement, "Big Tobacco" companies are no longer allowed outdoor advertisements such as billboards near stadiums or shop-

ping malls, nor are they allowed to use cartoons (e.g., Joe Camel) in the packaging and advertising of tobacco-containing products. In addition, the sale and distribution of clothing and merchandise such as caps and T-shirts with brand-name logos is no longer permitted (*Master Settlement Agreement* 1998). This settlement did not cover individual, federal, or class-action suits but only suits filed by the states themselves. In addition, the cigarette manufacturers that signed the settlement agreement agreed to establish a foundation to fund "the study of and programs to reduce youth tobacco product usage and youth substance abuse in the states" (*Master Settlement Agreement,* 1998).

Since 1985, numerous other reports on smoking and health by the U.S. Surgeon General have been issued; they invariably repeat the assertions about the devastating effects of cigarette smoking. For a historical summation of the developments between cigarette consumption and efforts to diminish cigarette use, see Figure 11.1.

SURGEON GENERAL'S WARNING: Quitting Smoking Now Greatly Reduces Serious Risks to Your Health.

SURGEON GENERAL'S WARNING: Smoking Causes Lung Cancer, Heart Disease, Emphysema, and May Complicate Pregnancy.

SURGEON GENERAL'S WARNING: Smoking by Pregnant Women May Result in Fetal Injury, Premature Birth, and Low Birth Weight.

SURGEON GENERAL'S WARNING: Cigarette Smoke Contains Carbon Monoxide.

FIGURE 11.2

Warnings on cigarette labels. Four warnings must be rotated on cigarette packages. The messages are based on the reports of the U.S. Surgeon General on *The Health Consequences of Smoking* (1985) and went into effect on October 12, 1985.

Pharmacology of Nicotine

NICOTINE ADMINISTRATION

In 1828, **nicotine** was discovered to be one component of tobacco. This colorless, highly volatile liquid alkaloid is one of more than 4000 chemicals found in the smoke from tobacco products such as cigarettes (NIDA 2004). When smoked, nicotine enters the lungs and is then absorbed into the bloodstream. When chewed (**tobacco chewing**) or dipped (**snuff dipping**), nicotine is absorbed through the mucous lining of the mouth.

The amount of nicotine absorbed into the body varies according to several factors:

KEY TERMS

nicotine
a colorless, highly volatile liquid akaloid

tobacco chewing
the absorption of nicotine through the mucous lining of the mouth

snuff dipping
placing a pinch of tobacco between the gums and the cheek

1. The exact composition of the tobacco used
2. How densely the tobacco is packed in the cigarette and the length of the cigarette smoked
3. Whether a filter is used and the characteristics of the filter
4. The volume of smoke inhaled
5. The number of cigarettes smoked throughout the day

Depending on how tobacco is taken, the rate at which it enters the bloodstream varies widely. Cigarette smoking results in rapid distribution of nicotine throughout the body; it reaches the brain within 10 seconds of inhalation. A typical smoker will take 10 puffs on a cigarette during the 5 minutes that the cigarette is lit. Thus, a person who smokes two packs (40 cigarettes) each day gets 400 "hits" of nicotine to the brain each day. In contrast, cigar and pipe smokers typically do not inhale the smoke; nicotine is absorbed more slowly through the lining of the mouth.

EFFECTS ON THE CENTRAL NERVOUS SYSTEM

Nicotine produces an intense effect on the central nervous system. Research has demonstrated that nicotine activates the brain circuitry in regions responsible for regulating feelings of pleasure. In particular, nicotine increases the release of the neurotransmitter dopamine in the so-called reward or pleasure pathways of the brain. This effect likely contributes to the abuse potential of the stimulant.

The pharmacokinetic properties of nicotine also enhance its abuse potential. Cigarette smoking allows nicotine to enter the brain rapidly, with drug levels peaking within 10 seconds of inhalation. The acute effects of this rapid increase in brain concentration dissipate within a few minutes, causing the smoker to continue to dose frequently throughout the day in an effort to maintain the pleasurable effects of the drug.

OTHER EFFECTS OF NICOTINE

In addition to its direct effects in the brain, nicotine increases the respiration rate at low dose levels because it stimulates the receptors in the carotid

(*text continues on page 336*)

Table 11.1 **Significant Developments Related to Smoking and Health, 1964–2001**

1964	• *Smoking and Health: Report of the Advisory Committee to the Surgeon General,* the first major U.S. report on smoking and health, is published. It concludes that cigarette smoking is a cause of lung cancer in men and a suspected cause in women, and identifies many other causal relationships and smoking–disease associations. The report calls for "appropriate" remedial action.
	• The National Interagency Council on Smoking and Health, the first national antismoking coalition, is formed.
	• Cigarette manufacturers establish a voluntary Cigarette Advertising Code for television and radio.
	• The American Medical Association (AMA) officially calls smoking "a serious health hazard."
	• The State Mutual Life Assurance Company becomes the first company to offer life insurance to nonsmokers at discounted rates.
1965	• Congress passes the Federal Cigarette Labeling and Advertising Act, requiring the following health warning on all cigarette packages: "Caution: Cigarette Smoking May Be Hazardous to Your Health."
	• The Public Health Service (PHS) establishes the National Clearinghouse for Smoking and Health.
1966	• A health warning label appears on all cigarette packages.
1967	• A report of the Surgeon General concludes that smoking is the principal cause of lung cancer.
	• The Federal Communications Commission (FCC) rules that the Fairness Doctrine applies to cigarette advertising. Stations broadcasting cigarette commercials must donate air time to antismoking messages.
	• The Federal Trade Commission (FTC) releases the first report on tar and nicotine yield in cigarette brands.
1968	• Action on Smoking and Health is formed to serve as a legal action arm for the antismoking community.
1969	• The National Association of Broadcasters (NAB) endorses phasing out cigarette ads on television and radio.
1970	• The Public Health Cigarette Smoking Act of 1969 is enacted, banning cigarette advertising on television and radio and requiring a stronger health warning on cigarette packages: "Warning: The Surgeon General Has Determined That Cigarette Smoking Is Dangerous to Your Health."
	• The World Health Organization (WHO) takes a public position against cigarette smoking.
1971	• The Surgeon General proposes a government ban on smoking in public places.
	• Cigarette advertising ends on radio and television. Fairness Doctrine antismoking messages also end.
	• Cigarette manufacturers' voluntary agreement to list tar and nicotine yield in all advertising becomes effective.
1972	• A report of the Surgeon General identifies involuntary smoking as a health risk.
	• Under a consent order with the FTC, six major cigarette companies agree to include a "clear and conspicuous" health warning in all cigarette advertisements.
1973	• Congress enacts the Little Cigar Act of 1973, banning little-cigar ads from television and radio.
	• The Civil Aeronautics Board requires "no smoking" sections on all commercial airline flights.
	• Arizona becomes the first state to restrict smoking in a number of public places and the first to do so explicitly because environmental tobacco smoke exposure is a public hazard.

(continued)

Table 11.1 *(continued)*

1975	• Cigarettes are discontinued in K-rations and C-rations to soldiers and sailors.
1977	• The American Cancer Society (ACS) sponsors the first national "Great American Smokeout."
1978	• The National Clearinghouse for Smoking and Health is renamed the Office on Smoking and Health. • Utah enacts the first state law banning tobacco advertisements on any billboard, streetcar sign, streetcar, or bus.
1979	• Minneapolis and St. Paul become the first cities to ban the distribution of free cigarette samples.
1980	• A report of the Surgeon General highlights the health consequences of smoking to women. • PHS announces "Health Objectives for the Nation," which include a goal to reduce the smoking rate to less than 25% of adults by 1990. • The FTC begins testing cigarettes for carbon monoxide yields.
1981	• A report of the Surgeon General focuses on *The Changing Cigarette.* It concludes that no cigarette or level of tobacco consumption is safe.
1982	• A report of the Surgeon General focuses exclusively on smoking and cancer. • Congress temporarily doubles the federal excise tax on cigarettes to 16 cents per pack, to take effect from January 1, 1983, to October 1, 1985. It marks the first such increase since 1951.
1983	• A report of the Surgeon General focuses exclusively on smoking and cardiovascular disease. • San Francisco passes a law to include smoking restrictions in private workplaces.
1984	• A report of the Surgeon General focuses exclusively on smoking and chronic obstructive lung disease. • Congress enacts the Comprehensive Smoking Education Act, requiring rotation of health warnings on cigarette packages and advertisements. • The FDA approves nicotine polacrilex gum as a "new drug." • The Surgeon General announces his goal of a smoke-free society by 2000.
1985	• A report of the Surgeon General covers smoking and occupational exposures. • Minnesota enacts the first state legislation to earmark a portion of the state cigarette excise tax to support antismoking programs.
1986	• A report of the Surgeon General focuses exclusively on the health consequences of involuntary smoking. • A special report of the Surgeon General documents the health consequences of using smokeless tobacco. • Congress enacts the Comprehensive Smokeless Tobacco Health Education Act of 1986. It requires rotation of three health warnings on smokeless tobacco packages and advertisements and bans smokeless tobacco advertising on broadcast media. • Congress extends permanently the 16 cents per pack federal excise tax on cigarettes. • Californians for Nonsmokers' Rights goes national, becoming Americans for Nonsmokers' Rights. It was originally formed as California GASP (Group Against Smoking Pollution) in 1976. • Minnesota enacts the first state law to ban free distribution of smokeless tobacco samples. • Congress imposes a federal excise tax on smokeless tobacco products.
1987	• The Department of Health and Human Services (DHHS) establishes a smoke-free environment in its facilities, affecting 120,000 DHHS employees nationwide. • The Minnesota Sports Commission votes to ban tobacco advertising in the Metrodome Sports Stadium effective in 1992, the first such action in the United States.

1988	• A report of the Surgeon General concentrates exclusively on nicotine addiction.
	• A congressionally mandated smoking ban takes effect on domestic airline flights scheduled for 2 hours or less. Northwest Airlines voluntarily bans smoking on all flights in North America.
	• ALA sponsors the first annual "Non-Dependence Day."
	• California voters pass a referendum raising the state cigarette excise tax by 25 cents per pack, the largest cigarette excise tax increase in U.S. history. Revenues are earmarked for public health purposes.
1989	• A report of the Surgeon General marks the 25th anniversary of the first *Smoking and Health* report; it focuses on progress since the first report.
1990	• The Environmental Protection Agency (EPA) issues a draft risk assessment on environmental tobacco smoke (ETS).
	• The Office of the Inspector General (OIG), DHHS, issues a report concluding that laws curtailing minors' access to tobacco are ignored. It proposes a minors' access to tobacco law for states.
	• The airline smoking ban goes into effect, banning smoking on all scheduled domestic flights of 6 hours or less.
	• The Secretary of the DHHS denounces "Uptown" cigarettes, a brand to be targeted to blacks; the manufacturer subsequently cancels its plans to market the cigarettes.
1991	• The National Institute for Occupational Safety and Health (OSH), part of the Centers for Disease Control and Prevention (CDC), issues a bulletin recommending that ETS be reduced to the lowest feasible concentration in the workplace.
	• The NCI and the ACS join together in the American Stop Smoking Intervention Study (ASSIST), funding 17 states over a period of 7 years at a cost of $165 million.
	• The federal cigarette excise tax increases to 20 cents.
1992	• The first federal legislation is enacted to require states to adopt and enforce restrictions on tobacco sales to minors. Penalties are to be imposed on state substance abuse funding without proper enforcement.
	• OIG, DHHS, issues a report documenting the widespread use of smokeless tobacco, particularly among young athletes.
	• A transdermal nicotine patch is introduced.
	• The Joint Commission on Accreditation of Healthcare Organizations (JCAHO) requires hospitals to be smoke-free as of January 1994 to maintain accreditation.
	• The FTC takes its first enforcement action under the Smokeless Tobacco Act, alleging that the Pinkerton Tobacco Company's Red Man brand name appeared illegally during a televised event.
	• The World Bank establishes a formal policy on tobacco, including discontinuing loans or investments for tobacco agriculture in developing countries.
1993	• The EPA releases its final risk assessment of ETS, classifying it as a "Group A" carcinogen.
	• Representatives of the tobacco industry file suit against the EPA related to the findings of its ETS risk assessment.
	• The OSH provides tobacco control resources to the remainder of states not funded under project ASSIST.
	• The FDA prohibits over-the-counter smoking-deterrent products because they have not been shown to be effective.
	• The U.S. Postal Service eliminates smoking in all of its facilities.
	• The federal cigarette excise tax increases to 24 cents.
	• Congress enacts a smoke-free policy for Women, Infants and Children (WIC) clinics.

(*continued*)

Table 11.1 (*continued*)

1993	• The Office of the U.S. Trade Representative and DHHS meet to discuss tobacco trade issues, creating the Task Force on Tobacco Exports to review the government's activities involving tobacco trade. • Congress enacts legislation requiring all American cigarettes to contain at least 75% American-grown tobacco and requiring a tariff on imported tobacco to help finance the federal tobacco crop subsidy program. • A working group of 16 state Attorneys General releases recommendations for implementing smoke-free policies in fast-food restaurants.
1994	• A report of the Surgeon General focuses on tobacco use among youth. • Congress enacts the Pro-Children Act of 1994, requiring all federally funded children's services to become smoke-free. • The Occupational Safety and Health Administration (OSHA) announces proposed regulations to prohibit smoking in the workplace, except in separately ventilated smoking rooms. • The six major domestic cigarette manufacturers testify before the U.S. House Subcommittee on Health and the Environment that they do not manipulate the nicotine levels in cigarettes. • FDA Commissioner Kessler testifies that cigarettes may qualify as drug delivery systems, bringing them within the jurisdiction of the FDA. • Mississippi becomes the first state to sue the tobacco industry to recover Medicaid costs for tobacco-related illnesses. • The Department of Defense (DOD) bans smoking in all of its workplaces. • The Robert Wood Johnson Foundation and the AMA launch the Smokeless States grant program to fund local initiatives for tobacco control and prevention.
1995	• *The Journal of the American Medical Association* publishes articles on documents from the Brown and Williamson Tobacco Corporation, indicating the industry's early knowledge of the harmful effects of tobacco use and the addictive nature of nicotine. • The Philip Morris Company recalls its cigarette brands due to the presence of contaminants. The CDC investigates reports of possible health effects. • FDA Commissioner Kessler declares tobacco use to be a pediatric disease. • The Department of Justice reaches a settlement with Philip Morris to remove tobacco advertisements from the line of sight of TV cameras in sports stadiums to ensure compliance with the federal ban on tobacco ads on TV. • The FTC reports that the cigarette industry spent $6 billion on advertising and promotions in 1993.
1996	• The Department of Transportation reports that about 80% of nonstop scheduled U.S. airline flights between the United States and foreign points will be smoke-free by June 1, 1996. • The FDA approves nicotine gum and two nicotine patches for over-the-counter sale. • The AMA calls for divestment of all tobacco stocks and mutual funds. • Philip Morris and U.S. Tobacco Company offer a proposal for federal legislation to ban vending machines, partial-pack sales, free samples to kids, and transit advertisements, among other things, in an effort to avoid FDA regulation of tobacco. • On August 23, 1996, President Clinton announces the nation's first comprehensive program to prevent children and adolescents from smoking cigarettes or using smokeless tobacco and beginning a lifetime of nicotine addiction.

1997	• The Liggett Group reaches a settlement with 22 state Attorneys General who have filed suits to recoup Medicaid costs to treat smoking-related illnesses.
	• Florida and Mississippi reach historic settlements with the tobacco industry to recoup losses related to Medicaid expenditures for tobacco-related illnesses as well as to fund public health programs focusing on tobacco-use reduction.
	• R. J. Reynolds voluntarily removes the highly controversial "Joe Camel" icon from all advertising.
	• Rep. Tom Bliley (R-VA) posts 843 sensitive Liggett documents on the House Commerce Committee web site. About 39,000 previously confidential tobacco industry documents are posted on the House Commerce Committee web site.
1998	• California becomes the first state to ban smoking in bars.
	• R. J. Reynolds's Mangini documents are released that appear to discuss targeting young people as young as 14.
	• *The Journal of the American Medical Association* publishes a major study that links both active and passive smoking with irreversible artery damage.
1999	• Texas settles its Medicaid lawsuit for more than $14 billion.
	• Tobacco executives testify before Congress that nicotine is addictive and smoking may cause cancer.
	• The tobacco industry reaches a $6.1 billion settlement with Minnesota and Blue Cross/Blue Shield. The industry agrees to the dissolution of the Council for Tobacco Research.
	• In the Master Settlement, the Attorneys General of 46 states and 5 territories sign a $206 billion agreement with tobacco companies to settle Medicaid lawsuits.
	• President Clinton issues a memorandum to increase access to, availability of, and research on previously secret tobacco industry documents released as part of the Minnesota and other court cases.
	• The American Legacy Foundation is established as part of the Master Settlement Agreement to develop a public education campaign that promotes tobacco control.
	• Four major tobacco companies agree to set up a $5.15 billion trust fund for growers to compensate them for lost income because of the Attorney General settlement (the National Tobacco Growers' Settlement Trust Fund).
	• The U.S. Department of Justice sues the tobacco industry to recover billions of dollars spent on smoking-related health care, accusing cigarette makers of a "coordinated campaign of fraud and deceit."
	• Philip Morris acknowledges scientific consensus on smoking: "There is an overwhelming medical and scientific consensus that cigarette smoking causes lung cancer, heart disease, emphysema, and other serious diseases in smokers." The Philip Morris web site states "there is no safe cigarette . . . cigarette smoking is addictive, as that term is most commonly used today."
	• Tobacco billboards come down and many are temporarily replaced by pro-health messages paid for by the tobacco industry as part of the Master Settlement Agreement.
2000	• A judge strikes down the portion of the Department of Justice lawsuit against the tobacco companies that deals with recovering Medicare expenses for ill smokers; the federal racketeering suit is allowed to proceed.
	• The Supreme Court rules against the FDA finding that the agency lacks the authority to regulate tobacco.
	• The DHHS releases *Healthy People 2010*, which includes tobacco as a priority area and as one of the 10 leading health indicators.
2001	• A Presidential Commission report makes recommendations on transitions for tobacco farmers.
	• President Clinton issues an Executive Order announcing the U.S. government's leadership on global tobacco control and prevention.

Source: Tobacco Information and Prevention Source, National Center for Chronic Disease Prevention and Health Promotion, Centers for Disease Control and Prevention (26 January 2005). Available http://www.cdc.gov/tobacco/overview/chron96.htm.

(text continued from page 330)

artery (in the neck) that monitor the brain's need for oxygen. It also stimulates the cardiovascular system by releasing epinephrine, which increases coronary blood flow, heart rate, and blood pressure. The effect is to raise the oxygen requirements of the heart muscle. Initially, nicotine stimulates salivary and bronchial secretions; it then inhibits them. The excess saliva associated with smoking is typically caused by the irritating smoke, not the nicotine itself.

Nicotine and perhaps other substances in tobacco smoke tend to inhibit hunger contractions in the stomach for as long as 1 hour. At the same time, this substance causes a slight increase in blood sugar and deadens the taste buds. These factors may explain the decreased feelings of hunger experienced by many smokers. Smokers have often reported that they gain weight after they stop smoking and that their appetite increases. In addition, when someone who smokes one or more packs per day quits, there may be a decrease in heart rate (two to three beats per minute) and as much as a 10% decrease in basal metabolic rate. The body is under less stress; therefore, it converts more food into fat.

Nicotine has been used as an insecticide, and at higher concentrations it can be extremely toxic. Symptoms of nicotine poisoning include sweating, vomiting, mental confusion, diarrhea, and breathing difficulty. Respiratory failure from the paralysis of muscles usually brings on death. The fatal dose for adults is 60 milligrams. Most cigarettes in the U.S. market today contain 10 milligrams or more of nicotine; through smoke, the average smoker takes in 1 to 2 milligrams of nicotine from every cigarette (NIDA 2004). It is virtually impossible to overdose, in part because a smoker feels the effects before any lethal amount can accumulate in the body (Schelling 1992).

Nicotine and other products in smoke, such as carbon monoxide, produce several other effects. As much as 10% of all the hemoglobin in smokers may be in the form of carboxyhemoglobin. This type of hemoglobin cannot carry oxygen, so as much as 10% of the smoker's blood is effectively out of circulation as far as normal oxygen–carbon dioxide exchange is concerned. This situation could easily cause a smoker to become breathless following exertion. It is a factor in heart attacks and in the lower birth-weights and survival rates of infants born to women who smoke during pregnancy (discussed later in this chapter).

CLOVE CIGARETTES

Indonesian **clove cigarettes** were first used by young Americans in the 1980s. In 1980, 12 million clove cigarettes were sold in this country; by 1984, sales had increased to 150 million. The popularity of clove cigarettes has diminished in recent years, however.

The aroma of clove cigarettes masks the negative physical effects of nicotine. As a result, adolescent and adult smokers often assume that these cigarettes are safer than tobacco cigarettes. In truth **eugenol**, the organic chemical that gives the clove its aroma, anesthetizes the back of the throat, reducing the apparent harshness of the smoke and allowing deeper inhalation. Further, these cigarettes consist of more than 60% tobacco and possess a greater amount of tar, nicotine, and carbon monoxide than regular cigarettes manufactured in the United States. Users have reported excessive wheezing, fluid retention in the lungs, and bloody phlegm after smoking clove cigarettes.

KEY TERMS

clove cigarettes
Indonesian aromatic-type cigarettes with more tobacco, tar, nicotine, and carbon monoxide than standard cigarettes in the United States

eugenol
the organic chemical in clove cigarettes that delivers the aroma when inhaled

Cigarette Smoking: A Costly Addiction

MORTALITY RATES

The past 25 years has been marked by a steady decline in cigarette consumption. Still, an estimated 46 million adults in the United States smoke cigarettes (CDC 2004b), even though this single be-havior will result in death or disability for many of its users.

As noted earlier, tobacco use is responsible for more than 440,000 deaths each year in the United States, or 1 in every 5 deaths. This includes ap-proximately 82,000 deaths from heart disease, 125,000 deaths from lung cancer, 31,000 deaths from other forms of cancer, 82,000 deaths from chronic lung disease, 17,000 deaths from stroke, and about 67,000 deaths from other diagnoses (see Figure 11.3). In fact, tobacco use is the lead-ing preventable cause of death in the United States (CDC 2002).

On average, adults who smoke die 13 to 14 years earlier than nonsmokers (CDC 2004a). The death rate increases with the amount smoked: A two-pack-a-day smoker has a mortality rate twice as high as the mortality rate for a nonsmoker. Over-all mortality rates are greater for those who smoke longer; death rates are directly proportional.

Cigarettes have different tar and nicotine con-tents; the effects they produce—and thus the mortality rates—vary as well. Smokers of low-tar and low-nicotine cigarettes have a mortality rate 50% greater than that of nonsmokers but 15% to 20% less than that of cigarette smokers as a group (DeAngelis 1989; U.S. Surgeon General 1981).

Overall mortality rates decline the longer ex-smokers abstain from smoking. People who stop smoking before age 50 reduce their risk of dying over the next 15 years by 50% (NCI 2004). The mortality rate for ex-smokers is related to the num-ber of cigarettes they used to smoke per day and the age at which they started to smoke. The mor-tality rate for cigar smokers is somewhat higher than that for nonsmokers and is related to the number of cigars smoked daily. The mortality rate for pipe smokers is slightly greater than that for nonsmokers.

CHRONIC ILLNESSES

Cigarette smokers not only tend to die at an ear-lier age than nonsmokers, but also have a higher probability of developing certain diseases, includ-ing cardiovascular disease, cancer, and broncho-pulmonary disease.

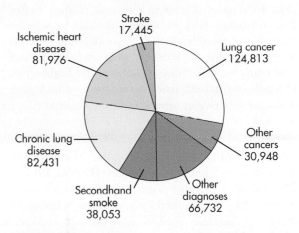

FIGURE 11.3

Annual deaths attributable to cigarette smoking, 1995–1999.

Source: CDC, Tobacco Information and Prevention Source, 2002.

Cardiovascular Disease

Overwhelming evidence shows that cigarette smok-ing increases the risk of cardiovascular disease. In fact, cigarettes caused almost 111,000 deaths per year from cardiovascular disease in the United States during the 1990s (CDC 2004a). Data col-lected for the United States, the United Kingdom, Canada, and other countries show that smoking is a major risk factor for heart attack. The proba-bility of heart attack is related to the amount smoked, which has a synergistic relationship to other risk factors, such as obesity.

Smoking cigarettes is a major risk factor for arteriosclerotic disease and for death from arterio-sclerotic aneurysm of the aorta (Palfai and Jan-kiewicz 1991). (An *aneurysm* is a weakened area in a blood vessel that forms a blood-filled sac and may rupture.) Smokers have a higher incidence of atherosclerosis of the coronary arteries that supply blood to the heart (the arteries become blocked with fat deposits), and the effect is dose-related. Both the carbon monoxide and the nicotine in cigarette smoke can precipitate *angina attacks* (painful spasms in the chest when the heart mus-cle does not get the blood supply it needs).

Smokers of low-tar and low-nicotine cigarettes have less risk of coronary heart disease, but their risk still exceeds that of nonsmokers. The risk goes down if the person quits; after about 10 years, the risk of coronary disease in ex-smokers approaches that in nonsmokers. Recovery time can be shorter or longer based on how long and frequently an individual smoked. Women who smoke and use oral contraceptives have a significantly higher risk of death or disability from stroke, heart attack, and other cardiovascular diseases than nonsmokers.

Cancer

Cigarette smoking is a major cause of cancers of the lung, bladder, pancreas, cervix, and kidney. The risk of cancer increases according to the number of cigarettes smoked each day, the number of years a person has smoked, and the age at which smoking began. For example, the risk of lung cancer in men who smoke two or more packs per day is 22 times greater than the risk for nonsmokers, while the risk for women is approximately 12 times greater (CDC 2004a).

There is no conclusive evidence of reduced health risks associated with low-tar cigarettes. Filtered cigarettes (i.e., those with small holes or perforations that dilute the smoke with air) reduce levels of tar, nicotine, and carbon monoxide at the mouth end of the filter and should be of some limited benefit. However, many smokers lose this benefit because they often smoke more cigarettes per day, increase puff number and volume, or block the filter holes with their fingers or lips (NCI 2001b). (See also "Here and Now," The Truth About "Light" Cigarettes.)

Pipe and cigar smokers are more likely to contract lung cancer than nonsmokers but less likely to do so than habitual cigarette smokers. Common types of cancers among cigar and pipe smokers include cancers of the mouth, larynx, and esophagus. The risk of cancer of the larynx is significantly higher in smokers compared with nonsmokers and is related to the amount smoked. A compounding effect has also been shown to exist between smoking and alcohol consumption and between exposure to asbestos and smoking, which increases a person's likelihood of developing cancer of the larynx. The risk of laryngeal cancer goes down if the person stops smoking; as with lung cancer, however, this form of cancer does not reach the level for nonsmokers until years following cessation.

Bronchopulmonary Disease

Cigarette smoking is the leading cause of bronchopulmonary disease, which includes a host of lung ailments. Cigarette smokers have higher death rates from pulmonary emphysema and chronic bronchitis and have impaired pulmonary function and other symptoms of pulmonary disease more frequently than nonsmokers.

Respiratory infections are more prevalent and more severe among cigarette smokers—particularly heavy smokers—than among nonsmokers. The risk of developing or dying from bronchopulmonary disease is higher among pipe or cigar smokers than nonsmokers but lower than for cigarette smokers. Ex-smokers have lower death rates from bronchopulmonary disease than do continuing smokers.

It is now understood how cigarette smoking causes one of the most common lung diseases, **emphysema**. Smoking produces inflammation of the lung tissue and increases the protein elastase in the tissue. Elastin, a structural material in the lungs, is broken down by the elastase enzyme. In the long run, the lung tissue becomes damaged extensively, causing emphysema (USDHHS 1995; U.S. Surgeon General 1984).

Cigarette smoking is the leading cause of bronchopulmonary disease.

KEY TERMS

emphysema
common type of lung disease often resulting from smoking

Here and Now

The Truth About "Light" Cigarettes

Many smokers choose "low-tar," "mild," or "light" cigarettes because they believe that these cigarettes may be less harmful to their health than "regular" or "full-flavor" cigarettes. Unfortunately, light cigarettes do not reduce the health risks of smoking. The only way to reduce risk to oneself and others is to stop smoking completely.

Common questions and answers pertaining to low-tar, mild, or light cigarettes follow:

Q: What about the lower tar and nicotine numbers on light cigarette packs and in ads for lights?

A: These numbers are determined using smoking machines that smoke every brand of cigarettes exactly the same way. These numbers cannot absolutely predict the amount of tar and nicotine a particular smoker may get because people do not smoke cigarettes the same way the machines do, and because no two individuals smoke the same way.

Q: How do light cigarettes "trick" the smoking machines?

A: Tobacco companies design light cigarettes with tiny pinholes on the filters. These vents are uncovered when cigarettes are smoked on smoking machines. As a result, these vents dilute cigarette smoke with air when light cigarettes are "puffed" on by the machines causing measurements of artificially low tar and nicotine levels. Many smokers do not know that vent holes are on their cigarette filters. Without realizing it and because they cannot avoid it, many block the tiny vent holes with their fingers or lips—which basically turns the light cigarette into a regular cigarette. Cigarette manufacturers can also make the paper wrapped around the tobacco of light cigarettes burn faster so that the smoking machines get in fewer puffs before the cigarettes burn down. The result is that the machine measures less tar and nicotine in the smoke of the cigarette.

Because unlike machines, individuals crave nicotine, they may inhale more deeply; take larger, more rapid, or more frequent puffs, or smoke a few extra cigarettes each day to get enough nicotine to satisfy their craving. This is called "compensating," and results in smokers inhaling more tar, nicotine, and other harmful chemicals than the machine-based numbers suggest.

Q: What is the scientific evidence about the health effects of light cigarettes?

A: The National Cancer Institute (NCI) has concluded that light cigarettes provide no benefit to smokers' health. According to its report, those people who switch to light cigarettes from regular cigarettes are likely to inhale the same amount of hazardous chemicals and remain at high risk for developing smoking-related cancers and other diseases.

Q: What do tobacco companies say about the health effects of light cigarettes?

A: The tobacco industry's own documents show that companies were well aware that smokers of light cigarettes compensate by taking bigger puffs. Industry documents also show that the companies were aware early on of the difference between machine-measured yields of tar and nicotine and the amount the smoker actually inhales. The NCI report concluded that strategies used by the tobacco industry to advertise and promote light cigarettes were intended to reassure smokers, to prevent them from quitting, and to lead consumers to perceive filtered and light cigarettes as safer alternatives to regular cigarettes.

Q: What is the bottom line for smokers who want to protect their health?

A: There is no such thing as a safe cigarette. The only proven way to reduce your risk of smoking-related disease is to quit smoking completely. Smokers who quit before age 50 cut their risk of dying in half over the next 15 years compared with people who keep smoking. Quitting also decreases your risk of lung cancer, heart attacks, stroke, and chronic lung disease.

Source: Adapted from Smoking.gov, a service of the National Cancer Institute, Centers for Disease Control and Prevention, National Institutes of Health, U.S. Department of Health and Human Services, and First Gov. (20 February 2005). Available www.smokefree.gov/lights-qa.html.

Heavy smoking can severely damage the lungs and cause emphysema. Left, a diseased lung due to smoking. Right, a healthy nonsmoker's lung.

EFFECTS WITHOUT SMOKING

The harmful effects of tobacco are not restricted to smokers. For example, women who use tobacco during pregnancy are more likely to have adverse birth outcomes, including babies with low birthweights, which is linked with an increased risk of infant death and with a variety of infant health disorders. Individuals who chew or dip tobacco run the risk of adverse consequences as well. Finally, the health of individuals who neither smoke nor chew is also adversely affected by tobacco—specifically, exposure to **environmental tobacco smoke** (ETS) that is inhaled by passive nonsmokers.

EFFECTS ON THE FETUS

Cigarette smoking during pregnancy has a significantly harmful effect on the development of the fetus, the survival of the newborn infant, and the

KEY TERMS

environmental tobacco smoke
the mixture of predominantly sidestream smoke and exhaled mainstream smoke that is inhaled by the passive smoker

sudden infant death syndrome (SIDS)
unexpected and unexplainable death that occurs while infants are sleeping

continued development of the child. Adverse effects on pregnancy range from increased risk for spontaneous abortion to impaired fetal growth, stillbirth, premature birth, and neonatal death. Babies born to mothers who smoke have a lower average body weight and length and have a smaller head circumference (Bartecchi et al. 1995). The amount a woman smokes affects the size of the child she bears. If a smoking woman gives up this habit for the entire duration of the pregnancy, her child will likely be of normal size and strength.

The below-average weight of babies born to smokers is caused by carbon monoxide and nicotine (Cook et al. 1990). Carbon monoxide reduces the oxygen-carrying capacity of the fetus's blood, just as it does the mother's. Fetal growth is retarded because the tissue becomes starved for oxygen. Inhaled nicotine enters the mother's blood from her lungs and rapidly constricts the blood flow to the placenta, reducing available oxygen and nutrients until the effect of the nicotine has worn off. In addition, nicotine crosses the blood–placenta barrier to reach the fetal bloodstream. It has the same effects on the fetus's nervous system and blood circulation as on the mother's. However, the fetus cannot metabolize nicotine efficiently; therefore, the effects last longer for the child than for the mother.

One known carcinogen in tobacco smoke, benzo(a)pyrene, crosses the placenta and enters the fetal blood. Experiments with pregnant mice exposed to benzo(a)pyrene showed that their offspring had a markedly higher incidence of cancer. The impact of smoking during pregnancy on the in-cidence of cancer in infants is not known. In addition, if the father smokes but the mother does not, the infant may still be affected by secondhand smoke.

Infants born to mothers who smoke have a reduced probability of survival. They are more likely to die from **sudden infant death syndrome (SIDS)** and other causes related to their retarded growth. Long-term effects may be observed in physical growth, mental development, and behavioral characteristics of those babies who survive the early weeks of life.

TOBACCO USE WITHOUT SMOKING

Although it is customary to associate the effects of tobacco use with smoking, in fact millions of non-smokers experience tobacco effects through their use of smokeless tobacco products.

Although a resurgence has occurred in the use of all forms of smokeless tobacco—plug, leaf, and snuff—the greatest cause for concern centers on the increased use of "dipping snuff." **Dipping snuff**, an act of placing tobacco between the gums and cheek, exposes the body to levels of nicotine equal to those obtained with cigarettes. **Chewing tobacco** and **snuff** are two types of smokeless tobacco products that are commonly referred to as "spit tobacco." Both types consist of tobacco leaves that are shredded and twisted into strands and then either chewed or placed in the cheek between the lower lip and gum. In this process, nicotine, along with a number of carcinogens, is absorbed through the oral tissue. In **snuffing**, tobacco is "snorted" instead of being chewed or placed in the cheek.

Smokeless tobacco contains powerful chemicals—including nicotine, nitrosamines, polycyclic aromatic hydrocarbons, and dozens of other carcinogens—that can injure tissues in the mouth and throat. The following findings have been made regarding smokeless tobacco:

- About 10.3 million Americans aged 12 or older used smokeless tobacco in 2003 (SAMHSA 2004).
- In 1986, the U.S. Surgeon General concluded that smokeless tobacco is not a safe substitute for smoking cigarettes for three reasons: (1) It can cause cancer, (2) it can produce a number of noncancerous oral conditions, and (3) it can lead to nicotine addiction and dependence.
- Oral cancer occurs several times more frequently among snuff dippers than among nontobacco users.
- Smokeless tobacco use is much higher among men (6.7%) than women (0.5%) (CDC 2004).
- An estimated 6.7% of high school students are current smokeless tobacco users; 3.7% of middle school users also use smokeless tobacco (CDC 2004c).

The popularity of snuff tobacco is largely due to more effective and persistent advertising campaigns depicting famous athletes using such products. During 2001, the five largest tobacco manufacturers spent $236.7 million on smokeless tobacco advertising and promotion (CDC 2004c). Some experts also believe that the increasing popularity of this tobacco product relates to its ability to satisfy the addiction to nicotine where smoking is prohibited. Thus, snuffing is perceived as an alternative to smoking in smoke-free environments.

How safe are smokeless tobacco products compared with cigarettes? The likelihood of getting oral cancer increases significantly for anyone who uses smokeless tobacco daily for 3.5 years or longer (Perry 1990; USDHHS 1995). Other evidence has shown that continued use of smokeless products can cause cancer of the pharynx and esophagus. The incidence of these cancers is related to the duration of use and the type of product used because "long-term snuff users have a 50% greater risk of developing oral cancer than nonusers" ("Smokeless Tobacco" 1990). Other, less serious effects of using smokeless tobacco include severe inflammation of gum tissue, tooth decay, receding gums, and tooth loss (Giovino et al. 1994; "Smokeless Tobacco" 1990).

In response to these developments, Congress enacted the Comprehensive Smokeless Tobacco Health Education Act of 1986. It requires rotation of three health warnings on smokeless tobacco packages and advertisements and bans smokeless tobacco advertising on broadcasting media.

KEY TERMS

dipping snuff
placing a pinch of smokeless tobacco between the gums and the cheek

chewing tobacco
tobacco leaves shredded and twisted into strands for chewing purposes

snuff
smokeless tobacco

snuffing
snorting chewing tobacco nasally

ENVIRONMENTAL TOBACCO SMOKE

Cigarette smoke drawn through the mouthpiece and inhaled directly from a cigarette is classified as **mainstream smoke**. **Sidestream smoke**, or second-hand smoke, refers to the smoke that comes directly from the lighted tip of a cigarette between puffs. **Passive smoking** refers to nonsmokers' inhalation of tobacco smoke. In addition, the term *ETS* is used to refer to the mixture of predominantly sidestream smoke and exhaled mainstream smoke that is inhaled by the passive smoker.

Studies of smoking and its effects have directed increased attention to sidestream smoke because the burning tobacco smoke that pollutes the air is breathed in by smokers and nonsmokers alike. This type of smoke contains much higher concentrations of some irritating and hazardous substances—such as carbon monoxide, nicotine, and ammonia—than inhaled mainstream smoke. Because it contains more particles of smaller diameter, sidestream smoke is more likely to be deposited deep in the lungs (Bartecchi et al. 1995).

Exposure to ETS causes an estimated 3000 non-smoking Americans to die of lung cancer and causes hundreds of thousands of children to suffer from lower respiratory tract infections each year (CDC 2004d). If several people smoke in an enclosed area, the carbon monoxide level may exceed the safe limit recommended by the Environmental Protection Agency. Under conditions of heavy smoking and poor ventilation, high concentrations of carbon monoxide can occur from sidestream smoke. Carbon monoxide gas is not removed by most standard air filtration systems. It can be diluted only by increasing ventilation with fresh air containing low levels of carbon monoxide. Formation of carbon monoxide can be reduced by increasing the amount of oxygen available during the burning of the tobacco. This goal can be achieved by using perforated cigarette paper and perforated filtertips. Regular and small cigars produce more carbon monoxide than cigarettes because the tobacco leaf wrapper reduces the amount of oxygen available at the burning zone. The levels of carbon monoxide created by smokers may cause nonsmokers with coronary disease to have angina attacks.

Who Smokes?

Given what we know today about the effects of smoking, it can be difficult to understand why people smoke. Lifetime users are understandably addicted; quitting is hard. Following are some recent statistics from SAMHSA (2004) that describe who is smoking:

1. In 2003, an estimated 70.8 million Americans reported current use of a tobacco product. This number gives a rate of 29.8% for the population aged 12 and older.
2. Males were more likely than females to report past-month use of any tobacco product. In 2001, 35.9% of males (ages 12 and older) were current users of any tobacco product compared to 24.0% of females.
3. In regard to smoking and racial and/or ethnic ancestry, American Indians and Alaska Natives were more likely than any other race/ethnicity group to report the past-month use of cigarettes. For past-month use (aged 12 and older), 41.8% of American Indians and Alaska Natives reported using at least one form of tobacco. The lowest current tobacco use rates were observed for Asians (13.8%).
4. Level of educational attainment was correlated with tobacco usage. The prevalence of past-month cigarette smoking decreased with increasing levels of education. College graduates were the least likely to report they smoked cigarettes (12.9%) compared with 29.4% of young adults aged 26 years and older with only a high school diploma and 32.2% of persons who lacked a high school diploma.

KEY TERMS

mainstream smoke
smoke drawn directly through the mouthpiece of a cigarette

sidestream smoke
smoke released into the air from a lighted cigarette

passive smoking
nonsmoker's inhalation of tobacco smoke

REASONS FOR SMOKING

Nicotine dependency through cigarette smoking is not only the most common form of drug addiction, but also the one that causes more deaths and disease than all other addictions combined (USDHHS 1994). Tobacco use continues despite the fact that, since the 1960s, medical research and government assessments have clearly proved that smoking leads to premature death.

If one asks tobacco users why they smoke, their answers are often quite similar:

1. It is relaxing.
2. It decreases the unpleasant effects of tension, anxiety, and anger.
3. It satisfies the craving.
4. It is a habit.
5. It provides stimulation, increased energy, and arousal.
6. It allows the manipulation of objects that have become satisfying habits (the cigarette, pipe, and so on).

In addition,

7. Female high school students smoke to lose weight (Rovner 1991; Wentz 1993).
8. Parents and/or siblings smoke (Rovner 1991; Wentz 1993).
9. A close friend or boyfriend/girlfriend smokes (USDHHS 1994).

Tobacco use fosters dependence for a number of reasons:

1. The habit can be rapidly and frequently reinforced by inhaling tobacco smoke (about 10 reinforcements per cigarette, or 200 with one pack).
2. The rapid metabolism and clearance of nicotine allows frequent and repeated use, which is encouraged by the rapid onset of withdrawal symptoms.
3. Smoking has complex pharmacological effects—both central and peripheral—that may satisfy a variety of the needs of the smoker.
4. Some groups offer psychological and social rewards for use, especially the peer groups of young people.

5. Smoking patterns can be generalized; that is, the smoker becomes conditioned to smoke with specific activities. For example, some smokers feel the need to smoke after a meal, when driving, and so on.
6. Smoking is reinforced by both pharmacological effects and ritual.
7. There is no marked performance impairment. In fact, smoking enhances performance in some cases. (Nicotine produces a state of alertness, prevents deterioration of reaction time, and improves learning.)

These reasons may not only explain why people continue to smoke, but also reveal why it is often difficult for them to stop (USDHHS 1994).

Smokers appear to regulate their intake of nicotine. For example, the smoker of a low-nicotine cigarette is likely to smoke more and inhale more deeply. The average one-pack-a-day smoker is estimated to self-administer thousands of pulses (one pulse per inhalation) of nicotine to specific nicotinic receptors in the brain per year. This rate greatly surpasses the stimulation rate of any other known form of substance abuse. A habit that is reinforced as frequently and easily as smoking is very hard to break.

Other factors responsible for creating the addiction to nicotine follow:

1. Cigarettes are readily available.
2. No equipment other than a lighter or match is needed.
3. Cigarettes are portable and easy to store.
4. Cigarettes are legal for individuals over age 18.
5. Other rewarding behaviors can occur while smoking (for example, drinking, socializing, and eating).

The Motivation Not to Smoke

When habitual smokers stop smoking on their own, without the use of smoking cessation aids, they may experience a variety of unpleasant withdrawal effects, including craving for tobacco, irritability, restlessness, sleep disturbances, gastrointestinal disturbances, anxiety, and impaired concentration, judgment, and psychomotor performance. The onset of nicotine withdrawal symptoms may occur within hours or days after quitting and may persist from a few days to several months. Frustration over these symptoms leads many people to start smoking again. The intensity of withdrawal effects may be mild, moderate, or severe; it is not always correlated with the amount smoked.

Research shows that smoking cessation should be a gradual process because this type of withdrawal eliminates the severe symptoms of craving for nicotine. According to the National Institute on Drug Abuse, "rates of relapse are highest in the first few weeks and months and diminish considerably after three months" (NIDA 1995; see Figure 11.4). The optimal treatment for smoking cessation also includes behavioral therapies (NIDA 1995). Behavioral modification treatments report 33% long-term abstinence with 50% recidivism. "Studies have shown that pharmacological treatment combined with psychological treatment, including psychological support and skill training to overcome high-risk situations, result in some of the highest long-term abstinence rates" (NIDA 1995).

ALTERNATIVE ACTIVITIES FOR SUCCESSFULLY QUITTING

The American Cancer Society has developed a list of alternative activities that the new ex-smoker might try as aids to get through the withdrawal period. When the craving for a cigarette arises, the smoker may engage in these behaviors:

- Nibble on fruit, celery, or carrots.
- Chew gum or spices such as ginger, cinnamon bark, or cloves.
- Use replacements in conjunction with quitting smoking, such as the nicotine patch or nicotine gum. (Such cessation smoking aids are discussed in greater detail in the next section.)
- Perform moderately strenuous physical activity, such as bicycling, jogging, or swimming (if the person's heart and lungs are not too badly damaged from smoking).
- Spend as much time as possible in places where smoking is prohibited, such as movie theaters, libraries, and other smoke-free environments.
- Associate with nonsmokers for long periods of time.

SMOKING CESSATION AIDS

Quitting smoking is easy. I've done it a thousand times.

—*Mark Twain*

There is no one "right" way to quit this habit. Successful cessation may include one or a combination of methods, including using step-by-step manuals, attending self-help classes or counseling, or using nicotine replacement therapy. A number of stop smoking aids are currently available, and they are discussed next.

Nicotine Gum

Nicotine gum can be purchased over-the-counter without a prescription. Chewing the gum allows the rapid absorption of nicotine through the mucous membranes of the mouth. Users chew the gum until noting a "peppery taste," and then hold it against the cheek to permit faster absorption. The user will chew on and off for about 20 to 30 minutes. Because food and drink can affect nicotine absorption, package instructions indicate that the user should avoid acidic foods and drinks such as soft drinks, coffee, or juices for at least 15 minutes before and during gum use.

Significant advantages afforded by nicotine gum are that it is easy to use and allows the user to control the dose of nicotine by controlling the number of pieces chewed each day. Nicotine gum is usually recommended for 1 to 3 months, with the maximum being 6 months. Individuals gradually decrease the number of pieces chewed each day, with a goal of complete abstinence from the drug. Side effects of the gum can include a bad taste, throat irritation, nausea (if the gum is swallowed), jaw discomfort (if chewed too rapidly), and racing heartbeat.

Nicotine Patches

Nicotine patches, also known as *transdermal nicotine systems,* are available without a prescription. The patch, which is directly applied and worn on the skin, releases a continuous flow of small doses of nicotine to quell the desire for cigarette-provided nicotine. The method of delivering nicotine to the skin reduces the withdrawal symptoms as the smoker attempts to quit. As the nicotine

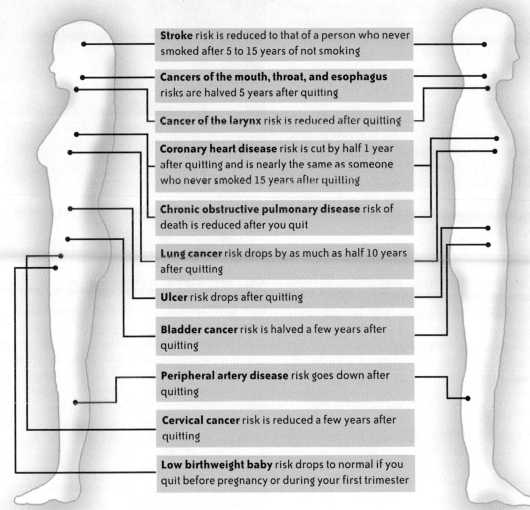

Compared to smokers, your . . .

Stroke risk is reduced to that of a person who never smoked after 5 to 15 years of not smoking

Cancers of the mouth, throat, and esophagus risks are halved 5 years after quitting

Cancer of the larynx risk is reduced after quitting

Coronary heart disease risk is cut by half 1 year after quitting and is nearly the same as someone who never smoked 15 years after quitting

Chronic obstructive pulmonary disease risk of death is reduced after you quit

Lung cancer risk drops by as much as half 10 years after quitting

Ulcer risk drops after quitting

Bladder cancer risk is halved a few years after quitting

Peripheral artery disease risk goes down after quitting

Cervical cancer risk is reduced a few years after quitting

Low birthweight baby risk drops to normal if you quit before pregnancy or during your first trimester

FIGURE 11.4
The Benefits of Quitting
After quitting, the body begins a series of changes that
continue for years.

Source: Centers for Disease Control and Prevention.

doses are lowered over a course of weeks, the smoker is weaned away from nicotine. The most common side effects are mild skin irritations such as redness and itching.

Nicotine Nasal Spray

Nicotine nasal sprays are available by prescription only. This form of administration rapidly delivers nicotine to the bloodstream as it is absorbed through the membranous lining of the nasal passages. It is easy to use and gives immediate relief of withdrawal symptoms. It is recommended for periods no longer than 6 months, tapering the dose at the end of 3 months. The most common side effects of using the spray include coughing, sinus irritation, runny nose, watery eyes, sneezing, and throat irritation. It is generally not recommended for individuals with asthma, allergies, or other pulmonary problems.

Nicotine Inhalers

Like nicotine nasal sprays, nicotine inhalers are only available by prescription. The nicotine inhaler is a small plastic tube that contains a nicotine plug. When the user puffs on the inhaler, the plug provides nicotine vapor into the mouth. One advantage to the inhaler is that the action of puffing it mimics some of the behaviors associated with smoking. Side effects associated with its use include coughing and throat irritation.

Bupropion

Bupropion is an antidepressant medication available only by prescription. In many individuals, this drug reduces symptoms of nicotine withdrawal. Individuals typically use the drug for 7 to 12 weeks, although the duration of therapy is generally individualized to the particular patient. Bupropion can be used alone or in combination with nicotine replacement therapies as just described.

KEY TERMS

gateway drug
drug whose use leads to the use of other drugs; alcohol, cigarettes, and marijuana are considered gateway drugs

patterns of behavior
consistent and related behaviors that occur together, such as marijuana use and euphoria, alcohol abuse and intoxication

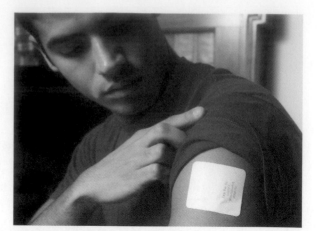

A transdermal patch, an example of a popular remedy for quitting smoking.

Social Issues: Looking to the Future

TOBACCO AS A GATEWAY DRUG

Recently, several research findings have indicated that tobacco is more of a serious **gateway drug** than previously expected. For example, nearly all heroin addicts initially began using gateway drugs such as alcohol and/or tobacco products. (Granted, most people who drink alcohol and use tobacco do not become heroin addicts.)

Biochemical evidence proving that the use of gateway drugs leads to the abuse of other substances is weak. However, some findings are quite interesting. "The decisions to use tobacco or other gateway drugs set up **patterns of behavior** that make it easier for a user to go on to other drugs" ("Nonsmoking Youth" 1991). In other words, smokers have developed the behavioral patterns that may lead them to experiment with and use other licit and illicit drugs.

Research indicates that cigarette smokers are more likely to use alcohol, marijuana, and cocaine than are nonsmokers (Giovino et al. 1994). Figure 11.5 shows a strong association between cigarette smoking and the use of illicit drugs and alcohol by 12- to 17-year-old smokers. "[I]n the 12- through 17-year-old group . . . those who smoked daily were approximately 14 times more likely to have binged on alcohol, 114 times more likely to have used marijuana at least 11 times, and 32 times more likely to have used cocaine at least 11 times than those who had not smoked" (USDHHS 1994, p. 36). Other studies have shown similar relationships between cigarette smoking and the prevalence of other drug use.

SMOKING PROHIBITION VERSUS SMOKERS' RIGHTS

In response to the percentage of the U.S. population that has effectively banned smoking from certain public facilities, people who desire to continue smoking have formed action groups to press their right to smoke. Through mailing lists, newsletters, and magazine promotions, the groups advocate and report on the following issues:

- How the rights of smokers have been eroded in public and private places
- How to write to members of Congress and other political leaders to urge them to uphold smokers' rights

- How to lobby effectively for smoking in the workplace
- How the harmful effects of secondhand smoke have been exaggerated or remain unproven
- How people who enjoy smoking have won major battles, preserving their right to smoke

Although some modest gains have been made by these groups, the trend toward restricting and banning cigarette smoking remains very strong. Antismoking groups have been highly successful in their own efforts, and restrictions on the sale of cigarettes and tobacco products remain very tight. The four primary aspects of tobacco control laws in each state are smoke-free indoor air, youth access to tobacco products, advertising of tobacco products, and excise taxes on tobacco products.

Smoke-Free Indoor Air

As of 1999, 45 states and the District of Columbia required some variation of smoke-free indoor air. Forty-one states and the District of Columbia limit smoking in state government worksites. In contrast, only 20 states have laws that restrict smoking in private workplaces. Many states have laws that

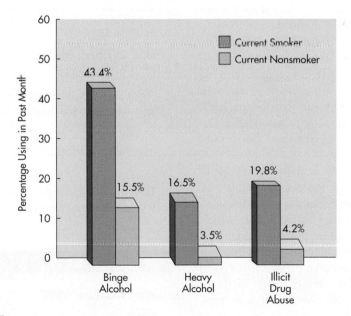

FIGURE 11.5

Use of illicit drugs and alcohol by smokers and nonsmokers, 2003.

Source: Substance Abuse and Mental Health Services Administration. (2004). *Results from the 2003 National Survey on Drug Use and Health: National Findings* (Office of Applied Studies, NSDUH Series H–25, DHHS Publication No. SMA 04–3964). Rockville, MD.

regulate smoking in restaurants, and some have laws that regulate smoking in other locations, such as day-care centers, hospitals, public transportation facilities, grocery stores, and enclosed arenas.

Youth Access to Tobacco

All 50 states have enacted laws that restrict the purchase, possession, or use of tobacco products by minors. Although no state has completely banned the sale of tobacco products through vending machines, none allows such sales to minors. In fact, many states have created additional restrictions intended to reduce youth access to vending machines. Some have banned the placement of vending machines in areas accessible to young people and allow their placement only in bars, liquor stores, adult clubs, and other adult-oriented establishments.

Licensing

Thirty-seven states and the District of Columbia require some form of retail licensure for the sale of tobacco products.

Taxing Cigarettes

All states tax cigarettes. In 2002, this tax ranged from less than 25¢ in 16 states to more than 50¢ per pack in 25 states. In addition, smokeless tobacco products are taxed in 42 states. Thus, statewide enforcement, preemptive legislation (legislation prohibiting any local jurisdiction from enacting reductions that are more stringent than the state law or restrictions that may vary from state law), court decisions, and federal legislation all influence and control the impact of state tobacco control legislation.

In short, the willingness of nonsmokers to speak up as firmly as necessary against smoking and exposure to secondhand smoke has inspired restrictive legislation against tobacco use, which in turn affects smoking habits. As stated earlier, a complete network of laws defines, controls, and restricts smoking, from the purchase of tobacco to the consumption of cigarettes or other types of tobacco products, such as smokeless and pipe tobacco, cigars, and the like.

Several organized groups of nonsmokers have made quite an impact, including Action on Smoking and Health (ASH), the Group Against Smokers' Pollution (GASP), the American Lung Association, the American Cancer Society, and medical and dental associations. These groups have been instrumental in passing legislation restricting or banning smoking in public places; banning cigarette commercials on television; and prohibiting smoking on commercial aircraft, on interstate buses, and in some restaurants, elevators, indoor theaters, libraries, art galleries, and museums.

Discussion Questions

1. If smoking is the most preventable cause of disease and premature death in the United States, why do people continue to smoke?

2. How effective are the health warning labels on cigarette packages? Interview two or three smokers about these warning labels.

3. List and define the diseases that cigarette smokers are most likely to contract.

4. What effects do cigarettes have on the fetus?

5. Why is smokeless tobacco perceived as safer than other forms of tobacco?

6. Who is most likely to smoke, and why?

7. Why do people who smoke become dependent on tobacco?

8. As tobacco markets in the United States have shrunk, what has happened abroad?

9. Assess the major methods for quitting smoking. Which methods are most likely to succeed?

10. Do you think smokers should have the right to smoke in public places? Explain.

Key Terms

Nicotiana tabacum   326

bright, flue-cured or Virginia   327

puffing   328

Summary

1 Nicotine is by far one of the most addictive drugs.

2 Approximately 29.8% of the U.S. population aged 12 and older reports current use of a tobacco product.

3 The quality of leaf tobacco has changed throughout the years of production. Since 1956, the amount of leaf tobacco in a cigarette has declined by approximately 25%. Most cigarettes today are low-tar and low-nicotine types.

4 Nicotine is the substance in tobacco that causes dependence. This drug initially stimulates and then depresses the nervous system.

5 The amount of tobacco absorbed varies according to five factors: (1) the exact composition of tobacco being used; (2) how densely the tobacco is packed in the cigarette and the length of the cigarette smoked; (3) whether a filter is used and the characteristics of the filter; (4) the volume of the smoke inhaled; and (5) the number of cigarettes smoked throughout the day.

6 Cigarette smoking is an addiction that is costly in several ways. For instance, each year 440,000 deaths in the United States are attributed to cigarette smoking.

7 Chewing tobacco and snuff are types of smokeless tobacco products that are commonly referred to as "spit tobacco." Both types consist of tobacco leaves that are shredded and twisted into strands and then either chewed or placed in the cheek between the lower lip and gum.

8 Research clearly shows that the tar and nicotine content of cigarettes affects mortality rates. Cigarette smokers tend to die at an earlier age than nonsmokers. They also have a greater probability of contracting various illnesses, including types of cancers, chronic bronchitis and emphysema, diseases of the cardiovascular system, and peptic ulcers. In addition, smoking has adverse effects on pregnancy and may harm the fetus.

9 Cigarette smoke is classified as either mainstream smoke, the smoke drawn directly through the mouthpiece of the cigarette, or sidestream smoke. Passive smoking refers to nonsmokers' inhalation of tobacco smoke. The term *environmental tobacco smoke* (*ETS*) is widely used to refer to the mixture of predominantly sidestream and exhaled mainstream smoke that is inhaled by the passive smoker.

10 The four primary aspects of tobacco-control laws in each state are smoke-free indoor air, youth access to tobacco products, advertising of tobacco products, and excise taxes on tobacco products.

References

Austin, G. A. *Perspectives on the History of Psychoactive Substance Use.* Washington, DC: National Institute on Drug Abuse, 1978.

Bartecchi, C. E., T. D. MacKenzie, and R. W. Shrier. "The Global Tobacco Epidemic." *Scientific American* (May 1995): 49.

"How Smoking Kills You." *Parade Magazine* 213 (December 1987): 209–211.

Centers for Disease Control and Prevention (CDC), "SAMMEC." *Morbidity and Mortality Weekly Report* 51 (2002): 300–303. Available www.cdc.gov/tobacco/overview/attradths.htm.

CDC. "Tobacco Use in the United States" (2003). Available http://www.cdc.gov/tobacco/overview/tobus_us.htm.

CDC. Tobacco Information and Prevention Source. "Tobacco-Related Mortality Fact Sheet" (February 2004a). Available www.cdc.gov/tobacco/factsheets/Tobacco_Related_Mortality_Factsheet.htm.

CDC. Tobacco Information and Prevention Source. "Adult Cigarette Smoking in the United States: Current Estimates" (May 2004b). Available www.cdc.gov/tobacco/factsheets/AdultCigaretteSmoking_FactSheet.htm.

CDC. Tobacco Information and Prevention Source. "Smokeless Tobacco Factsheet" (July 2004c). Available www.cdc.gov/tobacco/factsheets/smokelesstobacco.htm.

CDC. Tobacco Information and Prevention Source. "Secondhand Smoke Factsheet" (February 2004d). Available www.cdc.gov/tobacco/factsheets/secondhand_smoke_factsheet.htm.

CDC. Tobacco Information and Prevention Source (26 January 2005). Available at http://www.cdc.gov/tobacco/issue.htm.

"Cigars." *Encyclopedia Americana*. Danbury, CT: Grolier, 1988.

Cook, P. S., R. C. Petersen, and D. T. Moore. *Alcohol, Tobacco, and Other Drugs May Harm the Unborn*. Rockville, MD: U.S. Department of Health and Human Services, 1990.

Corti, E. C. *A History of Smoking*. London: Harrap and Company, 1931.

DeAngelis, T. "Behavior Is Included in Report on Smoking." *APA Monitor* 20 (1989): 1, 4.

Economic Research Service, USDA. "Briefing Room: Tobacco" (9 January 2004). Available http://www.ers.usda.gov/briefing/tobacco.

Federal Trade Commission (FTC). "Cigarette Report for 1999." (2001). Available www.ftc.gov/reports/cigarettes/1999cigarettereport.pdf.

Giovino, G. A., M. W. Schooley, B. P. Zhu, J. H. Chrismon, S. L. Tambour, and J. P. Peddicord. "Trends and Recent Patterns in Selected Tobacco-Use Behaviors. Surveillance Summary." *Morbidity and Mortality Weekly Report* 43 (SS-3) (1994): 1–43.

Heimann, R. K. *Tobacco and Americans*. New York: McGraw-Hill, 1960.

Langton, P. A. *Drug Use and the Alcohol Dilemma*. Boston: Allyn and Bacon, 1991.

Master Settlement Agreement Between the Settling States of the United States of America and the Participating Tobacco Manufacturers (1998).

National Cancer Institute (NCI). "Environmental Tobacco Smoke." (2000). Available http://cis.nci.nih.gov/fact/3_9.htm.

National Cancer Institute (NCI). "Research on Tobacco and Tobacco-Related Cancers" (2001a). Available http://plan.cancer.gov/public/tobacco.htm.

National Cancer Institute (NCI). (2001b). "Questions and Answers for Monograph 13: Risks Associated with Smoking Cigarettes with Low Machine-Measured Yields of Tar and Nicotine." Available http://www.cancer.gov/newscenter/lowtar QA.

National Cancer Institute (NCI). "Cancer Facts" (4 November 2004a). Available http://cis.nci.nih.gov/fact/10-14.htm.

National Cancer Institute (NCI). "Tobacco Statistics Snapshot." (26 November 2004b). Available: http//www.cancer.gov/cancertopics/tobacco/statistics snapshot.

National Institute on Drug Abuse (NIDA). *Cigarette Smoking*. CAP 42. Rockville, MD: National Institute on Drug Abuse, January 1995.

National Institute on Drug Abuse (NIDA). NIDA Research Report—Nicotine Addiction. (7 December 2004). Available www.nida.nih.gov/reserachreports/nicotine/nicotine.html.

"Non-smoking Youth Better Resist Other Drugs." *Prevention Newsline* (Spring 1991): 5.

O'Brien, R., S. Cohen, G. Evans, and J. Fine. *The Encyclopedia of Drug Abuse*, 2nd ed. New York: Facts on File and Greenspring, 1992.

Palfai, T., and H. Jankiewicz. *Drugs and Human Behavior*. Dubuque, IA: Brown, 1991.

Perry, S. "Recognizing Everyday Addicts." *Current Health* 2 (May 1990): 20–23.

Rovner, S. "Up in Smoke: Why Do So Many Kids Ignore All the Evidence Condemning Cigarettes?" *Washington Post, National Weekly Edition* (16–22 December 1991): 20–21.

Schelling, T. C. "Addictive Drugs: The Cigarette Experience." *Science* (24 January 1992): 430–433.

Schultes, R. E. "Ethnopharmacological Significance of Psychotropic Drugs of Vegetal Origin." In *Principles of Psychopharmacology*, 2nd ed., edited by W. G. Clark and J. del Giudice, 41–70. New York: Academic Press, 1978.

"Smokeless Tobacco, Think Before You Chew." (Leaflet). Chicago: American Dental Association, 1990.

Substance Abuse and Mental Health Services Administration (SAMHSA). *Results from the 2003 National Household Survey on Drug Abuse and Health: National Findings.* NSDUH Series H-25, DHHS Publication No. SMA 04-3964. Rockville, MD: Office of Applied Studies, 2004.

U.S. Department of Health and Human Services (USDHHS). *Preventing Tobacco Use Among Young People: A Report of the Surgeon General.* Atlanta: USDHHS, Public Health Service, Centers for Disease Control and Prevention, National Center for Chronic Disease Prevention and Health Promotion, Office on Smoking and Health, 1994.

U.S. Department of Health and Human Services (USDHHS). *Tobacco-Control Activities in the United States, 1992–1993: Biennial Report to Congress.* Atlanta, GA: USDHHS, Public Health Service, Centers for Disease Control and Prevention, National Center for Chronic Disease Prevention and Health Promotion, Office on Smoking and Health, 1995.

U.S. Department of Health and Human Services (USDHHS) and Centers for Disease Control and Prevention (CDC). "Current Trends: Mortality Trends for Selected Smoking-Related Cancers and Breast Cancer—United States 1950–1990." *Morbidity and Mortality Weekly Report* 12 (12 November 1993): 863–866.

U.S. Surgeon General. *The Changing Cigarette.* Publication No. PHS 81-51056. Washington, DC: U.S. Department of Health, Education, and Welfare, 1981.

U.S. Surgeon General. *The Health Consequences of Smoking.* Washington, DC: U.S. Department of Health, Education and Welfare, 1984.

U.S. Surgeon General. *The Health Consequences of Smoking: Cancer and Chronic Lung Disease in the Workplace.* Washington, DC: U.S. Government Printing Office, 1985.

Wentz, C. "22.2 Million American Women Just Don't Get It" (editorial). *Journal of Women's Health* 3 (4 November 1993): 127–128.

World Health Organization (WHO). Tobacco Free Initiative (2005). Available http://who.int/tobacco/health_priority/en/.

CHAPTER 12

Hallucinogens (Psychedelics)

Did You Know?

- Many ancient mystics used hallucinogens as part of their religious ceremonies.
- Hallucinogens were abused by relatively few people in the United States until the social upheaval of the 1960s.
- The Native American Church in the United States has special permission from the federal government to use the psychedelic mescaline as part of its religious sacrament.
- Some hallucinogens—such as LSD, MDA, and Ecstasy—have been used by psychiatrists to assist in psychotherapy with certain patients.
- Hallucinogens such as LSD do not tend to be physically addicting.
- The senses are grossly exaggerated and distorted under the influence of hallucinogens.
- Ecstasy abuse increased dramatically from 1996 to 2000 due to its popularity as a "club drug" and its use at "rave" parties, but recently its abuse appears to have diminished.

- For some users, hallucinogens can cause frightening, nightmarish experiences called *bad trips.*
- Phencyclidine (PCP) was originally developed as a general anesthetic, but because of its ability to cause psychosis it is no longer prescribed for use in humans.
- PCP is sometimes used as an additive in "street" hallucinogens.
- Intense use of PCP can cause psychotic episodes, making management of users by medical or law enforcement personnel very dangerous.
- Ketamine is related to PCP, was also developed as a general anesthetic, and is still used in children.

On completing this chapter you will be able to:

◎ Explain why hallucinogens became so popular during the 1960s.

◎ Describe how hallucinogens alter the senses.

◎ Outline how psychedelic, stimulant, and anticholinergic effects are expressed in the three principal types of hallucinogens.

◎ Describe why some psychotherapists believe that using MDMA for their patients may be beneficial.

◎ Explain the reason for Ecstasy's most recent popularity.

◎ Explain how hallucinogens differ from other commonly abused drugs in terms of their addicting properties and their ability to cause dependence.

◎ Describe the effects that environment and personality have on the individual's response to hallucinogens.

◎ Explain the term *club drugs* and describe their particular problems.

◎ Characterize how PCP differs from other hallucinogens.

◎ Explain the similarities between PCP and ketamine.

Drugs and Society Online is a great source for additional drugs and society information for both students and instructors.
Visit **http://drugsandsociety.jbpub.com** to find a variety of useful tools for learning, thinking, and teaching.

Introduction

I was doing acid [LSD] on Thanksgiving. The turkey begged my Dad not to carve it. Another time my James Dean poster told me to kill myself and I wasn't worth living. So I tried.
(From Venturelli's files, Val, age 17, 1996.)

This quote from a young adult illustrates the sensory and emotional distortions that can be caused by using hallucinogens. In this chapter, we begin with a brief historical review of the use of hallucinogens, tracing the trend in the United States from the 1960s to today. Next, the nature of hallucinogens and the effects they produce are examined. The rest of the chapter addresses the various types of psychedelic agents: LSD types, phenylethylamines (including Ecstasy), anticholinergics, and other miscellaneous substances.

The History of Hallucinogen Use

People have known and written about drug-related hallucinations for centuries. Throughout the ages, individuals who saw visions or experienced hallucinations were perceived as being holy or sacred, as receiving divine messages, or possibly as being bewitched and controlled by the devil. There are many indications that medicine men, shamans, witches, oracles, and perhaps mystics and priests of various groups were familiar with drugs and herbs that caused such experiences and today are known as **hallucinogens** (Research Report 2001).

Protests against the Vietnam War in the 1960s and 1970s often included the use of hallucinogens.

Before the 1960s, several psychedelic substances, such as mescaline from the peyote cactus, could be obtained from chemical supply houses with no restriction in the United States. Abuse of hallucinogens did not become a major social problem in this country until this decade of racial struggles, the Vietnam War, and violent demonstrations. Many individuals frustrated with the hypocrisy of "the establishment" tried to "turn on and tune in" by using hallucinogens as pharmacological crutches.

Psychedelic drugs became especially popular when some medical professionals such as then-Harvard psychology professor, Timothy Leary, reported that these drugs allowed users to get in touch with themselves and achieve a peaceful inner serenity (Associated Press 1999). At the same time, it became well publicized that the natural **psychedelics** (such as mescaline and peyote) were and had been for many years used routinely by some religious organizations of Native Americans for enhancing spiritual experiences. This factor contributed to the mystical, supernatural aura associated with hallucinogenic agents and added to their enticement for the so-called dropout generation.

With widespread use of LSD, it was observed that this and similar drugs may induce a form of psychosis-like schizophrenia (*DSM-IV-TR* 2000). The term **psychotomimetic** was coined to describe these compounds; it means "psychosis mimicking" and is still used in medicine today. The basis for the designation is the effects of these drugs that

KEY TERMS

hallucinogens
substances that alter sensory processing in the brain, causing perceptual disturbances, changes in thought processing, and depersonalization

psychedelics
substances that expand or heighten perception and consciousness

psychotomimetic
substances that cause psychosis-like symptoms

induce mental states that impair an individual's ability to recognize and respond appropriately to reality.

By the mid-1960s, federal regulatory agencies had become concerned with the misuse of hallucinogens and the potential emotional damage caused by these drugs. Access to hallucinogenic agents was restricted, and laws against their distribution were passed. Despite the problems associated with these psychedelics, some groups demanded that responsible use was possible and that they be allowed legal access to these substances.

THE NATIVE AMERICAN CHURCH

The hallucinogen peyote plays a central role in the ceremonies of Native Americans who follow a religion that is a combination of Christian doctrine and Native American religious rituals. Members of this church are found as far north as Canada. They believe that God made a special gift of this sacramental plant to them so that they might commune more directly with Him. The first organized peyote church was the First-Born Church of Christ, incorporated in 1914 in Oklahoma. The Native American Church of the United States was chartered in 1918 and is the largest such group at present (approximately 100,000–200,000 members).

Because of the religious beliefs of the members of the Native American Church concerning the

Timothy Leary advocated legalization of LSD in the 1960s.

powers of peyote, when Congress legislated against its use in 1965, it allowed room for religious use of this psychedelic plant. The American Indian Religious Freedom Act of 1978 was an attempt by Congress to allow the members of the Native American Church access to peyote due to constitutional guarantees of religious freedom. Due to controversy inspired by the original piece of legislation, an amendment to the 1978 act was signed in 1994, which specifically protected the use of peyote in Native American Church ceremonies. This amendment also prohibits use of peyote for nonreligious purposes (Associated Press 2003; Mims 2000). However, despite these efforts by Congress to resolve this issue, controversies continue to arise (see "Case in Point," Peyote and the Rights of Native Americans: How Far Should It Go?).

TIMOTHY LEARY AND THE LEAGUE OF SPIRITUAL DISCOVERY

In 1966, 3 years after being fired by Harvard because of his controversial involvement with hallucinogens (Associated Press 1999), Timothy Leary undertook a constitutional strategy intended to retain legitimate access to another hallucinogen, LSD. He began a religion called the League of Spiritual Discovery; LSD was the sacrament. This unorthodox religious orientation to the LSD experience was presented in a manual called *The Psychedelic Experience* (Leary et al. 1964), which

Peyote is used as a sacramental plant by members of the Native American Church as part of their religious ceremonies.

►Case in Point   Peyote and the Rights of Native Americans: How Far Should It Go?

Jonathan Fowler, a member of the Grand Traverse Band of Ottawa and Chippewa Indians, requested a judge allow his 4-year-old son to ingest peyote with him, as part of a religious ritual at the Native American Church of the Morning Star. The boy's mother opposed the request, fearing potential neurological damage to the boy. Although the use of peyote in Native American rituals is legal in all 50 states, the judge ruled against Fowler, stating that the boy could use peyote when he becomes old enough to comprehend its effects and with permission from both parents. Several Native American congregations who use peyote already have age limitations indicating who can take the substance during religious rites.

Source: "Court Says No Peyote for Native American Boy" (22 April 2003). Available www.cognitiveliberty.org/dll/peyote_boy.html.

was based on the *Tibetan Book of the Dead.* It became the "bible" of the psychedelic drug movement.

The movement grew, but most members used "street" LSD and did not follow Leary's directions. Leary believed that the hallucinogenic experience was only beneficial under proper control and guidance. But most members of this so-called religion merely used the organization as a front to gain access to an illegal drug. Federal authorities did not agree with Leary's freedom of religion interpretation and in 1969 convicted him for possession of marijuana and LSD and sentenced him to 20 years imprisonment (Stone 1991). Before being incarcerated, Leary escaped to Algeria and wandered for a couple of years before being extradited to the United States. He served several years in jail and was released in 1976.

Even in his later years, Leary continued to believe that U.S. citizens should be able to use hallucinogens without government regulation. He died in 1996 at the age of 75 years, revered by some but despised by others (Associated Press 1999; "Many Were Lost" 1996).

Hallucinogen Use Today

Today, the use of hallucinogens (excluding marijuana) is primarily a young-adult phenomenon (Johnston 1999). Although the use rate has not returned to that of the late 1960s and early 1970s (approximately 16%), in high school seniors lifetime use in 2004 was 9.7% (Johnston 2004). (See Table 12.1.) It has been speculated that this popularity reflects the ignorance of a new generation about the potential problems of the hallucinogens.

The Nature of Hallucinogens

Agreement has not been reached on what constitutes a hallucinogenic agent (O'Brien 1996), for several reasons. First, a variety of seemingly unrelated drug groups can produce hallucinations, delusions, or sensory disturbances under certain conditions. For example, besides the traditional hallucinogens (such as LSD), high doses of anticholinergics, cocaine, amphetamines, and steroids can cause hallucinations.

In addition, responses to even the traditional hallucinogens can vary tremendously from person to person and from experience to experience. Multiple mechanisms are involved in the actions of these drugs, which contribute to the array of responses that they can cause. These drugs most certainly influence the complex inner workings of the human mind and have been described as psychedelic, **psychotogenic**, or psychotomimetic. The features of hallucinogens that distinguish them from other drug groups are their ability to alter perception, thought, and feeling in such a manner that does not normally occur except in dreams or during experiences of extreme religious exaltation (Research Report 2001). We examine these characteristics throughout this chapter.

KEY TERMS

psychotogenic
substances that initiate psychotic behavior

Table 12.1 Trends (shown in percentages) in the Use of LSD and All Hallucinogens by 8th Graders through Young Adults, 1994–2004

	USED DURING LIFETIME				USED DURING YEAR				USED DURING MONTH			
	1994	1996	1999	2004	1994	1996	1999	2004	1994	1996	1999	2004
8th graders												
LSD	3.7	5.1	4.1	1.8	2.4	3.5	2.4	1.1	1.1	1.5	1.1	0.5
All hallucinogens	4.3	5.9	4.8	3.5	2.7	4.1	2.9	2.2	1.3	1.9	1.3	1.0
10th graders												
LSD	7.2	9.4	8.5	2.8	5.2	6.9	6.0	1.6	2.0	2.4	2.3	0.6
All hallucinogens	8.1	10.5	9.7	6.4	5.8	7.8	6.9	4.1	2.4	2.8	2.9	1.6
12th graders												
LSD	10.5	12.6	12.2	4.6	6.9	8.8	8.1	2.2	2.6	2.5	2.7	0.7
All hallucinogens	11.4	14.0	13.7	9.7	7.6	10.1	9.4	6.2	3.1	3.5	3.5	1.9
	1994	1996	2001		1994	1996	2001		1994	1996	2001	
Young Adults												
LSD	13.8	15.0	16.0		4.0	4.5	3.4		1.1	0.7	0.7	
All hallucinogens	15.9	15.4	18.3		5.1	4.9	5.4		1.6	1.4	1.2	
Ecstasy	3.8	5.2	13.0		0.7	1.7	7.5		0.2	0.3	1.8	

*For this survey, inhalants and marijuana were not considered as hallucinogens.

Sources: Johnston, L., P. O'Malley, and J. Bachman. "Monitoring the Future National Results on Adolescents Drug Use. Overview of Key Findings, 2002." Lansing, MI: University of Michigan, 2003.

Johnston, L. "Overall Teen Drug Use Continues Gradual Decline, But Use of Inhalants Rises" (2004). Available www.monitoringthefuture.org.

SENSORY AND PSYCHOLOGICAL EFFECTS

In general, LSD is considered the prototype agent against which other hallucinogens are measured (Research Report 2001). Typical users experience several stages of sensory experiences; they can go through all stages during a single "trip" or, more likely, will pass through only some. These stages are as follows:

1. Heightened, exaggerated senses
2. Loss of control
3. Self-reflection
4. Loss of identity and a sense of cosmic merging

The following illustrations of the stages of the LSD experience are based primarily on an account by Solomon Snyder (1974), a highly regarded neuroscientist (one of the principal discoverers of

endorphins; see Chapter 4), who personally experienced the effects of LSD as a young resident in psychiatry.

Altered Senses

In his encounter with LSD, Snyder used a moderate dose of 100 to 200 micrograms and observed few discernible effects for the first 30 minutes except some mild nausea. After this time had elapsed, objects took on a purplish tinge and appeared to be vaguely outlined. Colors, textures, and lines achieved an unexpected richness. Perception was so exaggerated that individual skin pores "stood out and clamored for recognition" (Snyder 1974, p. 42). Objects became distorted; when Snyder focused on his thumb, it began to swell, undulate, and then moved forward in a menacing fashion. Visions filled with distorted imagery occurred when his eyes were closed. The sense of time and distance changed dramatically; "a minute was like an hour, a week was like an eternity, a foot became a mile" (Snyder 1974, p. 43). The present seemed to drag on forever, and the concept of future lost its meaning. The exaggeration of perceptions and feelings gave the sense of more events occurring in a time period, giving the impression of time slowing.

An associated sensation described by Snyder is called **synesthesia**, a crossover phenomenon between senses. For example, sound develops visual dimensions, and vice versa, enabling you to see sounds and hear colors. These altered sensory experiences are described as a heightened sensory awareness and relate to the first component of the psychedelic state (Research Report 2001).

Loss of Control

The second feature of LSD also relates to altered sensory experiences and a loss of control (O'Brien 1996). The user cannot determine whether the psychedelic trip will be a pleasant, relaxing experience or a "bad trip," with recollections of hidden fears and suppressed anxieties that can precipitate neurotic or psychotic responses. The frightening reactions may persist for a few minutes or several hours and be mildly agitating or extremely disturbing. Some bad trips can include feelings of panic, confusion, suspicion, helplessness, and a total lack of control. The following example illustrates how terrifying a bad trip can be:

> I was having problems breathing [and] my throat was all screwed up. The things that entered my mind were that I was dead and people were saying good-bye, because they really meant it. I was witnessing my own

funeral. I was thinking that I was going to wake either in the back seat of a cop car or in the hospital. *(From Venturelli's files, interview with a 19-year-old male, 1995.)*

Replays of these frightening experiences can occur at a later time, even though the drug has not been taken again; such recurrences are referred to as "**flashbacks**" (Research Report 2001) or hallucinogen persisting perception disorder (Halpern and Pope 2003).

It is not clear what determines the nature of the sensory response. Perhaps it relates to the state of anxiety and personality of the user or the nature of his or her surroundings. It is interesting that Timothy Leary tried to teach his "drug disciples" that "turning on correctly means to understand the many levels that are brought into focus; it takes years of discipline, training and discipleship" ("Celebration #1" 1966). He apparently felt that, with experience and training, you could control the sensory effects of the hallucinogens. This is an interesting possibility but has never been well demonstrated.

Self-Reflection

Snyder (1974) made reference to the third component of the psychedelic response in his LSD experience. During the period when sensory effects predominate, self-reflection also occurs. While in this state, Snyder explained, the user "becomes aware of thoughts and feelings long hidden beneath the surface, forgotten and/or repressed" (p. 44). As a psychiatrist, Snyder claimed that this new perspective can lead to valid insights that are useful psychotherapeutic exercises.

Some psychotherapists have used or advocated the use of psychedelics for this purpose since the 1950s, as described by Sigmund Freud, to "make conscious the unconscious" (Snyder 1974, p. 44). Although a case can be made for the psychotherapeutic use of this group of drugs, the Food and Drug Administration (FDA) has not approved any of these agents for psychiatric use. The psychedelics currently available are considered to be too unpredictable in their effects and possess substantial risks (Abraham et al. 1996). Not only is their administration not considered to be significantly therapeutic, but their use is also deemed a great

KEY TERMS

synesthesia
a subjective sensation or image of a sense other than the one being stimulated, such as an auditory sensation caused by a visual stimulus

flashbacks
recurrences of earlier drug-induced sensory experiences in the absence of the drug

enough risk that the principal hallucinogenic agents are clasified (i.e., scheduled) as controlled substances (see Chapter 3).

Loss of Identity and Cosmic Merging

The final features that set the psychedelics apart as unique drugs were described by Snyder (1974) as the "mystical-spiritual aspect of the drug experience." He claimed, "It is indescribable. For how can anyone verbalize a merging of his being with the totality of the universe? How do you put into words the feeling that 'all is one,' 'I am of the all,' 'I am no longer.' One's skin ceases to be a boundary between self and others" (p. 45). Because consumption of hallucinogen-containing plants has often been part of religious ceremonies, it is likely that this sense of cosmic merging and union with all humankind correlates to the exhilaratingly spiritual experiences described by many religious mystics.

The loss of identity and personal boundaries caused by hallucinogens is not viewed as being so spiritually enticing by all. In particular, for individuals who have rigid, highly ordered personalities, the dissolution of a well-organized and well-structured world is terrifying because the drug destroys the individual's emotional support. Such an individual finds that the loss of a separate identity can cause extreme panic and anxiety. During these drug-induced panic states, which in some ways are schizophrenic-like, people have committed suicide and homicide. These tragic reactions are part of the risk of using hallucinogenics and explain some of the FDA's hesitancy to legalize or authorize them for psychotherapeutic use.

MECHANISMS OF ACTION

As with most drugs, hallucinogens represent the proverbial "double-edged sword." These drugs may cause potentially useful psychiatric effects for many people. However, the variability in positive versus negative responses, coupled with lack of understanding as to what factors are responsible for the variables, have made these drugs dangerous and difficult to manage.

Some researchers have suggested that all hallucinogens act at a common central nervous system (CNS) site to exert their psychedelic effects. Although this hypothesis has not been totally dis-

proven, there is little evidence to support it. The fact that so many different types of drugs can cause hallucinogenic effects suggests that multiple mechanisms are likely responsible for their actions.

The most predictable and typical psychedelic experiences are caused by LSD or similar agents. Consequently, these agents have been the primary focus of studies intended to elucidate the nature of hallucinogenic mechanisms. Although LSD has effects at several CNS sites, ranging from the spinal cord to the cortex of the brain, its effects on the neurotransmitter serotonin most likely account for its psychedelic properties (Nichols 2004). That LSD and similar drugs alter serotonin activity has been proven; how they affect this transmitter is not so readily apparent.

Although many experts believe changes in serotonin activity are the basis for the psychedelic properties of most hallucinogens, a case can be made for the involvement of norepinephrine, dopamine, acetylcholine, and perhaps other transmitter systems as well (see Chapter 4). Only additional research will be able to sort out this complex but important issue.

Types of Hallucinogenic Agents

Due to recent technological developments, understanding of hallucinogens has advanced; even so, the classification of these drugs remains somewhat arbitrary. Many agents produce some of the pharmacological effects of the traditional psychedelics, such as LSD and mescaline.

A second type of hallucinogen includes those agents that have amphetamine-like molecular structures (referred to as *phenylethylamines*) and possess some stimulant action; this group includes drugs such as DOM (dimethoxymethylamphetamine), MDA (methylenedioxyamphetamine), and MDMA (methylenedioxymethamphetamine or Ecstasy). These agents vary in their hallucinogen or stimulant properties. MDA is more like an amphetamine (stimulant), whereas MDMA is more like LSD (hallucinogen). In large doses, however, each of the phenylethylamines causes substantial CNS stimulation.

The third major group of hallucinogens comprises the anticholinergic drugs, which block some of the receptors for the neurotransmitter acetylcholine (see Chapter 4). Almost all drugs that antagonize these receptors cause hallucinations in high doses. Many of these potent anticholinergic hallucinogens are naturally occurring and have been known, used, and abused for millennia.

TRADITIONAL HALLUCINOGENS: LSD TYPES

The LSD-like drugs are considered to be the prototypical hallucinogens and are used as the basis of comparison for other types of agents with psychedelic properties. Included in this group are LSD itself and some hallucinogens derived from plants, such as mescaline from the peyote cactus, psilocybin from mushrooms, dimethyltryptamine (DMT) from seeds, and myristicin from nutmeg. Because LSD is the principal hallucinogen, its origin, history, and properties are discussed in detail, providing a basis for understanding the other psychedelic drugs.

Lysergic Acid Diethylamide (LSD)

LSD is a relatively new drug, but similar compounds have existed for a long time. For example, accounts from the Middle Ages tell about a strange affliction that caused pregnant women to abort and others to develop strange burning sensations in their extremities. Today, we call this condition **ergotism** and know that it is caused by eating grain contaminated by the ergot fungus. This fungus produces compounds related to LSD called the *ergot alkaloids* (Goldstein 1994; NIDA Infofax 1999b). Besides the sensory effects, the ergot substances can cause hallucinations, delirium, and psychosis.

In 1938, Albert Hofmann, a scientist for Sandoz Pharmaceutical Laboratories of Basel, Switzerland, worked on a series of ergot compounds in a search for active chemicals that might be of medical value. Lysergic acid was similar in structure to

Albert Hofmann created LSD in 1938 while trying to synthesize a drug to study psychosis.

a compound called *nikethamide*, a stimulant, and Hofmann tried to create slight chemical modifications that might merit further testing. The result of this effort was the production of lysergic acid diethylamide, or LSD. Hofmann's experience with this new compound gave insight into the effects of this drug (Research Report 2001).

Soon after LSD was discovered, the similarity of experiences with this agent to the symptoms of schizophrenia were noted, which prompted researchers to investigate correlations between the two. The hope was to use LSD as a tool for producing an artificial psychosis to aid in understanding the biochemistry of psychosis (Research Report 2001). Interest in this use of LSD has declined because it is generally accepted that LSD effects differ from natural psychoses.

The use of LSD in psychotherapy has also been tried in connection with the treatment of alcoholism, autism, paranoia, schizophrenia, and various other mental and emotional disorders. Therapeutic use of LSD has not increased to any great extent over the years because of its limited success, legal aspects, difficulty in obtaining the pure drug, adverse reactions to the drug ("bad trips" can occur under controlled as well as uncontrolled conditions), and rapid tolerance buildup in some patients.

Nonmedical interest in LSD and related drugs began to grow during the 1950s and peaked in the 1960s, when LSD was used by millions of young

KEY TERMS

ergotism
poisoning by toxic substances from the ergot fungus
Claviceps purpurea

Americans for chemical escape. Occasionally, a "bad trip" would cause a user to feel terror and panic; these experiences resulted in well-publicized accidental deaths due to jumping from building tops or running into the pathway of oncoming vehicles (U.S. Department of Justice 1991).

As with other hallucinogens, the use of LSD by teenagers declined somewhat over the 1970s and 1980s but began to rise again in the early 1990s. The reason for this rise was thought to relate to a decline in the perceived dangers of using LSD and an increase in peer approval (Johnston 1999). However, a recent survey demonstrated a dramatic drop in LSD use in 2004 that has not been explained (Johnston 2004; Table 12.1). Of high school seniors sampled in 1975, 11.3% had used LSD sometime during their life; that number declined to 8.6% in 1992, rebounded to 12.2% in 1999, and tumbled to 4.6% in 2004. LSD users are typically college or high school students, white, middle-class, and risk-takers (Johnston et al. 1996; Johnston 2004).

Synthesis and Administration LSD is a complex molecule that requires about 1 week to be synthesized. Because of the sophisticated chemistry necessary for its production, LSD is not manufactured by local illicit laboratories but requires the skills of a trained chemist (U.S. Department of Justice 2002; National Drug Threat Assessment 2003).

Small quantities of LSD are applied to squares of absorbent blotter paper to be chewed or swallowed.

Because of LSD's potency, it has been difficult to locate the illicit LSD labs; small quantities of LSD are sufficient to satisfy the demand and can be easily transported without detection.

The physical properties of LSD are not distinctive. In its purified form, LSD is colorless, odorless, and tasteless. It can be purchased in several forms, including tiny tablets (about one-tenth the size of aspirins, called *microdots*), capsules, thin squares of gelatin called "window panes," or more commonly dissolved and applied to paper as "blotter acid" and cut up into 0.25-inch squares for individual dosing (Publishers Group 2002). Each square is swallowed or chewed and represents a single dose. One gram of LSD can provide 10,000 individual doses and be sold on the streets for $50,000. Although LSD usually is taken by mouth, it is sometimes injected.

Physiological Effects Like many hallucinogens, LSD is remarkably potent. The typical dose today is 20 to 30 micrograms, compared with a typical dose of 150 to 300 micrograms in the 1960s. This difference in dose likely explains why today fewer users of LSD are experiencing severe side effects (NIDA Infofax 1999b). In monkeys, the lethal dose has been determined to be about 5 milligrams per kilogram of body weight.

When taken orally, LSD is readily absorbed and diffused into all tissues. It passes through the placenta into the fetus and through the blood–brain barrier. The brain receives about 1% of the total dose.

Within the brain, LSD is particularly concentrated in the hypothalamus, the limbic system, and the auditory and visual reflex areas. Electrodes placed in the limbic system show an "electrical storm," or a massive increase in neural activity, which might correlate with the overwhelming flood of sensations and the phenomenon of synesthesia reported by the user (Research Report 2001). LSD also activates the sympathetic nervous system; shortly after the drug is taken, body temperature, heart rate, and blood pressure rise, the person sweats, and the pupils of the eyes dilate. Its effects on the parasympathetic nervous system increase salivation and nausea (NIDA Infofax 1999b). These systemic effects do not appear to be related to the hallucinogenic properties of the drug.

The effect of LSD begins within 30 to 90 minutes after ingestion and can last up to 12 hours. Tolerance to the effects of LSD develops more rapidly and lasts longer than tolerance to other hallucinogens (Research Report 2001). Tolerance develops very quickly to repeated doses, probably because of a change in sensitivity of the target cells in the brain rather than a change in its metabolism. Tolerance wears off within a few days after the drug is discontinued. Because there are no withdrawal symptoms, a person does not become physically dependent, but some psychological dependency on LSD can occur (NIDA Infofax 1999b).

Behavioral Effects Because LSD alters a number of systems in the brain, its behavioral effects are many and variable among individuals (Goldstein 1995). The following sections address common CNS responses to this drug.

Creativity and Insight. A question often raised by researchers interested in experimenting with LSD is this: Does LSD help expand the mind, increasing insight and creativity? This question is extremely difficult to answer because no one has ever determined the origin of insight and creativity. Moreover, each of us views these qualities differently.

Subjects under the influence of LSD often express the feeling of being more creative, but creative acts such as drawing and painting are hindered by the motor impairment caused by LSD. The products of artists under the influence of the drug usually prove to be inferior to those produced before the drug experience. Paintings done in LSD creativity studies have been described as reminiscent of "schizophrenic art."

In an often-cited study, creativity, attitude, and anxiety tests on 24 college students found that LSD had no objective effect on creativity, although many of the subjects said they felt they were more creative (McGlothin et al. 1967). This paradox is noted in several studies of LSD use: The subjects believe they have more insight and provide better answers to life's problems, but they do not or cannot demonstrate this increase objectively. Overt behavior is not modified, and these new insights are short-lived unless they are reinforced by modified behavior.

In spite of these results, some researchers still contend that LSD can enhance the creative process. For example, Oscar Janigar, a psychiatrist at the University of California, Los Angeles, claimed to have determined that LSD does not produce a tangible alteration in the way a painter paints; thus, it does not turn a poor painter into a good one. However, Janigar claimed that LSD does alter the way the painter appraises the world and allows the artist to "plunge into areas where access was restricted by confines of perceptions" and consequently becomes more creative (Tucker 1987, p. 16).

Adverse Psychedelic Effects. It is important to remember that there is no typical pattern of response to LSD. The experience varies for each user as a function of the person's *set*, or expectations, and *setting*, or environment, during the experience (Publishers Group 2002). Two of the major negative responses are described as follows (NIDA Infofax 1999b; Pahnke et al. 1970):

1. The psychotic adverse reaction, or "freakout," is an intense, nightmarish experience. The subject may have complete loss of emotional control and experience paranoid delusions, hallucinations, panic attacks, psychosis, and catatonic seizures. In rare instances, some of these reactions are prolonged, lasting days.
2. The nonpsychotic adverse reaction may involve varying degrees of tension, anxiety, fear, depression, and despair but not as intense a response as the "freakout." A person with deep psychological problems or a strong need to be in conscious control or one who takes the drug in an unfavorable setting is more likely to have an adverse reaction than a person with a well-integrated personality.

Severe LSD behavioral toxicity can be treated with tranquilizers or a benzodiazepine.

Perceptual Effects. Because the brain's sensory processing is altered by a hallucinogenic dose of LSD, many kinds of unusual illusions can occur. Some users report seeing shifting geometrical patterns mixed with intense color perception; others observe the movement of stationary objects, such that a speck on the wall appears as a large blinking

This head was sculpted by a university student while under the influence of LSD.

eye or an unfolding flower. Interpretation of sounds can also be scrambled; a dropped ashtray may become a gun fired at the user, for instance. In some cases, LSD alters perceptions to the extent that people feel they can walk on water or fly through the air. The sensation that the body is distorted and even coming apart is another common effect, especially for novice users. Thoughts of suicide and sometimes actual attempts can be caused by use of LSD as well (NIDA Infofax 1999b; U.S. Department of Justice 1991).

Many LSD users find their sense of time distorted, such that hours may be perceived as years or an eternity. As discussed earlier, users may also have a distorted perception of their own knowledge or creativity; for instance, they may feel their ideas or work are especially unique, brilliant, or artistic. When analyzed by a person not on LSD or explained after the "trip" is over, however, these ideas or creations are almost always quite ordinary.

In sum, LSD alters perception such that any sensation can be perceived in the extreme. An experience can be incredibly beautiful and uplifting. However, sometimes the experience can be very unpleasant.

The "flashback" is an interesting but poorly understood phenomenon of LSD use. Although usually thought of as being adverse, sometimes flashbacks are pleasant and even referred to as "free trips." During a flashback, sensations caused by previous LSD use return, although the subject is not using the drug at the time.

There are three broad categories of negative LSD-related flashbacks:

1. *"Body trip":* recurrence of an unpleasant physical sensation
2. *"Bad mind trip":* recurrence of a distressing thought or emotion
3. *Altered visual perception:* the most frequent type of recurrence, consisting of seeing dots, flashes, trails of light, halos, false motion in the peripheral field, and other sensations

Flashbacks are most disturbing because they come on unexpectedly. Some have been reported years after use of LSD; for most people, however, flashbacks usually subside within weeks or months after taking LSD (NIDA Infofax 1999b). The duration of a flashback is variable, lasting from a few minutes to several hours (Fleckenstein 2000).

Although the precise mechanism of flashbacks is unknown, physical or psychological stresses and some drugs such as marijuana may trigger these experiences (Goldstein 1995). It has been proposed that flashbacks are an especially vivid form of memory that becomes seared into the subconscious mind due to the effects of LSD on the brain's transmitters.

Treatment consists of reassurance that the condition will go away and use of a sedative such as diazepam (Valium), if necessary, to treat the anxiety or panic that can accompany the flashback experience.

Genetic Damage and Birth Defects Experiments conducted in the mid-1960s suggested that LSD could cause birth defects, based on the observation that, when LSD was added to a suspension of human white blood cells in a test tube, the chromosomes of these cells were damaged. From this finding, it was proposed that, when LSD was consumed by human beings, it could damage the chromosomes of the male sperm, female egg, or cells of the developing infant. Such damage theoretically could result in congenital defects in offspring (Dishotsky et al. 1971).

Carefully controlled studies conducted after news of LSD's chromosomal effects were made public have not supported this hypothesis. Experiments have revealed that, in contrast to the test tube findings, there is no chromosomal damage to white blood cells or any other cells when LSD is given to a human being (Dishotsky et al. 1971).

Studies have also shown that there are no carcinogenic or mutagenic effects from using LSD in experimental animals or human beings, with the exception of the fruit fly. (LSD is a mutagen in fruit flies if given in doses that are equivalent to 100,000 times the hallucinogenic dose for people.) Teratogenic effects occur in mice if LSD is given early in pregnancy. LSD may be teratogenic in rhesus monkeys if it is injected in doses (based on body weight) exceeding at least 100 times the usual hallucinogenic dose for humans. In other studies, women who took street LSD but not those given pure LSD had a higher rate of spontaneous abortions and births of malformed infants; this finding suggests that contaminants in adulterated LSD were responsible for the fetal effects and not the hallucinogen itself (Dishotsky et al. 1971).

Early Human Research In the 1950s, the U.S. government—specifically, the Central Intelligence Agency (CIA) and the army—became interested in reports of the effects of mind-altering drugs, including LSD. Unknown to the public at the time, these agencies conducted tests on human beings to learn more about such compounds and determine their usefulness in conducting military and clandestine missions. These activities became public when a biochemist, Frank Olson, killed himself in 1953 after being given a drink laced with LSD. Olson had a severe psychotic reaction and was being treated for the condition when he jumped out of a 10th-story window. His family was told only that he had committed suicide. The connection to LSD was not uncovered until 1975. The court awarded Olson's family $750,000 in damages in 1976.

In 1976, the extent of these studies was revealed: Nearly 585 soldiers and 900 civilians had been given LSD in poorly organized experiments in which participants were coerced into taking this drug or not told that they were receiving it. Powerful hallucinogens such as LSD can cause serious psychological damage in some subjects, especially when they are unaware of what is happening.

The legal consequences of these LSD studies continued for years. As recently as 1987, a New York judge awarded $700,000 to the family of a mental patient who killed himself after having been given LSD without an explanation of the drug's nature. The judge said that there was a "conspiracy of silence" among the army, the Department of Justice, and the New York State Attorney General to conceal events surrounding the death of the subject, Harold Blauer.

Mescaline (Peyote)

Mescaline is one of approximately 30 psychoactive chemicals that have been isolated from the peyote cactus and used for centuries in the Americas (see "Here and Now," Peyote: An Ancient Indian Way). One of the first reports on the peyote plant was made by Francisco Hernandez to the court of King Philip II of Spain. King Philip was interested in reports from the earlier Cortés expedition about strange medicines the natives used and sent Hernandez to collect information about herbs and medicines. Hernandez worked on this project from 1570 to 1575 and reported on the use of more than 1200 plant remedies as well as the existence of many hallucinogenic plants. He was one of the first to record the eating of parts of the peyote cactus and the resulting visions and mental changes.

In the 17th century, Spanish Catholic priests asked their Indian converts to confess to the use of peyote, which they believed was used to conjure up demons. However, nothing stopped its use. By 1760, use of peyote had spread into what is now the United States.

Peyote has been confused with another plant, the mescal shrub, which produces dark red beans that contain an extremely toxic alkaloid called *cytisine*. This alkaloid may cause hallucinations, convulsions, and even death. In addition, a mescal liquor is made from the agave cactus. Partly because of misidentification with the toxic mescal beans, the U.S. government outlawed the use of both peyote and mescaline for everyone except members of the Native American Church (Mims 2000). Mescaline has been used for decades by this group as part of their religious sacrament.

Here and Now

Peyote: An Ancient Indian Way

Members of the Native American Church use the buttons of the hallucinogenic peyote cactus to brew a sacramental tea as sacred to them as the bread and wine of the Christian Eucharist. As described by one member, "Peyote is a gift given to the Indians, but its ways cannot be obtained overnight. It has to be done with sincerity. It becomes part of your way of life. One has to walk that walk." Those who accept this form of worship believe that respectful use of peyote can be a gateway to the realm of the spirit, visions, and guidance. The use of peyote as part of the latest New Age craze is very disturbing to members of this church and is viewed almost as a form of sacrilege.

Source: Mims, B. "Peyote: When the Ancient Indian Way Collides with a New Age Craze." *Salt Lake Tribune* 258 (1 July 1999): A-10.

Mescaline is the most active drug in peyote; it induces intensified perception of colors and euphoria in the user. However, as Aldous Huxley said in *The Doors of Perception* (1954), his book about his experimentation with mescaline, "Along with the happily transfigured majority of mescaline takers there is a minority that finds in the drug only hell and purgatory." After Huxley related his experiences with mescaline, it was used by an increasing number of people.

Physiological Effects The average dose of mescaline that will cause hallucinations and other physiological effects is from 300 to 600 milligrams. It may take up to 20 peyote (mescal) buttons (ingested orally) to get 600 milligrams of mescaline.

The peyote cactus contains a number of drugs. The best known is mescaline.

Based on animal studies, scientists estimate that a lethal dosage is 10 to 30 times greater than that which causes behavioral effects in human beings. (About 200 milligrams is the lowest mind-altering dose.) Death in animals results from convulsions and respiratory arrest. Mescaline is perhaps 1000 to 3000 times less potent than LSD and 30 times less potent than another common hallucinogen, psilocybin (Mathias 1993). Psilocybin is discussed later in this chapter.

Mescaline's effects include dilation of the pupils (**mydriasis**), increase in body temperature, anxiety, visual hallucinations, and alteration of body image. The last effect is a type of hallucination in which parts of the body may seem to disappear or to become grossly distorted. Mescaline induces vomiting in many people and some muscular relaxation (sedation). Apparently, there are few aftereffects or drug hangover feelings at low doses. Higher doses of mescaline slow the heart and respiratory rhythm, contract the intestines and the uterus, and cause headache, difficulty in coordination, dry skin with itching, and hypertension (high blood pressure).

Mescaline users report that they lose all awareness of time. As with LSD, the setting for the "trip" influences the user's reactions. Most mescaline users prefer natural settings, most likely due to the

KEY TERMS

mydriasis
pupil dilation

historical association of this drug with Native Americans and their nature-related spiritual experiences (often under the influence of this drug). The visual hallucinations achieved depend on the individual. Colors are at first intensified and may be followed by hallucinations of shades, movements, forms, and events. The senses of smell and taste are enhanced. Some people claim (as with LSD) that they can "hear" colors and "see" sounds, such as the wind. Synesthesia occurs naturally in a small percentage of cases.

At low to medium doses, a state of euphoria is reported, often followed by a feeling of anxiety and less frequently by depression. Occasionally, users observe themselves as two people and experience the sensation that the mind and the body are separate entities. A number of people have had cosmic experiences that are profound—almost religious—and in which they discover a sense of unity with all creation. People who have this sensation often believe they have discovered the meaning of existence.

Mechanism of Action Within 30 to 120 minutes after ingestion, mescaline reaches a maximum concentration in the brain. The effects may persist for as long as 9 or 10 hours. Hallucinations may last up to 2 hours and are usually affected by the dose level. About half the dose is excreted unchanged after 6 hours and can be recovered in the urine for reuse (if peyote is in short supply). A slow tolerance builds up after repeated use, and there is cross-tolerance to LSD. As with LSD, mescaline intoxication can be alleviated or stopped by taking a dose of chlorpromazine (Thorazine), a tranquilizer, and to a lesser extent by taking diazepam (Valium). Like LSD, mescaline probably exerts much of its hallucinogenic effects by altering serotonin systems (Aghajanian and Marck 2000).

Analysis of street samples of mescaline obtained in a number of U.S. cities over the past decade shows that the chemical sold rarely is authentic. Regardless of color or appearance, these street drugs are usually other hallucinogens, such as LSD, DOM, or PCP. If a person decides to take hallucinogenic street drugs, "let the buyer beware." Not only is the actual content often different and potentially much more toxic than bar-

gained for (they are frequently contaminated), but the dosage is usually unknown even if the drug is genuine.

Psilocybin

The drug psilocybin has a long and colorful history. Its principal source is the *Psilocybe mexicana* mushroom of the "magic" variety (Goldstein 1994; U.S. Department of Justice 2002). It was first used by some of the early natives of Central America more than 2000 years ago. In Guatemala, statues of mushrooms that date back to 100 B.C. have been found. The Aztecs later used the mushrooms for ceremonial rites. When the Spaniards came into Mexico in the 1500s, the natives were calling the *Psilocybe mexicana* mushroom "God's flesh." Because of this seeming sacrilege, they were harshly treated by the Spanish priests.

Gordon Wasson identified the *Psilocybe mexicana* mushroom in 1955. The active ingredient was extracted in 1958 by Albert Hofmann, who also synthesized LSD. Doing research, Hofmann wanted to make certain he would feel the effects of the mushroom, so he ate 32 of them, weighing 2.4 grams (a medium dose by Native American standards) and then recorded his hallucinogenic reactions (Burger 1968).

Timothy Leary also tried some psilocybin mushrooms in Mexico in 1960; apparently, the experience influenced him greatly. On his return to Harvard, he carried out a series of experiments using psilocybin with student groups. Leary was

The *Psilocybe* mushroom is the source of the hallucinogens psilocybin and psilocin.

careless in experimental procedures and did some work in uncontrolled situations. His actions caused a major administrative upheaval, ending in his departure from Harvard.

One of Leary's questionable studies was the "Good Friday" experiment in which 20 theological students were given either a placebo or psilocybin in a double-blind study (that is, neither the researcher nor the subjects know who gets the placebo or the drug), after which all attended the same 2.5-hour Good Friday service. The experimental group reported mystical experiences whereas the control group did not (Pahnke and Richards 1966). Leary believed that the experience was of value and that, under proper control and guidance, the hallucinatory experience could be beneficial.

Psilocybin is not very common on the street. Generally, it is administered orally and is eaten either fresh or dried. Accidental poisonings are common for those who mistakenly consume poisonous mushrooms rather than the hallucinogenic variety.

The dried form of these mushrooms contains from 0.2% to 0.5% psilocybin. The hallucinogenic effects produced are quite similar to those of LSD, and there is a cross-tolerance among psilocybin, LSD, and mescaline. The effects caused by psilocybin vary with the dosage taken. Up to 4 milligrams cause a pleasant experience, relaxation, and some body sensation. In some subjects, higher doses cause considerable perceptual and body image changes, accompanied by hallucinations, as illustrated in the following quote:

> The first time I 'shroomed, everything looked like it was made of plastic, like everything could be folded up or something. Whatever somebody told me, I would believe it to be true. Like if I was drinking a beer and someone told me it was tequila, I would taste tequila. *(From Venturelli's files, interview with a 20-year-old male, 1995.)*

In extreme cases, psyilocybin can even induce the first stages of schizophrenia-like psychosis (Vollenwelder et al. 1998). Psilocybin stimulates the autonomic nervous system, dilates the pupils, and increases the body temperature. There is some evidence that psilocybin is metabolized into psilocin,

which is more potent and may be the principal active ingredient. Psilocin is found in mushrooms, albeit in small amounts. Like the other hallucinogens, psilocybin apparently causes no physical dependence.

Tryptamines Some compounds related to the tryptamine class of drugs (molecules that resemble the neurotransmitter serotonin) have hallucinogenic properties and can exist naturally in herbs, fungi, and animals or can be synthesized in the laboratory. Most of these compounds are Schedule I drugs and illegal (DEA 2002a). Two examples are discussed in this section.

Dimethyltryptamine (DMT). DMT is a short-acting hallucinogen found in the seeds of certain leguminous trees native to the West Indies and parts of South America (Schultes 1978). It is also prepared synthetically in illicit laboratories. For centuries, the powdered seeds have been used as a snuff called *cohoba* in pipes and snuffing tubes. The Haitian natives claim that, under the influence of the drug, they can communicate with their gods. Its effects may last less than 1 hour, which has earned it the nickname "the businessman's lunch break" drug.

DMT has no effect when taken orally; it is inhaled either as smoke from the burning plant or in vaporized form. DMT is sometimes added to parsley leaves or flakes, tobacco, or marijuana to induce its hallucinogenic effect. The usual dose is 60 to 150 milligrams. In structure and action, it is similar to psilocybin although not as powerful. Like the other hallucinogens discussed, DMT does not cause physical dependence.

Foxy. The synthetic substance chemically named 5-methoxy-*N,N*-diisopropyltryptamine (Foxy) is a relatively new hallucinogen. Despite the fact this drug is sometimes used at raves and clubs in Arizona, California, New York, and Florida, it is not yet scheduled by the DEA. At lower doses, Foxy can cause euphoria; at higher doses, its effects are similar to LSD (DEA 2002a).

Nutmeg High doses of nutmeg can be quite intoxicating, causing symptoms such as drowsiness, stupor, delirium, and sleep. Prison inmates have known about this drug for years, so in most prisons use of spices such as nutmeg is restricted.

Nutmeg contains 5% to 15% myristica oil, which is responsible for the physical effects. Myristicin (about 4%), which is structurally similar to mescaline, and elemicin are probably the most potent psychoactive ingredients in nutmeg. Myristicin blocks release of serotonin from brain neurons. Some scientists believe that it can be converted in the body to MDMA (a close relative of MDA, discussed later), which also affects the CNS. Mace, the exterior covering of the nutmeg seed, also contains the hallucinogenic compound myristicin.

Two tablespoons of nutmeg (about 14 grams) taken orally cause a rather unpleasant "trip" with a dreamlike stage; rapid heartbeat, dry mouth, and thirst are experienced as well. Agitation, apprehension, and a sense of impending doom may last about 12 hours, with a sense of unreality persisting for several days (Claus et al. 1970).

PHENYLETHYLAMINE HALLUCINOGENS

The phenylethylamine drugs are chemically related to amphetamines. Phenylethylamines have varying degrees of hallucinogenic and CNS stimulant effects, which are likely related to their ability to release serotonin and dopamine, respectively. Consequently, the phenylethylamines that predominantly release serotonin are dominated by their hallucinogenic action and are LSD-like, whereas those more inclined to release dopamine are dominated by their stimulant effects and are cocaine-like.

Dimethoxymethylamphetamine (DOM or STP)

The basic structure of DOM is amphetamine. Nonetheless, it is a fairly powerful hallucinogen that seems to work through mechanisms similar to those found with mescaline and LSD. In fact, the effects of DOM are similar to those caused by a combination of amphetamine and LSD, with the hallucinogenic effects of the drug overpowering the amphetaminelike physiological effects.

KEY TERMS

entactogens
drugs that enhance the sensation and pleasure of touching

"Designer" Amphetamines

"Designer" amphetamines were discussed in Chapter 10 but are presented again here owing to their hallucinogenic effects. Their hybrid actions as psychedelic stimulants not only make them a particularly fascinating topic for research, but also provide a unique experience described by drug abusers as a "smooth amphetamine" or **entactogens** (implying that the pleasurable sensation of touch is enhanced). This characterization likely accounts for the popularity of the designer amphetamines (Drug Abuse USA Home 2000).

3,4-Methylenedioxyamphetamine (MDA) MDA, first synthesized in 1910, is structurally related to both mescaline and amphetamine. Early research found that MDA is an *anorexiant* (causing loss of appetite) as well as a mood elevator in some persons. Further research has shown that the mode of action of MDA is similar to that of amphetamines. It causes additional release of the neurotransmitters serotonin, dopamine, and norepinephrine.

MDA has been used as an adjunct to psychotherapy. In one study, eight volunteers who had previously experienced the effects of LSD under clinical conditions were given 150 milligrams of MDA. Effects of the drug were noted between 40 and 60 minutes following ingestion by all eight subjects. The subjective effects following administration peaked at the end of 90 minutes and persisted for approximately 8 hours. None of the subjects experienced hallucinations, perceptual distortion, or closed-eye imagery, but they reported that the feelings the drug induced had some relationship to those previously experienced with LSD. The subjects found that both drugs induced an intensification of feelings, increased perceptions of self-insight, and heightened empathy with others during the experience. Most of the subjects also felt an increased sense of aesthetic enjoyment at some point during the intoxication. Seven of the eight subjects said they perceived music as "three-dimensional" (Naranjo et al. 1967).

On the street, MDA has been called the *love drug* because of its effects on the sense of touch and the attitudes of the users. Users often report experiencing a sense of well-being (likely a stimulant effect) and heightened tactile sensations (like a hallucinogenic effect) and thus increased pleasure through sex and expressions of affection. Those under the influence of MDA frequently focus on interpersonal relationships and demonstrate an overwhelming desire or need to be with or talk to people. Some users say they have a very pleasant "body high"—more sensual than cerebral, and more emphatic than introverted. For these reasons, MDA is sometimes used by persons attending raves much like MDMA or Ecstasy (Kalant 2001).

The unpleasant side effects most often reported are nausea, periodic tensing of muscles in the neck, tightening of the jaw and grinding of the teeth, and dilation of the pupils. Street doses of MDA range from 100 to 150 milligrams. Serious convulsions and death have resulted from larger doses, but in these cases the quantity of MDA was not accurately measured. Ingestion of 500 milligrams of pure MDA has been shown to cause death. The only adverse reaction to moderate doses reported is a marked physical exhaustion, lasting as long as 2 days (Marquardt et al. 1978).

An unpleasant MDA experience should be treated the same as a bad trip with any hallucinogen. The person should be "talked down" (reassured) in a friendly and supportive manner. The use of other drugs is rarely needed, although medical attention may be necessary. Under the Comprehensive Drug Abuse Prevention and Control Act of 1970, MDA is classified as a Schedule I substance; illegal possession is a serious offense.

Methylenedioxymethamphetamine (MDMA) MDMA is a modification of MDA but is thought to have more psychedelic and less stimulant activity (for example, euphoria) than its predecessor. MDMA is also structurally similar to mescaline. This drug has become known as *Ecstasy*, *XTC*, and *Adam* (Zickler 2000). (Ecstasy was also discussed in Chapter 10.)

MDMA was synthesized in 1912, but it only became widely used in the 1980s (Cami et al. 2000). This designer amphetamine can be produced easily (DEA 2002b). Although the synthesis can be done by local illicit laboratories (Hyslop 2000), most of the MDMA supplies in this country are smuggled in from outlaw drug laboratories in European countries such as the Netherlands (Cloud 2000). The unusual psychological effects it produces are part of the reason for its popularity. The drug causes euphoria, increased energy, increased sensitivity to touch, and lowered inhibitions. Many users claim it intensifies emotional feelings without sensory distortion and that it increases empathy and awareness both of the user's body and of the aesthetics of the surroundings (Farley 2000). Some consider MDMA to be an aphrodisiac. Because MDMA lowers defense mechanisms and reduces inhibitions, it has even been used during psychoanalysis (Cloud 2000).

MDMA—popularized in the 1980s by articles in *Newsweek* (Adler 1985), *Time* (Toufexis 1985), and other magazines—is again being touted on the national newstands as a drug with euphoric effects, potential therapeutic value, and lack of serious side effects. MDMA is popular with college-age students and young adults (ONDCP 2004). Because of its effect of enhancing sensations, MDMA has been used as part of a countercultural "rave" scene, including high-tech music and laser light shows. Observers report that MDMA-linked rave parties are reminiscent of the "acid parties" of the 1960s and 1970s.

Because of the widespread abuse of MDMA, the DEA prohibited its use by placing it on Schedule I in 1985 (ONDCP 2004). At the time of the ban, it was estimated that as many as 200 physicians were using the drug in psychotherapy (Greer and Tolbert 1990) and an estimated 30,000 doses per month were being taken for recreational purposes.

Ecstasy is frequently used at "raves" to increase sensory stimulation and the pleasure of touching.

Currently, MDMA is classified as a "club drug" because of its frequent use at rave dances, clubs, and bars (ONDCP 2004). A dose of this drug is readily affordable at $10 to $20 (Hegadoran et al. 1999).

MDMA is usually taken orally, but it is sometimes snorted or even occasionally smoked (Taylor 1994). After the high starts, it may persist for minutes or even an hour, depending on the person, the purity of the drug, and the environment in which it is taken. When "coming down" from an MDMA-induced high, people often take small oral doses known as "boosters" to get high again. If they take too many boosters, they become very fatigued the next day. The average dose is about 75 to 150 milligrams; toxic effects have been reported at higher doses (Cami et al. 2000).

There is disagreement as to the possible harmful side effects of MDMA. Use of high doses can cause psychosis and paranoia (Parrott 2000a). Some negative physiological responses caused by recreational doses include dilated pupils, dry mouth and throat, clenching and grinding of teeth (resulting in the use of baby pacifiers), muscle aches and stiffness (in 28% of users), fatigue (in 80% of users), insomnia (in 38% of users), agitation, and anxiety. Some of these reactions can be intense and unpredictable. Under some conditions, death can be caused by hyperthermia (elevated body temperature), instability of the autonomic nervous system, and kidney failure (Burke 2001).

Several studies have demonstrated long-term damage to serotonin neurons in the brain following a single high dose of either MDMA or MDA, which may result in impaired memory, diminished ability to process information, and heightened impulsivity (Parrott 2000b; Williams 2002). Although the behavioral significance of this damage in people is not clear, at the present time caution using this drug is warranted (see "Here and Now," MDMA's Casual User).

There has been considerable debate as to the addictive properties of MDMA. Some claim this drug is like LSD with little likelihood of causing physical dependence, whereas others claim its properties are likely to be more amphetamine-like. Part of the difficulty in sorting out this controversy is that most moderate MDMA users also use other drugs, making it difficult to determine which effects are specifically attributable to the MDMA. The potential to cause addiction and dependence by MDMA is likely somewhere between that of amphetamine and LSD. Because of its ability to cause euphoria and release of dopamine in the brain, it is very probable that use by smoking or injection can cause significant dependence.

ANTICHOLINERGIC HALLUCINOGENS

The anticholinergic hallucinogens include naturally occurring alkaloid (bitter organic base) substances that are present in plants and herbs found around

Here and Now

MDMA's: Casual User

A study examined 15 regular Ecstasy users, 15 novice (first-time) Ecstasy users, and 15 controls who attended a Saturday night rave. The regular users consumed, on average, 1.8 MDMA tablets, the novice users took 1.4 MDMA tablets, and the controls had no drug except alcohol. All groups reported positive moods during the dance. However, 2 days later, the Ecstasy users felt significantly more depressed, unsociable, unpleasant, and less good-tempered than the controls. Verbal recall was also diminished in MDMA users, who remembered only 60% to 70% of the words remembered by the control subjects. Those who used Ecstasy regularly had the most difficulty remembering.

Source: Parrott, A., and J. Lasky. "Ecstasy (MDMA) Effects Upon Mood and Cognition: Before, During and After a Saturday Night Dance." *Psychopharmacology* 139 (1998): 261–268.

the world. These drugs are often mentioned in folklore and in early literature as being added to "potions." They are thought to have killed the Roman Emperor Claudius and to have poisoned Hamlet's father. Historically, they have been the favorite drugs used to eliminate inconvenient people (Marken et al. 1996). Hallucinogens affecting the cholinergic neurons also have been used by South American Indians for religious ceremonies (Schultes and Hofmann 1980) and were probably used in witchcraft to give the illusion of flying, to prepare sacrificial victims, and even to give some types of marijuana ("superpot") its kick.

The potato family of plants (Solanaceae) contain most of these mind-altering drugs. Three potent anticholinergic compounds are commonly found in these plants: (1) scopolamine, or hyoscine; (2) hyoscyamine; and (3) atropine. Scopolamine may produce excitement, hallucinations, and delirium even at therapeutic doses. With atropine, doses bordering on toxic levels are usually required to obtain these effects (Schultes and Hofmann 1973). All of these active alkaloid drugs block some acetylcholine receptors (see Chapter 4).

These alkaloid drugs can be used as ingredients in cold symptom remedies because they have a drying effect and block production of mucus in the nose and throat. They also prevent salivation; therefore, the mouth becomes uncommonly dry and perspiration may stop. Atropine may increase the heart rate by 100% and dilate the pupils markedly, causing inability to focus on nearby objects. Other annoying side effects of these anticholinergic drugs include constipation and difficulty in urinating. These inconveniences tend to discourage excessive abuse of these drugs for their hallucinogenic properties. Usually, people who abuse these anticholinergic compounds are receiving the drugs by prescription (Marken et al. 1996).

Anticholinergics can cause drowsiness by affecting the sleep centers of the brain. At large doses, a condition occurs that is similar to a psychosis, characterized by delirium, loss of attention, mental confusion, and sleepiness (Carlini 1993). Hallucinations may also occur at higher doses. At very high doses, paralysis of the respiratory system may cause death.

Although hundreds of plant species naturally contain anticholinergic substances and consequently can cause psychedelic experiences, only a few of the principal plants are mentioned here.

Atropa belladonna:
The Deadly Nightshade Plant

Knowledge of this plant is very old, and its use as a drug is reported in early folklore. The name of the genus, *Atropa,* is the origin for the drug name atropine and indicates the reverence the Greeks had for the plant. Atropos was one of the three Fates in Greek mythology, whose duty it was to cut the thread of life when the time came. This plant has been used for thousands of years by assassins and murderers. In *Tales of the Arabian Nights,* unsuspecting potentates were poisoned with atropine from the deadly nightshade or one of its relatives. Fourteen berries of the deadly nightshade contain enough drug to cause death.

The species name, *belladonna,* means "beautiful woman." In early Rome and Egypt, girls with large pupils were considered attractive and friendly. To create this condition, they would put a few drops of an extract of this plant into their eyes, causing the pupils to dilate (Marken et al. 1996). Belladonna has also enjoyed a reputation as a love potion.

Mandragora officinarum: The Mandrake

The mandrake contains several active psychedelic alkaloids: hyoscyamine, scopolamine, atropine, and mandragorine. Mandrake has been used as a love potion for centuries but has also been known for its toxic properties. In ancient folk medicine, mandrake was used to treat many ailments in spite of its side effects. It was recommended as a sedative, to relieve nervous conditions, and to relieve pain (Schultes and Hofmann 1980).

The root of the mandrake is forked and, viewed with a little imagination, may resemble the human body (as portrayed in the *Harry Potter and the Chamber of Secrets* movie in 2002). Because of this resemblance, it has been credited with human attributes, which gave rise to many superstitions in the Middle Ages about its magical powers. Shakespeare referred to this plant in *Romeo and Juliet.* In her farewell speech, Juliet says, "And shrieks like mandrakes torn out of the earth, that living mortals hearing them run mad."

Hyoscyamus niger: Henbane

Henbane is a plant that contains both hyoscyamine and scopolamine. In A.D. 60, Pliny the Elder spoke of henbane: "For this is certainly known, that if one takes it in drink more than four leaves, it will put him beside himself" (Jones 1956). Henbane was also used in the orgies, or bacchanalias, of the ancient world.

Although rarely used today, henbane has been given medicinally since early times. It was frequently used to cause sleep, although hallucinations often occurred if given in excess. It was likely included in witches' brews and deadly concoctions during the Dark Ages (Schultes and Hofmann 1980).

Datura stramonium: Jimsonweed

The *Datura* genus of the Solanaceae family includes a large number of related plants found worldwide. The principal active drug in this group is scopolamine; there are also several less active alkaloids.

Throughout history, these plants have been used as hallucinogens by many societies. They are mentioned in early Sanskrit and Chinese writings and were revered by the Buddhists. There is also some indication that the priestess (oracle) at the ancient Greek Temple of Apollo at Delphi was under the influence of this type of plant when she made prophecies (Schultes 1970). Before the supposed divine possession, she appeared to have chewed leaves of the sacred laurel. A mystic vapor was also reported to have risen from a fissure in the ground. The sacred laurel may have been one of the *Datura* species, and the vapors may have come from burning these plants.

Jimsonweed gets its name from an incident that took place in 17th-century Jamestown. British soldiers ate this weed while trying to capture Nathaniel Bacon, who had made seditious remarks about the king. Although still abused occasionally by adventuresome young people, the anticholinergic side effects of jimsonweed are so unpleasant that it rarely becomes a long-term problem (Tiongson and Salen 1998).

OTHER HALLUCINOGENS

Technically, any drug that alters perceptions, thoughts, and feelings in a manner that is not normally experienced except in dreams can be classified as a hallucinogen. Because the brain's sensory input is complex and involves several neurotransmitter systems, drugs with many diverse effects can cause hallucinations (Research Report 2001).

Four agents that do not conveniently fit into the principal categories of hallucinogens are discussed in the following sections.

Phencyclidine (PCP)

PCP is considered by many experts as the most dangerous of the hallucinogens (*DSM-IV-TR* 2000; Maier 2003). PCP was developed in the late 1950s as an intravenous anesthetic. Although it was found to be effective, it had serious side effects that caused it to be discontinued for human use (Research Report 2001). Sometimes when people were re-

Datura stramonium, or jimsonweed, is a common plant that contains the hallucinogenic drug scopolamine.

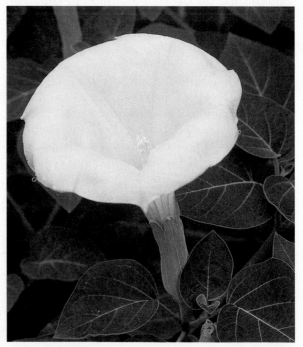

KEY TERMS

jimsonweed
a potent hallucinogenic plant

covering from PCP anesthesia, they experienced delirium and manic states of excitation lasting 18 hours (*DSM-IV-TR* 2000). PCP is currently a Schedule II drug, legitimately available only as an anesthetic for animals but has even been banned from veterinary practice since 1985 because of its high theft rate. Most, if not all, PCP used in the United States today is produced illegally (U.S. Department of Justice 1991).

Street PCP is mainly synthesized from readily available chemical precursors in clandestine laboratories. Within 24 hours, "cooks" (the makers of street PCP) can set up a lab, make several gallons of the drug, and destroy the lab before the police can locate them. Liquid PCP is then poured into containers and ready for shipment (Maier 2003).

PCP first appeared on the street drug scene in 1967 as the *PeaCe Pill*. In 1968, it reappeared in New York as a substance called *hog*. By 1969, PCP was found under a variety of guises. It was sold as *angel dust* and sprinkled on parsley for smoking. Today, it is sold on the streets under many different slang names, including *angel dust, supergrass, killerweed, embalming fluid, bobbies, dippies, hydro a,* and *purple haze,* to mention a few (Dewan 2003; Maier 2003).

In the late 1960s, PCP began to find its way into a variety of street drugs sold as psychedelics. By 1970, authorities observed that phencyclidine was used widely as a main ingredient in psychedelic preparations. It is still frequently substituted for and sold as LSD, mescaline, marijuana, and cocaine (Maier 2003).

One difficulty in estimating the effects or use patterns of PCP is caused by variance in drug purity. Also, there are about 30 **analogs** of PCP, some of which have appeared on the street. PCP has so many other street names that people may not know they are using it or they may have been deceived when buying what they thought was LSD or mescaline (Dewan 2003). Users may not question the identity of the substances unless they have a bad reaction.

PCP is available as a pure, white crystalline powder, as tablets, or as capsules. However, because it is usually manufactured in makeshift laboratories, it is frequently discolored by contaminants from a tan to brown with a consistency ranging from powder to a gummy mass (U.S. Department of Justice

1991). PCP can be taken orally, smoked, sniffed, or injected (NIDA Infofax 1999c). In the late 1960s through the early 1970s, PCP was mostly taken orally, but it is now commonly snorted or applied to dark brown cigarettes, leafy materials such as parsley, mint, oregano, marijuana, or tobacco and smoked (National Drug Threat Assessment 2003). By smoking PCP, the experienced user is better able to limit his or her dosage to a desired level. After smoking, the subjective effects appear within 1 to 5 minutes and peak within the next 5 to 30 minutes. The high lasts about 4 to 6 hours, followed by a 6- to 24-hour "comedown" (*DSM-IV-TR* 2000).

In the 1979 national drug survey performed by the National Institute on Drug Abuse, about 7% of the U.S. high school seniors had used PCP in a 12-month period; however, in 2004, that rate had declined to 0.7% (Johnston 2004).

Physiological Effects Although PCP may have hallucinogenic effects, it can cause a host of other physiological actions, including stimulation, depression, anesthesia, and analgesia. The effects of PCP on the CNS vary greatly. At low doses, the most prominent effect is similar to that of alcohol intoxication, with generalized numbness. As the dose of PCP increases, the person becomes even more insensitive and may become fully anesthetized. Large doses can cause coma, convulsions, and death (*DSM-IV-TR* 2000).

The majority of peripheral effects are apparently related to activation of the sympathetic nervous system (see Chapter 5). Flushing, excess sweating, and a blank stare are common, although the size of the pupils is unaffected. The cardiovascular system reacts by increasing blood pressure and heart rate. Other effects include side-to-side eye movements (called *nystagmus*), muscular incoordination, double vision, dizziness, nausea, and vomiting (NIDA Infofax 1999c). These symptoms occur in many people taking medium to high doses.

KEY TERMS

analogs
drugs with similar structures

Psychological Effects PCP has unpleasant effects most of the time it is used. Why, then, do people use it repeatedly as their drug of choice?

PCP has the ability to markedly alter the person's subjective feelings; this effect may be reinforcing, even though the alteration is not always positive. Some say use of PCP makes them feel "godlike" and powerful (Maier 2003). There is an element of risk, not knowing how the trip will turn out. PCP may give the user feelings of strength, power, and invulnerability (NIDA Infofax 1999c). Other positive effects include heightened sensitivity to outside stimuli, a sense of stimulation and mood elevation, and dissociation from surroundings. Also, PCP is a social drug; virtually all users report taking it in groups rather than during a solitary experience. PCP also causes serious perceptual distortions. Users cannot accurately interpret the environment and as a result may do what appear to be absurd things such as jump out of a window thinking they can fly (*DSM-IV-TR* 2000).

Chronic users may take PCP in "runs" extending over 2 to 3 days, during which time they do not sleep or eat. In later stages of chronic administration, users may develop outright paranoia, unpredictable violent behavior, and auditory hallucinations (*DSM-IV-TR* 2000). Law enforcement officers claim to be more fearful of suspects on PCP than of suspects on other drugs of abuse. Often such people seem to have superhuman strength and are totally irrational and very difficult—even dangerous—to manage (NIDA Infofax 1999a).

PCP has no equal in its ability to produce brief psychoses similar to schizophrenia (Jentsch and Roth 1999). The psychoses—induced with moderate doses given to normal, healthy volunteers—last about 2 hours and are characterized by changes in body image, thought disorders, estrangement, autism, and occasionally rigid inability to move (**catatonia**, or catalepsy). Subjects report feeling numb, have great difficulty differentiating between themselves and their surroundings, and complain afterward of feeling extremely isolated and apathetic. They are often violently paranoid during the psychosis (*DSM-IV-TR* 2000; *Medical Letter* 1996). When PCP was given experimentally to hospitalized chronic schizophrenics, it made them much worse not for a few hours but for 6 weeks. PCP is not just another hallucinogen—many authorities view it as much more dangerous than other drugs of abuse (Dewan 2003; Maier 2003).

Medical Management The diagnosis of a PCP overdose is frequently missed because the symptoms often closely resemble those of an acute schizophrenic episode.

Simple, uncomplicated PCP intoxication can be managed with the same techniques used in other psychedelic drug cases. It is important to have a quiet environment, limited contact with an empathic person capable of determining any deterioration in the patient's physical state, protection from self-harm, and the availability of hospital facilities. "Talking down" is not helpful; the patient is better off isolated from external stimuli as much as possible.

Valium is often used for its sedating effect to prevent injury to self and to staff and also to reduce the chance for severe convulsions. An antipsychotic agent (for example, haloperidol [Haldol]) is frequently administered to make the patient manageable (Jaffe 1990).

The medical management of a comatose or convulsing patient is more difficult. The patient may need external respiratory assistance and external cooling to reduce fever. Blood pressure may have to be reduced to safe levels and convulsions controlled. Restraints and four to five strong hospital aides are often needed to prevent the patient from injuring himself or herself or the medical staff. After the coma lightens, the patient typically becomes delirious, paranoid, and violently assaultive.

Effects of Chronic Use Chronic PCP users may develop a tolerance to the drug; thus, a decrease in behavioral effects and toxicity can occur with frequent administration. Different forms of dependence may occur when tolerance develops. Users may complain of vague cravings after cessation of the drug. In addition, long-term difficulties in memory, speech, and thinking persist for 6 to 12 months in the chronic user (NIDA Infofax 1999c). These functional changes are accompanied by personality deficits such as social isolation and states of anxiety, nervousness, and extreme agitation (*DSM-IV-TR* 2000).

Ketamine

Ketamine has received attention lately as a "club drug." Its annual use in 2004 by high school seniors was 1.9% (Johnston 2004). Ketamine, like PCP, was originally developed for its general anesthetic properties (Research Report 2001). Its effects resemble those of PCP except they are more rapid and less potent (Research Report 2001). Depending on the dose, ketamine can have many effects, ranging from feelings of weightlessness to out-of-body or near-death experiences. Ketamine, often referred to as "Special K," has been abused as a "date rape" drug like other CNS depressants, such as Rohypnol or gamma-hydroxybutyrate (GHB) (see Chapter 6; Research Report 2001). Abuse of ketamine has been reported in many cities throughout the United States, and the drug is sometimes snorted as a substitute for cocaine. Several deaths have been linked to ketamine overdoses (NIDA Infofax 1999a).

Dextromethorphan

Dextromethorphan is the active ingredient used in many OTC cough medicines because of its ability to suppress the cough reflex (Research Report 2001). However, when consumed in high quantities (approximately 10 times the recommended dose), it can cause some hallucinogenic effects much like PCP and ketamine do. These effects can vary and have been described as ranging from a mild stimulant effect to a complete dissociation from one's body. The effects can last for several hours. Abuse of dextromethorphan is typically done by teenagers and is sometimes referred to as "roboing" (Schulz 2004).

Marijuana

In high doses, marijuana use can result in image distortions and hallucinations (Nunez and Gurpegui 2002). Some users claim that marijuana can enhance hearing, vision, and skin sensitivity, although these claims have not been confirmed in controlled laboratory studies.

Although typical marijuana use does not appear to cause severe emotional disorders like the other hallucinogens, some experts suggest it can aggravate underlying mental illness such as depression. Each month, thousands of people seek professional treatment due to marijuana-related problems (McRae et al. 2003). In contrast to other hallucinogens that have a combination of stimulant and psychedelic effects, high doses of marijuana cause a combination of depression and hallucinations and enhance the appetite (Fleckenstein 2000). Marijuana is discussed thoroughly in Chapter 13.

■ NATURAL SUBSTANCES

Naturally Occurring Hallucinogens

Many plants contain naturally occurring hallucinogens. As already discussed, examples of such substances include mescaline from the peyote cactus, psilocybin from psilocybe mushrooms, and anticholinergic drugs such as atropine from the deadly nightshade plant, mandrake, or jimsonweed. Although some of these plants have been used for medicinal purposes for centuries, typically the therapeutic benefit has not been a consequence of the hallucinogenic effects of the substance. For example, anticholinergic drugs usually cause CNS

Ketamine is frequently used as a general anesthetic for veterinarian procedures.

depression and induce sleep; therefore, herbs that contain these drugs have been used as sleep potions. The hallucinogenic properties of some natural products, such as peyote, are viewed as positive by some cultures. As already mentioned, peyote is employed in a religious context as a sacrament for the Native American Church. In the United States today, the hallucinogen-containing natural substances are generally not viewed as therapeutic and are more likely to be used for their mind-altering properties as "recreational" drugs by adolescents (see "Case in Point," Jimsonweed Abuse in Idaho). Some users claim because these are "natural" rather than "synthetic" sources of a hallucinogenic episode, that somehow it makes the experience more rewarding and desirable. There is no evidence that the natural-versus-synthetic features of a hallucinogen are responsible for "the quality" of a drug-induced hallucination.

Salvia divinorum

Occasionally, obscure hallucinogenic herbs make their way into the culture of hallucinogenic substance users. This migration has become easier because of the Internet and specialized web sites that provide information (some accurate and much anecdotal) and the means to acquire these typically "natural" substances. For example, a relatively recent hallucinogenic fad has been the use of the Mexican herb *Salvia divinorum*. This relatively unknown plant is referred to as "diviner's mint" and is legal in the United States despite its ability to cause intense hallucinations, "out-of-body" experiences, and short-term memory loss (Jones 2001; Pienciak 2003). Promotions for these products include advertising claims such as "The Mazatec people have preserved *Salvia divinorum* and the knowledge surrounding its use for hundreds of years. We are privileged to have them share their sacred herb with us" (Jones 2001, p. A14). The dried herb can sell for as much as $120 per ounce. The drug typically makes the user introverted while "altering the conscious in unusual ways" (Jones 2001). Although national drug information sources and law enforcement officers are not well informed about this and other similar obscure hallucinogenic herbs, they claim to be watching carefully to see whether their use will cause significant health or social problems (Jones 2001; Shiner 2003). This herb can have dramatic effects on perception, causing hallucinations when chewed or smoked (Leinwand 2003). It typically is not used in social settings and often is used only once because the effects can be quite unpleasant, often triggering a lack of coordination and frightening perceptions (Simmie 2003). Because of its frequent negative consequences, this herb is not viewed as particularly addicting (Pienciak 2003).

Discussion Questions

1. Why were substances with hallucinogenic properties used by ancient religions and cults?

►Case in Point   Jimsonweed Abuse in Idaho

Jimsonweed is a natural herb whose medicinal purposes include treatment for asthma, muscle spasms, and whooping cough. Its dangerous side effects include hallucinogenic actions and induction of a rapid heartbeat. Because of the effects jimsonweed has on the body, and because it is a legal, uncontrolled substance, adolescents have been known to take this herb for its psychedelic properties. For example, a new wave of jimsonweed abuse in eastern Idaho recently resulted in several teenagers entering the emergency room in drug-induced comas. Jimsonweed is a fairly accessible and somewhat inexpensive herb that is dangerous not only because of its biological effects, but also because of the variability of its side effects' intensity from batch to batch.

Source: "Jimson Weed Abuse in Idaho" (2003). Available www.drug-rehabs.org/content.php?cid=1097&state=Idaho.

2. Would you expect "natural" hallucinogens such as peyote to have less adverse effects than other hallucinogens? Why or why not?

3. Why would a drug with both stimulant and hallucinogenic effects have peculiar abuse potential?

4. Why do some users find psychedelic experiences terrifying while others find them desirable?

5. Do you think the federal government is justified in lying to the public about the dangers of hallucinogens to convince people to stop using these drugs? Defend your answer.

6. How do the side effects of LSD compare with those of the CNS stimulants?

7. Why has MDMA become so popular?

8. Why is PCP more dangerous than LSD?

9. How do PCP and ketamine compare?

10. What is the best way to convince people that hallucinogenic drugs of abuse can be harmful?

11. What is a flashback and how is it caused?

Key Terms

hallucinogens 354

psychedelics 354

psychotomimetic 354

psychotogenic 356

synesthesia 358

flashbacks 358

ergotism 360

mydriasis 365

entactogens 368

jimsonweed 372

analogs 373

catatonia 374

Summary

1 Many drugs can exert hallucinogenic effects. The principal hallucinogens include LSD types, phenylethylamines, and anticholinergic agents. The four major effects that occur from administering LSD include (1) heightened senses, (2) loss of sensory control, (3) self-reflection or introspection, and (4) loss of identity or sense of cosmic merging.

2 Hallucinogens exaggerate sensory input and cause vivid and unusual visual and auditory effects.

3 The classic hallucinogens, such as LSD, cause predominantly psychedelic effects. Phenylethylamines are related to amphetamines and cause varying combinations of psychedelic and stimulant effects. Anticholinergic drugs also produce psychedelic effects when taken in high doses.

4 One of the prominent effects of hallucinogens is self-reflection. The user becomes aware of thoughts and feelings that had been forgotten or repressed. It is claimed that some experiences help to clarify motives and relationships and cause periods of greater openness. These effects have been promoted by some psychiatrists as providing valid insights useful in psychotherapy.

5 The classic hallucinogens do not cause physical dependence. Although some tolerance can build up to the hallucinogenic effects of drugs such as LSD, withdrawal effects are usually minor.

6 The environment plays a major role in determining the sensory response to hallucinogens. Environments that are warm, comfortable, and hospitable tend to create a pleasant sensory response to the psychedelic effects of these drugs. Threatening, hostile environments are likely to lead to intimidating, frightening "bad trips."

7 In some users, high doses of LSD can cause a terrifying destruction of identity, resulting in panic and severe anxiety that resembles schizophrenia. Another psychological feature commonly associated with LSD is the "flashback" phenomenon. LSD use can cause recurring, unexpected

visual and time distortions that last a few minutes to several hours. Flashbacks can occur months to years after use of the drug.

8 Designer amphetamines such as MDMA (Ecstasy) have been included in the "club drug" phenomenon. MDMA is frequently used by young people to enhance the sensory experience of "raves" and the nightclub scene. Although viewed by some as harmless and even therapeutic, evidence of potentially serious negative consequences suggests that these drugs can be extremely dangerous in high doses and under some conditions.

9 Hallucinogens purchased on the "street" are often poorly prepared and contaminated with adulterant substances. This practice of cutting the pure drugs with other substances also makes use of street hallucinogens very dangerous.

10 PCP differs from the other traditional hallucinogens in several ways: (1) It is a general anesthetic in high doses. (2) It causes schizophrenia-like psychosis. PCP can produce incredible strength and extreme violent behavior, making users very difficult to manage. (3) Management of the severe psychological reactions to PCP requires drug therapy, whereas treatment of other hallucinogens often requires only reassurance, "talking down," and supportive therapy. (4) Reactions to overdoses include fever, convulsions, and coma.

11 Other substances also abused for their hallucinogenic properties include ketamine, a veterinary general anesthetic; dextromethorphan, a common OTC anticough medication; and some natural herbs, such as *Salvia divinorum,* that are promoted over the Internet.

▌References

Abraham, H., A. Aldridge, and P. Gogia. "The Psychopharmacology of Hallucinogens." *Neuropharmacology* 14 (1996): 285–298.

Adler, J. "Getting High on Ecstasy." *Newsweek* (15 April 1985): 15.

Aghajanian, G., and G. Marck. "Serotonin Model of Schizophrenia Emerging Role of Glutamate Mechanisms." *Brain Research Review* 31 (2000): 302–312.

Associated Press. "60s Icon Timothy Leary Cooperated with the FBI." *Salt Lake Tribune* 258 (1 July 1999): A-10.

Associated Press. "Judge Rules Boy, 4, Can't Take Peyote." *The Washington Post* (23 April 2003): A-2.

Burger, A., ed. "Quotes from Albert Hofmann." Drugs Affecting the Central Nervous System. *Psychotomimetic Agents,* vol. 2. New York: Dekker, 1968.

Burke, J. "Ecstasy Death Toll Set to Go on Rising." *Guardian Unlimited* (2001). Available http://society.guardian.co.uk.

Cami, J., M. Farre, M. Mas, and P. Roset. "Human Pharmacology of Ecstasy: Psychomotor Performance and Subjective Effects." *Journal of Clinical Psychopharmacology* 20 (2000): 455–466.

Carlini, E. "Preliminary Note: Dangerous Use of Anticholinergic Drugs in Brazil." *Drugs and Alcohol Dependence* 32 (1993): 1–7.

"Celebration #1." *New Yorker* 42 (1966): 43.

Claus, E. P., V. E. Tyler, and L. R. Brady. *Pharmacognosy,* 6th ed. Philadelphia: Lea & Febiger, 1970.

Cloud, J. "The Lure of Ecstasy." *Time* 155 (5 June 2000): 62.

Dewan, S. "A Drug Feared in the '70s Is Tied to Suspect in Killing." *The New York Times* (6 April 2003).

Diagnostic and Statistical Manual of Mental Disorders. 4th ed., Text Revision (*DSM-IV-TR*). Washington DC: APA, 2000.

Dishotsky, N. I., W. D. Loughman, R. E. Mogar, and W. R. Lipscomb. "LSD and Genetic Damage." *Science* 172 (1971): 431–440.

Drug Abuse USA Home. "Entactogens: MDA, MDMA and MDEA." (25 April 2000). Available www.drug-abuse.com/information/mdma/mdma4.html.

Drug Enforcement Agency (DEA). "Trippin on Tryptamine." *Intelligence Brief* (October 2002a): Document # DEA-02052.

Drug Enforcement Agency (DEA). "September 2002 Highlight." *Domestic Strategy* (December 2002b): Publication # DEA-02060.

Farley, C. "Rave New World." *Time* 15 (5 June 2000): 69.

Fleckenstein, A. "Pharmacological Aspects of Substance Abuse." In *Remington: The Science and Practice of Pharmacy,* 20th edition, edited by A. Gennaro, 1175–1182. Baltimore, MD: Lippincott Williams & Wilkins, 2000.

Goldstein, A. *Addiction from Biology to Drug Policy.* New York: Freeman, 1994.

Goldstein, F. "Pharmacological Aspects of Substance Abuse." In *Remington's Pharmaceutical Sciences,* 19th ed., edited by A. R. Gennaro, 780–794. Easton, PA: Mack, 1995.

Greer, G., and R. Tolbert. "The Therapeutic Use of MDMA." In *Ecstasy: The Clinical, Pharmacological and Neurotoxicological Effects of the Drug MDMA,* edited by S. J. Peroutka, 28. Boston: Kluwer, 1990.

Halpern, J., and H. Pope. "Hallocinogen Persisting Perception Disorder: What Do We Know After 50 Years?" *Drug and Alcohol Dependence* 69 (2003): 109–119.

Hegadoran, K., G. Baker, and M. Bourin. "3,4-Methylenedioxy Analogues of Amphetamine: Defining the Risks to Humans." *Neuroscience and Behavioral Review* 23 (1999): 539–553.

Huxley, A. *The Doors of Perception*. New York: Harper, 1954.

Hyslop, M. "Townsend Spearheads Campaign to Curb Rising Use of Ecstasy." *The Washington Times* (29 September 2000): C-1.

Jaffe, J. "Drug Addiction and Drug Abuse." In *The Pharmacological Basis of Therapeutics*, 8th ed., edited by A. Gilman, T. Rall, A. Nies, and P. Taylor, 522–573. New York: Pergamon, 1990.

Jentsch, J., and R. Roth. "The Neuropsychopharmacology of Phencyclidine: From NMDA Receptor Hypofunction to the Dopamine Hypothesis of Schizophrenia." *Neuropsychopharmacology* 20 (1999): 201–225.

Johnston, L. University of Michigan News Release (17 December 1999), citing the National Survey on Drug Abuse.

Johnston, L. "Overall Teen Drug Use Continues Gradual Decline; But Use of Inhalants Rises." Available http://www.monitoringthefuture.org.

Johnston, L., P. O'Malley, and J. Bachman. *National Survey Results on Drug Use from Monitoring the Future Study, 1975–1994*, vol. 2. University of Michigan, NIDA, NIH Publication No. 96-4027. Washington, DC: National Institute on Drug Abuse, 1996.

Jones, R. "New Cautions About an Herb That's Hip, Hallucinogenic and Legal." *The New York Times* (9 July 2001): A-14.

Jones, W. H. S. *Natural History*. Cambridge, MA: Harvard University Press, 1956.

Kalant, H. "The Pharmacology and Toxicology of 'Ecstasy' (MDMA) and the Related Drugs." *Canadian Medical Association Journal* 165 (2001): 917–928.

Leary, T., R. Metzner, and R. Alpert. *The Psychedelic Experience*. New Hyde Park, NY: University Books, 1964.

Leinwand, D. "Teens, and Now DEA, Are on Trail of Hallucinogenic Herb." *USA Today* (23 June 2003): 1.

Maier, T. "PCP Is Rearing Its Ugly Head Again." *Insight on the News* (17 February 2003): 4–6.

"Many Were Lost Because of Leary" Letters (to the editor). *USA Today* 14 (3 June 1996): 12-A.

Marken, P., S. Stoner, and M. Bunker. "Anticholinergic Drug Abuse and Misuse." *CNS Drugs* 5 (1996): 190–199.

Marquardt, G. M., V. DiStefano, and L. L. Ling. "Pharmacological Effects of (S)-, and (R)-MDA." In *The Psychopharmacology of Hallucinogens*, edited by R. C. Stillman and R. E. Willette. New York: Pergamon, 1978.

Mathias, R. "NIDA Research Takes a New Look at LSD and Other Hallucinogens." *NIDA Notes* 8 (March/April 1993): 6.

McGlothin, W., S. Cohen, and M. S. McGlothin. "Long-Lasting Effects of LSD on Normals." *Archives of General Psychiatry* 17 (1967): 521–532.

McRae, A., A. Budney, and K. Brady. "Treatment of Marijuana Dependence: A Review of the Literature." *Journal of Substance Abuse Treatment* 24 (2003): 369–376.

Medical Letter. "Phencyclidine (PCP)." 38 (10 May 1996): 45.

Mims, B. "Peyote: When the Ancient Indian Way Collides with a New Age Craze." *Salt Lake Tribune* 260 (12 August 2000): C-1.

Naranjo, C., A. T. Shulgin, and T. Sargent. "Evaluation of 3,4-Methylenedioxyamphetamine (MDA) as an Adjunct to Psychotherapy." *Medicina et Pharmacologia Experimentalis* 17 (1967): 359–364.

National Drug Threat Assessment 2003. "Other Dangerous Drugs, Hallucinogens." *National Drug Intelligence Center*, U.S. Department of Justice (2003): Product No. 2003-Q0317-001.

Nichols, D. "Hallucinogens." *Pharmacological Therapeutics* 101 (2004): 131–181.

NIDA Infofax. Club Drugs (November 1999a). Available 165.112.78.61/Infofax/clubdrugs.html.

NIDA Infofax. LSD (November 1999b). Available 165.112.78.61/Infofax/lsd.html.

NIDA Infofax. PCP (Phencyclidine) (November 1999c). Available 165.112.78.61/Infofax/pcp.html.

Nunez, L., and M. Gurpegui. "Cannabis-Induced Psychosis: A Cross-sectional Comparison with Acute Schizophrenia." *Acta Psychiatry Scandinavia* 105 (2002): 1173–1178.

O'Brien, C. "Drug Addiction and Drug Abuse." In *The Pharmacological Basis of Therapeutics*, 9th ed., edited by J. Hardman and L. Limbird, 557–577. New York: McGraw-Hill, 1996.

ONDCP. "MDMA (Ecstasy)." *Drug Policy Information Clearing House Fact Sheet* (February 2004). Available www.whitehousedrugpolicy.gov/publications/factsht/mdam/.

Pahnke, W. N., A. A. Kurland, S. Unger, C. Savage, and S. Grof. "The Experimental Use of Psychedelic (LSD) Psychotherapy." In *Hallucinogenic Drug Research: Impact on Science and Society*, edited by J. R. Gamage and E. L. Zerkin. Beloit, WI: Stash, 1970.

Pahnke, W. N., and W. A. Richards. "Implications of LSD and Experimental Mysticism." *Journal of Religion and Health* 5 (1966): 175–200.

Parrott, A. "Human Research on MDMA Neurotoxicity: Cognitive and Behavioral Indices of Changes." *Neuropsychobiology* 43 (2000a): 17–24.

Parrott, A. "Psychobiological Problems in Heavy 'Ecstasy' (MMA) Polydrug Users." *Drug and Alcohol Dependence* 60 (2000b): 105–110.

Pienciak, R. "DEA Issues Warning for Legal Herb Stronger Than LSD." *Daily News (NY)* (25 July 2003).

Publishers Group. "Street Drugs." 2805 Alvarado Lane North, Plymouth, MN 55447 (2002).

Research Report. "Hallucinogens and Dissociative Drugs." *NIDA Research Report Series* (March 2001): NIH Publication # 01-4209.

Schultes, R. E. "The Plant Kingdom and Hallucinogens (Part III)." *Bulletin on Narcotics* 22 (1970): 25–53.

Schultes, R. E. "Ethnopharmacological Significance of Psychotropic Drugs of Vegetal Origin." In *Principles of Psychopharmacology*, 2nd ed., edited by W. G. Clark and J. del Giudice. New York: Academic Press, 1978.

Schultes, R. E., and A. Hofmann. *The Botany and Chemistry of Hallucinogens.* Springfield, IL: Thomas, 1973.

Schultes, R. E., and A. Hofmann. *The Botany and Chemistry of Hallucinogens,* 2nd ed. Springfield, IL: Thomas, 1980.

Schulz, S. "Dextromethorphan—A Dangerous Trip" (14 March 2004). Available www.theindependent.com/stories/031404/new_dextro15.shtm.

Shiner, S. "Mystic Herb Catches Fire." *The Washington Times* (28 March 2003).

Simmie, S. "Herb Inspires High Expectations." *Toronto Star* (28 July 2003).

Snyder, S. H. *Madness and the Brain.* New York: McGraw-Hill, 1974.

Stone, J. "Turn On, Tune In, Boot Up." *Discover* 12 (June 1991): 32–33.

Taylor, J. "All-New MDMA FAQ." *Usenet News* (27 May 1994). Available sci.med.pharmacy.

Tiongson, J., and P. Salen. "Mass Ingestion of Jimsonweed by Eleven Teenagers." *Delaware Medical Journal* 70 (1998): 1–6.

Toufexis, A. "A Crackdown on Ecstasy." *Time* (10 June 1985): 64.

Tucker, R. "Acid Test." *Omni* (November 1987): 16.

U.S. Department of Justice. "Let's All Work to Fight Drug Abuse." Pamphlet from DEA published by L.A.W. Publications and distributed with permission by International Drug Education Association, 1991.

U.S. Department of Justice. "Drugs, Youth, and the Internet." *Information Bulletin* (October 2002): Product #2002-L0424-006.

Vollenwelder, F., M. Vollenwelder-Scherpenhuyzen, A. Baber, N. Vogel, and D. Nell. "Psilocybin Induces Schizophrenia-like Psychosis in Human via a Serotonin-2 Agonist Action." *NeuroReport* 9 (1998): 3897–3902.

Williams, J. "Prenatal Exposure to Ecstasy May Impair Memory and Cognition." *NIDA Notes* 17 (October 2002): 8.

Zickler, P. "NIDA Launches Initiative to Control Club Drugs." *NIDA Notes* 14 (2000): 1.

CHAPTER 13

Marijuana

Did You Know?

- Marijuana contains hundreds of chemical compounds but only a few found in the resin are responsible for producing the euphoric "high."

- In the 1930s, one early belief about marijuana was that smokers turned into killers.

- In the 1930s, marijuana was brought across the U.S. borders by Mexican laborers who migrated into the United States seeking jobs.

- George Washington grew marijuana plants at Mount Vernon for medicine and rope making.

- Out of 19.5 million illicit drug users in the United States, marijuana was used by approximately 75% of current illicit drug users, or approximately 14.6 million people.

- In some states, marijuana is one of the largest cash-producing crops.

- Marijuana still grows wild in many American states today.

- Research shows that many users have difficulty learning and remembering what they have learned when they are "high."

- "Although two-thirds of the U.S. population opposes legalizing marijuana, almost three-quarters think it should be made legally available to physicians to prescribe to patients for reducing pain and suffering" (Robert Wood Johnson Foundation 2001, p. 78).

- Approximately 90% of senior high school students report that marijuana is "very easy" to get.

- A typical "high" from one "joint" may last from 2 to 3 hours.

- Marijuana has been found to impair many skills required for safe driving: alertness, ability to concentrate, coordination, and reaction time.

- In June 2000, Hawaii became the first state to approve a medical marijuana bill.

- Tetrahydrocannabinol (THC) reaches the brain within 14 seconds after inhalation.

- Surveys indicate that 60% to 80% of marijuana users sometimes drive when "high."

- Cannabis has been used to treat extreme nausea, glaucoma, pain, depression, and convulsions.

- THC is stored for a long period in body fat; complete elimination can take up to 30 days.

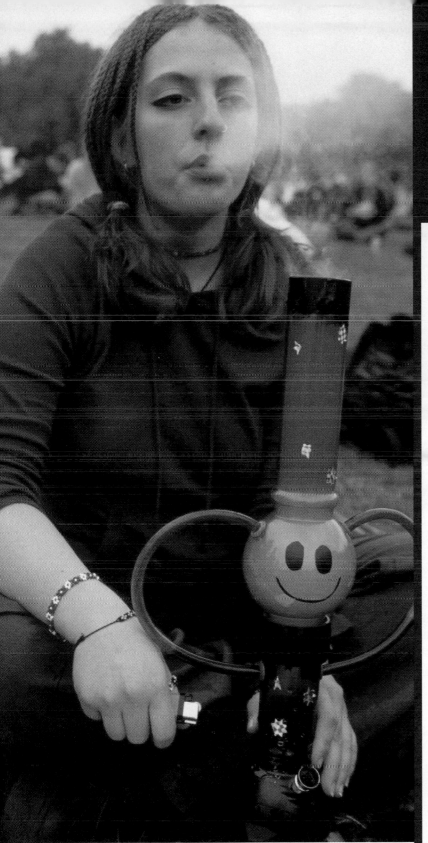

On completing this chapter you will be able to:

◎ Explain what marijuana is and why it remains so controversial.

◎ Differentiate between the effects of low and high doses of marijuana.

◎ List and explain the potential effects marijuana use has on the body.

◎ Describe how tolerance and dependence affect the response to marijuana and its use.

◎ Explain the medical uses of marijuana.

◎ Explain what age groups are most likely to use marijuana.

◎ Explain how the percentages of first-time users of marijuana changed from 1994 to 1997.

◎ Explain how the perceived danger of marijuana use has changed with regard to high school seniors and younger age groups.

◎ Differentiate between prior and current beliefs regarding the effects of chronic marijuana use.

Since I was in college and tried my first hit, I have always been a connoisseur of what we used to call grass, now it's weed or even "the ganja." I first went through a period of using it a lot—it was a different way to get a buzz. Then I got married and my wife did not like me smoking it, and we had kids, so except for a few occasional puffs from my neighbor, I just about gave it up. Then I got divorced from [my wife] and I married a woman who does not object to me smoking a little weed every now and then, even though she does not do it herself. So sometimes on weekends, I will roll a joint before going to bed and take a few puffs off of it. I know it is illegal, but big deal, who knows about it? I used to watch that program "Cops" and just found it silly when police officers would arrest someone (usually a young kid) for possession. Big bust, I would think. Isn't it silly to charge someone with possession of marijuana? I consider it to be like alcohol and cigarettes. I don't think it should be illegal anymore. I know so many people who do it and there are dozens of people who probably use this drug that I am not even aware of their using it. What happens if two-thirds of our population uses this drug? Are we going to charge and arrest all these people? The whole illegality of it is silly. *(From Venturelli's research files, interview with a 48-year-old male working as a restaurant owner, residing in Reno, Nevada, June 10, 2000.)*

We used to have one great big bong and fill it with dope [referring to marijuana], and all of us in someone's fraternity room would each take hits from the bong. Today, it's a different life altogether. I am working three different jobs, one teaching at a junior high school, [one] working at a film production studio, and my third claim to fame is my job as a part-time waiter. . . . I feel that I wasted many nights by just "smokin'," "dopin'," and "drinkin'" back during those college days. I sometimes think that I could have accomplished a lot more if I would not have inhaled so much dope. If I had to do it over again I would not have wasted so much time. *(From Venturelli's research files, interview with a 28-year-old male, August 9, 1996.)*

The preceding interviews illustrate two contrasting views regarding marijuana usage as a subcultural phenomenon. The first interview presents a "die-hard" user who refuses to relinquish his use of this drug. This individual has been using marijuana for many years and considers it an essential recreational drug. Conversely, the second interviewee expresses some regret over the time "wasted" while becoming intoxicated with marijuana when he could have been pursuing other, more career-oriented activities.

Introduction

Although marijuana is potentially less addictive than other drugs, such as cocaine, crack, heroin, and barbiturates (to name a few), it remains one of the few drugs that is controversial. It is difficult to wade through the emotion, politics, and rigidity found in the writings on marijuana to tease out the objective, clinical reality. In the United States, extreme views go back to the 1930s, when the film *Reefer Madness* portrayed an after-school marijuana "club" for high school students in suits and ties who became hallucinatory, homicidal, violent, and suicidal; such symptoms were highly exaggerated. As a complete contradiction, in the same decade, the Rastafarian religion spread among Jamaican agricultural workers, who named marijuana a *holy plant*.

[In] *Ganja in Jamaica* (Rubin and Comitas 1975) [the book] focused its findings to refute the claim that marijuana users damaged their productive capability. The study found that most rural Jamaicans who smoked ganja (marijuana) were extraordinarily diligent peasants who invested impressive amounts of time and energy in multiple income-bearing schemes every day of the year. Starting before sunrise, they tended livestock and poultry; farmed gardens; hired out their labor for wages; exchanged goods and services in an indigenous marketing system; maintained churches, self-help associations, political parties, guilds, schools, and households; and sometimes, at night, clandestinely cleared acres of forest to cultivate marijuana. They listened to the radio, watched television, and read newspapers to perform better as citizens in a modern democracy. These active, clear-sighted economic strategist and community builders depended on a heavy daily intake of ganja for nourishment as "brain food," and relied on it specifically to improve production. Adult Jamaican marijuana smokers consumed some six or more large "spliffs" (hand-rolled cigars) of ganja a day, or a few ounces. They also consumed it in teas, tisanes, and tonics. As employers, they preferred to pay their employees ganja rather than money and encouraged its use in the workplace. (Rubin and Comitas 1975, cited in Hamid 1998, p. 61)

Marijuana is simply the hemp plant, *Cannabis sativa,* which has been cultivated for thousands of years. When smoked, the dried and crushed leaves, stems, and seeds of cannabis produce sedative and mind-altering effects, which vary according to the potency of the variety of plant used. Usage in the United States began in the 1920s, rose during the 1960s and 1970s, and fell in every year from 1978 until 1991. From 1991 on, however, usage began to climb. In this chapter, we review the history, past and current usage trends, attitudes, and controversies surrounding marijuana (including the amotivational syndrome and the recent debate inspired by proposals for medical legalization), and its physiological and behavioral effects on the user.

History and Trends in Marijuana Use

In many societies, marijuana has historically been a valued crop. It is called *hemp* because the woody fibers of the stem yield a fiber that can be made into cloth and rope. The term *cannabis* comes from the Greek word for hemp. Initially, the Spaniards brought cannabis to the Western Hemisphere as a source of fiber and seeds. For thousands of years, the seeds have been pressed to extract red oil used for medicinal and euphorigenic purposes (Abood and Martin 1992; Iversen 1993). The plant (both male and female) also produces a resin with active ingredients that affect the central nervous system (CNS). Marijuana contains hundreds of chemical compounds, but only a few found in the resin are responsible for producing the euphoric "high."

Even the original uses of marijuana remain controversial. Botanists have never been able to trace cannabis to its origins, although some think it originated in Asia. Ancient Chinese documents contain the earliest record name of hemp—*ma*, meaning fiber producing plant. In the late 1970s, during an archeological dig in Gansu, the seat of Chinese civilization, workers uncovered cannabis seed stored in an earthen jar.

Ayurvedic documents from 600 B.C. describe an intoxicating resin from the plant. The fifth century B.C. Greek historian Herodotus recorded that the Scythians burned the tops of the plant, producing a narcotic smoke. And a first-century Greek physician wrote that hemp was made into intoxicating cakes, perhaps the forerunners of the marijuana brownies of 1960s fame. (Pollan 1998, p. 39)

Other sources report that the first known record of marijuana use is the *Book of Drugs* written about 2737 B.C. by the Chinese Emperor Shen Nung; he prescribed marijuana for treating gout, malaria, gas pains, and absentmindedness. The Chinese apparently had much respect for the plant. They obtained fiber for clothes and medicine from it for thousands of years. The Chinese named the plant *ma* (maw), which in the Chinese language can also mean "valuable" or "endearing." The term *ma* was still used as late as 1930.

Around 500 B.C., another Chinese book of treatments referred to the medical use of marijuana. Nonetheless, the plant got a bad name from the moralists of the day, who claimed that youngsters became wild and disrespectful from the recreational use of *ma*. They called it the "liberator of sin" because, under its influence, the youngsters refused to listen to their elders and did other scandalous things. Although the Chinese recognized *ma*'s medical usefulness, they eventually banned it because of its unpredictable intoxicating effects. Later, because of rampant use, it was legalized again.

India also has a long and varied history of marijuana use. It was an essential part of Indian religious ceremonies for thousands of years. The well-known Rig Veda and other chants describe the use of *soma*, which some believe was marijuana. Early writings describe a ritual in which resin was collected from the plants. After fasting and purification, certain men ran naked through the cannabis fields. The clinging resin was scraped off their bodies, and cakes were made from it and used in feasts. For centuries, missionaries in India tried to ban the use of marijuana, but they were never successful, because its use was too heavily ingrained in the culture. From India, the use of marijuana spread throughout Asia, Africa, Europe, and the Americas—English settlers brought it to the U.S. colonies.

Assyrian records dating back to 650 B.C. refer to a drug called *azulla* that was used for making rope and cloth and was consumed to experience euphoria. The ancient Greeks also knew about marijuana. Galen described the general use of hemp in cakes, which, when eaten in excess, produced narcotic effects. Herodotus described the Scythian custom of burning marijuana seeds and leaves to produce a narcotic smoke in steam baths. It was believed that breathing the smoke from the burning plants would cause frenzied activity. Groups of people stood in the smoke and laughed and danced as it took effect.

One legend about cannabis is based on the travels of Marco Polo in the 12th century. Marco Polo told of the legendary Hasan Ibn-Sabbah, who terrorized a part of Arabia in the early 1100s. His men were some of the earliest political murderers and he ordered them to kill under the influence of hashish, a strong, unadulterated cannabis derivative. The cult was called the *hashishiyya*, from which came the word *hashish*. (The word *assassin* may be derived from the name of Sheik Hasan, who was a political leader in the 10th century.)

It is unlikely, however, that using hashish can turn people into killers. Experience suggests that people tend to become sleepy and indolent rather than violent after eating or smoking hashish or another of the strong cannabis preparations available in Arabia (Abel 1989).

Napoleon's troops brought hashish to France after their campaign in Egypt at the beginning of the 19th century, despite Napoleon's strict orders to the contrary. By the 1840s, the use of hashish, as well as opium, was widespread in France, and efforts to curb its spread were unsuccessful.

In North America, hemp was planted near Jamestown in 1611 for use in making rope. By 1630, half of the winter clothing at this settlement was made from hemp fibers. There is no evidence that hemp was used medicinally at this time. Hemp was also valuable as a source of fiber for clothing and rope for the Pilgrims at Plymouth. To meet the demand for fiber, a law was passed in Massachusetts in 1639 requiring every household to plant hemp seed. However, it took much manual labor to work the hemp fiber into usable form, resulting in a chronic shortage of fiber for fishnets and the like (Abel 1989).

George Washington cultivated a field of hemp at Mount Vernon, and there is some indication that it was used for medicine as well as for making rope. In his writings, Washington once mentioned that he forgot to separate the male and female plants, a process usually done because the female plant gave more resin if not pollinated.

In the early 1800s, U.S. physicians used marijuana extracts to produce a tonic intended for both medicinal and recreational purposes. This practice changed in 1937 with passage of the Marijuana Tax Act. The Marijuana Tax Act was modeled after the Harrison Act of 1914 in that marijuana was now considered a narcotic and subject to the same legal controls as cocaine and the opiates (see Chapter 3). Like these opiates, marijuana distributors had to register and pay a tax to legally import, buy, or sell this drug (Musto 1999). As a result, the Marijuana Tax Act prohibited the use of this drug as an intoxicant and regulated its use as a medicine.

Most of the abuse of marijuana in the United States during the early part of the 20th century took place near the Mexican border and in the ghetto areas of major cities. Cannabis was mistakenly considered a narcotic, like opium, and legal authorities treated it as such (Abood and Martin 1992). In 1931, Harry Anslinger, who was the first appointed head of the Bureau of Narcotics and later would become responsible for the enforcement of marijuana laws, believed that the problem was slight (Musto 1999). By 1936, however, he

FIGURE 13.1

This antimarijuana poster was distributed by the Federal Bureau of Narcotics in the late 1930s.

claimed that the increase in the use of marijuana was of great national concern (Anslinger and Cooper 1937; see Figure 13.1). Anslinger set up an informational program that ultimately led to the federal law that banned marijuana. The following sensationalized statement was part of Anslinger's campaign to outlaw the drug:

> What about the alleged connection between drugs and sexual pleasure? . . . What is the real relationship between drugs and sex? There isn't any question about marijuana being a sexual stimulant. It has been used throughout the ages for that: in Egypt, for instance. From what we have seen, it is an aphrodisiac, and I believe that the use in colleges today has sexual connotations. (Anslinger and Cooper 1937, p. 19)

In addition, during this time, some usually accurate magazines reported that marijuana was partly responsible for crimes of violence. In 1936, *Scientific American* reported that "marijuana produces a wide variety of symptoms in the user, including hilarity, swooning, and sexual excitement. Combined with intoxicants, it often makes the smoker vicious, with a desire to fight and kill" ("Marijuana Menaces Youth" 1936, p. 151). A famous poster of the day, called "The Assassination of Youth," was effective in molding attitudes against drug use.

Largely because of the media's influence on public opinion, Congress passed the Marijuana Tax Act in 1937. However, as a result of the discussions and debates before the passage of the 1970 Comprehensive Drug Abuse Prevention and Control Act, which replaced or updated all other laws concerning narcotics and dangerous drugs, the Marijuana Tax Act of 1937 was declared unconstitutional in 1969 because it classified marijuana as a narcotic. (For further historical details, see Chapter 3.) Marijuana has not been classified as a narcotic since 1971.

In the early 1900s, marijuana was brought across the U.S. borders by Mexican laborers who entered the United States seeking jobs. From the border areas of the United States, recreational use of marijuana spread into mainly the southwestern region of the United States. Such use reached major cities in Texas and surrounding states as well as a number of African American communities in these cities. Heavy users of marijuana included a subpopulation of jazz musicians as well as other "bohemian types" who led more of an unstructured existence in unconventional jobs and occupations (artists, entertainers, poets, criminals, and so on). Thus, before the 1960s, marijuana use was largely confined to small segments of African American urban youth, jazz musicians, and particularly artists and writers who belonged to the 1950s Beat Generation. Use rose tremendously in the 1960s, when it was closely associated with the hippie counterculture, in which marijuana was categorized as a psychedelic (consciousness-expanding) sacrament. It spread into other youth categories during the 1970s, until approximately 1978. In each year from 1978 until 1991, marijuana use fell. After 1991, researchers and prevention specialists were astounded to see a rise in usage among youth.

Marijuana still grows wild in many American states today. Curiously, one reason for the survival of this supply is that, during World War II, the fiber used to make rope (sisal) was hard to import, so the government paid subsidies to farmers who grew hemp. Much of today's crop comes from these same plants. Another reason for the spread of the plants is that, until recently, the seeds were used in birdseed. Leftover seed was discarded in the garbage and thus spread to landfill dumps, where it sprouted. Birdseed containing marijuana seeds is still available, but the seeds are sterilized so that they cannot germinate.

The Indian Hemp Drug Commission Report in the 1890s and the 1930 Panama Canal Zone

Report on marijuana stressed that available evidence did not prove marijuana to be as dangerous as it was popularly thought; these reports were given little publicity, however, and for the most part were disregarded. In 1944, a report was issued by the LaGuardia Committee on Marijuana, which consisted of 31 qualified physicians, psychiatrists, psychologists, pharmacologists, chemists, and sociologists appointed by the New York Academy of Medicine. They stated in one key summary that marijuana was not the killer many thought it to be:

> It was found that marijuana in an effective dose impairs intellectual functioning in general. . . . Marijuana does not change the basic personality structure of the individual. It lessens inhibition and this brings out what is latent in his thoughts and emotions but it does not evoke responses that would otherwise be totally alien to him. . . . Those who have been smoking marijuana for years showed no mental or physical deterioration that may be attributed to the drug. (Solomon 1966, p. 37)

Much of the early research conducted did not consider the potency of marijuana. As a result, findings from various studies are often conflicting and difficult to compare. Because the quality of marijuana varies so greatly, it is impossible to know the amount of drug taken without analyzing the original material and the leftover stub, or "roach." Conditions such as type of seed, soil moisture and fertility, amount of sunlight, and temperature all have an effect on the amounts of active ingredients found in the resulting marijuana plant.

Current Use of Marijuana

The National Survey on Drug Use and Health (NSDUH) in 2004 reported that marijuana is the most commonly used *illicit* drug (14.6 million past-month users) (SAMHSA 2004). In 2003, out of an estimated 19.5 million Americans aged 12 or older who were current users of any type of illicit drug, marijuana was used by 75.2%.* An estimated

54.6% of current illicit drug users used only marijuana, 20.6% used marijuana and another illicit drug, and the remaining 24.8% used an illicit drug but not marijuana in the past month (see Figure 13.2). About 45.4% of current illicit drug users in 2003 (8.8 million Americans) used illicit drugs other than marijuana and hashish, either with or without marijuana.

Other current findings are as follows (SAMHSA 2004):

• There were an estimated 2.6 million new marijuana users in 2002 (see Figure 13.3). This means that each day on average 7000 Americans tried marijuana for the first time. About two-thirds (69%) of these new marijuana users were younger than age 18, and roughly half (53%) were female.

• The annual number of marijuana initiates generally increased from 1965 until about 1973 (see Figure 13.3). From 1973 to 1978, the annual number of marijuana initiates remained level at slightly more than 3 million per year. After 1978, the number of initiates declined,

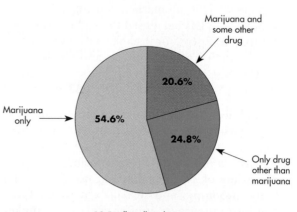

19.5 million illicit drug users

FIGURE 13.2

Types of drugs used in the past month, aged 12 or older in 2003.

Source: Substance Abuse and Mental Health Services Administration (SAMHSA). *Results From the 2003 National Survey on Drug Use and Health: National Findings.* Rockville, MD: Office of Applied Studies, 2004.

---

*Current drug use is defined as having used an illicit drug in the month before the NSDUH surveys were conducted.

FIGURE 13.3

Annual number of new users of marijuana, 1965–2002.

....

Source: Substance Abuse and Mental Health Services Administration (SAMHSA). *Results from the 2003 National Survey on Drug Use and Health: National Findings.* Rockville, MD: Office of Applied Studies, 2004.

reaching a low point in 1989, then rose again until 1995. From 1995 to 2002, no consistent trend was observable, with estimates of new users varying between 2.4 million and 2.9 million per year. The proportion of marijuana initiates younger than age 18 (69% in 2002) has generally increased since the 1960s, when less than half of initiates were younger than age 18. The average age of marijuana initiates was around 19 in the late 1960s and was 17.2 in 2002.

- Among all youths aged 12 to 17 in 2003, 11.2% were current illicit drug users: 7.9% used marijuana, 4.0% used prescription-type drugs, 1.3% used inhalants, 1.0% used hallucinogens, and 0.6% used cocaine.
- Rates of marijuana use were highest among young adults (18 to 25 years) at 20.3%, with 17% using marijuana.
- Among adults aged 26 or older, of the 5.6% who reported current illicit drug use, 4% used marijuana.
- Boys had a higher rate of marijuana use than girls (8.6% versus 7.2%).
- In 2003, 12.2% of past-year marijuana users used marijuana on 300 or more days in the past

12 months. This rate translates into 3.1 million persons using marijuana on a daily or almost daily basis over a 12-month period. This total was the same number as found in 2002. However, the number of youths aged 12 to 17 who used marijuana daily or almost daily declined from 358,000 in 2002 to 282,000 in 2003. The number of youths who used marijuana on 20 or more days in the past month declined from 603,000 in 2002 to 482,000 in 2003.

As Table 13.1 shows, the frequency of marijuana use is strongly correlated with age. The age group reporting the highest lifetime (53.9%), past-year (28.5%), and past-month (17%) was 18- to 25-year-olds. For the 26 and older age group, marijuana use sharply drops during the past year (6.9%) and past month (4.0%).

Table 13.2 shows the number of people who first used marijuana from 1999 to 2002 by average age and age-specific rate of first use. In comparing Table 13.1 with Table 13.2, it becomes apparent that although drug use remains highest among youth, first use of marijuana is highest among 12- to 17-year-olds, fluctuating from 86.5% in 1999 to a high of 98.2% in 2000. The next highest

Table 13.1 **Marijuana Use Reported in 2003 by Americans During Lifetime, Past Year, and Past Month, According to Age**

AGE (YEARS)	LIFETIME (%)	PAST YEAR (%)	PAST MONTH (%)
12–17	19.6	15.0	7.9
18–25	53.9	28.5	17.0
26 and older	41.2	6.9	4.0

Source: Results from the 2003 National Survey on Drug Use and Health: National Findings. Rockville, MD: Department of Health and Human Services, Substance Abuse and Mental Health Services Administration, Office of Applied Studies, 2004.

rate of first use of marijuana is found among 18- to 25-year-olds, ranging from 59.8% in 1999 to a low of 49.4% in 2002. Although not shown in Table 13.2, overall the percentage of new "recruits" using marijuana for the first time is highest for people younger than 26 years of age as compared with other age groups beyond 26 years of age. In particular, Table 13.2 indicates that although the percentages of first-time users have been decreasing for 18- to 25-year-olds, 12- to 17-year-olds do not show the same downward trend from 1999 through 2002. In summary, while a modest pattern of declining initial use of marijuana is evident for the 18- to 25-year-old first-time users, the 12- to 17-year-old first-time users do not show the same trend.

TRENDS IN USE

As stated previously, marijuana is by far the most widely used illicit drug. Nearly half of all seniors (46%) in high school report some marijuana use in their lifetime, 35% report some use in the past year, and 21% report some use in the past month. Among 10th graders, the corresponding rates are 36%, 28%, and 17%, respectively. Even among 8th-grade students, marijuana has been used by more than one in six (18%), with 13% reporting use in the prior year and 8% reporting use in the prior month. Current daily marijuana use (defined as use on 20 or more occasions in the past 30 days) is also noteworthy. One in 17 12th graders (6%) uses marijuana daily, as do one in 28 10th graders (3.6%) and about one in 100 8th graders (1%) (Johnston et al. 2004).

More recent findings also indicate that of all students in each grade who report some illicit drug use in their lifetime, half have used only marijuana: 40% of all 8th-grade users of any illicit drug (9% of the total 8th-grade sample), 52% of all 10th-grade users of any illicit drug (22% of the total 10-grade sample), and 46% of the 12th-grade

Table 13.2 **Estimated Number (in Thousands) of Persons Who First Used Marijuana During 1999–2002, Their Age of First Use, and Annual Age-Specific Rates of First Use**

YEAR	INITIATES (1000'S)	MEAN AGE (YEARS)	AGE-SPECIFIC RATE OF FIRST USE	
			12–17 YEARS	18–25 YEARS
1999	2,175	17.5	86.5%	59.8%
2000	2,862	16.9	98.2%	56.1%
2001	2,806	17.3	93.6%	56.3%
2002	2,573	17.2	87.0%	49.4%

Source: Results from the 2003 National Survey on Drug Use and Health: National Findings. Rockville, MD: Department of Health and Human Services, Substance Abuse and Mental Health Services Administration, Office of Applied Studies, 2004.

(A) Percentage using marijuana in the last 12 months

(B) Percentage perceiving harmfulness from marijuana use

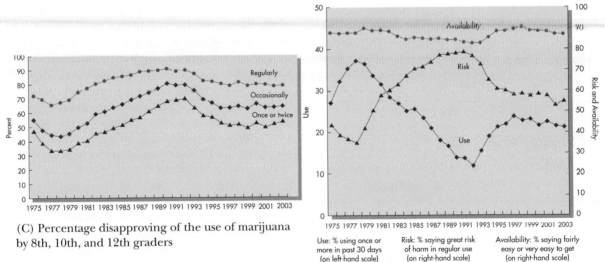

(C) Percentage disapproving of the use of marijuana by 8th, 10th, and 12th graders

Use: % using once or more in past 30 days (on left-hand scale)

Risk: % saying great risk of harm in regular use (on right-hand scale)

Availability: % saying fairly easy or very easy to get (on right-hand scale)

(D) Percentage of 12th graders perceiving the availability and risk of regular use, and reporting use of marijuana in the past 30 days

FIGURE 13.4

Trends in annual use, perceived risk, disapproval, and perceived availability, risk, and use of marijuana among 8th, 10th, and 12th graders.

Source: Johnston, L. D., P. M. O'Malley, and J. G. Bachman, and J. E. Schulenberg. *Monitoring the Future: National Survey Results on Drug Use, 1975–2003: Volume 1, Secondary School Students.* Bethesda, MD: National Institutes of Health, National Institute on Drug Abuse, 2004.

users of any illicit drug (23% of the total 12th-grade sample). Put another way, more than half of the 8th and 12th graders and nearly half of the 10th graders who ever used an illicit drug have used something in addition to, or other than, marijuana (Johnston et al. 2004).

ANNUAL USE

Figure 13.4 illustrates trends in annual use, perceived harmfulness, disapproval, and perceived availability, risk, and use of marijuana among 8th, 10th, and 12th graders. Figure 13.4A indicates that annual and 30-day prevalence (not illustrated) of marijuana use leveled off between 1978 and 1979, following a steady rise in the preceding years. In 1980, there was a drop in both statistics for the first time. These rates continued to decline every year through 1992, except for a brief pause in 1985. Following this 12-year decline, annual use of marijuana among 12th graders rose sharply beginning in 1993. Indeed, this rate nearly doubled between 1992 and 1997, from 22% to 39%. It was not until 1998 that this trend turned around, although annual use did not decline a significant amount. By 2003, annual use had declined to 35%, still only modestly lower than the recent peak level of 39% in 1997.

PERCEIVED HARMFULNESS

Figure 13.4B shows that in 1978 the percentage of 8th, 10th, and 12th graders perceiving "great risk" from using marijuana was at a low point (approximately 34% for 12th graders). From 1979 to 1991, the percentage identifying this drug with "great risk" continued to rise to approximately 78% of 12th graders. Since 1992 to 2003, the percentage of 12th graders perceiving "great risk" has been dropping to its current low of approximately 55%. **Perceived risk** is a leading indicator of change in

use. When the amount of risk associated with marijuana use decreases, a resurgence of use follows shortly. Similarly, when perceived risk increases, a decrease in use usually follows.

DISAPPROVAL

Figure 13.4C shows that the percentage of youths saying they "disapprove" of using marijuana was at a low point in 1977. Disapproval percentages have been increasing since 1977, peaked in 1990, showed a very moderate downward trend from 1992 through 2003. Thus, there is less disapproval of using marijuana today than in previous years.

PERCEIVED AVAILABILITY, RISK, AND USE

From 1975 through 1978, the degree of harmfulness perceived as being associated with all levels of marijuana use declined as use increased sharply; see Figure 13.4D. For the first time in 1979, the proportion of high school seniors seeing risk to the marijuana user increased. In 1992, perceived risk began to drop again, which presaged a sharp increase in use beginning in 1993. As perceived risk continued to decline, use rose in tandem until 1997. The association between perceived risk and use generally goes hand-in-hand: That is, perceived risk decreases as use increases, and vice versa. Perceived risk peaked in 1991, but continually declined from 1992 through 2002, with a slight increase beginning in 2003.

Figure 13.4D also indicates that from 1975 through 2003 a steady proportion of 12th graders (90%) believed that marijuana is fairly easy or very easy to get. One interview revealed a common belief at many of U.S. public schools:

What, weed? It's so easy to get. In fact, many times, I didn't even have to buy, it would be offered in the morning, at lunchtime, and whenever we get together, even after school it is there. Among the users (and we know each other real well), it's as common as sharing candy. (*From Venturelli's research files, 15-year-old male, first-year high school student residing in a medium-size town in the Midwest, June 19, 2000.*)

Marijuana: Is It the Assassin of Youth?

In the late 1930s, the poster "Marijuana: Assassin of Youth" made a clever play on words, bringing up reminders of the Middle Eastern "hashashin" cult, whose terrible exploits were attributed to their use of hashish (marijuana resin).

At the time, marijuana was even incorrectly classified as a narcotic, like opium and morphine. Amotivational syndrome, lassitude, poor driving skills the day after smoking, educational failure, and dependence may not quite add up to "assassination," as wildly exaggerated in *Reefer Madness*. The poster was right, however, in associating use of this drug with young people, among whom marijuana is popular in both local peer groups and broad youth cultures.

MAJOR FACTORS AFFECTING MARIJUANA USE

As discussed in the beginning chapters of this text, the mass media, parental role models, perceived risk, availability, and peers have the most direct influence on the development of youths' attitudes regarding drug use. Just recently, parental use of marijuana has been found to be a significant influence on teens' use of this drug.

In a study by Kandel et al. (2001), when parents had used marijuana at some time in their lives, their teen children were 40% more likely to have used the drug in their lifetime than teens whose parents had never used marijuana. Moreover, when parents had used marijuana in the past year, their children were *twice* as likely to have used in the same time period than were teens whose parents had not used in the past year. This same study also found that when parents had used marijuana in the past year, their teen children were more likely to have used marijuana in the past year when compared with the children of parents who had used at some time in their life, but not in the last year. Similarly, parental use of other drugs, such as alcohol, nicotine, and cocaine, was also found to have an impact on their teen children's use of marijuana. More importantly, the perceived risk of use is the most important influence on teen marijuana use. In the Kandel et al. (2001) study, it was found to be *five* times more important than parental use.

When comparisons are made between 8th, 10th, and 12th graders, the perceived availability of marijuana rises sharply with grade level. In 2003, 45% of 8th graders said marijuana would be "fairly easy" or "very easy" to get, versus 74% of 10th graders and 87% of 12th graders (Johnston et al. 2004). Children in lower grades are less likely to have friends and access to friends who use marijuana (as well as access to other major drugs of abuse). Marijuana has been almost universally available to American high school seniors (from 83% to 90%) over at least the past 28 years (Johnston et al. 2004).

Beginning several years before age 13 (early adolescence), peers and peer groups begin to exert the most influence (Greenblatt 1999; Heitzeg 1996; Tudor et al. 1987; Venturelli 2000). Research shows that it is unlikely that an individual will use drugs when his or her peers do not use them. Marijuana use, in particular, is a group-motivated behavior that is strongly affected by peer pressure and influence. In effect, habitual drug users are likely to belong to drug-using groups. In contrast, people who do not use drugs belong to groups in which drug use is perceived as an unacceptable and devious form of social recreation. Learning theory (see Chapter 2) explains how peers can influence one another; drug-using peer members serve as role models, legitimizing use. Peers in such groups are saying, in essence, "It's perfectly normal to use drugs"; in turn, this justifies usage.

A common example of polydrug use (alcohol and marijuana).

In addition to these major factors (the mass media, parental role models, perceived risk, availability, and peer influences), four other factors must be taken into account as influencing drug use:

1. Structural factors, such as age, gender, family background, and religious beliefs
2. Social and interactional factors, such as the type of interpersonal relationships, friendship cliques, and drug use within the peer group setting
3. Setting, such as the type of community and neighborhood (physical location of drug use)
4. Attitudinal factors, such as personal beliefs and attitudes regarding drug use, and personality factors, such as self-esteem, level of security versus insecurity, and maturation level

Keep in mind these factors can easily overlap; they are not separate and distinct.

Sociologists have long studied "youth cultures" (Coleman 1961). In the 1970s, sociologists began to examine different subcultures of youth in terms of the behaviors that symbolically represent the group, in which participation in drug use is a ritual that marks off entrance into the group and out of childhood—a "rite of passage." Typically, American high school culture includes a "leading" clique, often associated with team sports, whose members might be called "jocks," "collegiates," or "rah-rahs," and a marginal, deviant, or rebellious group (Eckert 1989). In some cases, the latter group is associated with marijuana use. In the mid-1960s, hippies were perceived as a group whose members were part of a counterculture committed to unconventional values, pacifism, and communalism in addition to psychedelic drugs. By 1970, this name denoted broader segments of youth who adhered merely to hippie styles of clothing and drug use (Buff 1970). By the 1980s, marijuana use was identified with subgroups of youth often called "burnouts." In many communities that were studied by

sociologists, "burnouts" came from all social levels, but were often overrepresented in upper-middle classes, and they were marginal and/or rebellious within the educational system, if not dropouts (Eckert 1989; Gaines 1992). Membership in such marijuana-using subcultures often bonds the youth to persistent drug use.

Is Marijuana Really a Gateway Drug?

Gateway drugs are drugs that serve as the "gate" or path that usually precedes the use of illicit drugs, such as marijuana, heroin, and LSD. Gateway drugs, or drugs-of-entry, serve to initiate a novice user into the drug-using world. Although the linkage is not biochemical, common gateway drugs include tobacco, inhalants, alcohol, and anabolic steroids.

The claim that marijuana use most often leads to the use of other more serious drugs, such as heroin, remains controversial (Gardner 1992). A recent Rand press release reports that the gateway theory does not explain the progression to other more addictive drugs; instead, "The people who are predisposed to use drugs and have the opportunity to use drugs are more likely than others to use both marijuana and harder drugs. . . . Marijuana typically comes first because it is more available" (Rand Drug Policy Research Center 2002). Thus, instead of assuming that marijuana, alcohol, and other, more commonly used drugs are simply gateway drugs responsible for leading to other, more serious drugs, it is more likely that other factors such as (1) the age when teens have opportunities to use marijuana and other drugs, (2) associated opportunities, and (3) the willingness to use drugs are better predictors of the progression from less addictive to more addictive and powerful types of drugs.

For example, the gateway theory cannot explain the fact that although it is true many heroin addicts began drug use with marijuana, it is also true that many, if not most, also used coffee and cigarettes. Millions of marijuana users never go beyond the gateway drugs used. "There are only a few thousand opiate addicts in Great Britain, yet there are millions who have tried cannabis" (Gossop 1987, p. 9).

KEY TERMS

gateway drugs
drugs that often lead to the use of more serious drugs; alcohol, tobacco, and marijuana are the drugs most commonly believed to be gateway drugs

Nevertheless, some explanation is needed for the small percentage of marijuana users who do progress to hard drugs such as heroin. It is unlikely that the use of marijuana is the *principal* cause of moving to harder drugs.

As described in Chapter 16, youths who turn to drugs are usually slightly to seriously alienated individuals. Thus, progression from marijuana to other drugs is more likely to depend on peer group composition, family relationships, social class, and the age at which drug use begins (Indiana Prevention Resource Center 1996).

It is important to note, however, that many, if not most, young drug users do eventually leave drug-using groups and abandon their drug-using behavior, a process sometimes called *maturing out.* An example that often typifies maturing out is found in the following interview:

> Sure, smoking dope and tripping on acid was a way of life when I was a teenager. But then I graduated college and had to join the real world—that everyday work world that my dull parents lived in. *(From Venturelli's research files, 28-year-old female, working for a national private security firm, August 12, 2000.)*

Other research further documents some young "burnouts" quitting marijuana smoking without sacrificing group membership (Eckert 1989).

Misperceptions of Marijuana Use

In a world in which marijuana can be considered either an "assassin" or a "sacrament," and in which it is associated with membership in prized or despised peer groups, it is not surprising that estimates of its use vary widely and inaccurately. Parents, for example, tend to underestimate their children's use of drugs. Findings from one study indicated that, "only 14% of the parents interviewed thought their children had experimented with marijuana while 38% of the teenagers said they had tried it" (Wren 1996, p. 1). In the same survey, 52% of teenagers reported having been offered drugs, while 34% of the parents thought their children might have been offered drugs.

Interestingly, another report by the former president of the National Center on Addiction and Substance Abuse at Columbia University stated the following with regard to baby boomer parents (parents born between the late 1940s through late 1950s):

> Almost half know someone who uses illegal drugs; a third have friends who use marijuana. Almost half expect their children to try illegal drugs, and 65 percent of those who smoked pot regularly when young believe their kids will try drugs . . . almost half of the parents don't think they can have much influence on whether their kids will use drugs. (Califano 1996, p. 19)

Even with regard to users' perceptions of other users, beliefs about marijuana remain distorted. College students tend to have exaggerated misperceptions of use, believing that their peers use marijuana much more than is true (Berkowitz 1991). For example, at one campus in northern New Jersey, two-thirds of students reported never using marijuana, yet most students polled believed that the average student uses marijuana once per week. Thus, with regard to marijuana users, interest in using remains persistently strong for the time being. In the early years of this millennium, high usage of marijuana remains stubbornly persistent.

Characteristics of Cannabis

In 1753, Carolus Linnaeus, a Swedish botanist, classified marijuana as *Cannabis sativa* (see Figure 13.5). *Cannabis sativa* is a plant that grows readily in many parts of the world. Most botanists agree that there is only one species (*sativa*) and that all the variants (*indica*, *Americana*, and *africana*) belong to that species, whereas others believe that the variants are three distinct species (Schultes 1978). *Indica* is considered to have the most potent resin, but climate, soil, and selective plant breeding all influence potency. The world's record

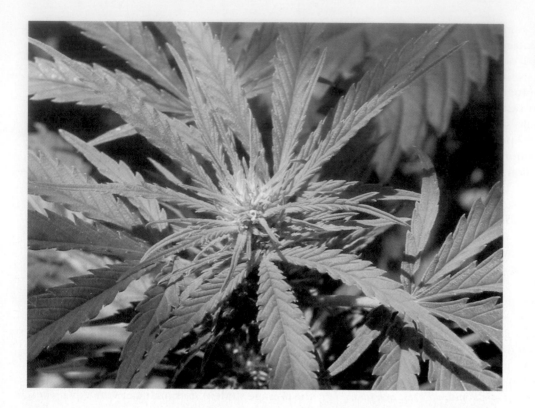

FIGURE 13.5
Marijuana plant.

marijuana plant was 39 feet tall, and its woody stem was nearly 3 inches in diameter.

Cannabis is *dioecious*, meaning that there are male and female plants. After the male plant releases its pollen, it usually dies. In any case, even before the male plant dies, cultivators of marijuana often eliminate or remove the male plants after the female plant has been pollinated.

There are more than 421 different chemicals in the cannabis plant, many of which have not yet been identified. Tetrahydrocannabinol, or THC, is the primary mind-altering (psychoactive) agent in marijuana (Abood and Martin 1996; Swan 1996) and appears to be important for the reinforcing properties of this substance (Kelly et al. 1994). THC is most highly concentrated in the flowering tops and upper leaves of the female plant. When crushed or beaten, these flowering tops produce a resin in which the psychoactive ingredient THC is found.

In cultivated marijuana crops, male plants are eradicated from the growing fields so that they cannot pollinate the female plants. The lack of pollination makes the potency of female plants increase dramatically. **Sinsemilla** (meaning "without seeds" in Spanish) is one of the most potent derivatives of the cannabis plant known in the United States, with an average of 7.5% and a range as high as 24% THC. *Sinsemilla* is made from the buds of flowering tops of female plants (NIDA 1998). Other known types that have a much higher THC content include "hydro" (which means grown in water) and "kine bud."

In the United States, the amount of THC found in street-sold marijuana ranges broadly from 0.5% to 11%. Reports indicate that the amount of THC in marijuana has risen dramatically since the 1960s (Kaplan and Whitmire 1995; NIDA 1998). "More efficient agriculture—new methods of harvesting and processing marijuana plants—has made pot about 20 times more potent than the

KEY TERMS

sinsemilla
meaning without seeds, this marijuana is made from the buds and flowering tops of female plants and is one of the most potent types

marijuana on the street in the 1960s and 1970s, drug treatment experts and law officials say" (Henneberger 1994, p. F-18). Further, the quantities of other, more potent types of marijuana such as sinsemilla as well as hydroponic types of marijuana ("hydro") are more readily available in illegal drug markets. The actual potencies of the more generic types of marijuana have remained the same in the past 30 years.

The latest reports indicate the following:

> Marijuana produced in Mexico remains the most widely available in the United States. High potency marijuana has also entered the U.S. drug market from Canada. Another source for marijuana in the United States is domestically grown marijuana, which includes both indoor and outdoor operations. Groups operating from Mexico employ a variety of transportations and concealment methods to smuggle marijuana into the United States. Most of the marijuana smuggled into the United States is concealed in vehicles—often in false compartments—or hidden in shipments of legitimate agricultural or industrial products. Marijuana is also smuggled across the border by rail, horse, raft, and backpack. Canada is becoming a source country for indoor-grown, high potency (15% to 25% THC) marijuana destined for the United States. Such indoor-grow operations have become an enormous and lucrative illicit industry, producing a potent form of marijuana that has come to be known as "BC Bud." (ONDCP 2003)

Native U.S. street-variety marijuana, often referred to as "ditch weed" *cannabis,* is sometimes considered inferior because of its low concentration of THC, usually less than 0.5%. THC levels in Jamaican, Colombian, and Mexican varieties range between 0.5% and 7%. This type of marijuana is made from parts of the cannabis plant that contain the least amount of THC. Some members of drug-using subcultures grind this type of marijuana (as well as more potent types of marijuana) into a powder and mix it into drinks, teas, and cookie and brownie batter.

Hashish (or hasheesh) is a second derivative of cannabis that contains the purest form of resin. This type of marijuana consists of the sticky resin from the female plant flowers and has an average THC level of 3.6%, but can go as high as 28% (NIDA 1998). Historically, hashish users have represented a somewhat small percentage of the cannabis user population in the United States, whereas in Europe use is much more prevalent. Hashish is produced in Lebanon, Afghanistan, and Pakistan.

A third derivative of the cannabis plant is *ganja,* which is produced in India. This preparation consists of the dried tops of female plants.

The Behavioral Effects of Marijuana Use

THE "HIGH"

The then widely held belief of the 1930s that marijuana is a destructive assassin of youth is no longer considered valid for casual or occasional users of this drug. In most individuals, low to moderate doses of cannabis produce euphoria and a pleasant state of relaxation (Goldstein 1994). What are the common effects experienced from marijuana use? After a few minutes of forcibly holding the smoke in the lungs, most users suddenly experience the "high." In this state of euphoria, the user experiences a dry mouth, elevated heartbeat, and some loss of coordination and balance, coupled with slower reaction times and a feeling of euphoria (mild to elevated intoxication). Blood vessels in the eyes expand, which accounts for reddening of the eyes. Some people experience slightly elevated blood pressure, which can double the normal heart rate. These effects can become intensified when other drugs, such as LSD and/or psychedelic ("magic") mushrooms, are combined with the marijuana.

The state of euphoria that results from the "high" is usually mild and short-lived; a typical high from one joint may last from 2 to 3 hours. Subjectively, the user experiences altered perception of space

KEY TERMS

hashish
sticky resin from the female plant flowers, which has an average THC level of 3.6% but ranges as high as 28%

and time, impaired memory of recent events, and impaired physical coordination (more of these subjective effects are discussed at length in the next section; Abood and Martin 1992). An occasional high is not usually hazardous unless the person attempts to drive a car, operate heavy machinery, fly a plane, or function in similar ways requiring coordination, good reflexes, or quick judgment (Nahas and Latour 1992). Even low doses of marijuana adversely affect perception, such as being able to judge the speed of an approaching vehicle or how much to slow down on an exit ramp. One interview revealed the following:

> In trying to describe the high, it's not like an alcohol high. In an alcohol high, you are a lot more uncoordinated if drinking a lot. With weed, it's like reality changes—you add a lot more base so-to-speak to what you see, hear, think, and feel. The reality is tempered with some distortion that to me and many others is pleasurable. You know how you feel after three or four very strong drinks [referring to alcoholic beverages]. Well take two more of those drinks and then look around the room you are in. Now, the difference between alcohol and weed is that you can walk to the bathroom quite well while under the influence of weed, while with alcohol you walk carefully so that no one notices that you are just about drunk. Weed is a mind high while alcohol is more of a body high. *(From Venturelli's research files, May 19, 2000, 23-year-old female, professionally employed and residing in San Francisco.)*

Two other interviews (same interviewee on two different occasions) also attempted to compare the "high" from marijuana with the effects of alcohol:

> The marijuana high is also not nearly as harsh on the body. Being high doesn't give you that painful hangover as alcohol does. The actual high is very functional; I tend to do some of my best work (after burning a "dubbie") in that state [of mind]. It is part of the lifestyle of mari-

juana. [In contrast], alcohol makes me (and most people I know) very unproductive when the "buzz" is reached. *(From Venturelli's research files, "Lectus Ferberger," 21-year-old male, undergraduate student at a Midwestern university, August 10, 2000.)*

> There seems to be a small misconception about the effects of marijuana and alcohol. For me, anyway, in looking at the physical "buzz" you get from alcohol, it is very physically disabling. You get drunk and stumble around, your lips loosen up, and you say things that you would not normally say. I find that marijuana has more of a calming effect. It makes you relaxed and a little more perceptive to some stimuli and obviously less perceptive to other stimuli. It is a light feeling, but not overwhelming to the equilibrium. *(From Venturelli's research files, same student as above, August 11, 2000.)*

An acute dose of cannabis can produce adverse reactions, ranging from mild anxiety to panic and paranoia in some users. These reactions occur most frequently in individuals who are under stress or who are anxious, depressed, or borderline schizophrenic (Nahas and Latour 1992). Such effects may also be seen in normal users who accidentally take much more than they feel they can handle.

Extreme reactions can also occur because of ingesting marijuana treated (or "laced") with such things as opium, PCP, or other additives. Based on limited evidence from survey studies, mild or often adverse reactions are experienced on one or more occasions by more than one-half of regular users; they are mainly self-treated and usually go unreported (see "Case in Point," Specific Signs of Marijuana Use).

SUBJECTIVE EUPHORIC EFFECTS

Subjective euphoric effects associated with marijuana use are the ongoing social and psychological experiences incurred while intoxicated by marijuana. These effects of intoxication include both the user's altered state of consciousness and his or her perceptions.

Subjective effects also include a general sense of relaxation and tranquility, coupled with height-

KEY TERMS

subjective euphoric effects
ongoing social and psychological experiences incurred while intoxicated with marijuana

►Case in Point   Specific Signs of Marijuana Use

- A sweet odor similar to burnt rope in room, on clothes, and so on.
- Roach: The small butt end of a marijuana cigarette.
- Joint: Looks like a hand-rolled cigarette; usually the ends are twisted or crimped.
- Roach clips: Holders for the roach could be any number of common items such as paper clips, bobby pins, or hemostats. They could also be of a store-bought variety in a number of shapes and disguises.
- Seeds or leaves in pockets or possession.
- Rolling papers or pipes, usually hidden somewhere.

- Eye drops: For disguising red eyes.
- Excessive use of incense, room deodorizers, or breath fresheners.
- Devices for keeping the substance such as film canisters, boxes, or cans.
- Eating binges: An aftereffect for some marijuana users.
- Appearance of intoxication, yet no smell of alcohol.
- Excessive laughter.
- Initial use (first hour): Animated behavior (loud or excessive talking).
- (Hours later): Fatigue or drowsiness.

ened sensitivity to sound, taste, and emotionality. Some users report occasional similarities to the typical hallucinogenic high. How closely the marijuana high resembles a hallucinogenic high depends on the amount of THC absorbed from marijuana. For example, higher amounts of THC found in more potent plants of marijuana, like *sinsemilla*, hydro, and kine bud more clearly mimic a hallucinogenic high. These effects are especially evident when considering the extent to which the senses of hearing, vision, sound, and taste are distorted by use of highly potent forms of marijuana.

Among marijuana users, some become very attached to these euphoric effects (in search of reexperiencing these effects). Such users often pride themselves on their extensive knowledge of this drug and maintain interest in discussing past experiences of "when I was really high" or "let me tell you about that night we smoked hydro. . . ." Devotees stay current with developments in the marijuana field by avidly reading monthly issues of magazines devoted to marijuana (the "art" of marijuana use) and frequently scan the Internet for information and conversations in chat rooms about the best varieties of marijuana, best growing techniques, announcements of hemp festivals, advice, and information regarding current laws, fines, and other information.

Why is marijuana so attractive to many individuals? One quote from an interview illustrates the extensive psychological and social reinforcement experienced by marijuana users:

It's the high that I particularly like. Everything becomes mellower. Everyday tensions are released or submerged by more inner-like experiences. I can review the day and how happy or miserable I feel. Actually, when I am thinking and I am high on grass, I always feel that my thoughts are profound. You think from another perspective, one that numbs the more reality-based everyday strains. On the other hand, there are moments when this drug affects your mood and channels it [in] different ways. You have moments when you either feel sad, happy, angry (in a more contemplative way), or worried. These moods are both good and bad. If for the moment you feel good, then your mood is positive. If you feel down, your mood is negative in a particular way. If I am with friends and we are all sharing the bong or joint or pipe, we laugh a lot together. It's a type of drug that makes you more jovial, more introspective, and friendly, gregarious. . . . *(From Venturelli's research files, 40-year-old male personnel manager, August 20, 1996.)*

Intense attachment to passionate feelings surrounding the use of marijuana is quite common. As explained in Chapter 2, largely through the reinforcement of pleasurable feelings, psychologists believe the drug user becomes attached and habituated to the drug. If these subjective euphoric experiences were to become largely negative, attachment to and repeated use of this drug would cease. Thus, the theory of differential association applies to the two interviewees. Developed by Edwin Sutherland in 1939 and revised in 1947, this theory attempts to explain delinquent behavior. Sociologists define the term **differential association** as the process by which individuals become socialized into the perceptions and values of a group. The application of this concept can be redefined as differential association with respect to drug use. In the case of marijuana, the drug-using group or even a fellow drug user rewards such behavior. It can include the perception that marijuana relieves boredom, stress, or is the "perfect" drug for just "hanging out" or "partying" and "getting high." Specifically, the definition of differential association is the behavioral satisfaction derived from friends who use marijuana. Psychologically, the high with others is the positive reward that cements the user to his or her friends and the drug.

DRIVING PERFORMANCE

Evidence shows that the ability to perform complex tasks, such as driving, can be strongly impaired while under the influence of marijuana (Goldstein 1994; Mathias 1996). Research indicates that "Cannabis consumption impairs motor coordination, reaction time, sensory perceptions and glare recovery" (Teen Challenge 2000, p. 1). This effect has been demonstrated in laboratory assessments of driving-related skills such as eye–hand coordination and reaction time, in driver simulator studies, in test course performance, and in actual street driving situations (Chait and Pierri

1992; Mathias 1996; Teen Challenge 2000). Another study tested the effects of known amounts of marijuana, alcohol, or both on driving. The subjects drove a course rigged with various traffic problems. There was a definite deterioration in driving skills among those who had used either drug, but the greatest deterioration was observed in subjects who had taken both. In another test, 59 subjects smoked marijuana until they were intoxicated and then were given sobriety tests on the roadside by highway patrol officers. Overall, 94% of the subjects did not pass the test 90 minutes after smoking, and 60% failed at 150 minutes, even though the blood THC was much lower at this time (Hollister 1986). Other studies on driving show this same inability to drive for as long as 12 to 24 hours after marijuana use.

In surveys, from 70% to 80% of marijuana users indicate that they sometimes drive while high. A study of drivers involved in fatal accidents in the greater Boston area showed that marijuana smokers were overrepresented in fatal highway accidents as compared with a control group of nonusers of similar age and gender. A 1998 study found that, of nearly 1800 blood samples taken from drivers arrested for driving while intoxicated, 19% tested positive for marijuana.

Further, "figures from previous studies of automobile accident victims show that from 6% to 12% of nonfatally injured drivers and 4% to 16% of fatally injured drivers had THC . . . in their bloodstream" (Mathias 1996, p. 6). Another study showed that 32% of drivers in shock trauma units had marijuana in their bloodstream. One problem with this study, however, is that individuals testing positive for THC also had alcohol in their bloodstream, making it impossible to determine whether THC or alcohol directly caused the car accident.

One notable interview presents us with a negative experience regarding use of marijuana and driving experiences:

One time I smoked some real strong dope at my friend's house, then had to drive back home, which was 2 miles in one direction. I remember wigging out (panicking) in trying to get home. There were moments when I did not know where I was until I would see the next marker of my neighborhood. I remember

KEY TERMS

differential association
behavioral satisfaction derived from friends who use marijuana

having seconds of panic because I did not know where I was; then suddenly, I would notice a neighborhood restaurant or some other marker that said I was right around my neighborhood. I took smaller streets on the way home and even took a longer way home because I was freaking out about the cops— what if one would spot me? This was bogus thinking because how the hell would anyone suddenly spot me while driving home? Well, that's an example of wigging out on weed. But, I still don't think that even that time I would be getting into an accident. I was so freaked out that I was extra careful not to speed, pass stop signs, or violate any law for fear of being seen. If anything, I drive slower when I am really high, not more dangerously. *(From Venturelli's research files, 20-year-old male college student in a Midwestern town, July 19, 2000.)*

In contrast, more scientific research indicates that some perceptual or other performance deficits resulting from marijuana use may persist for some time after the high, and users who attempt to drive, fly, operate heavy machinery, perform surgery, and so on may not recognize their impairment because they do not feel intoxicated. States such as California have established testing procedures to detect the presence of THC in urine or blood samples from apparently intoxicated drivers.

If the use of marijuana becomes more socially acceptable (or perhaps even legal) and penalties for simple possession become more lenient, it is likely that individuals will feel less inclined to hide their drug use. Unfortunately, it follows that these individuals may also be more inclined to drive while high, endangering themselves and others.

CRITICAL THINKING SKILLS

Marijuana has been found to have a negative impact on critical thinking skills. Recent research by NIDA shows that heavy marijuana use impairs critical skills related to attention, memory, and learning. Another study showed that even alertness, coordination, and reaction time were impaired by marijuana usage (NCADI 1998). Impairment continues even after discontinuing this drug's use for at least 24 hours (Brown and Massaro 1996).

In the same study, researchers compared 65 *heavy users* (using approximately every other day) with *light users* (using once or twice per week). Heavy users made more mistakes and had greater difficulty sustaining attention, shifting attention to meet demands of challenges in the environment, and registering, processing, and using information (Brown and Massaro 1996) compared with the light users. In addition, heavy users had greater difficulty completing the tests, which specifically measured aspects of attention, memory, and learning, such as intellectual functioning, abstraction ability, attention span, verbal fluency, and learning and recalling abilities (Brown and Massaro 1996; Teen Challenge 2000). One researcher stated, "If you could get heavy users to learn an item, then they could remember it; the problem was getting them to learn it in the first place" (Brown and Massaro 1996, p. 3). The researchers surmised that marijuana alters brain activity because residues of the drug persist in the brain or because a withdrawal syndrome follows the euphoric effects of the marijuana wear off. In another study, researchers tested the cognitive functioning of 65 marijuana-using college students. Residual impairments were seen on the day (24 hours) after use in terms of sustaining attention, shifting attention, and hence in registering, organizing, and using information (Pope and Yurgulen-Todd 1996). This study, which was undertaken during the 1990s, is significant because it was carefully controlled. The unresolved question is whether these memory impairments are short term or long term. These noteworthy findings complement many other similar findings that identified protracted cognitive impairment among heavy users of marijuana (NCADI 1998).

AMOTIVATIONAL SYNDROME

The so-called **amotivational syndrome** (sometimes referred to as "antimotivational syndrome") is a flashpoint of controversy about marijuana, although not as newsworthy as that regarding medical legalization. *Amotivational syndrome* refers to a belief

KEY TERMS

amotivational syndrome
a belief that heavy use of marijuana causes a lack of motivation and reduced productivity

Typical effects of amotivational syndrome

that heavy use of marijuana causes a lack of motivation and reduced productivity. Specifically, users show apathy, poor short-term memory, difficulty in concentration, and a lingering disinterest in pursuing goals (Abood and Martin 1992).

In the past, this syndrome received considerable attention. People who are high, or "stoned," lack the desire to perform hard work and are not interested in doing difficult tasks. There is some evidence of this behavior in regular marijuana users (Nahas and Latour 1992). Overall, although not solely the result of cannabis use, *chronic users* have lower grades in school, are more likely to be absent from classes, and are likely not to complete assignments and to drop out of school (Henneberger 1994; Liska 1997). In terms of age, the earlier someone begins smoking marijuana, coupled with heavier use, the more likely the amotivational characteristics will prevail and the more difficult it will be to cease using this drug.

Although the effects of marijuana per se are somewhat responsible for creating this syndrome, other factors contribute as well. For instance, is the lack of motivation caused by the drug itself or is it that poorly motivated people begin using marijuana, which then further exacerbates their lack of motivation? Surveys show that a sizable number of marijuana users and their peer groups tend to be alienated from society and are likely to be classified as nonconformists and/or rebellious youths. They may, in fact, select to emphasize pleasure and nonconformity rather than goal-directed behavior.

Advocates of marijuana legalization stress data that tend to debunk research on amotivational

syndrome. One institute that supports legalization, the Lindesmith Center, published a study asserting that college students who are users have higher grades than nonusers (Zimmer and Morgan 1997). How can we account for the discrepancies between this study and others, not to mention the clinical experiences of students, who often report academic repercussions of heavy use? One factor in the explanation is sociocultural:

> In the New York–New Jersey metro region, there are "druggy" schools and "drinking" schools. The "druggy" schools are more upper-middle class, liberal arts schools, artsy types, latter-day hippies, etc. The boozer campuses are filled with blue-collar and lower-middle-class kids—sometimes big fraternity schools. Frontloading at basketball games, comas after pledge parties . . . . Not as good educational backgrounds as the artsy potheads, who went to better schools, private schools, read a lot, or heard a lot at dinner before college, so they get by with their profs. However, the potheads ratchet down into easier majors, and they get crummier grades as they get into regular use. (*Interview with Pearl Mott, prevention specialist, Drug Prevention Programs in Higher Education, Washington, D.C., October 1994, for a prevention newsletter.*)

A second methodological factor complicating drug research among such students is simply that academic failures stay in "F" categories for only one or two semesters. Many then disappear from statistics entirely, via academic attrition.

A more serious challenge to the notion of amotivational syndrome comes from the same ethnographic research that was mentioned at the beginning of this chapter. The most well known of these investigations was carried out by Vera Rubin and Labros Comitas, as reported in their book *Ganja in Jamaica* (1975). Follow-up studies were done in Jamaica (Dreher 1982; Hamid 1998) and Costa Rica (Carter 1980; Pollan 1998). None of these works found that chronic use impaired occupational or other functioning; in fact, the main point of the Jamaican studies was that users defined this drug as helpful and motivating for work—a "motivational syndrome." This work is often cited to counter amotivational syndrome

▶Case in Point   Marijuana Use May Lead to a Life of Trouble

Dear Ann Landers: Twenty years ago, when I was in my early 20s, you printed a column about marijuana. You expressed concern that marijuana may have "taken a generation of doers and turned them into a generation of dreamers."

I used to smoke pot daily. I somehow managed to get through college and hold down a job, but I wasn't getting anywhere. Every night, I would get high and write down in a journal all the things I planned to do. After reading your column, I realized I had been doing the same thing year after year and was getting nowhere. I decided to quit smoking pot.

I can't begin to tell you how my life changed. I became bored with my party-animal boyfriend and later married a wonderful man. I went back to school, earned a master's degree and got an excellent position with a *Fortune* 500 company. I also developed much needed self-esteem. It was your column on marijuana that helped me turn my life around, and I want to write a belated "thank you."—*Margie in Tennessee*

Dear Tennessee: I very much appreciate your generous letter. Please keep reading for one that should be of special interest to you:

Dear Ann Landers: Last fall, my teen-age son began smoking marijuana and was soon out of control. I sent him away to a special program. He is much better now, but I could not understand how my son got into so much trouble. Two weeks ago, the truth came out.

Last summer, I sent my two teen-agers to visit their uncle and aunt across the country. I decided it would be a good way for my brother and his wife to get to know their niece and nephew. I was mistaken. He and his wife smoked pot in front of my kids and offered it to them.

I believe that my brother and his wife contributed to my son's problems, and I am considering suing them for the cost of the special program I put my son in. I am so angry about this that I am considering a break with the entire family. Please advise. *A Canadian Mom*

Dear Mom: Be thankful the "special program" was a success, and forget about a lawsuit and becoming estranged from the entire family. Mass retaliation is never a good idea.

Next summer, see that your son has a local job, and keep your eye on the companions he hangs out with.

Source: Ann Landers/*The Times of Northwest Indiana*, c/o Times Mirror, Los Angeles, CA 90053. Reprinted with permission of Esther P Lederer Trust and Creators Syndicate, Inc.

claims. By this logic, dropping out of the "rat race" is a cultural posture, with marijuana being secondary to, or, at most, reinforcing the drift away from a mainstream lifestyle. The Jamaican and Costa Rican subjects, however, were not observed engaging in an academic, cognitively complex, or rapid reflex activity, nor were they found in occupations that are competitive and striving for mobility. Rather, these subjects were involved in repetitive, physical labor such as sugar-cane cutting. In such a context, marijuana drug use functions to provide a pleasant sedation that counters the monotony and physical discomfort of such labor. When studies in other cultures contradict the largely American notion of amotivational syndrome, we are left to be cautious in making a direct assumption that marijuana use leads to such a syndrome. (For related information on how marijuana affects personality, see "Case in Point," Marijuana Use May Lead to a Life of Trouble.)

Therapeutic Uses and the Controversy over Medical Marijuana Use

In the last 7 years, new controversy about the medical uses of marijuana has begun to emerge. Basically, **medical marijuana use** involves using cannabis, primarily THC, as a drug to calm or to relieve symp-

KEY TERMS

medical marijuana use
use of the THC in cannabis as a drug to calm or to relieve symptoms of an illness

▶ Holding the Line   Cannabis Buyers' Club

In San Francisco, a small underground shop called the Cannabis Buyers' Club flourishes. Writer Richard C. Paddock describes a typical scene: "Dozens of people sit on rummage-sale couches and folding chairs, smoking high-grade marijuana. A dozen more line up at the counter, fingering the day's sample buds and buying their ration of weed." Although this setting may sound enticing to the average pot smoker, chances are he or she would be leery of partaking in this scene. As Paddock tells us, "doing your shopping here means you are sick or dying."

The Cannabis Buyers' Club is just one flourishing underground trend directed toward granting sick or dying people the right to use marijuana. Thousands of people stricken with such ailments as AIDS, cancer, glaucoma, epilepsy, and multiple sclerosis use marijuana every day to treat their sicknesses or allay their pains. Regarding the San Francisco scene, in 1995 Mayor Frank Jordan (formerly a police chief) said, "I have no problem whatsoever with the use of marijuana for medical purposes . . . we should bend the law."

Marijuana has been used for medical purposes for at least 5000 years, across cultures and generations; such a strong grounding in history would seem to grant a certain credibility to this drug as being medically beneficial. Unfortunately for proponents of medical cannabis use, the United States has been reluctant to permit studies on possible ways to allow open use of marijuana for medical reasons. For over 3 years, Donald Abrams of the University of California, San Francisco, a respected AIDS researcher, has been seeking government permission to conduct a "clinical trial to determine whether smoking marijuana can help patients overcome the deadly AIDS wasting syndrome." To date, Abrams has been unsuccessful in his attempts and predicts that he will be able to do his research if science can survive the politics.

Bob Randall, one of the eight people in the United States who can legally smoke marijuana, is quoted by Paddock as saying, "In a sane society, the prospect of an easy-to-grow plant that could ease suffering and prolong life would be a cause for celebration."

Source: Paddock, R. C. "'Drug Stores' Fill Prescriptions with Pot, Not Pills." *Salt Lake Tribune* 249 (1 March 1995): A-1.

toms of an illness. At the heart of this controversy is the use of an illicit drug for medical purposes. However, the desire to use cannabis in this fashion is nothing new. Between 1840 and 1900, European and American medical journals published more than 100 articles on the therapeutic use of the drug known then as *Cannabis indica* (or Indian hemp) and now as marijuana. It was recommended as an appetite stimulant, muscle relaxant, analgesic, hypnotic, and anticonvulsant. As late as 1913, Sir William Osler recommended it as the most satisfactory remedy for migraines (Grinspoon and Bakalar 1995).

Marijuana was used to treat a variety of human ills in folk and formal medicine for thousands of years in South Africa, Turkey, South America, and Egypt as well as such Asian countries as India, Malaysia, Myanmar, and Siam. Thus, marijuana, known as *cannabis* back then, has a 5000-year medical history that came to an abrupt end by passage

of the Marijuana Tax Act of 1937. When the Marijuana Tax Act became law, marijuana was legally classified as a narcotic, and at that time medical use of this substance effectively ceased. Only in the past decade has there been organized renewed interest in possible medical uses for cannabis. Because of potential clinical uses for marijuana, enforcement of laws prohibiting the use of this substance has been very controversial (see "Holding the Line," Cannabis Buyers' Club).

Marijuana has been shown to be effective in the treatment of certain types of medical conditions. However, because medicines are available that are at least as effective and without abuse potential, none of these applications is currently approved by the Food and Drug Administration (FDA). According to researchers (Abood and Martin 1992; Consroe and Sandyk 1992; Iversen 1993) and proponents for the medical uses of marijuana, the potential uses are as follows:

Reduction in intraocular (eye) pressure. Marijuana lowers glaucoma-associated intraocular pressure, even though it does not cure the condition or reverse blindness (Goldstein 1995). **Glaucoma** is the second leading cause of blindness, caused by uncontrollable eye pressure (Julian 1994).

Antiasthmatic effect. Some research indicates that short-term smoking of marijuana improves breathing for asthma patients. Marijuana smoke dilates the lungs' air passages (bronchodilation). Findings also show, however, that the lung-irritating properties of marijuana smoke seem to offset its benefits. Regardless, marijuana may still prove useful when other drugs are not effective because of a different mode of action in causing bronchodilation.

Muscle-relaxant effect. Some studies indicate that muscle spasms are relieved when patients with muscle disorders, such as multiple sclerosis, use marijuana.

Antiseizure effect. Marijuana has both convulsing and anticonvulsant properties and has been considered for use in preventing seizures associated with epilepsy. In animal experimentation, the cannabinoids reduced or increased seizure activities, depending on how the experiments were conducted. One or more of the marijuana components may be useful in combination with other standard antiseizure medication, although at present their value seems limited.

Antidepressant effect. Cannabis and the synthetic cannabinoid synhexyl have been used successfully in Great Britain as specific euphoriants for the treatment of depression.

Analgesic effect. Published testimonials have reported that marijuana can relieve the intense pain associated with migraine and chronic headaches or inflammation (Grinspoon and Bakalar 1995). In South Africa, native women smoke cannabis to dull the pain of childbirth (Hamid 1998; Solomon 1966). The pain-relieving potency of marijuana has not been carefully studied and compared with other analgesics, such as narcotics or aspirin-type drugs.

Appetite stimulant. The stimulant effects on appetite are seen as useful for patients with HIV and some eating disorders (Sewester 1993; see Chapter 16).

Arguments against using marijuana for medicinal purposes conclude that marijuana is a harmful substance for the following reasons:

1. It contains 421 chemicals.
2. It is stronger than it was 20 years ago, and this new, potent marijuana presents new dangers unrecognized years ago.
3. It is far worse for the lungs than tobacco.
4. THC and other components of marijuana are fat soluble and remain in the human body for a month.
5. It causes brain damage and a behavioral disorder known as "amotivational syndrome."
6. Any use of marijuana constitutes abuse, and marijuana has no medical value whatsoever (NORML 2000).

All of these reasons have either been disputed or shown to be exaggerated claims by proponents who are in favor of allowing marijuana to be medically used. Proponents for medical use argue that "its illegality (marijuana) . . . imposes much anxiety and expense on suffering people, forces them to bargain with illicit drug dealers, and exposes them to the threat of criminal prosecution" (Grinspoon and Bakalar 1995, p. 1876).

Even though the federal government maintains that such use is unlawful, in 1996, voters in the states of Arizona and California, and just recently voters in Arizona and Maryland together with the country of Canada, approved propositions permitting physicians to prescribe marijuana for medical problems, with the idea that terminally ill patients could be given the option of smokable marijuana as opposed to the already-approved **Marinol** (dronabinol). This event triggered a major response by

KEY TERMS

glaucoma
potentially blinding eye disease causing continual and increasing intraocular pressure

Marinol
FDA-approved THC in capsule form (dronabinol)

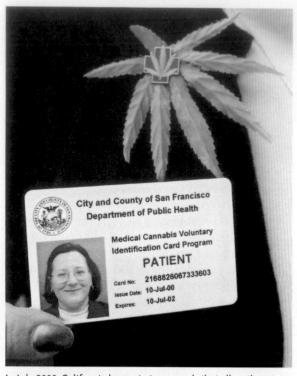

In July 2000, California began to issue cards that allow the users to purchase marijuana for medicinal purposes.

the federal government. Former President Clinton, the Secretary of Health and Human Services, and the U.S. Attorney General all made pronouncements reiterating the negative effects of marijuana, its abuse potential, and the danger of sending a "pro-use message" or one that suggested use was not outside the realm of accepted behavior (HHS 1996). The government warned that physicians who availed themselves of the permission given in these new state regulations would be prosecuted, lose their privilege of writing prescriptions, and be excluded from Medicare and Medicaid reimbursement. The entire legislative initiative was cast as being a smokescreen for legalization, with the federal government purporting that those who supported it were "closet" marijuana advocates or, at best, legalization advocates.

Physicians responded indignantly to what they considered a heavy-handed attempt to overrule their medical judgments and to smear them unfairly, especially when most of them were neither pro-use nor even pro-legalization, except in this one medical situation. An editorial in the prestigious *New England Journal of Medicine*, titled "Federal Foolishness and Marijuana" (Kassirer 1997), claimed that it was hypocritical to allow physicians to prescribe the highly addicting opiates morphine or meperidine, which cause death at doses not much greater than those that relieve pain, but not marijuana, which is far less addictive and does not cause death. The purpose of the legislative initiative, the editorial pointed out, was to alleviate the suffering of terminally ill patients, for whom long-term abuse potential is irrelevant. Many of these patients perceive the smokable form of THC as being more effective than Marinol, a factor that is difficult to measure in experimental procedures. As far as the governmental reasons for prohibiting the drug for medical purposes, a few joked, it was a rerun of *Reefer Madness*.

In June 2000, Hawaii became the first state to pass a medical marijuana bill that approved the possession and use of marijuana for medical purposes. Hawaii's governor, Benjamin J. Cayetano, "said it was one aspect of his effort to make Hawaii the health care center of the Pacific" (Associated Press 2000). Passage of this bill currently affects 500 to 1000 residents of Hawaii. The belief by the governor is that "Hawaii law will lead to similar legislation in other states" (Associated Press 2000). This means that anyone found in possession of marijuana would be exempt if he or she can verify medical usage. This same article mentioned that Alaska, Arizona, California, Maine, Nevada, Oregon, Washington, and the District of Columbia have approved medical marijuana laws even though the U.S. Justice Department is challenging those laws. In addition, in March 2000, London's conservative Tory party voted in favor of supporting an experiment in legalization by beginning to hold public debates on this matter (Hopps 2000). Members of the party were expecting to experiment with legalization. Interestingly, in England, cannabis possession carries up to a 7-year jail sentence, although such long sentences are rare. Time will tell what the outcomes in the United States, Canada, and the United Kingdom will be. As mentioned previously, several states are at variance with federal law, under which medical and recreational use of marijuana remains illegal.

The Physiological Effects of Marijuana Use

Although the literature on marijuana use repeatedly states that "in 5,000 years of medical and nonmedical use, marijuana has not caused a single overdose death" (Grinspoon and Bakalar 1995, 1875), the effects of marijuana use should not be overlooked. We begin by examining the effects of marijuana on the lungs.

When marijuana smoke is inhaled into the lungs, THC, the psychoactive ingredient, leaves the blood rapidly through metabolism and efficient uptake into the tissues. THC and its metabolites tend to bind to proteins in the blood and remain stored for long periods in body fat. Five days after a single dosage of THC, 20% remains stored, whereas 20% of its metabolites remain in the blood (Indiana Prevention Resource Center 1996; Kryger 1995). Complete elimination of a single dose can take up to 30 days. Measurable levels of THC in blood from chronic users can often be detected for several days or even weeks after their last marijuana cigarette (joint).

In smokers, lung absorption and transport of THC to the brain are rapid; THC reaches the brain within as little as 14 seconds after inhalation. Marijuana is metabolized more efficiently through smoking than via intravenous injection or oral ingestion. Smoking is also three to five times more potent than these two methods (Jones 1980; Kaplan and Whitmire 1995; Kryger 1995). Other findings that compare the amounts of marijuana with tobacco conclude that "three to four joints a day is about as harmful to your lungs as smoking a pack of cigarettes a day" (Reaney 2000, p. 1).

Some effects of cannabis described in the following sections are unquestionably toxic in that they can either directly or indirectly produce adverse health effects. Other effects may be beneficial in treating some medical conditions. The use of marijuana, THC, and synthetic cannabinoids, either alone or in combination with other drugs, is currently being investigated for treating pain, inflammation, glaucoma, nausea, and muscle spasms (Iversen 1993).

EFFECTS ON THE CENTRAL NERVOUS SYSTEM

The primary effects of marijuana—specifically, of THC—are on CNS functions. The precise CNS effects of consuming marijuana or administering THC can vary according to the expectations of the user, the social setting, the route of administration, and previous experiences (Abood and Martin 1992; Jaffe 1990). Smoking a marijuana cigarette can alter mood, coordination, memory, and self-perception. Usually, such exposure causes some euphoria, a sense of well-being, and relaxation. Marijuana smokers often claim heightened sensory awareness and **altered perceptions** (particularly a slowing of time), associated with hunger (the "**munchies**") and a dry mouth (Hubbard et al. 1999; Swan 1994).

High doses of THC or greater exposure to marijuana can cause hallucinations, delusions, and paranoia (APA 1994; Goldstein 1995; Hubbard et al. 1999). Some users describe anxiety after high-dose exposure. Due to the availability and widespread use of marijuana, psychiatric emergencies from marijuana overdose are becoming somewhat common. Long-term, chronic users often show decreased interest in personal appearance or goals (part of the amotivational syndrome discussed earlier in this chapter) as well as an inability to concentrate, make appropriate decisions, and recall information from short-term memory (Abood and Martin 1992; Block 1996).

The precise classification of THC is uncertain because the responses to marijuana are highly variable and appear to have elements of all three major groups of drugs of abuse. Consequently, marijuana use can cause euphoria and paranoia (like stimulants), drowsiness and sedation (like depressants), and hallucinations (like psychedelics). It is possible that THC alters several receptor or transmitter systems in the brain and this action would account for its diverse and somewhat unpredictable effects.

KEY TERMS

altered perceptions
changes in the interpretation of stimuli resulting from marijuana

munchies
hunger experienced while under the effects of marijuana

The recent dramatic discovery of a specific receptor site in the brain for THC, called the *cannabinoid* receptor, suggests that a selective endogenous marijuana system exists in the brain and is activated by THC when marijuana is consumed (Hudson 1990). Some researchers speculate that an endogenous fatty acid-like substance called **anandamide** naturally works at these marijuana sites; efforts are being made to characterize this substance, which perhaps is a neurotransmitter (Iversen 1993). It is possible that, from this discovery, a group of new therapeutic agents will be developed that can selectively interact with the marijuana receptors, resulting in medical benefits without the side effects that generally accompany marijuana use (Iversen 1993; Swan 1993).

EFFECTS ON THE RESPIRATORY SYSTEM

Marijuana is often smoked like tobacco and, like tobacco, it can cause damage to the lungs (Adams and Martin 1996; Consroe and Sandyk 1992). When smoking tobacco, nearly 70% of the total suspended particles in the smoke are retained in the lungs. Because marijuana smoke is inhaled more deeply than tobacco smoke, even more tar residues may be retained with its use.

Smoke is a mixture of tiny particles suspended in gas, mostly carbon monoxide. These solid particles combine to form a residue called *tar*. Cannabis produces more tar (as much as 50% more) than an equivalent weight of tobacco and is smoked in a way that increases the accumulation of tar (Jones 1980).

More than 150 chemicals have been identified in marijuana smoke and tar. A few are proven carcinogens; many others have not yet been tested for carcinogenicity. The carcinogen benzopyrene, for example, is 70% more abundant in marijuana smoke than in tobacco smoke. When cannabis tar is applied to the skin of experimental animals, it causes precancerous lesions similar to those caused by tobacco tar. Similarly, whenever isolated lung tissue is exposed to these same tars, precancerous changes result (Hollister 1986; Jones 1980; Turner 1980).

Special white blood cells in living lung tissue—alveolar macrophages—play a role in removing debris from the lungs. When exposed to smoke from cannabis, these cells are less able to remove bacteria and other foreign debris.

Smoking only a few marijuana cigarettes a day for 6 to 8 weeks can significantly impair pulmonary function. Laboratory and clinical evidence often indicate that heavy use of marijuana causes cellular changes and that users have a higher incidence of such respiratory problems as laryngitis, pharyngitis, bronchitis, asthma-like conditions, cough, hoarseness, and dry throat (Goldstein 1995; Hollister 1986). Some reports emphasize the potential damage to pulmonary function that can occur from chronic marijuana use (NIDA 1991). Evidence suggests that many 20-year-old smokers of both hashish and tobacco have lung damage comparable to that found in heavy tobacco smokers older than 40 years of age. It is believed that the tar from tobacco and marijuana has damaging effects, but it is not known whether smokers who use both products suffer synergistic or additive effects (Hollister 1986; Jones 1980).

EFFECTS ON THE CARDIOVASCULAR SYSTEM

In human beings, cannabis causes both *vasodilation* (enlarged blood vessels) and an increase in heart rate related to the amount of THC consumed (Abood and Martin 1992; NIDA 2000). The vasodilation is responsible for the reddening of the eyes often seen in marijuana smokers. In physically healthy users, these effects, as well as slight changes in heart rhythm, are transitory and do not appear to be significant. In patients with heart disease, however, the increased oxygen requirement due to the accelerated heart rate may have serious consequences. The effect of cannabis on people with heart rhythm irregularities is not known. Because of vasodilation caused by marijuana use, abnormally low blood pressure can occur when standing. In addition, if a user stands up quickly after smoking, a feeling of lightheadedness or fainting may result. Chronic administration of large doses of THC to healthy volunteers

KEY TERMS

anandamide
possible neurotransmitter acting at the marijuana (cannabinoid) receptor

shows that tolerance develops to the increase in heart rate and vasodilation.

People with cardiovascular problems seem to be at an increased risk when smoking marijuana (Hollister 1986). Marijuana products also bind hemoglobin, limiting the amount of oxygen that can be carried to the heart tissue. In a few cases, this deficiency could trigger heart attacks in susceptible people (Palfai and Jankiewicz 1991). The National Academy of Sciences' Institute of Medicine recommends that people with cardiovascular disease avoid marijuana use because there are still many unanswered questions about its effects on the cardiovascular system.

EFFECTS ON SEXUAL PERFORMANCE AND REPRODUCTION

Drugs may interfere with sexual performance and reproduction in several ways. They may alter sexual behavior, affect fertility, damage the chromosomes of germ cells in the male or female, or adversely affect fetal growth and development.

The Indian Hemp Commission (Taylor 1963, 1966), which wrote the first scientific report on cannabis, commented that it had a sexually stimulating effect, like alcohol. However, the report also said that cannabis was used by Asian Indian ascetics to destroy the sexual appetite. This apparent discrepancy may be a dose-related effect. Used occasionally over the short term, marijuana may act as an **aphrodisiac** by decreasing CNS inhibitions. In addition, the altered perception of time under the influence of the drug could make the pleasurable sensations appear to last longer than they actually do.

Marijuana affects the sympathetic nervous system, increasing vasodilation in the genitals and delaying ejaculation. High doses over a period of time lead to depression of libido and impotence—possibly due to the decreased amount of testosterone, the male sex hormone.

Cannabis has several effects on semen. The total number of sperm cells and the concentration of sperm per unit volume are decreased during ejaculation. Moreover, there is an increase in the proportion of sperm with abnormal appearance and reduced motility. These qualities are usually associated with lower fertility and a higher probability of producing an abnormal embryo should fertilization take place.

Despite these effects, there are *no* documented reports of children with birth defects in which the abnormality was linked to the father's smoking marijuana. It is possible that damaged sperm cells are incapable of fertilization (so that only normal sperm cells reach the egg) or that the abnormal sperm appearance is meaningless in terms of predicting birth defects. When marijuana use stops, the quality of sperm gradually returns to normal over several months.

Less reliable data are available on the effects of cannabis on female libido, sexual response (ability to respond to sexual stimulation with vaginal lubrication and orgasm), and fertile reproductive (menstrual) cycles (Consroe and Sandyk 1992; Grinspoon 1987). Preliminary data from the Reproductive Biology Research Foundation show that chronic smoking of cannabis (at least three times per week for the preceding 6 months) adversely affects the female reproductive cycle. Results with women were correlated with work in rhesus monkeys; it was found that THC blocks ovulation (due to effects on female sex hormones).

Data on effects of marijuana use during pregnancy and lactation are inconclusive. Some evidence suggests that the use of this drug by pregnant women can result in intrauterine growth retardation, which is characterized by increased fetal mortality, prolonged labor, low birthweight babies, and behavioral abnormalities in newborns (Fernandez-Ruiz et al. 1992; Nahas and Latour 1992; Roffman and George 1988). THC and other cannabinoids pass through the blood–placenta barrier and concentrate in the fetus's fatty tissue, including its brain. Ethical considerations prevent duplication of the experiment in humans.

Women who smoke marijuana during pregnancy also often use other drugs—such as alcohol, tobacco, and cocaine—that are known to have adverse effects on the developing fetus. Because

KEY TERMS

aphrodisiac
a compound that is believed to be the cause of sexual arousal

multiple drugs are used, it is difficult to isolate the specific effects of marijuana during pregnancy. Like many other substances, THC is taken up by the mammary glands in lactating women and is excreted in the breast milk. Effects of marijuana in the breast milk on human infants have not been determined (Christina 1994; Murphy and Bartke 1992).

In studies on mice and rats (but not humans), the addition of THC to pregnant animals lowered litter size, increased fetal reabsorption, and increased the number of reproductive abnormalities in the surviving offspring (Dewey 1986). The offspring of the drug-treated animal mothers had reduced fertility and more testicular abnormalities. The dose of cannabinoids used in these studies was higher than that used by humans. Clearly, pregnant women should be advised against using marijuana, even though there are few direct data on its prenatal effects in humans (Dewey 1986; Murphy and Bartke 1992).

TOLERANCE AND DEPENDENCE

It has been known for many years that tolerance to some effects of cannabis builds rapidly in animals—namely, the drug effect becomes less intense with repeated administration. Frequent use of high doses of marijuana or THC in humans produces similar tolerance. For example, increasingly higher doses must be given to obtain the same intensity of subjective effects and increased heart rate that occur initially with small doses (Abood and Martin 1992).

Frequent high doses of THC also can produce mild physical dependence. Healthy subjects who smoke several "joints" a day or who are given comparable amounts of THC orally experience irritability, sleep disturbances, weight loss, loss of appetite, sweating, and gastrointestinal upsets when drug use is stopped abruptly. However, not all subjects experience this mild form of withdrawal.

It is much easier to show psychological dependence in heavy users of marijuana (Abood and Martin 1992; Hollister 1986). Psychological dependence involves an attachment to the euphoric effects of the THC content in marijuana and may include "craving" for the drug. The subjective psy-

chological effects of marijuana intoxication include a heightened sensitivity to and distortion of sight, smell, taste, and sound; mood alteration; and diminished reaction time.

Diagnosis: Cannabis Dependence

In general, outright cannabis addiction, with obsessive drug seeking and compulsive drug-taking behavior, is relatively rare with low-THC cannabis. Contributing to this is the fact that the less potent forms of marijuana are most readily available in the United States, resulting in most chronic users in this country having little problem controlling or eliminating their cannabis habit if they so desired.

The Diagnostic and Statistical Manual of Mental Disorders, fourth edition (*DSM-IV*), recognizes a diagnosis of cannabis dependence. It is characterized by "compulsive use" and spending hours per day acquiring and using the substance. These users persist in their use despite knowledge of physical problems (for example, chronic cough related to smoking) or psychological problems (for example, excessive sedation resulting from repeated use of high doses; APA 1994).

CHRONIC USE

Research on *chronic use of marijuana* (repeated daily use of this drug) in the 1970s indicated the possibility of three types of damage: (1) chromosomal damage (Stenchever et al. 1974); (2) *cerebral atrophy* (shrinking of the brain) (Campbell et al. 1971); and (3) lowered capacity of white blood cells to fight disease (Suciu-Foca et al. 1974). These findings have all been found to be contradicted or refuted by subsequent research. The only finding that appears very credible is that heavy use of this drug impairs lung capacity (Bloodworth 1987; Henneberger 1994; Kaplan and Whitmire 1995; Oliwenstein 1988; Swan 1994).

Other evidence indicates that chronic, heavy use of cannabis can lead to unforeseen calamities in some users (see "Case in Point," Chronic Marijuana Use). We have pointed out that marijuana produces a variety of psychoactive effects. One of those effects is sedation of unwanted emotional states such as anxiety, which are inevitable given the conflicts and turmoil of living in our fast-paced

►Case in Point Chronic Marijuana Use

The following comments show how marijuana use can become a disturbing habit:

I guess you could say it was peer pressure. Back in 1969, I was a sophomore in college, and everyone was smoking "dope." The Vietnam War was in progress, and most students on college campuses were heavily involved in the drug scene. I first started smoking marijuana when my closest friends did. I was taught by other students who already knew how to enjoy the effects of "pot."

I recall that one of my fellow students used to supply me with "nickel bags," and many users nicknamed him "God." How did he get such a name? Because he sold some very potent marijuana that at times caused us to hallucinate.

I used pot nearly every day for about a year and a half, and hardly an evening would pass without smoking dope and listening to music. Smoking marijuana became as common as drinking alcohol. I used it in the same manner a person has a cocktail after a long day. At first, I liked the effects of being "high," but later I became so accustomed to the stuff that life appeared boring without it.

After graduating, my college friends went their separate ways, and I stopped using marijuana for a few years. A year later, in graduate school, a neighborhood friend reintroduced me to the pleasure of smoking pot. I began to use it again but not as often. Whenever I experienced some pressure, I would use a little to relax.

After finishing my degree, I found myself employed at an institution that at times was boring. Again, I started using pot at night to relax, and somehow it got out of control. I used to smoke a little before work and sometimes during lunch. I thought all was well until one day I got fired because someone accused me of being high on the job.

Soon afterward, I came to the realization that the use of marijuana can be very insidious. It has a way of becoming psychologically addictive, and you don't even realize it. When I was high, I thought that no one knew, and that I was even more effective with others. Little did I know, I was dead wrong and fooling no one.

Source: From Venturelli's files, interview with a 39-year-old male, May 1990.

society today. As with the chronic use of any psychoactive drug that produces sedating effects, normal emotional and psychosocial development can be arrested by heavy marijuana consumption. For example, a youth who is usually "high" at a party avoids the anxieties and embarrassments of introspective and critical interpersonal interactions, but instead will be interested in "thrill-seeking" behavior, such as romantic and sexual involvements, experimentation with and heavy use of other drugs, and other types of more daring experiences.

From years of research with this drug, we find that heavy and chronic use of marijuana can very easily compromise cognitive functions, such as short-term memory, concentration, moderately "taxing" problem solving, and even spiritual growth and development. Often, the more serious costs in using this drug are that the individual acquires a poor record for development and advancement of learning, as is often expected in educational settings (schools, colleges, trade

schools, and universities). Another cost that is more serious is the retardation in emotional development. Such types of development are often obscured by "being high all the time." Further, in such chronic use cases, much time is wasted seeking the pleasures and sometimes the longed-for thrills derived from the habitual use of marijuana.

The amotivational syndrome, in fact, can be "deconstructed" into the sedation, depression, and cognitive impairment discussed throughout this chapter. The user who is experiencing a subjective euphoric effect, enjoying the presence and social reinforcement of peers, "feeling no pain," and remaining cognitively unfocused finds it difficult to intellectually grasp the learned experiences from such developmental delays. Although many do "mature out" of use, this step may occur only after years of development have slipped away, never to be regained. Sometimes treatment interventions are necessary to get the subject into a drug-free state and reunited with non–drug-using peer groups.

In concluding this chapter, we note that the history of this drug indicates that usage and availability will remain widespread despite all the efforts to eradicate its existence. Despite all the prevention efforts to date, marijuana remains the most popular illicit drug, topped only by alcohol and tobacco, which are licit drugs.

Discussion Questions

1. What are the pharmacological, sociological, and psychological reasons why the very young continue to use marijuana at alarming rates despite the illegality of usage?

2. Do you believe that prosecution for marijuana possession should be more or less rigid than it currently is? Why?

3. Debate whether marijuana use adversely affects driving capabilities.

4. Either directly interview or imagine interviews of several users and nonusers of marijuana. How do you think they would answer the question of whether their critical thinking skills are adversely affected by this drug?

5. Among marijuana users, does the amotivational syndrome exist? Interview several users and try to either add to the characteristics of this syndrome from your interviews or modify the syndrome as explained in this chapter.

6. In light of the information in this chapter regarding medical marijuana use, do you believe in legalizing medical marijuana use? Why or why not?

7. What is your reaction to legalizing marijuana as a controlled substance like alcohol and tobacco products? Give reasons either for or against this statement.

8. Do you believe consistent use of marijuana changes personality? If so, how?

9. Summarize how marijuana affects the CNS, respiratory system, cardiovascular system, and sexual performance and reproduction.

10. Debate how much family upbringing and attachment to a religion contribute to later drug use.

11. From reading this chapter, try to explain why most heroin users have used marijuana, whereas the vast majority of marijuana users never advance to such highly addictive drugs.

12. Explain why a user of cannabis might develop psychological dependence.

13. Do you believe that use of marijuana is more or less harmful than use of tobacco products? Should they be regulated differently?

Key Terms

perceived risk   392

gateway drugs   394

Cannabis sativa   395

sinsemilla   396

hashish   397

subjective euphoric effects   398

differential association   400

amotivational syndrome   401

medical marijuana use   403

glaucoma   405

Marinol   405

altered perceptions   407

munchies   407

anandamide   408

aphrodisiac   409

Summary

1 Marijuana consists of the dried and crushed leaves, flowers, stems, and seeds of the *Cannabis sativa* plant. THC (tetrahydrocannabinol) is the primary mind-altering (psychoactive) ingredient in marijuana.

2 Marijuana remains very controversial for the following reasons: (1) a high percentage of the U.S. population uses this drug; (2) it remains

illegal; (3) several states, but not the federal government, have approved medical uses of marijuana; (4) marijuana accounts for a large number of arrests for simple possession; (5) it is one of the least addictive-type drugs; and (6) most marijuana users do not "graduate" to other more addictive illicit drugs.

3 Effects of marijuana can vary according to expectations and surroundings. At low doses, such as when smoked or ingested (eaten), marijuana often has a sedative effect. At higher doses, it can produce hallucinations and delusions.

4 As with tobacco, heavy use of marijuana can impair pulmonary function, cause chronic respiratory diseases (such as bronchitis and asthma), and promote lung cancer. Marijuana causes vasodilation and a compensatory increase in heart rate. The effects of marijuana on sexual performance and reproduction are controversial. Some studies have suggested this substance not only enhances sexual arousal but also promotes "risky" sexual behavior (unprotected sex).

5 Tolerance to the CNS and cardiovascular effects of marijuana develop rapidly with repeated use. Although physical dependence and associated withdrawal are minor, psychological dependence can be significant in chronic, heavy users.

6 The active ingredient in marijuana, THC, has been used for treating a variety of seemingly unrelated medical conditions. This drug is indicated for treatment of nausea and vomiting in cancer patients receiving chemotherapy and for treatment of anorexia (lack of appetite) in AIDS patients. Other potential therapeutic uses for THC include relief of intraocular pressure associated with glaucoma, as an antiasthmatic drug, for muscle relaxation, as prevention for some types of seizures, as an antidepressant, and as an analgesic to relieve migraines and other types of pain.

7 The age groups most likely to use marijuana are the following: (1) highest lifetime use, adults between 26 and 34 years of age (53.9%); (2) highest past-year and past-month use, 18- to 25-year-olds; and (3) sharp drop in use, 26 and older age group.

8 The rate of first use of marijuana is highest among 12- to 17-year-olds, fluctuating from 86.5% in 1999 to a high of 98.2% in 2000. The next highest rate of first users of marijuana is found among 18- to 25-year-olds, ranging from 59.8% in 1999 to a low of 49.4% in 2002.

9 Perceived risk is a leading indicator of change in use. When the amount of risk associated with marijuana use decreases, a resurgence in its popularity follows shortly. Similarly, when perceived risk increases, a decrease in use typically follows. In 1978, the percentage of 8th, 10th, and 12th graders perceiving "great risk" from using marijuana was at a low point (approximately 34% for 12th graders). From 1979 to 1991, the percentage identifying it with "great risk" continued to rise to approximately 78% for 12th graders. From 1992 to 2003, the percentage of 12th graders perceiving "great risk" from marijuana use declined to its current low of approximately 55%.

References

Abel, E. L. *Marijuana: The First Twelve Thousand Years.* New York: Plenum, 1989.

Abood, M., and B. Martin. "Neurobiology of Marijuana Abuse." *Trends in Pharmacological Sciences* 13 (May 1992): 201–206.

Abood, M. E., and B. R. Martin. "Molecular Neurobiology of the Cannabinoid Receptor." *International Review of Neurobiology* 39 (May 1996): 197–219.

Adams, I. B., and B. R. Martin, "Cannabis: Pharmacology and Toxicology in Animals and Humans." *Addiction* 91 (1996): 1585–1614.

American Psychiatric Association (APA). *Diagnostic and Statistical Manual of Mental Disorders,* 4th ed. [*DSM-IV*], chairman Allen Frances. Washington, DC: APA, 1994.

Anslinger, H. J., and C. R. Cooper. "Marijuana: Assassin of Youth." *American Magazine* 124 (July 1937): 19–20, 150–153.

Associated Press. "Hawaii Becomes First State to Approve Medical Marijuana Bill." *The New York Times on the Web* (15 June 2000). Available http://www.nytimes.com/library/national/science/health/061500hth-hawaii marijuana.html.

Berkowitz, A. "Following Imaginary Peers: How Norm Misperceptions Influence Student Substance Abuse." In *Project Direction,* edited by G. Lindsay and G. Rulf, 12–15 (Module No. 2). Muncie, IN: Ball State University, 1991.

Block, R. I. "Does Heavy Marijuana Use Impair Human Cognition and Brain Function?" *Journal of the American Medical Association* 275 (1996): 560–561.

Bloodworth, R. C. "Major Problems Associated with Marijuana Use." *Psychiatric Medicine* 3 (1987): 173–184.

Brown, M. W., and S. Massaro. "Attention and Memory Impaired in Heavy Users of Marijuana." Rockville, MD: NIDA, 20 February 1996. Available http://www.health. org pressrl/heavymar.html.

Buff, J. "Greasers, Dopers, and Hippies: Three Responses to the Adult World." In *The White Majority*, edited by L. Howe, 60–70. New York: Random House, 1970.

Califano, J. A. "Dangerous Indifference to Drugs." *Washington Post* (23 September 1996): A-19.

Campbell, A. G., M. Evans, J. L. Thomson, and M. J. Williams. "Cerebral Atrophy in Young Cannabis Smokers." *Lancet* 19 (1971): 1219–1225.

Carter, E. *Cannabis in Costa Rica.* Philadelphia, PA: Institute for the Study of Human Issues, 1980.

Chait, L., and J. Pierri. "Effect of Smoked Marijuana on Human Performance: A Critical Review." In *Marijuana/Cannabinoids, Neurobiology and Neurophysiology*, edited by L. Murphy and A. Bartke, 387–424. Boca Raton, FL: CRC Press, 1992.

Christina, D. *Marijuana: Personality and Behavior.* Tempe, AZ: Do It Now, 1994.

Coleman, J. S. *The Adolescent Society.* New York: Free Press of Glencoe, 1961.

Consroe, P., and R. Sandyk. "Potential Role of Cannabinoids for Therapy of Neurological Disorders." In *Marijuana/Cannabinoids, Neurobiology and Neurophysiology*, edited by L. Murphy and A. Bartke, 459–524. Boca Raton, FL: CRC Press, 1992.

Dewey, W. L. "Cannabinoid Pharmacology." *Pharmacological Reviews* 38 (1986): 48–50.

Dreher, M. C. "Working Men and Ganja: Marijuana Use in Rural Jamaica." Philadelphia, PA: Institute for the Study of Human Issues, 1982.

Eckert, P. *Jocks and Burnouts: Social Categories and Identity in the High School.* New York: Teachers College, Columbia University, 1989.

Fernandez-Ruiz, J., F. Rodriguez de Fonseca, M. Navarro, and J. Ramos. "Maternal Cannabinoid Exposure and Brain Development: Changes in the Ontogeny of Dopaminergic Neurons." In *Marijuana/Cannabinoids, Neurobiology and Neurophysiology*, edited by L. Murphy and A. Bartke, 118–164. Boca Raton, FL: CRC Press, 1992.

Gaines, G. *Teenage Wasteland: Suburbia's Dead-End Kids.* New York: Harper Perennial, 1992.

Gardner, E. "Cannabinoid Interaction with Brain Reward Systems: The Neurobiological Basis of Cannabinoid Abuse." In *Marijuana/Cannabinoids, Neurobiology and Neurophysiology*, edited by L. Murphy and A. Bartke, 275–335. Boca Raton, FL: CRC Press, 1992.

Goldstein, A. *Addiction from Biology to Drug Policy.* New York: Freeman, 1994.

Goldstein, F. "Pharmacological Aspects of Substance Abuse." *Remington's Pharmaceutical Sciences*, 19th ed. Easton, PA: Mack, 1995.

Gossop, M. *Living with Drugs*, 2nd ed. Aldershot, England: Wildwood House, 1987.

Greenblatt, J. C. *Adolescent Self-Reported Behaviors and Their Association with Marijuana Use.* Office of Applied Studies (OAS) of the Substance Abuse and Mental Health Services Administration (SAMHSA). Rockville, MD: National Clearinghouse for Alcohol and Drug Information, July 1999.

Grinspoon, L. "Marijuana." *Harvard Medical School Mental Health Letter* 4 (November 1987): 1–4.

Grinspoon, L., and J. B. Bakalar. "Commentary, Marijuana as Medicine: A Plea for Reconsideration." *Journal of the American Medical Association* 273 (1995): 1875–1876. Available http://www.commonlink.com~olsen/medical/lester.html.

Hamid, A. *Drugs in America: Sociology, Economics, and Politics.* Gaithersburg, MD: Aspen Publishers Inc., 1998.

Health and Human Services (HHS). "Substance Abuse—A National Challenge" (6 May 1996). Available www.os. dhhs.gov/news/press/1996pres/960506b.html.

Heitzeg, N. *Deviance: Rulemakers and Rulebreakers.* St. Paul, MN: West Publishing, 1996.

Henneberger, M. "Pot Surges Back, It's Like a Whole New World." *New York Times* (6 February 1994): C19.

Hollister, L. E. "Health Aspects of Cannabis." *Pharmacological Reviews* 38 (1986): 39–42.

Hopps, J. "Tory Press Open to Reform on Cannabis." *Reuters* (30 March 2000). Available http://dailynews. yahoo.com/h/nm/20000330/wl/Britain_drugs_1.html.

Hubbard, J. R., S. E. Franco, and E. S. Onaivi. "Marijuana: Medical Implications." *American Family Physician* 283 (1999): 231–240.

Hudson, R. "Researchers Identify Gene That Triggers Marijuana's 'High.'" *Wall Street Journal* (9 August 1990): B-2.

Indiana Prevention Resource Center. *Factline on: Marijuana.* Bloomington, IN: Indiana Prevention Resource Center, 1996.

Iversen, L. "Medicinal Use of Marijuana." *Nature* 365 (1993): 12–13.

Jaffe, J. H. "Drug Addiction and Drug Abuse." In *The Pharmacological Basis of Therapeutics*, 8th ed., edited by A. Gilman, T. Rall, A. Nies, and P. Taylor. New York: Pergamon, 1990.

Johnston, L., P. O'Malley, and J. Bachman. *Monitoring the Future: National Results on Adolescent Drug Use: Overview of Key Findings, 1999.* Bethesda, MD: National Institute on Drug Abuse, 2000.

Johnston, L., P. O'Malley, and J. Bachman. *Monitoring the Future: National Results on Adolescent Drug Use: Overview of Key Findings, 2000.* Bethesda, MD: National Institute on Drug Abuse, 2001.

Johnston, L. D., P. M. O'Malley, J. G. Bachman, and J. E. Schulenberg. *Monitoring the Future: National Survey Results on Drug Use, 1975-2003: Volume I, Secondary School Students*, Bethesda, MD: National Institutes of Health, National Institute on Drug Abuse, 2004.

Jones, R. T. "Human Effects: An Overview." In *Marijuana Research Findings: 1980*, NIDA Research Monograph No. 31. Washington, DC: National Institute on Drug Abuse, 1980.

Julian, B. S. "alt.hemp CANNABIS/MARIJUANA FAQ." FAG Maintainer (online publication). Amherst, MA: University of Massachusetts at Amherst, 1994. Available http://www.faqs.org/faqs/drugs/hemp-marijuana/.

Kandel, D. B., P. C. Griesler, G. Lee, M. Davies, and C. Shaffsan. *Parental Influences on Adolescent Marijuana Use and the Baby Boom Generation: Findings from the 1995–1996 National Household Surveys on Drug Abuse*. Department of Health and Human Services (DHHS). Rockville, MD: Substance Abuse and Mental Health Services Administration, 2001.

Kaplan, L. F., and R. Whitmire. "Pot—It's Potent, Prevalent and Preventable." *Salt Lake Tribune* 250 (21 May 1995): 9.

Kassirer, J. "Federal Foolishness and Marijuana" (editorial). *New England Journal of Medicine* 336 (1997): 11-32.

Kelly, T., R. Foltin, C. Emurian, and M. Fischman. "Effects of THC on Marijuana Smoking, Drug Choice and Verbal Report of Drug Liking." *Journal of Experimental Analysis of Behavior* 61 (1994): 203–211.

Kryger, A. H. *Preventive Medicine Clinic of Monterey: Marijuana Mental Disturbances*. Iowa City, IA: Virtual Hospital Home Page, 24 October 1995: 1–6. Available http://vh.radiology.uiowa.edu.

Liska, K. *Drugs and the Human Body*, 5th ed. Upper Saddle River, NJ: Prentice Hall, 1997.

"Marijuana Menaces Youth." *Scientific American* 154 (1936): 151.

Mathias, R. "Marijuana Impairs Driving-Related Skills and Workplace Performance." *NIDA Notes* 11, (January/February 1996): 6.

Murphy, L., and A. Bartke. "Effects of THC on Pregnancy, Puberty, and the Neuroendocrine System." In *Marijuana/Cannabinoids, Neurobiology and Neurophysiology*, edited by L. Murphy and A. Bartke, 539. Boca Raton, FL: CRC Press, 1992.

Musto, D. F. *The American Disease. Origins of Narcotic Control*, 3rd ed. New York: Oxford University Press, 1999.

Nahas, G., and C. Latour. "The Human Toxicity of Marijuana." *Medical Journal of Australia* 156 (1992): 495–497.

National Clearinghouse on Alcohol and Drug Information (NCADI). *Marijuana: Facts Parents Need to Know*. Quick Screen, At Home Drug Test. Rockville, MD: National Clearinghouse on Alcohol and Drug Information, revised November 1998. Available http://www.athome-drugtest.com/drugabusemarij.html.

National Institute on Drug Abuse (NIDA). *Drug Abuse and Drug Abuse Research*, DHHS Publication No. 91-1704. Washington, DC: U.S. Department of Health and Human Services, 1991.

National Institute on Drug Abuse (NIDA). *Marijuana: Facts Parents Need to Know*. NIH Publication No. 95-4037. Rockville, MD: National Clearinghouse on Alcohol and Drug Information, 1998. Available http://www.athomedrugtest.com/ drug abuse marij.html.

National Institute on Drug Abuse (NIDA) (Infofax). *Marijuana*. Bethesda, MD: U.S. Department of Health and Human Services, 29 March 2000. Available http://www.nida.nih.gov/infofax/marijuana.html.

NORML. *Marijuana and the Human Body*. NORML Common Sense Series (June 2000). Available http://www.timesoft.com/ncnorml/common.

Office of National Drug Control Policy (ONDCP), Executive Office of the President. *Chart Book: Illicit Drug and Drug Control*. Washington, DC: ONDCP, October 2002.

Office of National Drug Control Policy (ONDCP). "Drug Facts: Marijuana." Washington, DC: ONDCP, 2003. Available http://www.whitehousedrugpolicy.gov/drugfact/marijuana/marijuana_h.html.

Oliwenstein, L. "The Perils of Pot." *Discover* 9 (1988): 18.

Palfai, T., and H. Jankiewicz. *Drugs and Human Behavior*. Dubuque, IA: Brown, 1991.

Pollan, M. "Medical Marijuana: Can It Help You? Should It Be Legal? A Report from California." *Herbs for Health* (March/April 1998): 38–50.

Pope, H. G., Jr., and D. Yurgulen-Todd. "The Residual Cognitive Effects of Heavy Marijuana Use in College Students." *Journal of the American Medical Association* 275 (1996): 521–527.

Rand Drug Policy Research Center. "Rand Releases Study on Marijuana 'Gateway Effect.'" Press release. Santa Monica, CA: Join Together on Line, 26 December 2002. Available http://www.jointogether.org.

Reaney, P. *Getting High May Not Be So Harmless After All*. Reuters Limited (20 March 2000). Available http://dailynews.yahoo.com/h/nm/20000320/sc/health_marijuana_1html.

Robert Wood Johnson Foundation. *Substance Abuse: The Nation's Number One Health Problem*. Prepared by the Schneider Institute for Health Policy for the Robert Wood Johnson Foundation, Brandeis University, Princeton, NJ: Robert Wood Johnson Foundation, February 2001.

Roffman, R. A., and W. H. George. "Cannabis Abuse." In *Assessment of Addictive Behaviors*, edited by D. M. Donovan and G. A. Marlatt, 78–86. New York: Guilford, 1988.

Rubin, V., and L. Comitas. *Ganja in Jamaica: A Medical Anthropological Study of Chronic Marijuana Use*. Paris: Mouton, 1975.

Schultes, R. E. "Ethnopharmacological Significance of Psychotropic Drugs of Vegetal Origin." *Principles of Psychopharmacology*, 2nd ed., edited by W. G. Clark and J. del Giudice. New York: Academic Press, 1978.

Sewester, S. *Drug Facts and Comparisons*. St. Louis, MO: Kluwer, 1993: 259h–259k.

Solomon, D., ed. *The Marihuana Papers*. New York: New American Library, 1966.

Stenchever, M. A., T. J. Kunysz, and M. A. Allen. "Chromosome Breakage in Users of Marijuana." *American Journal of Obstetrics and Gynecology* 118 (January 1974): 106–113.

Substance Abuse and Mental Health Services Administration (SAMHSA), Office of Applied Studies (OAS). *Results from the 2001 National Household Survey on Drug Abuse: Volume I. Summary of National Findings*. Rockville, MD: SAMHSA, August 2002a.

Substance Abuse and Mental Health Services Administration (SAMHSA), Office of Applied Studies (OAS). *The National Household Survey on Drug Abuse (NHSDA): Marijuana Use and Drug Dependence*. Rockville, MD: SAMHSA, August 2002b.

Substance Abuse and Mental Health Administration (SAMHSA), Office of Applied Studies (OAS). *National Household Survey on Drug Abuse: The NHSDA Report: Characteristics of New Marijuana Users*. Rockville, MD: SAMHSA, January 2003. Available http://www.samhsa.gov/oas/2k3/newmj/newmj.htm.

Substance Abuse and Mental Health Services Administration (SAMHSA). *Results from the 2003 National Survey on Drug Use and Health: National Findings*. Rockville, MD: Office of Applied Studies, 2004.

Suciu-Foca, N., J. P. Armand, and A. Morishima. "Inhibition of Cellular Immunity in Marijuana Smokers." *Science* 183 (1974): 419–420.

Swan, N. "Researchers Make Pivotal Marijuana and Heroin Discoveries." *NIDA Notes* 8 (10 September 1993): 1.

Swan, N. "A Look at Marijuana's Harmful Effects." *NIDA Notes* 9 (February/March 1994): 3–4.

Swan, N. "Facts About Marijuana and Marijuana Abuse." *NIDA Notes* 11 (March/April 1996): 15.

Taylor N. *Narcotics: Nature's Dangerous Gifts.* New York: Dell, 1963.

Taylor, N. "The Pleasant Assassin: The Story of Marijuana." *The Marijuana Papers*, ed. D. Solomon. New York: Signet Books, 1966.

Teen Challenge. *Drugs: Frequently Asked Questions.* South Australia: Pragin Press, 2000. Available http://www.tc.sn.au/hoax2.asp.

Tudor, C. G., D. M. Petersen, and K. W. Elifson. "An Examination of the Relationships Between Peer and Parental Influences and Adolescent Drug Use." In *Chemical Dependencies: Patterns, Costs, and Consequences*, edited by C. D. Chambers, J. A. Inciardi, D. M. Petersen, H. A. Siegal, and O. Z. White. Athens, OH: Ohio University Press, 1987.

Turner, C. E. "Chemistry and Metabolism." In *Marijuana Research Findings: 1980.* NIDA Research Monograph No. 31. Washington, DC: National Institute on Drug Abuse, 1980.

Venturelli, P. J. "Drugs in Schools: Myths and Reality." In *The Annals of the American Academy of Political and Social Science*, edited by W. Hinkle and S. Henry, 72–87. Thousand Oaks, CA: Sage Publications, January 2000.

Wren, C. S. "Youth Marijuana Use Rises." *Themes of the Times, New York Times* (20 February 1996): 1.

Zimmer, L., and J. P. Morgan. *Marijuana Myths, Marijuana Facts: A Review of the Scientific Evidence.* New York: Lindesmith Center, 1997.

CHAPTER 14

Inhalants

Did You Know?

- More than 1000 different products are abused commonly in the United States.

- Ordinary household products are misused as inhalants: glues/adhesives, nail polish remover, gasoline, paint thinner, spray paint, butane lighter fluid, propane gas, typewriter correction fluid, household cleaners, cooking sprays, deodorants, whipping cream aerosols, marking pens, and air conditioning coolants.

- Inhalant abuse is typically a problem of adolescents and teenagers. By the time children reach 8th grade, 17% will have misused inhalants.

- Every year, young people in this country die of inhalant abuse, and hundreds suffer severe consequences, including permanent brain damage and destruction of the heart, kidney, liver, and bone marrow.

- Inhalant abusers can die suddenly and without warning; even first-time abusers have died from sniffing inhalants.

Introduction

Inhalants are **volatile** substances that elicit psychological or physiological changes when introduced into the body via the lungs. They are rarely administered by any other route. Most cause intoxicating and/or **euphorigenic** effects. Many of these substances were never intended to be used by humans as drugs; consequently, they are not often thought of as having abuse potential. However, abuse of inhalants is a serious public health problem: according to data derived from the 2003 National Household Survey on Drug Use and Health, 10.7% of youths aged 12 to 17 had misused an inhalant at least once in his or her lifetime; 4.5% and 1.3% had misused an inhalant in the past year and month, respectively (SAMHSA 2004). Use among adolescents is especially disturbing; approximately 17.3% of U.S. 8th graders have misused an inhalant at least once in their lifetime (Johnston et al. 2005). This frequency of inhalant abuse among 8th graders surpasses the frequency of abuse of such highly publicized drugs as cocaine (3.4%), amphetamines (7.5%), and marijuana (16.3%) in this age group (Johnston et al. 2005).

A widespread misconception is that inhalant abuse is a harmless "phase" that occurs commonly during normal childhood and teenage development and as such is not worthy of significant concern because young people will "grow out of it" without experiencing harm. On the contrary, hundreds of adolescents and teenagers in the United States die or are seriously injured each year as a result of inhalant abuse. Even first-time users may die from "sudden sniffing death syndrome" (SSDS), a condition characterized by serious cardiac **arrhythmia** occurring during or immediately after inhaling. Accurate statistics regarding the number of inhalant-associated deaths and injuries

each year are unavailable, in part because medical examiners often attribute deaths from inhalant use to suicide, suffocation, or accidents. Nevertheless, every year young people in the United States die from inhalant abuse, and hundreds more suffer severe consequences such as permanent brain damage, loss of muscle control, and damage to the heart, blood, kidney, liver, and bone marrow (U.S. Consumer Product Safety Commission 2005).

Most inhalants are household or commercial products composed of several different chemicals. These compounds can act alone or synergistically to exert toxic effects. The potential of these agents to cause harm is compounded by the high concentrations of these substances absorbed in the body by inhalation and the tendency for these often *lipid* (oil or fat)-rich substances to be retained in lipid-containing vital organs. Another important consideration is that the users are often developmentally immature and as such can be more susceptible to the toxic effects of inhalants. The summation of these factors makes inhalants dangerous substances of abuse.

History of Inhalants

The modern era of inhalant abuse can be traced to 1776, when British chemist Joseph Priestley synthesized nitrous oxide (Kennedy and Longnecker 1990), a colorless gas with a slightly sweet odor and no noticeable taste. Roughly 20 years later, he and Humphry Davy suggested correctly that the gas might be useful as an anesthetic, and experiments were conducted to test this possibility. Meanwhile, many people learned that inhalation of nitrous oxide produces a euphoria that lasts for minutes. Hence, during the decades between its discovery and clinical use, the inhalant was abused. Its abuse continued to be fashionable into the early 19th century because it served as a means of rapidly attaining drunkenness without consuming alcohol.

Dentists contributed greatly to the introduction of nitrous oxide as an anesthetic. At a stage show in the 1840s, Horace Wells, a dentist, noticed that one of the persons involved in the show injured himself while under the influence of nitrous oxide, and yet felt no pain. Wells was so impressed by this anesthetic effect that he subsequently allowed his own tooth to be extracted while under the influence of the gas. His experiment was a success: Wells felt no pain. He went on to attempt to demonstrate his discovery at Massachusetts General Hospital in Boston; unfortunately, the patient cried out during the operation and the experiment was deemed unsuccessful. Nevertheless, word of this demonstration and others like it spread, ultimately leading to the use of nitrous oxide and other volatile anesthetics as legitimate medical therapy (Kennedy and Longnecker 1990).

Over the years, it was discovered that many chemicals, in addition to nitrous oxide, could be inhaled so as to alter psychological function. Such abuse of inhalants came to public attention in the 1950s when the news media reported that young people were getting "high" from sniffing glue. The term *glue sniffing* is still used today, but it is often used to describe inhalation of many products besides glue. In fact, there are more than 1000 different products that are currently misused as inhalants (U.S. Consumer Product Safety Commission 2005), some of which are listed in Table 14.1. These chemicals are not regulated like other drugs of abuse; hence, they are readily available to young people. This category of drugs can be classified into three major groups: volatile substances, anesthetics, and nitrites.

Types of Inhalants

VOLATILE SUBSTANCES

Over the past 50 years, the number of products containing volatile substances has increased substantially. This category of agents includes aerosols (e.g., spray paints, hair sprays, deodorants, air fresheners), art or office supplies (e.g., correction fluids, felt-tip marker fluids), adhesives (e.g., airplane and other glues), fuels (e.g., propane, gasoline), and industrial or household solvents (e.g., nail polish remover, paint thinners, dry-cleaning fluids). Some volatile substances exist as gases (e.g., nitrous oxide; the propellant in whipping cream cans), and others as liquids that vaporize at room temperature (e.g., gasoline). In some cases, the abuser inhales vapors directly from their original containers (called *sniff-*

ing or *snorting*). Still others inhale volatile solvents from plastic bags (called *bagging*) or from old rags or bandannas soaked in the solvent fluid and held over the mouth (called *huffing*).

Table 14.1 Inhalants

VOLATILE SOLVENTS	
Adhesives	
Airplane glue	Rubber cement
Polyvinylchloride cement	
Aerosols	
Spray paint	Hair spray
Deodorant, air freshener	Analgesic spray, asthma spray
Solvents and Gases	
Nail polish remover	Paint remover
Paint thinner	Typing correction fluid and thinner
Fuel gas	Cigarette lighter fluid
Gasoline	
Cleaning Agents	
Dry-cleaning fluid	Spot remover
Degreaser	
Dessert Topping Sprays	
Whipped cream, whippets	
ANESTHETICS	
Gas	Liquid
Local	
NITRITES	
Nitrite Room Odorizers	
"Poppers" and "rush"	

Source: Adapted from National Institute on Drug Abuse (NIDA). Research Report Services—Inhalant Abuse, NIH Publication No. 94–3818. July 1999.

Acute effects of the volatile chemicals that are commonly abused include initial nausea with some irritation of airways causing coughing and sneezing. Low doses often bring a brief feeling of light-headedness, mild stimulation followed by a loss of control, lack of coordination, and disorientation accompanied by dizziness and possible hallucinations. In some instances, higher doses can produce relaxation and depression leading to sleep or coma. If inhalation is continued, dangerous **hypoxia** may occur and cause brain damage or death. In other cases, SSDS can occur. Other potential toxic consequences of inhaling such substances include hypertension and damage to the cardiac muscle, peripheral nerves, brain, and kidneys. In addition, chronic users of inhalants frequently lose their appetite, are continually tired, and experience nosebleeds. If use of inhalants persists, some of the damage becomes irreversible.

Aerosols

Chemicals associated with aerosol sprays are popular among young inhalant abusers. Aerosol sprays are often abused not because of the effects produced by their principal ingredients but rather because of the effects of their propellant gases. In addition, some aerosol sprays (i.e., those necessary to suspend metallic paints) are inhaled because of the psychoactive effects caused by the solvents used to dissolve the product (NIDA 1999). Inhalation of aerosol preparations can be dangerous because these devices are capable of generating very high concentrations of the inhaled chemicals, much greater than those released more slowly from liquid products.

Toluene

Aerosol preparations can contain a variety of chemicals. One such chemical is toluene. Toluene is found in some glues, paints, thinners, nail polishes, and typewriter correction fluid. It is a principal ingredient in "Texas shoe shine" (a shoe spray containing toluene). Toluene represents one of the more dangerous chemicals found in aerosols and other solvents. Because this molecule is highly lipid soluble and has a low molecular weight, it is rapidly absorbed by the lungs, brain, heart, and liver. Accordingly, toluene abuse can cause damage to the brain resulting in incoordination, impaired cognition, limb spasms, convulsions, behavioral abnormalities, and coma. In addition, chronic abuse of toluene-containing products can damage other organs, especially the liver and kidneys. Toluene inhalation can also cause heart arrhythmia.

Butane and Propane

Butane and propane are found commonly in aerosols (e.g., spray paints, air fresheners, hair sprays) and are used as fuel gas or in lighter fluid. Use of these agents is quite common among inhalant abusers. For instance, one survey of adolescents in a Virginia correctional facility reported that butane lighter fluid was the third most frequently used inhalant among members of that population (gasoline was the most frequently used, and Freons the second most commonly used [McGarvey et al. 1999]). These chemicals likely constitute the most common "sniffing death hazards" among U.S. students (NIDA 1999). Furthermore, these chemicals are highly flammable: Fires and serious burn injuries have resulted when inhalation has been combined with smoking.

Gasoline

Because of its widespread availability, gasoline is abused commonly by young people, particularly in rural settings. Gasoline is a mixture of volatile chemicals, including toluene, benzene, and tri-orthocresyl phosphate (TCP). As a mixture of chemicals, its intentional inhalation can be especially dangerous. Benzene is an organic compound that causes serious injury to the bone marrow and suppresses the immune system. TCP is a fuel additive that causes degeneration of motor neurons. Lead, formerly a common constituent of gasoline, can cause lead poisoning, which leads to persistent CNS damage. Furthermore, gasoline is highly flammable; as with butane and propane, fires and serious burn injuries have resulted when gasoline inhalation has been combined with smoking of marijuana, tobacco, or other drugs.

KEY TERMS

hypoxia
a state of oxygen deficiency

Here and Now

Chronic Solvent Abuse, Brain Abnormalities, and Cognitive Deficits

Chronic inhalant abuse has long been associated with neurological damage and cognitive abnormalities that can range from mild impairment to severe dementia. In fact, the severity of these problems can be greater than for drugs often considered by the general population as being more harmful. For example, a 2002 report published by Neil Rosenberg of the University of Colorado Health Sciences Center found that chronic solvent abusers performed worse than chronic users of other drugs (especially cocaine and alcohol) on tests of working memory and problem solving. In this study, abusers inhaled primarily vapors from spray paint containing toluene, and averaged more than 10 years of regular abuse. More than half of the group reported near-daily inhalant intoxication.

According to Rosenberg, "the extensive neurological damage and cognitive impairments we found among chronic solvent abusers in our study could limit their ability to control their behavior and perceive problems associated with their substance abuse.... Some of the brain damage and cognitive deficits seen in both primary inhalant and cocaine abusers in the study could stem from the heavy use of alcohol that was common

among both groups.... However, the diffuse white matter changes and abnormalities found in the thalamus have not been seen in alcohol abusers and are clearly from solvent abuse."

Sources: Robert Mathias, November 2002. "Chronic Solvent Abusers Have More Brain Abnormalities and Cognitive Impairments Than Cocaine Abusers." *NIDA Notes,* 17. Available http://www.drugabuse.gov/NIDA_notes/NNVol17N4/Chronic.html; Rosenberg, N., et al., *Clinical Toxicology* 40 (2002): 21–34.

Freons

Freons and other fluorinated hydrocarbons are used in a number of products including refrigerators, air conditioners, and airbrushes. Their inhalation can cause not only serious liver damage but also SSDS. Inhaling these agents also poses other dangers; freeze injuries can occur when individuals inhaling Freons lose consciousness, leaving unprotected skin in close proximity to cold. In one serious, but rare, case, a 16-year-old male attempted to "get high" by inhaling airbrush propellant. The patient lost consciousness. When he awoke, he discovered that his tongue and lips were frozen, and that he had suffered serious burns on

his larynx, vocal cords, trachea, bronchi, and esophagus (Kuspis and Krenzelok 1999).

ANESTHETICS

When used properly, other forms of inhalants with abuse potential are important therapeutic agents. Included in this category are anesthetics such as ether, chloroform, halothane, and nitrous oxide. Although all the anesthetic gases work much like the central nervous system (CNS) depressants, only nitrous oxide is available enough to be a significant abuse concern.

Nitrous oxide is a colorless gas that is used frequently for minor outpatient procedures in offices of both physicians and dentists. It is often referred to as "laughing gas" because it can cause giggling and laughter in the patient receiving it. Nitrous oxide produces a unique profile of stimulant, hallucinogenic, and depressant effects. Because it is readily accessible, health professionals themselves or their staff are most likely to abuse nitrous oxide.

In addition to being found in a clinical setting, nitrous oxide is sold in large balloons from which the gas is released and inhaled for its mind-altering effects. It is also found in small cylindrical cartridges used as charges for whipped cream dispensers. These cylinders and other plastic containers filled with nitrous oxide are referred to as "whippets." Although significant abuse problems of nitrous oxide are infrequent (Dohrn et al. 1993), there are occasional reports of severe hypoxia (i.e., a lack of oxygen) or death due to acute over-

doses or psychosis. For the most part, nitrous oxide does not pose a significant abuse problem for the general public.

NITRITES

Nitrites are chemicals that cause vasodilation. Owing to this property, the prototype of this group, amyl nitrite, is available by prescription to treat angina. Nitrites were first abused in the 1960s as ampules of the compound were available over-the-counter (OTC). The ampules were "popped" between the fingers (hence, the name "poppers") and held to the nostrils for inhalation. They have been abused by only a few, selective groups, such as some homosexual men, to enhance "sexual stamina and pleasure." Many of these chemicals were banned in 1991 (NIDA 1999). According to a recent survey, only 1.3% of 12th graders reported any nitrite use in 2004 (Johnston et al. 2005).

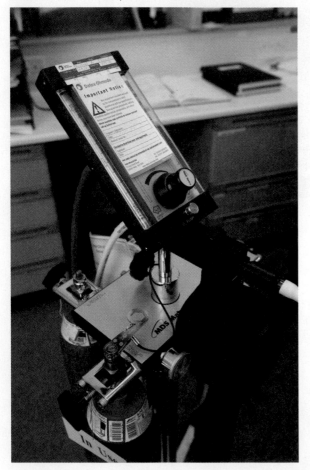

Anesthetics are an example of an inhalant.

Current Patterns and Signs of Abuse

Inhalants, particularly gases and aerosols, are often among the first drugs that young children misuse. The inhalants are popular for several reasons:

- They are legally obtained.
- They are readily available in most households and workplaces.
- They are inexpensive.
- They are easy to conceal.
- Most users are uninformed about the potential dangers.

In addition, inhalation is popular because it causes feelings of intoxication and euphoria much more rapidly than does the consumption of agents such as alcohol. Furthermore, the withdrawal ("hangover") is often less severe than with alcohol.

ADOLESCENT AND TEENAGE USAGE

Inhalant abuse is typically a problem of adolescents and teenagers. According to the Substance Abuse and Mental Health Services Administration (SAMHSA), in 2003, 1.3% of 12- to 17-year-olds reported current inhalant use, as compared with only 0.1% of adults aged 26 or older (SAMHSA 2004). Adolescents most commonly use inhalants, with usage decreasing as students grow older. For example, according to the 2004 *Monitoring the Future* study (Johnston et al. 2005), 4.5% of 8th graders reported using inhalants within the past month, whereas only 2.4% of 10th graders and 1.5% of high school seniors reported a similar pattern of use (see Table 14.2). One reason for this age difference is that older individuals often view use of inhalants with disdain and consider it unsophisticated and a "kid's" habit.

Inhalants were used by high percentages of 10th and 12th graders in 2004. Lifetime inhalant use among 12th graders in 2004 was 10.9%, compared with 12.4% among 10th graders (see Table 14.2).

Of considerable concern are reports that inhalant abuse can begin as early as the preschool years (Spiller and Krenzelok 1997). Researchers and poison information centers have described cases of 2- to 6-year-old children inhaling gasoline vapors. Imitation of older siblings or neighbors often accounts for this initial exposure. At least one study indicates that many 7- and 8-year-olds are familiar with the psychological effects of inhaling gasoline (Kaufman 1973). Hence, education efforts should be directed at very young children as well as adolescents and their parents.

Over the past 3 years, there has been a 17% decline in reported use of illicit drugs by 8th, 10th and 12th graders. In contrast, inhalant abuse has not shown this trend, especially among 8th graders (Volkow 2005; see also Table 14.2).

GENDER, RACE, SOCIOECONOMICS, AND ABUSE

According to the 2003 National Survey on Drug Use and Health, a greater percentage of men (2.6%) than women (1.5%) aged 18 to 25 have used an inhalant during the past year. However, that gender difference is diminishing as evidenced by recent findings that rates of past-year inhalant use were similar among females (4.6%) and males (4.3%) aged 12 to 17. White, non-Hispanic, and Hispanic individuals aged 12 to 17 were more likely than black or Asian individuals to have misused an inhalant at least once in their lifetime (11.7%, 10.6%, 6.8%, and 9.4%, respectively; SAMHSA 2004).

Chronic inhalant users frequently have a profile like that associated with other substance abusers. That is, often they live in unhappy surroundings with severe family or school problems, they have poor self-images, and sniffing gives them an accessible escape. Poverty, a history of child abuse, or poor grades are all associated with inhalant abuse (NIDA 2004). The problem of inhalant abuse is not unique to the United States. According to research data reported by the National Institute on Drug Abuse (NIDA), inhalant abuse is of worldwide concern. Low prices and easy access make inhalants as problematic in Asia, Africa, and Latin America as in the United States (NIDA 1999).

Table 14.2 Inhalant Use Among 8th, 10th, and 12th Graders
Data show the percentages of 8th, 10th, and 12th graders who used inhalants.

	8TH GRADERS			10TH GRADERS			12TH GRADERS		
	2002	2003	2004	2002	2003	2004	2002	2003	2004
Lifetime	15.2	15.8	17.3	13.5	12.7	12.4	11.7	11.2	10.9
Annual	7.7	8.7	9.6	5.8	5.4	5.9	4.5	3.9	4.2
30-Day	3.8	4.1	4.5	2.4	2.2	2.4	1.5	1.5	1.5

Source: Johnston, L. D., P. M. O'Malley, J. G. Bachman, and J. E. Schulenberg. *Monitoring the Future National Results on Adolescent Drug Use: Overview of Key Findings.* Bethesda, MD: National Institute on Drug Abuse, 2005.

SIGNS OF INHALANT ABUSE

Individuals under the influence of inhalants are often uncoordinated and disoriented and appear "drunken" as if having consumed alcohol. Red and watery eyes, slurred speech, nausea, headaches, and nosebleeds are also common. Rashes around the nose and mouth or unexplained paint on the hands and mouth can be signs of inhalant abuse. Other signs include smelling a chemical odor in the room or in unusual containers (e.g., soda cans, plastic bags), finding cans of aerosol whipped cream that will not foam, or discovering air conditioners that do not work. In addition, children who are frequent users of inhalants have the following characteristics:

- Often collect an unusual assortment of chemicals (such as glues, paints, thinners and solvents, nail polish, liquid eraser, and cleaning fluids) in bedrooms or with belongings
- Have breath that occasionally smells of solvents
- Often have the "sniffles" similar to a cold but without other symptoms of the ailment
- Appear drunk for short periods of time (15 to 60 minutes) but recover quickly
- Do not do well in school and are usually unkempt

Other signs of inhalant abuse can include the following:

- Sitting with a pen or marker near nose
- Constantly smelling clothing sleeves
- Hiding rags, clothes, or empty containers of the potentially abused products in closets, boxes, and other places
- Possessing chemical-soaked rags, bags, or socks
- Abusable household items missing

Dangers of Inhalant Abuse

The dangers of inhalant abuse stretch beyond simply the direct physical damage to the heart, lungs, liver, and brain. Other dangers include choking on vomitus, asphyxiation, and suffocation. In addition, abusers can seriously injure themselves or others while in an "intoxicated" state caused by the inhalant. In particular, frequent falls or accidents involving impaired driving occur in individuals under the influence of inhalants.

Other damage caused by inhalants include destruction of nerves that relay sound to the brain and thereby may cause deafness. The ability of the kidney to control the amount of acid in the blood can be impaired. Severe rashes around the nose and mouth may also result (ONDCP 2003).

Use of inhalants during pregnancy can also put newborns at risk of developmental deficits. Animal studies suggest that prenatal exposure to trichlorethylene (TCE) or toluene can cause delayed neurobehavioral development, reduced birthweight, and occasional skeletal abnormalities (NIDA 2004). Although it is not yet possible to link prenatal exposure to specific inhalants with a specific birth defect, case reports have documented developmental abnormalities in offspring of mothers who chronically abuse inhalants (NIDA 2004).

Another significant concern with inhalants is that these agents are considered gateway drugs because they are easy to obtain, inexpensive, and difficult to detect. According to Dr. Fred Beauvais, Tri-Ethnic Center for Prevention Research at Colorado State University, "children as young as 4th graders who begin to use volatile solvents also will start experimenting with other drugs, usually alcohol and marijuana" (NIDA 1999).

Discussion Questions

1. Name the three types of inhalants, and list examples of each type. List the dangerous side effects associated with the misuse of each type of inhalant.

2. Why are inhalants widely abused?

3. What is sudden sniffing death syndrome?

4. What chemical properties of inhalants make these agents particularly dangerous?

5. Who is most likely to abuse inhalants?

6. List several signs of inhalant abuse.

7. List several dangers of inhalant abuse other than the direct physical damage done by the chemical itself.

Key Terms

volatile **420**

euphorigenic **420**

arrhythmia **420**

hypoxia **422**

Summary

1 Inhalants are volatile substances that cause intoxicating and/or euphorigenic effects. Most were never intended to be used as drugs and are not often thought of as having abuse potential. However, inhalant abuse is a serious public health problem. Hundreds of adolescents and teenagers in the United States die or are seriously injured each year as a result of inhalant abuse. Even first-time users die from a condition referred to as sudden sniffing death syndrome (SSDS).

2 Most inhalants are household or commercial products composed of several different fat-soluble chemicals that can act alone or synergistically to exert toxic effects. These agents can be classified into three groups: volatile substances, anesthetics, and nitrites.

3 Volatile substances include aerosols, adhesives, fuels, and household solvents. Abusers inhale vapors directly from their original containers (called *sniffing* or *snorting*), from plastic bags (called *bagging*), or from old rags or bandannas soaked in the solvent fluid and held over the mouth (called *huffing*). Abuse of these agents can cause damage to the liver, brain, kidney, and immune system, as well as SSDS.

4 Anesthetics include ether, chloroform, halothane, and nitrous oxide. When used properly, these forms of inhalants are important therapeutic agents. However, their misuse can cause severe hypoxia and death.

5 Nitrites are vasodilators abused by only a few, selective groups to enhance "sexual stamina and pleasure." Their use has declined since many of these chemicals were banned in 1991.

6 Inhalants are popular because they are legally obtained, readily available, inexpensive, and easy to conceal.

7 Inhalant abuse is typically a problem of adolescents and teenagers, although it can begin as early as the preschool years. There has been a recent trend of decreasing inhalant abuse among young people. Nevertheless, one in every five 8th graders has abused an inhalant.

8 Signs of inhalant abuse include a "drunken" appearance, watery eyes, nausea, headaches, and nosebleeds. Rashes around the nose and mouth or unexplained paint on the hands and mouth can be signs of inhalant abuse. Other signs can include smelling a chemical odor in the room or in unusual containers (e.g., soda cans, plastic bags), finding cans of aerosol whipped cream that will not foam, or discovering air conditioners that do not work.

9 Dangers of inhalant abuse beyond those caused by the chemicals per se include choking on vomitus, asphyxiation, and suffocation.

References

Dohrn, C., J. Lichtor, A. Coalson, H. Uitvlugt, H. deWit, and J. Zachny. "Reinforcing Effects of Extended Inhalation of Nitrous Oxide in Humans." *Drugs and Alcohol Dependence* 31 (1993): 265–280.

Johnston, L. D., P. M. O'Malley, J. G. Bachman, and J. E. Schulenberg. *Monitoring the Future National Results on Adolescent Drug Use: Overview of Key Findings,* Bethesda, MD: National Institute on Drug Abuse, 2005.

Kaufman, A. "Gasoline Sniffing Among Children in a Pueblo Indian Village." *Pediatrics* 51 (1973): 1060–1064.

Kennedy, S. K., and D. E. Longnecker, "History and Principles of Anesthesiology." In *The Pharmacological Basis of Therapeutics,* edited by A. G. Gilman, T. W. Rall, A. S. Nies, and P. Taylor 269. New York: Pergamon Press, 1990.

Kuspis, D. A., and E. P. Krenzelok. "Oral Frostbite Injury from Intentional Abuse of a Fluorinated Hydrocarbon." *Journal of Toxicology and Clinical Toxicology* 37 (1999): 873–875.

McGarvey, E. L., G. J. Calvet, W. Mason, and D. Waite. "Adolescent Inhalant Abuse: Environments of Use." *American Journal of Drug and Alcohol Abuse* 25 (1999): 731–741.

National Institute on Drug Abuse (NIDA). *Research Report Series—Inhalant Abuse*, NIH Publication No. 94–3818. July 1999.

NIDA, *Research Report Series—Inhalant Abuse*, NIH Publication No. 00-3818, March 2004.

Office of National Drug Control Policy (ONDCP). Inhalants Fact Sheet (February 2003). Available www.whitehouse drugpolicy.gov/publications/factsht/inhalants/ (accessed 20 February 2005).

Spiller, H. A., and E. P. Krenzelok. "Epidemiology of Inhalant Abuse Reported to Two Regional Poison Centers" *Clinical Toxicology* 35 (1997): 167–173.

Substance Abuse and Mental Health Services Administration (SAMHSA). *Results from the 2003 National Survey on Drug Use and Health: National Findings.* NMSDA Series M-22, DMMS Publication No. SMA 04-3964. Rockville, MD: Office of Applied Studies, 2004.

U.S. Consumer Product Safety Commission. *A Parent's Guide to Preventing Inhalant Abuse.* Document 389. Available http://www.cpsc.gov/CPSCPUB/PUBS/389.html.

Volkow, N. D. Inhalant Abuse Is an Emerging Health Problem (updated 2 February 2005). Available www.nida.nih.gov/about/welcome/messageinhalants105.html.

CHAPTER 15

Over-the-Counter (OTC), Prescription, and Herbal Drugs

Did You Know?

- More than 700 of the current over-the-counter (OTC) drug products were available only by prescription 30 years ago.

- Pharmacists can provide useful counseling in selecting appropriate OTC products.

- Careless, excessive use of some OTC medications can cause addiction, physical dependence, tolerance, and withdrawal symptoms.

- When used together, prescription drugs or drugs of abuse can interact with OTC or herbal drugs in a dangerous and sometimes even lethal manner.

- Despite the marketing of hundreds of pain-relieving products, there are really only three different types of active analgesic ingredients found in oral OTC pain relievers.

- OTC cold medications do not cure the common cold but might temporarily relieve symptoms such as nasal congestion, muscle aches, and coughing.

- Most herbal remedies are very popular products that, despite containing drugs, are available without a prescription and by law are excluded from routine OTC regulation by the Food and Drug Administration (FDA).

- Many more people die in the United States from adverse reactions to legal medications than succumb to all illegal drug use.

- Most generic drugs are as effective as, but substantially less expensive than, their proprietary counterparts.

- Pharmacists are required by law to counsel patients concerning the use and safety of prescriptions that they fill.

On completing this chapter you will be able to:

◎ Outline the general differences between prescription and nonprescription drugs.

◎ Explain why the FDA occasionally switches prescription drugs to over-the-counter (OTC) status.

◎ Describe potential abuse problems with OTC, herbal, and prescription drugs.

◎ Identify some of the drugs that have been switched to OTC.

◎ Discuss the potential problems of making more effective OTC drugs available to the public for self-care.

◎ Describe the type of information that is included on the labels of nonprescription medicines.

◎ Discuss the rules for safe use of nonprescription drugs.

◎ Determine the difference between herbal products and OTC medications.

◎ Explain why the FDA has removed ephedrine and ephedra from its list of approved OTC products.

◎ Discuss the type of information that should be communicated between doctor and patient to avoid unnecessary drug side effects.

◎ Explain the advantages and disadvantages of generic and proprietary drugs.

Drugs and Society Online is a great source for additional drugs and society information for both students and instructors.
Visit **http://drugsandsociety.jbpub.com** to find a variety of useful tools for learning, thinking, and teaching.

Introduction

More than $44 billion is spent each year in the United States on prescription and nonprescription (over-the-counter or OTC) drugs (Just the Facts 2003). Prescription and OTC drugs have been viewed differently by the public since these classifications were formally established by the Durham-Humphrey Amendment of 1951. In general, we view OTC medications as less effective, relatively free from side effects, and rarely abused; in contrast, we often consider prescription drugs as much more potent, typically used for more serious medical conditions, and frequently dangerous. However, distinctions between prescription and nonprescription drugs, which at one time appeared to be obvious, have become blurred by changes in public demand and federal policies. Because of escalating health costs and a growing interest in self-care, people today want access to effective medications, and governmental agencies such as the Food and Drug Administration (FDA) are responding to their demands. Consequently, the FDA is actively involved in switching effective and relatively safe prescription medications to OTC status. In fact, more than 700 drug products sold OTC today were available only by prescription 30 years ago (CDER 2002). It is clear that in the future, many more drugs will be removed from behind the pharmacist's counter and made available for public access as nonprescription medications. These changes emphasize the arbitrary nature of classifying drugs as prescription and OTC and remind us that similar care should be taken with all medications to achieve maximal benefit and minimal risk.

In this chapter, we begin by discussing OTC or nonprescription drugs. The first topic encompasses policies regarding OTC drug regulation and is followed by a discussion of safe self-care with nonprescription drug products. Explanations of some of the most common medications in this category, including herbal remedies, conclude the section on OTC drugs. The second part of this chapter gives a general overview of prescription drugs. The consequences of misusing prescription drugs, as well as ways for you to avoid such problems, are discussed. A brief presentation of some of the most commonly prescribed drugs ends the chapter.

OTC Drugs

Each year people in the United States spend more than $14 billion on drug products that are purchased OTC, and this market is projected to reach $28 billion by the year 2010 (Covington 1993; Greenberg 1996). Today, more than 300,000 different OTC products are available to treat everything from age spots to halitosis; they account for 60% of the annual drug purchases in this country (Greenberg 1996). An estimated three out of four people routinely self-medicate with these drug products (Greenberg 1996). Some of the 80 major drug classes currently approved for OTC status are shown in Table 15.1.

OTC remedies are nonprescription drugs that may be obtained and used without the supervision of a physician or other health professional. Nevertheless, for some people, certain OTC products can be dangerous when used alone or in combination with other drugs. Although some OTC drugs are very beneficial in the self-treatment of minor to moderate uncomplicated health problems, others are of questionable therapeutic value, and their usefulness is often misrepresented by manufacturers.

ABUSE OF OTC DRUGS

A couple of high school students from Oregon became extremely ill from overdosing on multiple boxes of cold and cough OTC products that they had shoplifted while ditching school. The students were found stumbling around in an alley near their school, disoriented and lethargic. A local secondary education official implied that the practice was routine and referred to by the local kids as "popping skittles" because the cold medicine capsules are multicolored.

Although the consequences of abusing OTC drugs can be severe, relatively speaking the occurrence rate is low. For example, of the 44,000 hospital admissions in 1999 due to the medical consequences of abusing legal drugs, only 2% were associated with OTC products, whereas 98% were related to prescription medication (The Dasis Report 2002).

Because these drugs are usually available on demand, perceived as being exceptionally safe,

Table 15.1 **Some Major Drug Classes Approved by the FDA for OTC Status**

DRUG CLASS	EFFECTS
Analgesics and anti-inflammatories	Relieve pain, fever, and inflammation
Cold remedies	Relieve cold symptoms
Antihistamines and allergy products	Relieve allergy symptoms
Stimulants	Diminish fatigue and drowsiness
Sedatives and sleep aids	Promote sleep
Antacids	Relieve indigestion from rebound acidity
Laxatives	Relieve self-limiting constipation
Antidiarrheals	Relieve minor, self-limiting diarrhea
Gastric secretion blockers	Relieve heartburn
Topical antimicrobials	Treat skin infections
Bronchodilators and antiasthmatics	Assist breathing
Dentrifices and dental products	Promote oral hygiene
Acne medications	Treat and prevent acne
Sunburn treatments and sunscreens	Treat and prevent skin damage from ultraviolet rays
Dandruff and athlete's foot medications	Treat and prevent specific skin conditions
Contraceptives and vaginal products	Prevent pregnancy and treat vaginal infections
Ophthalmics	Promote eye hygiene and treat eye infections
Vitamins and minerals	Provide diet supplements
Antiperspirants	Promote body hygiene
Hair growth stimulators	Promote hair growth

Source: Walsh, P. *Physicians' Desk Reference for Nonprescription Drugs and Dietary Supplements.* 22nd ed. Montvale, NJ: Medical Economics, 2001.

and poorly understood by the general public, their abuse patterns differ somewhat from those seen with the so-called hard-core drugs of abuse, nevertheless, they can be equally harmful. Even though the OTC products generally have a greater margin of safety than their prescription counterparts, issues of abuse need to be considered. For example, many OTC drugs, when misused, can cause physical and psychological dependence. Nonprescription products that can be severely habit-forming include nasal and ophthalmic (eye) decongestants, laxatives, antihistamines, sleep aids, and antacids. Of particular abuse concern are the OTC stimulants, such as ephedrine, which can either be severely toxic by themselves or can be used as precursors to the synthesis of the extremely addicting and dangerous amphetamines. In fact, because of these concerns, the FDA recently ruled that ephedrine no longer can be included in OTC or herbal products.

Because use of OTC products is unrestricted, the patterns of abuse are impossible to determine accurately. However, these products are more likely to be abused by members of the unsuspecting general public who inadvertently become dependent due to excessive self-medication than by hard-core drug addicts who obtain the most potent drugs of abuse by illicit means.

FEDERAL REGULATION OF OTC DRUGS

In the United States, the FDA is responsible for regulating OTC drugs. Under direction of the FDA, the active ingredients in OTC drugs have been, and continue to be, evaluated and classified according to their effectiveness and safety (CDER 2002). At this time, the principal ingredients included in nonprescription drug products are category I (that is, they are considered safe and effective).

The FDA has attempted to make even more drugs available to the general public by switching some frequently used and safe prescription medications to OTC status. This policy is in response to public demand to have access to effective drugs for self-medication and has resulted in approximately 70 successful switches leading to more than 700 new OTC products (Snowbeck 2005). This policy helps to cut medical costs by eliminating the need for costly visits to health providers for treatment of minor, self-limiting ailments (Stolberg 2000). A few of the more notable drugs that have been switched from prescription to nonprescription status since 1985 (Slezak 1996; White-Sax 1998) are naproxen (analgesic, anti-inflammatory: Aleve); ketoprofen (analgesic: Orudis); hydrocortisone (anti-inflammatory steroid: Cortaid); loperamide (antidiarrheal: Imodium); tioconazole (vaginal antifungal: Vagistat-1); epinephrine (bronchodilator: Bronkaid Mist); miconazole (antifungal: Monistat 7); cimetidine (heartburn medication: Tagamet); increased-strength minoxidil (hair growth stimulant: Rogaine); nicotine patch (smoking cessation aid: Nicotrol); cromolyn (allergy medication: Nasalcrom); triclosan (antibacterial for gum disease: Colgate Total toothpaste); and loratadine (nonsedating antihistamine: Claritin).

A major concern of health professionals is that reclassification of safe prescription drugs to OTC status will result in overuse or misuse of these agents. The reclassified drugs may tempt individuals to self-medicate rather than seek medical care for potentially serious health problems or encourage the use of multiple drugs at the same time, increasing the likelihood of dangerous interactions (Stolberg 2000). Clearly, the FDA has slowed down this process: Since 2002, only five ingredients have been switched, including OTC versions of Claritin and the heartburn medication Prilosec (Snowbeck 2005).

It is likely that effective and safe prescription drugs will continue to be made available OTC, albeit at a slower pace. In fact, the FDA is considering other groups of drugs currently available by prescription for OTC status in the next several years. Drugs being evaluated for reclassification include those that lower cholesterol, new topical antibiotics, antivirals (to treat skin viral infections), and birth control pills (White-Sax 1998; Stolberg 2000; *USA Today* 2005).

OTC DRUGS AND SELF-CARE

Of approximately 3.5 billion health problems treated in the United States annually, almost 2 billion can be treated with an OTC drug (OTC Observations 1998). This fact demonstrates that the public frequently engages in medical self-care with OTC products. Self-care with nonprescription medications occurs because we decide that we have a health problem that can be adequately self-medicated without involving a health professional. Proper self-care assumes that the individual has made a correct diagnosis of the health problem and is informed enough to select the appropriate OTC product. If done correctly, self-care with OTC medications can provide significant relief from minor, self-limiting health problems at minimal cost. However, a lack of understanding about the nature of the OTC products—what they can and cannot do—and their potential side effects can result in harmful misuse. For this reason, it is important that those who consume OTC medications be fully aware of their proper use. This goal usually can be achieved by reading product labels carefully and asking questions of health professionals such as pharmacists and physicians.

OTC Labels

Information about proper use of OTC medications is required to be cited on the drug label and is regulated by the FDA. Required label information includes (1) approved uses of the product, (2) detailed instructions on safe and effective use, and (3) cautions or warnings to those at greatest risk when taking the medication. Recent FDA regulations require that this information be readily intelligible to the lay public and easily read (Nordenberg 1999) (see Figure 15.1).

Many consumers experience adverse side effects because they either choose to ignore the warnings on OTC labels or simply do not bother to read them. For example, excessive or inappropriate use of some nonprescription drugs can cause drug dependence; consequently, people who are always dropping medication in the eyes "to get the red out" or popping antacids like dessert after every meal are likely addicted. They continue to use OTC products to avoid unpleasant eye redness or stomach acidity, which are likely withdrawal consequences of excessive use of these medications.

Rules for Proper OTC Drug Use

The OTC marketplace for drugs operates differently than does its prescription counterpart. The use of OTC drugs is not restricted, and consumers are responsible for making correct decisions about these products. Thus, to a large degree, the consumer sets policy and determines use patterns.

Because there are no formal controls over the use of OTC drugs, abuse often occurs. In extreme situations, the abuse of OTC medication can be very troublesome, even causing structural damage to the body. Proper education about the pharmacological features of these agents is necessary if consumers are to make intelligent and informed decisions about OTC drug use. To reduce the incidence of problems, the following rules should be observed when using nonprescription products (CDER 2002):

1. Always know what you are taking. Identify the active ingredients in the product.

2. Know the effects. Be sure you know both the desired and potential undesired effects of each active ingredient.

3. Read and heed the warnings and cautions. The warnings are not intended to scare but to protect.

4. Do not use OTC drug products for more than 1 to 2 weeks. If the problem being treated persists beyond this time, consult a health professional.

FIGURE 15.1

OTC Label

Certain information must appear on the labels of an OTC medicinal product.

(a) Product Label Front

(b) Back of Label

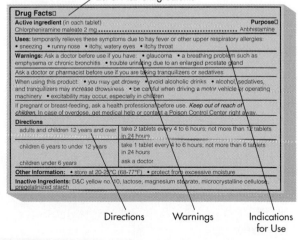

5. Be particularly cautious if you are also taking prescription or herbal drugs. Serious interactions between OTC drugs and these medications frequently occur. If you have a question, be sure to find out the answer.

6. If you have questions, ask a pharmacist. Pharmacists are excellent sources of information about OTC drugs. They possess up-to-date knowledge of OTC products and can assist consumers in selecting correct medications for their health needs. Ask them to help you.

7. Most importantly: If you don't need it, don't use it!

TYPES OF OTC DRUGS

It is impossible to provide a detailed description of the hundreds of active ingredients approved by the FDA for OTC distribution; however, the following includes a brief discussion of the most common OTC drugs available in this country.

Internal Analgesics

We spend more than $2 billion on internal (taken by mouth) **analgesics**, the largest sales category of OTC drugs in the United States. Most of the money is for **salicylates** (aspirin products—Anacin, Bayer), acetaminophen (Tylenol, Datril, Pamprin, Panadol), ibuprofen (Advil, Nuprin), and ibuprofen-like drugs such as naproxen (Aleve) and ketoprofen (Orudis). The composi-

tions of common OTC internal analgesics are given in Table 15.2.

Therapeutic Considerations The internal analgesic products are effective in treating several common ailments.

- *Analgesic Action.* The OTC analgesics effectively relieve mild to moderate somatic pain associated with musculoskeletal structures such as bones, skin, teeth, joints, and ligaments. Pains that are relieved by the use of these drugs include headaches, toothaches, earaches, and muscle strains. In contrast, these drugs are not effective in the treatment of severe pain or pain associated with internal organs, such as the heart, stomach, and intestines (*Drug Facts and Comparisons* 2005).

- *Anti-inflammatory Effects.* Use of high doses (two to three times the analgesic dose) of the salicylates and ibuprofen relieves the symptoms of inflammation such as those associated with arthritis (*Drug Facts and Comparisons* 2005). In contrast, even high doses of acetaminophen have little anti-inflammatory action. Because of this **anti-inflammatory** effect, these drugs are frequently compared with a group of natural, very potent anti-inflammatory compounds, the **steroids**. To distinguish drugs such as the salicylates and ibuprofen from steroids, these drugs are often called **nonsteroidal anti-inflammatory drugs (NSAIDs)**.

- *Antipyretic Effects.* The OTC analgesics, such as aspirin and acetaminophen, reduce fever but do not alter normal body temperature (*Drug Facts and Comparisons* 2005). Such drugs are called **antipyretics**. The frequent use of these drugs to eliminate fevers is very controversial. Some clinicians believe that low-grade fever may be a defense mechanism that helps destroy infecting microorganisms such as bacteria and viruses; thus, interfering with fevers may hamper the body's ability to rid itself of infection-causing microorganisms. Because no serious problems are associated with fevers of 102°F or less, they are probably better left unmedicated.

- *Side Effects.* When selecting an OTC analgesic drug for relief of pain, inflammation, or fever,

KEY TERMS

analgesics
drugs that relieve pain while allowing consciousness

salicylates
aspirin-like drugs

anti-inflammatory
relieves symptoms of inflammation

steroids
potent hormones released from the adrenal glands

nonsteroidal anti-inflammatory drugs (NSAIDs)
anti-inflammatory drugs that do not have steroid properties

antipyretics
drugs that reduce fevers

Table 15.2 **Compositions of OTC Internal Analgesics (dose per unit)**

PRODUCT	ASPIRIN (MG)	ACETAMINOPHEN (MG)	IBUPROFEN (MG)	OTHER
Anacin	400	—	—	Caffeine
Bayer Aspirin	325	—	—	—
Empirin	325	—	—	—
Alka-Seltzer, Extra Strength	500	—	—	Antacid
Ecotrin	325	—	—	Coated tablet
Excedrin, Extra Strength	250	250	—	Caffeine
Tylenol, Children's	—	80	—	—
Advil	—	—	200	—
Motrin IB	—	—	200	—
Motrin, Children's	—	—	100	—
Nuprin	—	—	200	—
Aleve	—	—	—	Naproxen (200 mg)
Orudis	—	—	—	Ketoprofen (12.5 mg)

Source: Walsh, P. *Physicians' Desk Reference for Nonprescription Drugs*, 22nd ed. Oradell, NJ: Medical Economics Data, 2001.

possible side effects should be considered. Although salicylates such as aspirin are frequently used, they can cause problems for both children and adults (see Table 15.3). Because of their side effects, salicylates are not recommended for (1) children, because of the potential for **Reye's syndrome**; (2) people suffering gastrointestinal problems, such as ulcers; or (3) people with bleeding problems, who are taking anticlot medication, who are scheduled for surgery, or who are near term in pregnancy, because salicylates interfere with blood clotting and prolong bleeding.

For minor aches and pains, acetaminophen substitutes adequately for salicylates, has no effect on blood clotting, and does not cause stomach irritation. In addition, acetaminophen does not influence the occurrence of Reye's syndrome, a potentially deadly complication of colds, flu, and chicken pox in children up to the age of 16 to 18 years who are using salicylates (*Drug Facts and Comparisons* 2005).

Caffeine and Other Additives A number of OTC analgesic products contain caffeine. Caffeine may relieve the aversion of pain due to its stimulant effect, which may be perceived as pleasant and energizing. The combination of caffeine with OTC analgesics may enhance pain relief (*Drug Facts and Comparisons* 2005) and be especially useful in treating vascular headaches because of the vasoconstrictive properties on cerebral blood vessels caused by this stimulant. In most OTC analgesic

KEY TERMS

Reye's syndrome
potentially fatal complication of colds, flu, or chicken pox in children

Table 15.3 Common Side Effects of OTC Nonsteroidal Anti-inflammatory Drugs (NSAIDs)

DRUGS	SYSTEM AFFECTED	SIDE EFFECTS
Salicylates (aspirin-like)	Gastrointestinal	Cause irritation, bleeding; aggravate ulcers
	Blood	Interfere with clotting; prolong bleeding
	Ears	Chronic high doses cause ringing (tinnitus) and hearing loss
	Pediatric	Cause Reye's syndrome
Acetaminophen	Liver	High acute doses or chronic exposure can cause severe damage
Ibuprofen (includes other, newer NSAIDs)	Gastrointestinal	Similar to salicylates but less severe
	Blood	Similar to salicylates but less severe
	Kidneys	Damage in elderly or those with existing kidney disease

products—for example, Anacin or Excedrin—the amount of caffeine is less than that found in one-fourth to one-half cup of coffee (about 30 milligrams/tablet). Other ingredients—such as antacids, antihistamines, and decongestants—sometimes included in OTC pain-relieving products have little or no analgesic action and usually add little to the therapeutic value of the medication.

A recent development for OTC analgesic products was FDA permission to advertise pain-relieving products effective in the relief of migraine headaches. Although these products have been found to provide relief from minor migraine headaches, they do not contain any new breakthrough drugs: These products contain previously available ingredients, such as aspirin, ibuprofen, and caffeine, just in higher doses (e.g., Migraine Extra Strength Excedrin).

Cold, Allergy, and Cough Remedies

At any one time, almost 5% of the population has a common cold. This adds up to billions of colds per year in the United States, at a cost of almost $5 billion annually (Dale 2000).

The incidence of the common cold varies with age. Children between 1 and 5 years are most susceptible; each child averages 6 to 12 respiratory illnesses per year, most of which are common colds. Individuals 25 to 30 years old average about 6 respiratory illnesses a year, and older adults average 2 or 3. The declining incidence of colds with age is owing to the immunity that occurs after each

infection with a cold virus; thus, if reinfected with the same virus, the microorganism is rapidly destroyed by the body's defense and the full-blown symptoms of a cold do not occur (Sause and Mangione 1991).

Most colds have similar general symptoms: In the first stage, the throat and nose are dry and scratchy; in the second stage, secretions accumulate in the air passages, nose, throat, and bronchial tubes. The second stage is marked by continuous sneezing, nasal obstruction, sore throat, coughing, and nasal discharge. There may be watering and redness of the eyes and pain in the face (particularly near the sinuses) and ears. One of the most bothersome symptoms of the common cold is the congestion of the mucous membranes of the nasal passages, due in part to capillary dilation, which causes these blood vessels to enlarge and become more permeable. Such vascular changes allow fluids to escape, resulting in drainage and also inflammation due to fluid-swollen tissues (Mackowiak 1999).

Decongestants The cold and allergy products we use are formulated with such drugs as decongestants (sympathomimetics), antihistamines (chlorpheniramine and pheniramine), analgesics (aspirin and acetaminophen), and an assortment of other substances (vitamin C, alcohol, caffeine, and so on). Table 15.4 lists the ingredients found in many common OTC cold and allergy products.

Antihistamines reduce congestion caused by allergies, but their effectiveness in the treatment

Table 15.4 **Compositions of Common OTC Cold and Allergy Products (dose per tablet)**

PRODUCT	SYMPATHOMIMETIC (MG)	ANTIHISTAMINE (MG)	ANALGESIC (MG)
Actifed	Pseudoephedrine (30)	Triprolidine (2.5)	—
Chlor-Trimeton Allergy	—	Chlorpheniramine (4)	—
Dristan Cold Multi-Symptom Formula	Phenylephrine (5)	Chlorpheniramine (2)	Acetaminophen (325)
Sudafed Sinus	Pseudoephedrine (30)	—	Acetaminophen (325)

Source: Walsh, P. *Physicians' Desk Reference for Nonprescription Drugs*, 22nd ed. Oradell, NJ: Medical Economics Data, 2001.

of virus-induced colds is controversial (Mackowiak 1999). In high doses, the anticholinergic action of antihistamines (see Chapter 4) also decreases mucus secretion, relieving the runny nose; however, this action is probably insignificant at the lower recommended doses of OTC preparations (Mackowiak 1999). An anticholinergic drying action may actually be harmful because it can lead to a serious coughing response. Due to anticholinergic effects, antihistamines also may cause dizziness, drowsiness, impaired judgment, constipation, and dry mouth; they sometimes are abused because of psychedelic effects resulting from high-dose consumption. Because of the limited usefulness and the side effects of antihistamine for treating colds, decongestant products without such agents are usually preferred for these viral infections. In contrast, antihistamines are very useful in relieving allergy-related congestion and symptoms.

The sympathomimetic drugs used as decongestants cause nasal membranes to shrink because of their vasoconstrictive effect, which reduces the congestion caused by both colds and allergies. Such drugs can be used in the form of sprays or drops (topical decongestants) or systemically (oral decongestants) (see Table 15.5). FDA-approved sympathomimetics include pseudoephredrine, phenylephrine (probably the most effective topical), naphazoline, oxymetazoline, and xylometazoline (Mackowiak 1999). Until recently, phenylpropanolamine was also included in OTC products and was one of the more popular system decongestant ingredients available without a prescription; however, in November 2000, the FDA requested that this mild stimulant be withdrawn from all OTC medications due to its association with strokes in women under the age of 50 years (Public Health Advisory 2000). Another substantial problem associated with the sympathomimetic decongestant ingredients in cold medicines is that they can easily be chemically converted into methamphetamine. For this reason, state and local governments are passing laws that require these decongestant products to be kept behind the counter and records to be kept of those who purchase these medications (see "Here and Now," Fighting the "Common Cold" Pills).

If you use decongestant nasal sprays frequently, you can experience **congestion rebound** due to tis-

Table 15.5 **Compositions of OTC Topical Decongestants (Drug Concentrations)**

PRODUCT	SYMPATHOMIMETIC
Afrin nasal spray	Oxymetazoline (0.05%)
Neo-Synephrine, 12 Hour	Oxymetazoline (0.05%)
Vicks Sinex, 12-Hour	Oxymetazoline (0.05%)

Source: Walsh, P. *Physicians' Desk Reference for Nonprescription Drugs*, 22nd ed. Oradell, NJ: Medical Economics Data, 2001.

KEY TERMS

congestion rebound
withdrawal from excessive use of a decongestant, resulting in congestion

Here and Now

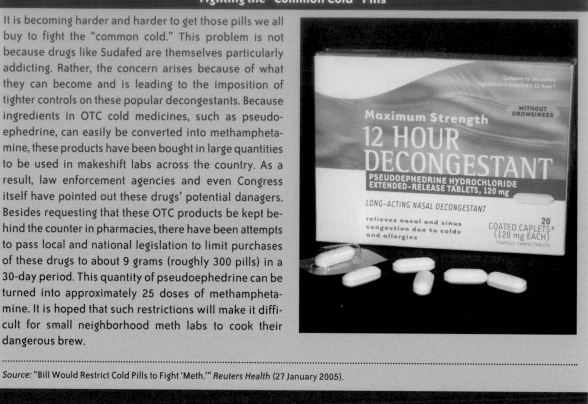
sue dependence. After using a nasal spray regularly for longer than the recommended period of time, the nasal membranes adjust to the effect of the vasoconstrictor and become very congested when the drug is not present. You may become "hooked" and use the spray more and more with less and less relief until your tissues no longer respond and the sinus passages become almost completely obstructed (Mackowiak 1999). Allergists frequently see new patients who are addicted to nasal decongestant sprays and are desperate for relief from congestion. This problem can be prevented by using nasal sprays sparingly and for no longer than the recommended time.

Orally ingested sympathomimetic drugs give less relief from congestion than the topical medications but are less likely to cause rebound effects. In contrast, systemic administration of these drugs is more likely to cause cardiovascular problems (that is, stimulate the heart, cause arrhythmia, increase blood pressure, and cause stroke).

Antitussives Other drugs used to relieve the common cold are intended to treat coughing. The cough reflex helps clear the lower respiratory tract of foreign matter, particularly in the later stages of a cold. There are two types of cough: productive and nonproductive. A *productive cough* removes mucus secretions and foreign matter so that breathing becomes easier and the infection clears up. A *nonproductive, or dry, cough* causes throat irritation; this type of cough is of little cleansing value. Some types of cough suppressant (antitussive) medication are useful for treating a nonproductive cough but should not be used to suppress a productive cough ("A Hacker's Guide" 1995).

Two kinds of OTC preparations are available to treat coughing:

- **Antitussives**—such as codeine, dextromethorphan, and diphenhydramine (an antihistamine)—that act on the central nervous system (CNS) to raise the threshold of the cough-coordinating center, thereby reducing the frequency and intensity of a cough
- **Expectorants**—such as guaifenesin and terpin hydrate—which theoretically (but not very effectively) increase and thin the fluids of the respiratory tract in an attempt to soothe the irritated respiratory tract membranes and decrease the thickness of the accumulated secretions so that coughing becomes more productive

Table 15.6 lists commonly used OTC antitussives and their compositions.

Often, the tickling sensation in the throat that triggers a cough can be eased by sucking on a cough drop or hard candy, which stimulates saliva flow to soothe the irritated membranes. Unless

The common cold accounts for 20% of all acute illnesses in the United States.

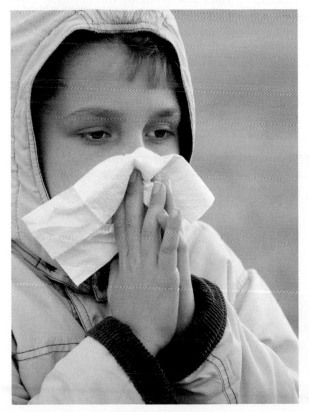

the cough is severe, sour hard candy often works just as well as more expensive cough lozenges.

Cough remedies, like other medications, have a psychological value. Many patients with respiratory tract infections claim they cough less after using cough remedies, even when it is objectively demonstrated that the remedies reduce neither the frequency nor the intensity of the cough. Cough remedies work in part by reducing patients' anxiety about the cough and causing them to believe that their cough is lessening. If you believe in the remedy, you often can get as much relief from a simple, inexpensive product as from the most sophisticated and costly one. If a cough does not ease in a few days, you should consult a doctor ("A Hacker's Guide" 1995).

Although not widely known, abuse of antitussive products by teenagers is a significant problem in some regions of this country. This abuse likely relates to the fact that the antitussive ingredient, dextromethorphan, in high doses can have a phencyclidine (PCP)–like effect (Research Report 2001b) (see "Here and Now," The Dextromethorphan Trip).

What Really Works? With all the advances in medicine today, there is still no cure for the common cold. In most cases, the best treatment is plenty of rest, increased fluid intake to prevent dehydration and to facilitate productive coughing, humidification of the air if it is dry, gargling with diluted salt water (2 teaspoons per quart), an analgesic to relieve the accompanying headache or muscle ache, and perhaps an occasional decongestant if nasal stuffiness is unbearable. Allergy symptoms, in contrast, are best relieved by antihistamines.

Sleep Aids

In 1995, an estimated 49% of the U.S. population experienced insomnia (the inability to fall asleep or stay asleep) at least 5 nights each month (Gill

KEY TERMS

antitussives
drugs that block the coughing reflex

expectorants
substances that stimulate mucus secretion and diminish mucus viscosity

Table 15.6 Compositions of Common OTC Antitussives (dose per unit)

PRODUCT	DEXTROMETHORPHAN (MG)	EXPECTORANT	OTHER
Comtrex Maximum Strength	15	—	Sympathomimetic; antihistamine; analgesic
Cheracol D Cough	10	Guaifenesin	Alcohol
Novahistine DMX	10	Guaifenesin	Sympathomimetic; alcohol
Robitussin CF	10	Guaifenesin	Sympathomimetic
Vicks NyQuil	10	—	Sympathomimetic; antihistamine; analgesic

Source: Walsh, P. *Physicians' Desk Reference for Nonprescription Drugs*, 22nd ed. Oradell, NJ: Medical Economics Data, 2001.

1999). About 1% of the adult population routinely self-medicate their insomnia with OTC sleep aids that are advertised as inducing a "safe and restful sleep." Described as nonbarbiturate and non–habit-forming, these low-potency products are frequently misused (Shuster 1996). For example, the parents of a young child were traveling cross-country. They knew the trip would be long and the child likely would grow tired and cranky. To keep the child quiet and manageable, the parents used Benadryl, an allergy medication, that contained an antihistamine to cause sedation (personal communication to Hanson, 2003). Use of these products in young children is inappropriate and can be dangerous.

The drugs commonly used in OTC sleep aids are antihistamines, particularly diphenhydramine (Gill 1999). Although antihistamines have been classified as OTC category I sleep aid ingredients (see Chapter 3), their usefulness in treating significant sleep disorders is highly questionable (Gill 1999). At best, some people who suffer mild, temporary sleep disturbances caused by problems such as physical discomfort, short-term disruption in daily routines (such as jet lag), and extreme emotional upset might experience temporary relief.

Here and Now

The Dextromethorphan Trip

Dextromethorphan is the antitussive ingredient frequently found in nonprescription cough medicine. Because of pharmacological properties that resemble those of PCP, OTC cough medicines are sometimes abused by teenagers. One such person, who had consumed almost an entire bottle of a popular anticough product, described his experience. He related that the effects of the drug hit first with lightheadedness and slight disorientation. After 1 hour, the disorientation became severe. He explained that it felt as though he were outside of himself looking in. The hallucinations were somewhat subtle with things appearing grainy and distorted. He found that breathing was sometimes constricted as though he were wearing a tight shirt collar. Then came hot flashes, which caused him to turn on a fan to cool down. He found walking was difficult, and time became distorted. The trip lasted 1 to 2 hours for the strong effects, but it seemed to continue forever. This person was an experienced user of acid (LSD) and mushrooms, but he had never been on a trip as scary as the one with the cough medicine. Several times he thought he was going to die. He found that coming down took a while. He decided that he would never do "dex" (dextromethorphan) again.

However, even for those few who initially benefit from these agents, tolerance develops within 2 to 4 days. For long-term sleep problems, OTC sleep aids are of no therapeutic value and are rarely recommended by health professionals. Actually, their placebo benefit is likely more significant than their actual pharmacological benefit. Usually counseling and psychotherapy are more effective approaches for resolving chronic insomnia than OTC or even prescription sleep aid drugs (Gill 1999).

Because antihistamines are CNS depressants, in low doses they can cause sedation and antianxiety action (see Chapter 6). Although in the past, some OTC products containing antihistamines were promoted for their relaxing effects (e.g., Quietworld and Compoz), currently, no sedatives are approved for OTC marketing. The FDA decided that the earlier products relieved anxiety by causing drowsiness, so, in fact, they were not legitimate sedatives. Because of this ruling, medications that are promoted as antianxiety products are no longer available without a prescription. However, antihistamines have been added to an array of other OTC drug products marketed for the purpose of causing relaxation or promoting sleep; such products include analgesics (Excedrin P.M.) and cold medicines (Triaminic Cold and Allergy). The rationale for such combinations is questionable, and their therapeutic value unsubstantiated.

Melatonin The hormone melatonin is currently being used by millions to induce sleep or to help the body's natural clock readjust after the effects of jet lag. Melatonin was referred to as the "all-natural nightcap of the 1990s." Although most users of this hormone want assistance in falling asleep, melatonin is also claimed to slow the aging process, stimulate the immune system, and enhance the sex drive. Melatonin is a naturally occurring hormone, also found in some foods. Under the 1994 Dietary Supplement and Education Act, melatonin is considered a dietary supplement and is not regulated by the FDA. Despite the popularity of melatonin products, little is known about the benefits or the potential adverse effects of this hormone; consequently, these products should be used cautiously, if at all (van den Heuval et al. 2005).

Stimulants

Some OTC drugs are promoted as stay-awake (NōDōz) or energy-promoting (Vivarin) products (Walsh 2001). In general, these medications contain high doses of caffeine (100–200 milligrams per tablet). (Caffeine and its pharmacological and abuse properties are discussed at length in Chapter 10.) Although it is true that CNS stimulation by ingesting significant doses of caffeine can increase the state of alertness during periods of drowsiness, the usefulness of such an approach is highly suspect.

For example, college students sometimes rely on such products to enhance mental endurance during cramming sessions for examinations. In fact, at one western U.S. university, the back page of a quarterly class schedule, printed and distributed by the university, included a full-page advertisement for the OTC stimulant Vivarin with the caption, "Exam Survival Kit." The implications of such promotions are obvious and disturbing. Due to the objections of the faculty, the advertisement was not run again at the university.

Routine use of stay-awake or energy-promoting products to enhance performance at work or in school can lead to dependence, resulting in withdrawal when the person stops using the drug. Most health professionals agree that there are more effective and safer ways to deal with fatigue and drowsiness—for example, managing time efficiently and getting plenty of rest.

Sympathomimetics Mild OTC sympathomimetics have been marketed as safe stimulants and as legal alternatives to cocaine and other illicit stimulants (Associated Press 2003). The principal drugs found in the mild stimulants are drugs such as phenylephrine and caffeine. The same drugs are also found in OTC decongestants and diet aids (Walsh 2001). Until recently, these products also contained the sympathomimetic phenylpropanolamine, but due to a link with strokes (see the earlier discussion in "Cold, Allergy, and Cough Remedies"), the FDA has required that this mild stimulant be withdrawn from all OTC products (Public Health Advisory 2000). Ephedrine has been similarly withdrawn from OTC use due to its potential toxicity on the cardiovascular system (FDA 2004).

Although much less potent than amphetamines, when used in high doses, the OTC stimulants can cause anxiety, restlessness, throbbing headaches, breathing problems, and tachycardia (rapid heartbeat). There have been reports of death due to heart arrhythmia, cerebral hemorrhaging, and strokes, as discussed earlier from excessive ephedrine use (see Chapter 10).

Gastrointestinal Medications

The gastrointestinal (GI) system consists principally of the esophagus, stomach, and intestines and is responsible for the absorption of nutrients and water into the body, as well as the elimination of body wastes. The function of the GI system can be altered by changes in eating habits, stress, infection, and diseases such as ulcers and cancers. Such problems may affect appetite, cause discomfort or pain, result in nausea and vomiting, and alter the formation and passage of stools from the intestines.

A variety of OTC medications are available to treat GI disorders such as indigestion (antacids), heartburn (gastric secretion blockers), constipation (laxatives), and diarrhea (antidiarrheals) (Walsh 2001). However, before individuals self-medicate with nonprescription drugs, they should be certain that the cause of their GI problem is minor, is self-limiting, and does not require professional care. Because antacids are the most frequently used of the GI nonprescription drugs, they are discussed here.

Antacids and Antiheartburn Medication More than $1 billion is spent annually on antacid preparations that claim to give relief from heartburn and indigestion caused by excessive eating or drinking and to provide long-term treatment of chronic peptic ulcer disease. It is estimated that as much as 50% of the population has had one or more attacks of **gastritis**, often referred to as "acid indigestion, heartburn, upset stomach, and sour or acid stomach." These attacks are often due to acid rebound, occurring 1 to 2 hours after eating; by

More than $1 billion is spent each year on antacid products such as this in the United States.

this time, the stomach contents have passed into the small intestines, leaving the gastric acids to irritate or damage the lining of the empty stomach. Heartburn, or gastroesophageal reflux, occurs after exposure of the lower esophagus to these very irritating gastric chemicals.

Some cases of severe, chronic acid indigestion may progress to peptic ulcer disease. Peptic ulcers (open sores) most frequently affect the duodenum (first part of the intestine) and the stomach. Although this condition is serious, it can be treated effectively with antacids, which are often combined with drugs available OTC or by prescription such as cimetidine (Tagamet), ranitidine (Zantac), and famotidine (Pepcid). A person with acute, severe stomach pain; chronic gastritis; blood in the stools (common ulcer symptoms); diarrhea; or vomiting should see a physician promptly and should not attempt to self-medicate with OTC antacids (Walsh 2001).

Most bouts of acid rebound, however, are associated with overeating or consuming irritating

KEY TERMS

gastritis
inflammation or irritation of the gut

foods or drinks; these self-limiting cases can usually be managed safely with OTC antacids (such as sodium bicarbonate, calcium carbonate, aluminum salts, and magnesium salts). Because of their alkaline (opposite of acidic) nature, the nonprescription products neutralize gastric acids and give relief.

Generally speaking, OTC antacid preparations are safe for occasional use at low recommended doses, but excessive use can cause serious problems. In addition, all antacids can interact with other drugs; they may alter the GI absorption or renal elimination of other medications. For example, some antacids inhibit the absorption of tetracycline antibiotics; thus, these products should not be taken at the same time. Consequently, patients using prescription drugs should consult with their physicians before taking OTC antacids (Walsh 2001).

Heartburn can be treated effectively with low doses of Tagamet, Zantac, or Pepcid. These drugs were switched to OTC status in the mid-1990s and help reduce gastric secretions (Walsh 2001).

Diet Aids

In U.S. society, being slim and trim are prerequisites to being attractive. It is estimated that approximately 33% of the people in the United States are *obese* (body fat in excess of 20% of normal) and 50% are overweight (Crespo and Arbesman 2003). Being obese has been linked to cardiovascular disease, some cancers, diabetes, chronic fatigue, and an array of aches and pains, not to mention psychological disorders such as depression (Sprague and Culbertson 1997). Popular remedies for losing weight often include fad diets advertised in supermarket journals, expensive weight loss programs, or both prescription and OTC diet aids.

Using drugs as diet aids is highly controversial (Sprague and Culbertson 1997). Most experts view them as useless or even dangerous. These drugs are supposed to depress the appetite, which helps users maintain low-calorie diets. The most effective of these agents are called **anorexiants**. Potent anorexiants, such as amphetamine-like drugs (including the once-popular diet aid, Phen-fen), can cause dangerous side effects (see Chapter 10) and are available only by prescription. The appetite suppression effects of prescription anorexiants are usually temporary, after which tolerance often builds. Thus, even prescription diet aid drugs are usually effective for only a short period. There are no wonder drugs to help the obese lose weight permanently.

The most potent and most frequently used OTC diet aid ingredient used to be the sympathomimetic phenylpropanolamine. Since the FDA required that this drug be removed from all OTC products (Public Health Advisory 2000), it is not clear which sympathomimetic will replace it in OTC diet aids. The OTC diet aids are minimally effective and of no value in the treatment of significant obesity. Despite their questionable value, frequent use of high doses of the OTC diet aid products is a common practice by weight-conscious female high school and college students. As one college sophomore who routinely carried a package of Dexatrim in her purse said, "Popping two or three of these before an important date helps me to eat like a bird and appear more petite" (from Hanson's files, interview, 1996). Interestingly, this same woman also occasionally induced vomiting after eating because of her fear that she was gaining weight. Such weight-management practices are extremely worrisome.

Approximately 25% to 30% of the people in the United States are obese and 50% are overweight.

KEY TERMS

anorexiants
drugs that suppress the activity of the brain's appetite center, causing reduced food intake

Skin Products

Because the skin is so accessible and readily visible, most people are sensitive about its appearance. These cosmetic concerns are motivated by attempts to look good and preserve youth. Literally thousands of OTC skin products with cosmetic and health objectives are available to consumers (Walsh 2001). Only a few of the most commonly used products are mentioned here: acne medications, sun products, and basic first-aid products.

Acne Medications Acne is the most common skin disorder affecting adolescents (Krowchuk 2000) and typically occurs during puberty in response to the secretion of the male hormone androgen (both males and females have this hormone) (Tatro 1998). Acne is usually chronic inflammation caused by bacteria trapped in plugged sebaceous (oil) glands and hair follicles. This condition consists of whiteheads, pimples, nodules, and, in more severe cases, pustules, cysts, and abscesses. Moderate to severe acne can cause unsightly scarring on the face, back, chest, and arms and should be treated aggressively by a dermatologist with drugs such as antibiotics (tetracycline) and potent **keratolytics**, such as Retin A (retinoic acid) or vitamin A or Accutane (isotretinoin). Usually, minor to moderate acne does not cause scarring or permanent skin damage and often can be safely self-medicated with OTC acne medications (Tatro 1998).

Several nonprescription approaches to treating mild acne are available:

1. *Sebum removal.* Oil and fatty chemicals (*sebum*) can accumulate on the skin and plug the sebaceous glands and hair follicles. Use of OTC products such as alcohol wipes (e.g., Stri-Dex) can help remove such accumulations.

2. *Peeling agents.* The FDA found several keratolytic agents safe and effective for treatment of minor acne: benzoyl peroxide (Oxy 5 and Oxy 10), salicylic acid (Oxy Medicated Pads), resorcinol, and sulfur (Acnemol), alone or in combination. These drugs help to prevent acne eruption by causing the **keratin layer** of the skin to peel or by killing the bacteria that cause inflammation associated with acne. If multiple concentrations of a keratolytic are available (such as Oxy 5 and Oxy 10 Advanced Formula), it is better to start with a lower concentration and move up to the higher one, allowing the skin to become accustomed to the caustic action of these products. The initial exposure may worsen the appearance of acne temporarily; however, with continual use, the acne usually improves.

Sun Products The damaging effects of sun exposure on the skin have been well publicized in recent years. It is now clear that the ultraviolet (UV) rays associated with sunlight have several adverse effects on the skin. It has been demonstrated that almost 1 million cases of skin cancer each year occur in the United States, most of which are a direct consequence of exposure to UV rays (American Cancer Society 2005). Almost 10,000 deaths occur from skin cancer each year, most of which are melanomas (American Cancer Society 2005).

The majority of these will be cancers of skin cells called basal cell or squamous cell carcinomas (White-Sax 2000). These cancers usually are easily removed by minor surgery, and patients have a good prognosis for recovery. About 0.5% of the population will suffer a much more deadly form of skin cancer called *melanoma*. Melanomas are cancers of the pigment-forming cells of the skin, called *melanocytes*, and spread rapidly from the skin throughout the body, causing death in 20% to 25% of patients (White-Sax 2000).

Another long-term concern related to UV exposure is premature aging. Skin frequently exposed to UV rays, such as during routine tanning, experiences deterioration associated with the aging process. Elastin and collagen fibers are damaged, causing a loss of pliability and elasticity in the skin

KEY TERMS

keratolytics
caustic agents that cause the keratin skin layer to peel

keratin layer
outermost protective layer of the skin

This skin cancer is melanoma and is caused by excessive exposure to ultraviolet light.

and resulting in a leathery, wrinkled appearance (White-Sax 2000).

Because of these damaging effects of sun exposure, an array of protective sunscreen products are available OTC. Most sunscreens are formulated to screen out the shorter UVB rays. These products have deliberately been designed to allow passage, in varying degrees, of the UVA rays because researchers once thought that these longer rays would help skin to tan without causing damage. Now it appears scientists were mistaken. Due to their deep penetration in the skin, UVA rays likely contribute to melanoma as well as chronic skin damage, causing skin to wrinkle, sag, and lose tone (White-Sax 2000).

The protection afforded by sunscreens is designated by an **SPF (sun protection factor) number**. This designation tells users the relative length of time they can stay in the sun before burning and includes ratings of 2 to 11 (*minimum*), 12 to 30 (*moderate*), and greater than 30 (*high*) (Schwartz 1999). For example, proper application of a product with an SPF of 10 allows users to remain in the sun without burning 10 times longer than if it was not applied. It is important to remember that the SPF designation does not indicate protection against UVA rays. Although there currently is no convenient rating system to assess UVA screening, products with SPF ratings of 15 or greater usually offer some protection against the longer UV radiation. In addition, a compound called *avobenzone* appears

to offer the fullest protection against UVA rays (*Medical Letter* 1999). If a product also protects against UVB and has an SPF designation of 15, it is classified as a broad-spectrum sunscreen ("Full Sun Protection" 1993).

Because the natural pigment in the skin affords some UV protection, people with fair complexions (less skin pigmentation) require products with higher SPF numbers than do dark-skinned people.

People who want complete protection from UVB exposure can use OTC sunblockers, which prevent any tanning. Sunscreen ingredients in high concentrations essentially become sunblockers. In addition, an opaque zinc oxide ointment is a highly effective and inexpensive sun-blocking product and is available OTC.

Skin First-Aid Products

A variety of unrelated OTC drugs are available as first-aid products for the self-treatment of minor skin problems. Included in this category of agents are the following products:

1. Local anesthetics, such as benzocaine (e.g., Dermoplast) to relieve the discomfort and pain of burns or trauma
2. Antibiotics and antiseptics, such as bacitracin (Polysporin), neomycin (Neosporin), betadine, and tincture of iodine to treat or prevent skin infections
3. Antihistamines (Benadryl) or corticosteroids (hydrocortisone [Cortaid]) to relieve itching or inflammation associated with skin rashes, allergies, or insect bites

These first-aid skin products can be effective when used properly. In general, side effects to such topical products are few and minor when they occur.

KEY TERMS

SPF (sun protection factor) number
designation to indicate a product's ability to screen ultraviolet rays

OTC HERBAL (NATURAL) PRODUCTS

There are approximately 500 herbal medicines currently available in the United States and other countries (Tan 2001). Herbal products are a unique category of OTC remedies that, with nutrients and dietary supplements, account for almost $15 billion a year in U.S. sales (Grady 2000). They are unique because, despite the presence of active ingredients, there is little or no federal regulation due to a 1994 law, supported by the dietary supplement industry, called the Dietary Supplement Health and Education Act (Frontlines 2000a; Tatro 1999). This law requires the government to demonstrate that substances in the herbal products are harmful before such products can be removed from the market; the burden of proof lies with the FDA, not the manufacturer (Tatro 1999).

This act also (1) makes the manufacturer responsible for its product's safety; (2) explains how product literature is used for product promotion; and (3) describes what can be included on labels. Due to these regulations, manufacturers cannot use terms such as *diagnose, treat, prevent,* or *cure.* Companies can, however, make claims about affecting body function. For example, manufacturers of glucosamine cannot claim their product helps cure arthritis, but they can say products with glucosamine help the joints function better (Tatro 1999). Because of the lack of regulation, these products often are not scientifically tested, and they vary considerably in both the quantity and quality of active ingredients (Frontlines 2000b; Tatro 1999). Herbal products have been viewed with considerable skepticism by many experts who argue that "assertions, speculation and testimonials do not substitute for evidence" when it comes to establishing the value of a drug (Slezak 1998, p. 38).

In the past few years, some changes in attitude toward herbal products have occurred. More people, including health professionals, have become convinced that some herbs may be useful in the treatment of minor health problems (*Consumer Reports* 2000). In fact, it has become quite common for doctors, nurses, and other formally trained health professionals to recommend herbal treatments for medical problems (*Consumer Reports* 2000). Despite greater acceptance, the fact that most people who use herbs to treat medical conditions still consider prescription drugs to be consid-

Herbal products have become very popular and widely accepted.

erably more effective suggests persistent skepticism regarding these products (*Consumer Reports* 2000).

Frequent uses of herbal products include treatment of anxiety, chronic fatigue, arthritis, and digestive problems (Innerself.com 2003). Another common use of these natural products is to elevate mood. The most popular herbs for this purpose are St. John's wort, S-adenosylmethionine (SAM-e), and kava kava (see "Here and Now," Herbal Options). It is generally thought that although these products do have some effect in the treatment of minor to moderate depression, there is no evidence they elevate a normal, undisturbed mood nor are they particularly effective against severe mood disturbances (*CBS Evening News* 2001). A major risk of self-administering these remedies for mood disorders is that some of the people self-treating their depression are severely emotionally unstable. Overall, depression leads to approximately 20,000 suicides in this country each year (Frontlines 2000a). Another considerable problem of self-medicating with herbal products for mood disorders is the lack of standardization for these substances. A recent survey revealed that the actual amount of active SAM-e per pill in products claiming to contain 200 mg active ingredient ranged from 80 to 250 mg. For these reasons, it is almost universally recommended that patients with serious emotional disturbances, especially depression, be diagnosed by a mental health professional even though some of these professionals may find use of the natural products to be acceptable for treatment of mild emotional problems (Frontlines 2000a).

Here and Now

Herbal Options

With the increasing popularity of herbal products, an array of choices have become available for dealing with many common, usually self-limiting health problems. The following is a list of some of the most popular of these medicinal herbs.

Echinacea

Common Claim: Stimulates immune system and helps fight infections.

Common Use: Reduce cold symptoms and help accelerate recovery.

Effectiveness: May shorten duration of cold, but does not prevent it; however, even this is controversial.*

Concerns: Relatively well tolerated, but fatigue and sleepiness occasionally occur.

Garlic

Common Claim: Inhibits production of cholesterol and reduces blood sugar.

Common Use: Treat diabetes and prevent cardiovascular disease.

Effectiveness: Most studies do not find garlic effective against serious diseases.

Concerns: Mild stomach discomfort and possible interaction with blood-thinning (anticlotting) prescription drugs occur.

Ginkgo Biloba

Common Claim: Improves memory.

Common Use: Often promoted to enhance memory for patients with Alzheimer's disease.

Effectiveness: At best helps to prevent some mental decline in Alzheimer's patients but does not appear to reverse memory loss or help normal or age-related memory losses.

Concerns: Can interact with blood-thinning medications such as aspirin.

Glucosamine and Chondroitin

Common Claim: Contributes to joint strength.

Common Use: Relieve the discomfort of arthritis.

Effectiveness: Provides moderate relief from the pain of arthritis and may help to slow progress of the disease.

Concerns: May interact with blood thinners and adversely affect adult-onset diabetes.

Saw Palmetto

Common Claim: Relieves discomforts associated with prostate gland.

Common Use: Shrink enlarged prostate and facilitate urination.

Effectiveness: Provides relief for most men within a month of use.

Concerns: Well tolerated by most men.

SAM-e

Common Claim: Helps regulate brain transmitters such as dopamine.

Common Use: Relieve symptoms of depression.

Effectiveness: Some evidence that it relieves moderate depression.

Concerns: Side effects are typically mild, such as stomach upset, insomnia, and nervousness. Can be very expensive, ranging from $55 to $260 per month.

St. John's Wort

Common Claim: Elevates mood.

Common Use: To treat mild to moderate depression.

Effectiveness: Appears to relieve some cases of mild depression for the short term.

Concerns: Recent alert from the FDA warns about interactions with numerous medications, such as birth-control pills and other antidepressants.

Ginseng[†]

Common Claim: Increases energy.

Common Use: Treat fatigue and enhance performance.

Effectiveness: There may be some mild stimulation, but there is no evidence of enhanced performance.

Concerns: Well tolerated for the most part, although there are some reports of minor addiction.

*Grimm, W., and H. Muller. "A Randomized Control Trial of the Effect of Fluid Extract of *Echinacea purpurea* on the Incidence and Severity of Colds and Respiratory Infections." *American Journal of Medicine* 106 (1999): 138–143.

[†]*Drug Facts and Comparison News* (October 1999): 74–78.

Other concerns with herbal products include the possibility of interaction with other OTC and prescription medications, especially in the elderly population (Dergal et al. 2002). This can be more problematic as the routine use of herbs becomes common, especially because unscrupulous manufacturers may deceive customers into thinking that these products are perfectly safe and do not really contain any drugs. Some interactions identified occur between products containing herbs such as garlic, ginkgo biloba, ephedra, and ginseng (Fugh-Berman 2000). A notable example of drug interactions has been reported with St. John's wort, which increases the metabolism and inactivates drugs used to treat heart failure, asthma, infections, or blood clots (Fugh-Berman 2000).

Finally, lack of regulation has encouraged such a lackadaisical attitude concerning herbs that their use has been trivialized to the extent that they and their associated active drugs are now being included in foods and marketed in both health-food stores and supermarkets. Recent snacks, cereals, and beverages spiked with medicinal herbs include ginseng ginger ale, kava kava corn chips, echinacea fruit drinks, and ginkgo-biloba chocolate bars (Frontlines 2000b). These products, sometimes referred to as "functional foods," are typically packaged in colorful containers with cartoon figures that are likely to appeal to kids and accompanied by subtle suggestive promotions implying that they can "support emotional and mental balance." The exact quantities of herbal substances added to such food and snack products

and their actual effects (if any) are difficult to monitor. Although concerned, regulator agencies are uncertain as to how to deal with the potential problems associated with this marketing strategy (Frontlines 2000b).

Herbals and Abuse

Despite the lack of governmental contol, drugs found naturally in plants or herbs can have serious side effects or can be abused (see "Here and Now," Herbs Can Make You Sick). In fact, some of the most powerful substances of abuse are extracted from plants and include drugs such as cocaine (*Erythroxylum coca*), marijuana (*Cannabis sativa*), peyote (*Lophophora williamsii*), and tobacco (*Nicotiana tabacum*). Because these substances are reviewed elsewhere in this book, they will not be discussed further here; they are mentioned to emphasize the point that being associated with herbs and natural products does not exclude a drug from being abused. Of concern in this section are unregulated herbal products and their potential for abuse and addiction. As a general rule, if a substance (including a natural product) elevates mood, causes a feeling of energy, or brings on a feeling of relaxation and relief from stress, it likely has potential for abuse (Tinsley 1999). Based on these principles, the herbal products most likely to be abused include those containing ma huang, ginseng, kava kava, and ephedrine (Gruber and Pope 1998; Tinsley 1999). Of course, with addiction typically comes high-quantity use and a greater chance of serious side effects—for example, the anorexia,

Here and Now

Herbs Can Make You Sick

Recently, a Chinese herb that is sold in the United States was linked to kidney failure and urinary cancer in a Belgian weight-loss clinic. The herb, *A. fangchi*, contains ingredients known to be potent carcinogens in laboratory animals. Illnesses related to the use of this herb have been reported in several European countries. *A. fangchi* has been used to treat asthma and has been included in weight-loss products as well. Episodes such as this strengthen the argument that the FDA should be more active in the regulation of herbal products and dietary supplements and argue against the common misconception that herbal products are always healthy and cannot hurt you because they are "natural."

Source: Sternberg, S. "Herb Raises Regulatory Alarm." *USA Today Health* (8 June, 2000). Available www.usatoday.com/life/health/alternative.

thought disturbances, insomnia, racing heart, and loss of sensation in the limbs sometimes experienced by users addicted to "Herbal Ecstasy," a product containing caffeine, kava kava, and ephedrine (Yates et al. 2000). Even though serious abuse of herbal products is possible, it does not occur frequently and, when it does occur, it is generally relatively easy to treat.

Prescription Drugs

The Durham-Humphrey Amendment of 1951 established the criteria that are still used today to determine whether a drug should be used only under the direction of a licensed health professional, such as a physician. According to this piece of legislation, drugs are controlled with prescriptions if they are (1) habit-forming, (2) not safe for self-medication, (3) intended to treat ailments that require the supervision of a health professional, or (4) new and without an established safe track record. There currently are more than 10,000 prescription products sold in the United States, representing approximately 1500 different drugs, with 20 to 50 new medications approved each year by the FDA (*Physicians' Desk Reference* 2003).

Because of their specialized training, physicians, dentists, and, under certain conditions, podiatrists, physician assistants, nurse practitioners, pharmacists, and optometrists are granted drug-prescribing privileges. The health professionals who write prescriptions are expected to accurately diagnose medical conditions requiring therapy, consider the benefits and risks of drug treatment for the patient, and identify the best drug and safest manner of administering it. The responsibility of the health professional does not conclude with the writing of a prescription; in many ways, it only just begins. Professional monitoring to ensure proper drug use and to evaluate the patient's response is crucial for successful therapy.

PRESCRIPTION DRUG ABUSE

According to the Substance Abuse and Mental Health Services Administration (SAMHSA), more than 11 million Americans use prescription drugs for nonmedical purposes each year (Narcotics Digest 2003). The three classes of prescription drugs most likely to be abused are narcotic analgesics, CNS depressants, and stimulants (used to treat obesity and attention-deficit hyperactivity disorder [ADHD]) (Research Report 2001a). Dealing with suspected abuse of prescription medication can pose a difficult management problem for physicians and pharmacists. It has become such a major issue that some third-party payers (that is, health insurance companies) have implemented tight monitoring procedures. Those who try to fraudulently obtain controlled substances with valid and invalid prescriptions include persons from all walks of life (CNN.com 2002). (See "Case in Point," Prescription Drugs Can Also Cause Addiction). Illicit use of prescription drug products may be prompted by any of several reasons (Longo et al. 2000; Wick 1995): (1) to relieve withdrawal caused by drug habits (e.g., benzodiazepines are used to relieve alcohol withdrawal); (2) to treat infections caused by drug abuse (e.g., antibiotics are used to treat injection infections); (3) to provide a source of fresh, clean needles for injecting drugs of abuse (e.g., via insulin syringes); and (4) to prolong the high caused by drugs of abuse (e.g., appetite suppressants are taken to enhance the effects of stimulants of abuse).

In the United States, young people frequently abuse prescription drugs. According to the Household Survey, in 2001 more than 10% of all 12- to 17-year-olds had used a psychotherapeutic agent at least once during their lifetime. However, young people rarely obtain the drugs by theft, fraud, or doctor shopping. Instead, they obtain their prescription drugs from peers, friends, or family members. In some areas, the problem is so severe that high schools have implemented programs to prevent such "sharing" (Information Brief 2002). Abusers of prescription drugs often have multiple addictions, including dependence on caffeine, alcohol, or nicotine. In addition, once a pharmacy is recognized as an easy target, word spreads and other abusers often begin to frequent the same store (Wick 1995). Signs of patients with drug-seeking behavior include the following:

- Use of altered or forged prescriptions
- Claims that a prescription has been lost and a physician is unavailable for confirmation

►Case in Point   Prescription Drugs Can Also Cause Addiction

Anne's grandmother was taken to the hospital after complaining of chest pains. When questioned, she could not recall which medications she had been taking, so the doctors instructed Anne to go to her grandmother's home to check her medicine cabinet. Anne came face to face with an emerging major problem: prescription drug use and addiction. Anne discovered a cupboard with several copies of *Physicians' Desk Reference,* a balance for weighing the pills, and shelves filled with 11 different prescription drugs, including 400 Valium tablets. In all, the street value of these drugs was estimated to approach $15,000.

To obtain the pills, Anne's grandmother would go from doctor to doctor complaining of anxiety or pain. The doctors didn't have the slightest idea they were being deceived. This tactic, known as "doctor shopping," is a common strategy used by both young and old to obtain prescription drugs that are abused and can cause dependence and addiction.

Sometimes the drug dependence can begin innocently enough, when a patient uses a drug to excess without good clinical supervision. What started for legitimate medical reasons can, however, become transformed into destructive abuse of prescription drugs with serious medical and legal consequences. Dealing with this form of drug abuse requires more finesse than force, and prevention typically can be realized through education of both patients and clinicians about the addiction potential of some prescription medications.

Source: Querna, E. "The Newest War on Drugs." *US News & World Report* (21 February 2005).

- Frequent visits to emergency rooms or clinics for poorly defined health problems
- Visits made to a pharmacy late in the day, on weekends, or just before closing
- Alteration of doses on a legitimate prescription
- Loud, abusive, and insulting behavior
- Use of several names
- Being particularly knowledgeable about drugs

PROPER DOCTOR–PATIENT COMMUNICATION

Many unnecessary side effects and delays in proper care are caused by poor communication between the health professional and the patient when a drug is prescribed. The smaller a drug's margin of safety (the difference between therapeutic and toxic doses), the greater the need for direction from a health professional concerning its proper use. The following is a brief overview of principles to help ensure that satisfactory communication takes place between the health professional and the patient.

Doctor–patient communication must be reciprocal. We tend to think that patients listen while doctors talk when it comes to deciding on the best medication for treatment. To ensure a proper diagnosis, precise and complete information from the patient is also essential. In fact, if a doctor is to select the best and safest drug for a patient, he or she needs to know everything possible about the medical problems to be treated. In addition, the patient should provide the doctor with a complete medical and drug history, particularly if there has been a problem with the patient's cardiovascular system, kidneys, liver, or mental functions. Other information that should be shared with the doctor includes previous drug reactions as well as a complete list of drugs routinely being used, including prescription, nonprescription, and herbal products.

The patient needs to be educated about proper drug use. If the doctor does not volunteer this information, the patient should insist on answers to the following questions:

- What is being treated? This question does not require a long, unintelligible scientific answer. It should include an easy-to-understand explanation of the medical problem.
- What is the desired outcome? The patient should know why the drug is prescribed and what the drug treatment is intended to accomplish. It is difficult for the patient to become involved in therapy if he or she is not aware of its objectives.
- What are the possible side effects of the drug? This answer does not necessitate an exhaustive list of every adverse reaction ever

In order to maximize benefit and minimize risk, there must be proper doctor-patient communication.

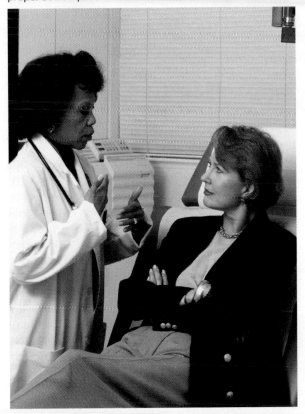

recorded in the medical literature; however, it is important to realize that adverse drug reactions to prescription drugs are very common. In the United States, more people die from adverse reactions to legal medications than succumb to all illegal drug use. It is estimated that approximately 100,000 people die while another 2.1 million are seriously injured in this country each year from reactions to legal medications (MacDonald 1998). In general, if adverse reactions occur in more than 1% of users, this should be mentioned to the patient. In addition, the patient should be made aware of ways to minimize the occurrence of side effects (e.g., an irritating drug should not be taken on an empty stomach to minimize nausea) as well as what to do if a side effect occurs (e.g., if a rash occurs, call the doctor immediately).

- How should the drug be taken to minimize problems and maximize benefits? This answer should include details on how much, how often, and how long the drug should be taken.

Although it is a health professional's legal and professional obligation to communicate this information, patients frequently leave the doctor's office with a prescription that gives them legal permission to use a drug but without the knowledge of how to use it properly. Because of this all-too-common problem, pharmacists have been mandated by legislation referred to as the Omnibus Budget Reconciliation Act of 1990 to provide the necessary information to patients on proper drug use (Waroholak-Juarez et al. 2000; Zak 1993) (see "Here and Now," OBRA '90). Patients should be encouraged to ask questions of those who write and fill prescriptions.

DRUG SELECTION: GENERIC VERSUS PROPRIETARY

Although it is the primary responsibility of the doctor or healthcare provider to decide which drug is most suitable for a treatment, often an inexpensive choice can be as effective and safe as a more costly option. This statement frequently is true when

Here and Now

OBRA '90: The Evolving Role of Pharmacists in Drug Management

In 1990, the U.S. Congress passed section 4401 of the Omnibus Budget Reconciliation Act (commonly referred to as OBRA '90), which substantially altered the role of pharmacists in drug management. This act designated the pharmacist as the key player in improving the quality of drug care for patients in this country. Because OBRA '90 is federal legislation, it can require drug-related services for Medicare patients only; however, most states have recognized that similar services should be made available to all patients and have enacted legislation to that end. OBRA '90 requires pharmacists to conduct a drug use review (DUR) for each prescription to improve the outcome of drug therapy and reduce adverse side effects. The DUR program describes four basic professional services that a pharmacist must render whenever a drug prescription is filled:

1. Prescriptions and patients' records must be screened to avoid problems caused by drug duplications, adverse drug–drug interactions, medical complications, incorrect drug doses, and incorrect duration of drug treatment.

2. Patients should be counseled regarding the following:

   · How to safely and effectively administer the drug

   · Common adverse effects and interactions with other drugs, food, and so forth

   · How to avoid problems with the drug

   · How to monitor the progress of drug therapy

   · How to store the drug properly

   · Whether a refill is intended

   · What to do if a dose is missed

3. Patient profiles, including information on disease, a list of medications, and the pharmacist's comments relevant to drug therapy, must be maintained. This information should be stored in computer files for future reference.

4. Documentation must record if the patient refuses consultation from the pharmacist, or if a potential drug therapy problem is identified and the patient is warned.

Source: Abood, R. "OBRA '90: Implementation and Enforcement." *NABP U.S. Pharmacists, State Boards—A Continuing Education Series.* Park Ridge, IL: National Association of Boards of Pharmacy, 1992.

---

choosing between generic and proprietary drugs. The term **generic** is used by the public to refer to the common name of a drug that is not subject to trademark rights; in contrast, **proprietary** denotes medications marketed under specific brand names (Vasquez and Vasquez 2000). For example, diazepam is the generic designation for the proprietary name Valium. Often, the most common proprietary name associated with a drug is the name given when it is newly released for marketing. Because

such drugs are almost always covered by patent restrictions for several years when first sold to the public, they become identified with their first proprietary names. After the patent lapses, the same drug often is also marketed by its less-known generic designation (Dighe 1999).

Because usually the pharmaceutical companies that market the generic products have not invested in the discovery or development of the drug, they often charge much less for their version of the medication. This situation contrasts with that of the original drug manufacturer, which may have invested as much as $500 million for research and development (see Chapter 3). Even though the generic product frequently is less expensive, the quality usually is not inferior to the related proprietary drug; thus, substitution of generic for proprietary products rarely compromises therapy

KEY TERMS

generic
official, nonpatented, nonproprietary name of a drug

proprietary
brand or trademark name that is registered with the U.S. Patent Office

(Dighe 1999). It should be noted that occasionally an inferior generic drug product is marketed to increase profit margins for the manufacturer and is not therapeutically equivalent to the proprietary drug product; however, physicians and pharmacists should be aware of these differences and prescribe accordingly. If a patient alerts the physician to concerns about drug costs, less expensive generic brands often can be substituted.

Because of reduced cost, generic products have become very popular. Currently, generic drugs account for more than 30% of all prescription drug sales, amounting to approximately $10 billion (CDER 2000). Because of the great demand, all states have laws that govern the use and substitution of generic drugs; unfortunately, the laws are not all the same. Some states have "positive laws" that require pharmacists to substitute a generic product unless the physician gives specific instructions not to do so. Other states have "negative laws" that forbid substitution without the physician's permission. Some physicians use convenient prescription forms with "May" or "May Not" substitution boxes that can be checked when the prescription is filled out.

COMMON CATEGORIES OF PRESCRIPTION DRUGS

Of the approximately 10,000 different prescription drugs available in the United States, the top 50 drugs in sales account for almost 30% of all new and refilled prescriptions ("Top 200 Drugs" 2000). As an example, a list of the 30 top-selling prescription drugs in 2003 is shown in Table 15.7. The following includes a brief discussion of some drug groups represented in the 30 most frequently prescribed medications. This list is not intended to be all-inclusive, but gives only a sampling of common prescription products.

Analgesics

The prescription analgesics consist mainly of narcotic and NSAID types. The narcotic analgesics most often dispensed to patients by prescription are (1) the low-potency agents propoxyphene (Darvon) and codeine, (2) the moderate-potency agents pentazocine (Talwin) and oxycodone (Percodan), and (3) the high-potency drug meperidine (Demerol). All narcotic analgesics are scheduled drugs because of their abuse potential and are effective against most types of pain. The narcotic analgesic products are often combined with aspirin or acetaminophen (e.g., Percocet is a combination of oxycodone and acetaminophen) to enhance their pain-relieving actions. For additional information about the narcotics, see Chapter 9.

The NSAIDs constitute the other major group of analgesics available by prescription. The pharmacology of these drugs is very similar to that of the OTC compound ibuprofen, discussed earlier in this chapter. These medications are used to relieve inflammatory conditions such as arthritis and are effective in relieving minor to moderate *musculoskeletal pain* (pain associated with body structures such as muscles, ligaments, bones, teeth, and skin). These drugs have no abuse potential and are not scheduled; several are also available OTC (see the discussion of OTC analgesics). Their principal adverse side effects include stomach irritation, kidney damage, *tinnitus* (ringing in the ears), dizziness, and swelling from fluid retention. Most prescription NSAIDs have similar pharmacological and side effects. Included in the group of prescription NSAIDs are ibuprofen (Motrin), naproxen (Anaprox), indomethacin (Indocin), sulindac (Clinoril), mefenamic acid (Ponstel), tolmetin (Tolectin), piroxicam (Feldene), and ketoprofen (Orudis) (McEvoy 2003).

Antibiotics

Drugs referred to by the layperson as "antibiotics" are more accurately described by the term *antibacterials*, although the more common term will be used here. For the most part, *antibiotics* are effective in treating infections caused by microorganisms classified as bacteria. Bacterial infections can occur anywhere in the body, resulting in tissue damage, loss of function, and, if untreated, ultimately death. Even though bacterial infections continue to be the most common serious diseases in the United States and throughout the world today, the vast majority of these can be cured with antibiotic treatment.

There are currently close to 100 different antibiotic drugs, which differ from one another in (1) whether they kill bacteria (*bactericidal*) or stop their growth (*bacteriostatic*), and (2) the species of

Table 15.7 The Top 30 Dispensed Prescription Drugs, 2003 (based on new and refill prescriptions)

RANKING	PROPRIETARY NAME	GENERIC NAME	PRINCIPAL CLINICAL USE
1	Hydrocodone	Same	Relieve moderate pain
2	Lipitor	Atorvastatin	Reduce cholesterol
3	Synthroid	Levothyroxine	Replace thyroid hormone
4	Atenolol	Atenolol	Open air passages
5	Zithromax	Azithromycin	Treat infection
6	Amoxicillin	Same	Treat infection
7	Furosemide	Same	Diuretic
8	Hydrochlorothiazide	Same	Treat high blood pressure
9	Norvasc	Amlodipine	Treat high blood pressure
10	Lisinopril	Prinivil	Lower blood pressure
11	Alprazolam	Same	Relieve anxiety
12	Zoloft	Sertraline	Antidepressant
13	Albuterol	Same	Open air passages
14	Toprol	Metoprolol	Treat heart disease
15	Zocor	Simvastatin	Reduce cholesterol
16	Premarin	Estrogen	Replace estrogen
17	Prevacid	Lansoprazole	Treat ulcers
18	Zyrtec	Cetirizine	Treat allergies
19	Ibuprofen	Several	Treat pain and inflammation
20	Levoxyl	Levothyroxine	Replace thyroid hormone
21	Propoxyphene	Same	Relieve minor pain
22	Triamterene	Several	Treat high blood pressure
23	Celebrex	Celecoxib	Anti-inflammatory
24	Ambien	Zolpidem	Sedative
25	Allegra	Fexofenadine	Treat allergies
26	Cephalexin	Same	Treat infection
27	Nexium	Esomeprazole	Relief from ulcers
28	Fosemax	Alendronate	Treat osteoporosis
29	Vioxx	Rofecoxib	Anti-inflammatory (removed from market)
30	Singular	Montelukast	Treat asthma attacks

Source: Internet Drug Index. "The Top 200 Prescriptions for 2003 by Number of U.S. Prescriptions Dispensed" (20 May 2004).
Available www.rxlist.com/top2000.

bacteria that are sensitive to their antibacterial action (McEvoy 2003). Antibiotics that are effective against many species of bacteria are classified as broad-spectrum types, whereas those antibiotics that are relatively selective and effective against only a few species of bacteria are considered narrow-spectrum drugs.

Although most antibiotics are well tolerated by patients, they can cause very serious side effects, especially if not used properly. For example, the penicillins have a very wide margin of safety for most patients, but 5% to 10% of the population is allergic to these drugs and life-threatening reactions can occur in sensitized patients if penicillins are used.

The most common groups of antibiotics include penicillins (e.g., amoxicillin—Amoxil, Augmentin, and Trimox), cephalosporins (e.g., cephalexin), fluoroquinolones (e.g., ciprofloxacin—Cipro), tetracyclines (e.g., minocycline—Minocin), aminoglycosides (e.g., streptomycin), sulfonamides (e.g., sufamethoxazole—Bactrim and Septra), and macrolides (e.g., erythromycin—E-Mycin).

Antidepressants

Severe depression is characterized by diminished interest or pleasure in normal activities accompanied by feelings of fatigue, pessimism, and guilt as well as sleep and appetite disturbances and suicidal desires (American Psychiatric Association 2000). Severe depression afflicts approximately 5% to 6% of the population at any one time, and it is estimated that about 17% of the population will become severely depressed during their life (Cooper 1998). This high prevalence makes depression the most common psychiatric disorder (Cooper 1998). According to the classification of the *Diagnostic and Statistical Manual of Mental Disorders* (*DSM-IV-TR*) of the American Psychiatric Association, several types of depression exist, based on their origin:

1. *Endogenous major depression,* a genetic disorder that can occur spontaneously and is due to transmitter imbalances in the brain
2. *Depression associated with bipolar mood disorder* (that is, manic-depressive disorder)
3. *Reactive depression,* the most common form of depression, which is a response to situations

of grief, personal loss, illness, or other very stressful situations

Antidepressant medication is typically used to treat endogenous major depression, although on occasion these drugs are used to treat other forms of depression if they are resistant to conventional therapy (Cooper 1998).

Several groups of prescription antidepressant medications are approved for use in the United States (McEvoy 2003). The most commonly used category is the **tricyclic antidepressants**. Included in this group are drugs such as amitriptyline (Elavil), imipramine (Tofranil), and nortriptyline (Pamelor). Although usually well tolerated, the tricyclic antidepressants can cause annoying side effects due to their anticholinergic activity. These adverse reactions include drowsiness, dry mouth, blurred vision, and constipation. Tolerance to these side effects usually develops with continued use.

The second group of drugs used to treat depression is referred to as the **monoamine oxidase inhibitors (MAOIs)**. Historically, these agents have been backup drugs for the tricyclic antidepressants. Because of their annoying and sometimes dangerous side effects as well as problems interacting with other drugs or even food, the MAOIs have become less popular with clinicians. These drugs can have deadly interactions with many of the stimulants of abuse such as methamphetamine, cocaine, and Ecstasy. Drugs belonging to this group include phenelzine (Nardil) and tranylcypromine (Parnate).

Agents from a third, somewhat disparate, group of antidepressants that are safer and with fewer side effects than the tricyclic or MAOI antidepressants are very popular. They include fluoxetine (Prozac), sertraline (Zoloft), paroxetine (Paxil), fluvoxamine (Luvox), bupropion (Wellbutrin), and trazodone (Desyrel). Although side effects and the margin of safety of these groups of antidepressants

KEY TERMS

tricyclic antidepressants
most commonly used group of drugs to treat severe depression

monoamine oxidase inhibitors (MAOIs)
drugs used to treat severe depression

may differ, in general they all appear to have similar therapeutic benefits. Of this third group of antidepressants, Prozac is the best known and the most frequently prescribed antidepressant; in 2003 it was the 11th most frequently prescribed drug in the United States (see Table 15.7). Although most commonly used to treat depression, Prozac has also been prescribed by physicians to treat more than 30 other conditions ranging from drug addiction (although not found to be generally effective) to kleptomania. The vast majority of these uses are not proven to be effective nor are they approved by the FDA.

Antidiabetic Drugs

Diabetes mellitus afflicts approximately 17 million people in the United States and is the result of insufficient or ineffective activity of insulin, a hormone secreted from the pancreas (Lamendola 2003). Due to the lack of insulin, untreated diabetics have severe problems with metabolism and elevated blood sugar (called **hyperglycemia**). The two major types of diabetes are type I (or juvenile type) and type II (or adult-onset type). **Type I diabetes** is caused by total destruction of the insulin-producing cells in the pancreas and usually begins in juveniles, but it occasionally begins during adulthood. In contrast, **type II diabetes** typically occurs after age 40 and is frequently associated with obesity. Recently, however, because severe obesity is occurring more often in younger persons, there has erupted an "epidemic" of type II diabetes

Insulin is self-administered by diabetic patients in subcutaneous injections.

in adolescents (McEvoy 2003). In type II diabetes, the pancreas is able to produce insulin, but insulin receptors no longer respond normally to this hormone (Gasbarro 1999). In both types of diabetes mellitus, drugs are administered to restore proper insulin function.

Because of the inability to produce or release insulin in the type I diabetic, these patients are universally treated with subcutaneous injections of insulin one to three times per day, depending on their needs. Usually the levels of sugar (glucose) in the blood are evaluated to determine the effectiveness of treatment. Insulin products are characterized by their onset of action and duration of effects. Two types of insulin are used: *short-acting* (regular) and *medium-acting* (NPH and lente) types.

The strategy for treating type II diabetics is somewhat different. For many of these patients, the symptoms of diabetes and problems of insufficient insulin function subside with proper diet, weight, and exercise management. If an appropriate change in lifestyle does not correct the diabetes-associated problems, drugs called **oral hypoglycemics** (meaning they are taken by mouth and lower blood sugar) are often prescribed. These drugs, which stimulate the release of additional insulin from the pancreas, include popular drugs such as metformin (Glucophage). If the diabetic symptoms are not adequately controlled with the oral hypoglycemic drugs, type II diabetics are treated with insulin injections, as are type I

KEY TERMS

diabetes mellitus
disease caused by elevated blood sugar due to insufficient insulin

hyperglycemia
elevated blood sugar

type I diabetes
disease associated with complete loss of insulin-producing cells in the pancreas

type II diabetes
disease usually associated with obesity; does not involve a loss of insulin-producing cells

oral hypoglycemics
drugs taken by mouth to treat type II diabetes

patients. There has been substantial improvement in the treatment of diabetes in the past few years due to new, more selective and effective drugs that control glucose blood levels (Marso 2002).

Antiepileptic Drugs

Approximately 1% of the population in the United States has some form of **epilepsy**. Although appropriate medication can control the disease in 80% of these patients, many people in this country with epilepsy are inadequately treated. Epilepsy is a neurological condition characterized by recurring seizures (that is, uncontrolled hyperactivity of the brain). Seizures are classified according to the region of the brain involved and the extent to which the hyperactivity spreads. Thus, seizures are considered to be either *partial* (brain involvement stays local) or *generalized* (brain involvement is widespread) and can involve severe motor activity (e.g., grand mal seizures) or few motor symptoms (e.g., petit mal seizures). Because of the diverse nature of different types of epilepsy, several drugs are used as antiepileptics. Thus, phenytoin (Dilantin), carbamazepine (Tegretol), and phenobarbital are prescribed to control partial and grand mal seizures, whereas ethosuximide (Zarontin) and valproic acid (Depakene) are used to treat generalized and petit mal seizures (McEvoy 2003).

Antiulcer Drugs

Peptic ulcers are sores that recur in the lining of the lower stomach (*gastric ulcer*) or most often in the upper portion of the small intestines (*duodenal ulcer*). It is apparent that secretions of gastric acids and digestive enzymes are necessary for ulcer development. Because gastric secretions are involved in developing peptic ulcers, several drug types are useful in ulcer treatment.

Antacids help to relieve acute discomfort due to ulcers by neutralizing gastric acidity. These drugs are discussed in greater detail in the OTC section of this chapter. Prescription drugs that block gastric secretion have been the mainstay of ulcer treatment. Because the endogenous chemical histamine is important in regulating gastric secretions, drugs that selectively block the activity of gastric histamine (called H_2 *blockers*) substantially reduce secretion of gastric acids and digestive enzymes. The very popular prescription drugs cimetidine (Tagamet), ranitidine (Zantac), and famotidine (Pepcid) function in this manner. Because Tagamet, Zantac, and Pepcid are used so frequently, they have been switched to OTC status by the FDA—not to treat ulcers, but to relieve heartburn (*esophageal reflux*) (White-Sax 1999).

Although the exact causes of peptic ulcers are not completely understood, a role for the bacteria *Helicobacter pylori* is now widely accepted. Because of the involvement of these microorganisms, most

Obesity in young children has reached epidemic status and is causing type II diabetes to occur at a younger age.

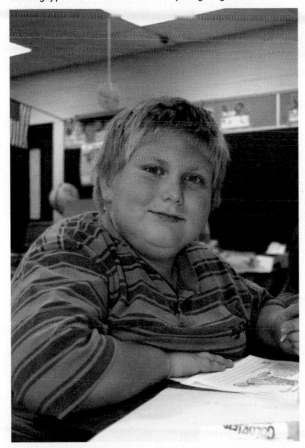

KEY TERMS

epilepsy
disease consisting of spontaneous, repetitive seizures

peptic ulcers
open sores that occur in the stomach or upper segment of the small intestine

clinicians treat patients with recurring ulcers with multiple antibiotics to eliminate these bacteria (Ford et al. 2003).

Bronchodilators

In 2003, the 13th leading drug for sales in this country was Albuterol, which widens air passages (*bronchi*) to facilitate breathing in patients with air passage constriction or obstruction (Internet Drug Index 2004). Such drugs are called **bronchodilators** and are particularly useful in relieving respiratory difficulty associated with asthma. Asthmatic patients frequently experience bouts of intense coughing, shortness of breath, tightness in the chest, and wheezing. Many of the symptoms of asthma are due to an increased sensitivity of the airways to irritating substances and can result in serious asthma attacks that are life-threatening if not treated promptly. Two major categories of bronchodilators are the sympathomimetics known as β-**adrenergic stimulants**—for example, isoproterenol (Isuprel) and albuterol (Proventil and Ventolin)—and xanthines (caffeine-like drugs) such as theophylline and its derivatives. These drugs relax the muscles of the air passages, cause bronchodilation, and facilitate breathing. In the early 1990s, some bronchial dilator medications were switched to OTC status, such as Bronkaid Mist and Primatene Mist.

Cardiovascular Drugs

Cardiovascular disease has been the number one cause of death in the United States for the past several decades. Consequently, of the 30 top-selling drugs in this country, seven are medications for diseases related to the cardiovascular system (Internet Drug Index 2004). The following are brief discussions of the major categories of cardiovascular drugs.

Antihypertensive Agents It is estimated that 15% of American adults require treatment for **hypertension** (persistent elevated high blood pressure) (Smith 2000). Because hypertension can result in serious damage to the heart, kidneys, and brain, this condition needs to be treated aggressively. Treatment should consist of changes in lifestyle, including exercise and diet, but usually also requires drug therapy. Two of the principal classes of antihypertensive agents are diuretics and direct vasodilators (Smith 2000):

1. *Diuretics* lower blood pressure by eliminating sodium and excess water from the body. Included in this category is hydrochlorothiazide (Dyazide).
2. *Direct vasodilators* reduce blood pressure by relaxing the muscles in the walls of blood vessels that cause vasoconstriction, thereby dilating the blood vessels and decreasing their resistance to the flow of blood. Drugs included in this category are calcium-channel blockers (diltiazem [Cardizem], verapamil [Calan], nifedipine [Procardia]); inhibitors of the enzyme that synthesizes the vasoconstricting hormone, angiotensin II (enalapril [Vasotec]); and drugs that block the vasoconstricting action of the sympathetic nervous system (clonidine [Catapre]; prazosin [Minipres]).

Antianginal Agents When the heart is deprived of sufficient blood (a condition called **ischemia**), the oxygen requirements of the cardiac muscle are not met and the breakdown of chemicals caused by the continual activity of the heart results in pain; this viselike chest pain is called **angina pectoris**. The most frequent cause of angina is obstruction of the coronary vessels (Kerin et al. 2001). Angina pectoris frequently occurs in patients with hypertension; left untreated, the underlying blockage of coronary vessels can result in heart attacks. All the drugs used to relieve or prevent angina decrease the oxygen

KEY TERMS

bronchodilators
drugs that widen air passages

β-adrenergic stimulants
drugs that stimulate a subtype of adrenaline and nonadrenaline receptors

hypertension
elevated blood pressure

ischemia
tissue deprived of sufficient blood and oxygen

angina pectoris
severe chest pain usually caused by a deficiency of blood to the heart muscle

deficit of the heart either by decreasing the amount of work required of the heart during normal functioning or by increasing the blood supply to the heart (Katzung and Chatterjee 1995). The three types of drugs prescribed for treating angina pectoris are (1) calcium-channel blockers (e.g., verapamil [Calan] and diltiazem [Cardizem]); (2) nitrates and nitrites (e.g., amylnitrite [Vaporate] and nitroglycerin [Transderm-Nitro]); and (3) blockers of the sympathetic nervous system, specifically classified as b-adrenergic blockers (e.g., atenolol [Tenormin] and propranolol [Inderal]).

Drugs to Treat Congestive Heart Failure When the cardiac muscle is unable to pump sufficient blood to satisfy the oxygen needs of the body, **congestive heart failure** occurs. This condition causes an enlarged heart, decreased ability to exercise, shortness of breath, and accumulation of fluid (**edema**) in the lungs and limbs (Katzung and Parmley 1995). The principal treatment for congestive heart failure consists of drugs that improve the heart's efficiency, such as digoxin (Lanoxin).

Drugs that cause vasodilation are also sometimes used successfully to reduce the work required of the heart as it pumps blood through the body. Among the drugs causing vasodilation are those already discussed in conjunction with other heart conditions such as hypertension and angina pectoris (e.g., enalapril [Vasotec] and captopril [Capoten]).

Cholesterol- and Lipid-Lowering Drugs Cholesterol and some types of fatty (*lipid*) molecules can accumulate in the walls of arteries and narrow the openings of these blood vessels. Such arterial changes cause hypertension, heart attacks, strokes, and heart failure and are the leading cause of death in the United States and other Western countries (Witztum 1995). These health problems can often be avoided by adopting a lifestyle that includes a low-fat and low-cholesterol diet combined with regular, appropriate exercise. However, sometimes lifestyle changes are insufficient; in such cases, cholesterol-lowering drugs can be used to prevent the damaging changes in blood vessel walls. The drugs most often used include lovastatin (Mevacor), cholestyramine (Questran), and niacin (vitamin B_3).

Hormone-Related Drugs

As explained in Chapter 4, hormones are released from endocrine (ductless) glands and are important in regulating metabolism, growth, tissue repair, reproduction, and other vital functions. When there is a deficiency or excess of specific hormones, body functions can be impaired, causing abnormal growth, imbalance in metabolism, disease, and often death. Hormones, or hormone-like substances, are sometimes administered as drugs to compensate for an endocrine deficiency and to restore normal function. This is the case for (1) insulin used to treat diabetes (see the earlier discussion for more details), (2) levothyroxine (Synthroid, an artificial thyroid hormone) to treat **hypothyroidism** (insufficient activity of the thyroid gland), and (3) conjugated estrogens (Premarin) to relieve the symptoms caused by estrogen deficiency during menopause.

Hormones can also be administered as drugs to alter normal body processes. Thus, drugs containing the female hormones, estrogen and progesterone (norethindrone, ethinyl estradiol [Ortho Novum]), can be used as contraceptives to alter the female reproductive cycles and prevent pregnancy. Another example involves drugs related to *corticosteroids* (hormones from the cortex of the adrenal glands), which are often prescribed because of their immune-suppressing effects. In high doses, the corticosteroid drugs (e.g., triamcinolone [Kenalog]) reduce symptoms of inflammation and are used to treat severe forms of inflammatory diseases, such as arthritis (McEvoy 2003).

Sedative-Hypnotic Agents

The sedative-hypnotics are discussed in considerable detail in Chapter 6. Because of the high incidence of anxiety and sleep disorders in the

KEY TERMS

congestive heart failure
heart is unable to pump sufficient blood for the body's needs

edema
swollen tissue due to an accumulation of fluid

hypothyroidism
thyroid gland does not produce sufficient hormone

United States (Shuster 1996), drugs that encourage relaxation and drowsiness are frequently pre-scribed and are usually included in the list of top-selling prescription drugs (Internet Drug Index 2004). Benzodiazepines commonly prescribed are clonazepam (Klonopin) and lorazepam (Ativan) (Internet Drug Index 2004).

Drugs to Treat HIV

Although not included in the top 30 list of pre-scription drugs (see Table 15.7), medications to treat HIV infection are of special relevance to drug abuse because of the high prevalence of infection by this deadly virus in intravenous drug addicts. The issue of AIDS and drug abuse is discussed at length in Chapter 17; of relevance to our discus-sion on prescription drugs are recent advances in pharmacological management of this disease. Al-though no cure for HIV or immunization against this virus is available yet, some drug therapies can delay the onset or slow the progression of this infection. The first drugs to be used effectively in AIDS therapy are the "transcriptase inhibitors" such as AZT (zidovudine) and Stavudine, which block a unique enzyme essential for HIV replica-tion (McEvoy 2003). Another group of anti-AIDS drugs called the *protease inhibitors* prevent HIV mat-uration; they include the recently approved drug, Saquinar. The protease inhibitors are particularly effective when used in combination with the tran-scriptase inhibitor drugs (McEvoy 2003). This combination is referred to by the acronym HAART (highly active antiretroviral therapy) (Stephenson et al. 2003).

Common Principles of Drug Use

Probably the most effective way to teach people not to use drugs improperly is to help them understand how to use drugs correctly. This goal can be achieved by educating the drug-using pub-lic about prescription, OTC, and herbal drug products. If people can appreciate the difference between the benefits of therapeutic drug use and the negative consequences of drug misuse or abuse, they will be more likely to use medications in a cautious and thoughtful manner. To reach this level of understanding, patients must be able to communicate freely with health professionals. Before prescription or OTC drugs are purchased and used, patients should have all questions an-swered about the therapeutic objective, the most effective mode of administration, and side effects. Education about proper drug use greatly dimin-ishes drug-related problems and unnecessary health costs.

To minimize problems, before using any drug product, the patient should be able to answer the following questions:

1. Why am I using this drug?
2. How should I be taking this drug?
3. What are the active ingredients in this drug product?
4. What are the most likely side effects of this drug?
5. How long should this drug be used?

Discussion Questions

1. Why are some prescription drugs appropriate for switching to OTC status?

2. What should the FDA use as a standard of safety when evaluating OTC and prescription drugs?

3. What role should the pharmacist play in pro-viding information about OTC and prescrip-tion drugs to patients?

4. What type of formal training should be required before a health professional is allowed to prescribe drugs?

5. What kinds of questions should be asked by a health professional to ensure that a patient has sufficient understanding concerning a drug to use it properly and safely?

6. What are the basic rules for using OTC drugs properly?

7. Should the FDA require that generic and pro-prietary versions of the same drug be exactly the same?

8. Even though some antibiotics have a wide margin of safety, currently there is no systemic antibiotic available OTC. Why is the FDA not willing to make some of these drugs available on a nonprescription basis?

9. Should herbal remedies be required to be safe and effective by the FDA like other OTC drug products?

10. What, if any, role should the FDA have in regulating herbal products?

Key Terms

analgesics 436

salicylates 436

anti-inflammatory 436

steroids 436

nonsteroidal anti-inflammatory drugs (NSAIDs) 436

antipyretics 436

Reye's syndrome 437

congestion rebound 439

antitussives 441

expectorants 441

gastritis 444

anorexiants 445

keratolytics 446

keratin layer 446

SPF (sun protection factor) number 447

generic 454

proprietary 454

tricyclic antidepressants 457

monoamine oxidase inhibitors (MAOIs) 457

diabetes mellitus 458

hyperglycemia 458

type I diabetes 458

type II diabetes 458

oral hypoglycemics 458

epilepsy 459

peptic ulcers 459

bronchodilators 460

β-adrenergic stimulants 460

hypertension 460

ischemia 460

angina pectoris 460

congestive heart failure 461

edema 461

hypothyroidism 461

Summary

1 Prescription drugs are available only by recommendation of an authorized health professional, such as a physician. Nonprescription (OTC) drugs are available on request and do not require approval by a health professional. In general, OTC medications are safer than their prescription counterparts but often less effective.

2 The switching policy of the FDA is an attempt to make available more effective medications to the general public on a nonprescription basis. This policy has been implemented in response to the interest in self-treatment by the public and in an attempt to reduce healthcare costs.

3 Drugs recently switched by the FDA to OTC status include ulcer medications, such as Tagamet and Zantac, and medications for asthma and allergies.

4 Potential problems that come by making more effective drugs available OTC include overuse and inappropriate use, leading to dependence and other undesirable side effects. For example, these more effective drugs could encourage self-treatment of medical problems that require professional care.

5 Information on OTC product labels is crucial for proper use of these drugs and thus is regulated by the FDA. Product labels must list the active ingredients and their quantities in the product. Labels must also provide instructions for safe and effective treatment with the drug as well as cautions and warnings.

6 Many herbal products contain active drugs and have become very popular. The lack of regulation makes these remedies difficult to assess for either efficacy or safety.

7 Although OTC drug products can be useful for treatment of many minor to moderate, self-limiting medical problems, when used without proper precautions, they can cause problems.

8 The principal drug groups available OTC are used in the treatment of common, minor medical problems and include analgesics, cold remedies, allergy products, mild stimulants, sleep aids, antacids, laxatives, antidiarrheals, antiasthmatics, acne medications, sunscreens, contraceptives, and nutrients.

9 For drugs to be prescribed properly, patients need to provide complete and accurate information about their medical condition and medical history to their physicians. In turn, providers need to communicate to patients what is being treated, why the drug is being used, how it should be used for maximum benefit, and what potential side effects can occur.

10 Proprietary drug names can be used legally only by the drug company that has trademark rights. Often, the original proprietary name becomes the popular name associated with the drug. Because the pharmaceutical company that develops a drug is trying to recover its investment, a newly marketed proprietary drug is expensive. Once the patent rights expire, other drug companies can also market the drug but under a different name; often, the common, generic name is used because it cannot be trademarked. The generic drugs are less expensive because the manufacturers do not need to recover any significant investment. Generally, the less expensive generic drug is as effective and safe as the proprietary counterpart.

11 Of the approximately 1500 different prescription drugs currently available in the United States, the most commonly prescribed groups are analgesics, antibiotics, antidepressants, drugs used for diabetes, antiulcer drugs, antiepileptic drugs, bronchodilators, drugs used to treat cardiovascular diseases, hormone-related drugs, and sedative-hypnotics.

12 Abuse of prescription drugs is a serious problem in the United States. Some patients try to persuade clinicians or pharmacists to make prescription medications available by using deceit or intimidation. Legal drugs obtained in this manner are often used to relieve drug dependence or to reduce withdrawal symptoms from illicit substances.

References

"A Hacker's Guide to Cough Remedies." *Wellness Letter* (UC Berkley) (October 1995): 3.

American Cancer Society. "Skin Cancer Facts" (2005). Available www.cancer.org/docroot/PED/content/ped_7_1_what_you_need_to_know_about_skin_cancer.asp?sitearea=PED.

American Psychiatric Association (APA). *Diagnostic and Statistical Manual of Mental Disorders*, 4th ed. revised [*DSM-IV-TR*]. Washington, DC: 2000.

Associated Press. "FDA Warns on Sales of Street Drug Alternatives." *The Washington Post* (1 April 2003): A-9.

CBS Evening News. "Study: St. John's Won't Cure Big Blues." National News (17 April 2001). Available www.cbs2chicago.com/now/story/0,1597,286149-225,00.shtml.

CDER. "Office of Generic Drugs." *FDA, Center for Drug Evaluation and Research* (November 2000). Available www.fda.gov/cder/ogd/index.htm.

CDER. "Over-the-Counter Medicine: What's Right for You?" Center for Drug Evaluation and Research, FDA (February 2002). Available www.fda.gov/cder.

CNN.com. "Jeb Bush's Daughter Charged with Prescription Fraud." CNN.com/U.S. (January 29, 2002). Available www.cnn.com/2002/us/01/29/jeb.bush.daughter.drugs.

Consumer Reports. "The Mainstreaming of Alternative Medicine." (May 2000): 17–24.

Cooper, C. "The Pharmacist's Role in Treating Clinical Depression." *Pharmacy Times* (June 1998): 39–42.

Covington, T. "Trends in Self-Care: The Rx to OTC Switch Movement." *Drug Newsletter* 12 (February 1993): 15–16.

Crespo, C., and J. Arbesman. "Obesity in the United States." *The Physician and Sports Medicine* 31 (November 2003): 1.

Dale, J. "The Common Cold." *Pharmacy Times.* Patient Education Colds (November 2000). Available www.pharmacy times.com/patedcold.html.

The Dasis Report. "Prescription and Over-the-Counter Drug Abuse Admissions." *Drug and Alcohol Services Information System* (24 July 2002). Available www.samhsa. gov/oas/2k2/otctx/otctx.htm.

Dergal, J., J. Gold, D. Laxer, M. Lee, M. Binns, K. Lanctot, M. Freeman, and P. Rochon. "Potential Interactions Between Herbal Medicines and Conventional Drug Therapies Used by Older Adults Attending a Memory Clinic." *Drugs and Aging* 19 (2002): 879–886.

Dighe, S. V. "A Review of the Safety of Generic Drugs." *Transplant Proceedings* 31 (3A suppl) (1999): 23S–24S.

Drug Facts and Comparisons, 59th ed. Central Analgesics, St. Louis: Wolters Kluwer Health, 2005: 978–1018.

Food Drug Administration (FDA). " Final Rule Declaring Dietary Supplements Containing Ephedrine Alkaloids Adulterated Because They Present an Unreasonable Risk. Final Rule." *Federal Registrar* 69 (2004): 6787–6854.

Ford, A., B. Delaney, D. Forman, and P. Moayyedi. "Eradication Therapy for Peptic Ulcer Disease in *Helicobacter Pylori* Positive Patients." *Cochrane Database of Systematic Review* 4 (2003): CD003840.

Frontlines. "Emotional 'Aspirin'." *Consumer Reports* (December 2000a): 60–62.

Frontlines. "Herbal Supplements, What's in the Chips?" *Consumer Reports* (December 2000b): 8.

Fugh-Berman, A. "Herb–Drug Interactions." *Lancet* 355 (2000): 134–138.

"Full Sun Protection." *Wellness Letter* (June 1993): 4–5.

Gasbarro, R. "Counseling the Patient with Diabetes." *Pharmacy Times* (October 1999): 53–66.

Gill, M. "The Pharmacist's Role in Sleep Disorders." *Pharmacy Times* (August 1999): 103–116.

Grady, D. "Chinese Herb Is Suspected in Cancer." *The New York Times on the Web* (8 June 2000). Available www.nytimes.com/library/national/science/health/06 0800hth-alternative-herb.html.

Greenberg, S. *Physician's Desk Reference for Nonprescription Drugs,* 17th ed. Oradell, NJ: Medical Economics Data, 1996.

Gruber, A. J., and H. G. Pope. "Ephedrine Abuse Among 36 Female Weightlifters." *American Journal of Addiction* 7 (1998): 256–261.

Information Brief. "Prescription Drug Abuse and Youth." U.S. Department of Justice (August 2002): Product #2002-L0424-004.

InnerSelf.com "Herbs and Their Use" (2003). Available www.innerself.com/Magazine?herbs_and_their_uses.htm.

Internet Drug Index. "The Top 200 Prescription Drugs for 2003 by Number U.S. Prescription Dispensed" (20 May 2004). Available www.rxlist.com/top200.

Just the Facts. "Prescription and Over-the-Counter Drugs." Alcohol and Drug Abuse Program, Alcohol and Drug Abuse Association Resource Center, 1030 E. Lafayette Street, Suite 100, Tallahassee, FL (2003).

Katzung, B., and K. Chatterjee. "Vasodilators and the Treatment of Angina Pectoris." In *Basic and Clinical Pharmacology,* 4th ed., edited by B. Katzung, 171–187. Norwalk, CT: Appleton & Lange, 1995.

Katzung, B., and W. Parmley. "Cardiac Glycosides and Other Drugs Used in Congestive Heart Failure." In *Basic and Clinical Pharmacology,* 6th ed., edited by B. Katzung, 188–204. Norwalk, CT: Appleton & Lange, 1995.

Kerin, D., R. Robertson, and D. Robertson. "Drugs Used for the Treatment of Myocardial Ischemia." In *The Pharmacological Basis of Therapeutics,* 10th ed., edited by J. Hardman and L. Limbird, 843–870. New York: McGraw-Hill, 2001.

Klein-Schwartz, W., and J. Hoopes. "Patient Assessment and Consultation." In *Handbook of Nonprescription Drugs,* 10th ed., edited by T. Covington, 11–20. Washington, DC: American Pharmaceutical Association, 1993.

Krowchuk, D. "Managing Acne in Adolescents." *Pediatric Clinics of North America* 47 (2000): 841–857.

Lamendola, C. "Early and More Vigorous Detection of Diabetes." *Journal of Cardiovascular Nursing* 18 (2003): 103–107.

Longo, L. P., T. Parran, B. Johnson, and W. Kinsey. "Addiction: Part II. Identification and Management of the Drug-Seeking Patient." *American Family Physician* 61 (2000): 2401–2481.

MacDonald, S. "Use with Care: Medicines Can Cure, or Kill." *Salt Lake Tribune* (3 September 1998): B-1.

Mackowiak, E. "The Common Cold: Prevention and Treatment." *Pharmacy Times* (November 1999): 95–106.

Marso, S. "Optimizing the Diabetic Formulary: Beyond Aspirin and Insulin." *Journal of American College of Cardiology* 40 (2002): 652–661.

McEvoy, G. American Hospital Formulary Service, American Society of Health System Pharmacists, Inc. AHFS Drug Information 2003. Bethesda, MD (2003).

Medical Letter. "Sunscreens: Are They Safe and Effective?" 41 (7 May 1999): 43–44.

Narcotics Digest. "Nonmedicinal Use of Prescription-Type Drugs Among Youth and Young Adults." (25 February 2003): Product #2003-R0485-008.

Nordenberg, T. "New Drug Label Spells It Out Simply." *FDA Consumer Magazine* (July/August 1999): Publication No. (FDA) 99-3232.

OTC Observations. "Facts and Figures About OTC Medicines." *Pharmacy Times* (suppl) (September 1998): 3.

Physicians' Desk Reference, 57th ed. Oradell, NJ: Medical Economics Data, 2003.

Public Health Advisory. "Phenylpropanolamine Advisory." FDA Center for Drug Evaluations (November 2000). Available www.fda.gov/cder/drug/infopage/ppa/advisory.htm.

Research Report. "Prescription Drug Abuse and Addiction." National Institute on Drug Abuse (April 2001a): NIH Publication No. 01-4881.

Research Report. "Hallucinogens and Dissociative Drugs." NIDA Research Report Series (March 2001b): NIH Publication #01-4209.

Sause, R., and R. Mangione. "Cough and Cold Treatment with OTC Medicine." *Pharmacy Times* (February 1991): 108–117.

Schwartz, R. "FDA Torches Sunscreen SPFs Greater than 30." *American Druggist* (July 1999): 22.

Shuster, J. "Insomnia: Understanding Its Pharmacological Treatment Options." *Pharmacy Times* 62 (August 1996): 67–76.

Simonsen, L. "Sun Exposure: The Stakes Are Rising." *Pharmacy Times* (May 1993): 25–31.

Slezak, M. "Steering Patients to Switches." *American Druggist* (July 1996): 32–35.

Slezak, M. "New England Journal Slaps 'Alternative' Industry." *American Druggist* (November 1998): 38.

Smith, S. "Treatment of Hypertension." *Pharmacy Times, ACPE Program* (November 2000). Available erpinfo.com/PTCE/content/Hypertension_CE.html.

Snowbeck, C. "FDA Raises Hurdle for Drugs to Move from Prescription to Over-the-Counter." *Post-Gazette.com Business News* (Pittsburgh, PA) (17 January 2005): Available www.post-gazette.com/pg/05016/442501.stm.

Sprague, J., and J. Culbertson, "Weight Loss: An Overview of Anorexia Agents." *Pharmacy Times* (June 1997): 65–74.

Stephenson, J., J. Imrie, M. Davis, and C. Mercer. "Is Use of Antiretroviral Therapy Among Homosexual Men Associated with Increased Risk of Transmission of HIV Infection?" *Sexually Transmitted Infections* 79 (2003): 7–10.

Stolberg, S. "F.D.A. Considers Switching Some Prescription Drugs to Over-the-Counter Status." *The New York Times on the Web* (28 June 2000). Available www.nytimes.com/library/national/science/062800-fda-otcdrugs.

Tan, A. "Herbs Need More Help to Go Mainstream: Experts." Reuters *Daily News* at Yahoo.com (29 May 2001). Available http://dailynews.yahoo.com/h/nm/20010529/hl/herbs_1.html.

Tatro, D. "Drug Therapy for Acne Vulgaris." *Druglink* (February 1998): 12–14.

Tatro, D. "Drug Interactions with Natural Product." *Drug Facts and Comparison News* (May 1999): 34–38.

Tinsley, J. A. "The Hazards of Psychotropic Herbs." *Minnesota Medicine* 82 (1999): 29–31.

"Top 200 Drugs of 1999." *Pharmacy Times* 66 (April 2000): 16.

USA Today. "FDA Delays Decision on OTC Emergency Contraception." Health and Behavior (14 February 2004). Available www.usatoday.com/news/health/2004-02-14-plan-b_x.htm.

van den Heuval, C., S. Ferguson, M. Macchiand, and D. Dawson. "Melatonin as a Hypnotic: Con." *Sleep Medicine Review* 9 (2005): 71–80.

Vasquez, C., and R. Vasquez. "Frequently Asked Questions About Generic Drugs." *GPR Patient Education* (November 2000). Available www.pharmacytimes.com/GPRpated.html.

Walsh, P. *Physicians' Desk Reference for Nonprescription Drugs and Dietary Supplements*, 22nd ed. Montvale, NJ: Medical Economics, 2001.

Warholak-Juarez, T., M. Rupp, T. Salazar, and S. Foster. "Effect of Patient Information on the Quality of Pharmacists' Drug Use Review Decisions." *Journal of American Pharmaceutical Association* (Washington) 40 (2000): 500–508.

White-Sax, B. "The Year in Review: OTCs of 1997." *Pharmacy Times* (March 1998): 42–46.

White-Sax, B. "Help for Heartburn." *Pharmacy Times* (February 1999): 17–18.

White-Sax, B. "Educating Consumers About Sun Protection." *Pharmacy Times* (May 2000): 48–50.

Wick, J. "Outsmarting Prescription Fraud." *Pharmacy Times* 61 (April 1995): 33–36.

Witztum, J. "Drugs Used in the Treatment of Hyperlipoproteinemias." In *The Pharmacological Basis of Therapeutics*, 9th ed., edited by J. Hardman and L. Limbird, 875–897. New York: McGraw–Hill, 1995.

Yates, K. M., A. O'Connor, and C. A. Horsley. "Herbal Ecstasy: A Case Series of Adverse Reactions." *New Zealand Medical Journal* 113 (2000): 315–317.

Zak, J. "OBRA '90 and DUR." *American Druggist* (October 1993): 57.

CHAPTER 16

Drug Use Within Major Subcultures

Did You Know?

- O Doping among world-class sports competitors is rampant.
- O Athletes are much more likely than other subcultural groups to take drugs that enhance physical attributes.
- O Approximately 500,000 teenagers use steroids and 52 thousand American children (12 and younger) use anabolic steroids.
- O Women express greater concern about drug use than men.
- O Overall, women consistently use fewer licit and illicit drugs than men do.
- O Drinking rates among adolescents are increasing more for girls than for boys.
- O In general, compared with men, women are more likely to become addicted to tobacco.
- O Approximately 70% of women in drug abuse treatment report histories of physical and sexual abuse with victimization beginning before 11 years of age and occurring repeatedly.
- O Adolescents usually learn their attitudes about drug use from family models.
- O More recently, a significant rising number of adolescents report drug use with family members.

- O Compared with adults who abuse drugs, drug-using adolescents are more likely to be involved in criminal activity.
- O Research shows that teenage gangs are major players in the drug trade.
- O Alcohol use is implicated in one-third to two-thirds of sexual assaults and acquaintance or date rape cases among teens and college students.
- O Among drug-using college students, 24% report using MDMA (Ecstasy) and psilocybin (mushrooms).
- O Twenty-three percent to 30% of all AIDS cases report injection drug use.
- O Approximately 72% of all people with AIDS who are currently alive are male; 28% are female.
- O African Americans account for 42% of all reported U.S. AIDS cases, white Americans account for 36%, and Hispanic Americans account for 20%.
- O An HIV-infected individual may not manifest symptoms of AIDS for as many as 10 to 12 years after the initial infection.
- O Ninety-eight percent of movies depict illicit drug use, alcohol, tobacco, or over-the-counter/prescription medicines.

Learning ◎bjectives

On completing this chapter you will be able to:

◎ Know which drugs are most likely to be abused by athletes and why.

◎ Describe the use of drug testing in athletic competitions.

◎ Determine where anabolic steroids come from.

◎ Describe the purpose and goals of the Adolescents Training and Learning to Avoid Steroids (ATLAS) prevention program.

◎ Explain the key differences between males and females regarding drug use.

◎ Explain two major ways women's history differs from men's history with regard to drug abuse.

◎ Explain the unique requirements that must be recognized and considered if women are to receive adequate treatment for drug dependence.

◎ Explain why adolescents use substances of abuse.

◎ Explain which types of parents are more likely to raise drug-abusing adolescents.

◎ List which types of drugs adolescents are most likely to abuse.

◎ Know the main factors motivating adolescents to join delinquent gangs.

◎ Know the major reasons why college students use drugs.

◎ List two major findings from research regarding drug use by college student subcultures.

◎ Know what "club drugs" are and how they are used.

◎ Explain how drug abuse contributes to the spread of AIDS.

◎ Know the key statistics regarding AIDS.

◎ List the major strategies to prevent contracting HIV infection.

◎ Know how the use of alcohol and other drugs is presented in popular movies and songs.

Introduction

Although similarities appear in the patterns of addiction among drug users, the development of initial use and eventual abuse varies immensely from individual to individual. When attempting to understand common causes and patterns of drug use, examining subcultures often provides a semblance of group commonalities. A **subculture** is defined as a subgroup within the population whose members share similar values and patterns of related behaviors that differ from those of other subcultures and the larger population. Even though many subcultures can be so broad and diverse that not all members may be consciously aware of one another, from an **outsider's perspective** (discussed in Chapter 1) they qualify as subcultures because they share similar behavior patterns. For example, sport, gender, age, and drug subcultures are often very large across the United States, and not all members of such subcultures can be aware of one another. However, from an outsider's perspective, they have similar patterns of behavior. When we refer to an insider's perspective, we are looking at a subculture from the inside and, therefore, expect the members to be aware of one another as a distinct group. An **insider's perspective** refers to viewing the subculture from the inside, just as members experience the ongoing activity. For example, a group of adolescents using drugs from a particular locality in a city or town and divorced women meeting to discuss coping with separation and being single qualify as distinct subcultures. Both insiders' and outsiders' perspectives include similar behavior patterns, just from different perspectives—inside and outside.

KEY TERMS

subculture
subgroup within the population whose members share similar values and patterns of related behaviors that differ from other subcultures and the larger population

outsider's perspective
viewing a group or subculture from outside the group and viewing the group and its members as an observer; looking "in" at the members

insider's perspective
viewing a group of subculture from inside the group seeing members as they perceive themselves

When defining a subculture, some sociologists refer to it as a "world within a world." Subcultures create and provide their members with lifestyle patterns that are observable, fairly consistent, and interwoven. Although it is a general perspective, viewing a group as a subculture offers a way to look at more generalized and distinctive patterns of drug use.

First, we examine why individuals within various subcultures might initially turn to drugs. The two types of forces that affect members of a subculture are internal and external forces, both of which affect these individuals' drug use behavior. *Internal subcultural forces* include

1. Shared attitudes about drug users and nonusers
2. Compatibility with other members of the peer group (often peer members share complementary personality traits)
3. Shared attitudes favorable to drug use despite conventional society's view that such behavior is deviant
4. Addiction to drugs or, at minimum, habitual drug usage
5. A common secrecy about drug use

External subcultural forces include

1. Preoccupation with law enforcement while procuring the drugs and while under the effects of illicit drugs
2. A desire to identify other users and sellers of illicit drugs such as verifying the dependability of the drug dealer (who best to "hook up" with)
3. Constant preoccupation regarding when more difficult-to-acquire-type drugs are available and seizing this opportunity
4. Preoccupation with being caught using or acting high in public, at work, at school, or at a social function at which drug use would be perceived as deviant social behavior

To further understand how similar patterns of drug use and/or abuse occur, in this chapter we look at drug users from both outsiders' and insiders' perspectives, from the vantage point of the members belonging to a distinct subculture. This chapter examines drug use and potential abuse in the following seven *drug-using* subcultures:

1. Sports/athletics
2. Women
3. Adolescents
4. College students
5. HIV and AIDS carriers
6. A certain percentage of professional actors, actresses, and entertainers who perform in movies
7. A certain percentage of Internet users who are seeking and purchasing illicit drugs

Athletes and Drug Abuse

Using performance-enhancing drugs for increased athletic ability is known as **"doping."** Current reports reveal that "'Doping' among world-class competitors is rampant, admit many athletes, and the governing bodies of individual sports, as well as the International Olympic Committee, turn a blind eye" (Begley et al. 1999, p. 49). Further, the reasons boil down to winning in sports, especially when millisecond differences exist between gold and silver medals. The differences between the two medals "can amount to millions in endorsement contract and appearance fees" (Begley et al. 1999, p. 49), and apparently the world of professional sports and "drugs [performance-enhancing drugs] go together like socks and sweat" (Begley et al. 1999, p. 49). Recently, Mr. Yesalis, an epidemiologist at Pennsylvania State University at University Park, stated that

> Elite athletes stay away from traditional anabolic steroids. They use testosterone creams or gels, which dramatically reduce the chance of being caught, in conjunction with insulin or insulin-like growth factor, and we don't even have a test for those. . . . The supplement industry has exploded since the passage of the Dietary Supplement Health and Education Act in 1994. . . . Anyone can buy substances like testosterone, human-growth hormone HGH, and insulin-like growth factor over the Internet. One site requires a doctor's prescription, but will sell one to any customer for $100. Or someone can just walk down to the local GNC, like Mr. Jackson's teammates at Florida State. There, one can buy muscle-building steroid "precursors" like androstene-

dione and creatine monohydrage. "Andro" is banned by the National Collegiate Athletic Association and other sports governing bodies, but it's legal to buy. They're not as effective as older anabolic steroids, but they do provide some benefits. . . . The law allows stores to sell vitamins, herbal remedies, and other supplements over-the-counter. (Suggs 2003, p. 36)

To understand why athletes are willing to risk using these drugs, it is necessary to further explore the sports mind-set. Young athletes receive exaggerated attention and prestige in almost every university, college, high school, and junior high school in the United States. Pressure to excel or be "the best" is placed on athletes by parents, peers, teachers, coaches, school administrators, the media, and the surrounding community. The importance of sports is frequently distorted and even used by some to evaluate the quality of educational institutions (Lawn 1984) or the quality of living conditions in a city. Athletic success can determine the level of financial support these institutions receive from local and state governments, alumni, and other private donors; thus, winning in athletics often translates into fiscal stability and institutional prosperity.

For the athlete, success in sports means psychological rewards such as the admiration of peers, school officials, family, and the community. In addition, athletic success can mean financial rewards such as scholarships, paid living expenses in college, advertising endorsement opportunities, and, for a few, incredible salaries as professional athletes. With the rewards of winning, athletes have to deal with the added pressures of not winning: "What will people think of me if I lose?" "When I lose, I let everybody down." "Losing shows that I am not as good as everyone thinks." These pressures on young, immature athletes can result in poor coping responses. Being better than competitors, no matter the cost, becomes the driv-

►Point/Counterpoint   How the "Juice" Is Flowing in Baseball ◄

We embrace instant gratification in the United States. We are a society that embraces "bigger, faster, stronger" and winning at all costs (in Dvorchak 2005). This concept now applies to professional sports with a devious outcome. A sampling from news sources reveals the following:

► Jose Canseco, a Major League Baseball player for the Oakland Athletics and Texas Rangers (among other teams), wrote a tell-all book titled *Juiced*, in which he exposed "not only the rampant use of performance-enhancing substances in baseball (with steroids replacing the amphetamines of Bouton's day) . . . A steroid devotee since the age of 20, Conseco goes beyond admitting his own usage . . . [to claiming that] . . . he often injected [Mark] McGwire while they were teammates . . . According to Canseco, steroids and human growth hormone gave McGwire and Sammy Sosa (whose own usage was 'so obvious, it was a joke') the strength, stamina, regenerative ability, and confidence they needed for [the] record setting home run duels often credited with restoring baseball's popularity after the 1994 strike" (Amazon.Com 2005).

► [S]everal star athletes, including New York Yankees slugger Jason Giambi, have reportedly told a federal grand jury investigating the [Balco] lab that they used illegal steroids, prompting Congress to hold hearings on the testing policies of all the major sports leagues" (Coile 2005).

► "Seattle Mariners minor-league outfielder Jamal Strong was suspended for 10 days Tuesday, making him the fourth player to test positive under Major League Baseball's new policy on performance-enhancing drugs" (Associated Press 2005).

► "Washington—How lawmakers introduced a bill Tuesday that would create a national standard for steroids testing for all professional sports and require a two-year suspension for the first positive test and a lifetime ban for a second offense" (Coile 2005).

► "The same anti-steroid rules that apply to badminton, billiards and bridge ought to apply to baseball, basketball and football, according to U.S. lawmakers who introduced a bill on Tuesday requiring American professional sports to adopt international drug testing standards" (Health Reuters and Yahoo! News 2005).

► "MLB's (Major League Baseball's) drug policy was denounced as laced with loopholes and lawmakers threatened to draft legislation calling for a national testing standard" (Health Reuters and Yahoo! News 2005).

► "McGwire's shameful refusal to answer questions about his alleged steroid use before a congressional committee and Bonds' unbelievable claim that he did not know that substances rubbed into his body were steroids clearly suggest deceit and dishonesty" (Eilek 2005).

► "Robert Eilek is a teacher at Temecula Middle School. He recently removed dozens of pieces of Mark McGwire memorabilia from his classroom in protest of McGwire's refusal to answer questions at a congressional inquiry on steroid use" (Eilek 2005).

ing motivation, and doing one's best is no longer sufficient. Such attitudes may lead to serious risk-taking behavior in an attempt to develop an advantage over the competition; this situation can include using drugs to improve performance.

The Canadian sprinter Ben Johnson, once known as the fastest human in history, was banned for life from competitive running in March 1993 (Begley et al. 1999; Hoberman and Yesalis 1995).

Five years earlier, at the 1988 Seoul Olympics, Johnson was stripped of a world's record for the 100-meter dash and forfeited the gold medal when his urine tested positive for steroids. Because of the first incident, Johnson was suspended from competition for 2 years. However, in 1992, the 31-year-old sprinter was attempting a comeback, with speeds that approached his world record times. In January 1993, a routine urine test

►Point/Counterpoint (continued)

These events bring up some questions to consider.

1. Are professional sports players entitled to claim records set if they were on drugs during their successful career? If they are entitled to their accomplishments regardless of their drug usage, how would it affect non–drug-using players? Is it fair to the sport and to the fans supporting the players? If they are not entitled to their accomplishments under drugged conditions, what should the penalty be?

2. Should *all* players in professional sports be continuously tested for drugs? Should this policy extend to both high school and college sport players? If so, what should the penalties for such drug violations be? If high school and college sports players should not be tested for drugs, why not?

3. What if we find clear evidence that some currently admired major sports figures who scored "big-time" records in the past were using steroids or other performance-enhancing drugs

while setting new and impressive records? Should anything be done about such evidence? If so, what penalties should the athletes receive? If not, why should we let them remain unblemished?

4. Are the real victims of this tragedy America's youth? Have athletes such as McGwire and Bonds betrayed the young who admire and emulate them? Do you think America's youth are affected by drug use in professional sports?

5. Does this scandal about professional sports and drug use suggest anything about the recent findings by the Centers of Disease Control and Prevention that steroid use among high school students more than doubled from 1991 to 2003?

6. As a high school teacher, is Robert Filek being overly severe regarding his treatment of McGwire's refusal to answer questions on steroid use at a congressional inquiry on steroid use?

Sources:

Amazon.com. "Editorial Reviews." Available http://www.amazon.com/exec/obidos/asin/0060746408/ref=bxgy (accessed 1 May 2005).

Associated Press. "Strong Suspended for Performance-Enhancing Drugs." *Sports ESPN* (26 April 2005). Available http://www.sports.espn.go.com/mlb/news/story?id=2046762&CMP=OTC-DT9705204233.

Coile, Z. "House Bill Seeks to Toughen Steroid Rules; Athletes in All Leagues Would Be Held to the Strict Standards Used in Olympics." *San Francisco Chronicle, Washington Bureau* (27 April 2005). Available http://www.sfgate.com/cgi-in/article.cgi?f=/c/a/205/04/27/steroids.tmp&feed=rss.n.

Dvorchak, R. "Former Steeler Courson Outlines Solutions for Steroid Use." *Post-Gazette.com* (27 April 2005). Available http://www.post-gazette.com/pg/05117/494862.stm.

Eilek, R. "Pro Sports Keep Heads in Sand on Steroids." *North County Times* (North San Diego and Southwest Riverside County columnists) (23 April 2005). Available http://www.nctimes.com/articles/2005/04/24/opinion/commentary/19_31_454_23_05.txt.

Health Reuters and Yahoo News. "Anti-steroid Rules Proposed for U.S. Pro Sports" (27 April 2005). Available http://news/yahoo.com/news?tmpl=story&u=/nm/20050427/hl_nm/steroid_rules_dc_1.

determined Johnson was again using steroids to enhance his athletic performance (Ferrente 1993). Widely publicized incidents such as this one concerning illicit use of so-called **ergogenic** (performance-enhancing) drugs by professional and amateur athletes have created intense interest in the problems of drug abuse in sports (Begley et al. 1999; Merchant 1992). (See "Point/Counterpoint," How the "Juice" Is Flowing in Baseball.)

DRUGS USED BY ATHLETES

Yes, the steroids I used certainly made me get bigger. I was going out for football and I had just made the team, so I kept using them and

KEY TERMS

ergogenic
drugs that enhance athletic performance

the results were phenomenal. Now, 2 years later, I won't be graduating. Several months ago, they removed a tumor on my liver, but they didn't get all the cancer. I am going home at the end of this semester. My parents want me to stay with them for the time I have left. When I go, I only have one wish—I want to die big and always be known as big Jim. *(From Venturelli's research files, interview with a 20-year-old male, December 13, 1996.)*

Studies have shown that athletes are less likely than nonathletes to use other drugs of abuse such as marijuana, alcohol, barbiturates, cocaine, and hallucinogens (Hoberman and Yesalis 1995; Samples 1989). However, athletes *are* much more likely than other populations to take drugs that enhance (physically or psychologically), or are thought to enhance, competitive performance; these drugs include stimulants such as amphetamines and cocaine and an array of drugs with presumed ergogenic effects, such as anabolic steroids

(Bell 1987). Some of the major drugs abused by athletes are listed in Table 16.1, along with their desired effects. The sections that follow discuss the drugs that are most frequently self-administered by athletes in an effort to improve their competitive performance.

Anabolic Steroids

Anabolic steroids consist of a group of natural and synthetic drugs that are chemically similar to cholesterol and related to the male hormone testosterone (Lukas 1993) and its artificial derivatives. Steroids are used for treatment of certain diseases such as specific types of anemia, some breast cancers, and testosterone deficiency. Although illegal when taken for nonmedical purposes, steroids have been illegally used by both athletes and nonathletes since the late 1950s to improve athletic ability and physical appearance because steroids have performance-enhancing and bodybuilding properties. Steroids are taken orally or

Table 16.1 **Partial List of Ergogenic Substances and Expected Effects**

DRUGS	EXPECTED RESULTS
Amino acids	Stimulate natural production of growth hormone
Amphetamines and cocaine	Increase strength, alertness, and endurance
Anabolic steroids	Increase muscle mass and strength
B-complex vitamins	Enhance body metabolism and increase energy
Caffeine	Reduce fatigue
Chromium	Enhance carbohydrate metabolism
Ephedrine	Improve breathing
Asthma medication	Improve breathing
OTC decongestants	Increase endurance
Thyroid hormone	Enhance metabolism and energy
β-blockers	Reduce hand tremor and stimulate growth hormone
Methylphenidate	Enhance alertness and endurance
Furosemide	Mask steroid use and enable rapid weight loss

Source: Harlan, R., and M. Garcia. "Neurobiology of Androgen Abuse." In *Drugs of Abuse,* edited by R. Watson, 185–201. Boca Raton, FL: CRC Press, 1992. Reprinted with permission. Copyright CRC Press.

injected into the muscles. Although males and females use steroids, males have higher rates of use (SAMHSA 1999c).

Naturally occurring male hormones, or **androgens**, are produced by the testes in males. These hormones are essential for normal growth and development of male sex organs as well as secondary sex characteristics such as muscular development, male hair patterns, voice changes, and fat distribution. The androgens are also necessary for appropriate growth spurts during adolescence (*Drug Facts and Comparisons* 1994). The principal accepted therapeutic use for androgens is for hormone replacement in males with abnormally functioning testes. In such cases, the androgens are administered before puberty and for prolonged periods during puberty to stimulate proper male development (*Drug Facts and Comparisons* 1994).

Abuse of Anabolic Steroids by Athletes Under some conditions, androgen-like drugs can increase muscle mass and strength; for this reason, they are referred to as **anabolic** (able to stimulate the conversion of nutrients into tissue) **steroids** (because chemically, they are similar to the steroids produced in the adrenal glands) and are used by many athletes to improve performance (Burke and Davis 1992). It is estimated that as many as 1 million Americans have used or are currently using these drugs to achieve a "competitive edge" or for other purposes (Welder and Melchert 1993; see Figure 16.1). Studies suggest that approximately 2% of college-age men and 6.7% of male high school students use anabolic steroids (Harlan and Garcia 1992). "A 2001 NCAA survey found that usage of stimulants, including ephedrine and amphetamines, and anabolic steroids had risen slightly since 1997. Between 3 and 4 percent of athletes surveyed admitted using stimulants, and 1.4 percent admitted using steroids" (Suggs 2003). Also realize that these percentages are much lower than what the survey revealed because athletes are inclined to hide drug usage for fear of jeopardizing their eligibility to play sports as well as other more personal reasons having to do with image in the eyes of others. Further, approximately 500,000 adolescents use steroids, and 52,000 American *children* use anabolic steroids; "a study in the journal *Pediatrics* last year found that 2.7% of Massa-

FIGURE 16.1

Reasons for nonmedicinal steroid use by college students.

Source: Harlan, R., and M. Garcia. "Neurobiology of Androgen Abuse." In *Drugs of Abuse,* edited by R. Watson, 186. Boca Raton, FL: CRC Press, 1992. Reprinted with permission. Copyright CRC Press.

chusetts middle-school athletes were using steroids" (Begley et al. 1999, p. 54). Another source indicates that males are more likely to use and abuse steroids than females (Johnston et al. 2004a), while "steroid abuse is growing most rapidly among young women" (NIDA 2000, p. 2). In a much larger nationwide study, the *Monitoring the Future* 2003 survey reports that 2.8% of 8th and 10th graders and 3.5% of 12th graders reported that they had taken anabolic steroids at least once in their lives (Johnston et al. 2004a). Competition for scholarships and entry into professional sports are major factors that influence young athletes to use steroids (Scott et al. 1996).

Although the vast majority of anabolic steroid users are male, women involved in bodybuilding and strength and endurance sports also abuse these drugs. Among seniors in high school, 3.2% of the males reported steroid use in the past year

KEY TERMS

androgens
naturally occurring male hormones, such as testosterone

anabolic steroids
androgen-like drugs that can increase muscle mass and strength

Besides risking their health, athletes who choose to dope should remember that they are role models. Seventy-three percent of youth want to be like a famous athlete; 53% of youth say it is common for famous athletes to use banned substances to get ahead.

compared with 1.1% of the females. These statistics are much lower among 19- to 32-year-olds—0.4%—with males accounting for all steroid use (Johnston et al. 2004a).

The first report of use of anabolic steroids to improve athletic performance was in 1954 by the Russian weight-lifting team. These drugs' performance-enhancing advantages were quickly recognized by other athletes, and it has been estimated that as many as 90% of the competitors in the 1960 Olympic games used some form of steroid (Toronto 1992). Because of the widespread misuse and associated problems with the use of these drugs, anabolic steroids were classified as Schedule III controlled drugs (see Chapter 3 for drug schedules) in 1991 (Merchant 1992).

KEY TERMS

"stacking"
use of several types of steroids at the same time

"cycling"
use of different types of steroids singly, but in sequence

"plateauing"
developing tolerance to the effects of anabolic steroids

"pyramiding"
moving from a low daily dose at the beginning of the cycle to a higher dose, then reducing use toward the end of the cycle

Due to federal regulations, individuals convicted of a first offense of trafficking with anabolic steroids can be sentenced to a maximum prison term of 5 years and a $250,000 fine. For a second offense, the prison term can increase to 10 years with a $500,000 fine. Even possession of illicitly obtained anabolic steroids can result in a 1-year term with at least a $1000 fine (U.S. Department of Justice 1991–1992).

Patterns of Abuse Geographical factors appear to have little to do with the use of anabolic steroids among athletes. In both inner-city and suburban schools, all are equally attracted to these drugs. However, some athletes are more inclined to abuse anabolic steroids than others. For example, football players have the highest rate of abuse; 9% self-reported out of 11 National Collegiate Athletic Association (NCAA) colleges and universities—in a survey conducted by the NCAA—whereas track and field athletes have the lowest rate of abuse (4% reported) (NIH/NIDA 1998). Another study using a more indirect method of interviewing found rates three times higher than the percentages just reported. In addition, the likelihood of abusing these drugs increases as the level of competition increases. Usage rates were approximately 14% in NCAA Division I athletes and 30% to 75% in professional athletes (Lukas 1993). In general, usage patterns for anabolic steroids vary considerably according to athletes' motivation, the level of competition, the type of sport, and the pressure for winning.

The pattern usually consists of self-administering doses that are 10 to 200 times greater than dosages used for legitimate medical conditions (Welder and Melchert 1993). Users take nonmedical anabolic-androgenic steroids in *cycles*, periods of use lasting 6 to 12 weeks or longer. **"Stacking"** these drugs means taking more than one at a time, which is common. The use of different steroids taken singly but in sequence is called **"cycling."** To avoid developing tolerance to a particular steroid (**"plateauing"**), athletes often stagger the various drugs, sometimes taking them in overlapping patterns or alternately. Users often move from a low daily dose at the beginning of a cycle to a higher dose, then reduce their use toward the end of the cycle (**"pyramiding"**). To combat the unwanted side effects of steroids, such as severe skin rashes and development of irreversible masculine traits in women, as well as sudden anger and explosive physical aggressiveness (known as "roid rage" in men), other drugs such as diuretics, antiestrogens, human chorionic gonadotropin, and antiacne medication are often taken concurrently (this pattern of use is referred to by users as an **"array"**). In general, power athletes prefer stacking, whereas bodybuilders prefer cycling.

Because steroid use has been prohibited by almost all legitimate sporting organizations, urine testing just before the athletic event has become commonplace (Lukas 1993). Steroid-using athletes attempt to avoid detection by trying to fool the tests. These highly questionable strategies include the following (Lukas 1993; Merchant 1992):

- Using the steroid only during training for the athletic events, but discontinuing its use several weeks before the competition to allow the drug to disappear from the body. Because oral steroids are cleared from the body faster than the injectable types, they are usually discontinued 2 to 4 weeks and the injection steroids are stopped 3 to 6 weeks before competition.
- Taking drugs, such as probenecid, that block the excretion of steroids in the urine. Probenecid inhibits the substance from reaching the urine. In addition, urine tests are all that the International Olympic Committee (IOC) requires (Begley et al. 1999).
- Using diuretics and drinking large quantities of water to increase the urine output and dilute the steroid so that it cannot be detected by the test.
- Adding adulterant chemicals to the urine, such as Drano, Clorox, ammonia, or eye drops to invalidate the tests.

Recent Developments in Evading Detection One serious problem today according to Prince Alexandre de Merode, who has been in charge of the IOC's Medical Commission for 31 years is that

the newest doping agents pose the risk of serious health problems, and even death. But a larger reason is that it is ridiculously easy to dope and not be caught. Doping and detection are like an arms race. First trainers discover a performance-enhancing drug. Then, sports officials develop a test for it. Trainers retaliate

by inventing a way to elude the detectors. So far, doping has stayed a lap ahead.

Other comments from the same source:

"Undetectable drugs are 90 percent of estimated doping cases," said Hein Verbruggen, head of International Cycling Union. (Begley et al. 1999, p. 50)

Chemists constantly use the 72 banned steroids to change the testosterone molecule. "All you have to do is take a steroid not on the list. Or, simply by going cold turkey a few weeks before competition, an athlete can get the muscle-bulking effects without getting caught" (Begley et al. 1999, p. 51).

Some of the most recent types of drugs that athletes use even though they are all banned by the NCAA are listed in Table 16.2. This table lists the class of performance-enhancing substances, examples, what these drugs do, who is likely to use such drugs, status regarding whether the drug is illicit or licit, and where athletes are likely to secure the drug (see Table 16.2).

Effects of Anabolic Steroids Low to moderate doses of anabolic steroids have little effect on the strength or athletic skills of the average adult. However, when high doses are used by athletes during intense training programs, these drugs cause significant gains in lean body mass (i.e., muscle) and strength while decreasing fat (Lukas 1993). Because most of these effects are transient and will disappear when steroid use is stopped, athletes feel compelled to continue using them and become psychologically hooked (Toronto 1992). The drugs are most likely to benefit athletes in contact and strength sports in which increased muscle mass provides an advantage, such as weight lifting and football; anabolic steroids are less likely to benefit athletes involved in sports requiring dexterity and agility, such as baseball or tennis.

The risks associated with anabolic steroids are not completely understood. Most certainly, the

KEY TERMS

"array"
use of other drugs while taking anabolic steroids to avoid possible side effects

Table 16.2 Performance-Enhancing Substances Banned by the NCAA

The following are among the substances many athletes use even though they are banned by the National Collegiate Athletic Association, and some are illegal under federal and state laws.

CLASS	EXAMPLES	WHAT DOES IT DO?	WHO USES IT?	IS IT LEGAL?	WHERE DO ATHLETES GET IT?
Steroids	Nandrolone, stanozol	Increases testosterone levels, thus building muscle.	Any athlete in a sport that requires strength and doesn't penalize muscle bulk can benefit. In an NCAA survey, football, baseball, rifle, and water-polo athletes admitted using steroids.	Not without a prescription.	Over the Internet or from a complicit doctor.
Steroid precursors	Androstenedione, 19-norandrostenediol	Can be converted into testosterone in the body.	Same as above.	Yes, under the Dietary Supplement and Health Education Act of 1994.	In drugstores, gyms, nutritional-supplement stores, and some grocery stores.
Hormones	Human growth hormone (HGH), erythropoietin (EPO)	HGH promotes growth in children and muscle development in adults. EPO increases production of red blood cells.	HGH is used by the same kinds of athletes who use steroids, while endurance athletes benefit from EPO.	Not without a prescription.	Over the Internet.
Stimulants	Ephedrine, caffeine (in excessive amounts)	Raises metabolic rate, giving a burst of energy.	Virtually all types of athletes. Not only do strength-oriented athletes like football players use them to get pumped up for workouts, but athletes like gymnasts use them to try to lose weight.	Yes. The Food and Drug Administration has banned ephedrine and caffeine (if the concentration in urine exceeds 15 micrograms/mL) as of 2001.	Generally available in drugstores and specialty stores.

Source: Suggs, W. "Deadly Fuel: As Supplements and Steroids Tempt and Endanger More Athletes, What Are Colleges Doing?" *Chronicle of Higher Education* XLIX (14 March 2003): A37. Copyright 2006, *Chronicle of Higher Education.* Reprinted with permission.

higher the doses and the longer the use, the greater the potential damage these drugs can do to the body. Some of the adverse effects thought to occur with heavy steroid use (10 to 30 times the doses used therapeutically) include the following:

- Increased "bad" blood cholesterol levels, which could eventually clog arteries and cause heart attacks and strokes (NCADI 1999)
- Increased risk of liver disorders, such as jaundice and tumors (Lukas 1993)

- Psychological side effects, including irritability, outbursts of anger ("roid rage"), mania, psychosis, and major depression
- Possible psychological and physical dependence with continual use of high doses, resulting in withdrawal symptoms, such as steroid craving (52%), fatigue (43%), depression (41%), restlessness (29%), loss of appetite (24%), insomnia (20%), diminished sex drive (20%), and headaches (20%) (Lukas 1993)
- Alterations in reproductive systems and sex hormones, causing changes in gender-related characteristics (Burke and Davis 1992): breast enlargement in males, breast reduction and bodily hair growth in females, infertility in both genders, and changes in genitalia—atrophy (shrinkage) of the penis and testicles in males and enlargement of external genitalia in females (Street et al. 1996)
- Changes in skin and hair in both genders: increased incidence and severity of acne, male pattern baldness, and increased body hair (Burke and Davis 1992)
- Persistent unpleasant breath odor (NCADI 1999)
- Swelling of the feet or lower limbs (NCADI 1999)
- Other changes, including stunted growth in adolescents, deepening of voice in females, and water retention, causing bloating (Burke and Davis 1992; Street et al. 1996)

Sources of Steroids Where do the anabolic steroids come from? About 50% of the anabolic steroids used in the United States are prescribed by doctors; the other 50% are obtained from the black market. Black market sources of steroids include drugs diverted from legitimate channels, smuggled from foreign countries—Brazil, Italy, Mexico, Great Britain, Portugal, France, and Peru (NIDA 1996)—that are designated for veterinarian use, or inactive counterfeits (U.S. Department of Justice 1991–1992). Recently, it was discovered that the primary source for steroids in the United States is the Baja, California, area of Mexico (Yesalis and Cowart 1998). The steroids are manufactured in Mexico City and shipped to pharmacies in the Baja region. Some health food stores and mail-order firms also offer products with names similar to the prescription anabolic steroids, such as Dynabdin, Metrobolin, and Diostero. These "sham steroids" contain only vitamins, amino acids, or micronutrients (Merchant 1992).

Most steroids used for nonmedical purposes are obtained illegally. A major federal report indicates that sources of illicit steroids fall into three rough categories: (1) smuggled steroids manufactured licitly or illicitly abroad, (2) drugs legally manufactured in this country and diverted to illicit sales at various places in the distribution chain, and (3) drugs clandestinely produced domestically. Small minorities of users obtain their drugs by prescription. Actual doses are often difficult to estimate because the product may have been produced in an uncontrolled laboratory with unknown quality control, may have been intended for veterinary use with its human equivalent doses not known, or may be counterfeit (NIH and NIDA 1998). Another source noted that the majority of young people report that steroids are easily available through their friends and coaches (McCaffrey 1999).

Stimulant Use Among Athletes

There are often reports in the media of football, basketball, or baseball players who have tested positive in a drug-screening evaluation or who have been suspended from competition due to drug abuse. In 1986, reports of cocaine-related deaths of sports figures included basketball star Len Bias and professional football player Don Rogers. Perhaps such sports tragedies helped convince some U.S. youth of the dangers of stimulant abuse and contributed to the decline in drug abuse in the late 1980s (Johnston et al. 1993). Clearly, no one—not even an athlete—is immune from the risks of these drugs.

Amphetamines and cocaine are abused to improve athletic skills (McDonald 1995). However, it is not clear if stimulants actually enhance athletic performance or merely the athlete's perception of performance. Many athletes believe these drugs promote quickness, enhance endurance, delay fatigue, increase self-confidence and aggression, and mask pain (Hoberman and Yesalis 1995). In fact, some studies have shown that stimulants can improve some aspects of athletic performance, especially in the presence of fatigue

(NIDA 1996). However, the risk of using stimulants in sports is substantial because these drugs mask extreme fatigue, increase the risk of heat exhaustion, and can have severe cardiovascular consequences, such as heart attacks and strokes (Bell 1987; see "Case in Point," When Drugs Enter the Boxing Ring).

Although some athletes would never consider using the hard stimulants, such as cocaine and amphetamines, milder stimulants that are legal and available over-the-counter (OTC) may be thought to be acceptable. Such stimulants include caffeine and OTC decongestants (for example, phenylpropanolamine and phenylephrine). These drugs can be a double-edged sword for the athlete. Their use can reduce fatigue, give a sense of energy, and even mask pain. Nevertheless, in high doses, especially when combined, they can cause nervousness, tremors, and restlessness, impair concentration, accelerate dehydration, and interfere with sleep ("OTC Drugs and Athletes" 1992). Some athletic competitions limit permissible blood levels of caffeine and do not allow the use of OTC stimulants such as decongestant drugs.

Miscellaneous Ergogenic Drugs

Most athletic organizations have banned the use of anabolic steroids and stimulants and are using more effective screening procedures to detect offenders. A result of this clampdown has been the search for alternative performance-enhancing drugs by athletes who feel a need for such pharmacological assistance. The following are brief discussions of a few of these substitute ergogenic substances (for a more complete list, see Table 16.1).

Clenbuterol At the 1992 Olympic Games in Barcelona, Spain, at least four athletes, including German world sprint champion Katrina Krabbe, were disqualified from competition for using the drug clenbuterol to enhance their athletic performance (Merchant 1992). Not available in the United States, this drug is known as "Doper's

▶Case in Point   When Drugs Enter the Boxing Ring

When Oliver McCall entered the boxing ring to fight for the heavyweight championship on February 7, 1997, he was not alone. With him came the spectre of years of drug abuse.

Just 7 weeks before, McCall had been arrested for swinging a Christmas tree around a hotel lobby while in a drug-induced haze. A few years earlier, he was found in a crack house after having been mugged by a fellow addict, to whom he lost the $1.5 million check he had carried with him in a sock to buy drugs. These events were just two of many drug-related occurrences on his record. His most recent arrest, however, had been followed by a drug treatment program, which he attended daily.

But something went wrong the night of February 7. After having announced to a friend, "I want my title. I'm fighting for my life," McCall seemed to want to get knocked out. In the third round, in the middle of the ring, in front of a packed audience, he listlessly walked around as his opponent, Lennox Lewis, threw punches at him. McCall dodged and bobbed his head, yet refused to fight back. After the fourth round, McCall stood alone, away from his corner, sobbing uncontrollably, seemingly having a nervous breakdown in front of a worldwide cable television audience. Fifty-five seconds into the fifth round, referee Mills Lane stopped the fight. Lewis was the winner. McCall, in more ways than one, was not.

While drugs have been an unwelcome part of sports in recent years, there are few cases where the consequences became more publicly evident. Here was a great contradiction for the world to see: Oliver McCall, the athlete who had never been knocked down, and Oliver McCall, the man floored by the pain and drugs in his life. McCall's trainer, George Benton, said, "It was hard to watch, but it could be the best thing that ever happened to the human race. Now a father can tell his kids, 'You see what you saw on T.V.? You see what happens on drugs?' It was a hell of a lesson."

Sources: Boston Globe (8 February 1997); *New York Times* (9 February 1997).

Delight" and is supposed to improve breathing and increase strength. Currently, most athletic urine examinations test for it.

Erythropoietin Clinically, erythropoietin is a drug used to treat patients with anemia. Because it stimulates the production of *red blood cells* (the oxygen-carrying cells in the blood), it is thought that this drug enhances oxygen use and produces additional energy. Erythropoietin is being used as a substitute for blood doping. *Blood doping* is when athletes attempt to increase their number of red blood cells by reinfusing some of their own blood (which has been stored) before an athletic event.

Erythropoietin is impossible to detect and has been reported to be used by athletes engaged in endurance activities such as long-distance cycling. The use of erythropoietin by athletes is extremely dangerous and is thought to be responsible for several deaths. It is also very expensive, which likely has helped to limit its abuse (Merchant 1992).

Human Growth Factor and Human Growth Hormone
Athletes have begun to abuse two types of steroids: **human growth factor (HGF)** and its "designer drug" synthetic version, **human growth hormone (HGH)**. HGF, also known as *somatotropin*, is a hormone naturally secreted by the pituitary gland at the base of the brain that helps to achieve normal growth potential of muscles, bones, and internal organs. Some athletes claim that release of natural HGF can be simulated by using drugs such as levodopa (used to treat Parkinson's disease), clonidine (used to treat hypertension), and amino acids. Athletes use commercially prepared HGF because it cannot be distinguished from naturally occurring HGF.

Use of this hormone by athletes is limited, however, by its high cost. The benefits of HGF to athletic performance are very controversial, although the potential side effects are substantial, including abnormal growth patterns (called *acromegaly*), diabetes, thyroid gland problems, heart disease, and loss of sex drive (Merchant 1992).

In recent years, the synthetic HGH has become available in the form of a newly structured steroid-type analog sold in vials; this product is used to build muscle tissue, with corresponding decreases in body fat, without exercise (McDonald 1995).

HGH is probably the most potent anabolic agent ever discovered, but it also one of the most expensive. In fact, HGH is so expensive that until the mid-1990s, "its use in the United States was confined to pediatric endocrinologists who used it to treat undersized children" (McDonald 1995, p. C1). To date, no tests have proved capable of detecting HGH in the blood or urine. In addition, the side effects of this drug remain largely unknown. As a result, this drug is highly vulnerable to abuse.

Beta (β)-Adrenergic Blockers The β-adrenergic blockers are drugs that affect the cardiovascular system and are frequently used to treat hypertension. They have been used in sports because they reduce heart rate and signs of nervousness, which in turn quiets hand tremors. Consequently, these drugs are most likely to be used by individuals participating in sports that require steady hands, such as competitive shooting. The use of these drugs is prohibited by most athletic organizations (Merchant 1992).

Gamma-Hydroxybutyrate The substance gamma-hydroxybutyrate (GHB) is found naturally in the brain and has been used in England to treat insomnia. Athletes and bodybuilders have used GHB to increase muscle mass and strength. Although the actual effects of the compound are not known, it has been reported to cause euphoria and increase the release of growth hormone. Acute poisoning with GHB has occurred, causing hospitalization; other adverse effects can include headaches, nausea, vomiting, muscle jerking, and even short-term coma, though full recovery has been universal ("Bodybuilding Drug" 1992; "Multistate Outbreak" 1994). Prolonged use may cause withdrawal (insomnia, anxiety, and tremor). GHB is especially dangerous when combined with central nervous system (CNS) stimulants such as amphetamines and cocaine.

KEY TERMS

human growth factor (HGF)
a hormone that stimulates normal growth

human growth hormone (HGH)
a "designer drug" synthetic version of HGF

PREVENTION AND TREATMENT

If the problem of drug abuse among athletes is to be dealt with effectively, sports programs must be designed to discourage inappropriate drug use and assist athletes who have developed drug abuse problems. Coaches and administrators should make it clear to sports participants that substance abuse will never give an athlete a competitive advantage in their programs and will not be tolerated. The Adolescents Training and Learning to Avoid Steroids **(ATLAS) program**, which was developed by Dr. Linn Goldberg of Oregon Health Sciences at the University of Portland, is one of the most successful prevention programs for steroid abuse. Athletes, coaches, and team leaders are trained to educate team members about the effects of anabolic steroid abuse. Because adolescents already know that anabolic steroids build muscles and can increase athletic abilities, both desirable and adverse effects of steroid use are taught. Research has shown that information about anabolic steroids that fails to acknowledge potential benefits creates a credibility gap that can make youths distrustful of the prevention program. The program consists of three components: classroom, weight training, and parent information components to "give the student athletes the knowledge and skills to resist steroid use and achieve their athletic goals in more effective, healthier ways" (Goldberg et al. 1996, p. 1555):

1. The classroom component consists of football coaches and student leaders conducting highly interactive sessions that explore the effects of steroids, the elements of sports nutrition, and strength training alternatives to steroid use. In this setting, while the coaches introduce topics and act as leaders, the students are exploring and learning from one another (Goldberg et al. 1996).

2. In the weight-training component, research staff members conduct seven hands-on sessions that teach the students proper weight training techniques (Goldberg et al. 1996).

3. The parent information component consists of discussions and information sessions with parents. The staff provides nutrition guidelines and seeks compliance while stressing the very best nutrition for the athletes and their families. Parents become more vigilant against steroid use and learn to enjoy well-balanced, nutritional meals (Goldberg et al. 1996).

Briefly summarized, results indicate that the students who participated in this program in comparison with the control group (a group of students not participating in the program) showed they (1) knew more about proper exercise, (2) had a clear understanding of the dangers of using steroids and had become much more sensitized to the harmful effects of such drugs, (3) held more unfavorable views of others' use of anabolic steroids, and (4) were more likely to avoid unhealthy eating (such as frequenting fast-food restaurants) (Goldberg et al. 1996).

Drug Use Among Women

Until recently, little was known about the patterns of female drug abuse. In general, most clinical drug abuse research, including treatment and rehabilitation outcomes, was either conducted in male populations and the results were extrapolated to women or the research was done in general populations with little regard to gender influences (Klee and Jackson 2002; USDHHS and NIDA 1999; Dicker and Leighton 1994; Lin 1994). Most researchers considered drug abuse to be a male problem. Today, the research focusing on women and drug use is better, but a greater amount of study is still needed. Even today, scientists performing even basic research with animals generally prefer male animal models to avoid the hormonal complexities of female animals. However, a growing concern for the importance of unique emotional, social, biochemical, and hormonal features in females has caused researchers to acknowledge the importance of gender differences.

KEY TERMS

ATLAS program
Adolescents Training and Learning to Avoid Steroids (ATLAS); an anabolic abuse prevention educational program that empowers student athletes to make the right choices about steroid use

WOMEN MORE CONCERNED ABOUT DRUG USE THAN MEN

Women are expressing greater concerns about drug use than men. When asked whether drug abuse is a greater problem now than 5 years earlier, 51% of women and 42% of men answered "yes" (Drug Strategies 1998). When asked whether drug use is a big concern among youth, 58% of women and 48% of men answered "yes" (Drug Strategies 1998). Further, 58% of women and 50% of men thought it was wrong to reduce prevention funds while increasing prison funds (Drug Strategies 1998). One reason for this discrepancy may be that women traditionally have been primary caregivers; therefore, they feel more responsible about issues that can plague their communities and their families and often feel the need to be more vocal and be in positions that maintain harmony within the family setting. Women also generally express more concerns about safety issues than men because they are more likely to be victims of violent crimes, such as muggings or sexual assaults.

PATTERNS OF DRUG USE: COMPARING FEMALES WITH MALES

Recent surveys comparing male and female drug use patterns confirm that differences exist among the licit and illicit drug-using populations. Table 16.3 compares annual female and male drug use among respondents ages 19 to 30. The research findings in this table indicate the following gender-related differences in drug use (Johnston et al. 2004b):

1. Overall, females consistently use fewer licit and illicit drugs (29% of females versus 34% of males use illicit drugs).
2. Males (84%) and females (83%) are nearly equal with regard to the consumption of alcohol. With regard to *binge drinking* (five or more drinks in a row in the last 2 weeks), greater differences exist between males (45%) and females (27%).
3. More males (31%) than females (24%) use marijuana on a yearly basis.
4. More males smoke cigarettes (39%) than females (36%).

5. Fewer females use cocaine (5%) compared to males (8.2%). The same is true for hallucinogens: 3.3% of females and 6.5% of males.

One finding that is often hidden by *current* drug use statistics is that nationwide surveys confirm that drug use is increasing among women, often more rapidly than among men (Drug Strategies 1998). From 1990 through 1996, the number of women seeking emergency drug treatment rose more rapidly than the number of men seeking such emergency treatment. Hospital records indicate that there were more women seeking emergency drug treatment for heroin and marijuana (Drug Strategies 1998). Other gender differences are that older women (over 60) tend to abuse tranquilizers, sedatives, and antidepressants (Drug Strategies 1998) and, in some cases, girls in junior high and high school are now surpassing boys with regard to alcohol and tobacco use. Drinking rates are increasing more rapidly for girls than for boys (Drug Strategies 1998), and women in general are more likely than men to become addicted to tobacco. Two factors that make smoking attractive to women (and girls) are that they believe it reduces stress and controls weight (Drug Strategies 1998).

Although some similarities appear between genders in drug usage rates for specific types of drugs, the general differences in the prevalence rates for females and males compel researchers to look for explanations so that we can better understand and deal with gender-related drug abuse problems.

FEMALE ROLES AND DRUG ADDICTION

Women are expected to take on more responsibilities than in my mother's day. Not only are we expected to work like men, but we also take care of the house, worry about the children, and get dinner on the table. If the house needs cleaning, everyone looks at the woman of the house. Men still have these expectations. I know things are changing with more equality between the sexes, but *real* equality of responsibilities has yet to occur. After everyone gets to bed on weekdays, I have a few drinks in order to calm me down before I go to bed. *(From Venturelli's research files, interview with a 43-year-old female, employed full-time, June 30, 1996.)*

Table 16.3 **Annual Use of Various Types of Drugs by Gender Among Respondent of Modal, Ages 19–30 (percent of total population)**

	FEMALES	MALES	TOTAL
Any illicit drug	28.9	34.0	31.0
Any illicit drug other than marijuana	15.8	18.8	17.0
Alcohol	83.3	83.8	83.4
Five or more drinks in a row in last 2 weeks	26.7	45.0	34.2
Cigarettes	36.2	38.5	37.1
Marijuana	24.4	30.7	27.0
Other narcotics	7.5	8.5	7.9
Tranquilizers*	6.3	6.5	6.4
Cocaine	5.0	8.2	6.3
Amphetamines*	4.7	6.1	5.2
Other cocaine	4.6	7.7	5.9
MDMA (Ecstasy)	3.5	4.7	4.0
Hallucinogens	3.3	6.5	4.6
Sedatives (barbiturates)*	3.2	3.9	3.5
Crack	1.0	1.1	1.0
Crystal methamphetamine (ice)	0.9	1.2	1.1
Inhalants	0.8	1.9	1.2
LSD	0.8	1.4	1.0
Heroin	0.3	0.5	0.3
PCP	0.3	0.2	0.3
Steroids	0.1	1.4	0.6

*Nonprescription use.

Source: Johnston, L. D., P. M. O'Malley, J. G. Bachman, and J. E. Schulenberg. *Monitoring the Future: National Survey Results on Drug Use, 1975–2003. Volume II: College Students and Adults.* Bethesda, MD: National Institute on Drug Abuse, 2004.

Another interview revealed the following:

My boyfriend does vacuum when I ask, but not much else. Of course, if his boss is coming to visit, then he appears concerned about cleaning the house. How many times is he fast asleep and I am having some hard liquor and a few puffs from a joint after cleaning everything before we get up the next morning. I used to complain but he does not really care about the housework, so I compensate by getting buzzed before going to sleep. *(From Venturelli's research files, interview with a 29-year-old female, employed part-time.)*

To appreciate the impact of drug abuse on women, it is necessary to understand the uniqueness of female roles in our society. Relative to drug abuse problems, women today are often judged by a double standard. Women suffering from drug addictions are often perceived less tolerantly than comparably addicted men (Erickson and Murray 1989). Because of these social biases, women are afraid of being condemned and are less likely to seek professional help for their own personal drug abuse problems. In addition, family, friends, and associates are less inclined to provide drug-dependent women with important emotional support (Klee and Jackson 2002; USDHHS and NIDA 1999).

The image of the alcoholic woman has always been that of one who is boisterous, flirtatious, effusive, and, sometimes, loudmouthed. This may be the person she might become on occasion, but more often she is secluded in the privacy of her apartment or home after getting the kids off to school or having just come home from the office, classroom, or business. She is shy, reclusive to a point, alienated, retrospective, and lacking in self-esteem. Later in her drinking, she may become self-pitying, resentful, and even childishly cruel because of the drug alcohol (Kirkpatrick 1999).

Due to their unique socioeconomic and family roles, women are especially vulnerable to emotional disruptions resulting from divorce, loneliness, and professional failures. Studies suggest that such stresses aggravate tendencies for women to abuse alcohol and other substances (Korolenko and Donskih 1990; Kirkpatrick 1999). More specifically, "women drink from a feeling of inadequacy and from a need for love, the kind of love not found within a sexual relationship but, rather, a love that is deeper and more primal" (Kirkpatrick 1999, p. 1).

In addition, drug addiction can occur in some women as a result of domestic adversities. Consequently, there is a high prevalence of drug dependence in women who are victims of sexual and/or physical abuse (Ladwig and Anderson 1989). "Approximately 70% of women in drug abuse treatment report histories of physical and sexual abuse, with victimization beginning before 11 years of age and occurring repeatedly" (SAMHSA 1999b, p. 1). These physical and emotional traumas result in, or are precursors to, factors leading to drug abuse,

such as low self-esteem, self-condemnation, anxiety and personal conflicts, dysfunctional dependencies, and overwhelming feelings of guilt (Kirkpatrick 1999). In addition, because of the crucial nurturing roles women hold, drug abuse problems can be particularly damaging to family stability.

Another unique role for women in drug abuse situations is that of a spouse, significant other, or mother to a drug addict. Often, in both traditional and nontraditional family relationships, women are expected to be nurturing, understanding, and willing to sacrifice to preserve the family integrity. If a family member becomes afflicted by drug dependence, the wife or mother is viewed as a failure. In other words, if the woman had maintained a good home and conducted her domestic chores properly, the family member would not have been driven to drugs (Klee and Jackson 2002; USDHHS and NIDA 1999).

Despite the disruption and considerable stress caused by drug addiction in the home, women continue to bear the burden of raising children, performing domestic chores, and keeping the family together. In addition, women in such circumstances are frequently put at great physical risk. The risk is from an addicted spouse who becomes abusive to his partner or from exposure to sexually transmitted diseases, such as HIV or hepatitis, transmitted by a careless infected partner. The anxiety and frustrations resulting from these stressful circumstances can encourage women themselves to become dependent as they seek emotional relief by using drugs.

WOMEN'S RESPONSE TO DRUGS

Research continues to lag regarding how women respond to substances of abuse. Although matters are slowly changing, the trend in drug abuse studies is still to avoid female populations; the effects of the drugs in men are still extrapolated to women. Even when drug abuse research is conducted on women, frequently the woman's response is not of primary concern; the objective is to determine the effects on a fetus during pregnancy or an infant during nursing (Klee and Jackson 2002; USDHHS and NIDA 1999).

Although it generally can be assumed that the physiological and drug responses of men and women are similar, some distinctions should be recognized. For example, a recent study compared the risk for lung cancer in men and women after a lifetime of cigarette smoking. It was found that female smokers were twice as likely to get lung cancer as males who had smoked an identical number of cigarettes in their lifetimes ("Women Smokers" 1994). Another study indicated that women are *three* times more likely to contract lung cancer than men when smoking the same amount of cigarettes (Kirkpatrick 1999). These differences clearly indicate that cigarette smoking is far more dangerous for women than for men. Finally, women's unique response to drugs includes a finding discovered by researchers at the University of California at San Francisco that women respond to a class of painkillers called kappa-opioids, which are ineffective in men (*Science Daily* 2000).

Drug Abuse and Reproduction

A very important physiological distinction that sets women apart from men about taking drugs is their ability to bear children. Because of this unique function, men and women have different endocrine (hormone) systems, organs, and structures, and women have varied drug responses according to their reproductive state. The unique features of women have a substantial impact on the response to drug abuse in the presence and absence of pregnancy.

Drug abuse patterns can influence the outcome of pregnancy even if they occur before a woman becomes pregnant. For example, women who are addicted to heroin are more likely to have poor health, including chronic infections, poor nutrition, and sexually transmitted diseases such as HIV infection, which can damage the offspring if pregnancy occurs. If substances are abused during pregnancy, they may directly affect the fetus and adversely alter its growth and development. The incidence of substance abuse during pregnancy is not known precisely, but undoubtedly hundreds of thousands of children have been exposed to drugs in utero. The effects of individual drugs of abuse taken during pregnancy are discussed in detail in the corresponding chapters, but several specific observations merit reiteration here:

1. Cocaine is a substantial threat for both the pregnant woman and the fetus. Although a number of specific claims for the fetal effects of cocaine are controversial (see Chapter 10), several observations appear legitimate: Cocaine use increases the likelihood of miscarriage when used during pregnancy; cocaine use in the late stages of pregnancy can cause cardiovascular or CNS complications in the baby at birth and immediately thereafter; and due to its vasoconstrictor effects, cocaine may deprive the fetal brain of oxygen, resulting in strokes and permanent physical and mental damage to the child.

2. The impact of alcohol consumption during pregnancy has been well documented and publicized (Mathias 1995). When alcohol is consumed by the mother, it crosses the placenta, but the effect of this drug on the fetus is highly variable and depends on the quantity of alcohol consumed, timing of exposure, maternal drug metabolism, maternal state of health, and presence of other drugs. A particularly alarming consequence of high alcohol intake during pregnancy is an aggregate of physical and mental defects called *fetal alcohol syndrome* (FAS). Characteristics of this syndrome include low birthweight, abnormal facial features, mental retardation, and retarded sensorimotor development. For additional details, see Chapters 7 and 8. In addition to its direct effects on the fetus, alcohol has played a major role in many unwanted pregnancies or has resulted in women's exposure to sexually transmitted diseases. As a CNS depressant, alcohol impairs judgment and reason and, in turn, encourages sexual risk taking that normally would not occur. The results are all too frequently tragic for women (SAMHSA 1999b).

3. Tobacco use during pregnancy is particularly rampant in the United States. Specifically, 20% of the smoking female adult population is pregnant. Some experts suggest smoking cigarettes during pregnancy may pose a greater risk to the fetus than taking cocaine. Tobacco use by pregnant women may interfere with blood flow to the fetus, deprive it of oxygen and nutrition, and disrupt development of its organs—particularly the brain. Also of significant concern is the possibility that ex-

posure of nonsmoking pregnant women to secondhand tobacco smoke may be damaging to the fetus.

4. Other drugs of abuse that have been associated with abnormal fetal development when used during pregnancy include barbiturates, benzodiazepines, amphetamines, marijuana, lysergic acid diethylamide (LSD), and even caffeine when consumed in high doses. Clearly, women should be strongly urged to avoid all substances of abuse, especially during pregnancy.

Women and Alcohol

Alcohol is the drug most widely used and abused by women in the United States. According to the 1999 *National Household Survey on Drug Abuse* among women aged 12 and older, 42.3% (SAMHSA 2002) used alcohol in the past month and 19.4% reported binge drinking (SAMHSA 1999a). Alcohol abuse is also a major problem for women on college campuses, even though male college students are more likely than their female counterparts to use alcohol on a daily basis.

As a rule, women are less likely than men to develop severe alcohol dependence; thus, only 25% of the alcoholics in the United States are female. Women are also likely to initiate their drinking patterns later in life than men (Klee and Jackson 2002; USDHHS and NIDA 1999). Interesting ethnic patterns of alcohol consumption have been reported in females, with black and white women manifesting similar drinking patterns. Although the proportions are similar, black women are more likely to completely abstain from alcohol than white women are.

Women who are dependent on alcohol are usually judged more harshly than men with similar difficulties. Alcoholic males are more likely to be excused because their drinking problems are often perceived as being caused by frustrating work conditions, family demands, economic pressures, or so-called nagging wives and children. In contrast, women with drinking problems are often perceived as spoiled or pampered, weak, deviant, or immoral. Such stigmas, referred to as labels in Chapter 2 (see labeling theory), cause women to experience more guilt and anxiety about their alcohol dependence and discourage

them from admitting their drug problems and seeking professional help (Kirkpatrick 1999).

The principal reasons for excessive alcohol consumption in women range from loneliness, boredom, and domestic stress in the "housewife drinker" to financial problems, sexual harassment, lack of challenge, discrimination, and powerlessness in the career woman. Depression is often associated with alcohol problems in women, although it is not clear whether this condition is a cause or an effect of the excessive use.

Women's Physiological Responses to Alcohol
Health consequences for excessive alcohol consumption appear to be more severe for women than for men. For example, alcoholic women are more likely to suffer premature death than alcoholic men. In addition, liver disease is more common and occurs at a younger age in female drinkers than in male alcoholics. In general, higher morbidity rates are experienced by alcoholic women than their male counterparts.

Several explanations have been suggested for the higher rate of adverse effects seen in female alcoholics. Their higher blood alcohol concentrations may be due to a smaller blood volume and more rapid absorption into the bloodstream after drinking. Alternatively, slower alcohol metabolism in the stomach and liver might cause more alcohol to reach the brain and other organs as well as prolong exposure to the drug following consumption (Goldstein 1995). Studies have shown that for a woman of average size, one alcoholic drink has effects equivalent to two drinks in an average-size man (see Chapter 7).

Dealing with Women's Alcohol Problems Alcoholic consumption varies considerably in women, ranging from total abstinence or an occasional drink to daily intake of large amounts of alcohol. Clearly, much is yet to be learned about the cause of some women's excessive drinking and dependence on alcohol. The role of genetic factors in predisposing women to alcohol-related problems is still unclear. The environment is certainly a major factor contributing to excessive alcohol consumption in women. It is well established that depression, stress, and trauma encourage alcohol consumption because of the antianxiety and amnesic properties of this drug. Because of unreasonable societal expectations and numerous socioeconomic disadvantages, women are especially vulnerable to the emotional upheavals that encourage excessive alcohol consumption.

As with all drug dependence problems, prevention is the preferred solution to alcohol abuse by women. Alcohol usually becomes problematic when it is no longer used occasionally to enhance social events but used daily to deal with personal problems. Such alcohol dependence can best be avoided by using constructive techniques to manage stress and frustrations. Because of unique female roles and society's expectations, women especially need to learn to be assertive with family members, associates in the workplace (including bosses), and other contacts in their daily routines. By expecting and demanding equitable treatment and consideration in personal and professional activities, stress and anxiety can often be reduced. Education, career training, and development of communication abilities can be particularly important in establishing a sense of self-worth (see also Chapter 17). With these skills and confidence, women are better able to manage problems associated with their lives and less likely to resort to drugs for an escape.

Women and Prescription Drugs

Women are more likely than men to suffer depression, anxiety, and panic attacks (Kirkpatrick 1999); be unable to express anger; be victims of physical and sexual abuse; and be subject to overwhelming guilt feelings (Kirkpatrick 1999). Consequently, they are also more likely to take and become addicted to the prescription drugs used in treating these disorders. Because these drugs are used as part of psychiatric therapy and under the supervision of a physician, drug dependence frequently is not recognized and may be ignored for months or even years. This type of "legitimate" drug abuse occurs most often in elderly women and includes the use of sedatives, antidepressants, and antianxiety medications. A recent study found that one in four women older than age 60 takes at least one of these drugs daily and that some of them develop serious drug problems (Drug Strategies 1998). Excessive use of these drugs by older women results in side effects such as insomnia, mood fluctuations, and disruption of cognitive

and motor functions that can substantially compromise the quality of life.

TREATMENT OF DRUG DEPENDENCY IN WOMEN

As previously discussed, women are less likely than men to seek treatment for, and rehabilitation from, drug dependence (Kirkpatrick 1999). Possible reasons for their reluctance are as follows:

1. In more traditional families, women have unique roles with high expectations. They are expected to assume demanding and ongoing responsibilities, such as motherhood, child rearing, and family maintenance that cannot be postponed and often cannot be delegated, even temporarily, to others. Consequently, many women feel that they are too essential for the well-being of other family members to leave the home and seek time-consuming treatment for drug abuse problems.

2. Drug treatment centers often are not designed to handle the unique health requirements of females—thus, women face more obstacles. These obstacles involve barriers to treatment entry, treatment engagement, and long-term recovery (NIDA 1999). Women have been shown to have greater health needs than men due to more frequent respiratory, genitourinary (associated with the sex and urinary organs), and circulatory problems. If drug treatment centers are not capable of providing the necessary physical care, women are less likely to participate in associated drug abuse programs.

3. Drug-dependent women are more inclined to be unemployed than their male counterparts and more likely to be receiving public support. The implications of this difference are twofold. First, because concerns about one's job often motivate drug-dependent workers to seek treatment, this issue is less likely to be a factor in unemployed women. Second, without the financial security of a job, unemployed women may feel that good treatment for their drug problems is unaffordable. (For more on treatment, see Chapter 18.)

The unique female requirements must be recognized and considered if women are to receive adequate treatment for drug dependence. Some considerations on how to achieve this objective include the following: (1) availability of female-sensitive services; (2) nonpunitive and noncoercive treatment that incorporates supportive behavior change approaches; and (3) treatment for a wide range of medical problems, mental disorders, and psychosocial problems (NIDA 1999). The role of motherhood needs to be used in a positive manner in drug treatment strategies. For most women, motherhood is viewed with high regard and linked to self-esteem. Approximately 90% of female drug abusers are in their childbearing years, and many have family responsibilities. Consequently, treatment approaches need to be tailored to allow women to fulfill their domestic responsibilities and satisfy their maternal obligations.

Women dependent on drugs often lack important coping skills. Because many women lead restricted, almost isolated lives that focus entirely on domestic responsibilities, they face limited alternatives for dealing with stressful situations. Under these restrictive circumstances, the use of drugs to cope with anxieties and frustrations is very appealing. To enhance their ability to cope, drug-dependent women need to develop communication and assertiveness skills. Further, they need to be encouraged to control situations rather than allowing themselves to be controlled by the situation. Specific techniques that have proven useful in coping management are exercise (particularly relaxation types), relaxing visual imagery, personal hobbies, and outside interests that require active participation. Many drug-dependent women require experiences that divert their attention from the source of their frustrations while affording them an opportunity to succeed and develop a sense of self-worth.

Finally, one research study found that the most effective treatment for women included a mutually supportive therapeutic environment that addressed the following issues: psychopathology (such as depression); a woman's role as mother; interpersonal relationships; and the need for parenting education. Another study found that cocaine-using women whose children were living with them during residential treatment remained in the treatment programs significantly longer than women whose children were not living with them at the facility. Thus, having the children in the treatment facility provides opportunities to assess and meet women's needs, which in turn affects the women's prognosis (NIDA 1999).

Prevention of Drug Dependence in Women

The best treatment for drug addiction is prevention. To help prevent drug problems in women as opposed to men, socioeconomic disadvantages need to be recognized as factors that make women more vulnerable to drug dependence, especially from prescription medication. Women need to learn that nondrug approaches are often more desirable for dealing with situational problems than prescribed medications. For example, for older women suffering loneliness, isolation, or depression, it is better to encourage participation in outside interests, such as hobbies and service activities. In addition, social support and concern should be encouraged from family, friends, and neighbors. Such nonmedicinal approaches are preferred over prescribing sedatives and hypnotics to cope with emotional distresses. Similarly, medical conditions such as obesity, constipation, or insomnia should be treated by changing lifestyle, eating, and exercise habits rather than using drug "bandage therapy."

When women are prescribed drugs, they should ask about the associated risks, especially as they relate to drug abuse potential. Frequently, drug dependency develops insidiously and is not recognized by either the patient or attending physician until it is already firmly established. If a woman taking medication is aware of the potential for becoming dependent and is instructed on how to avoid its occurrence, the problems of dependence and abuse can frequently be averted. (See Chapter 17 for more on prevention and education.)

Drug Use in Adolescent Subcultures

I love waking up in the morning and smoking a nice fat joint. I live above the garage now, and my mom lives across the yard from the garage. This is a great living arrangement! I go to my room a few hours before crashing on many school nights, get high, drink some vodka that my older brother buys for me, then finally crash. In the morning, I always wake myself up so my mom stays away from my room, and my hideaway stash box is always locked. I roll me a joint and get a little high before I greet mom in the morning for a quick breakfast. I think she gets high too, but if I ask her and she says "no," what if she then asks me and gets all suspicious and shit? Besides, my Uncle Prentice always gets high with me, so I still think my mom really does not care about smoking weed. In fact, I know she is more worried about me drinking and driving than my friend "Mary Jane" [nickname for marijuana]. That's just my private life and no one needs to know. *(From Venturelli's research files, male, age 18, residing in Chicago, July 10, 2000.)*

From ages 13 through 18, adolescents are more likely to experience heightened psychological, social, and biological changes. Often, such internal and external changes are manifested by emotional outbursts. Why do such changes and urges arise? The adolescent's body is stretching, growing, and sometimes appearing out of control due to the hormonal changes of puberty.

Adolescents are uncertain and confused about not knowing who or what they are becoming. They are often confused as to their worth to family, peers, society, and even to themselves (Kantrowitz and Wingert 1999). Adding to the frustration of growing up, the cultural status of adolescents is poorly defined. They find themselves trapped in a "no-man's land" between the acceptance, simplicity, and security of childhood, and the stress, complexities, expectations, independence, and responsibilities of adulthood. Not only do adolescents have difficulty deciding who and what they are, but adults are equally unsure as to how to deal with these transitional human beings. While the grown-up world tries to push adolescents out of

the secure nest of childhood, it is not willing to bestow the full membership and rights of adulthood upon them (Johnson et al. 1996; Kantrowitz and Wingert 1999).

Because of their uniquely rapid development, several developmental issues are particularly important to evolving adolescents (Elmen and Offer 1993; Johnson et al. 1996; Kantrowitz and Wingert 1999):

- Discovering and understanding their distinctive identities
- Forming more intimate and caring relationships with others
- Establishing a sense of autonomy
- Coming to terms with the hormone-related feelings of puberty and expressing their sexuality
- Learning to become productive contributors to society
- Feeling alone and alienated

Due to all this developmental confusion, "normal" behavior for the adolescent is difficult to define precisely. Experts generally agree that persistent low self-esteem, depression, feelings of alienation, and other emotional disturbances can be troublesome for teenagers. Most adolescents are relatively well adjusted and are able to cope with **sociobiological changes**. Emotionally stable adolescents relate well to family and peers and function productively within their schools, neighborhoods, and communities. The majority of adolescents experience transient problems, which they are able to resolve, but some become deeply disturbed and are unable to grow out of their problems without counseling and therapy. Those adolescents who are unable or unwilling to ask for assistance often turn to destructive devices, such as drugs or violence (Kantrowitz and Wingert 1999), for relief from their emotional dilemmas.

WHY ADOLESCENTS USE DRUGS

Although there is no such thing as a "typical" substance-abusing adolescent, certain physiological, psychological, and sociological factors are often associated with drug problems in this subculture (Johnson et al. 1996). In looking at an array of explanations regarding why adolescents use drugs, one recent study by Columbia University's

KEY TERMS

sociobiological changes
the belief that biological forces (largely genes) have a direct influence on the root causes of social psychological behavior

National Center on Addiction and Substance Abuse found that

> Children ages 12 to 17 who are frequently bored are 50% more likely to smoke, drink, get drunk and use illegal drugs. In addition, kids with $25 or more a week in spending money are nearly twice as likely to smoke, drink or use drugs as children with less money. Anxiety is another risk factor. The study found that youngsters who said they're highly stressed are twice as likely as low-stress kids to smoke, drink or use drugs. (Associated Press 2003)

It is important to remember that not all drug use by adolescents means therapy is necessary or even desirable. More traditional proven and accepted explanations stress that most excessive drug use that often leads to abuse by adolescents results from the desire to experience new behaviors and sensations, a passing fancy of maturation, an attempt to relieve peer pressure, feelings of alienation, or an inclination to enhance a social setting with chemistry (Kantrowitz and Wingert 1999). Most of these adolescent users will not go on to develop problematic dependence on drugs and, for the most part, should be watched but not aggressively confronted or treated. The adolescents who usually have significant difficulty with drug use are those who turn to drugs for extended support as coping devices and become drug-reliant because they are unable to find alternative, less destructive solutions to their problems. Several major factors can contribute to serious drug dependence in adolescents (Archambault 1992; Johnson et al. 1996; Walsh and Scheinkman 1992).

Research indicates that the most important factor influencing drug use among adolescents is peer drug use (Bahr et al. 1995; Kandel 1980; NIDA 1999; Swadi 1992; Winters 1997). Consequently, eventual transition to heavier substance use also directly correlates with peer use (Steinberg et al. 1994). Conversely, individuals whose peer groups do not use or abuse drugs are less likely to use drugs themselves (Venturelli 2000). Research has identified a correlation between strong family bonds and non–drug-using peer groups (NIDA 1999). "Adolescents with higher [stronger] family bonds are less likely than adoles-

cents with lower [weaker] bonds to have close friends who use drugs" (Bahr et al. 1995, p. 466). In addition, family bonding is highly correlated with educational commitment. In essence, family bonding influences choice of friends and educational goals and aspirations (Bahr et al. 1995).

Three noteworthy differences exist between male and female adolescents: (1) Males demonstrate a stronger association between educational achievement and family bonds; (2) among females, peer drug use is negatively associated with family bonds, so peer drug use and family bonds are not likely to influence the use of licit and illicit drugs by females; and (3) the impact of age on peer drug use (the younger the age, the more vulnerable to peer pressure) and on the amount of alcohol consumed can be predicted with slightly greater accuracy for males than females (Teen Challenge 2000).

Many adolescents use drugs to help cope with boredom, unpleasant feelings, emotions, and stress or to relieve depression, reduce tension, and reduce alienation (Teen Challenge 2000). Psychological differences among adolescents who are frequent drug users, experimenters, and abstainers often can be traced to early childhood, the quality of parenting in their homes, and their home environment. It has been suggested that certain types of parents are more likely to raise children at high risk for substance abuse (Archambault 1992). For example, an alcoholic adolescent usually has at least one parent of the following types:

Alcoholic. This parent serves as a negative role model for the adolescent. The child sees the parent dealing with problems by consuming drugs. Even though drinking alcohol is not illegal for adults, it sends the message that drugs can solve problems. The guilt-ridden alcoholic parent is unable to provide the child with a loving, supportive relationship. In addition, the presence of the alcoholic parent is often disruptive or abusive to the family and creates fear or embarrassment in the child.

Nonconsuming and condemning. This type of parent not only chooses to abstain from drinking but also is very judgmental about drinkers and condemns them for their behavior. Such persons, who are often referred to as *teetotalers,* have a rigid, moralistic approach to life. Their black-and-white attitudes frequently prove inadequate and unforgiving in an imperfect, gray world. Children in these families can feel inferior and guilty when they are unable to live up to parental expectations, and they may resort to drugs to cope with their frustrations.

Overly demanding. This type of parent forces unrealistic expectations on his or her children. These parents often live vicariously through their children and require sons and daughters to pursue endeavors in which the parents were unable to succeed. Particular emphasis may be placed on achievements in athletics, academics, or career selections. Even though the parents' efforts may be well intended, the children get the message that their parents are more concerned about "what they are" than "who they are." These parents frequently encourage sibling rivalries to enhance performance, but such competitions always yield a loser.

Overly protective. These types of parents do not give their children a chance to develop a sense of self-worth and independence. Because the parents deprive their children of the opportunities to learn how to master their abilities within their surroundings, the children are not able to develop confidence and a positive self-image. Such children are frequently unsure about who they are and what they are capable of achieving. Parents who use children to satisfy their own ego needs or who are trying to convince themselves that they really do like their children tend to be overly protective.

The principal influence for learned behavior is usually the home; therefore, several other family-related variables can significantly affect adolescents' decision to start, maintain, or cease a drug habit (Kinney 2000; Lawson and Lawson 1992). For example, adolescents usually learn their attitudes about drug use from family models. In other words, what are the drug-consuming patterns of parents and siblings? Adolescents are more likely to develop drug problems if other members of the family (1) are excessive in their drug (legal or illegal) consumption, (2) approve of the use of illicit drugs, or (3) use drugs as a problem-solving strategy.

Sociological factors that damage self-image can also encourage adolescent drug use. Feelings of rejection may cause poor relationships with family members, peers, school personnel, or coworkers. Ethnic differences sometimes contribute to a poor self-image because people of minority races or cultures are frequently socially excluded and are sometimes viewed as being inferior and undesirable by the majority population. This type of negative message is very difficult for adolescents to deal with. Sometimes, to ensure acceptance, adolescents adopt the attitudes and behaviors of their affiliated groups. If a peer group, or a gang, views drug use as cool, desirable, or even necessary, members (or those desiring membership) feel compelled to conform and become involved in drugs.

PATTERNS OF DRUG USE IN ADOLESCENTS

Growing minorities of younger aged teenagers are exposed to drug use within their own families. A recent study reported that "20% of . . . 600 teens in drug treatment in New York, Texas, Florida and California said they have shared drugs other than alcohol with their parents, and that about 5% of the teens actually were introduced to drugs—usually marijuana—by their moms and dads" (Leinwand 2000, p. 1). In 1999, Partnership for a Drug-Free America reported similar shocking findings (Leinwand 2000).

Jason, 17, a recovering addict from an upper-middle-class family in Simi Valley, California, says he wishes his father had been more of a parent and less of a buddy when it came to marijuana. "[Jason] made his drug purchase: a $5 bag of pot. Jason says his father walked by his room's open door as he was stashing it in a dresser drawer. [His father then] '. . . told about his marijuana use,' Jason says. 'We went into his [dad's] office, and he had a (water pipe) and we got high together.' [Jason reports that at the time, he] '. . . thought it was *sooo* cool'" (Leinwand 2000, p. 2).

In another example, La'kiesha, 15, of southern California, is the third generation of a family in which members have become addicted to drugs. La'kiesha said her grandmother smoked pot regularly and gave her a few puffs when she was 5 years old, to settle her down before bedtime (Leinwand 2000).

Teenagers being introduced to drugs or using drugs with parents, especially illicit drugs in middle- and upper-middle-class families, is a relatively recent phenomenon. Years ago, alcohol may have been shared between parents and their children in a low percentage of cases; however, today there are parents who either have been or are currently using illicit drugs and they appear to be influencing the use of these drugs by their children. Currently, this occurs in a small minority of families; nevertheless, it remains shocking.

Recent surveys regarding drug use patterns found that by 12th grade, (seniors in high school), approximately 51% of the teens had used alcohol, approximately 53% had used cigarettes, 45.7% had used marijuana, and 10.9% had used inhalants in 2004 (see Table 16.4). The 2004 *Monitoring the Future* study conducted by the National Institute on Drug Abuse (NIDA) reported the following findings (Johnston et al. 2004b).

1. The proportion of U.S. 8th-, 10th-, and 12th-grade students who reported lifetime, annual, or 30-day use of any illicit drug continued to show a gradual decline from 2001 to 2004.
2. Use of marijuana—by far the most widely used of the illicit drugs—showed a decline from 2001 to 2004.
3. Although high in percentage terms for such young ages, the use of alcohol among 8th, 10th, and 12th graders showed a very modest decline from 2001 to 2004.
4. Lifetime use of inhalants among 8th graders increased significantly from 2003 to 2004. These products are inexpensive, legal, and easy to obtain, making them more attractive to younger adolescents who have less ready access to illicit drugs.
5. Overall, teen substance use has been following a downward direction, although the declines have been very modest. A number of drugs show little or no change in their usage rates in 2004 compared to 2003, although use of most of them is at levels below their recent peak rates.

ADOLESCENT VERSUS ADULT DRUG ABUSE

Adolescent patterns of drug abuse are very different from drug use patterns in adults (Moss et al. 1994). The uniqueness of adolescent drug abuse means that drug-dependent teenagers usually are not successfully treated with adult-directed therapy. For example, compared with adults who abuse drugs, drug-using adolescents are (1) more likely to be involved in criminal activity and at earlier ages; (2) more likely to have other members of the family who abuse drugs; (3) more likely to be associated with a dysfunctional family that engages in emotional and/or physical abuse of its members; and (4) more likely to begin drug use because of curiosity or peer pressure (Bahr et al. 1995; Daily 1992b; Hoshino 1992; Steinberg et al. 1994; Teen Challenge 2000). Such differences need to be considered when developing adolescent-targeted treatment programs.

CONSEQUENCES AND COINCIDENTAL PROBLEMS

Researchers have concluded that the problem of adolescent drug use is a symptom and not a cause of personal social maladjustment. Even so, because of the pharmacological actions of drugs, routine use can contribute to school and social failures, unintended injuries (usually automobile-related), criminal and violent behavior, sexual risk taking, depression, and suicide (Curry and Spergel 1997).

It is important to realize that, because serious drug abuse is usually the result of emotional instability, consequences of the underlying disorders may be expressed with chemical dependence, making diagnosis and treatment more difficult. The undesirable coincidental problems may include self-destruction, risk taking, abuse, or negative group behaviors. Some of these adolescent problems and their relationship to drug abuse are discussed in the following sections.

Adolescent Suicide

Current research shows that although no cause-and-effect relationship exists between use of alcohol and/or other drugs and suicide, such drugs are often contributing factors (Minnesota Institute of Public Health 1995). Adolescents are particularly vulnerable to suicide actions; in fact, white males between 14 and 20 years old are the most likely to commit suicide in the United States (Daily 1992b). Further, the teenage suicide rate has doubled since 1980 (Siegel and Senna 1997).

Table 16.4 Drug Use Among 8th, 10th, and 12th Graders

Data show the percentages of 8th, 10th, and 12th graders who used both licit and illicit types of drugs in 2001, 2002, 2003, and 2004.

	8TH GRADERS				10TH GRADERS				12TH GRADERS			
	2001	2002	2003	2004	2001	2002	2003	2004	2001	2002	2003	2004
Any Illicit Drug												
Lifetime	26.8	24.5	22.8	21.5	45.6	44.6	41.4	39.8	53.9	53.0	51.1	51.1
Annual	19.5	17.7	16.1	15.2	37.2	34.8	32.0	31.1	41.4	41.0	39.3	38.8
30-day	11.7	10.4	9.7	8.4	22.7	20.8	19.5	18.3	25.7	25.4	24.1	23.4
Alcohol												
Lifetime	26.8	24.5	22.8	21.5	45.6	44.6	41.4	39.8	53.9	53.0	51.1	51.1
Annual	19.5	17.7	16.1	15.2	37.2	34.8	32.0	31.1	41.4	41.0	39.3	38.8
30-day	11.7	10.4	9.7	8.4	22.7	20.8	19.5	18.3	25.7	25.4	24.1	23.4
Cigarettes (Any Use)												
Lifetime	36.6	31.4	28.4	27.9	52.8	47.4	43.0	40.7	61.0	57.2	53.7	52.8
Annual*	—	—	—	—	—	—	—	—	—	—	—	—
30-day	12.2	10.7	10.2	9.2	21.3	17.7	16.7	16.0	29.5	26.7	24.4	25.0
Marijuana/Hashish												
Lifetime	20.4	19.2	17.5	16.3	40.1	38.7	36.4	35.1	49.0	47.8	46.1	45.7
Annual	15.4	14.6	12.8	11.8	32.7	30.3	28.2	27.5	37.0	36.2	34.9	34.3
30-day	9.2	8.3	7.5	6.4	19.8	17.8	17.0	15.9	22.4	21.5	21.2	19.9
Inhalants												
Lifetime	17.1	15.2	15.8	17.3	15.2	13.5	12.7	12.4	13.0	11.7	11.2	10.9
Annual	9.1	7.7	8.7	9.6	6.6	5.8	5.4	5.9	4.5	4.5	3.9	4.2
30-day	4.0	3.8	4.1	4.5	2.4	2.4	2.2	2.4	1.7	1.5	1.5	1.5
Amphetamines												
Lifetime	10.2	8.7	8.4	7.5	16.0	14.9	13.1	11.9	16.2	16.8	14.4	15.0
Annual	6.7	5.5	5.5	4.9	11.7	10.7	9.0	8.5	10.9	11.1	9.9	10.0
30-day	3.2	2.8	2.7	2.3	5.6	5.2	4.3	4.0	5.6	5.5	5.0	4.6
Hallucinogens												
Lifetime	3.9	3.3	3.2	3.0	6.6	6.3	5.9	5.8	10.4	9.2	9.0	8.7
Annual	3.4	2.6	2.6	2.2	6.2	4.7	4.1	4.1	9.1	6.6	5.9	6.2
30-day	1.6	1.2	1.2	1.0	2.1	1.6	1.5	1.6	3.3	2.3	1.8	1.9
Cocaine												
Lifetime	4.3	3.6	3.6	3.4	5.7	6.1	5.1	5.4	8.2	7.8	7.7	8.1
Annual	2.5	2.3	2.2	2.0	3.6	4.0	3.3	3.7	4.8	5.0	4.8	5.3
30-day	1.2	1.1	0.9	0.9	1.3	1.6	1.3	1.7	2.1	2.3	2.1	2.3

Table 16.4 (continued)

	8TH GRADERS				10TH GRADERS				12TH GRADERS			
	2001	2002	2003	2004	2001	2002	2003	2004	2001	2002	2003	2004
Crack Cocaine												
Lifetime	3.0	2.5	2.5	2.4	3.1	3.6	2.7	2.6	3.7	3.8	3.6	3.9
Annual	1.7	1.6	1.6	1.3	1.8	2.3	1.6	1.7	2.1	2.3	2.2	2.3
30-day	0.8	0.8	0.7	0.6	0.7	1.0	0.7	0.8	1.1	1.2	0.9	1.0
Steroids												
Lifetime	2.8	2.5	2.5	1.9	3.5	3.5	3.0	2.4	3.7	4.0	3.5	3.4
Annual	1.6	1.5	1.4	1.1	2.1	2.2	1.7	1.5	2.4	2.5	2.1	2.5
30-day	0.7	0.8	0.7	0.5	0.9	1.0	0.8	0.8	1.3	1.4	1.3	1.6
Heroin												
Lifetime	1.7	1.6	1.6	1.6	1.7	1.8	1.5	1.5	1.8	1.7	1.5	1.5
Annual	1.0	0.9	0.9	1.0	0.9	1.1	0.7	0.9	0.9	1.0	0.8	0.9
30-day	0.6	0.5	0.4	0.5	0.3	0.5	0.3	0.5	0.4	0.5	0.4	0.5

*Not available at time of printing.

Source: Johnston, L. D., P. M. O'Malley, J. G. Bachman, and J. E. Schulenberg. *Overall Teen Drug Use Continues Gradual Decline, But Use of Inhalants Rises* Ann Arbor, MI: University of Michigan News and Information Services, March 2005.

The result is that suicide is now the second leading cause of death among persons 15 to 24 years of age. Twenty percent to 36% of suicide victims have a history of alcohol abuse or were drinking shortly before their suicide. There are approximately 1800 teen suicides per year, approximately 8 or 9 per 100,000 living teens (ABC News 2000). Some experts have described severe chemical dependence as a form of slow, drug-related suicide. For clinicians, every case of serious drug addiction conceals a suicidal individual because all drug abuse inevitably constitutes a game of life and death very similar to "Russian roulette," which comes back into fashion at certain times and under certain circumstances (Bergeret 1981).

Clearly, many teenagers who abuse alcohol and other drugs possess a self-destructive attitude as this quote from an online chat with Dr. David Shaffer, a teen suicide expert, demonstrates: "[T]wo-thirds of all suicides amongst boys occur in boys who are abusing alcohol or other drugs; so the link between suicide and alcohol and certain drugs, like cocaine and Ecstasy and other stimulant drugs, is a very close one" (Schaefer et al. 1993, p. 39).

According to Shaffer, adolescents who attempt suicide are more likely to (1) have disciplinary problems, then abuse alcohol and feel even more depressed; (2) be very anxious and not display any bad behavior problems; or (3) have a perfectionist attitude and never be satisfied with their outcomes. Nearly all suffer from depression before their suicide attempts. Females generally differ from males in that they are prone to even greater amounts of depression with fewer cases of alcohol or other drug abuse (ABC News 2000).

Besides posing a direct health threat because of their physiological effects, drugs of abuse can precipitate suicide attempts due to their pharmacological impact. A number of studies have found a very high correlation between acute suicidal behavior and drug use (Buckstein et al. 1993). One report noted that adolescent alcoholics have a suicide rate 58 times greater than the national average. In another study, 30% of adolescent alcoholics had made suicide attempts, although 92% admitted to a history of having suicidal thoughts (Daily 1992b).

It has been speculated that the incidence of suicide in drug-consuming adolescents is high because both types of behavior are the consequence of an inability to develop fundamental adult attributes of confidence, self-esteem, and independence. When drug use does not make up for their need for these characteristics, the resulting frustrations are intensified and ultimately played out in the suicide act.

Most adolescents experiment with drugs for reasons not related to antisocial or deviant behavior but rather due to curiosity, desire for recreation, boredom, desire to gain new insights and experiences, or urge to heighten social interactions. These adolescents are not likely to engage in self-destructive behavior. In addition, adolescents from "healthy" family environments are not likely to attempt suicide. Specifically, Daily (1992b) stated that the families least likely to have suicidal members are those that

- Express love and show mutual concern
- Are tolerant of differences and overlook failings
- Encourage the development of self-confidence and self-expression
- Have parents who assume strong leadership roles but are not autocratic
- Have interaction characterized by humor and good-natured teasing
- Are able to serve as a source of joy and happiness to their members

Suicide is more likely to be attempted by those adolescents who turn to alcohol and other drugs to help them cope with serious emotional and personality conflicts and frustrations. These susceptible teenagers represent approximately 5% of the adolescent population (Beschner and Friedman 1985; Siegel and Senna 1997). Wright (1985) found that four features significantly contribute to the likelihood of suicidal thought in high school students:

1. Parents with interpersonal conflicts who often use an adolescent child with drug problems as the scapegoat for family problems
2. Fathers who have poor, and often confrontational, relationships with their children
3. Parents who are viewed by their adolescent children as being emotionally unstable, usually suffering from perpetual anger and depression

4. A sense of frustration, desperation, and inability to resolve personal and emotional difficulties through traditional means

Clearly, it is important to identify those adolescents who are at risk for suicide and to provide immediate care and appropriate emotional support.

Sexual Violence and Drugs

Alcohol use has been closely associated with almost every type of sexual abuse in which the adolescent is victimized. "For the perpetrator, being under the influence may remove both physical and psychological inhibitors which keep people from acting out violently. They may also use alcohol or drugs as an excuse for criminal behavior" (WCASA 1997, p. 13). For example, alcohol is by far the most significant factor in date, acquaintance, and gang rapes involving teenagers (Parrot 1988; Prendergast 1994). The evidence for alcohol involvement in incest is particularly overwhelming. Approximately 4 million children in America live in incestuous homes with alcoholic parents. In addition, 42% of drug-abusing female adolescents have been victims of sexual abuse (Daily 1992a). It is estimated that almost half of the offenders consume alcohol before molesting a child and at least one-third of the perpetrators are chronic alcoholics. Finally, 85% of child molesters were sexually abused themselves as children, usually at the same age as their victims, and the vast majority of these molesters abused drugs as adolescents (Daily 1992a).

These very disturbing associations illustrate the relationship between drugs and violent sexual behavior both in terms of initiating the act and because of the act. The effects of such sexual violence are devastating and far-reaching. Thus, incest victims are themselves more likely than the general population to abuse drugs as adolescents and to engage in antisocial delinquency, prostitution, depression, and suicide (Daily 1992a).

Gangs and Drugs

The very disturbing involvement of adolescents in gangs and gang-related activities and violence is a social phenomenon that first became widely recognized in the 1950s and 1960s. Hollywood, for example, introduced America to the problems of adolescent gangs in the classic movies *Blackboard*

Jungle and *West Side Story*. Although the basis for gang involvement has not changed over the years, the levels of violence and public concern have increased dramatically. Many communities consider gang-related problems to be their number one social issue. Access to sophisticated weaponry and greater mobility have drawn unsuspecting neighborhoods and innocent bystanders into the often-violent clashes of **intragang** and **intergang** warfare. Individuals and communities have been reacting angrily to this growing menace. To deal effectively with the threats of gang-initiated violence and crime, however, it is important to understand why gangs form, what their objectives are, how they are structured, and how to discourage adolescent involvement.

Children often join gangs because they are neglected by their parents, lack positive role models, and fail to receive adequate adult supervision. Other motivations for joining a gang include peer pressures, low self-esteem, and the perceived easy acquisition of money from gang-related drug dealing and other criminal activities.

In comparison to traditional, formal youth organizations, juvenile gangs may appear disorganized. Research shows, however, that verbal rules, policies, customs, and hierarchies of command are rigidly observed within the gang. Thus, common values and attitudes exist:

1. Gang membership is usually defined in socioeconomic, racial, and ethnic terms, and adolescents involved have similar backgrounds.
2. Gang members are distinguished by a distinctive and well-defined dress code. Violation of this code by members, or mimicking of the dress code by non-gang members can result in ostracism, ridicule, physical abuse, and violence.
3. Leadership and seniority within the gang are defined by vested time in belonging to the gang, age, loyalty, and demonstrated delinquent cleverness (often related to drug dealing and other crimes).
4. Gang members use gang slang to ensure *camaraderie* and group loyalty.

Although a stable home life does not ensure that an adolescent will not become involved with gang-related activity, a strong family environment and guidance from respected parents and guardians are clearly deterrents (Lale 1992). Many gang members are children from dysfunctional, broken, or single-parent homes. Many parents are aware of their children's gang involvement but they lack the skill, confidence, and authority to deter the gang or curtail drug involvement of their teenagers. To make matters worse, ineffective parents often discourage or even interfere with involvement by outside authorities due to misdirected loyalty to their children and/or to avoid embarrassment to their family and community.

Because troubled adolescents are often estranged from their families, they are particularly influenced by their peer groups. These teenagers are most likely to associate with groups whose members have similar backgrounds and problems and who make them feel accepted. Because of this vulnerability, adolescents may become involved with local gangs. In summary, gangs offer the following:

- Fellowship and camaraderie
- Identity and recognition
- Membership and belonging
- Family substitution and role models
- Security and protection
- Diversion and excitement
- Friendships and structure
- Money and financial gain for relatively little effort
- Ability to live the crazy life (*vida loca*) (Sanders 1994; Shelden et al. 2001) or *locura* (craziness) (Shelden et al. 2004)

In the United States, estimates of the total number of existing gangs vary widely. For example, in Chicago, estimates range from 12,000 to 120,000 gang members. Spergel (1990) provided the following percentages of those who are reportedly in gangs within a particular school population in the Chicago area: 5% of the elementary school youths, 10% of all high school youths, 20% of those in special school programs, and, more alarmingly perhaps, 35% of those between 16 and 19 years of age who have dropped out of school

KEY TERMS

intragang
between members of the *same* gang

intergang
between members of the *different* gangs

(Shelden et al. 2001). Keep in mind that these data are for just one city.

Research shows that teenage gangs are becoming major players in the drug trade (Siegel and Senna 1997). Two of the largest gangs in Los Angeles, the Bloods and the Crips, are examples of this trend. Estimated membership in these two gangs exceeds 20,000. In the past, organized crime families maintained a monopoly on the Asian heroin market. Today, youth gangs have entered this trade, for two reasons: (1) Recent efforts and successes in prosecuting top mob bosses by criminal justice officials have created opportunities for new players, and (2) demand has grown for cocaine and synthetic drugs that are produced locally in many U.S. cities. In Los Angeles and most major larger cities, drug-dealing gangs maintain "rock houses" or "stash houses" (where crack cocaine is used and sold) that serve as selling and distribution centers for hard drugs. The crack cocaine found in these "rock houses" is often supplied or run by gang members (Siegel and Senna 1997).

To a lesser extent, other, less violent gangs with smaller memberships are also involved in drug dealing. Recent research shows that the media may exaggerate the percentage of gangs involved in drug dealing. Citywide drug dealing by tightly organized "super" gangs appears to be on the decline and is being superseded by the activities of loosely organized, "neighborhood-based groups" (Siegel and Senna 1997). The main reason for this shift is that federal and state law enforcement of drug laws have forced drug dealers to become "flexible, informal organizations [rather] than rigid vertically organized gangs with . . . [leaders] . . . who are far removed from day-to-day action [on the street]" (Siegel and Senna 1997, p. 409).

Drug use and gang-related activities are often linked but the relationship is highly variable (Curry and Spergel 1997; Fagan 1990). Clearly, problems with drugs exist without gangs and gang-related activities can occur despite the absence of drugs; however, because they have common etiologies, their occurrences are often intertwined. Most adolescents who are associated with gangs are knowledgeable about drugs. Many gang members have experimented with drugs, much like other adolescents their age. However, the hard-core gang mem-

bers are more likely to be engaged not only in drug use, but also in drug dealing as a source of revenue to support the gang-related activities (Lale 1992; Siegel and Senna 1997). The types of drugs used and their significance and functions vary from gang to gang (Fagan 1990; Siegel and Senna 1997). For example, many Latino gangs do not profit from drug trafficking but are primarily interested in using hard-core drugs such as heroin and phencyclidine (PCP). In contrast, African American gangs tend to be more interested in the illicit commercial value of drugs and often engage in dealing crack and other cocaine forms.

PREVENTION, INTERVENTION, AND TREATMENT OF ADOLESCENT DRUG PROBLEMS

The most effective way to prevent adolescent gang involvement is to identify, at an early age, those children at risk and provide them with lifestyle alternatives. Important components of such strategies are as follows:

- Encourage parental awareness of gangs and teach parents how to address problems in their own families that may encourage gang involvement.
- Provide teenagers with alternative participation in organizations or groups that satisfy their needs for camaraderie, participation, and emotional security in a constructive way. These groups can be organized around athletics, school activities, career development, or service rendering.
- Help children to develop coping skills that will enable them to deal with the frustration and stress in their personal lives.
- Educate children about gang-related problems and help them understand that, like drugs, gangs are the result of problems and are not the solutions.

As with most health problems, the sooner drug abuse is identified in the adolescent, the greater the likelihood that the problem can be resolved. It can be difficult to recognize signs of drug abuse in teenagers because their behavior can be erratic and unpredictable even under the best of circumstances. In fact, many of the behavioral patterns that occur coincidentally with drug problems are also present when drugs are not a problem. However, frequent occurrence or clustering of these behaviors may indicate the presence of substance abuse. The behaviors that can be warning signs include the following (Archambault 1992):

- Abruptly changing the circle of friends
- Experiencing major mood swings
- Continually challenging rules and regulations
- Overreacting to frustrations
- Being particularly submissive to peer pressures
- Sleeping excessively
- Keeping very late hours
- Withdrawing from family involvement
- Letting personal hygiene deteriorate
- Becoming isolated
- Engaging in unusual selling of possessions
- Manipulating family members
- Becoming abusive toward other members of the family
- Frequently coming home at night "high"

Prevention of Adolescent Drug Abuse

Logically, the best treatment for drug abuse is to prevent the problem from starting. This approach, referred to as **primary prevention**, has been typically viewed as total abstinence from drug use (see Chapter 17). Informational scare tactics are frequently used as a component of primary prevention strategies. These messages often focus on a dangerous (although in some cases rare) potential side effect and present the warning against drug use in a graphic and frightening fashion. Although this approach may scare naive adolescents away from drugs, many adolescents today, especially if they are experienced, question the validity of the scare tactics and ignore the message.

Another form of primary prevention is to encourage adolescents to become involved in formal groups, such as structured clubs or organizations, in an effort to reduce the likelihood of substance abuse (Howard 1992). Group memberships can help adolescents develop a sense of belonging and contributing to a productive, desirable objective. This involvement can also provide the adolescent with the strength to resist undesirable peer pressures. In contrast, belonging to informal groups such as gangs—groups with loose structures and ill-defined, often antisocial objectives—can lead to participation in poorly chaperoned parties, excessive sexual involvement, and nonproductive activities. Adolescent members of such poorly defined organizations tend to drink alcohol at an earlier age and are more likely to use other substances of abuse.

Some experts claim that primary prevention against drug use is unrealistic for many adolescents. They believe that no strategy is likely to stop adolescents from experimenting with alcohol or other drugs of abuse, especially if these substances are part of their home environment (e.g., if alcohol or tobacco is routinely used) and are viewed as normal, acceptable, and even expected behaviors (Howard 1992). For these adolescents, it is important to recognize when drug use moves from experimentation or a social exercise to early stages of a problem and to prevent serious dependence from developing. This approach, referred to as **secondary prevention**, consists of (1) teaching adolescents about the early signs of abuse, (2) teaching adolescents how to assist peers and family members with drug problems, and (3) teaching adolescents how and where help is available for people with drug problems (Archambault 1992). Regardless of the prevention approach used, adolescents need to understand that drugs are never the solution for emotional difficulties, nor are they useful for long-term coping.

Treatment of Adolescent Drug Abuse

To provide appropriate treatment for adolescent drug abuse, the severity of the problem must be ascertained. The criteria for such assessments include the following:

- Differentiating between abuse and normal adolescent experimentation with drugs
- Distinguishing between minor abuse and severe dependency on drugs

KEY TERMS

primary prevention
prevention of any drug use

secondary prevention
preventing drug use, from either casual or recreational to drug dependence

• Distinguishing among behavioral problems resulting from (1) general behavioral disorders, such as juvenile delinquency; (2) mental retardation; and (3) drugs of abuse

There is no single best approach for treating adolescent substance abuse. Occasionally, the troubled adolescent is admitted to a clinic and treated on an inpatient basis. The inpatient approach is very expensive and creates a temporary "artificial" environment that may be of limited value in preparing adolescents for the problems to be faced in their real homes and neighborhoods. However, the advantage of an inpatient approach is that adolescents can be managed better and their behavior can be more tightly monitored and controlled (Hoshino 1992).

A more practical and routine treatment approach is to allow adolescents to remain in their natural environment and to provide the necessary life skills to be successful at home, in school, and in the community. For example, adolescents being treated for drug dependence should be helped with

• Schoolwork, so that appropriate progress toward high school graduation occurs
• Career skills, so that adolescents can become self-reliant and learn to care for themselves and others
• Family problems and learning to communicate and resolve conflicts

If therapy is to be successful, it is important to improve the environment of the drug-abusing adolescent. This aspect of treatment includes disassociation of the adolescent from groups (such as gangs) or surroundings that encourage drug use and promotes association with healthy and supportive groups (such as a nurturing family) and experiences (such as athletics and school activities). Although desirable, such separation is not always possible, especially if the family and home environment are factors that encourage abuse; the likelihood of therapeutic success is substantially diminished under these circumstances.

Often, therapeutic objectives are facilitated by positive reinforcement that encourages life changes that eliminate access to and use of drugs. This goal can frequently be achieved by association with peers who have similar drug and social problems but are motivated to make positive changes in

their life. Group sessions with such peers are held under the supervision of a trained therapist and consist of members sharing problems and solutions (Hoshino 1992). Some other recent options include holistic therapies such as acupuncture, homeotherapy, massage therapy, aromatherapy, yoga, nutrition therapy, and many more options that were once marginalized by the medical profession (Apostolides 1996).

Another useful approach is to discourage use of drugs by reducing their reinforcing effects. This result can sometimes be achieved by substituting a stronger positive or negative reinforcer. For example, if adolescents use drugs because they believe these substances cause good feelings and help them cope with emotional problems, it may be necessary to replace the drug-taking behavior with other activities that make the adolescent feel good without the drug (such as participation in sports or recreational activities). Negative reinforcers, such as parental discovery and punishment or police apprehension, may discourage drug use by teenagers who are willing to conform and respect authorities. However, negative approaches are ineffective deterrents for nonconforming, rebellious adolescents. Negative reinforcers also do not tend to discourage adolescent use of substances that are more socially acceptable, such as alcohol, tobacco, and even marijuana (Howard 1992).

Regardless of the treatment approach, adolescents must meet several basic objectives if therapy for their drug dependence is to be successful (Daily 1992b):

• Realize that "drugs do not solve problems"—they only make the problems worse.
• Understand why they turned to drugs in the first place.
• Be convinced that abandoning drugs grants them greater independence and control over their own lives.
• Understand that drug abuse is a symptom of underlying problems that need to be resolved.

SUMMARY OF ADOLESCENT DRUG ABUSE

Drug abuse by adolescents is particularly problematic in the United States. The teenage years are filled with experimentation, searching, confusion, rebellion, poor self-image, and insecurity. These attributes, if not managed properly, can cause inappropriate coping and lead to problems such as drug dependence, gang involvement, violence, criminal behavior, and suicide. Clearly, early detection of severe underlying emotional problems and application of effective early preventive therapy are important for proper management. Approaches to treatment of drug abuse problems must be individualized because each adolescent is a unique product of physiological, psychological, and environmental factors.

Almost as important as early intervention for adolescent drug abuse problems is recognizing when treatment is *unnecessary*. We should not be too quick to label all young drug users as antisocial and emotionally unstable. In most cases, teenagers who have used drugs are merely experimenting with new emotions or exercising their newfound freedom. In such situations, nonintervention is usually better than therapeutic meddling. For the most part, if adolescents are given the opportunity, they will work through their own feelings, conflicts, and attitudes about substance abuse, and they will develop a responsible philosophy concerning the use of these drugs.

Drug Use in College Student Subcultures

Chapter 8 includes a lengthy discussion of alcohol use and abuse by college students. This section focuses on college undergraduate use of alcohol not discussed in that chapter, with additional emphasis on the use and abuse of illicit drugs by college students currently attending institutions of higher education.

Table 16.5 compares trends in the annual use of various types of licit and illicit drugs by full-time college students with "others" who are the same age (1 to 4 years beyond high school) but are *not* attending college. Overall, full-time college students (36.5%) were slightly less likely to use any illicit drugs in 2003 than others (40.9%). The rates of annual drug use for college students and for others were equal with regard to hallucinogen use (7.4%). Table 16.5 also shows that college students were *more likely* to use alcohol (81.7% of college students versus 76.7% of others) and Ritalin (4.7% of college students using this drug com-

pared to 3% of others). With the exception of these two drugs, respondents not attending college were more likely to use all the other drugs listed in Table 16.5.

Table 16.6 shows yearly trends in drug use among U.S. college students from 2000 through 2003 (Johnston et al., 2004b). This table details the percentages of college students who used drugs in the past 12 months before the surveys were administered. The main finding is that the overall use of any illicit drugs remained fairly constant from 2000 to 2003—approximately 37%, when averaging the 4 years of surveying. From 1994 to 2000, some slight increases and decreases (depending on the drug) in the overall use of illicit drugs, including marijuana, MDMA, and opioids, were noted. Further, the following trends show modest increases, decreases, and not much change:*

Modest Percentage *Increased Usage* from 2000 to 2003 (unless noted otherwise)

- Any illicit drug other than marijuana
- LSD (steep drop in percentage using)
- Cocaine and crack use
- Other narcotics, OxyContin, and Vicodin
- Tranquilizers
- Sedatives (barbiturates)

Modest Percentage *Decreased Usage* from 2000 to 2003

- Cigarettes
- MDMA (Ecstasy)

Not Much Change (Stable Percentages) in Usage

- Alcohol
- Marijuana
- Hallucinogens
- Amphetamines

REASONS FOR COLLEGE STUDENTS' DRUG USE

Figure 16.2 shows the primary reasons why a sample survey of 1232 male and female college students used alcohol and other drugs. The major reasons cited in this sample survey were (1) to have

---

*Rates for many of the drugs listed as experiencing increases and decreases in use are very slight percentage differences from 2000 through 2003.

Table 16.5 Annual Prevalence of Use of Drugs, 2003: Full-Time College Students Versus Others 1 to 4 Years Beyond High School (entries are percentages, highest to lowest)

	FULL-TIME COLLEGE STUDENTS	OTHERS
Any illicit drug*	36.5%	40.9%
Any illicit drug* other than marijuana	17.9	23.6
Alcohol	81.7	76.7
Cigarettes	35.2	47.6
Marijuana	33.7	36.0
Other narcotics†	8.7	11.4
OxyContin	2.2	4.5
Vicodin	7.5	11.2
Hallucinogens	7.4	7.4
LSD	1.4	1.9
Amphetamines†	7.1	9.4
Ritalin	4.7	3.0
Methamphetamine	2.6	4.4
Ice	0.9	2.2
Tranquilizers	6.9	8.4
Cocaine	5.4	8.8
Crack	1.3	1.8
MDMA (Ecstasy)	4.4	6.7
Sedatives† (barbituates)	4.1	6.2
Inhalants	1.8	1.9
Rohypnol	0.4	0.9
GHBs	0.3	0.7
Heroin	0.2	0.6
Ketamine	1.0	1.4

*Use of "any illicit drug" includes use of marijuana, hallucinogens, cocaine, or heroin, or any use of other narcotics, amphetamines, sedatives (barbituates), or tranquilizers not under a doctor's orders.

†Only drug use that was not under a doctor's orders is included here.

Source: Johnston, L. D., P. M. O'Malley, J. G. Bachman, and J. E. Schulenberg. *Monitoring the Future National Survey Results on Drug Use, 1975–2003. Volume II: College Students and Adults Ages 19–45.* Bethesda, MD: National Institute on Drug Abuse, 2004.

Table 16.6 **Trends in Annual Use of Drugs Among College Students 1 to 4 Years Beyond High School (percentage who used in the past 12 months except as noted)**

	2000	2001	2002	2003
Approximate weighted *N*	1350	1340	1260	1270
Any illicit drug*	36.1%	37.9%	37.0%	36.5%
Any illicit drug other than marijuana*	15.6	16.4	16.6	17.9
Alcohol	83.2	83.0	82.9	81.7
Cigarettes	41.3	39.0	38.3	35.2
Marijuana	34.0	35.6	34.7	33.7
Hallucinogens	6.7	7.5	6.3	7.4
LSD	4.3	4.0	2.1	1.4
MDMA (Ecstasy)	9.1	9.2	6.8	4.4
Amphetamines†	6.6	7.2	7.0	7.1
Ritalin	NA	NA	5.7	4.7
Methamphetamine	1.6	2.4	1.2	2.6
Crystal methamphetamine (ice)	0.5	0.6	0.8	0.9
Cocaine	4.8	4.7	4.0	5.4
Crack	0.9	0.9	0.4	1.3
Other narcotics†	4.5	5.7	7.4	8.7
OxyContin	NA	NA	1.5	2.2
Vicodin	NA	NA	6.9	7.5
Tranquilizers	4.2	5.1	6.7	6.9
Sedatives (barbiturates)†	3.7	3.8	3.7	4.1
Inhalants	2.9	2.8	2.0	1.8
Heroin	0.5	0.4	0.1	0.2
Rohypnol	NA	NA	0.7	0.4
GHB	NA	NA	0.6	0.3
Ketamine	NA	NA	1.3	1.0

*Use of "any illicit drug" includes any use of marijuana, hallucinogens, cocaine, or heroin, or any use of other narcotics, amphetamines, sedatives (barbiturates), or tranquilizers not under a doctor's orders.

†Only drug use that was not under a doctor's orders is included here.

Source: Johnston, L. D., P. M. O'Malley, J. G. Bachman, and J. E. Schulenberg. *Monitoring the Future National Survey Results on Drug Use, 1975–2003. Volume II: College Students and Adults Ages 19–45.* Bethesda, MD: National Institute on Drug Abuse, 2004.

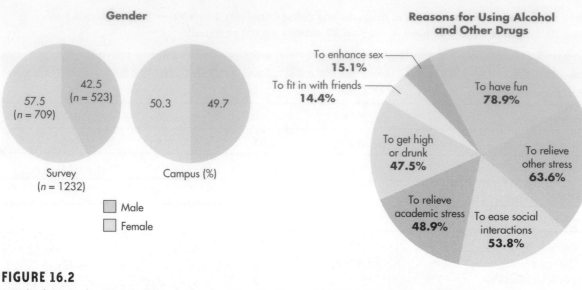

FIGURE 16.2

Sample of reasons for using alcohol and other drugs from the Campus Alcohol and Drug Resource Center at the University of Florida, 1999.

....

Source: Reprinted with permission from Campus Alcohol Drug Resource Center at the University of Florida, *Alcohol and Other Drug Use, 1999.* University of Florida, 2000. Available http://www.health.ufl.edu/shcc/cadrc.htm.

fun (78.9%), (2) to relieve stress (63.9%), and (3) to ease social interactions (53.8%). This sample also reveals that within the past 12 months, approximately 89% used alcohol, 37% used marijuana (or hash or hash oil), and 40% used cigarettes. Approximately 74% of respondents were white, 12% were Hispanic, and 12% were African American (Campus Alcohol Drug Resource Center 2000). This survey alone indicates that the use of alcohol and other drugs on most larger state universities continues to be rampant.

ADDITIONAL NOTEWORTHY FINDINGS REGARDING DRUG USE BY COLLEGE STUDENTS

The following sections describe the most recent significant studies and findings regarding the use of drugs by college students.

Patterns of Alcohol and Other Drug Use

Recent literature reviews of undergraduates' substance use and abuse and the prevalence patterns of alcohol and other drug use found that the most popular substance used by undergraduates is alcohol, which was used by about 90% of students at least once a year. Heavy alcohol use, which includes binge drinking, ranged from 20% to 40% in this group: "while binge drinking decreased by 6% among dormitory residents between 1993 and 1999, it increased by about the same amount among those living off campus. Nearly 80% of binge drinkers live in a fraternity or sorority house, often off campus" (Marklein 2000, p. 1). Other results showed that alcohol use was associated with serious and acute problems such as alcoholism, poor academic performance, drinking and driving, and criminalistic behavior (e.g., driving while intoxicated, vandalism, violence). From 1997 to 1998, alcohol arrests in the nation's colleges increased by 24.3%; this is reported as the largest increase in 7 years. In comparing the same 2 years, drug law violations on U.S. campuses increased by 11.1% (Nicklin 2000).

Summarized in the following list are other significant findings regarding alcohol and other drug use:

- During the 2 weeks before the survey, 39% of college students had "binged" on alcohol (Johnston et al. 2000b).

- Among college students, rates of binge drinking were highest among whites—43.3% for males and 24.4% for females. Among African Americans, the rates were 24.8% for males and 5.4% for females. Among Asians, the rates were 32% for males and 20% for females.
- Young adults ages 18 to 25 are most likely to binge or drink heavily; 54% of the drinkers in this age group binge and about one in four are heavy drinkers.
- "College students who frequently binge drink are more likely to smoke cigarettes and use illegal drugs as well" (Hitt 2001, p. 1).
- Past-month alcohol use was reported by 63.1% of full-time college students compared with 53.3% of their counterparts who were not currently enrolled full time. Binge and heavy-use rates for college students were 42.5% and 18.2%, respectively, compared with 37.7% and 12.1%, respectively, for other persons aged 18 to 22 (SAMHSA 2002).
- A clear relationship exists between alcohol use and grade point average (GPA) among college students: students with GPAs of a "D" or "F" equivalent drink three times as much as those who earn "A" equivalent GPAs.
- The National Household Survey on Drug Abuse (NHSDA) reports that youths who received grades of D or lower were more likely than those with higher grades to have used cigarettes, alcohol, or illicit drugs during the past month (NHSDA 2002).
- Almost half of college students who were victims of campus crimes said they were drinking or using other drugs when they were victimized.
- Researchers estimate that alcohol use is implicated in one- to two-thirds of sexual assault and acquaintance or date rape cases among teens and college students.

Predicting Drug Use for First-Year College Students

The best predictor of drug use for first-year college students was drug use during a typical month in the senior year of high school. Overall, college students responding to a questionnaire were found to use marijuana less frequently than they did in high school. Further, alcohol use increased early in the college years. Although the frequency of alcohol use increased, the number of times that college students got drunk did not rise. Most of these students found new friends in college with whom they got drunk. Alcohol and drug use depended on the choice of new college friends (Leibsohn 1994).

Dormitories for Non–Drug-Using Students

In 1988, Rutgers University was one of the first universities to create a dormitory for students who are recuperating addicts and who want to stay away from the alcohol-charged atmosphere of conventional dormitories. The dormitory at Rutgers maintains strict rules and careful management (Witham 1995). Other universities offer similar variations for on-campus living. In 1989, the University of Michigan opened a substance-free housing facility and set aside 500 dormitory spaces; 1200 students applied for these spaces (Belsie 1995).

Remaining Popularity of Certain Types of "Softer" Drugs

Marijuana and psilocybin mushrooms are two types of illicit recreational drugs whose popularity appeared to grow in the 1990s and to date remain sought after (popular) on most college campuses. Referred to as "soft drugs," these substances are commonly used on most college campuses (Ravid 1995).

> Weed and coke are great, but when the "shrooms" [referring to psilocybin mushrooms] are in town, it is a special treat. Friends on other campuses, the big state university campuses, are lucky to have more different types of drugs available. At our university, both "shrooms" and real hydroponic weed happen about one or two times a semester. *(From Venturelli's research files, male, 21 years of age, attending a smaller comprehensive university in the Midwest, June 12, 2003.)*

Nationwide surveys showed that in yearly drug use averages from 1984 through 1999, there was a steady progressive increase in the use of hallucinogens, which includes psilocybin mushrooms, Ecstasy, and LSD. In 1984 (the first year of the survey), 3.7% of college students used LSD; in 1999, 5.4% used this same drug. Similarly, in 1984, 6.2%

used hallucinogens (excluding LSD) and in 1999, 7.8% used these same hallucinogenic-type drugs (Johnston et al. 2000b). Concerning college students' use of MDMA (Ecstasy) in 2000, the annual use was 9% (Johnston et al. 2001).

According to a 1990 study, with the exception of marijuana, psilocybin mushrooms and Ecstasy/MDMA were the most widely used illicit drugs among first- and second-year, full-time college students. Through studies based on self-reporting (which is not a representative nationwide sample), a fair number of universities reported that about 24% of their drug-using students use psilocybin mushrooms. Use of Ecstasy/MDMA also increased from 16% to 24%.

The occasional use of cocaine (a "harder" drug) increased from 5.9% in 1995 to 6.7% in 1996 (Bennett et al. 1999). This increase was documented in a sample of 2710 students at an undergraduate university in the Southwest. More than likely, the high cost of cocaine keeps the "occasional use" from becoming "frequent use." Nevertheless, cocaine is another drug that appeared to be part of the drug scene on most campuses in the 1990s and in the beginning of the 21st century.

Steroid Usage Patterns

A study of 58,625 college students from 78 colleges and universities in the United States (Meilman et al. 1995) concluded the following:

- Steroid users consumed dramatically more alcohol and demonstrated higher rates of binge drinking than other students.
- A significantly higher percentage of steroid users than nonusers reported using tobacco, marijuana, cocaine, amphetamines, sedatives, hallucinogens, opiates, inhalants, and designer drugs.

- A higher percentage of steroid users than nonusers reported experiencing negative consequences because of substance abuse. Such negative consequences included arrest, public intoxication, driving under the influence, court-ordered community service, and disciplinary actions by university officials.
- A greater percentage of steroid users than nonusers reported family histories of alcohol abuse and other drugs.

Rohypnol and Date Rape

Rohypnol, also known as the "date-rape drug," is one of six drugs recently referred to as **club drugs**. The other club drugs are MDMA (Ecstasy), gamma-hydroxybutyrate (GHB), ketamine, methamphetamine, and LSD. Club drugs are used by individuals at all-night dance parties such as "raves" or "trances," dance clubs, and bars. All of these drugs are colorless, tasteless, and odorless. They can be added unobtrusively to beverages by individuals who may want to intoxicate or sedate others (NIDA 2000). In cases of sexual assault or rape, the small white Rohypnol pills are slipped into a person's drink, causing the person to black out and have no memories of events that occurred while he or she was under the influence of the drug. A minority of undergraduates also use the drug to intensify the effects of marijuana and alcohol. One problem with identifying whether this drug has been given to an unwilling recipient is that Rohypnol can be detected only for 60 hours after ingestion (Lively 1996).

Rohypnol (flunitrazepam) belongs to a class of drugs known as benzodiazepines (such as Valium and Xanax). Although this drug is not approved for prescription use in the United States, it is approved and used in more than 60 countries as a treatment for insomnia, as a sedative, and as a presurgery anesthetic (NIDA 2000).

KEY TERMS

Rohypnol
the "date-rape drug," used on many college campuses

club drugs
a new class of illicit drugs used on college campuses, at bars, in night clubs, and at "raves" where drinking and dancing occur; club drugs include MDMA (Ecstasy), GHB, Rohypnol, ketamine, methamphetamine, and LSD

HIV and AIDS

AIDS came to the attention of medical authorities in the United States on June 4, 1981, in a newsletter from the Centers for Disease Control and Prevention (CDC) in Atlanta, Georgia (Zuger 2000). HIV, the virus that causes AIDS, was not discovered until 1983. Since 1981, 830,000 cases of AIDS have been reported to the CDC (CDC 2004b). Of these cases, approximately 74% were males and 26% were females. Worldwide, more than 19 million people have died of AIDS, almost 25 million of them in sub-Saharan Africa. Currently, there are 34 million people living with AIDS, and 13 million children who have been orphaned by the disease (*USA Today* 2000, p. 1). Of the 34 million people living with AIDS, approximately 70% live in South Africa, and 1 million more were infected last year (CDC 2004a).

As of December 1999, the CDC reported that 113,002 adults, adolescents, and children were living in the United States with HIV and 290,542 were living with AIDS. Between 1997 to 1999, 367,965 males and 62,476 females died from AIDS (CDC 1999). The CDC estimates that approximately 950,000 people in the United States are infected with HIV, but one-fourth have yet to be diagnosed (MyDNA.com 2005).

NATURE OF HIV INFECTION AND RELATED SYMPTOMS

AIDS (acquired immunodeficiency syndrome) is caused by the human immunodeficiency virus (HIV).

AIDS is a disease in which the body's immune system breaks down and is unable to fight off certain infections, known as "opportunistic infections," and other illnesses that take advantage of a weakened immune system.

When a person is infected with HIV, the virus enters the body and lives and multiplies primarily in the white blood cells. These immune cells normally protect us from disease. The hallmark of HIV infection is the progressive loss of a specific type of immune cells called T-helper or CD4 cells.

As the virus grows, it damages or kills CD4 and other cells, weakening the immune system and leaving the individual vulnerable to numerous opportunistic infections and other illnesses, ranging from pneumonia to cancer. The CDC defines someone as having a clinical diagnosis of AIDS if he or she has tested positive for HIV and has one or both of these conditions:

- The person has experienced one or more AIDS-related infections or illnesses.

- The number of CD4 cells has reached or fallen below 200 per cubic millimeter of blood (a measurement known as a T-cell count) (Schernoff and Smith 2001).

As mentioned previously, the immune systems of HIV-positive individuals become severely compromised as important immune cells called CD4+ helper T lymphocytes and macrophages are destroyed (see Figure 16.3). Because these immune cells are crucial in identifying and eliminating infection-causing microorganisms such as bacteria, fungi, and viruses, their deficiency substantially increases the likelihood and severity of infectious diseases. Progression of the disease brings weight loss, infections in the throat ("thrush") and skin (shingles), and other opportunistic infections and/or cancer (e.g., Kaposi's sarcoma). A person with HIV is diagnosed with AIDS when the helper T-cell count in his or her blood falls below $200/mm^3$. Infections become increasingly difficult to control with medication, and consequently severe opportunistic infections, such as pneumonia, meningitis, hepatitis, and tuberculosis, occur and eventually lead to death. The likelihood of introducing these opportunistic infections into the body increases in patients who are injection drug users because they often share injection equipment, such as needles and syringes that are contaminated with disease-causing microorganisms.

An HIV-infected individual may not manifest symptoms of AIDS for as many as 10 to 12 years after the initial infection. Although the HIV infected individual may experience no symptoms, he or she is highly contagious.

After an individual has become infected, he or she may have a brief flu-like illness usually within 6 to 12 weeks. It is not known what determines the length of the latency period, when symptoms are not present. The asymptomatic period eventually ends, however, and signs of immune disorder appear. Initial symptoms of this disease include night sweats, swollen lymph glands, fever, and/or headaches.

DIAGNOSIS AND TREATMENT

It is crucial that HIV-infected people be aware of their condition to avoid activities that might transmit the infection to others. Testing for the

FIGURE 16.3

Disrupting the Assembly Line

HIV survives by invading white blood cells and turning them into virus factories. The process involves several steps, and each offers a potential target for therapy. This diagram shows how HIV does its work and how antiviral drugs do theirs.

·······································

Source: Crowley, G. "Targeting a Deadly Scrap of Genetic Code." C. Blumrich, graphic designer. *Newsweek* (2 December 1996): 69. Copyright © Newsweek, Inc. All rights reserved. Reprinted by permission.

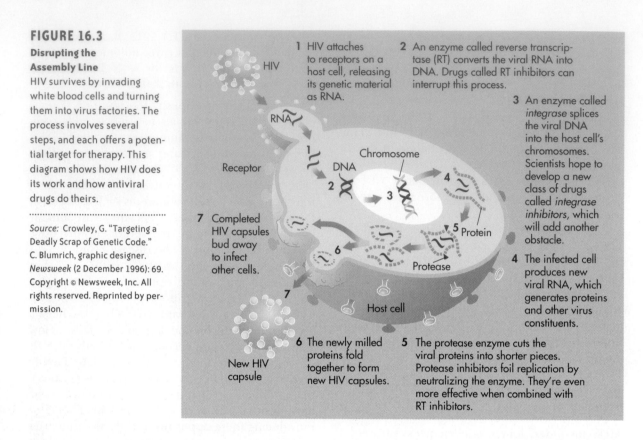

1 HIV attaches to receptors on a host cell, releasing its genetic material as RNA.

2 An enzyme called reverse transcriptase (RT) converts the viral RNA into DNA. Drugs called RT inhibitors can interrupt this process.

3 An enzyme called *integrase* splices the viral DNA into the host cell's chromosomes. Scientists hope to develop a new class of drugs called *integrase inhibitors,* which will add another obstacle.

4 The infected cell produces new viral RNA, which generates proteins and other virus constituents.

5 The protease enzyme cuts the viral proteins into shorter pieces. Protease inhibitors foil replication by neutralizing the enzyme. They're even more effective when combined with RT inhibitors.

6 The newly milled proteins fold together to form new HIV capsules.

7 Completed HIV capsules bud away to infect other cells.

presence of infection has been available since 1985 and is done by determining whether the body is producing antibodies against HIV. Further, since 1996, newspapers, magazines, radio, and television have been advertising a take-at-home HIV antibody test. The presence of these specific antibodies indicates HIV infection. If an individual is infected, it takes 6 to 12 weeks after the HIV exposure before the body produces enough antibodies to be detected in currently available tests. If the antibody is not present within 6 months after HIV exposure, it is likely that infection did not occur (Pietroski 1993).

Although the tests for HIV infection are reliable, false negatives (i.e., the test says no HIV is present even though the individual is infected) and false positives (i.e., the test says the individual

is infected even though no HIV is present) occur in 1 out of 30,000 tests. Because testing positive for HIV is currently perceived as eventually life-threatening and is a highly emotional diagnosis, great effort is made to ensure confidentiality of the test results. The blood specimens to be tested are coded, and the personnel conducting the tests are not allowed to divulge the results to anyone but the individual who was tested. The issue of confidentiality is very controversial, however. It is often difficult to decide who has the right to know when HIV has been detected (see "Point/Counterpoint," Who Should Know the Results of Your HIV Test *If* You Test Positive?).

After a positive HIV diagnosis, the best way to lengthen one's life is to immediately begin drug treatments. The first prescription drug treatment for AIDS, AZT, was introduced in 1987. In 1996, **protease inhibitors** came on the market. When combined with AZT and other drugs, protease inhibitors resulted in miraculous remissions of desperately ill AIDS patients (Zuger 2000). Further, it appears that with such drug combinations, HIV blood lev-

KEY TERMS

protease inhibitors
a major breakthrough class of drugs used to treat HIV-infected individuals

▶Point/Counterpoint

Who Should Know the Results of Your HIV Test *If* You Test Positive?

Most people would probably want to keep such results private, but consider the following. Would your opinion about HIV-positive people keeping their results confidential change in the following circumstances:

▶ You require first aid after a serious auto accident and the emergency medical technician assisting is HIV-positive?

▶ Your doctor is HIV-positive?

▶ Your dentist is HIV-positive?

▶ Your manicurist is HIV-positive?

▶ Your massage therapist is HIV-positive?

▶ Your severely handicapped daughter's elementary school teacher is HIV-positive?

▶ Your lover is HIV-positive?

▶ Your tattoo artist is HIV-positive?

▶ Your jeweler who is about to pierce your daughter's ears is HIV-positive?

▶ Your boxing partner is HIV-positive?

▶ Your jail cellmate is HIV-positive?

Arguments for *not* disclosing HIV-positive results to anyone other than the person undergoing HIV screening are that reporting such results to others would (1) force many people not to take the test for fear of disclosure to others; (2) possibly cause loss of employment (if the results require mandatory reporting to supervisors or managers); (3) unnecessarily stigmatize the HIV-positive person, exposing an infected person to social ostracism and gossip and potentially creating fear and panic in others; and (4) potentially destroy a partner or marriage relationship if the significant other or spouse is notified.

Arguments *for* mandatory disclosure to others potentially affected by the results of this disease include (1) to protect domestic or marital partners, (2) to protect others from HIV-positive workers who could infect them (such as surgeons who are involved in invasive bodily care or procedures), and (3) to honor the public's right to know of the threat of contracting this terminal disease.

Currently, employers cannot legally terminate a worker for being HIV-positive. In cases of direct potential threat to the public, an HIV-positive worker can be reassigned to a different position. Also, in most cases, employers cannot legally inquire about HIV test results. An exception to this is the military and prison, where mandatory testing is required (Atlanta Legal Aid Main Page 1999).

What is your opinion about this issue?

The sooner an HIV-positive person begins drug treatment, the more effective the treatment may be. Knowing this, should HIV-positive individuals be required to inform past sexual partners and people with whom they have shared needles so that these people can be tested (known as "partner notification" or "contact tracing")?

If an HIV-positive surgeon is going to operate on you, your mother, your father, or your child—do you have the right to know? What are the rights of the HIV-positive individual versus the rights of the public?

Source: Atlanta Legal Aid Main Page. *Should You Tell Your Employer That You're HIV Positive?* Atlanta: Emory University, 1999. Available http://www.law.emory.edu/PI?ALAS?disclosure.htm.

els in newly infected patients remain at exceedingly low levels (Zuger 2000). Although the drug combinations do not rid the body of infected cells, results indicate that HIV infections could become as manageable as diabetes (Cowley 1996).

Today, people in the United States and other developed countries can use a number of drugs to treat HIV infection and AIDS. Some of these are designed to treat the opportunistic infec-tions and illnesses that affect people with HIV/AIDS. In addition, several types of drugs seek to prevent HIV from reproducing and destroying the body's immune system. Reverse transcriptase inhibitors attach an HIV enzyme called reverse transcriptase. They include abacavir, delavirdine, didanosine (ddI), efavirenz, lamivudine (3TC), nevirapine, stavudine (d4T), zalcitabine (ddC), and zidovudine (AZT).

Many HIV patents are taking several of these drugs in combination—a regimen known as **highly active antiretroviral therapy (HAART)**. When successful, combinations or "cocktail" therapy can reduce the level of HIV in the bloodstream to very low—even undetectable—levels and sometimes enable the body's CD4 immune cells to rebound to normal levels (American Foundation for AIDS Research [amfAR] 2001, pp. 6–9).

> I take the famous drug "cocktail" and have to wake myself up in the middle of the night around 4 in the morning, then go back to sleep. I am used to it. I know it is a pain in the neck, but I think that despite this, the side effects can even be worse at times. I really don't want to go into it; it's depressing. The bright side: I am still alive after 9 years since diagnosed with AIDS; I am not dead yet. *(Interview with a 52-year-old male, working as a bartender in Chicago, May 18, 2000.)*

The most recent update on HAART indicates that this therapy regimen results in dramatic reduction in the incidence of AIDS and death in individuals infected with HIV (MyDNA.com 2005). Less than 5 years ago, patients took approximately 37 pills per day, a few years later it was a 14-pill-a-day regimen, and today in the majority of cases, only three pills have to be taken each day (Scripps Howard News Service 2003). The pills must be taken regularly each day to ensure effective therapy. The cost of the cocktail can be up to $2000 to $3000 per month. Unfortunately, many health insurance companies continue to actively issue restrictive amendments on their policies that cap reimbursement for such expensive drug therapies. As a result, infected individuals with extensive debt obligations and patients without health insurance are often unable to afford the latest drug therapy.

Some HIV-infected persons taking the current treatment regimens suffer side effects that are so severe they choose to stop taking some of the drugs

necessary to hold off the development of AIDS. Side effects can include diarrhea, bone-marrow suppression, an inability to tolerate the drugs, and tumor-like growths on the neck and other parts of the body. However, the overall success in treating HIV-positive patients has resulted in a 23% drop in HIV-related deaths in 1996 and a 40% drop in such deaths in 1997. Because the drugs halt the progression of HIV to AIDS, the rates of new AIDS cases fell 25% by 1998 (Zuger 2000).

A successful prognosis for HIV infection and AIDS relies on three factors: (1) initiation of a drug regimen as soon as possible after an HIV-positive diagnosis, (2) strict adherence to medical advice and treatment, and (3) maintenance of a healthy diet without drug use or abuse so as to avoid taxing the immune system.

Scientists are optimistic that eventually there will be a vaccine against HIV/AIDS. Although approximately 30 types of vaccines are being studied, the development of such a vaccine after clinical trials can take more than a decade (Fischer 2000). The key is to invent "killer" T cells to shut down or destroy HIV-infected cells (Fischer 2000).

Who Is at Risk for AIDS?

Although anyone can become infected with HIV, its routes of transmission are limited to blood, semen, vaginal fluid, and possibly some other body fluids (Grinspoon 1994). Before the advent of AZT, mothers were more likely to the pass the virus to their children prenatally or through breast milk. HIV is a virus that is not likely to survive outside of the body. Consequently, it is not spread by casual contact, such as by shaking hands, touching, hugging, or kissing (although "deep" kissing with an infected person is not recommended). In addition, it is not spread through food or water, by sharing cups or glasses, by coughing and sneezing, or by using common toilets. It is not spread by mosquitoes or other insects.

The following populations are at greatest risk for contracting AIDS:

1. Men with a history of having had multiple homosexual or bisexual partners
2. Injecting drug users and their sexual partners

3. Heterosexuals with multiple partners
4. Infants born to HIV-infected women (approximately 10% of all HIV-positive mothers have HIV-positive babies)
5. People who receive contaminated blood products, such as for transfusions or treatment of blood disorders (blood banks have nearly completely improved the screening of their blood supplies in the last decade)

See Figures 16.4 and 16.5 for a detailed breakdown of categories of U.S. AIDS cases by type of HIV exposure.

Figure 16.4 shows that approximately 54% of all adult/adolescent men with AIDS report sex with men, and another approximately 23% report injection drug use. An estimated 7% of cases are attributed to male-to-male sexual contact and injection drug use, 15% of male cases are attributed to heterosexual contact, and other risk exposures account for the remaining 1% of cases. Figure 16.5 shows that 68% of women with AIDS attribute their exposure to heterosexual contact, and 30% attribute their exposure to injection drug use.

Other findings regarding age at diagnosis of HIV infection and AIDS reported through 2003 follow (CDC 2004a).

- HIV is the fifth leading cause of death for all Americans between the ages of 25 and 44.
- By age group, 41% of persons living with AIDS were 35 to 44 years old.
- Among African American men and women between the ages of 25 and 44, HIV is the number one cause of death.
- In the United States, approximately 77% of all people who currently have AIDS are male and 23% are female. Worldwide, 73 women are infected for every 100 infected men.
- African Americans account for 42% of all reported AIDS patients in the United States, white Americans account for 36% of AIDS cases, and Hispanic Americans account for 20% of cases (CDC 2004).

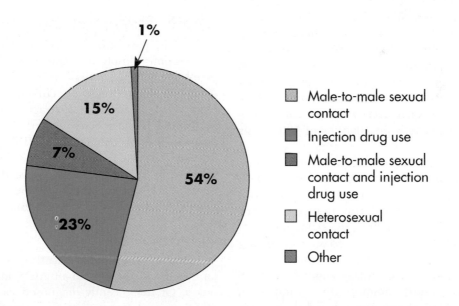

FIGURE 16.4

Approximate percentages of AIDS cases in adult/adolescent men, by risk exposure, United States, 1999–2003.

Source: Centers for Disease Control and Prevention (CDC). *HIV/AIDS Surveillance Report, 2003 (Volume 15).* Atlanta: U.S. Department of Health and Human Services, CDC, 2004.

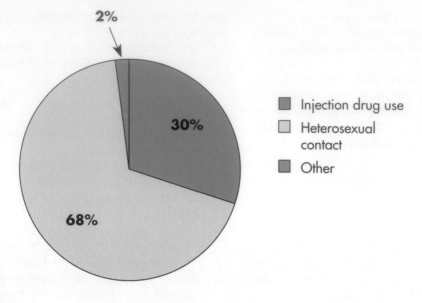

FIGURE 16.5

Approximate percentages of AIDS cases in adult/adolescent women, by risk exposure, United States, 1999–2003.

Source: Centers for Disease Control and Prevention (CDC). *HIV/AIDS Surveillance Report, 2003 (Volume 15)*. Atlanta: U.S. Department of Health and Human Services, CDC, 2004.

• By region, 39% of HIV/AIDS patients resided in the South, 29% in the Northeast, 19% in the West, 10% in the Midwest, and 3% in the U.S. territories. New York, Florida, Texas, and North Carolina reported the highest number of persons with HIV infection in 2003. Most people with AIDS are found in metropolitan areas with populations of 500,000 or more.

• From 1999 through 2003, the estimated number of AIDS cases decreased among injection drug users and among males having sex with males who were also intravenous drug users. From 1999 through 2000, the estimated number of AIDS cases decreased slightly among males having sex with males; however, from 2001 to 2003, the estimated number of AIDS cases increased among this population. Among persons exposed through heterosexual contact, the estimated number of AIDS cases increased each year from 1999 through 2003.

AIDS AND DRUGS OF ABUSE

During the past several years, the AIDS epidemic has become closely associated with drug abuse problems. As mentioned earlier, individuals addicted to illicit drugs are currently the second largest risk group for contracting AIDS. AIDS in women is particularly linked to drug abuse. Nearly 70% of the female AIDS patients are infected because of injection drug use by themselves or by a sexual partner (Glave 1994). Several reasons account for the high incidence of this deadly infection in the drug-abusing population.

Intravenous Drugs

Intravenous drug use has become the most important factor in the spread of AIDS in the United States. Of the recently diagnosed cases of AIDS, 29% resulted from injection drug use (CDC 2000c), with heroin, cocaine, or both being the primary drugs injected. Among severely addicted populations, intravenous drug use is often undertaken with little regard to hygiene, and injection para-phernalia such as needles, syringes, and cotton are frequently shared with other drug addicts (Millstein 1993). Sharing HIV-contaminated injection equipment can easily result in the transmission of this virus. The likelihood of an intravenous drug user contracting AIDS is directly correlated with (1) the frequency of drug injections, (2) the number of partners with whom injection equipment is shared, (3) the frequency of needle sharing, and (4) the frequency of injections in locations where there are high AIDS infection rates, such as in shooting galleries or crack houses (Booth et al. 1993).

Crack

Use of drugs such as crack (Ciba Foundation 1992) and alcohol (Colthurst 1993) tends to compromise judgment and encourage high-risk activities such as injection drug use or sexual risk taking (Beard and Kunsman 1993; Inciardi et al. 1993). In particular, the use of crack has been associated with high rates of HIV infection. Crack addicts often exchange sex for drugs or money to purchase drugs (Inciardi et al. 1993; Mathias 1993). These dangerous activities frequently occur in populations with an already high rate of HIV infection. Once infected, almost half of crack users continue to use sex to obtain their drugs and become a source of HIV infection for others (Diaz and Chu 1993).

ADOLESCENTS AND AIDS

Since the beginning of the HIV/AIDS epidemic, more than 2200 adolescent males ages 13 to 19 years have been reported to have AIDS. Approximately 27% of AIDS cases among adolescent males ages 13 to 19 occurred among those who had hemophilia and acquired their infection before blood products were heat treated to prevent HIV transmission. Injection drug use is more common among the 20- to 24-year-old men reported to have AIDs than among adolescents with AIDS, but less common than among men older than 24 years of age who have AIDS. Approximately 7% of AIDS cases among men ages 13 to 24 years reported heterosexual contact as their exposure category. In 2002, male adolescents between the ages of 13 through 19 who

were diagnosed with AIDS contracted the disease in the following ways (CDC 2004b):

- Male-to-male sexual contact: 41%
- Hemophilia: 27%
- Injection drug use: 10%
- Heterosexual contact: 8%
- Male-to-male sexual contact and injection drug use: 6%
- Other/not identified: 6%
- Transfusion recipient: 4%

Other recent important findings include the following:

- Black and Hispanic adolescents have been disproportionately affected by the HIV/AIDS epidemic. In the United States in 2002, 15% of the adolescent population was black, yet 65% of AIDS cases reported in 13- to 19-year-olds involved African Americans. Hispanics accounted for 16% of the total adolescent population, yet 20% of AIDS cases reported in adolescents involved Hispanic patients.
- Approximately two-thirds of AIDS cases among adolescent and young adult women were attributed to heterosexual contact as the mode of exposure to HIV. Cases among 13- to 19-year-old women (19%) were less likely to be attributed to injection drug use than were cases among 20- to 24-year-old women (29%).
- Most 13- to 19-year-old females reported contracting HIV followed by AIDS through heterosexual contact (66%), injection drug use (19%), and other/not identified causes (15%) (CDC 2004c).
- A recent United Nations Aids Report (UNAIDS) estimated that throughout the world, "one-third of those living with AIDS are aged 15–24" (MSNBC 2004). Further, most of these individuals who contract HIV do not even know they have the disease.
- HIV infection is spreading rapidly among younger urban gay men who are too young to recall the beginning of the AIDS epidemic two decades ago.
- Medical journalists from the University of Massachusetts Medical School in Worcester have reported positive outcomes for infants

born with HIV infection. "During the first 15 years of the epidemic, they note, 15,000 U.S. infants acquired HIV, mainly from their mothers. Today, fewer than 200 U.S. children acquire HIV in a year, and these infections occur largely because the mother did not have appropriate prenatal care to prevent transmission" (Yahoo! 2001; Reuters 2001).

- Nearly half of the roughly 40,000 Americans who become newly infected with HIV each year are younger than the age of 25. Approximately 25% of the people now living with HIV in this country became infected when they were teenagers. More importantly, many young people also use drugs and alcohol, which can increase the likelihood that they will engage in high-risk sexual behavior.
- Adolescents who are most vulnerable to HIV infection include those who are homeless or runaways, juvenile offenders, and school dropouts.
- Worldwide, sexual intercourse is by far the most common mode of HIV transmission. In the United States, as many as half of all new HIV infections are associated either directly or indirectly with injection drug use (i.e., using HIV-contaminated needles to inject drugs or having sexual contact with an HIV-infected drug user) (Body Health Resources 2004).

Three of the principal ways adolescents become infected with HIV are as follows: (1) high-risk sexual activity (unprotected sexual intercourse is reported by more than half of adolescents by the age of 17 years); (2) injection of substances of abuse; and (3) sex with multiple partners (Schaefer et al. 1993; CDC 2004a, 2004b). Clearly, young people must be better educated about HIV, its transmission, and potential consequences before this epidemic becomes even more disastrous in adolescents.

WHAT TO DO ABOUT HIV AND AIDS

What can I do about being HIV-positive? I was diagnosed 3 years ago, and so far, I am basically okay. I have started taking medication to slow down the rate of infection, but one never knows when the first symptoms will suddenly pop up. My lover is clear of the infection and we are careful—usually. I am worried about my condition, but nothing can be done about it. Life is full of good luck and bad luck; so far I have been spared. Regarding tomorrow, who knows. *(From Venturelli's research files, interview with a 32-year-old male hospital administrator, October 10, 1996.)*

To date, the combination of various types of protease inhibitors and antiretroviral therapy medications is the most promising treatment for remaining relatively healthy with HIV. Although protease inhibitors do not completely rid the body of HIV antibodies, this category of drugs is usually successful in holding the virus at low levels in the bloodstream. The current lack of a permanent cure makes prevention the most important element in dealing with the AIDS problem. There are two main strategies for preventing HIV:

- People should be encouraged to adopt safer sexual behavior. Some of the steps to help achieve this include (1) avoiding multiple sex partners, especially if they are strangers or only casual acquaintances; (2) avoiding risk-taking sexual behavior that may allow HIV transmission, such as unprotected vaginal, oral, and anal intercourse; and (3) encouraging individuals who choose to continue high-risk sexual behaviors to use condoms or insist that their sexual partner use a condom.
- Drug abusers should be educated about their risk of contracting AIDS. They should be encouraged to reduce their risk by (1) abstaining from injecting drugs; (2) not sharing injection paraphernalia or always using clean needles (if available through "needle exchange programs"); (3) not sharing drugs with groups with high rates of HIV infection such as those in shooting galleries or crack houses; and (4) disinfecting the equipment (cleaning and boiling equipment for at least 15 minutes) between uses if they continue to share injection equipment.

One of the major difficulties in controlling the AIDS epidemic is identifying where preventive efforts should be focused. Because of limited resources, it is impossible to personally educate everyone in this country about HIV and AIDS. Consequently, our most intense efforts must be targeted at populations and neighborhoods with particularly high HIV infection rates. The National Research Council has declared that, although anyone can acquire AIDS, a handful of neighborhoods have been devastated by this infection, whereas most of the nation remains relatively unscathed (Kolata 1993). It has been speculated that some 35 to 45 large neighborhoods in the United States fuel the AIDS epidemic throughout the country; if HIV infection could be controlled in these areas, the national epidemic would diminish significantly. Because of this hypothesis, it has been proposed that AIDS prevention efforts particularly be focused on younger gay men and injection drug users who have multiple sex partners in the high-density AIDS neighborhoods found in many large metropolitan cities throughout the United States. Even with this focused approach, no one should be fooled into thinking that the HIV/AIDS problem will be eliminated. Everyone should approach potential sexual partners with some degree of caution, especially because the carrier of HIV may be unaware of infection or be reluctant to admit being a carrier for fear of abandonment. One thing is evident: If any doubt exists, we strongly recommend getting tested several times in a row before engaging in potentially life-threatening sexual contact.

The Entertainment Industry and Drug Use

Musicians sing about guzzling liquor and movie stars puff cigarettes and take drugs on the big screen. However, federal officials ask: Where is the unglamorous side of substance use—like hangovers, slurred speech, or trouble with the law (*News Tribune* 1999)? Drug use has a tendency to be displayed or fueled (depending on your perspective) by popular culture. In this section, we discuss three important genres of popular culture—movies, music, and the Internet—as one electronic "subculture" that depicts and promotes drug use.

At the Lollapalooza music festival held in July 1997 in an amphitheater in Massachusetts, the mostly white, suburban teen crowd cheered wildly when rap group Cypress Hill pushed a 6-foot-tall *bong*, or water pipe, onstage. The group sold 5 million copies of its first two albums, one of which included songs titled "Legalize It," "Hits from the Bong," and "I Wanna Get High" (Winters 1997).

In a research study for Columbia's Center on Addiction and Substance Abuse, 76% of 12- to 17-year-olds indicated that the entertainment industry encourages illegal drug use. One 16-year-old daily marijuana user said, "All I know is that almost every song you listen to says something about [drug use]. It puts it into your mind constantly. . . . When you see the celebrities doing it, it makes it seem okay" (Winters 1997, p. 41).

Mel Gibson consuming a drug. Do such pictures have any effect on viewers?

Approximately 5 years ago, rock and rap music industries experienced a heroin epidemic. Although many other rock stars before Kurt Cobain used and abused drugs, Cobain's struggle with heroin and his 1994 suicide appear to have glamorized the use of this drug. "The number of top alternative bands that have been linked to heroin through a member's overdose, arrest, admitted use, or recovery is staggering: Nirvana, Hole, Smashing Pumpkins, Everclear, Blind Melon, Skinny Puppy, 7 Year Bitch, Red Hot Chili Peppers, Stone Temple Pilots, Breeders, Alice in Chains, Sublime, Sex Pistols, Porno for Pyros, and Depeche Mode" (Schoemer 1996, p. 50).

Together these bands have sold more than 60 million albums—"that's a heck of a lot of white, middle-class kids in the heartland" (Schoemer 1996, p. 50). Despite some factions in the music industry attempting to curtail heroin use by rock stars, many claim that the music industry still glamorizes heroin and other drug use.

How pervasive is drug use in today's popular movies and music? Recent research indicates that there is much substance abuse in popular movies and music. Studies revealed that 98% of movies reviewed depicted illicit drugs, alcohol, tobacco, or OTC and prescription medicines. Alcohol and tobacco appeared in more than 90% of movies, and illicit drugs appeared in 22%. About one-fourth (26%) of the movies that depicted illicit drugs contained explicit, graphic portrayals of their preparation and/or ingestion. Substance use was almost never a central theme, and very few movies ever specified motivations for use. Less than one-half (49%) of the movies portrayed short-term consequences of substance use, and about 12% depicted long-term consequences. Of the 669 adult major characters featured in the 200 movies studied, 5% used illicit drugs, 25% smoked tobacco, and 65% consumed alcohol. At least two major characters used illicit drugs in 12% of the movies, tobacco in 44%, and alcohol in 85% (ONDCP 1999).

In summarizing main findings from a study conducted by the Office of National Drug Control Policy (1999) regarding substance use in both movies and songs, the following results were found:

- Alcohol appeared in 93% of the movies and 17% of the songs; tobacco appeared in 89% of the movies but only 3% of the songs.
- Alcohol use was associated with wealth or luxury in 34% of the movies in which it appeared, with sexual activity in 19%, and with crime or violence in 37%.
- Alcohol use was associated with wealth or luxury in 24% of the songs in which it was referenced, with sexual activity in 3%, and with crime or violence in 13%.
- Sixty-three percent of rap songs contained references to substances; only 10% of songs in other categories did.
- In movies depicting illicit drugs, marijuana appeared most frequently (51%), followed by powder cocaine (33%); hallucinogens, heroin or other opiates, and miscellaneous others (each 12%); and crack cocaine (2%).
- In songs referring to illicit drugs, marijuana appeared most frequently (63%), followed by crack cocaine (15%); powder cocaine (10%); and hallucinogens, heroin or other opiates, and miscellaneous others (4% each).

These findings clearly indicate that both movies and songs continue to reflect widespread use of alcohol and other drugs in our culture. Furthermore, their influence on the public viewing audiences continues to have an impact on values and attitudes about the use and/or abuse of drugs. One executive director of a Washington, D.C., area youth group, said, "It's becoming increasingly difficult to administer our preventive drug programs because the youth culture has changed in a manner that a lot more of popular music idolizes the use of marijuana and hallucinogens and that has a profound effect on young people" (Haywood 1996, p. 14).

Another top administrator at the Center for Substance Abuse Prevention of the Substance Abuse and Mental Health Services Administration, agreed, "Our pop culture is sending a lot of pro-drug messages" (Haywood 1996). In addition to these observations, the major findings noted earlier with regard to substance use in movies and songs support the amount of alcohol and other drugs used in these two major types of electronic and audio mediums.

MORE RECENT PROMOTER OF DRUG USE: THE INTERNET

According to the UCLA Center for Communication Policy, for those who use online technology, the Internet is considered the most important source for information—more important than TV or radio. "Some 55% of Internet users said 'most' or 'all' information in cyberspace is reliable and accurate, while only a third of non-users agreed" (Reuters and CNN.com 2000a). A survey of 55,000 Internet users performed by a market research firm called Media Matrix discovered that low-income World Wide Web users are now the fastest-growing U.S. market (Reuters and CNN.com 2000b).

There is no question that pro-drug messages and detailed information are readily available over the Internet. The Internet maintains a unique subculture of drug enthusiasts. Drug use information found online includes how to roll super joints, bake marijuana-laced brownies, grow "magic" psilocybin mushrooms, and create formulas for making amphetamine-like drugs; where to purchase the latest equipment for indoor growing of marijuana; and where to obtain catalogs that offer drug paraphernalia for sale. Similarly, magazines such as *High Times* and *Hemp Times* claim growing numbers of subscribers. Such magazines devote most of their articles, features, advice columns, hemp festival information, and advertisements to the pleasures of drug consumption. Further, chat rooms devoted to finding, growing, purchasing, and making drug substances are growing in popularity. Often, chat rooms and exchange of information on the Internet remain oblivious to nonillicit drug users.

A more recent and alarming occurrence is the boom in illicit drug sales online. Prescription drugs are being sold without a prescription over the Internet. Often solicitations are in the form of spam (unsolicited emails), including multiple offers each day. The International Narcotics Control Board (INCB) reported recently, "90% of online drugs sales take place without a medical prescription" (Join Together.Online and BBC News 2005). The INCB said, "The illicit trade over the Internet has been identified as one of the major sources for prescription medicines abused by children and adolescents in certain countries such as the United States."

Billions of [doses of] controlled substances— some of them highly potent drugs such as oxycodone, equivalent to morphine, and fentanyl, which is many times stronger than morphine, [including Viagra, Xanex and OxyContin (to name a few)]—are being sold by unlicensed Internet pharmacies. (Join Together Online and BBC News 2005)

Clearly, the Internet is becoming a source of illicit drugs for anyone having access to computers, and this audience includes younger teens and adults. Legal suppliers appear to be fueling the trade by providing their products to unlicensed Internet pharmacies that then sell these legally restricted types of drugs (Join Together Online and BBC News 2005).

Although the Internet serves as an immensely valuable medium for learning, conducting business, communicating, and making information available, it is also used by a growing number of drug users as a forum for exchanging and learning about the latest information and techniques of drug consumption. Individuals who use the Internet for this type of information should be particularly wary because it is difficult if not impossible for harmful myths and fallacies posted on the web to be regulated.

Discussion Questions

1. What are two strengths and two weaknesses of studying subcultures from (1) an insider's perspective and (2) an outsider's perspective?

2. What are the principal drugs abused by athletes?

3. What are the principal effects and side effects of steroids?

4. What factors encourage drug use by athletes?

5. From the "world" of steroid abusers, define and give an example of the following terms: stacking, cycling, plateauing, pyramiding, and array.

6. Argue both for and against drug testing in sports.

7. What type of penalties do you think should be used against athletes who abuse drugs?

8. Review the ATLAS steroid prevention program. Can you improve its methods for lessening steroid use among adolescents? How effective do you think this program would be at your college or university?

9. List the reasons why women are more concerned about drug use and abuse than men. Can you add several additional reasons not mentioned in this chapter?

10. Do you believe that drug prevention programs should be created uniquely for males and females?

11. What factors in the unique female roles encourage the use of substances of abuse?

12. Should childbearing women who abuse drugs be punished? Why or why not?

13. Why are women who have been or are sexually abused more likely to become addicted to drugs?

14. Why are adolescents especially vulnerable to drug abuse problems?

15. List and explain three reasons why you think adolescents from upper-middle-class socioeconomic backgrounds become drug abusers.

16. What types of parents are most likely to have children who develop drug abuse problems?

17. How do adolescent drug abuse patterns differ from those in adults?

18. In what way are drugs of abuse associated with juvenile gang activity?

19. Should all adolescents who use drugs of abuse be treated for drug dependence? Explain your answer.

20. Do you think that it is realistic to expect drug abusers to change their habits to prevent the spread of AIDS? Why or why not?

21. Should prisoners who test positive for HIV be segregated from the non–HIV-positive popu-

lations? Should prisoners be given free access to condoms in prisons? Why or why not?

22. John was caught by campus or city police growing psilocybin (hallucinogenic) mushrooms in his off-campus college apartment. Should John be punished by his college or university in addition to the punishment that will be meted out by the criminal justice system? Why or why not?

23. What if you discover that your roommate is HIV positive? How would you handle this situation?

24. Do you think that the excessive use of alcohol and other drugs in movies influences viewers? Further, are people who enjoy rap music affected by the lyrics that refer to drug use and/or abuse? Why or why not?

25. Do you believe that drug information over the Internet, such as chat rooms devoted to the use of certain drugs (e.g., where to purchase equipment for growing marijuana, OTC stimulant pills, and the spores of psilocybin mushrooms), promotes drug use? Why or why not?

Key Terms

subculture `470`

outsider's perspective `470`

insider's perspective `470`

"doping" `471`

ergogenic `473`

androgens `475`

anabolic steroids `475`

"stacking" `476`

"cycling" `476`

"plateauing" `476`

"pyramiding" `476`

"array" `477`

human growth factor (HGF) `481`

Summary

1 The most common drugs abused by athletes are the ergogenic (performance-enhancing) substances. They include the anabolic steroids, for building muscle mass and strength, and the CNS stimulants, to achieve energy, quickness, and endurance.

2 Drug testing is conducted for most professional athletic competitions and usually includes screens for steroids and stimulants. However, some performance-enhancing drugs, such as erythropoietin and HGF, are undetectable. Yet, undetectable drugs are involved in 90% of the estimated doping cases. Athletes who use performance-enhancing drugs often go to great lengths to avoid detection by these drug tests.

3 About 50% of the anabolic steroids used in the United States are prescribed by doctors; the other 50% are obtained from the black market. Black market steroids include drugs diverted from legitimate channels smuggled from foreign countries—for example, Brazil, Italy, Mexico, Great Britain, Portugal, France, and Peru—designated for veterinarian use, or inactive counterfeits.

4 The ATLAS prevention program uses athletes, coaches, and team leaders who are trained to educate team members about the effects of ana-

bolic steroid abuse. They emphasize both desirable and adverse effects of steroid use. Presenting a balanced perspective is stressed because adolescents know very well how anabolic steroids build muscles and can increase athletic abilities.

5 In general, women are (1) more concerned about drugs and drug use than men; (2) more likely to believe in drug prevention programs, such as needle exchange and testing reckless drivers for drug use than men; and (3) more likely to speak with their children about drug use than men (Drug Strategies 1998).

6 There is a high prevalence of drug dependence in women who are victims of sexual and/or physical abuse. Approximately 70% of women in drug abuse treatment report histories of physical abuse with victimization beginning at 11 years of age and occurring repeatedly. Further, women and men have different endocrine (hormone) systems, organs, and structures, and women's responses to drugs vary according to their reproductive states.

7 For women to receive adequate treatment for drug dependence, certain considerations must be met: (1) availability of female-sensitive services, (2) nonpunitive and noncoercive treatment that incorporates supportive behavior change approaches, and (3) treatment for a wide range of medical problems, mental disorders, and psychosocial problems.

8 Most adolescents who use substances of abuse are going through normal psychosocial development and will not develop problematic dependence on these drugs. The adolescent users who have difficulty with drugs often lack coping skills to deal with their problems, have dysfunctional families, possess poor self-images, and/or feel socially and emotionally insecure.

9 Parents who are most likely to raise drug-abusing adolescents are (1) drug abusers, (2) non–drug-using coupled with being constantly condemning, (3) overly demanding, (4) overly protective, or (5) unable to communicate effectively with their children.

10 The substances adolescents are most likely to abuse are alcohol, cigarettes, inhalants, marijuana, LSD, Ecstasy, and prescription stimulants. High-frequency use is most likely to occur with cigarettes, alcohol, and marijuana.

11 People who become gang members were often neglected by their parents, lacked positive role models, and failed to receive adequate adult supervision. Other motivations for joining a gang include peer pressures, low self-esteem, and perceived easy acquisition of money from gang-related drug dealing and other criminal activities.

12 The major reasons cited by college students for their use of drugs were (1) to have fun, (2) to relieve stress, (3) to ease social interactions, (4) to relieve academic stress, and (5) to get high or drunk.

13 Two interesting findings from research regarding drug use by college student subcultures are that (1) the best predictor of drug use for first-year college students is drug use during a typical month in the senior year of high school, and (2) usually recreational drug use does not begin in college but has already been established in high school.

14 Club drugs include MDMA (Ecstasy), GHB, Rohypnol, ketamine, methamphetamine, and LSD. The phrase *club drug* is derived from the use of these drugs at all-night dance parties such as raves or trances, dance clubs, and bars. All these drugs are colorless, tasteless, and odorless. Individuals who may want to intoxicate, sedate, and later sexually take advantage of others can add them unobtrusively to beverages.

15 After homosexual men, individuals who are addicted to illicit drugs are the second largest group at risk for contracting AIDS. This risk results from sharing of blood-contaminated needles and syringes and increased involvement in sexual risk taking because of the effects of drugs or in securing payment for drugs.

16 In the United States, since 1981, 830,000 cases of AIDS have been reported to the CDC (CDC 2004b). Of these cases, approximately 74% were males and 26% were females. Worldwide, more than 19 million people have died of AIDS, almost 25 million of them in sub-Saharan Africa. About 34 million people are living with AIDS, most of them in Africa, and 1 million more were infected last year (Sternberg 2000, p. 1). To date, AIDS has caused 13 million children to be orphaned. South Africa, which in large part is poverty stricken, has more than 70% of the world's 34 million people with HIV/AIDS.

17 Major ways to prevent contracting HIV include (1) engaging in safe (protected) sexual behavior, (2) avoiding use of contaminated drug paraphernalia and especially use of intravenous drugs, (3) avoiding use of drugs in groups with high rates of HIV infection, and (4) frankly discussing past sexual histories with potential sexual partners and, if in any doubt, being tested for HIV several times in a row.

18 The extent of alcohol and drug use in movies and songs is startling. Overall, findings of one study revealed that 98% of movies reviewed depicted illicit drugs, alcohol, and tobacco or OTC/prescription medicines. In this same detailed study, alcohol appeared in 93% of the movies and in 17% of the songs; tobacco appeared in 89% of movies but only 3% of songs. The lyrics of 63% of rap songs versus about 10% of the lyrics in other categories had substance references.

19 The music industry has been setting up drug-using celebrities as teen role models. The message conveyed by much of the music and by many bands is that drug use is acceptable. After several drug-related deaths of celebrities over the past few years, the industry is working to change such perceptions.

20 New media influences contribute to drug use. The Internet is considered to be the latest source of information where knowledge about use of illicit drugs is burgeoning.

References

ABC News. "Suicide's Young Victims: A Chat with Teen Suicide Expert Dr. David Shaffer." *Talk City and ABCNEWS.Com* (12 April 2000). Available http://www.abcnews.go.com/onair/020/chat000329_teensuicide.html.

American Foundation for AIDs Research (amfAR). "Facts About HIV/AIDS, 2001." New York: Body Health Resources Corporation, 2001.

Apostolides, M. "How to Quit the Holistic Way." *Psychology Today* 29 (September/ October 1996): 30–43, 75–76.

Archambault, D. "Adolescence, a Physiological, Cultural and Psychological No Man's Land." In *Adolescent Substance Abuse, Etiology, Treatment and Prevention*, edited by G. Lawson and A. Lawson, 11–28. Gaithersburg, MD: Aspen, 1992.

Associated Press. "Boredom, Stress, Money Linked to Drug Abuse." *Chesterton/Valparaiso Post Tribune* (20 August 2003): 1, A8.

Bahr, S. J., A. C. Marcos, and S. L. Maughan. "Family, Educational and Peer Influences on Alcohol Use of Female and Male Adolescents." *Journal of Studies on Alcohol* 56 (1995): 457–469.

Beard, B., and V. Kunsman. "A Cause for Concern: Alcohol-Induced Risky Sex on College Campuses." *Prevention Pipeline* 6 (September–October 1993): 24.

Begley, S., and M. Brant with Dickey, C., K. Helmstaedt, R. Nordland, and T. Hayden. "The Real Scandal." *Newsweek* 133 (15 February 1999): 48–54.

Bell, J. "Athletes' Use and Abuse of Drugs." *The Physician and Sports Medicine* 15 (March 1987): 99–108.

Belsie, L. "Temperance Movement Hits College Dorms." *The Christian Science Monitor* 87 (30 August 1995).

Bennett, M. F., J. Miller, and W. Gill. "Drinking, Binge Drinking, and Other Drug Use Among Southwestern Undergraduates: Three-Year Trends." *American Journal of Drug and Alcohol Abuse* 25 (1999): 331–346.

Bergeret, J. "Young People, Drugs . . . and Others." Rockville, MD: United Nations Office for Drug Control Office for Drug Control and Crime Prevention (UN/ODCCP) (1 January 1981). Available http://www.undep.org/bulletin/bulletin_1981-01-01_4_page002.html.

Beschner, G., and A. Friedman. "Treatment of Adolescent Drug Abusers." *International Journal of the Addictions* 20 (1985): 977–993.

Body Health Resources. "Facts about HIV/AIDS." AmfAR AIDS Research. New York: Body Health Resources, 2004. Available http://www.thebody.com/amfAR2004.html.

"Bodybuilding Drug Yields 'High.'" *Pharmacy Times* (June 1992): 14.

Booth, R., J. Watters, and D. Chitwood. "HIV Risk-Related Sex Behaviors Among Injection Drug Users, Crack Smokers, and Injection Drug Users Who Smoke Crack." *American Journal of Public Health* 83 (1993): 1144–1148.

Buckstein, D., D. Brent, J. Perper, G. Moritz, M. Baugher, J. Schweers, C. Roth, and L. Balach. "Risk Factors for Completed Suicide Among Adolescents with a Lifetime History of Substance Abuse: A Case-Control Study." *Acta Psychiatry Scandinavia* 88 (1993): 403–408.

Burke, C., and S. Davis. "Anabolic Steroid Abuse." *Pharmacy Times* (June 1992): 35–40.

Campus Alcohol Drug Resource Center at the University of Florida. *Alcohol and Other Drug Use, 1999*. University of Florida (2000). Available http://ww.health.ufl.edu.shcc/cadrc.htm.

Centers for Disease Control and Prevention (CDC). *Facts About Adolescents and HIV/AIDS*. Atlanta, GA: CDC, March 1998. Available http://www.thebody.com/cdc/hivteen.html.

Centers for Disease Control and Prevention (CDC). "HIV/AIDS." *Surveillance Reports* 11 (1999): 1–3.

Centers for Disease Control and Prevention (CDC). *Age at Diagnosis of HIV Infection or AIDS, Reported Through 1999, United States*. HIV/AIDS Surveillance—General Epidemiology 178 Slide Series Through 1999, Slide 24 of 24. Atlanta, GA: National Center for HIV, STD, and TB Prevention, January 2000a.

Centers for Disease Control and Prevention (CDC). *AIDS Cases by Age and Sex Reported 1981–1999, United States*. HIV/AIDS Surveillance—General Epidemiology 178 Slide Series Through 1999, Slide 2 of 24. Atlanta, GA: National Center for HIV, STD, and TB Prevention, January 2000b.

Centers for Disease Control and Prevention (CDC). *Adult/Adolescent AIDS Cases by Exposure Category and Year of Diagnosis, 1985–June 1999, United States*. HIV/AIDS Surveillance—General Epidemiology 178 Slide Series Through 1999, Slide 8 of 24. Atlanta, GA: National Center for HIV, STD, and TB Prevention, January 2000c.

Centers for Disease Control and Prevention (CDC). *HIV/AIDS Surveillance Report, 2003 (Volume15)*. Atlanta, GA: U.S. Department of Health and Human Services, CDC, 2004a.

Centers for Disease Control and Prevention (CDC). *Estimated AIDS Cases Among Male Adolescents and Young Adults by Exposure Category, Diagnosed Through 2002, United States*. National Center for HIV, STD, and TB Prevention, Divisions of HIV/AIDS Prevention Surveillance Branch. Washington, DC: CDC, 2004b. Available http://www.cdc.gov/hiv/265/1265-5.htm.

Centers for Disease Control and Prevention (CDC). *Estimated AIDS Cases Among Female Adolescents and Young Adults by Exposure Category, Diagnosed through 2002, United States*. National Center for HIV, STD, and TB Prevention, Divisions of HIV/AIDS Prevention Surveillance Branch. Washington, DC: CDC, 2004c.

Ciba Foundation. "AIDS and HIV Infection in Cocaine Users." In *Cocaine: Scientific and Social Dimensions*, 181–194. New York: Wiley, 1992.

Colthurst, T. "HIV and Alcohol Impairment: Reducing Risks." *Prevention Pipeline* 6 (July–August 1993): 24.

Cowley, G. "Targeting a Deadly Scrap of Genetic Code." *Newsweek* (2 December 1996): 68–69.

Curry, D. G., and I. A. Spergel. "Gang Homicide, Delinquency, and Community." In *Gangs and Gang Behavior*, edited by G. Larry Mays, 314–336. Chicago, IL: Nelson-Hall, 1997.

Daily, S. "Alcohol, Incest, and Adolescence." In *Adolescent Substance Abuse, Etiology, Treatment and Prevention*, edited by G. Lawson and A. Lawson, 251–266. Gaithersburg, MD: Aspen, 1992a.

Daily, S. "Suicide Solution: The Relationship of Alcohol and Drug Abuse to Adolescent Suicide." In *Adolescent Substance Abuse, Etiology, Treatment and Prevention*, edited by G. Lawson and A. Lawson, 233–250. Gaithersburg, MD: Aspen, 1992b.

Diaz, T., and S. Chu. "Crack Cocaine Use and Sexual Behavior Among People with AIDS." *Journal of the American Medical Association* 269 (1993): 2845–2846.

Dicker, M., and E. A. Leighton. "Trends in the U.S. Prevalence of Drug-Using Parturient Women and Drug-Affected Newborns, 1979 Through 1990." *American Journal of Public Health* 84 (September 1994): 1433.

Drug Facts and Comparisons, 109–109c. St. Louis, MO: Kluwer, 1994.

Drug Strategies. *Keeping Score 1998, Drug Use and Attitudes.* Washington, DC: 1998. Available http://www.drugstrategies.org/ks/1998/use.html.

Elmen, J., and D. Offer. "Normality, Turmoil and Adolescence." In *Handbook of Clinical Research and Practice with Adolescents*, edited by P. Tolan and B. Cohler, 5–19. New York: Wiley, 1993.

Erickson, P. G., and G. F. Murray: "Sex Differences in Cocaine Use and Experiences: A Double Standard Revived?" *American Journal of Drug and Alcohol Abuse* 15 (1989): 135–152.

Fagan, J. "Social Processes of Delinquency and Drug Use Among Urban Gangs." In *Gangs in America*, edited by C. R. Huff, 183–213. Newbury Park, CA: Sage, 1990.

Ferrente, R. "Ben Johnson Retires from Running After Positive Test." *Morning Edition* on National Public Radio (8 March 1993).

Fischer, J. S. "Searching for That Ounce of Prevention: Promising Strategies for an AIDS Vaccine." *U.S. News and World Report* (17 July 2000).

Glave, J. "Betty Ford Got Help, But Addiction Stalks Thousands of Women." *Salt Lake Tribune* 248 (3 June 1994): A-1.

Goldberg, L., D. Elliot, G. N. Clarke, D. P. MacKinnon, E. Moe, L. Zoref, C. Green, S. L. Wolf, E. Greffrath, D. J. Miller, and A. Lapin. "Effects of a Multidimensional Anabolic Steroid Prevention Intervention: The Adolescents Training and Learning to Avoid Steroids (ATLAS) Program. *Journal of the American Medical Association* 276 (1996): 1555–1562.

Goldstein, F. "Pharmacological Aspects of Substance Abuse." In *Remington's Pharmaceutical Sciences*, 19th ed. Easton, PA: Mack, 1995.

Grinspoon, L. "AIDS and Mental Health—Part 1." *Harvard Mental Health Letter* 10 (January 1994): 1–4.

Harlan, R., and M. Garcia. "Neurobiology of Androgen Abuse." In *Drugs of Abuse*, edited by R. Watson, 185–201. Boca Raton, FL: CRC Press, 1992.

Haywood, R. L. "Why More Young People Are Using Drugs." *Jet* 90 (9 September 1996).

Hitt, E. "Binge-Drinking Students Use Other Drugs: Report." *Health—Reuters* (12 September 2001). Available http://us.news2.yimg.com/f/42/31/7m/dailynews.yahoo.com/h/nm/20010912/hl/students_2.hti.

Hoberman, J. M., and C. E. Yesalis. "The History of Synthetic Testosterone." *Scientific American* (February 1995).

Hoshino, J. "Assessment of Adolescent Substance Abuse." In *Adolescent Substance Abuse, Etiology, Treatment and Prevention*, edited by G. Lawson and A. Lawson, 87–104. Gaithersburg, MD: Aspen, 1992.

Howard, M. "Adolescent Substance Abuse: A Social Learning Theory Perspective." In *Adolescent Substance Abuse, Etiology, Treatment and Prevention*, edited by G. Lawson and A. Lawson, 29–40. Gaithersburg, MD: Aspen, 1992.

Inciardi, James A., D. Lockwood, and A. E. Pottieger. *Woman and Crack-Cocaine.* New York: Macmillian, 1993.

Johnson, R. A., J. P. Hoffmann, and D. R. Gerstein. *The Relationship Between Family Structure and Adolescent Substance Use.* Rockville, MD: SAMHSA, Office of Applied Studies, July 1996.

Johnston, L. D., P. O'Malley, and J. G. Bachman. *National Survey Results from the Monitoring the Future Study, 1975–1992.* Rockville, MD: National Institute on Drug Abuse, 1993.

Johnston, L. D., P. O'Malley, and J. G. Bachman. *National Survey Results from the Monitoring the Future Study, 1975–1994.* Rockville, MD: National Institute on Drug Abuse, 1996.

Johnston, L. D., P. O'Malley, and J. G. Bachman. *National Survey on Drug Abuse from the Monitoring the Future Study, 1975–1998; College and Young Adults;* The University of Michigan Institute for Social Research, National Institute on Drug Abuse, U.S. Department of Human Services, National Institutes of Health, 1999.

Johnston, L. D., P. O'Malley, and J. G. Bachman. *The Monitoring the Future National Results on Adolescent Drug Use: Overview of Key Findings, 1999.* The University of Michigan Institute for Social Research, National Institute on

Drug Abuse, U.S. Department of Human Services, National Institutes of Health, 2000a.

Johnston, L. D., P. O'Malley, and J. G. Bachman. *National Survey Results on Drug Use from the Monitoring the Future Study, 1975–1999. Vol. 2, College Students and Young Adults*, U.S. Department of Health and Human Services (USD-HHS), National Institute on Drug Abuse (NIDA). Washington, DC: U.S. Government Printing Office, 2000b.

Johnston, L. D., P. O'Malley, and J. G. Bachman. *National Survey Results on Drug Use from the Monitoring the Future Study, 1975–2000. Vol. 2, College Students and Young Adults*, U.S. Department of Health and Human Services (USD-HHS), National Institute on Drug Abuse (NIDA). Washington, DC: U.S. Government Printing Office, 2001.

Johnston, L. D., P. M. O'Malley, J. G. Bachman, and J. E. Schulenberg. *Monitoring the Future: National Survey Results on Drug Use, 1975–2003. Volume I: Secondary School Students*. Bethesda, MD: National Institute on Drug Abuse, 2004a.

Johnston, L. D., P. M. O'Malley, J. G. Bachman, and J. E. Schulenberg. *Monitoring the Future National Survey Results on Drug Use, 1975–2003. Volume II: College Students and Adults Ages 19–45*. Bethesda, MD: National Institute on Drug Abuse, 2004b.

Johnston, L. D., P. M. O'Malley, J. G. Bachman, and J. E. Schulenberg. "Overall Teen Drug Use Continues Gradual Decline But Use of Inhalants Rises." *Monitoring the Future National Survey Results on Drug Use*. University of Michigan and National Institute on Drug Abuse. Bethesda, MD: National Institute on Drug Abuse, 2004c.

Join Together Online and BBC (British Broadcasting Company) News. "Illicit Drug Sales Booming Online." Boston, MA: Boston University School of Public Health, 2005. Available http://org/y/0,221,576328,00.html.

Kandel, D. B. "Drug and Drinking Behavior Among Youth." *Annual Review of Sociology* 6 (1980): 235–285.

Kantrowitz, B., and P. Wingert. "Beyond Littleton: How Well Do You Know Your Kid?" *Newsweek* (10 May 1999).

Kinney, J. *Loosening the Grip*, 6th ed. Boston: McGraw Hill, 2000.

Kirkpatrick, J. *The Woman Alcoholic*. Quakertown, PA: Women for Sobriety, 1999. Available http://www.womenforsobriety.org/articles/wfs_leadstory12.html.

Klee, H., and M. Jackson. *Drug Misuse and Motherhood*. New York: Routledge, 2002.

Kolata, G. "Targeting Urged in Attack on AIDS." *New York Times* 142 (7 March 1993): 1.

Korolenko, C. P., and T. A. Donskih. "Addictive Behavior in Women: A Theoretical Perspective." *Drugs and Society* 4 (1990): 39–65.

Ladwig, G. B., and M. D. Anderson. "Substance Abuse in Women: Relationship Between Chemical Dependency of Women and Past Reports of Physical and/or Sexual Abuse." *International Journal of the Addictions* 24 (1989): 739–754.

Lale, T. "Gangs and Drugs." In *Adolescent Substance Abuse, Etiology, Treatment and Prevention*, edited by G. Lawson and A. Lawson, 267–281. Gaithersburg, MD: Aspen, 1992.

Lawn, J. *Team Up for Drug Prevention with America's Young Athletes*. Washington DC: Drug Enforcement Administration, U.S. Department of Justice, 1984.

Lawson, G., and A. Lawson, "Etiology." In *Adolescent Substance Abuse, Etiology, Treatment and Prevention*, edited by G. Lawson and A. Lawson, 1–10. Gaithersburg, MD: Aspen, 1992.

Leibsohn, J. "The Relationship Between Drug and Alcohol Use and Peer Group Associations of College Freshmen as They Transition from High School." *Journal of Drug Education* 24 (1994): 177–192.

Leinwand, D. "20% Say They Used Drugs with Their Mom or Dad. Among Reasons: Boomer Culture and Misguided Attempts to Bond." *USA Today* (27 August 2000). Available http://www.usatoday.com/usatonline/20000824/25790504s.htm.

Lin, A. Y. F. "Should Women Be Included in Clinical Trials?" *Pharmacy Times* 10 (November 1994): 27.

Lively, K. "The 'Date-Rape Drug': Colleges Worry about Reports of Growing Use of Rohypnol, a Sedative." *Chronicle of Higher Education* 42 (28 June 1996): A-29.

Lukas, S. "Urine Testing for Anabolic-Androgenic Steroids." *Trends in Pharmacological Sciences* 14 (1993): 61–68.

Marklein, M. B. "College Binge Drinking Heads Off Campus." *USA Today* (14 March 2000). Available http://www.usatoday.com/life/health/addiction/lhadd029.htm.

Mathias, R. "Sex-for-Crack Phenomenon Poses Risk for Spread of AIDS in Heterosexuals." *NIDA Notes* 8 (May/June 1993): 8–11.

Mathias, R. "NIDA Survey Provides First National Data on Drug Use During Pregnancy." *NIDA Notes* 10 (January/February 1995): 6–7.

McCaffrey, B. R. "McCaffrey Announces Strategy to Fight Drug Use in Sports." *Daily Washington File* (21 October 1999). Available http://www.usis.it/wireless/wf991021/99102114.htm.

McDonald, M. "Fast, Strong, Dead?" *Salt Lake Tribune* 250 (22 June 1995): C1, C8.

Meilman, P. W., R. K. Grace, C. A. Presley, and R. Lyerla. "Beyond Performance Enhancement: Polypharmacy Among Collegiate Users of Steroids." *Journal of American College Health* 44 (November 1995): 98–104.

Merchant, W. "Medications and Athletes." *American Druggist* (October 1992): 6–14.

Millstein, R. *Community Alert Bulletin*. Rockville, MD: National Institute on Drug Abuse, U.S. Department of Health and Human Services, 25 March 1993.

Minnesota Institute of Public Health. *Alcohol and Other Drugs & Suicide.* Anoka, MN: Spring 1995. Available http://www.mikph.org/area/fs8.html.

Moss, H., L. Kirisci, H. Gordon, and R. Tarter. "A Neuro-psychological Profile of Adolescent Alcoholics." *Alcoholism: Clinical and Experimental Research* 18 (1994): 159–163.

MSNBC. "East Europe HIV Cases Swell: UN." *Health News* (2004). Available http://www.msnbc.com/news/64383.asp.

"Multistate Outbreak of Poisonings Associated with Illicit Use of GHB." *Prevention Pipeline* 7 (May–June 1994): 95, 96.

MyDNA.com. "News Center: HAART Therapy Slows Progression to AIDS." Washington, DC: American Medical Association, 2005. Available http://www.mydna.com/health/sexual/aids/resources/news/20.

National Clearinghouse for Alcohol and Drug Information (NCADI). *Drugs of Abuse.* Rockville, MD: Substance Abuse and Mental Health Services Administration, 1999. Available http://www.health.org/pubs/catalog/rpos.htm.

National Household Survey on Drug Abuse. "Academic Performance and Youth Substance Use." Rockville, MD: Office of Applied Studies (OAS), Substance Abuse and Mental Health Services Administration (SAMHSA), 6 September 2002. Available http://www/drugabusestatistics.samhsa.gov.

National Institute on Drug Abuse (NIDA). *Anabolic Steroid Abuse.* Capsule 43. Rockville, MD: NIDA, 1996.

National Institute on Drug Abuse (NIDA). *Drug Abuse and Addiction Research: The Sixth Triennial Report to Congress.* Rockville, MD: U.S. Department of Health and Human Services, 1999.

National Institute on Drug Abuse (NIDA). "Club Drugs: Community Alert Bulletin." *NIDA Notes* 14 (30 March 2000).

National Institutes of Health (NIH) and National Institute on Drug Abuse (NIDA). *Drug Abuse and Drug Abuse Research: Executive Summary.* Rockville, MD: Substance Abuse and Mental Health Services Administration, 1998.

News Tribune. "Alcohol, Tobacco or Drugs Used in 98% of Popular Movies." (29 April 1999). Available http://www.newstribune.com/stories/042999/ent_0429990069.html.

Nicklin, J. L. "Arrests at Colleges Surge for Alcohol and Drug Violations." *Chronicle of Higher Education* (9 June 2000).

Office of National Drug Control Policy (ONDCP). *Substance Use in Popular Movies and Music.* Media Campaign, Campaign Publications. Rockville, MD: ONDCP Drugs and Crime Clearinghouse, 1999.

Olufs, C. "The AIDS Time Line: 20 Years, 20 Drugs, 20 Million Deaths—No Cure in Sight." *Women Alive* (Spring 2001). Available http://www.thebody.com/ws/spring01/timeline.html.

"OTC Drugs and Athletes." *Pharmacy Times* (June 1992): 16.

Parrot, A. *Date Rape and Acquaintance Rape.* New York: Rosen, 1988.

Pietroski, N. "Counseling HIV/AIDS Patients." *American Druggist* (August 1993): 50–56.

Prendergast, M. L. "Substance Use and Abuse Among College Students: A Review of Recent Literature." *Journal of American College Health* 43 (1994): 99–113.

Ravid, J. "The Hard-Core Curriculum." *Rolling Stone* 719 (19 October 1995): 99.

Reuters and CNN.com. "Users See Internet as Key Information Source." *Reuters* (16 August 2000a). Available http://www.cnn.com/2000/TECH/computing/08/16/internet.study.reut/index.html.

Reuters and CNN.com. "Study: Lower-Income Web Users Now Fastest-Growing U.S. Market." *Reuters* (22 August 2000b). Available http//www.cnn.com/2000/TECH/computing/08/22/internet.incomes.reut/index.htm.

Samples, P. "Alcoholism in Athletes: New Directions for Treatment." *The Physician and Sports Medicine* (17 April 1989): 193–202.

Sanders, W. B. *Gangbangs and Drive-bys.* New York: Aldine De Gruyter, 1994.

Schaefer, M. A., J. F. Hilton, M. Ekstrand, and J. Keogh. "Relationship Between Drug Use and Sexual Behaviors and the Occurrence of Sexually Transmitted Diseases Among High-Risk Male Youth." *Sexually Transmitted Diseases* 20 (November–December 1993): 39–47.

Schernoff M., and R. A. Smith. "HIV Treatments: A History of Scientific Advance." *Body Positive* XIV (July 2001): 1–7.

Schoemer, K. "Rockers, Models and the New Allure of Heroin." *Newsweek* (26 August 1996): 24–36.

Science Daily. "Pain Drug Reveals What Most Already Know—Men's and Women's Brains Are Simply Different." (15 March 2000). Available http://www.sciencedaily.com/releases/2000/03/000315075845.htm.

Scott, D. M., J. C. Wagner, and T. W. Barlow. "Anabolic Steroids Use Among Adolescents in Nebraska Schools." *American Journal of Health-System Pharmacy* 53 (1996): 2068–2072.

Scripps Howard News Service. "AIDS Fear: Complacency: Infection Rate Is on Rise for First Time Since 1994." Reported in *Post-Tribune* (21 August 2003): A-10.

Shelden, R.G., S. Tracy, and W. Brown. *Youth Gangs in American Society.* Belmont, CA: Wadsworth/Thomson Learning, 2001.

Shelden, R. G., S. K. Tracy, and W. B. Brown. *Youth Gangs in American Society,* 3rd ed. Belmont, CA: Wadsworth/Thomson Learning, 2004.

Siegel, L., and J. Senna. *Juvenile Delinquency*, 6th ed. St. Paul, MN: West, 1997.

Spergel, I.A. *Youth Gangs: Problem and Response.* Chicago, IL: University of Chicago, School of Social Service Administration, 1990.

Steinberg, L., A. Fletcher, and N. Darling. "Parental Monitoring and Peer Influences on Adolescent Substance Use." *Pediatrics* 93 (1994): 1060–1064.

Sternberg, S. "AIDS Apocalypse Expanding." *USA Today* (28 June 2000). Available www.usatoday.com/life/health/aids/Africa/lhafr008.htm.

Street, C., J. Antonio, and D. Cudlipp. "Androgen Use by Athletes: A Reevaluation of the Health Risks." *Canadian Journal of Applied Physiology* 2 (1996): 421–440, 1996.

Substance Abuse and Mental Health Services Administration (SAMHSA). *1999 Household Survey on Drug Abuse* (1999a) Available http://www.samhsa.gov/statistics/statistics.html.

Substance Abuse and Mental Health Services Administration (SAMHSA). *Making the Connection Between Substance Abuse and HIV/AIDS Prevention for Women of Color and Youth.* Rockville, MD: U.S. Department of Health and Human Services, 1999b.

Substance Abuse and Mental Health Services Administration (SAMHSA). *Tips for Teens: About Steroids.* Center for Substance Abuse Prevention. Rockville, MD: U.S. Department of Health and Human Services, 1999c.

Substance Abuse and Mental Health Services Administration (SAMHSA). *Results from the 2001 National Household Survey on Drug Abuse: Volume I. Summary of National Findings* (Office of Applied Studies, NHSDA Series). Rockville, MD: U.S. Department of Health and Human Services, 2002.

Suggs, W. "Deadly Fuel: As Supplements and Steroids Tempt and Endanger More Athletes, What Are Colleges Doing?" *Chronicle of Higher Education* XLIX (14 March 2003): A36–A38.

Swadi, H. "Relative Risk Factors in Detecting Adolescent Drug Abuse." *Drug and Alcohol Dependence* 29 (1992): 253–254.

Teen Challenge. *Drugs: Frequently Asked Questions.* South Australia: Pragin Press, 2000. Available http://www.tc.sn.au/hoax2.asp.

Toronto, R. "Young Athletes Who Use 'Enhancing' Steroids Risk Severe Physical Consequences." *Salt Lake Tribune* 244 (6 July 1992): C-5.

USA Today. "AIDS Likely to Devastate Teen Population." *USA Today: Health* (28 August 2000): 1. Available http://www.usatoday.com/life/health/1hd1.htm.

U.S. Department of Health and Human Services (USDHHS), National Institute on Drug Abuse (NIDA). *Drug Abuse and Addiction Research: The Sixth Triennial Report to Congress. NIDA Research Priorities and Highlights, Role of Research: Women's Health and Gender Differences,* Washington, DC: U.S. Government Printing Office, 1999.

U.S. Department of Justice. "Anabolic Steroids and You." Washington, DC: Demand Reduction Section, Drug Enforcement Administration, 1991–1992.

Venturelli, P. J. "Drugs in Schools: Myths and Reality." In *The Annals of the American Academy of Political and Social Science* 567, edited by W. H. Hinkle and S. Henry, 72–87. Thousand Oaks, CA: Sage, January 2000.

Walsh, F., and M. Sheinkman. "Family Context of Adolescence." In *Adolescent Substance Abuse, Etiology, Treatment and Prevention,* edited by G. Lawson and A. Lawson, 149–171. Gaithersburg, MD: Aspen, 1992.

Welder, A., and R. Melchert. "Cardiotoxic Effects of Cocaine and Anabolic-Androgenic Steroids in the Athlete." *Journal of Pharmacological and Toxicological Methods* 29 (1993): 61–68.

Winters, F. A. *Teen Addiction.* San Diego, CA: Greenhaven Press, 1997.

Wisconsin Coalition Against Sexual Assault (WCASA). *Sexual Violence and Sexual Abuse.* Madison, WI: WCASA, 1997.

Witham, D. "Recovery in the Dorm: Rutgers University's Special Housing for Addicted Students." *Chronicle of Higher Education* 42 (10 November 1995): A-33.

"Women Smokers Run High Risk for Lung Cancer." *Prevention Pipeline* 7 (May–June 1994): 7.

Wright, L. "Suicidal Thoughts and Their Relationship to Family Stress and Personal Problems Among High School Seniors and College Undergraduates." *Adolescence* 20 (1985): 575–580.

Yahoo! and Reuters. "HIV Drug Combinations Benefit Teens, Children Too." *Health—Reuters* (2001). Available http://dailynews.yahoo.com/h/nm/20011126/hl/teenhiv_.html.

Yesalis, C. E., and J. S. Cowart. *The Steroids Game.* Champaign, IL: Human Kinetics, 1998.

Zuger, A. M. D. "Epidemic: An Overview." *New York Times* (8 August 2000). Available http://www.nytimes.com/library/national/science/aids/aids-overview.html.

CHAPTER 17

Drug Abuse Prevention

Did You Know?

- Comprehensive prevention programs involving the community, school, and family are more effective than single-unit programs.

- The harm reduction drug prevention model that is practiced in the Netherlands is a preventive model that meets drug users on "their own turf" in dealing with drug use and/or abuse.

- The targeted audience of drug prevention programs must distinguish between early experimenters, nonproblem drug users, nondetected committed or secret users, problem users, and former users.

- A key decision in drug prevention programs is whether to stress total abstinence or responsible use.

- Students in drug prevention programs who do not know how to say "no" need refusal skills training or peer resistance training.

- Drug education actually began in the 1830s with the temperance movement.

- Family risk factors that often lead to drug use include being raised in a chaotic home environment, having parents with ineffective parenting skills, and having a lack of mutual attachments and nurturing.

- Information-only drug prevention programs increase the knowledge about drugs, but have little or no effect on habitual use.

- Peer-based drug prevention uses fellow students as educators, mentors, counselors, or facilitators of prevention and outreach work.

- DARE drug prevention programs are in approximately 70% of the United States' school districts and reach approximately 25 million students.

- Drug courts are considered as a newer form of drug prevention in which drug defendants are more likely to undergo treatment (rehabilitation) than incarceration (punishment).

- Other strategies for dealing with drug use include the alternatives approach and meditation.

On completing this chapter you will be able to:

◎ List the 10 most prominent factors influencing alcohol and other drug use surrounding the individual.

◎ List and briefly explain the three major types of drug prevention programs.

◎ List the five types of drug users that have to be considered *before* implementing a drug prevention program.

◎ List the four levels of comprehensive prevention programs for drug use and abuse.

◎ List the three family factors that can prevent initiation to drugs or extensive drug use.

◎ List four existing prevention programs largely found in higher education.

◎ Understand the main goals of the following large-scale drug prevention programs: BACCHUS and GAMMA Peer Education Network, DARE, and drug courts.

◎ Describe two other alternatives to drug use.

Drugs and Society Online is a great source for additional drugs and society information for both students and instructors.
Visit **http://drugsandsociety.jbpub.com** to find a variety of useful tools for learning, thinking, and teaching.

Introduction

When someone tells another person "Just don't do drugs" and if that person is addicted to, say, cocaine like I was, that comes across as a retarded answer. You cannot just quit when you are addicted because even the idea of addiction continually blocks the possibility of casually deciding to stop using the drug. A lot has to go into the day you actually stop using the drug. First of all, the craving for the drug continually reminds you to do it maybe just a few more times. Then, your life appears to be less engaging because your body is missing the chemical properties of the drug that it became accustomed to and this affects your level of depression. So you have to sort of go through that slow abstinence period—you are without the drug and sometimes you can only deal with abstaining 1 hour at a time for the first week or so. Then slowly, ever so slowly, for me at least, the addict has to rebuild her or his daily living without the drug. It's just not easy. If it were, most people addicted to drugs would probably quit on their own. Especially when you realize that you are not controlling the drug, the drug is controlling you. Just remember, most addicts continually deceive (lie) themselves and others that they are not "really" addicted. Do you know how hard it is to become aware that these lies are part of the addiction? Before the extended therapy I had, no one could convince me that the daily cocaine I was snorting and smoking was bad. *(From Venturelli's research files, female, age 37, academic administrator in higher education, who for the past 3 years has been drug free, June 21, 2000.)*

This chapter explores and provides information on doing *something* about drug use and abuse. With so many potential causes for the unnecessary and nonmedical use of psychoactive substances, it becomes increasingly important to discuss methods, programs, and strategies that prevent, delay,

KEY TERMS

AOD
alcohol and other drugs

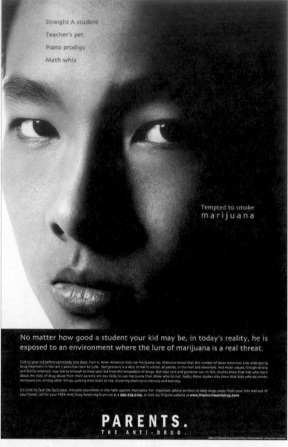

Straight A student
Teacher's pet
Piano prodigy
Math whiz

Tempted to smoke
marijuana

No matter how good a student your kid may be, in today's reality, he is exposed to an environment where the lure of marijuana is a real threat.

PARENTS.
THE ANTI-DRUG.

Example of an advertisement aimed at alerting parents about the dangers of early drug use.

or at the very least, moderate the habitual use of drugs.

Figure 17.1 shows many of the potential environmental factors involved in what influences alcohol and other drug use (**AOD**). The core in this figure starts with the individual, and each concentric "zone" represents clusters of factors that influence an individual's views, attitudes, and behaviors toward drug use. With so many factors, each having an independent potential effect on the individual, you can see why comprehensive prevention programs involving the community, school, and family are more effective than single-unit programs, such as having a mandatory drug education program in elementary grades without other complementary and overlapping drug programs in the community and the family. Prevention research clearly shows that "we must attend to

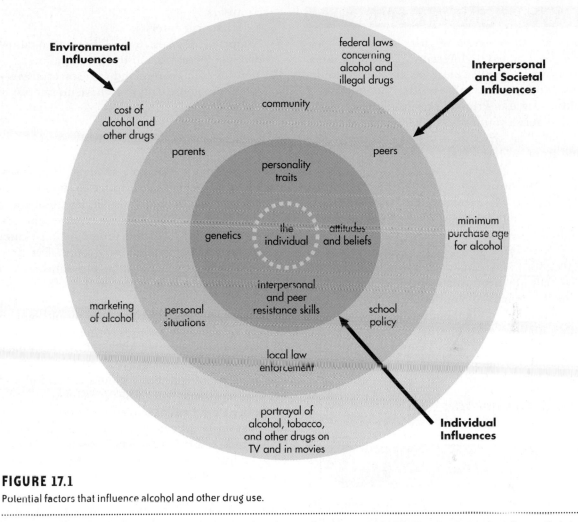

Environmental Influences

Interpersonal and Societal Influences

Individual Influences

federal laws concerning alcohol and illegal drugs

community

cost of alcohol and other drugs

parents

peers

personality traits

genetics

the individual

attitudes and beliefs

minimum purchase age for alcohol

interpersonal and peer resistance skills

marketing of alcohol

personal situations

school policy

local law enforcement

portrayal of alcohol, tobacco, and other drugs on TV and in movies

FIGURE 17.1

Potential factors that influence alcohol and other drug use.

Source: U.S. Department of Health and Human Services, Office for Substance Abuse Prevention (1989). Figure 2.1, Factors that Influence Alcohol and Other Drug Use. In *Prevention plus II: Tools for creating and sustaining drug-free communities* (p. 19). (DHHS Publication No. (ADM) 89-1649). Rockville, MD: Author. Distributed by the National Clearinghouse for Alcohol and Drug Information.

all factors; prevention that focuses on only one or two factors and ignores or discounts the rest is likely to fail to have a long-term, permanent impact" (Tinzmann and Hixson 1992, p. 3).

Through comprehensive prevention programs that are multifaceted and complementary, we are able to more effectively "tease out" which factors are most influential. The televised commercial in the early 1990s that showed two eggs frying in a pan: "This is your brain . . . this is your brain on drugs," sponsored by the Partnership for a Drug-Free America, was an early attempt at prevention through a disturbing analogy. Although its effect

was poor on drug users, who had never felt their brains frying, it was an initial step toward innovative prevention efforts. Was it worth the airtime? Can the success of these programs be adequately measured?

In 1997, 15 states thought prevention of alcohol and other drug abuse was important enough to maintain certified prevention specialist credentialing. Today, a bewildering variety of programs exist from coast to coast in school districts, churches, and other communities, all with the goal of preventing initial drug use or halting use before it becomes a problem ("Be Smart, Don't Start").

Drug Prevention Programs

There are three levels of drug prevention programs, each suited to different types of drug users. **Primary drug prevention programs** are aimed at nonusers, and the goal is to "inoculate" potential users against drug use. Primary prevention is often targeted at at-risk youth who may live in areas where licit and illicit types of drugs are rampant, may come from problem families, or are surrounded by drug-abusing peers.

The other two major types of drug prevention programs are (1) **secondary drug prevention programs**—their aim is toward newer drug users with a limited history of use; and (2) **tertiary drug prevention programs**—their goal is to focus directly on intervention and target chemically dependent individuals who need treatment.

Usually primary, secondary, and tertiary programs are used in combination because, in most settings, all three types of drug users constitute the targeted population. Table 17.1 further illustrates these levels of drug prevention and corresponding suggested activities; what can be accomplished is listed under each of the three types of prevention (primary, secondary, and tertiary).

Considering the Audience and Approach

It is important to be aware that drug users vary in their exposure and past histories of substance use and/or abuse. The audience for drug prevention comprises both users and nonusers. In analyzing the population of users, categories include the following:

- Nonusers
- Early experimenters
- Nonproblem drug users—those who abuse drugs on occasion, mostly for recreation
- Nondetected, committed, or secret users—those who abuse drugs and have no interest in stopping
- Problem users
- Former users

It is important that role models, counselors, teachers, and anyone else involved in drug prevention programs take into consideration that there are different types of substance users/abusers. Therefore, drug prevention programs must cater to the specific needs of these groups. For nonproblem users, drug education programs should examine the abuse of drugs and reinforce the message that uncontrolled use leads to abuse. For committed users, drug education should aim to prevent or delay drug abuse. Former users should be given information that will reinforce their decision to stop abusing drugs.

A number of questions should be considered by a professional planning a prevention program. To what type of audience should the drug information be targeted: Youths or adults? Peers or parents? Should information focus on knowledge, attitudes, or behavior? Should the program emphasize and recommend abstinence or responsible use?

In most cases, it is appropriate for drug prevention to focus on knowledge, attitudes, and behavior; the three are clearly related. For instance, if the goal is to increase knowledge, should we assume that attitudes and behavior will change accordingly, or should knowledge about the harmful effects of drugs be kept separate from attitudes and behavior? For example, if you learn that smoking marijuana is a health hazard, equal to or more destructive than smoking cigarettes, does this knowledge limit the satisfaction you derive from smoking marijuana with friends? Some would say "yes." Unfortunately, many would say "no." In fact, knowledge about the harmful effects of certain types of drugs has very little effect on the personal attitudes and habits of most people. Most cigarette smokers are aware of the health hazards before they start smoking, but this does not always stop them from starting or becoming addicted.

KEY TERMS

primary drug prevention programs
the very broad range of activities aimed at reducing the risk of drug use among nonusers and assuring continued nonuse

secondary drug prevention programs
targeting at-risk groups, experimenters, and early-abuse populations to reverse the progression of abusive behaviors, similar to "early intervention"

tertiary drug prevention programs
intervention at an advanced state of drug abuse; basically the same as drug abuse treatment

Table 17.1 Levels of Drug Prevention and Suggested Activities

Primary Prevention (risk reduction before abuse)	

Intrapersonal Factors	Affective education (emotional literacy)
	 Resilience training
	 Values clarification
	 Personal and social skills development
	   Assertiveness skills training
	   Refusal skills
	 Drug information and education

Small Group Factors	Peer mentoring, counseling, outreach, modeling Conflict resolution Curriculum infusion Activities demonstrating misperception of peer norms Alternatives to use: recreational, cultural, athletic Strengthening families
Systems Level	Strengthening school–family links Strengthening school–community group links Strengthening community support systems Media advocacy efforts, reducing alcohol marketing
Secondary Prevention (intervening in early abuse)	
	Assessment strategies: identification of abuse subgroups and individual diagnoses Early intervention coupled with sanctions Teacher–counselor–parent team approach Developing healthy alternative youth culture Recovering role models
Tertiary Prevention (intervening in advanced abuse)	
	Assessment and diagnosis Referral into treatment Case management Reentry

Drug education programs have to direct their attention to a small range of behavioral objectives. They will not be effective if they address too many issues.

Finally, drug prevention programs must decide whether they will stress total abstinence or responsible use. Abstinence is radically different from responsible use. A program cannot advocate both. Information and "scare tactics" alone have no effect on drug use. Educational prevention models have been modified lately to achieve the following goals:

- Convey the message that society is inconsistent concerning drug use. For example, certain drugs that cause serious harm to a large percentage of the population are legal, whereas other drugs that have less impact are illegal.

• Convey that the reasons for drug use are complex and that drug users vary.
• Demonstrate to youth that young and old alike are affected by role models, in that attitudes regarding drug use are often patterned from family members who are role models.
• Acknowledge that other influential role models in music, sports, art, drama, business, and education who use and abuse drugs can affect attitudes toward drug use (see Chapter 16).

AN EXAMPLE OF DRUG PREVENTION AT CENTRAL HIGH IN ELMTOWN

This section describes how a school-based prevention program is implemented and demonstrates that programs must be comprehensive and multifaceted to be successful.

Let us stand in the shoes of a parent and teacher committee trying to design a primary prevention program for students at Central High in Elmtown. The group has some prevention research materials that it received from the National Clearinghouse for Alcohol and Drug Information. After some thought, most members of the committee decide not to address individual, personal risk factors (discussed in Chapters 2 and 18) that may generate anxieties or conflicts or painful or threatening feelings. They have spoken with some students and ascertained that most of the 9th and 10th graders—even those who tend toward rebelliousness and avant-garde styles—are against taking drugs. Although many students feel this way, there are trends in the school that worry the committee members. Some popular 11th- and 12th-grade peer group leaders are drug users, and drug sales have been occurring on school grounds. The presence and availability of drugs and the beginning of a drug-using atmosphere make it more likely that some of the younger students will initiate use.

In brainstorming sessions, different committee members suggest ways to help these students avert initiation of drug use. Depending on their thinking, theoretical bent, and exposure to prevention models, members come up with the following ideas:

• Students need to be grounded in good, solid knowledge about the negative effects and dangers of drugs (1) as provided in a drug education course or (2) more subtly, in a curriculum concerning drug effects and drug-using behaviors (also covered later, in the section on higher education).
• Students with low self-esteem will feel uncomfortable asserting individual choices or points of view that deviate from those held by peers or peer leaders. Bolstering a positive self-image would allow such students to refuse drugs.
• Students who have low expectations regarding their ability to refuse drugs will be least likely to actually refuse. The school might try to increase their "self-efficacy"—that is, their belief that their behaviors are powerful and will have results.
• Students just do not know how to say "no" and need refusal skills training or peer-resistance training.
• Although a clique leadership may set a pro-use tone, it is probable that the quiet antidrug students represent a silent majority. They may misperceive the amount of drug use that occurs in their school. If the antidrug students are shown that their own attitudes and beliefs are actually in the majority, they will see that the "emperor has no clothes."
• A more confrontational approach involves removing drugs from the school environment by infiltrating the student body or using informants to gather information about who is distributing drugs. Dealers and users can then be identified or counseled and their parents notified. The school could make the decision to go as far as having the student arrested or expelling him or her.

With so many options put forth, some of the committee members become frustrated and fear that a sufficient program will never be created. Some of them have experienced alcoholism in their families and fear that many of these approaches are too "ineffective" for helping the students who are already experimenting.

Seeing a disaster brewing, the committee chair makes a call to the Division of Substance Abuse Services in the state Department of Health to inquire about drug prevention programs. The operator refers the call to the prevention specialists at the agency, who are linked to the National Prevention Network, which is part of the National Association of State Alcohol and Drug Abuse Directors. The specialist schedules a meeting with the committee, in which she makes the following points:

1. A prevention needs assessment is helpful, and necessitates using validated survey instruments to determine the patterns of behavior and attitudes regarding drug use among the student body.

2. A combination of primary and secondary prevention would be good for the majority of the student body, and group treatment for substance abuse should be made available at an adolescent outpatient clinic. The outpatient clinic will assess some students who are well on their way to addiction and refer them into inpatient treatment. Because this intervention occurs when the student is at an advanced abuse state, this is considered tertiary prevention.

Notice how all three types of approaches (primary, secondary, and tertiary) are necessary to implement a comprehensive prevention strategy.

The specialist brought along a staff member of the Local Council on Alcoholism and Drug Dependence, an affiliate of the National Council on Alcoholism and Drug Dependence (NCADD) branch serving a three-county region of the state. Thousands of branches of NCADD exist in the United States, and their goal is to help local groups design and implement prevention programs. Many branches have developed specialized programs for teens, children, women, and the elderly. The staff member conducts preliminary sessions with the prevention committee and arranges to sign an affiliation agreement with the school administration, whereby NCADD will act as consultants to the school, aiding it in designing a prevention program to fit its particular needs. It will design a project, which will be based on a needs assessment that incorporates a survey of chemical attitudes and use and interviews with parents, teachers, and students. The project design will include the program objectives, a method and management plan, a timeline, and an evaluation component.

To help those members bewildered by the many possible factors identified by the committee in its brainstorming session (such as self-esteem, self-efficacy, and refusal skills), the staff member invites the committee to sample a number of available, attractive packages of "user-friendly" activities such as the following:

- "Broad-brush" packages, which cover a variety of personal choice and primary prevention areas (Holstein et al. 1995)
- More targeted strategies, which might include a training package to be implemented by a consultant hired by the school district to address issues such as assertiveness training

Assertiveness training skills, which include a variety of personal and social skills, enable people to communicate their needs and feelings in an open, direct, and appropriate manner, while still recognizing the needs and feelings of others. They make people feel more powerful and better about themselves (less like "doormats"), and they offer strategies for saying "no" without hurting, provoking, or manipulating others (Alberti and Emmons 1988). Assertive behavior contrasts with hostile or belligerent behavior, passive and helpless behavior, and passive-aggressive or indirect manipulation. The exercises included in assertiveness training are nonthreatening, concrete, direct, and enjoyable.

Many intrapersonal prevention concepts, or personal and social skills development concepts, have come and gone, with a trendy "buzz word" accompanying each in the year it was introduced. Many of these concepts overlap, such as life skills training, self-esteem, self-efficacy, resilience training, and assertiveness training (McIntyre et al. 1990; Norman 1994). The danger lies in employing them as gimmicks or slogans that accomplish little. Nevertheless, as Botvin and others have shown, personal and skills training that are carefully based on known cognitive and behavioral change factors, if carefully put into place, can indeed make a difference (Botvin and Wills 1985; Shiffman and Wills 1987). It is also true that almost any positive lifestyle activity is likely to act as an alternative to participating in a drug-using subculture.

Comprehensive Prevention Programs for Drug Use and Abuse

HARM REDUCTION MODEL

At the broadest level is a society-wide prevention model that would entail a much more comprehensive approach. The **harm reduction model** is an approach to drug use and addiction practiced in some cites in the Netherlands and the United Kingdom. It is described by Westermeyer as an addiction model that connects "with the addicted community, by having an 'open door policy' that welcomes addicts to take part in services, regardless of level of motivation for change, goals or personal ideology" (Westermeyer n.d.). In a sense, it is a model that meets addicts on their own level.

Westermeyer identifies three central beliefs of the harm reduction model:

1. Excessive behaviors occur along a continuum of risk ranging from minimal to extreme. Addictive behaviors are not all-or-nothing phenomena. Although a drug or alcohol abstainer has a lower risk of harm than a drug or alcohol user, a moderate drinker is causing less harm than a binge drinker is; a crystal methamphetamine smoker or sniffer is causing less harm than a crystal injector.

2. Changing addictive behavior is a stepwise process, with complete abstinence being the final step. Those who embrace the harm reduction model believe that any movement in the direction of reduced harm—no matter how small—is positive in and of itself.

3. Sobriety simply is not for everybody. This statement requires the acceptance that many people live in horrible circumstances. Some are able to cope without the use of drugs; others use drugs as a primary means of coping. Until we are in a position to offer an alternative

means of survival to these individuals, we are in no position to cast moral judgment. The health and well-being of the individual are of primary concern; if individuals are unwilling or unable to change addictive behavior at this time, they should not be denied services. *Attempts should be made to reduce the harm of their habits as much as possible* (Westermeyer n.d.).

According to Westermeyer, the Dutch (who created this approach to drug use and abuse) have "an 80% connection rate with the addicted population," while in the United States we are 80% disconnected from our addicted populations. In fact, through our punitive model in dealing with drug users, the strongest connection we have with the addicted population in the United States comes when they are arrested and jailed.

COMMUNITY-BASED DRUG PREVENTION

Community-based programs are very broad and take into account the community's youth, parents, businesses, media, schools, law enforcement, religious or fraternal groups, civic or volunteer groups, healthcare professionals, and government agencies with expertise in the field of substance abuse. The primary goal of community-based prevention is to provide coordinated programs among the numerous agencies and organizations involved in prevention. Prevention requires communities to conduct a structured review of current prevention programs to determine (1) whether the programs in place were examined and tested according to rigorous scientific standards during their development and (2) whether these programs incorporate the basic principles of prevention that have been identified in research. Usually, prevention programs at the community level ask the following questions (Sloboda and David 1999):

- Does the program have components for the individual, the family, the school, the media, community organizations, and healthcare providers? Are the program components well integrated in theme and content so that they reinforce rather than duplicate one another?
- Does the prevention program use media and community education strategies to increase public awareness, attracting community sup-

KEY TERMS

harm reduction model
a society-wide approach to drug use and/or abuse that focuses on reducing the harm experienced by the drug user and/or abuser as well as the harm to society

port, reinforcing the school-based curriculum for students and parents, and keeping the public informed of the program's progress?

- Are interventions carefully designed to reach different at-risk populations, and are they of sufficient duration to make an impact?
- Does the program follow a structured organizational plan that progresses from needs assessment through planning, implementation, and review to refinement, with feedback to and from the community at all stages?
- Are the objectives and activities specific, time-limited, feasible (in terms of available resources), and integrated so that they work together across program components and can be used to evaluate program progress and outcomes?

Often, these programs set up prevention policy boards to oversee planning and implementation. Boards should include representatives from law enforcement, juvenile justice, education, recreation, social services, private industry, health and mental health agencies, churches, civic organizations, and other community agencies that serve youth and families. They should also include one or several youth members. "The community can be a target group, especially when there is extensive community denial or lack of awareness, lack of clear policies, poor law enforcement, and so on. Public awareness campaigns, political action, and similar efforts are appropriate at this level of prevention" (Tinzmann and Hixson 1992, pp. 2, 3).

Community prevention programs can also direct their attention to changing the legal and social environment regarding alcohol, tobacco, and other drug supplies (**ATOD**) and toward youth (CPRD 2000). This effort also includes individual and environmental strategies. For example, an environmental approach to reducing underage drinking might involve training clerks to insist on proper age identification when selling alcoholic beverages. An individual approach might involve education efforts, such as a media campaign, aimed at discouraging young people from drinking (Silver Gate Group and Robert Wood Johnson Foundation 2001).

Other community-based strategies include the following:

- Strengthening the enforcement of existing legal regulations of ATOD sales and use
- Educating merchants and servers about alcohol and tobacco sales laws
- Regulating legislation regarding the sale of alcohol and tobacco to minors
- Implementing "use and lose" laws, which allow for the suspension of the driver's license of a person younger than 21 years of age following a conviction for any alcohol or drug violation (e.g., use, possession, or attempt to purchase with or without false identification)
- Imposing regulations on location and density of retail outlets—that is, monitoring the number of unsupervised vending machines dispensing cigarettes to minors in a given community and monitoring the number of retail establishments selling alcohol and tobacco near schools

In conclusion, community prevention emphasizes comprehensive drug abuse prevention programs that include multiple components, such as the use of media, drug education in schools, parent education, community organizations, and formulation of drug-related health policy. In essence, community drug prevention seeks to reduce drug abuse by informing, coordinating, and increasing the level of drug use at the community level.

SCHOOL-BASED DRUG PREVENTION

Education has been used extensively in the past to control the use and abuse of drugs, especially alcohol and tobacco. Drug education actually began in the late 1800s, when most states required that the harmful effects of certain drugs be taught. An example of an early educational attempt to curb or stop drug abuse is the temperance movement in the late 19th century. The Women's Christian Temperance Union (WCTU) and the Anti-Saloon League taught that alcohol consumption was harmful and contrary to Christian morality.

KEY TERMS

ATOD
alcohol, tobacco, and other drugs

Years ago, when drug prevention was first attempted, most substance abuse experts thought that schools should be responsible for educating the public about the dangerous use and eventual abuse of drugs because education is school's main objective. Schools began teaching about drug use, but in the beginning, drug prevention focused on individual factors, such as the dangers of particular types of drugs, the dangers of trusting individuals who sell drugs, and other scare tactics. One problem with this approach was that students varied enormously with regard to their drug experiences. Often, the students had already tried the "dangerous" drugs and had experienced only pleasurable effects with few negative consequences. Their experiences occurred *before* their exposure to drug prevention programs that relied on negative information, which is generally known as the **scare tactic approach**. Many self-reported use surveys revealed that these programs were not successful. With such audiences of drug users, the warnings are short-lived, not believed, or perceived as exaggerations. Table 17.2 summarizes the most popular, common, school-based drug prevention programs by including the premise, strategies, and effectiveness of the following approaches: (a) cognitive, (b) affective, (c) combined cognitive and affective, (d) social learning/cognitive behavioral, and (e) normative education. Table 17.2 also details the strengths (if any) and weaknesses of each approach.

Curriculum-Based Drug Education Objectives

In an effort to educate students about the dangers of drug use, school-based drug education programs and objectives have been implemented in most U.S. school curriculums. Specific educational topics have been established for elementary, junior high, and senior high and college levels:

Elementary Level

Drugs versus poisons

Effects of alcohol, tobacco, and marijuana on the body

Differences between candy and drugs

Drug overdoses

Dangers of experimentation

How to say "no" to peers using drugs

Reasons for taking drugs: curing illness, pleasure, escape, parental use, and ceremony

Junior High Level

How peer pressure works

How to say "no" to peer pressure

How drugs affect the body, physiologically and psychologically

Where to seek help when needed

Attitudes toward drug use

How to have fun without drugs

Harmful effects of tobacco, alcohol, and marijuana on the body

Stress management and building positive self-esteem

How advertisers push drugs

Consequences of breaking drug laws

Differences between wine, beer, and distilled spirits

Family drug use

Family drinking problems and family members who may have drug addiction problems

Images of violence and drug use in rock and rap music

Teenage drug abuse and associated problems

Senior High and College Level

Responsible use of medications

How drugs affect the body and the mind

Legal versus illegal drugs

Table 17.2 **Summary of Common School-Based Drug Prevention Approaches**

APPROACH	PREMISE	STRATEGIES	EFFECTIVENESS
Cognitive	If youths understand the dangers of AOD, they will not use them.	Teach pharmacology of alcohol and other drugs, how they are used, long-range consequences of use—usually through scare tactics.	Seldom effective; sometimes detrimental—arouses curiosity and encourages experimentation. "Dire facts" are not credible; knowledge alone does not counteract peer pressure. Knowledge is necessary, but not sufficient; focus on more immediate physical/social consequences may work.
Affective	High self-esteem, values consistent with nonuse, and good problem-solving and decision-making skills help youth avoid AOD.	Raise self-esteem. Teach values and life skills. Typically, do not include AOD information.	Do not decrease rate of use. Some community members and parents protest teaching values and decision making. Need to include AOD information.
Combined cognitive and affective	Students need both information and life skills to avoid AOD use.	Teach problem-solving, decision-making, peer pressure resistance skills; and provide explicit information about AOD to connect life skills and AOD use and consequences.	Little consistent effect on reducing AOD use, although some successes have been reported.
Social learning/ cognitive-behavioral approach	AOD use usually begins in a social setting between grades 5 and 9, usually with peers, but sometimes adults; youth need skills for resisting these pressures. (Based on Bandura's social learning theory.)	Teach how to identify pressures from peers, media, advertising, families. Teach resistance skills, model counterarguments. Students role play pressure situations and actively practice resisting.	Sometimes effective, especially if peers are involved in instruction and when students already have other fairly well-developed social skills. Little evidence that effects last.
Normative education approach	Youth overestimate the extent of AOD use among peers and thus may use AOD to feel part of the group.	Correct misconceptions, demonstrate actual norms through discussion, develop nonuse norms.	Success with some drugs; not very effective with alcohol. Some youngsters may believe that fewer peers use AOD than actually do, and may come to feel AOD use is more acceptable than they did before entering the program.

AOD: alcohol and other drugs

Source: U.S. Department of Health and Human Services, Office for Substance Abuse Prevention (1989). Figure 2.1, Factors that Influence Alcohol and Other Drug Use. In *Prevention plus II: Tools for creating and sustaining drug-free communities* (p. 19). (DHHS Publication No. (ADM) 89-1649). Rockville, MD: Author. Distributed by the National Clearinghouse for Alcohol and Drug Information.

Drinking and driving

Drug effects on the fetus

Recreational drug use

Ways of coping with problems: anger and stress management

How to detect problem drug users

Drug education, prevention, and treatment

Positive and negative role models

How to build positive self-esteem

Criminal sanctions for various types of drug use

"Binge" drinking

Drugs and driving

Date rape

Addiction to drugs and alcoholism

Principal Questions for School-Based Programs

The following questions should be asked to improve the outcomes of drug education programs:

- Do the school-based programs reach children from kindergarten through high school? If not, do they at least reach children during the critical middle school or junior high years?
- Do the programs contain multiple years of intervention (all through the middle school or junior high years)?
- Do the programs use a well-tested, standardized intervention with detailed lesson plans and student materials?
- Do the programs use age-appropriate interactive teaching methods (modeling, role playing, discussion, group feedback, reinforcement, extended practice)?
- Do the programs foster prosocial bonding to the school and community?
- Do the programs teach social competence (communication, self-efficacy, assertiveness) and drug resistance skills that are culturally and developmentally appropriate?
- Do the programs promote positive peer influence?
- Do the programs promote antidrug social norms?

- Do the programs emphasize skills-training teaching methods?
- Do the programs include an adequate "dosage" (10–15 sessions in year 1 and another 10–15 booster sessions)?
- Is there periodic evaluation to determine whether the programs are effective?

FAMILY-BASED PREVENTION PROGRAMS

Primary family risk factors that predispose youth to find drugs attractive include the following:

- Chaotic home environments, particularly in which parents abuse substances or suffer from mental illnesses
- Ineffective parenting, especially with children with difficult temperaments and conduct disorders
- Lack of mutual attachments and nurturing

"Results from longitudinal studies of children, particularly those children most at risk for problems, indicate that families can protect children and youth against drug use and abuse through effective family management practices that impart skills young people can use in resisting social pressures to use drugs" (NIH and NIDA 1998, p. 49).

If the just listed risk factors are the primary risk factors, *protective factors*—the factors that can insulate against drug use—include the following:

- Strong parent–child bonds
- Parental monitoring with clear rules of conduct within the family unit and involvement of parents in the lives of their children
- Open communication of values within the family
- High levels of supervision and monitoring
- No inconsistent disciplining from lackadaisical to extreme enforcement of rules, and no "say one thing and then do another"
- Consistent high levels of parental warmth, affection, and emotional support

In addition, research shows that protective family factors can moderate the effects of risk factors. The risk of associating with peers who use drugs can be offset by protective family factors, such as parent conventionality, maternal adjustment, and strong parent–child attachment.

Prevention at the family level needs to stress parent–child interaction strategies, communication skills, child management practices, and family management skills. Research has also shown that parents need to take a more active role in their children's lives. This includes talking to their children about drugs, monitoring their activities, getting to know their friends, and understanding their problems and personal concerns (NIH and NIDA 1998).

Prevention Principles for Family-Based Programs

In conclusion, family-based prevention programs need to do the following:

- Reach families of children at each stage of development.
- Train parents in behavioral skills to
  - Reduce conduct problems in children.
  - Improve parent–child relations, including positive reinforcement, listening and communication skills, and problem solving.
  - Provide consistent discipline and rule making.
  - Monitor children's activities during adolescence.
- Include an educational component for parents with drug information for them and their children.
- Focus on families whose children are in kindergarten through 12th grade to enhance protective factors.
- Provide access to counseling services for families at risk.

Drug Prevention Programs in Higher Education

The seriousness of alcohol and other drug use on college campuses is underscored by the following findings (Phoenix House 2000):

- According to the Core Institute, an organization that surveys college drinking practices, 300,000 of today's college students will eventually die of alcohol-related causes, such as drunk driving accidents, cirrhosis of the liver, various cancers, and heart disease.
- Of today's first-year college students, 159,000 will drop out of school next year because of alcohol or other drug-related reasons.

- Almost one-third of college students admit to having missed at least one class because of their alcohol or drug use.
- One night of heavy drinking can impair a person's ability to think abstractly for up to 30 days, limiting the ability to relate textbook reading to classroom discussions or to think through processes such as football plays.

As we can see, the use of alcohol and other drugs is a serious problem within the college or university environment. Major problems on college campuses resulting from such drug abuse include property damage, poor academic performance, damaged relationships, unprotected sexual activity, physical injuries, date rape, and suicide (Perkins 1997).

It is obvious that with all these negative findings regarding alcohol and other drug use on college campuses, prevention programs are vital. Next, we review the major prevention programs that currently exist in higher education.

OVERVIEW AND CRITIQUE OF EXISTING PREVENTION PROGRAMS

Information-Only or Awareness Model

One of the earliest preventive interventions, this model is based on the belief that if people are given extensive information about the harmful effects of drugs, it will change their attitudes about use and abuse. This model assumes that people are rational enough to seriously curtail or stop drug use based on information. Obviously, today we know that, at most, the majority of drug users exposed to the **information-only or awareness model** become more knowledgeable about the effects of drugs, but this approach has very little influence on the use of habitual or addictive-type drugs.

KEY TERMS

information-only or awareness model
assumes that teaching about the harmful effects of drugs will change attitudes about use and abuse

Attitude Change Model or Affective Education Model

The **attitude change model or affective education model** assumes that people use drugs because they have poor self-esteem (Gonzalez and Clement 1994). As a result, prevention focuses on strengthening self-image, building up positive self-esteem, and boosting self-confidence. A problem with this model is that attitudes often are resistant to change and fluctuate depending on such environmental influences as peer and party settings. Attitudes that were formed in an educational setting (drug and alcohol classes) are abandoned in substance use settings.

Social Influences Model

The **social influences model** assumes that substance abuse results from multiple influences. Although "outside" influences are perceived as major influences, "inner" influences are also taken into account. Inner influences such as prior socialization, a vulnerability to please others, and a need to be accepted by friends and peers are likewise taken into account. This prevention strategy emphasizes peer resistance and "inoculation" techniques. Techniques primarily include the following (Gonzalez and Clement 1994):

1. Offering factual information about the consequences of drug use
2. Guiding development of skills to recognize outer and inner pressures to use drugs, methods, and techniques to resist usage
3. Communicating correct information about the extent of drug use by students of similar ages

KEY TERMS

attitude change model or affective education model
assumes that people use drugs because of lack of self-esteem

social influences model
assumes that drug users lack resistance skills

ecological or person-in-environment model
stresses that changes in the environment change people's attitudes about drugs

4. Modeling, rehearsing, and reinforcing skills for resisting drugs when friends or peers expect compliance
5. Persuading students to try these resistance approaches and techniques in classroom or group settings and in peer group settings away from the classroom

By far, this method has been more successful than the information-only and attitude change models. Although it works best when it begins at the junior high school level, refresher courses should be administered at least every 2 years. Some research findings indicate that although this method is least effective with alcohol consumption, it *is* effective with marijuana and cigarette smoking (Gonzalez and Clement 1994).

Ecological or Person-in-Environment Model

This model is one of the newest types of prevention programs. "Interventions based on this model have multiple components and are designed to address both individuals and the policies, practices, and social norms that affect students on campuses or in the community" (Gonzalez and Clement 1994, p. 3). Developed from human ecology, the **ecological or person-in-environment model** stresses that changes in the environment change people. Although the ecological or person-in-environment model does not ignore substance use from individual causes, such as personal beliefs and perception of risk, it does primarily focus on the causes from the social environment (Hansen 1997, p. 6). "The central tenet [beliefs] of social ecology is that individual behavior is mainly the result of socialization; to change the behavior, we must change the social institutions that shape it" (Hansen 1997, p. 6). Hansen also stated "the strongest predictors of alcohol and drug abuse among young people are social."

This perspective emphasizes that it is important to take into account all of the environments that may have an impact on drug use. Friends, acquaintances, roommates, and classmates in dorms, sororities, and fraternities, at parties, cafes, and nightspots can influence students.

As a result, this model advocates the following drug prevention strategies (Gonzalez and Clement 1994):

1. Dissemination of drug information
2. Cognitive and behavioral skills training for youth, parents, and professionals
3. Mass media programming
4. Development of grassroots citizen interest groups
5. Leadership training for key organization and community officials
6. Policy analysis and reformulation

The college campus has long served as an initiator and perpetuator for drug use and abuse. Fraternity drunkenness, for example, was decried as early as 1840 (Horowitz 1987). In 1988, an 18-year-old student attending Rutgers University died of alcohol poisoning at a fraternity party. In a television interview following the incident, then-Chancellor Edward Bloustein described fraternities as "organized conspiracies dedicated to the consumption of alcohol" (Hansen 1997, p. 5).

Chemical abuse on campus is linked to the vast majority of vandalism, fights, accidents, sexually transmitted diseases, unplanned pregnancies, racial bias incidents, and date rape, and at least one-third of academic attrition (Koss et al. 1987). Although campus prevention programs and research date back several decades, such efforts remained isolated and sporadic until the late 1970s. All campuses now have medium to extensive alcohol and other drug prevention programs in effect.

Examples of Large-Scale Drug Prevention Programs

BACCHUS AND GAMMA PEER EDUCATION NETWORK

In 1975, an organization known as BACCHUS (Boosting Alcohol Consciousness Concerning the Health of University Students) was developed as a national student organization. Soon BACCHUS realized that many of its affiliates were members of sororities and fraternities; therefore, it renamed the organization **BACCHUS and GAMMA** (Greeks Advocating Mature Management of Alcohol) **Peer Education Network**. Currently, there are approximately 1000 international BACCHUS and GAMMA peer education affiliates with approximately 25,000

active members (BACCHUS and GAMMA 2000a). In the United States, there are approximately 850 affiliates.

The original goal of this program was to prevent alcohol abuse. Today, the program has broadened its goals to include other student health and safety issues, such as sexual responsibility, tobacco use, marijuana use, and sexual assault. The mission of this organization is to actively promote peer education as a useful element of campus health education and wellness efforts (BACCHUS and GAMMA 2000b). Drug education and activities are created to increase awareness, development, and promotion of positive lifestyles and decision-making skills (BACCHUS and GAMMA 2000b).

Each campus affiliate group plans programs according to the needs of its specific campus. "Some members choose to focus on National Collegiate Awareness Week, Sexual Responsibility Week, Safe Spring Break programs, or tobacco prevention. Others use formal peer education training to present programs to the campus community" (BACCHUS and GAMMA 2000b, p. 1).

FUND FOR THE IMPROVEMENT OF POST-SECONDARY EDUCATION DRUG PREVENTION PROGRAMS

In 1987, a huge explosion of campus drug prevention programs began. It was spawned by a $14 billion annual budget for college drug prevention placed in the Drug-Free Schools and Communities Act of 1986 (now titled the Safe and Free Schools and Communities Act). The funding was parceled out by the Department of Education, Fund for the Improvement of Post-Secondary Education (FIPSE). FIPSE Drug Prevention Programs awarded about 100 grants per year from 1987 until 1996 via a grant competition that called

KEY TERMS

BACCHUS and GAMMA Peer Education Network
a national and international association of college and university peer education programs focused on alcohol abuse prevention and other related student health and safety issues

for colleges to mount institution-wide programs. The guiding philosophy included the following points:

- A small, isolated program was seen as making little difference, but a comprehensive program reaching into several areas of the institution could send many consistent anti-use messages that would eventually reach "critical mass" and change the campus environment.
- There should be well-known, top-down administrative support for prevention programming.
- There should be well-written and carefully implemented policies about chemical use on campus.

The hundreds of new programs, whose administrators met and interacted in annual grantee conferences, generated the sense that there was a national prevention movement in higher education. The Network of Colleges and Universities Dedicated to Prevention of Alcohol and Other Drug Abuse was founded, incorporating 900 institutions. The Network is supported by a new Higher Education Center for Alcohol and Other Drug prevention funded by the U.S. Department of Education, which provides a range of materials and newsletters (Ryan et al. 1995).

In 1989, FIPSE initiated a grant program for regional campus prevention consortia. By joining a consortium, colleges and universities could pool scarce resources, create support networks, and train new workers. In 1994, more than 100 regional consortia were listed on a database maintained by the Higher Education Center. In 1999, more than two-thirds of all 3300 institutions of higher education were affiliates of the Network, belonged to a regional consortium, or had started other programs under the aegis of FIPSE.

From a decade of experience, several exemplary approaches emerged. These strategies might be the predominant focus of a program or one of a number of complementary components of a comprehensive effort. The strategies are addressed next.

Peer-Based Efforts

Student peers can be involved in a number of ways: as educators, mentors, counselors, or facili-

tators of prevention and outreach work. Such an approach multiplies manpower tremendously, reaches the students who are apt to become lost in the flow, is not perceived as an outside or authoritarian intrusion, speaks the language of students, and works to change the predominant cultural tone on campus. Peers can conduct classroom presentations, work informational tables or drop-in centers, create prevention newsletters, and establish links to community groups. It is important to carefully train and supervise peer facilitators. Many peer programs are residence hall-based, taking advantage of the training of residence hall assistants and peer facilitators (BACCHUS and GAMMA 1994).

Curriculum Infusion

Infusion of a skill or topic across the curriculum has been used in conjunction with classes on writing skills, gender issues, and other areas. Curriculum infusion can be undertaken at individual institutions or as a consortium project. The advantage of curriculum infusion is that it involves faculty members, achieves open discussion of drug issues in the classroom as part of the normal educational process, and stimulates critical thinking about drug issues.

Improvisational Theater Groups

Improvisational theater groups that tackle health and wellness issues can be lively, stimulating, and provocative, often breaking through peer and institutional denial and bringing issues home to students with a dramatic emotional impact. Improvisational topics can include date rape, sexually transmitted disease, children of alcoholics on campus, and denial of chemical dependency.

Strategies to Change Misperceptions of Use

Social psychologists Alan Berkowitz and Wesley Perkins, both of Hobart and William Smith Colleges, have conducted influential research illustrating that students often have incorrect estimates (exaggerated misperceptions) of drug use by their peers (Perkins 1991 and 1997; Perkins and Berkowitz 1986). Thus, they misperceive the peer norms governing drug use, which may lead them to "follow imaginary peers." This idea is a modification of the traditional understanding that peers influence peers. It follows logically that activities demonstrating the accurate use pattern to students and correcting misperceptions will indirectly affect overall use patterns. These efforts have included simply publicizing the results of alcohol and drug use surveys and awarding prizes for coming up with correct estimates.

Alternative Events

Alternative events, such as "mocktail" parties, alcohol-free discos, and indoor rock climbing, especially as alternatives to pre-sporting events and holiday parties, help avoid some events that are traditionally associated with chemical abuse.

Programs That Change Marketing of Alcohol on and near Campuses

Institutions of higher education are a major focus of alcohol marketing. Alcoholic beverage producers sponsor many campus events, and these companies buy considerable newspaper advertising. The National College Magazine *U*, for example, had a 3-year advertising contract with Anheuser-Busch (Magnum and Taylor 1990). This publicity sends many pro-use messages. Prevention programs have recruited business and advertising majors to work on curtailing such marketing projects.

Finally, it is better to embed prevention messages within an overall wellness perspective. Students are concerned about health and wellness issues, not programs that come off as dogmatic or preachy, moralizing, exaggerating, and nagging—perhaps reminding them of life at home.

DARE (DRUG ABUSE RESISTANCE EDUCATION)

One major drug prevention program that had high hopes for success was the school-based drug education programs incorporated in approximately 70% of the nation's school districts—**DARE (Drug Abuse Resistance Education)**. DARE reaches 25 million students and has been adopted in 44 foreign countries (*Law Enforcement News* 1996). Recent evaluations of this program show that, on a short-term basis, DARE improved students' views of themselves and increased their sense of personal responsibility. However, the program has *not*

yielded a measurable, significant change in drug use (Rosenbaum and Hanson 1998; Vogt, 2003, p. 1). Moreover, this drug education program showed a strong inconsistency between students' self-reported attitudes about use and actual drug use (Clayton et al. 1991; Ennett et al. 1994; Vogt 2003). (See "Holding the Line" for more information on DARE and several other programs that attempt to prevent drug use.)

One major problem is that "over the past decade, a flurry of studies—by the U.S. surgeon general and the General Accounting Office, among others—found no significant difference in drug use between DARE graduates and students never exposed to the curriculum" (Vogt 2003, p. 1). Further, regarding graduates of the DARE program, one official said,

> I can't tell you how many kids told me DARE introduced them to drugs. The problem with DARE, other than that it's a multimillion dollar conglomerate in the business of selling T-shirts, is that it takes the burden off parents to raise their kids [drug free]. (Vogt 2003, p. 3)

Another major problem that has been identified is that the DARE drug education program is presented in the classroom by fully uniformed police officers. Although the officers are well intentioned and their efforts are commendable, they are hardly a mechanism for transmitting new norms that would find converts among students, except perhaps those already successfully socialized (Gopelrud 1991). More importantly, uniformed police officers used as teachers "sends the wrong message that drugs are a law enforcement issue, rather than a public health issue" (Zeese and Lewin 1998, p. 1).

DRUG COURTS

Although these courts of law vary in organization, in scope, and at what point intervention occurs, the underlying premise is that drug possession

KEY TERMS

DARE (Drug Abuse Resistance Education)
drug education program presented in elementary and junior high schools nationwide by police officers

▶ Holding the Line

Frustrating Results from National Drug Prevention Campaigns and Programs

In 1995, a disturbing study published by a group of researchers at the University of Michigan and backed by the U.S. Department of Health and Human Services (DHHS) and the National Institute on Drug Abuse (NIDA) showed that the use of illicit drugs by young people had been rising steadily since 1992. The results of this study were even more perplexing because overall drug use had been declining over the same period. The increase was happening despite several seemingly successful efforts to combat drug abuse with high-powered prevention programs.

Since the 1980s, most funds allocated for drug prevention have been spent in three areas: criminal justice, major advertising campaigns, and DARE (Drug Abuse Resistance Education). Law enforcement professionals for hard-core addicts, especially in poor urban neighborhoods, have favored compulsory preventive programs. According to William N. Brownsberger, Assistant State Attorney General in the Massachusetts Narcotics and Special Investigations Division, addicts who are forced against their will to enter and remain in therapy can overcome their addiction. Roughly 90% of all addicts are arrested at least once every year, giving the criminal justice system plenty of opportunities to help them kick their habits.

One highly visible persuasive effort to end drug abuse has been the advertising campaign created by the Partnership for a Drug-Free America. The nation's advertising industry developed the Partnership and funded it by collaborating with advertisers and a variety of health and educational agencies. The goal was to promote images designed to make drug use look "uncool," especially to younger people. In addition to the creative services donated by advertising agencies, media organizations donated more than $2 billion of public service and advertising space to the Partnership between the late 1980s and 1990s.

In the early 1990s, the Partnership commissioned surveys to measure the effect of its media campaign on students in the Los Angeles and New York City school systems. On both coasts, increased exposure to the Partnership's messages appeared to dramatically change students' attitudes toward drugs. At the same time, however, the number of students who admitted using drugs actually increased.

Another high-visibility persuasive effort has been the nationwide DARE program, which was launched in Los Angeles in 1983. "DARE's curriculum reflects mainstream theories about the best way to reduce drinking, smoking, and drug use by children. . . . The program began as a collaboration between Los Angeles Police Department and the city's school district" (Miller 2001, p. A14). Using role-playing techniques and resistance training, uniformed police officers become social workers, talking with students in their classrooms, educating them about the dangers of drugs, and giving them the tools to resist temptation or peer pressure. They generally teach 17 classroom sessions.

> Today most school-based prevention programs, including DARE, assume that adolescents need grown-ups' help in resisting social pressures to use [drugs]. Therefore, they try to correct children's exaggerated beliefs about the prevalence of drug use among their peers. They offer them information about the physical and social effects of using and they try to impart "resistance skills" for making and acting on thoughtful decisions. (Miller 2001, A14)

Although DARE is the most popular drug education program ever developed for children, increasing numbers of critics claim that its benefits, if any, are short-lasting. Most DARE training begins in the 5th grade. At this age, students accept most of what they hear. By middle school, however, the effectiveness of DARE begins to erode. By high school, many students resist participation in the program. According to a researcher from the Research Triangle Institute in Durham, North Carolina, which conducted a $300,000 study on the impact of DARE, "Unless there's some sort of booster session that reinforces the original curriculum, the effects of most drug use prevention programs decay rather than increase over time." The findings of numerous research studies conducted on DARE's effectiveness suggest that DARE students were no less likely to use drugs than students who had not gone through the program (Ennett et al. 1994; Vogt 2003, p. 3). Some have even claimed that the DARE program teaches kids to become curious about illicit drug use or actually motivates them to do drugs (Vogt 2003, p. 3). Further, "[a]s DARE America celebrated its 20th anniversary, the nation's most widely used school-based drug prevention program was struggling with a credibility crisis that has devastated the organization financially and threatens its survival" (Vogt 2003). Reports indicate that a number of school districts throughout the country have abandoned the program, finding DARE to be ineffective in curbing both licit and illicit drug use.

In light of the diminishing returns from various drug prevention programs, in late 1996 the Clinton administration proposed a compulsory drug test for teenagers who are applying for their driver's licenses. Like everything else, the proposal had both supporters and critics. Although this tactic may be part of the answer, prevention programs that have measurable, *long-lasting* effects remain difficult to find.

Sources: Brownsberger, W. N. "Just Say 'Criminal Justice.'" *Boston Globe* (20 October 1996).

Ennett, S. T., N. S. Tobler, C. L. Ringwalt, and R. L. Flewelling. "How Effective Is Drug Abuse Resistance Education? A Metaanalysis of Project D.A.R.E. Outcome Evaluations." *American Journal of Public Health* 84 (1994): 1394–1401.

Gordon, P. "The Truth About D.A.R.E." *Buzz Magazine* (July 1996).

Gordon, P. "Can Madison Avenue Really Save America by Making Illegal Drugs Totally Uncool?" *Buzz Magazine* (August 1996).

Miller, D. W. "DARE Reinvents Itself—With Help from Its Social-Scientist Critics." *Chronicle of Higher Education* 48 (19 October 2001): A12–14.

Vogt, A. "Now Many 'Just Say No' to DARE." *Chicago Tribune* (26 January 2003): 1, 3.

and use is not only a law enforcement/criminal justice problem, but also a public health problem (Sherin and Mahoney 1996). In **drug court** programs, criminal justice agencies collaborate closely with the substance abuse treatment community and other societal institutions to design and operate the program. Thus, the key goal is to divert substance abusers into supervised community treatment centers in an attempt to eliminate the destructive behavior. A committee usually composed of a judge, the district attorney, a public defender, the probation department, and treatment center officials determines whether treatment is needed and the type and length of treatment. At the first National Drug Court Conference, one researcher reported, "These courts rely on strong collaboration among judges, prosecutors, defense lawyers, and related supporting agencies (such as case management, corrections, pretrial services, probation, etc.), on the one hand, and a partnership with treatment agencies (or providers) and other community organizations and representatives on the other" (Goldkamp 1993, p. 33).

The treatment phase generally consists of: (1) detoxification (removal of physical dependence on drugs from body), (2) stabilization (treating the psychological craving for the drug), and (3) aftercare (helping the defendant obtain education or job training, find a job, and remain drug free). (OJP 2000)

To date, nearly every county in every state in the United States has implemented at least one drug court.

Overall, there have been lower rearrest rates for defendants participating in drug court sentencing and there were statistically significant differences in disposition between those assigned to drug court and the comparison groups. Those assigned to drug court were more likely not to face further prosecution and less likely to serve probation or short jail terms. Finally, using drug court and its system of administering treatment within a legal atmosphere is more cost-effective than criminal courts: between $1200 and $3500 per participant compared with approximately $5000 to incarcerate the same defendant (OJP DCCTAP 1999). Research shows, however, that we should be cautious

KEY TERMS

drug court
court designed to focus on treatment programs and options in place of punishment for drug offenses

for two reasons: (1) The research on the effectiveness of these courts was done very early—the courts were in operation fewer than 10 months, and (2) these courts were very selective of the defendants allowed to participate—the criticism being that the courts tended to select violators who would have a better chance for rehabilitation.

It is apparent that drug courts need more time to operate, and more evaluation research needs to be conducted. The most promising aspect of these courts is the emphasis on treating drug addiction instead of simply punishing without treating as has been the case historically.

Problems with Assessing the Success of Drug Prevention Programs

Both the National Institute on Drug Abuse (NIDA) and individual researchers have evaluated the multitude of drug abuse prevention programs in the United States. The general conclusions of these studies are as follows:

- Very few programs have demonstrated clear success or have adequately evaluated themselves.
- The relationships among information about drugs, attitudes toward use, and actual use are unclear in these programs.

Some factors that are key to developing successful programs include the following:

- Prevention must be coordinated at different levels. Successful programs involve families, schools, and communities. In some cases, these efforts are not coordinated.
- The program must be integrated into the ongoing activities of schools, families, and community organizations. Superficial introduction of drug prevention strategies has limited effects. For instance, distributing literature door-to-door, making in-class presentations of the harmful effects of drugs, and posting banners and slogans warning of the consequences of drug abuse in communities are not successful methods. Instead, programs that are comprehensive and community-wide, integrated into

neighborhood clubs, organizations, and church activities, are more likely to have a long-term impact on preventing drug use. A clear example is the yearly Great American Smokeout launched against tobacco use.

- Personal autobiographical and social experience accounts of former drug abusers should be included in drug information that is distributed. Recipients of drug prevention information should be given real-life accounts of use, abuse, despair, and successful drug rehabilitation. Just receiving drug information alone has little impact, either initially or over the long term.

Other Alternatives to Drug Use

It has been suggested that people have an innate need to alter their conscious state. This belief is based on the observation that, as part of their normal play, preschoolers deliberately whirl themselves dizzy and even momentarily choke each other to lose consciousness (Wilson and Wilson 1975). Some young children progress to discovering and using chemicals (such as sniffing shoe polish or gasoline) to alter consciousness and learn to be very secretive about this behavior. They learn to be circumspect or come to feel guilty and repress the desire to alter consciousness when adults catch them in these activities.

If this desire to alter the state of consciousness is inherent in human beings, then the use of psychoactive drugs, legal or illegal, in adulthood is natural. Drug abuse is, therefore, a logical continuation of a developmental sequence that goes back to early childhood (Carroll 1977; Weil 1972).

Other researchers question why, even if there is an innate desire to alter consciousness, only some people progress to abusing chemical substances. It appears that people who do not abuse psychoactive drugs have found positive alternatives to altering consciousness; they feel no need to take chemical substances for this purpose. Involvement in activities such as Boy Scouts and Girl Scouts, youth sports teams, music groups, the YMCA and YWCA, drug-free video game centers, drug-free dances, environmental and historical preservation projects, and social and service projects are viable alternatives to drug use. The rationale for these programs is that youth will find these activities engaging enough to forgo alcohol and drug use (Forman and Linney 1988).

This strategy is known as the **alternatives approach**. Workers in the drug abuse field tend to agree on its effectiveness. They note that young ex-abusers of common illicit drugs are more likely to stop when they gain satisfaction from exploring positive alternatives rather than from a fear of consequent harm. The alternatives approach assumes the following (Cohen 1971):

1. People abuse drugs voluntarily to fill a need or basic drive.
2. Most people abuse drugs for negative reasons. They may be dealing with negative feelings or situations, such as relieving boredom, anxiety, depression, tension, or other unpleasant emotional and psychological states. They may be rebelling against authority, trying to escape feelings of loneliness or inadequacy, or trying to be accepted by peers. Peer pressure is extremely important as an inducing force.
3. Some people who abuse drugs believe the experience is positive. They may feel that their sensual experiences or music enjoyment is enhanced, or that they have achieved altered states of consciousness, or they may simply experience a sense of adventure. Some people may want to explore their own consciousness and reasons for the attraction to drug use.

Whether the reasons for drug use are positive or negative, the effects sought can be achieved through alternative, nondrug means. Such means are preferable to drug use and more constructive because the person is not relying on a psychoactive substance for satisfaction; rather, he or she is finding satisfaction based on personal achievements. Ideally, this approach should lead to a lifetime of self-satisfaction.

Table 17.3 lists various types of experiences, the motives for such experiences, the probable drugs of abuse with which they are associated, and alternatives to these drugs. As shown in the table, any constructive activity can be considered an alternative to drug abuse. For example, a young person who needs an outlet for increased physical energy might respond better to dance and movement

training or a project in preventive medicine than to work on ecological projects. In a large alternatives program established in Idaho, the following activities were planned during a month: arts and crafts, karate, re-forestation, backpacking, Humane Society dog show, horseback riding, artwork for posters for various programs, astronomy, camping, and volunteering in a local hospital.

MEDITATION

Some of the most intriguing research about the brain is being done on the state of the mind during **meditation**. In certain countries, such as India, people have long histories of being able to achieve certain goals through meditation. The word *yoga* is derived from the Sanskrit word for union, or yoking, meaning "the process of discipline by which a person attains union with the Absolute." In a sense, it refers to the use of the mind to control itself and the body.

Meditation involves brain wave activity centered on ponderous, contemplative, and reflective thought. An individual who meditates is able to decrease oxygen consumption within a matter of minutes by as much as 20%, a level usually reached only after 4 to 5 hours of sleep. However, meditation is physiologically different from sleep, based on the electroencephalograph (EEG) pattern and rate of decline of oxygen consumption. Along with the decreased metabolic rate and changes in EEG, there is also a marked decrease in blood lactate. Lactate is produced by metabolism of skeletal muscle, and the decrease is probably due to the reduced activity of the sympathetic nervous system during meditation. Heart rate and respiration are also slowed.

KEY TERMS

alternatives approach
an approach emphasizing the exploration of positive alternatives to drug abuse, based on replacing the pleasurable feelings gained from drug abuse with involvement in social and educational activities

meditation
a state of consciousness in which there is a constant level of awareness focusing on one object; for example, yoga and Zen Buddhism

Table 17.3 Experiences, Motives, and Possible Alternatives for a Drug Abuser

EXPERIENCE	CORRESPONDING MOTIVES	DRUGS ABUSED	POSSIBLE ALTERNATIVES
Physical	Desire for physical well-being: physical relaxation, relief from sickness, desire for more energy	Alcohol, sedative-hypnotics, stimulants, marijuana	Athletics, dance, exercise, hiking, diet, carpentry, outdoor work, swimming, hatha yoga
Sensory	Desire to magnify sensorium: sound, touch, taste, need for sensual/sexual stimulation	Hallucinogens, marijuana, alcohol	Sensory awareness training, sky diving, experiencing sensory beauty of nature, scuba diving
Emotional	Relief from psychological pain: attempt to resolve personal problems, relief from bad mood, escape from anxiety, desire for emotional insight, liberation of feeling and emotional relaxation	Narcotics, alcohol, barbiturates, sedative-hypnotics	Competent individual counseling, well-run group therapy, instruction in psychology of personal development
Interpersonal	Desire to gain peer acceptance, break through interpersonal barriers, "communicate"; defiance of authority figures	Any, especially alcohol, marijuana	Expertly managed sensitivity and encounter groups, well-run group therapy, instruction in social customs, confidence training, emphasis on assisting others (e.g., YMCA or YWCA volunteers)
Social	Desire to promote social change, find identifiable subculture, tune out intolerable environmental conditions (e.g., poverty)	Marijuana, psychedelics	Social service community action in positive social change; helping the poor, aged, infirm, or young; tutoring handicapped individuals; ecology action; YMCA or YWCA Big Brother/Sister programs
Political	Desire to promote political change (out of desperation with the social-political order) and to identify with antiestablishment subgroup	Marijuana, psychedelics	Political service, lobbying for nonpartisan projects (e.g., Common Cause); field work with politicians and public officials
Intellectual	Desire to escape boredom, out of intellectual curiosity, to solve cognitive problems, gain new understanding in the world of ideas, research one's own awareness	Stimulants, sometimes psychedelics	Intellectual excitement through reading, debate, and discussion; creative games and puzzles; self-hypnosis; training in concentration
Creative-aesthetic	Desire to improve creative performance, enhance enjoyment of art already produced (e.g., music); enjoy imaginative mental productions	Marijuana, stimulants, psychedelics	Nongraded instruction in producing and/or appreciating art, music, drama, and creative hobbies
Philosophical	Desire to discover meaningful values, find meaning in life, help establish personal identity, organize a belief structure	Psychedelics, marijuana, stimulants	Discussions, seminars, courses on ethics, the nature of reality, relevant philosophical literature; explorations of value systems
Spiritual-mystical	Desire to transcend orthodox religion, develop spiritual insights, reach higher levels of consciousness, augment yogic practices, take a spiritual shortcut	Psychedelics, marijuana	Exposure to nonchemical methods of spiritual development; study of world religions, mysticism, meditation, yogic techniques

THE NATURAL MIND APPROACH

Some people who take drugs eventually look for other methods of maintaining the valuable parts of the drug experience. These people may learn to value the meditation "high" and abandon drugs. Long-term drug users sometimes credit their drug experiences with having given them a taste of their potential, even though continued use has diminished the novelty of drug use. After these individuals become established in careers, they claim to have grown out of chemically induced altered states of consciousness. As Andrew Weil (1972, p. 67) put it, "One does not see any long-time meditators give up meditation to become acid heads."

Although chemical highs are effective means of altering the state of consciousness, they interfere with the most worthwhile states of altered consciousness because they reinforce the illusion that highs come from external, material agents rather than from within your own nervous system.

Some people have difficulty using meditation as an alternative to drugs because, to be effective, meditation takes practice and concentration; in contrast, the effects of drugs are immediate. Nevertheless, it is within everyone's potential to meditate.

Discussion Questions

1. Figure 17.1 lists many factors that can influence drug use. Design a drug prevention program by selecting any one of the concentric circles and include all factors within that circle.

2. Comment on the harm reduction model as presented here and in other literature you may have. (For example, see http://www.habitsmart.com/harm.html; http://www.ennotes.com/legalizing-drugs/s716; and http://www.enotes.com/jax/index.php/enotes/search?q=drugs.) What are the major strengths and weaknesses of this model in comparison to the way the United States views drug users and/or abusers? Why do you think the U.S. government remains opposed to this approach? Speculate on how the United States would change if it were to adopt the harm reduction model.

3. What would you emphasize in a primary prevention program for junior high school students? High school students? College students?

4. How would you design a drug prevention program for nondetected committed or secret users? What would you emphasize?

5. What do you think is more likely to work today in drug prevention programs for America's youth: teaching moderate use or total abstinence? Why?

6. Your boss says, "We received a much smaller amount of money from the federal government to create a drug prevention program. I want you to focus on a community-based approach, school-based approach, or family-based prevention program." Which would you select and why?

7. How effective has BACCHUS and GAMMA Peer Education Network been on your campus? Can you give examples?

8. List and explain two potential strengths and two potential weaknesses of drug courts in comparison with traditional criminal courts in the United States.

9. Evaluate the DARE drug prevention program. What problems has this program encountered with regard to its effectiveness?

10. What is your assessment of using the alternatives approach and meditation for preventing drug use? Do you think it works? Why or why not?

Key Terms

AOD 528

primary drug prevention programs 530

secondary drug prevention programs 530

tertiary drug prevention programs 530

harm reduction model 534

Summary

1 The 10 most prominent factors affecting an individual's use of drugs are as follows: (1) genetics, (2) personality traits, (3) attitudes and beliefs, (4) interpersonal and peer resistance skills, (5) community, (6) peers, (7) school policy, (8) local law enforcement, (9) personal situations, and (10) parents.

2 Three major types of prevention programs are (1) primary, (2) secondary, and (3) tertiary prevention.

3 Five major types of drug users that drug prevention programs have to recognize before assembling a program are (1) early experimenters, (2) nonproblem drug users/recreational users, (3) nondetected committed or secret users, (4) problem users, and (5) former users.

4 The four levels of comprehensive prevention programs for drug use and abuse are (1) the harm reduction model, (2) community-based prevention, (3) school-based prevention, and (4) family-based prevention.

5 Proactive family factors can moderate the effects of drug risk factors. The risk of associat-ing with peers who use drugs can be offset by protective family factors, such as parent conven-tionality, maternal adjustment, and strong parent–child attachment.

6 Four primary prevention programs that exist in higher education are the (1) information-only or awareness model, (2) attitude change model or affective education model, (3) social influences model, and (4) ecological or person-in-environment model.

7 The main goals of three of today's large-scale prevention programs include (1) BACCHUS and GAMMA Peer Education Network—a national and international association of college and uni-versity peer-education programs focused on alco-hol abuse prevention and other related student health and safety issues; (2) DARE—a once-popular nationwide drug prevention program presented in junior high schools by police officers; and (3) drug courts—a newer nationwide approach to preven-tion in which the primary purpose is to focus on treatment programs and options instead of pun-ishment for drug offenses.

8 Two additional possibilities for lessening or eliminating drug use are the alternatives approach and meditation. Alternatives to drug abuse are based on replacing the euphoria and pleasure gained by being high with involvement in social, recreational, and educational activities. Meditation is producing a state of consciousness in which there is a constant level of very satisfying awareness that is rewarding in itself without artifi-cial inducements (drugs). Yoga and Zen Buddhism are examples.

References

Alberti, R. E., and M. L. Emmons. *Your Perfect Right.* San Luis Obispo, CA: Impact Publishers, 1988.

BACCHUS and GAMMA. *Community College Guide to Peer Education.* Denver, CO: The BACCHUS and GAMMA Peer Education Network, 1994.

BACCHUS and GAMMA. *Energy, Education, Support.* Den-ver, CO: The BACCHUS and GAMMA Peer Education Network, 2000a. Available http://www.bacchusgamma. org/contact.asp.

BACCHUS and GAMMA. *What Is BACCHUS and GAMMA Network?* Denver, CO: The BACCHUS and GAMMA

Peer Education Network, 2000b. Available http://www.bacchusgamma.org/tour_2.asp.

Botvin, G. J., and T. A. Wills. "Personal and Social Skills Training: Cognitive-Behavioral Approaches to Substance Abuse Prevention." In *Prevention Research: Deterring Drug Abuse Among Children and Adolescents*. NIDA Research Monograph 64. Rockville, MD: NIDA (U.S. HHS, PHS, ADAMHA), 1985.

Carroll, E. "Notes on the Epidemiology of Inhalants." In *Review of Inhalants*, edited by C. W. Sharp and M. L. Brehm. NIDA Research Monograph No. 15. Washington, DC: National Institute on Drug Abuse, 1977.

Center for Prevention Research and Development (CPRD). *Research Based Approaches in the Community Domain*. Champaign, IL: University of Illinois Urbana Champaign, 2000. Available http://www.cprd.uiuc.edu/publications/principles/community_domain.html.

Clayton, R. R., R. Cattarello, L. E. Cay, and K. P. Walden. "Persuasive Communication and Drug Prevention: An Evaluation of the D.A.R.E. Program." In *Persuasive Communication and Drug Abuse Prevention*, edited by L. Donohew, H. Sypepher, and W. Bukowski, 83–107. Hillsdale, NJ: Erlbaum, 1991.

Cohen, A. Y. "The Journey Beyond Trips: Alternatives to Drugs." *Journal of Psychedelic Drugs* 3 (Spring 1971): 7–11.

Ennett, S. T., N. S. Tobler, C. L. Ringwalt, and R. L. Flewelling. "How Effective Is Drug Abuse Resistance Education? A Meta-analysis of Project D.A.R.E. Outcome Evaluations." *American Journal of Public Health* 84 (1994): 1394–1401.

Forman, S. G., and J. A. Linney. "School-Based Prevention of Adolescent Substance Abuse: Programs, Implementation and Future Direction." *School Psychology Review* 17 (1988): 550–558.

Goldkamp, J. *Justice and Treatment Innovation: The Drug Court Movement*. Washington, DC: National Institute of Justice and the State Justice Institute, 1993.

Gonzalez, G. M., and V. V. Clement, eds. *Preventing Substance Abuse*. U.S. Department of Education. Washington, DC: U.S. Government Printing Office, 1994.

Gopelrud E. N., ed. *Preventing Adolescent Drug Use: From Theory to Practice*. OSAP Monograph #8, DHHS Publication No. (ADM) 91–1725. Rockville, MD: Office of Substance Abuse Prevention, 1991.

Hansen, W. B. "A Social Ecology Theory of Alcohol and Drug Use Prevention Among College and University Students." In *Designing Alcohol and Other Drug Prevention Programs in Higher Education*. Newton, MA: Higher Education Center for Alcohol and Other Drug Prevention, U.S. Department of Education, 1997. Available http://www.edc.org/hec/pubs/theorybook/Hansen.html.

Holstein, M. E., W. E. Cohen, and P. Steinbroner. *A Matter of Balance: Personal Strategies for Alcohol and Other Drugs*. Ashland, OR: CNS Productions, 1995.

Horowitz, H. L. *Campus Life*. New York: Knopf, 1987.

Koss, M. P., C. A. Gidycz, and R. Wisniewski. "The Scope of Rape: Incidence and Prevalence of Sexual Aggression and Victimization in a National Sample of Higher Education Students." *Journal of Consulting and Clinical Psychology* 34 (1987): 186–196.

Law Enforcement News. "When It Comes to the Young, Anti-drug Efforts Are Going to Pot." 22 (1996): 441–447.

Magnum, A., and P. Taylor. "Peddling Booze on Campus: How to Spot It, How to Fight It." *Eta Sigma Gamman* 22 (1990): 1.

McIntyre, K., D. White, and R. Yoast. *Resilience Among High-Risk Youth*. Madison, WI: University of Wisconsin, 1990.

National Institutes of Health (NIH) and National Institute on Drug Abuse (NIDA). *Drug Abuse and Drug Abuse Research*. Washington, DC: U.S. Government Printing Office, 1998.

Norman, E. "Personal Factors Related to Substance Misuse: Risk Abatement and/or Resiliency Enhancement." In *Substance Abuse in Adolescence*, edited by T. P. Gulotta, G. R. Adamds, and R. Montemayor, 47–56. Thousand Oaks, CA: Sage Publications, 1994.

Office of Justice Programs (OJP). *OJP Drug Court Clearinghouse and Technical Assistance Project: Summary of Drug Court Activity by State and County*. Washington, DC: U.S. Government Printing Office, 10 January 2000.

Office of Justice Programs (OJP) Drug Court Clearinghouse and Technical Assistance Project (DCCTAP). *Looking at a Decade of Drug Courts*. Washington, DC: Drug Court Clearinghouse and Technical Assistance Project, 1999.

Perkins, H. W. "Confronting Misperceptions of Peer Use Norms Among College Students: An Alternative Approach for Alcohol and Other Drug Education Programs." In *The Higher Education Leaders/Peers Network Peer Prevention Program Resource Manual*, Washington, DC: Texas Christian University, U.S. Department of Education (FIPSE), 1991: 18–32.

Perkins, H. W. "College Student Misperceptions of Alcohol and Other Drug Norms Among Peers: Exploring Causes, Consequences, and Implications for Prevention Programs." In *Designing Alcohol and Other Drug Prevention Programs in Higher Education*. Newton, MA: U.S. Department of Education, Higher Education Center for Alcohol and Other Drug Prevention, 1997. Available http://www.edc.org/hec/pubs/theorybook/perkins.html.

Perkins, H. W., and A. D. Berkowitz. "Perceiving the Community Norms of Alcohol Use Among Students: Some Research Implications for Campus Alcohol Education Programming." *International Journal of the Addictions* 21, (1986): 861–976.

Phoenix House. *School Daze?* (2000). Available http://www.factsontap.org/collexp/Stats.htm.

Rosenbaum, D. P., and S. Hanson. "Assessing the Effects of School-Based Drug Education; A Six-Year Multi-level

Analysis of Project DARE." Department of Criminal Justice and Center for Research in Law and Justice. Chicago, IL: University of Illinois at Chicago, 6 April 1998. Available http://www.tfy.drugsense.org/uic.htm.

Ryan, B. E., T. Colthurst, and L. Segars. *College Alcohol Risk Assessment Guide*. San Diego: UCSD Extension, University of California at San Diego, 1995.

Sherin, K. M., and B. Mahoney. *Treatment Drug Courts: Integrating Substance Abuse Treatment with Legal Case Processing*. Rockville, MD: U.S. Department of Health and Human Services, 1996.

Shiffman, S., and T. A. Wills, eds. *Coping and Substance Abuse*. New York: Academic Press, 1987.

Silver Gate Group and Robert Wood Johnson Foundation. *Prevention 2000: Moving Effective Prevention Programs into Practice*. Princeton, NJ: Robert Wood Johnson Foundation, 2001.

Sloboda, Z., and S. L. David. *Preventing Drug Use Among Children and Adolescents: A Research-Based Guide*. Washington, DC: National Institute on Drug Abuse and National Institutes of Health, April 1999.

Tinzmann, M. B., and J. Hixson. *What Does Research Say*

About Prevention? Oak Brook, IL: North Central Regional Educational Laboratory, 1992. Available http://www.ncrel.org/sdrs/areas/stw_esys/6prevntn.htm.

Vogt, A. "Now Many 'Just Say No' to DARE." *Chicago Tribune* (26 January 2003), 1, 3.

Weil, A. *The Natural Mind.* Boston, MA: Houghton Mifflin, 1972.

Westermeyer, R. W. "Reducing Harm: A Very Good Idea" (no date). Available http://www.habitsmart.com/harm.html [accessed 6 March 2005].

Wilson, M., and S. Wilson, eds. *Drugs in American Life, Vol. 1.* New York: Wilson, 1975.

Zeese, K. B., and P. M. Lewin. *The Effective Drug Control Strategy.* Washington, DC: Network of Reform Group and the National Coalition for Effective Drug Policies, 1998. Available http://www.csdp.org/edcs/edc.htm.

CHAPTER 18

Treating Drug Dependence

Did You Know?

- A variety of approaches to drug addiction treatment exist, including behavioral and pharmacological therapies.

- No single treatment approach is appropriate for all individuals.

- Medical detoxification is not a treatment, but rather a precursor to treatment.

- The most successful treatment programs provide a combination of therapies and other services to meet the needs of the individual abuser.

On completing this chapter you will be able to:

◎ List several principles that characterize effective drug treatment.

◎ List the advantages and disadvantages of several strategies to treat addiction.

◎ Discuss pharmacological strategies to treat addiction.

Drugs and Society Online is a great source for additional drugs and society information for both students and instructors.
Visit **http://drugsandsociety.jbpub.com** to find a variety of useful tools for learning, thinking, and teaching.

Treatment of Addiction

People who are addicted to drugs come from all walks of life. Many suffer from occupational, social, or psychiatric or other health problems that can make their addictions difficult to treat. Even in the absence of such complicating problems, the severity of addictions varies widely. Moreover, there are many types of addictive drugs, and the use and abuse of several drugs concurrently is common. As a consequence and by necessity, treatments for specific drug dependencies often differ.

A variety of approaches to drug addiction treatment exist. Some include behavioral therapy, such as counseling, psychotherapy, or cognitive therapy. Others include medications, ranging from treatment medications (i.e., methadone, LAAM [l-α-acetyl-methadol], nicotine patches, and nicotine gum) to those intended to treat co-occurring mental disorders (i.e., antidepressants or mood stabilizers). The most successful drug abuse treatment programs typically provide a combination of therapies and other services to meet the needs of the individual abuser. They incorporate adequate assessment of treatment needs required not only as a direct consequence of the physiological and psychological effects of the drug, but also from indirect problems, such as the need for housing, legal, and financial services, educational and vocational assistance, and family/child-care services. Such needs are often shaped by the gender, age, race, culture, and sexual orientation of the abuser.

Treatment facilities provide a variety of services to people dealing with substance abuse.

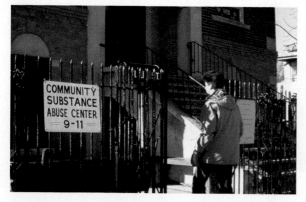

In the United States, thousands of specialized treatment facilities provide rehabilitation, counseling, behavioral therapy, medication, case management, and other types of services to people dealing with substance abuse. Treatment can take various lengths of time and can occur in many different forms in a variety of settings. Because drug addiction is generally a chronic disorder characterized by occasional relapses, a one-time, short-term treatment is often inadequate. Research has shown that good outcomes are contingent on adequate duration of treatment. Generally, for residential or outpatient treatment, participation for fewer than 90 days is of limited or no effectiveness; treatments lasting significantly longer are needed (NIDA 1999). For methadone maintenance, 12 months of treatment is often the minimum needed, and some individuals who are addicted to opiates require extended treatment lasting several years (NIDA 1999). Many individuals who enter treatment drop out before receiving all of its benefits; hence, successful treatment often requires more than one treatment experience.

To best target treatment for an individual, the type and goals of treatment must be determined. Consideration must be given to the fact that both the type and the goals of treatment largely depend on the view one holds of addiction. For example, if the disease model is applied to addiction, total abstinence is required because this model views drug abuse as a biological condition that is largely uncontrollable. The user is perceived as "ill" and thus irrational about continued drug use. On the other hand, if responsible drug use is the goal, then occasional and moderate drug use can be the intended end result.

Effective treatment allows addicts to stop abusing drugs, returns them to a drug-free state of existence, and transforms them into employable and productive members of society. Measures of effectiveness typically include assessing levels of family functioning, employability, criminal behavior, and medical condition. Overall, treatment of addiction is as successful as treatment of other chronic diseases such as diabetes, hypertension, and asthma (NIDA 1999).

Studies clearly show that treatment is much less expensive than continuing addiction. Treatment is also less expensive than simply incarcerating addicts. For example, the average cost for 1 full year of methadone maintenance treatment is approximately $4700 per patient, whereas 1 full year of imprisonment costs approximately $18,400 per person (NIDA 1999). According to several estimates, every $1 invested in addiction treatment programs yields a return of between $4 and $7 in reduced drug-related crime, criminal justice costs, and theft (NIDA 1999). Major savings to the individual and society also come from significantly fewer interpersonal conflicts, improvements in workplace productivity, and reductions in drug-related incidents (NIDA 1999).

Successful outcomes depend on retaining the person in treatment long enough to gain the full benefit. Several factors influence retention, including individual motivation to change drug-using behavior and degree of support from family and friends. Pressure from employers, the criminal justice system, or extensions of the court (i.e., child protective services) can also be important. Because individual problems such as mental illness or criminal involvement decrease the likelihood of retaining patients in treatment, broad-ranging programs (i.e., with medical and legal services) are important. It is also important for providers to ensure a transition to continuing care or "aftercare" following a patient's completion of formal treatment (NIDA 1999).

NIDA has delineated 13 overarching principles that characterize effective addiction treatment (NIDA 1999). These tenets, similar to those described by the majority of treatment researchers and providers, include the following:

1. *No single treatment is appropriate for all individuals.* Treatment settings, interventions, and services must be matched to each individual's particular problems and needs.
2. *Treatment needs to be readily available.* Individuals who are addicted to drugs are often uncertain about whether to seek treatment. Hence, it is crucial that services be available as soon as an individual makes the decision to seek help for his or her addiction. Opportunities for treatment can be lost if it is not immediately available or is not readily accessible.

3. *Effective treatment attends to multiple needs of the individual, not just his or her drug use.* To be effective, treatment must address the individual's drug use and any associated medical, psychological, social, vocational, and legal problems.
4. *An individual's treatment and services plan must be assessed continually and modified as necessary to ensure that the plan meets his or her changing needs.* A person undergoing treatment may require varying combinations of services and treatment components during the course of treatment and recovery. In addition to counseling or psychotherapy, medication, other medical services, family therapy, parenting instruction, vocational rehabilitation, and social and legal services may be required. Hence, continual monitoring is important.
5. *Remaining in treatment for an adequate period is critical for treatment effectiveness.* The appropriate duration for an individual depends on his or her problems and needs. As noted earlier, research indicates that for most patients, the threshold of significant improvement is reached at about 3 months in treatment.
6. *Counseling (individual and/or group) and other behavioral therapies are critical components of effective treatment for addiction.* In behavioral therapy, patients address issues of motivation, build skills to resist drug use, replace drug-using activities with constructive and rewarding non–drug-using activities, and improve problem-solving abilities.
7. *Medications are an important element of treatment for many patients, especially when combined with counseling and other behavioral therapies.* Methadone, LAAM, naltrexone, and nicotine patches are just some examples of medications that can be effective treatments. For patients with mental disorders, medications (i.e., antidepressants, anxiolytics) can be especially important.
8. *Addicted or drug-abusing individuals with coexisting mental disorders should have both disorders treated in an integrated way.* Because addictive and mental disorders often occur in the same individual, patients presenting for either

condition should be assessed and treated for the co-occurrence of the other.

9. *Medical detoxification is only the first stage of addiction treatment and by itself does little to change long-term drug use.* Medical detoxification (that is, the process of safely managing the acute physical symptoms of withdrawal associated with stopping drug use) can be an important first step toward abstinence. However, detoxification alone is rarely sufficient to help addicts achieve long-term abstinence.

10. *Treatment does not need to be voluntary to be effective.* Strong motivation can facilitate the treatment process. Sanctions or enticements in the family, criminal justice system, or employment setting can facilitate treatment entry and increase both retention rates and success of drug treatment interventions.

11. *Possible drug use during treatment must be monitored continuously.* Backsliding into drug use often occurs during addiction treatment. The objective of monitoring a patient's drug and alcohol use during treatment is that it can help the patient withstand urges to use drugs. Such monitoring also can provide early evidence of drug use so that the individual's treatment plan can be adjusted. Feedback to patients who test positive for illicit drug use is an important element of monitoring.

12. *Treatment programs should provide assessment for HIV/AIDS, hepatitis B and C, tuberculosis, and other infectious diseases and counseling to help patients modify or stop behaviors that place them or others at risk of infection.*

13. *Recovery from drug addiction can be a long-term process and frequently requires multiple episodes of treatment.* As with other chronic illnesses, relapses to drug use can occur during or after successful treatment episodes. Addicted individuals may require prolonged and multiple episodes of treatment to achieve long-term abstinence and fully restored functioning. Participation in self-help support programs during and following treatment often is helpful in maintaining abstinence.

Many treatment programs apply one or more of these listed principles as part of their therapeutic strategy.

Drug Addiction Treatment in the United States

THERAPEUTIC STRATEGIES

There is a wide array of general therapeutic strategies for treatment. Some involve pharmacological interventions, such as methadone maintenance or narcotic antagonist treatment. Other programs apply a drug-free approach. Programs can be short or long term, and can be individualized or involve group participation. The following is an overview of various treatment approaches. It is important to realize that many treatment programs blend one or more of these approaches as part of their therapeutic strategy.

HISTORICAL APPROACHES

Considerable effort has been expended to find treatments for substance abuse. Several approaches, or at least components of them, continue to be utilized today. These include:

Alcoholics Anonymous

Founded in the mid-1930s, Alcoholics Anonymous (AA) is now an international organization. The desire to stop drinking is the sole criterion required to join. The original founders of AA were strongly influenced by a religious movement known as the "Oxford Group" and the psychoanalyst Carl Jung. AA outlines 12 successive measures referred to as "steps" that alcoholics should accomplish during the recovery process. These steps include admitting that the person addicted to alcohol has no power over the drug. He or she must also believe in a greater "power" who can help him or her overcome shortcomings. Individuals must make initial and ongoing assessments of their life, and admit to others the character of their wrongs. In addition, individuals must make amends to those whom they have adversely affected, except in situations where such actions could harm others (Alcoholics Anonymous 2003).

It is difficult to assess the success of AA for four reasons:

1. AA insists on anonymity; it does not reveal names of members.

Common alcohol abuse–related problems are shared at AA meetings.

2. Membership is strictly voluntary. Those who want to join become members when they vow to give up drinking. Controlled studies are impossible.

3. Members are a homogeneous group. They tend to be middle class and socially conservative.

4. Some addiction researchers are of the opinion that the more severe, hard-core alcoholics who refuse to seek help generally do not go to AA, whereas a smaller percentage of problem drinkers who come to view themselves as addicted to alcohol take this path (see Rudy 1994 for further discussion of this and other related findings). In part, this self-selection may be responsible for the group's high success rate.

Regardless, AA has been, and continues to be, a very important method for treating many recovering alcoholics.

AA has two types of meetings: open and closed. **Open meetings** are open to anyone who has an interest in attending and witnessing these meetings, and they last approximately 45 minutes to 1 hour. **Closed meetings** are for alcoholics who have a serious desire to completely stop drinking. These meetings are not open to viewers or "shoppers." At closed meetings, recovering alcoholics address, through testimonials, how alcohol has diminished their quality of life.

Some outgrowths of AA include Al-Anon, Adult Children of Alcoholics, and Alateen. These are parallel organizations supporting AA. Al-Anon is for spouses and other close relatives of alcoholics, and Alateen is exclusively for teenagers whose lives have been affected by someone else's alcoholism. Both relatives and teen members of alcoholic families learn means and methods for coping with destructive behaviors exhibited by alcoholic members.

Rehabilitation Facilities

The first rehabilitation programs grew out of the work that AA members did with other active alcoholics. Known as "Twelfth stepping," this program involves reaching out to others in need and attempting to draw them in. The movement began in the early days of AA when the organization's founder, Bill W., had alcoholics trying to stop drinking or "dry out" living at his house in Brooklyn. At that time, "[his] home was stuffed, from cellar to attic, with alcoholics in all stages of recovery" (Al-Anon 1970). It was a natural transition to opening up "drying out houses" in the 1940s and 1950s.

Also during the 1950s, the **Minnesota model**, an inpatient rehabilitation model, was developed. It combined the AA philosophy with a multidisciplinary treatment team. A treatment plan was used, based on assessment of the individual and prioritization of goals. This model, which borrows from social work practice, is still used in treatment programs. Due to the vagaries of insurance reimbursement in Minnesota, the program lasted

KEY TERMS

open meetings
meetings to which anyone having an interest in attending and witnessing is invited

closed meetings
meetings to which only alcoholics having a serious desire to completely stop drinking are invited

Minnesota model
a major model in the treatment of alcohol and drug abuse, involving a month-long stay in an inpatient rehabilitation facility, a multidisciplinary treatment team, systematic assessment, and a formal treatment plan with long- and short-term goals

28 days because that was the length covered by insurance; therefore, alcoholism programs traditionally were roughly 1 month long.

GENERAL THERAPEUTIC STRATEGIES

In addition to the approaches mentioned previously, there are numerous strategies to drug addiction treatment. Although not all treatment programs fit perfectly into any one of these categories, the following provides an overview of the general types of services available (NIDA 1999).

Medical Detoxification

Medical detoxification is a process whereby individuals are systematically withdrawn from drugs, typically under the care of a physician. Medications are available for detoxification from benzodiazepines, alcohol, barbiturates, opiates, nicotine, and other sedatives. Detoxification can be medically necessary, as untreated withdrawal from some agents (that is, alcohol and barbiturates) can be fatal. Although "detox" is sometimes referred to as a distinct treatment modality, it is more appropriately considered a precursor to treatment because it is designed to treat the acute physiological effects of stopping drug use. It is not designed to address the psychological, social, and behavioral problems associated with addiction and, therefore, does not typically produce lasting behavioral changes. Detoxification is most useful when it incorporates formal processes of assessment and referral to subsequent drug addiction treatment (NIDA 1999).

Outpatient Drug-Free Treatment

The outpatient strategy varies in the intensity and forms of services offered. Such treatment often is more suitable for individuals who are employed or who have extensive family and/or community support. Low-intensity programs may offer little more than drug education, warnings, and advice. Other

outpatient models, such as intensive day treatment, can be comparable to residential programs in effectiveness and services. Group counseling is often emphasized (NIDA 1999).

Short-Term Residential Programs

Short-term residential programs provide relatively brief treatment based on a modified 12-step approach. These programs were originally designed to treat alcoholism, but have been used to treat other forms of addiction. The original residential treatment model consisted of a 3- to 6-week hospital-based, inpatient treatment phase, followed by extended outpatient therapy and participation in a self-help group, such as AA. Reduced healthcare insurance coverage for substance abuse treatment has resulted in a diminished number of these programs, and the average length of stay under managed care review is much shorter than in early programs (NIDA 1999).

Long-Term Residential Treatment Programs

Long-term residential programs provide care 24 hours per day, generally in nonhospital settings. The best-known residential treatment model is the **therapeutic community** (TC), but residential treatment may also employ other models, such as cognitive-behavioral therapy.

The typical TC resident has more severe problems compared with patients in other forms of drug treatment—sometimes with more co-occurring mental health problems and criminal involvement. His or her addiction is viewed in the context of his or her social and psychological deficits, and treatment focuses on developing personal accountability and responsibility. Research shows that TCs can be modified to treat individuals with special needs, including adolescents, women, those with severe mental disorders, and individuals in the criminal justice system (NIDA 1999).

Participation in a TC involves planned lengths of stay of 6 to 12 months. Treatment is highly structured and can at times be confrontational. Activities are designed to help residents examine damaging self-concepts, beliefs, and patterns of behavior and to find constructive ways to interact with others. The TC focuses on the "resocialization" of the individual and uses the other

KEY TERMS

therapeutic community
a program that advocates a complete change in lifestyle, such as complete abstinence from drugs, elimination of deviant behavior, and development of employable skills

residents, staff, and social context as active components of treatment. Many TCs also provide employment training and other support services on-site.

Treating Criminal Justice-Involved Drug Abusers and Addicts

Research has shown that combining drug treatment with criminal justice sanctions can decrease drug use and related crime. Treatment may be delivered prior to, during, after, or in lieu of incarceration. Individuals under legal coercion tend to stay in treatment for a longer period of time and do as well as or better than individuals who are not under legal pressure (NIDA 1999).

SPECIFIC THERAPEUTIC STRATEGIES

NIDA (1999) has described several scientifically based approaches to drug addiction treatment that are not described in detail in the previous sections. Some are designed to address the consequences of addiction for the individual, family, or society. All, according to NIDA, should supplement or enhance—but not replace—existing treatment programs.

Relapse Prevention

This approach is based on the theory that learning processes play a critical role in the development of maladaptive behavioral patterns. Thus, patients learn to identify and correct problematic behaviors. They learn strategies intended to enhance self-control so as to facilitate abstinence. Specific techniques include exploring the positive and negative consequences of continued use, self-monitoring to recognize drug cravings early on and identifying high-risk situations for use, and developing strategies for coping with and avoiding high-risk situations and the desire to use. An important element of treatment is anticipating the problems patients are likely to meet and helping them develop effective coping strategies.

The Matrix Model

The matrix model provides a framework for engaging stimulant abusers in treatment with the goal of achieving abstinence. Patients learn about

issues critical to addiction and relapse, receive assistance from a trained therapist, become familiar with self-help programs, and are monitored for drug use by urine testing. The model includes education for family members affected by the addiction. Other components include early recovery skills groups, relapse prevention groups, 12-step programs, relapse analysis, and social support groups.

The therapist functions simultaneously as teacher and coach, fostering a positive, encouraging relationship with the patient and using that relationship to reinforce positive behavior change. The interaction between the therapist and the patient is realistic and direct but not confrontational or parental. Therapists are trained to conduct treatment sessions in a way that promotes the patient's self-esteem.

A patient receives individual counseling in an alcoholism treatment center.

Supportive-Expressive Psychotherapy

This approach is a time-limited, focused psychotherapy that has been adapted for heroin- and cocaine-addicted individuals. Its two main components include (1) supportive techniques to help patients feel comfortable in discussing their personal experiences and (2) expressive techniques to help patients identify and work through interpersonal relationship issues (NIDA 1999). Particular attention is paid to the relationship between drugs and problem feelings and behaviors, and how problems may be solved without the use of drugs.

Individualized Drug Counseling

Individualized counseling focuses on stopping or reducing an individual's illicit drug use. Through weekly or biweekly sessions, the counselor helps the patient develop coping strategies and tools for abstaining from drug use and then maintaining abstinence. The addiction counselor often encourages 12-step participation and makes referrals for needed supplemental medical, psychiatric, and employment services.

Motivational Enhancement Therapy (MET)

MET is a patient-centered counseling approach for initiating behavior change by helping clients to resolve ambivalence about engaging in treatment and discontinuing drug use (NIDA 1999). Instead of guiding the patient through the recovery process, MET employs strategies to evoke rapid and internally motivated change in the client. Therapy consists of an initial assessment battery session, followed by two to four individual treatment sessions with a therapist. Feedback generated from the initial assessment battery is provided to the patient to stimulate discussion regarding personal substance abuse and to elicit self-motivational statements. Coping strategies for high-risk situations are discussed. In subsequent sessions, the therapist monitors change, reviews cessation strategies being used, and continues to encourage commitment to change or sustained abstinence.

Community Reinforcement Approach Plus Vouchers

This intensive 24-week outpatient therapy has been used for treatment of cocaine addiction. The treatment goals are (1) to achieve cocaine abstinence long enough for patients to learn new life skills that will help sustain abstinence and (2) to reduce alcohol consumption for patients whose drinking is associated with cocaine use (NIDA 1999). Patients attend weekly or biweekly individual counseling sessions in which they learn a variety of skills to minimize drug use. Patients also submit urine samples and receive vouchers for cocaine-negative samples. The value of the vouchers increases with consecutive drug-free samples. Patients may exchange vouchers for retail goods that are consistent with a cocaine-free lifestyle. Voucher-based reinforcement has also been employed in conjunction with methadone maintenance therapy.

PHARMACOLOGICAL STRATEGIES

Some treatment strategies employ pharmacological approaches to help patients with their addiction(s). These strategies are based on the properties of the drug to which they are addicted. Examples of these strategies are discussed in the following sections.

Opioid Agonist Maintenance Therapy

Treatment for opiate addicts is often conducted in outpatient settings using methadone. The use of methadone, an opioid **agonist** (that is, a drug that activates opioid receptors), is often referred to as methadone maintenance therapy (MMT). Methadone is a long-acting synthetic opiate medication administered orally for a sustained period at a dosage sufficient to prevent opiate withdrawal and decrease craving. Patients stabilized on adequate, sustained dosages of methadone or a related compound, LAAM, can function normally. They can hold jobs, avoid the crime and violence of the street culture, and reduce their exposure to HIV by stopping or decreasing injection drug use and drug-related, high-risk sexual behavior.

Patients stabilized on opiate agonists can engage more readily in counseling and other behavioral interventions essential to recovery and rehabilitation. The best, most effective opiate agonist maintenance programs include individual and/or group counseling, as well as provision of, or referral to, other needed medical, psychological, and social services (NIDA 1999).

One supervisor of a methadone clinic associated with a Brooklyn, New York, hospital explains the MMT process it employs:

> First of all, we test for alcohol, benzodiazepines [Valium-like substances], and other drugs. Clients with positive tox [who test positive for drugs] are administratively discharged. They come in at 6:30 for their dose, and then the vast majority go off to work! Methadone, job counseling, and GED classes allow them to get their lives together. Our goal is to taper them off to zero.

Although many criticisms have been levied against the use of methadone, other research findings contradict this skepticism. Since the 1980s, 65% to 85% of methadone-treated patients have not only remained in treatment for a year or more, but also dramatically ceased or strongly curtailed their criminal behavior and had strong records of gainful employment while receiving the drug (Swan 1994). In addition, methadone is reported to reduce the risk of HIV infection. This benefit alone is believed to lower the costs to society, especially those associated with providing health care to AIDS patients.

Nicotine Replacement Therapy

Nicotine was the first pharmacological agent approved by the FDA for use in smoking cessation therapy. As discussed in Chapter 11, nicotine replacement therapies, such as nicotine gum, transdermal patches, nasal sprays, and inhalers, are used to relieve withdrawal symptoms. An added benefit is that these forms of nicotine have little abuse potential because they do not produce the pleasurable effects of tobacco products.

Antagonist Therapy

An **antagonist** is a compound that suppresses the actions of a drug. Narcotic antagonists have properties that make them important tools in the clinical treatment of narcotic drug dependence. For instance, they counteract the central nervous system depressant effects in opioid drug overdoses.

Opiate antagonists are often used in the emergency treatment of opiate poisoning (overdose). Some physicians claim to perform instant detoxification with the use of an opiate antagonist during sedation. Two opiate antagonists, naltrexone and cyclazocine, block heroin from having an effect on the heroin addict. Further, naloxone (Narcan) is often used as an antidote for opioid overdose (commonly known as "narcotic poisoning"). It is also used as a component of a recently approved treatment for opioid dependence (see "Holding the Line").

Antagonists were developed as a by-product of research in analgesics. Scientists were interested in dissociating the dependence-producing and necessary pain-relieving properties of substances that could replace morphine. This research led to the development of nalorphine, the first specific opiate antagonist. Although its short duration of action and frequent unpleasant side effects limited its clinical usefulness, its properties stimulated further research into this class of drugs (Archer 1981; Palfai and Jankiewicz 1991).

Other Pharmacological Therapies

Clonidine (Catapres) is useful in treating opiate-dependent people during the difficult withdrawal stages (Ginzburg 1986). Studies thus far show the value of this drug for withdrawal from heroin, morphine, codeine, and methadone. Clonidine is not addictive and does not cause euphoria, but it does block cravings for drugs. It also makes the person feel better compared with the depression experienced by addicts using other methods of withdrawal.

Antabuse, whose generic name is disulfiram, is a drug used for treating alcoholics. This drug is perceived as a deterrent drug—it makes people violently ill if alcohol is used. "Antabuse interferes with the normal metabolism of alcohol, resulting

KEY TERMS

antagonist
a drug that blocks another drug from producing its effects; often used in detoxification from opiates

Holding the Line Expanded Options for Treatment of Heroin Addiction

Until 2000, opiate dependence treatments such as methadone could be dispensed only in a very limited number of clinics that specialize in addiction treatment. As a consequence of the Drug Addiction Treatment Act of 2000 (see Chapter 3), the FDA announced approval of Subutex and Suboxone tablets for the treatment of opiate dependence by specially trained physicians. Accordingly, the drugs can be prescribed in an office setting and, therefore, can provide greater access to patients needing treatment.

Subutex and Suboxone treat opiate addiction by preventing symptoms of withdrawal from heroin and other opiates. Subutex contains only buprenorphine (a partial opioid agonist) and is intended for use at the beginning of treatment for drug abuse. Suboxone contains both buprenorphine and the opiate antagonist naloxone, and is intended to be used in maintenance treatment of opiate addiction. Naloxone has limited effects if administered sublingually, but is effective as an antagonist if administered intravenously. It has been added to Suboxone to guard against intravenous abuse of buprenorphine by individuals who are physically dependent on opiates.

in serious physical reaction even if a small amount of alcohol is ingested" (McNeece and DiNitto 1994). The greatest asset in using this drug is its ability to deter impulsive drinking (McNeece and DiNitto 1994).

CURRENT TRENDS IN PROVIDING TREATMENT SERVICES

Certifying Qualified Counselors

Separate treatment models evolved for drug addicts and alcoholics. This, in turn, led to separate governmental and certification entities. Over the past two decades, most of these bodies have been merged into single-chemical dependency or addictions authorities and certification boards, although New York state accomplished this step in 1995–1996. Most recently, the recognition of the terrible health costs of tobacco consumption has spurred the addition of nicotine to the responsibility of addictions authorities and to the knowledge areas required of counselors.

Although qualifications for becoming addictions counselors once included merely being a recovering addict and having the enthusiasm, energy, and empathy to work with other addicts, the credentialing requirements became more rigorous in the 1970s. From the mid-1970s on, a credentialing system evolved that demanded increased levels of competency. Today, most states operate certification boards, which are linked in a national

consortium, and certification is also provided by the national addiction counselors' association.

Certification requirements include taking classes, passing a written examination, and undertaking service experience. The certification consortium generally requires an oral and written case presentation as well. Although minor variations in the state credentialing systems exist, counselors must be able to perform the following tasks:

- Screen candidates for eligibility and appropriateness.
- Follow intake procedures.
- Handle patient orientation and education.
- Practice case management.
- Assess patient strengths and weaknesses.
- Develop and implement a treatment plan in collaboration with the patient.
- Handle cases involving addiction-specific individual, group, and family counseling.
- Understand the pharmacology of addictive substances and the dynamics of addiction.
- Maintain ethical practices and patient confidentiality.
- Understand the role of the addictions counselor and how it differs from that of other professional roles.

One of the most important advances in the field has been the development of a subfield for addicts with concurrent psychiatric disabilities (mentally ill chemical abusers) (Kelly and Ramundo 1993). This field is particularly complex because many symptoms of mental illness share similarities with chemically induced organic brain syndromes (early in the days of crack cocaine, many patients were overdiagnosed with "paranoid schizophrenia" in public hospitals in New York City—especially by newly arrived, out-of-town physicians).

Patient Placement Criteria

Treatment professionals use **patient placement criteria** to match the severity of the addiction to the level of care needed, ranging from medical inpatient care, nonmedical inpatient care, and intensive outpatient care, to outpatient care (CSAT 1993). Unfortunately, managed care guidelines established by many health insurance carriers simply do not allow for treatment beyond outpatient care or brief inpatient detoxification. Matching the client's profile to a treatment modality is more likely to achieve lasting success. A person with severe attention deficit hyperactivity disorder, for example, tends to be disorganized and forgetful and is unsuited for the strict behavioral expectations of the TC. Likewise, an emotionally fragile individual is unsuited to confrontational groups.

Special Focus Programs

Programs have been created that are similar to AA but without the spiritual emphasis that some potential members find difficult to accept. These programs include Rational Recovery, which evolved from Albert Ellis's Rational-Emotive Therapy (Ellis et al. 1988), and the similar programs Smart Recovery and Secular Organizations for Sobriety (Christopher 1988). One of the principles behind these programs is early intervention. In contrast to past practices, in which the addict was scooped up off the street (fitting the description of the addict "hitting rock bottom"), treatment begins at an earlier phase of addiction.

Historically there have also been shifts to mandated or involuntary treatment. Two components of this practice include the following:

- Originally called *industrial alcoholism programs*, these programs have existed for some time. Their goal is to identify and refer addicted employees to treatment programs. This model has been adapted for use in school settings (*student assistance programs* [SAPs]) and in orga-

nizational settings such as labor unions or consortia of unions (*member assistance programs*). Some states now fund SAPs and certify SAP professionals.

- The TC has always counted on many court-mandated clients, but the trend accelerated tremendously in the 1990s, with demonstration programs established in Colorado, Texas, and New Mexico for collaborative planning of criminal justice and addictions treatment systems. Many treatment programs have retooled to accommodate convicts paroled or serving out their sentences, and treatment programs have been instituted in prisons.

Discussion Questions

1. List several principles that characterize effective addiction treatment.

2. Describe Alcoholics Anonymous and its approach to assisting individuals addicted to alcohol.

3. Describe several therapeutic strategies to treat addiction.

4. Describe the therapeutic community approach to treating substance abuse.

5. Describe three pharmacological strategies to treat opioid dependence.

Key Terms

open meetings **559**

closed meetings **559**

Minnesota model **559**

KEY TERMS

patient placement criteria
a system that allows the referring professional to match the assessed level of addictive severity with an appropriate intensity and level of care, ranging from an outpatient clinic to a medical center

Summary

1 One of the earliest real alcoholism recovery efforts was Alcoholics Anonymous (AA). Programs modeled on AA, known as 12-step fellowships, are major routes to recovery.

2 There are numerous approaches to drug addiction treatment, including outpatient and residential treatment. Medical detoxification is not a treatment per se, but rather a precursor to treatment.

3 Relapse prevention is a cognitive-behavioral approach based on the theory that learning processes play a critical role in the development of maladaptive behavioral patterns. According to this approach, to overcome addiction, patients must learn to identify and correct problematic behaviors.

4 Motivational enhancement therapy is a client-centered counseling approach for initiating behavior change by helping clients to resolve ambivalence about engaging in treatment and discontinuing drug use.

5 Addiction counseling has now become a true profession, governed by national and state certification.

6 A major approach to heroin and other opiate addiction has involved the provision of methadone, a synthetic opiate.

References

Al-Anon. *Al-Anon's Favorite Forum Editorials*. New York: Al-Anon Family Group Headquarters, 1970.

Alcoholics Anonymous. "AA's Twelve Steps" (2003). Available http://www.alcoholics-anonymous.org/default/en_about_aa_sub.cfm?subpageid=84&pageid=13.

Archer, S. "Historical Perspective on the Chemistry and Development of Naltrexone." In *Narcotic Antagonists: Naltrexone Pharmaco-Chemistry and Sustained-Release Preparations*, edited by R. E. Willette and G. Barnett. NIDA Research Monograph 28. Washington, DC: National Institute on Drug Abuse, 1981.

Christopher, J. *Unhooked: Staying Sober and Drug-Free*. Buffalo, NY: Prometheus Books, 1988.

CSAT. *Guidelines for the Treatment of Alcohol and Other Drug-Abusing Adolescents*. Treatment Improvement Protocol (TIP) Series 4. Rockville, MD: U.S. DHHS, PHS, SAMHSA, Center for Substance Abuse Treatment, 1993.

Ellis, A., J. F. McInerney, R. DiGiuseppe, and R. J. Yeager. *Rational-Emotive Therapy with Alcoholics and Substance Abusers*. Boston: Allyn and Bacon, 1988.

Ginzburg, H. M. *Naltrexone: Its Chemical Utility*. Rockville, MD: National Institute on Drug Abuse, 1986.

Kelly, K., and P. Ramundo. *You Mean I'm Not Lazy, Stupid, or Crazy?!* New York: Scribner, 1993.

McNeece, C. A., and D. M. DiNitto. *Chemical Dependency: A Systems Approach*. Englewood Cliffs, NJ: Prentice-Hall, 1994.

National Institute on Drug Abuse (NIDA). *Principles of Drug Addiction Treatment*. National Institutes of Health Publication No. 99-4180, October 1999.

Palfai, T., and H. Jankiewicz. *Drugs and Human Behavior*. Dubuque, IA: Brown, 1991.

Rudy, D. "Perspectives on Alcoholism: Lessons from Alcoholics and Alcohologists." In *Drug Use in America: Social, Cultural, and Political Perspectives*, edited by P. J. Venturelli, 23–29. Boston, MA: Jones and Bartlett, 1994.

Swan, N. "Research Demonstrates Long-Term Benefits of Methadone Treatment." *NIDA Notes* 9 (November/December 1994). Available http://www.nida.nihgov/NIDA_NOTES.

APPENDIX A

Federal Agencies with Drug Abuse Missions

Drug Enforcement Administration (DEA)

Because of the unique problems of drug abuse in 1930, Congress authorized the establishment of the Bureau of Narcotics in the Treasury Department to administer the relevant laws. This agency remained in the Treasury Department until 1968, when it became part of a new group in the Justice Department, the Bureau of Narcotics and Dangerous Drugs. Harry Anslinger served as head of the bureau for over 30 years, from its creation until his retirement in 1962. Anslinger was an agent during Prohibition, and later, as head of the bureau, he played an important role in getting marijuana outlawed by the federal government. In 1973, the Bureau of Narcotics and Dangerous Drugs became the Drug Enforcement Administration (DEA). Today, the DEA has the responsibility of infiltrating and breaking up illegal drug traffic in the United States, as well as controlling the use of Scheduled substances.

Special Action Office for Drug Abuse Prevention (SAODAP)

In 1971, President Richard Nixon set up a temporary agency, SAODAP, to initiate short-term and long-term planning of programs and to coordinate antidrug abuse programs with the states so that proper funding procedures and policies were followed. This office was located in the White House and was intended to advise the president. One major reason for establishing this organization was the initial report of a high heroin addiction rate in returning Vietnam veterans. The program was supposed to fight the increase in addiction in the United States. SAODAP was abolished, as planned, with most of its education, research, treatment, and rehabilitation functions going to a new agency, the National Institute on Drug Abuse (NIDA). An expert on the staff of advisors to the president, the domestic policy staff, assumed the duties of advising the president on drug-related matters and drug abuse programs. The advisor was to keep track of budgets for drug programs and coordinate policy with law enforcement groups. Under the administration of Ronald Reagan, further changes were proposed. A pattern of federal policy was established; that is, control and management of drug programs in the United States changed with each new "crisis."

Alcohol, Drug Abuse, and Mental Health Administration (ADAMHA)

In 1973, a new agency was formed after the Department of Health, Education, and Welfare Secretary Casper Weinberger stripped the alcohol and drug abuse sections from the National Institute of Mental Health (NIMH). This action formed the National Institute of Alcohol Abuse and Alcoholism (NIAAA) and the NIDA (see previous section). NIAAA, NIDA, and NIMH were under the agency ADAMHA (Alcohol, Drug Abuse and

Mental Health Administration). This shuffling and redesign was part of federal attempts to bring the post-Vietnam War heroin crisis under control and to address the perennial problems of alcoholism and dependence on other drugs. The mission of NIAAA and NIDA was and still is to coordinate both clinical and basic research directed at drugs of abuse. Today, these institutes support 80% to 90% of all drug dependence research conducted in the United States. During fiscal year 2005, these institutes controlled budgets of $1 million (NIDA) and $438 (NIAAA) million.

In October 1992, ADAMHA was reorganized, and both NIDA and NIAAA officially became Institutes of the National Institutes of Health (NIH) as mandated by the ADAMHA Reorganization Act of 1992 (Greenhouse 1992).

The Substance Abuse and Mental Health Services Administration (SAMHSA)

With passage of the ADAMHA Reorganization Act of 1992, the services programs of NIDA, NIAAA, and NIMH were incorporated into the newly created SAMHSA. This agency was given the lead responsibility for prevention and treatment of addictive and mental health problems and disorders. Its overall mission is to reduce the incidence and prevalence of substance abuse and mental disorders by ensuring the best therapeutic use of scientific knowledge and improving access to high-quality, effective programs (*SAMHSA Bulletin* 1992).

State Regulations

There have always been questions regarding the relative responsibilities of state versus federal laws and their respective regulatory agencies. In general, the U.S. form of government has allowed local control to take precedence over national control. Because of this historic attitude, states were the first to pass laws to regulate the abuse or misuse of drugs. Federal laws developed later, after the federal govern-

ment gained greater jurisdiction over the well-being and lives of the citizens and it became apparent that, due to interstate trafficking, national drug abuse problems could not be effectively dealt with on a state-by-state basis. Some early state laws banned the use of smoking opium, regulated the sale of various psychoactive drug substances, and, in a few instances, set up treatment programs. However, these early legislative actions made no effort to *prevent* drug abuse. Drug abuse was controlled to a great extent by social pressure rather than by law. It was considered morally wrong to be an alcoholic or an addict to opium or some other drug.

The drug laws varied considerably from state to state in 1932, so the National Conference of Commissioners on Uniform State Laws set up the Uniform Narcotic Drug Act (UNDA), which was later adopted by nearly all states. The UNDA provided for the control of possession, use, and distribution of opiates and cocaine. In 1942, marijuana was included under this act because it was classified as a narcotic.

In 1967, the Food and Drug Administration proposed the Model Drug Abuse Control Act and urged the states to adopt it on a uniform basis. This law extended controls over depressant, stimulant, and hallucinogenic drugs, similar to the 1965 federal law. Many states set up laws based on this model.

The federal Controlled Substances Act of 1970 stimulated the National Conference of Commissioners to propose a new Uniform Controlled Substances Act (UCSA). The UCSA permits enactment of a single state law regulating the illicit possession, use, manufacture, and dispensing of controlled psychoactive substances. At this time, most states have enacted the UCSA or modifications of it.

Today, state law enforcement of drug statutes does not always reflect federal regulations, although for the most part, the two statutory levels are harmonious. For example, marijuana has tentatively been approved for medicinal use in California and Arizona but is considered a Schedule I substance by federal regulatory agencies (as of this writing).

APPENDIX B

Drugs of Use and Abuse

The table that follows provides detailed information about the drugs listed. Note that the heading *CSA Schedules* refers to categorization under the Controlled Substances Act (CSA). The roman numeral(s) to the right of each drug name specifies each as a Schedule I, II, III, IV, or V drug. See Chapter 3, for more information on scheduling.

DRUGS	CSA SCHEDULES	MEDICAL USES	TRADE OR OTHER NAMES	SLANG NAMES
Narcotics				
Opium	II III V	Analgesic, antidiarrheal	Dover's Powder, Paregoric, Parepectolin	Opium
Morphine	II III	Analgesic, antitussive	Morphine, MS-Contin, Roxanol, Roxanol-SR	M, Morpho, Morph, Tab, White, Stuff, Miss, Emma, Monkey
Codeine	II III V	Analgesic, antitussive	Tylenol w/Codeine, Empirin w/Codeine, Robitussin A-C, Fiorinal w/Codeine	School Boy
Heroin	I	None	Diacetylmorphine	Horse, Smack, H, Stuff, Junk
Hydromorphone	II	Analgesic	Dilaudid	Little D, Lords
Meperidine (Pethidine)	II	Analgesic	Demerol, Mepergan	Isonipecaine, Dolantol
Methadone	II	Analgesic	Dolophine, Methadone, Methadose	Dollies, Dolls, Amidone
Other Narcotics	I II III IV V	Analgesic, antidiarrheal, antitussive	Numorphan, Percodan, Percocet, Tylox, Tussionex, Fentanyl, Darvon, Lomotil, Talwin*	T. and Blue's, Designer Drugs (Fentanyl Derivatives), China White

* Not designated as a narcotic under C.S.A. (Controlled Substances Act).

Source: Adapted from Drug Enforcement Administration, U.S. Dept. of Justice, *Drugs of Abuse.* 1989 Edition. Washington, DC: Government Printing Office, 1989; and "Let's All Work to Fight Drug Abuse." Dallas, TX: L.A.W. Publications, 1991.

DEPENDENCE PHYSICAL/ PSYCHOLOGICAL	TOLERANCE	DURATION (HOURS)	ADMINISTRATION METHODS	POSSIBLE EFFECTS	EFFECTS OF OVERDOSE	WITHDRAWAL SYNDROME
High/High	Yes	3–6	Oral, smoked			
High/High	Yes	3–6	Oral, smoked, injected	Euphoria, drowsiness, respiratory depression, constricted pupils, nausea	Slow and shallow breathing, clammy skin, convulsions, coma, possible death	Watery eyes, runny nose, yawning, loss of appetite, irritability, tremors, panic, cramps, nausea, chills and sweating
Mod./Mod.	Yes	3–6	Oral, injected			
High/High	Yes	3–6	Injected, sniffed, smoked			
High/High	Yes	3–6	Oral, injected			
High/High	Yes	3–6	Oral, injected			
High/High–Low	Yes	12–24	Oral, injected			
High–Low/ High–Low	Yes	Variable	Oral, injected			

(continued)

DRUGS	CSA SCHEDULES	MEDICAL USES	TRADE OR OTHER NAMES	SLANG NAMES
Depressants				
Chloral Hydrate	IV	Hypnotic	Noctec	—
Barbiturates	II III IV	Anesthetic, anticonvulsant, sedative, hypnotic, veterinary euthanasia agent	Amytal, Butisol, Fiorinal, Lotusate, Nembutal, Seconal, Tuinal, Phenobarbital	Yellows, Yellow Jackets, Barbs, Reds, Redbirds, Tooies, Phennies
Benzodiazepines	IV	Antianxiety, anticonvulsant, sedative, hypnotic	Ativan, Dalmane, Diazepam, Paxipam, Librium, Xanax, Serax, Valium, Tranxene, Verstran, Versed, Halcion, Restoril	Downers, Goof Balls, Sleeping Pills, Candy
Methaqualone	I	Sedative, hypnotic	Quaalude	Lude, Quay, Guad, Mandrex
Glutethimide	III	Sedative, hypnotic	Doriden	—
Other Depressants	III IV	Antianxiety, sedative, hypnotic	Equanil, Miltown, Noludar, Placidyl, Valmid	Tranquilizers, Muscle Relaxants, Sleeping Pills
Stimulants				
Cocaine†	II	Local anesthetic		Bump, Toot, C, Coke, Flake, Snow, Candy, Crack
Amphetamines	II	Attention deficit disorders, narcolepsy, weight control	Biphetamine, Desoxyn, Dexedrine	Pep Pills, Bennies, Uppers, Truck Drivers, Dexies, Black Beauties, Speed
Phenmetrazine	II	Weight control	Preludin	Uppers, Peaches, Hearts
Methylphenidate	II	Attention deficit disorders, narcolepsy	Ritalin	Speed, Meth, Crystal, Crank, Go Fast
Other Stimulants	III IV	Weight control	Apidex, Cylert, Didrex, Ionamin, Melfiat, Plegine, Sanorex, Tenuate, Tepanil, Prelu-2	—
Hallucinogens				
LSD	I	None		Acid, Microdot, Cubes
Mescaline and Peyote	I	None		Mesc Buttons, Cactus
Amphetamine Variants	I	None	2, 5-DMA, PMA, STP, MDA, MDMA, TMA, DOM, DOB	Ecstasy, Designer Drugs
Phencyclidine	II	None	PCP	PCP, Angel Dust, Hog, Peace Pill
Phencyclidine Analogues	I	None	PCE, PCPY, TCP	—
Other Hallucinogens	I	None	Bufotenine, Ibogaine, DMT, Det, Psilocybin, Psilocyn	Sacred Mushrooms, Magic Mushrooms, Mushrooms

† Designated as a narcotic under C.S.A.

DEPENDENCE PHYSICAL/ PSYCHOLOGICAL	TOLERANCE	DURATION (HOURS)	ADMINISTRATION METHODS	POSSIBLE EFFECTS	EFFECTS OF OVERDOSE	WITHDRAWAL SYNDROME
Mod./Mod.	Yes	5–8	Oral			
High–Mod./ High–Mod.	Yes	1–16	Oral	Slurred speech, disorientation, drunken behavior without odor of alcohol	Shallow respiration, clammy skin, dilated pupils, weak and rapid pulse, coma, possible death	Anxiety, insomnia, tremors, delirium, convulsions, possible death
Low/Low	Yes	4–8	Oral			
High/High	Yes	4–8	Oral			
High/Mod.	Yes	4–8	Oral			
Mod./Mod.	Yes	4–8	Oral			
Possible/High	Yes	1–2	Sniffed, smoked injected	Increased alertness, excitation, euphoria, increased pulse rate and blood pressure, insomnia, loss of appetite	Agitation, increase in body temperature, hallucinations, convulsions, possible death	Apathy, long periods of sleep, irritability, depression, disorientation
Possible/High	Yes	2–4	Oral, injected			
Possible/High	Yes	2–4	Oral, injected			
Possible/Mod.	Yes	2–4	Oral, injected			
Possible/High	Yes	2–4	Oral, injected			
None/Unknown	Yes	8–12	Oral	Illusions and hallucinations, poor perception of time and distance	Longer, more intense "trip" episodes, psychosis, possible death	Withdrawal syndrome not reported
None/Unknown	Yes	8–12	Oral			
Unknown/Unknown	Yes	Variable	Oral, injected			
Unknown/High	Yes	Days	Smoked, oral, injected			
Unknown/High	Yes	Days	Smoked, oral, injected			
None/Unknown	Possible	Variable	Smoked, oral, injected, sniffed			

(continued)

DRUGS	CSA SCHEDULES	MEDICAL USES	TRADE OR OTHER NAMES	SLANG NAMES
Cannabis				
Marijuana	I	None		Pot, Grass, Reefer, Roach, Maui Wowie, Joint, Weed, Loco Weed, Mary Jane
Tetrahydrocannabinol	I II	Cancer chemo-therapy antinauseant	THC, Marinol	THC
Hashish	I	None		Hash
Hashish Oil	I	None		Hash Oil
Inhalants		None	Gasoline, Airplane Glue, Veg. Spray, Hairspray, Deodorants, Spray Paint, Liquid Paper, Paint Thinner, Rubber Cement	Sniffing, Glue Sniffing, Snorting

DEPENDENCE PHYSICAL/ PSYCHOLOGICAL	TOLERANCE	DURATION (HOURS)	ADMINISTRATION METHODS	POSSIBLE EFFECTS	EFFECTS OF OVERDOSE	WITHDRAWAL SYNDROME
Unknown/Mod.	Yes	2–4	Smoked, oral	Euphoria, relaxed inhibitions, increased appetite, disoriented behavior	Fatigue, paranoia, possible psychosis	Insomnia, hyperactivity and decreased appetite occasionally reported
Unknown/Mod.	Yes	2–4	Smoked, oral			
Unknown/Mod.	Yes	2–4	Smoked, oral			
Unknown/Mod.	Yes	2–4	Smoked, oral			
None/Unknown	Yes	30 min.	Sniffed	Euphoria, headaches, nausea, fainting, stupor, rapid heartbeat	Damage to lungs, liver, kidneys, bone marrow, suffocation, choking, anemia, possible stroke, sudden death	Insomnia, increased appetite, depression, irritability, headache

INDEX

PHOTO CREDITS